I0328585

John Adams

The Monthly Magazine

John Adams

The Monthly Magazine

ISBN/EAN: 9783741117244

Manufactured in Europe, USA, Canada, Australia, Japa

Cover: Foto ©Andreas Hilbeck / pixelio.de

Manufactured and distributed by brebook publishing software (www.brebook.com)

John Adams

The Monthly Magazine

THE

MONTHLY MAGAZINE;

OR,

BRITISH REGISTER.

Including

MISCELLANEOUS COMMUNICATIONS FROM CORRESPONDENTS, ON ALL SUBJECTS OF LITERATURE AND SCIENCE.
MEMOIRS OF DISTINGUISHED PERSONS.
ORIGINAL LETTERS, ANECDOTES, &C.
POETRY.
LITERARY AND PHILOSOPHICAL INTELLIGENCE.
PROCEEDINGS OF LEARNED SOCIETIES.
REVIEW OF THE NEW MUSIC.
. . . . THE FINE ARTS.
. . . . ENGLISH, GERMAN, FRENCH, SPANISH, AND AMERICAN LITERATURE.
ACCOUNT OF ALL NEW PATENTS.
LIST OF NEW BOOKS AND IMPORTATIONS.
REGISTER OF DISEASES IN LONDON.
RETROSPECT OF PUBLIC AFFAIRS.
LIST OF BANKRUPTCIES AND DIVIDENDS
DOMESTIC OCCURRENCES CLASSED AND ARRANGED IN THE GEOGRAPHICAL ORDER OF THE COUNTIES.
MARRIAGES, DEATHS, BIOGRAPHICAL MEMOIRS, &C.
REPORT OF THE STATE OF COMMERCE, &C.
. . . . . OF AGRICULTURE, &C.
. . . . . OF THE WEATHER.

VOL. XII.

PART II. FOR 1801.

LONDON:

PRINTED FOR RICHARD PHILLIPS, No. 71, ST. PAUL'S CHURCH YARD:

By whom Communications are thankfully received.

(Price Twelve Shillings half-bound.)

[J. ADLARD, PRINTER, DUKE-STREET, WEST-SMITHFIELD.]

MONTHLY MAGAZINE.

No. 76. AUGUST 1, 1801. [No. 1, of Vol. 12.

On the 20th Day of July was published, the SUPPLEMENTARY NUMBER *to the Eleventh Volume of the* MONTHLY MAGAZINE, *containing—A comprehensive Retrospect of the Progress of* BRITISH LITERATURE *during the last six Months—and similar Retrospects of* GERMAN, FRENCH, *and* SPANISH LITERATURE; *with* INDEXES, TITLE, &c.

ORIGINAL COMMUNICATIONS.

For the Monthly Magazine.

ON THE AMOUNT OF THE NATIONAL DEBT.

THE Amount of the National Debt has lately been laid before the public in three separate statements, all of them in fact agreeing nearly with each other, but so differently arranged and modified as to lead an inattentive reader to very opposite conclusions respecting the real state of the public finances. In order, therefore, to have a just idea on this interesting subject, it will be necessary to reduce those statements to the same form, by which means an opportunity will be afforded, not only of ascertaining their accuracy, but of examining the principles on which they are founded.

The first statement has been given by Mr. Morgan, in his "Comparative View of the Public Finances," &c. and is as follows:—

Stock in the perpetual annuities, deducting the Irish loans .	£. 525,454,680	
Borrowed on a tontine in 1789	1,002,099	
977,141l. per ann. long annuities, worth, at 5 per cent. . .	18,444,260	
556,372l. per ann. life and short annuities, worth, at 5 per cent.	3,148,696	
		548,049,735
Imperial loan, consisting of stock in the 3 per cents.	7,502,633	
230,000l. annuity for 20 years, worth	2,866,260	
		10,368,893
		558,418,628
Deduct the stock redeemed by the Commissioners		52,281,656
	Debt remaining	506,136,972

The second statement was submitted to the House of Commons by Mr. Tierney, in the form of a Resolution, to the following effect:—

RESOLVED, That the total amount of the public funded debt, including the Irish and Imperial loans, and deducting the stock purchased by the Commissioners, and 16,083,802l. transferred to them on account of land-tax redeemed, was in February, 1801 . . .	£. 484,365,464
That the life and short annuities were about 540,000l. per ann. worth *	3,375,000
That the long annuities were 1,007,000l. per ann. worth, at 5 per cent.	21,978,132
	509,718,596
Deduct the Irish loans	19,708,750
Debt remaining, exclusive of the stock redeemed for the land-tax	490,009,846

On this and the other propositions of Mr. Tierney the previous question was put and carried. The following Resolution, which forms the third statement of the public debt, was then proposed by the Chancellor of the Exchequer and agreed to.

RESOLVED, That the total amount of the public debt, after deducting the stock purchased by the Commissioners, and 16,083,802l. transferred to them on account of the land-tax redeemed, was, in February, 1801	400,709,832
That the life and short annuities were 545,333l. per ann. worth	3,408,331
That the long annuities were 1,007,613l. per ann. worth, at 5 per cent.	21,989,702
Whole debt	426,207,865

* I have taken these annuities at 6¼ years purchase. No value is assigned to any of the temporary annuities in these resolutions.

It is to be obſerved, that the ſtock charged upon the income-tax and the Imperial loan (which are properly included in Mr. Tierney's and Mr. Morgan's ſtatements) have in this very conciſe account been entirely omitted. The former of theſe amounts to 56,445,000l. and the latter, excluſive of the annuity for 20 years, to 7,502,633l. making, together, the ſum of 63,947,633l. to be added to 426,207,865l. and conſequently the real amount of the debt, according to this ſtatement, is 490,155,498l. or rather greater than it is made to be in Mr. Tierney's ſtatement. But why is the ſtock redeemed on account of the land-tax excluded in theſe reſolutions? The produce of the tax is ſtill eſtimated by the Chancellor of the Exchequer at the uſual ſum of two millions, although it muſt have been leſſened by this redemption above 450,000l. a year. Either the revenue muſt be diminiſhed, or the debt muſt remain in its former ſtate. To ſuppoſe otherwiſe is to be guilty of the abſurdity which a perſon would commit, who, after having ſold ſome of his eſtates to pay his debts, made the rents of thoſe eſtates to conſtitute a part of his annual income. It is evident, therefore, that the fair amount of the public debt cannot be obtained without including this ſtock, which will make it, according to Mr. Tierney's ſtatement, equal to 506,093,648l. and, according to the reſolution of the Houſe of Commons, equal to 506,239,300l.—agreeing ſo nearly in both inſtances with its amount in Mr. Morgan's ſtatement, as to render it a matter of little conſequence which of them is the moſt accurate.

The impreſſion intended to be made by theſe reſolutions is obvious. They are ſo much in the ſtyle and ſpirit of the great prototype Mr. Pitt, that the public may ſafely conſole themſelves on his removal with having had his genuine diſciples for his ſucceſſors. By omitting 56 millions charged upon the income-tax, which will require ten years to be redeemed—between ſeven and eight millions lent to the Emperor, of which there is little probability that he will ever pay a farthing—about 25 millions, the values of the long and ſhort annuities—and 16 millions, commuted for one-fourth part of the annual produce of the land tax—the public debt has been reduced more than 100 millions below its real amount;—and yet even according to this very defective and mutilated ſtatement it ſtill exceeds 400 millions—a ſum which the moſt daring financiers before the adminiſtration of Mr. Pitt could not have contemplated without diſmay. But ſo ſtupendous is the magnitude of the debt, that the arbitrary omiſſion of 100 millions has little or no effect in diminiſhing its enormity. The nation, however, is ſoothed, by a new ſpecies of arithmetic, with the aſſurance, that its finances are in a condition three times better than they were before its debts had been doubled by the preſent war. In the year 1786 it is ſtated that the ſum annually applicable to the reduction of the public debt was one million, being about $\frac{1}{238}$th part of the capital. In the year 1801, by the addition of new taxes for the purpoſe, to the amount of three millions, this ſum is increaſed to 5,300,000l. ſo that it now forms $\frac{1}{76}$th part of the debt. From hence we are to infer, that the ratio of our proſperity is as 238 to 76, or as more than three to one;—in other words, that the nation is now three times richer with a debt of 500 millions, than it was in 1786 with a debt of 238 millions! It will follow then, by this mode of reaſoning, that the debt may be accumulated to more than 1200 millions before the public finances are reduced to the deplorable condition in which Mr. Pitt found them at the commencement of his adminiſtration. This is certainly a very conſoling proſpect for his ſucceſſors, and they appear duly influenced by the conſideration of it. The ſums to be raiſed in Great Britain for the year 1801 are coolly eſtimated at 69 millions, and the peace-eſtabliſhment of the country (if the war were now cloſed) at 34 millions a year! To thoſe who are ſatisfied with the arithmetic of the Treaſury, theſe eſtimates will probably afford no cauſe of alarm, and therefore it will be of little avail to prove to ſuch perſons that they are groſsly underrated. To thoſe, on the contrary, who are better informed on public affairs, they need no comment; for whether the *war*-expenditure be 69 or 75 millions a year, and the *peace*-eſtabliſhment be 34 or 36 millions, they muſt be equally convinced of the enormity of ſuch a ſyſtem, and of the ruin in which it muſt terminate.

M. N.

For the Monthly Magazine.

GENERAL OBSERVATIONS *on the* PERSEPOLITAN CHARACTERS, *with a* DESCRIPTION *and* REPRESENTATION *of ſome* BRICKS *lately ſent to* EUROPE, *from the* SITE *of* ANTIENT BABYLON.

ABOUT one day's journey from Shiras, in Perſia, appear the ruins of a magnificent ediſice, which ſtill attracts

tracts the admiration of every traveller. These ruins are called by the Persians Chehil-Minar; or, The Forty Columns, although there are always more or less to be seen than that number. The following travellers, Ives, Irwin, Figueroa, Pietro della Valle, Thevenot, Chardin, Gemelli, Le Bruyn, Kæmpfer, Otter, Niebuhr, and Franklin, have actually visited them; and among writers, the following—Hyde, Caylus, Murr, Langles, Herder, Witte, Wahl, Hageman, besides a number of others, have spoken of them; and several have attempted to explain the copious sculptures which are still visible on them. But it is chiefly the foreign and unusual characters and inscriptions joined to them which have long occupied the skill and exercised the penetration of many learned Orientalists, who have wearied themselves in fruitless attempts to discover the alphabet out of which they are composed.

These remarkable inscriptions appear to be regular variations and compositions of a right line, as Sir W. Jones well observes; and of an angular figure. They have, likewise, a striking resemblance to nails, for which reason the French writers commonly call them, *caractères à cloux*, or the nail-headed characters. They are also denominated Persepolitan, upon the supposition that these columns once formed a part of the royal palace of the sovereigns of Persia, called by the Greek writers Persepolis. Among others, this opinion is advanced by the learned M. Heeren, professor at Göttingen, in a work lately published on that subject; an opinion, however, which Mr. Tychsen attempts to refute, who supposes the palace, the ruins of which still remain, to have been built much later, by the princes who succeeded Alexander, and governed that country under the name of the Arsacides and Arsacidæ. Whether this be the case or not, or whether these ruins date from the time of the first and most antient dynasty of Persia, the Pishdadians, or whether, as others pretend, they were built by the famous Gemshid, who is said to have built the celebrated city of Issahar, is not the object of our present enquiry. It is more certain that the place of the inscriptions is to this day called Issahar, and also Tahti-Gemshid, or the Throne of Gemshid; and it is equally certain that the above-said inscriptions have been hitherto reckoned peculiar to these ruins; at least it is the general opinion of the literati, that they are only to be found on the marbles or gems dug up there, and not in any other part or province of Persia. More recently, however, the curious discovery has been made, that the same sort of characters are to be found, not only in the province of Fars, in Persia, but that they are copiously and usually met with near the Euphrates, in Chaldæa, amongst what are supposed to be the ruins of its antient capital, Babylon. This fact was, indeed, announced several years ago by M. Beauchamp, Correspondent of the Royal Academy of Sciences at Paris, who, on his return from Bagdad, where he had resided several years, brought to the learned Abbé Barthelemy specimens of unknown characters, which he discovered on the bricks, still remaining in great numbers near Helleh, on the Euphrates, on the identical spot where, according to D'Anville, Major Rennel, and other geographers, the antient Babylon was situated. Besides these bricks with inscriptions, M. Beauchamp likewise found several solid cylinders, three inches in diameter, composed of a white substance, and covered with very small writing, resembling the inscriptions of Persepolis, as described by Chardin; also a number of blue stones with inscriptions engraved on them. M. Beauchamp's correspondence was translated from the French of the *Journal des Sçavans*, published in the year 1782, into English, and inserted in the European Magazine for 1792.

M. Michaux also, a French botanist, (the same who has now again accompanied Captain Baudin in his voyage of discoveries) during the time of his being at Bagdat procured and lately brought to Paris a fine inscription, which was found in that neighbourhood, and which contained characters resembling the Persepolitan ones. Of this inscription, M. Millin, the present keeper of the Cabinet of Antiquities, has procured a plaster cast to be made, which is one foot and a half long, and one foot broad, for the purpose of sending copies for the inspection of the foreign literati; one of these is expected to arrive soon in London.

Our curiosity, however, is now still further and sufficiently excited by the twelve original bricks which have lately arrived in London, sent from Bagdad to the East India Company, and which contain inscriptions perfectly according with the Persepolitan ones, thus confirming M. Beauchamp's discovery. They are of two different kinds: one of those which were merely dried in the sun, the other of those which, like ours, were baked in a furnace. This circumstance wonderfully corresponds with the account given by Herodotus in his first book, in which he relates, that Babylon being in a situation deprived of stones, timber, and other materials for building, nature had abundantly provided for this defect by an inexhaustible store of clay, of the best quality, fit for preparing excellent bricks, which, either dried in the sun or burnt on the fire, acquired a strength sufficient to resist the injury even of many centuries. These bricks are in thickness three inches: their length and breadth is between twelve and thirteen inches, and it was with such bricks that not only Babylon, but, if we may believe Josephus, the famous Tower of Babel was constructed. This last historian further pretends, that after the deluge two columns were erected by the children of Noah; the one, like our Babylonian bricks, and the other of stone, in order to be able to resist both elements, the water and the fire, in case of a second catastrophe.

A principal question occurs here for solution, viz. whether the above inscriptions are to be read horizontally, and beginning from the left hand, like the characters of the Sanscrit, and other languages of India and Europe; or whether they are to be read from the right hand to the left, like the Hebrew, the Arabic, and other Oriental dialects; whether they must be read perpendicularly, either from the top to the bottom, like the Chinese, the Mungul, and the Japanese characters; or from the bottom to the top, as is related of the antient Mexicans, by the Jesuit Acosta, and of some nations in Asia at the present day. Niebuhr and Tychsen lean to the former opinion, viz. that they are to be read horizontally, and from the left to the right; whilst Raspe thinks they ought to be read perpendicularly, and Wahl pretends, that they run, at least sometimes, from the right to the left.

Another question, likewise, suggests itself, whether these nail-headed characters are of the alphabetic kind, like ours in Europe; whether they are of the syllabic kind, like the Habessinian, the Devanagari, and other Oriental alphabets; or lastly, whether they are hieroglyphical, like those on the Egyptian Pyramids, or, at least, expressing complete ideas by arbitrary signs, like the characters usual amongst the Chinese, and amongst a number of nations, different in language, in the south-east regions of Asia. Hyde, a hundred years ago, took them to be mere scrawlings or useless ornaments, totally destitute of any sensible signification; and indeed M. Witte, Professor at Rostock, in a pamphlet lately published, endeavours to prove the same; while others again will have it, that they contain great mysteries, and are even denotative of the secret doctrines of the Magi. Niebuhr, who has brought to Europe the most accurate drawings of these characters hitherto procurable, contends for their being alphabetical, and, to confirm his opinion, adduces no less than three different alphabets for the same kind of writing. One of these M. Tychsen, at Rostock, has made use of, with a view to decypher a part of these inscriptions. To this notion, however, he seems to have gained no proselytes, and the explanation which he has given in his essay, lately published in Germany, appears so forced and unnatural, that it has already in a manner lost all credit with the German literati.

It may be further observed here, that Colonel, now General, Vallancy, in his Irish Grammar, published in 1773, affirmed, that the Persepolitan characters bear a strong resemblance to that species of writing which the Irish call *Ogam*. But the characters are so complex, according to Sir W. Jones, in his Dissertation on the Persians, and the variations so numerous, as to preclude an opinion that they could be symbols of articulate sounds. For even the *Nagari* system, he observes, which has more distinct letters than any one known alphabet, consists only of forty-nine single characters, two of which are mere substitutions, and four of little use in Sanscrit or in any other language; while the more complicated Persepolitan figures, as exhibited by Niebuhr, must be as numerous, at least, as the Chinese keys, which are the signs of ideas only, and none of which resemble the old Persian letters at Istahar. Thus far Sir W. Jones.

Amongst these and other opinions I hope soon to lay before the public, my own, in a larger work, and, by that means if possible, throw some further light on a subject which has not been hitherto sufficiently elucidated.

London, J. HAGER.
June 4, 1801.

INSCRIP-

INSCRIPTION ON THE BABYLONIAN BRICKS.

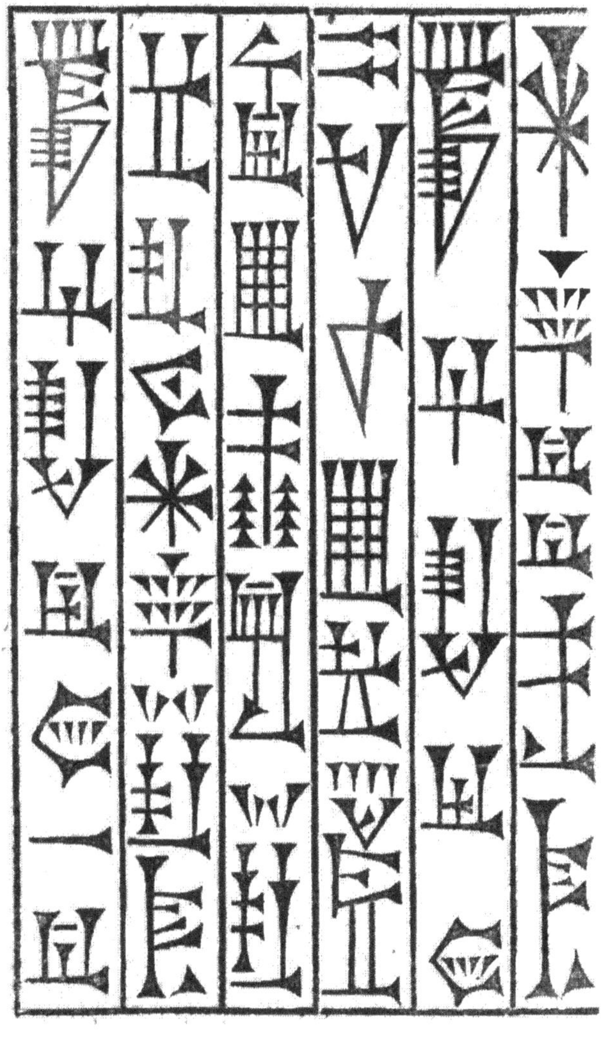

A VIEW, *shewing the* FACE *of a* BRICK. *All the* BRICKS *are composed of a* YELLOWISH CLAY, *somewhat redder in the Center, and they are in Thickness three Inches, and in Length and Breadth between 12 and 13 Inches.*

P. S. Mr. Montucci, *Occasional Chinese Transcriber*, has published proposals for a work *on the Characteristic Merits of the Chinese Language*, the title of which he has surrounded with Chinese characters, apparently to make a captivating shew of his learning, but which, however, more decidedly proves him to be merely what he styles himself, "*An Occasional Transcriber*." The upper line of these characters he has *transcribed* from a work published in England above thirty years since, namely, *the fifty-ninth Vol. of the Philosoph. Transact. Table* XXI. *line the 4th.*

The characters of the bottom line he has *transcribed* from Table XXIII. line 6th, of the same volume, where they occur in exactly the same order.

As to the two perpendicular columns, the one is *transcribed* from the other.

His Chinese motto—*Books do not exhaust words—words do not exhaust ideas*, he has *transcribed* from p. 323, of the first volume of the Memoirs of the Missionaries of Peking, where it is applied by Father Amiot to enforce the observation, that men of merit are sometimes slandered by obscure and base miscreants. "I am aware (says he) that the approbation of the truly learned and respectable is their security, but a Missionary, nevertheless, has the displeasure to see himself quoted in works of ignorance and falsehood; for *books do not exhaust words—words do not exhaust ideas.*"

Thus then has this *Occasional Transcriber* had the mal-adroitness of applying to another that which so aptly applies to himself.

The English reader should besides know, that, in all the fifteen 4to volumes of the Memoirs of the Missionaries of Peking, this is the only sentence expressed in Chinese characters. Is it not fair to conclude, that this critic, distressed for a motto on this occasion, was compelled to *transcribe*, not being able to find an original motto adapted to his purpose in the many Chinese books in Europe, which every where abound with such apothegms? Ought he not, at least, to have cited the author of his motto? Thus whilst this gentleman presumes to treat others only as smatterers in Chinese, he seems to prove himself, by the very title of his work, to be nothing but a literary plagiary, and a servile *Transcriber!*

July 11, 1801. J. H.

To

To the Editor of the Monthly Magazine.

SIR,

AS the public attention has lately been called to a dreadful abuse of that power with which the law entrusts, and must necessarily entrust, the masters of parish apprentices, in the case of Francis Jeveaux, of Greenwich, who was tried in the Court of King's Bench, on Friday the 22d of May, before Lord Kenyon, may I make a few observations on this method of disposing of poor orphan-children, and more especially of girls?

It appeared on the trial that this man had no less than seventeen miserable girls at one time in his power; that the two who had at length made their escape, were dreadfully emaciated by want of food, and other cruel treatment; and that five had actually fallen victims to his brutality.

Lord Kenyon very humanely observed, how much it was to be lamented that parish-officers, or even higher persons, did not look into these horrid abuses more than they did—that it was an employment worthy of the highest characters: and Mr. Justice Grose, on the 23d instant, in pronouncing the sentence of the law, very justly reprehends the parish-overseers, and even the magistrates, who signed their indentures, as partakers in the guilt, for never having given themselves the trouble to inquire what became of the unhappy victims whom they had thus consigned over to hopeless misery, and to an untimely grave.

The subject, it seems, excited, as it surely ought, the just indignation of the whole Court; and it has since been adverted to in many of the public papers, in which several humane proposals have been thrown out as hints for preventing such abuses in future; and Mr. Justice Grose expresses his satisfaction that "these points and topics have attracted the attention of the magistrates of that county (Kent), who have made an order, which if pursued may in future in some respects remedy the evil complained of:" but he does not state to the Court, (or at least the Sun, in which I read the account, does not mention the statement), what that order may be.

Every friend to humanity, Mr. Editor, must rejoice that this dreadful instance of abused power has excited such general attention, and some of the plans proposed to prevent such horrors in future are undoubtedly good, as palliatives. For instance, it would be well that the names of all poor parish-apprentices should not only be registered, but that these registers should from time to time be inspected by the clergyman, church-wardens, and other humane inhabitants of their respective parishes; that their regular attendance at church should be enforced, and that they should sometimes be personally visited. But are these proposals any thing more than palliatives? Do they strike at the root of the evil? Is there not something in the very nature of the contract itself, which by giving the power of exercising them with impunity, calls forth into action the very worst passions of the human frame?

It is not at all probable that Francis Jeveaux, of whatever atrocities he may since have been guilty, should have set out at first with the intention of treating these unhappy children in the manner he has done. That he must always have been an unprincipled character, we will readily admit, but it does not hence by any means follow that he was naturally cruel, much less that he was such a monster of cruelty as to have taken these unfortunate victims for the purpose of destroying them. His motive, in all probability, was simply the desire of gain from the produce of their labour; and although any view to their benefit can hardly be supposed, yet he may have persuaded himself, and would probably have replied to others, as many an Egyptian and West Indian task-master has done before him, that there could not be any fear of his ill-treating the children committed to his care, as it would counteract the very end he had in view, towards which the preservation of their life and health was essentially requisite.* It is even possible that at first his very nature would have revolted at the bare mention of such cruelty, and that with Hazael, when forewarned by the prophet of the effect on his mind which temptation and power would hereafter produce, he would have exclaimed, "Is thy servant

* To suppose of his previous character worse than is here stated, would indeed be to implicate the parish-officers, and even the magistrates, in an equal share of guilt; for to what less would their having placed unprotected children with such a monster have amounted, than consigning them to destruction of the most dreadful kind, merely to get rid of the expence of supporting them till they should be able to maintain themselves?

vant a dog, that he should do this great thing?"*

Where then shall we seek for the cause of this dreadful catastrophe, if not in the very nature of the contract itself? Are we not justified in supposing that this man, like many other unprincipled men, might have passed through life unstigmatized by any act of singular atrocity, had not a power like that which is given to a master over a poor unfriended parish-apprentice, supplied the temptation? And if such be its operation on the character of the master, and such the miseries which it may entail on the servant, what shall we say of the continuance of the practice?

That a suspicion of the fatal operation of contracts of this sort on the human heart, had struck the mind of Mr. Justice Grose when pronouncing sentence on the culprit, seems, I think, to be implied by his saying, that "the order made by the Kent-magistrates, if pursued, may, in *some respects*, in future, remedy the evil complained of."

Certain however it is, that the instance under contemplation is by no means a solitary instance. Children bound apprentice for their labour, and more especially girls, whether by a charity-school, by the Foundling-hospital, or by their respective parishes, are always liable to be, and in fact generally are, in some respect or other, unkindly, if not cruelly, treated; and the writer of this paper conceives herself fully authorized to affirm, having paid some attention to the subject, that how much soever, by the adoption of wise and humane regulations, their situation may be ameliorated, yet, that while human nature and the state of society remain what they are at present, children so bound will be less likely than others to conduct themselves well, and must always be exposed to improper and unkind, if not to very cruel, treatment. May she be permitted to refer, for the reasoning on which this assertion is founded, to an account of two charity-schools in the city of York, lately published by herself, in which the case of apprenticeships for labour is pretty fully considered; and the good effects exemplified of entirely abolishing the practice?

In hope of calling the attention of the liberal and humane to a subject which the first law authority in the kingdom has declared to be "an employment worthy of the highest characters." I am, Yours, &c.

York, June 30, 1801. C. CAPPE.

* 2 Kings, 10. 13.

To the Editor of the Monthly Magazine.

SIR,

I DARE say few literary men have been in company without hearing the question asked frequently, what would it cost to purchase all the new publications of a year? The work entitled *Annals of Philosophy and Literature* has enabled me to answer that question, and beneath will be found an account of the number and value of all the works, whether books or pamphlets, published in London in the year 1800. I cannot help remarking how nearly the total coincides with Wendiborn's Account, published in 1791, who estimated them at seven hundred. With respect to the value, it must be observed that the price is taken in boards.

Yours, &c.

A CONSTANT READER.

NUMBER *and* COST *of all the* NEW PUBLICATIONS, PUBLISHED *in* LONDON, *during the* YEAR 1800.

In Agriculture, 18 books, &c. amounting to	6	6	0
Antiquities, 15	27	3	0
Arts, Useful and Fine, 21	9	7	0
Biography, 13	4	7	0
Chemistry, ditto	3	16	0
Dictionaries, Grammars, and books of Education, 38	7	14	0
Dramatic, 42	6	12	0
Ethics and Metaphysics, 6	2	19	0
History, 24	20	17	0
Law, 24 } Trials at Law, 7 }	10	4	0
Mathematics, 5	2	12	0
Medicine, Surgery, &c. 60	15	17	0
Miscellaneous, 34	18	3	0
Natural History, 9	7	19	0
Novels, 40 about	20	0	0
Philosophy, 9	3	8	0
Philology, 12	2	12	0
Poetry (including Translations) 68	22	6	0
Politics and Political Economy 119	10	9	0
Theology, 43 } Sermons, 55 }	16	4	0
Voyages and Travels 20	15	10	0
Total number, 693.	£230	5	0

To

To the Editor of the Monthly Magazine.

SIR,

IF the following account of a district little known, and yet of no inconsiderable importance, should be thought acceptable to your readers, it is much at your service.

In that part of the principality of Saxe-Cobourg which is contiguous to the great forest of Thuringia, is situated the little canton of Sonnenburg, comprising an extent of about eleven square leagues. Of these nearly eight are taken up by a mountainous projection of the forest, exhibiting a striking assemblage of rocks, and torrents, and woods, with a few villages in the most fertile spots; while the great mass of the population is spread over the remaining three leagues. The whole number of inhabitants is about 13,000, occupying 2200 houses, which are collected into six small towns, and seventy villages and hamlets; their cattle and horses amount to 8500. Potatoes form the chief sustenance of the people, and provisions in general are very cheap.

Destitute of the convenience of water-carriage, and without any materials except those which are furnished by their own rocks and forests, it would be impossible for this little tract of country to support half its present population, without the most patient and unremitting industry. Much of the territory is not suited for the improvements of agriculture; the inhabitants have therefore from time immemorial applied themselves to manufacture, more especially of those various articles that are known over all Europe by the name of *Nuremberg wares*. At the fair of Frankfort they have long enjoyed peculiar privileges, for which they make a yearly acknowledgment to the chief magistrate of samples of their various manufactures. The value of these small articles amounts annually to about 8000l. of which the principal are pill-boxes, sieve-frames, looking-glass frames, chessboards, chessmen and draughts, hand-organs, slates to write on, gun-flints, and a variety of childrens' toys, such as whistles, fiddles, marbles, dolls, baby houses, horses, coaches &c. From the great division of labour many of these articles are sold surprisingly cheap: numbers of little whistles are made, and pass through the hands of three or four workmen, whose wholesale price at Sonnenburg does not exceed four shillings for seventy dozen. Besides the traffic in these small goods, there are three forges worked in the mountains, which, besides supplying the wants of the inhabitants, export tools and implements of wrought iron. Some heavy rough goods, as timber, potash, lamp-black, and pitch, the produce of their forests, are sent by land to Kronach on the Mayn, whence they are distributed to the districts down the river. At the village of Steinach is a manufacture of Prussian-blue, and at Hoemmern are vitriol works, and black, brown, yellow, red and white earths for the painters. Glückſthal and Lauscha possess glass-houses, where they make bottles, apothecaries' vials, beads, enamel buttons and looking glasses to the annual amount of about 5000l. A manufacture of porcelain has of late been established at Limbach, and already yields a profit of above 3000l. Such are the various methods in which the inhabitants of Sonnenburg render the public tributary to their industry: all the rough materials are the spontaneous produce of their own territory; their manufactures are articles of universal and regular demand in civilized society; industry is the hereditary portion of Germans, and therefore their prosperity is fixed upon as durable a basis as any thing human can be.

To the Editor of the Monthly Magazine.

SIR,

THE annual meeting of the subscribers to the charity for the Relief of Married Women during lying-in, and Sick Persons, established at Tottenham High Cross, Middlesex, in 1791, was lately held. From an inspection of the books it appears, that the first year only 14 persons were relieved—second year 35—third year 52—fourth year 64—fifth year 78—sixth year 79—seventh year 94—eighth year 91—ninth year 102—tenth year 94.

This useful institution is supported by the trifling subscription of six-pence, weekly, from each subscriber, which supplies linen to every inhabitant of the parish, male or female, who applies for it, in case of sickness; and enables each subscriber to give away two tickets in a year, to either a sick or lying-in person, whom it entitles to eleven shillings, besides the privilege of linen.

This charity was first formed on a very confined scale, under the auspices of eight ladies only; it is now patronized by a numerous and respectable list of subscribers, and has given birth to most of the similar establishments in different parts of the kingdom. P. W.

To the Editor of the Monthly Magazine.

SIR,

I HAVE read with pleasure the various descriptions of the State of Society and Manners in many Towns of this Island

Island and have pursued with delight the meandering paths which many of your Correspondents have led us in their topographical descriptions; but, whilst my eye dwelt with extacy on the happy state of their civilized inhabitants, and my imagination rioted on the romantic scenery, and feasted on the luxurious landscape which surrounded their abodes, I secretly regretted that I was not personally acquainted with many of the objects which excited such sensations of pleasure within me, and I was sorry that I could not join in rearing the monument of affection, to the witness of departed years, or boldly stand up in vindication of its rights. Permit me to avail myself of the improvement of late adopted in your work, by publicly paying a tribute of affection to a place, which, since my first acquaintance with the same, I have often revisited with increased satisfaction; and by attempting to pourtray a sketch of the manners of its inhabitants, the simplicity and unassuming amiableness of which I have often beheld with admiration, and which, though distant, I still remember with unabated pleasure. The subject of the present letter may perhaps to many appear trifling and unimportant; but, when I recollect that the more minutiæ every individual branch of knowledge embraces, the more its limits are extended, and the more perfect its system is rendered, I cannot but think that by far the greater part of your readers, who are convinced of the importance of Topographical History, will acknowledge the utility of such an attempt, nor condemn the description of a *Village* as despicable and insignificant.

In the West-Riding of Yorkshire, at a small distance from the high-road leading from Leeds to Bradford, and almost in the middle between both towns, lies the small, but neat village of *Fulnec*, a settlement of the *United Brethren*.* Situated on the slope of a rising ground, and assisted by the improvements of agriculture and the embellishments of the gardener, Fulnec presents a striking and agreeable view from the opposite hill; whilst the style and extensiveness of its principal buildings, together with the pleasing symmetry, so unusual in the plan of a village, arrests the attention, and rouses the curiosity of the inquisitive traveller. Unlike many of the settlements of the United Brethren on the continent, which, for the most part, seem to have been laid out, as chance or a relish for solitude directed, in the most dreary and uncultivated districts, Fulnec is not destitute of beautiful prospects: on the contrary, its situation is on that account peculiarly inviting; and the front view, which presents to the inhabitants a prospect of Tongstall, together with the range of an extensive park, and part of the village, situated on the gradual ascent of the opposite hill, is certainly very picturesque. The village itself consists principally of two long streets, neatly paved; and the buildings in particular of which the lower street is composed, exhibit an handsome appearance; amongst these, the chapel is particularly remarkable for its elegance and simplicity, with which the spacious buildings on either side, the one for the single men, and the other for the single women, agreeably correspond. Of late, several other buildings have been erected, between the chapel and the houses just mentioned; but although the symmetry of the view has, in a manner, been preserved, the effect is, in my opinion, totally lost. Before the front is an elegant terrace leading to the burying-ground; and lower still, is an extensive range of meadows, which in summer exhibit the most smiling appearance of verdure and fertility.

About the middle of the last century, the estate upon which Fulnec now stands bore all the marks of a dreary and uncultivated wild. The land, which now wears the appearance of a smiling Eden, was then partly a rocky and unfruitful soil, partly one continued swamp, overgrown with moss and bulrushes. But that adventurous spirit of enthusiasm which characterizes all the undertakings of the United Brethren—which has led them to explore the icy regions of Labradore and Greenland, and to penetrate into the burning desarts of Africa—was not to be daunted by such trifling obstacles. With indefatigable zeal, the ground was quickly cleared by the new settlers, many of whom had forsaken their families and connections on the continent, to enlist under the banners of the worthy founder of their sect; and, in a short time, the superior cultivation of the estate, on which the small colony was formed, exhibited striking proofs of the industry and unwearied diligence of its inhabitants. Nor was it long before many of the adjacent villagers, led either by curiosity or by a uniformity of principle, flocked to the place, and joined the Brethren. The name of *Lambshill*, which had, at first,

* Other settlements of the United Brethren in this country, are Oakbrook, in Derbyshire, and Fairfield, in Lancashire; besides which, they have *Societies* in many of the principal towns.

been given to the settlement, was soon changed into that of Fulnec, after a small village in Moravia, from which country the United Brethren were formerly, on account of their religion, obliged to emigrate; and in the space of a few years, the number of its inhabitants amounted to above 600. Various manufactories were erected, and the enterprising spirit and industry of the colonists were such, that they quickly found them productive of much profit. The cloathing-business, in particular, was carried on to a very large extent, the greater part of the single men, whose number amounted to above 150, being employed in that line; whilst the majority of the single-women, of whom, more than 200 inhabited the *sisters'-house*, gained their subsistence by spinning.

But, although the novelty of the doctrine* of the United Brethren, in conjunction with various other circumstances, had enticed many to settle in the place, a great part of the new-comers soon lost their relish for the principles of the Brethren, and found their regulations too rigorous and austere. Unaccustomed to any religious constraint, and unable to submit to the observance of orders and institutions, many of which they considered as a useless restraint, or even militating against the dictates of reason, a large number was induced to quit the Society, and to go elsewhere in quest of those advantages which they had vainly hoped to find amongst the United Brethren. Thus, by degrees, the number of inhabitants in Fulnec has dwindled away; and at present the place contains only 400 persons. In the present age, when nothing is more decried than the very appearance of religious controul, and when freedom of opinion and toleration of principle is fortunately growing daily more predominant, few will, perhaps, be tempted to join the society of a sect, whose principles, it cannot be denied, require, above all things, an implicit obedience to their Ministers, and an entire resignation of many things which a liberal mind is apt to consider as lawful and perfectly innocent.

It would, perhaps, sound ridiculous, were I to speak of the State of Literature in a village; and yet, even in this particular, Fulnec is, comparatively speaking, far beyond most villages. Whilst few, if any, of the wealthier part of the neighbouring village to which Fulnec belongs, have enjoyed the benefit of a university education, there are a tolerable number in this settlement of the United Brethren, who have prosecuted their studies with no small success in foreign seminaries of learning. Amongst these, the Rev. Mr. Hartley justly deserves to be named. His sermons from the pulpit are manly, eloquent, and persuasive; and the liberality of his sentiments, free from the smallest tincture of bigotry or mysticism, has justly gained him the applause of his small congregation, by whom he is universally admired and revered. Under the inspection of this worthy gentleman, whose talents as a scholar and divine are equally great, the boarding-schools of Fulnec have attained to a great and just repute in the neighbourhood. Convinced of the importance of the education of youth, Mr. Hartley has supplied his schools with able teachers, and has provided them, for the education of boys, with several gentlemen from the university; so that the youth have an excellent opportunity of acquiring, besides the usual branches of science taught at boarding-schools, a competent knowledge of the languages, both ancient and modern; of the mathematics, and of natural history, and natural philosophy in its fullest extent. In the regulations of this institution, he has wisely avoided those two disagreeable extremes, which so often characterize boarding-schools, and has exhibited a plan of education, the principles of which are equally remote from a barbarous severity and a licentious freedom. Nor have his labours been unsuccessful; the large number of young people of both sexes who have frequented the schools of Fulnec sufficiently prove that their parents and guardians are convinced of the utility of his plan, and approve of the means by which it is executed.——I was once the happy father of two hopeful children, whom, previous to my acquaintance with the settlement of the United Brethren, I placed, at the recommendation of a friend, in the school at Fulnec; and I had the inexpressible pleasure to see them, after having spent their time at school, return home to their family, with a considerable stock of learning; and, what was of more satisfaction to the fond parent, with minds uncontaminated by those vices which are so easily to be acquired at a public school.—There is one thing,

* For a full account of the religious principles of the Brethren, I refer your Readers to a work, entitled, "*An Exposition of Christian Doctrine, as taught in the Protestant Church of the Unitas Fratrum, or United Brethren, by A. G. Spangenberg.*"

thing, however, which I cannot pass over here without sensations of regret. It is undoubtedly highly beneficial for the moral conduct of the pupils in a boarding school, to be carefully attended by a great number of masters; but surely, whilst the teachers of a school are indefatigable in their zeal to promote the welfare of the youth intrusted to their care, they should not be suffered to languish in poverty, as I have been informed is the case in this settlement of the United Brethren.—— The school is possessed of a small but choice collection of books; and for the improvement and entertainment of such of the inhabitants who choose to read, a variety of periodical publications are regularly taken in.—Besides this, a Museum has lately been opened by Mr. Steinhauer, for public inspection; and as it is well supplied by the Missionaries in the English dominions abroad, it exhibits a tolerable collection of valuable curiosities.—Although it is in vain to expect to find in a village all the fashionable amusements of the town, such as plays, routs, assemblies, &c which are likewise contrary to the doctrine of the United Brethren, yet concerts are regularly performed every week in Fulnec; and I have more than once been present at a musical performance, which, though not to be compared to the efforts of a city-band, far surpassed my warmest expectations. The general taste for music, which prevails not only in this but in all the settlements of the United Brethren, is certainly to be attributed to the great part which music forms in their religious worship: nor have they been destitute of able composers, particularly in Germany, and the names of Worthington and Latrobe are in high veneration among their societies in this country.

As Philanthropy and universal Charity seem to be the leading principles of the United Brethren, it may easily be imagined, that the settlement of which I now write, is not remiss in exercising those noble duties, the due observance of which, the Divine Founder of the Christian religion so warmly enjoined to his followers. Indeed, so prudent and effective are the regulations which have been adopted by their congregations in general, to succour the distress and relieve the miseries of their oppressed Brethren, that a real mendicant has scarcely ever been known to dwell among them. Nor is their charity confined to persons of their own denomination alone; by an agreement of the leading persons in Fulnec, a soup-shop was opened during the late severe winter, and this nourishing article was liberally, though not without certain restrictions, distributed to the poor of the neighbouring villages. Since then, I have been informed, that a Sunday-school has likewise been begun for poor children of both sexes, which, from the well known perseverance of the undertakers, promises much success.

It is difficult for a person unacquainted with the nature of the establishment of the United Brethren to conceive the bare possibility of the astonishing regularity and order which are so conspicuous in every thing; but, if he reflects that a perfect unanimity in doctrine pervades the whole Society (for none but persons belonging to the United Brethren are permitted to live in their settlements), his astonishment will, perhaps, subside, and he will recognize the potent sway which congenial sentiments, particularly in religion, bear over mankind. Unbiassed by those petty animosities which so often originate among illiberal minds upon subjects of a religious tendency, the inhabitants of Fulnec and other settlements of the United Brethren are able to carry the most arduous undertakings into effect. Of this, their extensive missions in the remotest quarters of the globe, which could never have been executed without the joint concurrence and support of the whole community, is a convincing proof.——Their implicit obedience to their lot, and their resignation to submit to the decrees of the same, even in cases which reason or human prudence are sufficiently able to decide, evinces, in my opinion, a firm belief in the divine guidance of it, strongly tinctured with mystic enthusiasm.—How far the separation of the sexes can be approved, I shall not pretend to determine. The sentiments of the celebrated author of "*Hanley Penson; or, the Melancholy Man,*" upon this subject, are probably well known to the generality of your Readers. He speaks, if I mistake not, in favour of the *Sisters'-houses*, as an asylum for that sex, which is exposed to such numerous dangers; but condemns the *Brethren's-houses*, as an hindrance to marriage, and even as prejudicial to the interests of the state. The manners of the United Brethren, as described by this author, though certainly taken from life, are, however, far from being a faithful representation of the United Brethren of the present day, and can only be applied to the state of their congregations shortly after their establishment in this country. It is true, those principles are still in force among them, which di-

rect

rect an almost total separation of the sexes, and the division of the sexes again into choirs; nor have any of their religious ceremonies, as Love-feasts, the Pediluvium, &c. been abolished; but that strange appearance of mysticism, and that cold reserve towards strangers, which was formerly, and, I believe, justly imputed to the United Brethren, has almost totally subsided; and their language and hymns are, for the most part, free from that amorous and mystic enthusiasm which, at a certain epocha, characterized the writings and verses of many of their leaders, but to which their respectable Founder, Count Zinzendorf, was an entire stranger.

But it is not my intention, Mr. Editor, to trouble you with a tedious descant upon the doctrines and regulations of the United Brethren, a task, which I find myself equally incapable of executing and unwilling to attempt; I shall therefore crave your attention to a few remarks upon the present state of trade in Fulnec, and then beg leave to conclude.—With the decrease of inhabitants, as mentioned above, it is natural to suppose that the manufactures and other branches of trade in Fulnec were either entirely ruined, or materially injured. At present, no business of any kind whatever is carried on to so great an extent, as formerly. A great part of the single women (*single-sisters*), whose number, at present, amounts to about 100, are employed in making embroidery, with orders for which they are supplied by different houses in London; whilst the single men (*single-brethren*), who have, by degrees, dwindled away to 30, are employed in different businesses belonging to their house. One particular branch of trade deserves notice, I mean, the manufactory of spinning wheels according to Mr. J. Antes's* newest inventions, which is superintended by an ingenious mechanic, Mr. Planta. — It cannot, however, be expected, that the manufactures of Fulnec will ever attain to their former flourishing state, as long as the principles upon which they are chiefly conducted at present, remain in force. As few of the trades are suffered to remain in the hands of individuals, but are the joint property of the Society, to whom the sole profits devolve (which are appropriated towards defraying a variety of unavoidable expences); it is natural to suppose, that few persons are found willing to undertake the management of the same, upon the low terms which are usually proposed; nor can any thing be more pernicious to the interests of the community, than that strange custom of committing the concerns of different branches of trade, by way of reward for past services, into the hands of persons who are often wholly ignorant of the business. By adopting more liberal principles in this respect, and by encouraging trades of every kind, the greater part of the congregations of the United Brethren abroad have attained to a singular perfection in various branches, and display a state of prosperity far superior to what is seen in their settlements in this island. Nor can it for a moment be doubted, that the principles of the Societies of the Brethren in Germany are particularly favourable to the promotion of trade, when we reflect, that many of the foreign princes have so liberally encouraged their settlements.—Even the great King of Prussia, Frederick II. was so well convinced of the advantage which he derived from their colonies, that he invited them to settle in his dominions; and, almost contrary to the principles of the Prussian Government, gladly consented to exempt them from bearing arms.

Should any remarks in the present Essay be erroneous, or any assertions unfounded, for which, although I have made the strictest enquiries into the circumstances here detailed, I cannot sufficiently vouch, it will perhaps excite one or another of the community to rectify those mistakes, and correct those errors into which I may have fallen, by exposing them in a subsequent paper, through the medium of your valuable work.

Like most persons with whom I have conversed concerning the doctrines and manners of the United Brethren, I must confess, I was at first not a little prejudiced against the same, by the strange accounts which I had either heard or read of their Societies. A nearer acquaintance, however, with their principles, and with many respectable individuals belonging to their community, has sufficiently convinced me, that those accounts were, for the most part, false; and I gladly seize the present opportunity to subscribe myself,

A FRIEND OF THE BRETHREN.

May 20th, 1801.

* For an account of the same, see, "*Memoirs of the Royal Society.*" Mr. Antes has, of late made himself known to the literary world, by his "*Remarks upon Egypt.*"

For

For the Monthly Magazine.

The ENQUIRER, No. XXV.

ON HEREDITARY VIRTUE.

MAY not virtue become hereditary? May not the habits of morality, at first acquired by individuals through the continued influence of good government and good education, become, in the course of a few generations, so far *congenite*, as to affect the organization of the brain, and thus be transmissive to posterity? I am eager to answer in the affirmative.

There is not any dispensation of Providence so trying to the heart, and so unaccountable by the head of a philosopher, as the melancholy train of hereditary maladies which visit the innocent offspring of licentious parents; infants who are born to suffer, as it were, under a penal law of life, and to whom nature seems to deny the tranquil happiness that attends the mere consciousness of existence. The critics have been somewhat at a loss to account for the poetical injustice committed by Virgil, in placing the souls of infants at the entrance of the infernal regions.

Continuo auditæ voces, vagitus et ingens,
Infantumque animæ flentes in limine primo,
Quos dulcis vitæ exfortes, et ab ubere raptos,
Abstulit, atra dies, et funere mersit acerbo.

Might not the pious poet have intended particularly to describe the morbid progeny of vicious parents, and to have selected such a place for their doubtful and ambiguous criminality, confounding, in his uncertain ethics, the sufferings of the children with the sins of their progenitors? However conjectural this may be, I must add my conviction, that the debasement and degradation of our mental powers are liable in the same manner to descend by inheritance. He who habituates his nature to vice and servility will impress a proclivity, *anterior* to any possible effect of education, on his yet unborn child. Let every parent feel the truth!—And the nation, which for a series of years has naturalized its habits of indolence or corruption, will have little chance of regeneration by its internal energies. Let every people believe in this fact!

From such a view of human nature I feel refreshment and consolation in reflecting that health, and that virtue (the health of the soul), may, with equal certainty, be propagated to posterity. My idea is this: That by a proper manner of unfolding and perfecting the faculties and dispositions of the individual, the early custom (and education is nothing more) will, in time, become the moral habit, and the moral habit will at length grow into the physical constitution, which, after a few generations, will devolve in succession, with at least as great certainty as hereditary maladies, and by thus effectually counterbalancing the misery they occasion, will vindicate Providence, and console the heart that revolts at the sight of unmerited suffering. In the same way I think the manners of a people, which are nothing more than prevalent habits of the plurality, may become intimately and physically united with the morals, and consequently with the happiness, of a whole people, and being as it were incorporated into their nature, humanity may not only arrive at that state of perfection in which every individual becomes a law to himself, but in which the whole society may become like an individual, confident of the hereditary morality of his descendant. Thus human nature, in its personal or national character, may be bred downward, until the animal organization become so vitiated, that a public will as certainly tend to corruption, as a person will succeed to the inheritance of consumption; while, on the other hand, the individual and the public may be bred up to physical and constitutional virtue and happiness.

I wish to believe that this theory is practically exemplified among certain classes and descriptions of mankind; and I will venture to ask, if the family of Christians, called Quakers, do not illustrate, in no small degree, this doctrine of hereditary virtue, this innate innocence, this primitive purity and instinctive aptitude for the truth and the right, getting such an assimilation with the bodily frame, as to germinate with the first principles of existence? I know not whether it may appear the credulity of imagination, but I think that the distinguishing attribute of this sect—*Equanimity*—has been so long the principle of education, that it is now become not a second but an original nature, and is discoverable in that undisturbed regularity of features, particularly among the females—that placidity of countenance—by which I do not mean merely those irradiations of good-humour, equally superficial and evanescent, but an infelt serenity of soul—a deeply-charactered composure—which has impressed the more solid and permanent organization.

Quakers have been called the Jesuits of Protestantism; but I rather think they are, on the whole, the best copyists of their Master, and of primitive Christianity, in their practice, though, perhaps, not altogether

together so in doctrine. Jesuits indeed they are, for they live in the practice of that rightful equality which Jesus was sent to inculcate by his doctrine and example—an equality not merely a fiction in the ceremonial of public worship, but which goes abroad and mixes with the duties and relations of life—an equality built upon this truth, that my rights are your duties, and your duties are my rights; and thus it being impossible to take away a right from another without the violation of a duty, the vice and misery of mankind must proceed from the uneqnal distribution consequent upon one part having lost their rights, and therefore, of necessity, another part having forgotten their duties. Without distinctions of rank, of order—without supporting any priesthood, the Quakers prove their vital Christianity in their deportment—in their temperance, regularity, cleanliness (the virtue of the body, as virtue is the cleanliness of the soul)—in their serene chearfulness, in their domestic economy, in their maintenance of their own poor, in their parental care and attention to charities, in their bounty to the honest and unfortunate bankrupt, in their proper sense of the precariousness of life, by admonishing and enforcing the seasonable settlement of their property, in collecting together, at stated times, with the familiarity of friendship and the brotherhood of humanity, and, flowing from a long consistency of such moral habits, a character of countenance, a kind of reflected glory from the face of their Divine Master, which beautifies the external visage, and makes such men equally respected by the refined politician and the ferocious savage. Mirabeau bowed to them from the Chair of the Convention, ; and when the Indians meet them in the desert, the cry of battle ceases, the tomahawk drops out of the hand, and they say to one another—"These are the men of PEACE!"

As an instance of that inverted education, which in process of years has influenced the animal constitution, I would mention the Jews, in whose gloomy and anti-social visage, suspicious look, timid air, general diminutiveness, and mean physiognomy, I see the degradation of nature, and an instinct of servitude. Recollecting that I once was an Irishman, I contemplate with disgust and horror what humiliating effects may be produced by the loss of OUR COUNTRY, until at length we reluctantly cast our eyes on the place of our nativity, and disperse ourselves into every corner of the globe, to be tolerated only by the contempt of all nations. If the native Irish have been bred downward into a state of bigotry and barbarism, it is because, through the continued agency of a miserable maxim of government, they have been politically insulated in the island they inhabit, and expatriated in their own country. Their religious system has been (strange as it may sound) endeared to them by persecution, and the crimes of our ancestors in their misrule of Ireland are punished in the epidemical moral maladies—in the hereditary constitutional bias to riot and rebellion—which has been for so many years the political education of the country. The Jews may be said to remain, even in their dispersion, still insulated, by their manners, and their prejudices, but more than all by connecting, like the Mahometans, all knowledge, or every thing worthy to be known or regarded, with their religious system. While the Koran, the Talmud, or the Vedas, are supposed, in the estimation of their respective followers, to include not only the religious, but the civil and municipal law; all innovation must appear an impiety, and ignorance, credulity, with excessive proud predilection, will be the constant concomitants of character, and will have even a hereditary influence, noxious to posterity. This identity of the civil and religious code is in other countries only an alliance of church and state; but this system has been attended, in a great degree, with the same effect of throwing a sort of religious horror upon all political innovation, and making the Reformer be deemed an atheist as assuredly as he is accounted a rebel. It is this commixture of religious and political interests which has instilled into this war the venom of persecution; and while I in part agree with the writer who assigns the barbarities committed by the lower Catholics, in the late rebellion, to the ferocious bigotry of religion (the natural and necessary disease flowing from ignorance and political incarceration), I might ask, whether the peculiar exasperation of this war is not, in the first instance, ascribable to that *specific* rancour infused by another order of men, who have put whole classes of the people under the anathema of impiety and atheism. I might ask, whether there can be, in its effects on the manners of every rank, so truly an Anti-christian and Anti-social conspiracy, as that of an *exclusive* religion, whatever be its name, either that which

denounces

denounces the eternal sufferings of another life, upon all those of a different communion, and thus instigates the ferocity of a Popish populace; or that which restricts all the blessings and benefits of this life to one particular mode of worshipping God, and thus instigates to that unfeeling selfishness of character, which I consider to be the dissolution of the body political, as putrefaction is of the natural body.

Through the despotism of two penal codes, that of the priesthood in cultivating ignorance, and that of mal-administration in the political insulation of the Irish people, they have been so long kept, if I may use the expression, in a state of solitary confinement, as must influence the very construction of the national character. I think, if the new-born children of a Quaker, of a Jew, and of a wandering Gypsey, were nurtured and bred under the same roof, and in the same manner, they would, notwithstanding, manifest a hereditary and constitutional difference of both physical and moral character; and I believe a nation may be bred downward to such a degree, by design, or by neglect, that it will require the process of some generations, to re-ascend to that common perfectibility of human nature, which developes the seeds of knowledge and virtue. Or, "as to make a tree bear better fruit than it used to do, it is not any thing you can do to the boughs, but it is the stirring of the earth, and putting new mould about the roots that must work it;" so, may not great political revolutions be periodically necessary to diffuse, and intermingle the seed of society, and place it in such a soil of new circumstances, as is better suited to the growth and maturation of moral character?

For the Monthly Magazine.

DESCRIPTION *of the* GALLERY *of* ANTIQUES *in the* CENTRAL MUSEUM *of the* ARTS *in* PARIS.—*With a Plate.*

(Continued from p. 499.)

V. Salle d' Apollon.

THIS hall* is ornamented with four beautiful pillars of red oriental granite, (*ffff.*) each of which is four mètres, and one decimètre high, and forty-three centimètres in diameter. The two which stand on each side of the Apollo of Belvedere, came from the church at Aix-la Chapelle, in which was the mausoleum of Charlemagne. The floors of the first three halls are of inlaid work; but this, the Hall of Laocoon, and the next following, where the statues of the Muses stand, are paved with rare and beautiful marble. The ceilings of the preceding halls contain paintings in fresco: in this it is white. A beautiful large octagonal table, of oriental red granite, indicated on the plan by the letter *m*, occupies the middle of the apartment.

* Hall of Apollo.

No. 125. *Mercury*, known by the name of *Antinous* of the Belvedere, (or *Mercure Lantin.*)

No. 126. Over this statue they have fixed into the wall a bas-relief, representing the *Throne* of Saturn. On an architectonic base, in the middle of the bas-relief, stands a kind of throne, partly covered with drapery. On the *suppedaneum*, or foot-stool, there is a globe bestrewed with stars, and enriched with the zodiac. On the left, two winged Genii bear Saturn's crooked knife, or the *harpé*; on the other side, two other Genii seem to contend for the sceptre of the God. This bas-relief, of Pentelican marble, was many years in the Hall of Antiques of the Louvre. Italy possesses many such bas reliefs, of the same size, and in the same style. There are two in the choir of the church of San Vitale at Ravenna, and represent the Throne of Neptune; a third is in the church della Madonna de' Miracoli, in Venice; and a fragment of a fourth, representing the Throne of Apollo, is at Rome, in the Villa Ludovisi.

No. 127. A small statue of Grecian marble, *Apollo Sauroctonos*; or, The Slayer of Lizards: he is exactly in the same attitude as the one in the Museum Pio-Clementinum: only the sculptor who repaired the statue, has very improperly put a lyre into his hand.

No. 128. A small *Statue of Mercury*; remarkable on account of the various attributes which are united in it. It has wings on the head, the caduceus in the hand, the tortoise under the left foot, and leans on a small pilaster ornamented with arabesques, such as were placed at the barriers of the Gymnasia.

No. 129. A *Venus* coming out of the bath: in her left hand she holds a towel to wipe herself with, and with the right she covers her bosom. She stands in the attitude of the Venus sculptured by Menophant. At her side stands a small square box; instead of which, the Gnidian Venus, by Praxiteles, to which she in other respects bears a great resemblance, has a vase. This statue, of Grecian marble, was taken from the Gallery at Versailles. The left hand, only, is by a modern artist.

No. 130. A small statue of *Mars*, with helmet and buckler.—(Lunesian marble.)

No. 131. *A young naked Apollo*, of Parian marble, with the lyre in his left-hand. The torso of this statue is executed in an excellent style of workmanship: the rest has been well supplied by a modern artist.

No. 132. A statue commonly called *Urania*, because Girardon, who restored the head and arms that were lost, placed upon her head a crown a crown of ſtars, and put a roll into her hand. Her attitude, and the motion of her left-hand to hold up a part of her garment (as ſufficiently appears from the folds, which are executed with great taſte) might lead us to conjecture that it is a *Spes*. This ſtatue was taken from the Gallery at Verſailles.

No. 133. A well-preſerved ſtatue, of hard Grecian marble, which repreſents the *Delphic Apollo*, ſupported by the tripod, and with a branch of laurel in his left hand. The parts ſupplied by a modern artiſt have been executed agreeably to ancient Greek coins. This ſtatue ſtood formerly in the Chateau of Ecouen, near Paris.

No. 134. A *Tripod*, of Pentelican marble, found at Oſtia in 1775. Taken from the Muſeum Pio-Clementinum.

No. 135. An *Antinous*, in the ſame attitude as the Antinous from the Muſeum Capitolinum.

No. 136. *Iſis Salutaris*; from the Muſeum-Pio-Clementinum.

No. 137. A ſmall, well-preſerved ſtatue of *Minerva*, of Luneſian marble, with remarkable attributes. At her feet is the ſerpent, the often inviſible guardian of her temple at Athens: her ſhield reſts on a winged giant, with ſerpent-feet, and with the ſtem of a tree as a weapon in his hand:—probably the giant Pallas or Enceladus.

No. 139. *Mars Victor*, a ſtatue of Pentelican marble, into the hands of which the artiſt who repaired it, placed a globe of the world and a ſcepter, becauſe he believed it to be a Roman Emperor.

No 140. A ſmall *Melpomene*, found in Attica.—(Parian marble.)

No. 141. A ſmall ſtatue of *Juno*, of Pentelican marble, with the drapery moſt taſtefully executed. The arms are by a modern ſculptor.

No. 142. The *Capitoline Venus*.

No. 143. Above the laſt mentioned ſtatue a beautiful bas-relief is fixed into the wall. It repreſents a Suovetauril, and was formerly in the veſtibule of the Library of St. Mark, at Venice. Antonio Laſreri publiſhed a copper-plate-engraving of it in 1553, at which time it ſeems to have been in the Palace of St Mark in Rome.

No. 145. *The Apollo of Belvedere*. On the 16th of laſt Brumaire (two days before the opening of the Gallery), Bonaparte, accompanied by a numerous retinue, viſited it, and affixed between the plinth and pedeſtal, the following inſcription:

La Statue d'Apollon, qui s'élève ſur ce piédeſtal,
Trouvée à Antium ſur la fin du XVe Siècle,
Placée au Vatican, par Jules II, au Commencement du XVIe,
Conquiſe l'An V. de la République, par l'Armée d'Italie,
Sous les Ordres du Général Bonaparte,
A été fixée ici le 21 Germinal An VIII.
Première Année de ſon Conſulat.

On the back ſtood the following inſcription:

Bonaparte, Ier Conſul
Cambacérès, II Conſul
Lebrun, IIIe Conſul
Lucien Bonaparte, Miniſtre de l'Interieur.

The pedeſtal of the Apollo is on a perron two ſteps high, ſo that it is elevated above the ſtatues ſtanding near it, and may be ſeen from the Hall of the Laocoon by the admiring crowd which is conſtantly aſſembled before it.—In front, beſide the ſteps of the perron, ſtand;

No. 144 Two *Sphinxes*, of red oriental granite; both from the Muſeum Pio-Clementinum. The perron itſelf is paved with the moſt precious marble. In the middle, ſix tables of antique moſaic work are inlaid, repreſenting, beſides other ornaments, animals drawn by birds.

No. 146. *Venus of Arles*, which was found in that city in the year 1651, and had till now been preſerved in the Gallery at Verſailles. Of hard, rather aſh-coloured marble. When Girardon repaired it, he put a mirror into her left, and an apple into her right-hand By being placed ſo near to the Capitoline Venus, this ſtatue is rather thrown into the ſhade. Perhaps it would have a more pleaſing effect, if no ſtatue ſtood on each ſide of that of Apollo.

No. 147. Above the *Venus of Arles* a bas-relief is inſerted into the wall, repreſenting a *Conclamation*. It is of Luneſian marble, and has been for many years paſt in the Hall of Antiques in the Louvre. Maffei and Dom Martin ſaw it there, and publiſhed drawings of it. It ſeems however to be only an imitation of an antique work of art, and probably was made ſo late as the commencement of the 16th century.

No. 148. The *Indian Bacchus*, with the Greek inſcription "*Sardanapalus*;" from the Muſeum Pio-Clementinum. Mongez, member of the National Inſtitute, has endeavoured to prove, to the great aſtoniſhment of Viſconti, in a prælection, which is printed in the *Decade Philoſophique, l'an* IX. No. 5. page 265, that this image (executed in a beautiful Grecian ſtyle!) is a portrait-ſtatue of Elrogabalus, who, Herodian tells us, reſembled the beautiful image of Bacchus.

No. 149. *Hercules*, carrying the little Telephus in his arms:—or *Hercules Commodus*, as it is commonly called. From the Belvedere.

No. 150. An *Apollo*, of hard Grecian marble, which ſtood formerly at the *Boſquet de la Colonnade* in the Garden of Verſailles. It is in the ſame attitude as the Lycian Apollo deſcribed by Lucian; the right-arm lies on the head; and in the left, which reſts on a ſtump of a tree entwined with a ſerpent, he probably held his bow.

No. 151. The *Egyptian Antinous* which was dug out of the ruins of the Villa Adriani. This ſtatue is of Pentelican marble, and formerly ſtood in the Muſeum Capitolinum.

No. 152. *Bacchus*, in the attitude of reſt, cloathed in the *nebris*. This ſtatue, of excellent

cellent workmanship, and in a good state of preservation, was formerly in the Gallery at Versailles. Mellan published a print of it.

No. 153. A beautiful colossal *Bust of Serapis*; from the Vatican Museum.

No. 154. A *Mercury*, of Pentelican marble, exactly in the attitude of that of the Vatican, No. 125. This was still more clearly characterised by some attributes in the head, for instance, he had two holes, into which the wings had evidently been fixed; and part of the caduceus is likewise ancient.

No. 155. The *Capitoline Juno*; according to others, a *Melpomene*. From the Museum Capitolinum.

No. 156. One of the most beautiful statues of Bacchus extant, of Pentelican marble. He is quite naked, and in a careless manner rests his left arm on the trunk of a tree. The head, which is in a state of perfect preservation, and from which the long locks of hair flow down to the breast, is encircled with ivy and the Bacchic fillet.

No. 157. Over the Bacchus a bas-relief is fixed into the wall. It is modelled after one in the Villa Borghese, and represents five young women, holding one another's hands, and dancing round a temple.

VI. *Salles des Muses.**—No. 165. A head of *Bacchus*.

No. 166. A *pillar of Oriental granite*; somewhat dark-grey and green, with slight shadowings of rose-colour, and white spots. The base and capital are of bronze, gilded, and richly ornamented.

No. 167. A *Head of Hippocrates*, as it is called. Of Pentelican marble.

No. 168. *Calliope*.—From the Museum Pio-Clementinum.

No. 169. *Apollo Musageta*.—From the same.

No 170. *Clio*.—From the same.

No. 171. *Melpomene*.—From the same.

No. 172. A *Hermes* of Pentelican marble, with a head of *Socrates*. It is engraved and described in the VIth Vol. of the Museum Pio-Clementinum.

No. 173. *Polyhymnia*.—From the same Museum.

No. 174. *Head of an Indian bearded Bacchus*; long supposed to be a head of Plato.

No. 175. The *Bust of Homer*, from the Capitoline-Museum.

No. 176. *Erato*.

No. 178. *Euterpe*.

No. 179. *Terpsichore*.

No. 180. *Urania*.

No. 181. *Thalia*.—All five from the Museum Pio-Clementinum.

No. 177. A *Euripides-Hermes*, of Pentelican marble; stood formerly in the Academy of Mantua; as likewise,

No. 184. The *Head of Virgil*, as it is called.

No. 182. Another *Head of Socrates*.

No. 183. A very beautiful pillar of African marble.

These are the antiques which are at present placed in the six apartments which have already been opened. When the whole is completed, the principal entrance will be in front, immediately from the Place de Louvre into the Hall which in the Plan is called *Hall of the Torso*. Whether more apartments will be fitted up for the reception of antiques, is not yet determined upon; but it is very probable that there will, especially if all the relievos and smaller antiques, which are partly very disadvantageously placed in the upper rooms of the Gallery of Paintings, and partly in the National Library, should be united to the Central Museum.

In some of the rooms, as for instance in that of the Belvedere Apollo, the windows are built up breast high; denoted in the plan by parallel lines. In winter the rooms are well warmed, by means of flues or *tuyaux de chaleur*, as they are called. In the vestibule through which the visitors at present pass into the inner court, some modern bronzes are placed, *cccc* in the Plan. In the *Hall of Illustrious Men*, pillars stand on a breast-high wall, *b b*, by which the halls are separated from one another. During the first three decades after the opening of the Gallery, the afflux of gaping spectators was, as it might be expected, very great, and somewhat troublesome to artists and real amateurs. But the flood of public curiosity will soon subside, and then nothing can surpass the still enjoyment of the spectacle here presented to the man of taste.—The light, upon the whole, is excellent, and the distribution of the statues has been made with great judgment, as in general they occupy in the very high apartments the places where they may be viewed to the greatest advantage. The group of the Laocoon, in particular, when seen from the principal entrance, will have a more sublime effect, than even Apollo of Belvedere at present when viewed from the Hall of the Laocoon.—That the sculptors of the *New* French school are not unworthy of daily having before them the most perfect models of antiquity, will probably soon be proved, by the increasing excellency of their productions. At least we may augur well from the bas-relief, of four feet and a half, by *Moitte*, which, soon after the opening of the exhibition, was placed over the door that at present leads to the Gallery.

* Hall of the Muses.

lery. It represents Minerva, as the Patroness of the Arts and Sciences, holding a lyre in one hand, and a crown of laurel in the other. Both the purity of the design and masterly execution of this figure have met with general and well merited approbation.

For the Monthly Magazine.

EXTRACTS *from a* LETTER *of the Rev.* H. TOULMIN, *dated* CHILACOTHAC, *Territory North West of the* OHIO, *19th. of April*, 1801.

THIS place is on the Scioto river, about 40 miles from where it empties into the Ohio. It is beautifully situated, and, though laid off but four years ago, is become a considerable place. When I came down the Ohio, the Scioto was the most dangerous part of the western country for Indians. I passed it with dread. The settlements are now wonderfully extended and scattered over the whole country. I came hither to buy land for a gentleman in Massachusets and myself, which is selling for the taxes due on it; but fear it will be almost labour lost. We purchased between 70 and 80,000 acres at Frankfort last winter, of which I expect we shall save a good deal. But I shall be forced to sell when the titles are ascertained, as the taxes on so much will be very burthensome. I have been much concerned to hear of the extravagant prices you have been forced to give for provisions: with us, on the other hand, flour has been four dollars and a half a barrel of 196 pounds: Wheat half-a-dollar a bushel: Beef, by the carcase, one dollar and three-quarters per 100lb. Much flour has been sent to New Orleans for exportation; but we are told that some of your ships have blocked up the mouth of our river, the Mississippi. Often have I wished that the intercourse between this country and yours were such as to admit of my sending a few barrels to you. Enough flour has been sold to give us some little money among us; of which there is, at present, an amazing scarcity: as the poor officers of government have felt to their cost, their salaries being all reduced.

There is at present a wonderful stirr of religion (as the phrase is) in Kentucky. Hundreds of people are baptized in several neighbourhoods, sometimes twenty a day. But this, not because the understanding is convinced—not because they have read the Scriptures and admire them—not because they are convinced of the truth of Christianity, and deem it right to make a profession of their belief—but because they have once or twice dropped into a meeting-house, where the preacher has threatened damnation to the unconverted, and promised heaven to the baptised—where the groanings and lamentations of the minister—the screamings and clappings of the people—the experiences of the converted, and all the train of apparatus calculated to operate on the imagination, have assured them, that the only path to happiness is to be baptised, and to observe the great characteristics of conversion; viz. an abhorrence of dancing, music, and card-playing.

I am looking with a good deal of anxiety for Mr.———, &c. If he will prosecute his business here,* he may make a handsome property; for we must manufacture goods for our own consumption. Indeed, at present, industrious farmers make cloth enough to clothe their own families. Even our governor's daughters are spinners: and their example has its influence on others, who affected to feel themselves above it: but they all want the right implements.

Dr. ——— (Mr. ———'s friend) is at Lexington. He has repeatedly staid at my house. He came on account of his land here, which he purchased in London; I think it is 20,000 acres; but the greater part I fear very indifferent, and bought very dearly: being in a poor, mountainous part of the country.

To the Editor of the Monthly Magazine.

SIR,

THE facility with which my last communication received admission into your Magazine has induced me again to trouble you: and, in consequence, I now send you *A Sketch of a Journey from Copenhagen to Hamburg*, which, though containing little information, may perhaps be rendered interesting by the present political state of the North of Europe.

The distance from Copenhagen to Hamburg by land (as it is termed) is about 70 Danish miles.† There are three modes of going this journey, which are:

* That of a cotton-manufacturer.

† The Danish mile is 4½ English miles nearly, i.e. 14¾ Danish miles make a degree of 69½ miles. It is difficult to compute the exact distance in some parts of this route, as the road is only measured in the island of Zealand: but the whole may be reckoned at about 310 English miles. In the following sketch, when I mention distance, it will, to prevent calculations, be in English miles.

first, that of purchasing a carriage, and travelling with post-horses. This is the most expensive way of travelling; and though in this case it is usual to dispose of the carriage at Hamburg, yet it will hardly sell for half its cost. The *second* mode is travelling extra post: and the *third* is with the common post, which carries the mail, and which leaves Copenhagen twice a week. This latter is a very expeditious but disagreeable mode of travelling, as the passengers are allowed a very short time at each stage for refreshment. The post travels very quick; the whole journey is usually performed, in summer, in 54 hours, and the greater part of the way with only two horses. But the mode of travelling adopted by those who have cheapness for their object, is by water, in a packet-boat to Kiel, and from thence by land to Hamburg. After examining these several modes, I preferred that of extra-post, for these reasons; 1st because it is less expensive than purchasing a carriage; 2d, you are not liable to detention on the road; and, 3d, it is of course much more pleasant and agreeable than the common post. As I wished to see the country, the packet-boat was out of the question.

The journey extra-post is performed in an open carriage with four wheels, called a waggon (Dan. "*Woggon*"), the driver of which sits on a small seat in the front; and in the body of the machine, which is generally hung on leather, are two or three seats, with room also for the baggage. Some of these carriages are well hung, and not inelegantly made, but in general little can be said in their praise. They are called Holstein post-waggons; the style having been brought from that country. The extra-post is established by the Government for the accommodation of travellers; the charge is regulated, and the driver wears the king's livery (scarlet faced with yellow), with a small French-horn slung across his shoulder, which he blows when any carriages stop the way, and they immediately make room for him to pass. The post-houses on the road are obliged to provide horses; and in case the passengers insist upon it, they must not be detained more than a quarter of an hour at each post-house.

I left Copenhagen for Roskild, the 8th of April 1796, in a hackney-coach (if I may be allowed the expression), accompanied by a friend who was also going to England. These vehicles are as easily procured in Copenhagen as in London. There are about 180 in constant use; some of which are always ready in the stable-yards; the fare of them is moderate, the horses are not bad, and the coachmen are generally very civil. They do not go farther from Copenhagen than to Roskild.

In my last, I conducted you to the King's new market, instead of crossing which diagonally to the king's theatre, we, to avoid the ruins, kept to the right, along the side on which is the new town, and passed through *Gronné-gadé (Anglicè* Green street). This is a fine broad street, half a mile in length, containing some handsome houses*: it divides the old town, which is on the left, from the new town. At the upper end of this street are the ramparts, † at the foot of which is a road for carriages, extending round the greater part of the city. We proceeded along this road till we reached the West Gate, through which we passed over the fosse, by means of a draw-bridge, to the high road. The first object which strikes the traveller here, is the obelisk formerly mentioned, and a mile farther on the road is the *Skydé bån*, called by the English, the Shooting-house. This house is fitted up as a place of public entertainment; and is well attended, particularly on a Sunday-evening, by the citizens of Copenhagen. Near this a very excellent road turns off to the right; it is broad and straight, about a mile in length, and planted on each side with a double row of fine trees, something like the Mall in St. James's-park: it leads into the high road to Elsineur. About a mile and a half further, after ascending a hill, we arrived at the palace of Fredericksburg. Here we looked back and bade farewell to Copenhagen, which I could not do without feeling some regret, as the Danes by their treatment gave me every reason to be satisfied with my stay there. They are certainly hospitable to strangers, and appear to be particularly fond of the English.‡

* The reader would have a very good idea of Copenhagen, if he were to procure a plan of that city to refer to, when he peruses this as well as my former Sketch. Without this aid, I should despair of making any relation of this kind plain or perspicuous.

† The ramparts are the usual promenade in the summer season for the *beau-monde*: and for a trifling sum (4 or 5 rix-dollars) a ticket may be purchased, which enables the proprietor to ride on horseback on them without molestation.

‡ Indeed this was the case on most parts of the Continent, before this destructive war and its attendant consequences cut off all direct communication of the greater part of it with England.

The appearance of Copenhagen from this eminence is grand, though at the same time it could not be viewed with unmixed pleasure, as several of the fine churches were without their spires, and surrounded by scaffolding for the purpose of repairing the damage done by the late terrible fire.

Descending the hill we lost sight of the metropolis, and pursued our journey to Roskild. There is nothing worthy of relation on the road; the country is well cultivated, and at intervals we have a view of the sea. The boundaries of the fields are chiefly banks of clay. On a former journey I had occasion to remark that in this part of the country the fields were ploughed with horses yoked together, sometimes to the number of eight or more, when two or three would have answered the purpose. On our arrival at Roskild, which is 18 miles from Copenhagen, we discharged our coach, and found good accommodations provided for us by our servant, whom we had sent on before for that purpose, as it was our intention to remain here a few days.

Roskild, formerly called *Roeskilde*, is at present a small town, containing about 200 houses. Some centuries ago, when it was the metropolis of Denmark, it was situated immediately on the bay of *Isse fiord*, from which it is now half a mile distant. The court was held here, and it contained the kings' palace, the cathedral, and thirty other churches and monasteries. All that now remains of ancient Roskilde is the cathedral, where the royal families of Denmark have for many ages been buried, and the ruins of a royal palace.* The cathedral, which is not large nor magnificent, was built A. D. 930: its architecture is more simple than the Gothic style. It contains some monuments which are worth attention; particularly four elegant *mausolea* in alabaster of late kings and queens. These were executed in Italy, and the workmanship does great credit to the abilities of the artist. A book is given to those who view the cathedral, which contains an account of the royal personages buried here, and of the great actions which they performed in their life-time. (Of course the battles which they gained are not forgotten). By this book it appears that the first king who was buried here was Harold Blaaetand,* A.D. 980. and the last was Frederic V. (surnamed the Great,) buried A. D. 1766. There is little in the churches in Denmark, or indeed in any of the reformed churches in other countries, which attracts attention, as they have no paintings, and the sculpture that sometimes makes its appearance is seldom above mediocrity. This want of decoration is not a subject of complaint in the Roman Catholic churches on the Continent, in which the eye is often wearied by the continual and unvaried round of altars, paintings, and sculptures. This town is famous for a treaty of peace having been signed here, between the Swedes and Danes in 1658, which is called "the peace of Roskild." The houses are old, and no trade is carried on except by the country-people for their implements of agriculture, &c. During our stay a fair was held, at which, as the French would say, we *assisted*; there was a good shew of horses, of which a few were saddle-horses, but the bulk consisted of those calculated for labour. A good draught-horse might have been purchased for 30 or 40 rix-dollars (6l. or 8l. sterling). The Danish horses are in general bony and sure-footed, but (according to the horse-dealers' phraseology) they have no blood. In Copenhagen and in the army, German and English horses are much in use.

We left Roskild the 12th of April in an extra-post-waggon, and we now had cause to congratulate ourselves on the goodness of the roads in this part of the country. I had formerly travelled in Holland, Flanders, &c. and I found that the *pavé* rendered the jolting of the carriages almost intolerable; but here this was not the case, as the roads are kept in such perfect order that they are as smooth as the floor of a room. There are no guards to the travelling vehicles in this country; they are not requisite, as highway robberies are seldom if ever heard of. The roads are always safe, which may be attributed to the Danes not having arrived at the height of civilization of more southern countries; and by this

* The person who shews the *curiosities* of the *ci-devant* metropolis assured me, that one of their kings, of the name of *Hamlet*, was poisoned by his brother in the garden belonging to this palace. Whether this be true or false, or whether the man had heard the story immortalised by the pen of our dramatic poet, and wished to impose upon us, I cannot determine.

* Some modern travellers say that this is Harold, (surnamed Harefoot), king of Denmark, England, and Norway; but the date will not agree with this: as Harold Harefoot succeeded to the throne of England in 1035.

this means, though they remain in ignorance of the conveniences and elegancies attendant on a higher ftate of cultivation, they have alfo the confolation to know that they avoid many of the vices infeparably joined with luxury. Their wants (I fpeak of the middling and lower claffes) are few, and thofe they have are eafily gratified.

Our next ftage was *Ringfted*, 18 miles from Rofkild. When the latter was the metropolis, this was a large city; it is now degenerated into a very fmall and inconfiderable town. But ftill it retains fome of its old privileges. The church, dedicated to St. Canute, which may be feen at a great diftance, is now in ruins; it is of Gothic architecture, and has been magnificent in its time. It contains the tombs of feveral of the royal familie. of Denmark. While we ftopped to change horfes, I obferved in the inn a fett of prints, called the *Kiobenhavn Skildere* (*Ang.* Copenhagen Magic-lantern): thefe are political caricatures,—fatires on the court of Copenhagen; they fhew that the Danes are not deficient in fpirit, nor incapable of properly appreciating the fooleries of courts and courtiers. At this town a road turns off to the village of Köge, lying on the bay of that name.*

The next ftage is generally a very long one, it reaches as far as Slagelfe, which is a diftance of 27 miles; but as we wifhed to vifit Soröe, where my friend was well acquainted, we difcharged our waggon at the *Krébs'-büfet* (*Ang.* Crabs'-houfe), an inn within a mile of that place, and 9 miles from Ringfted.

The *Krébs'-büfet* is very pleafantly fituated on the banks of a lake, which in this time of the year is always well ftocked with cray-fifh (Dan. *Krébs*), from which the inn takes its name. The gentry who live near this place fometimes refide here a few days in the fummer feafon, to eat this fifh in perfection, with which alfo excellent foup is made. The inn, though fmall, has good accommodations; and, what is of as much confequence, the people are very civil and attentive to their vifitors, and their charges are moderate.

The town of *Soröe* is in a very retired fituation; it is built on the fide of a large piece of water; the air is pure, and the country round is beautifully variegated with hill and dale; it is woody and in fome parts highly cultivated; but the boundaries of the fields being of ftone, give that part of the country a heavy appearance. There are feveral fmall farms about this town, which we vifited, and found the inhabitants very comfortable, and to appearance happy; but they are not in that fituation fo as to exclude all anxiety for the future, as the great landholder ftill has the power to remove them from the fields which they have exerted their induftry in cultivating and bringing to perfection, to other parts of his eftate which require their labour. The benevolent Count de Bernftorff, though he did much for this ufeful and induftrious clafs of men, could not do all he wifhed. He well knew that the reformation of longftanding abufes, if intended to be of permanent utility muft be gradual.* That much has been done for thefe poor people cannot be doubted, when we compare their prefent ftate with what they were formerly†, and with that of their northern neighbours. The peafantry of Denmark are hofpitable, at leaft as far as their means extend; they are unpolifhed, but not rude; neither have they that inquifitivenefs which has been remarked as fo very obtrufive and difgufting in other countries‡. The fimplicity of the Danifh as well as of the Norwegian peafantry is that of nature, and not of depraved or premature

* Kiöge-bay is celebrated latterly as the rendezvous of the fleet of Admiral Parker, after the *famous* battle off Copenhagen: a battle which will doubtlefs caufe the Englifh as well as the Danifh name to be *recollected*, and *properly eftimated* by pofterity.

* For the abolition of the Slave-trade in the Danifh Weft India Iflands, which this great man projected and endeavoured to accomplifh, he caufed a law to be enacted, impofing a penalty (fufficient to amount to a prohibition) on any one concerned in this infamous traffic after the year 1803. So that, unlefs *recent events* prevent it, we may have caufe to hope that this unfortunate race in thefe iflands will be emancipated from their galling yoke, and in due time reftored to their rightful place in fociety. Of the man who does not rejoice at this information, the *negro himfelf* may truly fay—Hic Niger *eft*; *hunc tu caveto!*

† On this fubject a writer of veracity, at the beginning of the 18th century fays, "The peafants of Denmark are as abfolute flaves as any in Barbadoes, but not fo well fed; they are fold with the land to which they belong, as timber is with us: fo that the land-holders eftimate their riches not by the number of acres, but by the number of boors." See "Molefworth's Hiftory of Denmark."

‡ I allude more particularly to the lower claffes in the United States of America.

premature civilization, aiming at independence of character, though hardly emerged from the ignorance of a state of barbarism. But the character of these people is of course much influenced by past times: from the state of servitude in which they have been kept, they appear to look up to the higher classes with that kind of awe which is generally observed by those who travel through countries where the feudal system has been carried to such an extent as in Denmark. The peasants are in general cleanly in their dress, and they wear wooden shoes. Few, if any, can read or write,—they have no spirit of inquiry or of enterprize,—no wish for improvement—and, with respect to intellect, they appear, like the inhabitants of Hindústàn, to have remained stationary for ages. This digression will, I trust, not appear impertinent, as it serves to throw some light on the character of a people but little known.

Soröe, which was in former times, like Ringsted, a place of considerable note, is now only the size of a small village, containing about 80 houses. Its famous academy, which had indeed the title of an university, and which was founded by Frederic II. for educating young noblemen, and hence called *Academia Equestris**, is now no more than a lodging-house for two or three young men, sons of merchants at Copenhagen, who are kept here by their friends that they may be away from the vices of the capital. The grounds about the academy are extensive, and kept in better order than could have been expected. The church, which is all that remains of the monastery of Soröe, where the famous Saxo Grammaticus was educated, is a fine piece of Gothic architecture deserving of notice.

During our stay at the Krebs'-hüset we amused ourselves in the day-time with shooting, as the country abounds with forests, in which there is plenty of game of every kind†; and the evenings were agreeably spent at Soröe, where we were very hospitably entertained, as well in the Academy as in the town.

On the 24th of April, we proceeded on our journey, through a pleasant and well-cultivated country, in which the prospect is charmingly diversified with country-seats, farms, woods, and pieces of water, but no rivers. We arrived at the small town of *Slagelsé*, at 4 o'clock, where we dined and changed horses. In this town there is nothing remarkable: the houses are ill-built, and the whole place has an appearance of poverty and decay. We strolled through the church-yard, and diverted ourselves with reading the epitaphs, which we found to be as puerile, though not so illiterate, as those in the country-church-yards in England, but enough so to shew that men will not scruple to make themselves appear ridiculous to posterity, rather than remain

——"to dumb forgetfulness a prey."

From Slagelsé to Korsöer, which was our next stage, is ten miles and a half. Three or four miles of the latter part of this stage is through waste-land.

Korsöer is a fortified town lying at the mouth of a small bay, forming a well-protected harbour, on the Great Belt. It has a few good houses which belong to merchants, as some trade is carried on from hence up the Baltic and in the vicinity. The fortifications are in ruins, and the town is chiefly inhabited by fishermen and sea-faring people.

Though it was night when we arrived here, we only stayed long enough to get our passes counter-signed*, and to procure a boat to proceed across to Nyebürg. We now found that we had saved ourselves much trouble and some expence by not purchasing a carriage at Copenhagen, as we first intended to do.

* Charles Gustavus, king of Sweden, was educated at this academy, on which account he spared both it and the town when he invaded the island in 1658.

† The game in Zealand is plentiful. The venison is *en haut goût*, but very lean, so much so that it is always larded when brought to the table. Indeed, the meat in general is not fat, though well-flavoured; but it is spoiled in the dressing. The poultry is good, but they have an absurd custom of killing chickens for the table when only three or four weeks old, which of course prevents the increase of this kind of poultry. The fish is excellent, particularly at Roskild and Soröe, where it is dressed immediately after it is caught. A sauce which the Danes eat with boiled fish is very palateable; it is made with horse-raddish grated small, mixed with cream and sugar.

* During our stay at Soröe we sent to Copenhagen for passes, which foreigners are obliged to take out, and are not allowed to remain in the island more than eight and forty hours from the date. It is the custom for strangers when they purpose leaving Copenhagen, to put an advertisement in the public papers; mentioning their names, places of abode, &c. and that they intend leaving that city on a certain day. This custom, for obvious reasons, would not be much relished by some of the numerous class of strangers who visit London.

The

The breadth of the Great Belt between Korsöer and Nyehörg is about 22 miles, but the wind being light and variable we were seven hours in crossing, and landed at Nyehörg in the island of Funen (or Fyën) at five o'clock in the morning. Three of the crew of our boat were old Danish seamen; and though they had been many years at sea, their manners were yet simple and to appearance uncontaminated. I have had opportunities of being well acquainted with Danish sailors, and I have almost invariably found their characters to be that of good seamen; as they are very hardy and possess a great degree of courage, they are also attentive to their employments, and always obedient to the commands of their officers. R. STEVENS.

N. B. In my Sketch of Copenhagen, which you had the goodness to insert in your Magazine for May last, the height of the Round Tower is erroneous; it should have been 80 feet instead of 180 feet.

(*To be continued.*)

For the Monthly Magazine.

VIEW *of* RELIGION, MANNERS, &c. *in the* ISLAND *of* CORFU.

(*Continued from Page* 489, *Vol. XI.*)

THE number of churches in Corfu is very considerable. Each officiating priest is annually elected by the assembled parishioners; but he has no fixed salary. The greater number of those churches, especially those in the country parts, have been built by private individuals, who, as proprietors, nominate the *papa*. The priest thus appointed is upon the same footing with the others, except that he usually holds his office for life.

The richest of those churches is that in which are deposited the reliques of St. Spiridion, to whom the Greeks bear a peculiar devotion. The descendants of the family which possessed his venerated remains have always enjoyed a sort of apparent property in the church, to which they have the privilege of nominating the officiating *papa*. That benefice, as being one of the best, is always conferred on one of their own family.

The festival of Saint Spiridion is celebrated with the greatest pomp. A week previous to the day, the doors, windows, and steeple of the church are adorned with myrtle and laurel branches. Round the top of the steeple runs an iron balustrade, at the four corners of which are erected four long poles bearing four flags: that of St. Marc, the Russian, and the English, are always of the number; for the fourth, the Danish or Swedish or Dutch, &c. is indiscriminately chosen, but never the Turkish, nor that of France, which was not admitted even when France was a monarchy. The bells are kept incessantly ringing during the whole week. At length, on the eve of the festival, amid the sound of all the bells in all the churches, and the report of firing, the priests expose to the veneration of the multitude the sacred shrine containing the saint's body entire and in good preservation. The shrine is of ebony, covered with gilded silver plates of very neat workmanship, and enriched with precious stones. The front consists of a large glass plate, through which the saint is discovered, standing in an erect posture, and arrayed in his pontifical robes.

The governor and his household repair in a body to assist at this ceremony, which is performed with greater tumult than devotion. A detachment of sixty soldiers find a difficult task in maintaining order among the crowd of people who, during three successive days and nights, eagerly throng to the spot, to implore the protection of the saint. After this, comes a procession, in which the clergy of Corfu are joined by a host of *papas* from the neighbouring isles, and even from the Morea. The shrine is carried on a bier by six *papas* in sacerdotal array, under a canopy alternately supported by the governor and the other chief officers and magistrates. They are preceded by the governor's band of music, who, as well as his servants, are dressed in their state-liveries. The whole garrison are all the while under arms; and the chief part of them accompany the procession. So soon as, in the course of its stated round, it has reached the ramparts which cover the city on the side fronting the sea, all the ships of war, with their flags displayed, pay it a salute of cannon and musketry: the gallies and galliots, with their colours likewise flying, advance from their usual station, and sail along the shore under the ramparts, keeping pace with the march of the procession above.

During all this time the air resounds with the report of cannon and mortars: and the port of Corfu presents a most pleasing spectacle, especially if it happen to contain a great number of foreign vessels. In the streets through which the procession passes, the windows of the houses are decorated with tapestry of various colors.

The ceremony is necessarily of long duration on account of the slowness of the march.

march. It is besides frequently interrupted by the approach of sick persons whom their friends carry under the shrine in full confidence of an infallible cure. It usually happens that several of those sick persons fall into frightful convulsions, and cause great confusion: but such of the *papas* as are in the secret dextrously avail themselves of the circumstance to levy contributions on the credulity of the devotees. During the whole time that the body of the saint continues to be exposed to public veneration, the church is crowded with sick persons, who lie there stretched on their beds, patiently awaiting a cure, for the promise of which they are obliged to pay.

So long as the festival lasts, the *papas* are busily employed in gratifying the public devotion; one devotee earnestly praying them to read him a portion of the gospel, another equally desirous to obtain a wax-candle, a handkerchief, a ribbon, or any other object which had touched the saint's body. All these favors are paid for.

The reliques of Saint Spiridion are exposed with the most religious confidence in every season of public calamity. His church has been enriched by private donations; and the devotion of the islanders is a productive source of wealth to him: the mechanic, the mariner, fancy that they insure the success of their undertakings by devoting a part of the profit to Saint Spiridion. Not a barque sails from their port, in the profits of whose voyage the saint is not interested: the Greeks even of the Morea and the Archipelago are equally zealous in paying tribute to him.

The night between Holy Thursday and Good Friday is remarkable for the number of processions which perambulate the city. Every church, every chapel, has its own, in which is triumphantly carried a sepulcre previously prepared with the greatest possible munificence; for in this point there is a certain emulation between the different churches. Each sepulcre is surrounded by a great number of lighted tapers, each *papa* holding one of very large size in his hand, and each person who accompanies the procession being also provided with one. All these different processions, after having perambulated the streets, unite on the esplanade, where the light of their numerous tapers equals the splendor of day. All the churches are open: all the streets and public squares are crowded with people running from church to church, from procession to procession. The women, who on other occasions, do not appear at church except in a close-railed gallery, now enjoy full liberty. This night is the time when they contract new acquaintances or renew their old.—On every side people are seen going in parties to enjoy the spectacle of the processions, and to visit the churches: devotion serves as a cloke to curiosity, or to the accomplishment of preconcerted plans. These pious rambles are usually succeeded by feasts, which do not always terminate peaceably. The events of the night furnish an ample fund of conversation for the ensuing day.

The night of Holy Thursday is further remarkable for a superstition of a singular kind. Some people cause a shirt to be made for them on that night. The work must be performed by an odd number of maidens all named Mary; and the shirt, begun at midnight, must be cut out, sewed, washed, and ironed before day: all which conditions being punctually observed, it is believed to possess the inestimable virtue of rendering the wearer invulnerable. Such shirts are very scarce.

During the first days of April, a sort of banner is carried about the streets, presenting the figure of Lazarus in the moment of resurrection, and loaded with the most ridiculous ornaments, such as necklaces of mock pearls, handkerchiefs, ribbons of various colors, small looking-glasses, little pictures in frames, even children's toys and dolls. The dress of the man who carries this extraordinary banner is not less whimsical: Over his masculine attire he wears a red petticoat fastened with knots of ribbon. He frequently interrupts his march to perform a very lively dance, during which he waves his banner, and sings in vulgar Greek the resurrection of Lazarus. A wretched haut bois of very shrill note, exactly the same as is used by the itinerant bear-dancers, together with a large drum, serve as accompaniments to his song, of which the burden is repeated by several spectators, who sometimes also join in the dance. This banner and its escort do not fail to stop before the doors of men in office or persons distinguished by superior opulence. The dance and the song are repaid by a pecuniary donation: one of the assistants carefully picks up the pieces of money thrown from the windows, and puts them into a box, but not till he has shewn them to the standard-bearer and his musicians, who are to share the sum collected. On paying a small sum, people are permitted to kiss the banner, of which, after it has been thus carried through

through the city during several days, the decorations are sold to the devotees. The purchasers respectfully preserve those baubles, which they place at their bed-heads.

Each *papa*, especially in the rural parts of the island, is ambitious to celebrate the festival of his church* with as great pomp as possible. Some days before the time, he ornaments the doors, the windows, the inside of the church with flowers and foliage, of which the devotion of his parishoners saves him not only the expense but even the trouble of collection and arrangement. In front of the church, a square inclosure is formed of very lofty poles planted at small intervals from each other. On these is laid a platform of boards covered with a carpet, and surmounted by a roof made of ships' sails. At the four angles stand four poles much more elevated than the rest, and each bearing a flag. The entire palisade is decked with foliage, and ornamented on the inner side with different pictures lent for the occasion by various individuals. Nothing can be conceived more whimsical than the collection here exhibited, in which sacred and profane subjects are promiscuously confounded. Beside a weeping Magdalen or a Madona, a Laïs is seen displaying her charms: after having feasted his eyes on the consolatory picture of peace, the spectator suddenly beholds the bustle and carnage of a battle scene; or, after quitting the portrait of a king or queen, he next beholds the representation of a group of topers in a tippling-house. In this booth, the young folk assemble and dance to the sound of the haut bois and tabor. A game much in vogue on those festive occasions is the *pente me mia*, or five and one. It is played at a table on one side of which rises a hollow pillar having at the bottom a hole communicating with the table. Into the top of the pillar is thrown a ball, which, on coming out below, must stop at a card bearing the number five, to entitle the gamester to win.

At these festivals the butchers expose their meat to sale, and at the same time act as *traiteurs*. The repast is prepared in the open street or road: it is a sheep roasted whole, almost as soon as killed. The entrails are rolled round the body; and, before it has hardly had time to be sufficiently cooked, the guests seat themselves on the ground, and receive each his portion of the sheep. Barrels of wine stand ready broached at a short distance; and the same butcher acts moreover as vintner. At these feasts a strong patrol find it difficult to maintain the public peace: it is frequently disturbed by quarrels, which are the more dangerous as the Greeks of those isles are in the constant habit of wearing arms. During the whole time of the festival, the *papa* is busily employed in repeating prayers at the request of one or another of his flock; which prayers being paid for, he is seldom heard to complain ot being overburthened with employment.

In the isle of Corfu are several Greek convents of men and women, which are, in general, a dead weight on the shoulders of society. Some few indeed of the feminine convents receive boarders, who remain there until their friends think of establishing them in the world. The whole of their education consists in learning to spin and knit: it rarely happens that any of them is taught to sew, and still more rare that any one learns to read and write her native language, however imperfectly. Girls who return home endowed with such accomplishments are accounted prodigies.

The ignorance of the Greek clergy in general is so great, especially in the rural parts, as to have become proverbial; the most learned among them being barely capable of reading and writing their own language. Some of them, destitute even of those humble qualifications, know but one mass and a few prayers which they have learned by heart, and which they indifferently use on every occasion. For example, if there is question of praying for rain, and the *papa* happens not to be acquainted with the proper form of prayer for that purpose, he boldly supplies its place by a prayer for fair weather. This trifling mistake does not prevent him from receiving payment; and the ignorant *papa* succeeds as well as the most learned of his brethren.

The generality of the Greek priests, especially in the towns, practise a kind of painting which affords them an additional opportunity of levying contributions on the devotion of the faithful. The painting is executed on wooden tablets primed with a thick coat of white paint: the colors are prepared with white of egg. The subjects are all of a religious nature, the Madonna, Saint Spiridion, Saint George, &c. but not even a trace can be discovered in them of the principles of design; and

* The festival of the saint to whom it is dedicated.

and the colouring is the same in all: the flesh is every where of a blackish hue, and the ground is usually gilded. The *papas* sell these sacred pictures after having blessed them: and the sale is tolerably productive, since there is not a Greek, especially a female, who is not anxious to purchase them; every individual being desirous of ornamenting the head of his bed with a number of such pictures, before which a lamp is carefully kept burning, night and day. The *papas* would not easily pardon a foreigner who should attempt to rival them in that branch of the fine arts, as appears from the following anecdote which is given in the words of the traveler already quoted——

"I had a Greek servant, who had long teased me for a Saint Spiridion, to be substituted in the place of a Saint Michael overthrowing the devil under the figure of a winged dragon. The devil's head had been defaced: and my Greek, who bore equal devotion to both of the characters in the painting, no longer reposed the same confidence in its virtue after that accident. At length I was obliged to perform my promise of procuring him a Saint Spiridion, equally miraculous, at least, as his old Michael and his mutilated devil. I bespoke the interesting picture from a *papa*, whom I requested to paint it in my own house, and afford me an opportunity of admiring his talents. He very obligingly complied with my request, came with all the necessary apparatus, and immediately commenced his work. For his model, he had another Saint Spiridion, which he assured me that he had already above a hundred times copied with the most perfect accuracy of resemblance. The painter having, during an occasional absence, left his pencils and unfinished performance under my care, I took a fancy to try my hand in that style of painting: I succeeded beyond my expectations; and the *papa*, on his return, found his picture almost completed. Conceiving that I had performed a wonderful exploit, I was not a little astonished to find that the painter became quite angry, and bitterly complained of my behaviour. My servant, on the other hand, was deeply afflicted, as he could not suppose that a Saint Spiridion of my production possessed any efficacy. I appeased the priest by liberally paying for the picture which I had presumptuously dared to touch; and I consoled the servant by furnishing the expense of a new painting, which now was not executed in my house."

(To be continued.)

To the Editor of the Monthly Magazine.

SIR,

FROM the many discussions occasioned by the late frequent returns of scarcity, we have learned little more, than that our annual produce is far short of our annual consumption, and that, with seven millions of uncultivated acres, and all the incitement to improvement afforded by high prices, the annual deficit continues to increase to an alarming degree. Having had these facts established, we must conclude that there exist some very powerful obstacles, capable of thus counteracting the progress which might naturally be expected in such circumstances.

To investigate, and if possible to ascertain, what it is that can thus impede the natural progress of the country, would, I conceive, be an object highly worthy of the attention of the most enlightened correspondents of your excellent and useful miscellany. I will therefore, Sir, with your permission, invite them to the discussion, and venture to offer for their consideration, in the form of queries, a few ideas which have occurred to me upon the subject.

First. Whether the present laws of succession do not accumulate large tracts of country in the hands of those who possess little floating capital, and whether the impossibility of proprietors under such circumstances accomplishing any plan of extensive cultivation, be not a principal bar to the progress of improvement?

Second. What effect on the cultivation of the soil might be expected from the abolishing the right of primogeniture, so that heritable property might be allowed to circulate in the same free manner that personal property does at present? and whether it is probable, under such circumstances, that individuals would generally continue to hold more land than they could profitably employ?

Third. Would not every part of the soil thrown thus into a natural course of circulation, soon have the portion of improvement bestowed upon it of which it might be found capable? For does not daily experience shew us the important changes operated upon the face of any part of the country, which passes into the hands of new proprietors; changes most probably to be attributed to that ardor with which every man prosecutes new undertakings?

Fourth. If entails either virtual or positive are supposed to be absolutely necessary to the present construction of our society,

society, might not the purpose be equally well attained by permitting the entails to be made upon money in place of land, and is there not reason to think that the public funds might be sufficiently permanent to become the subject of such entails?

A CITIZEN OF GLASGOW.

For the Monthly Magazine.

An Account of RAVENSTONEDALE, *in the* COUNTY *of* WESTMORLAND.

THE almost universal approbation with which statistical inquisitions have been lately received, and their manifest utility in discovering the real state and nature of a country, and thereby directing to the different practical improvements of which it is capable, are considerations that have induced the writer of this article to submit to the public the following observations. It is also his intention, to extend his inquiries to the several districts of which this county is composed, and, if proper and authentic information shall be obtained, to continue his reports in some of the subsequent numbers of the Monthly Magazine.

Ravenstonedale, in all probability, derived its name from the great quantity of *raven* or *grey stones*, which abound in the southern extremity of the parish; though the late Dr. Burn, in his history of Westmorland, has traced it to a different origin. The river *Raven* however, from which he supposes the appellation to have been received, must certainly have existed in the Doctor's imagination only; as a river of that name is now wholly unknown. In a charter made in the time of Henry II. it is called *Ravenstandale*, which seems partly to confirm the derivation we have given; *stane* being still, as is well known, the provincial word for *stone*, throughout the counties of Westmorland and Cumberland. The extent of the parish is about seven miles from north to south; and at its greatest breadth, five miles from east to west. It is sixteen miles from Kendal, and twelve from Appleby: is bounded on the east by the parish of Kirkby Stephen; on the south by the parishes of Kirkby-Stephen and Sedbergh; on the west by the parish of Orton; and on the north by the parishes of Crosby Garret and Kirkby-Stephen.

The nature and quality of the soil have one grand division, formed by some rivulets that intersect and divide the eastern from the western part of the parish. These waters are also the boundaries which separate the various kinds of stone that are found here, and the disposition and inclination of the different strata. On the east side of the parish and of these rivulets, the soil is generally upon a fine limestone, but in some situations a sandy loam may be observed. On the west-side, the soil, though of an excellent quality and scarcely inferior to the other, is nevertheless totally dissimilar: it lies upon a hard kind of stone, provincially denominated *rag*, which continues to some distance westward without interruption, and with little or no variation. The difference in the disposition of the strata appears to be very remarkable: on the one side, they incline to the east; whilst on the other, they uniformly verge to the west. As a map of this parish has not perhaps ever been made, it is next to an impossibility, to ascertain with any degree of exactness the number of acres that Ravenstonedale contains. The inclosed lands have, however, been computed to consist of about two thousand five hundred acres; but this computation seems to be erroneous, and to fall short of the precise number.

From its elevated situation, and the vicinity of the mountains by which it is surrounded, it might naturally be supposed, that the atmosphere of this part of the country could have little to recommend it, and that the climate in winter would be very severe. That this is really the case, the inhabitants have sufficient experience. Great falls of rain and snow are very frequent. But during the months of January, February, and March, the cold is perhaps most intense; and at this season of the year the hills are generally covered with snow, which renders the air very chill and piercing. It does not however oft happen, that there is rain here when the wind blows from the east; the clouds being generally dissipated and broken on the high ridge of mountains, which separate Westmorland from Yorkshire. In the year 1777, the small pox was very mortal, and a great number of people died, all of whom, one excepted, had the disease naturally; since that time inoculation has been more generally adopted, and its beneficial effects have been highly visible. The vaccine or cow-pox was also introduced during the last winter, and was proved to be a more mild and easy disease than the small-pox, and a complete preventative against the infection of that disorder. Nor has inoculation for the cow-pox been confined to the practice of medical men only. Many have been inoculated by others, with great success. And in some instances, parents themselves have inoculated their

own

own children, and always perfectly succeeded. The inhabitants of this parish are in general a healthy and hardy race of people, of a robust and muscular form of body, subject to no particular disease, and many of them attain to an advanced age. There is one person ninety three years of age, who nevertheless enjoys at this time a good state of health. And there are others so stout and healthy at the age of eighty five, or eighty-six, as to be able to perform a great deal of work. It cannot however be denied, but that where the person is formed by nature with a weak and sickly habit of body, this country is by no means suitable for his constitution.

It is generally believed, that very good free-stone might be procured on some of the lands belonging to the Earl of Lonsdale, but at present there are no quarries of this kind wrought. In the hill called Clouds, some small and inconsiderable veins of spar and lead ore have been found. There are stones got in the parish, which are appropriated by the inhabitants to the uses of flooring and slating houses. Some of these stones are smooth, and will receive a polish, others are rough and contain veins of flint, and they are in general of a brown and darkish hue. Coals are brought from the Stanemore pits, a distance of eighteen miles, and sell at the rate of 5s. 6d. per cart load.* Peats also, which are got on the neighbouring common, are used for fuel by many families, and sell for 1s. 6d. the cart in summer, and for 2s. in winter.

According to Dr. Burn, whose history of this county was published in 1777, this parish contained 225 families, of which 59 were dissenters. The following is a copy of the late report made by the parish-officers on this subject:

Inhabited houses, in 1801, 224.—Uninhabited ditto 5.—Families 280.—Males 498.—Females 640—Employed in agriculture, 232.—Employed in trades, 54.—Other classes, 846.—Total, 1138.

It appears therefore that since 1777 there has been an increase of 55 families; and that the average number of persons composing a family, is 4 $\frac{1}{16}$ nearly. There are at this time in the parish, 43 families of Calvinist Dissenters, consisting of 172 individuals; and 4 of quakers, making 17 persons. There are also a few methodists, but they have no meeting-house, nor any constant preacher. Accustomed as I am to consider religion as the great basis of morality, and of the happiness of mankind individually and collectively; and more especially as the evils and calamities which have of late years pervaded and desolated Europe, appear to have originated from a contempt and dereliction of all religious worship; it is with the utmost concern and regret that I behold the increasing infidelity of the present age, already extended to the most retired and sequestered situations. Formerly, and perhaps also at no great distance of time, the church and the different dissenting meeting-houses in the parish might have been seen attended on a Sunday by a very numerous and respectable assemblage of people, and this when the population of the place was evidently less than at present. But

Tempora mutantur, et nos mutamur in illis.

Not to say worse, an apathy, or blameable indifference, respecting the sublime doctrines of Christianity and the rites and ceremonies of religion has pervaded the mass of the people. The church is very much deserted; and at the distribution of the sacrament, which according to custom takes place six times in the year, there are seldom more than twenty persons present.

The farms are very small, few being above 60l. a year, and varying from that to 10l. and under. Indeed the number of farmers in this parish is few, in comparison of the number of proprietors of land, who live on their own estates, and follow husbandry; there being generally reckoned three land-holders, or as they are here denominated *statesmen*, for one farmer. The number of yeomanry is however of late years much diminished, and the land is divided into greater portions, and has become the possession of a more opulent, but less numerous, set of people than formerly. To the man used to associate ideas of general plenty and prosperity with the increased affluence of a few individuals, and who knows not that wealth may possibly exist in a country, and nevertheless that misery and want may also exist in a still greater degree, a change of this nature will doubtless appear pleasing. But nothing is more certain, than that the comforts and conveniences of the people at large have decreased, in proportion as the influence and riches of a few have been augmented. The mode of cultivation in use, is probably not much different from that which was practised nearly a century ago. Men are naturally attached to ancient customs; and when their local situation contributes to render their attachments more strong, it requires much time, before improvements in

* The cart-load here mentioned, consists of 25 pecks of coals, and the peck contains 16 quarts, Winchester measure.

in agriculture of any considerable importance can be effected; since it is by slow and almost imperceptible degrees they will be communicated and adopted. And it must be from much experience and repeated observation, that the attentive agriculturist will learn to pursue that plan of cultivation which is most congenial to the soil and climate of his grounds, and best adapted to promote his own interest. Very little of the land in this parish is in tillage. Mr. Pringle in his Agricultural Survey of the County of Westmorland, published in 1794, says that in Ravenstonedale there are not sixty acres of corn. And I can very readily believe there would be no such number at that time; since at present, when the dearness of grain might be supposed a sufficient inducement to attempt the culture of this necessary article on every soil and in every climate, where any probability of success should present itself; and when more land is in tillage, than can be remembered at any former period; there are nevertheless not more than one hundred acres sown with corn. Those whose grounds are in tillage, take three or four crops of oats from the same land without intermission; and afterwards the land thus impoverished is left to recruit itself, without sowing upon it for this purpose any artificial grasses, as is customary in other countries. It seems astonishing that the coldness and moisture of the climate should be considered by the inhabitants as insurmountable difficulties attending the cultivation of corn, when it is well known, that in Norway, Sweden, and some other northern situations, where the cold is far more intense, and where the soil is in many places naturally unfertile, they nevertheless grow great quantities of grain. The cause of superiority in the culture and production of corn in those bleak and dreary regions appears to be the use of a kind of seed that ripens at a very early period, and which requires not for so great a length of time the warmth and nutriment of the sun to bring it to perfection. And were the same kind of seed of universal request here, the crops would, I doubt not, be much more prolific than at present, and be also sooner ready for the sickle. It is not so much the elevation of the country, or the vicinity of the mountains, as many suppose, that hinders the corn from ripening and being productive, but the use of a grain which cannot attain to perfection until the year be far advanced, when the great falls of rain that generally happen at that season, destroy the hopes of the husbandman, and render the crops of comparatively small value. With respect to potatoes, there are very few grown in this parish; and perhaps not more than two or three families plant a quantity sufficient for their own supply. The potatoes that are chiefly consumed here, are therefore brought from Appleby, for the carriage of which, in addition to the exorbitant price this article has lately fetched, and exclusive of impositions which are not unfrequent, they pay nine-pence for every eight Winchester pecks; insomuch that, during the last year, the Winchester bushel of potatoes was often sold for six shillings. It is impossible to assign any plausible or satisfactory reason, why an article that has been cultivated in almost every part of the country with the greatest profit and success ever since its first importation, and which is perhaps the most useful root that was ever imported into this or any other country, should be so much neglected in Ravenstonedale. It has been computed that an acre of ground planted with potatoes, will yield on an average three hundred and twenty Winchester bushels, which, if sold at the rate of two shillings per bushel, will leave 32l. for the rental of the land and other incidental expences. And if every landholder and farmer were to appropriate one acre of ground yearly to the raising of potatoes, than which nothing can be more profitable, there would not only be a quantity sufficient for the use of all the inhabitants, but a great provision for the support of horses and cows during the winter season would be also thereby effected.* Turnips also have been very little attempted. The general opinion of agriculturists, founded on I know not what foundation, is that they are a crop which will not succeed here. One person has this year sown a small field with turnip seed, the greatest quantity of land that has perhaps ever been set apart for this purpose. Ravenstonedale is most remarkable for its excellent meadow and pasture-ground; and, in this view of it, perhaps excels every other parish in Westmorland and Cumberland. It is probable, that two-thirds of this district may

* Before quitting this subject, it is not perhaps either improper or unnecessary to notice the method by which potatoes are usually cultivated here. They neither dig nor plough the ground destined for this purpose; but having placed upon it the intended manure, plant the potatoes, and spread over them a light covering of soil. A method very reprehensible.

con$\int$t

consist of meadow; and the rest which is not in tillage, of pasture-land. They generally reckon, that to pasture a cow five or six months will make her very good beef, and sufficiently fat for the market; and in some instances not so much time is allowed. Twenty yards of well got hay are also deemed fully competent for a like purpose, during the winter season: nor is corn or any thing else made use of in feeding cattle. The great price which fat cattle have fetched of late, has made the business of a grazier very lucrative, as some of those fed here have been sold for upwards of thirty guineas each. In instances however of this kind, the time required for fattening was generally much longer than is mentioned above; and a cow bought into the pastures for nine or ten pounds, is, after having remained there five or six months, usually estimated at eighteen or nineteen pounds. Sheep are commonly supposed to be sold from ten to sixteen shillings in advance, after pasturing. The number of sheep pastured here, does not probably exceed five hundred. They are denominated, from the great length of their wool, the long Scotch sheep, in contradistinction to the Cheviot-hill breed, the wool of which, though finer, is of a shorter nature. It is computed that four fleeces of those sheep will make a stone, and the stone sells for nine shillings and sixpence. When the sheep are fat, they weigh from ten to fourteen lbs. per quarter. Very good mutton is also sometimes killed off the common. Ravenstonedale, from its fine meadow and pasture-ground, is also noted for the excellent butter and cheese it produces. Much of this butter is carried into the counties of Yorkshire and Lancashire, and some of it into Northumberland. Butter is therefore the cheapest article sold here. For some time past however, on account of the high prices of provisions, the profits of the dairy have been likewise very great, and the value of land has thereby much advanced. It may be said with certainty and propriety, that the rents and advantages arising from farming and the cultivation of land, are in a great measure obtained from the quantity and excellency of the butter and cheese which this parish produces. In most counties they wash their butter with water, but here they do not; and nevertheless, greater neatness and skill cannot be exhibited, nor butter of a more excellent taste and flavour be obtained. The land in this parish pays no tithes; the landholders having purchased them of the then lord of the manor, a predecessor of the present Earl of Lonsdale. "In Ravenstonedale," says Mr. Housman, "where no tithes are paid, there are between 2000 and 3000 acres inclosed, four-fifths of which are let at the rate of four shillings to eleven shillings the acre, and the remainder at from twenty shillings to forty shillings." But this is certainly a mistake: the land lets *in general* for between thirty and forty shillings per acre, and some of it for more. The last year, some estates were let to farm at more than forty-five shillings per acre. The lands are seldom leased for a longer term than six years; and generally the leases are much shorter. This undoubtedly prevents all ideas of improvement, and the farmer, unless some agreement be previously made to the contrary, cannot be expected to advance the condition of the land he occupies.

(To be continued.)

MEMOIRS OF EMINENT PERSONS.

ACCOUNT *of* M. OESER, PROFESSOR *of* PAINTING, *and* DIRECTOR *of the* ELECTORAL ACADEMY *of* PAINTING *at* LEIPZIG, *in* SAXONY.

M. OESER, was born at Presburg, in Hungary, in 1717. He was destined to be a confectioner, but he never could find any relish in this sweet occupation. His first master in the arts was called *Kamanf*, who tormented him very much by employing him to copy prints, treated him often with boxes on the ear when he wished to follow his own ideas, and caused him thereby to run away from his apprenticeship. *Oeser* often related, in a humorous manner, the pedantry of the old man, and his own youthful tricks. At Vienna, where he properly got his first instruction in the arts, he lived with an old good-natured uncle, with whom the young, sprightly, and ingenious nephew might do whatever he pleased. There he acquired by his productions, not only the esteem and friendship of the then living artists of distinction, particularly of the Director *Von Scupen* and of M. *Meytanz*, but likewise the favour and affection of many great men. The youth who, together with the greatest liveliness, was possessed of much amiable modesty, was quite surprised, when his *Sacrifice of Abraham* won

won the first prize in the academy. Being of the Protestant religion, he had, according to the spirit of the times, much trouble to endure from the rage of making proselytes, by which the pious ladies and their confessors were infected; but he adhered constantly to the Protestant religion, and often beat off the converters by repartees, when he was not disposed to argumentation. The crowning of his *Sacrifice*, a subject equally interesting to the Christians of all parties, was probably the occasion of his taking the highest concern in this favourite subject of his youth, during his whole life. For a quite different reason, the *Family of Lot* engaged him in perpetual trials, how such a subject might be treated in a noble manner. His rash and sprightly temper entangled him in many disagreeable affairs, out of which he always got happily by his address in bodily exercises, and his presence of mind. In every thing he undertook, he was above the ordinary rate. He played with superior skill at billiards, fenced in a masterly manner, and as well with his left hand as his right; knew how to manage a horse with elegance, was an excellent shot, and often hit a swallow or a lark in its flight with a pistol. One of his most intimate friends at Vienna, was *Rafael Danner*, of whom he spoke always with emotion till his death, particularly when he looked at the portrait of his friend, or shewed it to others

The brilliant Court of the Augustus, at Dresden, the collections of the monuments of arts, and several of his countrymen, drew him towards the end of 1739 to Dresden; and from that time Saxony became his second mother country, where he only thought with a longing wish of Italy, whither he had always felt an inexpressible desire to go. At Dresden, *Winkelmann* and *Hagedorn* became his friends; and the former is, perhaps, mostly indebted to Oeser for his taste in the arts. Oeser made his eye sensible of what is beautiful or deformed; he taught him to see, as he used to express himself. The whole description of Rafael's Madonna is taken from the mouth of Oeser. In 1744 he was called to Petersburg, and was about to go thither, when the death of the Empress Anna frustrated his expectations. During this period, he got acquainted at Dresden with Miss *Orleburg*, whom he afterwards married, who had the most beneficial influence upon his whole subsequent life, and whose excellent qualities the old man often praised with a thankful emotion. Economy, a quality too often wanting in men of genius, was not a virtue of Oeser's; he seldom worked for money, except after he had spent his last ducat; whenever he could, he followed his own whims and ideas. In the seven years' war, he for the most part lived at Dahlen, with the learned Count of Bünau, whose apartments he painted, as he had been previously engaged to do. This Count of Bünau is a very high character amongst the German literati. He wrote a "*History of the German Empire*," full of matter and deep researches; and bequeathed his library, the catalogue of which, in six volumes in quarto, is still in high estimation, to the Electoral Library.

Towards the end of the war, Oeser went to live at Leipsig, where he had already made several valuable acquaintances. The Elector Christian establishing an academy at Leipzig for the improvement of arts, and leaving Oeser to chuse between Dresden and Leipzig; he preferred Leipsig, and was appointed Director of the Academy of Painting. He looked upon the time he passed at Dresden, and the first years of his abode at Leipzig, as the best period of his life, as well as of his performances of art. "Saxony has spoiled me," he would often say, in order to intimate that he often was obliged to comply with what modern taste required, and on that account he neglected, in some degree, the beautiful antique. His old friends were of the same opinion. He finished, some days before his death, a Head of Christ, painted in oil, which still shows the unimpaired glow of its master. The Sleeping Nymphs of Diana were his last production, which he painted while Schnorr, one of his most worthy disciples, read to him some scenes of Schiller's Don Carlos; they do not betray the trembling hand of a man of eighty two years. He died the 18th of March, 1799, and preserved his jovial, truly philosophic disposition of mind to the last moment. The former liveliness of his youth had subsided to an amiable frank serenity, which, as his character was naturally open and honest, made him a most interesting character. As a man he was, perhaps, still more remarkable than as an artist. His long-life was full of original traits of all kinds; and his friends found always something ingenious, laconic, caustic or whimsical, to mention of *old Oeser*. An anecdote of him when he was still at Vienna, is, perhaps, worth relating. The worm, which injured so much

much the ships under the water, was then the general subject of conversation, and every one was desirous to know it. Young Oeser imagined a quite peculiar kind of a worm, furnished at one extremity with a kind of saw, and at the other with a borer, and found out means to put this production of his own brain with a mysterious air into the hands of some curious print-mongers. A few days afterwards a seller of curiosities brought him, with an important air, this new worm for copying, and recommended to him to be silent; and so Oeser was fully occupied in copying his own worm, till the true one was brought to Vienna, with an ample description, exposing the supposititious one to general ridicule. He used to speak his opinion on all subjects, particularly on politics, with great frankness, and often with vehemence. In this style he had probably spoken with the Prussian General Seydlitz, when he at the end of the seven years war came home late in the night, threw away his hat and stick, and said, "Now, if General Seydlitz is not an honest man and my friend, I must lose my head." His family, of course, spent the night in anxious expectation, and was first tranquillised, when Seydlitz came the next morning with his ordinary kindness, spoke of the arts and of works of arts, and then went gaily with him to walk.

M. Oeser's lasting monuments will be the pictures with which he has decorated St. Nicholas's Church, at Leipzig, one of the most magnificent fabrics in Germany; immense sums having been spent in the last twenty years by the magistrates of Leipzig, in ornamenting the inside of this old Gothic structure. M. Oeser displayed all the skill of his invention and colouring in six great pictures, the subjects of which are taken from the Gospel of St. John, and in adorning the *battisterio*, which is, indeed, the finest to be found in Germany. The statue of the present Elector of Saxony, placed in the midst of a public walk before the Gates of St. Peter, at Leipzig, has also been executed by M. Oeser; and the ceilings in the great assembly-room, in a public edifice, at Leipzig, called the Merchants' hall, (*Gewand-haus*) has been painted by the same artist, who, but for the transient faintness of his colouring, would have excelled in fresco painting.

As Oeser had not studied in Italy, and, perhaps, by nature was little inclined to observe punctually the rules of the art, it would be unjust to submit his works to the severity of a critical examination. As for invention, they are not distinguished by elevated thoughts, well chosen poetical ornaments, or happy allegories. They are, besides, negligently drawn; their disposition is only calculated for composing a whole, but does not extend to the single parts, in which good and bad, agreeable and offending, strokes, continually and mutually balance each other. The expression wants life and force, and the whole management exactness and accuracy; the colouring ought to be stronger in the light places and less dark in the *chiaro-scuro*; but in other respects his works are most sweet and delightful images, and productions of innocent simplicity and of genius. He was undoubtedly a man endowed with the greatest talents, and, if compared with *Mengs*, we would say, that Mengs has given a wonderful example of the cultivation of indifferent talents, by the greatest efforts and by continual assiduity, but that Oeser had arrived at the point where he stood, as it were playing, and by the free favour of nature. If he had lived in times more favourable to the arts, and had enjoyed the advantage of instructing himself in a good school, he would, without doubt, have shone among the first artists. In every part of his works we are struck with the display of an eminent disposition for the arts. He is of a free and easy spirit, seldom sublime, but always rich in ideas, and adorned with an amiable grace, which attended him through his whole life, and remained with him even in his most advanced age. He shews us children as sweet and natural as those of Corregio; young girls with the soft and lovely feminine grace of Albano's nymphs; charming landscapes coloured with the purple of Aurora, or tinged with the glowing red of the evening. The negligence of management could easily have been changed by culture into that beautiful facility which is so much valued in the works of many a great artist. Light and shade are often distributed by him too arbitrarily, but are however, for the most part, like the drapery, employed in large masses and to an agreeable effect. Another proof of the extent of his faculties, his free spirit and the easiness to bend his mind to every line of business, may be taken from his etched plates, some works in marble, and the architectural ornaments in the inner-part of St. Nicholas' Church, at Leipzig. These last are particularly elegant, imagined with taste, and fitted to the place as well as to their destination. It is finally to be mentioned, that Oeser shewed, on every occasion, a decided aversion to grotesque ornaments, which certainly is not to be approved of, but which, however, must not be interpreted to his disadvantage. For modes of taste revolve, like days and seasons, in a continual circle, and in one is abundantly brought forth what in another does not prosper. It might be difficult to shew that such an immoderate a use of those ornaments, as is made in the present times, is more laudable or useful than an unlimited rejecting of them; nor will it be long before they grow disgusting. But true art, and a pure genuine taste, will never declare exclusively for or against any thing; they will rather examine every thing, choose the best, and adapt it to their intended purpose.

MEMOIRS of CARDINAL MAURY.

JEAN SIFFREIN MAURY, a celebrated French ecclesiastic, and cardinal of the Roman church, was born at Valeras, June 26, 1746, of a family which acquired considerable wealth by trade. Discovering a strong turn for the church, he received an education accordingly, and soon became distinguished as an excellent preacher. His talents were so generally admired, especially by persons of the first distinction, that preferments flowed in upon him in abundance; and, at the commencement of the Revolution, he was prior of Lyons and preacher to the king. The clergy of Peronne appointed him their Deputy to the Assembly of the Estates in 1789, and in that situation he greatly distinguished himself as an orator. In the chamber of the clergy he opposed vigorously the re-union of the orders; and when that measure was carried into effect, he quitted Versailles and went to Peronne, where he was arrested, but was released by order of the Legislative Body. He afterwards returned to the National Assembly, where he displayed great powers of eloquence in defence of royalty, the privileges of the nobility, the rights of the clergy, and the whole ancient regimen of France. Amidst all the wild uproar of political confusion, and the violence of the populace, agitated by the revolutionary spirit, and having the most alarming and shocking scenes constantly exhibited before his eyes, the Abbé Maury preserved his courage and asserted his principles, without the least reserve, till the fury of the storm could no longer be stemmed; and, therefore, he prudently withdrew into Italy, where the Pope gave him a bishopric, and, in 1792, sent him in quality of his nuncio to Frankfort, to assist at the coronation of the emperor.—Some time afterwards he was made archbishop of Nice, and, in February 1794, he received a cardinal's hat.

The literary talents of the Cardinal are equal to his powers as an orator, and he possesses a most penetrating judgment, with a vivid imagination. His mind is firm and undaunted; and, while he was a member of the National Assembly, the thunder of his eloquence oftentimes struck those with confusion who hated both him and his order.

He is the author of a Treatise on the Eloquence of the Pulpit, a subject which he has treated with the hand of a most skilful master, and, as one, who excels himself in the art which he teaches. But, though his book cannot be read without material advantage by every theoretical student, it must be admitted that the ingenious author has evinced too great a partiality to the oratory and pulpit compositions of his own countrymen. To the English in particular he will scarcely allow any merit, and it will be seen that divines of the Protestant communion are all little in the estimation of his Eminency. He appreciates the merits of our own most distinguished writers with a critical severity that shews either a mind warped by extreme prejudice, or one that is but slightly acquainted with the productions he condemns.

MEMOIRS of COUNT DE HOMPESCH.

THIS nobleman, who was grand master of Malta at the time when it yielded to the French, is a German by birth, and the first of that nation who ever enjoyed that distinguished office.

Military renown seems to have been the constant characteristic of the Maltese knights, and the history of this order certainly exhibits some of the most gallant exploits that are to be found in the records of mankind. But in the capture of Malta, in 1798, the glory of the order was tarnished, and it affords a striking contrast to the illustrious siege of Rhodes, which brought these military monks into the possession of this island. The letters written by the Count to Bonaparte on that occasion are filled with adulatory submissions and pusillanimous expressions, far beneath the character of a soldier, much more of the representative of a chivalrous order so illustrious as that of St. John.

Extracts from the Port-folio of a Man of Letters.

CHINESE TELEGRAPH *and* STOVES.

IN the "Travels of *John Bell*, of Antermony," from St. Petersburg to Pekin, in 1720, he describes two ingenious inventions, which were then in use in China; and the reader will probably recognize in them, the telegraph of modern days, and the flue-stoves of the celebrated culinary economist.—"Near the populous city of Siang-fu, (says our author,) we met with many turrets upon the road, called post houses, erected at certain distances from one another, with a flag-staff, on which is hoisted the Imperial pendant.—These turrets are so contrived as to be in sight of one another, and by signals, they can convey intelligence of any remarkable event. By this means the court is informed, in the speediest manner imaginable, of whatever disturbance may happen, in the most remote provinces of the empire. These posts are also very useful, by keeping the country free from highwaymen; for should a person escape at one house, on a signal being made, he would certainly be stopped at the next." What was the peculiar construction of these signals Mr. Bell does not inform us; but as they were capable "of conveying intelligence of *any* remarkable event in the speediest manner imaginable," they must have been something more than mere pendants on a flag-staff. But to return to our author, who now writes from a village within four miles of the capital of China: "My lodgings in this village happened to be at a cook's-house, which gave me an opportunity of observing the ingenuity of these people, even on trifling occasions. My landlord being in his shop, I paid him a visit; where I found *six kettles, placed in a row, on furnaces*, having a separate opening under each of them for receiving the fuel, which consisted of a few small sticks and straw. On his pulling a thong he blew a pair of bellows, which made all his kettles boil in a very short time. They are, indeed, very thin, and made of cast-iron, being extremely smooth, both within and without. The scarcity of fuel near such a populous city, prompts people to contrive the easiest methods of dressing their victuals and keeping themselves warm during the winter which is severe for two months."

PORTRAITS *of* CHAUCER *and* GOWER.

The following Poetical Portraits of those venerable English poets, CHAUCER and GOWER, have never appeared in print. They were copied many years since out of a manuscript collection of no great antiquity; however, the language bespeaks the composition to be ancient.

Edgware Road, July 10, 1801.

JEFFERY CHAUCER.

HIS stature was not very tall;
Lean he was—his legs were small,
Hosed within a stock of red;
A button'd bonnet on his head,
From under which did hang, I ween,
Silver hairs, both bright and sheen;
His beard was white, and trimmed round;
His count'nance blithe, and merry found;
A sleeveless jacket, large and wide,
With many plaits and skirts beside,
Of water-camblet did he weare;
A whittle by his belt he beare;
His shoes were corned, broad before;
His inkhorn at his side he wore;
And in his hand he bare a book;
Thus did this ancient Poet look.

JOHN GOWER.

LARGE he was—his height was long;
Broad of breast, his limbs were strong;
But colour pale, and wan his look,
Such as they that ply'n their book;
His head was grey, and quaintly shorne;
Neatly was his beard yworn;
His visage grave and stern, and grim,
Cato was most like to him;
His bonnet was a hat of blue,
His sleeves were strait of that same hue;
A surcoat of a tawney dye
Hung in plaits across his thigh;
A breeche close unto his nock,
Handsomed with a long stock;
Peeked before were his shoone,
He wore such as others donne;
A bag of red was by his side,
And by that his napkin ty'd.
Thus John Gower did appear,
Quaint attired as you hear.

DUCKING-STOOL *in* FRANCE.

I read not long since in a newspaper, the following paragraph: "A woman was ducked in the Thames, at Kingston, in Surry, in a chair preserved in the town for that purpose, pursuant to sentence, on an indictment for being a common scold." Although this appears somewhat like what in the cant of the present day is called a *hoax*, or what used to be named a *take-in* or *banter*; yet that *ducking* was a punishment by the common law of England for the like offences is very certain. The same punishment was inflicted in France, especially in those parts which were in possession of the English, as I have now a proof before me in an ancient

ancient manuscript, of the usages there in the reign of Richard Cœur de Lyon. The law runs in the following words: "Si feme est conveincue d'estre tenfose ou medisans, ele sera liée ob une corde sos les ayselles et sera gitée par iij fes en l'aigue, et si aucuns lo y reprochet cils paiera x. s. et si feme lo y reproche ele paera x. s. ou sera colée iij fes en l'aigue et cis x. s. sunt au besoig de la cite;" which I thus render in English: "If a woman be convicted of scolding or abuse, she shall have a cord fastened under her arm-pits, and be cast three times into the water; and if any one upbraid her with it, such person shall pay ten-pence; and if it be a woman that upbraids, the woman shall pay ten-pence or be ducked three times: and this sum of ten-pence shall be for the use of the public."

The following very singular CASE *is related by* DR. CHEYNE, *of* BATH, *in his* TREATISE *on the* ENGLISH MALADY.*

"*The Case of the Hon Colonel Townshend.*—Colonel Townshend, a gentleman of excellent natural parts and of great honour and integrity, had for many years been afflicted with a *nephritick* complaint, attended with constant vomitings, which had made his life painful and miserable. During the whole time of his illness he had observed the strictest regimen, living on the softest vegetables and lightest animal foods, drinking asse's-milk daily, even in the camp; and for common drink, Bristol-water, which, the summer before his death, he had drank on the spot. But his illness increasing, and his strength decaying, he came from Bristol to Bath in a litter in autumn, and lay at the Bell-inn. Dr. Baynard, (who is since dead,) and I, were called to him, and attended him twice a day for about the space of a week; but his vomiting continuing still incessant, and obstinate against all remedies, we despaired of his recovery. While he was in this condition he sent for us early one morning: we waited on him, with Mr. *Skrine*, the apothecary: we found his senses clear, and his mind calm: his nurse, and several servants were about him. He had made his will, and settled his affairs. He told us, he had sent for us to give him some account of *an odd sensation*, he had for some time observed and felt of himself, which was, —that *composing himself, he could die or expire when he pleased*; and yet, by an effort, or somehow, he could *come to life again*: which it seems he had sometimes tried before he sent for us. We heard this with surprise, but as it was not to be accounted for upon *common principles*, we could hardly believe the fact as he related it, much less give any account of it, unless he should please to make the *experiment* before us, which we were unwilling he should do, lest in his weak condition he should carry it too far. He continued to talk very distinctly and sensibly above an hour about this, (to him,) surprising sensation, and insisted so much on our seeing the trial made, that we were at last obliged to comply. We all three felt his pulse first: it was distinct, though small and thready; and his heart had its usual beating.

"He composed himself on his back, and lay in a still posture some time; while *I* held his right hand, Dr. *Baynard* laid his hand on his heart, and Mr. *Skrine* held a clean looking-glass to his mouth. I found his pulse sink gradually, till at last I could not feel any by the most exact and nice touch. Dr. Baynard could not feel the least motion in his *heart*, nor Mr. Skrine perceive the least soil of breath on the bright mirror he held to his mouth; then each of us, by turns, examined his *arm*, *heart*, and *breath*, but could not, by the nicest scrutiny, discover the least symptom of life in him. We reasoned a long time about this odd *appearance* as well as we could, and all of us judging it inexplicable and unaccountable, and finding he still continued in that condition, we began to conclude that he had, indeed, carried the experiment too far, and at last were satisfied that he was *actually dead*, and were just about to leave him. This continued about half an hour, by nine o'clock in the morning, in *autumn*. As we were going away, we observed some motion about the body, and upon examination found his pulse and the motion of his heart gradually returning; he began to breathe gently, and speak softly: we were all astonished to the last degree at this unexpected change, and after some further conversation with him, and among ourselves, went away fully satisfied as to all the particulars of this fact, but confounded, and puzzled, and not able to form any rational scheme that might account for it.

"He afterwards called for his *attorney*, added a codicil to his will—settled legacies on his servants—received the sacrament—and calmly and composedly expired about five or six o'clock that evening."

* Page 307. Second Edition.

Th

The Doctor goes on by saying, the body was opened, and his complaints were found to have proceeded from a *nephritick* cancer, and concludes with the following strong testimony; which, from a man of his character, must be deemed conclusive as to the truth of his statement.

"I have narrated the *facts*, as I saw and observed them deliberately and distinctly, and shall leave to the philosophic reader to make what inferences he thinks fit: *The truth of the material circumstances I will warrant.*"

REMARKABLE CHARACTERS.

Mr. GUY, who was the founder of the noble hospital that bears his name in the borough of Southwark, was as remarkable for his private parsimony as his public munificence. He invariably dined alone, and a soiled proof-sheet, or an old newspaper, was his constant substitute for a table-cloth.

It is recorded of him, that as he was one winter evening sitting in his room, meditating over a handful of half-lighted embers confined within the narrow precincts of a brick-stove, and without any candle, a person who came to enquire for him was introduced, and after the first compliments were passed, and the guest requested to take a seat, Mr. Guy lighted a farthing-candle, which lay ready on the table by him, and desired to know the purport of the gentleman's visit. The visitor was the famous Vulture Hopkins, immortalised by Pope, in the lines—

"*When Hopkins dies, a thousand lights attend*
"*The wretch, that living, sav'd a candle's end,* &c."

"I have been told, (said Hopkins) that you, Sir, are better versed in the prudent and necessary art of *saving*, than any man now living, and I therefore wait upon you for a lesson of frugality; an art, in which I used to think I excelled, but am told by all who know you, that you are greatly my superior."—"And is that all you come about? (said Guy,) why then, we can talk this matter over in the dark:" So saying, he with great deliberation extinguished his new-lighted farthing-candle. Struck with this instance of economy, Hopkins rose up, acknowledged himself convinced of the other's superior thrift, and took his leave.

A boiled egg was the usual dinner of Sir HANS SLOANE. When he once complained to Doctor Mortimer that all his friends had deserted him, the Doctor observed that Chelsea was a considerable distance from the residence of most of them, and therefore they might be disappointed when they came, to find he had so slight a dinner. This gentle remonstrance put the old Baronet in a rage, and he exclaimed, "Keep a table! Invite people to dinner!—Would you have me ruin myself? Public credit totters already, and if, (as has been presaged,) there should be a national-bankruptcy, or a sponge to wipe out the National-debt, you may yet see me in a workhouse." His landed interest was, at that time, very considerable, and his Museum worth much more than the twenty thousand pounds, which was given for it by Parliament.

Pope has recorded the rapacity of PETER WALTERS, but there are some circumstances in his life not generally known. He was of a low origin, but acquired an immense estate; the principal part of which arose from his knowledge of the world, and careful attention to the follies and vices of young noblemen and gentlemen of fortune, whose wants he was, *on proper terms*, always ready and willing to supply.

He was first an Under-steward to the great Earl of Uxbridge, whom he had the address to manage with such dexterity, that to his dying hour, no man stood so well with that nobleman as Peter Walters. The Earl himself was a great usurer, and Peter was privy to all his bargains. When they were alone and disengaged, their custom was to compare notes, and then a question somtimes arose about which of them had pocketed the greatest number of peers. Pope calls Walters *a person eminent in the wisdom of his profession, a dexterous attorney, and a good, if not a safe, conveyancer.* It happened one night that Anthony Henley, who was as remarkable for his *wit*, as Peter was for his *money*, met together at an inn on the road and joined company. In the course of the evening's conversation, Henley heartily rallied his new companion, on his immoderate love of money, and threw out some sarcastic hints on his manner of getting it. Walters was no less severe upon Anthony for his sovereign contempt of that precious metal, and his ways of squandering it. "At best, (Henley said,) every-body knows, Walters, how you got your *money*,—but do be frank for once, and tell me how the devil you came by your *wit*, for they very rarely go together."—

"Why,

"Why, as to that, (said Peter,) *I thank my stars I am not indebted to nature for a grain of it—but you must know I' have lately bought a good many estates from men of a bright fancy and high genius, and they gave me their wit into the bargain.*"

Mr. LAW, projector of the Mississippi-scheme, was a Scotch gentleman of narrow fortune but great ambition; he had travelled through great part of Europe, and subsisted chiefly by gaming, by which he acquired considerable sums, particularly in Italy, where he first hatched his paper project, which afterwards gave birth to those detestable bubbles that brought both England and France to the brink of ruin. He offered his scheme first to the King of Sardinia, who told him his dominions were too small for such a project; adding, *If I know the humour of the French, I am sure they will relish your plan!* Mr. Law took his Majesty's advice, and it succeeded. The Regent Duke of Orleans came into his views. In December 1719, Law abjured the Protestant religion, and in the January following was made Comptroller-general of the Finances; in which situation he so managed *and controlled*, that he amassed almost all the cash of the kingdom and brought it into the King's coffers, and was himself nominally worth half a million; but not having the prudence or foresight to secure a shilling of it in foreign banks, he was obliged to relinquish this immense treasure, and the very next year to fly secretly from France, to avoid being torn to pieces by the enraged people. Such a sudden elevation, and precipitate downfal, is scarcely to be paralleled. From being the first man in a great kingdom, on whom all the people gazed, as at a meteor, he was in the twinkling of an eye reduced to the low rank of a sorry vagabond, whom all men despised; for after wandering about Europe for some time, he died at Munich, very poor. After his decease, his widow lived at Utrecht in a private manner; but his son was so fortunate as to procure a cornetcy of horse, and his daughter, a very amiable young lady, married the Lord Wallingford, son to the Earl of Banbury.

ORIGINAL POETRY.

The CLOSE *of* DAY.

NO breeze disturbs the summer leaves,
That sleep refresh'd with evening dew;
An amber cloud the moon receives,
And veils her crescent from the view.

The voice of neither herd nor flock,
With tones of love, salutes my ears,
In echoes from the mountain rock,
That wears the mossy robe of years.

New hay and honeysuckles lend
Their fragrance to the breathing vale,
And nameless flowers their odors blend,
And with their sweets the smell regale.

As on I travel through the gloom,
That dims the closing eye of day,
Glow worms, with silvery lamps, illume
The verdant borders of my way.

The lark, sweet minstrel of the skies!
His carol ended, sinks to rest,
And by his feathery partner lies,
So happy in their humble nest!

Thus, in a green sequestered dell,
Safe from the frowns of wealth or care,
In smiles of peace my soul would dwell
With her, my fairest of the fair!

But now I mourn her, absent far,
My blooming flower of sweet delight!
Whose presence, like the evening star,
Would cheer the lonely brow of night.

W. EVANS.

To MARIA.

SHOULD Phœbus e'er forsake my mind,
Their favour should the Nine refuse,
Yet I, propitious fair, could find
A theme in thee—in thee a Muse.

Thy native charms, thy moral grace,
The pow'r of fiction far excel;
Each beauty decorates thy face,
Within thee all the virtues dwell.

Such melody thy notes to me
As sweetest poet never sung;
And true perfection would it be
To sing thy merits with thy tongue.

Let Phœbus, then, desert my mind,
Their succour let the Nine refuse,
I, matchless maid! shall ever find
A theme in thee—in thee a Muse.

T. OLDHAM.

A TRI-

From ANACREON.

COME, thou beft of painters, come!
  Mafter of the Rhodian art,
While mem'ry with her image glows,
  Paint the miftrefs of my heart.

Firft her gloffy ringlets trace:
  —Paint them foft, and black as jet;
And, if fuch thy mimic pow'r,
  Paint them breathing every fweet.

From the full luxuriant cheek,
  Peeping thro' her dufky hair,
Let the ivory forehead rife
  Brightly glittering, fmooth, and fair.

Her eye-brows trace with fteadieft hand;
  With care the graceful arch defign:
Part not the bewitching curves,
  Nor yet unite the waving line.

Shaded by a jetty lid,
  Paint me next her eye of fire,
Sparkling bright with rays of fenfe,
  Melting too with foft defire.

Rofes blend with whiteft milk—
  Tint her lovely cheeks with this;
And her foft perfuafive lips
  Challenging the lufcious kifs.

Round her alabafter neck
  Let the wanton graces play;
Shade, with a robe of purple dye,
  The brighter charms that fhun the day.

But gently through the carelefs folds
  Let the fnowy bofom break:
—Enough! 'tis fhe! I own thy power;
  It breathes—it lives—it foon will fpeak!

W. SHEPHERD.

BALLAD.

'TWAS on a cliff, whofe rocky bafe
  Baffled the briny wave;
Whofe cultur'd heights their verdant ftore
  To many tenant gave;

A mother, led by ruftic cares,
  Had wander'd with her child;
Unwean'd the babe—yet on the grafs
  He frolick'd and he fmil'd.

With what delight the mother glow'd
  To mark the infant's joy;
How oft would paufe, amidft her toil,
  To contemplate her boy.

Yet foon, by other cares eftranged,
  Her thoughts the child forfook;
Carelefs he wanton'd on the ground,
  Nor caught his mother's look.

Cropt was each flow'r that caught his eye,
  'Till, fcrambling o'er the green,
He gain'd the cliff's unfhelter'd edge,
  And pleas'd furvey'd the fcene!

'Twas now the mother, from her toil,
  Turn'd to behold her child—
The urchin gone!—her cheeks were flufh'd!—
  Her wand'ring eye was wild!

She faw him on the cliff's rude brink—
  Now carelefs peeping o'er—
He turn'd, and to his mother fmil'd,
  —Then fported as before.

Sunk was her voice—'twas vain to fly—
  'Twas vain the brink to brave—
Oh Nature! it was thine alone
  To prompt the means to fave!

She tore the kerchief from her breaft,
  And laid her bofom bare:
He faw delighted—left the brink,
  And fought to banquet there.

H. R.

The DARTMOOR COTTER; or, the WIDOW and her PONY.

I. MORE favage than the howl
  Of winter on the moor,
His voice, who once a widow drove
  At midnight from his door.

II. The hills were clad with fnow,
  And glimmer'd in the moon,
Which, through the clouds, feem'd like the fun
  Obfcur'd with mift at noon.

III. From noon to midnight hour,
  The Dame her way purfued
O'er hill and dale, o'er moorland wild,
  And mountain folitude.

IV. Her pony with the cold
  Begins to droop and fink;
The fnow deny'd him grafs to eat,
  And ice, a pool to drink.

V. The inn is nigh: fhe knocks,
  And calls aloud for aid,
To lift her pony from the fnow,
  Where proftrate he was laid.

VI. "Away"—a voice replies;
  Nor has fhe anfwer more;
But, fhiv'ring, liftens to the wind
  O'er Dartmoor-foreft roar.

VII. She thinks of home—fo far!
  With tears, and heaves a figh,
When, lo! a found of horror fwells
  The gale that whiftles by.

VIII. A hollow groan refounds,
  And ftops her panting breath;
Alas! her pony's plaintive moan
  Bids her farewel in death!

IX. A cot in fight fhe reach'd,
  Heartlefs again to knock;
But, at her call, a fwain unbars
  The door, without a lock.

X. Unlike

X. Unlike that Publican,
Who rudely cry'd—"depart"—
This cottager compassion breathes,
And feels a tender heart.

XI. He lights a blazing fire,
To yield her sweet relief,
And mingles with her tale of woe
His sympathy of grief.

XII. With morn around the door
The Cotter's children smil'd,
Or gambol'd in the heath, as blithe
As bees that haunt the wild.

XIII. This tale they love to tell
The stranger on the green,
And show him where the pony fell,
And where his bones are seen.

XIV. The Father of the dew
Accepts the Widow's tears
That drop in pity for the beast,
Who serv'd her days and years.

Tavistock, W. EVANS.
April, 1801.

COURTLY ADULATION.

From Ariosto's Satires.

RASH is that fool, who 'gainst his sovereign lord,
Presumes to proffer one opposing word;
Should he at noon see stars! then grope your way;
The sun, at midnight! blinking shun his ray.
Where'er at random falls his praise or blame,
Consenting courtiers echo back the same.
Nay, e'en the rear of slaves, who look and quake,
Nor ever dare their humble silence break,
With ev'ry grinning muscle seem to cry,
We, if we durst, would sanction too, the lie.

Hackney. J. M.

LINES, *translated from the* IRISH *of* THADY RUDDY, *an* UNTUTORED BARD.

WHY does that rose shine forth with so much pride?
In all the glories of an Eastern bride?
Is it because she decks fair *Selin's** bow'rs?
Is it because she's called the Queen of Flow'rs?
Is it because she scents the verdant plain,
And lives in ev'ry poet's love-sick strain?
Is it because she breathes in Homer's Greek,
And shares the charms of lovely Nora's cheek?
Is it because the plaintive bird of night
Woos her in strains that lend e'en saints delight?
But mark yon humble lily of the vale,
Content to flourish in the past'ral tale;
Content in her own native shade to breathe,
Or bloom at times in some young shepherd's wreathe;
Yet thou art dearer to my lowly breast,
Than yon proud rose in all her radiance drest.
The purest emblem of the modest maid,
Who flies the wanton eye, and courts the shade.

* An extensive vale in the county of Leitrim.

A TRIBUTE *to the* MEMORY *of a* YOUNG GENTLEMAN, *who died on the 10th of June, in early life, eminent for his worth and diligence in his profession as Surgeon of a Dispensary.*

IN haste to thee the fatal mandate came,
And quick thy spirit fled its languid frame.
Farewel! 'tis finished! Heaven requir'd no more;
Thy days of labour, studious nights, are o'er.
Yet, silent now upon thy lowly bed,
Thou sleepest not with the forgotten dead;
No, gentle shade, justice thy name shall raise,
And o'er the cypress spread the verdant bays:
Bid it survive a fair example shown,
And may the young compare it with their own.
In all *their* time, (thy treasure of rich use,)
Are no regretted moments of abuse?
As thee devout, say, have they minds as free,
And, blest by science, humble found as thee?
Of gentle manners, are their morals pure;
In them does misery meet a friend as sure?
Does filial duty's pure affection glow,
And faith seal every claim the good can know?
Is aught revers'd? reverse the erring plan,
These are the graces that adorn the man.
For gold and honours vain the giddy strife—
The first of honours is an useful life.
Lamented shade, farewel! thy labour's done,
And Heaven, high prize for virtue! early won.
External gifts the Muse deems toys of earth,
But pays just tribute here to modest worth.

Lancaster,
June 18, 1801.

MONTHLY RETROSPECT OF THE FINE ARTS.

(Communications and the Loan of all new Prints are requested.)

Bonaparte. Engraved from a bust modelled by Ceracci, by H. Richter. Published for Richters, Newman-street, Price 10s. 6d. Plain, 1l. 1s. in Colours

THE resemblance of a man who has performed so conspicuous a character in the great theatre of the world, at this most eventful period, naturally excites curiosity; and to gratify that curiosity, we have been treated with several of his portraits. This is said to be a very striking resemblance, and the circumstances that attended the modelling the bust, are collateral proofs that it is so. About twenty years ago, Ceracci an Italian, who was the sculptor, resided in Margaret-street, Cavendish-square, and was considered by many of the best judges as a young artist of great promise. At this time he gave some instructions to Mrs. Damer. He modelled the heads of the Marquis of Buckingham, Admiral Keppel, General Paoli, and many other eminent characters. He was also the sculptor of the figures on the top of Somerset House; and one very curious specimen of his taste and talents he presented to Mr. Goubert, at whose death it was purchased by Mr. Raphael Smith, in whose possession it now is.

With all this, Ceracci did not find encouragement in this country, which he therefore left in about four or five years, and went to reside in Vienna; where he staid a short time, but was on some account or other ordered to quit the empire. He then went to America, where he was noticed and employed; and to purchase marble for a monument which he had an order for, he took a voyage to Italy. Bonaparte, previously to his going with the troops to Egypt, happened to be in the same city at the same time, and Ceracci obtained permission to make a model of his head. With this the General was so much pleased, that he told the sculptor if he came to Paris he would endeavour to serve him. Ceracci went to Paris, and afterwards repaid his countryman's kindness by being a principal contriver of the plot to destroy him by the Internal machine; and for this he was guillotined.

This copy is correctly drawn, and admirably engraved. In the general outline of the head, and spirit of the eye, it bears a strong resemblance to a large medallion that has been lately engraved at Paris. On one side of this is the Chief Consul's head, inscribed *An.* ix. 1801. *Bonaparte Consul de la rep. Fran.* On the reverse is a globe, with the rays of the sun shining upon that part of the Continent in which France is situated, and a heavy cloud hovering over the part in which is Great Britain! Motto, *Bonheur au Continent, Paix de Luneville.*

Masquerier's Portrait of Bonaparte is removed from Piccadilly to Macklin's Gallery, Fleet street.

Poetry and Painting have been considered as sister-arts. The name of Gessner of Zurich stands very high in the former; his son, who is an inhabitant of this country, has embraced the latter; and whatever may be his defects, has certainly an abundant portion of fire. Wherever this is found we augur improvement. The fleet courser, that sometimes flies out of the beaten track, may be checked in his wild career, and brought into the proper bounds—but the sluggish animal that drags on at the same dull pace, without daring to deviate to the right or left, can never be spurred into speed.

This gentleman, (Mr. Gessner jun.) has lately made a number of designs, relative *to bloody battles, and to bruising arms.* Forty or fifty of these are in the possession of Mr. Ackermann of the Strand, who intends to publish them. The following subjects, which bear strong marks of a vigorous mind and abound in savage grandeur, are already engraved, and are sold at 6s. the Pair. In Colours 12s.

Saxon Dragoons patroling in a Storm. Ziegler sculpt.—Austrian Hussars in pursuit of the Enemy. Ziegler sculpt.

The contrast between these two prints, is in an eminent degree striking. The light-coloured cloaks of the Saxons, and the chilling and violent wind and storm in the distance, is marked with the hand of a master, and appears to be felt by both the horses and their riders. The heat of the whole surrounding scenery, which is in a perfect blaze, forms a very strong opposition.

English Light Horse attacking French Artillery. Merke sculpt.—Prussian Hussars on a Night Piquet. Ziegler sculpt.

These are two spirited prints.

Russian Hussars and Cossacks attacked by French Horse and Foot. Merke sculpt. Austrian Hussars charging the Enemy through a Town. J. Bluck sculpt.

This pair of prints display war in all its horrors.

An Officer of Cuirassiers leading on his Troops. J. Bluck sculpt.—Hessian Hussars, on a Night Patrol. C. Ziegler sculpt.

The effect of the peasant's lanthorn in the last of these prints, though rather violent in the blaze, is striking.

Saxon Hussars attacked by French Infantry from an Ambuscade. J. Bluck sculpt.—A Reconnoitring party of Austrian Dragoons retreating from the Enemy. J. Bluck sculpt.

These two prints, like the others, have great spirit, but would not have been injured by being, in the painters phrase, *a little kept down* both in drawing and colouring.

To the gentlemen of the army, these subjects have peculiar interest, and we are told that among the military the sale has been considerable.

Swearing-in the Lord Mayor. Painted by Miller. Engraved by B. Smith. Published by Messrs. Boydell, Cheapside, and the Shakespeare Gallery. Price 3l. 3s.

This print is forcibly engraved, and derives a large portion of its interest from the number of portraits; a greater number, we believe, than were ever inserted in any one print. A key-plate with references to them all, is delivered with the print. The internal view of Guildhall is correct, and comprizes the full length portraits of Sir Matthew Hale, and the other Judges, who, after the dreadful fire in 1666, regulated the rebuilding of London by such wise rules as to prevent the endless train of law suits which might otherwise have ensued, and would have been little less chargeable than the fire had been. These portraits were painted by Michael Wright, a tolerably good painter. The key-print describes many of them.

Agrippina landing with the Ashes of Germanicus. Burney del. Agar sculpt.—Sophonisba receiving her Nuptial Present from Massinissa. Burney del. Agar sculpt. Published for Ackermann, 101 Strand. Price 3s. Plain. Coloured 7s.

These are two very elegant little vignettes. In the first of them, the figures are antique, though that of Agrippina, if she stood upright, would be above the height of a British beauty. The figure of Sophonisba in the second, is voluptuous, but the displaying a cornucopia as the nuptial torch, though it may be warranted in the Court of Paphos, would, in an English Court, excite some whimsical ideas, which might lead to Doctors' Commons, and the Court of King's Bench. We are at a loss to conceive how the loose drapery, to which the horn and garland are suspended, is supported. If we suppose it the wind, it must be Boreas, for Zephyrus would not have sufficient power. Notwithstanding all this, it is a light and tasteful design, and very neatly engraved.

A Drawing-book, consisting of Four Heads. Maria Cosway del. Samuel Phillips sculpt. Published for R. Ackermann, Print Warehouse, No. 101, Strand. Price 10s. 6d. Plain. 21s. Coloured.

These heads are in the antique style, and intended for Bacchus, Ariadne, Innocence, and Simplicity.

The face of Bacchus is rather feminine, though the profile, which is perfectly Grecian, resembles a figure that was some years since at the late Mr. Hamilton's gardens at Cobham, in Surrey. The head of Ariadne is in a singular position, but is a good model to draw from. The heads of *Innocence* and *Simplicity* are characteristic, and well display the two passions they are intended to personify. The whole are admirably engraved in the chalk manner, by Mr. Samuel Phillips, whom we have had former occasions to notice, and who displays marks of improvement, that we expect will in time raise him to eminence.

While we are on the subjects designed by Mrs. Cosway, we cannot resist noticing a design which Agar has lately engraved, as a vignette to a bill of Ackermann, Suardy and Cos. Water-proof Manufactory at Chelsea. The process which cloth or wearing-apparel undergoes at this place, renders it impenetrable to rain, and Mrs. Cosway has well described this by a whimsical and poetical *concetto*.

A figure, which by the courtesy of allegory, and the practice of allegorical painters, must we believe be called a dolphin, is represented swimming in the ocean, and spouting water to a considerable height from each of his nostrils. Upon the animal's back, stands a little Cupid, holding a piece of light drapery, which the wind very complacently blows a little higher than his head. It is inscribed *Rain defied—Health preserved.* Partly enveloped in a cloud immediately above it, is a little Genius pressing between his hand hands somewhat that must be considered to be a sort of sponge, charged with water, till it descends in a violent torrent upon the water-proof canopy—under which the little Cupid, perfectly secure, "*Rides in the Whirlwind, and defies the Storm.*"

This is all very prettily imagined, but it would have had a lighter and more airy effect, if the figure in the clouds had been raised higher, so as to have been more above the canopy.

Mr. Holloway is engaged in an arduous undertaking; making large prints from Rafaelle's cartoons. The history of these grand models of grace and greatness, is singular and curious.

Leo X. employed Rafaelle to delineate them as designs for tapestry, to ornament the pontifical apartments at Rome. For this, (according to Panvinio,) he agreed to pay 50,000 *scudi doro*, to the proprietor of a large tapestry manufactory in Flanders. The work was finished and sent to Rome, but the money agreed to be paid was not returned, and these inimitable productions were left in the hands of the tapestry merchant and his successors for near a century, when they were purchased by either the parliament of Great Britain, or Charles I. for a very large sum: it has been said, near ten thousand pounds.

Soon after the decollation of this prince, his very fine collection of pictures, statues, tapestry, jewels, &c. was sold; and by a catalogue which was discovered some years since in Moorfields, and fell into the hands of the late Sir John Stanley, it appears that the cartoons were purchased by his highness (Cromwell,) for 300l. This, considering the price at which they had been so recently purchased, was a very small sum; but the temper of the times was too harsh and gloomy to set much value upon elegant embellishments, and paintings of religious subjects were held in such abhorrence, that previous to the sale, an order was made to burn all such pictures as contained any representations of the Second Person in the Trinity, or the Virgin Mary. Be the cause what it would, this unfortunate monarch's valuable collection of pictures, statues, jewels, plate, and the furniture of nineteen palaces, sold for 18,000l.

The cartoons were, after this, deposited in Hampton-court-palace. From thence they were several years since removed to the Queen's-house; and from the Queen's-house they are removed to Windsor, where Mr. Holloway has been permitted to copy them; for which purpose he has for several months had a scaffolding erected, and is now sedulously applying to making the drawings. From his former productions there is every reason to think he will produce a set of prints that will not only do honour to himself but to the country.

The cartoons have been several times copied. Twice by Sir James Thornhill. The larger set were purchased at Sir James's sale, by the late Duke of Bedford, for 200l. and have been lately presented by the present Duke to the Royal Academy, at Somerset-house.

The first set of engravings that were ever made of them, were by Dorigny, to whom Queen Anne allotted apartments in the palace, during the progress of the work, and afterwards knighted the artist. The second set were very neatly engraved in smaller size by Simon Gribelin, with an internal view of the room as it appeared at Hampton-court. Another set were wretchedly wrought by Kirkhall, and are usually printed in blue, green or red. Mr. Simon is engaged in a copy, and one of the prints we are told is finished.

The print of the Siege of Valenciennes, engraved by Bromley, from Loutherbourg's capital picture, is finished, and will be published early in the winter. The subscribers will have ample reason to be satisfied that though they have waited long, they have not waited in vain, for it is a most correct and spirited copy, and admirably engraved.

Mr. Mitchell, of Newman-street, has published a book on Grecian, Roman, and Gothic Architecture, price to subscribers four guineas. The plates exhibit several buildings that have been erected by the author; and his aim, in those that he has planned for families, seems to be to unite, in a compact and elegant villa, all the comforts of a house to live in. This is good sense, but has not always been adopted; for we have often seen comfort and convenience sacrificed to splendour and show. A section of the Panorama, which Mr. Mitchell built, will be very curious to those who have not considered the subject, as it completely elucidates the principle, by which this *triumph of perspective* is effected.

Windsor Castle is to undergo a thorough repair, and to have, throughout the whole building, Gothic windows, similar to the architecture of the time of Edward III. Mr. Wyatt is the architect, and expects that it will take about three years to compleat it.

LIST OF DISEASES IN LONDON.

Account of Diseases in an Eastern District of London, from the 20th of June to the 20th of July, 1801.

ACUTE DISEASES.	No. of Cases.
Typhus	22
Febris Intermittens	1
Pneumonia	7
Cynanche Tonsillaris	8
Acute Rheumatism	3
CHRONIC DISEASES.	
Cough	18
Dyspnœa	9
Cough and Dyspnœa	12
Phthisis Pulmonalis	3
Pleurodyne	1
Hydrothorax	2
Apoplexia	1
Paralysis	2
Cephalalgia	5
Dyspepsia	7
Anasarca	4
Ascites	2
Amenorrhœa	3
Menorrhagia	2
Chlorosis	5
Asthenia	2
Hypochondriasis	2
Hysteria	3
Scrophula	2
Diarrhœa	5
Hæmorrhois	3
Scabies	1
Herpes	3
Chronic Rheumatism	12
PUERPERAL DISEASES.	
Menorrhagia Lochialis	3
Low Puerperal Fever	2
Abscessus Mammarum	1
INFANTILE DISEASES.	
Febris Infantilis	2
Rachitis	1
Aphthæ	5
Herpes	8

It will appear from the annexed list, that the fever, which has long formed a large proportion in former lists, continues to prevail, and that the number of patients under its influence is still large.—This disease has propagated itself to a considerable extent, particularly amongst the lower orders of society; so that there is hardly a family that has been visited by it, in which almost every member of it has not been more or less affected. Together with the other symptoms of this disease, which have been frequently recited, some affections of the throat have of late, in several instances, been experienced. In these cases, there has been a slight inflammation of the mucous membrane of the fauces, and some enlargement of the tonsils, occasioning a degree of pain and difficulty in deglutition. These symptoms have, however, soon yielded to the inhaling of the steam of warm water; or frequently sipping some tepid emollient liquor, or the use of moderately astringent gargles.

Similar affections of the throat, but in a higher degree, have, in some instances, constituted the primary disease. The patient has first complained of stiffness and fulness about the throat, the tonsils, and the whole of the internal fauces have been much inflamed, and the degree of fever, indicated by the fulness and frequency of the pulse and the heat of the skin, has been considerable.

The use of aperient medicines, keeping up a determination to the skin by antimonials, and the use of emollient gargles have generally been attended with success, and in a few days the disease has been removed.

NEW PATENTS LATELY ENROLLED.

MR. WHITBY, *and others, for a* MILL *to grind* BARK *for the* USE *of* TANNERS.

THIS mill consists of a number of cutters fixed upon arbors or axles, which cut the bark to pieces; after which the bark falls through an eye, and passes between two large cast-iron plates, with grooves or furrows, cut either hollow or levelled square. The under plate is made to move round, which is found to facilitate the entrance of the bark into the eye more than if the upper plate moved.

The upper plate may, however, be made to move round, if the situation in which the mill stands requires it; and, in this case, the grooves or furrows are reversed.

A perpendicular shaft rests upon brass, fixed upon the bridge-tree, which, by means of two screws, is raised or depressed to grind the bark finer or coarser as may be wished.

These two cast-iron plates (for which the patent is particularly granted, and which appear to constitute the chief invention in this mill,) are set in motion by common mill machinery, such as used in horse, water, wind, or steam mills.

This mill, when moved by a horse, will grind

grind three hundred-weight of bark in an hour; but as the plates may be made of any circumference, varying with the power by which they are moved, the quantity ground by the mill in a given time will be in proportion to the size of the plates, and consequently to the power which moves the machinery. The advantages promised by this invention are, a saving of bark, and an acceleration in the process of tanning, as it is said that bark, ground fine by this mill, without being pulverized, spends more rapidly and more completely in the pits.

MESSRS. WHITE *and* SMETHURST *for an* IMPROVED LAMP-BURNER.

This is an improvement on the burner of the common Argand lamp, the object of which is to cause a more free and plentiful supply of oil to the ignited part of the wick, by which means it may burn better, require snuffing less frequently, and will burn with oil of an inferior quality. These advantages are obtained simply by leaving more space between the two tubes within which the wick is confined than is usually done, and in this the whole improvement of the Patentee appears to consist. It is necessary however to reduce to the usual size the space at the top of the wick, in order that the burnt crust may be more conveniently brushed off. This may be done by putting on a ring conically shaped, so as to bring the space at top to the requisite dimension.

The principle of improvement here is to take away the close adhesion between the sides of the unburnt wick and the tubes between which it is confined; for, as this part of the wick is constantly soaked in oil, it thereby adheres closely to the sides of the tubes, and the capillary attraction by which the oil is drawn up into the burning circle of the wick, is thus much less than it would be if the wick were simply hanging down loosely to the oil reservoir. At the same time all the important advantage gained by the Argand construction is preserved equally well merely by the ring at the top of the wick-tube. The Patentees suggest other methods of constructing the supporters of the wick, as for instance, by supporting a ring upon pillars or bars, or by making slits or openings in the sides of the tubes, and the like, all of which will ensure the same advantages.

One of the most important benefits which the Patentees assert will be derived from their improved lamp, is to enable the wick to burn common whale or seed-oils, which are sold nearly at half the price of the best spermaceti oil, and it is probable that, if the lamp burns well, little, if any, of the offensive smell occasioned by these oils, when burnt in the common way, will be perceived.

[*The following Patents have lately been obtained in America.*]

MR. JAMES COX, *of Rahway, in East Jersey, for a* MACHINE *to save* LABOUR *in* TAN-YARDS.

It consists of sets of frames adapted to the vats on which the hides are to be stretched, and secured in such a manner as to be both in a situation to be acted upon by the fluid in which they are immersed, and to be easily lifted out for airing, by the strength of one or two men. Thus in the operations of soaking in common water, in lime water, &c. the hides are *handled* with very little expenditure of time or strength.

MR. WILLIAM YOUNG, *of Connecticut, for a* NEW MODE *of raising* SASH-WINDOWS.

This is performed by means of cork, &c. in the simplest possible manner, with scarcely any expence. The contrivance is the following: Three or four holes are bored in the sides of the sash, into which hole common bottle-corks are inserted, projecting about the sixteenth of an inch. These press against the window-frames, along the usual groove, and by their elasticity support the sash at any height which may be required.

LIST OF NEW PUBLICATIONS IN JUNE.

AGRICULTURE.

The Case of the Farmers; with a Dedication to the Board of Agriculture; and an Address to all Present and Future Writers on Agriculture, by a Hertfordshire Farmer, 8vo. 2s. Badcock.

BIOGRAPHY.

Memoirs of the late Mrs. Robinson, written by herself; including Anecdotes of many distinguished Persons of the present Period; with Poems and Letters never before published, written by herself, or addressed to her

her by various Persons, 4 vols, foolscap 8vo. 1l. 1s. in boards. Phillips.

A Narrative of the Life of Sarah Shade, containing many well-authenticated and curious Facts, more particularly during her Voyage to the East Indies, in 1769, and in traversing that Country with the Army at the Siege of Pondicherry, Vellore, Negapatam, &c. 2s. Hatchard.

CHEMISTRY.

Synoptic Tables of Chemistry; intended to serve as a Summary of the Lectures delivered on that Science in the Public Schools in Paris, by A. F. Fourcroy, royal folio, 1l. 1s. boards. Cadell and Davies.

DRAMA.

Mutius Scævola; or, the Roman Patriot; an Historical Drama, as adapted for Representation, by W. H. Ireland, with a Preface by Mr. Feltham, 2s. 6d. Badcock.

EDUCATION.

Introduction to the English Reader; or, a Selection of Pieces in Prose and Poetry, calculated to improve the younger Classes of learners in Reading, by Lindley Murray, 3s. bound. Longman and Rees.

Aphorisms for Youth; with Observations and Reflections, Religious, Moral, Critical, and Characteristic, original, or selected from the most distinguished Writers; interspersed with original Poetry, 5s. boards.
Lackington, Allen, and Co.

The Adventures of Kamoula; or, a Vindication of the Ways of Providence, exemplified in the Triumph of Virtue and Innocence over Corruption and Malice, 1s. 6d.
Lackington, Allen, and Co

The Order and Method of Instructing Children; with Strictures on the Modern System of Education, by G. Crabb, 12mo. 3s. 6d. boards. Longman and Rees.

The Amiable Tutoress; or, the History of Mary and Jane Hornby; a Tale for young Persons, 2s. Hurst.

HISTORY.

The History of England, from the earliest Dawn of Record, to the Peace of 1783, by C. Coote, L. L. D. 9 vols. 8vo. 3l. 3s. boards. Kearsley.

Memoirs of the Reign of George III. from the Year 1796, to the Commencement of the Year 1799, by William Belsham, 1 vol. 4to. 1l. 1s. boards, and 2 vols. 8vo. 18s. boards. Robinsons.

LAW.

The Statutes at large, Anno 41. Geo. III. being the fifth and concluding Session of the eighteenth and last Parliament of Great Britain, with a copious Index to the Volume, 4to. 6s. 6d. boards. Butterworth.

Tabula Judicum; a complete Register of the Judges of the Superior Courts, with the Attornies and Solicitors General, for the Eighteenth Century, including the subsequent Alterations to the 5th of June, 1801, with Biographical References, 3s. 6d.
Ogilvy and Son.

MISCELLANIES.

Remarks by T. Ludlum on the Scurrilous Reflections cast upon the Rev. W. and T. Ludlum, by Dr. Milner, 1s. Wilkie.

A General System of Equestrian Education, by Mr. Astley, sen. Professor of the Art of Riding, &c. with Engravings, 10s. 6d.
Creed.

The Letters between the Marquis of Blandford, and Lady Mary Anne Sturt; the Report of the Trial; and Mr Sturt's Vindication of himself from the Charge of having connived at the Adulterous Intercourse between the Parties, 5s. Ridgway.

The Persian Moonshee; containing the Grammatical Rules, the Pund Nameh of Sadi, Forms of Address, select Tales, Lives of the Philosophers, Dialogues, some Chapters of St. Matthew; with Notes by the late William Chambers, Esq. all in Persian, with English Translations by Henry Gladwin, Esq. of Calcutta; illustrated with Plates, containing exact Imitations of Persian and Arabic Manuscripts; and containing every requisite Instruction for obtaining a thorough Knowledge of the Persian Language, and to render the most difficult Hand-writing perfectly familiar. royal 4to. 3l. 3s. bds.
Debrett.

The Method of Educating the Deaf and Dumb, by the Abbé de l'Epée, translated from the French, 8vo. 7s. 6d.
Cadell and Davies.

The Boa Constrictor; an Illustration from the Natural of what has appeared in the Political World; suggested in consequence of a Recollection of Events, which were provoked by a late French demi-official Publication in the Moniteur; concluding with some Considerations respecting Negociation, by the Author of the Theory of Chess, 1s.
Hatchard.

The Theological, Philosophical, and Miscellaneous Works of the Rev. William Jones, with an Account of his Life and Writings, 12 vols. large 8vo. with Portrait, 5l. 8s. bds.
Rivingtons.

The Philosophical Transactions of the Royal Society of London, for the Year 1801, Part I. Elmsley.

A Week's Conversation on the Plurality of Worlds; translated from the French of M. de Fontenelle, with considerable Improvements, by J. Hughes, Esq. to which is added, Mr. Addison's Defence of the Newtonian Philosophy, 3s. boards. Jones.

Dodsley's Annual Register for the Year 1799, 10s 6d. boards.
Otridge and other Proprietors.

Letters addressed to a young Man, on his Entrance into Life, and adapted to the Circumstances of the Times, by Mrs. West, Authoress of a Tale of the Times, &c. 3 vols. 12mo. 16s. 6d. boards. Longman and Rees.

Six Picturesque Views in North Wales, engraved in Aquatinta by Alken; with Poetical Reflections on leaving that Country, by the

the Rev. Brian Broughton, M. A. royal 4to. 12s. Mawman.

An Introduction to the Theory and Practice of Plane and Spherical Trigonometry, and the Orthographic and Sterographic Projections of the Sphere; including the Theory of Navigation, illustrated by Practical Examples, and applied to the Mensuration of Heights and Distances; to determine the Latitude by two Altitudes of the Sun, the Longitude by the Lunar Observations, and to other important Problems on the Sphere, and in Nautical Astronomy, by Thomas Keith, Teacher of Mathematics, 10s. 6d. boards. Longman and Rees.

Canterbury Tales, by Harriet Lee, volume 4, 8s. boards. Robinsons.

Second Edition of a New Table of all the Stamp-duties, completed to the 9th of July, 1801. by T. Edwards, Law-stationer, an open sheet, 1s. Edwards.

Account of the Emancipation of the Slaves of Unity Valley Pen, in Jamaica, by David Barclay, 6d. Phillips.

Part of a Letter to a Noble Earl, containing a Comment on the Doctrines and Facts of Sir Richard Musgrave's Vindicatory of the Yeomanry and Catholics of the City of Cork, by Thomas Townsend, Esq. 1s. 6d. Booker.

The Sincere Huron; or, Pupil of Nature; translated from the French of Voltaire, 1s. 6d. Bone.

Lectures on the Elements of Commerce, Politics, and Finances, peculiarly calculated to qualify young Gentlemen for Public Situations, and for Parliamentary Business, by Thomas Mortimer, Esq. 8vo. 9s. boards Longman and Rees.

An Appeal to the Public on the Controversy between Hannah More, the Curate of Blagdon, and the Rev. Sir A. Elton, by Thomas Bere, A. M. 2s. Robinsons.

The Elements of Gaelic Grammar, by the Rev. A. Stewart, 8vo. 4s. boards. Vernor and Hood.

The Magus; or, Celestial Intelligencer; forming a Complete System of Occult Philosophy and Magic; to which is added, the Lives of the most eminent Magi, &c. by Francis Barrett, 4to. 1l. 7s. Lackington, Allen, and Co.

The Principles of Morality, by George Ensor, Esq. 8vo. 6s. boards. Jordan.

Prose on various Occasions, Literary and Political, collected from the Newspapers, 8vo. 3s. 6d. Hurst.

Lloyd's Monthly List of the Commercial Shipping belonging or trading to Great Britain and Ireland; containing the following interesting Particulars respecting every ship, viz. her Name, Tonnage, Class, or Condition and Age; her Captain, Owners, and Brokers Names; present Trade or Employment, Station, Situation, and other recent Information concerning her; the Port where built or registered, and her Number of Guns; with Miscellaneous Observations, &c. In the above Description, nearly 12,000 Vessels are included. To which is added, a correct List of the Royal Navy of the United Kingdoms of Great Britain and Ireland, with the first Lieutenants, and the Agents of the Captains, 1s. 6d. Hurst.

MILITARY.

Observations on the Establishment of a Royal Military College for the Instruction of the Officers of the British Army, as proposed by the Secretary at War, 1s. Egerton.

The English Bowman; or, Tracts on Archery; containing the History, Character, and Military Career of the English Long Bow, including Sir John Smith's Discourse on Weapons, &c. &c. with many Notes and Historical Illustrations: to which is added, the Bowman's Glory, a very scarce Tract, by T. Roberts, with Frontispiece, 10s. 6d. Egerton.

MEDICAL.

The second Volume of the Institution of the Practice of Medicine, by Joseph Baptist Buserius de Kanifeld; translated from the Latin by William Cullen Brown, 8vo. 8s. boards. Cadell and Davies.

Medical Researches and Observations; being a Series of Essays on the Practice of Physic: Essay I. on the Nature, Cause, and Cure of Fever, with extraneous Prescription, by Dr. Andrew Ferguson, of Aberdeen, 8vo. 6s. boards. Hurst.

A Letter to Sir Walter Farquhar, Bart. on the Subject of a particular Affection of the Bowels, very frequent and fatal in the East Indies, 2s. Cadell and Davies.

Two Memoirs on the Cesarean Operation, by M. Baudelocque, sen. translated from the French. With Notes, an Appendix, and Engravings, by John Hull, M. D. 6s. Bickerstaff.

A Supplement to Practical Observations on the Natural History and Cure of the Lues Venerea; containing Remarks on the Application of the Lunar Caustic to Strictures of the Urethra; on the Use of Sedatives in Gonorrhœa, and their dangerous Consequences in Lues Venerea; with an Examination of those Effects of Mercury which are decisive in the Cure of this Disease, by John Howard, Surgeon, 2s. Baldwin.

Observations on the Medical and Domestic Management of the Consumptive; on the Powers of Digitalis Purpurea; and on the Cure of the Scrophula, by Thomas Beddoes, M. D. 9s. boards. Longman and Rees.

NATURAL HISTORY.

The Cabinet of Natural History, 2 vols. 12mo. 9s. boards. Vernor and Hood.

POLITICAL.

The Political Interests of Great Britain; in which are included the necessary Measures for procuring an advantageous and permanent Peace with France and her Allies; for terminating our Differences with the Northern Confederate Powers, concerning the Freedom

Maritime

of Neutral Maritime Commerce, and restoring Plenty to the United Kingdoms, by George Edwards, Esq. 7s. boards. Johnson

The Sound and Baltic considered in a Political, Military, and Commercial View, intended to illustrate the relative Connections and Maritime Strength of the Northern Powers; containing also Observations upon Egypt, and the Trade of India, as connected with the East Sea or Baltic; translated from a German Pamphlet published at Berlin in April last, 2s. 6d. Debrett.

POLITICAL ECONOMY.

The Means of Reforming the Morals of the Poor, by the Prevention of Poverty; and a Plan for meliorating the Condition of the Parish Paupers, and diminishing the Expence of maintaining them, by John Hill, Member of the Royal College of Surgeons. Hatchard.

POETRY.

Epistle to Count Rumford, by Peter Pindar, 4to. 2s. 6d. West and Hughes.

A Satirical Epistle in Verse to the Poet Laureat, on his Carmen Seculare, containing some Strictures on Modern Times and Characters. Ginger.

The Wedding and Bedding; or, John Bull and his Bride fast Asleep; a Satirical Poem, by T. Canning, 2s. Jordan.

Alonzo and Cora, with other original Poems, principally elegiac, by Elizabeth Scot; to which are added, Letters in Verse, by Blacklock and Burns, 8vo. 10s. 6d. Rivingtons.

Juvenilia; a Collection of Poems, written between the Ages of 12 and 16, by J. H. L. Hunt, late of the Grammar School of Christ's Hospital, 12mo. 6s. boards. Rivingtons.

Lines on the Death of the late Sir Ralph Abercromby, by the Author of the Conspiracy of Gowrie, 1s. Bell.

The Poetical Works of Hector Macneil, Esq. 2 vols. 12mo. with beautiful Engravings. Longman and Rees.

Rodolpho, a Poetical Romance, 4to. 2s. Phillips.

Beauties of British Poetry, selected by Sidney Melmoth, Esq. 12mo. 5s. boards. Vernor and Hood

TRAVELS.

Travels in Portugal, and through France and Spain; with a Dissertation on the Literature of Portugal, and the Spanish and Portuguese Languages, by Henry Frederick Link, Professor at the University of Rostock; translated from the German, by J. Hinckley, Esq. with Notes, 8vo. 9s. boards. Longman and Rees.

THEOLOGY.

Unwelcome Thoughts to the Religious World in the Nineteenth Century, on the Birth, Health, Sickness, and certain Death of the Protestant or visible Gentile Church in the present Century; including Strictures on the last General Fast; with a Religious Proposition to the Church for Political Relief to Groaning Europe, by J. Carter, 6s. V. Griffiths.

Addresses to the Inhabitants of the several Parishes in the Districts of Louth and Horncastle, on the Duty of Family Prayer, and on the Reading the Holy Scriptures, with Forms of Prayer, by a Committee of the Clergy in the aforesaid Districts. Rivingtons.

The Wise and the Foolish Builder; a Sermon preached before the University of Cambridge, June 21, 1801, by Robert Luke, B.D. 1s. Rivingtons.

Eis Theos, eis Mesites; or, an Attempt to shew how far the Philosophical Notion of a Plurality of Worlds is consistent, or not so, with the Language of the Holy Scriptures, 8vo 8s. boards. Rivingtons.

The Duties of Men in Public Professions considered, in a Charge to the Clergy of the Archdeaconry of St. Albans, at a Visitation, held May 27, 1801, by Joseph Holden Pott, Prebendary and Archdeacon, 1s. 6d. Rivingtons.

Horæ Mosaicæ; or, a View of the Mosaical Records, with respect to their Coincidence with Profane Antiquity, their internal Credibility, and their Connection with Christianity; comprehending the Substance of eight Lectures read before the University of Oxford in the Year 1801, pursuant to the Will of the late Rev. John Bampton, by George Stanley Faber, A. M. 2 vols. 8vo. 14s. boards. Rivingtons.

Thoughts on the Religious Observance of the Sabbath, and on Private Prayer, by George Vanbrugh, L. L. B. second Edition, inlarged, 1s. 6d. Robson.

A Dialogue between a Country Gentleman, and one of his Poor Neighbours, who had been led away from the Church, under the Pretext of hearing the Gospel, and attending Evangelical Preachers, 1s. Rivingtons.

An Apology for the Sabbath, by John Prior Estlin, 1s. 6d. Johnson.

An entirely New Collection of Hymns, sung in all the Chapels of the late Countess of Huntingdon, with a Portrait of her Ladyship, square 12mo. 3s. Jones.

Pious Thoughts concerning the Knowledge and Love of God, and other Holy Exercises; to which is prefixed, Directions for a Holy Life, and the attaining Christian Perfection, 18mo. 1s. Jones.

On Preaching the Word; a Discourse delivered at the Visitation of the Archdeacon of York, at Doncaster, June 1801, by John Lowe, M. A. 1s Mawman.

Divine Authority of the Bible; or, Revelation and Reason opposed to Sophistry and Ridicule; being a Refutation of Paine's Age of Reason; with Observations on other Writers on the same Subject, written in France, by Robert Thomson, 2s. sewed. Higham.

Self-sufficiency incompatible with Christianity; a Sermon delivered at the Visitation of of the Bishop of Peterborough, at Daventry, June, 1801, by T. J. Twisleton, A. M. 2s. Rivingtons.

Thoughts on Modern Religion, and its Influence on Modern Manners, 1s. Rivingtons.

Notes, Critical and Dissertatory, on the Gospel and Epistles of St. John, by the Rev. R. Shepherd, D. D. F. R. S. 4to. 1l. 5s bds. Mawman.

Practical Sermons, by the late Rev. Joseph Milner, M. A. to which is prefixed, an Account of the Life and Character of the Author; second Edition, revised and corrected, by the Rev. Isaac Milner, D. D. Large Additions are made to the Life of the Author; with further Animadversions on Dr. Haweis's Misrepresentations of Mr. Milner's History of the Church of Christ; and two Sermons, not before published, 8vo. 6s. Mawman.

The further Animadversions may be purchased separately, price 6d. Mawman.

Hosea; translated from the Hebrew, with Notes, Explanatory and Critical, by Samuel Lord Bishop of Rochester, 4to. 1l. 1s. boards. Robson.

Lectures on the Church Catechism, more particularly appropriated to the Sundays in Lent, by the Rev. G. Glasse, D. D. 1s. Rivingtons.

A Practical Exposition of the Ten Commandments, with an Introduction, adapted to general Use, by the Rev. G. Glasse, D. D. 3s. 6d. fine, 2s. common, boards. Rivingtons.

The Evidence and Design of Christianity considered, 1s. Rivingtons.

A Sermon, preached before the Hon. Society of Lincoln's Inn, on the Fast Day, Feb. 13, 1801, by William Jackson, D. D. 1s. 6d. Rivingtons.

The Song of Songs, which is Solomon's; a new Translation, with a Commentary and Notes, by T. Williams, Author of the Age of Infidelity, &c. 8vo. 6s. bds. Williams.

The Practical Efficacy of the Unitarian Doctrine considered, in a Series of Letters to the Rev. Andrew Fuller; a second Edition, much inlarged, with a Defence of the same, in Letters to a Friend, 3s. Johnson.

VETERINARY ART.

An Enquiry into the Structure and Animal Economy of the Horse, comprehending the Diseases to which his Limbs and Feet are subject; with Directions for Shoeing, and pointing out a Method for ascertaining his Age, with an Attempt to explain the Laws of his progressive Motion; illustrated by Plates, by Richard Lawrence, Veterinary-surgeon, 4to. 1l. 11s. 6d. boards. Wallis.

VARIETIES, LITERARY AND PHILOSOPHICAL.

Including Notices of Works in Hand, Domestic and Foreign.

**** Authentic Communications for this Article will always be thankfully received.*

IN consequence of the ruinous and oppressive duty upon paper, the booksellers have been obliged to abandon their design of reprinting a new and complete edition of the British Poets. The new duty upon paper, so far from encreasing the revenue, threatens to destroy the consumption almost altogether. All Literary Projects which were not far advanced, are necessarily laid aside, and the stagnation in this branch of business begins already to be severely felt by Printers, and the inferior agents of literature.

Mr. JOHN NICHOLS will speedily publish an improved edition, in 18 vols. large octavo, of the Works of Dean Swift. It will be enriched with Notes by sundry persons and by the editor.

A translation is in forwardness of Citizen OLIVER's Travels in the Ottoman Empire, Egypt, Syria, and Persia.

Mr. CRUTWELL, author of several useful publications, has in the press a Tour through Great Britain, in six volumes; it is intended to exhibit a complete view of the domestic state of Great Britain.

Sir HENRY ENGLEFIELD has in the press, *A Walk through Southampton*, which comprises an interesting Survey of the long neglected Antiquities of the Town, and will contain Engravings of some of the most remarkable.

A third volume of MEDICINA NAUTICA is nearly ready for publication; which, for original matter, and more careful selection, will surpass the preceding volumes. The medical department, as well as others in the navy, acquired fresh activity from the flag of Lord St. Vincent appearing in the Channel; new facts and observations have been recorded to more advantage; and as the present volume is likely to bring down the occurrences of the fleet, to the conclusion of the war, the whole will exhibit a wider field of Medical Practice in the Navy than has ever been reaped by others. Communications for this work, may be addressed to the author.

The Rev. SAMUEL LOWELL, of Bristol, has a volume of Sermons in the press, which will be published with all convenient expedition.

Doctor HAGER is about to publish a Description of the *Assyrian History*, lately brought from the Ruins of *Babylon*, and has permission to dedicate it to the East India Company.

Dr. GARNETT, who has resigned his situation

situation as Professor of Natural Philosophy and Chemistry in the Royal Institution, (as we noticed in our last Number,) intends, we understand, in future, to devote his time to the practice of the profession to which his studies have been particularly directed, that of medicine. He also intends to deliver Lectures on the Theory and Practice of Medicine, and on the Animal Economy, as well as on Chemistry, and those branches of Natural Philosophy connected with medicine.

Mr. MUSHET, of the Clyde Works, to whom Science is indebted for several excellent Memoirs on the Manufacture of Iron, and the Assay and Reduction of its Ores, has lately taken out a patent for a new and expeditious method of converting iron into steel, by combining it with more precision than heretofore with various proportions of carbon, and by subsequent cementation to give to the steel the valuable properties of welding and malleability. Of this valuable discovery we shall hereafter give a more detailed account in the article of New Patents.

Although the influence of solar-light is so essential to the well-being of plants and animals, yet some late experiments of Dr. MICHELOTTI, of Turin, seem to prove that the sun's rays are a stimulus too strong to be supported, for any considerable length of time, by vegetables and insects in their embryo state. Having collected moth's eggs, in December, (the *Phalæna dispar. Linn.*) he put a few into two bottles coated with black-wax, and an equal number into two transparent bottles; a pair of each, viz. an opaque and a transparent one, were placed on the outside of a window, exposed to the full sun; and the other pair was so situated in a northern aspect, as only to receive the light by reflection. On the 21st of April, the eggs in the first opaque-bottle were mostly hatched, and the little caterpillars had crawled to the top of the bottle, while on the same day only one of the eggs in the transparent-bottle had hatched—as this was the first so it was also the last. On the next day a few caterpillars made their appearance in the opaque-bottle exposed to the North, and it was five days after before any eggs were hatched in the transparent one: the next year a similar experiment was tried with four more bottles, of which one was covered with black-varnish, another with red, a third with white, and the other was left transparent; into each of these some moth's-eggs were put and the bottles were exposed to the sun. Those in the black-bottle were first hatched, then those in the red and lastly those in the white one; all the eggs in the transparent-bottle perished. Similar experiments were tried with corresponding results on the seeds of vegetables; those selected for the purpose were the lupin, kidney-bean, and chich-pea: these were kept moistened with water till the process of germination commenced; their cotyledons were then stripped of their opaque skin, and some of each were put in thin tubes with wet cotton, of which some were transparent and others coated with thin lead; all the tubes were then placed in the same bottle of water and exposed to the sun. The process of germination went on at first rapidly in all the tubes, and the cotyledons assumed a yellow colour; at this period all those in the transparent tubes died, whereas those in opaque ones became green, and vegetated vigorously till they had filled the tubes.

It is now three years since Citizen DISPAN, of Toulouse, announced the discovery of a new acid exuding from the pods of the chich-pea, and which therefore he called the *ciceric-acid*: Citizen DEYEUX soon after published, in the *Journal de Physique*, a Memoir to shew that this new acid was merely the oxalic. A quarter of an acre of chich-peas having lately been cultivated by Citizen Dispan, for the purpose of obtaining a sufficient quantity of this acid for a complete analysis, it has now been subject to the rigorous examination of Vauquelin, and appears to consist of malic-acid, mixed with a small quantity of oxalic and a slight trace of acetic.

Citizen MOURGUE has lately published a Statistical Essay, which contains the result of twenty-one years observations on the relative and actual number of births, deaths and marriages, at Montpellier, from 1771 to 1792. The average of the whole population, during the above twenty-one years, is 32,897. During the three-autumnal months there are *one-fourth* more births than during the three spring-months; yet the greatest number of births is in January, and the least in June. The annual births are 1197, or 1-27½th of the whole population. The number of males born is to that of females, as 20 to 21¼: the illegitimate children form *one-ninth* of the whole annual reproduction, whereas at Paris they compose *one-fourth*. The number of marriages is 282, which is, to the whole population, as *one* to 118: of those that are born, one in 2⅓th is married. The number of deaths each year is 1112, and their proportion to the whole population is as *one* to 29¼. Of these, 546 are children under ten years old. Winter and spring are the healthiest seasons; the burials in August are to those in May, as 3½ to 2. In 1774, 1778, and 1783, the small-pox was epidemic, and in those years the annual mortality was encreased by 421 children. In the 21 years above-mentioned, three men and thirteen women died at the age of 100 and upwards; and *one* person in 7½ arrives at the age of 70.

Citizen SEGUIN has communicated to the National Institute, a Memoir on the Manufacture of *Paper from Straw*; he presented, at the same time, several specimens of the paper, some of which had been printed on and proved to be very strong and good.

A new and easy method of *purifying rape-oil* has been published by C. THENARD—it is as follows: to 100 parts of oil add 1½ or 2 of concentrated sulphuric-acid, and mix the whole well by agitation: the oil immediately becomes turbid and of a blackish green colour; in about three quarters of an hour the colouring matter begins to collect in clots; the agitation should then be discontinued, and clean water, twice the weight of the sulphuric-acid, must be added: in order to mix the water with the oil and acid, a further agitation of half an hour must be had recourse to, and the mass may afterwards be left to clarify for eight days: at the end of this time three separate fluids will be perceived in the vessel, the upper of which is the clear oil, the next is sulphuric-acid and water, and the lowest is a black mud or fecula: the oil should be separated by a syphon from the acid and water, and filtered carefully through cotton or wool; it will then be nearly without colour, smell, or taste, and will burn clearly and quietly to the very last drop.

According to a letter lately addressed by C. HUMBOLDT to Cit. FOURCROY, it appears, that during sixteen months he has been traversing the vast territory between the coast, the Orenoquo, Rio-Nigro, and the river of the Amazons. His companion, C. Bonpland, has dried, with duplicates, more than six thousand plants, and he has described with him on the spot, twelve hundred species, great part of which appeared to them to belong to genera not described by Aublet, Jacquin, Mutis, or Dombey. They have collected insects, shells, and different kinds of wood proper for dyeing; dissected crocodiles, lamantins, apes, and the gymnotus electricus, the fluid of which is absolutely galvanic and not electric; and they have described a great many serpents, lizards, and fish. Amidst the thick forests of the Rio-Nigro; surrounded by ferocious tygers and crocodiles; his body tormented with the stings of the formidable moskitos and ants; having had for three months no other aliment than water, bananas, and manioc, among the Otomaque Indians, *who eat earth*; or on the banks of the Casquiara, under the equator, where, in the course of a hundred and thirty leagues, no human being is seen;—in all these embarrassing situations he says he never repented of his undertaking. When he left Spain he intended to proceed directly to Mexico, thence to Peru and the Philippines; but a malignant fever, which broke out in the frigate, induced him to remain on the coast of South America; and, thinking it possible to penetrate thence into the interior, he undertook two journeys, one to the missions of the Chayma Indians of Paria, and the other to that vast country situated to the north of the river of the Amazons, between Popayan and the mountains of the French part of Guyana. They twice passed the grand cataracts of the Orenoquo, and those of Atures and Maypura, in lat. 50° 12' and long. 5° 39', W. dep. from Paris 4° 43' and 4° 41' 40". From the mouth of the Guaviara and the rivers Atabapo, Temi, and Tuamini, he caused his pirogua to be carried by land, as far as the Rio-Nigro, while they followed on foot through forests of Hevea, Cinchona, and Canella Winterana. He ascended the Casquiara inhabited by the Ydapaminares, who eat nothing but ants dried in the smoke, and penetrated to the sources of the Orenoquo, even beyond the volcano of Duida, or as far as the ferocity of the Guaica and Guaharribo Indians would permit him to venture. The river of the Amazons, he observes, has been inhabited for 200 years by Europeans; but on the Orenoquo and the Rio-Nigro, it was only about thirty years ago that the Europeans ventured to form a few settlements beyond the cataracts. Those which exist do not comprehend above 1800 Indians, from the eighth degree to the equator; and there are no other whites than six or seven missionary monks. From St. Thomas, the capital of Guyana, lat. 8° 8' 24", long. 4° 25' 2", he crossed once more the great desert called Llanos, inhabited by wild-cattle and horses. At the time he wrote he was em-

employed in constructing a map of the country through which he had travelled, having been so fortunate as to make astronomical observations in fifty-four places. He was about to embark for the Havanna, whence he intended to proceed to Mexico. Among the Permilano and Paragini Indians, he saw musical instruments made of the *caoutchouc*, and the inhabitants told him they found it in the earth. The *dapitche* or *zapir* is really a spongy white mass found under the roots of two trees, which appeared to them of a new genus, the *jacio* and the *curvana*, and of which they will one day give a description. The juice of these trees is a very aqueous milk, but it appears that it is a malady in these trees to lose the juice by the roots. This discharge causes the tree to perish, and the milk coagulates in the moist earth, where it is preserved from the contact of the air. He has sent the *dapitche* itself, and a mass of *caoutchouc* made from it, merely by exposing it to heat or dissolving it over the fire. In regard to the earth of the Otomaquas he observes, that this nation, so hideous by the paintings which disfigure their bodies, for three months, when the Orenoquo is very high, and they can find no tortoises, eat scarcely any thing but a kind of fat earth. There are some of them who eat a pound and a half of it per day. Some of the monks assert that they mix with it the fat of the tails of crocodiles: but this he found to be false. They found among the Otomaquas stores of the pure earth which they eat: they prepare it in no other way than burning it slightly, and rendering it moist. It is astonishing that any people can be healthy and robust, and eat a pound and a half of earth daily.

One of the prejudices which most strongly oppose the propagation of sheep with superfine wool, is the opinion, too generally diffused, that this race cannot succeed in our climate and with our ordinary pastures. The useful voyage that Citizen LASTEYRIE has recently made in the north of Europe, has already enabled us to announce that even the excessive cold does not contribute to the degeneration of wool, as the Spanish race is preserved pure in the most northern parts of Sweden and Denmark. A fact lately observed by Citizen RICHARD D'AUBIGNY, even enables us to advance, that bad food and pasturage in humid places, although they injure the health of the animals themselves, do not impair the beauty of the wool. That Citizen, called to particular functions elsewhere, has been obliged to abandon to the care of inferior agents, the flock of the pure race which he kept on his own property. This flock has been, for ten years past, managed like all those of the department of the Allier, that is to say, shut up at nights in close, narrow stables, the dung of which is only taken away once a year, and led out at days by children into the most marshy pastures and without any precaution against epizootic diseases. Citizen RICHARD, on returning to his farm, found his sheep in the worst possible state of health, but the wool had not, by any means, degenerated; and he has presented the Society of Agriculture some patterns of very fine cloth, which he has caused to be manufactured with this wool in many of the best manufactories. Citizen TESSIER had recognized the same fact in an experiment which he had tried at Rambouillet. He has abandoned, for many years together, a male and female of pure race, in a meadow very moist and all encompassed with water. Those animals had become completely savage; they took them in order to shear them with snares or gins, and in spite of such a long and unfavourable residence, their wool and that of their young which they had produced, had not degenerated. These facts acquire a great degree of importance, if it be considered that by supposing the Spanish race should come to spread itself over all France, it would be ill-looked after in a great number of places, and could only find an aliment but little adapted to make it prosper. But even in that case, the wool would still be preserved in its purity, and if the proprietors should not be able to draw all the advantage possible from this naturalization, with respect to the beauty of the individuals and the quantity of the wool, which a better order of things might procure for them, they would always preserve the invaluable advantage of selling their fleeces at a much superior price, and be enabled to deliver to our manufacturers stuffs of the first quality in that kind.

Professor GOETLING of Jena, proposes a new composition of metal to be used instead of the silver in the celebrated experiment, lately discovered by Mr. Volta. This composition consists of one part of *regulus antimonii martialis* and two parts of lead, which, being very fusible, may be easily formed into plates of any size. The effect in using this metal is not so strong as with silver, and about 100 pairs of zinc plates, and plates of that composition will

will only have the same effect as 80 pairs of silver and zinc plates. This composition however is less expensive, and not so easily oxydable. The metallic composition for making types has nearly the same effect.

The French General VIAL, who is lately returned from Egypt to France, has presented to the Chief Consul an antique *torso* of the greatest beauty. It represents the body of a youth of 15, worked quite anatomically. It was found in the Delta, and is supposed to originate from the Babylonian temple. Connoisseurs value it as the most exquisite piece of sculpture that has been found by the French in Egypt. The hieroglyphics, with which it is covered, are perfectly well preserved.

By Order of General MENOU an Arabic Journal is printing at Cairo, in order to publish the transactions of the French government throughout Egypt, to banish the prejudices and fears of the inhabitants, and to establish more confidence between them and the French. It is entitled *Tombeyéb* (accounts) conducted by the Secretary of the Divan, *Chrik Leyd Ismael el Kbarbab*, and printed in the national office at Cairo. The chieftains of the different caravans that resort to this place receive several copies, and are to take every opportunity of spreading this publication through the medium of trade to Yemen, Syria, and the interior part of Africa. Previously to its being printed, it passes the censure of the Ulema, that nothing contrary to the religious and civil laws may be inserted in it. It consists of the following sections: 1, Transactions of the French Government. 2, Transactions of the Divan. 3. Account of the Nautical Affairs of Europe and Asia, as far as they possess any interest to the Egyptians. 4. Papers and treatises relating to arts, sciences, morals and politics. The superintendance of this journal is intrusted to Citizen FOURIER, chief of the law administration.

Several Members of the Philological Society of Leipsic have formed themselves into a society, with a view of publishing a new Journal of Philology, written in Latin, and edited by professor BECK. It will appear under the title of *Commentarii Societatis Philologicæ Lipsiensis*, and will contain Memoirs on Philology in general, critical observations on authors and ancient monuments, with the method of investigating and explaining them. It is also intended to be a repository for interesting passages, and extracts from works on philology, which, on account of their shortness, are often too soon forgotten or neglected. This work will also contain extracts and translations from foreign journals, notices of new works, and, in short, every thing which may promote the study of this interesting branch of science. One number of this Journal, containing twelve sheets, 8vo. will appear every three months, beginning from 1801.

The Epidemic Distemper, which ravaged Andalusia, has entirely disappeared. This is attributed, in a great measure, to the fumigations with muriatic acid, recommended by C. GUYTON. The flattering reception given to the three physicians sent by the French government to these distressed countries, do honour to the choice of the School of Montpelier. These three Professors, on their return from Andalusia, experienced the most honourable attentions at Madrid. M. DE MASDEWAL, first Physician to the King, presented them to the Prince of Peace, and afterwards gave a fraternal dinner, at which all the most celebrated physicians of Madrid were present. M. de Masdewal did not hesitate to declare, that he owed his rank and fortune in the profession to the education which he received at Montpelier, under the celebrated practitioner CHAPTAL, uncle to the present minister, and eminent chemist.

A young botanist in Saxony, Dr. SCHWŒGRICHEN, is about to publish two volumes of the posthumous works of HEDWIG, with a great number of coloured plates.

Three numbers of a valuable work have appeared, published by the Count of WALDSTEEN and Dr. KITAIBEL, intitled *Plantæ Rariores Hungaricæ indigenæ*. They contain a number of interesting plants, with plates, nearly in the style of JACQUIN, that is to say, some of them very good, others indifferent. It is remarkable that these skilful botanists have found, in the spring-head of a mineral-water in Hungary, the *Nymphæa Lotus*, a plant which has hitherto been thought to belong exclusively to Egypt and the East Indies.

TH. DE SAUSSURE has been making some very interesting experiments on the combination of alumine with carbonic acid, and with water. Respecting the existence of carbonated alumine, very different opinions have been entertained by chemists of the first eminence. FOURCROY affirms, that, if to a solution of common alum, carbonated potash be carefully added, there will be a copious precipitate, without any considerable extrication of carbonic acid; and that if the precipitate, after

after being washed, be thrown into nitrous acid, an entire solution takes place, accompanied by a strong effervescence; hence, he infers, that the precipitate was an artificial combination of alumine and carbonic acid. GREN, on the other hand, asserts, that by a careful decomposition of a solution of alum, a non-effervescent precipitate is obtained; and hence infers that alumine has no affinity for carbonic acid. These differences of opinion, and contradictory facts, Saussure has harmonised, and by an excellent series of experiments has thrown much additional information on this interesting subject. Having prepared an effervescent alumine, by decomposing a solution of alum by carbonated ammonia, re-dissolving the precipitate in muriatic acid, and again precipitating it by carbonated ammonia, he divided it into two portions, the one finely pulverised, and the other in lumps; these were exposed to the open air for eighteen months, at the end of which period, it was found, that the pulverised alumine was no longer effervescent, but that the portion in mass was considerably so. By digesting them in pure potash, some ammonia was disengaged from the effervescent alumine, but not from the other; hence Saussure infers, that the effervescence was owing to carbonated ammonia which remained in the precipitate in mass, but had evaporated from that which was pulverised. To a solution of alum, a little carbonated potash was added, but not so as to decompose the whole of it: the precipitate hence resulting was a pure non-effervescent alumine; the effervescence, therefore, of common precipitated alumine, as in Fourcroy's experiment, was owing to its retaining some carbonated potash. A completely neutralized nitrat of alumine was prepared, to which was added a small piece of calcareous spar; a decomposition took place, accompanied by the extrication of carbonic acid, and the precipitate was pure non-effervescent alumine. Some pure non-effervescent alumine was diffused in water, which was afterwards impregnated with carbonic acid: the clear filtered liquor, upon exposure to the air, gave out its carbonic acid, and a few grains of pure non-effervescent alumine were deposited. An immediate turbidness and precipitate was also occasioned in another portion of the liquor, by a few drops of pure ammonia. The pure crystallised clay of Halle, in Saxony, which is generally reckoned a native carbonat of alumine, dissolved in sulphuric and nitric acid, *without any effervescence*. Hence it follows, that the native carbonats of alumine do not contain carbonic acid; that the artificial alumines owe their effervescence to a portion of mild alkali still remaining mixed with them; that alumine is combinable with carbonic acid through the medium of water, but their mutual affinities are so slight, that the acid is separated by the pure alkalies, and even by atmospheric acid.

From some experiments of M. ACHARD, it appears, that the germination of seeds is considerably hastened, by placing them in a condensed atmosphere, the quickness of their evolution, *ceteris paribus*, being according to the specific gravity of the atmospheric air in which they are placed. Various small animals being placed in determinate quantities of compressed air, it was found that they lived longer in this than they would have done if the same weight of air had been only at the ordinary atmospheric pressure; thus the same quantity of air that would support a bird for an hour, when compressed to a third of its bulk, will support it for an hour and forty minutes.

HUMBOLDT, who is at present engaged in a scientific journey through the Spanish South American dominions, has been making some barometrical observations near the equator, from which it appears, that there are four regular atmospheric tides every twenty-four hours, seemingly dependent on the attraction of the sun, upon which winds and storms have no influence; the mercury falls from nine o'clock in the morning till four in the evening; it rises from four till eleven; it falls from eleven till half past four in the morning, and re-ascends from that time till nine o'clock. A similar fact had been previously observed at Bengal, where the barometer rises and falls regularly every twenty-four hours.

Citizen MARGUERON, of the Military-hospital at Strasburgh, has discovered a new species of oil in the berries of the dogwood (*cornus sanguinea* of Linnæus). Having procured ten kilogrammes of the ripe berries, which, when in a state of maturity, are of a blackish colour, they were laid in a heap to soften, and heat a little; being then washed to a pulp, and submitted, without further preparation, to the press, two litres of a fat viscous oil were procured, of a clear green colour, without smell, and without taste. When mixed with sallad, it could not be distinguished from the best olive oil; various methods were tried to free it from its green colour, but without success; with the

the alkalies, it forms soap; it dissolves litharge by being boiled upon it, and thereby becomes drying: when spread upon the surface of water, and exposed to the air for a month, it assumed a solid consistence, and a white colour like wax: it burns by help of a wick, with a white flame, and without any sensible smell or smoak; a small lamp being filled with it, and properly trimmed, lasted two hours and a half; whereas, the same quantity of olive-oil, in the same lamp, and with a similar wick, lasted only two hours and a quarter; and rape-oil, in the same circumstances, lasted only two hours. In addition to these valuable properties, it is found not to congeal by a considerable degree of cold. It is probable, therefore, in those districts where the dogwood abounds, that it would be well worth while to collect the berries for manufacture.

Spanish Botanists.—Among other learned Spanish botanists, Don ANTONIO JOSEPH CAVANILLES is celebrated for the different works which he has published; he is sedulously employed in advancing the progress of his favourite science. The prints of his works have the merit of being designed by himself. He lives at Madrid.

Don JOSEPH CELESTINO MUTIS is Director of the Royal Botanic Expedition in the new Kingdom of Granada, in South America. Hitherto he has published nothing; but he has almost finished the *Flora of Granada*, which will comprehend some thousands of plants, and a great number of new genera, with good descriptions. The plates of this work are magnificent, and have all been made by artists of the country, formed by Mutis. They excited the admiration of the great Linnæus, to whom Mutis usually sent specimens of his labours in botany. This learned Professor has spent forty years in America, which he has almost entirely consecrated to botany, and traversing those rich mountains. Among other works of Natural History, he has terminated a very curious History of Ants. His descriptions are filled with amenity, and with useful philosophical views. He is indefatigable in his labours, and if his works have not yet seen the light, it must be attributed to his excessive modesty, which makes him consider them as always imperfect. However his Flora of Granada will be published on his return to Santa Fé.

Don F. A. CEA, a favourite pupil of Mutis, is at present at Paris, where he is learning from JUSSIEU, VENTENAT, &c. a number of new discoveries, which illustrate the science. He has published some ideas of his master, on the different species of quinquina, in the Annals of Physical Sciences of Madrid, and he is at present employed in decisive experiments to confirm them.

Don HYPOLITE RUIZ and Don S. PAVON, Disciples of ORTEGA, after having travelled to Peru with M. DOMBEY, and traversed that country and Chili for ten successive years, have returned to Madrid, where they are publishing their *Flora of Peru and Chili*, of which there has already appeared one number of new genera, and one of new species, on large paper, with beautiful cuts; these Professors are men of talents, and describe well; their third volume of species is finished, and is ready to be printed.

Don LOUIS NEE has made a voyage round the globe, in the expedition of MALESPINA, and has collected, with an indefatigable ardour, a great number of plants. His Herbary is very rich and curious. Cavanilles has published some of his plants, principally those of New Holland, and has rectified some errors of the English botanists, who had described them before. There are other Spanish botanists, as well in the kingdom of Spain, as in America, and in the Philippine Islands; but they are less celebrated than those here noticed.

PROCEEDINGS OF LEARNED SOCIETIES.

NATIONAL INSTITUTE OF FRANCE.

NOTICE *of the* LABOURS *of the* CLASS *of* MATHEMATICAL *and* PHYSICAL SCIENCES *during the first Quarterly Sitting of the* YEAR 9, *by* CIT. DELAMBRE.

THE limits of this sitting, and the desire of husbanding the time for readings of a kind less austere, and consequently of a more general interest, oblige us to pass rapidly in review the different Memoirs of Mathematics which have appeared during this quarter.

Citizen PRONY has published a plan which gives the rationale of that part of the instruction of the Polytechnic School, which has for its object the equilibrium and the movement of bodies.

Citizen

Citizen LACROIX has communicated his views respecting the necessity and the means of making new experiments on the resistance of fluids.

Citizen DUC LA CHAPELLE, an Associate Member, has sent us a very circumstantial Memoir on the winter of the year 8, which destroyed half of the harvest in the South of France. He finds the principal causes of this calamity in the want of snow, the false thaws, and the very abundant white frosts.

In spite of the almost continual rains, we have been able to observe, in the entire circle, the solstitial declination of the sun. These observations, although few in number, have confirmed the singular result, which has made us already find many times the obliquity of the ecliptic less, by some seconds, in winter than in summer. This singularity appears to accord with the yet imperfect knowledge, both of absolute refraction, and of the variations which it experiences in the different states of the atmosphere.

Citizen LEGENDRE has given a third edition of his Geometry, and Citizen LACROIX, the second of his Elements of Algebra. The rapidity with which these re-impressions succeed each other, at the same time that it proves the merit of these works, shews likewise how far the study of the mathematics is spreading in France.

The Executive Commission of Piedmont, to whom Citizen VASSALA has carried the models of the metre and of the kilogram, writes to the Institute, that they are about to nominate Commissaries, authorized to establish, with the greatest precision, the relations of the measures and weights of Piedmont, with the new measures of France. They announce, also, that they will contribute, with all their power, to make known the advantages of the new system, the effect of which will be to approximate the relations which ought to unite more nearly the two nations.

Two numbers of the Egyptian Decade have procured us some notices of the labours of the Institute of Cairo; we distinguish in it—1. A Memoir of Citizens LANCRET and CHABROL, on the means of re-establishing the Canal of Alexandria, the restoration of which would be no less useful to agriculture than to commerce.—2. A Table of the Latitude and Longitude of different points of Upper and Lower Egypt, by Citizen NOUET, and the observations of the same astronomer to determine the course of the Nile from Syene to Cairo; a new and important labour, executed in the most exact manner.—3. A Memoir on the Mekyas of the Isle of Raoudah, by Citizen LEPERE. This monument, constructed by the Caliph Almamon, in the year 211 of the Hegira, is a well, which communicates, by a subterraneous canal, with the Nile, and whose waters are, consequently, always on a level with those of the river. In the middle of the well rises a column of marble, divided into cubits, palms, and digits, which indicates the rise of the water. The observation is made commodiously, by means of a stair case, which winds about the interior, next to the inner wall of the well. At the arrival of the French, this well was almost filled up by the deposits of the Nile, so that it only communicated with the river by filtration. Citizen Lepere has thoroughly cleansed it; the column has been entirely laid bare, and the divisions have been found more equal than had been commonly reported. The medium size of each of the 16 cubits is 0°. 54′.—The preceding details on the Mekyas or Nilometer have been given by Citizen Monge. To perpetuate the utility of prior observations by the Mekyas, in case this monument should happen to be destroyed, Citizen Lepere presents to posterity an invariable rule to appreciate the ulterior exhaustments of the Nile, and of the level of the valley. This point is taken on the socle or foundation at the north angle of the calcareous layer or stratum, which serves for a base to the great pyramid, and it is more elevated by 42°. 5′. than the chapiter of the column of the Mekyas.—

4. And lastly, an extensive Memoir on the agriculture and commerce of Upper Egypt, by Citizen GIRARD, who terminates it thus:—"What success ought we not to hope for from the labours undertaken for the amelioration of Egypt, which, placed in the centre of the antient Continent, may collect all its productions in one, as it is, by its position, the most natural *entrepôt* of the commerce of the world?"

In the physical part, the allowed time has only permitted an arid nomenclature of the important labours of the Class; but, in Chymistry, Citizen BERTHOLLET has proved, that the propagation of chymical action is moderated—1. by the weakness of that action, and—2 by the changes of constitution to which the substances that exercise it are subject. He has established the limits of the chymical knowledge which has been hitherto acquired in vegetable physiology—And lastly, he has shewn that motion accelerates the communication of heat, by the near approach

proach of the parts which are at a distant temperature, so that their reciprocal action becomes, by that means, more lively and more instantaneous; but that we have not, therefore, a right to conclude, that elastic liquids and fluids are incapable of transmitting heat.

Citizen GUYTON has been employed in ascertaining the means of purifying infected air, and stopping the progress of contagion. He scrupulously examines all the methods pursued to our days, not excluding his own, and determines those which ought to inspire the most confidence. The same Citizen has read a Memoir on the preparation of mortars, of lime, of *beton*, and of the different species of puzzolani; he compares these different methods of construction, and gives the result of some experiments made on a large scale, even under the water of the sea, with materials which he proposes to substitute for the puzzolani of Italy.

In Experimental Physics, Citizen HALLE has given an account of the experiments relative to Galvanism, which have been repeated or made, for the first time, in the School of Medicine, by means of the apparatus of Volta. Their general result is, a demonstration of the identity of the galvanic principle with electricity.

In Meteorology, Citizen TESSIER has presented a series of questions to be proposed to the Constituted Authority, and to the Correspondents of the Institute in the departments, to procure from them all the documents necessary to ascertain the extent and the effects of the tempest of the 18th Brumaire.

Citizen LAMARCK has been endeavouring to fix the nomenclature of certain meteors; according to him, storms, hurricanes, and gusts of wind, only operate under certain clouds, which conceal the cause, traverse a band in a right line, in the direction of the wind which impells them, they have only transient effects, and lower the barometer very little or nothing at all. On the other hand, tempests are felt at a great distance, and in all directions at once; they do not last less than ten or twelve hours, and may go beyond 36—do not surprize all at once, and cause the barometer to fall considerably. According to these definitions, the winds of the 18th Brumaire last were the result of a real tempest, and not of a hurricane.

In Botany, Citizen VENTENAT, in a Memoir on the plants named *arum*, or calves-foot, (*pied de veau*) has shewn, that many of those which the botanists have given an account of hitherto, differ from it so much by their fructification, as to form a particular genus, the characters of which Citizen Ventenat has determined, and which he has named *caladium*.

Citizen BEAUVOIS has presented many designs of plants of the countries of Oware and of Benin, of which he intends shortly to publish the Flora. He has described more particularly a new genus of the family of cucurbitaceæ, which he names myrianthus, the only one of that family which is a tree properly so called. It might be called, with propriety, the tree-melon (*melon en arbre*.)

Citizen RAMOND has discovered, in the Pyrenees, a new kind of plant, which approaches to the colchici, to the bulbocodia, and the crocuses, or saffrons; he has named it *minderera*, after the Spaniards, and he has communicated the figure and the description of it. He has also made a curious observation, and even unique, hitherto; he has found the aquatic ranunculus flourishing, not as is usual, on the surface of the water, but under the water, at a certain depth.

Citizen PICOT LA PEYROUSE has announced proposals to publish a particular description of the plants named Saxifrages, and he has communicated the motives which have determined him to it, and the basis on which he proposes to establish it. The leaves, according to which he had distinguished these plants, till now afford no constant characters; there are, besides, in this genus, more hybrid species, that is to say, sprung from a mixture of the two others, than was commonly thought. Citizen La Peyrouse has sought distinctive marks in the figure; the proportion and the relations of the parts of fructification; he has divided the entire genus into many natural groupes, and he has collected, in the works of the antient botanists, and in their herbals, a more exact synonymy than had hitherto appeared.

In Zoology, Citizen LACEPEDE has described a serpent, to this day unknown to naturalists, of which he makes a genus, and which he names *erpeton tentaculé*. Its characters are, having a row of large laminæ underneath the body, and the under part of the tail covered with small scales, like those of the back.

Citizen CUVIER has made known the actual state of his researches relative to quadrupeds; he has found, at this moment, twenty-three species of those animals, not one of which has yet been seen alive on the surface of the earth.

In Medicine, Citizen HALLE has given an account of the contagious malady which

which lately devastated a part of Spain. He has proved that it was not the plague of the Levant, but the malady known in America by the name of yellow fever.

Citizen LAFOSSE has read some observations on the different ligaments considered in men and in animals; and he has shewn, by practical arguments and examples, that there are cases in which the section of those ligaments may be very advantageous.

Besides these manuscript Memoirs, several Members of the Class have published, in this trimestre, a number of printed works; but we have not time at present, says the Secretary, even to quote the titles.

Present State of the New Science of Galvanism, being the Report of a late Commission of the National Institute, by C. CUVIER.

Accident, the parent of most discoveries, has lately favoured the philosophical world in a manner which will render the present period remarkable in the history of the sciences. Some pieces of metal brought into contact have manifested phenomena which no sagacity could foresee, and a new field has been opened as vast as it is fertile in important applications. The influence of these phenomena becomes more and more extended. Being at first confined, according to every appearance, to the animal œconomy, it seems now to act an important part in chemistry. It was to the genius of VOLTA, that we were indebted for this new discovery. His opinion, that galvanism was only an application of electricity to the animal œconomy, having been confirmed by several men of science, he endeavoured to find out the means of increasing its effects, so far as to render the real nature of them evident to every body. He found that, by multiplying the pairs of metals, disposing them always alternately, and keeping them moist—certain attractions, repulsions, and commotions, perfectly similar to those occasioned by the electrical jar, are produced; and that, in general, a pile, formed of pieces of silver, zinc, and moistened pasteboard, placed alternately, one above the other, immediately manifested all the appearances of positive electricity at the extremity where the silver is, and of the negative electricity at that end where the zinc is placed. There was, however, this difference, that a Leyden phial, once discharged, exhibits no further effects, unless it be charged again; whereas Volta's pile constantly charges itself, and its effects are continually renewed; it is only by discharging it with very large conductors that its effect can be diminished even for a single moment. The Leyden phial always discharges, if there be the least moisture in continuity between its two surfaces; but if the pasteboard pieces of Volta's pile are impregnated with ever so much water, its effects lose none of their intensity: the phenomena do not cease till the pile is entirely immersed in water. These differences have excited some doubts respecting the perfect identity of galvanism with electricity; and other phenomena, still more extraordinary, have increased these doubts.

If the ends of two metallic wires be immersed in water, one of which communicates with the resinous or negative extremity of the pile, and the other with the vitreous or positive; and if they be kept at a little distance from each other, there are disengaged from the extremity of the former bubbles of hydrogen gas, and from that of the other oxygen gas, which becomes fixed in the metal when the latter is oxidable, or, if it be not so, rises in bubbles; and this action continues as long as the apparatus remains in this state. But it is not in this that the great singularity of the phenomena consists, and it is here that galvanism begins to enter the province of chemistry. It would have been very natural to consider this gas as the product of the decomposition of water, if a particular circumstance had not excited doubts in regard to this explanation. That the disengagement may take place, the ends of the wires must be at a certain distance; if they touch, no bubbles are seen. How comes it that the oxygen and hydrogen, arising from the same molecule of water, should appear at points so far distant? And why does each of them appear exclusively at the wire connected with one of the extremities of the pile, and never at the other?

Such was the knowledge respecting the phenomena of galvanism at the time of the report made to the Class in the last quarter. All the experiments made in France and other countries, arranged and confirmed by the commission, have tended to confirm the three following results:—1. An augmentation of intensity, according to the number and extent of the metallic surfaces brought into contact:—2. A continued renewal of the action:—3. A production of the two gases by the communication of the two extremities of the pile through water.

During the last three months, philosophers have redoubled their efforts; their curiosity has been excited, above all, by the

the last phenomenon: some have imagined they could distinguish in it the foundation of a new system of chemistry; others, more prudent, have suspended their judgment, or have endeavoured to refer the facts to the theories already known. But, whatever might be their individual system, they ought all to have begun by a similar research—by trying to produce the two gases in separate quantities of water. If the two quantities of water are perfectly insulated, the gas does not appear: if they are made to communicate by a metallic wire, there is only a double production of gas; that is to say, each extremity of the intermediate wire acts in the portion of water in which it is immersed, as if the wire came immediately from the extremity of the pile opposed to that which communicates with that portion, so that each portion gives, at the same time, two gases. But if sulphuric acid be interposed between the two quantities of water, the gases manifest themselves each on its own side. The case is the same if a communication be established between the water by the means of a living body, such as the hand. Thus, the production of each gas in the separate quantities of water is completely proved.

It is evident that there are only three possible ways of explaining these facts: either the galvanic action tends in each quantity of water to take away one of its constituent parts, leaving the other in excess; or it decomposes the water, and, suffering one of the gases to be disengaged at the end of one of the wires, conducts the other, in an invisible manner, to the extremity of the other, to suffer it to be there disengaged; or, in the last place, the water is not decomposed, but its combination with some principle or other, emanating from the positive side of the pile, produces oxygen gas, and with that emanating from the negative side, hydrogen.

The two first opinions have been advanced in the Class by Monge, and the other in a Memoir by Fourcroy; the third belongs to some foreigners, and particularly Professor Richter, of Jena. It appears to be so much in contradiction with the whole of the other chemical phenomena, that it would have been impossible to admit it, even if the experiment in question could not have been satisfactorily explained in another manner.

The Memoir of Fourcroy is the result of very numerous experiments made by Vauquelin and Thenard; and he adds to a very ingenious explanation of the principal fact, a multitude of circumstances before unknown. These authors admit the existence of a peculiar fluid which they call the galvanic, and which circulates from the positive side of the pile towards the negative. According to them, this fluid, on issuing from the positive side, decomposes the water, and suffers the oxygen to escape in bubbles; but it combines with the hydrogen to form a liquid which traverses the water, or the sulphuric acid, or the human body, in order to reach the extremity of the negative wire, where the galvanism abandons its hydrogen, and, in its turn, suffers it to escape in the form of gas, while it itself penetrates the wire. The following is the experiment by which the authors prove that such is the secret progress of the phenomenon:—If well washed oxide of silver be interposed between the two waters, the negative wire, near which the hydrogen gas ought to manifest itself, produces no effervescence, and the oxide is in part reduced on the positive side: the reason of this, say these authors, is, because the galvanic fluid, charged with hydrogen, loses it in traversing the oxide, the oxygen of which takes it up in re-forming the water.

The new experiments and discoveries in this interesting science will be regularly inserted in the *Varieties* of the Monthly Magazine.

REVIEW OF THE NEW MUSICAL PUBLICATIONS.

A Collection of Favourite Songs, sung by Mr. Dignum, Mr. Denman, Mrs. Franklin, Miss Daniels, Miss Howells, and Mr. Townsend, at Vauxhall Gardens. Composed by Mr. Hook. 3s. *Bland and Weller.*

THE present collection comprizes six songs, and, considering how constantly Mr. Hook is obliged to re-tread the same ground in this species of composition, exhibits as much variety and novelty as we are fairly entitled to expect. "Flatt'ring Lovers often swear," sung by Miss Howells, is an agreeable artless little ballad, and "Love and obey," sung by Mrs. Franklin, is sprightly and pointed. "Anna of the Tyne," sung by Miss Daniels, is a pleasant Scotch melody, and by no means void of originality, though not equal to the succeeding song—"Tho' Fortune shuns my Love," sung by Mr. Dignum,

Dignum, in which we find much of that striking and distinct character which marks a creative fancy, and forms the first requisite in ballad music. "The Rights of Woman," sung by Mrs. Franklin, is a plain, simple, and free air, containing several passages highly favourable to the turn of thought in the words; and "Neptune's Prophecy," sung by Mr. Dignum, is bold, firm, and animating.

Twelve Anthems, particularly calculated for Families, or small Choral Societies, by S. Webbe. 8s. *Birchall.*

These useful and improving little compositions, are intended, as the ingenious author informs us in his preface, for the perusal "of those who, on days set apart for devotion, may wish to take the aid of music in raising the mind to a contemplation of the Divine Goodness to man." The words are wholly selected from holy writ, and the general construction of the harmony requires only three voices. The tenor parts are written in the treble cliff, except in the chorusses, and the thorough-bass figures are purposely omitted, unless where the harmony might appear to be doubtful.

The different subjects consist of "Morning Devotion, Deliverance, Divine Bounty, Assembling to Worship, the Church, Wisdom, Praise, Penitence, Christ's Birth, Christ's Passion and Death, Evening Devotion, and Christ's Resurrection." Mr. Webbe has treated these several interesting and sublime subjects with much force and propriety; and those vocal amateurs, who are partial to the performance of sacred harmony, but have not leisure to study the more abstruse compositions, will derive much gratification and advantage from the practice of these familiar, but excellent, pieces.

Three Sonatas for the Piano-forte, in which are introduced Favourite Airs; with an Accompaniment for a Flute or Violin. Composed, and dedicated to Miss Graham, by James Fisin. 6s. *Goulding, Phipps, and D'Almaine.*

These sonatas are written in an easy, pleasant style, and, though by no means elaborate, are tasteful and novel. The themes are, for the most part, conceived with liveliness and feeling, and the digressive matter affords in general a just and happy relief. A favourite Welsh Air, and Queen Mary's Lamentation, are here formed into very engaging and improving exercises, and are calculated to please the general, as well as the cultivated, ear.

"For o'er the Western Ocean," a Ballad; the Words by R. C. Dallas, Esq. Composed, and inscribed to Mrs. Hall, by Joseph Major. 1s. *Lavenu.*

The appropriate simplicity of this Air cannot but greatly recommend it to the lovers of good ballad music. The melody moves throughout with nature, ease, and smoothness; and the base is, for the most part, chosen with judgment. With the unaffected plainness of the whole, we are particularly pleased: indeed, we do not know of many instances in which so much effect is produced by so few notes.

The Overture to the Iron Tower; or, Cell of Mystery; as performed with universal Applause at the New Royal Amphitheatre. Composed, and arranged for the Piano-forte, by J. Sanderson. 2s. *Riley.*

This Overture consists of four movements, which the composer has arranged in a clear and familiar style. The effect, when we heard it in the band, was strikingly good; and Mr. Sanderson has adapted it for the piano-forte with so much judgment, as to strongly remind us of the pleasure it afforded us at the Amphitheatre. The passages in general lie well for the finger, and the *execution* is calculated for its improvement.

The Farewell, a favourite Ballad; with an Accompaniment for the Piano-forte or Harp. 1s. *Preston.*

We find in the melody of this little song a great deal of sweetness and pathos, but are obliged to remark, that the accent is not always just, nor the accompaniment constructed with that science and skill necessary to the producing the best effect. The words are written with much of the true spirit of lyric poetry, and calculated to touch the finer feelings of every sensible heart.

The favourite Irish Air introduced in the second Pantomime of Harlequin Amulet, at the Theatre-royal Drury-Lane. Arranged as a Rondo for the Piano-forte, by A. Betts. 1s. *Rolfe.*

Mr. Betts, by the additional ideas which he has thrown into this old favourite of the public, has rendered it a strikingly pleasing Rondo. Where the improvement of the practitioner forms the chief object of the master, we greatly approve the adoption of popular airs, convinced that they assist both the ear and the finger, and facilitate the acquisition of a just and accurate idea of time.

Numbers

Numbers XI. and XII. of Handel's Overtures for the Piano-forte and Flute. Adapted by J. Mazzinghi.
Goulding, Phipps, and D'Almaine.

The present Numbers of this useful work, complete Mr. Mazzinghi's plan, and we congratulate him on the success with which he has executed his undertaking. We here find the Overtures to Alexander Balas, Messiah, the fourth and eighth Anthems, the Jubilate, and the whole of the Grand Coronation Anthem, which, together with those in the previous Numbers, comprize all the most popular and eligible Overtures of the great German composer, and form a most valuable little library in the grand style of organ and piano-forte music.

"Come Peace Repose with Me," a Canzonet. Set to Music and Inscribed to Miss Colburn, by J. B. Adams. 1s. *Skillern.*

The chaste and plaintive style of this Canzonet, will interest those who are fond of pathos and simplicity. The distances are natural, and characterised by a mellifluency highly favourable to the sentiment of the words.

"The Lassie of the Glen," a Scotch Song, composed by W. P. Cope. 1s. *Riley.*

"The Lassie of the Glen," is one of those little efforts, in which, though nothing scientific or classical is expected, yet we find much ease, sprightliness, and pleasantness of effect. The melody, not strikingly novel, is for the most part greatly engaging, and partakes throughout of the true Scotch style.

The Nightingale, a Canzonet. Set to Music and inscribed to Miss [illegible], by J. B. Adams. 1s. 6d. *Skillern.*

The "Nightingale" is a charming little air, and the accompaniment is ingeniously constructed in imitation of the bird, which forms the subject of the words.

[We apologize to Dr. Clarke, for the *erratum* of the press, in our critique last month, of his excellent Glee; and request the public instead of "Composed by John Cambridge, Mus. Doc." read "Composed by John Clarke, Mus. Doc. Cambridge."]

STATE OF PUBLIC AFFAIRS,

In July, 1801.

FRANCE.

On every point of the French coast, immense preparations are still advancing for a pretended invasion of the British empire. We are well aware that when we use the word *pretended* we are perfectly correct; but we regret that we are, by these means, compelled into a vast and overwhelming expence.

The divisions of flat-bottomed boats, which lately sailed from Havre, we understand, eluded the vigilance of the English cruizers; and, it is supposed, arrived at their destination.

With respect to the general state of affairs on the Continent, if we may believe the French official papers, the continental intrigues are on the point of being amicably adjusted at last. The plan of indemnities is to be extended still farther; and by suffering several of the dissatisfied powers to partake of its *blessings* themselves, the storm is once more likely to be averted. The Pope will, certainly, and with the consent of the more powerful of the Catholic States, be dispossessed of all his temporal dominions, which, there is little doubt, will be conferred on the late King of Sardinia; who, it is said, is now to be known by the new-fangled title of the King of Etruria, and who will once more be suffered to keep possession of his new gift of a crown, just as long as France or Austria shall graciously condescend to permit. There is a degree of natural reserve in the conduct of the First Consul, probably the effect of profound and perpetual meditation, which is totally uncongenial to the manners of the people of France, and which we already find has disgusted some of the diplomatic corps. Cobentzel and Lucchesini, the Austrian and Prussian Ministers, have requested to be recalled, from this cause alone, as it is said, and are to leave Paris shortly.

Paris journals, of the 8th of July, announce the arrival of the Lodi brig on the 28th of June at Nice from Egypt, which she left on the 19th of May, having taken a Turkish vessel, loaded with horses, on her passage. She brings no dispatches from the French General; as he forwarded, some days before the Lodi sailed, by three different advice-boats, accounts of the military operations up to that period, which boats are not yet arrived, and supposed, of course, to be captured. The French were in possession of Cairo

Cairo and Alexandria at the time she failed, and General Menou commanded in the latter city; and, they say, is supplied abundantly with ammunition and provisions for several years. The step taken by General Hutchinson, of inundating the country round Alexandria to the extent of fifty miles, by cutting the dyke of Lake Wadje, and opening a passage for the waters into Lake Mareotis, at the same time that it considerably fortifies his position at Aboukir, will render the fortifications of Alexandria impregnable, the waters making approaches impossible. It likewise totally prevents any intercourse between the French armies at Cairo and Alexandria.

The French treasury has, for some time, been very much distressed. The receipts were unequal to the expenditure, and some extraordinary measure was deemed necessary. The Chief Consul, who has for some time laboured under a severe illness, notwithstanding, attended a Council of Finance, and the following expedient is said to have been determined upon. Some Members of the Council were deputed to go on the 29th of June, at night, to the *Banque de la France*, the *Caisse d'Amortissement*, and the *Caisse d'Escompte*. From these three banks they obtained, by *strong representations*, about eight millions of livres in cash, being all the specie they possessed. The mode of repayment was by bills on the receivers of the revenue, at fourteen months date. The draining these banks of their specie, was likely to be productive of the most serious inconveniences. Accordingly the next morning a deputation waited upon the Chief Consul, and represented to him that the banks must stop their payments unless the specie was restored. They obtained about a million and a half of the eight millions. A negociation afterwards commenced for a loan of five millions sterling, to be redeemed by the produce of the taxes. Orders on the receivers of the revenue were to be given to the persons furnishing the loan. The negociation was attended with considerable difficulties, for the orders on the receivers were to be at fourteen months date, and it was impossible for the bankers to get their orders discounted. A hope was then held out of paying off the loan at an earlier period, with the contributions which Portugal would furnish.

By the Hamburgh mail which arrived on the 10th of July, the Turks, it seems, feel uneasy at the slow expulsion of the French from Egypt, and are under great anxiety, least an attack may be made on some of their coasts in the Morea by the French; they have refused the liberty of trading in the Black Sea to the New Republic of the Seven Venetian Islands, though solicited by the Russian Ambassador. Count Cobentzel, it is said, is to be replaced at Paris by Count Staremberg, the Austrian Envoy at the Court of London; the same accounts add, that Paswan Oglou had defeated an army of Turks near Widden, and taken one thousand prisoners. From Milan we are informed that a corps of French troops are assembling in Tuscany, their destination unknown; and that the English take the greater part of the ships bound for the Italian ports in the possession of the French. From Brussels, that the troops of Luxemburgh consisting of ten thousand men, have received orders to hold themselves in readiness to march for the coast, on the projected invasion. And from the Hague, that General Angereau, with an adjutant only, set out from thence for Paris, leaving the whole of his staff behind.

The reigning Duke of Wurtemburgh has positively refused to set at liberty the state-prisoners who conspired against his person and government. They are still confined in irons in the fortress of Asperg, and will be immediately brought to trial.

The Paris journals have arrived to the date of the 14th of July, but being published early on that day, could not contain any account of the Anniversary then in celebration. They state that the restoration of Bonaparte's health, and his appearance in public, has had the effect of raising the French funds two per cent. Various reports were in circulation respecting Gantheaume, but all enveloped in mystery. They quote a letter from Messina, saying, "that a large English vessel, richly laden, had arrived there, being captured by Gantheaume's squadron, thirty leagues west of Candia, in the beginning of June."

A proclamation addressed to the French by the Consuls of the Republic, previous to the celebration of the Anniversary of the Revolution, is to the following purport. "This day is destined for the celebration of that epoch of hope and glory, in which you witnessed the downfal of barbarous institutions, and you ceased to be divided into two people, the one condemned to lead a life of humiliation, and the other selected for the enjoyment of distinctions and grandeur; in which your property was rendered free like your persons—in which the feudal system was destroyed

destroyed—and with that system all the numerous abuses which centuries had accumulated upon your heads. You celebrated that epoch in 1790, with an union of the same principles, the same sentiments, and the same wishes.—You celebrate it this day under the happiest auspices." It concludes with, "Enjoy, Frenchmen, your situation, your glory, and the hopes of the future;—be ever faithful to those principles and those institutions which have constituted your successes, and which will accomplish the greatness and the happiness of your children."

The Official Journal of Paris, of the 11th of July, speaks of a peace with England in the following terms: "A Member of the English Parliament, lately a Minister, informs us, in a few words, of the policy of the late Administration. He wishes to make peace with France, and to keep all the colonies taken by the English, while all the allies were engaged in the continental war. By this mode of reasoning, all the Venetian territories, Styria, Carinthia, Dalmatia, &c. should have been united to the French Republic, by the preliminaries of Leoben; half of Germany, and the kingdom of Naples, should have shared the same fate by the treaty of Luneville. Batavia, the Cisalpine, and Switzerland, would have formed, long ago, French departments, and Portugal a Spanish province. On the contrary, of all these conquests France keeps only a small part. Let the English Minister imitate this conduct, and peace will speedily be made. Batavia, Helvetia, and the Cisalpine, are independent. Naples and Portugal are in the number of powers. France has only acquired an encrease of five millions of people, which is only an equivalent for the four millions of population acquired by Austria by the partition of Poland.

"Russia, Sweden, Denmark, and Prussia, have been, and still are, in a hostile state against England. Were it not for the death of Paul the First, the battle of Copenhagen would have had very different consequences; but, if the embarrassments of a new reign, and a generous wish for general peace, have induced the Emperor Alexander to soften the measures of his predecessor, he does not feel the less the obligations which the nation, at the head of which he is placed, imposes upon him; and Lord St. Helen's, however well qualified, is very far from finding at Petersburg the disposition with which the English Administration flattered itself."

GERMANY.

The Cabinets of Germany are still agitated, it appears, by the grand affair of indemnities, the dismemberments necessary to be effected in the empire, the shares to be adjudged to the principal powers of Germany, to the Grand Duke of Tuscany, and to the Stadtholder.

Those cited, and those whose lands are still undivided, redouble their activity and their courage in attempts to secure their existence; and providing against future contingencies, endeavour to make provision for that great crisis which changes the forms of states. Here there is the Counsellor of an Ecclesiastical Prince, who fearing, with some reason, for the political safety of his master, seeks to attach him to another sovereign, and to divine what will be the power he may possess; what may be his means—his projects—his political system, when he shall have submitted to the new modifications. Nor is it merely principalities, nor confined to the simple inhabitants of hamlets, that conjectures are formed as to their future destiny. The Imperial cities seem secure, but it is extremely possible that even among these cities, those which are of less importance may be incorporated with the states in whose vicinity they are placed, and that those only will be preserved whose opulence and commerce give them rank in the empire.

PORTUGAL.

Portugal has found herself under the necessity of concluding a peace with the hostile army by which she was invaded; and we have since learned, by dispatches from the British Minister at Lisbon, that Bonaparte has refused to accede to the terms which have been ratified by the Spanish Court; and it should seem, that the articles of capitulation are still a secret, in consequence of such refusal. The Spaniards, indeed, appear to have been precipitate; and yet the cause of so hasty a pacification is obvious. The Court of Madrid has uniformly manifested a reluctance to hostilities with Portugal. Spain had no effective army of her own, or rather, perhaps, chose to have none; and she might have contemplated the fall of Portugal as the prologue to her own ruin. Something of the Court intrigues, therefore, that are still playing off in the North of Europe, has been also exhibited in the South; and France appears, hitherto, to have been the dupe of the game. From the whole prospect of the dispute, there can be no doubt that the Courts of Spain and Portugal have maintained a secret understanding

derstanding with each other; the former has prevaricated and forborne from the attack as long as it was practicable; the advance of a French army, however, to effect the business which the Spanish Cabinet seemed to decline, rendered a mock aggression necessary: Spain, therefore, with an apparent desire to please her republican ally, but in reality to prevent a greater mischief still, commenced the aggression; she took the field with an army hastily collected together, and ridiculously destitute of provisions and stores; and had an army sent to oppose her of the same paper complexion, and equally devoid of energy: the mummery of a battle or two deceives the French into a belief, that both parties are seriously at war; the republican forces, *so kindly promised*, are expedited to assist the victorious career of their ally: but the moment they arrive on the frontiers of the seat of action, terms are proposed by the Portuguese Court, acceded to by that of Spain, and the French army is perplexed and paralysed.

Letters received at Hamburgh from Lisbon state, that the secret articles of the Treaty of Badajos will not be made public until the Portuguese possessions in South America are secured from invasion on the part of England, by a reinforcement of French troops.

EGYPT.

A dispatch has been received from Lord Elgin, dated Constantinople, May 23, stating the arrival of an officer from the Captain Pasha, with intelligence, that General Hutchinson had marched from Rosetta on the 18th of May, with 4000 British troops, in company with a corps of Turks of equal force, under the command of the Captain Pasha, and on the 9th attacked the French near Rahmanich. The French were driven in, and in the course of the night they retired towards Cairo, having left a small garrison in the entrenchments of Rahmanich. On the 10th the fort surrendered, and the combined force then proceeded towards Cairo, having concerted their movements with the Grand Vizir, who was at El Hanka, a position four leagues distant from Cairo, in a north-east direction. The English loss at Rahmanich is stated not to exceed 30 men. The Turkish officer reports, that a reinforcement of 3000 British troops had arrived at Aboukir about the 6th of May.

We are enabled to confirm the report of the arrival of Admiral Blanket at Suez, but instead of being capable of affording any effective aid to the British expedition, he stood himself in need of every assistance from the natives, or he must have perished from actual want, having been separated from the rest of his squadron in the dangerous and difficult passage of the Red Sea, and being totally without stores or provisions. The remainder of the ships were so much injured, as to be compelled to relinquish the undertaking altogether. The British forces, however, will be immediately joined, and probably are so already, by the Condean corps, consisting of not less than five or six hundred, from Malta.

A second dispatch has been received from Lord Elgin, dated Constantinople, June 5, to the following purport:—The French, after quitting Rahmanich, made a wonderful march, and reached Cairo on the 12th of May. It is supposed they then advanced to attack the Vizir at Belbeis. General Hutchinson, who was in his progress from Rahmanich towards Cairo, had, by the aid of the Arabs, taken a convoy of five hundred camels, with their escort of six hundred men. It was destined for Alexandria, which is understood to be in great want of some articles of provisions and of water. General Hutchinson, in his march up the country, observes, that the inhabitants were, in the highest degree, incensed against the French, putting to death every one that falls into their hands.

Admiral Blanket, in his letter to Lord Keith of the 6th, acquaints him with the arrival of the reinforcements from India, under the command of General Baird, Colonel Wellesley, Colonel Murray, &c. After the surrendering of Damietta, a corps of seven hundred men embarked on the Lake Burlos, for France, and were taken by Lord Keith.

Lord Elgin further informs, that a messenger was that moment come in from Lord Keith, dated off Alexandria, May 23, that he, (Lord Keith) had received a letter from the Captain Pasha, dated at Kemesheriff, on the 19th, that his Excellency informs him, that the Secretary of the Grand Vizir had arrived with the agreeable intelligence of the French and Copths having moved forward from Cairo to attack the Vizir's army, but that his Highness had advanced with his artillery and cavalry, defeated the enemy, and forced them to retreat. Lord Keith appears to have had no further details of this important action.

GREAT BRITAIN.

It is at length fixed, that the Duke of Portland should deliver up the seals in the latter end of July. A Council will be held

held at Weymouth about that time, to swear in Lord Pelham, who succeeds his Grace as one of the Secretaries of State.

The Royal Assent has been given by Commission, on the 27th of June, to the following Bills:—An Act for extending the Period of Preference granted, and continued by several Acts, to Bodies Corporate and Persons, for the Redemption of the Land-tax, and to amend an Act of the Thirty-eighth Year of the Reign of his present Majesty, for granting an aid to his Majesty by a Land-tax.—An Act for regulating, until the 20th Day of May, 1802, the Allowance of Drawback on the Exportation from Ireland of British Plantation Sugar, and for allowing certain Drawbacks on Sugar exported from Ireland, and for allowing British Plantation Sugar to be warehoused in Ireland. An Act to permit the Exportation of Tea to Ireland, without Payment of any Duty, under certain Restrictions. An Act for transferring the Receipt and Management of the Duties on Licences for using or exercising the Trade of a Horse-dealer, from the Commissioners for the Affairs of Taxes, and also for making further Provisions in respect to the said Duties so transferred. An Act for allowing, until the 1st of August, 1802, the Importation of certain Fish from Newfoundland, and the Coast of Labrador, and for granting a Bounty thereon. An Act for the Relief of certain Insolvent Debtors. An Act for the better Regulation of Public Notaries in England. An Act for making and maintaining a Navigable Canal from near the Town of Croydon, in the County of Surrey, into the Grand Surrey Canal, in the Parish of St. Paul, Deptford, in the County of Surrey, and for supplying the Towns of Croydon, Streatham, and Dulwich, and the District called Norwood, in the Parish of Croydon, in the said County of Surrey, and the Town of Sydenham, in the County of Kent, with Water from the said Canal. An Act for amending, widening, improving, and keeping in repair, the Road leading from Paddington to Harrow-on-the-Hill, in the County of Middlesex.

On the Motion of Mr. Abbott, an Account was ordered to be laid upon the Table, under the Act of the present year of his Majesty's reign, for ascertaining the Population of this Kingdom.

On the 2d of July an end was put to the Session of the Imperial Parliament by Commission.

The Lord Chancellor then addressed the two Houses to the following purport:—"The brilliant and repeated successes of his Majesty's arms, by sea and land, important as they are in their immediate consequences, are not less satisfactory to his Majesty's mind, as affording fresh and decisive proofs of that vigorous exertion, undaunted valour, and steady perseverance, which distinguish the national character, and on which the chief reliance must be placed for respect abroad, and for confidence and security at home. Events so honourable to the British name, derive, at the present moment, peculiar value in his Majesty's estimation, from their tendency to facilitate the attainment of the great object of his unceasing solicitude, the restoration of peace on fair and adequate terms. They furnish, at the same time, an additional pledge, that if the sentiments of moderation and justice, which will ever govern his Majesty's conduct, should be rendered unavailing, in this instance, by unreasonable pretensions on the part of his enemies, the spirit and firmness of his people will continue to be manifested by such efforts and sacrifices as may be necessary for asserting the honour of his Majesty's Crown, and for maintaining the permanent interests of the empire."

We are sorry to state, that on the 9th of July the Ambuscade Dutch frigate, Capt. V. Vois was lost at the Nore. Having got under weigh about 8 o'clock, with a strong wind to the S. W. by W. in order to proceed to the Downs, she was observed, by the spectators from the batteries, and some remarks were made, that she carried a great deal of sail, and was too much by the head; she, however, carried sail till she came near a sand, called the Middle, which is about seven miles from Sheerness, when a leak sprung; the water coming in at the hawseholes, was discovered by some women on the lower deck, (it is supposed a plank in her bows had given way) they immediately gave the alarm, and assistance was directly sent down, to put in the plugs; but it was too late, the water gaining so fast, that in less than five minutes she was upon her beam-ends, and drifted upon the Middle Sand, where she now lies, with her yard-arms above water, and her head to the southward. Boats were immediately sent from the different ships to save the people, and most of them, we are happy to state, were fortunately preserved. By what we can learn, the loss is about twenty-two, who have perished. The Ambuscade was an old frigate, and was going to join the other three Dutch ships that are coming with convoy from Ireland.

ALPHABETICAL LIST *of* BANKRUPTCIES *and* DIVIDENDS *announced between the 20th of June and the 20th of July extracted from the London Gazettes.*

BANKRUPTCIES.

(The Solicitors' Names are between Parentheſes)

ARTAUD, S. jun. Finner, ſhopkeeper. (Jones, Duke ſtreet, Lincoln's inn fields)
Angus, J. Strand, carver, &c. (Pickering, Pudding lane)
Allport, T. Lawrence Poultney hill, merchant. (Alpinal, Quality court)
Adcock, E. Birmingham, grocer. (Kinderley and Long, Symond's inn)
Bird, W. B. Yarmouth, linen-draper. (Charter, Printer ſtreet)
Bailey, W. Briſtol, linen-draper. (Blandford and Sweet, Temple)
Bibby, T. Stockport, grocer. (Wright and Reynolds, Temple)
Breton, W. March, millwright. (Miller, Carey ſtreet)
Bridge, S. Sible Hedingham, plumber. (Holmes, Mark lane)
Burchall, L. Southampton, draper. (Walker, Serjeant's inn)
Cornish, F. Taunton, cooper. (Kinglake, Taunton)
Connard, J. Piccadilly, cutler. (Wright and Bovil, Chancery lane)
Cutler, N. White's Grounds, Spaniſh-leather-dreſſer. (Fowler, Lambeth road)
Cooke, N. Charles ſtreet, Weſtminſter, army-broker. (Monkhouſe, Howland ſtreet)
Chapman, W. Rugby, ſcrivener.
Cole, B. Strand, innkeeper. (Benton, Swan yard, Blackman ſtreet)
Cougull, A. Sun ſtreet, floriſt. (Bloomfield and Foy, Manſel ſtreet)
Cohen, J. Haydon ſquare, chair-manufacturer. (Bloomfield and Foy, Manſel ſtreet)
Chigiven, W. Weſt lane, merchant. (Iſaacs, Bury ſtreet)
Campbell, J. Mortimer ſtreet, painter. (Wood, St. Bartholomew's Hoſpital
Cother, B. Wootton-under-Edge, clothier. (Price and Williams, Lincoln's inn)
Collins, J. St. Paul's Church yard, confectioner. (Wild, Warwick ſquare)
Cockayne, N. Derby, baker. (Bromley and Bell, Gray's inn)
Deacon, J. E. New Bond ſtreet, linen-draper. (Sherwood and Farrell, Canterbury ſquare)
Daſh, E. Walcot, riding-maſter. (Edmunds, Lincoln's inn)
Dearlove, J. Walworth, corn-dealer. (Smith, Hatton garden)
Dawſon, J. Hyde ſtreet, ſteel-manufacturer. (Warrand, Arundel ſtreet)
Evans, J. Mansfield Woodhouſe, hoſier. (Macdougal and Hunter, Lincoln's inn)
Evans, T. Worceſter, merchant. (Platt, Bride court)
Earle, R. Chicheſter, ſpirit-merchant. (Dally, Chicheſter)
Emmens, J. Abingdon, carrier. (Blagrave, Salisbury ſtreet)
Fearon, J. Birmingham, tin-plate-worker. (Dolphin, Birmingham)
Farquhar, C. Madox ſtreet, builder. (Buxton, Great Marlbro')
French, H. Broad ſtreet, St. Giles's, card-maker. (Bennett, Dean's court, St. Paul's)
Gidd, E. Taunton, druggiſt. (Tarrant, Chancery lane)
Girling, D. Beccles, ſhopkeeper. (Loxley, Cheapſide)
Gale, J. Bradford, clothier. (Debary and Cope, Temple)
Gilman, J. Great Yarmouth, linen-draper. (Swain and Stevens, Old Jewry)
Howard, S. Bradford, carpenter. (Shephard and Adlington, Gray's inn)
Hawkins, E. Kingſton, Hull, cabinet-maker. (Sandwith, Hull)
Hawkins, J. Newbury, dealer. (Bexwell, George ſtreet, Minories)
Halſtead, R. Horſham, victualler. (Smith, Furnival's inn)
Hill, J. Maidſtone, glaſs-ſeller. (Wilkinson, Temple)
Harding, W. and F. Mellor, Derby, mercers. (Barber and Brown, Fetter lane)
Jones, S. J. Milſom, and S. Howard, Bradford, clothiers. (Debary and Cope, Temple)
Lucey, S. Tooley ſtreet, oilman. (Gregory and Brookes, Wax-chandler's hall)
Marſh, T. Old Compton ſtreet, taylor. (Barber, Thanet place)
Myers, J. Sunderland, hardwareman. (Sanſum, Ely place)
Nicklin, E. and J. Tipton, maltmen. (Johnſon, Temple)
Olivant, A. Stamford, miller (Redifer, Stamford)
Occarſon, A. Fenchurch ſtreet. (King and Setree, Cutler's hall)
Perry, J. and G. Rigge, Bread ſtreet, warehouſemen. (Jopſon, Lincoln's inn)
Pugh, W. Worceſter, merchant. (Platt, Bride court)
Peacock, J. and C. Gill, London, merchants. (Baxters and Martin, Furnival's inn)
Phillips, C. Halifax, merchant. (Wrigleſworth, Gray's inn)
Risk, J. Drury lane, currier. (Rouſhell, Bouverie ſtreet)
Robinſon, E. Dudley, carrier. (Fellows, Dudley)
Richardſon, P. Portſea, bookſeller. (Conſtable, Symond's inn)
Rudduck, N. Monkwearmouth ſhore, butcher. (Raiſbeck, Stockton)
Rawſon, J. Leiceſter, hatter. (Keerton, Gray's inn)
Smith, R. Bradford, victualler. (Williams, Caſtle ſtreet, Holborn)
Stewart, J. Watford, mariner. (Dann and Teaſdale, Threadneedle ſtreet)
Symons, E. P. and P. W. Crapp, Plaiſtow green, weolers, (Tilbury and Sanford, Ely place)
Wilſon, R. Bread ſtreet, merchant. (Davies, Ely place)
Weller, W. W. Deptford, miller. (Lambert, Hatton garden)
Woolley, D. Carrhill, clothier. (Coulthurſt, Bedford row)
Wood, J. Wedneſbury, gunlock-maker. (Bourne, Dudley)

DIVIDENDS ANNOUNCED.

Anderſon, A. and D. Robertſon, Coleman ſtreet, merchants, July 25
Armitage, M. Newport, miller, Aug. 4
Atkinſon, R. Kingſton, Hull, merchant, Aug. 10
Bourn, S. Spalding, grocer. July 17
Baker, J. Staines, coach-maſter, Aug. 1
Banner, E. Liverpool, brewer July 21
Barratt, J. Worſley, fuſtian-manufacturer, July 28
Bradbury, S. Baſinghall ſtreet, broker, July 20
Baker, C. jun. Preſcott, tanner, Aug. 3
Buddicom, R. J. Liverpool, merchant, Aug. 7
Bamber, W. Chorley, muſlin-manufacturer, Aug. 13
Bentley, W. and W. Britain, Aſhton, lamp-manufacturers, Aug. 14
Barrs, W. and S. Birmingham, linen-drapers, Aug. 10, (final)
Cooper, J. Wild court, printer, July 14
Cooper, T. jun. Liverpool, horſe-dealer, July 21
Cook, J. Leeds, builder, July 31
Duffin, J. and R. Chipping Norton, and F. Duffin, Thame, drapers, July 28
Davis, O. Vine ſtreet, brewer, July 28
Dinividdie, J. Pendlebury, W. Dinividdie, Collyhurſt, L. Dinividdie, Mancheſter, and H. Bewicke, Lawrence lane, merchants, Sept. 15
Dixon, J. Mancheſter, merchant, Aug. 11
Eldridge, C. Cheltenham, victualler, July 30
Edwards, T. New Bond ſtreet, haberdaſher, Sept. 5
Fiſher, S. Sheffield, ſcrivener, Aug. 1
Foxcroft, M. and E. Nottingham, milliners, July 31
Fearon, H. St. Mary Axe, factor, Aug. 11
Glaſsbrook, T. Wigan, ſhopkeeper, July 25
Grimſditch, W. Liverpool, blackſmith, July 21
Greaves, J. ſenior, Walworth, inſurance-broker, July 25
Gowan, G. Great Ormond ſtreet, merchant, Aug. 11
Graham, W. P. Bread ſtreet, merchant, July 28
Grimſhaw, R. Gorton, and J. Grimſhaw, Mancheſter, merchants, July 30
Green, J. ſenior, Chorley, calico-manufacturer, Aug. 12 (final)
Holroyd, H. Greenwich, hoop-bender, July 18
Harriſon, T. Lancaſter, merchant, July 22
Heap, W. and T. Burton, Mancheſter, dealers, July 18
Harris, S. and J. Clarke, Wormwood ſtreet, ironmongers, July 18
Hair, J. Spur ſtreet, merchant, July 25
Hall, J. Weſt Bromwich, buckle-chape-maker, Aug. 21, (final)
Higgins, T. Throgmorton ſtreet, merchant, Aug. 18
James, J. Old Burlington ſtreet, taylor, Aug. 8
Kirk, G. and J. Ford, Grocers Hall court, merchants, July 25
Lawſon, S. Rotherhithe, carver, Aug. 11
Morton, G. Long Acre, coach maker, July 14
Morrell, N. Newton on Ouſe, dealer, July 23
Mawbey, J. Long Buckley, cordwainer, July 20
Maclean, W. Golport, ſlopſeller, July 20
Mardon, J. Moreton, hampſtead, ſerge-maker, July 16
Mure, H. P. and W. Mure, Fenchurch ſtreet, merchants, July 25
Mills, T. Marbank, potter, Aug. 4
Milne, A. Hatton garden, merchant, July 21
Maillard, J. J. Lime ſtreet, merchant, Aug. 1
Marriott, S. Paul's head Tavern, vintner, Sept. 12
Freeman, W. Great Tower ſtreet, cooper, July 14
Perkins, T. and J. Lazarus, Marybone ſtreet, mercers, July 18
Power, J. Nuneaton, malſter, Aug. 13
Page, C. Croydon, taylor, Aug. 4
Perry, S. Malmeſbury, linen-draper, Aug. 12
Richardſon, R. Corporation row, merchant, July 21
Roberts, R. and W. Williams, Great Tower hill lane, warehouſemen, July 25
Rogers, E. and J. Rodd, Bread ſtreet, woollen-factors, Aug. 11
Robſon, J. Berwick, grocer, Aug. 13. (final)
Scudamore, C. and A. W. Collard, Mancheſter, manufacturers, July 18
Sheldrick, W. Witham, coach-maſter, July 21
Sedgewick, M. Darlington, grocer, July 25
Sweatman, W. Briſtol, linen-draper, Aug. 4
Shaw, J. Fongewith-Haulgh, and W. Shaw, and J. Boyes, Mancheſter, fuſtian-manufacturers, July 29
Smith, T. Tunſtall, potter, Aug. 4
Smither, J. Bath, hatter, Aug. 4
Stocken, O. F. jun. Parſon's Green, coal-merchant, Aug. 8
Thompſon, J. Craven ſtreet, victualler, July 14
Thorns, J. Broadway, Weſtminſter, cordwainer, Aug. 4
Terry, J. and W. Richards, Birmingham, button-makers, Aug. 18
Towſey, G. Letcomb-Regis, miller, Aug. 11
Wilkinſon, E. and W. Dudley, Charing Croſs, vintners, July 14
Webb, J. Drury lane, taylor, Aug. 1
Watſon, T. Oxford ſtreet, dealer, Aug. 8
Woodward, T. Barnard Caſtle, ſpirit-merchant, July 28
Wilkinſon, J. Kingſton, Hull, block maker, July 31
Wyberg, J. Mancheſter, ſhoemaker, Aug. 1
Wilkinſon, E. and W. Dudley, Charing Croſs, vintners, Aug. 11. (final)
Waldo, J. J. Francis, and J. J. Waldo, Birmingham, Briſtol, and Boſton, in America, merchants, Aug. 8
Young, G. and G. Glennie, Budge row, merchants, July 25

MARRIAGES AND DEATHS IN AND NEAR LONDON.

With Biographical Memoirs of distinguished Characters recently deceased.

The number of prisoners under confinement in the metropolis, who have given notice in the Gazette of July 4, of their intentions to take the benefit of the recent Act of Parliament for their liberation is as follows:—69 in Newgate, 146 in the King's Bench, 177 in the Fleet, 31 in the Poultry, 19 in the Marshalsea, 9 in Tothill Fields Bridewell, 31 in the New Jail, Southwark, 41 in Giltspur-street Compter, and 19 in Ludgate.

Not less than *one hundred and twenty one* inclosure bills have passed during the late session of parliament; the greatest number ever passed in any former session was *eighty-seven*.

The late Secret Committee of the House of Commons, having discovered many imperfections in the corn-trade, and particularly in the corn-market of London, have, in consequence, recommended the following regulations, as conceiving that the London-market must affect all the corn-markets in the kingdom. That the present corn-market of London be inlarged, and a regular clerk appointed under the corporation, and a register kept of the proceedings. That factors shall not be allowed to deal on their own account, but be placed on the footing of brokers in other trades carried on in the City of London, by obliging them to give bonds to the same effect. That, to prevent jobbing, no corn should be sold a second time, before the payment on the first sale; and that the factors should exhibit *all* their samples at the same time, on opening of the market at a fixed hour.

With a view to remedy these material inconveniences, the Committee recommend, that effectual measures should be adopted early in the next Session of Parliament, for enlarging and opening the corn-market in London, either by removing it to the west side of Tower Hill, near the river, or by extending the Exchange in Mark-lane, by the purchase and pulling down of some of the warehouses and premises surrounding it; for appointing a proper clerk, to be responsible to the corporation; and for establishing a correct public register of transactions therein, and regular hours for opening and closing the same.

Married.] Mr. Serjeant Onslow, to Lady Drake, relict of Sir Francis Samuel Drake, bart. and only daughter of George Onslow, esq. late of Dunsborough House, in the county of Surrey.

Mr. Storr, silversmith, of Air-street, Piccadilly, to Miss E. Berger, youngest daughter of Mr. Berger, of Hampstead.

Mr. W. Saxton, of Weymouth, to Miss Branth, of Berkeley-square.

At St. George's, Hanover-square, H. M. Gould, esq. to Miss E. Hawkins, youngest daughter of the late T. Hawkins, esq. of Nash-court, in Kent

Captain Archibald Campbell, of the 88th regt. to Miss Macdonald, of Devonshire-street, Portland place.

J. Wilkes Hill, esq. surgeon, to Miss Pinkney, both of Great Tower-hill.

At St. George's, Hanover-square, the Rev. R. F. Onslow, eldest son of the Dean of Worcester, to Miss Harriet Foley, third daughter of the Hon. A. Foley, M. P.

C. Rainsford, esq. of Farnborough, Berks. to Miss M. de Dompiere, of Grenville-street.

R. S. D. Light, esq. to Miss H. Miller, second daughter of the late J. Miller, esq. of Carey-street.

T. Probert, esq. of Gray's-inn, to Miss Macdonald, of Dublin.

Mr. J. Jardine, of Gloucester terrace, Hoxton, to Miss Brown, of Estwick, Herts.

Mr. W. Daniel, of Howland-street, to Miss Weston, of Upper Charlotte-street.

The Right Hon. Lord Ongley, to Miss Burgoyne, only daughter of the late Sir John Burgoyne, bart.

Lord Pelham, to Lady Mary Osborne, daughter of the late Duke of Leeds.

Mr. F. Brewin, of Surry-square, to Miss Addison, of Sudbury.

Mr. Mason, of London-street, to Miss Swaine, of the Borough.

T. Nesbitt, jun. esq. of Kingsland, to Miss Sally Preston, niece to the late Sir John Call, bart.

At Mary-le-bonne Church, Major William Armstrong, to Miss Dana, daughter of the Rev. Mr. Dana, and niece to Lord Kinnaird and Sir W. Pulteney, bart.

Died.] W. Lee, esq. of Old Broad-street.

In King-street, Westminster, Mrs. Gibbons, relict of T. Gibbons, esq. of the Treasury.

At Kew, Mrs. M. Aylesworth.

In Quality court, Chancery-lane, in his 24th year, Mr. J. M'Culloch.

At Lockley's, near Welwyn, Herts, T. Le Blanc, esq.

In her 26th year, Mrs. Palmer, of Putney.

In Charles-street, Berkeley-square, the Hon. F. Levison Gower, widow of the late Rear-admiral Gower, and daughter of the late Admiral Boscawen.

In John-street, Fitzroy-square, in her 75th year, Mrs. E. Phipps, relict of F. Phipps, esq. of the Island of St. Christopher.

At Greenwich, in her 77th year, Mrs. Taylor, relict of W. Taylor, esq. formerly surgeon of Greenwich Hospital.

F. Wheatley, esq. R. A. of distinguished talents as a painter.

The Hon. Miss A. Ryder, daughter of Lord Harrowby.

Mrs. Whitfore, of Great James-street, Bedford row.

At Chessington, in Surry, aged 48, Mrs. Dalrymple.

PROVINCIAL OCCURRENCES.

WITH ALL THE MARRIAGES AND DEATHS,

Arranged geographically, or in the Order of the Counties, from North to South.

**** Authentic Communications for this Department are always very thankfully received.*

NORTHUMBERLAND AND DURHAM.

Lately at Brancepeth, two bats were accidentally caught in the hollow of an ancient oak, and being brought into the castle, were put under a glass case for an hour or two; when one of them was delivered of a young one, which immediately on its birth appeared very active, and clung to the mother's breast, where it continued as if in the act of sucking. This incident proves, beyond a doubt, that the bat is not oviparous, as has been sometimes thought by naturalists.

The projected improvements of Tyne Bridge commenced June 30. The completion of the work is stipulated for August 1802, when about 10 feet of commodious passage will be added to the internal width of that valuable structure.

Population of the parish of Wickham, in the county of Durham. Males 1739—females 1920—total 3659.

Population of the town of Berwick upon Tweed; males 3009, — females 4178. Tweedmouth; males 771,—females 937. Spital; males 421, — females 579,—total number of inhabitants, 9695.

An act has lately passed for the establishment of schools for the education of poor children, in the county palatine of Durham.

Married.] At Sunderland, Mr Smith, wine merchant, and adjutant to the Sunderland volunteers, to Miss Graham, daughter of Mr. J. Graham.—Captain Wilson of the volunteer corps, to Miss E Horn, daughter of Mr. T. Horn, coal fitter.—Mr. Mountain, of Knaresborough, in Yorkshire, to Miss E. Robson, daughter of Mr. Robson, taylor, of Newcastle.

At Crondale, in Surrey, G. S. Camden, esq. of Hursham, to Miss M. Gaull, second daugter of the late major Gaull, of Newcastle.—Mr. R. Rowell, farmer, of the Warrener's house, near Morpeth, to Miss E. Common, of Morpeth North Bar.—The Rev. J. Ireland, jun. of West Routon, in Yorkshire, to Miss Cunningham, of Tynemouth.

In Durham, R. Surtees, esq. to Miss Robinson.—Mr. J. Reynoldson, of North Shields, to Miss Heron, daughter of Major Heron, of South Shields.—Mr. Bell, of Walwick, near Mexham, to Miss White, of Nillstone House, near Langley Mill.—Mr. Irving, surgeon, of Hesket, Newmarket, to Miss Dawson, of Greystock.

Died.] At Newcastle, Mrs. M. Bulman, dealer in household furniture.—Mr. G. Veitch, taylor.—Miss M. Newton, daughter of Mr. W. Newton, grocer, of Gateshead. Mr. J. Dodds, architect. — Aged 80, Mr. N. Wallis, master mariner.—Aged 84, Mrs. Lake.

At Stockton, in her 66th year, Mrs. Atkinson, widow.

At Alnwick, Mr. T. Harrison, an eminent plumber and glazier.—J. Stephenson, esq. of North Shields.

At Sunderland, Mrs. A. Davie, wife of Mr. J. Davie, sail-maker.—Mr. A. Thompson, formerly an opulent butcher.

At Bishop's Aukland, aged 78, Mrs. Rawling, relict of Mr. Rawling, surgeon.—

Mr. Pawsey, of the horse shoe, Haverill. From some unknown cause, for several weeks previous to his death, he refused every kind of sustenance, and literally starved himself to death.

At Edinburgh, Mr. J. Bruce, tacksman of Kelso Mills, and an officer in the Kelso volunteers.

At Windlestone, Mr. G. Watts, gardener to Sir John Eden, Bart.

In his 62d year, while on a visit at Kerrfield, near Peebles, in Scotland, Mr. J. Robertson, goldsmith and jeweller, of Newcastle.—Captain J. White, son of R. White, esq. of Morton, near Stockton.

At York, in his 28th year, Mr. H. Guy, of Newcastle. He arrived there in the Mercury coach, on his way to the latter town, and was found dead in bed on the following morning, at the Black Swan inn. He was in a deep decline.

Mr. Wetherall, a very promising young man of Whitby, in Yorkshire. He had served his apprenticeship at South Shields, and bathing in the sea, near Sunderland, ventured too far in and was drowned.

At Stella, aged 95, Mrs. Dunn.

At Tynemouth, in his 28th year, J. Yeoman, esq. eldest son of the late H. W. Yeoman, esq. of the Woodlands, near Whitby, justice of the peace for the North Riding. He served as captain in the 23d regiment of foot in Ireland, and on the Continent.

At Corbridge, aged 76, of an apoplexy, Mr. W. Glazonby, formerly an eminent boat builder, at South Shields.

At Newwater Haugh, near Berwick upon Tweed, aged 74, Mr J. Hall, late of Fordhill, Northumberland.—Mr. Dixon, master of the Bridge Inn, Claypath.

At Westacomb, near Hexham, Mrs. Mewburn.

CUM-

CUMBERLAND AND WESTMORLAND.

A mushroom was taken up on Underbarrow common, near Kendal, on the 10th of June, which measured 2½ inches in height, without the stalk, 6¼ in diameter, 20½ in circumference, and weighed 3½ pounds!

Married.] Mr. J. Hewer, of Sebergham, to Miss Scott, of Hesket, Newmarket.

At Workington, Mr. E. Parkins, mate of the brig Industry, to Miss Lawson.—Mr. J. Armstrong, officer of excise of Castletown, Derbyshire, to Miss Tye, daughter of Mr. J. Tye, Taylor.—Mr. H. Carr, to Miss Christopherson, both of Seaton.

At Whitehaven, Mr. C. Wilkinson, merchant, of Ulverstone, to Miss Vowart. Mr. R. Sanderson, cooper, to Miss D. Hudson.

At Kendal, Mr. C. Gardner, brazier, to Miss Garnett, of Kirkland.—Mr. R. Atkinson, to Miss Hewitson.—Mr. Coward, of Elter Hall, to Miss Jackson, of Yewdales, near Coniston.

Died.] At Carlisle, aged 55, Mrs. M. Lawrie, relict of Mr. M. Lawrie, clockmaker.—In the bloom of youth, Henry, the youngest son of J. O. Yates, esq. of Skiruth Abbey.

At Whitehaven, aged 63, Mrs. Stitt, widow.—Aged 25, Mrs. E. Jefferson.

At Workington, in the prime of life, Mrs. Ellwood, wife of Mr. R. Ellwood, of Cross Hill.

At Wigton, in the prime of life, J. W. Augustus Elliott, esq.

At Kendall, at the house of Mr. Romney, aged 65, Mr. W. Cockin, late of Burton, in Kendal. In the former part of his life he taught writing and Arithmetic at St. Bees, and afterwards for many years in Lancaster, and at Nottingham. As a teacher, he was universally allowed to be at the head of his profession; nor was he more remarkable for the solidity, depth and vigour of his understanding, than for a peculiarly happy and original method of conveying instruction. Though the author of several publications of very superior excellence, yet such was his modesty and diffidence, that, excepting his arithmetic, and a single volume of poems, published solely for the use of a few select friends, no persuasions could ever induce him to prefix his name to any of them. Notwithstanding this studied solicitude to pass through life in obscurity, his essay on delivering written language, with other philosophical essays, his volume of poems, intitled Ode to the Genius of the Lakes, his Fall of Scepticism and Infidelity Predicted, his Revision of West's Guide to the Lakes, with notes, addenda, &c. his Theory of the Book on Arithmetic, &c. probably will hand his name and reputation down to the latest posterity. But though thus indifferent to the praises of men, he was by no means inattentive to his better interests: in the practice of moral and religious duties, he arrived at the greatest perfection: self-government and duty with him went hand in hand. He was the admirer, the friend and the champion of the church of England, which he defended with manly spirit and resolution, against the attacks of the doubtful sceptic, as well as against the more openly daring infidel. Had he lived, it was his intention to give the world a work, now ready for the press, on miscellaneous subjects. It is to be hoped, that some friend to deceased merit will not suffer such a literary treasure to be buried in the tomb with its author.

The Rev. J. Coward, M. A. of Queen's College, Oxford, and master of the free grammar school of Kendal.

At Ennerdale, Mr. J. Tyson, paper-maker.

At Keswick, aged 34, Mr. J. Clark.

In her 14th year, Miss Armstrong, daughter of the Rev. J. Armstrong, of Unthank.

YORKSHIRE.

On the night of June 19, between the hours of 12 and 1, a most beautiful phenomenon was observed at Hull, towards the S. W. part of the horizon, resembling, on being first seen, an immense moon, with a black bar across; it seemed then gradually to form itself into seven small distinct moons, or globes of fire, which disappeared for the space of a few seconds. Its re-appearance was equally brilliant, at first shewing itself like what we are told of the face of the moon; afterwards into 5 circular balls, and lastly like several small stars, which gradually faded away, leaving the whole atmosphere beautifully illumined and clear. During the time of its being visible, a faint blue light fell upon the surrounding objects, like that of distant torches, but when entirely gone, the appearance was serene, like a fine summer's morning.

The ship Brothers, captain Marshall, of Hull, having lately arrived there, from Davis's Straits fishery, (with 600 butts, a quantity of loose blubber, and about 13 tons of whale fins, the produce of 20 fish) reports that there has not been in the annals of the whale fishery a success so great as what has occurred this year. Eleven ships in Davis's Straits and the adjoining seas, took 128; and probably the whales were taken in the space of little more than a month. Reckoning each of these whales to produce about 30 butts of blubber, which may be considered a moderate computation, as the whales of those seas are considerably larger than what are taken in Greenland, the cargoes of these eleven ships will amount to 3840 butts of blubber, which, at the rate of 3 butts to one ton, will be found to yield, on the article of oil alone, a clear gain to the country of 44,800l.

There is now growing in the garden of Mrs. Bethell, of Rise, a cucumber seventeen inches long, and six in circumference.

The names of *sixty-five* persons, in different places of the West Riding—shopkeepers, grocers, badgers, millers, meal-sellers, &c. through

through the spirited conduct of the justices, have been lately advertised in the Leeds papers, as being convicted of having in their possession false weights, or unequal balances.

It appears that the late Mr. Thomas Hanby, of London, merchant, by his will, bearing date January 12, 1782, gave the interest of 800l. three per cent. consolidated bank annuities to the master, wardens, &c. of the company of cutlers of Hallamshire, to dispose of the clear yearly dividends of 500l. (part of the said 800l.) for the benefit of poor housekeepers, resident in the parish of Sheffield, of the age of fifty or upwards, as far as the dividends would extend, to relieve, two-thirds men and one-third women, with one blue-cloth coat or cloak, one black hat, and twenty shillings in money, to each such poor man and woman. The greater part of the residue was disposed of for maintaining, educating, and cloathing as many poor boys and girls, in the charity school of Sheffield, as the said residue of the dividends would extend to maintain, &c.

Population of the Township and Parish of Halifax.—Halifax 8886; Skircoats 2338; Southowram 3148; Raistrick 2053; Fixby 346; Elland in Greetland 3385; Staniland, including Old Lindley 1800; Norland 1181; Barkisland 1799; Rishworth 960; Soyland 1888; Sowerby 4275; Warley 3546; Midgley 1209; Wadsworth 2801; Heptonstall 2983; Erringden 1315; Stansfield 4768; Langfield 1170; Ovenden 4513; Northowram 4887; Shelf 1306; Hopperholme cum Brighouse 2879;—total 63,134. In 1764, by a statement then taken, the inhabitants amounted to only 41,135; there is, therefore, an increase of 22119, in the course of seventeen years. The number of females exceeds that of the males by 2358.

Population of Barnsley.—Males 1791; females 1815;—total 3606.

Since the commencement of the York Female Friendly Society, instituted in 1778, for the benefit of the young women educated in the Grey Coat and Spinning Schools, there has been distributed among the members in sickness, the sum of 161l. and in addition to that sum, from a separate fund, supported solely by the subscription of honorary members, the sum of 127l. has been distributed, as rewards for good conduct, in presents for funerals, and relief in cases of peculiar distress, towards which the general fund could not apply. It appears further that a fund was established in November, 1800, for allowing, by accumulation, small annuities to such of the members of the above society as may live to arrive at old age.

The royal assent has been lately given by commission to an act for paving, cleansing, lighting, watching, and otherwise improving and regulating the streets, squares, lanes, and other public passages and places within the parish of Sculcoates, adjoining to Hull; and for removing and preventing nuisances, annoyances, encroachments, and obstructions; and for licensing and regulating hackney-coaches, chairs, porters, coal-carriers, and water-carriers, trucks, carts, and other carriages within the said parish. The royal assent has been also given to an act for enabling Charlotta Bethell, widow, to make and maintain a navigable canal from the river Hull, at a point in the parish of Leven, near the boundary between Eske and Leven Carrs, in the East Riding, to Leven Bridge, in the said Riding.

A correspondent of the Leeds Mercury endeavours to point out to its agricultural readers, the many and very great advantages of the early mowing of grass, which, he remarks, are unhappily noticed but by few,—urging, that if grass stands till it is ripe, all the virtue goes into the seed, and the hay is then little better than straw. On the contrary, if grass is cut in due time, when the sap is equally distributed from bottom to top, and before it all gets to the top, then we have the whole virtue of the herb, and the end will be effectually answered, both with respect to cows kept for milking, in producing much and excellent milk, and for horses, as the hay cut in June is to them at once both hay and corn. The objection about the bulk or quantity, and letting hay stand in order to increase its weight, he attempts to remove, by adducing a well-known fact, that cows or horses will not eat clean up hay mown on the 20th of July; whereas, of what is mown before June is over, they will literally gather up the fragments, that nothing will be lost.—To this, he adds the loss in the *spirituous* part; likewise bringing into the account, the very great damage by loss of fog, &c. On the whole, he recommends mowing grass by the 20th, or, in backward seasons, by the end of June, wherever the ground is in tolerable condition; but where the land is poor, and the occupier has neither money, skill, nor industry to improve it, it will doubtless require some longer time.

A three-shear wether sheep was lately exhibited to a great concourse of people in York Market, which was esteemed the greatest phenomenon of the kind ever seen, both for symmetry and fatness. The above extraordinary animal, when alive, weighed 21 st.; when killed and dressed, the fore-quarters weighed 49 lb. each; and the full weight of the four quarters was 182 lb. He was fed by Mr. Kirby, of Catton, was remarkably small boned, and was, thought, by the best judges, to have carried more mutton for his bone, than any sheep ever produced in this county.

The committee of the meeting established at Driffield, for encouraging the breed of sheep and cattle, in the East Riding, have announced

nounced their determination to give the following premiums, at the annual shew to be held on the 25th of August of the present year, the day before the fair-day at Driffield.—For the best shearling tup, from any part of England, 10l. 10s.; for the best shearling tup, bred in the East Riding, 10l. 10s.; for the second best shearling tup, bred in ditto, 8l. 8s.; for the third best ditto, ditto, 6l. 6s.; for the fourth best ditto, ditto, 4l. 4s.; and for the fifth best, 2l. 2s. Also, for the best year-old bull, bred in ditto, 5l. 5s; for the second best ditto ditto, 3l. 3s.; and for the third best ditto ditto, 2l. 2s. Also, for the best two-year old heifer, bred in ditto, 3l. 3s.; and for the best boar, bred in ditto, 3l. 3s. Certificates will be required, that the sheep shall have been fed upon green food or hay only. No sheep will be permitted to be shewn which are coloured or besmeared, or are clipped partially on any part of the body, the tail only excepted.

At the annual shew of tulips held by the Florists' Society, at Mrs. Cawood's, in Colliergate, York, May 21, the first prize was adjudged to Mr. Ardington's Incomparable O; the second to Mr. Barker's Incomparable Miller; and the third to Mr. Meynell's Atlas.

The Rev. J. Graham, treasurer to the York Charitable Society, has been publicly called upon in a letter which appeared in the York Herald of May 30, signed W. Dunsley, to produce explicitly, fairly, and regularly, all the papers, accounts, &c. in his possession, relative to the receipt and expenditure of the monies subscribed, the suspected misapplication of some part of the fund of the society having, it is alleged, become the subject of general conversation, &c.

Married.] G. Anderson, esq. late major in the 34th regiment of foot, to Miss L. A. Croft, third daughter of S. Croft, esq. of Stillington. They immediately set off on an excursion for the Lakes.—C. Maughan, esq. captain in the regiment of York Fencibles, to Miss Cuningham, of York.

At Hull, Mr. R. S. Clark, master mariner, to Mrs. M. Huntingdon.—Mr. P. Forrester, to Miss Weddell.—Mr. Skelton, taylor, to Miss Scoresby, of Whitby.

Mr. G. Thompson of Sculcoats, near Hull, to Miss Stickney, of Drypool.

At Easingwould, Mr. T. Driffield, to Mrs. Wise.

At Thornton-le-Beans, Mr. W. Dighton, surgeon, of Northallerton, to Miss Surr.—Mr. R. Toothill, of Doncaster, to Miss Swinden, of Tinsley.

At York, Mr. J. Wolstenholme, bookseller, to Miss Roebuck.—Mr. Sturdy, auctioneer, to Miss E. Lawn.

At Halifax, Mr. M. Oddy, to Miss Mc Kinnel.—Mr. Joel Bates, to Miss A. Chambers.

Mr. W. Walker, of Bramhope, to Mrs. Hargreave, of the Red Lyon Inn, Wetherby.—Mr. Kirkpatrick, brandy merchant, of Clitheroe, to Miss Boocock, of Skipton.—Mr. J. Lupage, to Miss S. Hutchinson; both of Thorner.

At Leeds, Mr. J. Cussons, officer in the excise, of Birstall, to Miss E. Robinson.—Mr. T. Carr, farmer, of Berwick, to Miss E. Perfect.—Mr. J. Atkin, plumber and glazier, to Miss S. Wilson.—Mr. J. Spencer, of Halifax, to Miss H. Carter, of North Owram.—Mr. J. Goodhall, innkeeper, to Mrs. M. Bradley, both of Boothtown.—Mr. W. Jessop, of Sheffield, to Miss Jermyn, of Drake House, near Eckington.

At Selby, J. Forster, jun. esq. to Miss Schofield, of Howden.—R. Shepherd, esq. of Lebberston Hall, near Scarborough, aged 81, to Mrs. A. Watson, widow, aged 24. By this marriage Mr. S. becomes brother to his son, and uncle to his grandson, the father and son having married two sisters.

Died.] At Hull, in his 28th year, the Rev. Jos. Rodwell, M. A. lecturer of Trinity Church, master of the free grammar school, in Hull, and vicar of North Ferriby, in the East Riding.

In her 45th year, Mrs. Richardson, widow of the late Mr. W. Richardson.—Aged 67, Mr. J. Bird, father of Mr. Bird, surgeon. Mrs. Greenwood, wife of Mr. Greenwood, merchant.

At Sheffield, aged 20, Miss Mathewman. At the Tontine-inn, Mr. A. Elliot. He had for a great number of years been employed as a commissioner for the different inclosures in the neighbourhood.

At an advanced age, Mrs. Carr. Her death, however, was unfortunately hastened by one of those melancholy accidents, which, of late years, have too frequently cut off both the old and the young. In approaching the fire; her clothes caught the flames, and she was burnt so severely that she only survived for a few days.

Aged 66, Mr. T. Taylor, cutler.—Mrs. J. Roberts, of the White Bear inn.

At Leeds, Mrs Tottie.

At York, suddenly, Mr. C. Smith, sadler.

In her 27th year, Mrs. Laycock, of Appleton Roebuck, near York; only child of Mr. Wilkinson, of Mellington, and niece to J. Wilkinson, esq. the present lord mayor of York.

At Tickhill, at an advanced age, Mr. R. Parnell, tanner.—Mr. Needham, of Bolton, near Doncaster.

At Selby, in his 77th year, Mr. W. Richardson, a man very valuable from his great skill in farriery.—Mr. J. Lees, schoolmaster, of Austerlands, in Saddleworth.

At Rushforth Hall, near Bingley, Mrs. Willett.

At Halifax, Mr. R. Mitchell, publican.—Mr. J. Mitchell, cloth dresser.

At Whitby, aged, 65, Mr. W. Hustler, ship owner.—J. Yeoman, esq. justice of peace for the North Riding, and formerly a captain in the army.

At

At Scarborough, aged 40, Mr. J. Short, of the New Inn.—Aged 25, Mr. W. Clarkson, jun.—Aged about 60, Mr. R. Jefferson, many years proprietor of the waggons from Scarborough to York.—Mrs. Hugill, widow.—Mr. R. Robinson, ship owner. —Miss Woodhall, sister of J. Woodhall, esq. banker.

At Chigwell, in Essex, aged 67, Mrs. A. Pead, sister of the late B. Pead, esq. of Hull.

Mr C. Willis, son of Mr. Willis, of Linton Lock; he was unfortunately killed by the passing through of a vessel, in consequence of the lower gate cloughs being drawn up before the upper gates were shut, by which he was caught between the clipping part and gate swing, and crushed instantly to death.

At Malton, in his 63d year, Mr. C. Hall, merchant.—In her 94th year, Mrs. Leake, mother to Mr. Leake, of Hard Farm, near Leeds.—Miss J. Ward, youngest daughter of Mr. Ward, of Chapel Allerton, near Leeds.

In Russia, Mr. B. Goodwin, late ship-chandler, of Hull.

At Blubber House, where she had gone for the benefit of her health, Mrs. Cryer, wife of Mr. Cryer, druggist.

Aged 65, J. Waterhouse, esq. of Well Head, near Halifax.—Mr. T. Hirst, of Clayton, near Bradford.—Mrs Wilson, relict of the late W. Wilson, esq. of Allerton, Gledhow, in the West Riding.—At Heeley, near Sheffield, Mr. T. Chapman; he has left the principal part of his property in charitable legacies.

At Rothwell, near Leeds, Mr S. Smithson, attorney, and many years steward to the R. H. Viscountess Irwin.—Mr. S. Musgrave, of Allerton Grange, near Leeds.—Mr. J. Braithwaite, of Askbank, near Bedale.—Mr. S. Crompton, eldest son of Joshua Crompton, esq. of Echolt Hall, near Bradford.

At Ribstone Park, the seat of Sir H Goodricke, bart. Mrs. Orby Sloper, wife of O. Sloper, Esq. pay-master of the 4th regiment of light dragoons.—R. Carr, esq. of Gilling, near Richmond.

At Castleford, near Leeds, very suddenly, Mr. J. Hartley, of Swillington.

At Rotherham, in the prime of life, Mrs. Robinson, wife of Mr. Robinson, officer of excise.

In the twenty-third year of his age, Mr. John Ross.—The untimely death of a youth of worth and talents is always an interesting subject of contemplation! but the circle which loved and respected him, though they acutely feel his loss, may think it proper to mourn in silence. When his worth and talents were of so eminent an order as to render their possessor secure of a distinguished place in the scale of moral and intellectual merit, and were so directed as to promise extensive usefulness to society, philanthropy mourns over the loss, and friendship feels a right to perpetuate his memory, to hold him up as an object deserving of imitation. Such was the subject of this Memoir. His character well deserves an abler delineator; correctness, however, shall supply the deficiency of judgment. John Ross was born at Rotherham, Nov. 19, 1778. His parents have no title to distinction from the station they hold in society; but their honest industry and modest excellence have obtained, what riches alone could never have secured—the esteem of all who know them. John was the fourth son of fourteen children. At his birth he had no apparent signs of life, and was laid out for interment; but the accoucheur, who had been immediately called away, returning after some time, exerted himself successfully in restoring suspended animation. He was afterward a very healthy child, and never had any illness till nearly sixteen years old.—When he was three years old, he could not articulate a word; and if, when he made the attempt, he was noticed by any of the family, his bashfulness prevented him from repeating it for hours. When about five or six years of age, he had the habit of applying the masculine pronoun to females, and the feminine to males. This, with other peculiarities, induced the neighbours to suspect that he would prove an idiot: even his parents seem to have fallen into the same opinion. At that age he was first taken to school, rather that he might be out of the way at home, than from any expectation that it would be advantageous to him. The fears of his friends proved groundless. He soon became extremely desirous of acquiring knowledge; and during the whole time he remained at that school, (which was nearly nine years), his uninterrupted application rendered unnecessary even the common injunctions to attention. Mr. Ramsbottom, the teacher under whose tuition he was placed, considers him as the best pupil he ever had. His parents are members of a society of Wesleyan Methodists. John was of course brought up in their persuasion; and so early as his eighth year, began to have very serious impressions.—The candid philanthropist, however hostile his tenets to those of the Methodists, must respect them for their unwearied and beneficial zeal; their advocates, however, must admit, that there have been periods when that zeal was intemperate. Such was the period we are speaking of; and their frequent and vehement denunciations of eternal torments, had so strong an effect upon John's mind that he was thrown into the most dreadful agonies.—If any have experienced the horrors of religious melancholy, they, and they only, will be able to estimate the mental sufferings which the poor child endured. He always went to bed with reluctance, fearing that in the morning he should open his eyes in hell—he deemed it a sin to allow himself the slightest degree of levity—he used frequently to leave his friends, that he might

might weep in solitude; and, at times, thought it criminal, in such a wretch as he, to dare to address the God whose unrelenting justice he imagined was pursuing him. How long he continued in this horrid state is uncertain; but there is reason to believe that these feelings remained in their utmost violence for more than three months. He could not say to what cause he ought to assign the restoration of his tranquillity—probably the growing strength of his mind may be considered as the principal, aided, no doubt, by the more pleasing representations given of the God "whose darling attribute is mercy," by those whose zeal was tempered with knowledge. To the latest period of his life he could not look upon this part of it without considerable emotion; and, it is not improbable, that this circumstance laid the foundation of a disposition to melancholy, which at times overpowered him, and which the strong energies of his mind, aided by the most rational considerations, were not able entirely to subdue. At nine years of age he was admitted a member of the society; and, at twelve, delivered his experience at one of their public love-feasts. Though naturally diffident, he spoke with such glowing animation of the goodness of God as excited the admiration of his crowded audience.—Previously to this event he had been very much distinguished for his piety. In the youthful associations for religious exercises he was regarded as the guide and instructor. If any disagreement arose, John was the peace-maker: his exertions were usually attended with success, and his reproof was esteemed so severe a punishment, that the offending party appeared before him with nearly as much reluctance as a criminal before the bar of justice. A striking proof, surely, of his excellence, that at so early an age he met with such respect from his equals. Religious pursuits seem to have engaged the greatest share of his attention till 1791, when he was in his 14th year. He had, however, learnt the usual rudiments, and made considerable proficiency in the practical parts of mathematics. Accidentally meeting with Hawney's Mensuration, he was so highly pleased with the specimens of geometrical demonstrations which he found there, that he soon made himself master of a considerable number of them. He then got one of the Gentlemen's Diaries; but most of the demonstration there required a greater acquaintance with mathematics than he then possessed. This, instead of damping his ardour, served only to encrease it; and having determined to learn algebra and geometry, his brother, (who has communicated most of the foregoing, and several of the following particulars), taught him to solve simple equations, and procured him Keil, Barrow, and Simson's Editions of Euclid, with Hamilton's Conic Sections, McLaurin's Algebra, &c. These works John regularly studied through three times, without any assistance. So indefatigable was he in the pursuit of mathematical knowledge, that he would scarcely allow himself time to eat or sleep. His brother used frequently to rise with him in winter at two o'clock in the morning to light him a fire, that he might pursue his favourite study with comfort. Such merit could not escape notice: Mr. Allard, a Dissenting-minister, then at Rotherham, struck with his serious deportment, and his eagerness in the acquisition of knowledge, urged him to direct his thoughts to the ministry. His attention was at this time so wholly absorbed by mathematics, that the proposal was agreeable to him, solely, or, at least, principally, because he hoped it would afford him an opportunity of continuing his scientific pursuits. Receiving the consent of his parents, and the approbation of a gentleman of Mr. Allard's congregation, the plan was finally fixed upon in 1792. Nearly from this period till his departure to the academy his time was equally divided between mathematics and the languages, &c. The former, however, still continued his grand object. In the beginning of 1793, he spent three months with a school-master in the neighbourhood; and was in the habit of demonstrating 15 or 16 propositions during the half-day he attended him. (He was at this time little more than 14 years old.) With him John went thro' a course of algebra, geometry, and trigonometry; and afterwards studied at home the higher parts of algebra, and Newton's Universal Arithmetic. On these he wrote notes, which prove that his acquaintance with them was by no means superficial. The same year, he was placed for three months under the tuition of Mr. Rotheram, an eminent mathematician who had long declined public teaching on account of his health. With this teacher he went through a regular course of all the branches of mathematics. Mr. Rotheram used to say, that "John surpassed all the boys he ever knew--that he had been all his life seeking for an old head upon young shoulders, and that he had, at last, found one when he was himself departing out of the world."—He wrote in both the Diaries for 1794, and in the Ladies' Diaries for 1795, 96, and 97. His first geometrical demonstrations for the Diaries, were produced when he was about fourteen years old, before he had any farther knowledge of geometry than what he had acquired by his own industry. The interest of the gentlemen already mentioned had procured him admission as a student in the Dissenting-academy then at Northampton, under the direction of the Rev. John Horsey, and a small exhibition to assist in supporting him there. He went to Northampton in the autumn of 1795; and during the three sessions he spent there, pursued with unremitting diligence the studies to which he was directed by the academical course,

course. His turn for investigation had now a wider range. Though he always retained a decided partiality for mathematics, they ceased to engross his whole attention, or even, (except, perhaps, during his first session), to be considered as his principal object. While engaged in the metaphysical course, which formed part of the second year's business, he read Locke's Essay, and Hartley's Observations. These admirable works were well calculated to please his thinking mind. He became the disciple of Hartley; and though he sometimes thought he had reason to differ from that profound philosopher, the leading principles received in his mind continual confirmation from the observations which occurred to him in the course of his after-reflection. Possessing to a considerable extent the means of knowledge—respected and beloved by Mr. Horsey, his family, and the students—(and the respect and affection were reciprocal)—his situation was highly agreeable to him, and he would have been happy in retaining it during the remainder of his preparatory course. The dissolution of the academy in 1798 prevented this, and threw a temporary gloom over his prospects. The trustees, conceiving that a defect in his pronunciation, which is allowed to have been considerable, and apparently incurable, totally disqualified him for the ministry, refused to grant him the same assistance with other students. They sent him, however, an exhibition (which they were afterwards prevailed upon to encrease considerably), and left him to pursue whatever line of life he might think most eligible. Ross had not originally undertaken the preparatory studies for the ministry with any direct view to the interest of others: this now regulated his decision. The situation of a Dissenting-minister is by no means enviable in a pecuniary view, but he considered it as affording the means of more extensive usefulness than any other in his power. This determined his choice; and, at the application of his friends, he was admitted an exhibitioner upon Dr. Williams's fund, as a student in the University of Glasgow; a seminary which, unlike the English universities, holds out all its literary advantages, unshackled by any religious tests. Thither he removed, with three of his fellow students, in Oct. 1798, and continued there till his final departure last April. He intended to have entered the Divinity-hall; but his exhibition rendered it necessary to join the philosophy-classes, as a public student, and theological studies engaged less of his attention than they otherwise would have done. His principal pursuits were, the philosophy of the human mind, philosophical philology, history, fluxions, chemistry, anatomy, physics, scripture-criticism, and composition, partly of class exercises, and partly of sermons for his private improvement. The classes he joined were not numerous: but attendance upon, and after study of, the lectures, were by no means the boundary of his exertions. To all the pursuits he engaged in, he gave his close and vigorous attention; and this was uninterrupted, except for very short intervals, during the long vacations of six months. Most of the subjects mentioned had more or less come before him previously to his attendance upon the university; but he eagerly seized the excellent opportunities afforded him of extending his knowledge. To philology he was directed by attending the private Greek course of Professor Young. These most interesting lectures opened a new field of enquiry to his philosophic mind; and he entered upon it with ardour and considerable success. He *studied* the lectures he attended, and thus rendered himself capable of pursuing, in private, the plan of investigation laid down by the Professor. It would be unpardonable to omit mentioning, that during the last year of his residence in Glasgow, by a perseverance of which there will be found few examples, he had so far overcome the impediment in his speech, as to be able to pronounce distinctly every letter, and almost every word.—Sheridan's Lectures on Elocution, first suggested the idea. They convinced him of the great importance of propriety in elocution, and furnished the means of attaining it. He had nearly overcome all his difficulties; and, had he lived, there is little doubt that he would have been completely successful in his grand object, and, at the same time, have acquired the habit of correct reading. During the last session of the college, his disorder was making a slow but too certain progress. He had joined only the natural-philosophy classes; and his illness prevented him from giving that regular attendance to which his inclination strongly prompted him. He studied Helsham and Mc Laurin, however, privately; and thus endeavoured to supply the deficiency. He had uniformly held a high place in the public classes which he had previously attended, and received the warm approbation of his class-fellows, and of those Professors who had an opportunity of appreciating his merit. During his short and irregular attendance on the public natural-philosophy class, the Professor saw enough to convince him of his abilities—the class to ascertain that, had not illness prevented, he would have held the first post of honour. Little more need be stated to convince the reader that the assertion was perfectly correct, that Ross was "secure of a distinguished place in the scale of intellectual merit."—He was not, perhaps, peculiarly remarkable for great quickness of apprehension; but he thought deeply, and seldom adopted opinions of whose truth he had not convinced himself by a rigorous examination. He read few books; but those were well selected, and, what is of the first importance, he reflected on what he read, and made his own

own what he found reason to approve. His compositions did not discover brilliancy of imagination, nor much elegance of expression; but they were distinguished by perspicuity and correctness, and displayed habits of just reasoning and close investigation, and, not unfrequently, great originality of thought. At the beginning of April his complaints had assumed so serious an aspect, that his friends thought it adviseable for him immediately to return home. He did not leave the university without the regret of all who were acquainted with him. These all respected him; but a thorough knowledge of his worth required intimacy, and this, owing to his natural reserve, and latterly, the attention he paid to his speaking, was confined to his fellow-students from Northampton. A friend accompanied him to Leith, whence, after a considerable delay, Ross took shipping for Hull. After a tedious and uncomfortable voyage he arrived there, May 2, in a condition which left every thing to fear, scarcely any thing to hope. One of his old fellow-students received him at Hull; and he remained there two or three days till his father came to conduct him home. The meeting with his family could not but be extremely affecting. A beloved son and brother, languid, pale, emaciated, in the last stage of a fatal disorder, returned, after a long absence, to die in the bosom of his family. Minds of sensibility will require no more; but the following particulars must be interesting. "He embraced us all," says his brother, "with an affection and tenderness which were inexpressibly striking. His mother was, at the first sight of him, so affected as to render her speechless. He saluted her, and, grasping her hand, and looking earnestly in her face, said, 'Why, mother, you do not speak to me! Do not be alarmed.—I am got home—I shall soon be better, you will see.'—She burst into tears." His friend Dr. Warwick pronounced the disorder to be a pulmonary consumption. He gradually grew worse; and, on the evening of May 24, he departed without a sigh or a groan. His pious resignation during the whole of his afflictive illness was in the highest degree exemplary. Not a discontented expression escaped him; but the benevolence of the Deity was the subject on which he delighted to dwell. When asked if he would not rather live than die, he answered, 'If it pleased the Almighty I should wish to live to be made useful to mankind; but I feel perfectly resigned." The same wish had animated him in his preparatory studies. A firm believer in what he considered the leading truths of Christianity, the hope of extending the practical conviction of them was a feeling which he indulged with earnestness.—To be the instrument of encreasing the virtue and happiness of his fellow creatures—what an animating thought! When he spoke of it, it was with a glow of feeling, of which those who were but slightly acquainted with him would not suppose him susceptible; his looks, his language, strongly expressed the ardent benevolence of his soul. Dr. Warwick once enquired of him the state of his mind. He replied, "I bless God, I have the testimony of a good conscience." At another time he said, "I do not feel that extatic joy which some do, but I have confidence in God." And, most assuredly, if warm, but rational and unassuming, habitual devotion—if sterling benevolence of the first order—if unspotted integrity—if the most amiable humility, and the most exemplary temperance and fortitude, can give a right to look back without regret, and forward with well-grounded hope, the friend whose loss we mourn possessed that right.—There is here no exaggeration. The writer has long been acquainted with his worth; and, enjoying his intimacy, has studied his character, with admiration indeed, but not with blind partiality. Ross had fixed high his estimate of excellence. Nothing lower than this would satisfy him. He had not attained it; but his inferiority was not observable in his conduct. He could not always repress his thoughts; he sometimes had feelings which rigid benevolence disapproved; but here his deviation from the strictest integrity ceased, and this would have been unknown had not his candour imparted and lamented it in the ear of friendship. His situation had not allowed him to bring into action all the virtues which are requisite for the perfect character; he had yet many trials to undergo; and of this he was perfectly sensible: but his correct principles of excellence—his ardent desire to act consistently with them—his firmness and perseverance—promised the fairest success.—An All-wise Providence, however, saw fit to call him hence. "I am going home—I am going to Heaven," were the last words he addressed to his mother.

Reader, dost thou wish to possess the same eminence in moral estimation with this excellent youth? (and, if the picture give thee any idea of the original, thy heart must be depraved if thou dost not *wish* it;) follow his example: take nothing short of perfection for thy object, consult the dictates of religion as thy guide, let its sanctions cooperate as motives to constancy in thy exertions; remember, that no well-directed efforts will be lost, and be not discouraged if they do not always appear successful.—Live like him, and thou mayest then hope to die like him.

LANCASHIRE.

The model of a new invented machine for printing calicoes, linens, stuffs, &c. was lately shown at Manchester. It consists of two parts; by the first any number of colours, not more than seven, may be printed at the same time; the other is an application to the cylinder, and will print three colours at once.

By these inventions the expence of block-cutting and engraving is saved.

A very singular entertainment was given lately (June 20) by Mr. W. Smith, of Sunny Bank, near Bolton. He on that day invited all the descendants of his father and mother, who were within a proper distance. Nine brothers and sisters, and two hundred and ten nephews and nieces attended, making, with himself, a company of two hundred and twenty persons, who partook of a very handsome and plentiful cold collation, in a barn neatly fitted up for the occasion. After dinner, the whole of this interesting assembly were seated on benches in an adjoining field, ranged in regular order of descent, the oldest member of the family being placed first, with her numerous progeny, consisting of seventy-one persons, and the rest in succession, each separate family being also collected together. This extraordinary feast was witnessed by a great concourse of spectators from Bolton and the neighbourhood, who were highly pleased with the scene, and generally struck with the very respectable appearance of this family meeting, which contained a large proportion of persons in those circumstances of easy mediocrity and competency, that are probably most favourable both to the moral disposition and character, and the real comfort and enjoyment of life. It is worthy of notice, that in so extensive a family, not one individual was prevented from attending the meeting, by sickness, although a typhus fever, has for some time been prevalent where a great proportion of its members reside, and it may be further regarded as a distinguished favour of Providence, that among so many relatives, there should be none deprived of the use of a single limb or sense, except one who has lately lost her sight. The whole number of persons now living to whom Mr. Smith is uncle, in the different degrees of that relation, is not less than two hundred and twenty five; which is the more remarkable, as he is himself a bachelor, and has consequently, only one line of relations to enumerate.

The Lancaster canal has at length been compleated to the Rev. Mr. Walton's estate, at Altham, by which the adjoining country will now be plentifully supplied with coal.

An act has lately passed for making and maintaining a road from the turnpike road leading from Bolton to Blackburn, at or near the Lamb Inn, in the township of Sharples, in the parish of Bolton, to the turnpike road leading from Preston to Blackburn, at or near to Bridle-lane end, in the township of Houghton, in the parish of Leyland, all in this county.

Eleven proprietors of fire engines in the town of Manchester, were lately fined in the sum of 10l. each, for not having their engines constructed in such a manner as to consume their own smoke.

Married.] At Liverpool, Mr. J. Holmes, to Miss Board.—Mr. J. E. Harrison, M. D. to Mrs. Mitchener.—Mr. Webb, to Miss Ashton, of Huyton.—R. Carus, esq. to Miss Terry.—Mr. J. Littlewood, of Archer Lodge, near Manchester, to Miss S. Swanwick, of Shropshire.—Mr. Lloyd, druggist, to Miss Johnson, daughter of Mr Johnson, brewer.—Mr. Special, hosier, to Miss E. Button, linen-draper.—Mr Hayes, draper, to Miss Steele.—C. Tayleur, esq. to Miss Hill.—Mr. R. Taylor, to Miss Knowles.—Mr. Munro, of the regiment of the Isles, to Miss A. Fletcher, of Whitehaven.

At Manchester, Mr J. Rutherford, to Miss S Merton.—Mr. J. Davies, hat-manufacturer, to Miss C. Barton, daughter of Mr. J. Barton, cotton merchant.—Mr. J. Buck, drug-broker, of Liverpool, to Miss Powell, daughter of Mr. Alderman Powell, of Chester.—Mr. J. Walker, attorney, to Miss A. Cheshyre, of Salford.—Mr. T. Addison, to Miss A. Tudesbury, of Salford.—Mr. J. Collier, of Salford, to Miss A. Wilson, of Manchester.

At Hartmel, Mr. T. Butler, of Outhwaite Hall, Lancaster, and Ulverstone, carrier, to Miss Bispin, of Cark Hill, near Cartmel.—Mr. S. Manley, merchant, of Tildesley, to Miss Rowe, of Culchelth.

At Willingdon, in Sussex, Mr. L. Cooper, sadler, of Lancaster, to Miss H. Putland.—Mr. Georgeson, of Liverpool, to Miss J. Porteous, of Dumfries.

At Garstang, Mr. Lawrence Threlfall, of Poulton, to Miss E. Thornton, of Catteral Hall.—Mr. T. Robinson, of Croxteth Hall, to Miss M. Hunt, of West Derby.

At Winwick, Dr Mather, to Miss M. Williamson, both of Newton.

Died.] At Lancaster, Mr. R. Edmondson.—Suddenly, Mr. M. Goth, one of the royal Lancaster artillery corps of volunteers.—Mr. J. Sutton, sail-maker.

In the prime of life, greatly esteemed, Mr. Parkinson, many years surgeon to the dispensary. The lingering consumptive complaint which brought on his death, was occasioned by his great attention to the duties of his station.

At Liverpool, Mr. Hewitson, wine-merchant.—Mrs. Bridge, wife of Mr. Bridge, gardener.—Mrs. Dawson, wife of Mr. Dawson, household-broker.—Mrs. Walthew.—Aged 77, Mr. J. Blackstock.—Mrs. Somerville, wife of Mr. J. Somerville, merchant.—Aged 81, Mr. J. Brocklebank, father of Mr. W. Brocklebank.—Aged 36, Mrs. Brocklebank, wife of Mr. W. Brocklebank.—Mr. T. Ashcroft.—Mr. J. Hayes, jeweller.

Aged 13, on her way to Bath, Miss Wakefield, daughter of Mr. J. Wakefield, jun. of Kendal.

At Cross Ford, Mrs. Langstone, wife of Mr. R. Langstone, cotton merchant.—At an advanced age, Mr. E. Holme, of Ardwick.

Mr. J. Greenwood, of Colne, who for several years had lived in the open avowal of atheism, but in his last sickness, declared himself fully convinced of the existence and

attributes

attributes of the Deity, and spoke much of the horrors of Atheism. A few days before his death, he ordered four elegant volumes, on atheistical subjects, to be brought to him, which he immediately committed to the flames. He died likewise with every mark of a true penitent, professing his firm belief in the Christian faith.

At Gorton, near Manchester, in the 42d year of his age, the Rev. Wm. Dodge Cooper; for many years minister of a numerous and respectable congregation of Protestant Dissenters there, and previously at Stand in the same county. He received his education for the ministry at Hoxton, under the care of Doctors Kippis, Rees, and Savage. Here by his assiduity and thirst after learning, and by his excellent deportment, he endeared himself to his tutors, and to all the wise and good of his acquaintance; and had the opportunity of storing his mind with those acquirements—that useful and improving knowledge—for which he had before a very strong desire, and lively relish. He was much and deservedly respected through life, not only by the objects of his ministerial care, and by his numerous acquaintance, but almost without exception by every one who had any knowledge of him. He was an highly acceptable preacher; young as he comparatively was, his services had long been esteemed invaluable by both young and old in the surrounding congregations; always inclined to expatiate on subjects serious and moral; and always careful to exemplify in his conduct the truths he delivered from the pulpit He was in opinion an Unitarian; but he did not appear fond of controversy or controversial subj ects. Liberality of sentiment formed a striking feature in his character, which the writer well knows him to have extended, even to those who deny the supernatural origin of Christianity; though he would complain indignantly of such attacks as manifested indecency or virulence. To the poor he was charitable and kind; to the lowly condescending and friendly; yet to the rich respectful and courteous. His temperance was exemplary, and in some instances, from his love of virtue, approached an extreme of abstinence. While as a man and as a minister, as a scholar and as a saint, few have shone more conspicuous, none ever entered into the friendly and domestic relations of life with more simplicity, sweetness of temper, cheerfulness, and true affection. In patience and fortitude, under sufferings, he was enabled to copy him whose minister he was. This disposition was eminently tried by the loss of an amiable, beloved, and affectionate wife, in the bloom of youth and beauty, accomplished and virtuous, when they had enjoyed each other's society but a little while; and when, according to the common course of events, they must have looked forward to many happy years of heart-felt enjoyment and felicity the highest that earth can afford. His last affliction was extended and severe; he enjoyed no sound and stable health for the last four years of his life; yet little complaining was heard, little anxiety observed; but, during the long afflictive period he constantly maintained such chearfulness and such spirits as rather to amuse his visitors, than depend on their conversation for amusement under his sufferings. Doubtless he was supported on the one hand by the influence of Christian principles, pointing his view to a happy immortality beyond the grave, and on the other by the exhilarating recollection of a virtuous, useful, and pious life. These outlines of his character are drawn by the hand of friendship; but all who knew him will acknowledge their truth and justness.

CHESHIRE.

Married.] At Chester, J. Hill, esq. of Lincoln's inn, London, son of the Rev. R. Hill, of Hough, in this county, and nephew of Sir Richard Hill, Bart. to Miss Wilkinson.

At Stockport, Mr. J Hardy, cotton manufacturer, to Miss Horrocks.—Mr. A. Britain, woollen draper of Chester, to Miss R. Britain, of Upton, near Chester.—Mr. J. Evans, to Mrs. A. Thomas, both of Alford.

At Knutsford, the Rev. P. Davis to Miss Long.

Died.] At Chester, Mrs. Stringer—Mr. Sortog, many years an eminent merchant of the city.—Mrs. Jones, wife of Mr. Jones, pawn broker—Mrs Lumber, wife of Mr. Lumber, of the Custom House. Miss Kay, of the ship.—Mr. Dicas, hardwareman.—Miss M. Manning, daughter of Mr. Manning, sadler.—Mrs. Jones, wife of Mr. Jones, pawnbroker.—Very suddenly, Mr. E. Frodsham, son of the late Mr. Frodsham, of Eccleston-hall.—Mr. J. Harper, of Pettywood, Middlewich.—Mr. J. Adams, of Christleton, near Chester.

Lately at Jamaica, of the yellow fever, aged 25, Mr. J. Wright, son of Mr. C. Wright, of Chester, mercer. He was a good and thorough sailor, of tried and approved courage, steadfast in duty, firm in danger, and unshaken by distress; he was likewise a dutiful son, an affectionate brother, and a kind friend. His disconsolate parents have to lament, in the short space of three weeks, the premature loss of two hopeful young men, torn from them in the flower of their youth, and whom, they had flattered themselves, would have been the stay of their declining years, and smooth before them, in their latter days, the thorny path of life.

At Aston Hall, near Derby, J. Walker, esq. one of the proprietors of the Lead Works, lately erected near Chester.

Mr. Shaw, miller, of Trafford.—Mr. Adams, of Christleton, near Chester.

At Cornbrook, Mrs. Starkey, late of Knutsford.—Mr. J. Harper, of Petty Wood, near Middlewich.

DERBYSHIRE.

DERBYSHIRE.

Married.] Mr. C. Taylor, of Dronfield, to Miss M. Smith, of Bannercross, near Sheffield.—Mr. Barker, of Chesterfield, to Miss Shaw, of Birmingham.

At Buxton, J. Bentley, Esq. merchant of the City road, to Miss M. Cheetham.—Mr. W. Jessopp, of Sheffield, to Miss Jermyn, of Drake-house, near Eckington, in this county.—Mr. J. Oldham, of Morton, to Miss H. Bowen, of Matlock.

At Foremark, Mr. S. Dudley, trumpeter in the fifth troop of Derbyshire yeomanry cavalry, to Miss C. Brown, of Ingleby.

Died.] Aged 62, Mrs. Topiis, of Wirksworth.

At Repton-Hays, in his 53d year, Mr. S. Smith, a respectable tradesman.—Mrs. Orgill, of Chapel-in-le Frith.

At Edensor, at the parsonage house, Mrs. Peake, wife of the Rev. Mr. Peake.

At Weston-under-wood, aged 66, Mrs. Hunt.

At Shirley Lodge, Miss S. Woolley.

NOTTINGHAMSHIRE.

Married.] At Nottingham, Mr. G. Gill, hosier, to Miss S. Butcher.—Mr. Woolley, hosier, to Miss E. Trueman.—Mr. Surplice, builder, to Miss Heyrick.

Mr. Fisher, mercer and draper, to Miss Tullents, both of Newark.

At Elston, Mr. J. Harpham, to Miss Hall, of Sibthorp.

Died.] At Nottingham, Mr. Watt, an ingenious mechanic.—Aged 74, Mrs. Frost, relict of the late T. Frost, esq.

Miss Bardsley, only daughter of James Bardsley, esq. This amiable young lady fell a martyr to that irremediable disease, consumption: a malady, which frequently deprives the world of some of its best and fairest ornaments. In fulfilling the various duties of her situation, few have exceeded the lamented subject of this brief memorial. Sincere and obliging as a friend, kind and endearing as a sister, and dutiful and affectionate as a daughter, she enjoyed the cordial love and esteem of her relatives and friends. To a good understanding, she united engaging and polished manners, and a scrupulous regard to decorum in her conduct and actions. Thus while preserved from levity and indiscretion, by the rectitude of her heart, her good sense and the delicacy of her feelings, she not only afforded an useful example to the younger part of her own sex, but was qualified to aid, by her discreet advice, the more mature and experienced of her friends and relatives. But the brightest trait of her character remains to be pourtrayed—her unaffected piety, and firm hope in the great truths and consolations of Christianity had long been known and felt by her friends. Yet, during the course, and especially at the termination of her lingering and painful sickness, did her Christian virtues appear with increased lustre!

At Newark, Mr. W. Anderton, of Nether Edge, near Sheffield.

In London, G. Wragg, esq. attorney of Mansfield.

At Wyverton, near Bingham, aged 37, Mr. J. Marriott.

At Collingham, near Newark, advanced in years, Mrs. Toyne, widow.

LINCOLNSHIRE.

The grammar school at Gainsborough which was founded by Queen Elizabeth, was either not endowed by her Majesty, or time and negligence have suffered the endowment to flow into other channels; but though the want of royal munificence has been, in part, compensated from other sources, still the establishment is found to be too small for the comfort of the pupils, and the master's own family; and it has been, therefore, determined to enlarge it by subscription. On this occasion, a liberality has been evinced not often paralleled. Almost all the principal inhabitants have voluntarily come forward to support the plan, among whom Mr. Hickman has subscribed 40 guineas, the Master of the School 30 guineas, Messrs. Wm. Hornby, J. Smith, G. Parnell, W. Barnard, W. Etherington, and J. Nettleship, each 20, the late Mr. Whitehouse 20, and J. Wetherall, esq. 10l. Though some conveniences have been given up in consequence of the increased price of building materials, yet still it is hoped that the subscription will be fonnd adequate to the erection of a lofty and spacious school-room, with chambers over it, in communication with the present house, which will furnish accommodations for an assistant, &c. &c.

Married.] At Gainsborough, Mr. L. Williamson, to Miss E. Manknell.—The Rev. Mr. Jackson, fellow of St. John's college, Cambridge, to Miss Willan, both of Stamford.

At Boston, Mr. Watson, builder, to Miss Flint.

Mr. J. Snow, to Miss Redhead; both of Metheringham, near Lincoln.

Died. At Lincoln, Mrs. Fowler, widow, daughter of the late Alderman Threkstone, Mrs. E. Lake, a lady far advanced in years,—Mr. G. Flower, grocer.—Suddenly, whilst at dinner in the city, Mr. Radley, of Heapham, near Gainsborough.—Aged 89, Mrs. E. Hales, daughter of the late Sir Christopher Hales, bart.—Aged 55, Mr. T. Taylor, master of the House of Industry.—Mr. Nettleship, of the Dolphin inn.

At Boston, very suddenly, Mr. George, many years master of the Indian Queen, public house.—Mr. Squire, merchant. In him the beautiful words of the Royal Psalmist are fully exemplified: "Mark the perfect man, and behold the upright, for the end of that man is peace."

At Louth, aged 75, Mr. S. Brown, hair-dresser.—Suddenly, Mrs. Orrell.—Aged 74, Mrs. Sewell, widow.

At Gainsborough, in his sixtieth year, very suddenly, J. Turner, esq. for many years a respectable merchant, but had lately retired from business, having built a neat mansion in the town, with the intention of enjoying the fruits of his persevering industry. He drank tea and was very chearful, but after walking out, finding himself unwell, had only just time to walk into a shop, sit down, and call for a glass of peppermint-water, before he expired.

Aged 88, Mrs. Bellamy, widow.—Mrs. Coates, wife of J. Coates, esq. wine merchant.

At Stamford, aged 36, Mrs. Boughton, wife of Mr. Boughton, grocer.—Aged 17, Mr. Robinson, eldest son of Mr. Robinson, coach-maker. His death was occasioned by his incautiously going into the river, a few days before, when in a state of high perspiration

At Spilsby, Mr. L. Barker, butcher.—Suddenly, aged 51, Mrs. H. Hill.

Advanced in years, Mr. J. Birt, of Welbourn, near Leadenham, a quaker; he was a kind friend and neighbour, receiving pleasure in doing good to all his acquaintance.

Mrs. Kitchen, wife of Mr. T. Kitchen, farmer, of Greatwell, near Lincoln.

At Sibsey, near Boston, aged 92, Mrs. Bromfleet.

At Freiston, near the same place, aged 93, Mr. Parvin.

At Donington, Mr. Shilcock, quarter-master of the Falkingham troop of yeomanry.

At Uffington, near Stamford, aged 77, Mrs. Cuthbert, widow.—Mr. J. Newman, of Easton, near Stamford.—Mrs. Key, wife of Mr. Key, attorney, at Holbeach.

At Barrowby, near Grantham, Mrs. Turner, widow.

LEICESTERSHIRE.

A stone was taken out of the bladder of a female patient at the infirmary in Leicester, who died of the disease (having applied too late to undergo the operation) of the enormous weight of 27 ounces. The above stone is supposed to be the largest ever found in the human bladder.

Married.] Mr. S. Timms, of Ashby-de-la Zouch, to Miss Clarke, of Packington.—Mr. Vernon, of Pailton, to Miss Davenport, of Wigstone.—Mr. C. Hewitt, merchant, of Manchester, to Mrs. F. Adcock, widow, and eldest daughter of Mr. H. Wotton, of Poulteney Lodge.

Died. At Leicester, in her 29th year, Miss Louisa Arnold, youngest daughter of Dr. Arnold.—Aged 84, Mrs. Anderson, mother of the Rev. Mr. Anderson.

At Belgrave, Mr. Palmer, of the Wheat Sheaf public house.—Mr. Mobbs, of Hampstead, formerly of Leicester.—Aged 53, Mrs. S. Pares, wife of Mr. C. Pares, butcher, of Kegworth.

STAFFORDSHIRE.

The Staffordshire Agricultural Society, R. Digott, esq. President, T Anson, esq. Vice-president, have offered the following premiums to be paid at their next meeting to be held at Litchfield, on July 21. To the person who shall produce the best shear hog ram, a gold medal; for the second best ditto a silver medal.—For the best two-shear ram, a gold medal; for the second best ditto, a silver medal.—For the best three-years old fat wether sheep, a gold medal; for the second best ditto, a silver medal.—For the best two-years old fat ditto, a gold medal; for the second best ditto, a silver medal.—For the best boar pig, a gold medal.—For the best gelt-in pig, a gold medal.—For the best yearling bull, a gold medal; for the second best ditto, a silver medal.—For the best two-years old bull, a gold medal; and for the second best ditto, a silver medal.

The bill for inclosing Needwood forest, in this county, having been lately enacted into a law, gives an increase of 10,000 acres of fine corn land for the benefit of the state.

Married.] At Wolverhampton, Mr. J. L. Donlon, to Miss E. Ryley.

Died. At Stafford, at the house of his brother A. Campbell, esq. M. D. the Rev. R. Campbell, A. M. rector of Mordeford, near Hereford.—Aged 84, Mrs. Wetwood, widow.

At Litchfield, Mrs. Simpson, wife of S. Simpson, esq.

At Uttoxeter, Mrs. Smith, wife of Mr. Smith, saddler.

Mr. E. Warner, of Broad Oaks, near Uttoxeter.

At Cheadle, aged 63, G. Spencer, gent.—Mrs. Hubball, of the Brick House, near Stafford.

At Wednesbury, in his 28th year, the Rev. Moses Taylor, Dissenting minister. His death was very unexpected, by which a widow and three small children are left in a destitute situation.

WARWICKSHIRE.

It appears that a PENNY CLUB was established about two years ago, at Harbourne, a parish nearly adjoining that of Birmingham, the members of which are principally composed of poor children, every one of whom subscribes one penny per week: once in two years the stock is laid out in cloathing, and then equally distributed among such poor members as are at that time on the list. The most pleasing effect has been already produced in consequence of this institution, and the charming spectacle was lately presented of more than 200 children neatly cloathed by this weekly deposit of money. The children subscribers are about 220, and the fund is increased by about 100 neighbours, who, friendly to the cause, subscribe the like sum, as as honorary members. The money is placed in a friendly hand, who allows 5 per cent. interest for it. In the parish of Painswick, Gloucestershire, a similar measure was set on foot in 1786, where it has produced the same happy effects as in the above-mentioned parish.

The advantage recently derived to the proprietors of the Birmingham Union-mill, upon the average price of bread and flour, for four weeks consecutive, compared with that of the town price, is stated to have been no less than 7d. ½ per peck, the aggregate amount of which for that period, is to the body of subscribers nearly 500l. ! !

Married.] At Dudley, Mr. J. Horton, to Miss E. Sutton, both of Tipton.

At Birmingham, Mr. T. Fox, to Miss A. Freeth.—Mr. J. H. Bolton, to Miss E. Edwards.—Mr. T. Allchurch, of Cradley, to Miss Scofield.—J. Smith, esq. of Penzance, to Miss M. S. Law.—Mr. T. Buckton, of Deritend, to Miss Owen.—Mr. Johnson, to Mrs. Beddowes, of the Green Man public-house. —Mr. J. Preston, to Miss A. D. Tutin.—Mr. J. Pratt, of Hempstead, to Miss Crocker, of Handsworth.—Mr. T. Barnes, to Miss Moulton, both of Kenilworth.—Mr. D. Maling, of Deritend, to Miss Brown, of Hall-end, near Polesworth.

Died.] At Birmingham, Mrs. Forest, relict of the late Mr. Forest, hair-dresser.—Aged 25, Mr. J. White, miniature-painter.

At Coventry, Mrs. Hook, widow.—Mrs. Ashbourne.—Mr. Rogers, of Summer-hill, near Birmingham.—Aged 76, W. Harrison, gent. of Kingsbury.

At Lutterworth, Mrs. Steward, wife of the late T. Steward, esq. formerly of Birmingham.—Mrs. Maullin, of Coseley.—Mr. J. Hawkes, of Wellibourn, a serjeant in Capt. Shirley's troop of Warwickshire Yeomanry Cavalry.

At Hampton, in Arden, Mrs. Lillington, wife of the Rev. R. Lillington, vicar.—Mr. Brown, a respectable farmer of Brinklow.

SHROPSHIRE.

Married. Mr. Holland, shoe-maker, to Miss Dodd, both of Whitchurch.—Mr. W. Davis, of Birmingham, to Miss S. Crowther, of Beobridge, in this county.—Mr. R. Grosvenor, attorney, of Market-Drayton, to Miss Emery, of Stone.

At Madeley, J. Purslow, esq. to Miss Boden, of Dawley.

At Dawley, Mr. Crumpton, to Miss Hornblower, of Madeley-Wood.—Mr. B. Whitehead, grocer, of Bridgnorth, to Miss N. Poolton, of Belton.

At Wentnor, Mr. R. Finch, aged 17, to Mrs. A. Wigley, aged 89.—The Rev. A. Wheeler, minor canon of Worcester cathedral, to Miss S. Harwood, of Burford, in this county.

Died.] Mr. J. Hallis, steward to the family of the Smythes at North Nibley, Gloucestershire, and at Condover in this county, upwards of forty-five years.

Mrs. Blower, wife of Mr. Blower, miller, of Hanwood.—Aged 74, Mrs. Cartwright, of Leighton.—Mrs. Jones, of Crow Meole.—In his 74th year, R. Dodd, esq. of the Bark Hill, Whitchurch.

At Shrewsbury, aged 78, Mrs. R. Stanier.

In the prime of life, after a few moments illness, Mrs. Briscoe, of Kington House; of great affability and beneficence among the lower class of her neighbours.

At Wem, after a long and very severe fit of the stone in the kidnies, Mr. J. Drury, tanner, deservedly lamented as the honest man, the good husband, the fond father, and sincere friend.

At Ludlow, much respected by his neighbours and friends, Mr. J. Rogers, of the Feathers inn. In attempting to separate two persons who were quarrelling, he was thrown down, and unfortunately received a wound in his head from the fall, which occasioned his death.

At Bitterley, T. Mathews, esq.—Aged 74, Mrs. Cartwright, of Leighton.—Mr. Marsh, of the Marsh near Westbury.

In Colebrook Dale, Mrs. A. Horton, a quaker.

WORCESTERSHIRE.

Married.] R. Pigot, esq. of Hounsil, to Miss M. Williamson, third daughter of the late J. Williamson, esq. of Stafford.—Mr. Gardiner, of Cotheridge, to Miss Mee, of Himley.—Mr. J. Chillingworth, of Inkberrow, to Miss M. Bardin, of the Rudgway.

At Warwick house, in this county, J. E. Cooper, esq. M. P. for the county of Sligo, in Ireland, to Miss E. Lindsay, of Loughry, county of Tyrone.

Mr. J. Berkley, to Miss Cooke, both of Longdon.

Died.] At Worcestershire, Mr. J. Scandret, gent.—Mrs. M. Robson, wife of Mr. Robson, sollicitor, of Castle-street, Leicester square, London.

In the Cottage-church yard, J. Deane, esq. of Berkeley, in Wexford, and many years M. P. for the county of Dublin.

Miss J. Hay, eldest daughter of Mr. Hay, of the Angel.—Of a decline, in her 22d. year, Miss S. Roberts, youngest daughter of Mr. Roberts.

Mrs. Turbill, of Bessford.

In London, Mrs. C. Barfoot, a quaker, daughter of the late Mr. J. Corbin, of Worcester.

At Broomsgrove, Miss M. Sheffield.

In Sansom Fields, Mrs. Baker, widow.

At Tenbury, Mrs. A. Lewis, tallow-chandler and soap-boiler.

At Offenham, the lady of the Rev. W. Digby, and sister to Lord Viscount Falkland.

HEREFORDSHIRE.

A correspondent of the Hereford Journal, who has devoted much of his time to the culture of potatoes, recommends that the blossom should not be suffered to seed; as in perfecting the seed a large portion of the substance and strength of the plant is drawn from the root.

The committee of the Hereford subscription flour company have lately purchased the building at Hereford, called the Friars, with all the property in the buildings, wharf, and adjoining meadow, so that it is now reserved to the sole use and benefit of the subscribers at large. In order to augment the beneficial purpose of this institution as much as possible, another class of subscribers is to be admitted, as well to the property as to the privileges of the original subscribers.

At the meeting of the Herefordshire Agricultural Society, June 1, the Earl of Oxford President. Among the rams exhibited were some very fat and fine Leicestershires; some real Rylands, crosses of the two sorts, and some of the South Downs. Many of the heifers were much admired, and the boar which gained the first premium, was highly approved of. The premiums were adjudged as follows:—to Mr. E. Yeld, of Wharton, for the best boar, a silver goblet, value 5l. 5s. To Mrs. E. Packwood, of Clehonger, for the second best ditto, a silver plate, value 3l. 3s. To Mr. J. Tully, of the Hay-wood, for the best three years old heifer, a silver goblet, value 5l. 5s. To T. C. Smith, of Street-court, esq. for the best fine woolled ram, three years old, a silver goblet, value 5l. 5s. The premium for the best yearling heifer was adjudged to Mr. Williams, of Thinghill, with a condition annexed, if it be proved to the satisfaction of the committee, that his heifer is not above the age required by the rules of the society.

Married.] At Linton Mr. T. Jones, attorney, of Coleford, to Miss Powell, of Linton-Point.

Died.] At Hereford, Mr. J. Pewtriss, butcher.

At Kington, Mr. G. James, surgeon and apothecary.

At Pencoyd, Mrs. Fisher.

At Stafford, the Rev. R. Campbell, A. M. chaplain to the Prince of Wales, and rector of Dore and Mordiford, in this county.

GLOUCESTERSHIRE.

Married.] The R. H. Lord John Thynne, M. P. for Bath, to Miss M. A. Master, second daughter of T. Master, esq. of Cirencester Abbey, in this county.

Died.] At Gloucester, Mrs. Stephens, wife of Mr. Stephens, banker.

At Stonehouse, aged 82, T. White, esq. —C. Edwin, esq. of Clearwell, many years M. P. for the county of Glamorgan.

OXFORDSHIRE.

Married.] At Oxford, the Reverend T. P. Mathews, of Magdalen College, to Miss Hughes

Died.] At Oxford, Miss Cross of Woodstock.—Aged 36, Mr. Parker, baker.—Aged 60, Mrs. E. Slaughter, wife of Mr. W. Slaughter, master of the King's Arms Inn.—Aged 67, Mrs. A. Carpenter, wife of Mr. J. Carpenter, sadler.—Mr. W. Morris, jun. of Enstone. As he was walking with a friend in this city, he complained of a giddiness in his head, dropped down and instantly expired.

The Rev. J. Alt, late Fellow of Trinity College Cambridge and Rector of Mixbury in this county.—In the prime of life, G. Dashwood, esq. late of Steeple Aston in this county.

At Headington, Mrs E. Mather.

At Henley, upon Thames, Mr. W. Bradshaw, a magistrate and one of the oldest members of the corporation.

BERKSHIRE.

Died.] At Reading, Mrs. Spalding, widow.

At Windsor, Mr. Robinson, many years gardener to the Castle-gardens.

BUCKINGHAMSHIRE.

The branch of canal leading from the bason in Buckingham, to the Grand Junction Canal, was opened, with great rejoicings on the 1st of May last. A number of the principal proprietors, including the Marquis of Buckingham, Mr. Praed, and Mr. Selby, gentlemen of the committee; Mr. Box, the treasurer, and a large party of ladies and gentlemen were in a barge, which led the way to 12 other barges laden with coals, slate, and a variety of other merchandize. This branch, which is 9½ miles in length, has been completed in about eight months' time, and will secure to an extensive district of country, the most substantial benefits.

Married.] In London, J. Dupré, esq. of Wilton Park, in this county, to Miss Maxwell, second daughter of Sir William Maxwell, bart. of Monreith.

BEDFORDSHIRE.

A Mr Ferryman has invented a machine for blanching wheat, that is, taking off the outward coat of the grain of wheat, previously to its being ground, by which the whole of the grain may be used in bread, without any of the inconveniences that have hitherto been found in bread made from the whole of the meal. By this machine, Mr. Ferryman can separate the outer coat of the wheat at the rate of 20 bushels per hour; and it is found that blanched wheat may be ground in two thirds of the time sooner than the same kind of wheat in its perfect state. Damaged wheat is also capable of being blanched. Satisfactory experiments to ascertain whether this method of blanching wheat was so far practicable as to become likely to be of general utility, have been lately made at the Duke of Bedford's seat at Woburn. Very great advantages are expected to attend this new process of blanching wheat. A principal benefit would be the getting off the outer coat of the wheat entirely free from pollard or flour, which has never been done yet by any mode of grinding. By this process, likewise, the dirt, that is always more or less attached

tached to the grain, and which first attracts the moisture which injures the grain, is taken off. Wheat blanched in this way, may be kept for any length of time, without risque, and might be laid 20 feet thick, or any depth, in the warehouse; whereas, at present, wheat is frequently in that state that it ought not to be laid more than a foot thick, and even then it will require the expence of frequent turning. It is believed that three pair of stones will grind as much as four pair in the common way; the grain will not heat so much in the grinding, and if ground altogether for brown bread, it may be ground as fast again as in the common way. The machinery may be applied to all water-mills, and likewise to every mill on a large scale, and does not require quite the power necessary for working a pair of stones. In erecting a new mill, no additional expence would be created, except the building of a kiln.

Died.] Rev. G. Freeman, L. L. D. and Rector of Shelton in this county.

CAMBRIDGESHIRE.

Married.] The Rev. G. Millers, minor-canon of Ely, and late of St. John's College, Cambridge, to Miss M. Forby, sister of the Rev. R Forby, of Fincham, in Norfolk.

NORFOLK.

On June 25, an alarming fire broke out in the roof of the west-end of Norwich Cathedral, which destroyed, in about an hour's time, a great part of its noble roof, towards the western extremity of the nave. The lead, which poured down in streams of liquid fire, together with the falling of the burning spars and beams, presented the most dangerous obstacles to those ascending the parapets; however the lead was cut away, and the flames were, at length, happily extinguished. The fire is believed to have been occasioned by a live coal falling from the iron-pan in which the plumbers were melting their lead to repair the roof.

Married.] Mr. J. Read, of Rickinghall Superior, to Miss Quantrill, of Walsham le Willows.—Mr. W. Green, miller, of Fakenham, to Miss Case, of Toftrees.—Major Ottley, late of Bury, but now of Swaffham, to Miss Styan, of Lombard-street, London. —Mr. Burton, publican, of Tombland, to Miss Dunham, of Buxton.—The Rev. C R. Dade, to Miss Powell, both of Yarmouth.

Died.] At Lynn, Mr. Vincent, grocer.—Mrs. Swan, wife of Mr. Swan, upholsterer.

At Yarmouth, Mr. T. Broodbank, miller. —Aged 82, Mr. T. Hurry, merchant; his character is pourtrayed by this description, that he was "an honest, an independent, and a virtuous man."

In China, aged 32, Mr. E. Syball, brother of Mr. Syball, of South Walsham.

Aged 50, Mr. J. Foulger, farmer, of Burnham.—The Rev. J. Standerirck, rector of Carnfield, and vicar of Shropham, both in this county.

SUFFOLK.

Married.] At Bury, Mr. M. Spilling, to Mrs. Adkin, widow and publican.

Mr. B Bolton, of Ipswich, to Miss Adams, of Hadleigh.

Mr. Boult, surgeon, of Walworth, near London, to Miss Denny, of Yoxford.

Died.] At Bury, Mr. R Smith, fellmonger.—Aged 23, Mrs. C. Mayhew, of Debenham.—Mrs. Jones, of Beccles.—Mrs Millington, of Rushford-lodge.—Mr. J. Mallows, of Wattisfield—Aged 84, R. Prettyman, esq. of Wingfield Castle.

At Ipswich, W. Ivory, esq. formerly a Captain in the East Norfolk Militia.—Mr. B. Cooper, builder, of Coddenham.—Master R. Wood, third son of Mr. J. Wood, of Woodbridge.

The Rev. J Sharpe, A. M. perpetual curate of Brightwell and Kesgrave, near Ipswich, and ordinary of the county jail; his memory will be long revered in the circle of his friends and acquaintance, as he was an honour to his sacred profession, and a pattern of Christian piety.

ESSEX.

Married.] Mr. C. Milburn, of Prittlewell, to Mrs. Suckling, of Great Baddow.

Mr. T. Goodenough, of Bishopsgate-street, London, to Miss Wilson, of Rumford.

Mr. N. Mead, of Writtle, to Mrs. Stevens, of Abridge.—Mr. S. Ratcliffe, of Sandon, to Miss S. Joslin, of Bures.—Mr. Mickelton, butcher, of Layer, to Miss White, of Mounts Farm, Great Saling.

At West Ham, Mr. West, to Miss Baker, both of Postwick, Suffolk.

T. Simpson, esq. of Norton, near Bury, to Miss C. Scarlett, 3d daughter of J. Scarlett, esq. of Halstead.

In London, Mr. T. Brook, jun. to Miss S. Ellington, both of Mildenhall.

Died.] At Colchester, at an advanced age, Mr. Tayspill, shopkeeper, and father of the Collector of the Customs.—Miss Wall, daughter of Mr. H. Wall, of Willingale Doe.

At Braintree, in his 17th year, Mr. C. Joslin.—Mr. W. Stebbing.

In London, the Rev. R. Moreton, vicar of Great Canfield

Mrs. Delhorne, widow, and a Quaker, late of Stanway Hall.—Miss S. Curtis, daughter of the late Rev. Mr. Curtis, of Linton.—Aged 65, Mr. J. Davison, eldest son of the late Mr. J. Davison, draper, of New Market.

KENT.

Lately at Canterbury, the workmen began to dismantle one of the fairest, and the last but one remaining of the six ancient gates of the city, which defended a principal entrance from the eastward; a strong and very handsome

some structure, built about the year 1470, coped and quoined with stone, and flanked by two lofty round towers, the whole embattled and furnished with a projecting gallery; and formerly a massy portcullis contributed to its further strength. Its early name was Newingate, but in later times it was better known by that of St. George. In the towers, large reservoirs were made about forty years ago, for supplying the markets and other public places with water; which are to be placed in the old watch-tower, on the north of the gateway, nearly opposite Ivy lane.

On May 31, Mr. Hodgman, engineer at Folkstone, made an experiment with his submarine apparatus. At five o'clock in the afternoon, he walked into the sea from the shore, opposite South-street, attended by a small boat; after remaining under water eighteen minutes, and traversing the bottom in various directions, considerably more than a quarter of a mile, he ascended in about eighteen feet water, was taken into the boat, and rowed ashore, amidst the acclamations of about 2000 persons assembled on the occasion.

Married.] D. Addison, gent. to Miss S. Whiting, both of Maidstone.

At Dover, Capt. J. Rutter, to Miss Roberts.

At St. Lawrence Church, in Thanet, Mr. T. Rummell, grocer, of Ramsgate, to Miss Spurgen.—Mr. J Wood, to Miss E. Culder, both of Hearn.—Mr. Channell, grazier, to Miss S. Brunger, both of Tenterden.—S. Margrie, esq. of Weymouth, to Miss Johnson, niece of Gen. Johnson, of Woolwich.

At Canterbury, Captain Robays, of the Estafette Troop, Royal Waggon Train, to Miss Rolfe.

Died.] At Canterbury, Mr. Cordall, many years master of the Dover Castle Inn.—Mr. Webster, chemist.

At Ramsgate, Mr. A. Brook, many years town-cryer.

At Rochester, in her 78th year, Mrs. Le Grand.

At Tenterden, in his 57th year, Mr. Lord, master of the barracks at Reading.

At Winchester, Mr. W. Gradidge, formerly a chemist in Canterbury.

At Dover, in his 71st year, P. Stringer, esq.—Mrs. Huntley.

At Goodhurst, suddenly, in an advanced age, the Rev. R. Polhill, many years minister of that parish.

In her 29th year, at Ashford, Mrs. R. Prebble, wife of Mr. J Prebble, blacksmith, and only daughter of Mr. J. Miller, of Ramsgate.

SUSSEX.

A gannet or Solan goose was lately taken alive on the beach near Seaford. It seemed to be in a state of torpitude, supposed to have been occasioned by fatigue from long flight, as it did not make the least effort to escape. It is now in the possession of Mr. Gwynne, attorney, and is still living, as it feeds heartily on fish or flesh. This bird exhibits a beautiful specimen of its species, and, in most particulars, agrees with the description given of it by Edwards and other ornithologists. The gannet is a bird of passage, and one of its most favourite resorts is the island of St. Kilda, the inhabitants of which are principally supported by them and their eggs, throughout the year. This is the first instance in the recollection of the people of Seaford and Lewes, of a gannet being seen on the Sussex coast.

"It would seem by the public prints, that the fact of woodcocks breeding in England, had been but lately found out, though it has long since been established in this county, where a year seldom passes without the discovery of several nests; the present season has produced not less than four, with eggs and young, that have come to our knowledge." *Lewes Journal, June* 8.

Married.] At Hastings, E. H. Columbine, esq. naval-officer, to Miss A. Curry, second daughter of T. Curry, esq. of Gosport.

Died.] Mr. Betsley, tanner, of Stapleford Common; he was found drowned in a pond near the dwelling-house of his mother. The deceased wanted only a few months of being of age, when he would have been entitled to a considerable landed property.

Miss M. Bushby, of Arundel.

HAMPSHIRE.

At Winchester summer assizes, which commenced July 14, the eleven following prisoners received sentence of death:—C. G. Williams, for forgery; W. Knight, G. Lomax, and W. Atkins, for robbing the Portsmouth and Winchester Mail; W. Freeman, for a rape; B. Noyes, for sheep-stealing; J. Leverett, for street-robbery; J. Botton and A. Everard, for horse-stealing; P. M'Guire, for highway-robbery; and W. Seward, for cutting hop-vines.

There are already forty-two members of the Experimental Farming Society at Clanville, who advance forty pounds each, which is the whole expence attending an undertaking of great public benefit, and probably also of private advantage. Eight shares yet remain undisposed of. It will require at least four years to survey the progressive state of the farm, and judge of the comparative merits of the drill and broad-cast husbandry, &c. Mr. Minchin, of Gosport, is the secretary.

Married.] Mr. Johnson, tanner, of Alresford, to Miss J. Rivers, of Bishop's Sutton.

Died.] At Southampton, Mr. Turner, an eminent carpenter and measurer.

At Andover, Mr. M Moore, master of the White Swan-inn.

Mr. J. Cawd, of Hassar-farm, near Winchester.

Mr. H. Midlane, plumber and glazier, of Havant.

Mr. J. Cordery, of Haseley-farm, near Twyford; his death, unfortunately occasioned

by

by galling his feet with new shoes, which brought on a mortification, will be a great loss to the poor, as he was of a very charitable and humane disposition.

WILTSHIRE.

Married.] Mr. Smith, farmer, of Teffonty to Miss S. Martin, eldest daughter of Mr O. Martin, of Fovant.—J. Bennett esq. of Pye-house, to Miss Lambert, of Boyton.

Died.] At Salisbury, in her 80th year, Mrs. Higginson, wife of W. Higginson, esq.—Aged, 77, J. Edgar, esq. alderman of this city.

At his seat, at New Park, near Devizes, J. Sutton, esq brother-in-law to Mr. Addington, the present Chancellor of the Exchequer, and formerly M. P. for many years, for the Borough of Devizes.

Mr. J. Barnes, of Chiston.—Mrs. Moulton, wife of Mr. Moulton, builder, in Fisherton.

At Amesbury, suddenly, Mr. J. Barnaby.

At Bradford, aged 90, Mrs. Tugwell.

SOMERSETSHIRE.

Married.] At Clifton, W. K. Crawford, M. D. to Miss Emily O'Connor, second daughter of Sir Patrick O'Connor, of Cork.—Mr J. Vowles, baker, to Miss M. Rymer, both of Bristol.

At Bristol, Mr. T. Rankins, sugar-refiner, of Newcastle-upon-Tyne, to Miss Wright, daughter of the late Rev. Mr. Wright, Dissenting Minister, at Atherstone, in Warwickshire.

At the Quaker's Meeting-house, Mr. J. Foiglase, merchant, of Helstone, in Cornwall, to Miss A. Ring, daughter of Mr. R. Ring, cooper.

Mr. J. Richardson, stationer, to Miss Powell.—Mr. J. Dando, baker, to Miss Murch.

At Bath, Mr. E. Barker, of Old Sodbury, Gloucestershire, to Miss M. Witchell.

At Bedminster, Mr Smith, mealman, to Miss Jane, both of Bristol.—Mr. J. Collison, of Widcombe, near Bath, to Miss D. Biggs, of Bristol.

Died.] At Bristol, Mrs. Coulson.—In his 77th year, S. Munckley, esq. of a truly exemplary character.—Miss M. Gill.

At Swanwick, near Bath, in her 82d year, Mrs. Jane Danvers, a lady of a truly charitable disposition.

DORSETSHIRE.

The total amount of the earnings of the prisoners confined in the county jail, and employed in different manufactures for one year, ending June, 1800, was 495l. 1s. 4½d. The number of prisoners for that year was sixty-two.

Married.] At Norton Fitzwarren, Mr. A. Turner, to Mrs. E. Norman, widow.

At Sydling, Mr. J. Hopkins, to Miss Devenish.—Mr. W. Saxton, of Weymouth, to Miss Brent, of London.

Died.] At Sherborne, Miss A. Bennett, of a worthy and strictly honest character.

At Bishop's Mall, Mr. J. Patten, sen.

At Grange, in his 63d year, F. R. Drewe, esq.

At Maiden Newton, aged 95, Mr. F. Dawe.—Mrs. Andrews, of Shroton.

At Thorverton, Mr. A. Forrest; of exemplary humanity, and equal attention to every description of his patients, in the exercise of the medical art.

DEVONSHIRE.

Died.] At Exeter, G. W. Carrington, esq. comptroller of the customs of that port.—Mr. R. Howell, many years master of the Swan-tavern. S. Tolfrey, esq. a gentleman of the most amiable manners.—Mrs. Davis, wife of Mr. Davis, mercer and woollen draper.—Aged 99, Mrs. J. Drew. She retained her rational faculties to the last, and, till within a few days of her decease, was regularly moving about with a basket of small wares for sale; during the winter season she was a carrier or retailer of almanacks for the Printer of the Exeter and Plymouth Gazette.

The Rev. H. Distin, vicar of Bishop's Teignton.

At South Molton, in an advanced age, Mr. Gould, surgeon and apothecary.—Mrs. Devels who lived a few miles from Exeter. As she was returning home, on the top of a waggon, a sudden jerk threw her from her seat and killed her on the spot.

At Maisonette, near Totness, T. Hicks, esq. Rear Admiral of the Blue, a very worthy man and brave officer.

At Exmouth, aged 86, Mrs. Howe.

At Awliscombe, near Honiton, Mrs. E. Roskilly, wife of the Rev. T. Roskilly, vicar.

At Aikerswell, aged 92, full of good works, the Rev. Mr. Burr, M. A. and rector of Dunterton.

At Topsham, in her 72d year, Mrs. R. Phillips, widow of the late Rev. H. Phillips, an affectionate sister and a truly pious Christian.

CORNWALL.

A mare, the property of Mr. W. Laynon, of St. Buryan, foaled lately a fine filley, with only one eye, and that in the middle of her forehead, and without nostrils. In other respects, it was perfect, came at its proper time, and lived two days.

Lord de Dunstanville, has, we learn, determined on building a pier, at Green Bank, in the town of Falmouth. The stones for the quay-work are actually contracted for, and railing. The new quay-work is to run out 50 feet from the cellars now occupied by Mr. Edwards; and the space between those cellars and the present Green Bank Quay, is to be filled up. An arm will be run from the southern point of this work, parallel with the extremity of Pye's Cellars, which will form a noble bason for the reception of vessels to unload in. The bason and pier, with the houses now building at Green Bank, and the Terrace Walk in front of those buildings, contribute handsomely to the embellishment of that part of of the town, and will make it by far the most pleasant spot in the neighbourhood.

WALES.

Married.] Mr. J. Rees, of Carmarthen, to Miss E. Williams, niece of J. Alexander, esq. of Wedhampton, Wilts.

R. Ellis, esq. of Cornist, Flintshire, to Miss Speed, of Chester, late of Holt, Denbighshire.—Mr. R. Gibbon, cornfactor, to Miss Jenkins, both of Haverford West.

Died.] At Swansea, T. Maddox, esq. sen. alderman.

In the prime of life, Mr. T. Owen, of Mathraval Hangynis, Montgomeryshire.

At Upton Castle, Pembrokeshire, the Rev. T. Wooles.

IRELAND.

Upon a diligent survey, made by the clergy of Dublin, on the 2d of June, six parishes in that city were found to contain 20,400 poor, in the most abject state.

Married.] In Dublin, the Hon. J. Cavendish, second son of Sir H. Cavendish, bart. to Lady A. Gore, third daughter of the Earl of Arran, and sister to the Marchioness of Abercorn.

Died.] In Dublin, J. Lyster, esq. late captain in the Independents.

Of an apoplectic stroke, at the seat of Mr. Latouche, county of Wicklow, Lieutenant-general Eustace, an honest soldier, and an honourable gentleman; he had ridden from Dalton that morning, and was apparently in perfect health.

DEATHS ABROAD.

[*Additional particulars relative to Cimarosa, whose death we announced in page 474, of our Magazine for June last.*]—This distinguished character was born at Capodi Monte, in Naples; he studied at the Conservatory of Loretto and was a pupil of the incomparable Durante. He had a liberal education, was uncommonly sober, and drank neither wine nor any strong liquors. At his quitting the Conservatory, he was received by Madame Ballante, who, then rich, employed all her means and interest to give reputation to young Cimarosa; she did more, she gave him her daughter in marriage, who soon died, leaving him a son. He married again, thro' the assiduous care of the respectable Madame Ballante, a young lady brought up under her care, and of her own household. This second wife died also after giving him a son and a daughter. Cimarosa had an extraordinary genius, an imagination always new, always brilliant; when he accompanied it was with the most exquisite taste, and he sung like the most skilful professors; but we are not to compare even these valuable talents with the enchanting gift of composition which he had received from nature, and which he displayed at the social table, without appearing the more serious or less amiable on that account. In a word, his loss is irreparable, even by the other original masters in music that the revolution has left in Italy. He was a good husband, a good father, and a zealous and grateful friend. Madame Ballante has lost her own fortune; but Cimarosa had the gratitude to receive his benefactress into his house, where she disposed of his property at her pleasure.

At Auxerre, Citizen Laire, librarian to the central school of the department of Yonne. His acquaintance with bibliography was very extensive; he had been the friend of Barthelemy, Rive, St. Leger, Caperonnier, Brunck, Debure, &c. and had travelled a great deal in France and Italy, to augment his fund of bibliographical knowledge. He has left behind him in this kind, five or six valuable works, and, among others, the one entitled, "Index librorum ab inventâ typographia ad annum 1500. An Index of books from the invention of typography, to the year 1500, printed at Sens, 1792, 2 vols. 8vo. He had laboured, in conjunction with Cardinal de Leomenie, on the work entitled: Serie dell' edizioni Aldine, A Series of the Aldine Editions which have been successively printed at Pisa, at Padua in 1790, and at Venice in 1792.

At Berlin, Christian Theophilus Selle, Doctor in Medicine, Intimate Counsellor and Director of the College of Medicine and Chirurgery, Member of the Academy of Sciences at Berlin, Director of the Class of Philosophy of the same Academy, and Member of the Academy of Stockholm and of the Society of Physicians of London and Switzerland. He was born at Stetting in Pomerania, on the 7th of October, 1748. He accompanied, in quality of physician, the Landgrave of Hesse Darmstadt; during his voyage to Petersburgh. Afterwards, he was named Physician to the Bishop, Primate of Ermeland, now the Archbishop of Gnesen. The king of Prussia, Frederick, made him his private physician, and soon after the death of that prince, Selle published a very well written history of his malady. King Frederick William II. confirmed him in that dignity, and directed him to investigate an epidemic disorder which had spread throughout Southern Prussia, during the war. The present king also honoured him with his confidence. His writings prove his profound knowledge in speculative philosophy and the art of healing. He possessed considerable merit as a moral philosopher, and his character excited the esteem of all who knew him. Unfortunately he was of a feeble constitution, he prescribed, himself, his last remedy and foretold the moment of his death; in this last matter, he was only mistaken in somewhat less than a quarter of an hour. He ordered his body to be opened after his decease. By that the immediate cause of his death was shewn to be an exulcerated pulmony.

ERRATA.—In our Magazine for May, in the Account of the Population of Salford, the total amount of both sexes is 1359, for which read 13,593; and the total amount of both sexes in Manchester and Salford is 71,819, instead of 84,053, the true numbers instead of "*great improvements have lately been made in Oxford-street*," read, *great improvements have lately been made in Oxford-street, Manchester.*

TO

MONTHLY COMMERCIAL REPORT.

EVEN in the midst of a war by which so much of our population is fruitlessly wasted, and so much of the natural and artificial produce of these isles is consumed, without replacing itself by any reproduction, still the *internal trade* of Great Britain continues, in spite of every obstacle, to become more extensive and more active. The number of new *canals* which have been lately completed or begun, the *highways* and *cross-roads* now in formation in every part of the country, and in every variety of direction, the new *trading companies* which associate in such numbers for the transaction of different branches of our domestic business, are so many remarkable and unequivocal proofs of the general truth.

The *Grand Junction Canal* was opened early, last month, at Paddington. Its completion has perfected a system of navigable communication between London and the midland counties, from which advantages incalculably great must arise, both to the capital and to all the inland districts through which the ramifications of these canals are extended. The *Grand Surrey Canal* is now in a train for execution. It is reasonably expected to contribute greatly to the benefit both of private trade and of the British navy, by the communications which it is to open between the southern part of this metropolis and the south-east counties. The *Tunnel under the Thames* has ceased to appear impracticable: suitable means have been adopted to surmount the first difficulties of the attempt, and we have now every reason to believe, that in as short a time as the nature of such a work can permit, this singular and most convenient channel of communication between Kent and Essex will be opened. In the North, the *Crinan Canal* has been, at length, completed; and the advantages which it must infallibly give to all navigation between the Mersey, the Solway Frith, the Clyde, and the Hebredean Isles, are likely, even within a few years, to accomplish an extraordinary advancement of trade and industry, especially on the north-west coast of Scotland. *Fuel and Salt*, in particular, must henceforth be considerably cheaper on these coasts. In the north east of Scotland, the foundation stone was, within these few weeks, laid, of a bridge over the Spey, at Fochabers, the erection of which has long been exceedingly wanted to open the counties of Bamff, Moray, Ross, Cromartie, and Caithness, to the intercourse of inland *traffic* with the south.

Such an improvement of the channels of inland trade might be supposed to lessen our coasting navigation; but this still increases. More than 10,000 vessels in the *coast trade* sail to and from the port of London only. It is estimated that these are little more than one third of the whole number of coasting vessels which the home trade of these isles employs.

The *whale fishery* on the Coast of Greenland, and especially in Davis's Streights, has been this year unusually successful. *Eleven* vessels returned with a quantity of blubber, which, exclusively of the spermaceti and the whalebone, will yield a clear profit of above 44,000l. sterling. Others have since returned to Newcastle, Hull, and Leith, and others are, as we learn, at Stromness, on their way, with ladings not less considerable. The prospect of a profitable year in the herring-fishery on the north east and north west coasts already begins to be extremely promising. That fishery is calculated to yield to the fishermen of the Frith of Forth only, an annual profit of above 200,000l. sterling, of which there was not, twelve years since, a single farthing among the ordinary returns of industry on those shores. We are informed that, for *turbot* alone, above 1000 guineas a week have, for many weeks past, been paid from London to the fishermen on the Dutch coast. It is good, that articles of subsistence at once so wholesome, and such favourites with the luxurious, are to be had at the present moderate price of turbot from any quarter. But we should certainly be much better pleased, if the thousand guineas a week went only in the English fishermens' pockets.

Our late differences with the nations on the Baltic threatened to deprive us of the raw materials for some of our principal manufactures. For these last two months our *Baltic Trade* has been beginning to revive. Since the conclusion of the Treaty at St. Petersburgh, by Lord St. Helens and the Russian Minister, every step has been taken to restore to full activity the ancient trade between Russia and this country. A number of ships have already arrived from the Baltic with grain, timber, iron, flax, hemp, &c. Fleets of merchant-ships have sailed for the Baltic from the ports on the east side of this island. But, as the use of English capital was withdrawn, for the last season, from the Russian merchants, it is not to be expected that the supply of Russian and Swedish commodities can be, for some months to come, so ample in the English market, as if no interruption in this branch of our commerce had taken place.

The Germans have, for a number of years, been, to a prodigious degree, gainers by the interruption of the wonted commercial intercourse between Britain and France. They are, this year, already, great gainers by the temporary cessation of our trade with the Baltic. At the last fairs of *Frankfort* and *Leipsic*, vast quantities of British goods were purchased for the Russian market. Even at late the fair of *Strasburgh* great quantities of our manufactures were clandestinely produced, at great risk, to be smuggled into France. The cotton-manufacturers of Germany, though they take a great deal of cotton yarn from this country, are not yet able to produce muslins, calicoes, and other cotton-stuffs, in the markets, at the low price of our British manufactures. The Emperor of Germany has just forbidden the exportation of tin from his dominions. And whatever tends to hinder this valuable metal from being readily procured from the tin mines of other countries, must, of course, favour the working and the exportation of tin from Cornwall.

Our trade with the Mediterranean, though greatly checked, is not destroyed by the war. Great quantities of wines have been recently imported from Gibraltar, St. Lucar, Lisbon, and Oporto, not only into the port of London, but to Cork, Dublin, Liverpool, Greenock, Leith, &c. Of Lisbon and Port wine alone, nearly 80,000 gallons were entered in the port of London between the 10th and the 17th of July. The Venetian ports in Italy preserve an intercourse, still open to us, with that country. Our trade with the States of Barbary increases: a[illegible]rnish us with provisions for our fleets and garrisons, in return for our woollens, and works

in

in metal, &c. With the Turkish dominions we have still a great commercial intercourse. Woollens, watches, arms, &c. are among our exports. Raw silk and cotton, wool, goats hair, &c. are goods which we import from those parts. The failure of the great commercial house of Bratis and Co. at Smyrna, has sensibly affected the merchants in different parts, who have trading connections with that emporium.

The West India Fleet, of 157 ships, laden with sugar, cotton, rum, melasses, coffee, pimento, indigo, cocoa, mahogany, &c. &c. has arrived safe at the different ports of London, Bristol, Liverpool, Greenock, and Port Glasgow, Newcastle, and Leith, for which its ships were destined. The prices of these goods are, of course, for the present, somewhat lower, but since our intercourse with Archangel and the Baltic is renewed, and as the Danish and Swedish intercourse with the West Indies, has been, for some months, deranged and interrupted; the sales will, in all probability, be sufficiently brisk to prevent any such fall in the prices as might be seriously alarming to the merchants or planters.

The *United States of America* have been encouraged by our late differences with Denmark, Sweden, and Russia, to pay more regard than they had lately done to the supply of this country with tar, and the other staple commodities of the Baltic. The American tar has been usually much mixed with sand and water. Of late they have used great precautions to free it from these impurities.

We are concerned to state, that the cotton-manufactures are, in different parts of this country, in a very languishing condition. In this manufacture, sooner than in any other capital one, is there danger of our being rivalled on the Continent. In the shires of Renfrew and Lanerk, many workmen have been lately discharged, and a spirit of emigration begins to become very prevalent. In 1799, there were imported into the Clyde 27,122 packages of unwrought cotton—in 1800,—22,450 packages. Since the beginning of the present year, 15,130 packages have already been imported.

The woollen manufacture is still flourishing. At the late fair of Ayr, both yarn and cloth were sold at high prices. A just alarm has been excited among the manufacturers, in regard to the clandestine exportation of yarn and wool from this country to the Continent. Several English manufactures are introduced into France, by Englishmen, who went thither for political reasons.

MONTHLY AGRICULTURAL REPORT.

THE late rains, and the fine sunny weather that has succeeded them, have been of the utmost importance to all the different kinds of grain-crops: they have not only been rendered more full in the ear, but considerably forwarded in other respects, so that, at present, there is every appearance of a very abundant harvest. In some of the more southern districts, the reaping of Rye and Oats has already commenced, and the produce, in such cases, has, in most instances, been large. The advantages that have been produced in the Potatoe, Turnip, and other root-crops, have been equally great, so that there can be little doubt but that each of these very important crops will be highly productive. The early Potatoes have, indeed, turned out remarkably well in most of the midland and southern parts of the kingdom.

Hops have, likewise, been greatly benefited by the same causes, and seem, at present, in a promising situation.

Some injury has, however, been done to the Hay, in many places, by the very heavy and frequent showers in the early and middle part of the month, but they must have been highly useful in promoting the aftermath, and in refreshing the pasture and grass lands.

But notwithstanding the appearances of almost all sorts of crops are extremely promising, the prices of grain still keep up —Average price throughout England and Wales, for the week ending July 18, Wheat, 136s. 11d.; Barley, -1s.; Oats, 37s.

Cattle of all kinds are likewise high —At Smithfield, beef sells from 4s 6d. to 5s. 4d.; mutton, from 5s. to 5s. 8d.; veal, from 4s. 4d. to 5s. 6d.; pork, from 5s. 4d. to 6s. 8d.; and lamb, from 5s. to 6s.—In Newgate and Leadenhall Market, beef sells from 3s. 10d. to 4s. 8d.; mutton, from 4s. 4d. to 5s. 7d.; veal, from 3s. 8d. to 5s.; pork, from 5s. 5d. to 6s. 8d.; and lamb, from 4s. 6d. to 6s.—Sheep, of the fat kind, are rather lower.—Store Hogs fetch high prices.

Hay still keeps up.—Price of Hay at St. James's Market, 5l. 3s. to 6l. 16. 6d.—At Whitechapel, 4l. 18s. 8d. to 6l. 8s.

Straw, as usual, is dear.—At St. James's Market, 2l. 14s. 6d. to 3l. 3s.—At Whitechapel, 2l. 10s. to 3l. 3s.

METEOROLOGICAL REPORT.

Observations on the State of the Weather, from the 24th of June, to the 24th of July, inclusive, 1801, two miles N. W. of St. Paul's.

Barometer.			*Thermometer.*		
Highest 30. 03. June 28, Wind W. N. W.			Highest 80°. July 21 and 22, Wind E.		
Lowest 29. 26. July 16, Wind N. E.			Lowest 54°. July 2, 10, 18, W. S. W.		
Greatest variation in 24 hours.	3.5 tenths of an inch	Between the mornings of the 9th and 10th of July, the mercury in the barometer rose from 29.3. to 29.65.	Greatest variation in 24 hours.	12°.	Between the hottest part of the day, on the 17th inst. and the same time on the 18th, the thermometer rose from 64°. to 76°.

The quantity of rain fallen during this month is equal to 3.46 inches of depth.

From

From the period of our last Report to the 29th ult. the barometer gradually rose: the heat of the atmosphere was, also, during the same period, increasing. On the 30th, at noon, the mercury in the barometer had fallen three tenths of an inch, when the metropolis and the neighbouring villages experienced one of the most violent storms, of rain, accompanied with thunder and lightning, that ever were known. The rain fell in sheets; many of the streets in London resembled, for several minutes, navigable canals; and in those which lead down to the Thames, the torrents of water were such, as it is said, no man living ever remembered before. In our rain-gauge, which is elevated 11 feet from the ground, more than two inches in depth of rain fell in less than an hour.

This storm was succeeded by 17 days in which it rained more or less every day, with the exception of the 5th inst. During the greater part of the 15th, which, in the Calendar, is called St Swithin, the rain was very heavy, and, according to an old prediction, with the origin of which we are unacquainted, many people were looking forward to 40 successive days of showery weather. Fortunately, however, for the state of agriculture, the Saint has deceived his adherents, and out of the first nine days, we have had six without any rain at all.

In the course of this month we have had 12 days without any rain, and the wind has been easterly eight days.

A NEW PLANET.

An important circumstance in Astronomy has just occurred, no less than the Discovery of ANOTHER NEW PLANET!!! This celestial phenomenon moves between the orbits of Mars and Jupiter, and is an intermediate Planet between them. It was discovered by M. PIAZZI, an Italian Astronomer, on the 1st of January, 1801. He concealed the discovery, to preserve all the honour and observations to himself, till after six weeks close watching, he fell ill. It will not be in a situation, with regard to the Sun, to be observed again, till a month or two hence. It is but a small Planet, ranking only as a Star of the eighth magnitude, and therefore not visible to the naked eye. Its motion is nearly parallel to the ecliptic, at present about 4½° to the north of it, and nearly entering the sign Leo. The distance from the Sun is about 2⅔ times that of the earth, and the periodical time nearly four years and two months.—Other particulars shall be given in our next.

TO CORRESPONDENTS.

We beg leave to close the controversy concerning Greek and Latin Prosody, which, we believe, has already been thought too protracted by the generality of our readers.

The topic of the Scarcity has been so much discussed in publications of every kind, that we have thought it advisable to suppress many of the letters which have been sent to us on this subject.

We have received a letter from Mr. Whitehead, in reply to the charge brought against him in our Magazine, by Dr. Falconer, in relation to the Portland-powder. We should certainly, in conformity to our usual practice, have inserted his defence, had not the whole turned upon a supposed *improvement* upon the medicine made by Mr. Whitehead, which, by placing it at once in the class of empirical nostrums, renders it no longer an object of proper medical discussion.

We beg leave to suggest to some of our many *Querists*, that, with a little pains, they might have their inquiries answered in a shorter way than by the circuitous mode of our publication; also, they will please to consider, that, when they invite our Correspondents to the discussion of a particular topic, they take it for granted, that we should choose to fill our pages with the matter in question, which is often far from being the case.

Neither the German Epigram, nor the Welsh Version of Gray, will suit our poetical department.

The Account of Lynn is not of a kind that will suit our Miscellany.

The Dissertation on the different Parts of Speech will be returned on being applied for.

The Discussion on Dr. Stewart's Philosophy would probably interest few of our Readers.

The Writer of Battologia commences a controversy with which we do not wish to occupy our pages. The paper to which he replies may be considered as an amusing specimen of conjectural criticism, which will probably have no serious effects.

THE
MONTHLY MAGAZINE.
No. 77. SEPTEMBER 1, 1801. [No. 2, of Vol. 12.

ORIGINAL COMMUNICATIONS.

For the Monthly Magazine.

REMARKS *on the* RETURNS *which have been made under the* ACT *for ascertaining the* POPULATION *of* GREAT BRITAIN.

THE returns, though at present very incomplete, shew, what there has long been great reason to suspect, that the total number of persons is considerably greater than it could be *proved* to be before the account was taken. The previous estimates, formed by different persons, were unavoidably vague and unsatisfactory, being founded chiefly on the returns of the number of houses charged to the house and window-duty: these returns were known to be incorrect, but the extent of the deficiency was not easily ascertained; there was no reason to believe that the number of *taxable* houses returned was considerably less than the truth; but it required very little attention to the state of the country, to perceive, that the number of houses not paying these taxes must greatly exceed the returns made by the surveyors, of houses excused for poverty, which in 1759, appeared to be only 282,422; and in 1781, 284,459. If the number of charged and chargeable houses does not at present very much exceed what it was in 1781, the number of houses excused must be, *at least*, 650,000, and will appear much greater when the returns are complete.

Another circumstance, which rendered most of the computations on this subject below the truth, was, that the average number of persons to a house was generally taken less than it now appears to be. Mr. G. King, in 1690, allowed rather more than four and a half to a house in London, and the bills of mortality; four and three-tenths in the cities and market-towns; and four in the villages and hamlets: if this was near the truth at the time, it has certainly since become very much otherwise. Dr. Price asserted, "that six to a house for London, and five to a house for all England is too large an allowance;" this assertion seemed to be justified by the accounts he had collected; but it now appears that, even excluding the army and navy (as many such persons may have been returned with their families), the proportion is about seven and a quarter to a house for London, and more than five and a half for all England and Wales. If the army, navy, and merchant-seamen are added to the total of inhabitants, it appears proper to add the empty to the inhabited houses, as most of the houses at present uninhabited, or probably a greater additional number, would be occupied, if all the persons serving out of the country were to return and reside here: the average proportion of inhabitants to a house will thus appear to be very near five and three-quarters.

In the adjoining counties of Northampton, Leicester, and Rutland, the proportion of inhabitants to a house is less than in any of the other counties, although in the two first the number of inhabitants, in respect to the extent of the counties, exceeds many others.

Exclusive of Middlesex, the number of persons to a house is less than six in all the counties except Suffolk, where it appears to me more than six and a half; possibly when the returns are complete, the apparent difference may be somewhat reduced; at present it excites some doubt respecting the accuracy of the number of houses returned for this county.

The maritime counties do not, on the whole, appear more populous than the inland counties: the manufactories, which are mostly established in the latter, contributing as much as the sea-ports of the former to an increase of inhabitants.

The supporters of the assertion, that since the commencement of the last century, the population *declined* considerably, have in general founded their opinion on the comparison of an Account, published by Dr. Davenant, of the total Number of Houses in England and Wales at Lady-day, 1690, according to the Hearth books, which makes them amount to 1,319,215

with, The returns since made by the surveyors of house and window-duties, according to which, the total number of houses in England and Wales in 1759 was - - 986,482

And in 1777 - - 952,734

Those whom the general appearance of the country, or other presumptive evidence, had induced to adopt a contrary opinion, knowing they could not defend it if the above numbers were correct, readily allowed there were great omissions in the late returns, and endeavoured, though with

with little success, to invalidate the account of 1690, which, upon examination, and a consideration of the circumstances attending it, will appear highly probable to have been, at least, as correct as the present account is likely to be. It was not from the number of houses having been over-rated in the account of 1690, but from the great omissions in the subsequent returns of houses not paying the tax, that the opinion of *depopulation* arose.

Upon comparing the number of houses, according to the account of 1690, with the total of the returns that have been made under the late act, there appears (even in the present defective state of the returns) an increase of more than 60,000 houses, and therefore probably of at least 330,000 inhabitants; that the increase *is very considerably greater* than this number *is certain*, as there are four English and six Welch counties wanting, and above 630 returns deficient in those included; but *how much* greater the number will appear, when the account is complete, must at present be mere conjecture.

The following are the Counties from which the Returns are complete; with the Number of Houses annexed, as they appeared in the Account of 1690.

	No. of Houses in 1690	*Inhabited Houses in 1801*	*Uninhabited*	*Proportion of uninhabited Houses*	*Total of Persons*	*Persons to a House*
Durham with Northumberland -		27,447	1,175	1 in 24	161,666	6
Westmoreland -	6,691	8,014	315	26	42,387	5¼
Lancaster -	46,961	101,723	3,115	34	588,711	5¾
Nottingham -	17,818	25,256	529	49	133,727	5¼
Derby - -	24,944	31,822	1,369	24	161,147	5
Stafford -	26,278	46,002	2,010	24	244,851	5¼
Warwick -	22,700	40,258	2,916	15	204,651	5
Rutland -	3,661	3,266	87	39	16,300	5
Huntingdon -	8,713	6,814	135	51	37,449	5½
Essex - -	40,545	38,407	1,027	38	226,638	6
Hertford -	17,488	17,531	491	37	96,770	5½
Bedford -	12,170	11,888	185	65	63,393	5¼
Devon - -	56,202	57,955	3,235	19	342,987	6

That there has been a decrease of inhabitants in some of the counties, is evident: this has happened chiefly in Huntingdon, Cambridge, Norfolk, Suffolk, Essex, and Somerset; and has been much more than counterbalanced by a great increase in other parts, particularly in Lancashire, Yorkshire, Nottingham, Derby, Chester, Warwick, Stafford, &c.

Although there has been a decrease of houses since the commencement of the last century, in Suffolk, Cambridge, and Huntingdon, it does not appear that the population of those counties is declining *at present*, for they contain fewer uninhabited houses in proportion to their whole number, than any other counties except Bedford.

In a note to the account laid before parliament, it is remarked, that 'of the houses returned "uninhabited" many are ruinous and uninhabitable; and in many counties the uninhabited houses are said to be mostly houses now building, and consequently not yet habitable.' Wherever those of the former description are numerous, it strongly shews, that the population has been declining for some years past; while, on the other hand, a considerable number of new houses (if not merely built in the place of old ones) is a pretty certain indication of an increasing population. There is, however, much reason to believe, that a great majority of the houses returned as uninhabited are really habitable houses unoccupied, as in most parts, where they appear particularly numerous, there are obvious causes to which it may be ascribed; thus in Warwick, where the proportion is greater than in any other county, being more than one out of fifteen, there can be little doubt that it arises, in a great measure, from the distressed state of the trade of Birmingham, and its neighbourhood; and in Devonshire, where they amount to somewhat more than one out of nineteen, it may be readily accounted for from the great decline

decline of the woollen trade in those parts.

It is probable, that when the returns are complete, there will appear, upon comparing the extent of the country with the whole number of inhabitants, about four acres to each person in all England, but a much greater proportion in Wales and Scotland. Such a comparison, however, will not by any means give an accurate idea of the increase of population, which the country is capable of sustaining; of which a better opinion might be formed, by comparing the quantity of grain and other provisions which it has been found necessary to import for some years past, with the increase of subsistence which the present waste and improveable land of the country is capable of producing.

Aug. 8, 1801. J. J. GRELLIER.

To the Editor of the Monthly Magazine.

SIR,

I HERE send a continuation of the Meteorological Journal for the first six Months of the Year 1801—See Monthly Magazine for February, 1801.

1801	Barom.	Therm. without	Therm. within	Rain	Evaporation	N.	E.	S.	W.	[illegible]
	Inch.	Deg.	Deg.	Inch.	Inch.					
January -	29.453	37.9	39.5	1.452	0.908	13	14	67	30	
February -	29.415	36.8	39.1	1.329	1.095	34	6	57	15	
March -	29.497	43.1	45.8	2.219	1.726	17	10	64	33	
April -	29.687	44.2	47.3	0.463	3.012	45	31	19	25	
May -	29.449	54.2	56.3	0.886	4.360	27	20	50	27	
June -	29.707	59.3	61.9	2.780	4.175	34	24	25	37	
Mean -	29.535	45.9	48.3							
			Total	9.124	14.276	170	105	282	167	

A friend of mine, Mr. Farey, the Duke of Bedford's agent at Woburn, has requested me to communicate, along with my journal, the results of some observations, which, during the last six months, he has made with six rain-gauges of a similar construction to mine.

Near to the efflux of every river into the sea, a ridge of high land, more or less elevated, begins on each side, and, proceeding on towards the source of the river they at last join and surround it, forming the *partage* or separation of the water that falls by rain to supply that river from that which goes to other rivers. The same holds good exactly, though on a smaller scale, of every brook, beginning with its junction with the river into which it falls.

This gentleman has it in contemplation to compare, by actual experiment, the quantity of rain which falls within the limits of the ridge of hills which surround Woburn, and that forms the supply of water to its brook, with the quantity of water which that brook actually discharges at a bridge some miles below Woburn; for which purpose the exact line of the summit of the ridge, in its whole circuit from the bridge (where a water-gauge is intended to be placed on the brook) is intended to be traced out, and an exact survey made of the land which it incloses, which amounts to about eight or ten thousand acres.

On the first of January last, three rain-gauges were placed at different points on this ridge of hills, numbered I. III. and V, and three others in different places in the vales, within the circuit of these hills, numbered II. IV. and VI. No. I. is placed on the ridge of the White House, farm-house, the top of the tunnel being twenty-four feet from the ground; No. III. is placed on the top of the riding-house at Woburn Abbey, at thirty-eight feet from the ground; No. V. on the steeple of Bow-brickhill Church, fifty-four feet from the ground; No. II. is placed on the ridge of Crawley Water-mill (being within about a mile from the bridge above-mentioned, and is twenty-seven feet high; No. IV. is placed on the ridge of a house, called Waterman's Lodge, in the vale below Woburn; and No. VI. is placed on an island in Cowhill-pond, in Woburn Park, about four feet above the ground. The first four months, this No. VI. stood on a building in Mr. Farey's yard, seven feet from the ground.

The *relative* heights of each of these different gauges, with mine, is intended to be given in some future communication, and also their heights above the sea, deduced from Captain Mudge's Trigonometrical Survey, for which calculation he has politely furnished us with ample data.

The Quantity of Rain fallen in the above-mentioned Places, for the last six Months, is as follows.

	On the Summit			In the Valley.		
	I.	III.	V.	II.	IV.	VI.
	Inches.	Inches.	Inches.	Inches.	Inches.	Inches.
January -	0.788	0.744	0.744	0.639	0.650	1.115
February - -	1.232	1.362	1.018	0.895	1.002	2.294
March - -	1.096	1.517	1.026	1.386	1.237	2.097
April - -	1.166	1.766	1.067	1.454	1.339	2.473
May - -	1.295	1.444	0.963	0.763	1.168	1.621
June - -	1.560	1.727	1.793	1.807	1.676	1.746
Total -	7.147	8.560	6.611	6.944	7.072	11.346

Mr. Farey requests me also to mention, that being at the village of Ridgemont, near Woburn, on Wednesday, the first of this month, about noon, a storm came on, attended with distant thunder. At first, it hailed pretty smartly, after which there was a heavy fall of rain for fifteen or twenty minutes; near the conclusion of which, remarking an uncommon appearance in the lower extremity of a blackish cloud towards the west, he attentively observed it, and saw a *water spout* proceed from this cloud; it continued visible nearly a quarter of an hour, frequently lengthening itself to a great distance below the cloud; again contracting, it was tapered towards the lower end, where it appeared to terminate in a blunt point. It rained all the time at Ridgemont, or probably the rain could have been seen descending below it. It did not project vertically from the cloud, but inclined considerably towards the wind, then about north east, and was not straight, but curved, with the convex side towards the wind. A little time before it disappeared, it lengthened out to nearly double its former length, and became cylindrical or nearly so, with its edges defined like a pipe: during this time it varied from its former horn-like appearance to a waving or serpentine line. It appears to have passed over the village of Aspley, and part of Wavenden, and at these places, and in the intervening fields, it rained in torrents for a few minutes. It is rather remarkable, that on the next day, about the same hour, another water-spout passed over Maulden, near Ampthill, in this county.

I am, Sir, your's, &c.
B. Bevan.

To the Editor of the Monthly Magazine.

SIR,

IT having been suggested to me by some friends and readers of your Magazine, that the following incident is not unworthy of a place amongst your miscellaneous articles, and as there is perhaps no probability that it will be inserted in any of the newspapers circulated in these parts, I have taken the liberty of sending you an account of it.

Yesterday, in the afternoon, came on here a most tremendous storm of thunder and lightning, that took at first a north-easterly direction, but which afterwards returned, and sent forth its sonorous and awful rumbling from different quarters of the heavens. A fine ash-tree, nearly thirty yards in height, belonging to Mr. John Fothergill, of Brounber, and growing upon his estate at Cross-gates, in this parish, was suddenly struck with the lightning, and shivered almost to pieces. The trunk of the tree, measuring ten yards and a half in length, and two yards and three quarters in circumference, was split from the top to the bottom, and broken into a thousand

thousand fragments. The length of that part of the tree, which was separated from the trunk by the force of the lightning, measured upwards of eighteen yards. Huge fragments were thrown in every direction, to the distance of sixty or eighty yards. And though the turnpike-road, between this place and Kendall, led close by the tree, and the farm house, in which were people, was at a very inconsiderable distance, and not further than where the broken pieces reached, yet happily no other mischief was done.

Ravenstonedale, J. ROBINSON.
July 9, 1801.

To the Editor of the Monthly Magazine.

SIR,

IN page 483 of your Magazine for July, Mr. Carey has attempted, with his usual ingenuity and acuteness, to reconcile the numbers of two *parinumeral* distichs in a Greek epigram by conjectural emendations, to which sober criticism, I think, must refuse her assent.

To suppose the N in εμεθεν to be merely paragogical, without producing a single example of such use, or any vestiges of such example, in this word, or its parallels, σεθεν and εθεν, from any poet or grammarian whatever, is an outrage surely to all rational probability; and we might, I think, with equal justice conceive the N in εν, ειν, τυπτομεν, and whatever words you please, to be also paragogical and not an essential letter, as well as in εμεθεν.

I consider his reasonings on αιν as no less destitute of probability: for, in this province of emendatory criticism, with respect to words so familiarly employed, a reader has a right to be satisfied, not only by what *analogy* and *orthography* may render plausible, but by what the unexceptionable *use* of approved writers has *actually* sanctioned. Otherwise, if no difficulty remained beyond this word, we might safely substitute αει for αιει, since the Attic writers undoubtedly follow that orthography without variation, whether they mean to lengthen or shorten the former syllable; though in the former case the iota might probably be subscribed.

With regard also to the substitution of μιμνοι for μιμναι, I may presume your readers to revolt at once from such an arbitrary and unauthorised transmutation of a most common word.

But, as I profess myself dissatisfied with the solution of Mr. Carey, I may be deemed perhaps unjustifiably censorious by some for this freedom, if unable to propose a better. Without allowing the reasonableness of this requisition, I shall submit, with deference to Mr. Carey and your readers, what appears to myself a simple and decisive adjustment of the inconsistency in the present readings of the epigram.

I need not mention the improbability of *no* error in the former distich, and not less than *three* in the latter.

Upon the former distich I observe thus:

Αλλος απο στελλων, ὁ δ' απ' αγρος, ὡς δ' απο ποντου,
Ευπολι, σοι πεμπει δωρα γενεθλιδια:

If the nominative case had been *definite*, and not indefinite, Παυλος suppose, instead of αλλος, the present tense πεμπει would have been proper and unexceptionable; but with the indeterminate words αλλος, ὁ, and ὡς, a *supposition* is absolutely necessary to the exigencies of legitimate composition, and πεμψη therefore should be substituted for πεμπει: *Others perhaps* MAY SEND *such and such things: it is sufficient for me, if I send*—This most obvious and reasonable alteration brings the numbers of the distich from 5953 to 5946, according to Mr. Carey's computation; or, including the iota, to 5956.

Again, in the latter distich:

Αλλ' εμεθεν δεξαι Μουσων στιχον, ὡς τις εις αιν
Μιμνοι και φιλιης σημα και ευμαθιης:

the subjunctive μιμνη is a form more regular and legitimate after δεξαι with ὡς, than the optative μιμνοι: in which correction the numeral difference between η and οι changes the total sum of the latter distich from 6018 to 5946 without reckoning the subscribed iota; and, with that addition, to 5956: so as to effect the required arithmetical correspondence in both cases between the distichs of the epigram.

However, though I am compelled to dissent with much reluctance from Mr. Carey's decisions on this occasion, I should not forgive myself, if I neglected this opportunity of expressing the pleasure and improvement, which I, in common, I am persuaded, with all your classical readers, never fail to reap from the critical remarks of this gentleman; and to avow my satisfaction at seeing your repository enriched by such communications of so sagacious and accurate a scholar.

Hackney July 3, GILBERT WAKEFIELD.
1801.

To the Editor of the Monthly Magazine.

SIR,

THE XIVth section of the second volume of Warton's History of English Poetry, closes with the following remarkable paragraph:—

"A well-

"A well-executed History of Scottish Poetry, from the thirteenth century, would be a valuable accession to the general literary history of Britain. The subject is pregnant with much curious and instructive information, is highly deserving of a minute and regular research, has never yet been uniformly examined in its full extent, and the materials are both accessible and ample. Even the bare lives of the vernacular poets of Scotland have never yet been written with tolerable care, and at present are only known from the meagre outlines of Dempster and Mackenzie. The Scotch appear to have had an early propensity to theatrical representations; and it is probable, that in the prosecution of such a design, among several other interesting and unexpected discoveries, many anecdotes, conducing to illustrate the rise and progress of our ancient drama, might be drawn from obscurity."

From the first perusal of this interesting passage, I have never ceased to think of the project it recommends; and it is now twelve years since I drew up a plan of the different particulars that seemed to be requisite to the complete execution of such a work; and which, though stated separately, for the sake of precision, were meant to be intimately blended together, in their proper proportions, throughout the whole. Of this plan I shall now proceed to lay an abridgement before your readers.

I. The first of these requisites I shall term Critical History, which exhibits the progress of poetry and taste through the various stages of improvement or decline, and includes, what is intimately connected with the subject—the state of learning at every different period.

II. The National History may next be mentioned, which describes that constant and powerful influence, which the administration of government, and the state of public affairs, have over the art of composition.

III. The History of Manners comes next to be considered, which includes an almost infinite variety of objects, down from the revolutions of religious opinion, to the changes in dress, and in the economy of the table.

IV. Another requisite is Biographical Anecdote, which gratifies the curiosity we naturally feel to be acquainted with the fortunes and characters of those whose productions pass in review before us.

V. Analytical Criticism may next be taken notice of, in which we are presented, in a summary manner, with the plan of every original performance, whose length or importance seems to merit this distinction; and in which are exhibited the thread of narration, the train of sentiment, or the succession of imagery, freed from all tedious superfluity of language, and from all the impertinence of useless digression.

VI. General Criticism stands next in order, which estimates the merit of every different production, and fixes, with precision, what degree of genius each different writer appears to have possessed, that he may not receive praises which are not his due, but be assigned a proper rank among his poetical brethren.

VII. Particular Criticism naturally follows, whose province it is to point out to the reader the beauties and blemishes of every composition, and to select such a number and variety of specimens, as may give him a lively and distinct idea of the style and manner in which it is executed.

VIII. Nor must Comparative Criticism be forgotten, which takes notice of the resemblances, whether intended or accidental, between our Scotch writers and those of other nations, either in the general plan of the performance, or in any detached and particular passage.

IX. The last of these requisites is Verbal Interpretation, whereby every word, which could not be comprehended by a person unacquainted with the dialect of Scotland, is explained by a synonimous expression in English.

With regard to the mere mechanical division of the work, it will naturally arrange itself in the following manner:—

The history of our poetry, from the earliest notices, down to the reign of James IV. will constitute the subject of the first book, which, with some preliminary dissertations on the language, will be amply sufficient for the first volume.

The brilliant reign of James IV. that Augustan æra of our vernacular poetry, will occupy the second book and the second volume, and will probably, to the reader of classical taste, be the most interesting portion of the whole.

The reign of James V. of the unfortunate Mary, and of James VI. till his removal to England, will require each of them its separate book, but may probably be comprized in a single volume.

The sixth book will treat of the seventeenth century, and the seventh of the one which has just closed; both may be comprehended in a fourth volume; for although the latter of these periods is richly distinguished by the illustrious names of Ramsay,

Ramfay, Rofs, Ferguffon, and Burns, the former is almoft a mere blank, and fupplies, to the hiftorian of our vernacular poetry, fcarcely any materials for difcuffion.

Of fuch an extenfive and multifarious defign, I have hitherto only been able to execute the Critical part of the firft volume; comprehending an account of Barbour's Bruce, of the Original Chronicle of Winton, the Poetical Remains of King James I. Blind Harry's Wallace, the Houlat of Holland, the Metrical Romances of Gawan and Gelegras, and Sir Gawan and Sir Galaron of Galloway, and the Three Tales of the Three Priefts of Peblis. Thefe will, indeed, conftitute the body of the volume; but there are yet many refearches to be made, and much laborious reading to be gone through, before I can be able to fill up, properly, the hiftorical, antiquarian, and biographical departments.

The chief difcouragement to fuch an undertaking, is the great fcarcity of Biographical materials; fo great, indeed, that it may, perhaps, be afferted, that of all our ancient vernacular poets, the account of Gawen Douglas is almoft the only one that has ever been written in a fatisfactory manner. Of his great cotemporary, Dunbar, whom I have always confidered as the firft of them all, on account of his union of fancy and humour, fo little is certainly known, that even the idea which had been generally adopted, that he was a native of Salton, in Eaft Lothian, upon a more accurate infpection of manufcripts, has lately been difcovered to be wholly erroneous. This want, however, is the lefs to be regretted, as a full detail of their lives and characters belongs more directly to a biographical performance, and is what, in a work of this general nature, could fcarcely have been admitted with any propriety. It is a want, alfo, which, though much to be lamented, muft not be laid to the charge of the hiftorian, who muft find it impracticable, in many cafes, to throw much light on the characters of thofe about whom their contemporaries were fo carelefs, or to give any certainty to thofe circumftances which time has fo long covered with the mifts of oblivion.

In the profecution of this undertaking, I fhall be much obliged to any correfpondent, who, through the medium of your ufeful mifcellany, may have it in his power to furnifh me either with notices of fcarce manufcripts or books, or any other thing connected with the fubject.

Edinburgh, I am, your's, &c.
March 30, 1801. ALEX. THOMSON.

To the Editor of the Monthly Magazine.

SIR,

THOUGH, as individuals, Dr. Montucci and Dr. Hager, be equally indifferent to me, I confefs the retort of the latter upon the former, in your laft Magazine, gave me pleafure, when confidered as the repulfe of an infult. I have lived long enough to remember many a literary conteft, but do not recollect any inftance of an attack fo illiberal as Dr. Montucci's. Having perufed Dr. Hager's work with fingular fatisfaction, I am glad to fee that my own opinion of it is confirmed by that of *the firft Orientalift in Europe*: faying thus much, it is fcarcely requifite to add the name of SILVESTRE DE SACY, who, after an elegant fummary of the volume in the *Magafin Encyclopédique*, thus concludes:

"We will clofe this article, by obferving, that the beauty of the execution of this volume perfectly correfponds with the importance of the work. We earneftly wifh Dr. Hager may fpeedily find all neceffary encouragement to expedite the publication of this important Dictionary; and we doubt not that his name, already juftly celebrated, will be enrolled in the number of the learned who have powerfully contributed to the glory of their own age, by extending the limits of the dominion of literature."

I am, Sir, your's, &c.
R. L. Y.

To the Editor of the Monthly Magazine.

SIR,

IN confonance with the laudable wifhes of Dr. Watkins, permit me to folicit, through the medium of your Mifcellany, fome particulars of the Life of Mr. WILLIAM DUDGEON; a name not yet, I believe, to be found in the records of biography. His "Philofophical Works" are comprifed in one volume 12mo, printed (though not announced in the title) at Glafgow, in 1765, and confift of "The State of the Moral World confidered; or, a Vindication of Providence in the Government of the Moral World;"—"A Defence of the State, &c." (i. e. a view of the nature and origin of moral good and evil);—"A View of the Neceffitarian; or, Beft Scheme;"—"A Catechifm founded on Experience and Reafon (i. e. the *law of Nature*), collected by a Father for the Ufe of his Children;"—"Philofophical Letters on the Being and Attributes of God," &c. &c. The Letters are addreffed to the Rev. Mr. JACKSON, a difciple of Dr. Clarke, and author of "Exiftence and Unity of God, proved from his Nature and Attributes;" and a "Defence, &c." whofe name is, I believe, likewife unknown in the annals of literary exiftence, istence. Mr. Dudgeon also corresponded with the celebrated Bishop Headly. Of his profound philosophical labours, which are perhaps the most elegant, correct, and intelligible disquisitions on the nature of moral good and evil extant, we shall decline mentioning, till some of your Correspondents favour us with even the parish register of his existence.

Your's,
Chapter Coffee-house, J. A. B.
July 16, 1801.

To the Editor of the Monthly Magazine.

SIR,

SOME years since, I copied the following inscription from the monument of the pious Dr. Martin Benson, Bishop of Gloucester, which I hope you will cause to be inserted in your Magazine. At the same time, I shall be obliged to any of your numerous Correspondents for some particulars of this worthy prelate.

I am, your's, &c.
J. WATKINS.

"Reader, be admonished by this marble to imitate Martin Benson, late Bishop of this Diocese. A rational piety raised the views of this excellent man above the world, and formed his whole temper into a truly Christian spirit of resignation. An uncommon warmth of benevolence made it the business and pleasure of his life to go about doing good, by instruction in righteousness, and by works of charity. He watched the flock of Christ as a faithful shepherd, from a sense of his own duty, and a disinterested concern for their common welfare: and he maintained the dignity of his authority by the meekness with which he exercised it. He felt a deep compassion for the vicious, and shewed it even while he was exposing the folly and wretchedness of vice, with a strength and turn of language peculiar to himself. His reproofs, being dictated by friendship, qualified by candour, and delivered with a natural delicacy of manners; were sincere, without roughness; and endearing, without dissimulation. He was, by constitution, liable to a depression of spirits; but innocence of heart enlivened his mind and his conversation with a cheerfulness that created a more affectionate regard for his superior worth, by rendering it more familiar and amiable. Under the most acute pains of his last tedious illness, he possessed his soul in patience, and, with a firm trust in his Redeemer, calmly resigned his spirit to the Father of Mercies."

To the Editor of the Monthly Magazine.

SIR,

I TAKE the liberty of sending, for insertion in your valuable Repertory, some interesting documents, hitherto unknown to the world in general, respecting the first introduction of Christianity into this island. They consist of extracts from the *British Triads*, printed in the *Myvyrian Archaiology of Wales*, vol. ii. page 60, and of which you were pleased to insert examples, in the Magazine for April last, page 219.

In a Triad, entitled the Three Hallowed Families of the Isle of Britain; the first family in order is mentioned thus:

"Gwelygorz Brân Vendigaid ab Llyr Llediaith: sev, y Brân hwnw á zug y fyz yn Nghrist gyntav i yr ynys hon o Ruvain, lle y bu ev yn ngharçar, trwy vrâd Aregwez Voezawg, merç Avarwy ab Lluz."

In English thus:

The family of BRAN, THE BLESSED, son of LLYR OF BARBAROUS SPEECH: that is to say, this BRAN brought the faith in Christ first into this island from Rome, where he was in captivity, through the treachery of AREGWEZ VOEZAWG, daughter of AVARWY son of LLUZ.

What follows is an extract from a Triad, called *Tri Meuwedigion deyrnez Ynys Prydain*; or, the THREE BLESSED PRINCES OF THE ISLE OF BRITAIN, the first of which is mentioned in these words:

"Brân Vendigaid ab Llyr Llediaith, à zygwys gyntav fyz yn Nghrist i genedyl y Cymry o Ruvain, lle y bu eve saith mlynez ei vab Caradawg, à zug gwyr Rhuvain yn nghарçar, gwedi ei vradycu, trwy hud a thwyll, a cynllwyn Aregwez Voegawg."

This is,

BRAN THE BLESSED, son of LLYR OF BARBAROUS SPEECH, who first brought the faith of Christ to the nation of the *Cymry* from Rome, where he was for seven years in hostage for his son CARADAWG, whom the men of Rome carried away a captive, after he had been betrayed through the allurement and deceit and plotting of AREGWEZ VOEZAWG.

The Triads record several other curious facts respecting *Brân*, and respecting *Caractacus*, his son, so celebrated in the world, which are capable of affording much light, in tracing out the system of government amongst the Britons; and of which, at a future opportunity, I may be able to furnish you, Mr. Editor, with some detail, I remain, &c.

August 7, 1801. MEIRION.

For

For the Monthly Magazine.

DESULTORY COMMENTS *on* MASON'S SUPPLEMENT *to* JOHNSON'S DICTIONARY.

(*Continued from Page 505, Vol. XI.*)

CANAKIN.

ITALIAN diction owes much of its peculiar beauty to the variety of its modificatory syllables. From its nouns are formed at pleasure augmentatives and diminutives; and these subdivide again into terms of disgust and approbation. *Albero* a tree, *alberone* a great tree, *alberonaccio* a great overgrown tree, *alberetto* a little tree, *alberettino* a nice little tree, &c. A like latent power of forming diminutives resides indeed in the northern tongues; but they are not equally profuse in its display: our own language especially in this respect is meanly sparing.

The Gothic dialects are mostly provided with three distinct diminutive affixes: 1 *chen*, *kin*, or *ke*, which is merely lessening; 2 *lein*, *lin*, or *le*, which has an endearing caressive character, 3 *ling*, which is applied to persons, not to things, and has a contemptuous signification.

Instances of the first are—German: *becher* a beaker, *becherchen* a small beaker; *lamm* a lamb, *lämmchen*, a small lamb; *haus* a house, *häuschen* a small house; *ball* a ball, *bälchen* a small ball. Low Dutch: *lam* a lamb, *lammeken* a small lamb; *man* a man, *manneke* a little man. Danish: *lade* a shed, *ladike* a small shed. English: lamb, *lambkin*; hood, *hutkin*; gourd, *gherkin*; man, *mannikin*, or mankin; hill, *hillikin*, or hillock; and perhaps a few others. Shakespeare has still *ladykin*, or la'kin, and *maudkerkin*; but these are now obsolete; and so is *canakin*, or cankin: *pipkin* is still heard.

Instances of the second are—German: *rose* a rose, *röslein* a rose bud; *weib*, a woman, *weiblein* a nice little woman; *kind* a child, *kindlein* a sweet little child; *buch* a book, *büchlein* a pretty little book. Danish: *bid* a bite, *bidling* a little bit; *due* a dove, *dulie* a little dove. English: first, *firstling*; cat, *kitling*; young, *younglin*; goose, *goslin*; duck, *ducklin*; dump, *dumplin*; and, if Wallis be right in his derivation, sack, *satchel*. In the English diminutives of this class the final *g*, altho' usual, is a corrupt addition, and has been the cause of throwing this whole order of words out of use, by confounding the caressive with the disparaging affix.

Instances of the third are—German: *flucht* flight, *flüchling*, a run away; *find* a find, *findling* a foundling; *buck* a hump, *bückling* one who is hunchbacked; *dichter* a poet, *dichterling* a poetaster; *witz* wit, *witzling* a witling. Anglosaxon: *hyra* hire, *hyrling* a hireling; *habban* to have or hold, *hæftling* a captive; *fremd* strange, *fremdling* an outcast. English: found, *foundling*; wit, *witling*; hire, *hireling*; fond, *fondling*; nest, *nestling*; dear, *darling*; suck, *suckling*; change, *changeling*; king, *kingling*; prince, *princeling*; world, *worldling*; man, *manling*; cringe, *cringeling*; and many others. This affix is in English so familiar, and so precisely understood, that it may still be applied to the formation of new words. Ben Jonson indeed ventured to coin *airling*, which has not been received; but this arises from the strange signification by him assigned to it: he uses it for a *topling*. *Earthling* would naturally mean a contemptible inhabitant of the earth, and might by a theologian be applied to man; *airling* would naturally mean a contemptible inhabitant of the air, and might in the Rape of the Lock, have been addressed by the chagrin of Ariel to the incautious Crispissa; but, by substituting an arbitrary to the essential signification, the word is rendered anomalous, and has therefore incurred the usual fate of such words—desuetude.

4. To the *kin* and *lin* of the northern dialects usage has now substituted the *et* or *let* of the southern, which is employed with increasing freedom in the mintage of English diminutives: as *circlet*, *hamlet*, *streamlet*, *ringlet*, *runlet*, *floweret*, *pocket*, *baronet*, *dragonet*, *coronet* and *coronet*, *riveret*, *riverlet* and *rivulet*, *pullet*, *cygnet*, and many others.

Dr. Geddes, in his new Translation of the Bible, which for purity of diction generally excels the old one, rashly hazards the word *wristlet*. He evidently supposes *bracelet* to mean an ornament for the arm, and to be derived from the French *bras*, arm; and *wristlet* to be likewise coined in the legal die of domestic analogy, and to mean an ornament for the wrist. This is surely a skip-over in etymology. From *bras* comes the verb *to brace*, to surround as with the arms; and from this verb descends the substantive *a brace*, that which embraces. Of this secondary substantive *brace*, a girt, *bracelet* is the diminutive; it means therefore a small girt. Dr Geddes might correctly have employed the terms *arm-bracelet*, and *wrist-bracelet*; or he might have used the more familiar *wrist-band*, which, although commonly applied to the unornamented termination of a shirt-sleeve, does not exclude the idea of ornament. *Armlet* and *wristlet* can only signify a small arm, and a small wrist.

Whence ſpring this *kin*, this *lin*, this *ling*, this *et*, or *let?* The origin of formative ſyllables can ſeldom be traced ſatisfactorily: coming into currency before the art of writing, the early ſhape of their courſe uſually lies behind the furtheſt ſummits of hiſtorical etymology: it is with the ſpying-glaſs of conjecture, not with the way-wiſer of record, that the bearing of their ſources muſt be made out. Take gueſs then inſtead of proof.

1. and 2. In Angloſaxon *blaen*, in Swediſh *klen*, in Swabian *clain*, in Lowſaxon *kleen*, and in Teutonic *chlein*, ſignify *little*. The Engliſh adjective *lean*, thin, is of the ſame family: and, as every word muſt at firſt have been the name of a ſenſible object, it probably denoted ſomething ſmall and ſlender, ſuppoſe *a ruſh*, or *a twig*. This *chlein* may among ſome Gothic tribes or provinces have dwindled into *chen* and *kin*; among others into *lein* and *lin*; and have been received in both forms after a remixture of the ſeparated clans. All diminutives eaſily acquire a careſſive character, as *animula*, *ocellus*, &c. the Greeks even called their diminutives ὑποκορισμα; and the ſofter form, *lin*, rather than *kin*, would moſt naturally be ſo appropriated.

3. Fetch Spelman's Gloſſary. Turn to the word *Adelingus*. It is there aſſerted that, in the early provincial dialect of Weſſex, *ling* ſignified an image, or idol. The firſt idols were little elſe than poſts, trunks of trees ſlightly faſhioned by the carver: *ling* then is likely to have ſignified the ſtem of a tree, before it came to ſignify an idol. Now in all languages a miſhapen or ſtupid individual is commonly compared with wood. What a ſtump of a man! What a blockhead! What a wooden pate! What a log! How ſtubborn! Metaphors theſe of the ſame claſs, and natural everywhere, becauſe founded in the qualities of things. Manling, Witling, Kingling, might thus be analyzed into Stump of a man! Block of a wit! Log of a king! The mould once formed would ſoon be employed to caſt ſubſtantives to which it was leſs adapted. The Daniſh *ling* left, left-handed, aukward, is perhaps connected etymologically with this affix: to call the left hand, the clumſy hand, or the wooden hand, is not unnatural.

4. The Engliſh *et* (or *let* as for ſound's ſake it is ſometimes written) deſcends from the French *ette*, which deſcends from the Italian *etto*: thus *floweret* is modelled after *fleurette*, and this after *fioretto*. But whence have the Italians their *etto*; for it is not obvious in the Latin? The academicians della Cruſca ought to have undertaken the inveſtigation at the word *agnelletto*, which was their firſt glaring opportunity. Did this ſyllable originally acquire a diminutive ſignification by being appended to certain adjectives, as *acerbetto*, ſouriſh, from *acerbo*, ſour? In its adjectival form can it be a corruption of the Latin *aptus*, which ſeems to be an abbreviation of *adpoſitus* to have *contiguity* for its primary idea; and to be etymologically allied with *apud*; it ſignifies therefore *cloſe to*, *near to*, *approaching?* Thus Cicero: *Facilius eſt apta diſſolvere quam diſſipata connectere.* *Acerbetto* then would mean approaching to ſour: *deſchetto* approaching to a table: *balenetto* very like a whale: *orcioletto* a canakin.

Capricious.—Mr. Maſon makes an article of this word merely to ſupply an authority or two for its uſe. He might have added to Dr. Johnſon's information a better account of its origin. Who underſtands the word from hearing that it means *whimſical*, *fanciful*, *humourſome?* Can it be ſaid of the melancholy hypochondriac that he is capricious, becauſe he is whimſical; of Milton's Comus that it is capricious, becauſe it is fanciful; or of conſpiratory clubs that they are capricious, becauſe they are humourſome? Certainly not. It is neceſſary to trace back the word to its radical idea: it means *friſky*, bounding or ſpringing like a gazel with unmotived irregularity. Ceva rightly tells us ſo.

Cum levis in nimbo delapſa volucribus alis
Lætitia in terras ſtellato ex æthere venit:
Cui comes ille ciens animos, et pectora verſans
Spiritus*, a capreis montanis nomen adeptus,
Ignotum Latio nomen: pictoribus ille
Interdum aſſiſtens operi, nec ſegnius inſtans
Vatibus, ante alios Muſis gratiſſimus hoſpes.

Captivance.—Words in *ance* were formerly more common in the language than they are now; and were oftener uſed in the plural number. We no longer, with Jeremy Taylor, ſay *purſuances*. The ſyllable *ance* comes directly from the French *ance*, and mediately from the Latin *antia*; and is uſed for the inflection of verbs: ſuffer, *ſufferance*, perſevere, *perſeverance*; equiponderate, *equiponderance*; abound, *abundance*; comply, *compliance*. In conſequence of their verbal origin, an idea of time, of continued, or of tranſitive action commonly clings about theſe words; ſo that *captivance* ſeemingly ſhould mean *the proceſs of taking captive*; whereas *captivity* being derived from the adjective, ſhould

* Vulgo *Capriccio*.

should mean *the quality of being captive*. If this observation be well founded, it accounts in some degree for the reluctance felt at employing this whole class of substantives in the plural number: that which is going on without interruption is as insusceptible of plurality as *warmth* or *beatitude*. Still we can say: the disagreeing warmths of mineral springs; the beatitudes promised in the sermon on the mount; the contrivances of the knights to follow Armida, and the want of variety in their captivances.

Catso.—A lady was complimenting Dr. Johnson on the omission of all indelicate words in his Dictionary. "I perceive, Madam, you have been poaching for them," was the reply of the shrewd cynic. The recorder of this word, and of its derivative, but ill imitates surely the caution of his predecessor: is it not a familiar oath or exclamation of the Italians, analogous in meaning to the Latin *pubes*, and, like it, used occasionally for an adolescent, a blood: does not *catzerie* therefore mean subserviency to libidinous gratification? Thus Ben Jonson:

These be our nimble-spirited *catsos*, that have their evasions at pleasure.
Every Man in his Humour.

And Marlow:

He looks like one that is employed in *catzerie*.
Jew of Malta.

Mr. Mason makes these words synonimous with *swindler* and *swindling*.

Celestin.—Why not distinguish between the substantive and the adjective; between Pope Celestin and the Celestine Friars? Does any one write *masculin*, *feminin*? Usage has established the *e* final in all adjectives formed by this rule of analogy: one always reads the 'Clementine constitutions,' the 'Benedictine editions.' This remark would have been better placed at the word *Benedictin*.

To chaldese.—Is a verb so anomalous to be received on such authority as that adduced by Mr. Mason? Is the passage from Butler's Remains any thing short of nonsense?

That men so grave and wise
Should be *chaldes'd* by gnats and flies.

In what respect can gnats *chaldese*, or *chaldaize*, mean; for the word is allowed to be formed from *chaldee*, a syriac dialect of the Hebrew. In Butler's sense of the word: He who chaldaized the book of Daniel chaldesed many a divine. See Hudibras, I. 1010.

Cloud-top'd.—This is a vitious though a common way of spelling: for it is a bull in orthography to describe the unutterable. A hard and a soft consonant cannot by any human organs be pronounced in immediate succession in the same syllable. Rob'd, robb'd, ribb'd, are possible sounds; so are soapt, stopt, lipt: but to unite in one termination *b*, *d*, *g*, *v*, or *z*, with *p*, *t*, *k*, *f*, or *s*, is inarticulable. Those who write top'd or topp'd, lip'd or lipp'd, stopp'd and ripp'd, propose to the organs of speech this impossible coalition. The reason why the Germans never learn to distinguish in speaking between *d* and *t*, *b* and *p*, is that the orthography of their language habitually confounds the difference, presenting the letters *b* and *d* when they must be pronounced *p* and *t*, and conversely. Thus the Germans absurdly write *Abt* and *Stadt*, which must be pronounced either *Abd* or *Apt*, either *Statt* or *Stadd*; the hard and the soft consonant cannot be both sounded in one exhalation. There is a difficulty in writing the participle *striped* in its contracted monosyllabic form: the *p* must in pronunciation be followed by *t*, yet it should not be confounded with *stript*, the regular contraction of *stripped*. Why not place an apostrophe before the letter *t*, as readily as before a *d*, and write *strip't*?

Committee.—This word is the regular personal substantive passive of the verb *to commit*, and means primarily, *One to whom any thing is committed*, as in the instances properly adduced by Mr. Mason. The parliamentary use of the word is anomalous: it there means the collective body of persons to whom any thing is committed; and, in that baragoinish sense, is accented on the second syllable.

Constituent.—In the established language of English polity *constituent* has long signified *he who deputes another*: it is thus defined by Johnson, it is thus employed by Burke. In this sense the *primary* are the *constituent* assemblies of the French. But some gallicizing writers have introduced an inconvenient practice of translating the French participle *constituante* (derived from the verb *constituer* to constitute) by the word *constituent* instead of the word *constituting*; they have called the first national assembly of France the *constituent* instead of the *constituting* assembly; and thus they have prepared our ears for the doctrine that parliament is the fundamental constituent authority, and electors the creatures of its fiat.

Constitutionalist. Mr. Mason unaccountably defines this word *an innovator of the civil constitution*; whereas it must by its structure mean, and in the adduced passage does mean, *a partizan of the constitution*.

Cooperage.—Mr. Mason defines cooperage, *a place where coopers work is done*, whereas it ought to mean *the price of cooper's work*: and *coopery* ought to designate *the place where coopers work is done*. Stallage, poundage, wharfage, pontage, murage, &c. signify the tolls levied for a stall, a pound, a wharf, a bridge, a wall, &c. Brewery, foundery, smithy, indicate the place where brewers, founders, smiths, do their work.

Corival.—As the word *rival* includes the idea of competition, the *co* is redundant: Shakespeare's authority has been impotent to protect a word manifestly improper: it is now disused.

Corrigible.—There are two ways of obtaining verbal adjectives: 1. by domestic analogy; adding to the infinitive the affix *able*, as *disputable*, *answerable*, *movable*, *vitrifiable*: 2. by importation from the French or Latin; as *admissible*, *applicable*, *irrefragable*, *soluble*. Of this latter class, so many are of doubtful purity, both in French and Latin, that it is perhaps safer to prefer, when both forms exist, the English form; as *admittable*, *applicable*, &c. *correctable* however does no where occur.

These adjectives all have, or should have, a passive signification: able *to be* disputed, answered, moved, vitrified; able *to be* admitted, applied, refused, dissolved, corrected. Those words are impurely employed, to which an active sense is sometimes assigned. *The Ephesian matron was a comfortable widow*: but not *Warm baths are most comfortable*: where *comforting*, or *comfortive*, is intended.

Cotqueenity.—Another proof, if proof were wanting, that there is a tendency in our language to purge itself of every thing anomalous: the affix *ity* is not appliable to words of Saxon origin; a Saxon word inflected by means of it is therefore suffered to obsolesce, although minted by Ben Jonson. Cot-queen is the queen of his own home or cot, where he ought to be king; the master Betty, the husband in petticoats. "A stateswoman, (says Addison,) is as ridiculous a creature as a cotqueen."

Coure.—Chaucer thus spells to cower:

Ferre from these other up in an halke
There lurked and there coured she.
R. R. v. 463

And again:

Kings mote to hem knele and coure. *P. Tale.*

Both words probably derive from the French *couvrir* to cover, and were first applied to the squatting of a hen to cover her chickens, and by degrees to squatting in general. Spenser seems to have preserved this primitive sense in the passage,

At last him turning to his charge behight,
With trembling hand his troubled pulse gan try,
Where finding life not yet dislodged quite,
He much rejoiced, and cour'd it tenderly,
As chicken newly hatcht.

Junius is for deriving the word from the Welsh *cwrrian*, to crouch on the pasterns; and Johnson from the manner in which a *cow* sinks on her knees. Neither of these projects of derivation will account for Spenser's use of the word.

Craple.—Few words are common to so many nations as the name of the crab. The Greeks have Καραβος; the French *Crabe*; the Swedes *Krabba*; and all the other Gothic dialects an orthographic variety of the same term. *Ecrevisse* is but a modification of the northern crabfish or crayfish. This animal being remarkable for its bent-in pincers-claws, has supplied in many languages the denomination of a hook, or crook. Thus in German *Krapf*, in Italian *Graffio*, in French *Agraffe* designates that hook which receives the bucket of a well. The French *griffe*, a claw, and the English verb *to gripe* have a common Gothic origin, and descend from the same stem. From *to gripe* comes the frequentative *to grapple*.

The motion of the crab is no less remarkable than its form: another set of derivatives very numerous, have this movement for their radical idea. In English *to creep*, in German *krauen*, *krableln*, and again, *to crawl*; as well as the Italian *grappare*, *grappeggiare*, and the French *grimper*; also *to scrape*, and its frequentatives *to scrabble*, *to scramble*, are no doubt of the same family.

Words denoting instruments are in all the Gothic dialects constructed by adding the affix *el*, which in Mæso-gothic signifies the primitive and commonest instrument, *the arm*, and occurs in the English word *elbow*, the bow or bend of the arm; and in *ell*, a measure of an arm's length. Thus, *shovel*, from to shove; *girdle*, from to gird; *heavel*, from to heave; *flail*, from to flay; *needle*, from A.S. *nestan*, to sew; *gabel*, a fork, from *to gape* (whence the gable-end, or forked-wall, of a house); *chisel*, from to chase, or enchase; *awel*, from A. S. *agan*, to begin; *spindle*, from to spin; *treadle*, from to tread; *trundle*, from

from to trend; *muzzle*, from mouth; *nozzle*, from nose; *handle*, from hand; *thimble*, from thumb; and many others: as, *kettle*, *pestle*, *sickle*, *saddle*, *easel*, *stopple*, &c. With the same affix the Germans form *gartel*, *hebel*, *flegel*, *nadel*, *gabel*, *spindel*, *kessel*, *sattel*, *stoppel*, &c. To this class of words *crable* appears to belong: it means therefore an instrument for creeping. It is to be lamented that the practice has not prevailed of spelling all these substantives with *el* instead of *le*, in order to distinguish this affix from that which serves to form frequentative verbs: such as *joust*, *jostle*; *hurt*, *hurtle*; *stray*, *straggle*, &c.

Culprit.—When a prisoner is brought to the bar, enquiry is made of him whether he pleads guilty or not guilty: on his answering "Not guilty," the clerk of the arraigns says, "*Qu'il paroit*, let it appear so." Hence originates the vulgar practice of calling a prisoner *the culprit*: it was mistaken by the croud for the legal denomination of a criminal.

Curiet.—For this word no sufficient authority is produced: probably it is an error of the press for *curiasse*.

(*To be continued.*)

To the Editor of the Monthly Magazine.

SIR,

THE article in your Magazine for April last (p. 230), respecting the Patent of the Artillery Company, appears to be incorrect. The game enquired after is not Popyemaye, but Popinjay; a game which is still annually played by a society of archers at Kilwinning, a small town of Ayrshire, in Scotland, where, however, from an evident error or provincialism, it is called "*Papingoe*."

According to Bailey, "Popinjay," (papejay, Fr. papejayo, Span. papegoy, Dan.) is a parrot of a greenish colour. In the game of *Papingoe*, a figure, resembling a parrot, is placed at a considerable height upon the church-steeple of Kilwinning, and the archer who brings down the figure with his arrow is immediately declared president of the society for the ensuing year. I have been informed, however, that it is not now requisite to be possessed of considerable skill in order to attain the office of president, and that shooting at the Popinjay is observed merely in conformity to ancient custom.

Glasgow, I am, your's, &c.
July 4, 1801. A. P.

To the Editor of the Monthly Magazine.

SIR,

THE enormous rise which has of late years taken place in the price of almost all the necessaries of life, has produced considerable distress in various departments of the community. It has reduced thousands of the lower ranks, who were once able to support themselves and their families by the produce of their industrious exertions, to the odious necessity of accepting parochial relief. The case of these meritorious sufferers, who in fact constitute the sinews of the state, has deservedly occupied a considerable share of the attention of the legislature, and in numerous instances their employers have laudably stept forward to alleviate their wants. But the pressure of distress is by no means confined to the lower orders of the community. The circumstances of the times have caused a melancholy change in the condition of a class of society whose feelings, though peculiarly acute, are in general too slightly regarded—I mean those females of reputable families and good education who were formerly enabled to make a decent and handsome appearance by the economical management of a small income. The labourer demands and receives an increase of wages in some degree proportioned to the encreasing dearness of provisions—the manufacturer may obviate his growing expences, by affixing a higher value on his article, and the landed gentry may raise the rents of their estates: but in this general race, this flight from poverty, those who have no resources but a scanty and unimprovable income, are left behind. They pay double for every thing which they consume, while their revenue remains stationary. In this case what prospect have they of future comfort, and by what means can they maintain themselves in that rank in society which they have been accustomed to hold.

The philosopher may inculcate the vanity of human distinctions, and the statist may coolly inform us, that society will be benefited by the annihilation of these lilies of the valley, which neither toil nor spin; and that events which compel a number of idle people to adopt some useful calling, are so far productive of general advantage. But the man of feeling will commiserate the situation of those, who having, in the earlier period of their lives, been taught to expect that they would be enabled to live independently of personal labour; are now bending beneath the heavy pressure of of the times, and are either unqualified by their habits and their experience for the conduct of business, or are prevented by a false shame, which, however culpable in the eye of stern philosophy, is excited and fostered by general prejudice, from taking a step which will instantly throw them out of that line of social connexion in which their views and sentiments have been formed. Whoever duly considers the case of these ill-starred individuals, will rejoice to hear of a scheme which bids fair to remunerate the services, without hurting the feelings of the industrious, and to provide a vent for the little manufactures of the ingenious, without imposing on them the necessity of making public profession of a trade. By the meritorious exertions of a few ladies, in whose characters are happily united maturity of understanding, zealous perseverance, and benevolence of heart, such an institution has been lately established in Manchester, under the denomination of the Repository.

The object of this institution is to provide well educated people, the amount or the value of whose incomes is distressfully reduced, with the means of earning a respectable livelihood, without losing the rank which they hold in society.

To obtain this desirable object, a repository or shop is opened, in which is received and sold any species or piece of workmanship, the executor or proprietor of which is inclined to adopt this medium of sale.

To every article sent to the Repository must be affixed a ticket, expressing the price at which the maker or owner proposes to sell it: on this ticket room must be left for the insertion of a number, under which it is registered in the books of the institution. With each article a bill is to be delivered, to which bill those who do not wish to appear as traffickers may affix their initials, or any convenient mark.

The agent and the visitors of the institution attend every Saturday morning from ten till twelve o'clock, for the purpose of taking in works, and accounting with those proprietors whose works are already sold. These may either apply in person, or by duly authorized representatives.

From the amount of the price of the articles sold, one penny in the shilling is deducted. This deduction is appropriated to the disbursement of the expences of the institution, which is further supported by voluntary subscriptions, not exceeding 10s. 6d. each.

The sales are managed by a salaried superintendant or shopwoman.

The conduct of the institution is regulated by visitors, two of whom undertake its inspection for the space of a month.

These visitors attend at the Repository every Saturday, not only to take in works, &c. as has been before mentioned, but also to inspect and balance the accounts.

It is obvious, that in an institution of this description, the minutest accuracy of book-keeping is indispensably requisite, and as the accounts to be opened are very numerous, the assistance of a hired clerk must in general be necessary. Fortunately for the Manchester Repository a lady, well versed in the practice of book-keeping, has generously offered her services, and actually regulates this important department of the establishment.

If the managers of this institution find that they have any surplus at the end of the year, they propose, in the first place, to strike off the deduction which they at present make from the amount of sales of works, and secondly, to purchase cloaths for the poor, and sets of child bed-linen to be lent for the month, on a subscriber's recommendation.

The institution derives some aid from contributions in work, to be sold for the benefit of the Repository. This aid has, however, been hitherto very trifling, as those ladies of independent property, who send in articles to be sold, generally appropriate the product to the relief of some individual, with whose circumstances of distress they are personally acquainted. And here is opened a most agreeable and interesting mode of bestowing charitable assistance. Many ladies have pages in the ledger of the Repository, who appropriate their profits to this most laudable purpose. Children, likewise, bring into the Repository their little works, and thus earn their portions of pocket-money.

The following are the principal articles which have hitherto been offered for sale at this Repository:—

Shirts of various sizes and descriptions, cravats, pocket-handkerchiefs, stays, cloaks, spencers, ladies dressing gowns, pockets, caps, tippets, frilled handkerchiefs, ruffs, &c.—Children's robes, vests, frocks and caps, socks, shoes, gloves, mitts, garters, petticoats, housewives, work-bags, all sorts of fancy-work, &c.

It has already been ascertained, that the Manchester Repository has been productive dustive of much good. With a view of promoting the establishment of similar institutions this outline of its plan is laid before the public through the medium of your valuable Magazine, by

BENEVOLUS.

A PEDESTRIAN EXCURSION *through* ENGLAND *and* WALES, *during the* SUMMER *of* 1797.

(Continued from page 125. of Vol. II.)

BURGER.* At the entrance of this village, we observed some substantial houses and cottages of stone: the latter mostly thatched. The extensive gardens of the public house (the Arundel Arms), are ornamented in the *Islington* stile, with leaden statues; a species of foppery we did not expect in so remote a situation. Being informed that the grounds about

Wardour Castle, were open to the *untaxed* observation of every one who chose to walk in them, we entered accordingly, and pursuing the principal walk to the left, which is shady and winding, arrived first at a beautiful, though somewhat mutilated, tri-corned little altar of earthenware, and then at a sylvan temple in which is a cast of Diana. In pursuing this walk our attention was occasionally attracted by urns, and fragments of buildings that had been suffered to go to decay, and by seats of rude rock-work, that commanded fine openings to the rich champaign spread before us. Of this the summit of a hill to which the meandering paths at length conducted us, afforded a still more extensive view. But the principal object of our search was the ruins of the old castle; whose shattered towers, overgrown with ivy and elder, as they first broke upon our sight, excited our veneration, but a nearer approach somewhat damped these enthusiastic sensations; nor could we behold without disgust the tasteless patch work of modern ruins, old walls, and grotto-work, Grecian arches, trim parterers and smooth-shaven green. Here are also some remains of the Mansion that was built soon after the destruction of the castle, and which, in its turn, was destroyed by the present lord, when he built the present residence. The lower part of these remains are now converted into a stable; above is a room which we were shewn, and which contains several prints, from subjects taken from the civil war, in the time of Charles I. and also two paintings, one of Socrates instructing Alcibiades, the other of his Brother Philosopher, throwing away his Wooden Dish on seeing a Poor Man drink, still more philosophically, out of the palm of his hand.

As it was now past five o'clock we could not see the house: that is to say, the whole of it could not be shewn to us: to those apartments that were at liberty however we had access. The chapel is, I believe, considered as the finest place of Catholic devotion in England; and it is certainly very beautiful — if beauty be indeed an epithet reconcilable with that imposing awe, which the decorations here accumulated irresistibly produce. The paintings, six in number, are mostly copies. Of these "The Marriage in Cana;" The Altar Piece, "Christ taken down from the Cross;" and particularly "The Assumption of the Virgin," appeared to us to be the best.

Among the other paintings that particulary interested us, were two fine Sea-pieces in the drawing-room, "Moonlight contrasted with the effects of Fire," and "A Shipwreck," by Vernet, "An Old Man," by Titian, and "John the Baptist," by Raphael. But that which above all arrested our attention, was "Joseph of Arimathea and the Virgin, begging the Body of Christ." The whole picture, according to my untutored taste at least, is masterly; and that passion and feeling which constitute the soul both of painting and poetry, are here most powerfully concentrated. The countenance of Mary in particular is perfectly thrilling. I gazed till the whole scene was realized before me, and I felt the artist in every nerve.

The farms in this neighbourhood, if we were rightly informed, like those every where else, are getting into fewer hands. There are, however, still some small ones, at about 30l. or 40l. a year. Wages from 6s. to 7s. per week. Little or no spinning for the women and children: the latter of which, till they are able to follow the plough, can earn nothing, some of them may then at ploughing-time get 4d. per day.

Lord Arundel, during the dear season, relieved their distresses by donations of bread; and parish assistance eked out the scanty

* In the former part of this Article, Monthly Magazine, for March, p. 125 misprinted *Bangor*. For "*course grounds*," in the same Article, p. 124, l. 23, *read*, "*course of the grounds*."

scanty hire of the labourer. Some few farmers raised the wages during the scarcity, but when the evil was somewhat abated, the wages were again reduced. The cottagers keep no cows; and a drop of milk is hardly to be procured by any means.

From Fonthill to Wardour Castle, our way had lain entirely through cross-country road; nor was the case altered in our way to East-Knoyle, through which we were conducted, over commons, lanes and farm-yards, by a peasant, of whom we enquired the way to Mere. From him we learnt that the farms in that neighbourhood were not in general very large. Few were above 3 or 400, more of them not above 100l. a year; and there were some perhaps (though very few) as low as 50l. or 40l. The cottagers have mostly a bit of garden; some of them a pig; but none of them a cow; and the farmers understood œconomy better than to *sell* their skim milk. Wages 7s. per week; in hay-time 8 or 9s. in harvest from 10s. to 12s. Hay-time and harvest usually occupy together from 8 to 10 weeks. The village of East-Knoyle, like all the cottages sprinkled in our way, is built of stone, and mostly covered with thatch.

Here we met with another instance of rustic civility. An old man, attentive to our enquiries, conducted us thro' the church-yard, and pointing out a steep path which we were to ascend, and a mill on the summit which we were to leave to the right, gave us one of those clear and distinct directions, so rarely to be expected from the peasantry of this country. From the summit, thus pointed out to us, we commanded one of the most pleasing views I had ever seen. Hills and vallies, rich, fertile, and variegated, were seen finely interspersed with woodlands and cottages, and here and there some prouder mansions; while other hills, dimly descried through the mists, bounded the prospect and mingled with the horizon. Beautiful slopes and dells and climes, cloathed with fern and coppice, formed the rough foreground of the picture; and the sky, cloudy, but rather wild and sublime than monotonous, formed a *sombre* but not unsuitable accompaniment: while a shower of rain gave additional freshness to all the nearer objects, and deepened the emerald tint of the short close turf we trod. Anon the moving curtains of the sky were rent, and the beams of the sun, breaking through the interstices of dark clouds, brightly illuminated the distant western hills, whose mitigated splendours, seen through the misty veil of an intervening shower, gave a finishing tho' transient beauty to the whole. One of the distinguished features of this scene, is the high ridgy hill near Stourhead, with Alfred's tower on the summit.

Evening was now approaching, and we had yet six or seven miles to walk. Yet it was with some reluctance that we quitted this commanding eminence for the downward path that led to Upton. Still, however, both the atmosphere and our own organs were in a favourable state for the enjoyment of the picturesque, and the beauty and fertility of the home-scene, in the lowlands, with their embowered and scattered cottages, seemed to rival the extensive diversity of the bird's-eye prospect. Nor was it long before we again ascended, and regained our former view, with some heightening additions: and now, once more, we descended through a deep slope, fertile and well coppiced, to a little hamlet, called

The Green; and thence, under luxuriant hedgerows and across fields, no less inviting, to

Usham, Upton, or *Upon* (for so variously it is called). This is a pretty village of stone, retired and tranquil. But its beauty is all without: and perhaps the advantages of stone built cottages are more to the beholder than the occupant. In one of these, where we went to inquire our farther way, of a poor double bent woman, who was seated at her wheel, we saw perhaps as much wretchedness as we could well have encountered in the mud-cottages of the fenns of Lincolnshire.

Our way was still cross-road—wild, neglected, unspoiled, cross-road--unfit indeed for chaises of all kinds, curricles, gigs, or tandems—But then it was variegated—it was wild—it was unfrequented—just such as suited the taste of two excentric pedestrians who abjured "towered cities," and were sick of "the busy haunts of men;" and away we thridded down pleasant lanes, over stiles, and along faint foot-tracks, by the side of another part of that fine range of hills, whose more commanding views had this day so often delighted us. My companion fell into deep musing and pursued the path undeviating; but my spirits were alert. I bounded to the summit, and pursued my way along its sharp ridge, for more than a mile, to its termination.

The principal scene commanded from this ridge, was the same in which we had twice before luxuriated—but it appeared here with increased advantages of extent, variety and beauty; and as this part of the ridge over-peers the neighbouring hills, it it has the additional advantage of commanding the whole circle of horizon. Alfred's tower again obtrudes itself upon observation from this new point of vision.

West Knoyle, to which I immediately descended, (to join my companion) from the extremity of this ridge, is an extensive though scattered village; but offered no particular food for our observation.

From hence the road winds, over a chain of hills, through narrow lanes, shady and delightful to the eye, with now and then a cottage or two, a farm-house, or a blacksmith's shop, till coming to a place where the road divides point-blank to right and left. Here we were at some loss which path to pursue; till luckily catching a glimpse of the church over a stile, we fixed our eyes upon this as our north-star, and directed our course accordingly, over fields and quags, till at last weary and hungry we arrived at

Mere; where the circumstance of our being on foot, and perhaps the *additions* made to our appearance by the last part of our journey, procured us but a cold reception. At the first inn we applied to *the house was full*; and at the second (the Angel) the good landlady eyed us with some evident signs of jealously, before she yielded her reluctant assent to our inquiries. Some cold leg of lamb, however, some lamb-chops, and a sallad, soon satisfied the cravings of the inward man, and restored us and ultimately mine hostess of the *Angel* to good humour; and we were sumptuously lodged in an apartment, hung not indeed with modern chintz—nor with ancient tapistry—no; but with cloths, daubed with a profane hunting-match, and a sacred legend in imitation of that once famous cloth of Arras. But as Balaam's ass only brayed and the hounds only yelped on canvas, we contrived to sleep very soundly till nine o'clock

Thursday, July 6. Mere is but a straggling sort of town, indifferently built. The little cross, or market-house, is a mean edifice; and the greatest curiosity we remarked was a publick-house sign, which exhibits a sorry black dog, with a coronet round his neck, and a chain; over which is written "The Old George!"

A manufactory of ticks is carried on here, at which women earn upon an average from 4s. to 4s. 6d. per week—though there are some who get 7s. and even 7s. 6d. Men from 8s. to 9s. 6d. It furnishes no employment for children. Labourers in husbandry receive 7s. per week. The farms are mostly large, from 3 to 7 or 800l. a year. Scarcely any from 50 to 100l. None of the cottagers (as might be expected) have any cows.

Having taken our morning repast and our morning lounge, we quitted Mere; and having passed the house of Mrs. Grose (widow of the famous Antiquary), we turned off to the right, to

Stour-head, the justly celebrated seat of Sir Richard Hoare. Having passed some time in admiring the paintings, (several of which—particularly "The Wise-men's Offerings," and "The Death of Dido," though a copy, deserve more particular notice) our attention was next directed to the gardens, the least interesting object in which (because so theatrically artificial—for it only performs by command of the turn-cock) is the cascade. Barring this foppery, the grounds are in good taste; and the decorations (the Doric temple on the lake, the Chinese bridge, the fine hanging plantations, the arch leading to the grotto, the grotto itself, and the nymph sleeping there, the antique Gothic cross (formerly an ornament to the city of Bristol), the urn, embossed with Bachanalian revels, the temple of the sun, and the pantheon, all deserve their separate portions of attention. In this last in particular, are some very fine statues. They are as follows "Peace" and a "Diana," two casts in metal; a "Flora," charming from the beautiful simplicity of its drapery; a "Hercules," truly Herculean; sublime in strength, without bombastic distortion of muscle—(some of our *sublime* painters of the *new* school would do well to study it.) a "Livia Augusta, as Ceres," equally captivating from the beauty of the features and fine representation of the simplicity of ancient drapery. These are in marble by Rysbach. "Meleager," and the "Egyptian Isis," are in plaster of Paris.

The terrace, an extensive ride, commanding a rich variety of prospect; and Alfred's tower, a modern triangular building of brick, and of very great height, were the next objects of our attention. From the top of this we commanded one of those extensive prospects, which fill the eye with present wonder, but from the indistinctness of their objects leave but few traces on the remembrance.

After these birds-eye prospects we would gladly have reposed ourselves in some scene of humble sequestration; and Arthur's vale, of which we had heard talk, as one of the beautiful objects of these extensive grounds, seemed by its name to promise what we wished; but in our search for this, we only lost ourselves in entangling

gling and pathless mazes, and at last were obliged to give over the pursuit.

We now crossed a common to Norton Ferris; whence, through a narrow defile, we passed to

Maiden Bradley; where we refreshed ourselves with some tea and rashers of bacon: our repast being accompanied with a concert of vocal music, which though not performed in the same room where we sat, effectually prevented us from hearing the sound of our own voices. This delectable performance was no other than a Cornish song, giving the French and all Revolutionists to the devil, and exalting "George the Great," with all due veneration, to the skies. The performers were a company of colliers (not very angelic indeed in their appearance), but they joined in the apotheosis with such Stentorian force of lungs, that I think it may be safely affirmed that never conqueror or mighty potentate had his praise more loudly celebrated.

The sortie from Maiden Bradley, as we directed our course towards the Bath road, presented a pleasing picture, terminating in blue distant hills; but whose principal beauty was undoubtedly derived from the brightness and serenity of the evening. The road continued to be very interesting for the first three miles, and through the twisted branches of some fine romantic trees afforded several beautiful views. The beauty of the evening however was over before we arrived at Frome (the place of our destination) which we entered at about half past nine, and where we were hospitably entertained by the relations and friends of my fellow-traveller.

(To be continued).

To the Editor of the Monthly Magazine.

SIR,

THE spirit of true poesy has been so long laid among the tombs of our literary fathers, that even the apparition of Genius is and ought to be considered, in our days, highly miraculous. The little volume containing the poetical works of the late T. Little, esq. is a phenomenon of this kind. The editor, in a very ingenious preface, abounding with classical remark and polite criticism, gives a brief account of the author, who, as it appears, was his particular friend, and a young man of the most ardent sensibility and refined passion. His eulogium on CATULLUS is elegant and accurate; but I do not coincide in the too favourable opinion he seems to entertain of the "sentimental levity, the '*grata protervitas*' of a Rochester or a Sedly." The amatory writers of an *earlier* date were certainly more fanciful, and, at the same time, more natural; I shall only instance the names of a RANDOLPH, or a DRAYTON, poets, with whose works I doubt not that MR. LITTLE himself was particularly intimate. To those I do not scruple to add SUCKLING, as much superior in delicate simplicity to his more famous contemporaries. In describing the warmer emotions of the heart, there is a chastity of expression required, which can alone give a durability of colouring to performances of a nature generally evanescent, or at least liable to decay with their subject. Who, at this period of comparative purity, is delighted with the mythological extravagance of WALLER, or the polished pedantry of LANSDOWN? Their admirers are departed with our grandames, or only exist in maiden-aunts, and antiquated beauties, who, happily, know very little of the matter. As for the so much celebrated elegies of HAMMOND, they are, though modern, even less sufferable; the stiff, affected exercises of a school-boy, not the spontaneous and animated effusions of a lover; and I can hardly determine, whether even the mad flights of the DELLA-CRUSCA tribe, wild and inconsistent as they are, may not be *more* appropriate to the delineation of those sentiments which owe their very birth to the temporary frenzy of an overheated heart, and, sometimes, of an overheated head. Though some may style this apathy, it is certainly the apathy of reason; and cannot be refuted by the chymerical enthusiasm of any metaphysical inamorato, from the time of PETRARCH himself to the present. After this short digression, I shall enter more minutely into a detail of the pieces which so forcibly demand our attention, first pointing out their peculiar characteristics.

Although they may, casually, betray the inconsiderate levity and effervescence of youth, they are, generally, correct and finished; there is much versatility of measure, but the diction and style are uniformly splendid. The playful archness of MATT. PRIOR has been, in some places, happily imitated, as in the lines, beginning "Yes, I think I once heard of an amorous youth, &c. in the SONG, p. 39; in the "Kiss;" and in "FANNY of TIMMOL." Many poems, of a more sublime or affecting order, remind us of that simple sweetness which LANGHORNE once so frequently evinced. The "SHIELD" is nothing inferior

ferior to the best of GRAY's minor odes, and, consequently, will admit of no sort of comparison with the monstrous productions of the day, for which the editor expresses a commendable distaste. "It screams for the guilt of days that are past," is awefully fine, and worthy of a poet, as is, likewise,

"While the damp boughs creak, and the swinging shield
Sings to the raving spirit of night."

The SONG, p. 115. is infinitely beautiful, and contains much real wit, blended with exquisite tenderness. I shall present it as a specimen.

If I swear by that eye, you'll allow
Its look is so shifting and new,
That the oath I might take on it now,
The very next glance would undo!
Those babies that nestle so sly,
Such different arrows have got,
That an oath on the glance of an eye
Such as your's, may be off in a shot!
Should I swear by the dew on your lip,
Though each moment the treasure renews,
If my constancy wishes to trip,
I may kiss off the oath when I choose!
Or a sigh may disperse from that flow'r
The dew and the oath that are there,
And I'd make a new vow ev'ry hour,
To lose them so sweetly in air!
But clear up the heav'n of your brow,
Nor fancy my faith is a feather;
On my heart I will pledge you my vow,
And they must be both broken together!

It would be easy to produce specimens of similar excellence, but I forbear to trespass upon the limits of your miscellany, and remain,

Yours, &c.

To the Editor of the Monthly Magazine.

SIR,

GIVE me leave to request, through the medium of your Magazine, some or one of those *who can*, to publish, by subscription, or otherwise, an engraving of the Hon. Thomas Erskine; thereby giving those an opportunity of sitting under his auspicious representation, who revere his professional character and abilities, his humane disposition and goodness of heart, and his disinterestedness, and you will oblige, Sir,

Your constant Reader,

IMIC.

Colchester, Aug. 6, 1801.

For the Monthly Magazine.

SKETCH *of a* JOURNEY *from* COPENHAGEN *to* HAMBURG, *&c.*

(Continued from Page 24.)

NYEBORG is an ancient town, situated on a bay where none but small vessels can enter, as the depth of water is not great. It is about three miles from the point of the promontory which extends itself into the Great Belt. It has been, what was called in former times, well fortified; but the fortifications, as well as the castle, are at present in a state of dilapidation; and a palace, which was formerly the residence of the Kings of Denmark, is now also in ruins. In 1659, a victory was obtained over the Swedes under the guns of the castle. This town, like many others in Zealand and Fünen, is falling fast to decay: it has but little commerce, and perhaps it would have none, if it were not that the revenue is collected here from the vessels which pay toll as they pass through the Great Belt. We were detained at Nyebörg several hours, until the commandant thought proper to rise, and countersign our papers: we were much mortified by our detention, as the accommodations of the inn were very indifferent; for we could only procure a cup of bad coffee, which we found but a sorry substitute for a breakfast, after travelling all night in an open boat. It would be supposed, that Nyebörg, though but a very small town, contained many poor, as in two inns which we entered, we saw boxes fixed in a conspicuous place in each, to receive charitable donations from travellers; similar lines were written on them, which were to the following effect:—"*Les Aumones sont agréable à Dieu.—Donnez en, sans Distinction de Nation, ni de Religion.—Nous sommes tous Frères.—Donnez à l'humanitié.*" This energetic demand we complied with, by dropping our "mite;" but we afterwards felt alarmed, when, on enquiry, we learned that a priest came every Saturday and unlocked the box, the contents of which he deposited in his pocket, and we could not find that any account was rendered of its application.

The road from Nyebörg to Odensee, the capital of Fünen, is through a flat, well-cultivated country. Indeed this islan is said to be better cultivated than Zealand: in the latter, corn-land chiefly abounds, but in Fünen there is more cattle than in Zealand, and of course more ground

ground set apart for meadow and pasture. Zealand is less populous in proportion than Fünen, which contains about 150,000 inhabitants. We arrived at Odensee, which is seventeen miles from Nyebörg, in four hours, and were glad to find good accommodations at the post house, where we stopped to refresh ourselves, and change horses.

We ran through *Odensee*, which is a large and populous town, and has much more appearance of trade than any we had passed through since we left Copenhagen. It lies on a river, which discharges itself into a bay in the Cattegat: its chief commerce consists in a leather manufactory of army accoutrements; there are also several mills for grinding corn, and three or four large breweries. The beer which is brewed here is as good as any in Denmark; indeed the Danish strong-beer is sometimes excellent, and when bottled and kept, it is nearly equal to London porter*. It is exported to the Danish settlements in the East and West Indies, and these hot climates greatly improve its flavour. Odensee has three churches, and a town-house, where the states of the kingdom formerly met to chuse a king, before the crown was made hereditary. In 1658, the Swedes possessed the island of Fünen, which they evacuated at the treaty of Roskild. King Charles Gustavus had his head quarters here. There are several printing-houses in this town, and two newspapers are published during the week†.

The next stage is Assens, which is twenty-two miles from Odensee. The beginning of the road of this stage is good, and the country is well cultivated: many gentlemen of respectability have country-seats about this part of the island, which have a pleasing effect on the surrounding scenery. We had not proceeded far on this road, before we were surprised and gratified, in seeing the fields for several miles round us covered with poultry, particularly with geese, and an innumerable quantity of goslings. About seven miles from Odensee is the small village of Dalem; here the roads begin to lose their smoothness and consistency, and for the last nine or ten miles they are very heavy. We drove into Assens in the evening, almost as weary as our horses, which had run all the way from Odensee.

Assens is a small town lying on the Little Belt, chiefly inhabited by fishermen. We ordered our boat, and immediately as we had drank our coffee, we stepped into it, and in two hours landed on the continent, in the province of South Jutland, or duchy of Sleswick, at a small place called Aaresünd, the distance of which from Assens is ten miles.

We found it would be difficult to procure post-horses this evening, and therefore, at the solicitation of our landlord, we took up our lodging here for the night; he promised that our supper and accommodations should repay us for our time, and he was as good as his word. We afterwards learned, that it was customary for the boats to go up to Hadersleben; but it being night, our boatmen wishing to save themselves trouble, landed us here, not perhaps without the concurrence of our inn-keeper.

We had now taken our leave of the Danish islands, and we found that Danish money would no longer pass current, except at this place, which has a direct communication with Fünen: we were prepared for this, and had accordingly supplied ourselves at Copenhagen with dollars, called Sleswick and Holstein specie-dollars; a silver-coin, with much alloy, which passes for about 4s. 6d. sterling. This coin has a general circulation all over Sleswick and Holstein, even including Hamburg itself. The specie dollar is divided into halves, quarters, &c. On the journey from Copenhagen to this place, the regular charge for a waggon and two horses is three marks, eight skillings Danish currency (i. e. 2s. 4d. sterling), per Danish mile: for the passage of the Great Belt, we paid six rix-dollars, four marks (i. e. 26s. 8d. sterling); and for the passage of the Little Belt two rix-dollars: making in the whole, for a journey of 144 miles, 4l. 11s. sterling, not reckoning the expences on the road, at the inns, &c. which are in general very moderate.

Aaresünd is not laid down on the maps which I have seen of this country; it lies at the mouth of a small river, and contains only about half a dozen houses, of which the inn makes by far the most respectable appearance. The master of it, a very civil man, informed us he had been in England, and that he had cultivated his garden

* I speak of London porter *in former times*, I do not mean to degrade the Danish strong-beer, by a comparison with the execrable trash that is now (1801) retailed under the name of porter in London.

† For a good account of the Danish newspapers, see the Monthly Magazine for April, 1800.

garden in the English style, which he wished us to see. We found it perfectly neat, but that it had more the appearance of a Dutch or a Flemish garden than of an English one. Those who have travelled in Holland and Flanders will know to what I allude, which I cannot illustrate better than by using the words of the poet:

"Grove nods at grove, each alley has its brother;
And half the platform just reflects the other."

The Danish gardens have generally a kind of wild fertility, and not that unnatural regularity and sameness which our landlord erroneously supposed to be the characteristic of an English garden*.

Early in the morning of the 26th of April, we left Aaresünd for Haderfleben, distant about nine miles. On each side of this road, the fields are divided by fine luxuriant hedges of black-thorn, which are also the boundaries of the road. These had to us a new and pleasing appearance, as we had been accustomed for some time past to see clay or large stones used for these purposes, except in some parts of Fünen, where there are low-kept hedges. The morning was so fine, that we got out of our vehicle, and walked the greater part of this post. We had occasion to remark, that the vegetation was much forwarder here than in England, though the latitude of the place is 55° north. In these countries, there is scarcely any spring or autumn; the transition from cold to heat is quick; there will sometimes be a hard frost, and a few days afterwards every thing will burst forth into vegetation, as if from the bosom of the snow. In the country which we were now travelling through, the grass was cut, and on the ground.

We arrived at Haderfleben in excellent spirits, prepared to enjoy a good breakfast, in the Danish meaning of the word. It is the custom in these countries to take a cup of coffee at seven o'clock, and at nine or ten breakfast is served, which consists of cold savoury meat, dried fish, eggs, bread, butter, and cheese, with Danish strong-beer, and French brandy, which of course cannot be dispensed with. *Haderfleben* is a small pleasant town, lying at the bottom of a hill. The most conspicuous object in it is a high pillar, with the figure of a man, with a large rod in his hand, on the top; this is the whipping-post, and from the situation in which it is placed, it would seem as if the rod was held in *terrorem* over the heads of travellers, who cannot avoid being struck with this object immediately on entering the town. While we were at breakfast, we heard psalm-singing in the street, which we found proceeded from a priest in canonicals, walking before four boys (paupers); the people informed us, that this was the custom morning and evening. The post-master here obliged us to take four horses, thinking, or pretending to think, that two were not sufficient to draw us and our baggage, though one strong English or German horse would actually have run away with the waggon (which is very light) and its contents: however, as these gentlemen are absolute in their way, we were obliged to submit to the imposition for the remainder of our journey.

From Haderfleben to Apenràde is twenty miles; the country is rather flat the greater part of this post, but on approaching the latter town, it has a more bold and mountainous appearance than any we had yet seen.

Apenràde is situated on a small bay, called Apenràde-fiörd; the houses are built of a light-coloured brick, which has a singular neat appearance, and the streets are kept very clean. Ships of 300 tons come up to this port from the Baltic, as it carries on a considerable trade with the islands in that sea. Its exports are chiefly corn, timber, and naval stores. It is a pleasant mercantile town; and the hilarity which we observed in the countenances of the inhabitants, bespoke that kind of contentment which is generally produced by honest industry. Apenràde reminded me of an English sea port town, but the comparison was greatly in its favour; for the people here are neater and cleaner, and have more the appearance of honesty and sobriety than is to be seen in the same kind of towns in England, where dirt and squalid wretchedness appear in every corner, and where the lower class of people are certainly as debauched as they are in any part of the world*. On leaving Apenràde, we have a view of the sea, and a small promontory, covered with a fine wood,

* The best garden I saw in Denmark was at the country-house of Mr. de Coninck (a merchant of great respectability), about fifteen miles from Copenhagen. The house and grounds lie upon one of the fine lakes with which Zealand abounds; the gardens are laid out with great taste, which does credit to the hospitable owner of the mansion, who is a Dutchman.

* I allude to Plymouth, Plymouth-dock, Portsmouth, and latterly Yarmouth, &c.

wood, to the left: the *coup d'œil* brought to my recollection the south-east end of the Island of Fayal, one of the Azores, of which it struck me as an almost exact resemblance.

From Apenrade, the road, for about a mile, runs along the sea-shore, when it turns off to the right into the country, which is fertile and well-cultivated. Near the road, we saw a small church, with the steeple about twenty yards from it; I wished to try the quickness of our driver, and accordingly I told him, that I supposed it had been blown off in a gale of wind, as it stood rather awry: to this, after taking his pipe from his mouth, and looking attentively at the church, he assented with a solemn nod. The ignorance and stupidity of the drivers of these vehicles is remarkable; we could never get a satisfactory answer to even the most plain question: they are like that class of people in Ireland, and in some parts of England (particularly in Norfolk and Suffolk), where it is extremely difficult for travellers to get a direct answer to any enquiry.

The next stage is Flensburg (distant from Apenrade twenty miles) which we reached in the evening. It is nearly surrounded with mountains on the land side, and lies on a gulph which runs up from the Baltic, and is a good harbour for small vessels, being completely sheltered from the wind. The town is well built, containing many substantial houses, chiefly of red brick; the principal street is broad and straight, and, upon the whole, it has the appearance of having been formerly a town of some consequence, but it has now nothing remarkable or worthy the attention of a traveller. We slept here, and in the morning proceeded on our journey.

From Flensburg to Sleswick is twenty-two miles: the roads are in general sandy and very heavy, and gave us a *presentiment* of what we were to expect for nearly the remainder of our journey. The village of *Angelen* lies between these towns, in the district of that name, from whence came the East Angles, who, it is said, gave the name to our country*. This village, as well as most of the villages in this country, consists of a few straggling houses†, or rather barns, which make a poor appearance on the outside, but are in general very comfortable and cleanly within.

We arrived at Sleswick about noon; but were previously obliged to go through the degrading ceremony (which fortunately but seldom occurs in this country) of being examined by the guard at the Castle of Gottorp. This was the first place at which we had been interrogated by a centinel, who, seeing us in an extra post waggon, gave himself all the airs of a man of consequence; and after making a number of enquiries, which could answer no other end than to shew his self-importance, but which we were obliged to answer, he discharged us with a supercilious look, saying, in a surly tone (in German) "*You may pass.*" From Gottorp to Sleswick, the road is planted with a fine row of high trees, which have really a magnificent appearance.

Sleswick (Dytch *Schleswig*), which has the honour of giving the name to this province, is a very well built town, about a mile and a half in length, lying in a semi-circle on the Gulph of Sley. It is a completely aristocratic, German city, which we were not long in discovering. Old-fashioned carriages, with tall men in tarnished liveries, behind them, were driving up and down the streets: the inhabitants were stiff in their dress, and formal and ceremonious in their behaviour; in fact, pomp and parade appear here to take place of that industry and commercial independence which we had with pleasure observed in the other towns of this province. The people of the inn were disgustingly inattentive to us because we had not an equipage and the appearance of noblemen; and on this account we found it hardly possible to procure accommodations even for the short time which we staid here. In this city they boast that the German language is spoken with as great accuracy as at Vienna; but it was perhaps fortunate for them, as it might save their credit, that we could not criticise on the purity of their diction. This city has very little trade, as none but small boats can come up to it, the passage of the Sley being long since choaked up with mud and sand; before this event it was a flourishing and populous place. It is now chiefly inhabited by the officers of the castle, and the poorer class, i.e. the

* The Britons asked their aid against the Scots and Picts, in consequence of which they came over in great numbers to this country, which now bears their name, e.g. *Angle-terre*, i.e. Angle-land, or England.

† Those who have been in Holland, and remarked the villages there, are apt to be fastidious, as perhaps none in the world can equal them for neatness, and, I may say, elegance; yet these have not that rural appearance which the villages in England have, but look rather like towns in miniature.

attendants

attendants on the court, and the attendants on them. It contains about 5000 inhabitants.

Proceeding on our journey, we went back to the Castle of Gottorp, the grounds about which are extremely well laid out; our driver, being perhaps connected with some of the domestics, wished us to see the Castle; but this we declined. It is surrounded with a ditch, and is a large, gloomy, proud-looking mansion, which appearance well suits with the character of the present possessor—the Prince Charles of Hesse Cassel, who is Governor of Sleswick and Holstein, and Commander in Chief of his Danish Majesty's Troops in these Provinces. He is, I am informed, almost universally disliked, for his proud, overbearing deportment, and the contempt in which he holds persons who are in inferior situations, particularly the lower orders of society*. From Gottorp to Rendsburg is seventeen miles, through a country abounding with heavy sands, where, if land-marks were not set up in the waste to direct the traveller, the half-formed roads would not have enabled our driver to discover the route, and we might probably have wandered about for many hours. This extensive tract is covered with sand (except here and there a small spot of rank grass) for many miles; and we sought in vain for the agreeable and enlivening prospect of agricultural industry, with which we had hitherto been much delighted. At length, after a most disagreeable and wearisome journey, we reached Rendsburg, and passed through the gates without being molested by the centinel, which we accounted for by its being garrisoned by Danish troops; indeed the commandant behaved with much attention and politeness, as he not only ordered the gates to be kept open two hours later than usual to accommodate us, but on our sending him our names, with thanks for his civility, he requested, if we remained in the town till the morning, that we would favour him with our company to breakfast.

Rendsburg is the frontier town in Holstein; it is regularly built, and its fortifications are the best of any in the Danish dominions. It lies on a canal, which runs from the Baltic. This is a work of great commercial importance, and deserves particular notice. It commences three miles north of Kiel, and forms the present boundary of Holstein and Sleswick. The distance, from its commencement to the last sluice, at Rendsburg, is 27 miles; by it ships of 120 to 140 tons can come up to this town from the Baltic. It is intended that this canal, which was begun in 1777, shall extend across the whole peninsula; the utility of which will be fully estimated by those who are acquainted with the great importance of inland navigation, in facilitating mercantile intercourse, which *sometimes* tends to civilise those countries through which its influence extends*. Rendsburg is a place of some trade, and contains about 2800 inhabitants, including the garrison.

The direct road from hence to Hamburg, which is distant eighty miles, is through the towns of Neüminster and Bramstede; but, as business called me to Glückstadt, we took the road to that place. We intended to proceed on to Remmels, a small village about fifteen miles from Rendsburg, the same night, but the rain disconcerted our plan, and we were glad to procure beds at the first place we reached on the road, which was a farm-house. We drove into the middle of the house, or rather barn, for so it appeared, as it contained the hay and corn; and, as the weather was unfavourable, was also occupied by the cattle and all the live stock which the farmer possessed. These barns are very spacious; the rooms for domestic purposes are on each side. We found this to be a good specimen of the farm houses in Holstein: the rooms and beds were remarkably neat and clean, and the whole of the family, which consisted of the farmer, his wife, and seven or eight grown-up sons and daughters, appeared to be honest, industrious, good humoured, attentive to each other, and particularly so to strangers.

Sylvester-row, ROBERT STEVENS.
Hackney.

(To be continued.)

* An anecdote is told of this Prince, which, if true, is highly illustrative of his pride and ignorance. His daughter, who is very amiable in her manners is (as formerly mentioned) married to the Crown-prince of Denmark; previous to which event, during her residence at Gottorp, she was kept almost in strict confinement by her father, who never suffered her to move out, except in a carriage, as he said "*the ground was not good enough for her to walk upon.*" This would hardly be believed but by those who are acquainted with the characters of petty German princes. The ludicrous story of "*the Old Grey Ass,*" as lately related (July, 1801) in the London newspapers, is particularly applicable.

* I am sorry to observe, that daily observation teaches us that this is not *always* the case.

To

To the Editor of the Monthly Magazine.

SIR,

AS in the observations which I wish to offer on some of Mr. Horne Tooke's etymologies, I have not the least design of controverting the general principles of his excellent system, for which I entertain as warm a respect as the most obsequious of his disciples; there is no occasion for me to preface them with explanations or apologies. Whatever improvements or whatever corrections may be made in the detail of the Diversions of Purley, the entire and undisputed merit must for ever remain with its author, of having alone conferred that importance on the science of etymology, from which all future discoveries must derive their value.

I proceed to state a few miscellaneous remarks on some points of his work, which I conceive to stand most in need of further investigation.

BY.—Mr. Tooke calls this preposition the imperative of *beon*, to be; and explains its use in most cases by the ellipsis of some such word as *cause*, *instrument*, &c. That such an explanation can be worthy of the author of Επεα πτεροεντα I am unable to reconcile with the following considerations.

1. The supposition of such an ellipsis is itself entirely gratuitous. Mr. Tooke does not, and, I will venture to say, cannot, give a single instance of *by*, in its sense of instrumentality, having been ever expressed by a compound of the verb *be* with such a word as he imagines.

2. The fundamental principle of the Diversions of Purley is, that the signification of every particle is to be sought in the distinct meaning which originally belonged to it, as either a noun or a verb. And it is implied in every step of this system that, for any verb or noun to be qualified to exercise the functions of a preposition, it must have a meaning expressive not of abstract but of some specific existence or action. To refer the preposition *by* to such a word as *beon* is to call it a word of no meaning. To refer its meaning to a word formerly associated with *beon*, but of which no remnant now remains, appears to me little better. The supposition is without the least authority of fact, and the allowance of it must be at the expence of the most important principles of Mr. Tooke's system. It must be to suppose that of such two words by which the meaning of *by* was originally expressed, the only one which could denote any specific relation has been dropped and forgotten, and nothing retained but a word which can have no title to rank as a preposition, but among those *unmeaning particles* for which Mr. Tooke so justly ridicules the author of Hermes. But,

3. Mr. Tooke has misrepresented the meaning of *by* in his attempts to trace it to its primitive form. The expressions of agency and instrumentality to which it is now principally appropriated, and which he chiefly labours to illustrate, were entirely foreign to its original signification. The Anglo-Saxons employed for the former of these ꝼꞃom and oꝼ; for the latter þuph and mid (middle, thence denoting by *means* of): and it was only along with the disuse of mid that *by* became invested with so great a share of the offices which it at present holds. The Germans, who retain their *mit*, still confine their *bey* within the bounds of its original import. To "support himself *by* labour," is, "sich nähren *mit* seiner arbeit." The original import of *be* or *bi* chiefly comprehended those of the latin, *secundum*, *juxta*, *versus*.

4. Mr. Tooke seems to consider his etymology of *by* supported by the frequent correspondence of its meaning with that of the preposition *with*; to which, when so used, he assigns a similar derivation, viz. from ƿyþþan, to be. In answer to this, I shall only observe that this confusion in the use of *with* and *by* never occurred in the Anglo-Saxon—that it took place only in consequence of these two sharing between them the functions of mid—that Mr. Tooke's introduction of ƿyþþan to explain the signification of *with* appears, as I shall further notice hereafter, without either use or foundation, and is morover liable to the same general objection I have already urged against his derivation of *by*. To this same objection I shall have further occasion to recur. In the meantime, let any one take any of Mr. Tooke's examples of the use of *by* or of *with*, where he professes to explain them by substituting the simple imperative *be*, and say whether such explanation conveys to him a single idea of their use.

It may be thought that I should not have thus contraverted Mr. Tooke's etymology of *by*, without having one of my own to offer in its room.

I may truly say, however, that the defects of the one had struck me long before I thought of their removal by the other. And though this, which I offer merely

as

as a conjecture, should be rejected, the objections to Mr. Tooke's etymology will still remain.

I have already mentioned the Latin prepositions which express the meaning of *be* or *bi* in the original Anglo Saxon. In a more general way it may be said always to specify *direction*. And to this sense the following instances (from the Saxon Chronicle), which may serve to illustrate its ordinary employment, are easily referred. Unfriþ scipa lægen *be* Westan, hostile ships lay *towards* the west; þa scipu foran *be* suþan east, the ships went south-east; sume men sædon *be*-Haralde, some men said by (*respecting*) Harold; ealla þa þing *be* Godes mynstran, þa wæron gesette *be* Wihtgares dæge, all those things *respecting* God's churches, that were appointed *in* the days of W.; *be* his broðra ræd, *according to* his brother's advice. I think it probable that it derives this signification from the verb began, bigan, bugan, Goth. BIUGAN to bow

1. By using the intransitive verb *turn or incline* in the above passages we obtain a very satisfactory interpretation of the meaning of *be*. And it is in this sense that the Anglo-Saxon verb was employed: him to beah Malcolm, Malcolm turned to him (Chron. An. 1031); Eadgar—beah þa fram him, Edgar turned from him (An. 1085) Cristina beah into mynstre (Do.), Christina turned into (entered) the monastery.

2. The Latin prepositions *secus*, *secundum*, from *sequor*, and *versus*, from *verto*, by which the import of *be* is most nearly expressed, support such an etymology, especially the latter, by the analogy of their own.

3. The original orthography of this preposition seems to have been big, which would correspond with the imperative of bigan.—Our old noun *bye*, I may remark, signifying a turning, digression, (by-the-*bye*, *bye-road*, &c.) is a derivative of the same origin.

To follow up this derivation of *be* through the very numerous train of its combinations, especially with verbs, would require more dilatation than can here be allowed; and, inasmuch as regards the examination of Mr. Tooke's etymology, is perfectly unnecessary. There is only one compound of *be* therefore which I shall here notice.

The usual derivation of the word *because* is thought so obvious that it may be deemed captious to call it in question. What I have already said, however, may explain on what grounds I would substitute the word *by*, as above interpreted, for the verb *be* in the resolution of this as of other similar compounds. I have selected this in particular for the sake of offering a remark on the latter member of the word.

The etymology of *cause* has puzzled philologists as much as its signification has exercised metaphysicians: and probably both would have derived advantage from pursuing their investigations in concert. Even without the assistance of Hume, however, the analogies of common language might, one would imagine, have suggested a much more plausible etymology of the word than any hitherto offered. There can be little doubt, I think, that it is originally the same with *case*, and has a similar origin as well as import with the word *occasion*, viz. from the Latin *cado*. The word *case* denotes the *be-falling*, the connected occurence of events: and let the scholastic metaphysician tell us what more he can understand by *cause*. This explanation might be illustrated by observing the analogous origin of the words *reason*, *account*, &c.: but I shall only add that the identity of *case* and *cause*, is exemplified as matter of fact both in the French *cause*, which is frequently employed to express the former as well as the latter, and in our English law courts, where the word *cause* is daily used in the acceptation which in common discourse we appropriate to *case*.

July 11, 1801.

For the Monthly Magazine.

ACCOUNT *of* PORTSMOUTH.

(Continued from p. 402 of Vol. 11.)

IN getting behind my spectacles to resume my account of Portsmouth, I fear that I have fallen into a sort of reverie on the subject.

With all the improvements Portsmouth has recently undergone, and notwithstanding its increased population, the various advantages that have accrued to it, and the progress it has made in refinement, it seems to me, that, if these things are properly appreciated, the place has much less reason to pique itself on acquirements than one is generally apt to suppose.

It is true that both Portsmouth and Portsea are better paved than formerly: they are no longer disfigured by obtruding signs, shew-boards, and barbers' poles; and many other obstructions equally unsightly and improper have been removed. Our streets have, in many parts, been widened: sharp and aukward corners have been rounded off: crooked lanes and alleys have been made straight: many other nuisances and annoyances have been done away: and our ambling nymphs may now fairly venture abroad without the antiquated lumber of pattens and clogs. And it is a fact, that this is chiefly owing, in Portsea, to the indefatigable industry and unbending perseverance of one individual. As to commerce, our case is certainly mended. As numbers have swoln our population, our trade has increased beyond all bounds, and we have made rapid strides towards establishing our name as a great commercial people. We have several merchants who may now rank as importers, if not as exporters; and we have already a manufactory for pipes, and another, very near a-kin to it, and of equal moment, for herb-tobacco. Besides this, we dress more *à-la-mode*: the fashions are not much above a month travelling down to us from the west end of the Town, and even some of our tradesfolk and the very rear ranks of our publicans make no small figure. They sport their horses and equipages; and of these Portsmouth-point has its share; and on the skirts of the town they boast their fine gravel-walk, gardens, and variegated parterres. Here they have their chateaus, their villas, and bowers, and in these they display more than Attic taste and Arcadian simplicity. The ornaments they have lavished on them are of the chastest order; vases, golden balls, lions' heads, Venuses, dolphins, and floating banners, are highly appropriate and emblematical; and their *fêtes-champêtres* on fine-weather Sundays, their principal *dies festæ*, are truly pastoral and amusing. But to turn to more general objects—our theatre, which is an improved one, and not small, is fitted up decently. The performers do not complain of playing to empty benches. Modesty and immodesty have for some time been distributed separately into upper and lower boxes. The riotous sons of Neptune and of Mars are at length overawed by the strengthened and uplifted arm of civil authority. We have the new pieces played to us as soon as the managers find it necessary to their interest. And our company is not without *some* performers of dramatic merit. We have balls and assemblies of the first order, notified at our corners, in crown-folios, at so cheap a rate as "2s. 6d. tea included." We have concerts, without much inclination for them, and now and then a sumptuous Jew's wedding. We make dull visits, play at cards to keep ourselves awake, and have a few jovial dinner-parties. We have elections and swearings-in of mayors, choosings of parliament-men, sessions, grand juries, clubs, charities, and armed associations of *royalists*, *loyalists*, and *loyal-independents*, and observe great anniversaries, and consequently have some feasting. We have several general evening rendezvous, where we take our pipes and our porter, listen to our oracles of instruction, regularly dissect the news of the day, and get our cues for the next; and a few of us pass our summer-afternoons very innocently and playfully at the bowling-green. We fill our fifteen or sixteen churches on Sundays pretty fairly, and keep the Sabbath otherwise as strict as the fourth commandment can be legally enforced upon us. Our play-folk are constrained to keep good hours: nine-pins, skittle-alleys, and whirligigs, have been lately proscribed: *hops* are denounced as contraband, the language of our streets must bear judicial criticism: disorderly vagabonds must fly to covert: and the wild excursions of our Jack-tars, on their jaded hacks, and with their drunken doxies and fidlers, on the wrecks of foundered coaches, are, to the great triumph of decency, no longer permissible. This is certainly consoling. It is equally true, that, though we have made concessions, we are yet unsold to the Mammon of unrighteousness—that our borough is represented in the Senate by the Cicero of the age, and Lord Hugh Seymour—that we have some goodly preachers and worthy pastors who labour to instruct us—that many of us, *incog.* have a *penchant* for the *belles-lettres*—that the Pursuits of Literature is a puny, though a malicious libel against our charter, and our incorporated wisdom—that some of our citizens have arrived at great and enviable civic and military honours—that by conspicuous loyalty and meritorious conduct others have been elevated to the rank and dignity of high sheriffs of the county—and, to crown the whole, that more than once (twice, or thrice, since my remembrance) the King and Royal Family have deigned, for days together, to honour us with their residence within this their loyal and *independent* burgh! Yet, Mr. Editor, methinks, after all, we are not one jot the better off than we were formerly. Though many of our boasted improvements have been made by virtue of Acts of Parliament, and various annoyances have been put an end to under the same high authority, I do not know that we live longer on account of it. Death certainly visits us at the same period as heretofore. His

ravages

ravages are not less frequent or considerable. Our old church-yards almost yearn from reflection, and our gardens have been curtailed of their fair proportion to make more room for the dead. Disease and the doctors are still in co-partnership. The trade of physic flourishes *supremely*; and physicians, surgeons, apothecaries, and quacks, are in abundance. Besides this, our poor-houses are crammed and grown larger. Our brothel-houses are become numerous; and our alehouses, and gin-shops, and pawn-shops, now almost defy calculation. Lawyers have multiplied upon us exceedingly. Malefactors are more numerous. We have greater need of constables and bumbailiffs. Our county sessions and assizes are chiefly occupied by our suits and litigations, and the misdeeds done amongst us. Our town-sessions are intolerably long.—Our county-gaol has been rebuilt on an enlarged plan, partly, I suppose, on account of our supplies to it; and our borough-gaol has for some time past been voted insufficient to accommodate the number of its tenants; and, upon the whole, Mr. Editor, I verily believe, there is more irreligion, more feuds, and political animosities, and consequently less urbanity, to be found amongst us.

From what I have heard of the state of the place about a century ago, and of the character of many of its then inhabitants, and of the manners of those times, it really appears to me that we are a much-altered people. From the relations that have been given to me of those days of yore, and from what I have seen of their manners in the last stage of their declension, I am become as much enamoured of them as the Abbé de Marolles was of the golden days of his youth, under Henry IV. of France; and in recollecting the beautiful manner in which the Abbé describes them, I cannot avoid the influence of his sentiments on my own as to the days of our good ancestors. I will not pretend that his delightful picture is suited to their more recent times; yet the tone of its colouring accords with my present temper on the subject, and there may be some parts that may bear an analogy to the period I have mentioned. Be that as it may, I cannot help thinking that we are neither so happy nor contented as we were formerly. If our manners are not of so rude a cast as they were, they are more factitious. Our morals, from being once sound and sturdy, are become lax and flimsy. There is not the same strength of character about us as heretofore, nor so much of originality in our composition, nor, with all the advances we have made in this age of reason and refinement, am I able to discover that we possess a larger stock of sterling sense than existed in the days of our predecessors and progenitors, when there was no boast or parade of learning or acquirements. But this, perhaps, is not the greatest evil. The fashionable vices of the day have laid hold of us. Our young men are rakes or *petit-maitres*, and our females do little else than dress, flirt about, club round the card-table, and read novels. Our high street, our walls, and our parades, are infested by courtezans. Six days out of seven are insufficient to prepare the engines of human destruction. Sunday is no day of rest in our naval arsenal. Its sanctity is broken up by martial sounds and military arrangements. Thus a day, peculiarly dedicated to a God of Peace, is grossly violated; its serenity is disturbed by tumultuous amusements, and the sobriety and decorum that ought, at least, to characterise it, are destroyed by vulgar and unseasonable revelries. I wish I could suppose that these observations, and several others here made, were peculiar to the place I have been describing; but I fear they are equally applicable to other towns, where there may be less to approve, and more to condemn, than at Portsmouth. Notwithstanding all the imperfections that belong to it, I have yet to speak of it in several points that will by no means discredit it; but as I have already reached my limits, I must satisfy myself with requesting the indulgence of continuing my account to a conclusion, in your next Number.

Portsmouth, W. N.

July 4, 1801.

(To be continued.)

To the Editor of the Monthly Magazine.

SIR,

I SHALL be greatly obliged to you for inserting in your valuable Magazine, and to any of your Correspondents for answering the following queries.

I am Sir,

A CONSTANT READER.

Cornwall, July 13, 1801.

Is the forfeit of ten pounds, which the law of the 8th and 9th W. orders to be levied for refusing to take a parish apprentice, to be considered as a fine for refusing to take only at that time, or as a legal pecuniary compensation for not providing for it?

In the former case, it is apprehended the parish has a right to put another appren-

 tice

tice on such person, as soon as the fine is levied; but in the latter, it is thought such person cannot be required to take another till it comes regularly to his turn; i. e. till all persons liable to take, have been supplied with one.

It is thought the letter of the law will admit of either; if so, does not the consideration of the *equity* of allowing a *pecuniary compensation* in such case, and the *extent* of the penalty, determine in favor of the latter?

If a parish has been in the custom, for time immemorial, of taking ten pounds as a compensation for refusing to take an apprentice, can it, consistently with justice, though agreeably to the civil law, adopt a different mode, by immediately putting another apprentice in the case where the penalty had been levied?

It may not be amiss to remark that the person on whom such an apprentice is put, is a real sufferer by the former proceedings of the parish, as it thereby falls to his lot to take an apprentice much sooner than it otherwise would have done; and hence it seems but reasonable that the parish should in honor allow such a person all the relief in its power.

To the Editor of the Monthly Magazine.

SIR,

A READER of your Magazine from its earliest publication, presumes to hope for information from some of the numerous correspondents of your justly celebrated Miscellany.

A few years ago, I was presented to a crown living under 50l. per ann. Upon it was a small parsonage in a most shattered condition, and some glebe land in a very neglected state. The late incumbent left no representatives from whom I could demand dilapidations. I have expended near two years income in clearing the glebe, repairing a barn, stable, cow-house, and fitting up the only room that could by any means be made habitable in the parsonage; in the ruins of which I am in imminent peril of being buried every time I occupy it. By the act which impowers me to raise money for rebuilding the parsonage, I am directed to procure leave from the patron. To whom, and in what manner will it be most adviseable to apply for such leave? The Governors or Directors of Queen Anne's Bounty are also empowered to lend 100l. free of interest for repairs on such small livings. In what manner, to whom, or through whom, is this application to be made, with most probability of success? Survey, estimates, certificate, plan, elevation, &c. are all prepared as the act directs, and the concurrence of my Diocesan can readily be procured.

Clear, explicit answers to these questions, and any other directions which may tend to forward or facilitate this business, may be of essential service to others, as well as Your humble Servant,

A WELCH PARSON.

To the Editor of the Monthly Magazine.

SIR,

I HAVE lived a considerable time in the city of Cork, and have long studied the manners of its inhabitants; but to make use of an expression of Mr. Burke's, they exhibit "so variegated a piece of Mosaic," that I believe it will be a difficult task to delineate their portrait.

One hundred thousand souls constitute, very nearly, the population of this city, which is built without any attention to order or regularity, some of the best edifices in it being often contiguous to the meanest hovels, and a row of well-built houses succeeded by salting-sheds and merchants' cellars. As commerce is the principal support of Cork, this last inconvenience cannot be done away without material injury to the trade of the place. The merchants form the richest and most powerful class of men here; they are generally engaged either in the West India and Lisbon trades, or in supplying government with provisions for the navy and army. In their manners they much resemble those of Hamburg: they have the same taste for expence and wasteful profusion, the same love of society, the same passion for shew; nay, the same rapid succession of riches and poverty may be observed here as in the above-mentioned place; and in some measure arises from the neglect of convoys and insuring, which, although fatal to some considerable houses, has given immediate affluence to others.

The Corkonians, as I remarked before, love society. Dinner-parties take place every day. Their entertainments are in the first style of expensive elegance; and owing to the intimate connection they have with Portugal, and the lowness of the duties, their wines are always excellent. The ladies remain in company after dinner longer than they are accustomed to do in this country; and then they take leave of the gentlemen, whom they see no more for the day: for the pleasures of the bottle are here considered in higher estimation than the conversation of the fair sex. However

However, cards make the latter some amends for the absence of the men, and the mistress of the house always takes care to provide a female party above stairs when her husband is engaged below. Whist is the principal game played, though of late casino has had some influence. Large sums are not often lost, for they mostly play low, and but very seldom. Dancing is the next principal amusement; and I must say, that the ladies of Cork dance gracefully and well; they are in general handsome and accomplished, for female education is, in some particulars, carefully attended to, and you find few who are not informed in the modern polite languages, and skilled in the science of music. But morality and philosophy are neglected. Easy freedom and gaiety are the characteristics of the women; they are open and unsuspicious: a stranger, if any way respectable, finds himself agreeably surprised at being intimately acquainted with those whom he has only known a few days. This good fortune invariably attends gentlemen who wear red coats.

The shopkeepers and tradespeople who form the middling order are a well informed industrious set of men; generous, spirited and brave—for they are all soldiers, and on many occasions, during the late troubles, signalized themselves for loyalty and cool intrepidity: like most of their countrymen, they love the bottle, and indulge themselves in the delirium of happiness which it bestows after the hour of business, that is, after five o'clock, for nothing is transacted posterior to this hour; and as they do not dine until it arrives, this indulgence is the more excuseable. Beggars are here innumerable, though there are several charitable institutions; but (as in other places) by having too many officers and overseers, and too many good regulations, it happens that these institutions are not regulated at all; and the most disgusting objects of human misery are suffered to implore charity in every street. You often meet a young man in rags, with a few books in his satchel thrown over his shoulder, and a pen in his hat, who asks charity, for the purpose of prosecuting his studies. This is a description of mendicant no where else, I believe, to be met with, but which, in Ireland, is common; and I understand that several of the lights of the Romish Church have originated from hence.

It was not until very lately that lunatics were considered as being worthy of the public care; they were permitted to wander about the city, to the terror of the weak, and to the horror of the humane. But by the advice and authority of the present Sir S. Rowland (then Mayor), a receptacle for them was built, and they are now properly confined and attended to.

It is during the assizes, which are held twice a-year, that Cork appears in all its splendour. Then the country is deserted, and all the people of consequence in the neighbourhood hasten to town, for the purpose of displaying their equipages, and partaking of the theatrical spectacles exhibited. The theatre, situated in George-street, is something larger than that in the Hay-market (London). It is handsomely decorated; the internal part forms a semicircle. The second tier of boxes are denominated *lattices* (I do not know for what reason); the third, pigeon-holes.—These last places are the resort of the Cyprian corps—composed of the most horrid and the ugliest wretches that ever offered their persons for sale.

Every one in Cork pretends to taste in theatricals, and you sometimes do meet with people of judgment in these matters; but the general pretension ill accords with the facts of empty bottles being flung at Madam Mara on her first appearance, and of Miss Farren being pelted with apples at her own benefit; whilst any of the London performers remain, the play house is crowded, but as soon as they withdraw, it is universally deserted. Astley very lately opened a theatre here for his exhibition, but he is not supported, and will very shortly be obliged to give it up.

At this period (the assizes) the public ball-rooms are open, and filled twice a week with dancers and card-players. But etiquette is so much regarded, that merchants, merchants' wives, and people of independent property, are only admitted. I have known many instances when the disapprobation of the company obliged several respectable shopkeepers to quit the room, who wished to break through the barrier that pride had raised between them and pleasure. For although wholesale dealing is the most honourable profession in this city, yet the retail business is thought to attach vulgarity to the conductors of it. It is for this reason, also, that the lower boxes at the theatre are set apart for the same haughty class.

A broad street, paved with small sharp stones (no flagged way), forms the fashionable promenade of Cork; every evening when the weather permits, this is crowded with young and old, handsome and ugly, of all descriptions. Here the businesses of love, of scandal, and of trade, are transacted

acted—here compliments are paid and returned, invitations given and received, and all the little *et cetera* of fashion performed. As I have mentioned scandal, I cannot help observing, that, owing to the great number of maidens who have felt the pangs of slighted love, and have been "unbroken in upon by kisses," this vice is too common, and often usurps the place of attic salt at their *conversations*. And few are found charitable enough to correct its venom, and turn its shaft from innocence and beauty; which, fragile in their natures, soon feel its fatal effects.

The fine arts are here in a most deplorable situation. There is one miniature-painter, who gives something like a human head for a guinea; and although several artists of merit have attempted to settle in this city, yet the want of being supported, the necessary consequence of want of taste, obliged them to fly to more genial climes.

Five statues (I recollect no more) ornament Cork—one of William the Third, in the Mansion-house, of lead, on a wooden pedestal, painted in colours to resemble life—An equestrian one of his late Majesty, on the Grand Parade, also of lead, emphatically denominated, King George on Horseback—A most famous representation of that celebrated patriot, Alderman Lawton (who kept the city very clean) in his robes, adorns the Exchange. The upper part of this old elegant building, when I was in Cork, was painted yellow, the lower part black.

In the church of St. Nicholas is a very fine monument, by Bacon, erected in memory of the late Lord Tracton, which was refused admittance into the Cathedral by the Dean, lest it should revive Popish ideas; and behind the Court-house is a headless figure of James the Second, which loyalty once erected, and which loyalty, ever varying, pulled down again.

Although the fine arts are thus neglected, yet Cork has produced some artists who honour their profession—For instance, Mr. Barry, late professor of painting at the Royal Academy, whose pictures in the Adelphi immortalise his name, as they stigmatise the Society for which they were painted: Mr. Burk, one of the most elegant and correct drawers we have at present, and who, in my opinion, is the only modern painter who seems to possess clear notions of the beautiful ideal. The late Mr. Butt, the Claude of Ireland, was also a native of this place, as is the present Mr. Grogan, excellent in depicting scenes in low life. I have seen several of his pictures no way inferior to the productions of *Hemskirk*.

Poetry is much indebted to the late learned Dr. de la Cour, of this place, whose Prospect of Poetry is admirable. This gentleman had the honour of his works so much at heart, that having two of his lines parodied, he became insane, and continued so till his death.

The lines were parodied thus:—

The northern blast envelopes the schologue,
And whistles through his leathern malevogue.

Your's, &c.
A. C. B.

For the Monthly Magazine.

Account of RAVENSTONEDALE, *in* WESTMORLAND.

(*Concluded from page 31 of our last.*)

THE church, though small, and not sufficiently capacious for containing a greater number than six hundred people, is nevertheless a very neat and beautiful structure, fully adequate to the population of the place, and capable of receiving a much larger congregation than almost ever assembles here for divine worship. This church was rebuilt in 1744, is very light, and admits a good circulation of air. The chancel measures four paces in length, and two and one-half in breadth. The whole length of the nave is thirteen paces, and its width eight. There are eight windows to the south, eight to the north, and two to the east. There is only one aisle, which is seven feet wide. The pulpit is erected against the north side of the church, and exactly at the half length of the nave. The seats are made of oak, and rise regularly and beautifully one above another. At the west end of the church is a gallery. The steeple is in the form of a square tower, and has three bells. It is said, that the church here was formerly dedicated to St. Oswald. Although a parish church, it is only a perpetual curacy; and is in the patronage of the Earl of Lonsdale as lord of the manor. The present incumbent is the Rev. Mr. Bowness. The stipend appertaining to the curate, and arising from the ancient salary paid out of the rectory, from lands given to the church or purchased with money left for that purpose, and from certain sums bequeathed to it as annuities, was estimated by Dr. Burn, in 1777, at 35l. per ann. Since that time, two augmentations, of 400l. each, have been obtained from queen Ann's and a private bounty in London, and lands purchased therewith; insomuch that

that the yearly value of the curacy must at this time be upwards of 70l. The dwelling-house belonging to the curate, which is but a small edifice, was built in 1781.

Here is also a handsome meeting-house for dissenters of calvinistic principles. And it is not more than justice to observe, that this meeting-house is pretty well attended, that the people in general who frequent it, are studious respecting the doctrines of religion, and that the minister is a zealous and laborious preacher. The minister has lately established a sunday school for the education of youth in the principles of christianity, at which fifty or sixty scholars frequently attend; and he regularly superintends their instruction during the intervals of preaching. The revenue of this meeting-house is something more than 40l. per ann. a sum certainly inadequate to the maintenance of a clergyman's family, and which, especially during the present exorbitant prices of the necessaries of life, it is the indispensable duty of the congregation properly to consider.

The grammar-school at Ravenstonedale was founded and endowed about the year 1688; and in 1758, a very good new school-house was built; adjoining to which a dwelling-house for the master was also erected. Board and education being here reasonable, and, as yet, not exceeding together eighteen guineas a year, there are at present several boys from other counties, who lodge in the village, and are instructed at this school in the different branches of literature. The boys belonging to the parish, who learn the Latin and Greek languages, are in consideration of the stipend of the school, which at this time amounts to nearly 35l. per ann. taught free of expence, but for instruction in any other department they pay accordingly. This school might have been of much more value than at present, and its revenue would scarcely (if at all) have been less than that of any other seminary in the county, had not the trustees imprudently, and perhaps illegally, converted two estates, purchased with the bequests of the founders, into rent-charges or annuities. This was done almost a century ago. One of the estates is now worth 70l. a year, or upwards; whereas the annuity is only 6l. and the other rent charge is, no doubt, proportionably inadequate to the real value of the estate. The continual decrease in the value of money, and consequently increase in the value of land, render all fixed sums, in process of time, very defective. It is greatly to be regretted, that no public-spirited individuals should have attempted the recovery of these estates; since, besides other illegalities attending actions of this nature, there is a special clause in the deed of settlement, that the trustees shall apply the rents and profits of the said estates to the use of the schoolmaster, and shall not make any lease thereof for a longer term than twenty-one years*. The number of scholars, upon an average, is about thirty-six. There are very few of the inhabitants, that are natives of this parish, who cannot read; and the greatest part of them are able to write, and understand the common rules of arithmetic; and in many instances, the more substantial landholders procure their children a very good education. Instruction is so cheap, that it is not placed beyond the reach of the poorest; and the anxiety expressed by the people for the instruction of their children, proves that they are impressed with a due sense of the importance and utility of education, in almost every department and transaction of life: nay, they have often been known voluntarily to undergo hardship and fatigue, that they might procure their children useful and virtuous instruction; and many have been sufficiently requited for such care and attention by their sons thereby rising to affluence and eminence, and acquiring the respect and esteem of mankind.

Ravenstonedale, though divided into what are here denominated *angles*, is nevertheless all one constablewick: it provides for its poor conjointly, and has no subordinate or independent townships. The number of poor upon the roll for last year, amounted to 156; and the sum expended for their relief was upwards of 500l. which, at an average, might probably be 1s. 3d. for each person, per week. No one received more than 4s. 6d. per week, and none had less than 1s. 6d. a month; and distribution was made according to the nature and circumstances of the case. Stock to the amount of 583l. 6s. 8d. was sometime ago purchased in the three per cent. consol. annuities, for the benefit of the poor of this parish; and the interest of this sum is regularly applied to their relief. At the time of Bishop Nicolson's parochial visitation in 1703, he was informed by the church-wardens of Ravenstonedale, they had not had a beggar in the parish within the memory of man;

* Dr. Burn.

and

and between thirty and forty years ago, the poor-rates did not amount to 20l. per annum.

The price of labour, as perhaps in all other places, is very unequal to the present prices of provisions. Men servants with victuals have from 6l. to 10l.; and maid servants from 3l. to 4l. a year. Common labourers have in summer 12d. and in winter 8d. a day and their victuals. Carpenters and masons have 2s. per day, without victuals. Taylors have 1s a day, and victuals. During the hay-harvest, which for the most part commences here towards the end of June or beginning of July, men have 2s. or 2s. 6d.; women 1s.; boys 1s. per day, and their victuals. Men, who hire for a month in the hay-harvest, have from 2l. to 3l.; women, from 16s. to 1l. 7s.; boys, from 12s. to 1l. 4s.; and they are also allowed victuals and drink. After the hay-harvest is finished, the greatest part of the men, women, and children betake themselves to the knitting of worsted stockings for Kendal, and some of them will earn by this business five or six shillings a week. The number of stockings knit in Ravenstonedale has been computed at upwards of one thousand pairs per week, one week with another through the year. Oatmeal is at present 2s. 6d. the Winchester peck. Flour is 5s. 9d. a stone. During the last winter and spring, beef sold at 7d.; mutton at 7d.; veal at 6d.; and pork at 8d per pound. The oatmeal is chiefly supplied from the market of Kirkby-stephen.

To the north and north-east of the church is a pretty large park, the wall of which appears to have been ten feet high, or upwards; but there is no remembrance, that deer were ever kept in it: it was fenced about by Philip Lord Wharton, in the year 1660. Of the land taken for the formation of this park, tradition says (and we must also confess, there are some facts, which seem strongly to favour a report of this nature), that it was the property of the inhabitants, and the then lord of the manor deprived them of it; but as a small compensation for the injury thereby sustained, he allowed them to inclose and cultivate part of the adjacent common. In this park, it is said, formerly stood the village of Ravenstonedale.

Anciently this parish had very great and extensive privileges conferred upon it, by some of the popes, and the kings of this realm. These privileges appear to have been granted, in consideration of the manor and advowson being annexed to the priory of Walton in Yorkshire, which was of the order of Sempringham in Lincolnshire. By these grants the inhabitants had not only a freedom from toll and other personal or pecuniary charges, but they had also the privilege of sanctuary, throughout the whole of their possessions; insomuch that the sheriff, or any other of the king's officers, could not enter to apprehend offenders, but the criminals were to be tried before the steward of the manor, by a jury of the tenants, and punished or acquitted according to the sentence of that court. Exceptions were however made in cases of life and member, when the culprits were to be tried within the manor, by commissioners appointed by the crown; and the priory was entitled to the goods and effects of the felons attainted. In pursuance of these grants and privileges, a manuscript of Mr. Anthony Fothergill of Trannahill, in this parish, written in the year 1645, sets forth, that if a murderer fled to the church or sanctuary, and tolled the holy bell (as it was called), he was free; and that if a stranger, who had offended, came within the precincts of the manor, he was safe from any pursuer. And he also adds, "Of our own knowledge, and within our own memory, no felon (though a murderer) was to be carried out of the parish for trial." And at this time, there is a place within the lord's park, in sight of the ancient highway leading from Kirkby-stephen to Kendal, commonly called and known by the name of the gallows-hill, which was undoubtedly the spot allotted for the execution of criminals. Amercements for bloodshed and other crimes, not felony, were frequent not very many years ago; and the jurisdiction relative to offences of this nature indisputably still exists, for no act of parliament hath ever abolished it. But the privilege of sanctuary, in this and all other places, was annulled in the reign of James I. and the other privileges have become extinct. The lord of the manor, however, still exercises the jurisdiction of proving of wills and granting letters of administration, which is a privilege of prior origin to any of the aforesaid ancient grants; and the steward of the lord's court administers the oath of office to the churchwardens of the parish; but in all other particulars, this place hath no peculiar exemption. All the land here is held of the lord of the manor by customary tenure; and what may be reckoned a remnant of ancient vassalage, the tenements cannot be broken or divided without the previous consent of the lord.

At a place called Rasate (the word *rase* probably

probably denoting a hill or rising ground), not far from Sunbiggin tarn, are two *tumuli*, which were opened, and many human bodies found in them. It was observed, that the bodies were placed in such a manner that all the heads extended to the summit of the hill, and that the hands were stretched over their breasts. At Newbiggin, a village, in this parish, there was formerly a chapel, supposed to have been dedicated to St. Helen; and at the north end of the village, is a field called chapel garth, and a spring known by the name of St. Helen's well. On the highway from Kirkby-stephen to Sedberg, and near Rawthey bridge, is a circle of large stones, supposed to be the remains of a Druidical temple. Mr. Fawcett Hunter had a house lately, remarkable for its situation, which was very descriptive of the nature and elevation of the country. The water that fell off one side of this house, ran into a brook that joins the river Eden, which empties itself into the sea below Carlisle; whilst the water that descended from the other side of the house, flowed into the rivers Rawthey and Lune, which fall into the sea below Lancaster.

Of persons that deserve to be particularly mentioned, and who were once eminent and distinguished characters, and natives of this parish, we may perhaps properly reckon the following. 1. Sir William Fothergill, who lived in the reign of king Henry VIII. and was standard-bearer to Sir Thomas Wharton, at the famous rencounter at Sollom Moss, where a very few English routed a Scotch army of fifteen thousand men. 2. George Fothergill, esq. of Tarn-house, who lived in the time of Charles II. and was clerk of the peace for the county of Westmoreland. 3. Thomas Fothergill, B. D. master of St. John's College in Cambridge, and founder of the grammar-school in Ravenstonedale. 4. Mr. Anthony Fothergill of Brounber, who, without any assistance from a liberal education, and by the mere force of natural endowments, was the author of several considerable tracts, religious and controversial. 5. George Fothergill, D. D. late principal of St. Edmund-hall in Oxford, who favoured the public during his life with several sermons preached before the university on particular occasions, and left behind him two volumes of sermons for publication, which exactly pourtray the life and manners of the author. He was a person of the greatest piety and virtue; and whilst fellow of Queen's College, in the same university, was universally esteemed one of the most learned and eminent tutors of his time*. He died in 1760, aged fifty-four. 6. Thomas Fothergill, D. D. late provost of Queen's college in Oxford, prebendary of Durham, and a younger brother of the above-mentioned Dr. George Fothergill. He succeeded his brother as tutor in the college, and in every respect imitated his amiable and laudable example. He was author of several sermons; and died in 1796, in the eighty-third year of his age. Both brothers were great benefactors to the public institutions here; and their memories will be long held in reverence and esteem.

The public roads in this parish, and indeed throughout the whole county, have been considerably improved of late years. In Ravenstonedale three pence per pound, according to valuation, is paid annually out of all landed property, as a modus or prescription for the making and repairing of roads; and as excellent materials are near at hand, they are not only well made, but kept in good repair. There are two large turnpikes, with several cross roads, in the parish; and some others are at present under contemplation. It is to be hoped, that no prejudices shall operate to counteract any improvements that may be deemed necessary, and which, however considered in the mean time, must ultimately conduce to the comfort and the advantage of the people.

A book-society was set on foot here, about seven or eight years ago; but in the space of two or three years, it was found necessary to be dissolved. The subscription money, which was only five shillings per ann. was certainly very inadequate to an undertaking of this nature. But independent of this, the genius and circumstances of the people, who from their occupation cannot be supposed greatly inclined to pursuits of a literary tendency, were perhaps the most serious difficulties, with which this institution had to contend. In giving a general character of the inhabitants, however, it is only just to say, that they are a sensible, sober, and industrious people; and though possessing a competent share of the comforts and conveniences of life, they have not arrived at such a state of civilization and refinement, as to depart from that pleasing simplicity which characterizes and adorns rural scenes.

In this parish are about 180 horses of all descriptions; and 10170 sheep upon the

* "See Public Characters of 1799 and 1800," in the life (I think) of Dr. Harrington.

the commons. In the river Lon or Lune, which has its rise here, and in the rivulet that runs through the parish, are very good trouts. In a tarn also, at the head of the village of Ravenstonedale, are trouts and a great number of eels. The wild quadrupeds here are foxes, otters, hares, wild cats, pole-cats, ermines and weasels. The birds are partridges, plovers, wild ducks, teals, snipes, and a great number of moor game. Of migratory birds there are the cuckow, the goatsucker, the swift, the house and window swallow, the sand martin or river swallow, the curlew, the lapwing, the tewit, and the sandpiper. There is also great plenty of the rarer species of birds, as the land and water rail, the missel thrush, the goldfinch and bulfinch, the willow-wren, the redstart, the fly-catcher; with the dun, the grey, and the barn owls.

The cuckoo usually appears here about the 20th of April, and departs about the 5th of July; the house and window-swallows about the 20th of April, and depart from the 4th to the 30th of September; the sand-martin from the 15th to the 31st of March, and departs about the 1st. of September; the curlew and lapwing about the middle of March and depart about the middle of August; the swift and goatsucker arrive at the commencement of continued daylight, which is about the 9th of May, and depart at the end of it, which is about the 2d of August; the sandpiper visits and stays through the whole of the breeding season; and the tewit is often found here in winter, when the weather is mild.

On the top of Wildboar-fell, the highest mountain in the parish, and perhaps not much inferior to any in the county, is frequently a very remarkable phenomenon, called a helm-wind, which probably nowhere exists in the kingdom, but in the north-east part of Westmoreland, and on the confines of the counties of Yorkshire and Lancashire. A rolling cloud, for three or four days incessantly floats on the summit of this mountain, when the sky is clear in every other part. This cloud is called by the country people the *helm*, which is said to be an Anglo-Saxon word, signifying a covering for the head, and from whence comes the diminutive *helmet*. This helm is not dispersed or blown away by the wind, but remains in its station, although a violent and roaring hurricane issues with incredible fury down the sides of the mountain, and threatens to destroy all before it. On a sudden ensues a profound calm; and then again alternately the tempest; which seldom extends into the country, more than a mile or two from the foot of the mountain.

To the Editor of the Monthly Magazine.

SIR,

IN your Number, published last month, I observe a detailed account of the National Debt, and a terrifying view of our Financial Situation. If I can make it appear to the writer, who has subscribed himself M. N. that, through haste, or inadvertence, he has fallen into any mistake, I venture to presume that he will hold himself under an obligation to me; but this is far from being my strongest motive for requesting you to insert this letter in your valuable Repository. I shall endeavour to supply the public with a more correct statement of its present debt, than has appeared in any former publication. Should I fail in the undertaking, you will find me, Sir, most willing to acknowledge, and rectify my error.

"It is to be observed (says M. N.) that the stock charged upon the income-tax, and the Imperial-loan, which are properly included in Mr. Tierney's and Mr. Morgan's statements, has, in this very concise account (Mr. Addington's) been entirely omitted." But a reference to the resolutions submitted to the House of Commons, will clearly shew, that Mr. Tierney, as well as Mr. Addington, deducts the advances to the Emperor. Mr. Tierney states (as M. N. has justly observed) "that the total amount of the public funded debt was, on the 1st of February, 1801, 484,365,464l. of which sum 27,211,383l.* is on account of Ireland and the Emperor of Germany;" but what are the remaining words of the resolution? They are, as follows—" *leaving a funded debt charged upon Great Britain of* 457,154,081l. including 56,445,000l. the interest of which is to be defrayed, and the capital redeemed, by the tax on income."

484,365,464l.
27,211,383l. to be deducted on account of Ireland, and the Emperor of Germany.
————
457,154,081l.

---

* 7,502,633l. Three per cent. stock created by advances to the Emperor.
19,708,750l. Capital stock on account of Ireland.
————
27,211,383l.

Thus

Thus it appears that Mr. Tierney concurs with the Chancellor of the Exchequer in excluding the Imperial-loans, and the loans to Ireland from his computation of the funded debt of *Great Britain*; but does not agree with him in omitting the stock, charged upon the income-tax. Whether the Imperial-loans ought to be deducted, will, before I conclude, be made the subject of consideration.

Having noticed this oversight in M. N. I proceed briefly to give the respective statements of Mr. Addington, Mr. Tierney, and Mr. Morgan, annexing a particular reference to the votes of the House of Commons, and to Mr. Morgan's "Comparative View, &c." all of which are now spread upon the table before me.

Public Funded Debt.

Mr. Addington, 400,709,832l. as it stood Feb. 1, 1801. Resolution 3d, carried—Vide votes.

Mr. Tierney, 457,154,081l. as it stood Feb. 1, 1801. Resolution 3d, not carried—Vide votes.

Mr. Morgan, 558,418,628l. as it stood April 5, 1801—"Comparative View, &c." p. 71.

By this statement you perceive, Sir, that there is a wide difference between these three gentlemen; Mr. Tierney's account exceeding Mr. Addington's more than 56,000,000l.; Mr. Morgan's exceeding Mr. Tierney's more than 101,000,000l. and outstripping Mr. Addington's more than 157,000,000l. The difference between Mr. Addington and Mr. Tierney is thus explained—the latter avowedly includes 56,445,000l. the interest of which is to be defrayed, and the capital redeemed, by the tax on income—the former avowedly excludes it—vide votes. It will be seen that the following statement makes the figures nearly the same.

457,154,081l. Mr. Tierney's statement.
400,709,832l. Mr. Addington's ditto.

56,444,249l. Excess of Mr. Tierney's.

56,445,000l. Charge upon income-tax.

The difference between Mr. Tierney and Mr. Morgan can have no reference to the small variation in the dates of their respective statements; neither does it consist in the charge upon the income-tax, for both gentlemen have included it, but in the following particulars, making a part of Mr. Morgan's, but not of Mr. Tierney's computation.

52,281,656l.	Redeemed by Commissioners for reducing the National Debt.		
16,083,802l.	Redeemed land-tax.		
21,592,956l.	Present value of life and temporary annuities.		
1,002,099l.	Borrowed upon tontine in 1789.		
10,368,893l.	Imperial-loans—3 per cent.	7,502,633l.	
	Ditto, 230,000l. per ann. for 20 years	2,866,260l.	Present value.
101,329,406l.		10,368,893l.	

558,418,628l. Mr. Morgan's statement.
457,154,081l. Mr. Tierney's ditto.

101,264,547l. Excess of Mr. Morgan's.

The difference between Mr. Addington, and Mr. Morgan consists in Mr. Morgan's including the charge on the income-tax, which Mr. Tierney has, likewise, included, but which Mr. Addington has excluded, and in all those items, which occasion the variation between the statements of Mr. Morgan and Mr. Tierney.

56,445,000l. Charge upon income-tax.
101,329,406l. Variation between the statements of Mr. Morgan, and Mr. Tierney—*Vide supra.*

157,774,406l.

558,418,628l. Mr. Morgan's statement.
400,709,832l. Mr. Addington's ditto.

157,708,796l. Excess of Mr. Morgan's.

Thus, Sir, have I endeavoured to shew, by an examination of the votes of the House of Commons, and of Mr. Morgan's last pamphlet, not only the difference in the amount of the several computations of the funded debt by Mr. Addington, Mr. Tierney, and Mr. Morgan, but from what causes that difference proceeds.

The next question, which naturally follows, is—whose mode of calculation ought to be preferred? This is the most interesting, as well as the most difficult part of the inquiry. It appears, if my representation be correct, that Mr. Morgan has not, after the example of the two senators, deducted the 52,281,656l. purchased by the Commissioners. I am aware that he has taken slight notice of that sum in a *note*, in which he says, that "of this stock (the 558,418,628l.)

558,418,628l.) 52,281,656l. have been redeemed by the Commiſſioners," &c. Certainly, this word *redeemed* ſeems to imply, that Mr. Morgan allows the deduction of that ſum; but why, therefore, has he not deducted it from his total, or omitted, in drawing up his account, capital ſtock to that amount, in the ſame manner as he has omitted the debt incurred by loans to Ireland? Nay, in p. 71 he affirms, that "the capital of the public debt, which, at the commencement of Mr. Pitt's adminiſtration, amounted to 232,000,000l. has been accumulated to the enormous maſs of 558,000,000l. and the peace eſtabliſhment," &c. &c. Here, Sir, is a poſitive aſſertion, that 558,000,000l. is the amount of the funded debt, without making any deduction whatever. Since, therefore, Mr. Morgan has only mentioned, in a ſhort note, the ſtock bought by the Commiſſioners, and does not ſubſtract it from his ſtatement, as he has done in other inſtances, when he makes any allowance; and ſince, in the paſſage I have quoted, he has, in ſo unqualified a manner declared the funded debt to be 558,000,000l.; am I not warranted in ſuppoſing that he wiſhes it ſo to be conſidered by the public, and in having ſet down his ſtatement at that ſum? Let me now ſubmit one queſtion, Sir, to your conſideration. As Mr. Morgan's title-page profeſſes to be a "Comparative View of the Public Finances, from the Beginning to the Cloſe of Mr. Pitt's Adminiſtration," ought he not, agreeably to his general character for fairneſs and candour, qualities for which he deſerves to be admired, no leſs than for his eminent talents, to have deducted all the ſavings made by that miniſter? Will it be contended, for an inſtant, that the 52,000,000l. thus redeemed, ought not to be placed to the credit of the nation? I cannot conceive that any perſon will venture to ſupport ſuch a poſition. If the public were, at this moment, to apply that ſtock to the reduction of the debt, would it not, by cancelling a portion to the ſame amount, diminiſh the claim of the national creditor? It cannot, ſurely be denied.

With reſpect to the 16,000,000l. of land-tax redeemed, I muſt confeſs that here, alſo, I agree with the two former gentlemen. True it is, as M. N. has remarked, that the Miniſter ought not to calculate, in his Ways and Means, upon 2,000,000l. as the annual produce of the land tax, and, at the ſame time, deduct that part of it, which has been redeemed, from the public debt: but it is only in over-rating his Ways and Means, that he has erred. He ſells an eſtate, and appropriates the purchaſe-money to the payment of debts; and then reckons upon the rents of the eſtate as a reſource for future debts, which he may incur. In eſtimating the means of diſcharging the ſervices of an enſuing year, he ſhould only calculate the unredeemed reſidue of the land tax; but in eſtimating the public debt, he has ſurely a right to deduct the ſtock, created by that portion of the land tax, which has been redeemed, and purchaſed. It is deſtined for the reduction of the debt, and is capable of being inſtantly applied to that purpoſe.

As to the 56,445,000l. charged upon the income-tax, I cannot but obſerve that this ſum properly makes a part of the national debt. If the nation were in the ſituation of an individual, called upon to ſatisfy the demands againſt him, the 56,000,000l. muſt immediately be diſcharged. Vain would it be to ſay that the Exchequer poſſeſſes ſuch, and ſuch reſources, which, if not interrupted by the courſe of events, would, after a certain number of years, gradually liquidate the debt. This conſideration would deſerve attention, if the queſtion were, what are the means of cancelling the debt, and not what is its preſent amount. Mr. Morgan has moſt judiciouſly obſerved, that, "if the mortgage upon the income tax be not reckoned, becauſe in 10 or 11 years after peace the 56,000,000 would be diſcharged, the Chancellor of the Exchequer ought, upon the ſame principle, to inſiſt, that there is no national debt, becauſe the ſinking fund would, in proceſs of time, accompliſh its complete redemption. This obſervation is ſtrong, and concluſive. It does not belong to the preſent inquiry to calculate whether it be probable that, in 10, or 11 years after the concluſion of the war, this burthen upon the country will be removed by the protracted operation of the income-tax; otherwiſe I would expreſs all my reaſons for thinking that no event is more unlikely. When it is conſidered that the number of years of war, during the laſt century, has been in an almoſt equal proportion to the years of peace; and that, provided Europe were, at this moment, to put an end to the exiſting war, a ſettled, and durable calm, in times ſo troublous, and revolutionary, could not reaſonably be expected, what chance is there, let me aſk, of a continued application of the income-tax for 10 years to the liquidation of the ſtock, with which it is charged. Or may it not, if unhappily the conteſt

contest should be prolonged, be loaded with additional burthens?" &c. &c. &c.

It appears that Mr. Morgan, in his estimate of the funded debt, has given the present value of the life and temporary annuities, and also of the Tontine in 1789, which is of the same nature. Mr. Addington and Mr. Tierney have merely stated these several annuities, without computing the price of their redemption. In this step, Mr. Morgan seems to have judged rightly. Suppose the national debt were now to be discharged, the annuities must be valued, and the cost of them, in principal money, be paid by the Government. Most strange would it be in an individual, who owed various sums upon mortgage, bond, &c. and had, also, granted many annuities, to overlook, in an estimate of his debts, the several annuities, and to consider them as no part of the demands against him, because they were one day to expire. This would be thought a ridiculous proceeding: while, on the contrary, it would be deemed wise, and fair, when he employed himself to ascertain the actual amount of his debts, to calculate what sum of money would induce another person to take the annuities upon himself. Government, like an intelligent individual, should pursue the same line of conduct. On this ground, I give, without scruple, the preference to Mr. Morgan's statement, in this particular article.

The last item, which calls for examination, is the money advanced, by way of loan, to the Emperor of Germany. Mr. Addington, and Mr. Tierney have deducted these loans, but Mr. Morgan has included them in the debt of Great Britain. True it is that we are only guarantees in this case; but is it not equally true, that this country has, hitherto, paid all the dividends. Is it probable that Austria will ever satisfy the debt she has contracted to Great Britain? She engaged to pay the interest regularly upon the sums which were advanced, and to invest annually a certain sum, in our funds, for the replacement of the capital, which was created by our loans in her behalf. Has she performed either part of this contract? Certainly not. It may be said that the Treasury of the Emperor has been exhausted by a long, and ruinous war, but that when his finances are recovered, he will not fail to observe his engagements. It may be so; he is not doubted. He never imitated the conduct of that European Potentate, who detained a subsidy, without performing the stipulated services; neither did he ever attempt to evade the acknowledgement of a just debt by contending, in opposition to the plain, and unambiguous terms of a positive Convention, that the money he had received was not a loan, but a subsidy. But though the present Emperor be strict in the fulfilment of his treaties, yet his reign may close 'ere he become able to satisfy our demands against him, and another Prince, less honourable, and less conscientious, may ascend the throne of Germany. The question therefore is—what, under all the circumstances, would any prudent man give to Government for the purchase of this debt? Nothing I fear: and, therefore, the advances, which have been made by this country for the sake of assisting the Emperor in the *common* cause, as it is *usually* called, ought not to be deducted from the amount of our national debt.

I have now, Sir, reviewed the statements of Mr. Addington, Mr. Tierney, and Mr. Morgan, and given my humble opinion upon the articles which constitute the difference in their respective accounts. If then the reasoning, which I have adopted, be just, the funded debt is different from what it is made by either of the three gentlemen, and, to attain correctness, two sums only should be deducted from Mr. Morgan's computation, namely, the stock redeemed by the Commissioners, and the redeemed land tax.

52,281,656l.	Stock redeemed by Commissioners.
16,083,802l.	Redeemed land-tax.
68,365,458l.	
558,418,628l.	Mr. Morgan's statement.
68,365,458l.	
490,053,170l.	Present amount of funded debt, as far as the same can be made out.

But I ought not, Sir, to stop here. My object is to furnish the public with the amount of its debt, upon a supposition that it is, at this moment, to be discharged. I ought, therefore, to add to the funded debt the total of the unfunded debt, and demands outstanding, for which no provision has been made, amounting, according to Mr. Addington, to 17,946,186l. according to Mr. Tierney, to 20,946,186l. and, according to Mr. Morgan, to 25,407,203l. The difference between Mr. Addington, and Mr. Tierney, seems to to admit an easy explanation—the former excludes the sum "advanced by the Bank, without interest, for the renewal of their Charter, and to be repaid in 1806"—the latter includes it.

20,946,186l.	—Vide Mr. Tierney's Motion in June, 1801—not carried.
17,946,186l.	—Vide Mr. Addington's Motion at the same time—carried.
3,000,000l.	

The difference between Mr. Tierney, and Mr. Morgan, can have no relation to the different periods of their statements, the account of the latter being made up to April last, that of the former to the June following, as far as it was then known; nor can it have any relation to the 3,000,000l. lent by the Bank, for both those gentlemen have included it. In what the difference actually consists I have, in vain, endeavoured to discover, as Mr. Tierney's Resolution, though not given in a way quite so general as Mr. Addington's, does not enumerate the specific arrears of each service. Let it, however, be recollected, that it is far more difficult to calculate outstanding demands, which are unprovided for, than to make a statement of the funded debt; and hence a considerable variation, in the estimates of different gentlemen, is more likely to happen. Let it, also, be recollected, that the difference between Mr. Tierney, and Mr. Morgan, is scarcely 4,500,000l. a sum which, I grant, is not trifling in itself, but which weighs lightly in the scale, when a debt exceeds 500,000,000l. That I may not be accused of a wish to swell the national debt beyond its actual amount, I will suppose that this sum of 4,500,000l. ought to be deducted. It is my intention, also, to omit, as my statement is formed entirely upon the hypothesis of immediate payment, the 3,000,000l. advanced by the Bank of England. If I were called upon in 1806 to give a statement of the public debt, I certainly should not overlook that article. For these reasons I shall adopt Mr. Addington's computation of the unfunded debt, and then the account will be as follows:—

490,053,170l.	Funded debt.
17,946,186l.	Unfunded debt.
507,999,356l.	*Present Amount of the National Debt as far as the same can be made out.*

I imagine, Sir, that you think this statement scarcely less deplorable, than the representation of M. N. It is most true, I agree with him, that the national debt, however I may differ with him as to its amount, has, in the course of a very few years, accumulated to a very alarming degree. Like him I tremble, when I perceive that it has increased in a proportion infinitely beyond the produce of all the boasted means for its reduction; like him, when I advert to the annual expenditure of Great Britain, amounting, in the estimates both of Mr. Addington, and Mr. Tierney, to 68,923,970l. (a sum, which according to the income-tax returns, far exceeds the whole income of the country, with an exception to such, as is under 60l. per annum) I dare not form the hope of any favourable change in our financial prospects. Many former writers on political economy predicted the very time, when the nation was to fall into a state of insolvency; but, happily, their prophecies have been falsified by the event. I will not be so absurd as to tread in their steps; but I will be bold enough to affirm, that perseverance in such a system of expence leads, sooner, or later, to ruin. When the maximum of taxation is arrived, the Exchequer will be no longer able to borrow, and bankruptcy must ensue. Will not the rapid, and continued increase of our enormous public debt finally plunge us into this horrid abyss? To avoid this fatal calamity, one change only is left. War must be exchanged for peace, and profusion for a rigid and invariable course of economy in every department of the state.

O. P.

Alnwick, Northumberland,
August 8, 1801.

To the Editor of the Monthly Magazine.

SIR,

IN a former Monthly Magazine, page 320, an enquiry is instituted about the *Life-boat* at Shields.—A perfect model of that boat is said to be kept at Northumberland House in the Strand, near Charing Cross, for the inspection of the curious; the Duke of that name, having been at the expence of a similar boat, on a larger scale, which has saved the lives of many valuable seamen. I am, Sir,

Your's, &c. S. R.

Extracts

Extracts from the Port-folio of a Man of Letters.

CRUEL USAGE *of the* JEWS *in* FORMER TIMES.

THE situation of the Jews from the time of their dispersion, after the destruction of Jerusalem, about the year of Christ 70, was truly deplorable. Of those who survived the siege of that city, some were sold for slaves and carried to different countries; yet their numbers increased, and by their address and application to traffic they acquired wealth, and, consequently, had always money to supply the necessities of the sovereigns of the country wherein they resided. In France they were imprisoned, accused of magic, of crucifying children, and of poisoning the public wells, in order to extort money from them. Their wealth was at one time confiscated if they embraced Christianity; and their bodies at another committed to the flames, if they persisted to follow the religion of their fathers. In England our king John imprisoned the rich Jews to possess himself of their riches. The story is well known of the seven teeth which he caused to be plucked out of a Jew's head, to make him give up his wealth. His son, Henry the third, followed his example, and laid an imposition upon the Jews for their *redemption*, and received at times from Aaron, a Jew of York, thirty thousand marks of silver, an immense sum in those days! Yet not contented with *fleecing* the Jews himself, he "let them out to farm (so Daniel the historian terms it) to his brother, the rich earl of Cornwall." According to Mathew of Paris, *(ut quos rex excoriaverat comes evisceraret,)* "that he *might cut them up altogether*." In an ancient manuscript of laws and customs established in the reign of Richard the first, for the government of the dominions belonging to the crown of England in France, I find the following instruction respecting Jews coming into the Isle of *Oleron*. It is contained in these words: "Ceu est lou peage des Jues. Chascuns Jues et Juere non estant en Oleron par chascune fois qúil venent en oleiron devent de lor chef iüj d' do piage au rey. E si la Jueve est prainz ele endeit vüj por sey et por leffant dau ventre. Et dit hom que guarners chasteaus quant il fut seneschaus doleyron juja quant li Jues ou la Jueve sen aluit ob lo dit peaage il sereit qualez en la mer une foyz por legage dau dit peage et la Jueve prainz iseit qualce does fez por sey et por leffant. Quar por ceu que tout laver aus Jues sont aus grans seignors daus terres sor cuy il eston: et ne sereit pas corteisie quon en prist lor deners por gage, mas au meisme cors dau Jue quit fait la malefaite en tort lo demage." Which may be thus translated: "This is the toll for the Jews—Every Jew and Jewess, not settled in Oleron, must pay each a tax of four deniers to the king, for every time he or she comes to Oleron. And if the Jewess be pregnant, she must pay eight for herself and the child in her womb. And it is said that when Guarners Chasteaus was seneschal in Oleron, he adjudged that a Jew or Jewess, not paying the said toll, should be once ducked in the sea, as a fine for non payment; and the Jewess that was pregnant should be ducked twice; once for herself, and once for her child. For, inasmuch as all the possessions of Jews, belong to the chief lords of the places where they dwell, it were not justice that money be taken from them, by way of fine for their offences; but that they should receive corporal punishment for them." Thus far this extract from this ancient manuscript. Péage is a word still in use in France, if not now, at least under the old government; it is defined, "*Droit pour un passage*," "A toll for passing through a place." The Jews, in the age of Richard the first, or Cœur de Lion, and before and since, were considered as serfs, or constituting, like villains and cattle, part or parcel of the estates of the great lords whereon they were settled, and possessing no property but what was subject to their arbitrary will and pleasure. Hence was derived the right these lords exercised of calling upon the Jews for whatever monies they thought proper. On this ground the property of Jews was confiscated upon their conversion to Christianity; because, as Montesquieu has observed, the lord had no right to continue his exactions after a Jew was converted, as he was no longer serf main mortable; that is to say, "a vassal commuting with money the services he owed and could not render in person."—This confiscation therefore was in the nature of an alienation-fine, or purchase of those rights. On the like ground our kings laid those heavy fines beforementioned on the rich Jews; that is to say, by way of redemption of the taxes due from the whole of the nation within their dominions; which redemption, however, was

was of no longer continuance than suited the necessities of their treasury, or the caprices of their will. In aftertimes the eyes of princes were opened to their true interests, and the Jews began to be treated with more moderation. The sovereigns of Europe from north to south, found them a useful body of people, whom they could not well do without. To say nothing of the Grand Duke of Tuscany, England and Holland granted them the protection of their government, with the free exercise of their religion. Spain has found the bad policy of driving them out of that country, as France has done of the persecution of the Protestants. Thus the Jews are at present spread over all Europe, living in ease and security; and are become the instruments, by means of which nations at the greatest distance communicate with each other, and thereby become connected; in which respect, the Jews resemble the nails and wooden pegs whereby a vast edifice is held together: and this toleration is certainly agreeable to the principles and doctrine of Christianity, which inculcates love and charity towards all mankind.

ORIGINAL LETTER *relative to* CHARLES *the* 12*th*.

The following authentic documents relating to the Swedish hero, Charles the XII. were found some years ago in the castle of Blarney in Ireland, which at present belongs to the descendant of the Mr. Jefferies mentioned in them, and of whom Voltaire speaks (in his Life of Charles the 12th.) in very high terms. In the official note from M. de Mullern may be perceived that implacability against Peter the Great, which marked every action of Charles; and although reduced to the utmost extremity, and a royal beggar, yet he still holds his accustomed dictatorial style, and speaks as if in the plenitude of power. The letter to my lord ambassador Sutton is a copy of that which was sent to him. In one corner of it are some Turkish words, of which I do not know the meaning.

"MY LORD,

"Though I have not much to add to the trouble I gave your Lordship the 27th past; yet I would not omitt so favourable an opportunity as this, of assuring your Lordship of my most humble respects, and at the same time begging your excuse for having sent a copy of the late conditions of peace between the Turks and the Muscovites, which I find is deficient in some particulars; but the fault is rather the interpreters than mine, who, not understanding the Turkish language, must take every thing translated from thence on trust: the enclos'd copy, I hope, will make some amends for the faults of the other, it being a translation from the original Turkish treaty, and communicated to me by some of the Swedish Chancery."

My Lord Ambassador Sutton.

"The Swedes begin now to abate somewhat of their great expectation of a new rupture between the Port and the Czar of Muscovy; but still flatter themselves that they will be powerfully assisted against king August: what ground they have for such hopes I can't comprehend, especially since the Turks have declar'd they will not engage in any warr against Poland; and, since they so much neglected the interest of the Swedes, when they might with one word have procur'd them all the advantages they reasonably could have desir'd: As to the 10m Spahis and some thousand Tartars, which 'tis said the Grand Vizier has offered the king of Sweden, I do not hear 'tis with any other design than to conduct him to some place of safety, whence he may with ease come to his own dominions. In short, had the king of Sweden a summ of money to throw away among these people, somewhat might be hop'd for from them; but I assure your lordship that *nervus rerum ger.* fails us to such a degree, the Swedes are themselves so miserably poor that unless the Swedes gett supplys from the Port they will not be able to stirr one stepp from Bender. I have taken occasion, from the ill usage the king has mett with here, to insinuate to these Ministers how much more it would be for his Majesty's advantage to rely upon his Christian allys, and to give them assurances not to invade Saxony, then to spend his time in courting the 168, by whom he may be sure to be xywycox at last; but having no orders from England to advance any such proposition, and finding the Swedes still insist on obligations and treatys without giving us any hopes of the desir'd assurance, I have desisted to urge it farther.

"Yesterday a letter from the Grand Vizir to the king of Sweden was communicated to me, which was conceiv'd in very unbecoming terms, viz. That his Majesty must now prepare to gett himself hence out of the country; that he had rather repair to his own dominions, where his presence is necessary, than by his cabals endeavour to embroil affaires here; that this is the last offer that will be made him, and that he will have reason to repent

pent of his willfulness in case he should refuse it.

"Eight or tenn days ago the Niester overflowed its banks to that degree, that the king with all his followers were oblig'd to quit their houses (which are now entirely ruin'd) and encamp under a village, which lyes half an English mile from Bender, by which it appears that the very Turkish elements *are tired of us and will have us from hence.*"

"Sacræ Regiæ Majestatis responsum ad libellum memorialem Armigeri et Ministri serenissimæ reginæ Magnæ Britanniæ de Jefferyes, literis fiduciariis et mandatis pariter instructi a serenissimo Romanorum Imperatore et celsis ac præpotentibus Ordinibus Generalibus Uniti Belgii, die 28 Aprilis, A° 1711, in castris ad urbem Benderam oblatum.

i.—Quod altè memoratæ summæ potestates sibi curæ esse ostendant pacem in Septemtrione inter partes belligerantes reconciliari, lubens percipit Sac. Reg. Majestas, earumque officia ad eam rem perficiendam perquam grata sibi futura esse declarat: sed et juxta desiderat, ut in tam arduo negotio ultra verba procedatur ab ipsis sponsionum pactorum religione obligatis ad opem ferendam hostesque, præter Czarum Moscoviæ (cum quo nulla amicitia restitui potest, nisi quæ nexu suo Portum Ottomanicum simul comprehendat:) ad æquas pacis conditiones adigendos.

Quantacumque enim fuerint amica ipsorum officia in reconcilianda pace, longe tamen efficacior futura erit eorum opera, si ex fœderum legibus vim repræsentare velint cæteris hostibus.

ii.—Quæ ad conservandam tuendamque Germaniæ tranquillitatem Hagæ-comitum anno superiore a confederatis potestatibus sancita sunt, nullo quidem sibi nocendi proposito facta este credit Sacra Regia Majestas: Quoniam autem decretum illud mala (ipso inscio et invito initum) ipsi multa, hostibus vero plurima commoda, adfert: per Ministros suos bis, et tertia demum vice, scripto Regio sua manu signato declaravit, se illius legibus nequaquam teneri posse aut velle. In qua sententia Sacra Regia Majestas persistit.

iii.—Quæ jussu et mandato Majestatis Britanniæ Dominæ suæ clementissimæ et Dominorum Ordinum Generalium Uniti Belgii proposuerat Armiger Jefferyes, de inoffensa libertate navigandi et commerciandi in portubus ad Mare Balticum a Czaro occupatis, talia esse judicat Sacra Regia Majestas ut cum tenore Tractatus Commerciorum ac recepto apud amicas gentes usu haud quaquam consistere possunt; atque proinde confidit serenissimam Magnæ Britanniæ Reginam atque celsos et præpotentes Ordines Generales uniti Belgii, amicos et confederatos suos, non amplius desideraturos rem tam noxiam sibi tamque fructuosam hostibus suis quam utique Sacra Regia Majestas neutiquam concedere potest, prætertim postquam per Ministros suos ad aulas ipsorum residentes notum fecerat, mandata abs se dudum data esse collegio ammiralitatis ut classem ad omnes illos portus ab hoste captos claudendos, arctèque obsidendos mittat.

Quam benevolam Sacræ Regiæ Majestatis mentem Armiger de Jeffereyes decenter renunciandam habet; cui de tero ipsa semper manet faventissima.

Dat: ad Urbem Benderam die 2 Mensis Maij An° 1711. Admandatum,

H. G. DE MULLERN.

ACADEMIC FLATTERY.

Clermont Tonnere, bishop of Noyon, a man ridiculous for his attachment to high birth, gave an annual prize to the French Academy, to be bestowed on the best poetical composition; but the only subject to be treated of was the praise of Louis XIV. After all the ordinary topics of adulation had been exhausted, the Academy proposed, for the year 1700, the following text for the prize-poem: "That the king possesses all the virtues in so eminent a degree, that it is impossible to judge by which of them he is principally characterised." When this topic was shewn to the king for his approbation, (for this was always done previously to its being given out; and his Majesty, moreover, sat to hear the piece recited) enured as he was to flattery, he felt that it was *rather too much*, and put his negative upon it. The Academy then, by advice of the bishop, let it down a little in the following manner: "That the king unites in his person so many great qualities, that it is difficult to judge which forms his principal character." Even this qualified dose of incense proved too strong for his Majesty's relish. The Academy and bishop, almost reduced to despair, tremblingly proposed their third edition: "That the king is not less distinguished by the virtues of a man of worth, than by those of a great prince." This luckily did not offend the monarch's modesty, and he suffered it to pass without further alteration.

MEMOIRS OF EMINENT PERSONS.

MEMOIRS OF GENERAL ACTON.

JOHN ACTON was born at Besançon, in Franche Comté. His father was an Irish gentleman, in the service of the French. He was sent to Toulon at an early age, to serve in the navy, where, having made an apprenticeship, he entered into the service of the Grand Duke of Tuscany. He at first obtained the command of a frigate, and was afterwards preferred to that of a ship of the line. This was his condition, when early in the year 1779 he was appointed Minister of Marine to his Sicilian Majesty. Two things only are to be noticed of him before this period, which prevented his name from sinking into obscurity. A foreign power, of the first rank, had, ever since a remarkable event in 1769, projected the idea of acquiring, in the Councils of his Sicilian Majesty, as well as in the internal administration of the two kingdoms, a preponderance which might be a counterpoise to the inveterate influence of other courts connected by the family compact. This scheme was always systematically conducted, and the first steps towards it were an attempt to take into the Council of State a young person, who by his age was unqualified to partake in state affairs. The attempt was baffled, whilst the venerable old Minister Tanucci held the reins of government. The interested parties were sensible of the necessity of his dismissal in order to attain their object; this respectable man was actually, by their influence, removed from the Ministry, at the end of the year 1776. He was replaced by the Marquis of Sambuca, a Sicilian Nobleman, formerly Ambassador at the Court of Vienna, and wholly dependent upon the foreign Court which was the promoter of the changes. This done, the young person obtained a share in the State Council. The next steps towards the desired objects were, some changes in the organization of the Councils of State. This venerable body, consisting of men who had passed through the most eminent places in the civil and military departments, usually attended his Majesty on stated days, in every week, to assist at the several reports of the Ministers, and to give their votes occasionally. It was resolved, under the appearance of saving those respectable men the trouble of assiduous attendance, that their assistance should be required only when the Court might be in the metropolis; and that the Ministers only should attend to the state affairs, in the country-seats and in the hunting-matches. Soon after another resolution was taken, that the attendance even of the Ministers should be dispensed with, and they promised to send their respective budgets to the first Minister, who usually and indispensably accompanied their Majesties wherever they chose to live. This was evidently calculated to render the Marquis Sambuca sole organ of sovereignty, sole administrator of public affairs, and the sole dispenser of every favour and bounty. It is a justice due to this minister to say, that, although he was entirely devoted to the person who had been, and still was, his protector, and howsoever great may have been his ambition and cupidity, he never appeared to lose sight of his own dignity, and of a proper patriotic spirit. He was obsequious to the will of the above person to a certain degree; beyond it he never exposed himself to censure. It was obvious that no one could so well answer the artful purpose as a foreigner bereft of the feelings of country, and who might treat the kingdoms of the Two Sicilies as conquered countries; and as it would have been improper to dismiss the Marquis of Sambuca too soon, as well as others of his colleagues, who were supported by the unanimous voice of public opinion, a new ministerial department was created. The Ministry of War and Navy was previously one only, but it was resolved that they should now be separated, and that, in order to render the Two Sicilies a naval power, a Flag-officer of distinction, Mr. Acton, should be called from abroad.

The appointment took place in January 1779, and was the subject of conversation all over the two kingdoms. The lower classes flattered themselves that the new establishment would tend to create a powerful navy, and give to the Monarchy of the Two Sicilies a due degree of ascendancy in European politics; some threw out the most violent censures on the Cabinet for having taken an obscure person, as they said, from the service of a petty Prince, rather than some distinguished English or French Admiral; others scoffed at the incongruity of Government in thinking of a navy before endeavouring to create and settle a commerce, and establishing some colonies to protect it.

It was, however, not long before that the Chevalier Otteio had been the Minister of

War

War and Navy, before the late separation of the two departments. He continued in that of war, at the appointment of Mr. Acton. Towards the end of 1779, under pretence that the Chevalier's old age did not allow him to bear the toils of office, and that dignified repose ought to be the reward of his past services, he was removed from the Ministry, and appointed Superintendant of the Royal Seat at Caserta. Mr. Acton succeeded to his place.

In the year 1780, a captain of infantry living in the district of *Le Virgini*, in Naples, having been noted for his free sentiments on religion, and being on his death bed, the rector and vicar of the parish waited on him, for the sake of reminding him of his *Christian duties*. The officer ordered them to be turned out of doors, and uttered several invectives against religion in general. The clergymen, presuming he was in a fit of delirium at that time, did not fail to call on him again and again. The officer would not hear their admonitions, and died in his sentiments. According to the canon-laws of the kingdom of Naples, and of other *Catholic* countries, persons who willingly and conscientiously choose to die *out of the bosom of the church*, are deprived of ecclesiastical sepulture. This was actually the case with this officer, who was buried in the open fields, *by the consent and direction of the clergy of the parish*, and with the authority of the Archiepiscopal Court of Naples. Mr. Acton, at the request of the Captain's family, and upon an information from the Judge of the district, ordered the corpse to be taken up again, and it was carried in pomp to a large church, and the expences ordered to be defrayed by the rector and his vicar, who were also to be banished from the royal dominions. This was by the clergy deemed a piece of Vandalism.

The other instance was this:—One of the docks designed by Mr. Acton for the construction of ships, was that of Castelamare, a small town on the Neapolitan gulf, 18 miles from Naples. The town was not capable of affording great conveniences to the military and naval officers, to the architects and other persons who directed the works. Mr. Acton ordered that they should be lodged, with all their families, in the several convents of the city. This resolution was hardly credited at first; as besides the violation of the canon laws, and of the constitution of monastic orders, forbidding the introduction of women into cloysters of monks, they were shocked that the officers, in so considerable a number, carrying with them their wives, sisters, and daughters, should live in a religious community. The chiefs of the several orders, of course, made the strongest remonstrances to Mr. Acton on this indecent resolution. His answer to them was, "*You must be obliged to me, Reverend Fathers, that I give you the company of so many ladies! Their friends may, if they like, take care of their conduct. As for you, I dare say you will be merry, and in no case losers by their society.*" These two facts rendered Mr. Acton odious to the ecclesiastical dignitaries, and to the Neapolitan clergy.

During the years 1780 and 1781, Mr. Acton occupied himself with a plan of the reform of the army, which was calculated to awaken the kingdom of Naples. That plan was never made public, nor did any tidings of it transpire. It was commonly ascribed to General Acton's natural taciturnity and reserve. The time, however, soon arrived, in which he gave his Majesty to understand that it was absurd that the army and the navy should depend upon the general treasury and on the pay-orders from the Minister of Finance, as they, and as other branches of public expenditure, had done hitherto. This system, he added, was still more objectionable, with respect to season and schemes of reform, as these operations required occasional and extraordinary expences not to be ranked among the established disbursements of government. He concluded, that it was better to enact a law, purporting, that the Minister of Finance should convey to the Minister of War and Marine a certain number of millions every year, for providing every thing required in that department, of which the latter Minister only should be administrator, and be considered responsible. The King, however, was dissuaded by the Marquis Guizueta, Minister of Finance. This old man made his Majesty sensible of the dangers likely to be brought on the royal treasury by such an innovation, as also of the perfect humiliation to himself were he to submit to such invasions upon his department. The project was, therefore, postponed, but only while the Marquis of Guizueta continued alive. The Marquis died in August 1782, and General Acton conceived another *plan*, tending to appoint a permanent Committee of Finance, whose President might be the organ of the royal will, with regard to the dispatches directed to the inferior administrators, but without the power of assisting at a Council of State, or having a right to make any verbal report to his

Majesty. This, as his enemies said, was evidently calculated to destroy the Minister of Finance, and to throw the Committee which exalted him entirely upon the dependence of so powerful a Minister. This Committee was honoured with the title of *The Great Council of Finance*. The chief Members of it were M. *Corradini*, whose stupidity, although concealed under the mask of Jesuitical taciturnity, had already become proverbial—M. *Mazzocchi*, whose revelling mind and manners had gotten him the name of *Capuchin of Magistracy*—and the President, the Prince of *Cimiti*, who, some years before, had been displaced from the Roman Embassy for want of capacity. The organization of that Council was a compound of Ministry and Magistracy; a combination of many unsettled and irregular jurisdictions; a repartition of business among the several members and inferior clerks and agents, acting and counteracting in so confused a manner, as to make us believe Mr. Acton had done all that in order to have the army, the navy, and the finances, at his sole disposal. We do not mean to cast any reflections on the defects of a government, much less are we inclined to give any unfavourable prepossession of this Minister, whom we believe as untainted as any person in his line. We shall only relate the reports of that time. The funds allotted to the support of the army and navy were, if we recollect rightly, four millions and a half of ducats (about 800,000l. sterling). The arrangements prescribed, that the navy should have a stated number of ships built every year, and the army consist of 30,000 troops of the line, and 46,000 militia. It is a fact fully established, that this number of men did not exist, *except in the pay-tables*, and as if this had not been sufficient, it is also an incontrovertible truth, that from the year 1782 to 1786, very few, if any, promotions took place in the army, owing, as the Minister said, to the near approaching promulgation of the new plan; and when some preferments among the superior officers were unavoidable, for preventing the total failure of military service, the commission was sent to the candidate six or seven months after his Majesty's appointment; in the mean while such officer received pay according to the old rank, whereas in the accounts his pay was charged as that to which he was about to succeed. It was supposed that more than two millions (nearly 400,000l. sterling) were saved every year, and the public voice had already pronounced a sentence which it is unnecessary to relate in this place. These proceedings are said to have cast an unfavourable opinion on General Acton in the eyes both of the army and navy; the individuals of which (generally very poor) had consecrated the prime of their life to the royal service, under the prospect of enjoying some comfort in their advanced age, but which they were thus disappointed of. Meantime another scene was opened to flatter further his ambition. He would attempt an usurpation of power on his two colleagues, the Ministers of Justice and that of Ecclesiastical Affairs, the only Ministers who still preserved their authority undiminished. By an ancient law of the kingdom of Naples (as well as in many other countries) some persons, and especially the officers of the army and navy, and of the King's Houshold, enjoyed the *privilegium fori*. For each of these orders there was a magistrate distinct from the body of the law, and all those three were independent of the Minister of Justice. Mr. Acton resolved to convert these individual Magistracies into Collegial Tribunals, dependent on his office, so as to give himself a further influence over the magistrates and lawyers of the kingdom. Had the matter stopped here, he would, they say, have gratified his ambition with little inconvenience to the public, except the additional expenditure for the support of these newly-established colleges of judicature. They were, however, it is said, productive of three signal inconveniences. —1. The Minister and his subaltern agents found, every day, new classes of people, to whom the *privilegium fori* ought to be extended, and thus they gradually divested the national magistracy of their jurisdiction.—2. As the judicial proceedings of the ancient courts of justice in Naples moved with great regularity, owing to a long practice and experience of past ages, and as such judicial customs were not easily to be grafted on a newly raised tribunal, consisting of people influenced by a Minister and his officers, unacquainted with civil and common law, there never passed a single day without blunders, which disgraced common sense, and sometimes excited laughter——3. What was worse than all, certain crafty and ambitious lawyers, without merit, intrigued in Mr. Acton's office for the purpose of getting a footing in the newly-raised tribunals, and under pretence of merit and reward, obtained, through him, a passage, or rather an intrusion, into the great courts. By this means the venerable body of the ordinary magistracy was insulted by the intrusion of a considerable number of unworthy persons

sons, and thereby the profession was rendered contemptible in the eyes of the nation.

The Nobility had not yet sufficient reasons to proclaim their dislike to this Minister, from any glaring injuries done them, either individually or collectively. The Neapolitans, more than any other people, are renowned for hospitality, and their attachment to foreigners. They are, perhaps, the only nation in Europe who have, in less than sixty years, suffered nine foreigners to be Ministers of State. In return they think themselves entitled to some degree of respect, and require that a foreigner exalted above them in their own country should be a person of merit. General Acton's new military *plan* was brought to an issue in the year 1786: but as it was deemed proper to effect the destruction of the army, and its execution would have given the highest offence to the nobility, it was resolved that a foreign officer should be invited to Naples to carry the plan into execution, and upon whom, in case of need, the whole odium of the innovation might be thrown. A German officer would certainly have been employed in this task, had it not been for fear of giving farther umbrage to the Bourbon Courts, already disgusted with the Neapolitan Government. Baron de *Salis*, a Swiss officer of distinction in the service of the French army, was the person appointed for the reform, and accordingly he repaired to Naples in December, 1786. Here again we are obliged to cast a veil over many disagreeable occurrences, which took place at the arrival of this officer in Naples, as well as on his operations, and confine ourselves to the nature of the disgust excited in the nobility.

Baron de *Salis* brought with him to Naples about fifty French officers of different rank, who were to co-operate under him in the great work of reform. These were men of little consideration, and what was worse, of still less ability. Intoxicated, however, with the character of reformers, and not reflecting whether the intended reform was a serious undertaking or a pantomime, to draw attention from other interested designs, they gave themselves a domineering air, and began to treat the Neapolitan officers belonging to the Nobility with indifference and contempt. Many instances could be given of their insolence, but we shall only remark, that one of the *soi-disant* reformers addressed, with improper language, one of the youngest sons of Prince Stigliano, of the illustrious House of Colonna. Baron de *Salis* himself, one day, arrogantly summoned to his presence the Marquis Mauri, Governor of Capua, a venerable man, 84 years old; and Prince de Sangro (son of the celebrated General of this name, and one of the Noblemen most devoted to the reigning House) after having been deprived of his prerogatives, as Colonel of a regiment, and having given in his resignation, was, by a dispatch from Mr. Acton, confined in the Castle of St. Elmo! This last event is said to have rendered the Minister not a little odious to the Nobility.

From the year 1787 to 1789 new attempts were made upon the banks of the metropolis, upon public credit, and the charitable foundations.—1. The seven banks of Naples, founded about two centuries ago, had always been the depository of a considerable part of the national money, and delivered their notes to their respective creditors. It was natural that many of these notes should be left in the hands of the possessors, especially by expatriation, sudden deaths, or neglect in the heirs of the possessors. In the course of two centuries, these notes, never claimed, had made a considerable sum, and were deemed a natural acquisition to the banks. But General Acton, according to the maxim in the Roman laws—*Bona vacantia Fiscus occupat*, confiscated the money.—2. From the very foundation of the banks, it was a custom constantly observed, that each person, on exchanging their notes, should pay a penny to the banks. This was, perhaps, originally intended to defray the expenditure of the administration. But as the banks had, in process of time, grown rich, these pence so accumulated during two centuries, (being never touched) that they amounted to some millions. *Bona vacantia Fiscus occupat!*—3. A considerable addition had been made to the national debt in the course of this century, and the state creditors of this description had lent their money at 4 per cent. The present rate of money in the ministerial financial aids, was much inferior. An order was issued, that the creditors and their heirs should declare, within one month, whether they would be paid the capital, or consent to receive 3 per cent. This order, which, in the supposition of a necessary execution, would have required upwards of 8,000,000 in ready cash, was issued at a time when not a single farthing was to be found in the

the treasury. The consequence was obvious. The better informed among the capitalists being inclined to believe that this financial manœuvre was little better than a fraud, declared that they stood in need of their capital. The timid and credulous part consented to the abatement; and thus in a debt of the same origin, nature, condition, and stipulation, some parts were paid in the proportion of four and some of three!—4. No pawn-brokers being in Naples, pious foundations, endowed with an immense wealth, receive pledges without interest. As their wealth was much above the public wants in this line, secret orders were given to the governors of these *Monti di Pietà* to convey to court the superfluous money!—5. Numberless other pious foundations, all over the kingdom, were intrusted with charitable distributions, such as dowries, subsidies, alms, &c. These wealthy masses had been, perhaps, ill governed for so many centuries—The time of philosophical and political reforms was come, and it was thought better to amalgamate all these heterogeneous elements into one homogeneous body, to be administered by the court under the direction of the Minister. This attempt, however, was not carried into execution, as they were afraid that such an unjustifiable spoliation would unavoidably lead to a rebellion in the metropolis, and perhaps throughout the whole kingdom The only result was, that all these fiscal operations rendered the name of the Minister odious to bankers and merchants, as it already was to some other classes of the people.

The more, however, General Acton seemed guilty of misconduct, the more the Sovereign favoured him. In June, 1789, after the death of Marquis Caracciolo, he attached to his other appointments the vacant Ministry of Foreign Affairs. This is the date of his meridian grandeur, unrivalled in any period of the Monarchy of the Two Sicilies, even without excepting Admiral Majone and Ser Gianni Caracciolo. The French Revolution extended its effects—no one's mind was occupied on inferior objects, and much less towards a Minister governing an insignificant state. His operations are, therefore, buried under a mass of those events which have afflicted Europe. We cannot, however, help noticing, that in the year 1794, he was near exposing his Sovereign to an aggression from the Court of Sweden. Baron d'Armfeld, one of the chief conspirators against the Regent, Duke of Sudermania, had taken refuge in Naples. The Regent sent his agents there in order to claim him, and to seize him, with the permission of the Government. Mr. Acton not only denied the request, but helped the Baron to effect his flight through Apulia for Manfredonia, and from the latter place to Trieste. This behaviour exposed him to the Philippics of M. Piranesi, the Swedish Consul at Rome; however, in the end it proved favourable to him. For the matters between the two Courts being arranged, on condition that he should be displaced from the Ministry of Foreign Affairs, he was created First Minister and Counsellor of State, in which station he held all the other Ministers under the same dependence as before.

If we should give credit to certain public papers, his Sicilian Majesty, on his arrival at Palermo, had removed Mr. Acton from his Councils, into which he had taken the most eminent persons from among the Sicilian clergy, nobility, and magistracy.

Yet we are happy to state, that General Acton has never been convicted of rapacity; satisfied with the immense emoluments of his places, and with the generous and extraordinary bounties and pensions of his Master, he has never been suspected of enriching himself in an unlawful way!

General Acton is upwards of 60 years of age, tall, and thin, of a pale complexion, a forbidding look, a piercing eye, and remarkably serious and reserved in his conversation.

London, March 20, 1801.

ORIGINAL POETRY.

ANACREONTIC.

CARE, caitiff wretch! begone from me,
And let me gaily quaff my bowl;
Haste from my presence, quickly flee,
To joy alone I yield my soul.

My hours I dedicate to mirth,
Then "let the liquid ruby flow,"
Which gives to new ideas birth,
And bids the soul with rapture glow.

Supremely

Supremely bleſt while thus I quaff,
My mind in airy regions roves,
I ſport the ſong, the toaſt, the laugh,
And think of Venus and the Loves.
A. P.

THE following Eſſay is from the claſſical pen of Dr. Geddes; and the Tranſlation which accompanies it, from that of his friend Mr. Good.

IN OBITUM
HONESTISSIMI, INTEGERRIMI, MEIQUE AMICISSIMI VIRI,
DOMINI DE PETRE.

ERGONE abripuit mihi mors crudelis Amicum,
Dulce decus, columen præſidiumque meum!
Abripuit, medio vix lapſo temporis ævo
Quod dare terrigenis fata benigna ſolent.
Heu! heu! quam ſubitò mortalis labitur ætas;
Quam celeri greſſu Nex inopina venit!
Nex atrox! nulli parcens, et neſcia flecti!
Sic mihi delicias tu, truculenta! rapis?
Non Petri pietas, nec fervida vota ſuorum
Lethalem poterant jam cohibere manum!
Duræ adſunt Parcæ, truncantes ſtamina vitæ;
Nobilis ac animus corpus inane fugit.
Quam tibi tum fuerat, quam vivus, Julia, ſenſus;
Tali, tam juvenis, væ! viduata Viro?
Sed tibi ſunt caſti cariſſima pignora amoris;
Hæc tibi triſtitiæ dulce levamen erunt.
Qui dolor excrucians invaſit pectora Nati,
Cum Pater, ante oculos, jam moriturus erat!
Sed Nato eſt ſuavis conjux, ſuaviſſima proles:
Proles et conjux dulce levamen erunt.
Ast mihi mœroris non ullum eſt dulce levamen;
Fomento nullo plaga levanda mea!
Non mihi ſubridens *ſoboles*, ſon blanda *ſodalis*,
Quæ queat ærumnas extenuare meas.
Pro ſponſa, ſobole et, defunćto proque parente,
Inſtar cunćtorum, ſolus Amicus erat:
Solus amicus erat—ſed qualis?—non mihi Frater
Germanus tam, quam Petrus amatus erat!
Scilicet, Is, princeps, eſt me dignatus amare;
Et locuples, inopem me cumulare bonis.
Bis decies Phœbus cœleſtia ſigna peregit;
Ex quo permiſſum eſt ejus amore frui:
Sum ſemper fruitus, dum fallax vita manebat:
Noluit, ac moriens, non meminiſſe mei.
Illius alma manus, ſtudiorum fida meorum
Fautrix—his ſtudiis otia grata dedit.
Plangite, Pierides! et longos ducite planćtus:
Muſarum conſtans Petrus amicus erat.
Tu, tu, præcipuè, quæ carmina ſacra Zionis
Pangis, tu gemitus ingeminato meos.
Quis tua, nunc, memet veſtigia, Diva, legentem
Per vepres, feſſum quis relevare velit?
Me prope cum piguit tantos tolerare labores,
Dejećtos animos ſuſtulit ille meos.
Me cum mordaci lacerarent dente maligni,
Et contrà fremeret cæca ſuperſtitio;
"Putida tu ſperne illorum convicia (dixit)
"Cura tibi tantùm, perficiatur opus."
Ah! ſi, Te vivo, melior Fortuna dediſſet
Huic operi ſummo ſummam adhibere manum;
Et Tibi poſtremos, ut primos, Petre, labores
Sors mea donaſſet poſſe dicare meos:
Gaudia quæ? quanta ac eſſet mea pura voluptas?
Hoc deſiderii ſumma, caputque mei!
Aſt aliter viſum Superis—forteṁque ſubire
Convenit—at fletus quis prohibere poteſt?
Omnibus es flendus, queis notus, Petre, fuiſti:
Mî flendi finem non feret ulla dies.
Ah! quotiens ſubiit Dilecti dulcis imago,
Rugoſas tingunt flumina ſalſa genas!
Singultus tremuli ſpirantia viſcera pulſant;
Rodit et occultus mollia corda dolor!
Sed ſecura quies tua ſors! ſedeſque beatæ
Te capiunt—Fruere O! ſorte, Beate! tuâ.
Et, ſi res liceat quondoque agnoſcere noſtras,
Sis bonus—et nobis, qua pote, Petre, fave!
A. G.

Scribebam in lectulo, dolens et infirmus;
Prid. Non. Jul. 1801.

ELEGY,
ON THE DEATH OF THE RIGHT HON. LORD PETRE,
Tranſlated from the Original Latin of
DR. GEDDES.

HAS cruel Death, then, robbed me of my friend!
My guide, my guard, my firſt and deareſt boaſt!
Robbed—ere he ſcarce had half-way reached his end,
Had Heaven allowed the days allowed to moſt.
How ſwift, alas! this mortal being flies;
How eager Death his heedleſs prey to gain!
Dread Death! remorſeleſs! deaf to human ſighs!
Thou, barbarous! thou! who all my ſweets haſt ſlain.
Vain Petre's wiſhes; vain the holy ſtrife,
Of prayers profuſe, to ſave him from the dead.
The preſent fates, relentleſs, claimed his life,
And from the fleſh his generous ſpirit fled.

How

How, how severe, O Julia, then thy grief,
Widowed so young, so vast the loss sustained!
But in thy children shalt thou find relief;
These are thy balm, the pledge of love unfeigned.

What felt the son! how deep his filial groan
When the last pang he saw his father seize!
Yet wife beloved, yet offspring are his own;
And wife and offspring shall his wound appease.

But nought of balm does Heaven to me assign;
No solace sweet, with healing influence, flows:
No smiling infants, bland companion, mine,
With deeds of love to mitigate my woes.

Spouse, sire, companion—he was all to me;
Though but a friend:—a friend? yet, ah, how dear!
E'en with less joy my brother's face I see,
Less feels my heart affinity so near.

And well my utmost love did Petre claim,
Who, rich himself, my poverty endowed;
Twice ten times traced the Sun th' etherial frame,
While Heaven to me his tender love allowed:

'Twas mine perpetual—long as life remained;
Mine, e'en in death, till ceased his heart to beat;
His fostering hand, my studies that sustained,
Gave to those studies recreation sweet.

Weep, Muses! weep—long sighs your bosoms fill!
Patron of verse was Petre ever found:
But chiefly thou, O Muse of Zion-hill,
Groan with my groans, and loud our griefs resound.

Who now shall soothe me as my path I wind,
Thy footsteps following, through entangling briars?
When, faint, at times the task I half resigned,
He cheered my soul, and roused my latent fires.

When malice grinned, with fang so oft that daunts,
When bigots, blind, o'erflowed with frantic foam,
"Spurn, spurn," said he, "these vile opprobrious taunts,
"Care but for this—to close th' important tome."

Oh that, while Heaven allowed thee yet to be,
This utmost work my utmost hand had past;
That fate had given to dedicate to thee,
As my first labours, so alike my last:

What joy, what rapture had I then revealed!
This my chief wish, the summit of my prayer!
But Heaven denied:—to Heaven our hearts should yield,—
But who, meantime, from weeping can forbear?

All must bewail thee, Petre! all who knew;
For me, my sorrows never shall subside;
As the loved image of my friend I view,
Down my ploughed cheeks how flows the briny tide!

Deep, trembling sobs convulse my labouring breast,
And secret anguish every nerve corrodes,
But rest is thine—secure, unsullied rest,
The songs of angels, and their bright abodes,

Enjoy, blest saint! enjoy the sweets that flow!
Unmingled sweets, whose fountain ne'er shall fail!
And, if thy powers can reach to man below,
O stoop, benign—let friendship still prevail.

SONNET, TO HOPE,

(Suggested by the Perusal of HUGH TREVOR, *vol. iii, chap. 12.)*

SWEET Hope! that still with fond delusive dreams
Cheer'st the sad heart, surcharg'd with grief and care,
My anguish'd mind longs for those healing streams
Which flow from thee, and charm beyond compare.

Oh deign to visit then my lonely cell,
And breathe thy influence on my wearied soul;
Come, pleasing flatterer, and smiling tell,
That yet my hours in happiness shall roll:

That Fortune's copious tide again shall flow;
That friends shall smile, and enemies repent;
That as in years I shall in wisdom grow,
And find each moment crown'd with sweet content;

Tell me that yet OLIVIA shall be mine,
And let the blest illusion be divine.

A. P.

LINES,

ADDRESSED TO A FRIEND.

AH! what avails it that the face of day
Wears the bright verdure of returning spring?
On me, alas! it sheds no genial ray—
No soft sensations its approaches bring.

My cherish'd hopes are wither'd in their bloom,
And expectation is for ever seal'd;
My fairest joys have met an early tomb,
And all my prospects are alike repeal'd.

O! why fond memory didst thou ever dwell
On scenes more fickle than the showery bow?
Or why did hope my anxious bosom swell
With bliss I never was ordained to know?

Imagi-

Imagination to my fancy drew
  A profpect happy in its every fhade,
Illum'd with gaiety was every hue,
  And every beauty was unknown to fade.

But 'twas an imbecility of mind
  That gave admiffion to a vain defire,
That painted human happinefs combin'd
  With the pure effence of celeftial fire.

Had caution ftrove to limit the defign,
  And fram'd it, fubject to a cloudy fky,
Serenity, at leaft, had then been mine,
  'Till taught by reafon forrow to defy:

Perhaps, Eliza, thy fuperior aid,
  Thy ready counfel and thy precepts wife,
Thy valued friendfhip in its truth array'd,
  And void of every fpecies of difguife—

Perhaps by thefe I may be taught to know,
  The calm ceffation that from virtue flows,
Perhaps thy dictates may relieve my woe,
  And guide my ruffled fpirits to repofe.

SONNET,

Tranflated from the Italian of SANNAZARIUS.

FALSE fleeting hopes and vain defires fare-
    well;
  Fond anxious wifhes that within my breaft
With fighs and unavailing anguifh dwell,
  Leave me, O leave me, to my wonted reft.

O, if oblivion on my troubled mind
  His gently foothing balm will ne'er beftow,
In death, at leaft, a refuge let me find,
  And with my being lofe the fenfe of woe.

Now let the fates their utmoft vengeance
    pour,
  Secure, their utmoft vengeance I defy;
Nor can affliction's darkeft gloomieft hour
  E'er from my bofom force another figh:

Nor Love himfelf another pang impart,
To deepen the defpair that rends my tortured
    heart. J. B.

PROCEEDINGS OF LEARNED SOCIETIES.

NATIONAL INSTITUTE OF FRANCE.

NOTICE *of the* LABOURS *of the* CLASS *of* MATHEMATICAL *and* PHYSICAL SCIENCES *during the fecond Quarterly Sitting of the* YEAR 9.

MATHEMATICAL PART.

CITIZEN LALANDE has read a notice *on the longitude of Alexandria in Egypt*; which he has determined by an emerfion of the ftar Antares, compared with the complete obfervation of the fame eclipfe, made at Marfeilles, by Citizen THULIS, affociate member of the Inftitute. It refults from this datum that the difference of the meridians is 1° 50′ 25″; which differs very little from that which Citizens NOUET and QUENOT had eftablifhed; thus, therefore, the pofition of this point appears to be now well known.

Citizen PRONY has read a notice on *large trigonometrical decimal tables*, calculated on the cadaftre or regifter, under his direction, by a method entirely new, and which had this advantage, that an indefinite number of calculators might be employed by it at once, from the moft of whom no other knowledge could be required than that of addition and fubtraction. The clafs having nominated commiffaries to render a detailed account of this extremely important work, important from its extent as well as from the care which has been applied in the execution, has heard with much intereft a report on the fubject, which it adopted, and which it ordered to be printed, in the notice of its labours, during the quarter juft finifhed.

Citizen DESFONTAINES has communicated to the clafs fome interefting details on the culture of the bread-fruit-tree.—This valuable tree, *Artocarpus incifa*, belongs to the family of *urtica*, and has much affinity with the genus of mulberry-tree. Its organs of fructification are well known, and have been accurately defcribed by FORSTER and other botanifts. It is to Citizens LABILLARDIERE and LAHAYE, in the colonies, that France is indebted for them. On their return from the voyage in fearch of La Peyroufe, they depofited feveral live fhoots of it in the Ifle of France, which they had brought from the Friendly Iflands; and we have lately learned, by a letter from Citizen MARTIN, director of the colonial nurferies in French Guiana, that the plant fent thither from France three years ago, fucceeds perfectly well, that it has multiplied, and is on the point of flowering, and that, in all probability, it will produce fruit in the courfe of this year. We muft not confound the bread-tree of the Friendly Iflands with the wild fpecies that grows in the Moluccas, and which we have already poffeffed for fome time in many of our colonies, although the one be only a variety of the other. Every full grown plant of the wild bread-fruit [illegible] bears above thirty or forty [illegible] are, at the same time, much smaller, less succulent, filled with large kernels, and difficult to digest. The variety in the Friendly Islands produces from three to four hundred, which succeed one another on the same tree during eight months of the year. They are of an oval form, and are about three decimetres in length, by two in breadth. The seeds, which all prove abortive, are replaced by a savory and very nourishing pulp. This abortion is, doubtless, owing to the practice which they have had from time immemorial, in the Friendly Islands, of multiplying these trees by shoots, which equally happens to many other plants, such as the ananas, the banana tree, &c. which they propagate in the same manner. The fruit of the bread-tree is the principal food of the inhabitants of the Friendly Islands, and of many other tribes in the South Sea Islands. It is eaten, baked under the ashes, and in water. According to Citizen Labillardière, it is much preferable to the *ignames*, or yams, and this naturalist assures us that the crews of the two vessels sent in search of La Peyrouse, voluntarily gave up the biscuit, and a small portion of good fresh bread, which was distributed to them every day, to live on the apples of the bread-fruit-tree, during a month of their stopping at the Friendly Islands. The English government has so well known the importance of this tree, that it has ordered two successive expeditions for the sole purpose of procuring it to enrich their colonies with it. The bread-fruit-tree might be cultivated to advantage in Egypt, and perhaps it would be possible to naturalize it in Corsica and in our southern departments; it grows under the same latitude as the paper mulberry tree *(murier à paper)* which resists the rigour of our winter.

Citizen Tessier has presented an account of the condition of the flock of Choisi, purchased by our late fellow member, Gilbert, in Spain, and now established in a national *bergerie*, at Perpignan. From the comparison he has made of the animals of this flock with that of Rambouillet, the original flock of which was brought into France, in 1786, it results that sheep of the same age and same sex, of the flock of Rambouillet, are larger sized, better shaped, and have a longer and a better furnished wool, although as fine as that of the flock of Perpignan, or, which is the same thing, as that of the flocks of Spain. Citizen Tessier concludes, from hence, that the race, far from having degenerated in our climate, has acquired perfection in it, an important truth, since it assures to us a means of prosperity for our agriculture and our manufactures.

The use of the tubercles or those kinds of calluses, vulgarly called *chataigne* and *ergots* in horses, has been hitherto unknown: Citizen Lafosse, an associate member, is convinced, from the anatomical researches he has made on this subject, that they serve to give attachment to the aponeuroses of the portion of the muscle which covers the cuticular limbs. He has likewise discovered that there exsudes from it a fat and strong-scented humour; and as he has found calluses, nearly similar, in different parts of the legs of other animals, he thinks it probable that the scent of the humour which they produce is that which directs dogs and other carnivorous animals in pursuit of their prey.

For a long time is has been admitted that the class of worms established by Linnæus, comprehended beings very dissimilar, and that his subdivision was not conformable to the analogy of the organization of the different species. The author of the present notice having long laboured on this object, proposed a general distribution of white-blooded animals, founded on their anatomy; he divided them into five classes, the molusca, crustaceous, insects, worms, and zoophites, which he reduced afterwards to three, and subdivided them into many orders: but it was yet far from being a compleat system of these animals which ought to comprehend their genera and species. Citizen Lamark has been lately occupied with a part of this labour, that which concerns the genera. After having discriminated two new classes, the *arachnides* and the *radiarii*, of the five first established, he subdivides one part of these classes in a particular manner, and afterwards forms genera so numerous and so well determined, that there no longer remains any ambiguity in their characters; this valuable labour leaves us only to desire the determination of the species, Citizen Lamarck only citing under each of his genera a part of those which are related to it. This work is the best proof that no one is more capable than he of successfully employing himself in what remains to be done, in order to terminate the methodical arrangement of this important part of the animal kingdom.

The memoir of Citizen Boucher, an associate member, which has for its object a marine bird, called *Grand Fou*, is not susceptible of extract. It is sufficient to say that it describes, in detail, all that concerns the forms and the habits of that species.

The history of minerals by Buffon is one of those works which the discoveries of late years rendered antique, in spite of the immortal charms of his style. Citizen PATRIN, charged with this part for one of the editions now publishing of the Natural history, has been obliged to make an entire new book of it; he there examines minerals principally with relation to the place which they occupy in the great edifice of the globe, to their order, in respect of antiquity, to the materials which compose them, and to those which accompany them: he gives the analysis and the description of each species, and indicate its uses in the arts and medicine.—What give a merit quite particular to this work, are the new and interesting facts, with which the extensive travels of the author have enabled him to enrich it.

MONTHLY RETROSPECT OF THE FINE ARTS.

(Communications and the Loan of all new Prints are requested.)

WE in a former Retrospect noticed that Bromley's engraving, from Loutherbourg's very fine picture of the Siege of Valenciennes, was in a forward state. It is now finished, and every subscriber who is a judge of the arts, will think the time he has waited for the completion of the work, amply compensated in the uncommonly masterly and spirited style in which it is executed; for, without at all derogating from the merit of other works, it is indisputably superior to any engraving, on a similar subject, that has hitherto appeared in this country. To take off the necessary number of impressions will be a work of some months; that done, it will be published for Cribb, Holborn, &c. Price to subscribers, common impressions, 3l. 3s. proofs, 5l. 5s.

Mr. Loutherbourg went to Valenciennes a short time after it was in the possession of the combined forces, to take a view of the ruins, the entrenchments, &c. so that this may be considered as a very faithful representation of the place. Mr. Gillray accompanied him in his tour, and took the portraits of the most distinguished officers, Austrian, &c. that were engaged in the siege, and thus there is every probability of the portraits being resemblances.

In subjects where force and spirit are requisite, where action and energy are the leading features in the merit of a picture, and where the scenery is diversified by a number of figures combined in one great action, and busily aiming at one great end, Mr. Loutherbourg is unrivalled. In the picture from which this is engraved he has exerted all his powers; and it is highly to the honour of Mr. Bromley, that he has transferred the spirit of the master from the canvas to his copper.

The group on the dexter-side of the picture, composed of his Royal Highness the Duke of York, and the English officers, is well balanced by a party of German officers on the opposite side; among the latter, several Hungarians, and three or four Pandours, with fierce and savage visages, and *bearded like the pard*, form a striking contrast to the rest of the troops. One of these ferocious personages has a pair of pistols and a dagger stuck in his girdle. This, we are informed, is the portrait of an officer whose conversation was wholly made up of a narrative of the bloody battles in which he had been engaged, and of the multitudes whom he had slain with *his red right-hand.*

Two or three bearded soldiers reclining on the foreground in the front, have an admirable effect: one of them has a short pipe in his mouth, and, it seems, belongs to an Austrian regiment, who never go to battle without this appendage; and who, except when eating, drinking, or sleeping, are always smoking.

The horses are admirably drawn and properly discriminated; from the spirited chargers of the Duke of York and his Royal Brother, and the German general officers, to the strong-built animals that draw the artillery. The foreground is extremely rich, and admirably broken, and the view of the blazing ruins of the city has a more awful and impressive effect than we have often witnessed in a print. As far as we recollect, a large portion of the merit of the original picture was comprised in the colouring; and though that seems a branch of excellence which cannot be transferred to the copper, yet the brilliancy and spirit with which this is engraved, gives an idea, and a very strong idea, of Mr. Loutherbourg's peculiarly splendid tints. In this, and other particulars, Mr. Bromley has evinced uncommon skill and knowledge of his profession;

fession; and taken as a whole, it may be fairly classed as one of the finest specimens of the graphic art, that has ever been produced. It brought to our recollection some of the very best views of sea-ports, engraved after the fine designs by Vernet,—but the figures in this are upon a much larger scale, and the style of engraving is infinitely more forcible. Admitting that the proofs of the Death of General Wolfe are worth the immense sums for which they have been repeatedly sold, it is not easy to say what sum a proof of this very fine piece of art will produce, after the lapse of a few years. A key-plate will be engraved and delivered to the purchasers, and subscribers, or in a future Retrospect the portraits shall be enumerated.

His Majesty Reviewing the Volunteer Corps assembled in Hyde Park in honour of the Birthday, June 4, 1799. Drawn and etched by R. Smirke, jun. Aqua tinta, by R. Earlom. Published by Messrs. Boydell, Shakespeare Gallery, and Cheapside. Size, 36 by 26. Price, plain, 1l. 11s. 6d. In colours, 4l. 4s.

This is a very accurate and pleasing representation of the different corps that were assembled on this occasion; the companies are distinguished by various colours, which are explained in a key-plate, and the innumerable little figures with which the print is peopled, are drawn with a vigour and effect that does great honour to the young artist who designed and etched it. They have a large portion of the spirit and fire of Callot. The part which has been alotted to Mr. Earlom, is executed with a judgment that marks all his productions, and greatly adds to the general effect, which, in the coloured impressions, is equal to a drawing.

The Battle of Copenhagen. N. Pocock, Esq. del. Stadler, sculpt. Published by R. Ackermann, No. 101, Strand. Drawn from a Sketch, made by R. Kittors, Esq. Secretary to the Admiral. Prints, 1l. 6s. Proofs, 2l. 2s. In colours, 2l. 12s. 6d.

The drawing from which this print is copied, was, previous to its being engraved, submitted to the inspection of Admiral Graves, R. Kittors, esq. and the principal officers who were in the engagement, and they all concurred in acknowledging it to be a perfectly correct representation of the places, the order of the ships, and the line of battle. It has, during its progress, been honoured by a most respectable list of subscribers, among whom we mark Lord Nelson, Admiral Graves, Earl Spencer, Earl of Liverpool, and most of the officers that were in the action.

In an island whose naval superiority is its pride, glory, and best defence, a representation of such scenes as tend to the honour of those gallant spirits, whose prowess has obtained, and still preserves, that superiority, is a very proper subject for the pencil. Marine-painting, by this means becomes, in a degree, historical and biographical, and at the same time that it commemorates our victories, is an honourable monument to the memory of those heroes who have fallen for their country. Much of the merit of such representations depends upon the fidelity with which they are executed; and in point of accuracy, this print is, by all who have seen it, acknowledged to have every claim to praise. Size of the print, 30½ inches, by 20½.

The Milk-maid. W. Pearce, pinx. Charles Turner, sculpt. Published January 1st, 1801, by S. Morgan, Margaret-street, Cavendish-square.

This print is well engraved in mezzotinto, but the very essence of designs of this description, lies in their simplicity, and proper selection of nature; and in those particulars we cannot say much in its favour. The girl has a vulgar character, and the cattle are not well drawn.

Lord Keith. Painted by Danloux, and engraved by S. W. Reynolds. Published by Danloux, Charles-street, Middlesex Hospital. Price, 1l. 1s.

Previous to the time of Sir Joshua Reynolds, the portraits of our Statesmen, Generals, or Admirals, were, with few exceptions, drawn in attitudes so similar, and with countenances so little appropriate to their characters, that though we had a tolerable correct *map of the face*, yet, unless we knew the points by which the man was distinguished, little was found to denote his employment, except the truncheon, the flowing periwig, or the long robe.

It was the glory of our late lamented President, (in his latter portraits especially), to take the peculiar turn of feature which was most favourable to the leading circumstances that had marked the character of the man he delineated; and by adding to this some little accompaniment, he frequently rendered his picture, in a degree, historical. This is strongly exemplified in his portrait of the late Lord Heathfield, firmly grasping the key of the

the fortress he so long, and so ably defended.

Since the death of this great Artist, Sir William Beechey, and some of our first-rate painters have displayed a portion of his spirit; but the mass of them have invariably drawn figures that seem *sitting for their pictures*. In this portrait that common and glaring error is avoided, for the figure is put in action, and in an action very naturally and well-chosen; it represents him in the engagement at the Cape of Good Hope, and is intended as a companion to that of Admiral Lord Duncan, and is extremely well engraved in mezzotinto.

A Series of highly-finished Engravings from Shakespeare's Seven Ages of Man, by Mr. W. Bromley, from Designs, by Mr. Stothard, R. A. accompanied with Descriptions, Historical, Moral, and Entertaining. By an eminent Literary Character. Published in Four Numbers, Price 7s. 6d. each, by H. D. Symonds, Paternoster-row.

This very beautiful work, which we ought to have noticed in a former Number, consists of seven exquisitely fine engravings, eleven and half inches, by eight, characteristic of the Seven Ages of Man, and a highly finished vignette, evidently taken from Pope's Essay. Without entering, at large, into the merits of each plate, all of which are done in a very superior style, we cannot help recommending, to public notice, the *School boy*, in the first Number; and the picture of *Second Childishness*, in the last, as two of the finest pieces of composition we have seen; the tardiness of the former, in his road to school, and the debility of the latter, "sans teeth, sans eyes, sans taste, sans every thing," cannot fail of leaving deep impressions in the mind of every spectator of the taste and execution of the artists. The illustrations are well adapted to the different subjects: as an introduction, the commentator has traced the different authors of Antiquity, as well as those of more modern times, who have divided the round of human existence into separate ages.

The other plates are illustrated by historical observations and by quotations from ancient and modern Poets. In contemplating the second period of life, the author has, we think, successfully combated the common notion, that childhood is the happiest part of mortal existence, and has thrown out hints for the improvement of that part of education which is devoted to the attainment of the dead languages. The *lover* is illustrated principally by references to Anacreon, Horace, and our own Poet, Thomson. In the two next scenes he has made Shakespeare his commentator, and has shewn that the description of the soldier was evidently taken from the character of Hotspur. The observations on *old-age* and *childishness*, are highly appropriate to the impressions naturally excited in every feeling breast by Mr. Bromley's plates. They are such as tend to awaken the tenderest emotions of the human heart; to inculcate filial piety in the young towards those in declining years, and to excite and encourage patience and chearfulness, and at that period of life when old-age and infirmities disqualify a man for the active scenes of the world. The whole work is executed in a manner that is highly creditable to the present improved state of the Fine Arts in this country.

Four Prints, engraved from Designs, by Mrs. Cosway, from the Ballad in Indigestion, which was sung by Mrs. Jordan. The Words by Mrs. Plowden. Published by Ackermann, No. 101, Strand. Price, 3s. 6d. each. Coloured, 7s. each.

This must be considered as exhibiting a sort of *trio* of female genius. The designs are from the following verses, divided into four parts, two lines to each.

"I rise with the morn, I gaze on the sun,
Aurora's bright lustre I see;
But I sigh with regret when day-light is gone,
For night brings no comfort to me.

I wander at night where the nightingales sing;
I traverse the sands of the sea;
They hear not my sighs, so no comfort they bring,
For what can bring comfort to me."

These prints are neatly engraved; the first, by *Mirian*, represents a female figure, recumbent on the ground and gazing on the rising sun, while a figure of Aurora, of Guido's family, is flying and scattering flowers in the air. The second is by *Cardon*, and represents a female leaning on a rock, with the ocean in the distance, and a figure of night throwing out her sable-robe. The third, engraved by *Delatre* is a moonlight scene; on the sands of the sea, beaten by the surge, an elegant female is represented as flying from the tempestuous scene. The fourth, and last is by *Cardon*, and exhibits a female in apparent grief, leaning upon a rock, and wringing her hands. The attitude of this figure is expressive, but borders on the extravagant, and though it may, on the whole,

whole, be correct in the drawing, the quantity of hair, and disposition of the drapery, give the head an appearance of being too large for the body. The prints, considered as a whole, are poetically conceived, and by the admirers of Ossian, will be considered as *chef d'œuvres* of art: by the admirers of easy and flowing versification, they may possibly be thought rather overcharged.

On the first of September Mr. RIEBAU proposes to publish, at 10s. 6d. No. I. of *Views on the Paddington Canal*, containing two plates, in *aqua tinta*, and handsomely coloured. The 1st View is from the Entrance at the Bason, with the Warehouses now erecting, and the Passengers Setting-off in the Packet-boat. The 2d plate is a View of the Grand Procession at the Opening, on the 10th of July.

Mr. VANDENBERGHE has issued proposals for publishing, by subscription, two prints, from a much-admired picture from Liss's Collection at Antwerp, painted by Dietricy, and mentioned by Sir Joshua Reynolds in his works; the subject of which represents Diana and the Shepherdess. The companion, (painted by the same Master), represents Nymphs Bathing; which will be ready for delivery in the month of February, 1802. The size of the prints, 29 inches in length, by 22 inches in height; and the price to subscribers, 5l. 5s.; of proof-impressions, 10l. 10s.

VARIETIES, LITERARY AND PHILOSOPHICAL.

Including Notices of Works in Hand, Domestic and Foreign.

*** *Authentic Communications for this Article will always be thankfully received.*

DR. BEDDOES has announced for publication, on Monday, November the second, the first number of *a Series of Essays on Health*. A number to appear on the first day of every month, till the work is compleated; the price of each number not to be below *One Shilling*, nor above *Two Shillings*; the number of Essays not to fall short of *Twelve*, nor to exceed *Sixteen*.

Mr. PRATT's pen is at this time employed on a subject the most interesting to the community. It is on a poem, intitled BREAD; or, the POOR; addressed to the RICH; a theme worthy the Muse of "Sympathy." It is expected to make its appearance at the close of the month.

The second volume of Miss EDGEWORTH's Moral Tales for Young People is just finished.

Mr. BOYD, the translator of DANTE's INFERNO, is now employed upon a translation of the ARAUCANA, in which he has made considerable progress.

The third and fourth volumes of the Scientific Dialogues are now in the press, and will be published in the course of the next month. These volumes will contain complete, but very familiar, introductions to the sciences of hydrostatics and pneumatics, illustrated by a great variety of experiments, and eight plates by Mr. LOWRY. The whole work will be finished in the course of a few months, and will comprise a complete system of natural and experimental philosophy and chemistry, adapted to the use of young people.

A second edition of Mr. HENRY's Epitome of Chemistry is now ready: the first was sold off in a few days.

Dr. WILLAN has just completed the second order of his Description and Treatment of Cutaneous Diseases. This order contains scaly diseases of the skin, and is illustrated with thirteen coloured plates.

Mr. T. CLIO RICKMAN has in the press two volumes of Poems, which he intends to publish at a subscription of half a guinea.

Dr. R. HALL has completed a translation of MORVEAU's recent Treatise upon the Means of Purifying Infected Air, Preventing Contagion, &c. &c.

The proprietors of the libraries at BATH have, with great justice and propriety, advanced their terms to half a crown per week, a crown per month, half a guinea per quarter, and one guinea per annum. An advance in the terms of subscription to circulating-libraries, book-societies, and public-libraries, is rendered indispensible by the new duty upon paper, and the consequent advance in the price of new publications. To keep pace with the price of paper and that of books, the subscriptions ought universally to be increased creafed one half, and we are confident lovers of literature are too liberal not to acquiefce in a meafure fo reafonable.

The Winter Courfe of Lectures at the MEDICAL SCHOOL of ST. THOMAS's and GUY's HOSPITALS will commence in the following order:—*Anatomy and Surgery*, by Mr. CLINE and Mr. ASTLEY COOPER, on Thurfday, October 1, at one o'clock —*Practice of Medicine*, by Dr. BABINGTON, on Friday, October 2, at ten o'clock in the morning—*Midwifery, and Difeafes of Women and Children*, by Dr. LOWDER and Dr. HAIGHTON, on Saturday, October 3, at eight in the morning—*Chemiftry and Experimental Philofophy*, by Dr. BABINGTON and the Rev. Mr. ROBERTS, on the fame morning, at ten—*Phyfiology, or Laws of the Animal Economy*, by Dr. HAIGHTON, on Monday, October 5, at a quarter before feven in the evening—*Theory of Medicine, and Materia Medica*, by Dr. CURRY, on Tuefday, October 6, at feven in the evening—*Principles and Practice of Surgery*, (illuftrated by felect cafes, under his care, in the hofpital) by Mr. ASTLEY COOPER, on Monday, October 12, at eight in the evening—In addition to thefe, Dr. SAUNDERS will, early in October, begin *A Courfe of Clinical Lectures on Select Medical Cafes*, under his care, in the hofpital.——N. B. The Lectures given at thefe hofpitals are fo arranged, that no two of them interfere with each other in the hours of attendance; and the whole is calculated to form a complete circle of Medical Inftruction. Terms, and other particulars, to be had at the hofpitals, or of Mr. Cox, bookfeller, St. Thomas's-ftreet, Southwark.

At the Medical Theatre, LONDON HOSPITAL, the Lectures on Anatomy, Phyfiology, and the Principles and Operations of Surgery, with Practical Anatomy, as ufual, will commence on the 1ft of October, by Mr. BLIZARD, Mr. J. BLIZARD, and Mr. HEADINGTON, Surgeons of the hofpital.

The following Courfes of Lectures will be delivered at the Medical Theatre, ST. BARTHOLOMEW's HOSPITAL, during the enfuing feafon: on the *Theory and Practice of Medicine*, by Dr. ROBERTS—*On Anatomy and Phyfiology*, by Mr. ABERNETHY—*On Comparative Anatomy*, by Mr. MACARTNEY—*On the Theory and Practice of Surgery*, by Mr. ABERNETHY—*On Chemiftry and the Materia Medica*, by Dr. POWELL—*On Midwifery, and the Difeafes of Women and Children*, by Dr. THYNNE.

Dr. DENNISON and Dr. SQUIRE, Phyficians and Men-midwives to the Lying-in Charity for delivering Poor Women at their own Habitations, early in the month of October, will begin a Courfe of Lectures on the Theory and Practice of Midwifery, and the Difeafes of Women and Children. In addition to a conftant fupply of labours, for practical improvement, gentlemen will have frequent opportunities of vifiting patients in diforders during pregnancy, and the advantages of feeing the treatment of difeafes incident to the ftate of child-birth and early infancy.

Dr. BATTY's Lectures on Midwifery will commence, at his houfe, in Marlborough-ftreet, on Monday, October 5, at eleven in the morning.

Dr. BRADLEY will commence his Autumnal Courfe of Lectures on the Theory and Practice of Medicine, on Monday, October the 5th, at the Lecture-room, No. 101, Leadenhall ftreet, at fix in the afternoon. The Courfe will confift of about feventy Lectures. Terms, three guineas. Private Courfes, for the accommodation of young Surgeons in the Navy or Army, are continued every morning at Dr. Bradley's, Delahay ftreet, Weftminfter.

M. CHEVALIER, Surgeon to the Weftminfter General Difpenfary, will commence his Autumnal Courfe of Lectures on the Principles and Operations of Surgery, on Monday, the 5th of October, at feven o'clock in the evening, at his houfe, No. 20, South Audley-ftreet, Grofvenor fquare, where a printed plan of the Courfe may be had, or at the Difpenfary, in Gerrard-ftreet, Soho.

Mr. PEARSON, Surgeon of the Lock Hofpital and Afylum, and of the Public Difpenfary, will begin his Autumnal Courfe of Lectures on the Principles and Practice of Surgery, on Monday, October the 5th, at feven o'clock in the evening. In this Courfe he will deliver an extenfive Account of the Hiftory and Treatment of Scrofula and Lues Venerea.

Dr. OSBORN's and Dr. CLARKE's Lectures on the Principles and Practice of Midwifery, and the Difeafes of Women and Children, will begin on Friday, October 2, at half paft ten in the morning, and they will be given in future only at Dr. Clarke's houfe, New Burlington-ftreet.

On the 5th day of October, Mr. T. POLE will commence his Courfe of Lectures

tures on the Theory and Practice of Midwifery, including the Diseases of Women and Children, at his house, No. 102, Leadenhall street, near the Royal Exchange, where printed particulars may be had.

At the Theatre of Anatomy, Great Windmill-street, two Courses of Lectures are read by Mr. WILSON during the Winter and Spring Seasons; one Course beginning on the 2d day of October, and terminating on the 18th Day of January; the other Course beginning on the 19th Day of January, and terminating towards the Middle of May. In each Course is explained the Structure of every Part of the Human Body, so as to exhibit a Complete View of its Anatomy, as far as it has been hitherto investigated; to which are added, its Physiology and Pathology; after which follow Lectures on the Operations of Surgery; and the Course concludes with the Anatomy of the Gravid Uterus. A Lecture is given daily from two until four o'clock in the afternoon. A room is likewise open for Dissections, under the direction of Mr. WILSON and Mr. THOMAS, from nine o'clock in the morning till two in the afternoon, from the 10th day of October till the 20th of April; where regular and full demonstrations of the Parts dissected are given; where the different Cases in Surgery are explained, the Methods of Operating shewn on the Dead Body; and where also the various Arts of Injecting and making Preparations are taught. Further particulars may be known, by applying to Mr. Wilson, at the Anatomical Theatre; or at his house, in Argyll-street, Hanover-square; or to Mr. Thomas, Leicester-square.

On Monday, October 12, Dr. CRICHTON will commence his Autumnal Course of Lectures on Medicine and Chemistry, at his Lecture-room, in Clifford-street, Bond-street. The Lectures on the Theory and Practice of Physic will be delivered every morning (Sundays excepted) at eight o'clock, those on Chemistry every Monday, Wednesday, and Friday, at nine; and those on Materia Medica every Tuesday, Thursday, and Saturday, at the same hour. Further particulars may be obtained by applying to Dr. Crichton, at his house, No. 15, Clifford street.

The Medical Lectures in the University of Glasgow will begin on Tuesday, the 3d of November, at the following hours:—*Dieteticks, Materia Medica, and Pharmacy*, by Dr. MILLAR, at ten o'clock in the forenoon — *Midwifery*, by Mr. TOWERS, at eleven—*Theory and Practice of Physic*, by Dr. FREER, at twelve—*Anatomy and Surgery*, by Dr. JEFFRAY, at two o'clock in the afternoon—*Chemistry and Chemical Pharmacy*, by Dr. CLEGHORN; at seven—*Clinical Lectures on the Cases of Patients in the Royal Infirmary*, by Dr. FREER and Dr. CLEGHORN. The first Lecture by Dr. Freer, on Thursday, the 12th of November, at six o'clock in the evening—Dr. BROWN will begin his Lectures on Botany, about the beginning of May next.

Citizen GEOFFROY, of the National Institute of Egypt, in a second journey which he has made to Sakkara, has been particularly employed in the study of the less apparent catacombs. He has observed some wells of but little depth, which only terminate in a very small cavity, and some excavations still less considerable, appropriated to the indigent. Their bodies, penetrated with bitumen, were enveloped in their mantles made of the same woollen stuff as the Felahhs now make use of; branches of date tree were placed in the folds of this stuff, and stalks of maize or Indian wheat formed the last covering; the whole was fixed by cords of date tree. This rude mummy was deposited in a fosse cut out of the rock; and the stones proceeding from this excavation, were laid in a heap on the body and cemented together with a fine plaster. The naturalist whose observations are here reported and abridged, was afterwards convinced that the catacombs of Memphis have all been as much explored by digging as those of Thebes. There are found on the surface of the rock, and buried under the sands which the winds have since carried there, mummies extracted from the subterranean galleries, different small figures, that of the Typhon, particularly pottery-ware, some of which are of elegant forms, and like the vases of Herculaneum, small masses of natron, carefully and curiously wrapt up in linen, gums, bitumens, and leaves transpierced by cords of palm-tree and disposed in the form of chaplets.

It appears from a report communicated to the Lyceum of Arts at Paris, on the *Rheum Palmatum*, a root imported into France, by Citizen COSTE, that this species of rhubarb is preferable to what is usually vended in commerce. The utility of this importation has been completely demonstrated. The Lyceum has decreed a medal and a crown to the importer.

It appears from a paper read at the private sitting of the Free Society of Sciences, Letters

Letters and Arts of Paris, by Citizen Bouvyer des Mortiers, that an individual, whoſe name is not mentioned, had made for ſale, a pretty large quantity of blue for painting, with a mixture of ceruſe, Pruſſian-blue, and oil of walnuts. He covered it up with water ſeveral inches to prevent its deſiccation, and laid it by till occaſion ſhould require it. After a certain time, ſome one calling on him in want of this paint, he was very much ſurpriſed to find it all white, except the ſurface, the colour of which was well preſerved. He was inclined to put ſome Pruſſian blue into the paint, when, by grinding or mixing it in the open air without addition, he ſaw the colour come again of itſelf, and in effect, by this operation he reſtored it to its former intenſity. He then covered it again with oil, imagining that it would keep better than under water. But his expectation was diſappointed, as the colour diſappeared a ſecond time, throughout the whole maſs. The Society of Medicine and Arts at Nantes, to which ſome of this diſcoloured and very white paint was brought, cauſed ſome to be ſtretched on white paper, upon wood, and on the wall of a caſement, and in a ſpace of time longer or ſhorter, the colour appeared again in its luſtre; that of the white paper was the ſloweſt in its regeneration. Here Citizen Le Bouvyer inquires what is the cauſe of this phenomenon? Is it the oil, which, by changing, diſcolours the Pruſſian-blue? Is it the air in maſs, or ſome one of its principal conſtituents, or any other ſubſtance found to be mingled or diſſolved in it, which recalls the colour? To theſe queſtions the author of the paper attempts to reply, by publiſhing the different intereſting experiments which he has made on this ſubject, and from which he deduces the following reſults: 1. That the diſcolouration of the paint is not owing to the decompoſition of the oil, but to the change of ſurfaces occaſioned by the retreat of the matter upon itſelf, and by the extinction of the luminous globules in the ſmall laminæ and in the pores of the colouring ſubſtance: 2. That neither the air in maſs nor any of its conſtituent principles, nor any thing contained in it, is neceſſary to regenerate the colour, ſince it is regenerated as well in vacuo as in the open air: 3. That caloric, without the contact of light, impedes the return of the colour, inſtead of contributing to it, and even deſtroys it: And, laſtly, that the interior movement of the parts, in whatever manner it be excited, and the action of the light, are ſufficient to re-produce the colour more or leſs rapidly, according as there is more or leſs of light and of movement.

Cit. Bernard preſented to the ſame aſſembly the copy and demonſtration of a machine of his own invention, by the help of which a man deprived of one hand may cut a pen.

Citizen Geoffroy, of the National Inſtitute of Egypt, has in his poſſeſſion three mummies, extremely well preſerved. They have been taken from the ſubterranean reſearches made at Sakkara, and are the firſt that have been found entire ſince the arrival of the French in Egypt. Each is incloſed in a coffer of ſycamore-wood, which is itſelf incloſed in ſeveral folds of linen wrapper, glued together; two of the coffers are ſculptured, the third is without ornaments in relievo, and the wrapper of this laſt is covered with hieroglyphics. In another mummy the hieroglyphics are deſigned on the wooden coffer which is tapeſtried with fine pointed linen, and the outer fold of linen is only covered with inſignificant paintings, which, however, have preſerved all their luſtre and freſhneſs. Citizen Geoffroy propoſes to depoſit his mummies, as likewiſe the great collection of which they make a part, in the Muſeum of Natural Hiſtory and Antiquities of Paris. The profeſſor, it is added, ſpares neither care nor expence, to procure and preſerve objects, the acquiſition of which may be uſeful to the progreſs of Natural Hiſtory.

We learn that the ſeveral departments of the *Bibliothèque Françoiſe*, a periodical, critical work, conducted by Charles Pougens, are filled by the following eminent perſons: Natural Hiſtory, Chemiſtry, and Surgery, by Berthollet, Desmarets, Labillardiere, Lassus, Members of the Inſtitute; Fortin, d'Urban, &c. Political and Rural Economy, by Tessier, of the Inſtitute, Legiſlation, &c. Delamalle, Juriſconſulte; P. Ustery. Hiſtory, Antiquities, and Travels, by Langles, Laporte-Dutheil, Leblond, E. Toulongeon, Members of the Inſtitute; Chardon la Rochette, P. H. Marron, &c. Philoſophy, Literature, Poetry, Romances, &c. by Boufflers, Segur; Meſdames Beaufort, d'Haussoul, Henriette Bourdie Viot, Louise St. Leon, Helen Maria Williams, &c.

The following is a general and comparative reſult of the bills of mortality of Cairo, during the years VII. and VIII. of the new French æra, preſented to the National

tional Institute of Egypt, by Citizen DES-GENETTES, on the 1st of Nivose, year IX.

Year VII.

Months.	Men.	Women.	Children.	Total.
Vendemiaire 29 and 30 Brumaire - .	2	5	10	17
Frimaire -	67	96	138	301
Nivose -	62	101	198	361
Pluviose -	97	102	197	396
Ventose -	98	139	253	490
Germinal -	103	152	263	518
Floreal -	116	139	320	575
Prairial -	71	138	330	539
Messidor -	91	148	365	604
Thermidor	96	118	517	731
Fructidor -	81	132	404	617
Complementary Days -	14	29	76	119
Total -	898	1299	3071	5268

Year VIII.

Months.	Men.	Women.	Children.	Total.
Vendemiaire -	113	112	325	550
Brumaire -	99	147	380	626
Frimaire -	128	171	564	863
Nivose -	102	160	813	1075
Pluviose -	77	117	499	693
Ventose -	7	7	37	51
Germinal -				
Floreal -	71	86	117	274
Prairial -	122	167	285	574
Messidor -	107	163	197	467
Thermidor -	83	133	128	344
Fructidor -	76	92	143	311
Complementary Days -	18	21	28	67
Total -	1003	1376	3516	5895

The tables of the year VII. were only commenced on the 29th of Brumaire; and the circumstances of the siege, in the year VIII. prevented the collecting of the exact results of Ventose, Germinal, and Floreal.

In Egypt, the General of Division, FRIANT, Commandant of the fifth District, has made an excursion to the Arabian Tower, situated about ten leagues from Alexandria. This monument appears very ancient, but it is extremely decayed, especially in the part exposed to the north. About three hundred toises from this tower is a vast square building, of about 120 feet on each front; the walls are of a great height, and of a thickness beyond all the usual proportions. This monument likewise appears very ancient, and seems to have some relation with the antiquities of Upper Egypt. No traveller has spoken of it, and General Friant exceedingly regrets the not having had with him in his journey any one, who, more conversant than himself in the knowledge of antique monuments, could assign the epoch in which the one here alluded to was built, and the use to which it was appropriated. General Friant has found many other ruins in the tour that he has made to a part of the coast of Barbary. He has explored almost all the antient extent of the lake Mareotis, and the canton of Mariouth, inhabited by a number of Arabian tribes.

According to a report of Citizen DESMARETZ, of the National Institute and of the Lyceum of Arts, read to the latter assembly, on the manufacture of Bauwans, at Passy, cotton is now brought to as great perfection in France as in England, and it is no dearer. Some superb patterns were handed about to the members. The Lyceum have granted to the author of this establishment a crown and a medal.

Professor SCHUMACHER, of Copenhagen, has just published the first volume of his *Medico-Chirurgical Observations*. As the author is attached to the service of the hospital, he must naturally have occasion to make curious remarks and such as are worthy of record. His zeal, has led him to endeavour to substitute the use of indigenous plants, to that of foreign vegetables: for example, he usually employs the gratiola in lieu of ipecacuanha. When this herb does not operate sufficiently alone, he recommends to assist it by the addition of a little rhubarb. He has likewise, discovered that in wounds and ulcers with inflammation, the *cortex hippocastani* or *salicis* has the same effect as the *cortex Peruvianus*, which is much dearer. The *carex arenaria* may be substituted with equal success to sarsaparilla. In intermitting fevers, with the help of such another *cortex*, there is no longer occasion for the *cortex regius*. And, lastly, it results from his experiments that the *Faba Pichurim* is an efficacious remedy against the *fluor albus (fleurs blanches)* especially when the malady is inveterate, and proceeds from imbecility.

REVIEW

REVIEW OF NEW MUSICAL PUBLICATIONS.

Three Figures and nine Voluntaries for the Organ or Piano-forte, interſperſed with ſeveral Interludes, by various Authors. The Figures and moſt of the Voluntaries originally compoſed by the late John Erneſt Eberlin, Organiſt at Saltzbourg. The whole arranged with ſome additions and alterations for the Uſe of Organiſts and Practitioners in general, and reſpectfully inſcribed to Doctor Buſby, by Joſeph Diettenhofer. 7s. 6d.

Goulding, Phipps, and D'Almaine.

THE preſent publication is the counterpart of one arranged from the ſame author, and publiſhed ſome time ſince, by Mr. Diettenhofer. Of that firſt part our muſical readers will remember that we ſpoke in high terms; the ſecond part is, in every reſpect, equally worthy of the ingenious and ſcientific Eberlin, and in its arrangement does much credit to the taſte and judgment of the editor.

The ſubjects of the figures are in general truly original, very ingeniouſly fancied, and worked with a ſkill only found in the really great maſters. The Voluntaries are cloſely conſtructed, and the Interludes are written with taſte. Eberlin's ſtyle, to uſe the words of the editor, in his advertiſement prefixed to the work, may be regarded as a true ſpecimen of organ compoſitions and organ performances, (eſpecially as practiſed in Germany), and exhibits a *ſtrong* likeneſs of Handel's figures and extemporary voluntaries.

Of the firſt part of this claſſical publication, a ſecond edition is already announced, and we do not heſitate to predict that the preſent will have an equally rapid ſale.

A new and complete Preceptor for the Clarinet, containing a ſhort and eaſy Treatiſe on Muſic, the Art of acquiring a fine tone, including forty-two Leſſons on the relative Notes, peculiar to the Clarinet; on the Chalumeau and Fingering the Inſtrument; on counting the Time, &c. by John Mahon. 10s. 6d.

Goulding, Phipps, and D'Almaine.

After peruſing the preſent publication with that ſedulous attention which didactic works of this magnitude demand, we can have the pleaſure to announce it to practitioners on the inſtrument, for the cultivation of which it is written, as containing an elaborate and well digeſted ſeries of inſtructions, progreſſively diſpoſed and clearly laid down, and which, if duly ſtudied, cannot fail to produce a correct and comprehenſive idea of the characters and powers of the clarinet, and a rapid advance in its practice and execution.

The author opens his preceptive matter with a view of the nature and capacity of this attractive inſtrument, and then proceeds to the management of the mouth or *embouchure*, explaining the method of acquiring a firmneſs in the lips, and a proper government of the reed, which, he juſtly obſerves, is the foundation of a good tone.

After ſome uſeful and judicious inſtructions reſpecting the poſition of the arms and head, we find ſome remarks ſo illuſtrative of the beſt method of acquiring a free and juſt ſtyle of performance, that we cannot do better than extract the ſenſe of them. "The great beauty of the clarinet, (ſays Mr. Maton,) conſiſts in a fine mellow tone, and a judicious expreſſion, to acquire which the practitioner ſhould not attempt too ſoon to move the finger rapidly, but, on the contrary, ſhould play the gamut, ſwelling and diminiſhing the notes, till the tone becomes ſteady and confirmed. He may thus proceed to the practice of ſuch of the favourite Scotch airs, as are adapted to the clarinet."

In the body of the work we find the ſcale and a drawing of the inſtrument, the doctrine of time, an explanation of the words commonly uſed in muſic, an aſcending and deſcending ſeries of twelling notes, *lepas* for the *chalumeau* and clarinet notes, and a ſcale of the *corno baſſetta*, with a drawing of the inſtrument. The practitioner is alſo furniſhed with twelve eaſy leſſons for two clarinets; twelve favorite airs, ſelected from the beſt Scottiſh, Iriſh, and French muſic, adapted for two clarinets; eight exerciſes for acquiring neat execution, from *concertanti duetto*, and a variety of *cadenzas* or preludes in different keys.

Journal de Muſique pour les Dames; or, Elegant Selections, compriſing the moſt favourite Compoſitions of Haydn, Mozart, Pleyel, &c. arranged for the Piano forte and Harp. In two Volumes folio. Volume 1. 10s. 6d.

Rolfe.

The firſt volume of this work, which now lays before us, contains ſixty-four pages, and exhibits an extenſive and reſpectable catalogue of vocal and inſtrumental muſic. Amongſt nearly thirty articles, most of which are popular favorites, either in this or other countries, we find two rondos by Paesiello, extracted from a collection expressly composed for the late Empress of Russia, General Kosciusko's Grand March, with variations by Mozart; "A Pity to Tender Anguish," by Haydn; a favorite rondo by Pleyel, and a celebrated air by Gluck. The whole forms a handsome folio volume, and should the remaining part of the work be selected with equal judgment, and printed with the same accuracy as the present, the "Journal de Musique" will contain a valuable collection of modern music.

"*Little Sue,*" *a Ballad, as sung by Miss Daniels, at Vauxhall Gardens, composed by W. P. R. Cope.* 1s. *Clementi and Co.*

Mr. Cope, in this little composition, has scrupulously attended to the turn and sense of the words, and produced all that variety and relief intended by the poet. The descent of the voice at "O then I'm forced to beg for more," is judicious, and the changes of the time at "Do sweet Lady," and at "Remember little Sue," are particularly proper and expressive. The words are written by Mr. C. Dibdin, jun. and by their characteristic ease and simplicity do credit to their author.

"*It is Night, and I am alone,*" *Composed by the late John Percy.* 2s. 6d. *Clementi & Co.*

We find in this song some traits of genius and just conception, much above the general cast of modern compositions. The words are from Ossian, and the composer has entered into their spirit, fervor and wild rudeness with an enthusiasm worthy of that talent and feeling which he had already displayed in so many similar instances. The variation of the movements produces a conspicuous and forcible effect, and the piano forte accompaniment is judiciously and expressively constructed.

Numbers 19 and 20 of Apollo et Terpsichore, forming a Collection of the most celebrated Songs, Duets, Rondos, Airs, &c. selected from the Works of Mozart, Haydn, Pleyel, Paesiello, &c. &c. Adapted for the Piano-forte, Harp, Violin, or German Flute. 1s. *Rolfe.*

The present numbers of this pleasing and useful work contain a variety of well-chosen matter, and cannot fail to contribute to the improvement of juvenile practitioners, both vocal and instrumental. Among other attractive little articles we find Madame Hilligsberg's Scotch Reel; "Sweet sung the Lark," composed by Martino; a celebrated Welsh air; "Haste the Joys of Life to share," by Reichardt; a minuet by Mozart; a cradle song, by Calpoth, and a favorite rondo by Pleyel.

Sonata for the Piano forte, composed by an Amateur. 1s. *Goulding, Phipps, and D'Almaine.*

We give Messrs. Goulding and Co. due credit for republishing a sonata at once so beautiful in its style, and so improving to the juvenile finger as the present, but cannot conceive by what means they have been led into the fallacy of announcing it as the production of an *Amateur.* It is from the pen of the late truly ingenious John Christian Bach, and will be found in one of his sets of familiar pieces for the piano-forte.

We have not the slightest intention to insinuate any intended imposition, but feel ourselves obliged to remark, that publishers cannot be too circumspect as to the originality of what is offered to them for the press, or the propriety of the titles and names they adopt.

"*When Sappho Tun'd the Raptur'd Strain.*" *A Glee, first composed by Mr. Danby, for three Voices, now arranged for four Voices, viz. a Treble, Countertenor, Tenor, and Bass, as a regular Fugue, with alterations, additions, and a thorough-Bass, by Joseph Diettenhofer.* 2s. *Preston.*

Though Mr. Diettenhofer cannot in the present publication claim the merit of an original composer, much praise is due to him for the mastery and judgment with which he has arranged and newly harmonized this popular glee. The *fugue* he has constructed from the subject of the second movement evinces considerable science, and much happy contrivance; the answers are every where introduced with so much meaning and effect, and exhibit such proofs of talent in this species of composition, that we hope Mr. Diettenhofer will, ere long, favor the public with some original productions.

Richer's favorite Hornpipe, arranged as a Rondo for the Piano-forte, by A. Betts. 1s. *Rolfe.*

This is one of those little compositions which it is become so much the fashion to form on known and popular subjects, and on which we are always inclined to look with a favourable eye, because, while they are so greatly calculated to allure the young practitioner to that application, without which little advance in execution can be expected, they chiefly consist of passages which give a due and proper exercise to the fingers.

Our

Our musical readers will be pleased to learn that Messrs. Clementi and Co. have invented a new species of barrel organ, which to the usual properties of that instrument adds the advantages of a double drum, tabor, triangle, flageolet, and pedal movements, all of which may be blended together, or introduced separately at the momentary will of the performer. At our examination of this curious and original piece of mechanism, we were not less struck with the various effects of power and sweetness which it produces, than with the simplicity and permanency of construction under which the whole is compiled, and by which it is not only calculated for an easy conveyance to any part of the united kingdom, but for exportation to the most distant parts of the globe.

LIST OF NEW PUBLICATIONS IN JUNE.

ANTIQUITIES.

The Sports and Pastimes of the People of England; including Rural and Domestic Recreations, Processions and Pompous Spectacles, &c. from the earliest Period to the present Time, illustrated by Engravings from ancient Paintings, by Joseph Strutt, 4to Plates coloured, 5l. 5s. Plain 3l. 3s. bds. White.

EDUCATION.

An English Alphabet for the Use of Foreigners, wherein the Pronunciation of the Vowels, or Voice-letters, is explained in twelve short Rules; abridged from a larger Work (for the Use of Omai), by Granville Sharp, 1s 6d. White.

The Child's First Book improved; with a Preface addressed to all affectionate Mothers and Teachers of Children, 1s. White.

A New Introduction to the Latin Tongue, on the Plan of the Grammar used at Eton, with considerable Additions, and explanatory Observations, 3s. Rivingtons.

HISTORY.

History of the Rebellion in Ireland, in the Year 1798, &c. containing an Account of the Proceedings of the Irish Revolutionists from the Year 1782; with an Appendix to illustrate some facts, by the Rev. James Gordon, Rector of Kilíigup, 8vo. 8s. boards. Hurst.

Historical Sketch of the Invasions on the British Isles, from the Time of William the Conqueror; translated and *continued* from the French; with a coloured Chart of Great Britain and Ireland, on which each Descent is delineated, 4to. 2s. 6d. Stockdale.

LAW

A Copious and Correct Abstract of the Act of Parliament passed June 27, 1801, for the Relief of certain Insolvent Debtors, by a Barrister at Law; to which is subjoined a Complete Alphabetical List of all the Persons who have taken, or intend to take, the Benefit of the said Act, 1s. 6d. Symonds.

An Addenda to the Fourth Edition of the Bankrupt-laws; containing the Determinations to the End of the Year 1800, by William Cooke, Esq 5s sewed. Brooke and Rider.

MEDICAL.

A New Edition, containing upwards of twenty Sheets of New Matter, of Motherby's Medical Dictionary, revised and corrected; with Additions, by George Wallis, M. D. with Copper-plates, Folio, 3l. 3s. boards. Johnson.

The Medical Assistant; or, Jamaica Practice of Physic, designed chiefly for the Use of Families and Plantations, by Thomas Dancer, M. D. 4to. 1l. 1s. boards. Murray and Highley.

History of Animal Magnetism; its Origin, Progress, and Present State; its Principles and Secrets displayed, as delivered by the late Dr. Demainauduc; to which is added, Dissertations on the Dropsy, Spasm, Epileptic Fits, St. Vitus's Dance, Gout, Rheumatism, and Consumption; also, Advice to those who visit the Sick, with Recipes to prevent Infection; a Definition of Sympathy, Antipathy, the Effects of the Imagination on Pregnant Women; of Nature, History, and on the Resurrection of the Body, by George Winter, M. D. 8vo. Newbery.

Observations on the Cancerous Breast; consisting chiefly of Original Correspondence between the Author and Dr. Baillie, Mr. Cline, Dr. Babington, Mr. Abernethy, and Dr. Stokes; with an Introductory Letter to Dr. Pitcairn, by Joseph Adams, M. D. 8vo. 3s. 6d. sewed. Longman and Rees.

MISCELLANIES.

The Indian Guide! or, Traveller's Companion through Europe and Asia, by Lieutenant-colonel Taylor, Part I. vol. 1, 12mo. 12s. boards. Wallis.

New Introduction for Playing Billiards; with an Historical Account of the Game, and some Account of distinguished Players, 1s. 6d. Hurst.

The Flowers of Persian Literature; containing Extracts from the most celebrated Authors, in Prose and Verse; with a Translation into English; to which is prefixed, an Essay on the Language and Literature of Persia, by S Rousseau, 4to. 18s. Sewell.

Hierogamy; or, an Apology for the Marriage of the Roman Catholic Priests without a Dispensation, in a Letter to the Rev. J. A. from the Rev. John Anthony Grigg. 1s 6d. Thorgood.

Report

Report of the Debates in the two Houses of Parliament during the present Year, 1801; with Notes and Illustrations, by William Woodfall, 3 vols. 2l 2s. Stockdale.

A Statement of Facts relative to Mrs. H. More's Schools, occasioned by some late Misrepresentations, 6d. Cadell and Davies.

Analytical Hints relative to the Process of Ackermann, Suardy, and Co's Manufactories for Water-proof Cloths and Wearing Apparel, 1s. Hurst.

The New East India Kalendar for 1801, compiled by Robert Hudson; with a Map of India, 4s. sewed. Debrett.

A Letter from the Right Hon Henry Dundas to the Court of Directors of the East India Company, on the Indian Debt, June 30, 1801, with official Documents, 5s. Debrett.

The Tooti Namah; or, Tales of the Parrot; in the Persian Language, with an English Translation, royal 8vo. Debrett.

An Account, shewing, in numerical Order, the Tickets entitled to Prizes in the Lottery, Anno 1800 (drawn in March last), with the Sums annexed; published by Order of the Managers, 1s 6d. Woodfall.

A Catalogue of Foreign Books, imported, and on Sale, by V. Griffiths, No. 1, Paternoster row, London, Price 1s. but *gratis* to Purchasers to the Amount of 2l. Griffiths.

MATHEMATICS.

A Treatise on Fluxions, by Colin Maclaurin, A. M. late Professor of Mathematics in the University of Edinburgh, and Fellow of the Royal Society; the second Edition; to which is prefixed, an Account of his Life; the whole revised and carefully corrected by an eminent Mathematician; illustrated with forty-one new Copper plates, in 2 large vols. 8vo. 1l. 8s. boards. W. Baynes.

MILITARY.

An Address to the British Volunteers and my Countrymen, respecting the threatened Invasion of England by French Usurpers, by a Volunteer and a plain Englishman, 1s Hatchard.

Proceedings of a General Court Martial, held at Gibraltar, in May, 1801, on William Hall, Paymaster of the Prince of Wales's Fencible Infantry, 2s. 6d. Cawthorn.

A Brief Discourse—"What Orders were best for Repulsing of Foreign Force, if at any Time they should Invade us," by Thomas Digges, first printed in 1590, 1s. Hatchard.

The British Commissary; comprising a System for that Office on Foreign Service; and an Essay towards ascertaining its Duties at Home, by Haviland Le Mesurier, Esq. 8vo. Egerton.

The Campaigns of General Suworow, written by an Officer, 2s. Hurst.

NOVELS.

The Knight and Mason; or, He who Runs may Read, 12mo. 4 vols. Crosby and Letterman.

The Confession; a Novel, by Agnes Musgrave, 5 vols. 12mo. 20s. boards. Cawthorn.

POETRY.

A Rainy Day; or, Poetical Impressions during a Stay at Brighthelmstone, in the Month of July, 1801, by James Boaden, 2s. Egerton.

A New Edition, revised and enlarged, with a New Preface, and with the Citations translated, of the Pursuits of Literature, a Satirical Poem, large 8vo. 12s. 6d. boards. Becket.

Crim. Con. a Pindaric Ode, to the Marquis of Blandford, 2s. 6d. West and Hughes.

Elegant Extracts; or, selected Pieces of Poetry; a New Edition, greatly enlarged, royal 8vo. 18s. boards. Johnson.

POLITICAL.

Considerations on the Right of the Clergy of England to a Seat in Parliament, by a Member of Lincoln's Inn, 1s. 6d. Cadell and Davies.

Adresse aux Vrais Hommes de Bien; à ceux qui Gouvernent, comme à ceux qui sont Gouvernés, 8vo. 5s. sewed. Spilsbury.

POLITICAL ECONOMY.

The first Part of the third Volume of the Reports of the Society for Bettering the Condition of the Poor, containing the thirteenth, fourteenth and fifteenth Reports, 1s. Hatchard.

An Investigation of Mr. Morgan's Comparative View of the public Finances, from the Beginning to the Close of the late Administration, by Daniel Wakefield, Esq.

TRADE AND COMMERCE.

An Address to the Public relative to the Wonderful Extension, and Flourishing Condition, of the Commercial and Shipping Interests of Great Britain, founded upon the complete and authentic Materials contained in Lloyd's Monthly Shipping List; to which are added, a Variety of Comparative Tables, proving that we are not yet ruined, by a Merchant, 1s. 6d. West and Hughes.

TOPOGRAPHY.

Cambrian Itinerary; or, Welsh Tourist; containing an Historical and Topographical Description of the Antiquities and Beauties of Wales, minutely describing, according to their geographical and modern Divisions, all the different Counties, Towns, &c. likewise a Colloquial Vocabulary in English and Welsh; and an Appendix, containing the ancient Welsh Alphabet; illustrated with Maps, by Thomas Evans, 8vo. 10s. 6d. boards. Hurst.

THEOLOGY.

The Anniversary Sermon of the Royal Humane Society, preached at Kensington, April 19th, and at St. Lawrence, Reading, June 17th, 1801, by W. Langford, D. D. with an Appendix, by the Society, on Shipwrecked Mariners, Resuscitation, &c. 1s. Rivingtons.

An

An Anfwer to an Anonymous Letter (dated Sept. 18, 1777) on Predeftination and Free Will; with a Poftfcript on Eternal Punifhments, 1s. White.

God's Approbation of our Labours neceffary to the Hope of Succefs; a Sermon, delivered at the annual Meeting of the Bedford Union, May 6, 1801, by Andrew Fuller, 6d. Button.

Familiar Inftructions to Young People, relating to the Feftivals of the Church of England, 4d. Rivingtons

Sermons on the Doctrines and Duties of Chriftianity, addreffed to a Country Congregation, 8vo. 5s boards. Cadell and Davies.

The Beauties of Hervey; or, Defcriptive, Picturefque, and Inftructive Paffages felected from the Works of that admired Author; to which is prefixed Memoirs of his Life, with a Portrait, 12mo. 3s. 6d. boards. Hurft.

Sermons by the late William Stevens, D. D. 3 vols. 8vo. 1l. 1s. boards. Cadell and Davies.

VETERINARY ART.

The firft Number of the Veterinary Tranfactions; containing Obfervations on the Effect and Treatment of Wounds of Joints, &c. to which are added, the Rules and Regulations of the Veterinary College, by Order of the general Meeting of Subfcribers of the Veterinary College, 3s. 6d. Debrett.

French Books publifhed by Dulau and Co. Soho-fquare.

French and Englifh Idioms compared; wherein the Idiomatical Difficulties of the French are introduced in a Sentence, and elucidated in a Manner entirely new, by Bellenger, 12mo. 2s. 6d.

Epitome of the French Elegant Extracts; or, Abrégé de la Bibliothèque Portative des Ecrivains François, en Profe et en Verfe, à l'Ufage des Ecoles, par M. Moyant, 5s.

La Boucle du Cheveux enlevée, Poëme Heroi-comique de Pope, traduit en Verfe, par M. Defmoulines, 4to, vellum paper, 7s.

Firft and fecond Volume of Davila, 8vo. being the two firft Volumes of the felect Collection of the moft claffical Italian Hiftorians, which will be printed in an uniform and convenient Size, on two Papers, with a new Type, and propofed by Subfcription.

Ariofto, new Edition, 4 vols. 12mo. 1l.

Ditto, fine Paper 1l. 11s. 6d.

Ditto, Caftigate, for the Ufe of Schools, 4 vol. 1l.

Imported by the fame.

Le Buffon de la Jeuneffe, 4 vol. 12mo. fig. 16s.

Mémoires et Voyages d'un Emigré, 3 vol. 12mo. 10s. 6d.

Rofetta; ou, l'Effet du Romance fur l'Efprit des Femmes, 4 vol. 12s.

Recherches fur la Vie et la Mort, par Bichat, Profeffeur d'Anatomie et de Phyfiologie, 8vo. 7s.

Obfervations Littéraires, Critiques, Politiques, Militaires, Géographiques, fur les Hiftoires de Tacite, avec le Texte Latin corrigé, avec 6 Cartes, gravées par Tardieu, et un Tableau de Mouvement du Legion Romain, pour fervir à l'Intelligence des Opérations Militaires, par Ferlet, 2 vol. 8vo. 14s.

Hiftoire de l'Etabliffement des François dans les Gaules, Ouvrage inédit du Préfident Hénault, 1 vol. 8vo. 10s. 6d.

Effai fur la Conduite du Pretres, appellés à travailler au Rétabliffement de la Religion Chrétienne en France, par Cofte, 8vo. 7s.

Idée de l'Homme, Phyfique et Moral, pour fervir d'Introduction à un Traité de Medicine, 12mo. 3s. 6d.

Anecdotes Chrétiennes; ou, Recueil de Traits d'Hiftoire choifis parmi les Grands Exemples de Vertu qu'ont donné les Catholiques François pendant la Révolution, 12mo. 3s. 6d.

Books imported by T. Boofey fince the Publication of his Catalogue of Foreign Books.

Dictionnaire de la Fable, par Noel, 2 vols. 8vo. 16s.

Dictionnaire Univerfelle de la Langue Françoife, par Bofei et Baftiew, 10s. 6d.

Siècles Litteraire; ou, Nouveau Dictionnaire Hiftorique, par Deleffarts, 6 vols. 8vo. 2l. 2s.

Origines Gaulaifes, &c. par La-Tour d'Auvergne, 8vo. 6s.

Campagne; ou, Voyage de 40 Jours, 8vo. 1s. 6d.

Paris à la Fin du 18me Siècle, par Pujoulez, 8vo. 6s.

Memoires de Le Kain, 8vo. 6s.

Guerre de Troie, par Tourlet, 2 vols. 8vo. 12s.

Conqueftes de Naples, 3 vol. 8vo. 15s.

Œuvres de Geffner, Traduction Interlineare 2 vols. 8vo. 12s.

Œuvres de Rulhiere, 8vo. 5s.

Exercifes Botanique à l'Ufage des Commencans, par Phillibert, 2 vols. 8vo. 157 fig. 2l. 2s.

Hiftoire du Directoire Executif, 2 vols. 8vo. 14s.

De la Litterature, par Mad. Stael, 2 vols. 8vo. 12s.

Satyriques Epigrammes, &c. de 18me Siècle, 8vo. 1l. 8s.

Traité de la Diftillation, 2 vols. 12mo. 7s.

Metamorphofes d'Ovide, par Defaintange, 2 vols. 8vo. 16 graveires, 16s.

Poefies Diverfes de De Lille, 12mo. 3s. 6d.

VOYAGES.

Voyages Phyfiques dans la Campagne, par L. Brulac, fig. 2 vols 8vo. 14s.

Voyages dans la Finifterre, 3 vols. 8vo. fig. 15s.

Voyages dans la Haut Penfilvanie, 3 vols. 8vo. fig. 24s.

Voyages

Voyages Pittoresque dans la Jura, par Lequino, 2 vols. 14s.

Voyages de Constantinople à Bassora, 8vo. 6s.

Premier Voyage autour de Monde, par Pigafetta. fig. et cartes, 8vo. 9s.

Voyage dans la Côté Occidentale de l'Afrique, par De Grandpre, fig. et cartes, 3 vols. 18s.

MEDICINE.

Memoires sur plusieurs Maladies, par Portal, 2 vols. 8vo 12s.

Medicine du Voyageur, 3 vols. 8vo. 18s.

De la Nature et l'Usage des Bains, par Macard, 8vo 6s

Recherches sur la Vie et la Mort, par Bichat, 8vo. 7s.

Dictionnaire de la Conversation de l'Homme, 2 vols 8vo. 18s.

Traité du Diabetes Sucré, avec les Notes, &c. Fourcroy, 6s.

Traité des Maladies Veneriennes, par Berlingheiri, 8vo. 6s.

Traité des Infections de l'Air, par Guyton, 8vo. 6s.

By H. Escher, Gerard-street.

Kotzebues neue Schauspiele 5ter und 6ter Band, von denen auch die Stüche einzeln zuhaben sind

Schiller's Maria Stuart, in German, 6s.

Linnei Species Plantarum, ed. Willdenow, tomi 3tu, pars 1ma, 14s

Tunh's Cryplogamische Gewächse, 2 Gefle, 10s.

Heyne Termini Botanier Fascio. 5 and 6 3s. each

Göethes neue Scriften, 7r. Band, 12s.

Tibulli Carmina, ed. Heyne, 12s.

Diodorus Siculus, ed. Eichstædt, tom. 1, 16s.

Euripidis Hecuba, ed. Hermann, 6s.

——— Eumenides, 2s.

Plauti Trinummus, 3s.

Aristophanis Nuber, 9s.

Jacob's Anthologia Græca, tom. xmus, 9s.

By C. Geisweiler, Parliament-street.

Homer nach Antiken Gezeichnel, von H. W. Tischbein mit Erklærungen, von C. G. Heyne, folio, 1801, Nr. 1 and 2, 4l 5s.

Virgilius Maro Varietate Lectionis, et Perpetua Adnotatione illustratus a C. G. Heyne, Editio novis curis, emendata et aucta, cuts, 1800, 6 vols 8vo. carta scripta, 8l. 18s. 6d.

Lexicon Nosologicum Polygloton Omnium Morborum, Symptomatum Vitiorumque Naturæ, &c. Auctore, Nemnich, folio, 1801, 1l. 5s.

P. Camperi Icones Herniarum, editæ a S. T. Soemmering, folio, 1801, 3l. 13s. 6d.

Campes Historisches Bilderbüchlein, 1801, cuts very neat, 18s.

Ossian's Cedrichte, von Rhode, 3 vols. 1800, 16s 6d.

Kotzebue neue Schauspiele, 6ter Band, 1801, 8s. 6d.

Dafontaine Leben eines armen Landpredigers, 2 vols. cuts 1801, 17s. 6d.

Engels Scriften, 2 vols. velin, 1801. 1l. 10s.

——— Lorenz Starh, ein Charaktegemalde, velin, 1801, 15s.

Vitæ T. Hemsterhusi et D. Ruhn Kenii, 1801, 4s. 6d.

Les Chevaliers du Lion, Histoire du Douzieme Siècle, d'apres l'Allemand. 4 vol. 1800, 1l. 1s.

Meisneri, J H. Nova Veteris Test. Clavis, 2 vols. 1801. 1l. 10s.

STATE OF PUBLIC AFFAIRS,

In August, 1801.

FRANCE.

THE French, in their marine adventures, have undoubtedly been more fortunate since the publication of our last Number than at almost any former period of the war, they have captured two ships of the line and the Jason frigate, which unluckily ran a-ground in the bay of St. Malo, and, together with her crew, was immediately taken possession of. With respect to their internal situation we seem to know but little. The reports circulated some time since of disputes existing between the First Consul and Carnot and Talleyrand, are now sufficiently proved to have been falshoods: on quitting Paris, they seem to have been merely entrusted with missions of a private nature, which having accomplished, they have again returned to their respective posts, the former still directing, through the medium of his brother, who resides there, the extraordinary preparations which are advancing at Boulogne.

As little truth there appears to have been in what has been alleged of a serious misunderstanding between the King of Prussia and Bonaparte; for, with a stretch of royal authority, which few people in this country will be disposed to countenance, he has ordered to be crushed, at the instigation, it is supposed, of the Chief Consul himself, a whole Committee of French Royalists, who have long been resident in the Prussian dominions, and have lately been suspected of fomenting intrigues in the interior of France. Prussia, as well as Sweden and Denmark, formerly notified

notified her acceſſion to the late treaty concluded at Peterſburg; but ſhe diſcovers very little inclination to retire from Hanover, and probably will not quit it at all.

The following are the details of the action of Algeſiras the 6th of July, and the ſubſequent engagement between that bay and Cadiz on the 12th and 13th of July, as given in the French papers:

Rear Admiral Linois, ſays the Miniſter of Marine, was apprized at half paſt ſeven in the morning, that the Engliſh ſquadron, which was cruizing before Cadiz, had paſſed the Streights. It was compoſed of ſix ſhips of the line, following in the wake of the leader, which ſteered for the Formidable, the ſhip more to the northward of the Deſaix, the Indomptable, and the frigate the Murion, to the ſouth. At a quarter paſt eight the battery of Iſle Verte fired upon the enemy. At half after eight the Indomptable began the fight, which ſoon became general. At half paſt nine Adm. Linois made the ſignal to cut the cables. The breeze from the land had fallen, and as the calm continued, the movement of the ſailing off of the ſhips was very tedious, and rendered more critical the poſition of the three ſhips, whoſe fire, however, did not ſlacken. At eleven o'clock the Formidable touched the ground, and the leader of the enemy's line touched alſo in front of her. Two Engliſh ſhips bore up with ſprings upon their cables, within a ſhort diſtance from thoſe of the Republic. The battery of Iſle Verte had almoſt for two hours ceaſed its fire, and the Engliſh boats, and other ſmall craft, threatened to poſſeſs themſelves of it. A captain of infantry, at the head of 130 ſoldiers, paſſengers on board the Formidable, went on ſhore to prevent the enemy from landing; they juſt arrived in time. An Engliſh boat was ſunk, and another taken. The captain of the Deſaix alſo ſent people to that battery, which was alſo ſerved with great activity. An Engliſh ſhip touched the ground oppoſite the battery, the fire of which we ſuſtained, as alſo that of the Indomptable. Her flag was ſtruck, but ſome of the boats towed her off. The battery of St. Jacques, ſituated to the north of the line, having ſlackened its fire, the General of Brigade, Devaux, who was on board the French ſquadron, haſtened into it with troops from the Deſaix, and poured ſome well-directed diſcharges upon the enemy. Seven Spaniſh gun-boats took ſuch an active part in the engagement, that five of them were ſunk or totally diſabled. The Engliſh ſhips were unable to reſiſt. Thoſe which were moored cut their cables, and the ſhip that was aground near the Formidable ſtruck her flag at two o'clock. In half an hour after, the battle ceaſed, the enemy having tacked, leaving the Hannibal, of 74 guns, behind. Admiral Linois, who takes no notice of his own ſervices in this glorious day, applies himſelf only to the praiſe of all thoſe who aſſiſted him; and it is with enthuſiaſm that he ſpeaks of the valour and diſcipline of the officers and ſoldiers, both by land and ſea. In the evening of the 6th of July ſeveral boats of the enemy's diviſion came on board the Hannibal to take away the wounded. As they had not a flag of truce, and were armed, Admiral Linois detained them and made them priſoners. The 7th of July he perceived at Gibraltar two of the ſhips that had been obliged to return into the port; the three others were in the road, but only one appeared fit to put to ſea." The Miniſter of Marine continues to ſay. "the battle laſted ſix hours, without intermiſſion; each French ſhip had to contend in ſucceſſion againſt three or four Engliſh. The loſs of the Engliſh he ſtates as amounting to 1500 men, killed and wounded, and that of the French 180 men killed, 300 wounded, of whom 13 are incurable, and 40 very ſeverely wounded.

The Spaniſh Admiral, Moreno, gives the following details of the engagement of the 12th and 13th of July.

"On the 9th of July, (ſays the Admiral) a diviſion of five Spaniſh ſhips of the line, one French ſhip of the line, and two frigates moored at Algeſiras, under his command, and joined the ſquadron of Vice Admiral Linois, encreaſed by the Hannibal, taken from the Engliſh. On the 12th, at one in the afternoon, Admiral Moreno gave the ſignal for preparing to return to Cadiz. During the night the ſquadron divided, the Formidable and Antoine, with two Spaniſh ſhips, aſtern. The night was very dark, and the wind freſh. The Engliſh ſquadron, which had been repaired at Gibraltar, and which failed at the ſame time with his, had been ſeen to windward in the evening. Two Spaniſh ſhips, three deckers, taking each other for enemies, fired and engaged upon each other in a terrible combat. They fell on board each other, one of them took fire, and both blew up. The St. Antoine, which was near theſe ſhips, ſeparated immediately on perceiving the fire, and thus fell to ſome diſtance from the ſquadron. The Admiral had not yet heard any ſure account of her. The Formidable perceiving

ceiving the mistake of the two Spanish ships, received their shots without firing again, and avoided so melancholy a combat. Admiral Moreno, with three Spanish and two French vessels, was at break of day to the westward of Cadiz. The Formidable, having steered directly for Cadiz, was at break of day on the Spanish coast, within reach of the English squadron. The battle began; alone against three ships and a frigate, the Formidable must have been taken; but the crew, glorying in the laurels of Algesiras, swore to sink with the vessel rather than strike. Victory smiled upon this intrepid resolution. Some cannon, well-pointed, kept the frigate at a distance. The Formidable manœuvred, and directed herself against the Pompee, which, at the second discharge, lost her three masts and was rendered naked as a boat. Two vessels still remained; the Formidable, fired upon on both sides, obliged them to quit her, and entered triumphantly into Cadiz."

In the Paris papers of the beginning of August, we find an official order, addressed to the prefects of the different departments throughout France, by Citizen Fouche, the Minister of General Police, relative to the incorrigible obstinacy of the French clergymen, who, by the indulgence of the laws, were suffered to return to the bosom of their country. It recapitulates the various indulgencies granted by the new Constitution to those emigrant Priests; such as the unmolested exercise of their clerical function in the respective communes to which they belong, as well as the emoluments arising therefrom. It then proceeds to state the ungrateful requital made by some of them to an indulgent Government; such as fomenting disunion and animosity among the people; quarrelling personally with the resident clergy, who were amicable to the laws of the Republic, and finally encouraging disaffection and resistance to the established order of things now in France. It concludes with three particular remedies: first, to seize the seditious and hitherto refractory priests, and banish them out of the territories of the Republic; next to remove those emigrant bishops, vicars, or curates, who have returned under the indulgencies granted; and lasty, to maitain in each commune the priest only who meets the approbation of the majority of the inhabitants.

RUSSIA.

The Petersburg Gazette of the 30th of June contains the following intelligence: The ecclesiastical princes are, in the Constitution of the German Empire, a part full as legitimate as the secular princes. The one and the other have for their support the peace of Westphalia, which has placed the shaken empire upon a basis, on which repose the rights of the ecclesiastical princes. This peace has strong guarantees, none of whom has as yet made known his opinion. The wise Catherine the Second took care to support with a firm hand the bond of the Germanic Constitution. Her successor upon the throne wishes to follow her system, and the ecclesiastical princes may confide in his powerful mediation. The delay in deciding the business of the indemnities affords ground to believe, that the peace of the empire will be yet subjected to a great many changes. Prussia herself, notwithstanding the friendship that unites her to France, does not treat this important affair with precipitation, &c.

The Emperor of Russia seems desirous of maintaining the relations of amity and peace with the Republic of France as well as other powers, as appears by a circular letter, dated 19th of June, signed by the Prince.

"All the relations of policy, commerce, and correspondence with France, which were interrupted, in consequence of the Revolution in that country, have not yet been re-established in their full extent; but as at the present moment negociations are going on to effect a reconciliation with that power by every means consistent with the dignity of the Emperor and the interests of his people, his Majesty has been pleased to charge his Ministers to apprize his foreign Ambassadors and Agents, that he is willing to renew the usual course of connection with the Government, and that the conferences respecting that object are in full activity. In the situation in which this matter stands, therefore, it is no longer proper that the Ambassadors of his Imperial Majesty should continue to observe any distance towards the Ambassadors of the French Government."

A similar letter has been sent respecting the Agents of the Batavian Republic.

DENMARK.

General Macdonald, in his speech to the King of Denmark, on being introduced to him as Minister for the French Republic, paid a high compliment to the late resistance of the Danes to the naval force of England.—"The Chief Consul of of the Republic (says he,) could confer on me no more flattering proof of confidence than in giving me charge to keep up that good understanding with your Majesty, and at the same time to be the interpreter of the French people and of their armies, in communicating to your Majesty the expressions of the admiration raised in the minds of the French people, by the noble and magnanimous resistance displayed by the Danish nation in defence of their violated rights, a resistance which will raise to them a lasting monument of fame."

PORTUGAL.

Intelligence has arrived from Lisbon, dated July the 14th, that peace has been a second time signed at Badajos. The Portuguese fortresses are to be garrisoned by French and Spanish troops; English ships to be excluded from the ports; and the naval magazines of England are embarked for Gibraltar. About thirty English persons, long resident in Lisbon, went on board the packet, having been allowed but twenty-four hours for their departure. The King of Spain, the Prince of Peace, and Lucien Bonaparte, are on their way from Badajos to Madrid; as is M. Pinto to Lisbon; and General St. Cyr is hourly expected there as Ambassador from the Republic of France.

ITALY.

The convention entered into with Cardinal Gonsalvi, on the part of the Pope, relative to the adjustment of all religious differences and discussions, was communicated by the First Consul to the Council of State, on the 6th of August, at Paris. It is, therefore, presumed that the feuds, fomented by the priests, will soon entirely cease; and that peace and harmony will characterize their Ministry in future.

From Florence, it is reported, that the Count de Ventura, having arrived there by order of his Majesty, Louis I. king of Tuscany, to receive, in his name, the oath of fidelity on the part of the Tuscans, and to take possession of his new states, that official act accordingly took place on the 2d of August, with uncommon pomp, and amidst the acclamations of a numerous and contented people.—The king will soon arrive, and preparations are making to receive him with a splendour suitable to his dignity. A proclamation was issued by his Tuscan Majesty, empowering the Count de Ventura to be his representative in Tuscany until his arrival; and another proclamation was published by General Murat, announcing the act of taking possession.

WEST INDIES.

Toussant L'Ouverture has arrived at Cape François, from the city of St. Domingo, after having organized and garrisoned with black troops all that part of the island which originally belonged to the Spaniards. Several engineers are now employed by him in fortifying the different ports at the east end of the island; and at Port Plata they have thrown up a long range of batteries, and mounted all the guns of the English frigate, Tartar, wrecked there in 1795.

EGYPT.

From the Extraordinary Gazette, published on the 21st of July, it appears that the defeat of the French army at Cairo, by that of the Grand Vizier, was nothing more than a check given to their progress.—It was the object of the French, by a very rapid motion from this city, to assault the Ottoman camp, disperse the army, and then, perhaps, endeavour to advance towards Alexandria, and relieve it from its blockade. All this might have been accomplished, had it not been for the fortunate presence of Colonel Murray, and several other British officers of a high degree of bravery and tactical knowledge, at this very moment in the Ottoman camp itself, and who had become apprised of the intentions of the enemy. Instead of waiting to receive the assault, surrounded by the usual incumbrances of women, and vast bodies of men unconnected with arms, they advised the Vizier to be in readiness for the enemy, by a select and advanced detachment; and, by the introduction of other military manœuvres of equal importance, completely succeeded in frustrating the intentions of the French, compelling them to retire, with the loss of about fifty killed, against thirty killed and eighty wounded on the part of the Turks. In this action the number of French are stated to have amounted to 4600, including cavalry; and that of the Turkish forces to about 9000. Fort Lesbie has been since evacuated, so that the whole of Damietta is now in possession of the Allies. We find also confirmed the important capture of the convoy of 550 camels, together with 600 French prisoners, which we mentioned in our last number; and, what is of more consequence, still we learn that Osman Bey, the successor of Murad Bey, has

has completely decided for the British, and has actually joined Sir J. Hutchinson with a corps of 1500 excellent cavalry, the kind of force in which the British army was most deficient.

From the inactivity which has of late been manifested by Sir J. Hutchinson, there appears to be difficulties of considerable moment; for, between the 10th of May and the 1st of June, he does not seem to have advanced above forty or fifty miles, having at the former period been at Rhamanie, and at the latter at Alkam. As to the assistance to be derived from the Bombay army, it is even yet doubtful; the inaccuracy of Lord Elgin's general statements we have formerly animadverted upon, and we now find, by Sir J. Hutchinson's dispatch, that, instead of the whole of this force having reached Suez, Colonel Murray, with the first division alone, had arrived, not at Suez, but at Cassir, a port at a considerable distance: and that General Baird, with the remainder of the troops, had not arrived any where, but was daily expected.

By intelligence from Vienna, of the 1st of August, we understand that Lord Minto, the English Ambassador, received a courier from Lord Elgin, at Constantinople, and immediately published the important official news, that the city and fort of Cairo, with the whole of the French troops in that garrison, part of whom were in an entrenched camp, had agreed, by a convention, to evacuate Egypt to the united Turkish and British forces. The French troops were not made prisoners; but were to be transported to France at the expence of Great Britain, with their arms, artillery, baggage, effects, &c. &c.

The result of this affair is, that the whole of Upper and part of Lower Egypt is in the power of the Allies. After the entrance of the Grand Vizier into Cairo, General Hutchinson wished to proceed against Alexandria with the English, and the whole of the forces that could be spared.

GREAT BRITAIN.

The plan of defending this country against any hostile attack on the part of France is still persevered in; it is, nevertheless, questioned by many, whether France ever had any serious intention of making a descent. Upon an impartial survey of what has been ascertained by Lord Nelson in his coasting excursions, it does appear to us very obvious, that the Chief Consul has had no real intention of hazarding so mad an enterprize as a serious descent upon the British Empire, for he does not appear to have made any adequate preparations for so formidable an undertaking. In the inner harbour, of Boulogne indeed, we are told that there are not less than a fleet of an hundred gun-boats ready for sailing. This, however, in the first place, is all conjecture; and, secondly, allowing it to be a fact, and that each of them will accommodate eighty men, which is being very liberal in our concession, we still should have from this chief magazine of attack not more than 8000 men, a force that would be destroyed before they could accomplish any one object of serious moment. But we are told the official French journal, the *Moniteur*, has publicly avowed these preparations for a long time, and decidedly stated it to be the intention of Bonaparte to attempt an invasion; and there has been a perpetual marching and countermarching of gun boats from port to port in the sight of our own fleets. For these very reasons we disbelieve the whole affair; when Bonaparte is serious in his intentions of a descent, he will be cautious and private—he will not employ his own printer to trumpet forth to all the world the object he has in view, nor proceed with his plan of preparation in the full face of the British navy. His object was, unquestionably, if he could have carried it, to frighten the Ministry and the People on this side of the water, that he might the more easily have obtained his proposed terms of pacification.

All the coast on the eastern part of Kent is in a state of great preparation to repel the threatened invasion. The Sea Fencibles have been several times exercised on board the Redoubt, Captain Shepherd, laying at Shelness Point, for the protection of that part of the coast, and the opposite shore of Whitstable and Hern Bay.

The German Journals speak of the approaching descent on England with as much certainty as the English themselves. They have already placed at the head of this important expedition, Generals Massena, Augereau, Lannes, and Bernadotte. They besides announce the formation of a permanent War Council, of which Moreau is to be president.

The military preparations along the Flemish coast are continued with undiminished activity. A corps of 1000 light cavalry for some secret expedition, has been lately selected from the troops at Brussels; and Carnot, Inspector General of Engineers, the brother to the Ex-director,

tor, has inspected Bruges, Ostend, and Nieuport.

The whole coast of *ci-devant* Flanders, the mouths of the Scheldt and the Meuse, and the ports of Holland, are however blockaded by the English squadrons and cruizers. All these extraordinary exertions evince the fears of the English Government at the formidable preparations carrying on from the Texel as far as Havre.

Authentic intelligence arrived at the Admiralty, July the 28th, from the Hon. William Cornwallis, Admiral of the Blue, informing the Lords Commissioners that his Lordship had received a letter from Captain Brisbane, of his Majesty's ship Doris, who commands the frigates employed in watching the enemy's fleet at the entrance of Brest harbour.

Captain Brisbane informs the Admiral that a most daring and gallant enterprize was, on the night of the 21st of July, undertaken by the boats of his Majesty's ships, entirely manned by volunteers, under the direction of Lieutenant Losack, of the Ville de Paris, whose gallantry on the occasion is better felt than expressed, who succeeded in boarding and carrying the French national ship, La Chevrette, mounting twenty guns, manned and completely prepared with 350 men, under the batteries in the Bay of Cameret, and in presence of the combined fleets of France and Spain. Captain Brisbane says, any comments of his would fall short of the merits due to those gallant officers, seamen, and marines, employed in this service. He concludes with regretting the loss of the killed and wounded; but says, when compared with that of the enemy, it is comparatively small. The total of the killed was eleven, and of the wounded fifty-seven, and one missing. The total of the enemy killed was the captain and ninety-one seamen and troops, and of the wounded sixty two.

Rear Admiral Sir James Saumarez has sent a letter to Mr. Nepean, dated on board his Majesty's ship Cæsar, at Gibraltar, the 6th of July, of the following purport: He stood through the Streights, with his Majesty's squadron under his orders, with the intention of attacking three French line of battle ships and a frigate, which were at anchor off Algesiras: On opening Cabareta point, he found the ships lay at a considerable distance from the enemy's batteries, and having a leading wind up to them, afforded every reasonable hope of success in the attack. He had previously directed Captain Hood, in the Venerable, to lead the squadron, which he executed with his accustomed gallantry; and, although it was not intended he should anchor, he found himself under the necessity so to do, from the wind's failing, (a circumstance so much to be apprehended in this country) and to which circumstance he has to regret the want of success in this well intended enterprize. Captain Stirling anchored opposite to the inner ship of the enemy, and brought the Pompée to action in the most spirited and gallant manner, which was also followed by the commanders of every ship in the squadron.

Captains Darby and Ferris, owing to light winds, were prevented for a considerable time from coming into action; at length the Hannibal getting a breeze, Captain Ferris had the most favourable prospect of being along-side one of the enemy's ships, when the Hannibal unfortunately took the ground, and he was extremely concerned to acquaint their Lordships, that after having made every possible effort with this ship and the Audacious to cover her from the enemy, he was under the necessity to make sail, being at the time only three cables length from one of the enemy's batteries.

The total number of officers and men killed, wounded, and missing, in this action, was 375.

Another dispatch from Rear Admiral Sir James Saumarez, dated on board the Cæsar, off Cape Trafalgar, July 13, was received at the Admiralty, August the 3d, acquainting the Commissioners that the three French line of battle ships disabled in the action of the 6th of July, off Algesiras, were on the 8th, reinforced by a squadron of five Spanish line of battle-ships under the command of Don Juan Joaquin de Moreno, and a French ship of seventy four guns, wearing a broad pendant, besides three frigates, and an incredible number of gun boats and other vessels, and got under sail on the morning of the 12th of July, together with his Majesty's late ship Hannibal, which the French had succeeded in getting off the shoal on which she struck.

The Admiral says, "I almost despaired of having a sufficient force in readiness to oppose to such numbers, but, through the great exertions of Captain Brenton, the officers, and men, belonging to the Cæsar, the ship was in readiness to warp out

out of the Mole yesterday morning, and got under weigh immediately after, with all the squadron, except the Pompee, which ship had not had time to get in the masts." The Admiral says he was determined, if possible, to obstruct the passage of this very powerful force to Cadiz. Late in the evening he observed the enemy's ships to have cleared Cabareta Point, and at eight he bore up with the squadron to stand after them. His Majesty's ship Superb, being stationed a-head of the Cæsar, he directed Captain Keats to make sail and attack the sternmost ships in the enemy's rear, using his endeavours to keep in shore of them. At eleven the Superb opened her fire close to the enemy's ships, and on the Cæsar's coming up, and preparing to engage a three-decker, that had hauled her wind, she was perceived to have taken fire, and the flames having communicated to a ship to leeward of her, both were seen in a blaze, and presented a most awful sight. No possibility existing of offering the least assistance in so distressing a situation, the Cæsar passed to close with the ship engaged by the Superb, and by the cool and determined fire kept upon her, which must ever reflect the highest credit on that ship, the enemy's ship was completely silenced, and soon after hauled down her colours.

The Venerable and Spencer having, at this time, come up, he bore up after the enemy, who were carrying a press of sail, standing out of the Straits, and lost sight of them during the night. It blew excessively hard till day-light, and in the morning the only ships in company were the Venerable and Thames, a head of the Cæsar, and one of the French ships at some distance from them, standing towards the shoals of Conil, besides the Spencer astern, coming up.

All the ships immediately made sail with a fresh breeze; but, as we approached, the wind suddenly failing, the Venerable was alone able to bring her to action, which Captain Hood did in the most gallant manner, and had nearly silenced the French ship, when his main mast, (which had been before wounded) was unfortunately shot away, and it coming nearly calm, the enemy's ship was enabled to get off without any possibility of following her. The French ship was an 84, with additional guns on the gunwale.

The enemy's ships (he adds) are now in sight to the westward, standing in for Cadiz. The Superb and Audacious, with the captured ship, are also in sight, with the Carlotta, Portuguese frigate, commanded by Captain Crawfurd Duncan, who very handsomely came out with the squadron, and has been of the greatest assistance to Captain Keats, in staying by the enemy's ship captured by the Superb.

The Spanish Admiral's ship, the Real Carlos, and the Sans Hermenegildo, were the two ships that took fire and blew up. The San Antonio, of 74 guns, under French colours, was taken by the Superb.

Sir James Saumarez received the following statement from Captain Keats:—

The Captain informs the Admiral, that in consequence of his directions to make sail up to and engage the sternmost of the enemy's ships, he, at half past eleven, found himself abreast of a Spanish three-decked ship, which, having brought in one with two other ships, nearly line abreast, he opened his fire upon, at not more than three cables' length; this evidently produced a good effect, as well in this ship as the others abreast of her, which soon began firing on each other, and at times on the Superb. In about a quarter of an hour he perceived the ship he was engaging, and which had lost her foretop-mast, to be on fire, upon which they instantly ceased to molest her, and she proceeded on to the San Antonio, of 74 guns, and 730 men, commanded by the Chief of Division, Le Rey, under French colours, and manned nearly equally with French and Spanish seamen, and which, after an action (the Chief being wounded) struck her colours. He learns from the very few survivors of the ships that caught fire and blew up, that in the confusion of the action, the Hermenegildo mistaking the Real Carlos for an enemy, ran on board her, and shared her melancholy fate. Fourteen seamen and marines have been wounded on board the Superb; this is the extent of the British loss in this action.

The Gazette of August 4 announces, that Lord Cochrane, of his Majesty's sloop Speedy, off Barcelona, May 6, after a mutual chace and warm action had captured a Spanish frigate of 32 guns, twenty-two long-twelve pounders, and two heavy carronades, named the Gamo, commanded by Don Francisco de Torris, manned by 319 naval officers, seamen, and marines. He says, the great disparity of force rendering it necessary to adopt some measure that might prove decisive, he resolved to board, and, with Lieutenant

nant Parker, the Hon. Mr. Cochrane, the boatswain, and crew, boarded, when, by the impetuosity of the attack, they forced them instantly to strike their colours. He has to lament, in boarding, the loss of one man only, and the severe wounds received by Lieutenant Parker and the boatswain.

Lord Cochrane says, the Speedy's force, at the commencement of the action, was 54, officers, men, and boys.

A letter received from Lord Nelson, dated on board his Majesty's ship Medusa, off Boulogne, the 4th of August, states, that the enemy's vessels, brigs, and flats, (lugger rigged) and a schooner, twenty-four in number, were that morning, at day-light, anchored in a line in the front of Boulogne; the wind being favourable for the bombs to act, he made the signal for them to weigh, and to throw shells at the vessels, but as little as possible to annoy the town; the Captains placed their ships in the best possible position, and in the course of the morning six were on shore, evidently much damaged; at six in the evening, before high water, five of the vessels which had been a-ground, hauled, with difficulty, into the Mole, the other remained under water: his Lordship believes that the whole of the vessels would have gone inside the pier but for want of water. What damage the enemy have sustained, beyond what his Lordship saw, it was impossible to tell.

The Noble Admiral anchored, on the 7th of August, in Margate-roads, with fixteen sail of gun brigs, and was received with well deserved honours.

Lord Nelson, on his arrival at Margate, dispatched an express to Captain Ruddell, Commanding Officer of the Ramsgate Sea Fencibles, to know whether he might rely on the assistance of that corps, if circumstances should render it necessary to call them forth; to which they unanimously answered, "that if his Lordship would send a gun-boat for them, they would immediately attend his Lordship whithersoever he pleased."

The following is the result of the authentic intelligence which has been received from Lord Nelson respecting a second attack upon Boulogne on the 18th of August.

Lord Nelson imputes the failure of success principally "to the darkness of the night, with the tide and half-tide, which separated the divisions, and to the circumstances of all the divisions not arriving at the same happy moment with Captain Parker, but he begs leave to be perfectly understood, that not the least blame attaches itself to any person." The plan of attack was as follows:—eight flat boats, with howitzers, were under the direction of Captain Conn; and six flat boats, armed with marines only, together with the boats belonging to the different ships and cutters in the squadron, were put under the command of Captain Somerville, of the Eugenie, who made four equal divisions of them, each consisting of flat boats, and about eleven six-oared boats. The first division, with himself; the second, under Captain Parker, of the Medusa; the third, under Captain Cotgrave, of the Gannet; and the fourth, under Captain Jones, of the Diligence. Each division having assembled on board the ships appointed, shoved off from them about eleven o'clock in the night of August the 15th. Each division having its proportionate number of the enemy's vessels to attack; the first beginning to the eastward, and so on in the order westward.

The second division got in first, the third soon after, which commenced a fire upon the enemy, but they were both soon obliged to retreat, having lost many men, particularly the former. The first division, owing to the strength of the tide, did not reach the part allotted them until a little before day-light, when, amidst a tremendous fire of shot, shells, and musquetry, from the shore, as well as from the gun-vessels, they very gallantly boarded the largest of the enemy's vessels, a brig, mounting long twenty-four pounders and carronades, two of which were upon the quarter-deck, pointing forwards. She was manned with 150 soldiers, besides seamen; her crew was strongly barricaded abaft the main mast, and kept an incessant fire upon our men; in the interim of boarding, being first obliged to clear away her strong boarding-netting, those allotted to cut the cables, to their great disappointment, found her moored with strong chains also, fixed to her keel. Owing to the heavy fire from the soldiers on board, which was spiritedly returned by our marines, they were not able to get entire possession of her, nor could they get at any means to set her on fire. After being three quarters of an hour on board and along side of her, they were obliged to abandon her, leaving a great number of their dead upon deck. The fourth division, notwithstanding every exertion of Captain Jones, and the officers and men in his division, to get into action, could not succeed, owing to the tide.

Amongst the wounded are Captain Parker,

Parker, and Lieutenant Langford.—Total, 4 officers, 33 seamen, 7 marines, killed; 14 officers, 84 seamen, 30 marines, wounded.—Total killed and wounded, 172.

Messrs. Williams and Gore two, Midshipmen of the Medusa, are since dead of their wounds at Deal.

The fate of Mr. Graves, Master of the Cæsar, the flag-ship of Admiral Saumarez's squadron, was very singular, and much to be lamented. He was standing on the poop between the Admiral and an officer, giving his directions for bringing the ship close to the enemy, along-side, in order that a single broadside might finish the contest, when a spent ball from a battery, seen in its approach by numbers, but not discerned by the unfortunate officer, took him in the neck, and severed his head from his body. He was buried next day at Gibraltar, with military honours.

We learn from Weymouth, that the King, on the 30th of July, declared his Grace the Duke of Portland, Lord President of his Majesty's Most Hon. Privy Council, and his Grace took his place at the Board accordingly. On the same day the King appointed the Right Hon. Thomas Pelham to be one of his Majesty's Principal Secretaries of State, in the room of his Grace the Duke of Portland.

LIST OF DISEASES IN LONDON.

Account of Diseases in an Eastern District of London, from the 20th of July to the 20th of August, 1801.

ACUTE DISEASES.	*No. of Cases.*
TYPHUS	28
Hepatitis	1
Acute Rheumatism	1
CHRONIC DISEASES.	
Tussis	10
Tussis et Dyspnœa	7
Pleurodyne	3
Phthisis Pulmonalis	2
Hydrothorax	2
Anasarca	3
Ascites	1
Cephalalgia	5
Paralysis	3
Vomitus	3
Diarrhœa	8
Dyspepsia	8
Chlorosis	4
Menorrhagia	4
Asthenia	4
Scrophula	3
Hæmorrhois	2
Hypochondriasis	3
Psora	4
Herpes	7
Lepra	1
Rheumatismus Chronicus	13
PUERPERAL DISEASES.	
Peritonitis	1
Mastodynia	2
Menorrhagia lochialis	3
INFANTILE DISEASES.	
Vermes	2
Herpes	5
Diarrhœa	4

Whilst we are under the necessity of again adverting to a subject, which we have long been obliged to consider—the prevalence of the typhoid contagion—we are at the same time happy to announce, that the symptoms of the disease are much less formidable than they have heretofore been, and that a fatal termination takes place much less frequently. The number of patients affected by it has indeed been rather increased, and it continues to propagate itself very extensively; but those affections of the brain, which formerly constituted so prominent a feature of the disease, occur less frequently and appear under a milder form.

The symptoms of angina also, which, in the last report, were mentioned as accompanying the disease, have disappeared. The disease therefore now appears under a form in which we have heretofore been accustomed to view it.

Complaints of the stomach and bowels have been very frequent. Diarrhæas have, in several instances, been troublesome, and have continued for a considerable time; but they have not been attended with any unpleasant consequences, unless when they have been injudiciously checked by astringents; or when, under the idea of supporting the strength of the patient, during the increased evacuation, recourse has been had to some warm cordial.—Upon a premature check to this evacuation we often hear of pains in the stomach and bowels, of which the patient did not before complain, and the removal of which is best accomplished by inviting the return of that discharge which nature had instituted with a view to relieve the constitution.

ALPHABETICAL

ALPHABETICAL LIST *of* BANKRUPTCIES *and* DIVIDENDS *announced between the 20th of July and the 20th of Aug. extracted from the London Gazettes.*

BANKRUPTCIES.

(The Solicitors' Names are between Parentheses)

ASHETON, T. N. Liverpool, merchant and underwriter. (G. Orrell, Liverpool)
Beveridge, T. Little street, factor. (Fishman and Pringle, Ely place)
Bradley, T. Wigan, shopkeeper. (Windle, Bartlett's buildings)
Bleffard, R. Great Bank, Bamford, Middleton, Lancashire, miller. (Messrs. Allen, Clement's inn)
Baldwin, W. Wigan, scrivener. (J. Hodgson, Chancery lane)
Crosby, J. Oxford street, mercer. (Auber, Elder street, Spital square)
Chamley, Wm. Liverpool, merchant. (Barrett, Manchester)
Chamley, Edm. Liverpool, merchant. (Barrett, Manchester)
Collin, M. and T. Lewis, Hatton Garden, navy agents. (Gale, Bedford street, Holborn)
Coleman, J. Bow street, Covent Garden, bricklayer. (Jones, Duke street, Lincoln's inn fields)
Clay, J. Batley, drysalter. (Battye, Chancery lane)
Collier, Geo. Shrewsbury, scrivener. (S. Stanley, Newport)
Davies, John, Callington, linen-draper. (Batten and Anstie, Temple)
Day, Wm. Cheapside, mans-mercer. (Bleasdale and Alexander, Hatton court)
Damerum, Jas. Portsmouth, baker. (Watts, Symond' inn)
Evans, John, Blackrod, victualler. (Sharpe and Eccles, Manchester)
Firth, J. Sowerby, Halifax, cornfactor. (Cardale, Hallward, and Spear, Gray's inn)
Field, Benj. Union street, Bishopsgate street, upholsterer. (Hall, Poultry)
Griffiths, Thomas Heusbridge, victualler. (Dyne, Serjeant's inn)
Gandar, Wm. St. John's street, plaisterer. (Welchon, Furnival's inn)
Griffin, Edw. St. Michael, in Bedwardine, grocer. (J. Allen, Worcester)
Gilks, T. Warwick, cornfactor. (Smart, Staple's inn)
Gore, Thomas, College Hill, London, warehouseman. (Boustead, Savage Gardens)
Harper, R. Newcastle-under-Lyne, scrivener. (Good, Tooting)
Holmes, T. Oxford, cordwainer. (Pallpot, Red Lion square)
Holmes, I. and J. Palmer, Craven street, army-brokers. (Dyne, Serjeant's inn)
Hardy, H. Snow hill, card-maker, (Leversedge, Fore street)
Horne, Jas. Jun. Woodbridge, corn merchant. (Bromley and Bell, Gray's inn)
Keighly, Jas. J. F Ferguson, and Wm. Armstrong, London, merchants. (Messrs. Shawe, Tudor street)
Kelly, Mich. Camden row, Pancras, warehouseman. (Allingham, St. John's square)
Macher, Wm. Parker's row, Bermondsey, baker. (Davies, Warwick street, Golden square)
Marsden, Wm. and C. Tonge, Liverpool, merchants. Lee, Temple, and Gregson and Smart, Angel court, Throgmorton street)
Motherhead, S. Manchester, cotton-manufacturer. (Edge, Manchester)
Marsden, W. Manchester, merchant. (Atcheson, Ely place)
Maddocks, R. Barge yard, Bucklersbury. (Hard, Furnival's inn)
Maddocks, R. and Wm. Barge yard, Bucklersbury, warehousemen. (Cruckshank, Basinghall street)
Miller, T and J. Hulme, Manchester, dealers in Weft. (Ellis, Cursitor street)
Mistlewood, Jas. Manchester, fruiterer. (Ellis, Cursitor street)
Mathews, J. Gargrave, Yorkshire, dealer. (G. and J. Crump, Liverpool)
Meany, W. Lamford, parish of Burrington, Somerset. (Blandford and Sweet, Temple)
Phillips, J. Walers, baker. (Sandys and Horton, Crane court, Fleet street)
Richardson, W. Sutwood, whitster. (Kaye, Bolton-le-Moors)
Robinson, Jas. Crosby square, merchant. (Smith and Lawson, Great St. Helens)
Stanley, J. Liverpool, merchant. (Barrett, Manchester)
Solomon, S. M. Birmingham, merchant. (A. Isaacs, Bury street)
Seagram, G. Tiverton, grocer. (Lys, Tooke's court, Chancery lane)
Swallow, D. Rotherhithe, victualler. (Willett and Annesley, Finsbury square)
Somervaille, Wm. Grange court, Carey street, taylor. (Windle, Bartlett's buildings)
Somervail, Jas. Liverpool, merchant. (Duree, Fenchurch street)
Sherrist, Jas. Hatton Garden, merchant. (Johnson, Ely place)
Thomas, J. Bathwick, dealer. (Shepherd and Adlington, Gray's inn)
Toy, Thomas, Penryn, linen-draper. (Cardale, Hallward, and Spear, Gray's inn)
Wilmot, T. Woolwich, linen-draper. (Netherfold, Essex street.
Wood, John and Joseph, Wednesbury, gunlock-makers. (Bourne, Dudley)

DIVIDENDS ANNOUNCED.

Allen, W. Birmingham, druggist, Sept. 15
Banton, Edm. Lancaster, merchant, Aug. 31.
Bastier, J. R. and J. J. Zurnlin, Devonshire square, merchants, Nov. 7
Bonney, W. Liverpool, soap-boiler, Aug. 28
Bratt, C. Warrington, linen draper, Aug. 29
Bennett, J. Wootton-under-Edge, carrier, Sept. 5
Beeston, J. Manchester, merchant, Sept. 9
Clifford, Geo. and J. Blanckenhagen, London, merchants, Aug. 29
Coals, J. Wellingborough, grocer, Aug. 17
Cooper, J. Epsom, brewer, Aug. 22
Carden, W. Bristol, merchant, Aug. 31
Davies, F. Bell yard, Doctor's Commons, coal-merchant, Aug. 15
Dade, T. Great Yarmouth, merchant, Aug. 26
Eldridge, C. Cheltenham, victualler, Aug. 28
Farloe, J. Hereford, mercer, Sept. 5
Farthing, R. Blakeney, merchant. Sept. 7
Glover, G. Paternoster row, warehouseman, Dec. 5
Glassbrook, T. G. and B. Wigan, grocers, Aug. 29
Gowan, Geo. Great Ormond street, merchant, Aug. 29
Gard, Josias, North Taunton, merchant, Sept. 10
Grint, J. Wandsworth, corn-chandler, Sept. 8
Harle, J. Buston, brewer, Aug. 22
Heathcote, F. Walsall, skinner, Aug. 31
Hampton, R. Rotherham, shopkeeper, Sept. 9
Hilman, Jos. Jun. Exeter, fuller, Sept 17
James, J. Old Burlington street, taylor, Aug. 31
Jardine, A. St. Mary, Haverfordwest, shopkeeper, August 29
Jones, Wm. Cheltenham, victualler, Aug. 28
Jackson, J. Temple Sowerby, banker, Aug. 27
Ireland, W. N. Calvert, J. Overend, and C. Tomlinson, Lancaster, merchants, Sept. 4
Kimble, S. and W. Spens, Norfolk street, Strand, merchants, Nov. 5
Kirkpatrick, T. Church passage, Carleton street, Aug. 28
Lane, J. Stratford, Essex, corn chandler.
Leabon, G. Stow Market, Draper, Oct. 14
Lowe, Wm. and Wm. Brooks, Pemberton, fustian-manufacturers, Sept. 18
Lawson, S. Rotherhithe, carver, Aug. 18
Martin, R. Bristol, mariner, Aug. 26
Mallam, J. Fleet street, merchant, Oct. 10
Nardon, J. Moretonhampstead, serge-maker, Aug. 31
Mure, H. R. Mure, and W. Mure, Fenchurch street, merchants, Aug. 29
Marshall, R. King's Lynn, bookseller, Aug 18
Mason, A. Lynn Regis, corn-dealer, Aug. 29
Macnamara, J. London, merchant, Sept. 19
M'Ewan, Jonah, Castle street East, Oxford market, cabinet-maker, Sept 8.
Needham, J. H. St. Neots, draper, Oct. 22
Platton, R. St. John's square, Clerkenwell, coachmaker, Sept. 5
Pendred, J. Wellingborough, leather-cutter, Aug. 18
Parry, T. Birmingham, haberdasher, Oct. 10
Party, T. R. Myrchall, and J. Tombs, Union street, Bishopsgate street, cotton-manufacturers, Oct 10
Priddle, Thomas, and John Osborne, Snow hill, cheesemongers, Sept. 8
Reilly, Jas. and Jas. Collins, Mead's court, Bond street, taylors, Aug. 29
Roberts, Wm. Robert-town, Yorkshire, blanket-maker, Sept. 8
Rogers, E. and J. Rodd, Bread street, Woollen-factors Sept. 5
Seaborne, G. W. Narrow street, Limehouse, mast-maker, Sept. 22
Salmon, J. Sunderland, coal-fitter, Sept. 26
Stringer, J. Stockport, cotton-manufacturer, Sept. 28
Sims, R. W. Liverpool, merchant, Sept. 14
Terry, J. and Wm Richards, Birmingham, button and buckle-maker, Aug. 31
Taylor, A. Wenlock street, thimble-maker, Sept. 8
Verfille, T. Leadenhal market, butcher, Oct. 10
Williats, Fred. Brewer-street, Golden square, cheesemonger, Sept. 5
Walton, J. Birmingham, rope-maker, Aug. 28
Whitty, G. New Malton, horse-dealer, Aug. 27
Willis, J. Pudding lane, merchant, Aug. 29
Wilkins, J. Paganhill, corn-dealer, Aug. 25
Zachary, H. Lawrence lane, Irish-factor, Aug. 29

*** *We shall in future comply with the suggestion of our Correspondent at Hull, and give the description, &c. of the Bankrupts more at large. Another Correspondent at Liverpool, who wishes us to insert a List of the Insolvent Debtors, who have taken advantage of the late Act, is informed that it would fill one Number of our Magazine; and if he turns to our List of New Publications, he will observe, that such an useful List has been published in the present month.*

MARRIAGES AND DEATHS IN AND NEAR LONDON.

With Biographical Memoirs of distinguished Characters recently deceased.

The Surrey Iron Rail-way, an Act for the erection of which has lately received the Royal Assent, promises to be one of the most useful public works that have of late been undertaken for the improvement of the county. These iron roads are excellent substitutes for canals, and, in some instances, superior to them. They are executed at one third of the expence, and by not obstructing the natural flow of rivers, all the evils with which canals are at times accompanied, are avoided. One horse, on an iron rail-way, will do the work of ten, and the speed with which carriage is performed, exceeds all other modes of conveyance. This iron rail-way, commencing at Wandsworth, will, in all probability, be extended to Portsmouth, by which, at all times of the year, and, in the severest frosts, when canals are locked up in ice, stores might be, in one day, conveyed from Woolwich-warren to our fleets at Spithead—a thing which it has been long in contemplation to effect.

The Grand Surrey Canal Bill has also lately received the sanction of Parliament. Perhaps a more important undertaking of this nature was never before attempted in these kingdoms. By a cut from the River Thames at Vauxhall, to Deptford, it penetrates the south part of the metropolis; collateral cuts extend to Rotherhithe, Peckham, Horsemonger-lane, and Blackman-street. The Royal Dock-yards and Victualling-office at Deptford, will also have the advantage of communications with this grand canal. The upper part of the canal, nearly in a south-east direction from Kennington-common, passes by Stockwell, Clapham, and Upper and Lower Tooting, to Mitcham. It will be, hereafter, continued to Portsmouth. It will be now speedily executed, under the direction of that very able engineer, Mr. Dodd, who was the author of the plan.

The Committee appointed by the Court of Common Council of London, to "take into consideration and report, if any, and what remedy can be applied to remove the extravagant high price of every necessary article of human sustenance," having reported their opinion thereon, among other particulars, state, that "the benefits proposed by the late Act of Parliament, for settling the assize of bread, have been defeated by various nefarious practices, and that the same should be repealed, and in lieu thereof, that an Act should be obtained for setting the assize upon the *weight and quality only*.

Married.] At St. George's, Hanover-square, the Rev. J. Scott, of Hull, to Miss Errington, of Newcastle.

W. Blackett, esq. only son of Sir Edward Blackett, bart. of Matsen, in Northumberland, to Miss Keene, eldest daughter of B. Keene, esq. of Westoe Lodge, in Cambridgeshire.

The Right Hon. Lord Aylmer, to Miss Louisa Call, second daughter of the late Sir John Call, bart.

Mr. R. Thrasher, to Mrs. Shapland, both of Cheapside.

F. T. Champneys, of Camden Town, to Miss Silk, of Hatton Garden.

Mr. J. Marks, builder, of Princes-street, to Miss Andrews, of Abridge.

At Layton, E. Goodhart, esq. jun. to Miss M. N. A. Dethmar, second daughter of G. Dethmar, esq. of Upton.

J. Grammar, esq. of Storey-street, Westminster, to Miss E. M'Comb, of Walcot-place, Lambeth.

L. Millington, esq. of Berner's-street, to Miss E. Shermer, of Lambeth Lawn.

T. Phillips, esq. of the City Chambers, to Miss C. Arbouin, fourth daughter of the late M. Arbouin, esq.

J. S. S. Smith, esq. of Lamb's Conduit-street, to Miss Turner, of Queen's-square, Bloomsbury.

Lieut. Col. Hutchinson, of the 49th regt. to Miss L. Vaillant, youngest daughter of Paul Vaillant, esq. of Pall Mall.

Died.] At his brother's, in Gerrard-street, Mr. Robert Christie, surgeon of his Majesty's ship L'Unité.

At his mother's house, Polygon, in Sommer's Town, aged 24, Ensign Charles Robert Harper, of the 2d battalion of the 9th regt. after a lingering illness, owing to the fatigues he underwent in the expedition to Holland.

At Chertsey, in Surrey, Lady Young, widow of the late Sir William Young, bart.

J. Powell, esq. author of a Treatise on the Law of Mortgages.

E. M. Mandeville, esq. author of several admired poems.

At his seat on Enfield Chase, General F. Mocher, Colonel of the 9th regiment of dragoons.

At his mansion on Blackheath, in his 71st year, the Right Hon. William Earl of Dartmouth, Viscount Lewisham, and Baron of Dartmouth. His Lordship was High Steward of the University of Oxford, Recorder of Litchfield, and a Governor of the Charter House. He is succeeded in his titles and estate by his son, Lord Lewisham, President of the Board of Controul.

On the 13th Inst. at Islington, Mrs. Jane Davies.

At Lambeth Terrace, ——— Price, esq. formerly of the city of London.

At Kensington, T. F. Saunders, esq. formerly of Exeter, Devon.

At

At his apartments, in the Admiralty, Mr. T. Sandford.

Mr. J. Lane, of Old Bond-street.

Mrs. Merry, of Queen Anne-street, West, relict of J. Merry, esq. of Micklefield, Herts.

Mrs. Browne, of Bridge-street, Blackfryars.

Mrs. Finch, of King-street, Covent Garden.

In Bedford-street, Covent Garden, Mrs. Ward, widow, late of Nuny Kirk, Northumberland.

Mrs. Haynes, of Clayton Place, Kennington.

Mrs. Bagshaw, of Duchess-street, Portland Place, widow of the late Colonel Bagshaw.

At his house, in Park-lane, aged 68, the Right Hon. Edward Lord Petre, a Roman Catholic Peer, and latterly considered as the head of that body of gentlemen. His Lordship had been for many years a martyr to the gout, which had produced a complication of disorders. This nobleman, whose virtuous character and upright conduct rendered him an object of universal admiration and esteem, was twice married, and has left a very numerous issue. He is succeeded in the title of Baron Petre by Robert Edward, his eldest son by his first wife, niece to the late Duke of Norfolk. Though a striking ornament of society, and a man who would have done honour to any situation, however high, he was prevented from ever taking his seat as a Peer of Parliament, on account of his adherence to the faith in which he was born. He was, like all his ancestors, a Roman Catholic by profession; but as a truly liberal Christian, he possessed a mind that nobly soared above all the unworthy notions of religious prejudice. Lord Petre annually expended about 5000l. in charity, a practice that was not discovered till after his Lordship's death.

At his house in Hatton Garden, Joseph Warner, esq. F. R. S. and the oldest Member of the Court of Examiners of the Royal College of Surgeons. This most respectable and valuable man was born in the Island of Antigua, in the year 1717, on the family-estate, which he inherited, together with that *ring*, famous in history, which Queen Elizabeth had given to the Earl of Essex, and which, in the hour of impending danger, he entrusted to the Countess of Nottingham, to be delivered to her Majesty. It is well known that the Earl was executed, and that the detention of the ring was acknowledged by the Countess on her death-bed, and then restored to the agonized and enraged Queen. The ring has, for very many years, regularly descended, together with the estate, in the Warner family. The subject of the present notice was sent to England at an early age, and entered at Westminster-school, where he continued six or seven years, and became an excellent classical scholar. At the age of 17 he was put apprentice to that very celebrated surgeon, Samuel Sharpe, with whom he resided seven years, he then was admitted Joint Lecturer in Anatomy at St. Thomas's Hospital, with Mr. Sharpe, after whose resignation Mr. Warner continued the lectures for a number of years. In 1746, during the Rebellion in Scotland, he volunteered his professional services, and joined the royal army under the Duke of Cumberland. In the course of that campaign, he was summoned to London, a vacancy having happened in the office of Surgeon to Guy's Hospital, and he was elected. In this very important situation, which he held during the unusually long period of forty-four years, he laboured assiduously and successfully: whilst he was employed in dispensing health to the numerous and afflicted objects, he was no less usefully engaged in communicating his knowledge to the students, who came from all parts of the country for instruction. His labours in the public service were, however, not confined to the wards and theatre of that noble hospital; as his valuable Treatises on the Cataract, on the Hydrocele, &c. and as his still more valuable volume of Cases, which has gone through several editions, amply testify. Mr. Warner's increasing and justly merited fame soon introduced him to an extensive practice amongst the most respectable and wealthy families of this metropolis; and by his brethren he was allowed to rank with the first ornaments of the profession. In 1756 he was elected a Fellow of the Royal Society, in whose Transactions a number of his communications have been published. In 1764, he was elected a Member of the Court of Assistants of the then Corporation of Surgeons, and in 1771, of the Court of Examiners, in which office he continued to discharge his duty most punctually, honourably, and usefully, until the 2d day of the month on which he died. His actual confinement by the last illness was very short, as his corporeal frame was literally worn out; but all his senses, and his understanding, continued, in an extraordinary degree, unimpaired to the end. This gave him the best opportunity of displaying that firmness of mind, for which, through his whole life, he was remarkable; for, although from the beginning, he was confident that he should not recover, and indeed predicted within a few days of when his death would happen, yet his whole conduct was unembarrassed, and he was even cheerful in the immediate prospect of that great change for which he was so well prepared. There are few situations in which an individual can be more eminently or extensively useful to mankind, than in that of a physician or surgeon to one of the hospitals of this great metropolis; those schools from whence anatomical, medical, and chirurgical knowledge is dispersed over the world. That Mr. Warner has fully acquitted himself of his share of this arduous but pleasing duty, the present and future generations will gratefully acknowledge. In appreciating his merits in this respect, it should not be forgotten that he was amongst the *early* teachers of anatomy in this country, whose labours have greatly contributed to render London, at the present day, the first chirurgical school in the world. Mr. Warner's education and manly understanding qualified him for the best society—he was a man of strict integrity, and punctiliously attentive to truth, even in small matters; and his manners were those of a polished gentleman. One who was honoured with his friendship during the last 19 years of his life, is desirous of paying this small but grateful tribute to the memory of a man in whose character nothing *mean* or *little* ever formed a part.

PROVINCIAL OCCURRENCES,

WITH ALL THE MARRIAGES AND DEATHS,

Arranged geographically, or in the Order of the Counties, from North to South.

*** *Authentic Communications for this Department are always very thankfully received.*

NORTHUMBERLAND AND DURHAM.

Lately, at Newcastle, at a special Court of the Governors of the Infirmary for the counties of Durham, Northumberland, and Newcastle upon Tyne, it was unanimously resolved that the Infirmary, in its present state, is but ill calculated to answer the benevolent purposes of such an institution; and that a subscription be entered into for the purpose of carrying into execution a plan proposed, in a report of their committee, for the *improvement and extension of the building of the Infirmary.* The Duke of Northumberland has transmitted a draft of 500l. as a contribution towards this useful purpose; Sir J. E. Swinburne, Bart. has given the sum of 100l.; as have also Sir M. W. Ridley, Bart.; Lady Ridley; Sir C. Monck, Bart.; Sir T. H. Liddell, Bart.; C. J. Brandling, esq.; W. Ord, esq.; and T. R. Beaumont, esq. There are other considerable benefactions, of fifty pounds, twenty guineas, ten guineas, five guineas, &c. &c.

At Durham assizes, which ended August 1, the following prisoners received sentence of death, viz. M. Sedgwick for a burglary, and A. Brown, Benjamin Simpson, William Saxton, and William Arthur, for sheep-stealing. They were all reprieved except William Arthur, who was left for execution.

Married.] At Newcastle, Mr. J. Lowes, draper, of Morpeth, to Miss A. Robertson, daughter of the late Rev. Mr. Robertson.—Mr. T. Snowball, tallow-chandler, to Miss A. Hastings, of Alnwick.—Mr. J. Watson, colliery viewer, to Miss Lawson, of Heaton.

Mr. Gregson, sail-maker, to Miss Allison, daughter of the late Mr. J. Allison, coal-fitter, both of Monkwearmouth.

At Durham, Mr. Mason, musician, to Miss Kemble, sister of Stephen Kemble, esq. Manager of the Theatre Royal, at Newcastle.

At Richmond, in Surrey, R. Riddell, esq. of Felton Park, Northumberland, to Miss Blount.

Mr. J. Forster, spirit merchant, of Hexham, to Mrs. Blackett, widow, of Wylam.

Mr. W. Harrison, of St. John's Chapel, Weardale, to Miss S. Todd, of Scorton, in Yorkshire.

At North Shields, Mr. R. Dodds, colliery viewer, to Miss A. Hutchinson.

Mr. W. Sanderson, son of Mr. Sanderson, Master of the Academy at Aberford, in Yorkshire, to Miss Bell, of Sunderland.

Died.] At Newcastle, in his 23d year, Mr. J. Grant, butcher. Mr. William Leadbeater, sadler and hardwareman.—In her 14th year, Miss M. A. Richardson, youngest daughter of Mr. J. Richardson, salt-merchant.

In her 67th year, Mrs. Gibson, relict of the late Mr. H. Gibson, surgeon.—Mrs. Lowrie, keeper of All Saints Workhouse; a woman much respected, for her benevolent attention to the poor over whom she presided.

Mrs. A. Fleming, of the Golden Anchor public house.—Mrs. Benson, widow of the late Mr Benson, warehouseman.—Aged 90, Mrs. Slater.—Mrs. M. Hall, widow of Mr. J. Hall, cheesemonger.

At North Shields, Mr. W. Cooper, of the custom-house.

At South Shields, aged 51, Mr. R. Harrison, master mariner.

At Ferry-hill, near Durham, Mrs. Bowlby, wife of Dr. Bowlby, register to the Dean and Chapter of Durham.

At East Herrington, Mr. J. Cummin, an eminent woodmonger.

At Battersea, near London, Mr. J. Kent, upholsterer, of Newcastle.

Mrs. C. Egerton, wife of the Rev. C. Egerton, rector of Washington.

At Peckham near London, Mrs. Powditch, formerly of North Shields.

At Toddridge, aged 60, Mr. W. Davidson, farmer.

At Hexham, aged 80, Mr. T. Cummins, who only survived his wife, Mrs. Elizabeth Cummins, aged 79, one day. They had been married

married fifty-four years, and were interred together in the same grave.

Aged 78, Mr. T. Emerson, of New-house, Weardale.

Mr. J. English, farmer, of Smalwell; he was accidentally killed by a stroke from a horse which he was dressing.

Mr. R. Urpeth, of Whickham he dropped down while loading a cart with hay, and expired immediately.

P. Darling, esq. of Bogan-green, Justice of Peace for the County of Berwick.

CUMBERLAND AND WESTMORLAND.

A correspondent of the Carlisle Journal, after noticing the prejudices of most farmers, in favour of old established systems of husbandry, and their aversion to the trying any new schemes, proceeds to observe that there are different plants, the culture of which is found very profitable in many of the southern counties, but which, it is generally supposed, would not succeed well in the northern counties—among these, he says the *vetch* seems not to have had due notice in these counties. According to this correspondent, the winter vetch will answer the most sanguine expectation, if properly cultivated and sown in a pretty good soil; a striking instance of which he points out in a field on the border of the river Petterill, near Newbiggin-hall. The luxuriance and weight of the crop is very astonishing, at least, to a Cumberland farmer. The soil is a deep sandy loam. It was plowed out of lea, in 1800, and sown with potatoe-oats. After harvest, the land was again plowed three times, and, about the beginning of October, was sown with the vetches, and well harrowed and should also have been rolled, but, in this instance, it was neglected. The plants flourished well all the winter, and about the latter end of April, the Rev. Mr. P——, by whose mode of culture this valuable crop was produced, began to cut the vetches, for the purpose of feeding his horses in the stable. This he has continued to do ever since, with good effect, and that part where the vetches were first cut, is again ready for the scythe. In short, the very large quantity which an acre of land, even in this county, is capable of producing of this excellent vegetable, the earliness in the spring, and lateness in the summer, when it is in use, the nutritiousness of the food, as well as the large quantity of manure which it produces, are considerations, which, in the opinion of this correspondent, ought to induce every farmer, at least, to try the experiment

The Museum at Keswick, of which Mr. Peter Crosthwaite is proprietor and founder, is visited by numerous parties of the nobility, gentry and others, and is still rapidly advancing in its usefulness and celebrity. He has lately published another edition of his maps of the lakes, and has likewise received a large donation of very great curiosities from the eastern world and other foreign climes; also a fine, healthy, ring-tailed eagle from the north, and fifteen new tunes for his celebrated organ, four of which are of his own composing. Mr. Crosthwaite claims the merit of having first invented, in the year 1768, the cork boat or life-boat, the model and papers relating to which, intended for the inspection of the Lords of the Admiralty, were lost or mislaid in London. In May 1800, he published in the Cumberland papers and in the Star, an advertisement which set forth forty-two capital inventions and discoveries, made by him, mostly aimed for the general good. He has, since its appearance, made two other discoveries, one of which is a copious spring of most extraordinary water, more pure than the celebrated medical springs of Malvern Hills, in Worcestershire, in the proportion of at least four to one; and it has been agreed by gentlemen of the faculty, that it is owing to their purity alone, that the Malvern waters cure the scurvy, scrophula, cancers, putrid and fœtid ulcers, with other diseases. Mr. Crosthwaite has tried this Keswick water upon four patients. It cured the first of the gravel and the stone, in a little time; the other three, who were also much afflicted with the same disorder, have but very lately begun its use and were considerably better in a few days. Water, impregnated with particles of stone and earth, and joined with acid and glutinous substances in the body, form the gravel and the stone, and plug up the minute vessels and strainers of the human frame, especially where the circulation is languid, and exercise is neglected:--the purest water, joined with exercise, it is now universally admitted, will dissolve the gravel and stone and the plugs too, and thus restore the natural circulation of the constitution, and if a due regard be paid to the use of this water and the non-naturals, Mr. Crossthwaite is of opinion, that it bids fair to subdue even the gout itself. Mr Crosthwaite exhibits a specimen of this water and some trophies of its healing power, in his Museum; he represents it as a pleasant medicine, and one of the most mild, and perhaps one of the most powerful, which art or nature ever yet produced. It is situated in the lordship of Brundholm, about 280 yards N.W. of Keswick-bridge, and nine yards from the Cockermouth road, and fronts the West; it is railed by a leaden pump (cased in oak and Skiddow slate) erected by Mr. William Jackson, for the use of his farms and his horses.

The depth of rain which fell in Carlisle last month, was 325 parts of an inch.—Greatest height of the barometer 30.25.—Least ditto 29 83. Greatest height of the thermometer 70° least ditto 32 $\frac{10}{11}$

Married.] Mr. Simpson, mercer and draper, of Workington, to Miss Hodge, of Cockermouth.

At Cockermouth, Mr. Dixon, to Mrs. Tolson.—The Rev. H. J. Hare, B. A. Fellow of Queen's College, Oxford, eldest son of the Rev. E. Hare, B. D. of Docking Hall, in Norfolk, and Rector of Workington, &c. in Cumberland, to Miss M. Patterson, of Melmerby Hall, in Cumberland.—Mr. C. Park, of the Globe public-house, in Carlisle, to Miss M. Bell, of Rose Tree.

At Gretna, Mr. W. Jackson, of Carlisle, to Miss M. Harding, of Bury, in Lancashire.

At Penrith, the Rev. W. Edmonson, of Scarby, in Lincolnshire, to Miss Jennings, of Thirlkeld.

Died.] At Carlisle, Mr Lothian, coachmaker. His death was occasioned by an accidental circumstance. Looking at some persons that were amusing themselves by throwing the hammer, about four days before, the hammer slipped from the hands of the person who was throwing it, and taking a wrong direction struck Mr. Lothian forcibly on the forehead.

At Whitehaven, aged 76, Mrs. A. Taylor, widow.

At Workington, in his 80th year, Capt. W. Thompson, many years master of the ship Diligence, of that port.—Aged 68, of an apoplexy, Mrs. A. Marshall. In the prime of life, of a malignant fever, Mrs. Armstrong, wife of Mr. Armstrong, officer of excise. Her marriage had been announced in the Cumberland packet only a few weeks before.

At Kendal, aged 68, Mr. T. Gandy, a quaker.—Aged 74, Mr. J. Dickinson, sadler.—Mr. Richard Conway.—Mrs. Js. Kemp.

At Penrith, Mr. A. Harrison, an eminent surgeon.

At Maryport, Master H. Bettleston, youngest son of Mr. Bettleston.

At Ambleside, advanced in years, Mrs. Taylor, widow, late of Abbots Hall, near Kendal.

In London, Mr. J. Barton, second son of the late M. Benjamin Barton, formerly of Carlisle.—Also, in the prime of life, Mrs. Smith, wife of Mr. Smith, merchant, and second daughter of the late Mr. J. Barnes, merchant, of Workington.

At Annan, Mr. G. Johnstone, late an officer of excise.

At Beckermont, Mr. H. Caddy, senior of Whitehaven.—Lately, Mrs. Taylor, relict of the late W. Taylor, esq. formerly surgeon of Greenwich Hospital, and only surviving daughter of the late J. Fletcher, esq. of Clea Hall, in Cumberland.

At Longburgh, aged 94, Mrs. A. Pattinson, widow.—On his passage from the West Indies, in his 23d year, Mr. J. Wynn, a native of Workington, and master of the ship Thetis, of Liverpool.

At Stanmore, the Rev G. D. Andrews, of Pembroke College, Oxford.

At Wigton, in an advanced age, Mrs. H. Wetherald, a Quaker; of a life truly exemplary and adorned with many excellent and endearing virtues, amonst which her charity to the poor shone always conspicuous.

YORKSHIRE.

Mr. Stavely has lately discharged from the prison in York Castle eleven poor debtors, out of the sum of 17l. 11s. left in his hands for that purpose, by the High-sheriff and Gentlemen of the Grand-jury.

The THIRSK AGRICULTURAL SOCIETY have announced their determination to give the following premiums on the 31st of August next, viz. for the best shearling sheep, 3l. 3s.; for the best two-shear sheep, 3l. 3s.; for the best heifer, 3l. 3s.; and for the best cow in milk, and bulled again, 3l. 3s.

The following is an Account of the Success of the Vessels that have lately arrived at Hull, from the Greenland and Davis's Straits Fisheries.

Ships.	*Captains.*	*Whales.*	*Butts of Blubber.*	*Tons of Fin.*
Brothers,	Marshall -	20	600	13
North Briton,	Edmonds -	10	330	6
Lynx,	Palmer -	14	470	9½
Symmetry,	Rose -	18	280	3
True Love,	Greenshaw	14	230	4
Oak Hall,	Colley -	9	106	1
Ariel,	Wilkinson	3	36	1
Minerva,	M'Bride -	9	106	1
Samuel,	Welbourn -	8	180	3
Blenheim,	Webster -	2	90	1
Manchester,	Matson -	16	270	3½
Molly,	Sadler -	29	350	4
Fanny,	Jennison -	11	255	4
Sarah and Elizabeth,	Hewitt -	10	123	1
Egginton,	Wray -	7	120	2½
Maria,	Mackiver -	9	150	2
Hunter,	Groat -	14	225	2½
Ellison,	Allen -	18	400	6
Lottery,	Rose -	9	210	3½
Elizabeth,	Tather -	19	360	5
Traveller	Armstrong	14	240	3
John,	Hutchinson		141	2
At Whitby.				
Volunteer,	Beolington,	11	270	4
Experiment,	Baxter,	15	250	4
Henrietta,	Kearsley,	10	270	4
Lively,	Case,		100	

At York assizes, which closed July 27, Sir Alan Chambre passed sentence of death on the following prisoners:—E. Hughes, for a

rape

rape; R. Grimshaw, E. Hill, and T. Coupland, for burglary; D. Whitaker, for forgery; G. Walker, for highway-robbery; and W. Foster, for horse-stealing.

Married.] Mr. A. Stansfield, of Stansfield, to Miss G. Sutcliff, of Langfield, both near Halifax.—Mr. W. Taylor, of Thornthorpe, to Miss West, of Norton, both near Malton.—Mr. J. Ware, flax-dresser, of York, to Miss D. Riplay, of Ingleby Manor, in the North Riding.—Mr. J. Wood, merchant, to Miss Nailor, daughter of Mr. T. Naylor, tobacconist, both of Bradford.

In London, Captain R. Barnes, of the ship Acton, of Hull, to Miss Willson, of Lynn, in Norfolk.

Mr. Mountain, of Knaresborough, to Miss E. Robson, of Newcastle-upon-Tyne.—Mr. J. Fielding, of the New-inn, Sheffield Moor, to Miss H. Colley.—Mr. G. Swinden, farmer, of Ecclesnall, to Mrs. A. Bustard, of Sheffield.

At Doncaster, Mr. Woofindin, of the Mail-coach public-house, to Mrs. E. Rackstraw, late house-keeper to G. Cooper, esq.

At York, Mr. R. Brown, confectioner, to Mrs. Clubley, of the same business.—Mr. W. Benson, to Miss E. S. Benson.

Mr. R. Dent, merchant, of Knaresborough, to Mrs. Wilkinson, of Manchester.

Mr. B. Dawson, woolstapler, of Apperley-bridge, to Miss Blackburn, of Bradford.

At Beverley, J. Foster, M. D. of Hornsea, to Miss Keld.

Mr. T. Gurnell, to Mrs. Gosway, both of Wakefield.—T. Robinson, esq. of Newcastle, to Miss A. F. Welbank, youngest daughter of the late C. Welbank, of Mount Pleasant, near Northallerton.—Mr. G. Danby, of Burlington, to Miss Butler, of Hornsea.

At Ripley, Mr. Bellerby, an eminent farmer, in Kilnwick Percy, to Miss Atkinson, of Killing Hall.—Mr. Parkinson, attorney, of Horncastle, to Miss H. Heald, youngest daughter of the late Mr. Heald, of Wakefield.

The Rev. F. Wrangham, vicar of Hunmanby, to Miss D. Cayley, second daughter of the late Rev. D. Cayley, rector of Thormanby.—Mr. T. Dennison, farmer, to Miss B. Wilson, both of Easingwould.—Mr. R. Bewlay, of York, to Miss Murfer, of Huntingdon.

At Sheffield, Mr. C. Brookfield, solicitor, to Miss Preston, eldest daughter of the Rev. M. Preston.—Mr. J. Hole, serjeant in the train of artillery, to Miss S. Gledhill.—Also, Mr. S. Mitchell, to Miss Brightmore.—Mr. W. Batt, maltster, of Wakefield, to Miss H. Bedford of Leeds.—G. W. Dowker, esq. of Salton, to Miss Chambers, of Kirk Ella.—Mr. Greenwood Bentley, attorney, of Bradford, to Miss Stockdale of Malton, near Skipton, in Craven.—Mr. Morris, apothecary, to Miss Holtby, both of Burlington.

At Hull, Mr. Milner, to Miss Wallis, daughter of Mr. C. Wallis, gunsmith.

Died.] At York, aged 29, Mr. T. Bell, son of Mr. Bell, builder.—Mrs. Peart, wife of Mr. Peart, tea-dealer.—The Rev. T. Pickard, vicar of St. Martin's, Coney-street, and one of the vicars-choral of the cathedral.—Aged 13, Master J. Champney, third son of Mr. Champney.—In her 68th year, Mrs. Duncanson, relict of Mr. R. Duncanson, bookbinder.

At Hull, aged 40, Mr. R. Jenkinson, glass and China-man.—Aged 68, Mrs. D. Sutton.—Miss J. Flower.—Aged 63, Mr. W. Hebblewhite, taylor.

At Wakefield, aged 24, after a very short illness, Mr. J. Bradley, jun. currier; he acted as fugle-man, to the corps of Royal Wakefield Volunteers.

At Whitby, aged 80, Mrs. Proud, widow.

At Beverley, aged 63, Mrs. Nelson, widow of the late M. Nelson, esq.—In the prime of life, Mr. Wilson, of the King's Head inn.

At Doncaster, aged 24, Mrs. Spink, late of the Blue Bell public-house.

In his 71st year, J. Roberts, esq. of Hill End, in Saddleworth; a man esteemed through life for his public spirit, testimonies of which will probably remain in Saddleworth, to late posterity; as likewise for his useful labours, true Christian exertion, and humane and charitable attention to the poor.

At Sharrowhead, near Sheffield, of an apoplexy, in his 73d year, Mr. W. Smith, of the City of Norwich.

At his lodgings, in London, Dr. T. Fowler, of York; a gentleman of distinguished professional abilities, which he exercised with great benevolence and humanity; also, a sincere Christian, a warm, disinterested friend, a kind brother, and a tender and truly affectionate husband.

Mr. C. Cook, of the Royal Oak inn, Northallerton; while perambulating his hayfield, he dropped down, and instantly expired.

At Pocklington, aged 94, Mrs. Calverley.

At Hessle, near Hull, aged 75, E. Johnson, esq.

Suddenly, Mrs. Payne, wife of W. Payne, esq. of Frickley, near Doncaster, youngest daughter of the late J. Arthington, esq. of Leeds.

Mrs. Sutcliffe, of Skircoat, near Halifax.

At Knottingley, Mr. W. Lee, many years a local preacher among the Wesleyan Methodists.—Miss J. Billam, second daughter of J. Billam, M. D. of Cotescue Park, and late of Leeds.

At Rainsbutt, near Thorne, Mr. J. Keighley.

Mrs. Cundall, late of Acomb Lodge, near York.

At Terreagles, near Dumfries, in an advanced age, the Hon. Lady Winifred Constable, only daughter of the late Lord Nithisdale, and relict of the late W. H. M. Constable, esq. of Everingham, in this county.

Mrs.

Mrs. Askwith, of Bishop Wilton, near Pocklington, mother of Mr. Askwith, proctor, of York.

At Epsom, in Surrey, after a few hours illness, Sir Griffith Boynton, bart of Burton Agnes, in this county, who, had he lived, would have attained his 32d year on the 17th of July; dying without issue, his very considerable property devolves on his next brother, now Sir Francis Boynton, bart. a captain in the North York Militia.

At an advanced age, Mr. F. Parker, of Copt Hewick, near Rippon.

At Tanfield Hall, in her 48th year, Mrs. Hart, wife of Col. Hart.

At South Cave, Miss R. Tapp, daughter of the Rev. W. Tapp.—In his 68th year, Mr. T. Agar, brother to Mr. Agar, of York, watchmaker, late of Heslington, near York.—The Rev. C. Wilkinson, curate of Thornton, near Pickering.—Mrs. Milner, wife of Mr. J. Milner, woolstapler, of Morley.

At Giggleswick, in Craven, in her 92d year, Mrs. P. Hodgson, a Quaker.

At Upper Edge, near Sheffield, in the prime of life, Mr. W. Anderton.

On the 12th of April, in the camp, near Alexandria, after three days illness, of a fever fatally prevalent in that country, Lieut. J. Brook, formerly of Killingbeck.

Mr. Foss, attorney, of Knaresborough.

Mrs. Hawkridge, relict of the late Mr. Hawkridge, apothecary, of Pateley-bridge.—Aged 51, R. Carr, esq. of Gilling, near Richmond.

At Howden, aged 19, Mr. G. Cumpstone, son of the late Rev. G. Cumpstone.

At Cork, in Ireland, J. Midgley, esq. of Cook Gate, near Haworth, in the West Riding.

In her 65th year, Mrs. A. Jackson, wife of Mr. T. Jackson, tanner, in Easingwould.

The Hon. and Rev. P. Howard, rector of Handsworth, and brother to the Earl of Suffolk.

LANCASHIRE.

The Lancashire Agricultural Society, at their late meeting, awarded a silver cup to each of the following gentlemen and farmers, viz, to Mr. Parker, of Hornby Hall, for improving the greatest quantity of land, by walled stone drains; to Mr. W. Robinson, his tenant, for ditto; to Dr. Campbell, for having his estate in the best manner of cultivation; to Mr. W. Robinson, his tenant, for ditto; to the Rev. J. Stainbank, of Scale Hall, for raising the best crop of hay-grass of the first year, with grass-seeds; to Mr. Gibson, for the best long-horned heifer, two years old; and to Mr. J. Salthouse, of Scotforth, for producing, and selling, in Lancaster Market, the greatest quantity of early potatoes (29 cwt.) on or before the 1st of July.

It is in contemplation to erect at Liverpool, either by subscription, or a tontine, a commodious building, including a large and spacious hotel and tavern, with suitable news-rooms, committee-rooms, offices for merchants, brokers, convenient warehouses, &c. &c. more particularly for the accommodation of the AMERICAN TRADE, as well as for other general purposes.

An ingenious mechanic at Chorley Moor has lately invented a machine, one of which has been erected in Kendal, Westmorland, for cutting all kinds of ivory combs.

In consideration of the great extent, population, and amount of the correspondence of the town of Liverpool, the post-master-general has lately ordered an additional number of letter-carriers to be employed, for the more speedy delivery of letters; and for the further accommodation of the public, a second delivery of letters has commenced at one o'clock in the afternoon.

Sixty-six insolvent debtors have been lately released from Lancaster jail, and thirty-one ditto, from the jail at Liverpool, having obtained their liberty under the late Insolvent Act.

The increased prosperity of the town and port of Liverpool, is a theme of admiration to every stranger who visits that place. It consists at present of no less than 580 streets, lanes, and courts, whilst immense buildings are daily going forward; and some idea may be formed of its flourishing commerce, from the vast number of merchant vessels cleared out from thence. It appears from the custom-house books, that from the 24th of June, 1800, to the 24th of June, 1801, no less than 5060 ships arrived there, of the united burden of 489,719 tons, which paid dock-duties to the amount of 18,365l. 18s 2d.

Married.] At Liverpool, Mr. J. Cook, merchant, to Miss Parkinson.—Mr. Barrowclough, of Manchester, to Mrs. Aldcroft of Bolton.—Mr. Boynton, engraver, to Miss Gorton.—Mr. R. Tatham, to Miss E. Lucas, daughter of Mr. Lucas, watch-engraver.

Mr. Heelis, of Bolton le-Moors, to Miss Harrison, of Thorlby, near Skipton, in Craven.

Mr. D. Hewitt, merchant, of Manchester, to Mrs. F. Adcock, widow, eldest daughter of Mr. H. Wotton, of Poultry-lodge, Leicestershire.

At Kirk Braddon, in the Isle of Man, E. Gaven, esq. of Ballagawn, to Miss Moore, of Peele.—Mr. T. Moore, surgeon, of Preston, to Miss Fisher, of Lancaster.—Mr. Garstang, attorney, of Preston, to Miss Raskell, of Charnock Green.—Mr. J. Cooper, of Beckfoot, to Miss Gilpin, eldest daughter of the late Rev. Mr. Gilpin, of Bolton-le-Moors.

At Manchester, Mr. H. R. Drake, to Miss H. E. Haverisher.—Mr. B. Roddes, to Mrs. E. Hulme.—Mr. N. Shelmerdine, to Miss Leeming, both of Salford.—Mr. R. Pendleton, to Miss Richardson.—Mr. Baker, of the post-office, to Mrs. Kynaston, widow of the late Mr. J. Kynaston, drysalter, of Salford.

Died.] At Liverpool, Mrs. M. Dean.—Mr. G. W. Watts, merchant.—Aged 51, Mr. J. Clare,

J. Clare, merchant.—Mrs Dowson.—Mr. T. Robinson, taylor.—Aged 52, Mr. A. Brockmann, merchant and broker.—Mr. J. Mears—Mr. J. Highfield, pocket-book-maker.—In his 42d year, Mr. J. G. Langguth, merchant.—In his 20th year, Mr. C. Hughes, brother to Mr. E. Hughes, currier.—Mrs. Drogheda, wife of Mr. Drogheda, joiner.

At Manchester, in his 22d year, Mr. H. Turner.

At Lancaster, M. Jones, esq.

Miss B. Whitehead, of Ainsworth Hall.—Mr. N. Tatham, of Kirkby Lonsdale.

At Ashton-under-Line, Mr. S. Hadfield; a member of the Society of Change-ringers, who, after the funeral-ceremony, rung a complete mourning-peal of grandsire-caters, consisting of 648 changes, composed by a member of the society, to correspond with the number of months the deceased had lived.

At Bolton, Mr. R. Gordon, spirit-merchant,—J. Hankinson, esq. of Preston.—Mrs. Cutts, of Wimslow.—T. Lovett, esq. of Chirk.

In the Month of September last, on board the Mentor, Captain Currie, on his passage from Jamaica, Mr. J. Swaine, late of Liverpool.—Mr. F. Wiatt, of Everton.

Early in March, on the coast of Africa, Mr. Nash, chief-mate of the ship William Heathcote, of Liverpool.

At Jamaica, June 19, Captain T. Smith, of the ship Trelawney, of Liverpool.

At Kirkham, aged 94, Mrs. Isabella Silcock.

At Greenalagh, near Kirkham, aged 92, Mrs. Burch.

CHESHIRE.

At the late annual Gooseberry-shew, at Chester, the following were adjudged to be the principal prizes, viz. of red, Mr. Bell's Alcock's King, 18 dwts. 19 grs.; of yellow, Mr. Warburton's Royal Sovereign, 14 dwts. 10 grs.; of green, Mr. Warburton's Langley Green, 14 dwts. 5 grs.; and of white, Mr. Warburton's Whitesmith, 16 dwts. 1 gr.

Married.] Mr. T. Weaver, of Mollington, near Chester, to Miss H. Hartley, of Blackburn.—Mr. G. Brookes, to Miss R. Taylor, both of Butley.

At Daresbury, Mr. J. Crowther, of Manchester, to Miss Bate, of Higher Walton, near Warrington.

Died.] At Chester, Mrs. Price.—In his 70th year, Mr. P. Heath, sen. clog-maker; of a strictly upright and pious character.—Mrs. Lawrence.—Captain Newton, formerly of Hallwood.

At Frodsham, Mr. A. Davies, officer in the customs.

At Warrington, J. Edwards, esq. of Chester; he had served nearly forty years in the Cheshire Militia.

At Nantwich, Mrs. Bulkeley, wife of Mr. J. Bulkeley, hair-dresser.—Mrs. Cawley, relict of the late Rev. Mr. Cawley, of Aldford.—Suddenly, of an apoplectic fit, Sir George Prescott, bart. of Theobald's Park, Herts, an eminent banker of London, and formerly of Chester.

Suddenly, Mr. J Higginbotham, thirty-five years steward to T. Patton, esq. of Bank.

At Liverpool, in her 80th year, Mrs. Brownent, widow of the late Mr. J. Brownent, of Frodsham; also, on the same day, aged 48, her daughter, Miss M. Brownent; they were both interred in one grave.

DERBYSHIRE.

At Derby assizes, eight prisoners were capitally convicted, and received sentence of dea h—James Gration, for burglary; Richard Raddish, John Dent, John Evans, and John Reader, for sheep-stealing; Joseph Hobson, for returning from transportation; and George L. Powell and John Drummond, for a highway-robbery.

Married.] The Rev. J. Shaw, minister of the Independent Congregation at Ilkeston, and late student of the Independent Academy at Rotherham, to Miss Mason of Ilkeston.

At Glossop, Mr. T. Turner, to Miss S. Wood, both of Hadfield.

At Derby, Mr. W. Clarke, Derby and Nottingham carrier, to Miss Woolley, of the Coppice, near Ripley.

Died.] At Derby, Mrs. Mellor, wife of Mr. Mellor, mercer and draper.—Miss S. Burton, of the Horse and Trumpet public-house.

At Quarndon, near Derby, aged 37, Mrs. Battelle, wife of Mr. R. Battelle, mercer and draper.

Aged 66, Mr E. Taylor, for thirty-four years the licensed master of the free school at Spondon.

In his 65th year, Mr. R. Moore, of Scropton.

At Alfreton, Mr. J. Taylor; he suddenly dropped down in a fit of apoplexy, and expired immediately.

At Stanton, near Derby, aged 19, of a consumptive habit, Mr. G. Greaves, eldest son of the Rev. G. Greaves, and an under-graduate of St. John's College, Cambridge.

NOTTINGHAMSHIRE.

Married.] Mr. J. Dowland, of Cuckney, to Miss Parsons, of Mansfield.—Mr. J. Wilcockson, druggist, of Spalding, in Lincolnshire, to Miss L. Pinckney, of Nottingham.

Mr. J. Eley, of the Nottingham Infantry, to Mrs. Ward, of the Sawyer's Arms, Nottingham.

Mr. Jefford, of the Nottingham Volunteers, to Miss Hewes, of the Balloon public-house, Nottingham.—Mr. H. Blagg, to Miss Chettle, both of Carcolston, near Bingham.

Died.] At Nottingham, aged 55, Mr. S. Eyre, hosier, late of Derby.—Aged 73, Mrs. Cresswell, wife of Mr. T. Cresswell, of Smalldale; and, two days after, aged 45, Mr. J. Cresswell, son of Mr. T. Cresswell.—Aged 50, Mr. T. Mason, of Bretton.—Mrs. Day, baker.

At Mansfield, Mr. Cook, chemist and druggist.

At Worksop, Miss Langley, daughter of the late Mr Langley, surgeon.

At Sherwood Hall, near Mansfield, in his 84th year, J Kellet, esq formerly Lieutenant-colonel of the Royal Regiment of Horse Guards Blue.

Aged 77, Mr. G. Miran, of Newthorpe, formerly a rope-maker, of Nottingham.—Miss M. Hutchinson, youngest daughter of the late Mr. N. Hutchinson, of Southwell.

At Newark, aged 56, Mr. J. Smith, formerly an eminent printer.

Mr. F. Radford, of Little Eaton.

At Burrowash, aged 74, the Rev H. Swindell, M. A —Aged 62, Mrs. Toplis, wife of Mr. R. Toplis, grocer, of Wirksworth.

At Repton Hages, in his 63d year, Mr. S. Smith.

LINCOLNSHIRE.

At Lincoln assizes, which terminated July 22d, J. Whitaker, for uttering a forged receipt for the sum of 400l; and M. Stubley, J. Chapman, and E. Taylor, were tried and capitally convicted of sheep-stealing, except Chapman, who was admitted King's evidence; also Elizabeth Lamb, and Susannah Mottershall, were found guilty of the murder of Mr. S. Glue, of Ipsworth: Lamb was admitted King's evidence.

At a late meeting, held at Market Raisin, in pursuant of public advertisement, to take into consideration the practicability of extending the Caistor line of navigation from its present head, along the original intended line of the said navigation; and thence along the foot of the Wolds, southwardly to Hambleton Hill, in the parish of Tealby, in this county, it was resolved, That the making a large navigation from the Caistor Canal, to Hambleton Hill, in the parish of Tealby, will be of great utility to the neighbourhood. That from the plan and estimate produced by Mr. Dixon, the sum of 6500l will be required for compleating the said undertaking; and, that to meet unforeseen contingencies, and to provide liberally for the completion of the work, it will be adviseable to take in subscriptions to the amount of 10,000l.

An act of Parliament has lately passed, for dividing, allotting and inclosing the open common-fields, meadows, pastures and other commonable-lands, in the parish of Louth, in this county.

Married.] Mr. E. Johnson, grazier, of Winteringham, to Miss H. Sleigth, of Gainsborough.—Mr R. Briggs, farmer and grazier, of Trusthorpe, to Miss Trolove, of Walmsgate.

Mr. Peck, farmer and grazier, of Apley, to Miss Bell, of Lincoln.—Mr. J. Williamson, of Lincoln, to Mrs. Williamson, of Marton, near Gainsborough.

At Stamford, Mr. Manley, to Miss Robinson, both of the company of comedians who frequent that town.

Mr. D. Hebb, of Claypole, to Miss Wriglesworth, of Lincoln.

Mr. J. Hyde, of Gainsborough, to Miss Tathwall, of Bawtry.—Mr. T. Holland, farmer, of Heckington, to Miss A. Wilkinson, daughter of Mr. Wilkinson, publican, of Lincoln.

Mr. Roper, farmer, of Sibthorpe, near Newark, to Miss Kenning, of Foston.

At Asgarby, Mr. A. D. Parkinson, attorney, eldest son of J. Parkinson, esq. to Miss H. M. Heald, of Horncastle, youngest daughter of the late Mr. Heald, of Wakefield.

Mr. T. Taylor, surgeon and apothecary, of Horncastle, to Miss Thompson, of Scrielsby.—Mr. J. Marfleet, to Miss M. Leak, both of Sleaford.

Died.] At Boston, aged 58, W. Robinson, gent. and alderman of that corporation.

In his 56th year, the Rev. T. King, D. D. chancellor of the cathedral church of Lincoln, &c. &c.

At Stamford, aged 62, Mr. Cave, alderman of that corporation.—Aged 65, Mr. Bass, taylor.

Mr. F. Holland, of Market Deeping, one of the coroners for this county.

Lieutenant Garnar, son of W. Garnar, esq. of Grantham.—Aged 36, Mr. E. Foster, collar maker, of Sleaford.

In London, aged 84, Mr. Barber, who lately kept hot-houses, in Stamford.

At Louth, Mrs. Utley.—Aged 18, Mr. W. Dunn, son of Mr. W. Dunn, merchant.

At Bourn, Mrs M. Roberts, relict of the late Mr. J. Roberts, grocer and chandler.

At Blandford, in Wiltshire, aged 87, the Rev. J. Basket, rector of Dunsby, in this county, which living he had held near 60 years.

At Aunsby, aged 55, Mrs. Jarvis, late of Sleaford.

At Saltfleet, aged 25, Mr. J. Stocks, grazier.—Mr. J. Mullor, of Barrowby, near Grantham.

Mr. Collinson, grocer, of Barton; as he was walking by the side of a loaded waggon, not far from the town, he unfortunately stumbled against a stone, and being unable to recover himself, fell under the wheels, which, going over him, killed him on the spot.

At Lea, near Gainsbro', Mrs. Maddison, relict of the late J. Maddison, esq. of Gainsbro'.

At Colsby, near Lincoln, aged 36, Mr. S. T. Garratt, grazier.—Aged 76, Mr. R. Goodwin, of Ealton.

Aged 13, Miss L. Fydell, niece of T. Fydell, esq. M. P. for Boston.

LEICESTERSHIRE.

At the assizes for the county and borough of Leicester, Thomas Chapman, and Thomas

mas Hanford, for burglary; Edward Dodson, and William Oram, for sheep-stealing; and William Brown, for house-robbery, were severally found guilty and received sentence of death. They were all reprieved before the judges left the town.

Thirteen insolvent-debtors have been lately released from the jail at Leicester, having taken the benefit of the Insolvent Act.

Died.] At Leicester, Mrs. Bruce, wife of Mr. Bruce, coach-proprietor.—Aged 50, Mr. C. Duncliff, grocer and tallow-chandler.—Much regretted, Mr. G. Peet, eldest son of Mr. Peet, taylor.—Mrs. Biggs.

At Walcote, Mrs. J. Smith, widow of the late Mr. W. Smith, brass-founder, of Birmingham.

The Rev. Mr Meyrick, rector of Lutterworth, and justice of peace for this county.

Major J. S. Browne, of the Leicestershire Militia, son of S. Browne, esq. of Leysthorpe; this gentleman was returning from London to join his regiment, at Yaxley barracks, and was found dead in the coach at Biggleswade.

At Kingston, island of Jamaica, Mr. S. W. Linwood, second son of Mrs. Linwood, of Leicester.

At Loughbro', in his 75th year, Mr. R. Wykes, of the Anchor-inn, which he had kept upwards of 30 years; a man of hospitable, obliging, and inoffensive manners, and a kind, indulgent master to his servants.

RUTLAND.

At the assizes at Oakham, July 24, John Exton, and Ann Baker, of Clipsham, for killing a sheep; and Anthony Yates, for stealing to the value of 40s. were capitally convicted and received sentence of death. Yates was reprieved, but Exton and Baker, were left for execution.

Married.] T. Tryon, esq. to Miss H. Brereton, youngest daughter of the Rev. W. Brereton, of Cottesmore.—Mr. Freeman, grocer, to Miss Baines, both of Uppingham.

At the Quaker's Meeting house, Great Bardfield, Mr. J. Burges, of Kidlington-park, to Miss E. Smith, of Bardfield-hall.

Mr. T. Dain, to Miss Ireland, both of Exton.

Died.] At Oakham, Mrs. Mould.—Mr. Charity, farmer, of Greetham.

Mrs. Frisby, wife of Mr. Frisby, horse-dealer, of Uppingham.—Mr. Branson, of Edith Weston.

STAFFORDSHIRE.

At the assizes at Stafford, thirteen prisoners were capitally convicted and condemned, of whom, five were left for execution, viz. G. Fearns, for passing forged notes; and J. Smith, T. Spittle, J. Palmer, and J. Harper, for horse-stealing.

Population of the Parish of Walsall, including the Borough and Foreign:—Borough. Inhabited houses, 1043—ditto uninhabited houses, 133—ditto families, 1080—ditto males, 2500—ditto females, 2677. Foreign of Walsall. Inhabited houses, 941—ditto uninhabited houses, 50—ditto families, 1004—ditto males, 2774—ditto females, 2448. Total number of inhabitants, 10,399.

Married.] The Rev. G. Barrs, B. A. curate of Rowley Regis, to Mrs. M. Haden, widow, of Haden Hill.—Mr. F. Smith, innkeeper, of Litchfield, to Miss Woolley, of Lullington.—R. Gildart, esq. of Norton Hall, to Miss Steers, of Liverpool.—Mr. S. Hathaway, of Stonnall, to Miss L. Sharratt, of Longdon.—Mr. Corser, of Munslow Aston, to Miss Bachus, of Wheaton Aston.

Died.] At Wolverhampton, aged 40, Mr. R. Henn, optician and factor. The most prominent virtues in his character were of the convivial cast—mirth, which could lighten sorrows, beguile care, and extend the limits of innocent pleasure, without trespassing on the boundaries of morality; he likewise deserves to be more particularly noticed for his candor—his equity—his prompt and liberal benevolence; in a word, for the mildness and rectitude of his life, and his fortitude and resignation under the stroke of death.

At Kidmore Green, near Wolverhampton, aged 63, Mrs E. Claredon, widow, late of Bridgwater, in Somerset.

At Penkhull, Miss Spode, eldest daughter of the late J. Spode, esq. of Stoke, near Newcastle.

At Longton Hall, near Lane End, in her 13th year, Miss A. Heathcote, third daughter of Sir J. Heathcote, bart.

Mrs. Broade, widow, of Little Fenton.—Mr. R. Wood, of Burslem, in the Potteries.—Aged 72, Mr. W. Ashton, of Billington Farm, near Stafford.

At Walsall, Mrs. Freeth.

At Uttoxeter, aged 77, Mr. B. Frear, formerly an officer of excise, in Derby.—Aged 24, Miss Taylor, of Coton.

WARWICKSHIRE.

The late act for the Improvement of the Town of Birmingham, among other clauses, providing for the better regulation of hackney coaches, waggons, carts, &c. &c. authorizes commissioners to widen the lower end of Bull-street, by taking down the Welsh Cross, and four adjoining tenements; to widen Swan-alley, by taking down four tenements and a range of shopping contiguous; to widen the lower end of Worcester-street, by taking down six tenements; to widen the lower end of Moor-street, by taking down eighteen tenements; to widen the Market-place, by taking down five tenements adjoining St. Martin's Church-yard, also twelve other tenements, with the remaining part of the shambles; and to widen the upper end of St. Martin's-lane, by taking down five tenements, &c.

At Coventry assizes, August 1st, W. Allen, for sheep-stealing, and W. Smith, for horse-stealing, were capitally convicted and received

received sentence of death, but were both reprieved before the judges left the town.

Married.] At Birmingham, Mr. C. Pain, baker, to Mrs. Millington —Mr. W. Hill, of Soho, to Mrs. M. Wetton, formerly cook to the gallant General Wolfe, but for many years last past, a truly, tender and respectable nurse, in the General Hospital of this town.

Mr. J. Green, to Miss S. Townshend.—Mr. J. Batham, plumber and glazier, to Miss Luity.—Mr. G. Morgan, plater, to Miss S. Hart, Mr. Barke, woollen-draper, to Miss Hart, of the Swan-inn.

In London, Mr. R. Boningdon, drawing-master, of Nottingham, to Miss Parks, of Birmingham.

At Tamworth, Mr. T Sheasby, of Fountain Hall, Glamorganshire, to Miss Birnes, niece to the late Mr. Barnes, collector of excise.

At Stoke, near Coventry, Mr E. Jeffery, to Mrs. E. Kimberley.—Mr. Gunn, tanner, to Miss Fallows, both of Great Barr.—Mr. Robinson, of Digbeth, to Miss C. Tonkinson, of Birmingham.

In London, Mr. R. Pountney, currier, of Birmingham, to Miss R Keeres, youngest daughter of J. Keeres, esq.

Mr. G. Taylor, of Birmingham, to Miss Allcocks, of Worcester.

Died.] At Birmingham, Mr. T. Lloyd, youngest son of Mrs. Lloyd, of New-street.—Mrs. Bewley, wife of Mr. Bewley, toy-maker.—Mrs. Soden.—Mrs. Byrne.—Mr. R. Holt, son of Mr. J. Holt, brushmaker.—Mr. Kemble, minister of the Catholic Chapel, at King Edward's-place.—Mr Poney, of the Woolpack public-house.—Mrs. Haynes.—Aged 80, Mrs. Penrose.—Mr. Oldchurch.—Master G. Simcox, second son of G. Simcox, esq.

At Coventry, Mrs. Collett, relict of the late Mr. Alderman Collett.—Suddenly, Mr. Baylis, land-surveyor.—Mr. Lea, permit-writer in the Excise Office.—Mr. H Cole, of the Toby's Head public-house.—Mrs. Cave.

At Hampstead, near London, aged 96, Mr. Mobbs, father of Mr. Mobbs, hatter, of Birmingham.

At Nuneaton, Mr. Powell, mercer and draper.

At Tamworth, Mrs. Blick, widow, formerly of Coventry.

Near King's Norton, where he went for the recovery of his health, J. Stewart, esq. lately an officer in the Warwickshire Militia.

At Sutton Colfield, aged 78, Mr. J. Spencer, mercer, and for several years master of the Three Tuns-inn.

At Long Island, in the Bahamas, aged 52, Mr. G. Hughes, third son of Mr. J. Hughes late of Berry Hall.

At Bordesly, aged 75, Mr. B. Freeth, much lamented by his friends, but particularly by his workmen, to whom he was the kindest and best of masters.

Mrs. Hodges, of Winnall, near Coventry.

SHROPSHIRE.

At Shrewsbury assizes, which ended July 29, the following prisoners were capitally convicted and received sentence of death: J. Nutts, alias Hayward, for sheep-stealing; (standing mute, he was found mute of malice, by an inquest of twelve men impannelled and sworn to enquire for the purpose); T. Bennet, and J. Pitt, for horse-stealing; J. Brown, and J. Randles, for sheep-stealing; L. Boyden, and S. Beetlestone, for burglary; and M. Millington, for stealing nine guineas and a silver-watch. Nutts and Bennett were left for execution—the rest were reprieved.

A potatoe-plant, dug up in a garden, at Shrewsbury, produced the astonishing progeny of seventy, from a single potatoe left in the ground accidentally, last season.

Married.] At Shrewsbury, Captain Storey, of the West Middlesex Militia, to Miss Keating.—Mr. S. Lee, butcher, to Miss M. Studley.—Mr. Ames, of Bouldon, to Miss Mapp, of Richard's Castle.—Mr J. Crowther, to Miss Towers, both of Cloverley.—Mr. J. Davies, of Leighton, to Miss S Wright, of Eyton upon Severn.—Mr. Wellings, of Much Wenlock, to Miss Hudson, of Morehall.—Mr. Burton, of Much All, to Mrs. Hinton, of the Talbot inn, Much Wenlock.—Mr. W. Leake, plumber and glazier, to Miss Whitford, daughter of Mr. Whitford, plasterer, both of Shrewsbury.

At Little Wenlock, T. Cleobury, esq. to Miss M. A. Humphries, eldest daughter of J. Humphries, esq. of Broseley.

Mr. J. Calcott, of Abbott's Betton Farm, to Miss M. Bennett, of Donnington.

At St. George's, Hanover-square, London, J. W. Broughent, esq. to Miss E. Farnworth, of Whitchurch.

Died.] At Shrewsbury, Mr. Maccalaster.—Of a decline, Miss Puttrell, eldest daughter of Mr. Puttrell.—Mr. Perkins, maltster.

G. Roberts, esq. of Wilmington.—Mrs. Bather, wife of B. Bather, esq. of Mitton.

At Liverpool, aged 61, J. Mason, esq. of Shrewsbury, truly exemplary as a husband and parent, a sincere friend, and an indulgent and truly generous benefactor to the poor; in short, he was esteemed and beloved by all who knew how to appreciate his worth.

At Ash, Mrs Benyon, widow; a lady of unexampled piety and benevolence.

At Dorrington, B. Pryce, esq. of Path.—Mr. T. Humpheys, of the Old Crow, public-house, in Frankwell.

Aged 84, the Rev. D. Williams, of Llanfairfechan, religious without ostentation, and of a uniformly virtuous life.

WOR-

WORCESTERSHIRE.

At Worcester assizes, July 20, the following prisoners, John Hopley, John Thomas, Thomas Wassell, and John Thorne, for sheep-stealing; and Robert Welland, for house-breaking, were capitally convicted and all left for execution. Three other prisoners, Susannah Pritchard, for sheep-stealing; John Stone, for house-breaking; and Thomas Green, the elder, for burglary, likewise received sentence of death, but were reprieved.

A subscription has been lately entered into at Worcester, for the repair of St. Andrew's spire, an ancient structure erected in the eleventh century, and now in a state of great decay, particularly the tower, which, unless it be cased and otherwise strengthened, must, in the course of a few years, sink beneath the weight of the spire, a piece of architecture justly considered as the chief ornament of the city and county, and scarcely to be rivalled by any of the most beautiful and admired structures of Europe. The height of the base or tower is 90 feet, and that of the spire, from its base, is 155 feet 6 inches—Total, 245 feet 6 inches. Upon a survey lately taken by an experienced architect, the necessary repairs will amount to more than 500l. As this structure is beautiful and elegant in itself, and highly ornamental to the city and surrounding country, and as the tower, in its present state, destroys, in a great measure, the effect of the beautiful structure it bears, the above laudable design will, no doubt, be carried into effect, agreeable to the general wish of the inhabitants, patronized as it already is, with the names of some of the leading characters of the county.

At Worcester, a fine cart-horse, the property of Mr. T. Allies, died lately, and, as he appeared, in good condition, the carcass was opened to discover the cause, when, to the surprise of those present at the investigation, near the stomach was found a solid brown stone, nearly the shape and size of a hatter's block, which weighed full eleven pounds and a half. On further inspection, another was taken out which weighed about three pounds, and two others yet smaller.

Married.] Mr. T. Bumford, of Wyre Piddles, to Miss J Summers, of Elmley Castle.

Died.] At Worcester, Mr. E. Nott, keeper of the city-prison.—In his 88th year, Mr. E. Brough.—Mr. Nicholls, of the Rising Sun public house.—In her 31st year, Mrs. Robson, wife of Mr. Robson, solicitor, of Castle-street, Leicester-square.

Suddenly, on a rupture of a blood-vessel in his lungs, Humphrey Littleton, esq Deputy Town-clerk of this city, and one of the Coroners for the county. As a public man, he was held in general estimation by all ranks, being a most able advocate of justice, though always inclined to mercy and humanity: despising sordid interest, he studied the welfare and happiness of mankind. His integrity was beyond corruption. He likewise shone conspicuous in the relative duties, through the whole tenor of his life, and in a word, may be ranked high in the list of honest and good men.

At Brockencott, in the parish of Chaddesley Corbett, aged 82, Mrs. Brettell, widow, late of Finstall House, near Bromsgrove.—Miss Millward, of Redditch.

At Bewdley, Mrs. Hunt.—Aged 80, Mrs. Godley.

At Evesham, Miss Wilkes, daughter of the late Rev. B. Wilkes, vicar of St. Constantine, in Cornwall.

At Bengworth, Mr. M. Cartwright, a Quaker.

At Chaddesley, near Kidderminster, Mrs. S. Prat, widow.—Mrs. Essex, of Leigh Sutton.—Aged 94, Mr. J. Barrett, of Stock and Bradley.

At Dudley, Mr. Gibbons, of the Bull's Head public-house, and Member of the band belonging to the Dudley Volunteer Association.

Messrs. T. and B. Woolley, brothers.—Mr. D. Hinton, liquor-merchant, late of Birmingham.

HEREFORDSHIRE.

Population of the City of Hereford.

	Males.	*Females.*	*Total.*
St. John Baptist	484	560	1044
All Saints	900	1040	1940
St. Peter	716	872	1588
St. Nicholas	304	490	794
St. Owen	354	504	858
St. Martin	265	339	604
			6828

Number of houses 1460, which leaves more than four inhabitants and a half to each family—Majority of females 781.

Married.] Mr. R. Lane, of Stretford, to Mrs. Proctor, relict of Mr. T. Procter, surgeon, of Leominster.

Died.] At Hereford, in his 86th year, Mr. W. Kinnersley, formerly of Birchin-Lane, London.

At Ross, in the prime of life, Mr. T. Dobson, currier.—Mrs. Evans, wife of Mr. Evans, brick-maker of Leominster.

At the advanced age of 99, Mr. R. Powell, father of Mr. W. Powell, a respectable farmer, of Titley.

GLOUCESTERSHIRE.

Married.] The Rev. C. Williams, vicar of Ixning, in Suffolk, to Miss E. Snell, third daughter of P. Snell, esq. of Wheatley Court, in this county.—The Rev. R. Waddy, minister

nister of the Northgate-street Chapel, in Gloucester, to Miss Mason, of Birmingham. —Mr. G. G. Thompson, eldest son of Mr. Thompson, woolstapler, of Fairford, to Miss Newman, of Latton, Wilts.—Mr. Halliday, an eminent clothier, of Stroud, to Miss Jones, of Wrington Court.

Died.] At Gloucester, Mr. Howes, of the King's Head inn.

At Wall's Hill, near Minchin Hampton, aged 83, Mr. S. Cambridge, clothier; a truly religious, charitable, and honest man.

At Thornbury, of a decline, Mrs. Morgan, wife of Mr. T. Morgan, watchmaker.

At Newent, Mrs. Elton, formerly of Westbury upon Severn.—Mr. Hall, of Bourton on the Water.

Mr J. Wyrhale, only son of G. Wyrhale, of Bicknor Court; a gentleman of strict integrity, and truly exemplary in the characters of husband, son, and brother. Although his fortune was but small, his hand and heart were ever open to the distresses of the surrounding poor.

OXFORDSHIRE.

Married.] At Oxford, Mr. J. Bally, of Bath, to Miss Penson, of Oxford.

At Burford, lieutenant-colonel Little, of the East India Company's service, to Miss S. Chavasse.—The Rev. W. Benson, B. D. of Queen's College, Oxford, rector of South Weston and Hampton Poyle, in this county, to Miss Harrison, of Daventry.

Died.] At Oxford, Mrs. M. Carson, wife of Mr. S. Carson, rum and brandy merchant. —Aged 22, Mr. R. Burton, of Worcester College, third son of the Rev. Dr. Burton, canon of Christ Church.

Aged 74, W. Bowles, esq. of Abingdon.

At her son's house, in Holywell, aged 87, Mrs. Meysey, widow of Mr. Meysey, formerly an eminent apothecary in Oxford.

BERKSHIRE.

Married.] Mr. J. W. Shackell, of Reading, to Miss Foster, of London.—The Rev. R. F. Godmand, M. A. of Brightwell, to Miss Humphreys, of Threadneedle-street, London.—Mr. Bunce, of the Upper Ship inn, Reading, to Miss Leach, of Caversham, Oxon. —Mr. Kirby, of South Moreton, to Miss Goddard, of Blount's Court.

Died.] At Reading, Mr. Worry, boot and shoe maker.—Mrs. Scott.

At Wokingham, aged 83, Mr. T. Wilmot, an eminent surgeon and apothecary.

Suddenly, Mr. D. Holton, shopkeeper; universally respected as a very worthy man.

BUCKINGHAMSHIRE.

At Aylesbury assizes, William Clisby was convicted of stealing a lamb, and received sentence of death, but was afterwards reprieved.

Died.] At Marlow, the Rev. T. Langley, rector of Whiston, Northamptonshire.

At Carswell House, Mrs. Perfect, niece to Sir John Harrington, bart.

HERTFORDSHIRE.

At Hertford assizes, W. Cox was found guilty of setting fire to a hovel of wheat, the property of Mr. J. Hilton, of Walkeen, and received sentence of death.

BEDFORDSHIRE.

At Bedford assizes, John Brown, for burglary; William Pepper, John Crawley, John Sharwood, and Joseph Clark, for sheep-stealing; James Dear, for felony; and John Carter, for stealing a quantity of rye, &c. were capitally convicted, and received sentence of death; but were all afterwards reprieved, except Brown and Pepper.

The Committee appointed for managing the affairs of the intended Bedford Infirmary, have lately fixed upon a spot of ground, south-west of the town, which appears to them extremely eligible for the situation of the building; and they have before them a plan, to the execution of which they hope the amount of donations, added to the handsome legacy of the late Mr. Whitbread, will be ultimately found adequate; but, as a considerable sum is still wanting to form an establishment proportioned to the extent and population of the county, contributions are earnestly solicited of such of the inhabitants, landed proprietors, and others, belonging to the county, as have not already subscribed to this highly beneficial institution.

Account of the WOBURN SHEEP SHEARING, 1801.*

No person who entertains an adequate idea of the national importance of agricultural improvements can have any doubt of the beneficial effects flowing from the annual meeting at Woburn established by his Grace the Duke of Bedford. Whatever some persons may be inclined to think of exhibitions of cattle fattened to a very extraordinary degree, and tending to push that part of the graziers' business to the extreme, none can question the propriety of comparing different races of cattle and sheep in various particulars, exclusive of excessive fatness; none can doubt the utility of premiums for promoting a more correct tillage, for bringing into use new and improved implements of husbandry; none can hesitate in admitting the importance of that extensive communication of ideas and emulation of excelling which necessarily flow from bringing the farmers of the remotest parts of the kingdom into contact with each other, to examine practices to many unknown, and to listen to sentiments equally novel and interesting. The drillers of Norfolk describe their system to the adherents of broadcasting from Cornwall and Kerry, the enemies of paring and burning are enlightened by the practice of Kent and Cambridge, and every effort in tillage may be expected when the

* We are indebted for this interesting article to Mr. Young's Annals of Agriculture.

bets

bets are in decision that shall decide the merit of the most important of all machines.

The sheep shearing this year was more numerously attended than on any former occasion, but the company was not so select and so strictly agricultural as formerly. In the whole there were 921 visitors present.

Leicestershire Tups let on Tuesday, June 16. No. 3, Lord Thanet, Kent 42l.—4, Lord Preston, Beds 73l. 10s—7, ——Standley, esq. Hants 63l.—8, Lord Talbot, Staffordshire 52l. 10s.—11, S. Whitbread, esq. Beds, 2-shrs. 52l. 10s—12, —— Spung, esq. Hants 31l. 10s.—13, Henry Budd, esq. Ditto 52l. 10s—14, Rev. Mr. Andsley, Northamptonshire, 3-shrs 31l. 10s.—15, Mr. Johnson, Norfolk 84l.—17, John Butfield, Potsgrove 42l.

South-Down Ewes sold on Wednesday Morning. Lot 1, Mr. Money Hill 20 ewes at 43s. per head 43l.—2, Ditto 20 at 42s.; 42l.—3, Ditto 20. at 65s; 65l.—4, Mr. Kingsley 20 at 28s.; 28l.—5, Sir J. Throgmorton 20 at 43s. 43l.—6, Mr. Johnson 20 at 50s; 50l—7, W. Northey, esq. 20 at 48s; 48l.—8, Mr. Money Hill 20 at 61s.; 61l.—9, Mr Kingsley 20 at 44s; 44l.

South-Down Tups let on Wednesday Evening. No. 2, Sir John Sebright, Herts 10l. 10s.—4, W. Anson, esq. Staffordshire 42l.—5, Mr. Runciman, Beds. 21l—7, Ditto, Ditto 21l. 8, Sir John Throgmorton 36l. 15s.—9, William Northey, esq. Wilts 42l.

Leicestershire Tups let on Thursday Morning. No. 1, Mr Luck, Beds 10l. 10s—3, John Higgins, esq ditto 10l. 10s.—6, Mr. Kingsley, Hants 10l. 10s.—7, Mr. Negus, Beds 21l. 5s.—8, Mr Barker, Kent 31l. 10s.—11, Mr. Greasham, Beds 15l. 15s.—12, Mr. Jennings, Ditto 26l. 5s.—14, Mr. Purser, Ditto 15l. 15s.—15, Mr. Davis, Northamptonshire 15l. 15s.—17, His Grace the Duke of Manchester, Hants 26l. 5s.

Leicestershire Ewes sold on Thursday Morning. Lot 1, Mr. Kingsley 5 at 8l. 8s.—2. Ditto 5 at 10l. 10s.—3, Lord John Russell 5 at 13l. 13s.—4, Mr. Purser 5 at 21l.

Herefordshire Heifers and Cows sold on Thursday Evening. No 1, Lord Preston a year-old 14l. 3s. 6d.—2, Hugh Hoare, esq. a 2-year-old 15l. 15s.—3, Ditto ditto 14l. 14s.—4, Mr. Ridgway a cow 21l.—5, Ditto ditto 28l. 17s. 6d.

Devonshire Heifers, &c. sold on Thursday Evening. No. 1, Sir Hugh Inglis an Alderney cow 14l. 14s—2, Hugh Hoare, esq. ditto 11l. 14s.—3, Mr. Bithrey a Devon heifer 18l 16s.—4, Mr Hewin ditto 16l. 16s.—5, Ditto ditto 21l.—6, Lord Preston ditto 15l. 15s—7, T. W. Coke, esq. ditto 16l. 15s.—8, Ditto ditto 21l.—9, Lord Preston ditto 13l. 2s. 6d.—10, Mr. Wellear ditto 17l. 17s.—11, T. W. Coke, esq. ditto 14l. 3s. 6d.—12, Hugh Hoare, esq. ditto 14l. 3s. 6d.—T. W. Coke, esq. a Devon bull 21l.—Total, 1637l. 3s. 6d.

In these four days, therefore, these breeds of sheep and cattle have been spread into the counties of Kent, Hants, Stafford, Hants, Northampton, Norfolk, Hert., Wilts, and Bucks: this must be esteemed a national benefit. Whatever may be the comparative merit of these and other breeds, it is certainly an object of importance to have them scattered about the kingdom in the hands of men who will, in all probability, give them that fair trial which shall ascertain their worth, and establish the race, if found better than the breeds of the county.

Premiums for encouraging the Introduction of the Leicester and South-Down Breed of Sheep into Bedfordshire.

I. To the person in Bedfordshire who shall, between June and Christmas 1800, expend the largest sum of money (not less than fifty guineas) in the purchase of breeding ewes or theaves of the New Leicester or South-Down breed—a premium of fifty guineas.

II. A premium of twenty guineas will be given to the person who expends the next largest sum in the same object, and on the same conditions.

Committee. LORD JOHN RUSSELL, SIR C. WILLOUGHBY, BART. ARTHUR YOUNG, ESQ. Opened the letters of the claimants for the premiums.

It appears by the certificates of Mr John Butfield and Mr. John Johnson, that Mr. Richard Gresham bought sheep as described in the advertisement to the amount of 84l. and 68l. 5s.—together, 152l. 5s.

It appears by the certificates of Mr. Francis Morland, Mr. Thomas Smith, and Mr. Richard Knight, that Mr. John Bithrey bought sheep as described to the amount of 23l. 2s.; 129l. 3s.; 32l.—Total, 184l. 5s. Mr. Bithrey's own certificate also.

It appears by the certificates of Mr. John Duckitt and Mr. A. W. Hodson, that Mr. W. Runciman bought sheep as described to the amount of 120l.; 73l.—Total, 193l. Mr. Runciman's own certificate also. And that pursuant to the conditions required, he put them to tups in 1800, and intends the same in 1801.

It appears by the certificates of Mr. John Johnson, Mr. R. Earle, and Mr. J. Tenny, that Mr. J. P. Cowley bought sheep as described to the amount of 49l. 10s.; 57l.; 21l.; 84l—Total, 211l. 10s.: and it appears that he hired rams of the same breed. His own certificate also.

Decision. It therefore appears to us that Mr. Cowley is entitled to the first premium, and that Mr. Runciman is entitled to the second premium; and that Mr. Bithrey and Mr. Gresham are entitled to the use of tups gratis, having expended more than the sum required. JOHN RUSSELL, C. WILLOUGHBY, A. YOUNG.

Premiums for Fat Wethers. I. To the person who shall breed, and produce at Woburn sheep-shearing, June 1801, the best two shear fat wether—the premium of a cup, value ten guineas.

II. To

II. To the person who shall breed in Bedfordshire, and produce at Woburn sheep-shearing 1801, the best two-shear fat wether, five guineas.—The same person not to have both premiums. The name of the breeder, together with the place where bred, to be duly certified, and given in at the time of shearing.

Committee. LORD SOMERVILLE, MR. BENNET, MR. T. CROOK.

Decision. The four prize wethers died well, and have done great credit to the breeders. The judges, taking into consideration the injury which results to the public from the practice of fattening animals on corn, are compelled to withold the first prize from Mr. Moore, and to give it to Mr. Bithrey. The second, or Bedfordshire prize is adjudged to Mr. Moore, carcass and wool considered. SOMERVILLE, J. BENNET, T. CROOK. Mr. Moore and Mr. Butfield, corn; Mr. Bithrey and Mr. Cowley, no corn.

Mr. Bithrey's Two year-old Wether.—Weight alive after shearing 183lb.; carcass 105lb. 8 oz.; wool 7lb. 12 oz.—20 alive, give 12 dead.

Mr. Cowley's.—Weight alive after shearing 153lb. 8 oz.; carcass 100lb. 8 oz.; wool 5lb. 12 oz.—20 alive give 13¼ dead.

Mr. Butfield's.—Weight alive after shearing 172lb. 8 oz.; carcass 112lb.; wool 4lb. 2 oz.—20 alive give 13¼ dead.

Mr. Moore's.—Weight alive after shearing 157lb.; carcass 105lb. 8 oz.; wool 6lb. 12 oz.—20 alive give 14 dead.

Wool—Butfield 4lb. 2 oz. at 14d.—4s. 9¾. Moore 6lb. 12 oz. at 11d.;—6s. 2½. Bithrey 7lb. 12 oz. at 10½—6s. 9¼. Cowley 5lb. 12 oz. at 9d.;—4s. 3¾.

Premiums for Theaves bred in Bedfordshire.

I. To the person who shall breed in Bedfordshire, and produce at Woburn sheep shearing 1801, the best theave—a cup, value ten guineas.

II. To the person who shall breed in Bedfordshire and produce at Woburn sheep-shearing 1801 the second-best theave—a cup, value five guineas.—The same person not to have both premiums.

Woburn Abbey, June 17, 1801.

Committee—T. W. COKE, ESQ. MR. STUBBINS, of Notts. MR. SKIPWORTH, of Lincolnshire.

Mr. Butfield, Mr. Moore, Mr. Platt, Mr. Cole, and Mr. Bithrey shewed for the premiums.

Adjudged the first premium to Mr. Butfield and the second to Mr. Moore.

Premium for encouraging Improvement in Implements of Agriculture.—To the person who shall produce at Woburn sheep shearing, 1801, the best and most useful newly invented implement—the sum of twenty guineas.

Woburn Abbey, June 18, 1801.

Committee.—LORD SOMERVILLE, T. W. COKE, ESQ. MR. JOHNSON, of Norfolk.

Decision.—Mr. Leicester's improved cultivator, being a heavy, four-horse power, entitled to no premium.

Mr. Greave's scuffler, three-horse power, not entitled to any premium.

Mr. Gooch's two-horse plough at length, not entitled to any premium.

There being one premium only, it is adjudged to Mr. Salmon, for his new-invented turnip drill, remarkable for the straightness of its work.

Mr. Lester, of Northampton, exhibited a chaff cutter, worked by two men and fed by a third, which cut eight bushels in nine minutes and a half. A patent machine.

ROBERT SALMON, Woburn, Bedfordshire, undertakes to make his improved drilling and sowing machines of different descriptions as under:

Machine principally applicable for turnips or small seeds, at nine inches asunder, or less if required, the feeders being capable of containing three quarters of a pint each 9l. 9s.

The same machine with the shares made to shift to different distances 11l. 11s.

The same machine with reservoirs to supply the feeders, applicable for sowing most kinds of grain, the reservoirs not less than one quarter of a peck for each drill 13l. 13s.

Exhibitions.—Mr. Wakefied*, of Burnham, in Essex, exhibited a Suffolk stallion, of the sorrel punch breed, which was much admired.

Mr. Inskip, of Old Warden, near Biggleswade, shewed a fat pig, half of the Suffolk and half of the Chinese breed, which rendered manifest to every eye the great improvement effected in swine.

Mr. Moore, of Bedfordshire, shewed a sow of the Suffolk breed, of a form much approved.

Mr. Chaplin, of Tathwell, in Lincolnshire, exhibited some Lincoln rams, the fleeces of which were much admired: one, a two-shear, weighed 17lb.; a three-shear, 15lb.; a five-shear, 12¼lb.; and of a seven-shear ewe, 10lb. Also a fat ewe, of which the following is an account—weight alive, after 24 hours fasting 181lb.; wool 12lb. 8 oz.; blood 6lb. 8 oz.; entrails 12lb. 8 oz.; pluck and head 10lb. 4 oz.; skin 17lb. 4 oz.; fat 15lb.; carcass 118lb.—Total, 179lb. 8 oz.—20 alive give 13 dead. 20 alive give 14½ fat included.

The Duke of Bedford killed the following South-Down ewe—Weight alive, after 26 hours fasting 140lb.; skin 8lb. 8 oz; head and pluck 8lb. 8 oz.; blood 5lb.; entrails 8lb. 8 oz; fat 13lb. 8 oz.—Total, 44lb. Net carcass 93lb. 8 oz.—Total, 137lb. 6 oz Lost 2lb.

* This gentleman is a very noted cultivator. That he conducts his business with no inconsiderable spirit may be conjectured from his having dibbled, in 1800, 348 acres of wheat, all on clover lay or bean stubbles, at 12s 6d. an acre, one row on a flag, for hand-hoeing, which cost him 30s. an acre: quantity of seed two to five pecks an acre.

8 oz.—20 alive give 13½ dead. 20 alive give 15, fat included.

Mr. Edward Smith, of Clothallbury, near Baldoc, exhibited a comparative lot of Hertford (Wiltſhire) and of South-Down ſheep which had gone together, and the ſuperiority of the latter was ſtriking. One was killed, ſhorn once, and not fed with any particular attention—Weight alive 151lb.; ſkin 12lb.; head 10lb. 8 oz.; blood 6lb. 8 oz; entrails 14lb.; fat 15lb. 8 oz.; carcaſs 92lb.—20 alive give 12½ dead.—20 alive give 14½, fat included.

The Hertfordſhire not fat enough to kill.

Mr. Bithrey, of Snelſham, Bedfordſhire, gave in an account of a three-ſhear ſheep by the Woburn A, out of an Ibſtock ewe, graſs fed, ſlaughtered December 21, 1800—Weight alive 272lb.; carcaſs 386lb.; ſkin 23lb.; blood 9lb.; head and pluck 13lb.; kele 17lb.; rough fat 7lb.; entrails 15lb.—Total, 270. Loſs (ſuppoſe) 2lb.—Total, 272lb.—20 alive give 11½ dead. 20 alive give 14½ fat included.

Mr. John Ellman, of Glynd, Suſſex, handed about an account of his flock at the laſt lambing:

Oct 17th, 1800, put rams to 607 ewes. Loſt in the winter 2; loſt in lambing 6; caſt her lamb 1; barren 21; produced lambs 577. —Total, 607.

Lambs living in June 1801, 744.

The converſation this meeting, as in all the former, was entirely agricultural; the breeds of cattle and ſheep were diſcuſſed. The plough cauſed no inconſiderable ſhare of debate, and gave riſe to the following *bets*.

Woburn June 17, 1801.

Mr. Coke propoſes, that at the next Woburn ſheep-ſhearing there ſhall be a trial of ploughs; and he challenges all England, with a Norfolk plough and a pair of horſes, to plough an acre, or half an acre, of any ſoil for fifty guineas; regard being had to the depth and cleanneſs of the furrow.—Four horſes allowed for a double-furrow plow. T. W. COKE.—Accepted, EDWARD WAKEFIELD, of *Burnham, Eſſex.*

No friend to the double-furrow plough ſtood forth.

Sir John Sebright offers to bet 50 guineas, that Mr. Coke will not plough an acre of land in one day, in a huſbandlike manner, with the wheel-plough commonly uſed in Norfolk, with two horſes; an acre of which Sir J. Sebright will plough in the ſame time with a Hertfordſhire plough and four horſes: the land to be fixed upon by Sir J. Sebright, near Beechwood in Herts, in the month of October. One perſon to be named by each of them, and they calling in a third if they do not agree. J. B. SEBRIGHT.—Accepted, T. W. COKE.

Relative to ſheep alſo the following took place:

Mr. Bithrey bets Mr Moore fifty guineas, that he ſhews this time twelvemonth a better two-ſhear wether at Woburn Abbey than Mr Moore, WM. BITHREY.—Accepted, J. MOORE.

Mr. Ed. Cowley bets twenty guineas, that Mr. Bithrey produce at next Woburn ſheep-ſhearing a better two-ſhear fat wether, of his own breed, than Mr. Moore. ED. COWLEY. —Accepted, J. MOORE.

Mr. Joſeph Cowley bets twenty guineas on the ſame, againſt Mr. Moore. J. P. COWLEY.—Accepted, J. MOORE.

Offer by Sir Thomas Carr.—Sir Thomas Carr, of Suſſex, will ſhow, in June 1802, 100 bullocks and 150 acres of wheat for any ſum not exceeding 100 guineas. The gentleman who accepts the challenge to poſſeſs the bullocks at this time. Not accepted by any one.

Mr. Ellman remarked on it, that the perſon who had the oxen might not have the wheat; he therefore recommended Sir Thomas to offer ſhewing 20 oxen; and as he had above 100, he would have the advantage of many to chooſe from, and the offer might then be accepted: but this was not Sir Thomas's object; he declined it.

The Duke announced the following premiums for the year enſuing:

Premiums for encouraging the Introduction of the Leiceſter and South-Down Breed of Sheep into Bedfordſhire.

I. To the perſon in Bedfordſhire who ſhall, between June and Chriſtmas 1801, expend the largeſt ſum of money (not leſs than ſixty guineas) in the purchaſe of breeding ewes or theaves of the new Leiceſter or South-Down breed, and put them to a tup of the ſame ſort, in the years 1801 and 1802—a premium of fifty guineas.

II. All other claimants of the preceding premium who appear to have expended a ſum not leſs than ſixty guineas ſhall have the uſe of a ram in the year 1802 of the ſame breed as the ewes purchaſed, gratis.

Premiums for Fat Wethers.—I. To the perſon who ſhall breed and produce at Woburn ſheep-ſhearing, June 1802, the beſt two-ſhear fat wether—the premium of a cup, value ten guineas.

II. To the perſon who ſhall breed in Bedfordſhire and produce at Woburn ſheep ſhearing, 1802, the beſt two-ſhear fat wether, five guineas —The ſame perſon not to have both premiums. The name of the breeder, together with the place where bred, to be duly certified and given in at the time of ſhearing.

Premiums for Theaves bred in Bedfordſhire.—I. To the perſon who ſhall breed in Bedfordſhire and produce at Woburn ſheep-ſhearing 1802 the beſt theave—a cup, value ten guineas.

II. To the perſon who ſhall breed in Bedfordſhire and produce at Woburn ſheep-ſhearing 1802 the ſecond-beſt theave—a cup, value five guineas. The ſame perſon not to have both premiums.

Sundry Premiums.—I. To the perſon who ſhall

shall produce at Woburn sheep-shearing 1802 the best boar—five guineas.

II. To the best sheep-shearer, five guineas—second-best, four guineas—third-best, three guineas—fourth-best, two guineas—fifth-best, one guinea.

Premiums for encouraging Improvements in Implements of Agriculture.—I. To the person who shall produce at Woburn sheep-shearing 1802 the best and most useful newly-invented implement—the sum of twenty guineas.

II. To the person who shall produce the plough which shall with the least force turn the deepest and cleanest furrow—a cup, value ten guineas.

For 1803.—To the farmer in Bedfordshire who shall produce the most satisfactory account of comparative trials between the drill and broadcast culture of wheat, barley, or oats, on not less than ten acres, being in the same field—thirty guineas.

On the Thursday, after dinner, the prize cups being placed before his Grace, he rose, according to the annual custom, and announced to the company the several decisions of the judges, which he read.

The Duke then remarked, that as the exertions in claim of the premiums for laying out money in the purchase of stock had been considerable, and many of the breeds were spread through the county, he had for the year ensuing proposed but one premium; and he should in future, probably, drop this class of premiums altogether. As the New Leicester and South-Down sheep were now in the farmers' hands, they must speak for themselves; he had no prejudices for any breed, and only wished that such trials should be made as might bring conviction which was really to be preferred. To attempt by premiums to force any thing further than this was not his object.

The farmers will now decide for themselves by experiment, and not by opinion. The laudable example of Mr. Smith, of Hertfordshire, proves that prejudices are giving way; nor can the Bedfordshire farmers do better than imitate such comparative trials.

Relative to the decision on the fat wethers his Grace observed, that the judges had suggested the propriety of rejecting corn-fed sheep; but he conceived that the decision would effect it, and deter any one from that practice. He was happy, however, to find, that both in the case of wethers and theaves the sheep shown were highly approved; and if the Bedfordshire farmers had heard all that had been said on the occasion, it would have stimulated them to become rivals to almost any county. A happy change: for it is well known that they once did not stand very high; but with such exertions as are now making, he trusted the reputation of the county would be established.

In explaining his motive for adding the premiums to the best shearers, his Grace remarked that it was an object of considerable consequence. There were some good ones in Bedfordshire, but not many, and by multiplying them much wool would be saved. Some gentlemen might think it a small object, but this was not the case; for on the mass of all clipping a few ounces per head would amount to a quantity that rendered it a national object. If any gentlemen of the county had very good shearers, it was to be hoped they would bring them.

The Duke then took notice of the discussion which had taken place upon ploughs; and said, that as it was an object which excited attention, he was glad he had added a premium for it. Competition is the only mean to ascertain which is the best; and should it be found that Bedfordshire is disgraced by its own plough, the sooner it is got rid of the better.

On the premium for the comparison of the drill and broadcast husbandry, he observed, that opinions were extremely at variance. Possibly these methods might not yet have been tried with sufficient accuracy. That from what he had seen, he was much inclined to prefer the drill, when well managed; but if there be not a determination to extirpate all weeds and keep the drills absolutely clean, it is better not to attempt that culture. The land should certainly be clean before any trial begins; then only annual weeds will be found, and the hoeings effective in destroying them.

His Grace then generally congratulated the county on the progress made, and expressed his hope that it would, year after year, advance; and that the Bedfordshire farmers would derive an increasing credit from their laudable exertions.

The first cup was then presented to Mr. Bithrey, and his health drunk in a bumper.

NORTHAMPTONSHIRE.

At the meeting of the Peterborough Agricultural Society, on the 5th of August, a premium of three guineas, offered by the society at their last annual meeting, to the person who should produce the best shearling ram, was adjudged to Mr. Smith, of Stoke Doyle; and a premium of one guinea, for the second best ditto, to Mr. A. Buswell, of Thetford; Mr Buswell likewise produced a two-shear ram for the premium of five guineas, but having no competitor, he was allowed a compensation in lieu of the premium.

Married.] Mr. St Gandern, of Morehay Lawn, to Miss Duncombe, of King's Cliffe.

Died.] At Northampton, Mr. W. Atterbury,—Mr. P. Agutter.

At Peterborough, Mrs. Flutter, wife of Mr. Flutter, seedsman.—Aged 7?, Mrs. Porter, a widow lady.—Aged 27, Mr. J. Beetham, second son of Mr. Beetham, apothecary.—In an advanced age, Mr. J. Calpert, formerly master of the Rose and Crown public-house.

Mr. Dolby, farmer, of Southwick, near Oundle;

Oundle; his death was occasioned by a sudden fall from his horse, in coming from Stamford-market.

At Pisford, near Northampton, in his 85th year, Mr. T. Underwood, upwards of fixty years a respectable inhabitant of that parish —Mr Busfyell, of Kettering.—Mrs. Brown, of Spratton.

Mr. Monday, first coachman to Earl Spencer; on his return to Althorpe from Spratton, he was unfortunately thrown from his horse, and killed on the spot.

At Oundle, in his 82d year, J. Paine, esq. formerly engaged in a very extensive line of business as an ironmonger, but had retired many years. He was greatly respected by all who knew him, for his uniform character of integrity and benevolence.

Mrs. Clark, of Bulwick.

At King's Thorpe, near Northampton, in her 81st year, Mrs Freemeaux, relict of J. Freemeaux, esq.

HUNTINGDONSHIRE.

At Huntingdon assizes, S. Witney received sentence of death, but was afterwards reprieved.

Died.] At Park House Farm, Mrs. Bond.

Mr. J. Godfrey, of Bluntisham; he was killed in attempting to stop a hay-cart, the horses of which were running away.

CAMBRIDGESHIRE.

At Cambridge assizes, which commenced before Lord Chief Baron Macdonald and Mr. Baron Hotham, July 20, J. Aubrey, for stealing an ewe lamb, was found guilty, and received sentence of death, but was afterwards reprieved. C. Kidman, capitally convicted at the last assizes, and afterwards reprieved, remains on his former order.

At the assizes for the Isle of Ely, held at Wisbeach, G. Baker was found guilty of having stolen a parcel, containing a large quantity of printed cotton goods, from out of a gang of lighters at Ely; he received judgment of death, which, however, was changed to transportation for life.

Married.] Mr. J. H. Jetson, surgeon, of Ware, in Herts, to Miss Edwards, daughter of the late Mr. Edwards, surgeon, of Newmarket.

At Cambridge, Mr. J. Sparrow, cook of Sidney College, to Miss Stevenson, only daughter of Mrs Cowling.—Mr. R. Cockerton, farmer, of Histon, to Mrs. A. Butler, of Girton.

Died.] At Ely, Mrs. Page, widow.—In his 23d year, Mr. J. Chambers, farmer, of Swaffham Bulbeck.

NORFOLK.

Abstract of the returns made unden the Population Act for this county; 130,249 males, 148,972 females—Total 279,221.

At the late Agricultural Meeting at Swaffham, Mr. Johnson, of Kempton, exhibited a capital Leicestershire tup; Mr. Beck, of Castle Rising, shewed a South Down shearling ewe, for which he had refused the sum of one hundred and fifty guineas; it was allowed by judges to be the finest picture of a sheep ever seen of its kind. M. Hill, esq. of Waterden, also produced a very fine South Down sheep, which weighed 28lbs. each quarter. The premiums were, accordingly, adjudged to these gentlemen for their excellent stock.

The machine for drilling turnips, which the Rev. Mr. Munnings exhibited at the late Holkham sheep-shearing, is represented to be nothing more than a perforated tin box, fixed to, and vertical with, the axis of a common wheel-barrow.

Married.] In London, Mr. Ferrant, merchant, to Miss F. Gillman, of Norwich.—Mr. R. Whiting, cabinet maker, of Cambridge, to Miss Page, of Lynn.—Captain S. Millington, of the ship Spectator, to Miss Dawson, both of Lynn.—Mr. R. Daniels, of Sprowston, to Miss Humphries, of Bramerton.

At Norwich, Mr. T. Boswell, of the canteen, at the horse barrack, to Mrs. Woods, of the Labour-in-vain public house.—Mr. T. Theobald, of Norwich, to Miss E. Colman, of Ashwelthorpe.—Mr. West, of Postwick, to Miss Baker, eldest daughter of J. Baker, esq. of West Ham, in Essex.—Mr. W. Brookbank, farmer, at Foxley, to Miss M. Mills, of South Pickenham.—Mr. T. Saunders, farmer, of East Tuddenham, to Miss Spicer, of Attleborough.—The Reverend J. Raven, of Litcham, to Miss Jones, of Ely.

Died.] At Norwich, in his 65th year, J. Tuthill, esq.—Aged 80, Mr. J. Norris, parish clerk of St. Benedict's.—In her 80th year, Mrs. M. Best, a maiden lady.—Aged 73, Mr. B. Hibgame, baker.—In her 36th year, Mrs. Blake, a lady remarkable for her cool and solid sense, her mild and engaging manners, and her strict and uniform attention to the various duties of life.

At Lynn, aged 21, Miss M. Lake, daughter of Mr. Lake, hatter.—Mr. H. Hubbard.—Mrs. Day.—Mr. J. Crisp, of the Star inn.—Mr. James Hull, of Wolverton, near Lynn.—Mrs. Bayly, widow, late of West Lexham, and sister of J. Marcon, esq. of Swaffham.—Mrs. Meux, wife of the Rev. Mr. Meux, rector of Swafield.—In his 56th year, Mr. J. Plaford, of Mannington.—Aged 56, Mrs A. Annison, of Westwick.—Aged 80, Mrs. M. Betts, a maiden lady, late of Norwich.—Miss Jackson, of Wattlefield, a quaker.

At Sheffield, (in Yorkshire), in his 73d year, Mr. W. Smith, of Norwich.

At Hardingham, in her 84th year, Mrs. Alpe, widow, late of Fransham.—Mr. J. Drake, surgeon and apothecary, of Horsford.—In his 21st year, Mr. B. Jolly, of Rickingham Superior.—Miss H. Berney, of

East Dereham.—In her 20th year, Mrs. Taylor, of Dilham.

SUFFOLK.

At the Bury assizes, which terminated July 29, the three following prisoners were capitally convicted and received sentence of death, viz. William Baldwin, a private of the 3d regiment of dragoon guards, for highway robbery; James Arnold for stealing a wether sheep; and John Hardingham, for stealing a fat calf. The two latter were reprieved, but Baldwin left for execution.

Married.] Mr. Woods, grocer, of Clare, to Miss Salmons of Norwich.—Mr. Brewin, of London, to Miss Addison, daughter of J. Addison, esq. banker of Sudbury.—Mr Poole, farmer, of Yeldham, to Miss M. Hubbard of Sudbury.—Mr. Fulcher, to Miss Nicholas; both of Eye.—In London, Mr. T. Brook, jun. to Miss S. Ellington; both of Mildenhall.—Mr. T. Simpson, of Newton, near Bury, Miss Scarlett, of Halstead, Essex.—Mr. Rodwell, of Denham, to Miss Gowing, of Eye.—Mr T. Haward, of Ringshall-hall, to Miss S. Cooper, of Sheepcoat Hall, Stowupland.

At Geldstone, Mr. Towell, to Miss Carver, of Beccles.

At Bungay, R. Camell, esq. to Mrs. E. Vandeput, widow of the late Admiral Vandeput.

Died. At Ipswich, Mrs. Brown, wife of Capt. R. Brown.—Mrs Skate, many years housekeeper to the late Dr. Gwyn, of this town.—Mrs Sawer, of the Post chaise inn. Mr. Cook, formerly of Bucklesham.—Mrs. Rich.—Mrs. Brame, wife of Capt. Brame.—In her 77th year, Mrs. E Stubbin, a lady unknown in the gay and fashionable world, but ever to be found in the more humble walk of private charity and benevolence.

In an advanced age, Mrs Russell, widow, of Shimpling.—Aged 77, Mr. W. Swaine, of Woodbridge.—Mr Frankleyn, farmer, of Drinkstone; on his returning home from church in the afternoon, he fell down in a fit, and expired shortly afterwards.

Mr. Limmer, miller of Tuddenham.

At Great Cornard, Mrs. Scott, wife of J. Scott, esq. of Stratford-green, Essex.

At her cottage in Little Saxham, in her 62d year, Mrs. M Canham, many years the faithful attendant on Mrs. Rushbroke, late of West Stow.

At Lowestoft, in his 80th year, J. Kitteridge, gent.—In his 67th year, Mr. James Nunn, of Burfield's farm, near Botesdale.—Mrs. Charlotte Syer, of Hadleigh.

At Lockleys, near Welwyn, Herts, T. Le Blanch, esq. formerly of Cavenham, near Bury.

At Eaton, aged 82, Mr. J. Pile, who had been forty-seven years clerk of that parish.

At Wallington Park, Suffolk, very suddenly, near 75 years of age, the Right Honourable Sir Grey Cooper, bart. Early in the morning Sir Grey rang the bell violently for his valet, whom he desired to saddle a horse, and ride over to the village, about a mile distant, for the doctor The man set off immediately and returned with the apothecary in less than half an hour; but they arrived too late, Sir Grey had breathed his last. The Rev. Mr. Cooper, in Wales, Sir Grey's eldest son, becomes possessed of the family estate, valued at about 9000l. per annum. Sir Grey Cooper was a benevolent and truly hospitable character; greatly regretted by all with whom he was acquainted, for the urbanity of his manners, the elegance of his conversation, and for the wit and anecdotes which so much enriched that conversation; and he was a scholar of the most polished and accomplished class. Indeed the effusions of his mind, which have been scattered among his friends, bear evident marks of a truly elegant mind, inspired by genius and cultivated by unremitting study. Sir Grey was a liberal benefactor to the poor; his household and friends were always entertained by him in the style of good old English hospitality.

ESSEX.

At Chelmsford assizes, which commenced July 21st, before Lord Chief Justice Kenyon and Mr. Justice Grose, the following prisoners were found guilty and capitally convicted, J. Hight, H. Harding, W. Worley, J. Butcher, and T Howard, the younger, soldiers of the first regiment of Guards, for burglary; T. Bishop, a soldier, for an assault and robbery; H Picket, a soldier, for burglary; E. Oldfield, a soldier, for an assault and robbery; J. Skinner and F. Armitage, soldiers of the first regiment for burglary; R. Taylor, G. Richards, J. Naylor, W. Eason, W. Moss, and T. Beddowes, all soldiers, for sheep-stealing. The prisoners were all young men. Three other prisoners were capitally convicted; but nine were reprieved before the judges left the town.

Married.] Mr. J. Bailey, of Earl's Colne, to Miss S. Woolman, of Sible Hedingham.—Mr. J. Hale, whitesmith, of Ballingdon, to Miss Webb, of Whickham-brook.

Died.] At Rivers-hall, Boxted, at an advanced age, Mrs. Milton, relict of the Rev. James Milton, rector of St. James's Colchester.

At Chipping Ongar, aged 56, the Rev. C. Louis Ratel, D. D. canon of the Cathedral-church of Vernon, in Normandy. In the late attempt to assassinate the Chief Consul at Paris, a priest concerned in that conspiracy took the name and designation of this gentleman, a circumstance which affected him so much that it is supposed to have occasioned his death

At Henham the Rev. F. Dixon, B. D. curate of that parish, and Rector of Bincome and Broadway, in Dorsetshire.

KENT.

KENT.

It is in agitation to form, by canals, a grand junction of the rivers, Thames, Medway, and Rother, in Sussex; or, in other words, to establish an inland communication with, or union of, the ports of London, Rochester, Maidstone, &c. with Rye, in Sussex. The great national utility, private advantages, &c. of such a navigation, will be obviously apparent, when it is considered, that Rye Harbour has been proved, from actual surveys, to be capable of improvement for the admission of vessels of much greater burthen than at present, and which, indeed, appears feasible, even from common observation; of course, a circuitous, and, at times, difficult, dangerous, and uncertain navigation from Gravesend, the Nore, North and South Foreland, the Downs, Goodwin Sands, and Dungeness, would be avoided, and thereby the loss of lives and property, to an incalculable number and amount. It would, likewise, be an expeditious, cheap, and safe conveyance of timber or naval stores, &c. in war-time, from out of the Wealds of Kent and Sussex, into five royal dock-yards, and as many private yards, in the river Thames, and in peace, would be a secure, near, and convenient intercourse from London to Rye, and, as far as it goes, to the western ports of the kingdom and to foreign parts.

At Maidstone assizes, which ended July 30, fourteen prisoners were condemned for death, and seven left for execution, among whom were the following:—T. Couchman, G. Mills, and R. Martin, for sheep-stealing, R. Smith, alias Jones, and Charlotte Green, for breaking open a dwelling house, and James Austin, for robbing the Mail.

Married.] At Eltham, W. S. D. Light, esq. to Miss Miller, second daughter of the late J. Miller, esq. of Carey-street, London.

At Canterbury, P. Barrard, esq. to Miss S. Naylor.—Mr. T. Minter, to Miss S. Silk.

Mr. Stunt, of Gillingham, to Miss Hughes, of Mersham.

At Lee, Captain Williams, of the 29th regt. of foot, to Miss Marsh, youngest daughter of the late S. Marsh, esq. of Belmont, in Middlesex.

The Rev. H. Rice, eldest son of the late H. Rice, esq. of Bramling Court, in this county, to Miss Lefroy, of Ashe, in Devonshire.

At Deal, Mr. I. C. Bach, in the service of the Swedish East India Company, to Miss S. Wells.

Died.] At Canterbury, Mr. T. Bliss — Mrs. Sankey, widow of the late Mr. T. Sankey, grocer.—Mr. Abbott, baker.—Serjeant-Major Stanfly, of the 1st, or regiment of Royal Dragoons.

At Rochester, in his 30th year, Mr. C. Paine, tin plate-worker.

At Chatham, Mr. W. Carter, builder.—Major Maubey, a superintendant of the Upper Barracks.

At Dover, in her 21st year, Miss M. A. Katnack.—Aged 65, Lieut. John Starr.

At Ramsgate, in his 85th year, Mr. J. Quince.

At Queensborough, R. Burgess, esq. Captain of the Sheerness Volunteer Cavalry.

HAMPSHIRE.

An ox was lately killed in Winchester, the weight of which was only 50 score, yet one of the kidnies weighed in fat no less than 110 pounds, and the other upwards of 70 pounds, a circumstance considered as truly extraordinary!

Married.] At Newchurch, Isle of Wight, Lieut. Coad, of the navy, to Miss Watts.—R. Shaftou, esq. of Newcastle-upon-Tyne, to Miss M Richman, of Lymington.

At Milton, J. Welch, esq of Woolcots, Dorset, to Miss Brewer, of Minchington.—E. H Columbine, esq Captain in the navy, and Commander of the Sea fencibles, at Hastings, to Miss A. Curry, of Gosport.

WILTSHIRE.

At Salisbury, Mr. E. King jun. of Winterslow, to Miss Marchmont, of Clarendon.—Mr. B. J. Harris, of Broughton Gifford, in this county, to Miss E. H. East, of Bath.—J. Pullin, esq. of Wick, in the parish of Brillington, to Miss B. Maundrell, second daughter of T. Maundrell, esq. of Blackland House, near Calne.—Mr. Vezey, to Miss Prosser, both of Box.

SOMERSETSHIRE.

Married.] Mr. J. Bally, bookseller, of Bath, to Miss Penton, of Oxford.—Mr. J. Stevens, glass-manufacturer, of Bristol, to Miss C. Brothington, of Tiverton.

Mr. J. Brine, of Temple Combe, to Miss Chaffey, of Stoke under Hamdon.

At Taunton St Mary, Mr J Beale, tobacconist, to Miss Betty.—J. Needham, esq. of Bickham, to Miss Havers, sister of T. Havers, esq. of Thelton Hall, Norfolk.—Mr. R. Corp, clerk at the War-office, to Miss F. Cottell, of Crewkherne.

At Frome, Mr. J. Cooke, aged 76, to Mrs. Pope, who, on the morning of her tender lacence to love and Hymen, attained her 80th year.

The Rev. Dr. Crossman, rector of Blagdon, in this county, to Miss Hannah More, of Bristol, a lady well known in the literary world.

At Bath, in his 72d year, Mr. Gramant, linguist, father of the young actress of that name.

In his 75th year, W. Oliver, esq. M. D. descended from ancestors, who have long flourished in that city, with medical and literary repute.

At Wrington, in advanced life, Mr. Coxe, of a truly respectable character; in his presence, afflictions were ever softened, and poverty lifted her head. He was exemplary in his duties, and in his death serene.

At Clifton, aged 18, J. Wadman, esq. of Imber House, near Warminster; his death was

was occasioned by the bursting of a blood-vessel, while hunting, in the month of September last.

DEVONSHIRE.

Married.] The Rev. N. Lightfoot, of Crediton, to Miss B. Prideaux, of Kingsbridge.—Mr. J. Clarke, surgeon, to Miss Gregory, both of Haberton ford, near Totness.—Mr. J. Browne, of Culmstock, to Miss H. Culverwell, eldest daughter of Mr. Culverwell, wholesale linen-draper, of Exeter.—Mr. J. Quick, of Brushford, to Miss Chilcott, of Dulverton.—Mr. G. Cooban, surgeon, of Plymouth, to Miss Rundle, of Tavistock.

Died.] Suddenly, at Sidmouth, Captain Whitter, of the royal navy.

CORNWALL.

Married.] At Truro, Mr. M. Shoal, to Miss J. Floyd.—Mr. C. Tippet, to Miss M. Miners.

Died.] Aged 34, Mr. T. Penberthy, brazier, of Penzance.

At Penryhn, Mrs. Corfield, wife of Mr. Corfield, supervisor of excise.

DEATHS ABROAD.

Died.] At Porto Bello, G. Stepney, esq. late of the King's County, Ireland.

Of the yellow-fever, in the West Indies, Lieut. T. Phelan, of the 4th or King's Foot, brother to the physician of that name, now serving with our army in Egypt. He was an amiable and intelligent youth.

MONTHLY COMMERCIAL REPORT.

THE BALTIC trade has been renewed with an eagerness in adventure, which may possibly lead to general losses and failures. Between the 27th and the 30th of July, not fewer than 315 ships passed up the Sound. Salt and pit-coal are carried, as ballast, by the ships from our Northern ports. The arrival of our West India fleets supplies West India produce for exportation both to the Baltic and the North Seas. The Russia merchants could make few purchases of British goods at the German fairs of Frankfort and Leipsic. Hence our cottons will be bought up with considerable avidity in the Russian markets. The Danes find it necessary to put their own ships from the West Indies upon quarantine, on account of the danger of an importation of the yellow fever.—And even this incident cannot but favour the reception of English West India goods in the Baltic; 560 cwt. of potashes, 1650 dozen lbs. of hog's bristles, 208 cwt. of feathers for beds, 108 tons of hemp, 413 tons of iron, 900 lbs. of isinglass, 207,300 yards of linen, 910 tons of tallow, and 4555 qrs. of wheat, are among our last imports from St. Petersburgh into the port of London. Many of the Baltic commodities begin to fall in price; they will fall still lower, as the season advances, and our ships, which have sailed thither, return with cargoes. Our trade to Russia, Sweden, Denmark, and Norway, drains us much less of our ready money, and takes off a much larger proportion of our manufactures, and of our West and East India produce, than it did 80 years since.

Our late Exports of cotton to Hamburg, especially from Glasgow, Leith, and Dundee, have been greatly too large; as the intercourse with the Baltic and the North Seas, was, for a short time, interrupted, the Scottish manufacturers knew not where to find a market; and, in their distress, sent out immense adventures to Germany. At the Frankfort and Leipsic fairs, British goods were sold cheap beyond any instance in the memory of man. The Russia merchants had been expected at these fairs; but there was not time for their coming, between the accession of the Emperor Alexander, and the periods when the fairs came on. Besides, as the prospects had opened of a renewal of their former intercourse with England, by the Baltic; they had hence the less inducement to think of supplying themselves with British goods by way of Germany. The British merchants and agents at the Frankfort and Leipsic fairs, were obliged to descend even to a sort of retail trade, and dispose of their cottons in half pieces.—They certainly sold with loss.—But, one good effect followed—the Saxon cottons remained unsold; as the manufacturers could not, without utter ruin, dispose of them at prices so low as those of the British manufactures of better colours, and superior fabrics. The rage of the Germans for adventuring in the manufacture of cottons, has certainly received a temporary check. It was even talked by French and German envy, that the British Government must have ordered the sales of our goods at prices so low, for the express purpose of ruining the competition of the German manufacturers. Four of the most opulent bankers in Vienna have joined to establish a bank at Hamburg, the principal business of which is to consist in the payment of those dividends upon the Imperial funds, which belong to foreigners. They have given sufficient security to the Austrian Government. Their establishment at Hamburg will be of advantage to the trade of that city. It will even afford some new accommodation to the commercial intercourse of Britain with Hamburg.

The fisheries continue to be most advantageously productive; 20l. in a single night, is no unusual gain to a single fisherman in the Moray frith, in the frith of Clyde, on the coast of the Isle of Man, in the friths of Tay and Forth, and at the mouth of the Tweed. Of the *herrings* thus taken, a large proportion are sold fresh, for the immediate subsistence of the manufacturing and agricultural labourers, and even as delicacies for the tables of the rich in all parts of the island. A large proportion is cured with salt, either in brine, or with smoke drying for domestic stores and for foreign exportation: oil is made from a part of the rest. Another part is, with lime and soda, employed, directly, in the manufacture of soap.

The two manufactures of *soap* and *glass*, are, on the whole, in a very thriving state at Newcastle, Leith, Dunbarton, Liverpool, London, &c. The kelp of our shores, the silicious sand which the same shores abundantly furnish, and the herrings and fish-oil which we procure in the greatest plenty, conspire to fix these among us, as two staple manufactures, of which, if we be not greatly wanting to ourselves, we shall not be soon deprived.

Between the 24th of June, 1800, and the 24th of June, 1801, 5060 ships, paying

£.28,365 18s. 2d. of dock-dues, and bearing 489,719 tons freight, appear to have entered the port of Liverpool. From Africa, from the West Indies, and from North America, cottons, ivory, sugars, tar, flour, &c. were brought into that port, in very large quantities, in the end of July. It has imported much timber from the Baltic since the restoration of peaceful intercourse between Britain and the nations on that sea. In the third week of July, not fewer than 480,000 herrings were brought into the port of Liverpool only.

Judicious and spirited efforts are now made, in consequence of the Union, to improve the trade, with the manufactures, and the husbandry of IRELAND. The agricultural societies for the improvement of the Irish breeds of cattle, have offered premiums to be distributed in October and April next, the most munificent which we remember to have seen proposed. *Linens* are now, in Scotland and England, somewhat lower in price than they have lately been; yet, the field for the sale of Irish linens is still vast, and it affords views of sufficient profit. We should hope, that the exertions of the Linen-Board and the manufacturers, will be directed to hinder both the coarse linens of Russia, and the fine linens of Germany, Flanders, Holland, and France, from being produced in any market with advantages which may give them a sale in preference to the Irish. The Irish participate considerably in the present success and industrious activity of the herring fishery. They prepare kelp on their shores. They are opening new coal-works. Several new canals are in a progress of execution. Their woollen manufactures begin to experience new prosperity; not properly in rivalship with those of England, but as an extension of them. Ireland is likely to participate continually more and more in the advantages of the American and the West India trade.

It is proper to state, for the information of the manufacturers and bleachers of Scotland, England, and Ireland, that both on the Continent, and in this country, very general complaints have been excited against the effects of the new modes of bleaching upon the cloths subjected to it. Our cottons, &c. bleached in this way, have been found to break out into holes very generally, and almost immediately after they began to be worn; and, they are also subject to be entirely discoloured after one or two washings.

All our West India goods, save sugar, have fallen in price, since the last arrivals from the West Indies. As the distillers are not yet permitted to resume the use of grain; it is probable, that their demand for sugar and melasses, will prevent these articles from falling very low in price for the present season. The consumption of coffee in this country, continues to be extended. The coffee plantations in the West Indies are also from time to time enlarged.

Stocks have not lately exhibited any extraordinary rise or fall in price. The English 3 per cents are, in London, at a market value, one third greater than that of the French 6 per cents on 'Change at Paris: in other words, the French *Tiers Consolidés*, bearing 6 per cent interest, is at 40, with a fluctuation of 1 or 2 per cent. upwards:—The English 3 per cents at 60 with a fluctuation upwards.

A keen competition has been lately excited in the trade of paper-money, between the Bank of England, and the country Banks. The trade requires regulation. The country bankers, if for the benefit of general commerce, encouraged, should be obliged to give full securities, and to submit to certain limitations.

English wool continues to be smuggled into Havre and other French ports. A great number of English workmen in our staple manufactures of cottons, woollens, leathers, and pottery, have found their way over to Normandy; and are now, under the auspices of the French Government, acting for the ruin of the manufactures in their mother country. The silk manufactures of the South of France are still in a state of extreme depression. The most extravagant rage for every thing that is English now prevails in France. The prohibitions of the Government are vain.—Horses, dogs, cottons, woollens, laces &c. &c must all be English.—Such is the voice of fashion. We give this information on authority the most unquestionable.

In the East, it appears, that the demand for British manufactures among the Chinese, continues to encrease.

Large quantities of grain are still imported. It is supposed, that by Christmas, six shillings a bushel may be the average price of good wheat.

MONTHLY AGRICULTURAL REPORT.

SINCE our last Report, every thing has proceeded in the most favourable manner for the purposes of agriculture. A heavy shower or two in the early part of the month, came extremely seasonable for the filling of the later sorts of grain crops in the more early districts, and for the whole, in such as are rendered more late from their situation. In most of the southern and midland counties, all the wheats and the greater part of the other sorts of crops are now secured. In many of the more northern counties too, the harvest has made considerable progress; most of the wheat crops being reaped, and a great part gotten in. The weather has been so particularly fine and suitable, that the harvest field perhaps seldom, if ever, displayed a greater scene of activity and bustle. The crops of almost every description are unusually good and abundant. In a journey of nearly 200 miles through the best grain districts in the kingdom, the Reporter scarcely observed a field that could be *justly* said to have a bad crop. In many he noticed crops of uncommon goodness both in respect to the quantity and quality of the grain. The oat and barley crops seemed in general to be equally good, and in many instances better than the wheat.—Average price of wheat for England and Wales from the returns, in the week ending August 15,—Wheat 124s 9d, barley 65s. 10d. oats 35s. 11d. rye 76s. 4d.

The

The potatoe crops, though in some places they appeared full strong and luxuriant in their growth, in many others they were observed to be thin, and as if stinted in their growth, by the dryness and heat of the weather. Those that have been taken up are however, in general, found to be of a good quality.

The bean and pea crops, on all the more stiff kinds of soil, seem to be very promising.

Turnips we remarked in many instances to be thin and patchy, though, on the whole, they may be said to have a favourable appearance.

Hops have gone on very well, and will probably afford a good and abundant crop in most of the districts where they are cultivated.

Apples in some of the cyder districts are likewise said to be a very foil crop; but in other places, they have almost wholly failed.

From the continued fineness of the weather, an unusual quantity of *Rowen* has been cut and made in the most perfect state.

The fallows and other lands in a state of preparation for wheat, have been put in the most suitable condition.

In the grazing districts there was seldom a greater abundance of grass at this period;—the prices of both fat and lean stock however, still keep high. At Smithfield Market, August 24, beef sold from 4s. 4d. to 5s. mutton, from 5s to 6s. veal, from 4s 8d. to 6s. pork, from 6s. to 6s. 3d.—At Newgate and Leadenhall Markets, beef, from 3s. 4d. to 4s. 6d. mutton, from 4s. 8d. to 5s. 6d. veal, from 4s. to 5s. 4d. pork, from 6s. to 6s. 8d.

Hay. At St. James's, 4l. to 6l.—At Whitechapel, 4l. 10s. to 6l 6s.

Clover. At Whitechapel, 6l. 10s. to 7l. 7s.

Straw. At St. James's, 2l. 17s. to 3l. 6s.—At Whitechapel, 2l. 12s. to 3l. 3s.

METEOROLOGICAL REPORT.

Observations on the State of the Weather, from the 24th of July, to the 24th of August, inclusive, 1801, two miles N. W. of St. Paul's.

Barometer.	*Thermometer.*
Highest 30. 15 Aug. 7 & 8, Wind E.	Highest 78°. Aug. 7, Wind changeable.
Lowest 29. 46. July 30 to Aug. 1. Wind very changeable.	Lowest 53°. Aug. 23, Wind E.
Greatest variation in 24 hours. 2.2 tenths of an inch. Between the mornings of the 29th and 30th ult. the mercury *fell* from 29.68 to 29.46: and between the 1st and 2d of the present month it *rose* from 29.46. to 29.68.	Greatest variation in 24 hours. 8°. The thermometer, at the hottest part of the day on the 29th of July stood at 68°. on the next day at the same hour it rose to 76°, or summer heat.

The quantity of rain fallen during this month is equal to 2.522 inches of depth.

Since our last report we have had a long series of fair weather. The principal part of the rain fell on the 2d and 3d instant, during the whole of which days, as well as on the preceding one, the barometer was gradually rising. Fair weather set in on the 4th, which, with the exception of a single day, has continued ever since. About 9 o'clock in the evening of the 13th, after the rain, the wind blowing from the east, the atmosphere swarmed with very small flies, which disappeared the next morning.

The thermometer has been at 78° on one day only, and on that day the wind shifted to all points of the compass *twice* in the course of eight or ten hours. In ten days the thermometer has been as high as 76°, or summer heat; and during the whole month the degrees of heat have varied but little from day to day.

We have remarked 22 days without rain; and in the course of the month the wind has blown either directly or partially from the east 26 days out of the 31.

THE
MONTHLY MAGAZINE.

No. 78. OCTOBER 1, 1801. [No. 3, of Vol. 12.

ORIGINAL COMMUNICATIONS.

For the Monthly Magazine.

OBSERVATIONS *on the* NAME *and* ORIGIN *of the* PYRAMIDS *of* EGYPT.

MY learned friend, *M. de Sacy*, has directed to me lately a copy of his Dissertation *upon the Name of the Pyramids**, at a time, when, as he says, whatever concerns *Egypt* seems to acquire a new interest. I perused his learned diatribe; but, as I am not of the same opinion about the etymology which he gives of that word, I shall take the liberty to propose another, at a time, when the same country, through the British victorious arms, has obtained for our capital an equal interest.

M. de Sacy, previous to his own etymology, has adduced those of several others. I shall here shortly produce them again; then, after proposing the reasons why I dissent from his, though very ingenious, derivation, I shall propose the reasons for mine. This will be done, I hope, not in an offensive way, or by abusing him, but in a polite manner, and obligingly, as it becomes men of letters and of education.

Concerning the word πυραμὶς, *M. de Sacy* observes first, that it was derived by some from πῦρ, *fire*. He quotes to that purpose *Ammianus Marcellinus*, where he says: *Pyramides sunt turres ab imo latis-timæ, in summitates acutissimas desinentes; quæ figura apud geometras sic appellatur, quod ad ignis speciem, τοῦ πυρὸς, ut nos dicimus, extenuatur in conum*†. But he very well observes, that this gives only a reason of the first syllable, which is πῦρ; not of the two others αμις, or, at least, of the syllable αμ (supposing it to be merely a *Greek* termination). Nevertheless, this is the common opinion, say the authors of the *Universal History*, that the word *pyramid* is derived from the Greek *pyr*, or *pur*, fire; and that these structures were so called from their shape, ascending from a broad base, and ending in a point like a flame‡.

But since, as it is said, there is no reason added by the ancients for the syllable *am*, *M. de Sacy* proceeds further, by quoting the *Etymologicon Magnum*, according to which, this word is derived from Πυρὸς, wheat, because they will have them to have been the Royal Granaries, constructed by the Israelitic *Joseph*. This etymology is adopted by *Vossius*, for this particular reason, because, he says, πυραμὶς has the same measure on the first syllable as πυρὸς, which is not the case in πῦρ and its derivations*. But πυρὸς, wheat, is as distant from πυραμὶς as πῦρ, fire; consequently it is equally insufficient.

Not finding a convenient etymology in the *Greek* language, from which we received this word first, and *Egypt* being the country where the pyramids stood, it is very natural to pass to the *Egyptian* one. Now, in this language, *piromi* signifies a man, and, if we believe *Herodotus*, it signified anciently a distinguished man, a very good man (καλὸς κἀγαθὸς). From thence, *Kircher*, and several others, quoted by *De Sacy*, derived then also the name *pyramis*. But *M. de Sacy* rejects this etymology, because, he says, *piromi* signifies in the *Coptic*, the daughter of the ancient Egyptian language, only a man, neither a good nor a bad one, and consequently there is no reason for believing that the *pyramids* were thus called, as if they were monuments or works of *great men*.

Although I myself am not of opinion, that *pyramis* was derived from *piromi*, yet I beg *M. de Sacy*'s leave to observe, that this seems to me not to be a reason founded enough for rejecting it. For I could adduce a number of words from ancient languages, which have thus deviated from their primitive signification, and bear now-a-days quite a different one. *Casa*, for instance, signified in the *Latin* language only a common house, and even a wretched one†; but to-day, in *Italian*, it may signify any house, even the most elegant and splendid. One may say, in the modern Italian, *una casa magnifica*; or, speaking of a family, *una illustre casa*, epithets which could never have been added to the Latin word *casa*. On the contrary, *Karl* signified, in the times of *Charles the Great*, when the German language began to be written, a strong, a valorous man. It is therefore that the illustrious son of *Pepin* was called

* *Sylvestre de Sacy, Observations sur le Nom des Pyramides.*

† Ammian. Marcellin. lib. 22. cap 15.

‡ History of Egypt, book 1. chap. 3. In Univ. Hist. Vol. 1.

* De Sacy, page 7.

† Gessner, Thesaur. Ling. Latin.

called *Karl*, *Karolus*, or *Charles**. But now-a-days, if the Germans choose to speak of a person of mean extraction, or of vulgar manners and behaviour, they call him *Karl*, or, after the modern dialect, *Kerl*. *M. Witte*, a learned of that country, has therefore very lately adopted again the etymology of *piromi*, for the pyramids, since *Herodotus*, an eye-witness, attests that the Egyptian priests called to him the *Colossus'* (τοὺς κολοσσοὺς) which represented their ancient sovereigns, *Piromi*†. And thus the pillars, which were placed on the borders of the roads, were called *Hermæ*, from *Mercury*, who presided over the roads; although the stones themselves were not *Mercuries*. But since Πυραμὶς is written with an *iotta*, instead of an *ipsilon*; and, as there is perhaps a better etymology to produce than *piromi*, we shall pass to other derivations.

Wilkins, in his Dissertation on the *Coptic Language*, thought that Πυραμὶς ought to be derived from the *Coptic* word ΠΟΥΡΟ, a king, and ΜΙΣΙ, a generation, as a building designated only for persons of a royal descendance; and *Iablonsky*, in his *Pantheon Egyptium*, derives it, with *la Croze*, from *Pire* or *Pira*, the sun, in *Coptic*, and *mue*, splendour; supposing that the *obelisks* anciently were called *pyramids*.

But *M. de Sacy* is displeased with both etymologies; the one for being too forced, as he says, and the other ill-founded; and thus he is likewise displeased with the etymology of *Mr. Adler*, who derives it from *pi*, the Egyptian article, and *rama*, height; because *rama* is not *Egyptian*. Finding therefore no convenient derivation in the *Egyptian* or *Coptic* language, he passes over to the *Arabic*.

It is well known that the *Arabic* language is at present as dominant in Egypt, as once the Egyptian. Now, in *Arabic*, a pyramid is called *Haram*‡; and this word must be written with a *he*, in order to distinguish it from another very usual, which is written with *ha*—*Haram* is derivated from a root, which signifies to be very ancient or decrepit—it consequently ought to signify a very ancient monument; and both *Herbelot* and *Michaelis*, quoted by *M. de Sacy*, were of the same opinion.

But here, *M. de Sacy* enters, and declares, that the word Πυραμὶς ought to be derived from *baram* indeed, but not written with a *he*, but with a *ba*, after which root, which signifies *to be sacred*, it ought to signify a sacred building or monument. *M. de Sacy* then supposes, 1. That the modern Arabian *he* ought to be changed into *ba*. 2. That the ancient Egyptians made use of the same expression. 3. That the Egyptian article *pi* ought to be prefixed. 4. That the *b* ought quite to be suppressed for pronouncing *piram*, instead of *pibram* or *pibaram*. 5. That the *ipsilon* of Πυραμὶς was only introduced by the Greeks, and that originally it was not so*.

But, with all the deference which I have for *M. de Sacy*'s eminent learning and character, I beg leave to observe, that it must be first better proved that the ancient Egyptians used such a word. For *Hermes*, which he adduces, is not a proof that this word was derived from *baram*; and, if it were, it would not follow that the pyramids were likewise called from *baram*. If we cannot find an original name for *pyramis* in the Egyptian language, we must search for it somewhere else. If the *Arabians*, their neighbours, had pyramids, we might derive this name from *Arabia*. But no such monument ever is mentioned by any historian. Let us then see whether there is not another neighbouring country, whence *pyramids*, as well as *obelisks*, could have been derived.

On casting a look towards *Assyria* or *Chaldea*, which, under the reign of *Semiramis*, extended as far as *Egypt*†, and, by its natural situation, was little distant from that country, I am of the firm opinion, that both *obelisks* and *pyramids* were derived to Egypt from *Babylon*.

That *Babylon* had a *square pyramid*, of the same height, if not higher, than the Egyptian ones, we know by the testimonies of *Herodotus* and *Strabo*‡. *Strabo* openly calls the tower of *Bel* a square pyramid, Πυραμὶς τετράγωνος. It was built of *brick*, indeed, not of *stone*, like the pyramids of *Ghize*. But the pyramids of *Sakhara*, in Egypt, which are more ancient than those of *Ghize*, are likewise built of *bricks*§. It consisted of several stories; but there are pyramids in *India*, now-a-days extant, which have a striking similarity with the Egyptian ones, and yet

* Adelung's Wörterbuch.

† Witte, Vertheidigung des Versuchs über den Ursprung der Pyramiden, &c. Leipzig, 1792, p. 62, et seq.

‡ Golius.

* Observations sur les Pyramides, p. 25, et seq.

† See *Polyænou Stratagemata*, in *Semiramis*; and *Frerct*, *Essai sur l'Hist. de la Chronolog. des Assyriens*..tom. 5, des *Mém. de l'Acad. des Inscript.*

‡ Herodot. lib. i. Strabo, lib. xvi.

§ *Grobert*, *Description des Pyramides*, *Paris*, *An* ix. *p.* 7.

consist

consist of stories. The pagoda of *Vilnour* has precisely the same number of stories, which *Herodotus* relates of the tower of *Bel**. The pagoda of *Tanjore* has even more stories than the tower of *Bel*.† And there are also some pyramids in *Egypt*, which consist of stories. *Grobert*, in his newest account of the pyramids of *Sakhara*, says, that these pyramids were less known, because the access to them was difficult; that they are more ancient than those of *Ghize*; that the largest is built of *bricks*; and that some of them are built with *stories*: *quelques unes sont construites en etages*‡.

All the pagodas in India, says *Le Gentil*, face the four cardinal points§. All the pyramids of *Ghize*, says *Grobert*, face the four cardinal points‖. The pagodas of *Deogur*, says *Hodges*, which are in the earliest stage of *Hindoo* buildings, are simple pyramids, without any light whatever within¶. That the pyramids of Egypt are without any light whatever within, is known long ago by the descriptions of *Pocock*, *Greaves*, and *Norden*. In a word, there is a striking similarity, as *Mr. Maurice* observes, between the pyramids of *Egypt*, and the more ancient pagodas of *India***; and as the tower of *Bel* had such a likeness with the pagodas of *India*, it seems, that the Indian *pagodas*, as well as the *pyramids* of Egypt, were an imitation of the *tower* of *Bel*.

That this tower faced the four cardinal points, it is an easy matter to prove. For, according to *Strabo*, it was like the Egyptian pyramids, and the Indian pagodas††; it was besides the *observatory* of the Chaldean astronomers‡‡: it stood in the midst of the temple of *Bel*, which was a square building; and this square building stood within the square walls of Babylon, which faced the four cardinal points: besides, its streets were all straight, and crossed by straight streets at right angles, consequently each house looked to the cardinal points§§.

* Le Gentil, Voyage dans les Mers des Indes, vol. 1. p. 537.

† Rennel's Geography of Herodotus, page 360.

‡ Grobert, cit. page 10 and 12.

§ Le Gentil, ibid.

‖ Grobert, page 18.

¶ Hodges' Select Views in India.—View of the Pagodas of Deogur.

** Maurice's Ind. Antiq. vol. 3, p. 419.

†† Strabo, lib. cit.

‡‡ Diodor. Sic. lib. ii.

§§ See Bochart, Phaleg, lib. i. cap. 17. and Univ. Hist. vol 3. Hist. of Babylon.

The modern towns in *China*, according to *du Halde*, are all in the same style. They are all squares, formed, like *Babylon*, by four straight walls, which unite at right angles; their walls look towards the four cardinal points; and the case is the same with their houses, the front of which must always face the south*.

But what is more curious, every Chinese town, according to the same *du Halde*, has one or more towers, remarkable for their high elevation, and consisting of from seven to nine stories. These stories go on decreasing (like a *pyramid*) so as they rise; that the *tower* of *Bel* had eight stories, and that these stories were decreasing as they rose, we know from *Herodotus* and *Strabo*. Thus the distance of places compenses the distance of times, and we find a curious analogy between *time* and *espace*.

But the *tower* of *Bel* seems also to have been dark at the inside: like the *pyramids* of *Egypt*. For its staircase was, according to *Herodotus*, on the outside; and no other place is mentioned that it contained, but a *chapel* on the top. This is not at all to be wondered at. For the *Shoemadoo*, or the great temple of *Pegu*, a *pyramidical* building, composed of *brick*, like the temple of *Bel*, and of a stupendous height, is, according to *Colon. Syms*, without excavation or aperture of any sort†. And this is not the only temple of this kind in *India* beyond the *Ganges*; for the largest and most celebrated temples, both in the kingdom of *Ava* and of *Pegu*, says *Dr. Buchanan*, are in the form of such *pyramids*‡.

If we now consider the antiquity of the *Babylonians*; if we call to mind that the tower of *Bel* was probably the same with the tower of *Babel*; and that *Sesostris*, who built the first *pyramid* in Egypt we know of, was much posterior to *Bel* and *Semiramis*; ought we not to believe the pyramids of *Egypt*, as well as the pagodas of *India* and *China*, derived from the tower of *Bel*, which was a temple, like the *Indian*, and a *Mausoleum*, or burial-place, like the *Egyptian* ones, where *Bel*, the first king and founder of *Babylon*, was buried, and worshipped?

All these observations lead me to search for the etymology of Πυραμὶς in the *Chaldaic* or *Hebrew* language; and, if possible, to derive it from thence.

There is no other name in both lan-

* Du Halde's Descript. de la Chine, tom. 2. page 8.

† Symes's Embassy to Ava, chap. v.

‡ Buchanan's Dissertation, in Asiat. Res. vol. 6.

guages for expressing a pyramid than *amud* or *amüd* (עמוד, with a *kibbutz*) a column, a pillar: for *thamar*, a palm-tree and some other words, are much less in use than *amüd**. A pyramid is, according to the ancients, a column representing *fire*: therefore the chemists, from time immemorial, have represented fire by a pyramid Δ. The *Scholiast* of *Horace* attests, that the pyramids were thus called from the figure similar to *fire*; he says that the pyramids are *regum Ægyptiorum sepulcra, ingenti mole construc ta, et in cacumen educta in modum flammæ assurgentis*: UNDE ET NOMEN ACCEPERUNT†. *Ur* signifies fire in *Hebrew* and *Chaldaic*; *amüd ur* is a column of fire, and *ur amüd*, a fire column. For although the genitive regularly ought to be after the nominative in *Hebrew*, we have instances enough of words being transposed; and after all, one might say, that the Greeks to distinguish a pyramid from another pillar, called it πῦρ αμἰς, a fire-column, as their language admits compositions of words, which is not the case in several other languages. But let us suppose the Chaldeans called it *ur-amüd*, for they were the oldest worshippers of *fire* we know, and *Bel*, which was the *sun*, and their *god*, was represented and worshipped by the *fire*. Now, if the Egyptians received the *ur-amüd* of the Chaldeans, their article, which they use to prefix to words, being a *p*, (as it is known) we shall have *pur-amüd*. The same might be the case with the *Greeks*; for some of them used to prefix, and even to insert, an F to several words. Thus they said Fεσπερα instead of ἑσπερα; ϝFις, instead of ὄις, &c. Besides that, *Fur* was the ancient name of *Fire*, we know not only from the Latin *furor*, but also from the most ancient *German*‡. The word πῦρ, fire, was, according to *Plato*, a foreign word, which the *Greeks* had taken from the *barbarians*§. F. and P. are two letters which continually are confounded, just like *t* or *d* and *s*. Thus the *Persians* were called by some *Fars*; and by others, *Parth*; consequently *ur-amüd*, *fur-amüd*, and Πυρ-αμὶς may be the same. The Greek accent on the last syllable confirms what I say: for it shews the ις not to be a mere additional Greek termination, but an essential syllable, belonging to the root. Nor is the change of *ü* into *i*, or of *d* into *s*, contrary to the rules of the most rigorous etymology. For we know how frequently the *vowels* are changed in different dialects; and thus also *dend* in Persian, is *dens* in Latin, or ὀδὺς in Greek.

But the *obelisks* afford a further proof of the *pyramids* being derived from *Babylon*. That *Semiramis* erected an *obelisk* one hundred and thirty feet high, is attested by *Diodorus Siculus**. This magnificent pillar was brought from *Armenia* (not from *Egypt*) *Assyria* being a flat country, and destitute of marbles. *Obeliskos*, is likewise not an *Egyptian* appellation: its root has hitherto as little been found in the *Egyptian* language, as that of *pyramis*. We received that name first from the *Greeks*—ισκος is the Greek diminutive; like βασιλίσκος, a little king, from βασιλεὺς; παιδίσκος, a little boy, from παῖς; κυνίσκος, a little dog, from κυὼν, &c. Besides, the Greeks used to prefix an *o* to words which originally had none.

Thus, instead of *nam*, in Persian; *nama*, in Samskrit; *nomen*, in Latin; a name, they have made ὄνομα; instead of *dend*, in Persian; *denda*, in Samskrit; *dens*, in Latin; a tooth; they have made ὀδὺς, ὀδόντος; and the case seems to have been the same with *O-bel-iskos*; or, they have corrupted it from *ba bel*, the god *Bel*, with the Hebrew and Chaldaic article *ba*: thus they seem also to have made *Assyria* from *Syria*, which was the common name of both countries.

Now the *obelisks* were, after the clear testimony of *Pliny*, pillars dedicated to the *Sun*; (*Solis numini sacrati*†); for they represented, as he says, the rays of the sun (*radiorum ejus argumentum in effigie est*); and therefore we find, in the Latin inscription, which is on a great obelisk still existant at *Rome*, that *Augustus* had dedicated it to the sun: *Soli donum dedit*‡. That the sun at *Babylon* was worshipped under the name of *Bel*, has been so often repeated, that it is superfluous to prove it here. The Phœnician coins found in Spain, prove, amongst other monuments, that *Baal* or *Bel* was the name of the *sun*§. The first obelisks in Egypt were also erected at *Heliopolis*, or in the town of the *sun*‖. There is then no wonder if an *obelisk* was called after *Bel*, whom it was to represent,

* See *Taylor's Hebr. Concord. Buxtorf. Lexic. Chald.* and other lexicographers.

† Apud *Jablonsky* in Prolegomen. ad Panth. Ægypt.

‡ Adelung's Wörterbuch.

§ Plato in Cratylo.

* Diodor. Sic. lib. ii.

† Plin. Nat. Hist. lib. xxxvi. cap. 14.

‡ The Obelisk of *Sesostris*, in *Piazza Colonna*.

§ See Court de Gebelin Monde Primitif, vol. 4.

‖ *Jablonsky* Prolegom. cit.

*O-be lisko*s,

O-bel iskos, or BEL, the Sun, diminutively.

To what has been said, I beg leave to add one proof more, by observing, that besides *Babylon* in *Chaldea*, there was also a *Babylon* in *Egypt**; and that this *Babylon*, as *Strabo* relates, was built by *Babylonians*†: *Diodorus Siculus*, who relates the same, adds, that they built a city, which, from their native place, they called *Babylon*‡. This is the same city which is now called *Old Cairo*; it is a suburb of the capital lately taken by the British arms. And what is more curious, both, the *pyramids* of *Memphis*, and the *Obelisks* of *Heliopolis*, are in its neighbourhood: the pyramids can to this day be seen from *New Babylon*, or Old Cairo, so near they are§.

All this seems to prove that the origin both, of *obelisks* and *pyramids* is to be derived from *Old Babylon*, consequently that their etymology also ought to be derived from the Assyriac or Hebrew language. Whether *Semiramis* and *Belus* were fabulous or not, this is no matter. It is enough, that *Belus* was worshipped by the *Babylonians*; that an *obelisk*, as well as a *pyramid*, existed at *Babylon* from the most ancient times; and that *Assyria* was a kingdom, situated near *Egypt*, on the way to *India* and *China*; and if not superior, certainly not inferior, in antiquity and culture to *India*, *China*, and *Egypt*.

St. Martin's street, *Sept.* 21, 1801. JOSEPH HAGER.

P. S. in ANSWER *to* MR. MONTUCCI'S *last* PUBLICATION.

Quid dignum tanto feret HIC PROMISSOR hiatu?
Parturiunt MONTES—nascetur *ridiculus mus!*
HOR. A. P.

IGNORANCE is in itself venial, since it falls not to the lot of every one to possess talents or leisure for the acquisition of learning; but ignorance combined with effrontery and presumption, is a fit subject of exposure. Of this, a most striking instance occurs in the example of Mr. Antonio Montucci, who, whilst he, by a most obstreperous pretence to Chinese learning, boasts on the one hand, that he has acquired *invaluable articles* (page 8.), and *inestimable treasures of Chinese literature* (page 2.), is, on the other, reduced to the beggarly necessity of proving the reverse by *transcribing*, from the *Philosophical Transactions*, published above thirty years since, his specimens of Chinese; and from the *Memoirs of the Missionaries of Peking*, his Chinese motto, which he most modestly sets forth as his own.

Mr. Montucci, in the beginning of his pamphlet, declares himself to be *actuated by a pure zeal for promoting Chinese literature in Europe*; and this zeal it was that made him run, no doubt, through all London, to obtrude his title-page on the booksellers, and suspend it in each of their shops. They were little aware of the libel it contains, in degradation of another who had most successfully preceded him in a publication on the subject.

Mr. Montucci, at the same time that he dilates with complacence on his *being able to copy Chinese characters*, has the impudent futility to say of himself (page 4.) that *it must be no small merit to copy them as he has done*; and hints pretty strongly, in what light he should be viewed, by observing, that *the most skilful in this art is most certain of promotion*, and *that the* CHINESE EMPERORS *are generally the most eminent in it*.

Does not this *transcribing Doctor* know the Latin adage, *Laus in ore proprio vilescit?* and therefore that he ought to intitle himself to the applause, before he should dare to claim it, instead of trumpeting about London, like a mountebank, that, *as the Chinese language is composed of characters all different from one another*, (what language is not?) *and of such a peculiar structure as to* BAFFLE THE IMITATION *of the* ABLEST EUROPEAN ARTISTS, therefore, DOCTOR ANTONIO MONTUCCI will himself mount his stage, to exhibit what no other European can perform. Thus much for the effrontery of this renowned transcriber.

Let us proceed to some proofs of his ignorance and presumption. Don Antonio Montucci (as we are told, page 8.) sees a copy of Dr. Hager's Chinese Keys, and observes a fault in the third character of the title-page. This character is of a size so large, as that every one may judge distinctly of its form, and was exactly copied by Mr. Coleman, the engraver, from one of the same magnitude, shape, and signification, brought from China by an English gentleman of the first respectability, and, with the proprietor's permission, may any day be referred to. So fastidious, however, is our new *Mandarin*, that even the elegancies of Chinese calligraphy are too full of errors to please him, though exemplified by instances of perpetual recurrence in their best executed writings; and so far does his ignorance extend, as not to know that the same Chinese character is often written with two, three, or even more, varieties; and thus ridiculous is he made in presuming to condemn altogether what he least understands.

Such too is the case in the instance of Fu (page 7.) *it will be proved*, he says, *that the monosyllable* Fu *has never a fifth tone*. The Don's qualification for correcting others will be obvious from the hardiness of this simple assertion; since not only the Chinese Dictionary of the *Propaganda*, brought by the French from Rome to Paris, and cited by M. Langlès, in his printed account of the Chinese Dictionaries, but also two Dictionaries of the late Mr. Fitz-hugh, one in Latin and the other

* Ptolom. Geograph. lib. iv.
† Strabo, lib. xvi.
‡ Diodor. Sic. lib. ii.
§ Grobert, cit.

ether in English, contain this very term *Fu* with the FIFTH, as given by the very Missionary to China, who was the author of it. Fu, however, must have no *fifth tone*; and why, because Mr. Montucci, the Infallible, says so. It does not occur in his Dictionary—a compilation, which, if those who have seen it may be credited, is a sorry one to a proverb!

Having thus far paraded with these ostents of learning, Mr. Montucci indulges the persuasion, that Dr. Hager will avail himself of the opportunity to add to his work, by appropriating the droppings of this omniscient Chinese. He, however, will pardon us, if we venture the conjecture, that the Doctor will still wait till *the invaluable articles* and *inestimable treasures* shall have made their appearance.

To the Editor of the Monthly Magazine.

SIR,

I SOME time since saw in your Magazine, a tribute of respect to the memory of Mr. George Cadogan Morgan, a person well-known to many of your readers, and by all who enjoyed his friendship, highly estimated, as well for the amiableness of his manners, and the purity of his morals, as for the extent of his knowledge, and his ardent attachment to the cause of human happiness. The writer, I remember, expressed concern, that no other poetical tribute had been paid to the memory of this valuable person; and I sympathized with the author, as I read the remark. If the following extract from a very imperfect poem, one of a small series of compositions of this kind, should be deemed worthy of a place in your Magazine, I may, probably, at a more convenient season, make a similar extract from a poem on the lamented death of the learned and estimable Mr. Gilbert Wakefield.

Extract from a Poem on the Death of the late Mr. GEORGE CADOGAN MORGAN.

BUT where the place for Superstition now?
For Fancy, where? Realities demand
A genuine strain—and could that strain but flow
As, Morgan, it should flow, not vainly then
Should it come back—then recollection strong,
Should be rekindled:—what thy brother was;
—The son, that could to age, consoling give
The lov'd attentions;—th' husband, that outstript
His partners wishes, the benignant sire,
Heart-tied, to his children;—and another self
To thee, of brother's kindest, and a friend,
Not of the vulgar or the narrow sort:—
Such should he live,—the patriot should live—
And above all, the friend of human kind:—
His principle should live;—his love of man
Spring in some breast, perhaps, estranged before
To the large passion, bath'd, as it might seem,
Into his very spirit, till he rose,
A baptiz'd soul, a new-created man.
His was the pastor's lot; and putting off*
The Shepherd's trim—he never could strip off,
—Nature had cloathed him there,—the pastor's heart—
The pastor, become tutor, now instill'd
With science principle, and love of truth,
Ardour for liberty, the proud contempt
Of pow'r, and priest-craft, and the fondling-wiles,
Link'd in a chain, to enslave human kind.—
And did he teach in vain?—No—Morgan,—No—
Love is a stirring principle, a seed
That silently works upward into life,
Of flower and fruit most fragrant, and a soil
The breast of youth, where Heav'n has lov'd to shed
The richest influence. G. DYER.

For the Monthly Magazine.

OBSERVATIONS *on the* IRRITABILITY *of* VEGETABLES, *by* T. GARNETT, M.D. F. L. S. &c. &c.

THAT the different functions of animals and vegetables depend upon the action of certain powers upon their irritability, has been shewn several years ago by Dr. Brown, who presented to the world the first specimen of just reasoning on the philosophy of living matter. This subject has since been elucidated by Dr. Darwin in his Zoonomia, as well as in his Phytologia, and by several other philosophers. I shall not here enter into the consideration of the principles of this doctrine, since that has been done at some length in my lecture on the Preservation of Health, which is now before the public: all that I intend here, is to mention a fact that fell under my observation this last summer, and which appears to admit of an easy explanation by the laws of irritability.

In the month of May last, the blossom on the gooseberry trees in the neighbourhood of Kirkby Lonsdale in Westmorland, was very luxuriant, and seemed to promise abundance of fruit; about the middle of that month however, a frosty night, succeeded by a very fine warm morning, frustrated all those promising prospects. In a few days the trees assumed the appearance of having been blighted, the blossoms dropt off, and very few gooseberries arrived at maturity. In this instance, the subtraction of heat had allowed the irritability of the vegetables to accumulate, and the heat in the morning, acting upon this morbidly accumulated irritability, had overpowered it, bringing on a state of exhausted irritability

* Mr. Morgan had been a Dissenting-minister.

lity, with gangrene or blight in several parts of the plant. This may perhaps be made more clear by an analogous instance which is better known. If a person, whose hands are benumbed with cold, and whose irritability is consequently accumulated by the subduction of the heat, bring the frigid limbs near a fire, the heat will act so powerfully on their accumulated irritability, that a violent inflammation and sometimes mortification will follow; whereas, if they had been exposed to warmth by degrees, the superabundant irritability would have been gradually exhausted, and no bad effects would have ensued.

That the effects produced on the gooseberry-trees must be explained in a similar manner, will appear from the following fact. My father's house is at the foot of a steep mountain, at the distance of about four miles from Kirkby Lonsdale. This mountain is to the eastward of the house, and intercepts the rays of the sun in such a manner that they do not shine on the garden for more than an hour after they have illuminated the town of Kirkby Lonsdale and the surrounded country. Though from this situation being cold and exposed, there is seldom abundance of fruit; yet this year the blossoms on the gooseberry-trees were very promising, and, contrary to what happened in other parts of the country, they were succeeded by great plenty of fine fruit. The frost had here been as severe to the full, as in the immediate neighbourhood of Kirkby Lonsdale; the situation of the house is high, and exposed; and the irritability would be accumulated here by the subtraction of the stimulus of heat, to the full as much as in the other situations; but then they were not immediately exposed to the direct rays of the sun: the atmosphere had become in some degree warmed by the effect of the sun on the surrounding country; the morbid irritability was then gradually worn off, and by the time that the sun's rays reached the garden, the vegetables were in a situation to bear their action without being overpowered.

A nearly similar effect took place with respect to the hazel: the blossoms were very abundant, but the prospect of nuts was in a considerable degree destroyed by the same change of temperature in the atmosphere; that night proved almost equally as destructive to the nuts as to the gooseberries; yet in situations where the trees were shaded from the morning sun, this fruit was to be met with in the greatest abundance. In warm, sunny situations however, scarce a single nut was to be found, and before the end of August, the autumnal tints had begun to vary the scene; a clear proof that a state of indirect debility, or exhausted irritability, had taken place. In short, I am pretty well convinced, not only from a number of facts which I have myself observed, and which I have stated fully in my lectures, but also from the observations of Uslar, that blight is almost always a species of gangrene or mortification, brought on by the action of the rays of the sun in the spring, on the morbidly accumulated irritability which had been produced by a considerable subtraction of heat during the night. A frosty night succeeded by a cloudy or misty morning is never attended with these effects, which almost certainly follow, if when the spring is considerably advanced, a frost should be succeeded by a fine, warm morning. If I have leisure, I may perhaps trouble you the next month with some more observations on this subject.

No. 51, Great Marlborough street,
September 13, 1801.

To the Editor of the Monthly Magazine.

SIR,

THE newspapers have announced that the Bank of England is about to adopt such alterations in the Bank-notes as will prevent forgeries.—I must be permitted to doubt this, if the alterations relate merely, as they state, to the watermarks in the paper. It is proposed to curve the perpendicular and horizontal wires in the paper moulds, and the figures expressing the value of the note to be water-marked. I have long been of opinion that the Bank does not understand the most effectual guard against forgery. It is quite a distinct object to have marks by which the Bank can detect forgery; to adopt such a note as may protect the public, has not yet been attempted. The engraving of the Bank-notes remains the most miserable specimen of the art, and the greatest care seems to be taken to copy exactly the rude example adopted at the first institution of the Bank.

In a former number of your magazine, there is a letter of Mr. Landseer the engraver, respecting a proposal made to the Bank, of a method of engraving the notes that could not be imitated. I have reason to believe that this proposal originates from a discovery of Mr. Foulis, of Edinburgh. He has revived the art of cross-

croſs-hatching on wooden cuts. This art was familiar to the old maſters 200 years ago, but even that excellent artiſt Neſbit could barely ſucceed in ſhewing a ſpecimen of it in two or three of his prints. To the old maſters it appears, however, to have been as eaſy as croſs-hatching on copper. Another diſcovery of Mr Fouis is the imitation of writing on wooden cuts, with the ſame eaſe and freedom of deſign as on copper. I preſume that the combination of theſe two diſcoveries for Bank note impreſſions, conſtituted the propoſal of the perſon mentioned by Mr. Landſeer. Water marks are much leſs uſeful to the public, than to the Bank for the detection of forgeries. A note that has been any time in circulation, becomes ſo blotted with ink, and tarniſhed, that it is difficult to diſtinguiſh the water-mark, and ſince 20 and 40 ſhilling notes are iſſued, we do not take time, nor can afford it, to look at every note between a ſtrong light. But the water mark is no check to forgery. I recollect that it appeared upon the trial of a forger ſome years ago, that he made the paper and water-mark in his room.

Had proper attention been paid to the engraving and deſign of notes, not a tenth part of the forgeries would have been committed on the Bank.

There are few firſt-rate engravers in any country; and the moſt effectual ſecurity is employing the very beſt, becauſe there will be ſo few that can imitate their workmanſhip. This appears to me a principle that every Bank ſhould follow.

Suppoſe the Bank of England notes were engraved by Bartolozzi, or Sharpe, with a view of the Bank buildings, in one of the upper corners, and an emblematic groupe of figures in the other, would not the forgery of ſuch an engraving be obvious at firſt ſight. Let me recommend thick paper; becauſe on thin paper the hand writing becomes faint with the leaſt damp, and the engraving is disfigured by the wrinkles of ſuch paper. The Scotch Banks are well aware of this, and all uſe thick ſtout paper. Wooden cuts have, however, an important advantage over copper-plates: they can bear, without injury to the cut, ten times the number of impreſſions; and when a proper engraving for a bank-note is fixed, ſimilarity in the impreſſions is a chief object.

Perhaps the beſt plan would be to have part of the note engraved on copper and part on wood; and the forgerer muſt then unite, in his own perſon, the art of engraving on both. I believe there is not an artiſt in Britain, who can engrave like Sharpe on copper, and like Anderſon or Neſbit on wood. MERCATOR.

To the Editor of the Monthly Magazine.

SIR,

I Confeſs myſelf one, perhaps of many, who have been mortified by your taking no notice of the New Planet in your laſt publiſhed number, although your preceding number announced a further account to be given of it in your next.*

I have ſeen a private letter, by which it appears, that ſince the diſcovery of it by PIAZZI at PALERMO, it has been ſeen by Profeſſor BODE at BERLIN: and I think there is no reaſon to doubt that it has been ſeen by the ASTRONOMERS at the NATIONAL OBSERVATORY at PARIS.

By the ſame letter it appears, that the diſcovery was communicated to the *Royal Profeſſor of Aſtronomy*, Dr. MASKELYNE. In the dearth of aſtronomical intelligence, which we generally ſuffer in the country, it would be kind, as early as poſſible, to fulfil your intimation, and to lay before the public, as much as can be learnt reſpecting this intereſting diſcovery at preſent.

I take this occaſion of mentioning, that the *ſpots* on the *ſun*, which have been ſeen within the laſt fortnight, have been remarkably large, very much diverſified in their outline, very numerous and extenſive.

By the time one of theſe cluſters took in paſſing over the edge of the field of my reflector, I judge it not to have been much leſs in breadth, than a tenth of the ſun's diameter. I remain,

Troſton Hall, Bury, Suffolk. Yours, &c.
September 6, 1801. C. LOFFT.

To the Editor of the Monthly Magazine.

SIR,

I SHALL be very much obliged to any of your numerous readers who will ſend me, through the channel of your valuable Magazine, ſome particulars of the life of Thomas Barker, author of a book now lying before me, entitled, "Dr. Wells's Letter to a Diſſenting Pariſhioner conſidered,' by Thomas Barker, V. D. M. London; printed for J. Clark, at the Bible and Crown in the Old Change, 1707." Who was Thomas Barker, and where is his life to be found?

Yours, &c.
A CONSTANT READER.

February 17, 1801.

* The account we promiſed exiſts in Von Zach's Geographical Ephemerides, which, from ſome accident, has not yet come to hand from Germany.

To

To the Editor of the Monthly Magazine.

SIR,

MRS. CAPPE's Letter, in your Magazine for August, has recalled my attention to a subject that has often greatly interested me, especially when I have witnessed the forlorn situation of orphans, abandoned by a parish to the uncertain treatment of an interested master. Warmly as I desire to promote the welfare and improve the condition of such children, I do not see how the practice of apprenticing them, as she contends, can be wholly abolished.

Domestic servitude will not occupy all the children of the poor; besides, in that line of employment, there are but few persons that will be troubled, for a number of years, with the requisite care and instruction, unless from compulsion, or for the sake of the bounty that is given with them as an apprentice-fee; nor can it be expected, that parish-officers will be burthened with transferring them continually from one place to another, as must be the case, were the master and apprentice not bound together by contract.

The claims of justice likewise demand that the master, who has had the wearisome task of initiating a child into the knowledge of a trade, or a mechanic-art, should reap some advantage from his labour, when able to perform it in a skilful manner.

The good of the community also seems to require that a numerous succession of mechanics and artists should be raised from amongst those children who are destined to earn their living by the labour of their hands; and what method can be pointed out so effectual for this purpose as apprenticeships?

The influence of custom is great in affairs of this nature; and, unless an entire new system of providing for the children of the parish poor should be adopted, there is greater probability of success, in proposing beneficial regulations, than in attempting to overthrow an order so long established, and so universally adopted, as that of binding these children for a term of years.

A legal restraint to prevent a mode of disposing of parish-children, now very general, would probably operate much in their favour. It has been a frequent practice of late years, when parishes are overburthened with children, to send them in numbers to Nottingham, and other manufacturing towns, where they are out of the reach of the care or inspection of those who should protect them. Without entering into the unfavourable circumstances of their situation to happiness, or moral improvement, whilst toiling from day to day, with but little remission for relaxation or instruction; I wish to draw the attention of those who have power to enforce a remedy, to the ill effects of removing them to a great distance from home, believing that the sufferings and corruption to which they are exposed, would be considerably diminished, were parish-officers compelled to place them within a certain number of miles from the boundaries of their own parish.

Let us suppose the limitation to be confined to six or ten miles at farthest, the distance would not exceed the possibility of investigation. It would operate as a powerful check upon masters, were parish-officers required to make an annual return of the state of all children placed out as apprentices. But it may be urged, that parish-business is already sufficiently burthensome, without the addition of so troublesome a task. Admit that it is so. The magnitude and importance of the object demand that persons be appointed in every parish, expressly to superintend the children belonging to it, who should be obliged to examine in person the situation of all apprentices, several times in a year, but not at stated periods. And here let me advert to the propriety of consigning the care of female children to inspectors of their own sex, as best adapted, in all points of view, for the office. What an extensive field for the exertions of benevolence would this scheme afford! the leisure enjoyed by women of a certain rank would enable them to render their visits of examination lessons of useful instruction: the good conduct, as well as the proper treatment, of the young people would be promoted, and many would be taught the value of character, who have now scarcely any stimulus to deserve one. The number of visitors might be regulated by circumstances and the population of the parish; and the parish might be distributed into districts, and one or more visitors appointed to each.

The benefits that would arise from the adoption of some such scheme, established on the principle of personal investigation, are so numerous, and of such importance, that I flatter myself, that persons qualified for the task will be excited to arrange and modify a plan that shall be both practicable and effectual, to prevent the possibility of a repetition of such criminal conduct towards parish children, as of late years

years has frequently disgraced the reputed humanity of the country. P. W.

Aug. 31, 1801.

For the Monthly Magazine.

Some ACCOUNT *of* DARTMOUTH; *its* SITUATION, STATE *of* SOCIETY, MANNERS, *&c.*

FROM the first appearance of the Monthly Magazine, I have read it regularly with pleasure and improvement; and having, in the course of the last spring, embarked on affairs of a commercial nature for the West Indies, I shipped, amongst other books, a complete set of them, to serve, in some measure, to amuse myself during the tedious hours of a long voyage.

Detained in our way down the Channel in Torbay, we were unfortunately exposed to a severe gale; the consequences of which were, that our vessel was driven a-shore, and greatly damaged, and with some difficulty brought into this port to be repaired; and here our ship's company, and myself among the rest, have been detained some months.

Amongst many of a very entertaining kind, the papers in your Magazine, giving an Account of the State of Society, Manners, &c. in various towns, have been to me peculiarly pleasing; and having leisure, and ample opportunities of collecting materials, I am induced to give you a sketch of this interesting place. I say *interesting*, because the *situation* of Dartmouth must be included in this sketch. It stands at the mouth of the river from which it takes its name, and which has its source in Dartmoor. From Dartmouth, the river is navigable for vessels of small burthen about *ten* miles, to the very pleasantly situated town of Totness. The beauties of this river have been celebrated by many a traveller; the scenery on each side, though greatly diversified, is in every respect beautiful; it consists of well-cultivated hills, formed into parks, gardens, and fields; elegant buildings, and delightfully romantic villages and cottages. Perhaps it does not abound in what may be termed *very bold scenery*, yet there are some appearances of a peculiarly grand kind, and the general richness and softness of the whole, must delight every contemplative and curious observer. The various windings of this beautiful river convey, at times, ideas which no language can fully express; and whether we go up or down it, the approach to the towns of Totness and Dartmouth is equally pleasing and romantic. To view it from the water, Dartmouth is a singularly pleasing object; it is equally so, whether we approach it by coming down the river, or by crossing the harbour at either of the passages, or entering it from the Channel. It is built on the side of a hill, extending nearly two miles from north to south, in the form of a crescent, and consists principally of three and four tier of houses rising one above the other, furnishing the idea of a most beautiful spot on which to have built a town, where uniformity and elegance could have been united. But all ideas of beauty, or even of convenience, vanish on becoming acquainted with Dartmouth. The new quay, on which are situated the principal inn, and a few other houses, is extremely pleasant, commanding the centre of the Harbour, the shipping, and the village of Kingswere, on the opposite side, built on a hill, perhaps as beautiful in its form, and as richly cultivated, as it is possible to conceive any spot to be. Adjoining to the New-quay is a spacious projection into the Harbour, denominated New-ground, having been at some former time gained from the water, on which are a few elm and oak-trees, but owing to the exposed situation at which they stand, they have never flourished; and though, at some previous period, the whole of that part of it which now forms a very pleasant walk, was planted, few of the trees have grown even to the diminutive size of those remaining. This piece of ground is surrounded entirely by water, a small bridge from the New-quay conducting you to it. Quitting this pleasant spot to view the town, the eye is disgusted, the smell offended, and the ear pained, at the vulgarity and prophaneness you are obliged to witness. The principal or lower street has a few good houses in it, but is so exceedingly narrow, that in *no part* can two carriages pass; the greater number of the buildings are very old, very lofty, and, in the upper stories almost permit the inhabitants to shake hands from the opposite sides. The houses on one side of this street have the advantage of a direct communication with the harbour, and for that reason have the preference for mercantile purposes, as vessels of considerable burthen can lie close to the cellars and stores. This street extends about half a mile south from the New-quay, and is terminated by the Custom-house-quay, on which are built the Custom-house, and the offices attached to it; and from this place, in addition to what constitutes the beauty of the former, you view

view the Castle, the parish-church of St. Petrox adjoining, and the mouth of the river Dart, where it empties itself into the English Channel.

You ascend from this to the higher street by flights of steps in various directions, excepting in one instance, where it is, I believe, *possible*, with great care and caution, to get up and down a small one-horse chair, but no other carriage can gain admission: and this street is worse in point of building, more confined, filthy, and offensive than the other. Proceeding in a southward direction, the houses are continued on *one side only*, when we get into what is called the South Town, where the buildings are mostly new, and very good; are inhabited by genteel families, and command an extensive and delightful prospect, including the Harbour and shipping, Kingswere, the Castle and Channel, the town, and some distance up the river. By this most pleasant walk, we are led to the Castle, situated on a charming spot, commanding an extensive sea-prospect, and protecting the entrance to the Harbour by two batteries, mounting each six eighteen-pounders. If we proceed northward from the New-quay, we pass through two or three narrow dirty streets, with here and there a good house, amidst many old and shabby ones. Ascending the hill, at this end of the town, we meet with several well-built, good houses, which command a more extensive and more beautiful and varied prospect, than those in the South Town, having not only a full view of the Harbour, shipping, town, Channel, &c. but also of a beautiful and highly cultivated valley at the western side of the town, presenting indeed to the eye the appearance of an extensive and richly adorned garden on both sides the river. In this truly romantic situation stands Dartmouth, so built, that the chimnies of one tier of houses are on a level with the entrances to those above them; and, what is both beautiful and singular, as you walk the streets, you see richly cultivated fields crowning the whole at a very considerable height.

The Harbour is very spacious, and the water very deep, capable of containing the whole of the English navy. The entrance is narrow, rendering it at times difficult for large vessels to come in or go out without warping or towing. Passing the town, about half a mile up the river is a very commodious dry-dock, capable of admitting two or three vessels at a time, built by a very public-spirited man, Mr. Seale; who has also contributed greatly to the enjoyment of the inhabitants, by permitting, at all times, a walk through a noble wood, by the side of the Dart, to be open for their accommodation. This delightful walk is terminated by a small fort, where a few cannon are placed, and fired on particular days. Of the commercial importance of this town, little can be said, and that little, unfortunately of an unpleasant kind. The Newfoundland trade has long been its chief dependance, and it has in times of *peace* been a flourishing and a wealthy place; but this disastrous war has completely effected its ruin. I assert it upon the authority of respectable men, merchants concerned in the trade, that there have been *at one time* three hundred sail of vessels belonging to Dartmouth employed in that trade; that, a very few years since, it had belonging to it a very large proportion of that number; and, in the present year, not *ten* have sailed to the land. Nor is it at all certain (and by some persons not thought probable), that *even peace*, considering the altered state of Europe since the commencement of the war, will restore to this town, either its trade, or its spirit for commercial speculations. The civil affairs of this town are managed by a mayor, a few aldermen, and freemen, who, as opportunity offers, elect two gentlemen to represent it in Parliament; and, in peaceable and flourishing times, are free and generous to their townsmen and neighbours, by giving public dinners and other entertainments. Its public buildings are few: a very ancient Guildhall, in an almost ruinous state; a neat brick-built Custom-house, erected about sixty years since; three parish-churches, and two Dissenting-chapels; one of the Baptist, and the other of the Presbyterian or Unitarian, denomination; the latter, however, is without a minister, and it is supposed will not be opened again.

There is likewise a house in the New Quay solely appropriated to public purposes, consisting of a coffee-room, where the London and provincial papers are taken in, and which is supported by subscription; an assembly-room, and card rooms: there is an assembly here once a fortnight during the winter, and public card-parties throughout the year; other public amusements there are none.

The state of literature and society is at a very low ebb in this town. I have long ago heard it remarked, that the further you remove from the metropolis, the less of a taste for literature, and a greater degree of indifference is observable respecting what books are published, and what takes place in in the learned world; and I have made the observation, that, in these respects, the West of England is inferior to the Eastern or Northern parts. To what particular cause it be owing, I cannot determine; but, certain it is, that a very considerable portion of mental debility, of intellectual supineness, of comparative ignorance of even the common civilities of polished life, is observable amongst the inhabitants of this town. That they should be less sensible of the varied beauties of nature by which they are surrounded than strangers, may easily be accounted for; as, however beautiful the scenery, it loses its effect upon those who perpetually behold it. Mercantile speculation—literary pleasures—the refinements of social life, are equally neglected.

To play the game of whist, and occasionally to employ a few hours in fishing, constitute the principal objects of pursuit. It may I think be admitted, that education in this town has never been thought of importance: certain it is, the objects of it have never been attained.

If however we may judge from appearances, a slight prospect of improvement is visible: there are now two boarding-schools for young gentlemen, both lately opened; one is kept by the curate of one of the parishes, and the other by a Dissenting minister; and, if proper encouragement be given to them, it is to be presumed, a considerable change for the better may be expected in the intellectual attainments of the rising generation.

It must not be forgotten, that there is a small book-society, principally confined to the circulation of pamphlets and reviews; and there was another formed upon a rather broader scale, but is has declined; because amongst its members no one could be found both willing and competent to manage its concerns. And as a proof that improvement may be expected, it is with pleasure I add, that I have heard a book-society has just been formed, composed entirely of ladies, with the exception of a clergyman, whom they have desired to act for them as treasurer and secretary. Public library there is none; and, except among professional men, no private ones. The inhabitants in general are to be classed among the middle rank in society: there are a *few* opulent families; a great many poor; but the poor are supplied with food, in the article of fish, at a very cheap rate. In other respects, provisions are higher than in the neighbouring towns. The population, lately ascertained, is about five thousand, exclusive of sailors; but the proportion of females is very large.

NAUTICUS.

Dartmouth, July 13, 1801.

For the Monthly Magazine.

WALKS *by the* FIRE-SIDE.

LET me retire at times from this bustle of life, and commune with myself in the closet of my heart. I now sit in the centre of a crowded city. Placed in the nave of this great wheel, it moves turbulently round, but I am still. A voluntary and temporary secession from society may have a tendency to brace and invigorate the mind, to give it a masculine independence, a happiness substantive and self denied. Yet, I ought to consider, that such seclusion may degenerate into a sullen and selfish estrangement from the world, which, after all that has been said of it, is, to use Voltaire's phrase, a very passable world. Certain it is, that terrestrial enjoyment can never result from a cynical isolation. Short retirements ought rather to urge a sweet return. Like an healthful excursion in the country, this self-sequestration will promote the better health of the heart, and refresh it with a purer air; for, were it more corrupt and contaminated than what common intercourse with the world affords, who would be so hardy as to talk with himself?

I once was alone upon the Lake of K—; alone—for the boatmen, as to any touch of society, were no better than their boat: indeed they were worse, for their indifference to the beauties of the place checked my feelings, and repressed the coming inspiration of the scenery. When I escaped from them, and stood alone in the midst of vast nature, I was sensible of a pleasurable elevation and expansion of soul; a feeling of being placed nearer to God, by being farther from man; a sensation of self-sufficiency, which kept me buoyed above the earth, yet in full prospect of its sublime beauties. I thought myself Lord of Inisfallan, with all its sweet variety of grateful green; and I walked through this garden of nature with a degree of that proud independence which distinguishes a most amiable savage, Jean Jaques Rousseau. But a drizzling rain began to fall, and, from the same moment, my enthusiasm began to cool. The Genius of the Lake deserted me, and I, who thought I could spend my life in this grand wooded amphitheatre, in a delightful dilation of mind over this fair expanse

of

of water, was glad, in little more than half an hour, to look out for company at the kitchen-fire. Ill calculated for general society, I should be a worse hermit, except I could support myself, as I believe hermits often did, by thinking that the world they affect to leave is talking of them. Even the mind of Rousseau might at times have been peopled with such ideas.

How well-fitted would Inisfallan have been for the burial-place of Rousseau, for the repose of the man of nature and of truth. I have seen a view of the Isle of Poplars, in the Lake at Ermenonville, where his body was, for a time, suffered to remain, until (I think, by a great want of taste and delicate feeling) it was transported to the Pantheon of *men* at Paris. This was taking him by violence from the beloved bosom of nature, to place her child on the breast of a hired and prostituted nurse. He was not able to give resistance; but, could he have done it, his free and indomitable spirit would have cry'd aloud—Leave—O leave me to repose! He who used to say, "That he never loved praying in his room; the walls, and other trifling works of men seemed to thrust themselves between God and him." He who said, "When you see me at death's door lay me under a shady oak; I promise you I shall be better." I repeat it, it was a great want of national taste, to squeeze the urn of such a man among their mob of immortals. The 'costume' of characters would have been much better preserved, by leaving him in a serene, sequestered spot, on which the eyes repose, and every part of the scene speaks for the hallowed inhabitant, and says,

"Placida *demum* in morte quiesco."

I lately saw another print, which I wished, for the sake of the moral contrast, to have placed near that of the tomb at Ermenonville. A little old man, with shoulders elevated above the head, sat in an arm-chair in the agony of death.—It was Frederic II. the late terrible warrior, and King of Prussia. Two grenadiers, one on each side, held, as high as their arms could extend, a large taper, and so exactly in the same attitude, that they still appeared to act under his word of command. The Prince of Prussia was kneeling with awe, rather than sorrow, at his side. No woman ventured to appear. Rousseau died in the arms of a woman, and that woman his wife. She has narrated his last conversation, which was beautifully characteristic. He desired the window that looked into the lawn to be opened, that he might take a last view of divine nature; and, after speaking to his wife in the language of endearment, and the kindest condolence, he got up to go to the window, fell down on the floor, and expired, while she supported him in her arms.

What has become of these opposite men?—this republican, and this despot; this man-hater with the most humane heart, and this man-destroyer, who affected to love philosophy and the Muses, but only wanted their panegyric and adulation. Where are ye now?

Is mind merely the result of material organization; and, that organization destroyed, is the mind dissipated and lost, to pass into some untried change, some new form of being? What is this breath of life, which animates the dust of the ground? Is the soul a mere quality, the result of organization; or, is it only the powers of life, or life itself? Does the brain secrete thought as the liver does bile, or as other secretions not less wonderful in their result? Are we immortal only in the sense of an implied indestructibility of the primary particles of matter, which are always changing from one combination to another, in the revolutions of the great wheel of existence? It appears, that there is no body, of which identity can be predicated for any ascertainable length of time, that the brain can never be in the same state any two given moments, and that permanent identity can be but partial similarity. "Thou'rt not thyself; for thou exists of many thousand grains, that issue out of dust." And when the whole organization of the brain is completely destroyed and dissipated, it seems hard to conceive how consciousness can continue, unless it adheres, as a quality, to the indivisible, indestructible atom, or is an element *sui generis*.

The doctrine of the Christian resurrection of the *whole* man seems most agreeable to the theory of mind being the result of organization; but the Gnostic doctrine of a soul distinct from the body, which in the first ages of Christianity was deemed heretical, became at length the general belief. The Gnostics themselves got it from the Platonic doctrine, and Plato himself from the philosophy of the East, which, in the Vedas, thus sublimely imagines the spiritual, ætherial principle: "All spirit is homogeneous, the spirit of God in kind the same with that of man, though differing infinitely from it in degree; and, as material substance is mere illusion, there exists, in this universe, only one

one generic, spiritual substance, the sole primary cause efficient, substantial, and formal, of all secondary causes and appearances whatever, but endued, in the highest degree, with a sublime, providential wisdom, and proceeding, by ways incomprehensible, to the spirits which emane from it." That spirit from which these created beings proceed, through which having proceeded they live, toward which they tend, and in which they are ultimately absorbed; that spirit is the Great One. Armstrong has made a poetical paraphrase:

There is, they say, (and I believe there is),
A spark within us of th'immortal fire,
That animates and moulds the grosser frame;
And, when the body sinks, escapes to Heav'n,
Its native seat, and mixes with the Gods.
Meanwhile, this heav'nly particle pervades
The mortal elements; in ev'ry nerve
It thrills with pleasure, or grows mad with pain;
And in its secret conclave, as it feels
The body's woes and joys, this ruling pow'r
Wields at its will the dull material world,
And is the body's health or malady.

It appears probable, that there are not in nature two substances of qualities so opposite, and even contradictory, as mind and body are supposed to be, which is nearly demonstrated from the impossibility of two such substances acting upon each other, without having one common quality between them. New elements are from time to time discovered, such as the electric, the magnetic, fluids, the *vis insita*, or principle of vitality inherent in the muscular fibre; the principle of acidity, called oxygen, which so long concealed itself from the European philosophers, but seems to have been early acknowledged in India, as a fifth element, under the name of "Ahass;" all these principles and elements lately discovered imply a yet unknown variety. The spirit of animation may be an element still more subtly material, even fire itself; the new caloric, and ancient *anima mundi*, which Voltaire has so well described in these comprehensive lines:

Ignis ubique latet, naturam complectitur omnem;
Cuncta parit, renovat, dividit, unit, alit.

Perhaps it is better not to think too much of our fate in futurity. It makes us once again children in the dark, and puts the mind into a state of terrifying ignorance, and hypochondriacal credulity, which makes it too subservient to those professing to be wiser, but, in reality, not a whit wiser, in those vast obscurities than ourselves: and, in truth, the general behaviour of the clergy, their personal worldly-mindedness, and political servility, make the heart revolt from the profession. Is not the existence of a clerical order inconsistent with the true principles of Protestant-dissenters, who take the New Testament as their plainest and best instructor, who are all equal as members of Christ's kingdom, and over whom such a distinction of spiritual rank must tend to introduce a human authority usurpatory of the right of Jesus as Christ? It is curious, that those who enjoy life the most, should fear death the least; and, certainly, that most vivacious breed of men, the French, seem to die, as they live, in more apparent good-humour than any other nation in Europe. The Turkish idea of its being an inevitable destiny blunts the sharpness of death; and, to my feelings, it gives a degree of social warmth to this chilling change, when I think how many thousands are, at the same instant, sharing in the companionship of mortality. Death, says Milton, is to life the crown or shame. Certainly it is most honourable, and may be sufferred with a sort of enjoyment in the field of battle, in the cause of our country. There it becomes *productive*, and has a value. Burns describes this beautifully:

Nae could faint-hearted doubtings teize him;
Death comes—Wi fearless eyes he sees him;
Wi bloody haund, a welcome gies him;
And when he fa's,
His latest draught of breathing leaves him
In faint huzzas.

For the Monthly Magazine.

A PEDESTRIAN EXCURSION *through* ENGLAND *and* WALES, *during the* SUMMER *of* 1797.

(Continued from p. 106.)

FROOME, SOMERSETSHIRE, *Friday* 7. To this place, and all its inhabitants, I was hitherto a perfect stranger. But I was not long permitted to remain so. My name soon transpired. It flew from house to house; and I found myself suddenly and unexpectedly in the midst of friends. I was too agreeably importuned to resist the temptation of a temporary delay. Excursions in the neighbourhood were planned; a cheerful party was formed for the evening; and the most flattering attention was paid to my comfort and my welfare.

In the morning, we rambled through the romantic dell, called *Vales Bottom*, into which the various branches of the river Froome empty themselves. Thence their collected waters flow onward beyond Freshford, between which and Bathford they are joined by another stream, and empty themselves into the Avon.

In this dell, we visited a cloth-mill, where we saw several women waiting for *spare-wool*, which they spin with the hand, at 2½d. per lb. Upon inquiry, I learned that it was great work to spin two pounds in a day. The children employed in the factory earn from 1s. 6d. to 2s. 6d. per week; for which, in the summer time, they work fourteen hours in the day. I need not add, their looks were pallid and miserable. The women, who pick knots off the work, earn from 4s. 6d. to 5s. per week, to which may be added the little perquisite of the wool picked off —perhaps, on an average, about 6d. per week more. From hence, we traced the dingle upwards to its abrupt termination or boundary, where, amidst a luxuriant bed of daffodils, the fairies of the fountains may be supposed to repose themselves. Here I was shewn a very curious and mysterious spring, which, I was informed, flows outward to the river for one half of the year, and inward from the river during the other half: and, it is affirmed by the neighbouring people, always to change its course (without the least respect to the act of parliament that altered the style) on Old Midsummer's Day.

Vales Farm is also another of the remarkables in the neighbourhood of this dingle. The house was formerly the manor house, and here are still the ruins of an antique parlour, and of a Roman Catholic chapel, now used as a woodhouse. The farm consists only of little better than 100 acres; yet, I was informed, that it paid 60l. a year direct taxes.

Having explored this dale to its upper extremity, we now returned to trace it downward, and amuse ourselves with its sinuous appendages, and expanding varieties; among which must not be forgotten its useful lime-kilns, nor its picturesque, half-ruined bridges—still less, the rude old excavation in the rock, to which we ascended, and at the mouth of which, sheltered by a fine screen of coppice wood, we set ourselves down to listen to the murmuring of the waters hastening over their broken bed, and mark the browzing flock, and here and there a cottage that diversified the sequestered scene. Descending still lower by some ruined and deserted buildings, we came to a considerable fulling-mill, over whose dam (after all not unfrequently the best of all *artificial* cascades, because, in fact, the least artificial), the wide sheet of water, now swoln by frequent rains, gushing with rude roar, and driving over its steep and craggy bed finely overshadowed with trees of all growths, presented us with some very interesting scenery, which, if not picturesque, was something more—was poetical, if I may be allowed the expression.

Pursuing now our road along the ridge of the dell to the *village of Elm*, we were presented with a new scene, of which the prominent objects were some iron-mills and cots, overhung by rocky and woody precipices on the one side, and the village itself situated on the opposite bank, under which the river rushed and foamed along; and the correspondent accompaniments of which were new ramifications of the dingle in the rear, one of which was cloathed and choaked up, as it were, with luxuriant trees and underwood, forming a sort of pent-up sea or torrent of waving foliage, through which the real stream that gushed was rather marked by its murmurings than its obvious course, till it rushed out to mingle itself with the main river.

Issuing from this romantic dingle, we crossed some fields to the neighbourhood of a leather-manufactory, and another fulling-mill, to amuse ourselves with the reverberations of a double echo.

We now returned to Froome, and devoted the remainder of the day to friendship and conviviality.

Saturday 8. *Froome.* The early part of this day was devoted to the factories, and to the different processes of card-making, carding, and spinning of wool, and other objects that seemed worthy of observation; among which must not be forgotten, the famous cask (at the sign of the Bell, if I recollect rightly) which is about as high as a two pair of stairs window, and holds I know not how many hundred hogsheads of ale. I need not add to this fact the remark, that Froome is a large and flourishing town. It is built upon very abrupt hills. The houses are of substantial stone, and the streets are paved, or rather pitched. Manufacturers earn from 10s. to 12s. per week—some more. Husbandmen not more than from 8s. to 9s. The church is spacious and neat; but the majority of the inhabitants are Dissenters. There are four meeting-houses; one Methodist, one Presbyterian, one of General, and one (the largest of all) of Particular Baptists: the Unitarians are few; and of known proselytes to "the Age of Reason" there are none.

After

After dinner, we walked to *Longlete*, in Wiltshire; a heavy, dull, and tasteless incumbrance, every thing belonging to which is in hideous taste, the Park excepted; and even that is but so-so. The canal is nothing better than a nasty stagnant pool; and the Aviary no longer contains any thing worthy of notice. But I forget that a great personage is reported to have thought, that this place was altogether *a very fine thing*. We returned to Froome, to spend the evening with a friend, from whose garden we had a view of the famous white horse cut out on the side of a hill.

Sunday 9. Beckington, through which we next passed, is a considerable manufacturing village, well built with stone. In it is a large boarding-school, the master of which was building himself a handsome new house.

Rode is another large, but less handsome, village; exhibiting many very mean cottages, and the appearance of much dirt and wretchedness. In the manufactures here, many men, women, and children are employed.

Farley, the next place we arrived at, is a little scattered village, but well-built with stone. At the entrance are some good old houses, particularly one, in the spacious garden of which a respectable clerical-looking man was diligently employed in collecting rose-leaves, probably for the medicinal purposes of his good lady, the Madam Bountiful of the village. The church is a plain, neat, little building.

Farley had once a castle, the memory of which is still preserved upon the map. Of this, a small fragment of the ruin, with the addition of much new work, is made into a farm-house. The other remains are parts of a very extensive wall, with fragments of three or four towers, of one of which the shell is tolerably entire, and finely vested with Time's venerable livery, the ivy; and a chapel, with a painted dormitory to the left, miserably out of repair. In this are some fine monuments of the Hungerford family: one very ancient; another bearing date 1648: the effigies are cut in white marble, in a good stile of sculpture. There are also some curious reliques; the armour of the Hungerford family, and Oliver Cromwell's saddle. In the vault are several old coffins, and some curious mummies, the leaden cases of which are molded to the forms and features of the respective faces.

Hence, by a foot-track, through a country at once wild and fertile, we proceeded to *Ivern* (or *Ifford*), which presented a scene of beauty and fertility; the river Froome, here a wide and rapid stream, and finely embowered, flowing through an antique stone bridge, between two hills, up one of which, by the road-side, the village is scattered. At the front of this picture, just beyond the bridge, are placed two handsome houses, the residences of Mr. Graysford and Mr. West. From hence (entering the county of Wilts) with little deviation from the course of the Froome, a diversified and somewhat romantic track conducted us to Freshford; the hills that rise from the borders of the stream being on one side finely wooded, and on the other sprinkled with hamlets and cottages, while the downs, with a range of ruins at the base, terminate the perspective.

Freshford. We approached this winding village through a hay-field, whose abundant crop did not appear much injured by the wetness of the season. At the entrance is an apparently good and spacious inn, built with stone, but which the taste either of the proprietor or the occupant has caused to be painted, to give it the resemblance of flaring red brick. The situation of this village is hilly and the buildings are straggling; but the appearance is altogether pleasingly romantic, and it commands prospects of a fine country.

We passed the works of a canal then cutting from Newbury to Bath, to communicate with the Coal-canal, whence the sinuosities of the Froome conducted us to

Stoke, a romantic and beautiful little village, scattered from the hill-top all the way down to the water-edge.

We now take our final leave of Wiltshire, and, following no further the course of the river Froome, mount, by a steep ascent, to *Claverton Down*, not without some indication in the appearance of the mansions we passed, of the elegance of that fine city we were about to approach; and of which, with all the luxuriant scenery around, we had presently a noble view from *Prior Park*.

(To be continued.)

For the Monthly Magazine.

REMARKS *of* PROFESSOR BŸGGE, *of* COPENHAGEN, *on the* NEW SYSTEM *of* WEIGHTS *and* MEASURES *adopted in* FRANCE.

THE learned Professor Bÿgge, of Copenhagen, was lately employed in a mission to Paris, the express object of which was to examine the merits of the new French metrical system, and the practicability of its introduction into foreign countries. His observations upon the various

various curiosities, and the collections relative to the arts and sciences, with which the metropolis of the French republic abounds, have already been presented to the British public in an English translation. A second volume has lately been published by the same author, containing, among other matter, remarks on the French system of weights and measures, which we shall give to our readers. Professor Bÿgge shews himself considerably averse to this system; and perhaps the time is come in which this important plan may be examined with more impartiality in France, as the first impressions produced by this bold and ingenious undertaking are very considerably worn off.

Professor Bÿgge begins by shewing the great inconvenience which was felt by the extreme variety of weights and measures in common use in France, which differed not only in distant provinces, but even in neighbouring towns; and he justly praises the wise intentions of the government, in reducing the whole to a common standard. "The easiest, simplest, and least expensive method of accomplishing this object," he observes, "would have been, doubtless, to have taken for the standard of length the French foot (*pied de roi*), the use of which was universal throughout France, and its relation with the measures of other countries most accurately ascertained. In like manner, for admeasurement of weight, the *poids de marc* might have been rigidly adhered to, as it is much used throughout Europe, and well known in commerce. The Paris pint, which legally contains forty-eight cubic inches, would have answered all the purposes of a measure for fluids; and the Paris bushel for dry goods. By these simple means, all the well known measures might have been preserved, which have been in constant use for centuries; and the public would not have lost the French foot, and the *poids de marc*, which have been employed in a vast number of mathematical, philosophical, and chemical calculations; and in a multitude of books, French and others. There would have been no difficulty in having accurate standards of these measures sent to the different departments, and their use enjoined by law.

"But this idea appeared too simple. It was wished not only to procure an equality of weights and measures for France, but to take a basis of admeasurement from nature herself, to introduce it in every country and to give to the whole world the same system of weights and measures. It was likewise supposed that their accuracy could never be impaired, or at least might always be restored, should the original standards be destroyed by fire or any other accidents, or injured by the lapse of time.

"The plan of the new French metrical system is certainly due to Borda, whose knowledge and ingenuity are well known. I have often observed to him that I was surprized that the simple pendulum under the latitude 45° should not be assumed as the unity for a measure of length, since this standard is so easy to be found, and to be fixed with rigorous exactness.

"His answer was, that it would not suit their purpose to use it, since it would be necessary, in determining its length, to employ the divisions of time, which themselves are arbitrary. But surely time and its divisions must be considered as fixed and unalterable in nature, as long as the globe continues to turn on its axis with an equal motion.

"The metre is the basis of the new French system of admeasurement. It is a ten millionth part of the arc of the meridian from the equator to the pole. The length of a degree of the meridian has been measured at 45° of latitude; every thing therefore depends on the accuracy with which this has been ascertained. Now, the imperfection of our mechanical instruments, joined to the comparative weakness of our organs of sight, the greater or less serenity of the atmosphere, the difficulty of well distinguishing the signals, and many other obstacles, all of these expose the most practised astronomer, when using the best instruments, to commit errors, which he is afterwards obliged to correct in an arbitrary manner. With the most accurate instruments, he may commit an error of one toise in ten thousand. This assertion is not founded merely on hypothesis, but on the experience of many years which I have had in trigonometrical surveys.

"Besides, the instruments made in France, not being constructed with as much accuracy as they are capable of being brought to, I think I am authorised to consider the error which I mentioned as more considerable; but allowing only this, it would make the difference of a twentieth of a line in the metre, and certainly this is not inconsiderable. But I am persuaded, from the dimensions of the meridian taken for the metrical basis, that the error may easily be double what I have mentioned, or the tenth of a line.

"The degrees to the north ought to be larger than the others; however, notwithstanding all the care and accuracy bestowed on this subject, it was found that under the latitude 43° 31′ the degree measured 57,048 toises; and in 45° 43′, it was 57,040 according to one measurement, and 57,050 according to another.

"This difference of ten toises shews that I have not exaggerated in supposing it possible, and even unavoidable, that an error might be committed, amounting to no less than six toises in a single degree.

"Hence it may be seen that even such accurate astronomers as Cassini and La Caille have not been able to come nearer the truth than one toise in ten thousand, and I suspect never will make a closer approximation; and from their own calculations the metre ought to be 3.0807 French feet.

"Since, however, the decree of the 18th Germinal fixed it at 3.0794 French feet, Bouguer's admeasurement of the meridian at Peru must have been adhered to, in which the elevation of the earth under the equator is reckoned at a three hundred and twentieth of its axis. But who is not struck with these arbitrary hypotheses, and with the difference which exists between these two bases for determining the metre, each of which appears as probable as the other, and yet differing the tenth of a line! In my opinion the true dimensions of the metre are still subject to a greater uncertainty than the length of the simple pendulum under a given latitude; and it cannot yet be affirmed with truth that the length of the metre is justly given, that it is invariable, and fixed by a natural standard.

"It has besides been taken for granted that the curvature of the arc of the meridian, from the equator to the pole, forms a perfect ellipsis. But this is still a mere hypothesis, for the degrees measured by Beccaria at Turin, by Liesganig in Hungary and Austria, and by La Caille on the coast of Africa, seem to prove that this curvature is by no means a perfectly regular ellipsis. This therefore would make it impossible to calculate the length of the whole meridian from the measurement of only a few degrees, and consequently would throw an equal difficulty on the valuation of the true length of the metre.

"In the new French system every division, from the highest to the lowest, is made by tens. This undoubtedly affords the greatest facility for calculations; but it may be doubted whether this mode of division is equally eligible for mechanics. I am of opinion that actual subdivisions of $\frac{1}{2}$, $\frac{1}{4}$, $\frac{1}{8}$, $\frac{1}{16}$, &c. may be made with much more accuracy than those of tenths. These last are a real school of patience for instrument-makers. In practical mechanics it is an undoubted truth that it is impossible to divide by tens and hundreds with the same exactness as by two; and this is shewn particularly in the construction of octants, quadrants, theodolites, graphometres, &c.

"If the new metrical system should come to be adopted universally, our successors would cease to have any connection with the science of their predecessors. Let us imagine our posterity employing the New Republican Calendar, using instruments divided into 100 degrees, and dividing the day into ten hours, undertaking to read astronomical, geographical, and nautical observations made in past times. To understand these observations, they must be reduced at every line, to translate our present language of calculation into their own idiom, and all their time will be taken up in reducing the antient divisions of time and space into correspondent modern terms. Soon they will be fatigued with these perpetually recurring calculations, and will reject altogether all books of the old style; and thus the fruit of so much laborious research made by our predecessors will be entirely thrown aside. The same will happen in works of natural philosophy and chemistry, in every case where weights and measures are concerned.

"This is a real and powerful obstacle to the progress of arts and sciences; for, to bring to perfection the sciences of astronomy, geography, and hydrography, it is particularly necessary to compare the result of antient and modern observations.

"Conformably to the new system the day was to be divided into ten hours, the hour into 100 minutes, and the minute into 100 seconds.

"The two excellent watch-makers, Berthoud and Breguet, along with some others, made however remonstrances with the directory, in the name of their whole body, on the great inconveniences which would ensue from such a division of time, and the particular injury which the whole trade would suffer thereby.

"This had the effect of obtaining from the government a resolution to postpone this innovation. I have only seen in Paris two clocks constructed on these divisions. One is a large clock set up in the middle

middle of the *Façade* of the Thuilleries, looking to the garden, which drew a good many gazers as an object of curiosity out of the common mode; the other is properly a time-piece, made by Berthoud, which has gone very regularly for these fifteen months.

"As to what concerns the Republican Calendar, difficulties likewise occur with regard to the precise period at which the French year begins. It ought to be on the day, in which, according to astronomical observations, the sun enters the first point of the sign Libra. Now the sun does not enter this sign every year on the same day and hour, and thus the republican year is equally subject to variations; and it is besides very difficult to determine this period, both for the past and the future. But, in the calendar of all other European nations, which is consecrated by long use and by the approbation of the greatest legislators and astronomers for its exactness, the computation of time, by the assistance of an easy intercalation, may be made for many centuries, past and to come; a computation which will not produce an error of a single day, compared with the true astronomical calculation, in less than 3200 years. It surely required more mature reflection, before a chronological system was to be abandoned, which possessed so much simplicity, facility in computation, and such rigorous exactness.

"The names adopted in this new system, such as, *metre*, *are*, *stère*, *litre*, and *gramme*, will long have a barbarous sound to the ears of the people; and it will be no less difficult for them to comprehend that the prefixed terms *deci*, *centi*, and *milli*, denote division by ten, an hundred, and a thousand, and that *deca*, *hecto*, *kilo*, and *myria*, signify multiplication by these numbers; and the fact is, that, notwithstanding the pains taken by the Directory to introduce the new system, by multiplying models of the standard weights, and distributing them to the departments, its use is almost entirely confined to the limits of Paris, and to the public officers, the latter using the new system merely in compliance with express orders. The greater number of the vast population of France neither know nor understand the new system, and continue in the old track; and it will probably require some centuries before this system has entirely displaced the use of the antient weights and measures.

"How great the difficulty then of introducing the new metrical system throughout Europe? There are reforms which are liable to too many obstacles in their introduction, and which entrench upon too powerful and multiplied interests, to be undertaken without the most serious inconveniences to the present state of society. It is in such cases however, that the necessity for such reforms may often be obviated by wise and prudent measures on the part of government."

To the Editor of the Monthly Magazine.

SIR,

MR. ALLARDYCE has taken much pains to shew that the conduct of the Directors of the Bank of England has been censurable, for not increasing the dividends upon Bank stock, and it must be confessed that his premises *appear* to warrant his conclusion, I was not, however, satisfied by the explanation which he gives of such paradoxical conduct, on the part of the Directors. Their interest in the concern was, I thought, too great to be despised, and to keep the dividend much below the point to which it could safely be carried, appeared to me an instance of negligence altogether unparalleled. I therefore consulted Dr. Adam Smith; and reflecting upon his observations, I felt convinced that the Bank-directors have not merited the blame imputed to them by Mr. Allardyce.

Perhaps I may be able to suggest to that gentleman the ground of his mistake.

He finds that private Bankers can divide yearly 13½ per cent. upon their capital, and *therefore* he considers that the Bank of England could increase their dividends either to that rate, or near it, or perhaps beyond it.

The capital of private Bankers, however, does not exceed what is necessary to keep by them for the discharge of their engagements, their notes, &c. as they come in. A private Banker, we may suppose, gains five per cent. per annum, upon the whole amount of the notes and bills which he can circulate. To support that circulation, it is only requisite that he should hold a certain proportion of cash in his hands. His profits are to be reckoned upon the amount necessary for that purpose. If, for instance, upon an average he circulates notes, &c. to the amount of a million, and the capital, or the quantity of money which enables him to do this, is a quarter of a million, he will gain upon that capital 20 per cent. per annum, deducting the expence of managing his business.

 That

A part of that capital, besides, may be deposited in his hands by others without any interest, or at a rate of interest lower than what he himself charges. In that case his profits will be still further increased according to the amount and nature of those deposits. The profits of London-bankers, who do not issue notes, seem entirely to arise from the advantageous employment of the money deposited in their hands. Upon any capital of their own which they may employ, common interest alone can usually be obtained, but when to this amount is added the interest yielded by the deposits of their customers, their profits may be sufficiently large.

But the Bank of England stands in a situation very different. Besides the capital in money which like other Banks it must hold (at least when it is not, as at present, restrained from paying in specie), the Bank of England has lent to Government a capital of above 11 millions, for which, instead of the profit which that capital, if it could be employed, would naturally yield, it receives only three per cent per annum.

Amount of accumulated capital supposed to be - -		£.4,000,000
Amount of deposits, ditto - - - - - -		2,500,000
		6,500,000
Lent by the Bank to Government for six years without Interest - - - - - -	3,000,000	
Amount of cash held for answering demands supposed to be - - - - - -	1,000,000	
		4,000,000
		2,500,000
Profit upon this disposeable sum of £2,500,000 - -		125,000
To which add profits stated above, - - - - -		1,150,000
		1,275,000
Deduct income tax - - - - - - - - - -		127,500
Remains as supposed total of profit - - - - -		1,147,500

The present circumstances of the Bank may yield a dividend of about 10l. per cent. which amount, in various ways, has actually been divided. But if payments were made in specie, the amount of Bank-notes circulated would be reduced in proportion to the specie so employed, and the profits of those notes must be reduced also, together with the profits upon the whole concern. It would not perhaps be prudent in the Directors to raise the dividend at once to its highest rate, when the continuance of that high rate must be very precarious. Probably one third part of the capital originally subscribed by the Bank-proprietors, would be sufficient to carry on their business to its present extent; and, *then indeed*, the dividends might be very much increased.

Mr. Allardyce claims a division of the sum which the Bank has accumulated. This accumulation, however, is the only real efficient capital that the Bank possesses. Divide it among the Proprietors, and in the first place their annual dividend would be diminished by the amount of the simple interest which that sum would yield;—in the next place, when payments were to be made in specie, the business could not be conducted with facility or security, and perhaps an absolute stoppage might take place.

I know not whether any one has considered, in a just point of view, the suspension of payments in specie by the Bank. Certainly no *injury* to the nation was to be apprehended if all the cash that it possessed had been sent to foreign countries by the operations of commerce.

To me therefore it appears, that, in adopting the measure in question, the Bank-directors were actuated by the view of extending their paper-circulation, and of augmenting in consequence their assistance to Government. On the part of Government, a minor consideration might be, that a quantity of specie was thereby reserved in the Bank-coffers, for a purpose to which so much was then applied—the payment of foreign subsidies. The measure, however, was of a desperate complexion; but the brave are said to be Fortune's favourites, and the rash are often indebted to her, for "hair-breadth escapes."

At a future opportunity, I will endeavour to shew in what manner and degree that measure has been detrimental to the nation.

Sept. 1, 1801. J. N. Hunt.

For

To the Editor of the Monthly Magazine.

SIR,

AS even your Magazine is not always pure from rhetorical flourishes against forestallers, regraters, and monopolizers, I feel an inclination to try, whether or not you will admit a little close reasoning in favour of those whom, after long and disinterested consideration, I regard, not only as absolutely incapable of doing harm, but as essentially requisite to the commerce of *all the necessaries of life*.

The reasons why any person buys any commodity to sell again; or, why any person sells any thing to another, knowing that the buyer intends to sell it again, are,

1. Because the person who buys to sell again, can improve the article by additional *labour*.

2. Because, with regard to the disposal of the article to the consumer, he possesses superior *information*.

3. Because he has more *time*.

4. Because he has more *capital*.

5. Because he will, in general, take more *care* of the article, when it is his own property, than if he were to sell it for another man.

Try any case of forestalling by the above positions, and you will find that the forestaller has benefited the public, by increasing the value of the commodity, in some one of those ways, or in several, or in all combined.

Again:

1. It is not for the advantage of the public, that the owner of any commodity should sell it to the consumer before it has received the requisite quantity of *labour*.

2. It is not for the advantage of the public, that he should sell for a lower price than he would otherwise sell for, in consequence of want of *information*.

3. It is not for the advantage of the public, that he should sell for a lower price, in consequence of want of *time*.

4. It is not for the advantage of the public, that he should sell for a lower price, in consequence of want of *capital*.

5. It is not for the advantage of the public, that any commodity should be sold for a lower price, in consequence of the want of *care*, or the dishonesty of a person selling on commission.

Try all political regulations that impede the free course of trade by the above rules, and you will find that they are disadvantageous to the public, in some one of the above ways, or in several, or in all combined.

This subject is not of temporary interest, from being at present under discussion; but, in a country where the prime article of subsistence is annually imported, and where, of course, the most abundant harvest is scarcity, it is a subject of high and perpetual importance. I am willing to illustrate these rules by examples; and, from time to time, to prove the theory by the practice from which it is taken, in as short and logical a manner as I can.

MISOPHETOR.

For the Monthly Magazine.

SKETCH *of a* JOURNEY *from* COPENHAGEN *to* HAMBURG, &c.

(Continued from Page 107.)

EARLY in the morning of the 28th of April, we left the farm-house at which we slept, and proceeded on our journey. We breakfasted at *Remmels*, a small and inconsiderable village, and from thence continued our journey to Itzehoe, which was our next stage, distant from Remmels fourteen miles. As we approached this town, the fields, which were chiefly sown with wheat and barley, were inclosed by hedges of black thorn, and the country appeared to be well cultivated; still the roads were very heavy, and the wheels of our vehicle were, for the greater part of the way, so enveloped in sand, that we were sometimes obliged to get out and walk, as the horses, though we had four, could with difficulty proceed. Immediately before we arrived at Itzehoe, the prospect from a mountain, or rather a hill (for nothing is here on a grand scale), at the foot of which lies the town, is very pleasing; the country before us appearing to be more populous, better cultivated, and graced with more trees than we had been accustomed to behold. At length, we arrived at Itzehoe, with our faces as sun-burnt as if we had been an India-voyage, which was occasioned by the reflection of the sun from the sand. We went to the Hamburg Coffee-house, where the accommodations were so good (indeed they were the best that we had met with since we left Copenhagen) and the people so very civil, that we were induced to stay two days to rest ourselves, as our journey for the last seventy miles had been extremely fatiguing.

Itzehoe has a very ancient origin: it is named from a fortress built the beginning of the ninth century, by order of Charles the Great, to repel the incursions of the Danes into Germany: this fortress was called Esseho or Isseho; in process of time, it was surrounded by a number of houses, which

which about the middle of the thirteenth century obtained the privileges of a town. It has since been several times destroyed, but is now a small, agreeable, and well-built town, partly situated on the river Stöer, which runs into the Elbe, and has been erroneously mentioned, by some travellers, as a canal cut from that river. It is distant from Hamburg forty seven miles. The church, which is in the market-place, is very small, but the steeple is high, and of a particularly light architecture; it stands on four small iron-pillars, which at a distance are hardly perceivable.

From Itzehoe to Glückstadt is twelve miles: part of the road is across a large heath covered with sand, between which and Krempt, is the village of *Steinburg*, consisting of about sixty large farm houses, the economy of which was the same as of that before described. The upper part of the gable-ends of the farm-houses in this part of Germany, like many of the houses in the West Indies, considerably overhang the lower part. Some of these farmers are rich; in one house which we visited, the rooms were not only neatly but elegantly furnished: I was told that the proprietor was worth 40,000 specie dollars, the whole of which he had accumulated by farming. On a rising ground, about a mile from this village, is a monument, in the form of an obelisk, which has a subterraneous passage leading to the palace of Count Rantzau, a mile distant, in the country of that name. Half way between Itzehoe and Glückstadt, is the small town of *Krempe* now only remarkable for the height of its steeple, which serves as a mark for seamen. It was formerly situated on the banks of the Elbe, and so strongly fortified that it sustained a siege of above twelve months, during the civil wars of Germany; its fortifications are now no more. The road from this town is the same as in France (*a chaussée* on each side of a *pavé*, rising in the middle), the country about here being low and marshy; it is in some parts highly cultivated, and scattered all over with farms of different sizes, which give pleasing ideas to the reflecting traveller, when he learns that it is only 150 years since this part of the country was a complete swamp, of no possible use to either man or beast.

Glückstadt, which we entered over a fine, broad draw-bridge, is fortified, but the fortifications are in want of repair. This is the Danish capital of Holstein; it contains a court of judicature and a court of chancery for that province. It may be said that Glückstadt is a small, well-built town; several canals run through it, the principal one crosses the top of the market-place, and is here connected with another, which divides the town into two nearly equal parts. The harbour is broad, and has water sufficient to admit large vessels; it is defended by a castle on the Elbe—if that may be called a defence, which would require some other fortifications to defend itself: indeed, in the opinion of those who have seen the fortifications in France and the Netherlands, such as those of Lisle and of Valenciennes, of Maestricht and of Breda, the defences of this country will almost dwindle into insignificant entrenchments; nevertheless, they are not to be despised, as in *these things* the name goes a great way. This town has not so much commerce as it formerly had, though it enjoys the same privileges as the Hans Towns; besides which, all religions are tolerated here, which is not the case in the latter places. The people of Glückstadt appear unpleasant to strangers, but, I am told, that they are very sociable amongst themselves: they imitate the Germans rather than the Danes, and their manners are, in consequence, a mixture of both. In their inattention to foreigners, they reminded me of my own countrymen, whose want of feeling and regard for men of other countries are proverbial on all parts of the Continent.

We remained several days at Glückstadt; and, as we had now arrived on the banks of the Elbe, I took a retrospective view of my journey from Copenhagen hither. I had been in Norway and Sweden, and found on this journey, that the bold and sublime scenery, with which those countries abound, was but ill-exchanged for the views in Denmark and its continental dominions; still in the latter places the picturesque sometimes occurred, but of romantic prospects we had none, unless those about Apenrade and Flensburg might be called such. In many parts of Sleswick and Holstein (as before mentioned) nothing was to be seen but large tracts of sand, with here and there a few brown furze-bushes, with hardly a spot of verdure to cheer the weary eye of the traveller: some parts of Holstein particularly reminded me of Salisbury-plain in England. Through the whole extent of this route, there is little to gratify the philosopher, the man of taste, or the man who travels for the purposes of information. Indeed the attainment of useful knowledge on this journey was placed farther from our reach, by not having the advantage that is found on other parts of the continent:

tinent: I allude to the public-tables, which so much enliven travelling in France, Flanders, Germany, &c. From this source much information is sometimes obtained, as men of education and science are frequently to be met with at the *tables-d'hôte* in these countries. Still we had not many inconveniences to encounter on our journey. In England, we are often stopped by toll-gates; in France and Flanders by the barriers; and in Holland and Germany, there is no end to the stoppages, either by the surly and supercilious centinel, the imposing custom house-officer, or the collector of the *passagée-gelt* (passage-money): nothing of this kind occurs in the journey from Copenhagen to Hamburg, if we except three or four turnpikes in Zealand and Fünen, and the interrogatories administered to us at the Castle of Gottorp. At each stage, we generally procured a bottle or two of wine, some cold meat and white bread; as there was nothing but black bread and French brandy to be had at the small inns, or barns, into which we drove between the stages, to refresh our horses and drivers. After we arrived on the Continent, particularly after we had passed Haderslében and Apenrâle, the change was very perceptible in the dress, manners, and language of the inhabitants. The dress of the higher classes was more stiff; and that of the lower classes (as we approached Germany) was less cleanly than we had been accustomed to see in the Danish isles. The manners and behaviour of both the higher and lower classes in Jutland and Holsteïn were repulsive, which made them appear to considerable disadvantage to us, particularly when contrasted with those of the Danes, who are in general hospitable, and attentive to strangers. The languages spoken in Sleswick and Holsteïn are Danish, *Plàt Dytch* (Ang. low German), and *Dytch*, i. e. German. In the northern parts of Slesvick, from our landing at Aaresünd, till we reached Apenrâle, the Danish language is generally spoken; but, from thence to Slesvick (the town of Flensburg excepted) we heard nothing but *Plàt Dytch*. At Slesvick, as before mentioned, the German language is spoken fluently, as it is all over Holsteïn*. The cultivation of the Danish Islands was far superior to that of the countries which we had last passed through; but natural causes operate greatly in favour of the former: yet, it is said, that Slesvick and Holsteïn contain more inhabitants on a square-mile than is to be found in either Zealand or Fünen.

The expence of a post-waggon and four horses from Aaresünd to Glückstadt, was at the rate of a specie dollar per Danish-mile, the whole amounting to twenty-eight specie-dollars (i. e. 6l. 6s. sterling). Had we gone direct from Copenhagen to Hamburg, the whole expence of only post-waggons and boats would have been 12l. 13s. sterling; to which, our expences on the road being added, the amount would have been about 24l. sterling. If a person have no business to call him to Hamburg, it would be adviseable for him to take our route (by which he will save forty miles in distance) and from Glückstadt proceed in a boat to Cuxhaven; the boat will cost about ten specie-dollars, including which, he will save at least from 8l. to 10l. sterling; as the expences at Hamburg, and from thence to Cuxhaven, are immoderately high. I have been thus particular in giving the regular rate of posting, as fixed by the government, because travellers who do not understand the languages are liable to be imposed on. To this it may be necessary to add, that the rate of travelling in Slesvick and Holsteïn, with *two horses* (for whether you travel in your own carriage, or in a post-waggon, the charge is the same) is two marks and four skillings, Holsteïn-currency (i. e. 2s. 10d. sterling) per Danish mile in Slesvick, and per German mile in Holsteïn.

From Glückstadt to Hamburg, through the villages of Elmshorne and Pinneberg, and the town of Altona, is about forty-three miles; the journey is generally performed in the same kind of vehicle as we travelled in from Copenhagen. Through the whole of this extent of country there is nothing interesting, or worthy the atten-

* I omitted to mention in my Sketch of Copenhagen, that the German and French languages are usually spoken in the polite circles of that city: the Danish language not being liked, on account of the disagreeable tone used in its pronunciation. The Danes, particularly the inhabitants of the capital, wish to be thought a polished nation, they therefore adopt the languages of that class of nations. English is not so much spoken as it was formerly. When the King returned home from his English tour, it was the fashion in the *beau-monde* to speak that language; but, like most fashions which are founded more in novelty than in reason, it has now lost much of the public estimation: there is at present (in 1796) but one English teacher in Copenhagen, and he has but little practice.

tion of the intelligent traveller. The entrance into Hamburg is through the Altona-gate; on the approach to the city, it has a grand appearance, but this is wholly forgotten, when you have been in it half an hour.

N. B. In my last Sketch, *Ritzebuttle* is stated to contain 80 houses, it should have been 200.

(To be continued.)

For the Monthly Magazine.

ACCOUNT *of a* JOURNEY *to the* SUMMIT *of* MOUNT PERDU, *one of the* UPPER PYRENNEES, *by* CITIZEN RAMOND, MEMBER *of the* NATIONAL INSTITUTE.

CIT. L. RAMOND, of the Legislative Body, of the National Institute, as likewise member of many learned societies, has lately published a Narrative of his excursion to Mount Perdu and the parts adjacent, on the crest, or most elevated summit, of the Upper Pyrenees; in which, (among other facts and discoveries sufficiently interesting to captivate the attention of the naturalist, and which, in a confused assemblage of ruins, shew nature acting by constant laws, and concealing a real order under apparent disorder), the most important object, next to tracing the different elements which enter into the composition of the Pyrenees themselves, is that great mass of organic fragments which reposes on the cimex or highest point of the Pyrenees. In those savage regions, where no one before himself had dared to penetrate, and where nature displays such fierce, terrible, and even horrid forms; the very dangers to which the author exposes himself, and the sensations which he experiences at the sight of so many extraordinary objects, add considerably to the value of his researches. Before the journey of Citizen Ramond, it was not unknown that there existed different fossil shells in that immense chain; but till then they had been only discovered in very small quantities, in a small number of places, and rather in the upper mountains than in the lower. It was undoubtedly known, but only as a singularity, to naturalists. They had, however, remarked the extreme abundance of calcareous matter, which predominates even in the upper regions of those mountains. Pallassou had made mention of it in his *Essay on the Mineralogy of the Pyrenees.* Without having ever reached the principal summits, he had judged of their nature by the strata which the torrents bring along with them, and by the same index be had ranged Vignemale, the Pic Blanc, and the Marboré, in the class of the last deposits of the sea. In the year 1786, Citizens Vidal and Reboul, having commenced operations which tended to determine exactly the height of the *Pic du Midi*, they inferred from thence, that of the different parts of the chain which are visible from the highest parts of that ridge; and so they judged that the principal summit of the Marboré was the most elevated point of the Pyrenees. But this summit is precisely the Mount Perdu, the height of which above the level of the sea is estimated at 3332 metres, or 1710 toises. They afterwards visited the valleys of Gavernie and of Estaubé, situated at the foot of Mount Perdu; and they ascertained so well the calcareous constitution of them, as to have no doubt that all the *fastigia*, or heights, supported on these vast bases, were formed of the same kind of stone; but to what order of revolutions do these immense deposits appertain? To resolve this question, sufficient data were wanting. In these circumstances, Citizen Ramond, in his turn, assailed the crest of the Pyrenees, rising to more than 3000 metres over the graduations or steps of the circus of Gavarnie, and, after an inspection of the places, came to this conclusion—*that the Pyrenees were finished when Mount Perdu was formed*—the inclination of the layers (coudres) towards the granitical axle of the chain, the nature of the rocks which cover it, and the order in which they succeed each other in proportion to their distance from it, had determined him to form this judgment. This however, was only a conjecture; for he had not as yet perceived, in the calcareous matter of these high regions, any trace of marine bodies. The moment of verifying this matter was now come; the Pyrenees, restored to peace, were likewise so to observation; and Citizen Ramond directed all his thoughts towards visiting again the Marboré, and opening himself a passage to Mount Perdu. But how must he arrive at this? At the entrance of the valley of Estaubé, its summit appears above the high walls that inclose it, like a cone all resplendent with snow. Citizen Ramond judged, that if he could scale those walls, or overturn them, he should have a view of the body itself of the mountain, and he decided to seek his route along the bottom or level of Estaubé. Provided with two excellent guides, and followed by some young pupils, full of zeal and courage, he set out from Bareges, the 25th Thermidor, year 5. In the evening, he reached the heights of Coumelie. At the break of day,

day, they took the route of the valley of Estaubé, and were not long in distinguishing the summit of Mount Perdu, which appeared above enormous rocks, cut perpendicularly like walls; but soon it disappeared behind those very walls, which seemed to rise higher in proportion to their nearer approach. At length, after four hour's journey, they found themselves at the foot of an intermediate glacier, covered with snow, and consequently accessible; this glacier, which conducted to a breach or opening that seemed to face Mount Perdu, they resolved to attempt by escalade. At length, after many attempts, the lessening of the cleft or breach, the ice concealed under snows of a pure white, the sinking of the high limits of the dell or valley, and the cold wind which rushes through the vast aperture of the cleft, again visible under gigantesque proportions, indicated the summit of the crest, and their arrival at the desired end; or, at least, the crest which they ascended is only separated from the summit of Mount Perdu by the erosion, or falling off, of a part of its flanks: this summit was before them, a little to the left, white, but shaded with grey, and envelopped in the bosom of a light cloud, which circulated slowly about it. Here, after a cry of joy, which announced the change of scene, a solemn silence succeeds, at the aspect of a new world, at the vast depth which separates the travellers from it, the glaciers which gird it round, and the snow which covers it; altogether presenting a frightful and sublime spectacle, with which all their faculties were overwhelmed. At their right, stood detached *the Cylinder* (another peak of the Marboré) more sombrous than the snow, more menacing than Mount Perdu itself, erect upon its base, and so near them, that it seems to touch Mount Perdu by the hand. At the foot of these two summits is a lake, still remaining iced, whence rises a band of rocks, which form here a long promontory; the figure of this band indicates a perfect similitude between its structure and that of the platform of the Cylinder. On their reaching the promontory, which was easily done, Citizen Ramond found its rock divided into horizontal strata, like those of the Marboré, and like the Cylinder and its platform. But were these strata or fissures? The first stroke of the hammer resolved the question: they were fissures, and the strata were vertical. All those which he had passed by, in mounting towards the crest, were more or less in the same direction: and now all the doubts of Cit. Ramond, with regard to the existence of shells and other marine-substances in the upper regions of the Pyrenees, were shortly to be removed; he was preparing to strike a second stroke into the heart of the rock, when he perceived, on its surface, a reddish projection; he looks at it more narrowly, and finds it to be a broken-off piece of the polypus kind (*un tronçon de polypier*) which he mistook at first for the celiular millepora. He examines further, and he sees the superior valve of an oyster filled with orthoceratites; afterwards he finds fragments of a fascicular madrepora; then other bruised or battered zoophytes, which he could not determine; and lastly some portions of échinites, which it was no less difficult to refer to their species. Here, an avalanche, or great drift of snow, falling from the summit of the mountain with a formidable noise, determined the departure of the travellers. It was necessary to descend; but to descend here—*hoc opus, hic labor est*—the very idea of returning over the snow, by which they had mounted, made them shudder. They search for an issue or egress at the eastern extremity of the basin; they turn the graduations of Mount Perdu; they slide, one after another, along a narrow cornice, suspended over abysses; from thence, they glide into a ravine; from that into another, and so from ravines to ravines, from precipices to precipices, they at length arrive at the bottom of the valley of Estaubé. Shortly there bursts forth one of those storms so terrible in the mountains; by the glare of the lightning they search for an asylum to pass the night; they arrive at a shepherd's hut, but too small to contain all the travellers. The weakest find a lodging here, and the most robust take shelter under the excavation of a rock. Towards the end of the same summer, Citizen Ramond resolved to revisit the same objects, under new appearances, and by another route. The glacier was then much changed; the snow was no more; but a field of ice, furrowed in all directions by large and vast crevices, where the foot could not rest on a single point; rocks lengthened into walls, curved into amphitheatres, cut out into graduations, rising into towers, to which the hand of giants seems to have applied the plumb and line, presented new and strange aspects to ravish the contemplation, at least, where the charm of enthusiasm is not wanting, which alone can conduct the traveller (through so many subversions, storms, torrents, avalanches, wrecks, and heaps of ruins; the revolutions of the earth, of the elements

elements, or, to borrow some of the interesting traits in the author's picturesque description, "Old rocks, all petrified with carcases; crests surcharged with the ices of an eternal winter; an august monument of venerable spoils; an immense cemetery of the inhabitants of the ancient world; a lugubrious-diadem and funeral-girdle of snow, where time passes on without ever growing young again; where death, by its substance and forms, is every where; from whose awful precincts every thing that lives is rejected," &c. &c.) to see these grand and terrible objects of nature. In this second expedition, the author made many important observations. By digging leisurely in the promontory of the lake, and in the rocks round about, he discovered a multitude of new testaceous animals, the specific characters of which he endeavoured to point out; he found others which he could not refer to any known genus; and, lastly, he thought he perceived even the bones of quadrupeds, exactly represented by the silex, both in their exterior and interior conformation. Fossil-bones on the highest mountains of the Pyrenees? This question opens a vast field of conjecture to Citizen Ramond, who, however, did not direct all his observations to the mineral kingdom only; the beautiful and rare plants of these mountains attracted likewise his regards, and this occupation made an agreeable diversion to his other researches. To study better the chain of the Pyrenees, he traversed the vallies of Gavarnie and of Héas; he visited *le Coumelie* and *le Pimené*; and, lastly, makes the following reflections on the chain of the Pyrenees, as distinguished from the Alps, and other mountains, the structure of which is better known. 1. The chain of the Pyrenees is essentially more simple. 2. There appears, however, to have been more trouble in the formation of the mountains superimposed on the primitive chain. 3. The calcareous matter, whether primitive or secondary, is here more sensibly abundant. 4. The secondary calcareous matter is here elevated to a more considerable height. And, 5. The ivasion (*l'ivasion*) has been effectuated in a contrary direction.

For the Monthly Magazine.

REMARKS *of some of* MR. HORNE TOOKE'S ETYMOLOGIES.

(Continued from p. 113.)

OF. The word aꝼoꝛa *offspring*, from which Mr. Tooke derives *of*, is merely a compound of *a from*, and ꝼoꝛan, *to go*; so that his whole explanation consists in referring our English preposition *of*, to the A. Saxon preposition *a*.

FOR. Notwithstanding the ingenuity which Mr. Tooke has displayed, in interpreting the use of this preposition by the noun ꝼaꝛꝛina, *cause*, I cannot agree with him in referring it to such an origin. In the first place, ꝼaꝛꝛina is a very obscure word, and far from having that vulgar notoriety, which Mr. Tooke himself teaches us to look for as the necessary qualification of words employed in so extensive a capacity. "All particles are in truth, in all languages, the signs of the most common and familiar ideas, and those which we have most frequently occasion to communicate. They had not otherwise become particles."—"The particles are always the words which were the most common and familiar in the language from which they came." Dio. of Purley, p. 334.

2. Mr. Tooke should have told us what we are to understand by the word which he thus employs in his interpretation of *for*. As he uses it, it certainly does not correspond with what either philosophers or the vulgar have been accustomed to understand by *cause*. Let us take only a few instances out of the numerous collection which he has given us. "*Christ died for us*, i. e. we being the *cause* of his dying." Surely no one can say that these expressions convey the same idea. "*Chelsea Hospital was built for disabled soldiers*, i. e. disabled soldiers being the *cause* of its being built." Whatever idea of cause Mr. Tooke may attribute to our Saxon ancestors, we surely must suppose, that when they spoke of one thing being caused by another, the necessary existence, at least, of that cause must have been implied. But Chelsea Hospital might be said, without the least impropriety, to have been built for disabled soldiers, though there had never been a disabled soldier in the world. "*He speaks one word for another*, i. e. another word being the *cause* of his speaking that word which he speaks." What species of causality this alludes to, I cannot divine. "*He sets down twelve acres for every man*, i. e. every, or each man, being the *cause* of his setting down twelve acres." But, if a narrator were to express himself so, would he not be immediately asked, whom they were set down *for*? "*Shall I think the world was made for one?*" Notwithstanding the depravity of the times, I should be sorry to believe this so popular a doctrine as Mr. Tooke's interpretation would make it. According to him

him, it muſt be the creed of every one who believes the exiſtence of one firſt *cauſe*. "*There is a natural, immutable, and eternal reaſon for that which we call virtue, and againſt that which we call vice*; or, that which we call virtue, we call virtue *for* a natural, eternal, and immutable reaſon; i. e. a natural, eternal, and immutable reaſon being the *cauſe* of our ſo calling it; or, there is a natural, eternal, and immutable reaſon, the cauſe of that which we call virtue." If *for* ſignify *cauſe* here, what is the meaning of *againſt*? It is evident, that the two words are directly oppoſed to each other: and, in ſuch a caſe, according to Mr. Tooke, "having once diſcovered one of the adverſe parties, the meaning of the other muſt follow of courſe," p. 347. It will not be very eaſy, however, to explain the meaning of a word denoting the *oppoſite of cauſe*.

Without going further into detail, I ſhall obſerve, that Mr. Tooke has frequently, in his interpretations, employed what many muſt think a very unauthorized periphraſis, and has, in a very few inſtances, given a ſynonimous explanation. The word which he makes to repreſent the cauſe is, in general, not the *cauſe*, but the *object*. If his explanation were juſt, the prepoſition *by* ſhould, in its ſenſe of cauſality for which we now ſo commonly employ it, be capable of ſupplying the place of *for* in the paſſages he has quoted; which it will not do in a ſingle inſtance. It muſt be remembered withal, that Mr. Tooke has advanced not a ſingle authority to ſhew that faſtna, or any obvious corruption of it, was ever employed in the office of *for*; and therefore it is a ſufficient objection to his opinion that

3. A much more ſimple and plauſible etymology offers itſelf in the noun for, *way, road*, the root or the offspring of foran, to go. Without uſing more latitude of conſtruction than Mr. Tooke has done with *cauſe*, ſuch a word will furniſh us with a much better illuſtration of the ſenſe of *for*. Our author has ſhewn this himſelf in one, at leaſt, of his interpretations. "*He quivered with his feet, and lay for dead*; i. e. as if death, or his being dead, had been the *cauſe* of his laying; or, he lay in that *manner* in which death, or being dead, is the *cauſe* that perſons ſo lay." Here he has given indeed an explanation of the meaning of *for*; but it is in the word *manner*, not in the word *cauſe*. *To lie for dead*, is to lie in the *manner* of one dead; or, as we ſay, elliptically, in a manner, or, in a *way*, dead. This, however, is not the moſt uſual ſignification of *for*, though its occaſional employment in this *way* is ſufficiently explained by our frequent uſe of the word *way*, at preſent in the ſenſe of *manner*.

The ordinary office of *for* is to repreſent the *road* to ſome object. So *Chriſt died for us*; we were the object in his *way* to which he died. Chelſea Hoſpital was built *by way of** (relieving) diſabled ſoldiers. "I write *for* your ſatisfaction;" or, by *way* of ſatisfying you. "He ſpeaks one word *for* another;" in his *way* to another, whilſt another is his object. "We ſailed directly *for* Genoa;" in the *way* to Genoa.

Sometimes *for* is uſed in appoſition with the word following it, which thus expreſſes not the object of the way, but the way itſelf: as in the inſtances, "hired *for* life;"—"Chemiſts have not been able, *for* aught is vulgarly known;"—"he lay *for* dead (as above noticed);"—"moral conſiderations can *no way* move the ſenſible appetite, were it not *for* (in the *way* of) the will."—"To die for a deſerter," denotes, according to Mr. Tooke, that the being a deſerter is the *cauſe* of my death. But would he not think it harſh to apply ſuch a conſtruction to the expreſſion—Horne Tooke was perſecuted *for* a traitor? The word, in both caſes, denotes not the *cauſe*, but the *way*, or manner, of my death, and of his perſecution.

The inſtances which Mr. Tooke has quoted from Tyrwhit of the uſe of *for*, in the ſenſe of *againſt*, admit of a very eaſy interpretation, if we conſider that one thing may ſtand in the *way* of another, either as the object to which it is directed, or as the obſtacle by which it is impeded†.

* The more proper form of this expreſſion ſeems to be *by way to*, as the words following it repreſent the object to which what goes before deſcribes the way.

† As we commonly employ *againſt* to denote the latter of theſe relations, the uſe of *for* is generally reſtricted to the former: and it is from this cuſtomary diſtinction that theſe prepoſitions have been uſually regarded as appoſites. A diſtinction, however, in ſo great meaſure arbitrary, was frequently overlooked, and many more familiar inſtances might be added to thoſe of Mr. Tyrwhit, in illuſtration of their interchange of capacity.

"*Againſt* my love ſhall be as I am now,
With Time's injurious hand, cruſh'd and o'erworn;
When hours have drain'd his blood, and fill'd his brow
With lines and wrinkles; when his youthful morn

 The

The Anglo-Saxon ꝼoꞃ is very frequently prefixed to verbs with the ſignification of *away*, as in ꝼoꞃ ᵹanᵹan, to go away; ꝼoꞃ-cyꞃꞃan, to turn away; ꝼoꞃ-meltan, to melt away. In old writers, ſuch compounds as *for-wear*, to wear away; *for-drive*, to drive away; continually occur; and the words *forget*, *forgive*, *forbid*, *forlorn*, &c. are eaſily traced to the ſame origin. Mr. Tooke's *cauſe* here deſerts us entirely; he has not even introduced the leaſt notice of this uſe of *for* in what he ſays on the ſubject. That he ſhould have omitted all mention of it in this part of his work is not, however, more ſurpriſing, than the manner in which he *has* alluded to it in two other paſſages. In a note to p. 331. (4to. ed.) where he has ſatisfactorily ſhewn that the French *hors* is a corruption of the Latin *foris*, we are told, that the words *forfeit*, *foreclose*, and many others where *for* occurs with this meaning, are derived from the French. And at p. 495. we have the following line of Chaucer:

"I ſe no more but that I am *fordo*."

introduced as an illuſtration of the word *forth*: "*fordo*, i. e. *forth done*, i. e. *done* to go *forth*, i. e. *out of doors*;" *forth* being derived from the French *fors* (now written *hors*), and that from the Latin *foris*. I ſhould have thought that every reader of Anglo-Saxon muſt have known that this uſe of *for* in our language was much prior to any of its acquiſitions from either the French or the Latin: and that no one, with the bare knowledge that the Gothic derivative ꝼoꞃ ſignifies *way*, and that *for* in compoſition is rendered by *a way*, could admit a doubt of their being the ſame word.

It is needleſs to ſhew, that the uſe of *for*, as a conjunction, is to be referred to the ſame import which belongs to it as a prepoſition. Mr. Tooke has ſufficiently ſhewn the abſurdity of ſuppoſing any characteriſtic diſtinction. As, however, its uſe in the former capacity was ſubſequent to its employment in the latter, we find its ſignification here more frequently obſcured by ellipſes, and diſtorted by corruption. The German *für*, which has deviated much leſs from its ſtrict primitive ſignification than our *for**, is ſtill confined to the office of a prepoſition.

To remove the etymology, which I have here been offering, ſtill further beyond the uncertainty of conjecture, it may be obſerved, that the Germans, beſides the prepoſition *für*, which they have in common with us, employ very frequently in the room of our *for* the word *wegen*, whoſe identity with *weg*, way, cannot admit of a doubt. "Dieſer ſache *wegen*," *for* (on account of) this matter; *deſwegen*, there-*fore*; *weſswegen*, where-*fore*. The Anglo-Saxon prefix they render by the ſame word: inſtead of ꝼoꞃ niman, to take away; ꝼoꞃ-ᵹan, to go away; ꝼoꞃ-ſendan, to ſend away; they have *weg-nehmen*, *weg-gehen*, *weg ſenden*.

FORTH. Mr. Tooke juſtly conſiders *forth* as the ſame with the prefix *for*†; and though he has given them an erroneous origin, he is nearer the truth probably in his etymology of theſe, than in that which he aſſigns to the prepoſition. Though we muſt not allow the French *fors*, and the Latin *foris*, to interfere with the direct Gothic extraction of our Engliſh *forth*, there ſeems plauſible reaſon for admitting them to be collateral branches of the ſame family. We know that a very conſiderable portion, at leaſt, of the Greek vocabulary is of Gothic derivation; and every probability indicates that the word πορος, the immediate origin of *foris*, *foramen*, our Engliſh *pore*, &c. is the ſame with the Anglo-Saxon ꝼoꞃ. Without inſiſting on the particular accuracy of the following table, it may ſerve at leaſt for a general

Hath travell'd on to age's ſteepy night;
And all thoſe beauties, whereof now he's king,
Are vaniſhing, or vaniſh'd, out of ſight,
Stealing away the treaſure of his ſpring;
For ſuch a time do I now fortify
Againſt confounding age's cruel knife."
SHAKESPEARE's Sonnets, v. 869.

With thoſe who adopt Mr. Tooke's explanation of *againſt* (as ſignifying *meeting*), this reciprocation of offices will add weight to the etymology which I have been aſſigning to *for*.

* The moſt frequent uſe of the German *für* is in ſuch expreſſions as "left *for* dead;" —"taken *for* granted;"—"ſhe paſſes *for* a virgin," &c. where Mr. Tooke's ſubſtitute, *cauſe*, is totally inapplicable, whilſt it receives a very ready interpretation from ꝼoꞃ. Thus they ſay, "Was *für* wein trinket ihr?" what do you drink for (in the *way* of) wine; "Was *für* bücher wollt ihr haben;"—what will you have for (in the *way* of) books.

† The Saxons ſeem to have employed them indifferently in compoſition; ꝼoꞃ-ꝼaꞃan and ꝼoꞃð-ꝼaꞃan were uſed alike for "to depart,"—"to die."

family,

comparative illustration of some of the principal branches of this very numerous family, in the principal dialects of Northern and Southern Europe.

FAIRRAN faran.	Πειρειν.
For (a way)	πορος, E. pore, L. foris.
For (preposition)	παρα (as παρα τι, wherefore).
—- (prefix)	—— (παραιρεμαι to take away†).
Fur, far	πορρω‡ L. porro.
Fore*	προ.
Forth	πορρωθεν.
Ford	πορθμος.
Ferry	περαω.

Sept. 6, 1801.

To the Editor of the Monthly Magazine.

SIR,

AS you make your useful Publication a vehicle of communication of opinion, as well on the arts, as on any other subject, I wish through it to convey some thoughts on the treatment shewn to a particular subject, in the annual exhibitions at the Royal Academy. The object I mean to direct attention to is architecture.

Does the Academy mean to intimate that it is a school for architecture, as well as for painting? Does it mean to imply, that because a few architectural drawings are hung any where in its yearly display of art, that it is a fostering-mother to it, as well as to painting?

The room appropriated to the hanging of the architectural designs is of itself as ineligible as it well can be for an exhibition of pictures of any kind; it surely need not be rendered worse by the introduction of any thing to obstruct an equal distribution of what little light there is, as is done by crowding this small room with large groups of statuary, which not only possess the very best situations for shewing the drawings to any advantage, but obscure them in that post they are suffered to occupy. Statuary is no more aiding to the effect of architectural drawings, than it is to painting; less so; and instead of filling and darkening that little room with an immense pedestal, comparatively, for statuary, it would be much more properly placed in the centre of the great room above, at a convenient distance from which, seats might be placed. But better than either would be to appropriate the room below, the model-academy, to statuary and models alone, and give the library and antique-room to the subjects of architecture, placing its miniature drawings nearest the light. If the Academy, continuing its present treatment, styles itself a school of architecture, surely none but boys will in future pay any deference to it; for it can be worthy the ambition of boys only to send designs there, and be proud of having their names inserted in their Catalogue, and their works contribute to swell their annual exhibition.

Architects are not to be told, how little architecture is known or regarded by portrait-painters; the one and the other is sufficiently indicated in their works and treatment. But it may be necessary that portrait-painters should be informed by architects, in what light they *should* consider their art, and be told that there is much more study and thought required in composing a structure combining taste, convenience, and durability, than in suiting the dress and back-ground of a portrait to the complexion and character of the human countenance; and that the study is of a much more exalted nature, requiring considerably more knowledge than is necessary to harmonize a few colours on a canvas, and to copy the different lineaments of the face.

Mere painters, from their unacquaintedness with architecture, judge of its merits only by its approximity to the effects of their own branch of art; and such compositions as by the glow and brilliancy of their colouring and finishing approach the

---

* The words *former*, *foremost*, generally considered as derivaties of *fore*, are the comparative and superlative degrees of the Anglo-Saxon Frum or From, beginning.

† The Latin *per* was employed as a prefix in the same sense with For and παρα. Thus *perjuro*, to forswear; *perdo*, to give away (as *perdere operam*, to lose one's labour), make away with, destroy, *pereo*, For-faran, to perish; *perverto*, For cyrran, to turn away, &c.

‡ πορρω also signified *beyond*, which Mr. Tooke shews to be a derivative of the participle *gone*.

the nearest to their gaudy productions, are placed in the best lights; while sober designs uniting taste and discrimination, and executed with the nicest attention, are treated as laborious trifles, and placed where they cannot have their merits estimated; some at the very top, others at the very skirting, of the room; and some with their backs to the light.*

Still more to express their indifference to architectural subjects, whatever is extraneous in the art of delineation, they associate with them; and they are mixed with drawings and paintings of botanical subjects, with flowers, and shells, and any branch of natural history. It is not in the present exhibition alone that this has been instanced, but every late year it has been increasing, and the present is worse than any former one.

Sir, I know the heads of the academy have been applied to on this subject, but it has not been attended to; on the contrary, the treatment has been worse; I have therefore made these few observations, to inform the public how ill architecture is treated by painters, and to intimate to them, that it is not the architects fault, that their works are made so little interesting, painters have turned them out of doors. The former having provided the latter a dwelling, they have taken possession of it, and have turned their protectors out into the street.

AN AMATEUR IN ARCHITECTURE.
May, 1801.

To the Editor of the Monthly Magazine.

SIR,

YOUR Journeyman-printer, (vol. x. page 437) bears very hard on us authors; and asserts that it is an *inviolate* rule with compositors never to take the unjustifiable liberty of deviating from an author's manuscript without his express permission. Of this extraordinary workman, I can only say *talis cum sis utinam noster esses*; for his typographic brethren have other habits; they are punctually, they are literally, they are verbally careless. I have tried experiments; I have been on the watch for several months past; I will now enumerate some grammatical blunders, which in communications of my own, have been carefully avoided in the manuscript, and as regularly introduced on the pages of the Monthly Magazine.

1. Farther for further. Dr. Johnson, long ago very justly observed that *further* being the comparitive of *forth*, and not of *far*, ought never to be written with an *a*: his remark has influenced general practice: to write or to set *farther* is to violate usage, as well as grammar.

2. Rhyme for rime. The word *rime* has no etymological connexion with the Greek *rhuthmos*: it derives from the Anglosaxon and Islandic *riem* or *rim*, which signifies the edge of a hide, a thong, a bond; hence the verb *rieman*, to tie with a thong, to bind. These words were metaphorically applied by the Skalds to designate that sort of tying by the edges, which lines, that rime, undergo: and from them all the Gothic dialects have the word. The Germans still distinguish verse and prose, by the names of *bound*, and *unbound* speech.

3. Upon for on. The preposition *notwithstanding* and the conjunction *inasmuchas* have not lost the meaning implied in their component parts, though they are often written as single words: neither ought *upon*. It can only be used with propriety where the words *up* and *on* may both be employed. *Set the sugar-basin upon the shelf*: but not: *Set down the coal-shoot upon the ground*. This blunder is so very common in the sacred books, that wherever a scripture style is aimed at, it must be purposely affected. The translators of the bible were better Hebraans, than Anglicists.

A similar remark might be applied to the words *unto* and *until*, which are compounded of *on* and *to*, and of *on* and *till*.

4. Ise for ize. The formative syllable *ize* being derived from the Greek *izō* should always be written with *z* not with *s*. All verbs therefore formed by the same rule of analogy as to *barbarize*, to *characterize*, to *proselytize* ought to terminate in *ize*: whereas the verbs formed from Latin supines,

* Particularly see the very beautiful drawings and designs in gothic architecture, by Messrs. Repton, placed in the very worst places and lights in the room, Nos. 855, 937, 942, and 1005, particularly 942. See also Mr. Alexander's exquisite miniature drawing of Waltham-cross, No. 1021. Also an elegant design and beautiful drawing, of a hall, in gothic architecture by Mr. J Dixon. No. 1032, which I had not seen, but by the accidental reflected light from a lady's white gown as she stood near it. And others of great, tho' less merit than these, to which I have willingly, though indignantly, gone on my knees to examine; and would some few of the portrait-painters do the same, they would but pay a just tribute to merit, and might by attention to such productions beget a just sense how unworthily, such works had been treated by being placed in such situations.

supines, such as to *promise*, to *revise*, to *manumise*, fitly end in *ise*.

To verbs of French origin neither of these rules apply, such as to *advertize*, to *recognize*, to *affranchise*: in these cases it is usual to spell by the ear; employing the z, or soft consonant, when the last syllable is accented, or long; and the *s*, or hard consonant, when the last syllable is unaccented, or short: for soft consonants, such as *b*, *d*, *g*, *z*, *v*, &c. more easily unite with long vowels: and hard consonants, such as *p*, *t*, *k*, *s*, *f*, &c. more easily unite with short vowels.

5. Forego for forgo, &c. The two inseparable prepositions *fore* and *for* differ in etymology as in meaning: the first has an anticipative, the second a privative signification: to *forego* is to go before; and to *forgo* is to go without. These two distinct syllables, which are prefixed to a great number of English verbs, have as studiously been confounded by your journeyman-printer, as they have been discriminated by me, so as in one place to have occasioned apparent nonsense.

This list of grievances could be extended * further; but I forgo the invidious task. Content that your type-setters should efface mere peculiarity (it is in them a natural influence of habit), and should every where substitute vulgar usage to recondite propriety.—I only wish that undisputed error and notorious incorrectness may not by them be woven into the text of

A PHILOLOGICAL CORRESPONDENT.

For the Monthly Magazine.

ACCOUNT *of* PORTSMOUTH.

(*Continued from page* 115. *of Vol.* 12.)

THAT the manners of a sea-port town have any strict relation to elegance I shall not attempt to prove; nor is it necessary to puff off our scanty fare of public amusements as composing "all the numerous *agremens* of polished society." Yet, Mr. Editor, as I would not have it considered that literature is at quite so low an ebb that a Latin inscription would be as inappropriate on a naval pillar at Portsmouth, as a boatswain's call in the hands of a regius professor at Oxford;† so neither would I have it supposed that all relating to us is coarseness, vulgarity and dullness; nor that Portsmouth is one of the kind of towns alluded to in the Sketch of a Journey from Copenhagen to Hamburg contained in your last number. To assert that it is a place "Where dirt and squallid wretchedness appear in every corner, and where the lower class of people are as debauched as they are in any part of the world," however such a description may agree with the state of other sea-port towns, is to betray a perfect deficiency of knowledge as to Portsmouth. We neither abound in wealth, nor are we surrounded by indigence or misery; and it may be certainly said of those, who compose the grand proportion of the inhabitants, and who rank as the inferior order, that they are generally industrious and hardworking people, and in a far better condition than the same class in towns and cities that display all the appendages of opulence and excessive luxury; and the appearance they make even in their working days garb is very different from debauchery and wretchedness. How far the description alluded to may suit the state of some of our inland and manufacturing towns, it is not my business here to enquire. It is worthy of remark that in our dock-yard the artizans in general are a fine healthy-looking body of young men, and that many of them with large families, acquire property, and live in some credit. Portsmouth has certainly its objects of wretchedness and infamy in common with other places, and some that are to be found in sea-ports only; yet there number is not so great as may have been imagined. Their abodes are mostly confined to particular districts, where, though our soldiers, by late regulations of our Lieutenant Governor, are debarred open communication, our jolly tars still seek recreation and amusement. As to our *Laises*, and *Thaises*, and *Phrynes*, with whom we can more than fill the upper boxes of our theatre, they are of course ladies of fashion, as well as of virtue and sentiment, and in these days of taste and refinement will not, I fancy, be imputed to us as a very *extraordinary* disparagement. With respect to cleanliness Portsmouth may vie with most towns. That, in spite of the most strict and regular measures resorted to, under the advice

---

* Retail for retale. A vulgarism borrowed from the painters of shop-boards: it is derived from *re* and *tale*, a selling out again. Owing for owen; the present participle active, for the past participle passive, an error very common in English writers. Scarce for scarse from the Italian *scarso*, &c.

† Vide Gentleman's Magazine. I had nearly forgotten to mention that notwithstanding we have schools and academies at home as well for classic lore, as the elegant and polite arts of drawing, fencing, &c. &c. we are the chief contributors to the boarding schools, both ordinary and extraordinary for many miles round.

and

and authority of Kings, Lords, and Commons, to purify every part of the two towns, and to keep our atmosphere properly oxygenated, there may be some filthy and noisome holes and corners, it is not worth while to deny; yet I do not see why this circumstance, even if true, should be thrown in our teeth, because Portsmouth forsooth happens to be a sea-port town of some note and consequence.

> "Such place hath Deptford, navy-building town,
> Woolwich, and Wapping, smelling strong of pitch;
> Such Lambeth, envy of each band and gown;
> And Twick'nam such, which fairer scenes enrich,
> Grots, statues, urns, and To—n's dog and bitch;
> Ne village is without, on either side,
> All up the silver Thames, or all adown;
> Ne Richmond's self, from whose tall front is ey'd
> Vales, spires, meand'ring streams, and Windsor's tow'ring pride."

As to our politics, I am not much disposed at present to enter into a history of them. Suffice it to say that we are upon the whole a very loyal people—that though the predominant sentiments of our corporation are not orthodox, they are nevertheless duly qualified by local and personal considerations—that even thus modified, they provoke some degree of rancour and hostility—and that at a contested election for the county, the uncourtly candidate, with all the clamour of his multitudinous friends, has but little chance of success against our numerous, well disciplined, and marshalled forces. Both our newspapers are of one faith, and inculcate the same political creed. We have three several volunteer corps; two belonging to Portsmouth: one of them, consisting of about 200 men, is composed of inhabitants of the town and custom-house officers; and the other, containing about the same number, has been raised from the garrison, generally by the individual who commands it. Portsea corps is somewhat less, and is made up chiefly of tradesmen within its walls. The corps seldom act in conjunction. Each has its peculiar spirit, of the nature of which their different titles already suggested, in addition to what is just stated of them, and of the place in general, may serve to give some idea. In Portsea there is a more popular interest than in Portsmouth, by which the corps of the former is doubtless influenced; and which, with their several different interests and other circumstances, and perhaps some prejudices, creates a marked distinction between the two towns, and in general disposes the one to keep aloof from the other. This, in some instances, may have the advantage of producing rivalship in good deeds, while on the other hand it may sometimes be of disservice to both.

From the want of a general public spirit, or else from the real difficulties that have been considered to be in the way of conveying water to us by means of aqueducts, we continue to be supplied with it by carts; and though what we get is excellent, the cry of "water" is so incessant in our streets, that, what with this offensive circumstance, and the jumbling noise of the carts, we suffer an almost intolerable nuisance from the mode through which we obtain it. It is certain that there is a sufficiency of good water in the vicinity of the towns for their regular supply; and I should suppose that this might be collected, into one or more reservoirs, from the different wells and springs from which we are at present supplied, if enough could not be obtained from one, and that it would afford an ample source for every purpose. It would save us the trouble and expence of such jobs and projects, as have been meditated and attempted, of bringing it through hills and from rivers twelve miles off; and besides this, perhaps, would supersede the necessity of sinking wells within our walls, to procure nothing but bad water, and ease us of part of the expence and of all the trouble attendant on our present means of supply. The materials of our present wells and pumps might perhaps be made to contribute their aid towards the expence of the undertaking. I must confess, I have not much considered the plan; but as it strikes as somewhat practicable, I am induced to suggest it.

The poor of Portsmouth and Portsea are differently managed in the two parishes. In the former, the poor-house is an old building, in a situation not chosen with any regard either to the health or the morals of the paupers. It is in one of the worst parts of the town, contiguous to a large barrack always occupied by soldiers, and without any sufficient yard or airing-ground, in the very centre of scenes of vice and prostitution. The parish poor-house of Portsea is a modern one, lately enlarged, about a mile from the town, at some distance from any buildings, in a very healthy spot, and in itself commodious. It has a large area within its walls, and a garden attached to it, from whence, I presume, it is supplied with a sufficient quantity of vegetables. In Portsmouth, the Overseers of the Poor are appointed yearly, as in other places, so that there is a continual change of persons in office, with no very strong interest to bind them to the regular discharge of its toilsome duties; and who, if they have every inclination to fulfil them, have not time to make themselves competent to the task, before they are succeeded by others, more insufficient than themselves.

In most cases the private concerns of the officer are chiefly attended to, and the business of the parish becomes a secondary consideration, or is even still less regarded. There may be some perhaps who think the worse they perform the office the more likely they are to avoid the trouble of it for the future. The parishioners of Portsmouth have felt these inconveniences, and have endeavoured to remedy them, by appointing a permanent governor or overseer of the poor; but the plan did not succeed, and they now go on as before. In Portsea, the parish officers have, for a long time past, held their appointment for life. They are shipwrights belonging to the dock, and being persons entitled to superannuation, or considered as deserving of preferment, they are relieved of all labour there, still receiving the King's-pay, and, at the nomination of one of the principal officers of the dock, are elected into the offices of church-wardens and overseers of the poor. They are re-chosen every year, but the election is mere matter of form. Portsea experiences the benefit of this plan, as well as the paupers, and Portsmouth I believe would be very willing to adopt the same. The poor-rates of the latter parish are much higher than those of Portsea, as will appear, with some other particulars I may be able to send you on this head, in a future statement. The work on which the poor of both parishes are generally engaged, is the picking of oakum, for which at a sea-port there is necessarily a large demand; and I have understood, that with respect to profit it answers very well. Gosport, which is situated opposite to us, on the west-side of our harbour, also employs its poor at present in the same manner; but is about to act differently, and in a large building, that is nearly finished, intends by their assistance to carry on a considerable manufactory. How far Portsmouth or Portsea may be benefited, and at the same time enabled to promote the health, comfort and morals of their poor, by employing them otherwise than they do at present, as in the cultivation of a few acres of garden-ground, the produce of which would unquestionably find a ready sale, I leave to the better judgment of those whom it may concern to determine.

Portsmouth is watched as well as lighted, under a particular act of parliament, the expence of which is defrayed by a rate. In Portsea, watch is kept under the old law, ordaining watch and ward; a certain number of the inhabitants watching every night, in turn, or finding substitutes. Its principal street, which is Queen-street, has of late employed additional watchmen for its security, the expence of which, and of lighting the street, together with several others, is defrayed by a voluntary subscription of the respective streets.

Our dock-yard, within the last twenty years, has undergone very considerable and important improvements, and they still continue to be carried on in the same style of grandeur and magnificence. Where such immense structures as first-rate ships of war are erected, and refitted in whole fleets, with a degree of expedition that may well excite astonishment, machines, workshops, and magazines, must necessarily be of relative size and consequence. One of the most grand and interesting spectacles that can be exhibited, or perhaps imagined, is the launch of one of these stupendous ships. To be present on such an occasion—to witness, with tens of thousands of spectators arranged around, place above place, as in a vast amphitheatre, the gigantic power of man displayed in this wonderful atchievement—to mark the anxiety and enthusiasm of the whole assembly—to perceive in them for some moments before the appointed stroke is aimed, that gives the stately vessel to her fate, almost delirium—to hear the tremendous crash of spars and shores, amid the loud pealing shouts that now burst forth, cheering the decorated ship to her destined element—the crowded decks joining in the heartfelt acclamations, with martial music playing in thundering notes the national air of "Rule Britannia," as she moves majestically onward in clouds of foam to meet the bounding main, itself a living spectacle—to hear and behold this, is undoubtedly sufficiently to affect most powerfully even him who never felt before.

If my limits would allow me to dwell on this part of my subject, I am conscious that I should be unable to do justice to it, or to give an adequate idea of the place as a naval arsenal.

The number of men at present belonging to the dock, including workmen under contracts, &c. is about three thouſand. With other new plans adopted, two ſteam engines have been lately ſet up, one of which I believe is on a larger ſcale than any ever before erected, and about three hundred convicts have been introduced into the yard, and are employed in different buſineſſes. This meaſure is of ſuch a nature that the policy of it may be ſomewhat doubted.—In 1756, the people of the dock, in order to ſupply their own families with bread and flour at a cheap rate, formed themſelves into a ſociety for the purpoſe of purchaſing land, erecting a mill, bakehouſe and other neceſſary buildings. Theſe have been for ſome time completed, and the plan I underſtand turns out a beneficial one. As well as in the dock, improvements are carrying on in the gun-wharf, which is of late conſiderably enlarged, and the ſtore-houſes of the victualling-office have been encreaſed.

The land throughout the iſland of Portſea is, as to holding, principally free. There is ſome leaſe-land under our corporation, and ſome under Wincheſter-college, to whom alſo belongs the rectory of Portſea.

We have no buildings deſerving of any note in the way of the antiquary; unleſs I take into my account Porcheſter-caſtle, a hiſtory of which, with the iſland of Portſea, I learn is in contemplation. The church of Portſmouth, with its tower, cupola, and lanthorn, may paſs as a ſtately edifice; but the ſtyle of its architecture is not remarkable for any beauty. The chapels in Portſea may be conſidered as neat buildings, and one of them is ſpacious and lofty. Our town-hall is chiefly noticeable as ſtanding in the way, in the midſt of our high-ſtreet, rendering the paſſage on each ſide narrow and inconvenient. Under and contiguous is our market-place, where, though living by the ſea-ſide, we get but a ſcanty ſupply of fiſh, and of courſe for that little pay extravagantly.—We have a fair in July, that continues a whole fortnight, the inſtitution of which muſt originally have been uſeful. It is now degenerated into mere ſtalls and booths for toys, trinkets, gew-gaws, and raree-ſhows; but it ſtill forms our jubilee, and there is a current tale that, while it laſts, Portſmouth is a ſor of ſanctuary. It extends further than along one ſide of our High-ſtreet, which, during its continuance, is a perfect ſcence of tumultuous revelry, din, hurly-burly, and confuſion.

If Portſmouth has not given birth to many characters of celebrity, yet there is one name connected with it, that may claim admiration and reſpect:—Jonas Hanway, of philanthropic memory, was born here, on the 12th of Auguſt, 1712.

In regard to views and proſpects I ſhall not now attempt a deſcription of them; Mr. Houſman may have ſaid enough, perhaps, to give your readers ſome idea of them. And here I beg leave to conclude.

Yours, &c.

Portſmouth, Sept. 8, 1801. W. N.

Population of Portſmouth and Portſea, taken under the Act; excluſive of the Army, Navy, and Militia.

	Inhabited houſes	Uninhabited houſes	Families	Males	Females	Total of Perſons	Employed in Agriculture	In trade & manufacture	Not of the preceding deſcription	Inns, taverns and Ale houſes
Portſmouth	1130*	4	1640	3148	4691	7839	0	958	6881	114†
Town of Portſea	2539‡	15	3263	6794	8149	14943	8	2294§	12744§	90
Liberty part of Portſea or vicinity within the Boro'	1641‖	10	2034	4367	5017	9384	360	1057§	7864§	23
Guildable part of Portſea or vicinity beyond the Boro'	231	0	227	535	525	1060	195	90	775	4
Total	5541	29	7164	14844	18382	33226	563	4399	28264	231

* High-ſtreet contains about 150 houſes—rents of them, and in Broad-ſtreet, on the Point, generally, from about 40 to 70l. per annum—The generality of the houſes in other parts from about 15 to 30l. a year.

† Fifty-ſix of theſe public-houſes are on Portſmouth Point, which is a part of the town, that at high-water is inſulated, communicating with the other part, by a draw-bridge; and where the total number of houſes is about 300, which I ſhould ſuppoſe have a greater number of perſons to each, than the other houſes of the town.

‡ Queen-ſtreet, the High-ſtreet of Portſea, contains about 180 houſes—rents in general, I ſuppoſe, from about 30 to 60l. per annum—In other parts of the town, they may be generally from about 12 to 16l. a year.

§ There is a miſtake of 103, in two of theſe ſums, in one or other of the columns.

‖ Rents moſtly from 10 to 14l.

Population of Goſport, taken under the Act; excluſive of the Army, Navy, and Militia.

	Inhabited houſes	Uninhabited houſes	Families	Males	Females	Total of perſons	Employed in agriculture	In trade & manufacture	No. of the preceding deſcription	Inns, Taverns and Alehouſes
Town of Goſport in Alverſtoke-pariſh	1440	26	2072	3466	4849	8315	0	1320	6995	84
Liberty part of Alverſtoke or Vicinity of Goſport	466	17	618	1287	1693	2980	244	404	2332	18
Total	1906	43	2690	4753	6542	11295	244	1724	9327	102

To the Editor of the Monthly Magazine.

SIR,

IN the ſecond book of the Jewiſh Chronicles (XXXV 25) it is ſtated that Jeremiah compoſed a funeral ſong on the death of king Joſiah, who was killed at Hadadrimmon in battle: that this dirge was regularly performed at Jeruſalem by the band of temple-ſingers: and that it was preſerved with his other elegies. No ſuch poem however occurs in this author's Lamentations, which all relate to the diſtreſs of Jeruſalem after its capture by the Perſians; ſo that it is commonly ſuppoſed, like the works the of bard Iddo, to have been loſt. All the reliques of Hebrew literature which have deſcended to theſe times, are preciſely the compoſitions preſerved in the temple-library; can it then have happened that a fragment, by its very deſtination neceſſary there, ſhould have undergone a ſeparate deſtruction? Beſides Joſephus (X Ant. V. 1.) ſtill knew the poem.

A dirge, the public performance of which by the ſinging-men and women was made an ordinance in Iſrael, muſt have been tranſcribed, it ſhould ſeem, with ſome ſolicitude of attention; and that too among the other poems appropriated for national ſolemnities and ſocial worſhip. Amid the Pſalms then is there no part at leaſt of ſo celebrated a compoſition?

The book of Pſalms is an anthology of poems, differing in antiquity, in merit and in matter: it conſiſts chiefly of hymns indeed, ſome perpetual and national, ſome occaſional and perſonal; but it alſo contains epithalamiums, war-ſongs and elegies. This book was certainly compiled after the reſtoration of the Jews; as ſome of the foremore poems celebrate the return from captivity. According to a tradition preſerved by Theodoret and others, it was probably compiled by Zechariah, to whoſe manner of compoſition the latter portions of the collection remarkably approximate.

David, having excelled as a harper, is likely to have bequeathed, through Aſaph (1 Chron. XVI. 5—7), many popular melodies to the band of temple-ſingers. If the ſuperſcriptions "of David," "of Aſaph," "of Heman," "of Ethan," were not intended merely to indicate the adapted *tune* of ſuch pſalms, the Editor, in affixing theſe titles, muſt have relied on deceptious tradition, or gueſſed with blundering raſhneſs; for, among the pſalms called "of David", a great many (V, XI, XVIII, XXIV, XXVII, &c.) allude to the temple as already built; and a great many more (XIV, LIII, LXIX, &c.) allude to the captivity as actual; although David died ſome years before the commencement of the firſt temple, and ſome centuries before the commencement of the Babylonian captivity. The ſuperſcription of a pſalm is therefore leſs to be relied on than internal evidence, in allotting it to a given author.

The ſtudier of Jeremiah's writings will frequently detect among the pſalms a reed analogous to his: for inſtance, in the XXII, XXXV, LV, LXIX, LXXI, LXXIV, LXXIX, LXXXVIII, LXXXIX, CII, and in many others. In ſome of theſe pſalms alluſions occur to Jeremiah's quarrel with his nephew Seraiah (LXIX 8) and with the prieſt Zephaniah (LV 13), who were both of the Ægyptian faction (2 Kings XXV 18); ſo that they were written during the ſiege of Jeruſalem. It is the more natural that compoſitions of Jeremiah ſhould have been induſtriouſly introduced into Jewiſh worſhip, as he was ſon to Hilkiah, the reviſer of the liturgy, as he bore an almoſt exceptionable allegiance to the Perſian or Babylonian party, was recompenſed by the beſiegers (Jeremiah XL. 5) after the capture of Jeruſalem, and at all times ſpoke the language of thoſe families under whoſe auſpices the reſtoration was effected. To the Ægyptian faction he was ſteadily hoſtile (M. M. VI 98 and 99); he even accompanied Johanan and his followers to Ægypt, rather to thwart than to aſſiſt their ſettle-

 ment

ment in that country (Jeremiah XLIII. 9); for his confidential secretary, Baruch, was shortly after dispatched (Baruch I. 1) to Babylon, whither Jeremiah appears to have ultimately* followed. After the captivity at least (Jeremiah XIII. v. 17 and 5) his walks were beside the Euphrates: so that the CXXXVII and some other similar psalms may probably, if not confidently, be also ascribed to him.

Of these elegiac psalms there is one, the eighty ninth, (it seems to have begun originally at the nineteenth verse) written with that carping disappointment which pervades every work of Jeremiah, and adapted exactly to the fortunes of king Josiah. His descent from David, his anointment (v. 20), his respite (v. 22), his piety (v. 26), his renewal of the covenant (v. 28) are first noticed. Then, with a somewhat querulous impiety, his desertion by Providence is bewailed. The irruption of Necho (v. 40), the plunder of the land (v. 41), the triumph of the adversary (v. 42), and the monarch's flight, wounded, from the battle (v. 43) is detailed. The consequent loss of the throne (v. 44), his early death (v. 45), at the age of thirty-nine, and the disgrace of his memory are successively lamented. The poem closes with another angry expostulation against Providence, as if the king had performed his part of the covenant, and had not been duly seconded by the Lord whom he worshipped. The various particulars enumerated do not all suit any other Jewish sovereign than Josiah: to him therefore they ought to be referred. The latter part of the LXXX psalm then is to be considered as Jeremiah's Lamentation for the death of king Josiah.

This dirge receives from Herodotus (Euterpe, 159) some light; and throws much on the often misinterpreted twelfth chapter of Zechariah, which is apparently out of its place, and should occur among the earlier fragments of Jeremiah. Here too is narrated the expedition of Necho against Jerusalem: for on no other occasion was Jerusalem threatened with a siege, full of exertion against the enemy, delivered finally from the danger, and yet filled with mourning after the event. The expression *there shall be as much mourning in Jerusalem as in the valley of Megiddo*, where Josiah and his companions fell, renders the application unequivocal. The six first verses of the ensuing chapter belong to the same oracle. It is no composition of Zechariah's, because it professes to have been written before the event, and he was born after: to say nothing of the allusion (Zechariah XIII. 6) to the painful punishment † incurred by Jeremiah (Jeremiah XX. 2, and Psalm XXII. 16,) which would suffice to identify the author.

ORIGINAL POETRY.

To the MEMORY *of the* REV. G. WAKEFIELD.

FRIEND of departed worth! whose pilgrim feet
Trace injured merit to its last retreat,
Oft will thy steps imprint the hallow'd shade,
Where Wakefield's dust, embalm'd in tears, is laid;
"Here (wilt thou say) a high undaunted soul,
That spurn'd at palsied caution's weak controul—
A mind by learning stor'd, by genius fir'd,
In Freedom's cause with gen'rous warmth inspir'd—
Moulders in earth; the fabric of his fame
Rests on the pillar of a spotless name!"
Tool of corruption—spaniel slave of power!
Should thy rash steps in some unguarded hour
Profane the shrine, deep on thy shrinking heart
Engrave this awful moral, and depart!

---

* The two books of Kings were apparently compiled and finished by Jeremiah; for they contain long passages also occurring in his acknowleged works (Compare 2 Kings XXIV and XXV with Jeremiah LII). These books were drawn up in Chaldea, since Babylonian names of months (1 Kings VI. 1), and other allusions to Persian religion (1 Kings XXII. 19), occur; and after the accession of Merodach, whose kindness to Jehoiachin is therein recorded. It is consequently probable that Jeremiah, under Merodach, was living at Babylon. One is dissatisfied to observe no mention of the fate of Jeremiah, in the book of his grand-nephew Ezra. The office allotted to Sheshbazzar (Ezra I. 11) would have been a natural reward of Jeremiah's loyalty. May it not have been the real one? Such Jews as were promoted at Babylon mostly assumed a new name or title; and the signature of Jeremiah occurs at Jerusalem, after the return, on the document quoted at length in the tenth and contiguous chapters of Nehemiah.

† A sort of stocks pierced to receive the hands and feet.

That

That not the shafts of slander, envy, hate,
The dungeon's gloom, nor the cold hand of fate,
Can rob the good man of that peerless prize
Which not pale Mammon's countless treasure buys—
The conscience clear whence secret pleasures flow,
And friendship kindled 'mid the gloom of woe,
Assiduous love that stays the parting breath,
And honest fame, triumphant over death.

For you, who o'er the sacred marble bend,
To weep the husband, father, brother, friend,
And, mutely eloquent, in anguish raise
Of keen regrets his monument of praise—
May Faith, may Friendship, dry your streaming eyes,
And Virtue mingle comfort with your sighs;
Till Resignation softly stealing on,
With pensive smile bid ling'ring Grief begone,
And tardy Time veil o'er with gradual shade
All but the tender tints you would not wish to fade!

L. A.

A SONG.

LET others boast the treach'rous art
The heedless fair to move;
I bear no base licentious heart,
But most sincerely love.

Let passion's wild impetuous beat
Their throbbing bosoms fire,
Be mine the mild and genial heat
Awaked by chaste desire!

I will not praise thy sparkling eyes,
Though there the graces dwell;
Nor will I sing with fond surprize
Thy bounding bosom's swell.

A cheek, a lip, may others gain,
Whom sense alone invites;
But short their joy allied to pain,
And vain their best delights.

Be mine to gaze upon thy face,
And matchless beauty find,
Nor there to mark one lovely grace
Unstampt upon thy mind.

Oh! can you nurse injurious fear
And cold suspicion know!
Let Love dispel the gelid tear
With his own gen'rous glow!

No fabled pow'rs will I attest,
That suits a man who feigns;
Can his but be an honest breast
Where your frank virtue reigns?

Let foolish men in labour's mine
Honour or wealth pursue,
The happy husband's arms be mine,
My only treasure you.

Unenvied, Lux'ry's lavish board,
Cold Grandeur's heartless life,
The bloody Warrior's impious sword,
The Statesman's crooked strife!

As Shepherds on a sea-beat shore
View Sailors tempt their fate,
We'll hear Ambition's tempest roar,
And pity them their state.

TRANSLATION,

From the German of SCHILLER, (*Die Ideale.*)

COMPANIONS of my earlier years,
For ever faithless will ye fly,
With all your train of hopes and fears,
Aspiring thoughts and warm desires,
Creative Fancy's magic fires
That warm'd my opening mind with distant scenes of joy?
Imagination's airy train,
Can nought your hasty flight retain?
Ah! never, never, shall I see
Those visions of my early prime,
Swept by the ruthless storms of time,
Lost in the ocean of eternity.

And are those suns for ever set in night,
That spread their lustre o'er my dawning day?
Those cherish'd visions of supreme delight
So oft invoked, no longer will they stay?
Each wish that fired my inexperienced mind,
And promised bliss and purity below,
Say must it still in Reason find a foe,
And leave a dull and dreary void behind?

As once the sculptured image fired
Pygmalion with an amorous flame,
Till breath and genial life inspired
The marble's cold and senseless frame;
So Nature to my opening soul
Appear'd in all her charms array'd,
Imagination lent her aid,
And mimic life inspired the wond'rous whole.

Responsive to my ardent mind,
The magic influence spread o'er all,
The tree, the flower, the water-fall,
The forest wild, the lawn, the grove,
All seem'd, to life and sense refined,
To echo back the song of boundless love.

Methought an influence divine,
Ruled with almighty power my mind,
And urged to every great design,
Form'd by the love of human kind!
How vast, how fair appear'd this wond'rous scene,
When Hope at first its opening buds display'd!
How dull and comfortless, how poor and mean,
Has Reason since this mighty world pourtrayed!

When first life's journey I begun,
Unburthen'd by the load of care,
In thought with mighty strides I ran
To scenes that Fancy painted fair;
Already would my wishes fly
To many a great and arduous height,
Nought was too distant, nought too high,
To tempt my fancy's daring flight.
How easy thence to snatch the prize
It seem'd amid the glorious strife,
While danced before my dazzled eyes
The forms that glitter in the morn of life.
Methought, obedient to my call,
That Love his roses in my path had strown;
That Fortune, with her golden crown,
And Fame, that hides in stars his lofty crest,
And Truth, in never-fading sun-beams drest,
On me had doom'd their choicest gifts to fall.

The

The fairy ſcenes are flown,
The bright enchantment vaniſhed in air;
Faithleſs, for ever are they gone,
Unmark'd, unheard my prayer.
On haſty wing has Fortune urged her flight,
Nor Knowledge grants me yet her gifts to ſhare,
While hid in clouds of doubt is Truth's immortal light.

I ſaw the palm of high renown
The undeſerving brow adorn;
I look'd—and lo! for ever flown
The opening ſweets of life's delicious morn!
And deeper ſtill and darker grew
The ſhades that gather'd round my lonely way,
While mid the dull and dreary view
Hope ſcarcely ſhed a feeble doubtful ray.

Of all the viſionary train
That Fancy erſt was wont to raiſe,
O ſay, which faithful yet remain,
To cheer the evening of my days!
Thou, Friendſhip, who alone haſt power
To heal each deeply-rankling wound,
And cheer affliction's darkeſt hour—
Thou whom I early ſought and found:
Employment, too, whoſe healing balm
Can ſtill the paſſions madding rage,
The tempeſt of the ſoul can calm,
And all life's ills aſſuage.
'Tis thou, who unappall'd by toil,
Canſt to perfection bring each nobler aim,
And atoms upon atoms pile,
To form a ſyſtem's mighty frame;
Led by thy hand in life's declining day,
Hours, minutes, months, and years, will ſoftly ſteal away.

J. B.

LINES

UPON THE DEATH OF THE REV. GILBERT WAKEFIELD.

IS Wakefield dead? I caught the paſſing tale
"Not warm affection's reſtleſs cares avail,"
"Nor healing ſkill, to ſtop his fleeting breath!"
Yet, yet, he lives; his mind has vanquiſh'd death.—
Long as the various literary ſtores
From ancient Rome, from claſſic Grecian ſhores,
Shall ſhare the vacant or the ſtudious hour—
Long as pure taſte and learning hold their power—
Long as the preſs exiſts, the ſoul to feed—
Wakefield ſurvives.—Ah! ſtill does Friendſhip bleed?
The huſband, father, friend, for ever loſt;
Thoſe hopes ſo late inſpir'd ſeverely croſs'd;
Hopes when again he breath'd in Freedom's air,
That years of happineſs might well repair
Of time and joy the cruel priſon's waſte—
But ſay, was his humane free ſpirit, plac'd
In earth's corrupted atmoſphere, at home;
This earth, where vice and war deſtroying roam?
No:—Heav'n in kindneſs ſnatch'd him from the ſcene
To dwell where love and truth are always green.

Sept. 11, 1801. J. N. H.

ERRATA—In the firſt of the introductory lines to Dr. Geddes's Latin Verſes, for "*Eſſay*," read "*Elegy*"—Line 1, verſe 3, of the Tranſlation to ditto, for "*wiſhes*," read "*virtues*,"—and in line 44, p. 136, for "*my* latent fires," read "*its* latent fires."

Extracts from the Port-folio of a Man of Letters.

NAUTICAL LITERATURE.

THE common and ſtatute law of ſea-matters (ſays the Monthly Review, vol. XI. p. 564) handed down by tradition, and by the Rhodian code from the ancients, was gradually modified into that ſyſtem of regulations known by the name of *Il Conſulato del Mare*, which received the papal ſanction in 1075, was re-enacted in moſt ſea-ports of the Mediterranean, but not till 1162 at Marſeilles. This work was firſt printed at Barcelona in 1502: it has been tranſlated into moſt European languages, our own excepted: the Dutch verſion of 1704 is the beſt.

The rules and orders taught by the circumſtances and experience of the Baltic ſailors were firſt reduced into a body of written law at Wiſby, one of the Anſeatic towns, and were printed at Copenhagen in 1505 in the Frankiſh tongue. Of theſe an Engliſh tranſlation appeared in 1536.

Surely a book containing theſe two primary codes of maritime law, in modern Engliſh, would neither be difficult to execute, nor difficult to ſell.

COALITION PROPOSED.

For a coalition between the churches of England and of Rome (ſays a commentator on Barry's Letter to the Society of Arts) no doubt the times are ripe: it would furniſh a favourable opportunity for increaſing the pomp of worſhip in our eſtabliſhed churches, and for converting them into galleries of the fine arts. It is for the learned among the catholics to ſtate the terms on which they could accept

benefices

benefices in the church of England. To the recognition of the Pope, as ſpiritual head of the church, there can be little objection: it would tend to weaken that alliance between the church and the ſtate, which is, by ſome, conſidered as hoſtile to civil liberty. But the celibacy of the clergy, that ceremony of the maſs which almoſt renders the prieſt himſelf an object of worſhip, and the practice of auricular confeſſion continued after the age of majority, ought, with the civil governor, to be obſoles. The obvious preparation for ſuch a change would be a repeal of the act of uniformity, and a marked patronage of thoſe among the Engliſh clergy, who, when thus ſet at liberty, ſhould be moſt active in conciliating their ſeveral hearers to this fraternal union. It is proper too, that the patrons of advowſons be conſulted about a public religion, which were beſt accompliſhed by leaving them at liberty to preſent to ordained prieſts of whatſoever particular tenets. Thus would any religion, to which the maſs of property may lean, become poſſeſſed of ſanctioned temples, in proportion to the opulence of its followers.

BARBARISM AND SOLECISM.

The Greeks called all foreign nations *barbarous*: to *barbarize* in language conſequently was to ſpeak or write like a foreigner, or *barbarian*; and a *barbariſm* was a vitious form of ſpeech worthy of a foreigner.

A king of Cyprus, by Solon's advice, founded a city called *Soloi*, in which ſo many Athenian emigrants came to ſettle that they permanently influenced the dialect of the natives. To *ſolecize* was to ſpeak or write like the inhabitants of *Soloi*, that is, to ape the Athenians affectedly; and a *Solœciſm* conſequently was an unſucceſsful attempt to copy the utmoſt refinement of phraſeology.

A barbariſm then is a fault of ſtyle originating in rudeneſs and ignorance; but a ſoleciſm is a fault of ſtyle originating in affectation and over-refinement.

Shakeſpeare ſometimes faulters into barbariſm, Ben Johnſon into ſoleciſm.

That the Greeks thus underſtood the words, may be further inferred from the circumſtance that, in morals, the derivative phraſes have been uſed metaphorically with the ſame relative ſenſe; barbariſm being applied to the ferocious, and ſoleciſm to the effeminate vices. Thus: *Tois de phronémaſin 'o baſileus bebarbarómenos 'ércketo.* And again: *Solœkizein 'ou monou epi phônés legetai, alla kai 'epi tón kata ton bion 'ataktós genomenón.*

A perverſion of the meaning of theſe terms began early among the Latin critics. Thus in a work which has been raſhly aſcribed to Cicero: *Vitia in ſermone, quominus is Latinus ſit, duo poſſunt eſſe, ſoleciſmus et barbariſmus. Solecijmus eſt cum verbis pluribus conſequens verbum ſuperiori non accomodatur. Barbariſmus eſt cum verbum aliquod vitioſe affertur.* Rhetor. ad Herennium, lib. iv. c. 12. This miſapplication of terms endures throughout the whole courſe of Roman literature; for Iſidorus Hiſpalenſis, c. xxxii. ſays: *Solœciſmus eſt plurimorum verborum inter ſe inconveniens compoſitio: ſicut barbariſmus unius verbi corruptio.*

WHY LIFT THE HAT?

Faſhions, like prejudices, have commonly ſome latent utility; this ſhould be inveſtigated and recorded, in order to prevent attempts to lay aſide the convenient. The old way of bowing had no ſuch merit. *Capita autem aperiri aſpectu magiſtratuum non venerationis cauſâ juſſêre, ſed, ut Varro auctor eſt, valetudinis, quo firmiora conſuetudine eâ fierent.* Nat. Hiſt. lib. xxviii. c. 6. According to Pliny then we pulled off our hats in ſalutation, that we might become leſs liable to catch cold: for our cuſtom, no doubt, has derived from the Romans. It did not anſwer this purpoſe; the Engliſh of the laſt generation were remarkable for catarrhous diſorders. Now that hats have neither taſſels nor corners, it is far more convenient only to touch than to lift them.

CRITICISM OF JOHNSON.

Dr. Johnſon's Criticiſm is not always ſo preciſe as eloquent: he ſays ſomewhere: "In the writings of other poets a character is too often an individual; in thoſe of Shakeſpeare, it is commonly a ſpecies." The diametrically oppoſite poſition would have approached nearer to truth. Shakeſpeare delights to individualize his perſons; and far from confining his imitation to thoſe traits of character which are common to whole claſſes, as Voltaire and other French dramatiſts have done, he officiouſly brings into notice all thoſe accidents of complexion, figure, habits, dialect, diſpoſition, which were traditionally ſuppoſed to peculiarize an Othello, a Richard, a Henry, a Shylock, a Macbeth. This practice is exactly what confers ſo much appearance of life on his portraiture —ſuch an air of reality on his perſonages; and what has given to the Gothic plays of England and Germany an intereſt ſo ſuperior to that excited by the ancient, or the French drama. The imitation of general nature, as it has been called, that is the omission of particulars from a fear of not making them harmonious and characteristic, resembles the practice of certain engravers, who have recourse to dotting, because they cannot draw correctly; and leave their outlines vague, least they should be detected in aberrations from truth and reality.

LESSING'S DRAMATURGY.

Lessing comments Aristotle, as divines the Bible; so as to extort his own critical opinions from the lips of the oracle.

VOLTAIRE.

Nicolai was praising Voltaire for having written so much that is new, and so much that is good. His good is not new—his new is not good: replied Lessing.

SALUTATION OF SNEEZERS.

Strada has written a dissertation on sneezing: he proves from Petronius and Apuleius that the custom of blessing sneezers was established among the Romans; from Aristenetus and Hippocrates that it prevailed among the Greeks; and from the Bible that it pre-existed among the Jews: but he is content to leave in its antient uncertainty the cause of a practice, to account for whose origin has vainly puzzled the encyclopedic information both of Pliny and of Aristotle.

Now for a pinch of snuff—and some attention (*chisha!*) to the associated recollections, which the consequent sternutation is calling up. When do I usually sneeze? On applying strong odors to the nose. When else? During the acme of that stimulation, which succeeds to a seasoned dinner and a cheerping pint; as Clemens Alexandrinus also had long ago observed. When else? If I sit unscreened with my back to the fire—and again, if I walk without my hat into the sun-shine.

The inference from these phænomena seems to be that sneezing indicates overaction, super-irritation, hyper-paroxysm; and that it is peculiarly characteristic of that excessive excitement, which is produced by the sudden or profuse radiation of heat or light on the face, head or back.

The disease called in France *coup-de-soleil* is the after weakness, or indirect debility, which succeeds to this peculiar form of excitement: it is in all hot countries very common, and often fatal. If therefore sneezing be naturally symptomatic of the *coup-de-soleil*, and a usual harbinger of its approach, it would, in all hot countries, almost inevitably be considered as a bad prognostic—as ominous of danger: it would consequently provoke a wish in every humane by-stander, that the head-aches and other symptoms of heliacal injury might not ensue. The ζῆθι or *salve* thus addressed to those who sneeze from sunshine, being an expression of real benevolence, would soon become a regular form of civility. The practice of such addrest would next be extended, by the apish inanity of politeness, to the voluntarily-provoked sneeze, and to the triumphant sneeze of culminating intoxication; and would at last be exported to those chilly climates, where to sneeze is never the fore-runner of danger, but rather the mark of a wholesome sensibility of fibre.

THE RULING CHARACTER.

What Pope has termed *the ruling passion*, is rather, in several of the instances himself has adduced, *character* formed by long habit. Thus, his dying courtier, who cries, "If, where I'm going, I can serve you, Sir!" is a man under the influence of an habitual practice of making unmeaning offers and compliments. I was used to think this example quite hyperbolical, till I met with the following story gravely related in the Saint-Evremondiana:—"Cardinal Mazarin on his death-bed requested an interview with the young king, Louis XIV. in which he assured him, that it had been his determination very speedily to have resigned his authority into his Majesty's hands, who was now so fully capable of governing for himself." He added, "that nothing in the approach of death afflicted him so much, as that he was to be deprived of the felicity of living under his Majesty's administration."

NAIVETE.

Writers sometimes, either through defect of judgment or excess of zeal, make voluntary confessions which an adversary could scarcely have extorted from them. Of this kind is a passage of Tillemont, quoted by Jortin in *Rem. on Eccl. Hist.* "Socrates (the ecclesiastical historian) was a lawyer, and very ignorant of the spirit and discipline of the church. Hence it comes to pass, that he commends equally either Catholics or Heretics, when they did things which seemed to him to be commendable."

Perhaps an English prelate, when in a charge to his clergy he told them that the popish clergy are "in very deed nearer and dearer to the Church of England than certain Protestant Dissenters," may be thought to have been surprised into a similar unlucky piece of sincerity.

Errata—In l. 29, p. 114, of last Number, *erase* the *Comma* after gravel-walk.—p. 115, l. 3. for "*reflection*" read "*repletion*."

MEMOIRS

MEMOIRS OF EMINENT PERSONS.

A TRIBUTE *to the* MEMORY *of* MR. WAKEFIELD.

LITERATURE has this month ſuſtained a ſevere loſs by the death of GILBERT WAKEFIELD, *B.A.* whom a fever carried off on September the 9th, in the 45th year of his age, to the unſpeakable regret of his family and friends. A perſon in various reſpects ſo diſtinguiſhed, is a proper ſubject for the contemplation of ſurvivors; and he had deſerved too well of the public not to be entitled to honourable and affectionate commemoration.

Mr. Wakefield, in "Memoirs of his own Life," publiſhed in 1792, has informed the world of all the circumſtances attending his education and paſſage through life down to that period, with a minuteneſs and frankneſs which render his work a very curious and entertaining piece of biography. I ſhall not make any tranſcripts from it, but, confining myſelf to a ſlight ſketch of the leading events, ſhall take that view of his character and conduct which ſuggeſts itſelf to the reflexion of a friendly but not a prejudiced by-ſtander.

GILBERT WAKEFIELD was born on February 22, 1756, at Nottingham, of which town his father was one of the parochial clergy. An uncommon ſolidity and ſeriouſneſs of diſpoſition marked him from infancy, together with a power of application, and thirſt after knowledge, which accelerated his progreſs in juvenile ſtudies. In his grammatical courſe he paſſed under the tuition of ſeveral maſters, the laſt and moſt reſpectable of whom was the Rev. Mr. Woodeſon, of Kingſton-upon-Thames, to which pariſh his father was then removed. He was uſed, however, to lament that he had not poſſeſſed the advantages of an uniform education at one of thoſe public ſchools, which undoubtedly, whatever may be their dangers and deficiencies, effect the point at which they excluſively aim, that of laying a ſolid foundation for claſſical erudition in its moſt exact form. In 1772 he was entered as a ſcholar of Jeſus-college, Cambridge; and it was ever a topic of thankfulneſs to him, that he became a member of *that* univerſity in which the love of truth met with ſome encouragement from a ſpirit of liberal enquiry, rather than of *that* which was devoted either to ſupine indolence, or to the paſſive inculcation of opinions ſanctioned by authority. During the firſt years, his attention was chiefly fixed upon claſſical ſtudies, always his favourites; and he was excited only by emulation and academical requiſitions to aim at that proficiency in mathematical knowledge which bears ſo high a value at Cambridge. Yet while he confeſſes himſelf deſtitute of a genuine taſte for ſpeculations of this kind, he ſcruples not to declare the infinite ſuperiority, in point of grandeur and ſublimity, of mathematical philoſophy to claſſical lucubrations. In 1776 he took his degree of B.A. on which occaſion he was nominated to the ſecond poſt among ſeventy five candidates; and ſoon after, he was elected to a fellowſhip of his college. In the ſame year he publiſhed a ſmall collection of Latin poems, with a few critical notes on Homer, at the univerſity-preſs. If not highly excellent, they were ſufficient to eſtabliſh the claim of a young man to more than ordinary acquaintance with the elegancies of literature. He had already obtained a knowledge of the Hebrew language, as preparatory to thoſe theological ſtudies which now became his moſt ſerious occupation; and it may ſafely be affirmed that no man ever commenced them with a mind more determined upon the unbiaſſed ſearch after truth, and the open aſſertion of it when diſcovered. The foundation which he laid for his enquiries was an accurate knowledge of the phraſeology of the Scriptures, acquired by means of attention to the idiom in which they were written. As at this time ſome of his moſt eſteemed academical friends manifeſted their diſſatisfaction with the articles of the church of England by a conſcientious refuſal of ſubſcription, it cannot be doubted that ſcruples on this point had already taken poſſeſſion of his mind; and ſo far had his convictions proceeded, that he has ſtigmatized his compliance with the forms requiſite for obtaining deacon's orders, which he received in 1778, as "the moſt diſingenuous action of his whole life." If, indeed, he could receive conſolation from the practice of others, there were ſeveral of his intimate aſſociates, who, by a ſuperiority to ſuch ſcruples, have ſince riſen to opulence and diſtinction in the church, without betraying any uneaſineſs for a ſimilar acquieſcence.

Mr. Wakefield left college after ordination, and engaged in a curacy at Stockport, in Cheſhire, whence he afterwards removed to a ſimilar ſituation in Liverpool. He performed the duties of his office with ſeriouſneſs and punctuality; but his diſſatisfaction

satisfaction with the doctrine and worship of the church continuing to increase, he probably considered his connection with it as not likely to be durable. The disgust he felt at what he saw of the practice of privateering, and the slave-trade, in the latter place of his residence, also awakened in his mind that humane interest in the rights and happiness of his fellow-creatures, which has made so conspicuous a part of his character. The American war did not tend to augment his attachment to the political administration of his country; in short, he became altogether unfit to make one of that body, the principal business of which, in the opinion of many, seems to be, acting as the satellites of existing authority, however exerted. His marriage, in 1779, to Miss Watson, neice of the rector of Stockport, was soon followed by an invitation to undertake the post of classical tutor at the dissenting academy at Warrington, with which he complied. That he was regarded as a very valuable acquisition to this institution—that he was exemplary in the discharge of his duty, and equally gained the attachment of his pupils, and the friendship and esteem of his colleagues—the writer of this account can from his own knowledge attest. Being now freed from all clerical shackles, he began his career as a theological controversialist, and, it must be confessed, with an acrimony of style which was lamented by his friends, and which laid him open to the reproach of his enemies. It is not here intended to vindicate what the writer himself cannot but disapprove; but the real and substantial kindness of Mr. Wakefield's temper, and the benevolence of his heart, were such, that this apparent contradiction must be solved by his warmth of zeal in what he thought the cause of truth, and perhaps by a familiarity with scholastic debates, which rendered him in some measure callous to the use, or rather abuse, of vituperative expressions from the press. In disputations by word of mouth no man was more calm and gentle, more patient in hearing, or more placid in replying; and if, in his writings, he has without hesitation or delicacy bestowed his censures, he has been equally liberal and decided in his praise. His applauses evidently came from the heart, free and unstinted, for envy did not possess a single particle in his composition; nor has he withheld them when he thought them deserved by particular laudable qualities, even in characters which he could not regard with general approbation. No man, perhaps, ever more fully gave way to the openness of his disposition in speaking *the whole truth* concerning men and things, unmoved by common considerations; whence it is not to be wondered at, that he frequently rendered himself more obnoxious to antagonists than the case essentially required, and roused prejudices which a more guarded conduct would have left dormant. A sentence which, in his Memoirs, he has quoted from Asgill, expresses (as it was probably meant to do) the spirit with which he wrote. "A blunt author in pursuit of truth, *knows no man* after the flesh, till his chace is over. For a man to *think* what he *writes*, may bespeak his *prudence*: but to *write* what he *thinks*, best opens his principles."

We shall not, in this sketch, attempt to give an account of all his publications, many of them small in bulk and temporary in their application. The most important of his theological labours will be allowed to be those in which he employs his singular erudition in the explanation of Scripture. Of these, the first was "A New Translation of the First Epistle of Paul, the Apostle, to the Thessalonians," printed in 1781. It was followed in the next year by "A New Translation of St. Matthew, with Notes, critical, philological, and explanatory," 4to. a work which obtained much applause, and amply displayed the extent of his reading, and the facility with which his memory called up its reposited stores for the purpose of illustration or parallelism. At this time he likewise augmented his fund for Scripture interpretation by the acquisition of various Oriental dialects. After quitting Warrington, at the dissolution of the academy, he took up his residence successively at Bramcote in Nottinghamshire, at Richmond, and at Nottingham, upon the plan of taking a few pupils, and pursuing at his leisure those studies to which he became continually more attached. While in the first of these situations, he published the first volume of "An Enquiry into the Opinions of the Christian Writers of the three first Centuries concerning the Person of Jesus Christ," a learned and elaborate performance, but which did not meet with encouragement sufficient to induce him to proceed in the design. A painful disorder in his left shoulder, with which he was attacked in 1786, and which harassed him for two years, interrupted the course of his employments; and he could do no more for letters during that period, than alleviate his sufferings by drawing up some remarks upon the Georgics of Virgil and the Poems of Gray, which he published with

with editions of those delightful compositions. As his health returned, his theological pursuits were resumed, and he again engaged in the field of controversy. He also, in 1789, made a commencement of a work, which promised much, as well for his reputation, as for the advantage of sacred literature. It was "an Union of Theological and Classical Learning, illustrating the Scriptures by Light borrowed from the Philology of Greece and Rome." Under the title of "Silva Critica," three parts of this performance have issued from the university press of Cambridge.

The formation of a dissenting college at Hackney, which, it was hoped, by the powerful aid of the metropolis, would become both more considerable and more permanent than former institutions of a like kind, produced an invitation to Mr. Wakefield to undertake the classical professorship. With this he thought proper to comply; and accordingly, in 1790, he quitted his abode at Nottingham, and removed to Hackney, upon the plan of joining with public tuition the instruction of private pupils. He has himself informed the public that "both of these anchors failed him, and left his little bark again afloat on the ocean of life." It is neither necessary nor desirable to revive the memory of differences between persons really respectable and well intentioned, but under the influence of different habits and views of things. We shall confine ourselves to a remark or two.

Mr. Wakefield was a person who derived his opinions entirely from the source of his own reason and reflection, and it will not be easy to name a man who stood more single and insulated in this respect throughout life than he. Although his principles had induced him to renounce his clerical office in the church of England, and he had become a *dissenter* from her doctrine and worship, yet he was far from uniting with any particular class of those who are usually denominated *dissenters*. He had an insuperable repugnance to their mode of performing divine service; and he held in no high estimation the theological and philosophical knowledge which it has been the principal object of their seminaries of education to communicate. It has already been observed, that the basis of his own divinity was philology. Classical literature, therefore, as containing the true rudiments of all other science, was that on which he thought the greatest stress should be laid, in a system of liberal education. This point he inculcated with an earnestness which probably appeared somewhat dictatorial to the conductors of the institution.

Further, in the progress of his speculations, he had been led to form notions concerning the expediency and propriety of public worship, extremely different from those of every body of Christians, whether in sects or establishments; and as he was incapable of thinking one thing and practising another, he had sufficiently made known his sentiments on this subject, as well in conversation, as by abstaining from attendance upon every place of religious assembly. They who were well acquainted with him, knew that in his own breast piety was one of the most predominant affections; but the assembling for social worship had for so many ages been regarded as the most powerful instrument for the support of general religion, that to discourage it was considered as of dangerous example, especially in a person engaged in the education of youth. Notwithstanding, therefore, his classical instructions in the college were received by the students almost with enthusiastical admiration, and conferred high credit on the institution, a dissolution of his connection with it took place in the summer of 1791.

The subsequent publication of his pamphlet on Public Worship deprived him (as he says) of the only two private pupils he expected. From that period he continued to reside at Hackney, in the capacity of a retired man of letters, employing his time partly in the education of his own children, partly in the composition of works which will perpetuate his name among those who have cultivated literature with most ardour and success. His "Translation of the New Testament, with Notes," 3 vols. 8vo. appeared towards the close of 1791, and was very respectably patronized. In language it preserves as much as possible of the old version. Its numerous deviations from that in sense, will be regarded as happy alterations or bold innovations, according to the prepossessions of the reader. A long list might be given of his succeeding labours, but we shall only particularize some of the most considerable. He printed (no longer at the Cambridge-press) two more parts of his "Silva Critica." He gave a new edition, much corrected, of his "Translation of the New Testament;" and besides, proved his zeal for Christianity, by enlarging a former work "On the Evidences of the Christian Religion," and by replying to Thomas Paine's attack upon it in his "Age of Reason."

To the works of Pope, as our most cultivated

tivated English poet, and the most perfect example of that splendour and felicity of diction which is not attained without much study of the poetic art, Mr. Wakefield paid particular attention. It was his design to have published a complete edition of his works; but after he had printed the first volume, the scheme was rendered abortive by Dr. Warton's edition. He, however, printed a second volume, entitled, "Notes on Pope," and also gave a new edition of Pope's "Iliad and Odyssey." In these publications he displayed all that variety of comparison and illustration, that power of tracing a poetical thought thro' different authors, with its successive shades and improvements, and that exquisite feeling of particular beauties, which distinguish him as an annotator of the writers of Greece and Rome.

As a classical editor he appeared in a selection from the Greek tragedians, in editions of Horace, Virgil, Bion and Moschus, and, finally, in his "Lucretius," a vast performance, which alone might seem the labour of many industrious years. Of his character, as a man of letters, I have been favoured with the following estimate by an able judge, the Rev. E. COGAN, of Cheshunt:

"In extent of erudition, particularly if an acquaintance with the Oriental languages be taken into the account, he was perhaps inferior to no man of the present age; and they who have been considered as having had the advantage over him in some of the less important *minutiæ* of Greek literature, have probably limited their attention to fewer objects, and certainly commenced their literary course with a more advantageous preparation. In conjectural criticism he exhibits much of the character of Bentley and Markland: men whom he esteemed according to their high deserts in that species of learning to which his own mind was peculiarly directed. Like these illustrious scholars, he is always learned, sometimes bold, and frequently happy. Like them he had a mind which disdained to be held in a servile subjection to authority; and in defiance of established readings, which too often substitute the dreams of transcribers for the gems of antiquity, he followed, without fear, wherever reason and probability seemed to lead the way. In his earlier critical works he exhibited, amidst some errors which his riper judgment discarded, the promise of his future greatness; and even his faults were the infirmities of genius; they flowed from that ardour and enthusiasm which cannot always wait for the slow decisions of cool enquiry. They were faults which, though they afforded a small consolation to dull malignity, did not diminish his praise in the estimation of one solid and impartial judge. His favourite study was poetry, and in an extensive acquaintance with the ancient poets, both Greek and Roman, few men since the revival of letters have equalled him, and no one ever surpassed him in the perception of their beauties. When he applies to them the hand of conjecture, he rarely fails to give new spirit and animation by his touch; and where we are obliged to dissent from his corrections, we are sometimes sorry for the credit of the poet that he does not appear to have written what the critic has suggested. He was peculiarly fond of tracing an elegance of poetical expression through the various modifications which it assumed in the hands of different writers, and in the illustration of ancient phraseology he did not overlook the poets of his own country, with many of which he was very familiar. His great work is undoubtedly his edition of "Lucretius," a work which ignorance may despise, at which malice may carp, and hireling scribblers may rail, but which will rank with the labours of Heinsius, Gronovius, Burman, and Heyne, as long as literature itself shall live. It will share the prediction with which Ovid has graced the memory of the great poet himself,

Carmina sublimis tunc sunt peritura Lucreti,
Exitio terras cum dabit una dies.

Besides its critical merit, it exhibits the richest display of the flowers of poetry that ever was presented to the world, and will amply reward the perusal of every man who has sensibility to relish the finest touches of human genius.

"Mr. Wakefield, even before this immortal specimen of his talents, was deservedly held in the highest estimation by the literati of Germany; and if his honours at home have not equalled his reputation abroad, the candid mind will easily find the explanation of this phenomenon in the violence of political party, and the mean jealousy which has too often disgraced the scholars of Great Britain. The name of Bentley is connected with proof enough of the justice of this insinuation."

I shall now proceed to an incident of his life which will be viewed with regret by the ingenuous of all parties; the *additional* sensations it inspires will, of course, be different according to the particular sentiments of individuals. It has already been hinted that Mr. Wakefield, from

from the time of his residence at Liverpool, had begun to imbibe a detestation of that policy which trampled upon the rights of mankind, and was founded upon unfeeling avarice and unprincipled ambition. His study of Christianity more and more convinced him that the maxims of the world and those of religion were in direct opposition: and, in common with many other excellent and learned men, he became persuaded of the absolute incompatibility of War with the Christian character. He had moreover received those principles of the origin and end of government, which, however they may now be regarded, were once thought fundamental to the British Constitution, and the basis of all civil liberty. He had occasionally, in the political contests of his country, publicly expressed his opinions upon these subjects; but the French Revolution was an event calculated to call forth all his ardour in the cause. His sanguine temper led him to consider it as the undoubted common cement of a better order of things, in which rational liberty, equitable policy, and pure religion, would finally become triumphant. He watched its progress with incredible interest, excused its unhappy deviations, and abhorred the combination of arbitrary power which threatened its destruction. It was impossible that he should refrain from employing his pen on the occasion, or that he should do it with a "cold and unperforming hand." In his "Remarks on the General Orders of the Duke of York," he had arraigned the justice of the war with France in terms which are supposed to have exercised the utmost forbearance of the Ministry. But in his "Reply to some Parts of the Bishop of Landaff's Address," he passed those limits. From that systematic progress in restraining the free communication of political opinions which may be traced in the acts of the late Ministry, it is not unreasonable to conclude, that a victim to the liberty of the press, of name and character sufficient to inspire a wide alarm, was really desired. Yet, as the Attorney-general solemnly protested that his prosecution of this pamphlet was spontaneous, and solely dictated to him by the heinous and dangerous nature of its contents, it would be uncandid to call his assertion in question. A man of sense, however, may be allowed to smile at the notion of real danger to supreme power, supported as well by public opinion, as by every active energy of the state, from a private writer, arguing upon principles so little applicable to the practice of the world, as those of the Gospel. Further, a man of a truly liberal and generous mind will perhaps view, not without indignation, the thunders of the law hurled upon a head distinguished for virtue and learning, without any humane allowance for well intentioned, if misguided, zeal. The attack commenced, not against the principal, who boldly and honestly came forward to avow himself, but against the agents; and the grand purport of it was sufficiently declared by the superior severity with which a bookseller was treated, who was not the editor, but only a casual vender of the work; but who had long been obnoxious as a distinguished publisher of books of free enquiry. Mr. Wakefield himself next underwent prosecution; and his sentence, upon conviction, was a two year's imprisonment in Dorchester gaol. There exists no other *measure* of punishment in such a case than comparison, and perhaps, upon the application of this rule, it will not be found inordinately severe. Two year's abode in a prison is, however, a most serious infliction! it is cutting off so much from desirable existence. Mr. Wakefield, notwithstanding his natural fortitude, felt it as such. Though, from his habits of sobriety and seclusion, he had little to resign in respect of the ordinary pleasures of the world; his habits of pedestrian exercise, and his enjoyment of family comfort, were essentially infringed by confinement. He likewise found all his plans of study so deranged, by the want of his library, and the many incommodities of his situation, that he was less able to employ that resource against tedium and melancholy than might have been expected. One powerful consolation, however, in addition to that of a good conscience, attended him. A set of warm and generous friends employed themselves in raising a contribution which should not only indemnify him from any pecuniary loss consequent upon his prosecution, but should alleviate his cares for the future support of his family. The purpose was effected; and it is to be hoped that Englishmen will ever retain spirit enough to take under their protection men who have faithfully, though perhaps not with due prudence and consideration, maintained the noble cause of mankind against the frowns of authority.

At length the tedious period elapsed, and the last day of May, in this year, restored him to liberty. He was received by his friends, many of whom had visited him in prison, with the most cordial welcome. He was endeared to them by his sufferings, and his character was generally thought to have received a meliorating tinge of mildness and moderation from the reflexions which had passed through his mind. He formed extensive plans for future literary labours, and he seemed fully capable of enjoying and benefiting that world to which he was returned. When—Oh what is man!—a fever, probably occasioned by his anxious exertions to fix himself in a new habitation, cut short all his prospects. From the first attack he persuaded himself that the termination would be fatal, and this conviction materially opposed every attempt of medicine in his favour. He surveyed death without terror, and prepared for it by tender offices to the survivors.

It is presumed that the character of Mr. Wakefield is sufficiently developed in the preceding sketch of his life. It may however be added, that there was in him an openness, a simplicity, a good faith, an affectionate ardour, a noble elevation of soul, which irresistibly made way to the hearts of all who nearly approached him, and rendered him the object of friendly attachment, to a degree almost unexampled. Let this be placed in balance to all that might appear arrogant or self-sufficient, harsh, or irritable in his literary conduct! His talents were rare—his morals pure—his views exalted—his courage invincible—his integrity without a spot. When will the place of such a man be supplied!

Stoke Newington, J. AIKIN,
Sept. 18, 1801.

PROCEEDINGS OF LEARNED SOCIETIES.

NATIONAL INSTITUTE OF FRANCE.

THE COMTE DE LIVOURNE (since King of Etruria) was present on the 1st Messidor (year 9) at the sitting of the Class of Mathematical and Physical Sciences of the Institute. He was accompanied by Citizen CHAPTAL, Minister of the Interior, and a Member of the Class; also, by the Chevalier AZARA, the Spanish Minister, and by two gentlemen of his suite. He took his place among the Members of the Institute, close to the President. The choice and the variety of the readings rendered this sitting very interesting.

Citizen HUZARD gave an account of the present state of the flock of Rambouillet, and of the product of the last shearing.

Citizen CHAPTAL read a memoir on different processes recently employed in the bleaching of cloth. They appear to be equally important by their celerity, their economy, and by the beauty of the results.

Citizen CUVIER read a memoir on the teeth of fishes. He presented some curious facts and important observations on this part of their organization; and detailed the motives which had obliged him to renounce the project of making use of them as a generical character, in the classification of this great order of animals.

Cit. LA PLACE read a memoir on the researches which have been hitherto made relative to the determination of the motion of the moon, and on their result. It was, doubtless, the province of the geometer who has so much contributed to perfect this important theory, to trace its history.

Citizen DOLOMIEU read a memoir on divers phenomena which accompanied the eruption of Mount Vesuvius in the year 2, or which are the consequences of it. This naturalist produced several fragments of iron utensils, of copper, of lead, and of glass, collected in the middle of the lava, and which, in its state of fusion, it had altered or mineralized in a very remarkable manner.

Citizen SAGE read a memoir on several new species of *belemnites*.

Citizen LALANDE read a note on the precise determination of the longitude, and consequently the position, of the city of Florence.

Citizen BERTHOLLET communicated a letter of the celebrated HERSCHEL, in which he intimates certain new opinions of his relative to the structure and the composition of the solar globe. The Institute seemed to think, like all the other sound European philosophers, that the observations of the learned Englishman are more valuable than his hypotheses.

The sitting was terminated by the reading of a memoir of Citizens FOUR-

CROY

CROY and VAUQUELIN, on Galvanism. It forms the series of the labours with which these chymists have already entertained the Class, and was accompanied with some new experiments, made with a galvanic pile or heap formed of metallic plates from eight to ten inches across.——It produced a lively scintillation and a brilliant inflammation in the atmospherical air, and in the oxygen gas.

Order of the Readings at the public Sitting of the Institute, held at the National Palace of Sciences and Arts, the 15th Messidor, year 9.

1. Distribution of prizes and announcement of new subjects for prizes. 2. Report on the Continuation of the *Dictionary of the French Language*, by Citizen ANDRIEUX. 3. A Memoir on the moral Writings of Cicero, by Cit. BOUCHAUD. 4. A Memoir on the last sale of Wool and Sheep of the Flock of Rambouillet, by Citizens TESSIER and HUZARD. 5. Extracts of a Memoir on the Bronze of the Antients, and on an antient Sword, by Citizen MONGEZ. 6. An Historical Notice on the Life and Works of Jean Baptiste Le Roi, by Citizen LEFEVRE GINEAU. 7. Extract of a Journey among the Creeks and Cherokees, by Citizen BEAUVOIS. 8. Extract of a Memoir on the Tribunals of Athens, by Citizen LEVESQUE. 9. A Memoir on the Bleaching of Linen, by Citizen SEGUIN. 10. *The Alchymist and his Children*, a Tale in Verse, by Citizen ANDRIEUX.

Notice of the labours of the Class of Mathematical and Physical Sciences, during the last quarterly sitting of the year 9.

The mathematical part by Citizen DELAMBRE.

Illustrations relative to a point of the history of the trigonometrical tables.

On the occasion of the great trigonometrical tables of the *cadastre*, or register, of which an account was given in the last Germinal, Citizen PRONY, to whom we are indebted for the first idea and the prompt execution of that immense work, read to the Class a Memoir on the *Opus Palatinum de Triangulis*, of RHETICUS. These tables, the most complete that have yet appeared for trigonometrical lines in natural numbers, had not been examined in all their parts with the same scrupulous attention. It was soon perceived that the tangents and the secants of the last degrees required considerable corrections: it was known in a vague manner that these corrections had been ordered, but it was not certainly known that they had been executed; at least, no trace was found of it in four copies, the only ones known at Paris of that extremely rare work. SCHULZE, in his Tables printed at Berlin, in 1778, had copied all the faults of Rheticus, and had contented himself with giving notice of it in his preface which seemed to imply the impossibility of finding a correct copy of the *Opus Palatinum*.

Citizen Prony had the good fortune to meet with one in which the tangents and the secants of the last degrees are of the same accuracy as all the rest. The title of the book is augmented with these words: "*Recens emendatus a Bartolomæo Pitisco, Silesio, &c.*" The seven last degrees have been calculated a-fresh, and this induced a necessity of printing again ninety pages, which were known by some differences in the paper and the characters; these last being more worn, and the former less beautiful, than in the rest of the volume. The Memoir of Citizen Prony contains the necessary *formulæ* to fix the quantity of the errors, exclusive of some tables of comparison which prove to what a point of exactness the corrections of Pitiscus have been carried.

To these researches of Citizen Prony we shall add, to satisfy those who, sometimes, make use of the tangents or natural secants, that these corrections, very important when extreme precision is required, become almost always imperceptible when we can be content with seven decimals; and, besides, the most generally known tables of this kind, such as those of Sherwin, Ozanam, Deparcieux, and more antiently that of Philip Lansberg, have been printed after a corrected copy, which will appear somewhat extraordinary when it is considered that Schulze and Vega, the editions of which are much more modern, have again produced faults which had long disappeared from the tables printed at London, at Paris, and at Middleburg. But of all the authors who have given exact secants and tangents, Lansberg is the only one that has every where established seven decimals, the others having only given 6 from 84° 16′ to 89° 25′, and only 5 in the 35 last minutes.

LIST OF NEW PUBLICATIONS IN SEPTEMBER.

EDUCATION.

The English Scholar's First Book, by John Commins, 3d. West and Hughes.

Surveys of Nature; the Sequel to Mrs. Trimmer's Introduction; being familiar Descriptions of Popular Subjects in Natural Philosophy, adapted to the Capacities of Children, by H. Ventum, Author of the Amiable Tutoress. Badcock.

HISTORY.

The History of Ancient and Modern Egypt; comprising a Comparison between the Ancient and Present State of Egypt, and a Philosophic View of those remarkable Productions connected with the History of that Country, volume 2d. 12mo. 5s. 6d. boards. West and Hughes.

MEDICAL.

A Treatise on Febrile Diseases, by A Phillips Wilson, M. D. volume 3d. 8vo. 9s. bds. Cadell and Davies.

The Institutions of the Practice of Medicine, by Joseph Baptist Burserius de Kanifield; translated from the Latin by William Cullen Brown, volume 3d. 8s. boards. Cadell and Davies.

Observations on the Cow-pox, by John Coakley Lettsom, M. D. with Engravings of the Sacred Cow, &c. &c. 8vo. 3s. sewed. Mawman.

An Account of a New Mode of Operation for the Removal of the Opacity in the Eye, called Cataract, by Sir James Earle, F. R. S. 3s. Johnson.

MILITARY.

The Duty of Officers commanding Detachments in the Field, by Colonel John Ormsby Vandeleur, of the 8th Dragoons, 5s. boards. Egerton.

METAPHYSICS.

Elements of the Philosophy of the Mind, and of Moral Philosophy; to which is prefixed, a Compendium of Logic, by Thomas Belsham, 9s. boards. Johnson.

MISCELLANIES.

The Third Part of Observations and Advices for the Improvement of the Manufacture of Muscovado Sugar and Rum; to which is added, a Description of a New Kiln for Drying Coffee; interspersed with Observations on this Business, by Bryan Higgins, M. D. 9s. boards Cadell and Davies.

A New Edition, elegantly printed, with a Portrait of the Author from an original Picture, engraved by Hopwood, of Essays, Moral, Economical, and Political, by Francis Bacon, Viscount St. Albans, &c. to which is prefixed, a Sketch of his Life, 6s. 6d. bds. Jones.

The Neological French and English Dictionary; containing Words of New Creation, not to be found in any French and English Vocabulary hitherto published, including those which form the Supplement to the fifth Edition of the French Academy's Dictionary, printed in 1798; with the New System of Weights, Measures, and Coins; and comprising a Short History of the French Revolution; a View of the Republic, with Anecdotes, &c. by William Dupré, 7s. 6d. bds. Clement.

Who are the Swindlers? a Query, by Miss Robertson of Blackheath, 1s 6d. Jordan.

Chronological Tablets, exhibiting every remarkable Occurrence, with Characteristic Traits of each Event, chiefly abridged from the French of the Abbot Lenglet du Fresnoy, and augmented to the present Time, particularly regarding British History, comprehending Accounts of Inventions and Discoveries in every Science, and Biographical Sketches of Illustrious or Notable Persons, 3s. Vernor and Hood.

Misère des Alpes; ou, Effets du Revolution Françoise en Suisse; observes dans un Voyage de Berne au Canton D'Underwald; containing a Description of the Vallies of Lauterbrunnen and Grindelwald, with the History of some of the most Unfortunate among the Inhabitants; to which is added the Music of the famous Air, "Ranz des Vaches de Suisse," 3s. 6d. sewed. Wright.

On the Influence attributed to Philosophers, Freemasons, and to the Illuminati, on the Revolution of France, by J. J. Mounier; translated by J. Walker, A. M. 8vo. 5s. sewed. Wallis.

A General Account of all the Rivers of Note, in Great Britain, with their peculiar Characters, the Countries through which they flow, and the entire Sea-coast of our Island, illustrated with Maps, by Henry Skrine, Esq. L. L. B. 8vo. 10s. 6d. boards. Elmsly and Co.

NOVELS.

Swedish Mysteries; or the Heroe of the Mine, a Tale; translated from a Swedish Manuscript, by Johanson Kidderslaw, 3 vols. 12mo. 15s. Lane.

Mysterious Husband, by the Author of the Mysterious Wife, 4 vols. 12mo. 1l. Lane.

A Plain Story, 4 vols. 12mo. 1l. Lane.

A New Edition, with a beautiful Vignette, of the Father and Daughter, a Tale, in Prose, by Mrs. Opie, 12mo. 4s. 6d. boards. Longman and Rees.

Concealment; or, the Cascade of Llantwarryhor, a Tale, 2 vols. 12mo. 8s. sewed. Lane.

The Dream; or Noble Cambrians, by Robert Evans, A. M. 2 vols. 12mo. 8s. sewed. Lane.

POLITICAL.

Considerations on the Momentous Subjects of Peace and War, and Negociation, in Answer to the Pretensions of France, by Mr. P. Pratt, 2s. Hatchard.

POLI-

POLITICAL ECONOMY.

The Corn-trade investigated, and the System of Fluctuation exposed; with a Proposition to remedy the alarming, fluctuating, Prices; and an Investigation of the Import and Export Laws; with some Remarks on the Landed Interest and Agriculture of this Country; clearly justifying the Farmers, vindicating the Dealers, and affixing the Stigma on the proper Objects, by Buxton Lawn, a new Edition, with large Additions, 3s. sewed. West and Hughes.

POETRY.

The Poetical Works of John Milton, with the principal Notes of various Commentators; to which are added Illustrations; with some Account of the Life of Milton, by the Rev. Henry John Todd, M. A. 6 vols. medium 8vo. 2l. 14s. boards; royal paper, 4l. 16s. boards. Rivingtons.

The Myrtle and Vine; or, Complete Vocal Library; containing a judicious Collection of the most popular Songs, interspersed with Originals; with an Essay on Singing and Song-writing; to which is added, Biographical Anecdotes of the most celebrated Song-writers, by C. H. Wilson, Esq. with many Copper-plates (Portraits), 4 vols. 12mo. 15s. West and Hughes.

The Free-school, a Poem, second Edition; to which is added, an Elegy on the Death of Edmund Jenney, Esq. and of Philip Bowes Broke, Esq. the former of whom died on the 22d of August, 1801, and the latter, suddenly, on the Day following, 1s. Robinsons.

A Translation of the Eighth Satire of Boileau on Man, written in the Year 1667. Phillips.

Poems, chiefly written in Retirement: the Fairy of the Lake, a Dramatic Romance; Effusions of Relative and Social Feelings; and Specimens of the Hope of Albion; or, Edwin and Northumbria, an Epic Poem, by John Thelwall; with Memoirs of the Life of the Author; and Notes and Illustrations of Runic Mythology, 7s. boards. Hurst.

Poems, by John Penn, Esq. containing several hitherto unpublished; those formerly published being revised and corrected, and the whole embellished with Plates, 2 vols. large 8vo. 1l. 5s. boards. Hatchard.

TRAVELS.

A Tour through Germany, particularly along the Banks of the Rhine, Mayne, &c. and that Part usually termed the Garden of Germany; to which is added, a Vocabulary of Familiar Phrases, &c. in German and English, for the Use of Travellers, by the Rev. Dr. Render, a Native of Germany, 2 vols. 8vo. 16s. boards. Longman and Rees.

A Tour from Downing to Ashton Moor, by Thomas Pennant, Esq. royal 4to with 40 plates, 1l 11s. 6d. bds. West and Hughes.

A Tour through the whole Island of Great Britain, with useful Observations for the Use of those who are desirous of travelling over England and Scotland, by the Rev. C. Cruttwell, 6 vols. 8vo. 2l. 8s. boards. Robinsons.

TOPOGRAPHY.

Views in Egypt, accompanied with a Descriptive History of the Antiquities, and of the Present Manners and Customs, of the Natives of that interesting Country; No. I to be completed in 10 Numbers, at one Guinea each. Bowyer.

A Picture of Petersburgh, from the German of Henry Storch, with plates, large 8vo. 14s. boards. Longman and Rees.

THEOLOGY.

The True Churchman ascertained; or, an Apology for those of the regular Clergy of the Establishment, who are sometimes called Evangelical Ministers; occasioned by several modern Publications, by John Overton, A. B. 8s. boards. Rivingtons.

The Books of the Apocrypha, with Critical and Historical Observations; and also Introductory Discourses explaining the Distinction between Canonical and Apocryphical Writings, ascertaining the Time when the latter were introduced into the Service of the Church, and illustrating the intimate Connection between the Old and New Testament; with a Sketch of the History of the Jews from the Cessation of Prophecy to the final Dissolution of their State, by Charles Wilson, D. D. large 8vo. 10s. 6d. boards. Cadell and Davies.

An Appeal to the Public Impartiality; or, the Manner in which the Dispute concerning "the important Question at Issue, &c." has been conducted, by Thomas T. Biddulph, M. A. 6d. Rivingtons.

A Sermon on the Sin of Adultery, preached at Weymouth, August 30, 1801, by the Rev. M. H. Luscombe, A. B. 1s. Rivingtons.

A Dialogue between a Minister of the Church and his Parishioner concerning the Christian's Liberty of Choosing his Teacher, 4d. Rivingtons.

A Plain and Practical Exposition of the Commandments; with an Introduction adapted to general Use, by the Rev. S. Glasse, D.D. 12mo. 3s. 6d. boards. Rivingtons.

An Essay on the unreasonableness of Scepticism, by the Rev. J. Hare, A. M. 12mo. 6s. boards. Rivingtons.

The Backslider; or, an Enquiry into the Nature, Symptoms, and Effects of Religious Declension; with the Means of Recovery, by A Fuller, 1s. Button.

A Scriptural Representation of the Abolition of the Fourth Command, so far as it related to the Observance of a particular Day; and a Vindication of their Conduct, who observe the First Day as the Sabbath, by T. Edmonds, 6d. Button.

Letters addressed to the Rev. John Graham, in Answer to his Defence of Scripture Doctrines as understood by the Church of England, and

and in Vindication of a Narrative of the Proceedings of a Society of Baptists in York in relinquishing Popular Systems of Religion, &c. by David Laton, 3s. Johnson.

The Amen to Social Prayer illustrated, a Sermon preached at Mr. Button's Meeting-house, by Abraham Booth, 1s. Button.

A Guide to Domestic Happiness, 5th Edition, greatly enlarged, 5s boards. Button.

The Refuge, by the Author of the Guide to Domestic Happiness, 4th Edition, with Additions, 5s. boards. Button.

A Sermon, preached at Norwich, Aug. 30, 1801, for the Benefit of the Norfolk and Norwich Hospital, by Pendlebury Houghton, 1s. Johnson.

An Appeal to the Society of Friends on the Primitive Simplicity of their Christian Principles and Church-discipline, and on some recent Proceedings in the said Society, Part I. 1s. Johnson.

By C. Geisweiler, Parliament-street.

Plantæ Rariores Hungariæ, col. fol. Vindob, 1801, Fas. I.—IV. 14l. 8s.

Wendland Plantæ Rariores que in Horto regio Herrenhusano coluntur, fol. col. Fas I. —IV. 3l. 3s. Hannoveræ, 1801.

Hoffmann Descriptio et Adumbratio Plantarum quæ Lichenes dicuntur, col. XII. Fas, Lipsiæ, 1789—1801, each Fas, 17s. 6d.

Histoire Naturelle des Oiseau Sauvages et Prive de la Franconie, col. folio, Nos. I. & II. 3l. 18s.

Meninsky Lexicon Arabico grersico Turcicum, 3 toms. fol. 15l. 15s. sheets.

Lucreti cari de rerum Natura Libri Sex. ed. Eichstaedt, 1801, tom. 1, 16s. sheets, com.

Diodori Siculi Bibliotheca Historica, ed Eichstaedt, 1800, tom 1, 16s.

C. Taciti Opera ed Oberlinus, 1801, tom. 1, 16s. sewed.

Quintilian de Institutione Oratoria, ed. Spalding, 15s. sewed.

Hermann de Emendanda Ratione Græcæ, accedunt Herodiani aliorumque Libelli, nunc primum Editi, 1801, 12s. 6d. sewed.

Schnurrer Dissertationes Philologico Criticæ, 8s. 6d. sewed.

Schleusner Novum Lexicon Græco Latinum in Novum Testamentum, tom. 1, 1801, 2l. 3s. sewed.

Paulus Philologisch, Kritischer, und Historischer Commentar über das neue Testament, tom. 2, 1801, 16s. sewed.

G. Abulpharagii sive Bar-hebræ Chronicon Syriacum ed Kirsch, 2 toms. 4°. 3l. 5s. sewed.

Cormon Dictionnaire Espagnol Français, et Français Espagnol, 1800, 2 toms.

Martens Recueil de Principaux Traites de Puissance de l'Europe, tom 7, et dernier Sup. Continuation jusqu'à la Paix de Luneville, 1801, 13s. sheets.

Martens Essai concernant les Armateurs, les prises, et sur tout les reprises, 8s. 6d. f. p. sewed.

French Books imported by Earle and Hemet, Albemarle-street.

Œuvres d'Homère, par Gin, 4 toms. 4°. proof plates.

Idylles de Théocrite, 2 toms. 4°. proof plates.

Œuvres de Xenophon, 2 vols. 4°. large paper.

Œuvres de Montesquieu, 5 toms. 4°. plates.

Le Sacre de Louis XV. imperial folio, primitive copy.

760 Sorts of Plays.

A large Collection of Novels.

Encyclopédie Methodique, 238 vols.

New French Books just imported by J. Deboffe, Gerrard-street, Soho.

Voyage Pittoresque en Syrie, Phénicie, et Basse Egypte, 19th livraison, proofs 2l. 12s. 6d. not proofs, 1l. 15s. each liv.

Histoire Naturelle des Colibris et Oiseaux Mouchés, coloured pltes, gilt lettering, 9th livraison, 1l. 15s.

Ditto, in 4to. 18s.

Histoire Naturelle des Oiseaux d'Afrique, par Vaillant, 15th liv. double plates coloured and uncoloured, 1l. 16s.

Ditto, in 4to. 18s.

Histoire Naturelle d'une Partie d'Oiseaux Nouveaux et Rares d'Amérique et des Indes, par Vaillant, double plates, coloured and uncoloured, 1l. 16s.

Ditto, in 4to, 18s.

Histoire des Chênes d'Amérique Septentrionale, par Michaux, folio, 4l. 4s.

Ditto, common paper, 2l. 2s.

Histoire Naturelle des Plantes Grasses, par Redouté, 12th livraison, folio, coloured plates, 2l. 12s. 6d.

Ditto, in 4to. 14s.

Description des Plantes Nouvelles, et peu Connues du Jardin de M. Cels, par Ventenat, folio, 4th liv. 1l. 11s. 6d.

Ditto, in 4to. 15s.

Plans, Coupes, et Elévations des plus Belles Maisons et des Hotels construits à Paris et dans les Environ, folio, plates, 4th and 5th liv. 10s.

Cabinet d'Histoire Naturelle de Seba, vol. 4, large folio.

Atlas Topographique des Environs de Paris, 16 sheets, and explanatory volume, 2l. 12s. 6d.

Galerie Antique des Chefs d'Œuvre d'Architecture, &c. 7th liv. 7s.

Traité des Arbres et Arbrestes, par Duhamel, 3d liv. large folio, fine paper, coloured plates, 1l. 16s.

Ditto, small paper, 1l. 1s.

Ditto, common paper, 12s.

Moniteur; ou, Gazette Nationale; for the first 6 Month of 1801 (complete sets of this work may be had from its commencement).

Bailey's German and English Dictionary, a new and improved Edition, 2 vols. 8vo. fine paper, 1l. 4s. in boards.

Carte de France, d'apres la Nouvelle Division en 103 Départements, 3s. 6d.

Traité

Traité de Mécanique Elemetaire, à l'Usage des Elêves de l'Ecole Polytechnique, par Prony, 8vo. 9s.

Recueil des Portraits des Miniſtres et Deputés au Congrès de Raſtadt pendant 1797 à 1799, the firſt 3 Numbers, 4to. 18s.

Rudimens de l'Hiſtoire; ou, Idée Générale et Précife des Peuples les plus célèbres tant Anciens que Modernes, par Demairon, 4 vols. 14s.

Les Jeandinaves, Poeme, trad. du Sévco-Gothique, ſuivi d'Obſervations ſur les Mœurs et la Réligion des Anciens Peuples de l'Ecrope Barbares, par Montbrun, 2 vols. 8vo. 12s.

Silvine Fille ſéduite au Général Blainville, ſon Séducteur, 3s.

Œuvres Philoſophiques de St. Lambert, 5 vols. 8vo. 1l. 1:s.

Tableau de l'Agriculture Soſcane, par Simonde, 6s.

Tableau Hiſtorique, Topographique, et Moral des Peuples des 4 Parties du Monde, par Sané, 2 vols. 14s.

Le Temps paſſé; ou, les Malheurs de Madame de M**, Emigrée, par Madame Mallarme, 2 vols. 6s.

Traité de l'Inoculation vaccine, 8vo. plates, 6s.

Traité de l'Orthographe Françoiſe, en Forme de Dictionnaire, par Reſtaut, nouvelle Edit. Augmentée, 2 vols. 18s.

Les Tombeax; ou, l'Influence des Inſtitutions Funébres ſur les Mœurs, par Gerard, 3s. 6d.

Table Analytique et Raiſonnée des Matures, continues dans les 70 volumes des Œuvres de Voltaire, par Chantreau, 2 vols. 16s.

Ditto, large paper, 1l. 4s.

Voyage dans la Haute Penſylvanie, et dans l'Etat de New York, par Crevecœur, 3 vols. 8vo. plates, 1l. 4s.

Voyage Pittoreſque en Suiſſe et en Italie, par Cambray, 2 vols. 12s.

To be had alſo of J. Deboffe.

Propoſals of all the ſumptuous Editions now printing by Didot l'Aîné, at Paris, viz. —Raime, 3 vols. folio (the firſt volume daily expected); Voyage dans la Haute et Baſſe Egypte, pendant l'Expédition du Général Bonaparte, 2 vols. folio, to be publiſhed about February next; Œuvres de Corneille, &c.

Imported by L'homme, Bond-ſtreet.

Fêtes et Courtiſannes de la Grece, 4 vols. 8vo. boards, 1l. 12s.

REVIEW OF NEW MUSICAL PUBLICATIONS.

Trois Grandes Sonatas pour le Piano-forte; compoſées et dediés à la Baronne de Kloeſt, née Jacobi, par J. B. Cramer. 8s. *Clementi and Co.*

MR. CRAMER has exercifed all his uſual addreſs in the preſent work, which abounds with ſtriking and maſterly paſſages, and every where evinces the real and great muſician. The modulations are in general highly artificial, without being forced; the combinations and reſolutions of the harmony are ingenious and juſt, and the rapid paſſages are conceived with much brilliancy of imagination.

The favourite Air of "Shepherds, I have loſt my Love;" adapted, with Variations, and a Violin accompamment (Obligato), by Joſeph Diettenhofer. 2s. *Riley.*

Mr. Diettenhofer has applied to this charming air ſix excellent variations, ſome of which poſſeſs that ſtyle and execution, which cannot fail to improve the practitioner. We wiſh, however, that Mr. Diettenhofer had not ſo rigidly adhered to the original baſs, as to preſerve the unprepared ſeventh in the ſixth bar of the theme. His judgment muſt have pointed out to him the falſity of the preſent conſtruction, and his acknowledged ſcience would have ſanctioned the liberty of an alteration.

"The Manly Heart," a Duett of Mozart's; varied for the Piano-forte, by A. Betts. 1s. *Rolfe.*

The variations and digreſſive matter thrown into this production by Mr. Betts do much credit to his taſte and imagination; but we cannot make this obſervation in his favour, without, at the ſame time, recommending to him a higher employment of his talents than that of arranging the works of other maſters. The compoſer who poſſeſſes the powers of originality, ſhould ſupport his own pretenſions, and leave the taſk of varying, arranging, and adapting, to inferior abilities.

A Second and Third Solo for a German-flute, with an Accompaniment for a Piano-forte; compoſed, and dedicated to John Jackſon, Eſq. by Gaetano Brandi. 2s. *Goulding, Phipps, and D'Almaine.*

Theſe ſolos, which are publiſhed ſeparately, and are to be ſucceeded by others monthly, are worthy companions of the firſt, the general excellencies of which we pointed out in a former Number of our Magazine.

Magazine. The melodies, for the most part, display considerable taste and fancy, and the passages are so arranged as to evince a thorough knowledge in the composer of the construction, genius, and powers of the instrument for which he writes.

Number I. of The Caledonian Museum; or, the Beauties of Scottish Harmony, intended to form a select Collection of the most esteemed Songs for the Piano-forte, Violin, and German-flute. Longman.

The plan of the *Caledonian Museum* is to collect, in twelve numbers, forming two volumes, octavo, all those Scottish melodies which have been so long sanctioned by their popularity, and which still continue favourites of the public. We find in this number a promising earnest of the goodness of the contents and execution of the future parts of this publication, and do not doubt but it will operate as a recommendation to the work.

Six Rondos from the Works of Pleyel, adapted for the Pedal-harp, by J. F. Bohlius. 1s. each. Riley.

These rondos are published separately; but being all from the same author, and similar in their style and tendency, we have classed them under one general head. Mr. Bohlius has selected and adapted the several pieces with that taste and judgment which cannot fail to recommend the undertaking to the lovers of good harp-music. Indeed each of the rondos is so well adapted for the piano forte, as well as the harp, that we would recommend the publisher to announce the future impressions for *both* those instruments.

A Sonata for the Piano-forte, with an Accompaniment for the Violin; in which is introduced, as an Adagio, Handel's favourite Song, "Lord, remember David;" composed, and dedicated to Mrs. Gregson, by F. Yaniewicz. 3s. 6d. Clementi & Co.

The prominent character of this sonata is that of an elegantly-conceived and regularly-constructed composition. The introduction of "Lord, remember David;" or, "*Rendi'l sereno al Ciglio*;" affords an admirable relief to the previous and succeeding movements, and gives an air of novelty to the whole, which adds much to its general attraction. The figure, occasionally added for the direction of the fingers, where the *time* fingering would be rather doubtful, is highly judicious, and affords so much assistance to the practitioner, that we hope to see the plan more generally adopted.

"Fair Arabella," a favourite Song, as sung by Mr. Dignum at Vauxhall-gardens; composed by W. P. R. Cope. 1s. Clementi and Co.

Mr. Cope in this little ballad has displayed much of that ingenuity and taste for which we have so repeatedly given him credit in our review of his former vocal compositions. The melody is smooth, graceful, and expressive; and the bass and modulation are easy and natural. We must, however, notice that in the transition of the harmony from the last bar but one to the last bar of the second page, we meet with an error of the engraver, which in the production of a less-informed musician we should have feared had been sanctioned by the manuscript.

Journal de Music pour les Dames; or, Elegant Selections; comprising the most favourite Compositions of Hadyn, Mozart, Pleyel, &c. arranged for the Piano-forte and Harp, in 2 vols. folio, vol. 2. 10s. 6d. Rolfe.

Of the merits of the first volume of this work we spoke in our last Number: the present number possesses an equal claim to our approbation, and completes one of the best-chosen collections of vocal and piano-forte music that the public have been furnished with for some years.

"The Maid of the Hay-stack," written on the recent Death of that unfortunate and lamented Female; composed by Theodore Smith. 1s. Goulding, Phipps, and D'Almaine.

Mr. Theodore Smith, who long since obtained so much reputation from his familiar piano-forte duetts, will lose nothing of his good name from the present composition. The melody, though not remarkably novel, is every where characteristic and impressive, and cannot fail to convey the pathos of this interesting tale to every feeling bosom.

Three Pieces, consisting of two Rondos and an Andante for the Piano-forte; composed by W. A. Mozart, 4s. Longman.

These pieces, though they do not rank amongst the greatest of Mozart's instrumental compositions, are of that pleasing and familiar construction, which must render them both desirable and useful to all young piano-forte practitioners.

ERRATUM.—In our Critique last month of Eberlin's Fugues and Voluntaries, for "The subjects of the *figures* are in general truly original," read "The subjects of the *fugues* are in general truly original."

VARI-

VARIETIES, LITERARY AND PHILOSOPHICAL.

Including Notices of Works in Hand, Domestic and Foreign.

*** *Authentic Communications for this Article will always be thankfully received.*

THE Booksellers of London have resolved to publish an uniform edition of such works as may be deemed *British Classics*. The work will extend to forty-five volumes, and be printed in a pocket size.

Miss AIKIN will publish in a few days a small volume of *Poetry for Children*; consisting of such pieces, partly original and partly selected, as may properly be committed to memory at an early age.

Dr. BEDDOES has deferred the publication of his Essays on Health till *the first day of December*, instead of the first of November, as was at first proposed.

Mr. HOLCROFT now resides at Paris, and there is some reason to hope that in the course of the ensuing winter he will favour the public with an account of his Travels in Germany and France. An account of the latter country, from so acute and enlightened a writer, could not fail to be very interesting to all Europe.

Miss HAY's large work of Female Biography will be printed this winter and be published early in the spring. It will include the lives of distinguished women of all ages and countries.

The Rev. J. BILDLAKE, Master of the Grammar-School at Plymouth, has in the press an Elementary Book of Geography, which promises to be *really* adapted to the practical business of education. All the existing works which profess to teach Geography, are either *too small*, and filled with nothing but proper names and technical phrases; or they are *too large*, and contain much extraneous, useless and obsolete matter. Mr. Bildlake's work will be divided into two parts; the one didactic, containing the divisions of the earth and the rationale of its motions; and the other, entertaining, to consist of popular accounts of the manners and customs of nations, decorated with nearly forty copper-plates.

Mr. BLAIR is collecting materials for an Historical Account of all the Hospitals, Infirmaries, Dispensaries, and Medical Societies in the Metropolis. Such a work cannot fail of being highly interesting to the public in general, as well as to the medical world in particular.

Mr. MONTEFIORE, a Notary-public of London, has in the press a quarto volume of Commercial and Notarial Precedents, which cannot fail to be of great use to merchants, and all persons connected with shipping and commerce in Great Britain and the colonies.

The new quarto edition of the great English Cyclopædia, by Dr. REES and assistants, will be commenced immediately after Christmas.

A Translation of GUITON MORVEAU's Treatise on the means of destroying Contagion, &c. has been undertaken by Dr. HALL, and will speedily be published.

Dr. PRIESTLEY writes from America in good health and spirits, describes in glowing terms the rapid state of improvement, and the wonderful increase in the population of that country, and leads his numerous friends in Great Britain to hope, that on the return of peace he may be induced to pay a short visit to his native country.

Cordage manufactured from the long beard which grows on the shells of cocoanuts, is found superior in every desirable point to that produced from hemp. The materials are collected in the Laccadive Islands, where it is produced in immense quantity, and some of the largest-sized cables have been made and tried on board the ships composing Admiral BLANKET's squadron. They answer perfectly well, and from their elastic nature are deemed more serviceable in a high swelling tide than those formed of the best hemp.

The object of the new voyage of discovery, (the Investigator, of 22 guns, Lieut. FLINDERS, which lately sailed from the Nore) is to examine the whole of the coast of New Holland, and to discover what large bays, especially rivers, are to be found there. Lieut. Flinders is accompanied by men of science; WESTALL, a brother of the celebrated artist, goes out as the draftsman.

An English Dramatic Library, by the Editor of the German Erato will soon make its appearance at Hamburg, and commence with Addison's Tragedy of Cato.

Mr. POPPLETON, an Englishman, has published a *Guide Pratique*, which is highly spoken of in the German papers.

HAYLEY's Life of Milton is republished, in English, *octavo*, at Strasburg:—A flattering proof of the extension of the English language upon the continent.

MONTAGUE's

MONTAGUE's Letters, GAY's and MOORE's Fables, STERNE's Journey and the Vicar of Wakefield, are the only English productions that have yet appeared from the Stereotype Press at Paris. They are in general of three qualities of paper, to suit every class of customers.

The Senate of Hamburgh is erecting a Monument, in the form of an obelisk, to the memory of their late Commercial Professor BUSCH.—His valuable library was disposed of in June last.—Its situation is on the banks of the Alster, on the ramparts.

Dr. CLARKE, in his "Survey of the Power and Opulence of Great Britain," gives, on respectable authorities, the total acres of land in the island at 73,178,627, of which 51,178,628 are in cultivation. Of this number, 2,837,000 have been cultivated since the revolution; of which, 2,804,000 have been taken into cultivation during the present reign, yet prices have advanced more during this reign than they have done for two centuries before. The Doctor supposes the average produce of an acre at three quarters of wheat; and a quarter he judges sufficient to supply one person with bread for one year.

One of the lionesses of the Botanical Garden at Paris whelped during the night between the 18th and 19th Brumaire (year 9) three young ones, alive and at the full time. This is the same lioness, which, having become pregnant, for the first time last year, hurt herself and miscarried on the 17th Messidor. On the day of her whelping she appeared languishing, and would not eat. She whelped her first young-one at ten o'clock at night, the second at eleven o'clock within a quarter, and the third at two o'clock in the morning. She uttered no cry, and was as gentle to her keeper as usual. These young lions, all three males, were at their birth about as big as adult cats, but they had a bigger head and their eyes were open; they crawled along the ground, and their cries were like the very loud mewings of a cat when exasperated. Their heads were void of mane and their whole bodies covered with a reddish hair, spotted with points and blackish bands; their tails were marked with black rings on a ground of tawny colour. These three young lions are well in health and grow stronger every day. The mother cherishes them with the greatest care. This is not the first time that lions have produced in Europe. An example of this is quoted in the *Ami de la Nature*, or *Choix d'Observations sur divers objects de la Nature et de l'Art*, which the author has taken from an English book, intitled *London in Miniature*, and printed in that city in 1755. "Entering the Tower of London, we were conducted to some iron-grated cells, in form of half-moons, inhabited by lionesses of different ages. The first shewn us was the Princess Dido, then in all the vigour of youth, about six years old, and handsome in every respect. The second was named Jenny; we were told she was about forty years old. This was the oldest lioness ever seen in the Tower, although for five hundred years this kind of animal has been kept there. She has been mother of nine young lions, all begotten by a lion named *Marco*, now dead. These nine young lions died in rearing, with the exception of *Nero*, who died about two years ago, having lived to be ten years old; and of *Nancy*, who lived double that age. It was not without extreme care that they could preserve these two last young lions, for no animals are more difficult to rear, on account of the convulsions which they are subject to at the period of dentition. They were kept for the first year in a warm chamber, and fed with milk. They were as gentle as sheep, but their natural ferocity was quickly developed with their growing strength."

They write from Milan, June 11, that General MIOLLIS has caused to be transported to Ferrara, in a public and honourable place, the bones of the immortal ARIOSTO, who was born in that city. The common opinion is that Ariosto was born at Reggio. But his family being allied to the Duke of Ferrara, and Duke Alphonso having invited him to his court, he built a house at Ferrara. This house indicated the simplicity of a philosopher. Being asked wherefore he was not more magnificently lodged, he who had built such superb palaces in his *Orlando Furioso*; he made answer "that *words were much more easily and sooner collected than stones.*" He died in the year 1535, at the age of 59 years.

For some years last past the public Library of the city of Hamburgh has made some important acquisitions. Besides the French works purchased for the sums that have been furnished by a subscription of many merchants; the cabinet of medals, attached to this library has been equally enriched by a pretty numerous series of coins of the city of Hamburg, which were in the possession of the heirs of M. AMSINK. The expence of this purchase has been likewise made by a Society of Merchants, by means of a voluntary subscription

scription. The burgomaster, CH. WIDOW, has greatly contributed to the enlargement of the library, especially while he was First Inspector of the Schools, in procuring for it many works of Natural History and of Medicine, in the sale of the library of a learned physician. It has been still further augmented with a complete collection of all the ancient physicians, by the liberality of an unknown person. In this department, few libraries will be better furnished than that of Hamburg; which induces a hope, that the treasures which it contains, will be soon put into order. As the apartments are too confined, the plan of the senator CORDES, is to join some contiguous buildings to it. During the little time that he has been charged with the functions of inspector, the library has already made several important acquisitions, such as the *Journal des Sçavans*, from its commencement, many large historical collections, and the best editions of the Greek classical authors. Pastor H. J. WILLERDING has induced the Ecclesiastical College of the church of St. Peter to grant it about sixty old manuscripts, and some first impressions, which were formerly preserved in that church. In the same library is preserved an excellent portrait of KLOPSTOCK, painted by ANTHONY HICKEL, a valuable artist, who died at Hamburg, and of which his brother, JOSEPH HICKEL, court-painter at Vienna, has made a present to the city in which that celebrated poet lived.

In the passage where MARIUS, the first bishop of Lausanne, makes mention, in the Annals of his own Time, of the pox (*variola*), there was then only one; and he observes that it particularly attacked horned cattle. It appears that it only attacked men in the following year, that is to say, in 571.* This shews that cows are susceptible of its attacks; it is singular enough that the same animal which first had this malady, should furnish to man the best preservative against the same malady. What appears still more surprising is, that from that remote epoch this malady has not been at all observed, or at least very seldom, upon cows.

* "A 570. Hoc anno morbus validus cum profluvio ventris et *variola* Italiam Galliamque valde afflixit. Et animalia bubala per ea loca maxime interierunt.—A. 571. Hoc anno infanda infirmitas et glandula, cujus nomen est pustula, in supra-scriptis regionibus innumerabilem populum devastavit."—Muller, in his History of Switzerland, compares with this another passage of Paul Warnefrid, where we read *de glandulis in modum nucis quas sequebatur febrium æstus*; and another of Anastasius, the librarian, who speaks *de percussione, scabierum, ut nemo posset mortuum suum interrogare*;—this, according to Muller, agrees with the small-pox, which in the first centuries, as well as the venereal malady, was more terrible and more deadly than in the sequel; among other reasons, because, at that time, they were unacquainted with the true methods of cure.

In a survey which has been lately made at Columbo, in the island of Ceylon, a species of palm has been discovered, called the *Palm Licualæ*, which produces very large leaves, and rivals in this respect the cocoa-tree itself. It is classed among the loftiest trees, and becomes still higher when bursting forth into blossom from its leafy summit. The sheaf which then envelopes the flower is very large, and when it bursts makes a loud report; after which it shoots forth branches on every side, to the very surprising height of thirty-six or forty feet.

We learn from a late statistical writer, that before the year 1770 there were not three books in the immense and overgrown Russian Empire upon medical subjects.

According to a list lately published by the Synod of Russia, there died, during the last year, in the thirty-two divisions of the Empire, 216 persons 100 years old; 153 between 101 and 110; 26 between 111 and 119; 9 aged 120; 1 aged 125; 2 aged 130, and 2550 above 90.

PIGNOTTI is well known to the readers of modern Italian poetry for fables, which borrow or reveal the most delicate graces of the language; and for metrical novels, and tales, which blazon or satirize the manners of polished society. His *La tomba di Shakespeare* has in Great Britain a patriotic claim to praise: the following extract will give some idea of its character. The author, after seeing in vision Apollo and the Muses, thus continues:—

Portati sulle piume della santa
Aura, che spira dal castalio fonte
Spiegavan l'ali i più sublimi cigni,
Che sul Tamigi un dì sciolsero il canto.
Venerabile in volto, e la canuta (Milton)
Chioma cinta d' alloro al Cielo ergea
I ciechi lumi, quei che sopra l' ali
Serafiche poggiò fino alle stelle,
E l' arbore vietata onde si colse
Dal primo genitor sì amaro frutto,
Coll' eroica cantò divina tromba.
Vedeasi accanto a lui della tebana
Lira l' erede, che spirar del Gange (Dryden)

Al Domator colla flessibil voce
Di Timoteo potè sì vari affetti:
E quei che il furto della chioma bionda (Pope)
Seppe cantare in sì soavi tempre.
Seguì colui che il sanguinoso scempio (Gray)
De' figli di Parnasso alto piangendo
Contro il Tiranno, del canuto vate
Di fulminante armò suono di morte
La profetica voce. Audace ingegno
Che della Gloria al faticoso monte
Due corsieri guidò fuoco-spiranti
Dalle fervide nari, il collo cinti
Della fiamma onde il folgor si disserra,
Che muovon strepitosi e da lontano
Romoreggianti passi. Appresso folta
Schiera di lieti spirti iva cantando
Inni di lode al cenere sacrato.

A work of very great importance to the lovers of painting has appeared at Bassano. *Storia Pittorica dell' Italia, dell' Abbate Luigi Lanzi*, 3 vols. 1795—1797. After the manner of Zannetti's *Pittura Veneziana* the author treats of each school separately; defines its peculiar character, and traces with punctuality its successive variations. The work is full of information, and very comprehensive; as not only painters of all kinds, but even engravers of eminence are introduced to notice. LANZI has long been known as a learned and industrious antiquary: his Essay on the Antient Language of Tuscany has been applauded by every philologer. His style is unaffectedly neat. Yet one desiderates, perhaps, that sagacity of discrimination, which never praises an imaginary merit, nor overlooks a latent blemish—that precision of judgment which constitutes the philosophical critic. This writer thus speaks of the cause of excellence in art. "*Il progresso in altre delle belle arti dipende sempre da certe massime adottate universalmente dal secolo, secondo le quali opera il professore e giudica il publico. A render communi ed a accreditare le migliori massime assai è conducente una storia generale che le suggelli. Così e gli artefici in operare, e gli altri in approbare o in dirigere, avranno principj non incerti, non controversi, non dedotti dal gusto di una o d'un altra scuola, ma certi e sicuri e fondati sull' esperienza costante di tanti luoghi, e di tanti secoli.*" Surely in attributing the progress of art to the maxims of the age (if by progress be meant progress toward perfection) this author errs. In the imitation of nature and in the selection of objects worthy to be imitated consists the whole duty of the artist: the rest is prejudice, is fashion, is opinion, transient, and fickle and convertible. The maxims of the age can never affect the fidelity of imitation; nor prevent forms of a finer growth, whether in men, or trees, or mountains, from being regarded with superior emotion. The number of excellent imitators will always bear, as it has always borne, a certain regular proportion to the whole number of imitators; so that whatever increases the demand for art, and thereby occasions a greater number of persons to devote themselves to the practice of it, must increase the chance for that higher order of excellence, which it is alone luxurious for the connoisseur to admire, and alone glorious for the artist to attain. O for the return of idolatry!

A new edition of MACCHIAVELLI's Works was printed in 1797, in six volumes, with the fictious date Philadelphia. It contains some hitherto unpublished reliques. 1. *Dell' ira e dei modi di curarla.* 2. *Descrizione della peste di* 1522. 3. *Istruzione a Raffaello Girolami.* 4. *Allocuzione fatta ad un Magistrato.* 5. Two dramatic trifles. 6. Two Latin wills, dated in 1511, and in 1522.

The following epitaph has been proposed for the late Pope Pius VI.

Perdita sub Sextis semper, testante* poeta,
Hoc quoque sub Sexto perdita Roma fuit.
Sed ne crede Pii culpa periisse, viator!
Perdidit heu Romam temporis impietas.

Opere in Verso e in Prosa, di G. S. DE COUREIL, 2 *vols. Pisa.* 1798 *e* 1799. This dashing writer has startled by his criticisms the acquiescent taste of the Italian journalists. "After Petrarch (he says) our poetry made no progress for two centuries.—Caro has been too much praised for his enervate prosaic unfaithful version of the Æneid.—Frugoni, except a few Anacreontics, has produced nothing but what is mediocre, or worse than mediocre.—Half Horace's Odes are only worthy of a schoolboy.—It is become a fashion to censure the tragedies of Alfieri; but Pepoli, who set the fashion, is a still feebler tragedian.—*La invenzione dell' Ariosto, che spesso è puerile affatto.—Bisogna, che un' opera infetta dalla monotonia, come per esempio i poemi d' Ossian.*—And how does this stingy critic write verses? Here is an Ode to Sleep: it is executed with taste.

Lascia le tacite
Fresche tue grotte,
Degli egri cori
Giocondo balsamo,
O sonno, O figlio
Dell' atra notte:

* Sannazarius made an epigram on Pope Alexander VI. which contained the observation:

Semper sub Sextis perdita Roma fuit.

E a queste

E a queste foglie
Rivolgi il piede,
Ove ti invoca
La mia Licoride,
E qualche tregua
Al duol ti chiede.

Vengan le immagini
Teco ridenti,
Venga la calma
D' oblio, che tempera
Gli acuti spasimi
Dei cur dolenti.

Teco la rosea
Salute antica
Venga; e s'è d'uopo,
Qualch ' ora involami,
E all' egra donala
Mia dolce amica.

There are at present in Paris 455 booksellers, 340 printers, 138 bookbinders, 41 stitchers of pamphlets, 327 engravers, 85 copper plate printers, 49 printsellers, and 71 old-book-shops; 240 sellers of lemonade, 200 keepers; of cook's shops, 630 wine-merchants, 146 perfumers, 154 lottery office-keepers; and 975 actors, actresses, singers, dancers, &c.

A recent census of the United States in North America makes their population amount to about 6,000,000; merchant shipping, above 100,000 tons; the value of their yearly exports, above 70,000,000 of dollars; and their public-revenue, 15,000,000 of dollars.

M. Castillo, Secretary to the Embassy of Spain, an enlightened friend of the sciences; and M. Zea, a naturalist, pensioned by his Catholic Majesty; have lately introduced the vaccine-inoculation at Madrid. The officers and ministers of state have been anxious to set the example, by submitting their children to this new kind of inoculation. The celebrated M. Alonzo, to whom natural history owes so much, accelerates the progress of this discovery, by assisting the physicians with all his means, and the credit which he derives from his place of Minister of Grace and Justice. M. Costa, a distinguished Professor of the Royal College of San Carlos, has been appointed to direct the operations; and M. Alonzo is to communicate the results to the learned societies of Paris.

The Theological Class on the Teylerian-foundation, at Harlem, proposes, for the subject of a prize, to be adjudged April 8, 1801—*the Inconveniences of a National Religion*; that is to say, *of a Form of Worship privileged and paid by the State*.—The foundation admits memoirs in Latin, Dutch, French, and English. The competition will be closed on the first of December, 1801. In the development of the proofs of the subject proposed, the class invites the candidates to join a plan of organization for different religious societies, founded on the grand principle of equality of rights.

The *Teylerian Society* has caused to be constructed, at its own expence, under the direction of D. Vanmarum, *a Digester of Papin*, in a complete style, for the purpose of making soups, to be distributed gratuitously to the poor. Sixty-two pounds of ox-bone boiled and boiled over again a second time, for two hours together, in this cauldron, have produced sixteen pounds of a very nourishing jelly.

A correspondent of the *Decade Philosophique* has lately communicated to the editors, a discovery which he made by accident, of a method of preserving mushrooms dry, without deforming them. Botanists, he observes, know how to collect and preserve plants, but he has never yet heard of their being able to preserve mushrooms. The author lives near the sea-shore, in a country, the soil of which is sandy, and where downs are formed which frequently shift their place. In traversing on foot one of these downs, he met with mushrooms buried under the sand, and which preserved their form. He made a collection of them, and found that they suffered no alteration afterwards; indeed they served him for an hygrometer; but if they soften in moist weather, they recover their hardness in dry weather; and, every principle of vegetation being destroyed, their form does not alter either by wrinkles or by rottenness. In imitating the process of nature, and drying these mushrooms in a stove of sand, moderately heated, as they dry flowers the shape and natural colour of which are intended to be preserved, it will be possible to form a collection of mushrooms. The only thing required will be to have sand very pure, deprived, by repeated washings, of all its terrene particles, to inclose the mushroom in it; dry it in the oven after the baking of bread, and afterwards secure it from dust and insects. Citizen de Cette, the discoverer, is of opinion, that the presence of a part of muriat of soda, contained in the salts on the sea-shore, is not necessary to the conservation of mushrooms; on the contrary, it may injure them, as it favours humidity, and humidity favours a vegetation, which requires to be checked. The sands under which Citizen Cette found

found the well-preserved mushrooms, were heaped together under tamarisk-trees, which sheltered them from rains and dews; and the sands with which he made his experiments no longer contained any saline parts, of which they had, doubtless, been deprived by the effect of the rains anterior to their change of place.

The manufacture at Passy, by Citizen Bawens, for speedily bleaching cotton-cloth, in which the process invented by Citizen Chaptal is employed, is the first in France which has been carried on on a large scale. The success has surpassed expectation; and the proprietors of that establishment are proceeding to multiply them on many points of the Republic, and especially in Belgium, where the manufacture of linen-cloth is considerable. The bleaching of these last is much easier, and the process has been extremely simplified by the intelligence of Citizen Bourlier, one of the manufacturers; two or three days suffice, at present, to give to the coarsest linen a degree of whiteness which the bleachers in general only obtain by long and expensive methods. The First Consul, accompanied by the Third Consul, and the Minister of Interior, went lately to visit this manufacture; he minutely inspected all the departments; traced the operation of combing, of spinning, and of weaving; and terminated his visit by examining the bleaching-machine, executed on the model of that of Citizen Chaptal. He saw wrought in this machine, by a single operation, [illegible]00 metres of cotton-cloth. Another very valuable experiment has been made, under the care of Citizen Chaptal, in the same manufacture, and its full success merits the greatest publicity: this is the ordinary washing of linen, proofs of which have been made, after many trials, on many hundred pairs of sheets, chosen among the dirtiest in the Hôtel Dieu at Paris. The uniform result of these experiments is, that it scarcely requires half of the ordinary expence; that two or three days are sufficient to terminate the operation; that the linen is neither altered by the liquor, nor rent, nor worn, as it only passes once through the hands, and that there is no necessity to beat it; and, lastly, that the alcaline liquor made use of, penetrating by the extreme heat of the apparatus, into the weft of the linen, all the foreign materials attached to it, and all infectious *miasma* introduced into it, are destroyed, which cannot be expected from ordinary lye, and which frequently becomes, especially in hospitals, the germ of dangerous maladies.

The Spanish nation, which has hitherto not kept pace with other cultivated nations in arts and sciences, begins now to emulate them very eagerly. The inoculation of the cow-pox is not only known in Spain, but already practised by several physicians with the greatest success, amongst which Dr. Francisco Peguillem particularly deserves to be mentioned, who procured himself the cow-pox matter from Paris, with which he has successfully begun to inoculate since December, 1800.—The Royal Economical Society has published, in the sixth volume of their *Memorias*, a translation of the Essays of Count Rumford, which are adapted for the use of Spain, by D. Domingo Agueira y Nagra, and separately sold in single numbers. The orders of the King, concerning the new weights and measures, are known from the newspapers, and in the new *Almanac Mercantile* (1801), we find, for the first time, a comparison between the French and Spanish measures, and likewise the French Almanac.—The sciences particularly cultivated in Spain, are natural philosophy, medicine, chemistry, and botany; for which a very good journal, the *Annales de Ciencias Naturales*, is established and appears every month. In the 6th, 7th, and 8th Numbers, we find the following memoirs: Botanical Treatises, by Broussonet; several Letters on Mineralogy, by Humboldt, directed to the Saxon Ambassador, Baron Forell, and to D. Joseph Clavijo, together with a Sketch of a Mineralogical History of Spain and its Colonies; Astronomical Observations from Madrid, Cadiz, &c. a Memoir on the Spanish Naturalists, and an Advertisement of the *Plantar. Rarior. Hungariæ Decad.* Another very useful journal is the *Semanerio de Agricultura y Artes*, begun under the protection of the Prince of Peace (*Principe de la Paz*), in which all inventions and discoveries made in foreign countries are collected and adapted for Spain. Thus we find in the 8th volume very good extracts on all Theories on Manuring; on the Method of Watering; on the Remedies for Preventing the Plague, &c. The new Chemical System begins to be likewise adopted, and several publications have appeared on this subject. Military Sciences are by no means neglected: the Campaigns of Bonaparte, and other Military Works are much

much in vogue. Shakespeare's works are also translated by Don PEDRO MONTENGON, who is at present publishing a Translation of Ossian in Verse: *El Fingal, y el Temora, T. 1 in 4. for Escribano.* The *Teatro Nuevo Espanol*, in three volumes, contains the best pieces of MOLIERE, DESTOUCHES, &c. and also of KOTZEBUE, who is here likewise severely criticised. There exist also Translations of *Arnauld's Delassements, Saint Pierre's Etudes*, and of *Quintilianus*; and a second edition of Blair's Lectures has been lately published.

NEW PATENTS LATELY ENROLLED.

MR. JAMES MANLEY, *of Great Budworth, in Cheshire, for a* NEW METHOD *of* MANUFACTURING SALT.

THE PATENTEE, in his specification, previous to the description of his several improvements, gives a short account of the method of manufacturing salt from brine, which is actually employed in Cheshire, and probably has continued the same, without material alterations, for a long course of years. It appears that every kind of brine contains in solution several foreign matters (besides the common salt, which is its largest saline ingredient), which are all to be considered as *impurities*, and, by mixing with the salt, impair its goodness. Several of these impurities are separable by heating the brine to a moderate degree, and these are the earths and the iron, which are held in solution by the carbonic acid. The whole process of boiling down the brine is performed usually in a single iron-pan, of large dimensions, but shallow, and heated by furnaces beneath it. The consequence of using a *single* pan is, that the impurities above mentioned fall down to the bottom of the pan, and foul the brine as soon as it is heated, and therefore they require to be raked out before the salt begins to separate by the continuance of the evaporation. This *raking-out* is represented as a troublesome process, and, moreover, very imperfect, since it is impossible entirely to separate the impurities by this method.

The first, and what appears to us the most material, of the three articles of improvement which are included in the specification, is the addition of another pan adjoining to the principal evaporating pan, and heated merely by an extension of the flues from the furnaces beneath the latter, which additional pan the Patentee denominates a *Preparing pan.* This pan is to hold as much brine as is generally used for one charge of the evaporating pan, and may be made of iron, or any other proper material. The dimensions are not specified, and the exact form is left to the experience of the manufacturer. It is the peculiar advantage of this preparing pan, that, whilst the common process is going on in the evaporating pan, the brine (which is drawn fresh and cold into the preparing-pan) is heated without any additional expence of fuel, to such a degree as to deposite the impurities separable by heat, and to be made clear, hot, and partly boiled down, before it goes into the evaporating-pan. This last, therefore, whilst it is finishing during one day the process of salting, is preparing, by its furnaces, the brine in the preparing-pan to be used the next day, and in a state much fitter for giving immediately a good salt, than if the brine were merely drawn up cold into a single evaporating pan, as in the usual method.

The great saving in the ingenious and simple means employed by the Patentee is certainly that of *fuel* (which is entirely coal in the Cheshire-works), and the consumption of which is so enormous as to form a very large share of the expences of the manufacture. The preparing-pan thus brings the brine to the same state for which, in the common process, a fire of several hours is requisite, without any additional expence of fuel, as it receives all its heat at second hand, from the flues of the fires of the evaporating-pan.

Among the lesser (though not unimportant) improvements mentioned by the Patentee are: An improvement in the quality of the manufactured articles, which is effected by causing many of the impurities to subside in the preparing-pan (out of which they are daily drained off through a waste-pipe), instead of mixing with the brine in the evaporating-pan, from which they can only be imperfectly removed by raking-out;—a saving of the time and trouble of raking out; and, by sending a purer brine into the salting pan, lessening the frequency of a necessary operation called *picking*, which is, to pick off from the bottom of the pan, from time to time, with an iron instrument, a thick sediment (a mixture of salt, selenite, and carbonate of lime), which gradually forms, and requires removal in this way every three or four weeks, though it increases the wear of the pans.

The second article in this specification is the use of alkalies added to the brine in certain quantities, in order to decompose the earthy-salts, and to render the salt purer. Any kind of fixed alkali is proposed by the Patentee, but no particular directions are given for their use by him, as both the time of adding them, and the quantity (he observes), must depend on the nature of the particular brine used, which differs much in different parts.

The third article is an ingenious contrivance for enabling the manufacturer to detain the fire under any pan, by using circuitous, instead of straight, flues. Several salt-makers have formed these circuitous or zig-zag flues, through which the flame of the furnaces has circulated very well till the brine began to boil; after which, the motion given to the pan by the violent ebullition, has always shaken and lifted up the pan, with all its contents, to a degree sufficient to raise it off the flue-walls, and thus to defeat the object of the circuitous-flues, by allowing the flame to pass straight on to the chimney through the space left by the heaving of the pan.

This is remedied by the Patentee, by fixing into the bottom of the pan long iron plates bent through their length at right angles, so as to form one flat surface to be laid on the pan, and there fixed by rivets, or any other mode, whilst the other part of the plate hangs down perpendicularly, and is received loosely into a groove in the bricks of the circuitous flue-walls. By this method, the lengthened course of the flame may still be preserved.

(We understand that this patent-right is disposed of to some salt-manufacturers at Northwich).

MR. LANT, *of Lincoln's Inn-square, London, for* GRADUATED MEASURING-GLASSES.

IT has been considered as a great improvement in the manual part of pharmacy, both for neatness and accuracy, to substitute, for the old pewter measures, glasses graduated from two or more ounces downwards to as small a quantity as is ever prescribed, except in the form of drops. Hence we now find no apothecary's shop unfurnished with these glasses, which are in constant and daily use. However, as no uniform standard of measurement has been resorted to, great inaccuracy in the graduation has crept into use, from the ignorance or carelessness of the makers. This the respectable Patentee, and inventor of the present corrected measures, had opportunity of ascertaining, when Warden of the Apothecaries Company, and it determined him to adopt the plan here given. "The weight of a gallon of distilled water is to be ascertained in troy-grains, whether of wine or beer measure, whereby, either by addition or division, the proper proportion of all the graduations requisite for any measure may be known in troy-grains, and parts of a grain, by having weights and scales adapted to the various purposes. To measures having a large surface, the surface is needful to be attended to, and the inaccuracy arising from thence is to be corrected by marks added to direct the eye to the same level as when they were first graduated. When made with glass, two surfaces being seen through glass containing transparent fluids, divisions are to be made corresponding with the upper and under surfaces if required. When lines are required for additional accuracy, the marks will serve as a guide whereby they may be described. When glass is not best adapted to the uses for which graduated measures may be wanted, they are to be made of other substances."

The Patentee, we find, has even attempted an accurate measure for dividing a portion of the wine-ounce into parts corresponding with what are considered as drops. He justly observes that drops are very unequal, the same liquid being used, when falling from unequal surfaces; and also vary from different liquids. This is certainly true; yet the latter circumstance is apparently of little consequence, since the practitioner, in ordering so many drops of any liquid, does not consider how much of the liquid *in weight* he wishes to give, but orders the *drop*, as a mode of division with which he is familiar, which is all that is wanted, could the equal size of the drop be always secured. We know not how the Patentee, in attempting to measure out from a very minute vessel so minute a quantity as a few drops (for, as he informs us, he has constructed measures from drops to pints, in vessels of respective sizes), has been able to make an accurate allowance for that portion which must always adhere to the sides of the vessel, and which, in such cases as these, must bear a considerable proportion to the whole: but, not having a full description of the whole apparatus, we cannot give any opinion with regard to the superiority, in this respect, to the usual method of measuring drops, corrected by the improvement which we believe has been attempted, of forming small phials for this purpose, the lips of which are ground exactly to the same dimensions in every respect.

The above measures, which will be distinguished by the name of Lane affixed to them, will be soon ready for sale at Mr. Blade's, Ludgate hill.

MONTHLY RETROSPECT OF THE FINE ARTS.

(*Communications and the Loan of all new Prints are requested.*)

The Birth-day Present to the Old Nurse. Bigg, del. Gaugain sculpt Published by Molteno, Pallmall. Price 1l. 1s.

Health and Sickness; the Companion Print to the above; the same Painter, Engraver, Publisher, and Price.

WE have had frequent occasion to notice Mr. Bigg's delineations, and very rarely without praise. They are almost invariably faithful and unsophisticated copies of nature. The praise to which his former productions are entitled may very fairly be extended to these two prints; their leading excellence is simplicity; though the sickly female figure in the last print, is very properly of a higher rank than those Mr. Bigg usually introduces; but, though pale, languid, and enervated, elegant and attractive. Both of the prints are neatly and carefully engraved, and are marked with the characteristic manner of the painter.

Mr. Molteno now possesses the plate of Hall's engraving from Sir Joshua Reynolds's very capital portrait of Mr. R. B. Sheridan, and has reduced the price from one guinea, at which it was originally published, to 15s.

The Prospects of Britannia, engraved from a Design by Thomas Martin. Published for Molteno, Palmall. Price in Colours, 2l. 2s.

During the time this plate was in Mr. Martin's possession, there were no impressions taken off in colours. The subject is allegorical, and represents Britannia arbitress of the world, and enjoying such blessings of peace and plenty, as we trust are in store for her at some future day; but like many other prophecies that have been gravely given out by Seers, who have flourished in this our day,—*we must wait for the period when they are to be fulfilled.*

Lieutenant General George Harris. Price 7l. 6s. Published for Jeffries, Clapham-road.

The portrait from which this is copied must be in the recollection of many readers; it was painted by Mr. Porter, and in the Royal Exhibition of last year. The picture was an *aggravated* likeness of a respectable-looking man, and rendered so fat, (in this representation) that it might have passed for Sir John Falstaff on his march to Coventry. In the print this is softened down, or melted down, which the reader pleases, and it is now a likeness of the original, and a tolerably good print.

Cleopatra on the Cydnus, going to meet Mark Antony.—The Trial of a Vestal Virgin, by carrying Water in a Sieve.—Drawn by Burney, engraved by Agar, and published by Ackermann, Strand. Price 5s. each, plain; 7s. each, coloured.

These are companion prints to *Agrippina*, and *Sophonisba*, which we have noticed in a former retrospect: the designs are airy and elegant, and the engravings neat and spirited.

The Birth of the Thames. Painted by Mrs. Cosway, and engraved by Mr. Tomkins, and published by Ackermann, Strand.

No. VII. of the Costume of China, by W. Alexander, No. 42, Newman-street, is published, as the preceding Numbers have been, for Messrs. G. and W. Miot, Pallmall.

This interesting work, from the manner in which it has been conducted, we ought to have noticed in a more particular manner than our room has yet allowed us. It is designed, engraved, and coloured in a style that does great honour to the taste and talents of the author; and has in no respect deviated from the original plan, but in some of the latter numbers we think rather improved upon it. Each number contains four coloured prints, and is sold at 10s. 6d. We shall take this opportunity of enumerating a few of the prints that have been published since the last retrospect of the work, and the subjects are of a nature that gives us a greater insight into the manners, customs, &c. of this singular people, than we can have from any thing hitherto published. In No. V. the first print is, "*A Soldier in Full Uniform.*" It is not easy to conceive a habit more clumsy, inconvenient, and inimical to the performance of military purposes, than that here exhibited; yet, from the gaudiness of the colour,

lour, and other circumstances, the writer informs us, that a battalion thus equipped, has at some distance, a splendid and even a military appearance.

II. A Group of Passengers, Watchmen, &c. Playing at Dice.

The Chinese are so much addicted to gaming, that they are seldom without a pack of cards or a set of dice in their pockets.

III. View of a Castle.

Is in a broad and good style.

IV. *A Sea Vessel under Sail.*

This will give some idea of Chinese naval tactics and ship-building. The main and foresails are of matting, strongly interwoven, and extended by pieces of bamboo, running horizontally across them. The mizen topsails are nankin.

Number VI, contains *a portrait of Chow Te Zhin.* He is attired in full court-dress, being a loose gown of silk or satin, and has a blue ball in his cap, to which is suspended a peacock's feather. The figure of an imaginary bird on his crest, denotes the wearer to be a Man of Letters, as the blazonry of a tyger would denote him to be military.

A Chinese Porter or Carrier.

The cart in which he deposits the goods he is to deliver has a sail, and when the wind is favourable, and the face of the country level, this is hoisted; and the exertions of the driver are thus lessened. When the wind is adverse, the sail is laid aside. Milton in his Paradise Lost, alludes to this practice.

———"On the barren plains
Of Sericana, where Chinese drive,
With sails and wind, their cany waggons light." Book 3, l. 437.

A Mandarin's Travelling-boat.

This is highly ornamented, and all the part occupied by the mandarin is enclosed by shutters.

The Habitation of a Mandarin.

The superior Chinese live in great privacy, their habitations are therefore generally surrounded by a wall, and their houses rarely exceed one story in heighth.

The first print in No. VII, is *a standard bearer.* His dress is nankin cotton, which is tied round the waist with the imperial and yellow girdle, and his legs are cross-quartered like those of Malvolio in the play. His hat is straw, neatly woven, and fastened under the chin.

A Sacrifice at the Temple.

The Chinese have no regular sabbath; their temples, constantly open, are visited by the supplicants on their commencing any important undertaking. Their idols are grotesque and frightful.

A Military Station.—A Fishing Boat.

The contrivance for raising their nets by *a lever*, the frame of which is composed of bamboo, which unite strength with flexibility, is good, and is made use of on almost every occasion. We have not room to add a more particular description, but on the whole recommend this work as worthy of particular attention.

The last number of Boydell's Shakespeare, will be published in a few weeks, and conclude a work of greater magnitude and importance, than any ever embarked in, in England, or any other country.

Westall has just finished a beautiful print from his admirable drawing of a storm in harvest; it is so exquisitely engraved, that without a very close inspection it cannot be distinguished from the original drawing.

The annual exhibition of the works of living artists in painting, drawing, and sculpture, was opened at Paris, on the 1st of September. The collection is less numerous than that of last year, in consequence of an universal determination to exclude every thing that did not possess striking merit. Three hundred painters have furnished three hundred drawings and paintings. The sculptors have supplied a much less proportion, though they have been employed in a number of works for government. There are few engravings, though the artists have given a number of plans for departments, columns, &c. A Battle, by Tauvray, and the Rape of Iphigenia, by Roland, are entitled to particular attention. The School of David continues to make greater progress every year, and promises to overcome prejudice and obtain additional support.

Rural Sports; in two volumes, by the Reverend William Daniel. Published for White, Fleet-street; Longman and Rees; Cadell and Davies; and Egerton. Price 4l. 4s.

This work is published by subscription, to be paid for on delivery: the first volume will be delivered this month, and the second in a short time. To country-gentlemen the volumes will be very interesting: they contain, the Natural History and Habits of the various Kinds

Kinds of Game:—alſo, Rules for Breeding and Breaking all the Species of Dogs uſed in its purſuit, with approved Remedies for the Diſorders, natural or incidental to them; numerous and experienced Methods for taking Fiſh, in Standing or Running Waters, with full directions for the Different Apparatus of Nets, Rods, &c. in Fiſhing; and of Guns, Powder, &c. in Shooting.

Of the Rules for *Breeding and Breaking Dogs, &c.* we do not profeſs to be proper judges: but as the reverend gentleman ſeems an adept in theſe ſciences, we dare ſay they are judicious. Be that as it may, the prints are executed in a very ſuperior ſtyle. They conſiſt of beaſts, dogs, fiſhes, birds, &c. and are from deſigns, by Stubbs, Gilpin, Reinagle, Chalon, S. Elmer, &c.

Mr. J. T. Smith, of Great Portland-ſtreet, has printed propoſals for publiſhing by ſubſcription, (to be paid on delivery), in the courſe of next ſpring, an Account and Explanation of the Paintings and other Ornaments and Decorations, diſcovered in September 1800, *on the Walls of the Houſe of Commons.* Including; beſides the Hiſtory of theſe Decorations and the Building, a variety of original particulars as to the ancient ſtate of the City of Weſtminſter, the Palace, &c; and the Principles and Hiſtory of Painting and Gothic Architecture, by John Sidney Hawkins, eſq. F. A. S. The Plates, of which there are to be ſeventeen, engraven by J. T. Smith, from drawings made by himſelf on the ſpot. The work is to be in quarto, and printed, by Benſley. The price, to ſubſcribers 3l. 13s. 6d. To non-ſubſcribers 4l. 4s.

This very curious and intereſting undertaking we have already ſlightly noticed, as intended, and are happy to find it is now in a ſtate of forwardneſs. The competency of Mr. Hawkins to the part that he has taken, is well known; and as we have ſeen the original deſigns before they were taken down to enlarge the Houſe of Commons, it is but juſtice to ſay, the copies made by Mr. Smith are in the ſtyle of drawing and colouring, and alſo in the ſtate of preſervation in which each ſubject was found, moſt ſingularly accurate.

Beſides the account of the chapel and paintings, the letter-preſs will neceſſarily include a variety of topics naturally ſpringing out of theſe ſubjects; and among other particulars, many obſervations on Gothic architecture, and paintings, eſpecially on glaſs. A great variety of original materials have been already communicated to the publiſher by his different friends, and he himſelf has been, and continues to be, indefatigable in his ſearch after every antiquity that remains in Weſtminſter; and he expreſſes his earneſt hope that any gentleman in whoſe houſe any curious veſtige *of other times* exiſts, will honour him by information, and a permiſſion to inſpect it. From this part of the work we expect much entertainment and information; for, except Stowe and Maitland, few writers have given us any intereſting particulars relative to Weſtminſter. The greateſt part of the remarks made by Mr. Pennant, are extracted from theſe two writers.

As Mr. Smith apprehends, that there may be gentlemen who would wiſh that the parts which were gilded in the original pictures, ſhould in like manner be gilt in his engravings, (which in other inſtances will be repreſented in yellow water-colour), the additional charge of 10s. 6d. will be made for this extra gilding.

Mr. Ackermann has juſt publiſhed a Treatiſe on Superfine Water-colours, with Directions how to prepare and uſe them, including a Catalogue of ſuch as, prepared with peculiar care, are ſold at his Print-warehouſe in the Strand.

In this little pamphlet, are many uſeful hints to ſuch ladies or gentlemen as are diſpoſed to ſtudy or practiſe this faſcinating art.

In a Retroſpect of the Fine Arts, it would be unpardonable to omit, a *Picture of Lady Macbeth*, which being engraved for one of the laſt numbers of Boydell's Shakeſpeare, is now exhibiting at the Shakeſpeare Gallery. It is drawn in a bold and broad ſtyle; and the ſoul of this fiend-like woman is diſplayed in her countenance—but the colouring, which is of the Venetian ſchool, has a rich warmth, and brilliant ſplendour, tempered with perfect harmony, that we have never ſeen equalled ſince the death of Sir Joſhua Reynolds.

CORRIGENDA.—In the Statement of the National Debt, in the laſt Number, p. 124, col. 1. l. 10. from the bottom, after "*redeemed*," add "*which are deducted from the debt by Mr. Addington and Mr. Tierney, but not by Mr. Morgan.*" P. 126, col. 2. l. 5. from the end, for "*change*," read "*chance*."

STATE

STATE OF PUBLIC AFFAIRS,

In September, 1801.

FRANCE.

THE Negotiation for Peace between this country and France has been long supposed to be on the point of closing, though from the continued meetings of Ministers upon this subject, and the communications which are yet maintained with M. Otto at home, and Mr. Merry at Paris, the final rupture cannot yet have taken place. The expectation of an invasion is still predominant: whether or not the English Ministry are serious in believing it to be the intention of the French to engage in so desperate an attack we know not, but thus much is certain at least, that if this be not the fact the extreme alarm, and precaution manifested on the occasion, is sufficient to induce the French to suppose that something may be effected, and to rouse them to the exercise of their powers.

A treaty has been concluded between the French Republic and the Pope, and since then the arrival of a nuncio at Paris has either taken place, or is daily expected. In this singular treaty one of the articles expressly stipulates that all the dignitaries of the French Church, who shall be acknowledged by the Pope, shall have previously taken an oath of allegiance to the subsisting government, and have received their appointments immediately from the Chief Consul himself. In consequence of his decision a brief has been received from his Holiness, addressed to the French Bishops and Archbishops resident in England, by which they are required, within ten days from the present period, to resign their dignities, or suffer certain canonical penalties. The Gallican Church has long disavowed the authority of the Pope as to pains and penalties, and affected its own independence; but it will scarcely, we think, be able to resist this authority and the call of Bonaparte to domestic duties. A meeting upon this subject was held on the 19th of September, at the Archbishop of Narbonne's house in London, and very numerously attended; its result has not yet appeared. It is not to be supposed that the present dignitaries of the church will be all of them re-appointed, and perhaps there are very few who will be thus fortunate. The Chief Consul, however, has engaged to provide handsomely for all who may not be re elected.

Bonaparte has at length concluded a peace with Portugal, the articles of which state, in the preamble, that the Plenipotentiaries of the *three* Belligerent Powers (meaning obviously France, Spain, and Portugal) having met together, have agreed to conclude *two treaties*, which, in their *essential parts*, will be but one, as the guarantee will be interchangeable, and will cease with respect to both treaties when either shall be infringed. It then proceeds to inform us of the name of the Plenipotentiary appointed by his Catholic Majesty, and of the Plenipotentiary appointed by the Prince Regent of Portugal to "carry this important object into full effect;" but no notice whatever is taken of the third Plenipotentiary alluded to in the commencement of the paper, and who ought to have been appointed by Bonaparte on behalf of the French Republic; nor does the signature of any French Plenipotentiary appear in conjuction with the names of the other two Ministers at its close. We have, it is true, received by the Hamburg mail a paper, which pretends to be a copy of the treaty of peace between Portugal and Spain. Where then is this *second* treaty referred to, and which is stated to have been concluded at the same time? What are its terms, and who are its subscribers? If we can form any judgment upon the present mysterious document, it is that the paper now published was drawn up between the two parties now affixing their signatures, who, in the first instance, added the name of Joseph Bonaparte, on behalf of the French Republic; but that Joseph Bonaparte not approving of either the one or the other, ordered his own name to be erased from the preamble, and refused to unite in the subscription. Our readers cannot have forgotten the demur on the part of the French Consul to the treaty as at first proposed, and actually signed by the other two Powers; the paper we now have, therefore, is probably the treaty as it, *at that moment*, existed, and which has now, for the first time, got abroad. But we have every reason to believe, that both the first and second treaties have been since ratified by France, and that a mutual understanding has taken place between all the contracting Powers. It is obvious, moreover, from the commencement of the Negociations gociation, that France had made demands, and that the two other contracting Powers had acceded to them on terms which it would be impolitic to communicate to the world at large, and more especially to Great Britain; and it is equally obvious, that the second treaty was meant to be a *secret* treaty, and to include the concessions of Portugal to the French Republic, as the first specifies more openly those she has made to Spain, and respecting which their was no necessity for concealment. All that relates to ourselves in the treaty now published, is contained in the following few words, which comprise the whole of Article II. "His Royal Highness (the Prince Regent) will shut the ports of his whole territories to the ships of Great Britain *in general*." This loosely worded prohibition is unquestionably regulated with minute precision by the treaty, yet carefully concealed behind the curtain, which at the same time provides under certain circumstances for the liberty yet allowed of an interchange of commerce between England and Portugal. By thus concealing, however, the engagements she is under to the French Republic, and the terms of her fidelity, she completely nonplusses the British Cabinet, who know not in what light to regard her.—Of this we have a sufficient proof already, in the mode in which the Island of Madeira has been taken possession of; it is not pretended to be by right of conquest, but for the generous purpose of affording protection to it against the nation that is now become its chief and most powerful ally.

By letters from Salem, in North America, of the 20th of July, we also learn that an expedition, consisting of not less than 100 sail of ships of different sizes, laden with stores and troops, to the amount of ten or fifteen thousand, had sailed from Bengal, under the escort of Admiral Rainier, to the Brazils.

The following is the purport of the circular letter of Citizen Desilles, the Prefect of the department of Angers, to the Subprefects and Mayors of his district.

"To conquer the continental peace the French people have exerted all their means. The conquest of the maritime peace now calls for all their thoughts and all their efforts. The task of our brave armies is fulfilled; but that of the sailors is beginning, and the moment approaches when they will make our flag illustrious, as the former have made our arms. Armaments are ordered in all the ports of the Republic. It is, therefore, necessary that the mariners answer the call of Government, and fly without delay to the post of honour.

"The Municipalities are responsible for the non-execution of the orders for raising men for the service of the ships of war, or for that of the ports and arsenals of the Republic, in case they should refuse to give to the syndics of the naval forces the assistance of which they may stand in need.

"Every citizen who has embraced the *maritime profession* is bound to the public service by sea and in the arsenals."

The Archbishop of Treves has dispatched one of his Vicars-General to inform the French Government, that he is now ready to take the oath of fidelity; that he will immediately issue orders for the opening of the churches, which were ordered to be shut by the command of the suffragan Bishops; and he will recommend to all who live under his superintendence the exact obedience to the laws of the Republic.

The French Government seem to be much at their ease upon the subject of the indemnifications in Germany, which naturally enough gives rise to great discussion there, tho' that discussion can have no chance of settling the question. It appears, from more than one article, as well as from the obvious probability of the case, that the great powers of Germany have negotiated separately at Paris; and the policy of the Chief Consul has given a decision upon their interest, which will scarcely be contradicted.

The First Regiment of Artillery, which had mutinied at Turin, and put to death the commander of the citadel, has been dissolved with ignominy, and the soldiers distributed among other corps. The circumstance is announced in a proclamation by Bonaparte, which, from the singularity of its sentiments, and the peculiarity of its phraseology, seems to have been penned by the First Consul himself.

From Rotterdam, August 19, it is reported that the gun-boats and other armed vessels destined to defend the mouth of the Meuse, and particularly the Isle of Goree; and the harbour of Helvoetsluys, are now stationed in those places most advantageous for repulsing the English, in case of attack. French and Batavian troops are continually arrivng at that part of the coast of Holland, where they will occupy several small camps which are already traced out. The squadron of Admiral Graves consisted of from fifteen to twenty ships of war of all sizes, and, according to the

the latest intelligence, is to be reinforced. On the other hand Admiral de Winter, Commander in Chief of the Dutch fleet, has been informed that numerous armaments are preparing at Margate, Harwich, and Yarmouth, which seems to announce that they are destined for some of the ports of the Batavian Republic. The same measures of precaution, however, have been adopted at the mouth of the Zuyder Zee, as well as at the entrance of the Texel.

According to accounts from Genoa, of the 31st of August, the French had not attempted any decisive measure against Porto-Ferrajo. They had, however, a battery and a corps of two thousand men in readiness for action. The two French frigates were still in the port of Leghorn; and the English had several frigates and armed ships cruizing in the channel of Piombino.

GERMANY.

It is generally believed that Prussia will receive the Bishopric of Munster as her indemnity. The acquisition of that bishopric would form a junction between the possessions of the King of Prussia on the Weser and the Embs, and those which remain to him on the Lower Rhine; to which, it is said, the Duchy of Berg is to be united by the arrangement between the Courts of Berlin and Munich.

The decease of the Elector of Cologne was an event which seems not to have been unexpected by the Cabinet of Berlin, and for which it appears to have been prepared. As soon as the fact was known, a courier was immediately dispatched to the Prussian Minister, at the Diet of Ratisbon, the Count de Goertz, who, on the very day he received his dispatches, invited several Ministers to a conference. He declared that his Court, having been informed of the decease of the Elector of Cologne, proposed to prevent the Chapters of Munster and Cologne from proceeding to the election of a new Elector or Bishop, and to employ the Duchy of Westphalia and the Bishopric of Munster, for the purpose of augmenting the mass of secularizations or indemnities. The Imperial Minister, without expressing any opinion, replied to the Count de Goertz, that he should send for instructions to his Court. The Ministers, however, of the Hereditary Princes, who were invited to the conference, declared unanimously that they adhered to the proposal of the Prussian Minister.

TUSCANY.

We hear from Florence, the 25th of August, that the day before the provisional Government was dissolved, and the senator Mozzi was appointed Prime Minister and Counsellor of State. The Minister of Finance opened a loan for 100,000 crowns, which was supplied by the nobility in less than three days. This sum is intended for the relief of those unfortunate persons who have been totally ruined by the war and revolution.

The Deputies of the Hebrew Nation, at Sinna had an audience of his Majesty on the 20th. He gave them a very gracious reception, and an assurance of his impartial protection, and an amelioration of their condition.

PORTUGAL.

A mail from Lisbon arrived on the 5th of September, by the King George packet. The letters contain no news of importance. The Harlequin packet, with the mail of the 5th ult. arrived at Lisbon on the 22d ult. and was expected to sail on the 31st ult. The Phaëton frigate sailed from Lisbon in company with the King George, and convoyed her as far as Cape Finisterre. The morning after they sailed from Lisbon, the Phaëton frigate spoke a Portuguese line of battle ship, the captain of which informed them, that during the night he had fallen in with one of Admiral Pole's squadron, which consisted of the St. George and Dreadnought, of 98 guns each; the Zealous, Powerful, Vanguard, and Ramilies, of 74 guns each. His Majesty's ship Warrior was expected at Lisbon, to lie as a guard ship.

The outward-bound Mediterranean and Lisbon fleets, consisting of nearly one hundred sail of vessels, under convoy, have put back to Torbay by contrary winds, being for some time off Falmouth.

ROME.

Bonaparte has at length prevailed upon the Pope to ratify the treaty he has so long proposed; and Cardinal Caprara, a descendent of one of the first families of Bologna, is appointed Legate to Paris. Almost all the French priests may now, therefore, be expected to return to their native country. Several of the Archbishops and Bishops have already consented to take the national oath.

RUSSIA.

It appears from a Treaty, signed at Petersburg, on the 11th of June, of Amity, Commerce, and Navigation, between Russia and Sweden, to continue for the space of twelve years from its date, that it allows the importation into Russia from Sweden, of Swedish allum, salt-herrings, and salt, on payment of one-half of the

present

present duties, and the produce of Swedish Finland, even wood, into Russia Finland duty free. Into Sweden, from Russia, hemp, linen, and tallow, at one-half, and linseed at two-thirds of the duties hitherto paid. Then follow some mercantile regulations relative to sailors, ships, and traders, in the respective ports of each country. In its political principle, it embraces and avowedly recognizes the basis of the famous convention entered into at Petersburg, on the 16th of December last, commonly called the Northern Confederacy, which caused the memorable bombardment of Copenhagen. This recognition is the more remarkable, as Lord St. Helens stands, we are told, so high in the good opinion of the Emperor Alexander at Petersburg. By the late settlement with Great Britain, there are two very material points which Russia has obtained; first, The limitation of the right of search: and secondly, The diminution of articles deemed contraband in war.

It is not only that the right of search is to be exercised in future by ships of war alone, and not by privateers (a very important concession): but the manner in which it is to be exercised is a much more important point gained by Russia. Each merchant ship of the neutral power, sailing under convoy, is to produce to the captain of the convoy before he sails, a passport, or sea-letter, in a certain form. The captain is to make no further enquiry. He is to take it for granted that the sea-letter gives a true description of the cargo, and he is not to make any search. Should this neutral fleet be met at sea by a ship of war of the other contracting party, that party being in a state of war, a boat is to be sent on board the captain of the convoy's ship, in order to verify the papers and certificates that are to prove that that ship is authorised to convoy such vessels, laden with such cargoes, and bound to such a port. This verification made, there is to be no pretence for any search, unless there be good ground for suspicion. But how can grounds of suspicion arise in the mind of the captain of the belligerent ship, unless he receives private intelligence from his own Government? But if his suspicions lead him to detain any ship, and if it shall be proved that it has been detained without just and sufficient cause, "the commander of the ship or ships of war of the Belligerent Powers shall not only be bound to make to the owners of the ship, and of the cargo a full and complete compensation for all the losses, expences, damages, and costs, occasioned by such a detention; but shall further be liable to an ulterior punishment for every act of violence, or other fault, which he may have committed, according as the nature of the case may require."

The second great point gained by Russia, is the diminution of the number of articles deemed contraband in war. In the articles enumerated as contraband, our readers will find not one which Russia exports, or which Russia, Sweden, or Denmark, produce. Iron, copper, timber, hemp, pitch, tar, sail-cloth, are not deemed contraband; though most, if not all, of those articles were formerly considered as such.

It appears therefore to us, that Russia has obtained not only all that the late Empress contended for in her declaration to the Courts of London, Versailles, and Madrid, in 1780, but several additional points of considerable importance.

The commerce of Russia appears now to have recovered its former splendour. The exportation from the city of Riga only, down to the end of July, amounted to 6,770,638 roubles; and England alone has had from that city Russian productions to the value of 2,509,853 roubles.

EGYPT.

Authentic intelligence was some time since received from General Hutchinson, dated at the Camp before Gizeh, June 21, by which we learned, that that General meant to erect batteries in the course of twenty-four hours, at Gizeh, which was on the opposite side of the river to Cairo. He says the place is weak, but it covers a bridge of communication which the French have over the Nile, and it is therefore essential to have it in their possession; then the General meant to cross the river, and join the army of the Grand Vizier, who was encamped near Cairo; it was his intention then to besiege that place, which was garrisoned by 4 or 5000 French; their works were very extended, and would require a much greater number of men to defend them. Great delays were occasioned in that operation, from the low state of the river, and from the bar of the Nile at Rosetta, which was frequently impassable for ten days together, so that the march of his men had been much retarded. The difficulty of procuring provisions for the army, and the obstacles which he encountered in bringing the heavy artillery up the river, he represents to have been very great.

The General has, however, sent intelligence since, from the same camp, dated the

the 29th of June, and from his letter we learn, that the British troops, and those of his Highness the Captain Pacha, invested Gizeh on the left bank of the Nile, whilst the army of his Highness the Grand Vizier moved forward, and took a position nearly within cannon shot of Cairo. On the 22d in the morning, the French sent out a flag of truce, and informed the General, that they wished to treat for the evacuation of Cairo, upon certain conditions. After a negociation of several days, they agreed to surrender the town and forts on the conditions which he had the honour to enclose. They then took possession of the gate of Gizeh at five o'clock in the evening of the 28th, and also of the Fort Sulkelki on the Cairo side of the river. Hostages have been mutually exchanged, and the final evacuation was to have taken place in about ten days. The General supposes that there were nearly 6000 troops of all kinds in the town. The troops, from the great heat of the weather, the difficulty of the navigation of the river, and the entire want of roads in the country, have suffered a considerable degree of fatigue; but the General says both the men and officers have submitted to it with the greatest patience, and have manifested a zeal for the honour of his Majesty's arms that was above all panegyric.

Then follow the conditions of the Convention, comprized in 21 Articles. In substance it stipulates, that the French army at Cairo, and its dependencies, shall be conveyed in ships belonging to, and at the expence of, the Allied Powers in Egypt, together with their baggage, arms, ammunition, and other effects, to the nearest French ports in the Mediterranean. Of this Convention, sent immediately to Alexandria, Menou is at liberty to avail himself, provided he signifies to the British General his assent thereto in ten days after its presentation to him.

The Moniteur gives extracts of accounts from Egypt down to the 14th of July, at which time the French still held out at Alexandria, where they are stated to be in such force as to defy any attempts that might be made upon them. They state the place to be also well stocked with provisions.

From Paris, the 8th of September, we learn that Citizen Lugan, Captain of the Heliopolis, left Egypt on the 14th of July, on board a small vessel called La Santa Madona Didra, manned with 20 good French sailors. It escaped the cruizers, touched at Cephalonia, and landed at Tarento. C. Lugan delivered to General Soult dispatches from General Menou, which were brought to Paris by a courier extraordinary. Generals Menou, Rampon, Friant, Songis, Delaing, Fauthier, &c. and all the other officers *Chefs de corps*, and superior officers of the garrison of Alexandria, had resolved to bury themselves under the ruins of the place rather than accede to a capitulation which they considered as disgraceful, because they did not believe it to be necessary.

Alexandria was defended by more than 600 pieces of artillery, was abundantly supplied with provisions, and particularly a large quantity of rice. The garrison had bread and biscuit to last them through the winter, and rice for several years. The soldiers were labouring incessantly, and with extraordinary activity, to augment the fortifications; they amounted to more than 9000 French, including the sailors and Members of the different Administrations, who had all taken up arms. General Menou bestows great praises on the zeal and activity of the Captains Villeneuve, Barré, and Richer. The Fort of Pompey's Pillar, by the extraordinary labour of four months, had acquired the same strength as Fort Cretin. They were masters of the Lake Mareotis, by means of forts constructed in different places, and of gun-boats transported thither from the ports of Alexandria.

The entrenched camp which General Menou had made choice of was secure from any *coup de main*, and defended the approaches to the place. The English could not approach but by the boyaux of the trenches.

The French Papers continue to say, that after the Convention of El Arisch was concluded between the Grand Vizier and General Kleber, it was asked which of the two armies had been victorious? The battle of Heliopolis, which took place two months after, furnished a sufficient answer. The Convention agreed upon by General Belliard, on the 28th of June, is precisely the same with that of El-Arisch. If Admiral Keith should fail of good faith, and refuse a passage by sea, as he did after the Treaty of El-Arisch, the spectacle would soon present itself of a new battle of Heliopolis. If the English (say the French Papers) had some success on the 21st of March, it was because all our General Officers did not demean themselves like the brave General Lanusse, and did not evince those heroic sentiments which alone can command victory. A cannon-ball carried off his thigh early in the action. He survived

vived the accident eight days. The Surgeon in Chief, Berrey, an officer of health of great merit, came to Alexandria to amputate the limb. He refused to submit to the operation. All his friends were assembled, and the experienced surgeon said, that he would be answerable for its success. It could not have put the life of the wounded General to hazard, and without it there was no possibility of his surviving. Fatigued, at length, by the solicitation of his friends—"No! (said Lanusse to them) I will not survive that dishonourable day."

EAST-INDIES.

Our late accounts from India intimate, that a new war is on the eve of breaking out in the Mysore Country. No sooner was Doondeah, one of Tippoo's adherents, defeated, than Cotione Rajah, by some hostilities, claimed the attention of the Mysore army. The conquest of this Chief will be a matter of some difficulty, owing to the natural defences of the country, as well as the extensive preparations made by the enemy.

The intended introduction of European laws into the Mysore Country caused no small degree of alarm; insomuch, that the right of fathers and masters of families, according to the Hindoo and Mahomedan laws, are recognized by the consent of the British Government. The additional revenue of the India Company, by their late treaties, amounts to about 25 lacks of pagodas, or near one million sterling per annum. The military establishment there will shortly be reduced, owing to the consolidation of empire, and the contraction of posts. The late General is, by order of the Government of Madras, succeeded by Col. Urban Vigors in the command of the subsidiary force serving with the Nizam, and Col. F. Gowdie succeeds the latter in the command of the Northern division of the army.

GREAT BRITAIN.

It appears that however close the connection may be, both in political sentiments and private friendship, between the late Minister and the present, we behold the latter, in every instance, acting in diametrical opposition to the system pursued by the former. We see him in the North of Europe acceding to the maritime code which Mr. Pitt haughtily rejected, as ruinous to the nation, and to resist which he plunged it into a bloody and expensive war; and in Egypt courting a convention which the late Administration sacrificed their honour to break, after it had been acceded to in their names; and to prevent a renewal of which, they have drained the country of its best soldiers and its last guinea.

The present Ministers affect great candour, and an earnest desire of throwing a veil over all distinctions of parties. This spirit is not, however, carried into any of the public offices, except the Admiralty. Earl St. Vincent, like a true seaman, knows no parties but the French and British, and labours most earnestly and ably to crush the one and exalt the other. His thoughts are wholly occupied in promoting the welfare and glory of our navy, not in discovering the politics of officers, that he may blast the hopes, whatever may be the merits, of those who differ in opinion from the Premier—not in distributing places and employments among the voters at rotten boroughs, in preference to men of merit and just claims—not in making the navy subservient to parliamentary interest! What must have been the indignation of a man of such generous and independent principles, on finding, as we are assured he has done, among the papers of his office, a memorandum, written by one of his predecessors, "Never to employ Admiral G—— because he voted for Mr. Fox at a Westminster election!"

A second and more considerable division of Lord Nelson's force sailed from the Downs for Boulogne on the 10th of September. It consisted of the York of 64 and Isis of 50 guns, with several other ships of war. His Lordship received intelligence the day before, that the enemy's flotilla had moved out of the harbour to Boulogne-roads, the winds having abated. Hence a suspicion arises of their having a design to put to sea.

The French Papers say, that the Lords of the Admiralty and Lord Nelson have asserted, in their official account, that the advanced guard of the light flotilla, by which Lord Nelson was beaten on the 15th of August, was chained to the land. It is said, also, in this account, that the English were repelled by the land-batteries, and that the English sailors were for a long time on board of the gun-boats. Both these assertions, they contend, are completely false. The advanced guard could not be moored to the bank, from which it was distant five hundred toises. Its anchors were attached by the ordinary cables. The English tried to board, but they were every where repulsed. The land-batteries never fired at all. How could they have done so, in the darkness of the night, without running the hazard of firing upon the French? The English were repulsed by the bayonets of the 42d, 57th, and 108th demi-brigades.

[illegible]tement of the Distribution of the BRITISH NAVAL FORCE, *exclusive of the Hired Armed Vessels, which are chiefly employed in protecting the Coasting Trade of Great Britain.*

	Line	Fifty's	Frigates	Sloops	Total
In Port and fitting - - - - -	9	1	80	84	174
Guard-ships, Hospital-ships, and Prison-ships, at the several Ports -	28	5	8	1	42
In the English and Irish Channels - -	46	—	44	51	141
In the Downs and North-Seas - -	12	4	28	84	128
At the West Islands, and on the Passage -	1	—	15	31	47
At Jamaica - - - - - -	3	1	24	9	37
In America, and at Newfoundland - -	—	—	7	6	13
East Indies, and on the Passage - -	8	7	8	13	37
Coast of Africa, and Secret Expedition -	—	1	7	4	12
On the Lisbon Station - - - - -	9	—	4	3	16
Gibraltar and Mediterranean - - -	27	4	56	33	120
Total in Commission	143	23	281	319	767
Receiving-ships - - - - - -	8	1	6	1	21
Serviceable, and repairing for Service -	6	1	3	3	13
In Ordinary - - - - - - -	19	—	15	25	59
Building - - - - - - -	20	2	5	—	27
Total	196	27	310	348	887

The Navy-list, published the 1st of September, contains 141 Admirals, 532 Captains, 418 Commanders, and 2274 Lieutenants.

General Distribution of the BRITISH ARMY, *September 1.*

	Cav.	Inf.	Fencibles Cav.	Fencibles Inf.	Mil.	Total Bat.	Inv. Com.
[illegible]land and Wales - - - - -	23	24	—	3	74	124	40
N[illegible] Britain - - - - - -	2	—	—	—	12	14	6
[illegible] - - - - - - -	6	12	—	32	—	50	6
[illegible], Guernsey, &c. - - - - -	—	5	—	2	—	7	20
[illegible] - - - - - - -	—	5	—	4	—	9	—
[illegible] - - - - - - -	—	1	—	—	•	1	—
[illegible] and Malta - - - - -	—	12	—	1	—	13	—
[illegible] - - - - - - -	3	22	—	—	—	25	—
[illegible], Nova Scotia, &c. - - - -	—	5	—	2	—	7	—
[illegible] Indies - - - - - -	1	34	—	—	—	35	—
[illegible] of Good Hope - - - - -	1	5	—	—	—	6	—
[illegible] Indies - - - - - - -	4	18	—	—	—	†22	—
[illegible] Sir H. Popham's Squadron -	1	—	—	—	—	‡1	—
[illegible] for Foreign Service in June -	1	3	—	—	—	4	—
[illegible] Passage from Abroad - - -	—	1	—	—	—	1	—
	42	147	—	44	86	319§	72

[illegible] And detachments. † The Company's Troops exclusive. ‡ With detachments.
[illegible] Exclusive of Artillery and Engineers at home and abroad, Independent Companies, Recruiting Corps, Volunteers, &c.

ALPHA-

ALPHABETICAL LIST *of* BANKRUPTCIES *and* DIVIDENDS *announced between the 20th of Aug. and the 20th of Sept. extracted from the London Gazettes.*

BANKRUPTCIES.

(The Solicitors' Names are between Parentheſes)

ALLCORN, Richard, Hampton, Middleſex. (Webb, St. Thomas's ſtreet, Southwark)
Ball, Wm. Derby, druggiſt. (Barbor and Browne, Fetter lane)
Beſwick, Jas. late of Hendon, baker. (Welch, Alderſgate ſtreet)
Beſton, John, Waſhwood Heath, Aſton, Warwick, factor. (Sanderſon, Palſgrave place)
Bamford, Samuel Paul, John Cooke, and Jas. Francis Clifford, Tiverton, worſted-manufacturers. (Conſtable, Symond's inn)
Bridgman, Edw. Higham Ferrers, Northampton, baker. (Hodſon, Wellingborough)
Brevitt, Wm late of Wedneſbury, Staffordſhire, butcher. (J. Lilley Parker, Stafford)
Baker, Thos. and John Shefland, Exeter, woollen-drapers. (Field, Friday ſtreet)
Bull, Jas. Edw. Bowyer, City Road, Old ſtreet, baker. (Gale, Bedford ſtreet, Bedford row)
Beaumont, Wm. late of Healey Butts, in South Croſland, pariſh of Almondbury, Yorkſhire, clothier, and Copartner with Rich. Beaumont and Stephen Vickerman. (Battye, Chancery lane)
Cantrill, Wm. Burton-upon-Trent, Staffordſhire, druggiſt. (Battera and Martin, Furnival's inn)
Deverell, Geo. Redbourn, Hertfordſhire, ſtraw-hat manufacturer. (Wild, Warwick ſquare)
Eccles, Thomas, Watling ſtreet, wholeſale-linen-draper. (Johnſon, Ely place)
French, Sam. jun. Hertford, mealman. (Allens, Clifford's inn)
Flinders, John, Nottingham, hoſier (Holmes, Mark lane)
Flux, Robert, Cirenceſter, Glouceſterſhire, carpenter. (Foulkes, Hart ſtreet, Bloomsbury)
Fox, Solomon, Wardour ſtreet, cabinet-maker. (Few, Red-lion ſquare)
Galliers, Jane, St. John ſtreet, Weſt Smithfield, baker. (Reeves, Nicholas lane)
Gardner, Samuel John, Pitt ſtreet, St. George's, Southwark, mealman (Tyler and Humphreys, Tooley ſtreet)
Garner, Thos. jun. Broad ſtreet, warehouſeman. (Ellis, Curſitor ſtreet)
Hanſon, John, Atherſtone, Warwickſhire, wine and ſpirit-merchant. (Barbor and Browne, Fetter lane)
Harling, Edw. late of Almondbury, Yorkſhire, merchant. (Battye, Chancery lane)
Hodſon, Jonathan, Stockport, ſhopkeeper. (Chetham, Stockport)
Hitchcock, Jas. late of Hatton Garden, dealer in prints, but now a priſoner in the Fleet. (Morris and Biggen, Inner Temple)
Keen, Henry, Cleeve Prior, Worceſterſhire, baker and maltſter. (Whitlow and Taylor, Gray's inn)
Lomas, Wm and Geo Needham market, Suffolk, hawkers. (Harding, Primroſe ſtreet)
Lomas, Wm late of Needham market, hawker. (Ellis, Curſitor ſtreet)
Levy, Lewis and Jonas, Oſborne place, Brick lane, Whitechapel, vermicelli-manufacturers. (Lee, Barnard's inn)
Mair, Jas. late of Graveſend, plumber. (Walker, Serjeant's inn, Chancery lane)
Morrice, Pierce, at Martin's court, St. Martin's lane, hoſier. (Eccleſton, Gray's inn)
Ockenden, Richard, late of Bexhill, Suſſex, ſhopkeeper. (Young, Milton and Powdall, Doctor's Commons)
Pickering, John, Lower Eaton ſtreet, Pimlico, dealer in wine and ſpirits. (Burman, Ormond ſtreet)
Pitt, Thos. Swanſea, haberdaſher. (Farrer, Lacey, Steadman and Wall, Bread ſtreet hill)
Quenby, John, Liverpool, tea-dealer. (Windle, Bartlett's buildings)
Quantrill, Jas. late of Duke ſtreet, Portland place, factor. (Noy and Templer, Mincing lane)
Rickets, Geo. Queen ſtreet, Cheapſide, warehouſeman. (Wild, Warwick ſquare)
Roberts, Hugh, late of Alderſgate ſtreet, ſilk-weaver. (Field, Friday ſtreet)
Stafford, Rob. jun. Huntingdon, grocer (Cooper and Lowe, Southampton buildings)
Scott, Mary, (widow of the late Joſeph Scott) Henry Scott, and Edw. Appleby, Hinkley, Leiceſterſhire, hoſiers. (Holmes, Mark lane)
Rowlands, John, Exeter, woollen draper. (Williams and Brooks, Lincoln's inn)
Stephens, Rob. Mancheſter, dealer in weſt. (Ellis, Curſitor ſtreet)
Simms, John, late of Sheepey Farm, Leiceſterſhire, miller. (Tebbut, Staple's inn)
Scarbrow, W. St. Neots, Huntingdonſhire, baker. (Cooper and Lowe, Southampton buildings)
Saul, T. and John Reynolds, Mancheſter, wool-ſtaplers. (Swan and Stevens, Old Jewry)
Sanderſon, Jas. Preſton, Lancaſhire, and N. Sanderſon, Houghton, Lancaſhire, cotton-manufacturers. (Hodgſon, Chancery lane)
Tolway, J. Motley, Eſſex, corn-merchant. (J. Ambroſe, Motley)
Tipper, B. Derby, patten-ring-maker. (Ward and Lockett, Derby)
Tubbs, D. late of Liverpool, merchant. (Daltera, Liverpool)
Woodward, J. Derby, callico manufacturer. (Forbes, Ely place)
Walter, Robt. Plymouth-dock, hatter. (Blandford and Sweet, Inner Temple)
Wimberley, T. Foſte, Huntingdonſhire, grocer. (Cooper and Lowe, Southampton buildings)
Wilkinſon, J. Bridlington, merchant. (D. Taylor, Bridlington)
Woodgar, W. Minories, brazier (Nind, Preſcot ſtreet)
Whitehead, W. Laceby, Lincolnſhire, ſhopkeeper. (Marris and Clarke, Barton upon Humber)
Wilſon, Jas. Birmingham, builder. (Kinderley and Long, Symond's inn)

DIVIDENDS ANNOUNCED.

Brown, Geo. Old Cavendiſh ſtreet, taylor, Nov 5
Birchall, John, Woore, Salop, dealer in ſalt, Sept. 22
Burnett, Edw. and Robt. Oliver, Mancheſter, linen-drapers, Sept. 29
Barton, John, Davies ſtreet, Hanover ſquare, dealer in horſes, Oct. 10
Burgess, Daniel, Blaby, Leiceſterſhire, victualler, Oct. 3
Bradley, Joſeph, Shawbank, callico manufacturer, Oct. 13
Barker, Wm. Simon Field and Abraham Field, Leeds, wool-ſtaplers, Oct. 13
Curtis, Jas. Swanſea, timber-merchant, Sept. 29
Corbett, Thos. late of Minchinhampton, clothier, Sept. 24
Croſs, Henry, Exeter, tobacconiſt, Sept. 30
Collins, Robert, jun. late of Union court, Broad ſtreet, carpenter and builder, Nov. 14
Denton, Wm. Elland, Halifax, merchant, Oct. 2
England, J. Wiſbech, St. Peter's, Ely, innkeeper, Sept. 22
Edwards, John, Kenſington, taylor, Oct. 17
Fiſhwick, Wm. Duke's court, St. Martin's lane, taylor, Nov. 21
Graeley, Joſeph Sherwin, Great Queen ſtreet, Lincoln's-inn-fields, merchant, Nov. 4
Gerrard, Jas. Cannon ſtreet, corn-factor, Oct. 20
Gillia, John, New Sarum, whipmaker, Sep. 24
Gowan, Geo. Great Ormond ſtreet, merchant, Dec. 5
Greenall, Wm. Hardſhaw, Lancaſhire, dealer, Oct. 5
Gaunt, John, Wandſworth, corn-chandler, Oct. 20
Holland, Wm. Southwark, linen-draper, Nov. 5
Hammond, Geo. Stamford, mercer, Sept. 24
Hunter, Margaret, H. Kruwen and Robt. Hunter, Briſtol, merchants, Oct. 1
Hunter, John, late of Rye, carrier, Oct. 24
Hawkins, John, Leiceſter, currier, Sep. 28
Hadfield, John, Sheffield, grocer, Oct. 1
Heap, Geo. Mancheſter, cotton-manufacturer, Oct. 3
Hobert, John, Crown ſtreet, Finſbury ſquare, ſhoemaker, Oct. 17
Johnſon, R. Joſeph, New Basford, mercer, Oct. 13, (final)
Lawſon, S. Rotherhithe, carver, Nov. 11
Long, Geo. jun Dewsbury, linen-draper, Oct. 4
Long, Wm. Pontefract, linen-draper, Sept. 28
Larkworthy, Ambroſe, Exeter, fuller, Oct. 1
Marriott, Sam. Paul's Head tavern, Cateaton ſtreet, vintner, Nov. 7
Mellor, Jas. jun. and John and Edm. Mellor, late of Wooldale, Town End, clothiers, Sept. 25
Morton, Thos. Raiſtrick, Halifax, dealer, Sept. 30
Mercer, Wm. Tunbridge, miller, Oct. 6
Madgwick, Thos. Buxted, tanner, Oct. 12
Newman, Holdſworth, Little Dartmouth, merchant, Sept. 19
Neale, Wm. Frome Selwood, innholder, Oct. 13
Niblock, Jas. and Geo. Burges, Briſtol, linen-drapers, Nov. 20
Pereira, Abm. Mendes, and Hermenegild Caſtellain, Old Bethlem, merchants, Dec. 8
Pye, John, Liverpool, merchant, Sept. 29
Paterſon, Thos. New Bond ſtreet, ſtone-maſon, Oct. 31
Potter, Geo Charing Croſs, haberdaſher, Nov. 7
Rachael and Jas. Biſhop, Briſtol, ſugar-bakers, Sept. 28
Rogers, John, Birmingham, ſaddler, Sept. 21
Rumſon, Robt. Chorley, grocer, Sept. 21
Reilly, Jas. and Jas. Collins, Mead's court, Bond ſtreet, taylors, Nov. 7
Radford, Wm. Liverpool, mercer, Oct. 3
Rowe, John, Sudbury, linen-draper, Nov 17
Sims, Robt. late of Walworth, grocer, Oct 6
Selby, Joſeph, Nottingham, baker, Sept. 30
Smith, John, St. Martin's lane, baker, Oct. 6
Uther, John William, Bowling-green lane, Clerkenwell, victualler, Sept. 26
White, M. Wm. Sunderland, wine and ſpirit-merchant, Sept. 14
Wagner, J. Michael, Briſtol, merchant, Sept. 30
Wade, J. Sheffield, factor, Sept. 15
Webb, Wm. Mancheſter, fuſtian-manufacturer, Sept. 25
Wallace, John, and Wm. Hawes, Hanwell, ſoap makers, &c. Nov. 7
Warren, Geo. Coventry ſtreet, Upholder, Nov. 21
Yale, John, Thos. Spencer Dunn, Sam. Helton Parker and Thos. Yate, Liverpool, merchants, Oct. 1
Zachary, Heath, of Lawrence lane Cheapſide, factor, Nov. 7

LIST

LIST OF DISEASES IN LONDON.

Account of Diseases in an Eastern District of London, from the 20th of August to the 20th of September 1801.

ACUTE DISEASES.

	No. of Cases.
TYPHUS	25
Febris Remittens	1
Variola	1
Peripneumonia	2
Acute Rheumatism	3
Dysenteria	10

CHRONIC DISEASES.

Tussis	8
Tussis et Dyspnœa	6
Peripneumonia Notha	2
Phthisis Pulmonalis	3
Hepatitis Chronica	2
Anasarca	7
Gastrodynia	3
Dyspepsia	4
Tenesmus	1
Diarrhœa	6
Enterodynia	4
Hæmorrhois	3
Menorrhagia	4
Fluor Albus	2
Scrophula	3
Vomitus	6
Vertigo	3
Paralysis	2
Impetigo	3
Lumbago	2
Rheumatismus Chronicus	12

PUERPERAL DISEASES.

Menorrhagia lochialis	4
Dolores post Partum	3

INFANTILE DISEASES.

Diarrhœa	6
Ophthalmia	2
Aphthæ	3

As the season of the year has arrived in which fevers of the typhous kind usually constitute a large part of the catalogue of diseases, the number in the present list will not excite any suprize. The principal occasion of regret is, that during those months in which, in the common course of things, this class of diseases does not make a conspicuous figure, it has lately very much engaged the attention of practitioners. In our last report we were happy to announce, that the disease had assumed a milder form, that the affections of the brain were less violent, and that the instances of a fatal termination were less frequent. In the cases which have since occurred, the delirium has been less violent: it has been rather of that low, muttering kind, which we have been formerly accustomed to observe in this species of fever. But though the brain has been less violently affected, the effects of the disease upon this organ have continued longer than usual.

In one instance, after the termination of the fever, the patient fell into that state of intellectual derangement which Nosologists have distinguished by the term Amentia.

A general inattention to surrounding objects, and an indifference to every person and to every thing about them, together with an indisposition to take in necessary food, are characteristics of this disease. The patient referred to, continued in this state for several days, but seems now to be gradually recovering from it. In one of the cases symptoms of hemiplegia occurred at the close of the fever; and in another, such a loss of recollection, and other symptoms of mental debility, as produced the appearance of premature old age.

Dysenteries have very frequently occurred during the last few weeks. These have been attended with the usual symptoms of a mild disease, and have not, in any of the cases referred to, proved fatal.

MARRIAGES AND DEATHS IN AND NEAR LONDON.

With Biographical Memoirs of distinguished Characters recently deceased.

At the late meeting of the Gloucestershire Society, M. Hickes Beach, esq. President, in the Chair, the sum of 170l. 5s. 6d. (including the liberal benefactions of absentees) was contributed for the purpose of apprenticing poor boys, sons of natives of that county, and for relieving, in the period of childbed, poor women natives, or the wives of natives, of the said county.

The effects of the East India Company in England and afloat, consisting of annuities, cash in the treasury, goods sold and not paid for, goods unsold, cargoes afloat, and other articles in their commerce, amounted, in the year 1800, to 16,185,950l.

The sale of the Company's goods, which, in the year 1793, were estimated, on an average, to amount to 4,988,300l. amounted, in the last year, to 7,367,727l.

By the list of the ships lost by the East India Company, from the year 1757, to the season of 1801, it appears that 11 have been burnt by accident, 10 taken by the French, and 33 wrecked at sea.

A late Gazette contained an Order in Council, declaring the port of La Valette, in the island

island of Malta, a free port, and allowing the same drawbacks and bounties as are allowed on the exportation of various articles to Minorca and Gibraltar.

It appears, that in the last 10 years, the revenue of Greenwich Hospital has been increased to the amount of 26,832l.; and in 13 years it has been more than doubled; the revenue of last year exceeded the expenditure by 32,645l. which is more than half the total amount of the revenue 13 years ago.

Married.] At St. James's Church, Sir Edward Crofton, to Lady Charlotte Stewart, fifth daughter of the Earl of Galloway.

P. Lee, esq. of Highbury Place, to Miss E. Arbouin.

At Tottenham, N. Harden, esq. to Miss H. Mecke.

Mr. Langhorne of Clapham, to Miss Box, only daughter of W. Box, esq. of Doctor's Commons.

R. Shaw, esq. of Dulwich Hill, to Mrs. A. Todd, of Gower street.

B. Montague, esq. of Gray's-Inn, to Miss Rush, eldest daughter of Sir William Beaumaurice Rush, of Wimbledon House, Surrey.

Brigadier General John Murray, to Miss M. Pasco, niece of W. Baker, esq Comptroller of the Customs at Montreal.

J. Bacon, esq. sculptor, to Miss Taylor, of High-street, Southwark.

J. Watkins, esq. of Charing Cross, to Mrs. Walker, late of Stafford.

Edmund Bacon, esq. eldest son of Sir Edmund Bacon, bart. to Miss Bacon, daughter of D. Bacon, esq. of Ottrey St. Mary.

Mr. Bent, bookseller, of Coventry-street, to Mrs. Hurford, widow of the late Henry Hurford, esq.

Died] Mrs. Rolls, wife of J. Rolls, esq. of Bermondsey; and a few days after, her husband, J. Rolls, esq.

E. Barnes, esq. Clerk of the Chester-road General Post-office.

At Chelsea, aged 47, T. Hammond, esq. Clerk in the Tellers-office, Exchequer, Agent in the Army, and for many years Deputy-agent to the Out-pensioners of Chelsea-hospital; a gentleman of pure principles, engaging demeanour, and unaffectedly candid practice. To the honour of a gentleman, and the warm benevolence of a philanthropist, Mr. Hammond happily united the active virtues of an enlightened morality, and the unassuming piety of a Christian.

W. Bulkeley, esq. Major of Chelsea College, universally lamented by every member of the houshold to which he belonged, from the Governor to the private pensioners, for whom he had been the means of procuring various additional comforts, and equally respected by his acquaintance for the suavity and urbanity of his manners, as a gentleman, and for his kindness and candour as a private friend, and an honourable and truly good man.

Mrs. Spring, wife of Lieutenant Spring, of Storey's Gate, Westminster.

In Soho-square, the Lady of L. Fowler, esq.

In her 29th year, Miss J. Baker, of Judd-place, West, Somer's Town.

At Dulwich, aged 72, Mrs. Flint, of London-bridge, Southwark.

Mr. J. Davenport, one of the assistant Pages to the Queen.

At Brompton Villa, Sir John Gresham, bart. the last male heir of that ancient family.

Mrs. Lawrence, of Church-street, Soho, widow of the late Mr. Lawrence, of the Strand.

At Weston, the seat of Lord Bradford, the Right Hon. Lady Lucy Bridgman, wife of the Hon. and Rev. G. Bridgman, and only daughter of the late Edmund Earl of Cork and Orrery.

W. Rix, esq. Town-clerk of the City of London, which place he held for 20 years, as likewise other offices for 40 years.

At Staines, in Middlesex, on his way into Devonshire, J. Bagshaw, esq. of the Oaks; by whose death Dr. Darling, late of Hull, but now of Brigg, in Lincolnshire, comes in to possession of very large estates in Derbyshire and Yorkshire.

[On Friday September the 18th, the remains of the late Rev. GILBERT WAKEFIELD, (see page 225) were conveyed from Hackney, to be interred with those of his father and mother, in the church of Richmond, Surrey. It was intended by the family that the funeral should be private, but the zeal and attachment of many of Mr. Wakefield's numerous friends, would not suffer them to decline the opportunity of paying their last tribute of personal respect to the memory of a man, who, while living, was beloved by them to a degree almost without example; accordingly they assembled at Hackney, to the number of about 50, in twelve mourning coaches, and accompanied the remains of their deeply lamented friend to the place of interment, and never were the genuine feelings of sorrow and regret more observable than on this melancholy occasion. The character of the deceased—his relationship to the minister of the parish—heightened by the consideration of his late long absence from his friends, and his hasty departure out of life—in short, every circumstance conspired to give uncommon interest to the solemnities of the day. Thus closed the career of a man, who, for ardour of mind, benignity of temper, persevering industry, and eminence in literary attainments, will, by all parties, be ranked among the most distinguished characters of the present age. We forbear going into detail here, another part of this Magazine being occupied with this melancholy subject. Mr. Wakefield has left an amiable and large family, to lament his loss, a widow and six children: an infant died during his confinement.]

PROVINCIAL OCCURRENCES.

WITH ALL THE MARRIAGES AND DEATHS,

Arranged geographically, or in the Order of the Counties, from North to South.

*** *Authentic Communications for this Department are always very thankfully received.*

NORTHUMBERLAND AND DURHAM.

It is in contemplation to open a more free communication through the western part of the county of Durham, by a new turnpike road from Barnard Castle, that shall proceed by way of Stanhope and Blanchland, to Corbridge or Hexham; with certain collateral branches, viz. one from Barnard Castle, by West Pitts and Redford, to Walsingham; one from near the Mill-stone quarries, on Stanhope Moor, that shall pass by Gold Hill and Healey Field, and meet the Lobley-hill road, near Dipton; one from a place further north, on the said Moor, that shall pass through Edmondbyers, and meet the branch of the Lobley-hill road, near Black-Hedley; and one from Blanchland, South Westwards, that shall pass by Rookhope Lead Mills, across the river Wear, near Westgate, and across the river Tees, near Winch-bridge, to communicate with the Stanmore road, near Brough. The proposed road, as above, will complete the shortest line from London to Edinburg, and, with the proper branches, as above, will be of the greatest advantage to the improvement of the country at large, as well as to the persons more immediately interested.

The following is an estimate of the expences which will be incurred in the completion of the design for improving and extending the building of the infirmary at Newcastle, as lately laid before the public by the committee, &c.—Contract for the new building 2925l.—Alterations and improvements in the old house, with iron bedsteads, water closets, &c. 890l.—total 3815l.

The heat at Newcastle has been lately excessive, both by night and day On Tuesday August 18, at 2 o'clock in the afternoon, Fahrenheit's thermometer, being exposed by Mr. Pringle, mathematician of North Shields, in the shade, in a northern aspect, stood at 77 degrees. The West India heat seldom exceeds 85.

The following vessels are arrived at Newcastle from Davis's Streights fishery. The Sarah, with 393 casks of blubber, and 10 tons of fins, the produce of 14 whales. The Everetta, with 414 casks of blubber, and 12 tons of fins, the produce of 15 whales and 1 seal. The Content, with 323 casks of blubber, and 10 tons of fins, the produce of 13 whales; and the Middleton, with 300 casks of blubber, and 10 tons of fins the produce of 14 whales.

Married.] At Monkwearmouth Shore, Mr. J. Ewbank, mercer and draper, to Miss Bushy, of Sunderland.

In London, Mr. F. A. Hellmers, merchant, to Miss H. Hunt, of Stockton upon Tees.

At Hampstead, J. Bird, esq of Howard street, Strand, to Miss M. Mole, of Newcastle.

In London, at St. Luke's church, Mr. J. Gibson, jun. of Barnard Castle, to Miss R. Wrigglesworth, daughter of Mr. B. Wrigglesworth, warehouseman.

At Newcastle, Mr. P. Paxton, builder, to Mrs. Ewart.

At Sydenham, Capt. A. Dixon, of the navy, to Miss J. Dixon, second daughter of Admiral Dixon.

At South Shields, T. Wallis, esq. to Miss Smith

At Durham, Mr. J. Watson, master of the Cock Inn, to Miss M. Nelson.

Died.] At Newcastle, Mr J. Hudson — Aged 95, Mrs Milburn, widow, late of Bywell.—Aged 51 years and one day, J. Wilkinson, esq. banker, and a captain in the Newcastle armed association.—Mrs. Verty, wife of Mr. Verty, draper.—Aged 41, Mr. D. Bell, woollen draper.—Mr. J. Talyntire, shoemaker.

In Gateshead, aged 90, Mrs. Wilson, relict of R. Wilson, esq. attorney.

At Sunderland, Mr. J. Colling, ship-builder.

At Durham, aged 68, Mr. J. Marshall, master of the Rose and Crown public house, in the market place.—Aged 65, Mr. J. Clark, coach-maker.—At an advanced age, Mr. A. Arthur, an honest industrious man, many years in the employment of the late Mr. Lewins, attorney.—Aged 57, Mr. J. Pearson, shoe-maker. — Suddenly aged 63, Mrs. Suddick, wife of Mr. W. Suddick, skinner.

At North Shields, aged 37, Mr. W. Adamson, a man of considerable ingenuity and uncommon industry. — Mr. R. Cuthbertson, hair-dresser. — Aged 68, Mr. W. Taylor, brewer.—Mrs French, wife of Mr. G. French, ship-owner. — Mr. H. Perry of the customs.

At Alnwick, Miss J. Foster, of the Queen's Head Inn.

At Stockton, Mrs. Teutin, of the Shakespeare Inn.—In her 76th year, Mrs. Ayres, wife of Mr. J. Ayres, of the Custom-house. —Mrs. Wray, wife of Mr. Wray, comedian. —Mrs. Jobson, widow, of Ogle, Northumberland.—Miss Bainbridge, youngest daughter of W. Bainbridge, esq. of the Riding.

At Harton, aged 37, Miss A. Oliver.

At High Shields, near Hexham, Mr. J. Ridley,

Ridley, a worthy servant to Mr. Bell; he unfortunately fell from a loaded cart of hay and was killed on the spot.

At the Brooms, aged 69, Mrs. S. Hedley.

At Hexham, aged 73, Mrs. Baty, of the Grey Bull Inn. On retiring to her apartment, the door of which was contiguous to that of the cellar, she, having no light, inadvertently entered the latter, and was precipitated to the bottom of the steps, where she was found, a short time afterwards, with her head dreadfully bruised, and struggling with the last remains of life, which she calmly yielded up in the morning.

Mr. H. Dooby, house steward and butler to W. Russel, esq. of Brancepeth castle; having engaged to drive a cart a small distance, the horse took fright and ran-away, when Mr. Dobby, in attempting to stop him, was unfortunately thrown down, and one of the wheels passing over his body, most severely bruised him. He was instantly taken to the castle, where he died within two hours.

At Jedburgh, in Scotland, Miss A. Bennett, of Chester.

At Barnard Castle, aged 67, Mr. R. Richmond, late Serjeant Major in the Durham militia

At Morpeth, Mrs. Beautiment, wife of Mr. W. Beautiment, mason.

CUMBERLAND AND WESTMORLAND.

A large plant of Indian corn is now growing in a garden belonging to Mr. Elgin, of Kendal; which was sown by some children in the month of May last. It is 6 feet high, 6 inches in circumference; and one of the leaves measures 3 feet 3 inches. It is not yet in flower, and to what height it may arrive cannot even be guessed at. It is certainly a most extraordinary plant, and numbers of people resort daily to see it.

Mr. Thomas Robinson, of Sedgwick, near Kendal, lately planted 13 grains of square barley, from which 147 stems or ears were produced. Each ear had 6 rows of grain; and, upon an average, 12 in each row! This species of grain will bear the winter's frost; and is well worth the attention of the farmer, on account of its productiveness.

Last Martinmas, Mr. Benn, of Preston house, near Whitehaven, planted 37 grains of Egyptian wheat, in an orchard. It was reaped about the 25th of August last, and produced as much fine corn as filled a quart!

This season a magnum bonum plum, of very extraordinary magnitude, grew in the open air, in the garden of Mr. T. Holmes, of Botcherby, near Carlisle; it weighed 4¾ ozs. and was 7½ by 7 inches in circumference!

Quantity of Rain which fell at the following Places in the Year 1800, in Inches and Decimals.

MONTHS	London.	Cambridge.	Lyndon, in Rutland.	West Bridgford, in Nottinghamsh.	Lincoln.	Ferriby near Kingston upon Hull.	Chatsworth, Derbyshire.	Lancaster.	Kendal.	Exeter.	Plymouth Hospital
January	3,64	2,93	2,41	3,99	——	3,59	4,01	4,04	6,59	4,59	6,38
February	0,24	0,25	0,29	0,35	0,37	0,30	0,52	0,54	1,77	1,17	2,19
March	0,46	2,04	1,62	1,35	1,81	1,45	1,71	1,50	2,72	2,96	1,74
April	3,34	2,49	3,06	2,46	2,41	3,83	2,84	5,50	6,49	2,65	4,11
May	1,42	1,53	2,39	1,93	3,41	1,77	1,67	3,79	4,34	3,24	3,97
June	1,00	1,81	1,83	1,11	1,82	1,24	0,02	0,67	0,97	0,25	0,25
July	0,00	0,00	0,14	0,43	0,32	0,01	0,15	1,03	1,61	0,07	0,23
August	1,52	2,38	5,08	2,50	3,32	3,00	0,95	0,94	0,89	0,73	1,28
September	3,08	3,24	6,66	4,71	3,22	5,75	5,78	4,67	5,89	1,62	2,64
October	1,52	1,62	1,72	2,12	2,32	1,82	3,64	5,00	8,24	1,28	2,14
November	4,66	4,49	4,98	4,25	4,03	4,63	2,76	5,00	4,51	2,74	7,43
December	2,10	2,78	2,12	1,70	1,08	2,09	2,03	3,25	4,13	3,32	3,09
	22,98	25,62	32,75	26,00	24,11	29,48	26,73	35,93	48,20	24,56	35,50

Married.] At Whitehaven, Mr. W. Sisson, of Millom, to Mrs. Bowman.—Mr. T. Dobson, ship-carpenter, to Miss S. Clementson.—Mr. J. Crossthwaite, of Bank End, in Lamplugh, to Miss J. Sheffield.—Mr. T. Lindall, ship carpenter, to Miss A. Westmorland.

At Kendal, Mr. R. Comstone, horse-comb-maker, to Mrs. Pennington, of the White Horse Inn.—Mr. J. Briggs, keeper of Sandy's hospital and library, and master of the charity school for boys, to Miss Harriton.

On the 24th of May last, at Kingston, in Jamaica, Mr. M. Hughes, master-mason, formerly of Whitehaven, to Miss E. Dykes, of Liverpool.

At Brampton, Mr J. Hetherington, flax-dresser, to Miss Thompson.—W. Allonby, M. D. son of W. Allonby, esq. of Flimby, to Miss N. Crossthwaite of Harrington.

At Workington, Mr. J. Brown, mariner, to Miss Ellen.—Mr. Brown, master of the brig Blessing, to Miss Whylie, of Moorclose.—The Rev T. Martin, assistant-minister of St. Nicholas, Whitehaven, to Mrs. Wilkinson, of Prospect hill.—Mr. T. Reed, of Bag-

 graw,

graw, to Miss S. Ray, second daughter of Mr. C. Ray, of Wigton, late an officer in the Cumberland Militia.

Died.] At Carlisle, in his 30th year, much respected, Mr. G. Hardelty, of the Crown and Mitre Inn. Returning home from visiting some friends in the country, he unfortunately fell from his horse, and his head struck against a stone with such violence as to fracture his skull, in a most dreadful manner. He was taken up apparently lifeless, and never after uttered an articulate word.

In the prime of life, Mr. J. Carrick, one of the partners in the Printfield of Donald and Co.—At an advanced age, Mrs. Howgill, schoolmistress —Mr. J. Wear, smith.—Mrs. C. Johnson, wife of Mr. M. Johnson, an eminent retail grocer and a quaker.—In her 31st year, Miss A. Lowthwaite; much lamented by her relations and acquaintance, as a very amiable and accomplished young lady.

Aged 58, Mr. W. Robson.

At Kendal, in an advanced age, Mr. Clementson —Mr. T. Holmes, woollen draper, &c. He was seized with a fit of apoplexy, of which he instantly expired.

In an advanced age, Mrs. Wilson, in the market-place.

At Braithwaite in Borrowdale, Mrs. Harrison, wife of the Rev. Mr. Harrison.

At Ullock, near Keswick, aged 57, Mrs. M Bell.

In the West Indies, on the passage between the island of Berbice, and St. Vincent's, Capt Walker, of the ship Alexandria, of Whitehaven; and at St. Christopher's, Mr. Backhouse, mate of the said vessel.

At Maryport, in the prime of life, Mrs. Huddlestone, wife of Captain J. Huddlestone.

At Rose-hill, near Whitehaven, in her 64th year, Mrs. Hartley, relict of the late J. Hartley, esq. whom she has survived only 6 months. She was a lady worthily esteemed through life by all her acquaintance.

At Fidler-hall, near Cartmel, Mr. J. Brockbank, chymist and druggist, of Kendal.—Mr. G. Willan, of Uphall, near Kirkby Lonsdale. His death was occasioned by a sudden fall.

At Stainburn, in an advanced age, Mr. J. Grave, many years a respectable butcher in Workington.—In the prime of life Mr. J. Holme, miller, at Beckmills, near Kendal.

At Caron, in North Britain, aged 81, Mr. J. Banks, late of Dalston, near Carlisle.

At Garsdale-head, near Sedburgh, Mr. T. Wind.

At Brough-under-Stainmore, Mr. J. Muncaster, fishmonger, of Cargo, near Carlisle. His death was occasioned by the horse taking fright, and the cart running over his body

At High Harseugh, near Kirk Oswald, aged 85, M. G. Arnison.

At Kirkoswald, of a consumptive complaint, in his 25th year, Mr. J. Wharton; highly respected by all who knew him as a young man of great promise. He came from London a few weeks ago to Kirkoswald, the place of his nativity, in hopes of recovering his health.

At Ecclefechan, in the prime of life, Mr. J. Fraser, writer.

YORKSHIRE.

At a late meeting of the West Riding Agricultural Society, held at Ferrybridge, premiums of 2 guineas were adjudged to the following persons, J. Colbeck, of Barkstone Ash, labourer in husbandry, for having brought up 8 legitimate children, without parochial assistance. To E. Barber, of Birkin parish, labourer in husbandry, for having brought up 6 legitimate children. To J. Barton, of Brotherton, labourer, for having had born to him 11 legitimate children, of whom 5 are now living, and has not received parochial relief; and to R. Simpson, for having lived 41 years in one service. Also a guinea and a half to R. Lee, for having lived 34 years in one service; also 2 guineas to Mary Scott of Brotherton, for rearing the greatest quantity of poultry; also to Mary Cousins, of Willow, a guinea and a half, for having this season hoed with the hand hoe, about 8 acres of broadcast turnips; also to B. W. D. Cooke, esq. 3 guineas, for shewing the best shearling tup; also to Sir John Ramsden, bart, 2 guineas for the second best ditto, and 4 guineas for the third best gimmer hog.

As the improvements of Agriculture have extended themselves over the face of the country, and cultivated and beautified it, the pleasures of the chace seem diminishing in proportion. In addition to this, the increasing price of all the articles of life, together with increasing taxes, are daily rendering the maintenance of a pack of hounds, and their consequent attendants, beyond the compass even of a noble fortune. Enclosures, however, are gradually increasing, and the great fox-covers disappearing. In short, there is every probability that a little time will see the end of fox-hunting, and that many men of the present age will live to be in at its death. In its place, grey-hound coursing has become, at least, in this county, the order of the day. Snowball, the property of Major Topham, (taken for every thing) is supposed to be the best greyhound that ever was; he has won four silver cups, and above 30 matches. Major, the brother of Snowball, given by Major Topham to Colonel Thornton, is imagined to be the best running dog now in England. He beat the famous bitch Dent, who was sold for 30 guineas. The Rev. Mr. Dudley's bitch Miss, of Bradwell hall, in Essex, which won the cup at the Tillingham-marsh meeting, in March last, is much spoken of.

A new coursing meeting has been lately established at Pentliver, by Captain Wellwood,

wood, who is remarkable in the feeding and training his greyhounds, which he does not trust to any one but himself. Also one in Ayrshire, and the other in Sterlingshire; all in Scotland. Flixton-Wolds have obtained the highest fame for coursing, as, likewise in point of breed, in fineness of skin and symmetry. The dogs bred here exhibit every sign of the highest blood possible; in comparison of these, what were formerly supposed to have been the fleetest greyhounds of their day, are much inferior, being large, coarse, wire-haired dogs. The greatest greyhound breeders, at present, are the Marquis Townshend and Mr. Hammond, in Norfolk; Mr. Mundy and Captain Swinfen, in Derbyshire; Mr. Stead, in Berkshire; the Rev. M. Corsellis, and Mr. B. Dudley, in Essex; Dr. Frampton, at Newmarket; Mr. Clark of Vauxhall, London; Col. Thornton, of Thornville Royal; Sir Rowland Wynne, of Nostal Park; Major Topham, of Wold Cottage, and Mr. Plumer of Bilton Hall, all in Yorkshire; and Captain Wellwood, of Pitliver, in Scotland.

Application is intended to be made to Parliament in the next session, for an act for building a bridge over the river Derwent, at or near Loftsome Ferry, from the parish of Wressel to the opposite shore of Hemingbrough, in the East Riding.

Preparations are making for carrying into execution an Act of Parliament lately passed, for dividing, enclosing, &c. the common and waste lands within the township of Hornsea, in the East Riding, and for making compensation in lieu of the tithes, and of ancient inclosed lands, in the same township.

Commissioners have been lately appointed to erect a new or outer pier at Scarborough, in which some progress has been already made, but there yet remains an extent of about 140 yards to be continued and finished. The above pier is to be built in from 9 to 11 feet depth of water, at low water, spring tides; and its base, up to that height, will be formed of large and small stones, thrown promiscuously, and will contain from 90 to 100 cubic yards, for each yard in length of the pier. Its superstructure, which will be formed of the same stones, laid for the greater part regularly, will contain nearly the same number of yards.

Two additional wings are to be made to the castle at York, for the further accommodation of prisoners, whom the increase of population renders yearly more numerous.

Medical State of the Lunatic Asylum at York.—Patients admitted from the first establishment of the Asylum, in 1777, to the 1st day of August, 1800, 1347; and from August 1800, to August 1801, 100—Total 1447.—Cured 661; relieved 341; incurable, and removed by desire of their friends, 173; died 145; remain in the house, 77 men and 50 women, among whom are 21 patients who enjoy the benefit of a considerable sum, arising annually from the enlarged payments of a few patients in easy circumstances—127.

State of the Asylum, from July 1, 1800, to July 1, 1801.

CREDITOR.—Balance in the hands of the House-steward and the two Banks at York, 87l. 18s. 11d.; from patients, and Lady Gower's Reduction fund, 2509l. 15s. 8d; interest on securities, and dividends in the funds, 152l. 5s. 10d.; Sale of 1000l. in the three per cent. consols. 643l. 15s.; legacies, from Mrs. Marsden 20l.; from Mrs. Legard 50l.; balance due to Wilson and Co.'s bank, 12l. 5s. 8d.—Total 3476l. 1s. 1d.

DEBTOR.—Weekly and house-bills, 2478l.; incidental tradesmen's bills, 968l. 5s. 8d.; balance remaining in the hands of the House-steward, 28l. 18s. 11d; due by Swan and Co. 7s. 2d.—Total 3476l. 1s. 1d.

Mr. Thomas Burton, gardener to Sir Rowland Wynne, Bart. of Nostal, near Pomfret, has lately announced, in the Yorkshire papers, his having found out a complete method of destroying insects, instantaneously, on the pine-apple-plants, without steeping them in any kind of liquor whatever: and without the least hurt or check to the plants; and particularly on the grape-vines, where the insects are so destructive to that fruit; and even all sorts of exotics, with the greatest safety. He likewise announces a remedy to prevent insects, and blight of mildew on the peach and nectarine trees. He purposes delivering receipts, shewing his method, as soon as he can obtain a sufficient number of subscribers, at five guineas each. The subscription is to close on the 31st of December.

A common horsebean, that had accidentally taken root in a corner of the Town-street of Northallerton, this year, produced from three stems, 103 pods, containing 314 full-grown beans!

Directors have been lately appointed for carrying into execution an Act of Parliament lately passed, for draining, embanking, &c. divers tracts of land, within the township of Muston, in the parish of Hunmanby, and also within sundry other parishes, townships, &c. adjoining or near to the rivers Derwent and Hartford, in the East and North Ridings of this county. Mr. Chapman, engineer for the above drainage, has advised that a number of cuts and other works of drainage, which he has set out, be made within the several townships of Willerby, Staxton, Flixton, Folkton, West Flatmanby, East Flatmanby, and Muston, previously to the completion of the main drain or channel, from Everley down to the sea.

The account lately published in a Leeds Paper, part of which has been copied into most of the other provincial papers, of a seditious meeting in the West Riding, countenanced and supported by persons of consequence, turns out to be an unfounded calumny upon

upon the gentlemen and magistrates of that district.

The spirited exertions of the gentlemen of the East Riding having produced, this year, a very large subscription, the late shew of candidate cattle for the East Riding was on a scale proportionably large. Mr. Dennison, of Kilnwick, was nominated steward of the day.—Tatton Sykes, Esq. whose judgment in sheep is universally acknowledged, was the tryer of the sheep-stock; Messrs. Wright and J. Hall were the judges of all the other stock produced. After a very minute inspection, the winners were declared to be as follow:—Mr. Wright, for the best shearling tup, from any part of England, 10l. 10s.; Mr. Cross, for the best ditto, bred in the East Riding, 10l. 10s.; Mr. Ward, for the best yearling bull, bred in ditto, 5l. 5s.; Mr. Coats, for the second best ditto, bred in ditto, 8l. 8s.; Mr. Ward, for the third best ditto, bred in ditto, 6l. 6s.; Mr. Marshal, for the fourth best ditto, bred in ditto, 4l. 4s.; Mr. Marshall, likewise, for the fifth best ditto, bred in ditto, 2l 2s; Mr. Outram, for the second best ditto, bred in ditto, 3l. 3s.; Mr. Philips, for the best two-year old heifer, bred in ditto, 3l. 3s.; and Mr. Robinson, for the best boar, bred in ditto, 3l. 3s.; Mr. Hall, of Scarborough, shewed some very capital ewes, both as to breed, condition, shape, and fleece. The prize-boar was of the Leicestershire breed. Among the gentlemen present were Major Osbaldeston, Colonel Creyke, Major Topham, Doctor Foord, Rev. Mr. Elliott, Mr. Best, Mr Dade, Mr. Pease, Mr. Grimstone, Mr. Digby Legard, Mr. Broadley, Mr. Bethell, Mr. Bryan Taylor, with a larger assembly of farming amateurs than any similar occasion ever before produced.

The Earl Fauconberg, Smith, arrived at Hull, from the Greenland-fishery, with 11 fish, about 203 butts of oil and blubber, and three tons of fins, is the only vessel belonging to th e port not before arrived.

In a garden, at Sheffield-moor, belonging to Mr. Watson, a single oat has, this year, produced 30 stems, containing in the whole 8500 grains!

Married.] At York, Mr. H. Bland, to Miss Ellis, only daughter of Mr. Alderman Ellis—Mr. J. Harrison, aged 78, formerly a tallow chandler, to Mrs M. Reif, aged 68.—Mr. F. Carter, wine-merchant, to Miss M. Worrall.—John Field, jun. esq. second son of J. Field, esq. of Heaton, to Miss Wainman, of Carr-head, in Craven.—Mr. J. Place, grocer, &c. of Witherby, to Miss Bellwood, of Sutton on the Forest.

At Hull, Mr. W. Fox, grocer, to Miss S. Parnel, of Newark.

At Wakefield, Mr. C. Cloyne, a preacher in the Methodist connection, to Miss Hadfield.

Mr. W. Barker, worsted-manufacturer, of Sowerby, to Miss A. Booth, of Soyland.—Mr. W. Kellet, to Miss M. Kitson, both of Skircoat, near Halifax.

At Halifax, Mr. W. Newby, to Miss E. Pearson.—Mr. J. Lees, merchant, to Miss E. Blagbrough.

Mr G. Beecroft, to Miss E. Booth, both of Seacroft, near Leeds.

The Rev. J. Burnett, M. A. to Miss Horsfall, of the Well, both of or near Huddersfield.—N. Jowett, esq. of Clock-house, near Bradford, to Miss Hodgson, of Bradford.—At Bramham, the Rev. J. Drake, A. M. to Miss Assheton, third daughter of the Rev. R. Assheton, D. D. Warden of Manchester.

At Gretna Green, Mr. W. Harrison, of St. John's Chapel Weardale, to Miss S. Todd, of Scorton, in this county.—Mr. A. Lees, woollen-manufacturer, of Bull House Hall, near Barnsley, to Miss J. Worthington, of Ashton-under-Line.—Mr. T. H. Faber, merchant, to Miss E. Atkinson, both of Bradford.

At Low Catton, Mr. R. Nixon, cheesemonger, &c. of London, to Miss Gray, of Stamford-bridge.—Mr. Wincup, of Hunsingore, to Miss Bird, of Weixley, both near Wetherby.—Mr. Thack, of Laund House, near Wetherby, to Miss Clark of Green Hammerton.

In London, Mr. S. H. Teush, to Miss Pollard, of Greenhill, near Halifax.

At Leeds, Mr. T. T. Morgan, of Litchfield, to Miss Butler, of Kirkstall Forge.—Mr. Land, distiller, to Miss Clapham.—Mr. J. Clapham, jun. to Miss Peele, late of London.

Died.] At York, aged 52, Mr. J. Barwick, farrier, and common-council-man for Micklegate Ward.—Mrs. Spink, widow, and dealer in spirituous liquors.—Mrs. Wright, wife of Mr. R. Wright, tea-man.—Very suddenly, Mr. T. Hardcastle, brother to the late Mr. Hardcastle, of the White Swan tavern.—In his 69th year, Mr R. Hearon.—L. Pickard, esq. many years steward to the late and the present Archbishop of York.—Mrs. Collinson, formerly of Scarboro'.—Mrs. Hesfay.—Aged 45, Mr. C. Masterman, butcher.—Mr. Schofield, jeweller.

At Hull, at an advanced age, Mrs. J. Spence, relict of Mr. J. Spence, ironmonger.

At Walthamstow, the Rev. F. Dixon, B. D. He held the sinecure chapelry of Rotheram, in this county.—Aged 18, Miss E. Fenton, of Spring Grove, near Huddersfield.

At Denton Park, suddenly, by a fall from his horse, J. Ibbetson, esq. third son of the late Sir James Ibbetson, bart.—Far advanced in years, Mrs. D. Wells, of Booth Ferry inn, near Howden.

At Hatfield, near Doncaster, aged 62, Mrs. Swainston.

At Ferry-bridge, aged 26, on his way from London to Nun Appleton, Mr. W. Hart, eldest son of Mr. H. Hart, of Nun Appleton, near York.

At Bath, Mrs. Eamonson, widow, formerly

merly of Lazingcroft, and late of Berwick, in Elmet, near Leeds.

At Morley, near Leeds, aged 30, Mr. J. Clough, formerly of Hill House, near Holmfirth

At Storrs, in Westmoreland, M. S. Grimstone, esq. eldest son of T. Grimstone, esq. of Grimstone and Kilnwick, in this county.

At Halifax, Mr. S. Appleyard, publican.—Suddenly, occasioned by a fall from a Scaffold, Mr. J. Briggs, publican.—Mr. J. Newill, confectioner.—J. Alexander, M. D. a gentleman as much admired for his professional skill, as he was respected for his private virtues.

At Wakefield, Miss A. Morgan.—Aged 68, Mrs. Ramsden.

At Whitby, Mr. F. Cooper, hardware-man.—Aged 30, Mrs. Walker, many years mistress of the Hare and Hounds tavern.

At Northallerton, or near it, Mr. G. Johnson. Having imprudently loaded his gun with small stones instead of shot, to shoot at some crows, the piece bursting, wounded him so severely in the left hand, as to occasion his death.

At Fulnec, near Leeds, Mr. J. Chambers, an active partner in the house of J. Haley and Co; a man of strict integrity and of a truly Christian character.

Miss Ward, of Chapel Allerton, near Leeds.

At Dronfield, the Rev. F. Cripps, minister of Trinity Church, in Leeds.

At Islington, near London, in his 29th year, Mr. R. Williamson, eldest son of Mr. H. Williamson, of York.

At Welton, in the West Riding, Mrs. E. Schames, widow.—Miss Howson, of Firbeck.—Miss Ward, of Chapel Allerton, near Leeds.—Mr. R. Flower, proprietor of the Hop Pole-inn, at Ollerton.

At Sessay, near Thirsk, aged 80, Mr. W. Pinkney.

Miss N. Ellis, of Hetton, near Skipton.—Mr. Atkinson, dry-salter, of Holbeck, son of Mr. T. Atkinson, tallow chandler, of Halifax.—Mr. J. Graham, of the New-inn, Armley.—Mrs. Parker, of North Hall, near Halifax.

At his son's house, at Morley, aged 90, Mr. J. Clough, formerly of Hill House, near Holmfirth.—Mr. Martin, of Headingley, near Halifax.

At Sheffield, Mr. Fairbank, land-surveyor, a Quaker.—Aged 73, S. Venner, esq. formerly Secretary to the Board of Customs in America.

At Bradford, Miss A. Morgan, late of the Sun-inn.

At Leeds, Mr. W. Teale, brazier.—Very suddenly, Mrs. De la Place.—In his 21st year, Mr. J. Binns, banker and bookseller.

LANCASHIRE.

Considerable improvements are intended to be made in the town of Liverpool, by widening, altering, &c. certain streets and passages—by supplying the town with fresh and wholesome water—by removing and preventing nuisances and annoyances—and by carrying into effect a plan for erecting certain buildings, near Chapel-street, and Tythe Barn-street, intended to be called the Exchange. It is also intended to supply the adjoining townships of Everton, Kirkdale, West Derby, and Toxteth Park, with good and wholesome water; by digging for, and collecting springs in any lands or grounds in the said several townships, and erecting reservoirs, engines, laying pipes, &c. for raising water in the said parishes.

A subscription has been lately entered into at Lancaster, to raise a sum of money, to erect proper buildings with suitable rooms, &c. for the accommodation of the High Sheriff, Grand Juries, and other gentlemen of the county, at the assizes and other public or general occasions. It is proposed to carry the plan into effect before the next assizes.

The plant called *Cactus Triangularis* is now in full flower at Standen Hall, near Clithero, which is justly reckoned a very great curiosity in this country.

Married.] At Lisbon, Mr. W. Harper, surgeon, on the Staff, son of Mr. Harper, hatter, of Manchester, to Miss A. Avelina Valudus, grand-daughter of the Marquis de Lorn, a nobleman of the first distinction in Portugal.

At Kirk Malew, Isle of Man, Mr. Holyman to Mrs Forsyth, of Castletown.—Mr. J. Smith, linen draper, of Hull, to Miss Greaves, of Mosley, near Manchester.

At Prestbury, Mr. Kitchen, to Miss Oliver, of Poynton.

At Preston, Mr. W. Corry, master-builder, &c. to Mrs. Parker, of the George Inn, widow.

At Liverpool, Mr. Coddington, to Miss Mitchell.—Mr. Pugh, stucco-worker, &c. to Mrs. Ripley, of the three tuns, public-house.—Mr. J. Diggles, to Miss Joynson.—H. B. Thornhill, esq. of Stanton, in Derbyshire, to Miss H. Pole.—Mr. Boys, to Miss M. Murray, daughter of Mr. J. Murray, painter.—Mr. J. Collins, to Mrs. M. M'Corley.—Mr. Fisher, surgeon, to Miss Musgrove.—Mr. W. Worrall, merchant, to Miss Diggles.—Mr. J. Castley, merchant, to Miss Williams.—Mr. T. Smith, tanner, to Miss B. Hatton, of Parbold.—Mr. R. Williams, pilot, to Miss P. Jones.

Mr. T. Lang, merchant, in Liverpool, to Miss Twigg, of Birmingham.

At Latham, T. H. Maud, esq. to Miss Marriott.

Mr. M. Ashcroft, of Walton, to Miss Rigby, of Melling.

Mr. Stephens, of Liverpool, to Miss Jackson, of Holyhead.

At Wigan, Mr. R. Marsden, taylor, to Miss Cleancross, mantua maker, of Ulverstone.

At Blackburn, Mr. J. Brogden, grocer, &c. to Miss Workman.

At Castle Douglas, Mr. J. M'Neilie, merchant, of Liverpool, to Miss Pew, daughter of J. Pew, esq. of Mavisbank.

Mr. Taylor, of Broad Oak, in Acrington, to Miss Fort, of or near the same place.

Died.] At Liverpool, aged 23, Mr. S. Gee, waiter at the Bull tavern, and universally esteemed for his civility, attention, integrity, and faithfulness.

In his 70th year, E. Butler, Esq. collector of the stamp duties for the Hundred of Lonsdale.

Mrs. M. Wilson.—Miss Huddlestone — Mrs. Urmson.—Mrs. Foxlow.—Mrs. Oliver, wife of captain T. Oliver, of the ship Mona. —In her 26th year, Mrs. Tarleton.

Mr. M. Dunn, a sincere Christian, a tender husband, and a faithful friend. His exemplary private life was well known to his numerous acquaintance, and he was a liberal benefactor to the poor of Liverpool and its vicinity.

Miss C. Shaw, daughter of the late captain Shaw, in the Dublin trade.—Mr. Ant. Burrow.

Mr. T. Parke, late one of the land waiters of this port.

Mr. Wyld, upwards of 20 years prompter of Covent Garden theatre.

At Manchester, aged 26, Miss E. Bray, daughter of Mr. W. Bray, of London.—Mr. Roberts, silversmith.—In his 83d year, Mr. P. Brooke, plumber and glazier.—Mrs. Alcock.

At Salford, Mr. J. Bennett.—Aged 17, Miss Charlton, daughter of Mr. Charlton, apothecary.

At Preston, Mr. R. Smith, tallow-chandler.

Mr. J. Kirkman: being a member of the lodge of Peace and Unity, No. 565, he was buried with Masonic honours.

At Lancaster, Mrs. Gaskell, widow of the late Mr. D. Gaskell, of Clifton, near Manchester.

At Blackburn, aged 90, Mrs. E. Wolstonecroft.—Mr. J. Cooke, many years servant to the gentlemens' concert in the above town.

At Rochdale, Mr. R. Holt, attorney, and clerk to the justices of peace for that district.

At Rivington, aged 82, Mrs. Dorning, late of Bolton.

At Sandbach, aged 59, Mrs. Dowe, relict of Captain M. Dowe, of Liverpool.

Mrs. Charnock, widow, of Fulwood, and mother to Mrs. J Montgomery, of Liverpool.

Mr. T. Taylor, merchant, of Blackley, near Manchester.

C. Baldwyn, esq. son of the late S Baldwyn, esq. of Manchester, and grandson of Dr. Thomas Lamplugh, formerly archbishop of York.

At Plat Bridge, near Wigan, in her 70th year, Elizabeth, wife of R Peters, esq.; a lady eminently distinguished by intrinsic goodness of heart, and the purest principles of religion. The solid endowments of her mind, and that elegant urbanity of manners, which rendered her conspicuous in a large circle of acquaintance, may be considered as minor virtues, if brought into comparison with her pious zeal in the cause of humanity and her active benevolence, which waited not for the solicitations of wretchedness, but led her to visit its dreary abodes. Her life was one continued scene of beneficence, and she was ever ready to extend the hand of charity to the poor, who have lost a real friend in this admirable woman.

The Rev. R. Mytton, of Eccleston.

At Ashton-under-Lyne, Mr. J. Harrop, fustian manufacturer.

At Mottram, in Longdendale, Mr. J. Bostock; a man deservedly respected and esteemed through life, for his hospitality to strangers and charitable disposition to the poor.

At Rivington Hall, aged 82, Mrs. H. Dorning, widow, late of Bolton; a lady of a mild and equal temper, of a meek and humble mind, and a warm, benevolent heart. Her character was formed upon the model of pure Christianity. Her friendships were select, sincere, and permanent; her charities discriminating, soothing and generous. To her it was more blessed to give than to receive, and she was ever ready to do more for others, than she would allow others to do for her. In the last period of her well-spent, long life, (the early periods of which had been peculiarly marked with severe and trying afflictions), she exhibited a picture of religious tranquillity and placid benevolence, at once consoling to virtue, and honourable to human nature.

At Vendue in Jamaica, on the 30th of April, Mr. W. Nichols, brother to Mr. T. Nichols, at Flixton.

At Aldingham, in the 83d year of his age, the Rev. Roger Baldwin, F. R. S. F. S. A. rector of Aldingham, and prebendary of Carlisle. He was born at Wigan in Lancashire, and studied physic for some years under the celebrated Boerhaave at Leyden. After his return to England he practised as a physician, with a high reputation, both at Cambridge (of which University he was a member, being a Fellow of Peter-house), and in his native town. Having, however, devoted a large portion of his time to Biblical Literature, and to the study of the Greek and Hebrew languages, about the age of forty he entered into the church. From that period, he resided principally at Aldingham, and divided his attention between literary pursuits, agriculture, and gardening. His information in almost every branch of knowledge,

knowledge, particularly history and languages, (both ancient and modern) was extensive and accurate, and in him there was an uncommon instance of a memory most wonderfully retentive being united to a clear judgment, and a lively imagination. Lord Willoughby of Parham; Hater, Bishop of London; Littleton, Bishop of Carlisle; Mr. Gray the poet; Dr Kennicott; the late Dr Heberden, &c. were among his intimate friends; and till within a few days of his death, he corresponded with many of the most learned men of the age. There is some reason to hope, that he may have left behind him works in a state fit for publication.

CHESHIRE.

Application is intended to be made to Parliament in the ensuing session, for an Act to inclose, &c. the lands commonly called Beam Heath, in the parish of Nantwich.

Twenty-seven insolvent debtors were lately liberated from the Castle at Chester.

Married.] At Chester, S. Thompson, esq. banker, of Liverpool, to Miss Hughs.—Mr. J. Monk, printer of the Chester Courant, to Miss Harrison, of Aldford.—Mr. J Cooper, woollen-draper, to Miss Hicks, sister of the late Major Hicks.—Mr. Poole, bookseller, to Miss Turner.

Mr. H. Harland, of Raynor, near Macclesfield, to Miss E. Birchinall, of Macclesfield.

Mr. Kitchen, check-manufacturer, of Prestbury, to Miss Oliver, of Poynton.

Mr. R. S. Clare, merchant, of Liverpool, to Miss Jones, of Weaverham.

Mr. T. Warburton, sail-maker, of Liverpool, to Miss Parsons, of Frodsham.

Mr. P. Bourne, of Newton, to Miss Holford, of Preston Hall.

Mr. F. Scattergood, of Stockport, to Miss M. Pownall, of Pullock-Smithy.

Died.] At Chester, Mr. Jones, shoemaker, and serjeant-major of the loyal Chester volunteers.

Mrs. Bowcock, wife of Mr. R. Bowcock, cotton manufacturer.—Aged 80, Mr. Bramwell, alderman of this city.—Mrs. Hill, aunt to J. Meacock, esq. major.—Aged 71, Mrs. Adams, of the Feathers inn.

At Dunham Massey, Mrs. Lowton, widow.

The Rev. C. Myton, A. M. rector of Eccleston, near Chester.

At Northwich, Mrs. Warburton, relict of Mr. J. Warburton, salt-proprietor.

In her 66th year, Mrs. Dodd, of Harthill.

Mr. Johnson, miller, of Neston.

DERBYSHIRE.

Application is intended to be made to Parliament in the next session, for an Act to make a communication, by canals and railways, or stone-roads, from the Cromford-canal, near Bull-bridge, to near Belper, and to near Black-brook-bridge; which canals, rail ways, or stone roads, are meant to pass through the parishes, &c. of Crick, Heage, Ashley Hay, Belper, and Duffield, all in this county; and also to confirm such agreement as may be made between the subscribers to such proposed canals, and the Cromford-canal Company, relative to such communication.

Married.] At Derby, Mr. W. Morley, to Miss M. Bromley.

In Sheffield, Yorkshire, M. C. Middleton, esq. of Leame, in this county, to Miss Althorpe, of Donington.

At Chesterfield, Mr. Radley, to Miss Nall.

At Oxford, G. Gardom, esq. of Bubrell, in this county, to Miss J. Dennis, of Cooper's-row, Tower-hill, London.

At Booton, near Derby, Mr. J Cantell, attorney, of King's Newton, to Miss Smith.—Mr. Wildgoose, to Miss M. Hancock, both of Dronfield.

Died.] At Duffield, in her 22d year, Miss M. Bradshaw, of Spondon; a young lady possessed of many accomplishments, but more virtues. Her worth and goodness were conspicuous, and her manners were most amiable and engaging.

NOTTINGHAMSHIRE.

A new fair, for the sale of cheese, to be held on the 25th of September next, and continued yearly on that day, has been lately appointed at Newark, by order of the Mayor.

The Retford Agricultural Society have offered a number of premiums for the present year, consisting of two of 10 guineas, one of 5, three of 2, three of 2, and five of 1 guinea, for the best short-horned bull, three years old or upwards, to be kept for the use of the neighbourhood, for one year at least; for the best stallion, to be kept for the use of the neighbourhood, for the season 1802; and for the second best short horned bull. These premiums to be determined at the spring meeting in 1802; also for the best tup shearling, for the best ewes, for the best wether-hog, and for the next best of each; also for the best boar, not less than one year old; and for the best sow: the sheep and pigs to be shewn on the 2d of July. Also for the greatest quantity of honey, and to the farming servant who shall have continued the longest time, not less than seven years, in the same family. Also a guinea and a pair of buck-skin breeches to the best ploughman; a guinea and a hat to the second best, and a guinea to the third best.

Married.] At Nottingham, Mr Fisher, to Miss Smith.—Mr. Morley, linen-draper, to Miss Bennett.—Mr Fothergill, of York, to Miss R. Bott, daughter of Mr Bott, dentist.

In London, J. Coleman, gent. to Mrs. Bramley, both of Nottingham

Mr. Nixon, saddler, of Newark, to Miss S. Mogg, of Thoroton.

At Bingham, Mr. W. Huckerby, schoolmaster, to Miss Robinson.

Died.] At Nottingham, at an advanced age, Mrs. Lockton, of the Old Angel public house.—Mrs. Butler, wife of Mr. Butler, baker.—Mr. Tate, cordwainer.—Mrs. Worthington, wife

wife of S. Worthington, esq. the present Mayor.—T. Moore, gent.

Mr. R. Flower, proprietor of the Hop-pole-inn, at Ollerton.

At East Bridgford, in consequence of a fall from a ladder the preceding evening, aged 45, Mr. M. Millington.

At Newark, Mr R. Hatfield.

LINCOLNSHIRE.

Special Commissioners have been lately appointed, agreeably to an Act of Parliament, for inclosing, draining, allotting, and improving, the commons and waste-grounds within the several parishes of Epworth, Haxey, Belton, and Owston, in the Isle of Axholme, in this county, and also for making a compensation for the tithes arising from the said commons, and from certain other lands within the said parishes.

Married.] At Grantham, Mr. J. Dorr, farmer, to Miss A. Partridge.

At Stamford, Mr. T. Manly, to Miss Robinson, daughter of Miss Taylor, a manager of the Nottingham Theatre.

In London, J. Hawkins, esq. of Sudbury, in Middlesex, to Miss Sibthorp, daughter of H. Sibthorp, esq. M. P. for Lincoln.

At Woolsthorpe, Mr. C. Smith, of London, to Miss Cooke.

Mr Preston, land-surveyor, of Keddington, near Louth, to Miss Hawling, of Horncastle.

At Brickingham, Mr. J. Horner, aged 66, to Miss S. Marshall, aged 20. This is the second time the bridegroom has entered into the connubial state, and in the choice of his partners has displayed much Christian charity—his present wife being extremely lame, and his former one blind.

Died.] At Lincoln, aged 60, Mr. R. Lowe, ironmonger.—At the Saracen's Head-inn, aged 45, Mr. W. Motteram, factor, late of Birmingham.

At Redbourne, aged 48, Mr. T. Sherlock, an eminent farmer and grazier.

At Louth, Mr. J. Hind, fishmonger.—Aged 66, Mr. W. Spavins, a pensioner on the Chatham-list, and author of a publication called The Seaman's Narrative.

At Benniworth, near Wragby, aged 98, Mr. J. Babington, farmer and grazier.

Mr. R Clarke, farmer, of Butterwick, near Gainsboro'. On his return home from Stockwith-fair, he was robbed of 13 guineas, murdered, and thrown into the river, a short distance from his own house. Two men are apprehended on suspicion of being perpetrators of this horrid deed.

LEICESTERSHIRE.

The Governors of the Leicester Infirmary, for the Sick and Lame of all counties, in consequence of the peculiar pressure of the times, were obliged, in the year 1796, to reduce the number of beds from 54 to 40, and, by the same cause, have been obliged to continue this reduction till last year. From the daily growing distresses, however, of the poor, and the annually increasing applications, the Governors have lately ventured to enlarge the extent of their charity, and have restored to suffering humanity some of those beds which, for the last five years, have remained unoccupied and useless. Last Midsummer they increased the number of beds from 40 to 46, and, trusting to the success of their intended pressing application to the public, have agreed, at their last annual meeting, to venture on an immediate addition of 10 beds, and to increase the number to 50. To the General Infirmary has lately been added another charitable institution, equally important and beneficial. An Asylum, in a separate building, has been opened for the reception of that most helpless and pitiable class of mortals, *poor lunatics*; but it is much to be lamented that it has not yet received that degree of encouragement which might have been reasonably expected, and, without which, it cannot long be supported in such a manner as the benevolent must wish. The asylum is capable of receiving twenty patients, but for *want of an adequate fund from donations and annual subscriptions*, it is, at present, opened upon a more contracted scale, and can receive only fourteen, for each of whom the Governors are obliged to demand a payment of ten shillings weekly, till such time as the bounty of the public shall have sufficiently increased their resources. They flatter themselves, however, animated by some recent symptoms of improvement, that they shall soon be enabled, gradually, to augment the number of patients, and, at the same time, to reduce the weekly demand for each, as was done in the similar institutions at York and Manchester. These improvements, when realized, will give the full advantage this charity is capable of producing.

Married.] Mr. Robert Heygate, of Market Harborough, to Miss Ann Garner, second daughter of Thomas Garner, of that place, esq.

At Leicester, Mr. Pegg, portrait painter, to Miss L. Harvey.

Died.] At Market Harboro', in his 85th year, J. Hands, gent. In business he was polite, attentive, and strictly just; in society an agreeable companion; and if religion, charity, sincerity, and friendship, united with unbounded hospitality, are the characteristics of a good Christian and an honest man, he certainly was both.

At Cossington, aged 28, Mrs Baguely.—Aged 86, Mrs. Burrough, wife of the Rev. S. Burrough, rector of Sipcote, and many years master of Rugby school.—Aged 18, Miss Lynes, of Kirkby Mallory.

RUTLAND.

Married.] B. Warren, esq. of Uppingham, to Miss Jackson, of Bromley, in Kent.

Died.] At Ketton, suddenly, Mr. Baxter an eminent land-surveyor.—Mrs. Mould, of Oakham.

STAF-

STAFFORDSHIRE.

At the late General Meeting of the Newcastle-under-Lyne and Pottery Agricultural Society, W. Sneyd, esq. president, in the Chair, a premium of one guinea was adjudged to Mr. J. Tilstone, of Newcastle, for cultivating the greatest quantity of early potatoes; also one guinea was adjudged to Mr. J. Shaw, servant to Mr R. Timmis, of Weston Hall, for having plashed upwards of 330 roods of quick fence, in a good manner; also a premium of two guineas was adjudged to John Cash, servant to Mr. Isaac Alton, of New Park, for having plowed 103 acres of land in a good manner; also one premium of five guineas, one of three, and two of two guineas, to different labourers in husbandry, for bringing up children without parochial assistance, &c.

Married.] At Wolverhampton, Mr. R. Farmer, factor, to Miss M. Smith.

Mr. Cope, of Ticknell, Derbyshire, to Miss Smith, of Oxgrove, in this county.

At Cheadle, Mr. Hubbard, attorney, to Mrs. Ward, widow.

Died.] At Wolverhampton, aged 80, Mr. J. Smith.—Mr. W. Ensor.—Mrs. E Wright. Mr. C. Setchell, currier.

At Walsall, aged 66, Mr. Clarkson, senior.—Of a decline, Mr. T. Marlow, bucklemaker, &c.—Mr. W. Clarke, of Ettingsall.—Mrs. Waldron, of Field House.—Mr. R. Farmer, of Dost-hill, near Tamworth.

At Tutbury, the Rev. R. Palmer.

WARWICKSHIRE.

Married.] At Birmingham, Mr. T. Lang, merchant, of Liverpool, to Miss M. Twigg.—Mr. Jordan, to Miss A. Johnson.—Mr. H. Laugher, to Miss Duplan.—Mr. W. Alder, to Miss E. Dawson.—G. Scale, esq of Coton Hall, Shropshire, to Miss H. Griffith, second daughter of J. D. Griffith, esq. of Birmingham-heath.—Mr. W. Bates, to Miss S. Gibson.—Mr. C. Horton, to Miss M. Mostyn.

Mr. J. Lillington, of Birmingham, to Miss Handford, of Biddeford, Devon.—Mr. H. Homer, jun. of Balsall-heath, to Miss A. Chambers, of Yardley.—Mr. T. Boyce, of London, to Miss Boyce, of Deritend.—Mr. J. Clarke, butcher, of Coleshill, to Miss Toon, of Shustock.

At Newnham Paddock, Lord Tara, of Ballinter, county of Meath, Ireland, to Miss Powys, second daughter of T. Jelf, M. P. esq. of Berwick House.—E. Dickenson, esq. of Dosthill House, near Tamworth, to Miss Crutchley, of Shenstone Lodge.—Mr. W. Phillips, of Birmingham, to Miss E. Smith, of Warwick.

Died.] At Birmingham, Mrs. S. Mobbs.

At Coventry, Mr. F. Soden, many years conductor of the Post-office; universally respected by those who knew him, for the ingenuous openness of his disposition, and the glowing charity of his heart. He was a pleasant companion, a sincere friend, ever ready to apply the healing balm to sharp affliction, and an honest man.

Mrs. Millar, relict of the late Mr. Millar, butcher.

Mrs. Daffron, of Trayford Hall, near Stichford.

At Handsworth, near Birmingham, aged 66, Mr. J. Millward, dealer in wire.—Mr. T. Askey, senior.—Aged 76, Mr. D. Thompson, of the Soho-manufactory.—Mrs. Siveter, of Sare-hole-mill, near Birmingham.

At Sutton Colfield, Mrs. Alcock, formerly of Birmingham. Mrs. Gamble

Master S. Frost, third son of Mr. Frost, of the Sand Pits, near Birmingham

At Berkswell, Miss Vale, daughter of the late Mr. Alderman Vale, of Coventry.

Aged 84, Mrs. Harvey, of Duddeston, near Birmingham. In her last moments she could revert to the transactions of her past life, with that high satisfaction which ever accompanies integrity and virtue.

At his son's house at Camphill, near Birmingham, A. Payton, esq. formerly an eminent linen draper in London.

At Tamworth, in his 72d year, Mr. R. Bage, a gentleman of the most kind and benevolent affections, and of the most scrupulous integrity, yet his mind was of a firm and manly cast. His gentle and unassuming manners formed a striking contrast to the vigour of his genius and understanding. He was distinguished by great mental acquirements, and was the author of Hermsprong, and other admired literary productions.—[*We hope some Inhabitant of Tamworth will evince a due regard to the worth of this excellent and most ingenious man, and favour us with a full account of him for our next Number.*]

SHROPSHIRE.

It is in contemplation to erect a bridge over the river Severn, at Hempton's Load, in this county, and to make proper roads therefrom to communicate with the Cleobury turnpike-road, near Billingsley, and the Dudley and Wolverhampton turnpike-road, near the Long Common, in the parish of Bobbington.

At the meeting of the Drayton Agricultural Society, Aug. 4, Sir Corbet Corbet, bart, President, in the Chair, there was a large shew of good stock, which, considering that this is only the second year of the institution, far exceeded all expectation. The prizes were adjudged as follow:—To J. Hill, esq. of Prees, for the best bull, for stock, 6l. 6s.;—to Mr. Bishop, of Shrewsbury, for the best cow, with her offspring, 3l. 3s.; to Sir Richard Hill, bart. of Hawkestone, for the best three-year old heifer, 2l. 2s.; for the second best ditto, 1l. 1s.; to Mr. Dicken, for the best New Leicester ram for stock, 2l. 2s.; to Mr. Davies, of Drayton, for the best two-shear ram bred, &c. 2l. 2s.; to Mr. W. Jellicorse, of Benthall, for the best three-shear ewe, new Leicester, 2l. 2s.; to Mr. J. B. Harding, of Oldsprings, for the best three-shear ewe of any sort, 2l. 2s.; to ditto, for the best two-shear New Leicester bred ditto, 1l. 1s.; to Mr. Eley, of Tyrley Castle, for the best three-

 year

year old draught filly, 3l. 3s.; and to Mr. J. B. Harding, for the best boar-pig, 1l. 1s.

There is now growing on the grounds of Mr. J. Perry, in the parish of Diddlestone, a nut-tree, planted by the present owner 52 years ago, which measures 36 yards in circumference—and, according to calculation, the above tree has on its branches about 250lbs. of nuts at this time

Married.] Mr. A. Enock, of Wellington, to Miss E. Hayward, of Trosnant, in Monmouthshire.

Mr. J. Smith, wheel-wright, of Meole, to Miss E. Moule, of Atcham.

Died.] At Shrewsbury, of a paralytic stroke, which she survived only about six hours, Mrs. Longmire, wife of Mr. Longmire, writing-master.—Aged 14, in the bloom of youthful beauty, Miss M. Davies.

At Chelmarsh, near Bridgenorth, the Rev. W. Nichols.

At Hurst, the Rev. P. Morris, rector of Sneade, Montgomeryshire, and many years justice of peace for the counties of Salop and Montgomery.

At Aston, in his 44th year, the Rev. J. R. Lloyd, rector of the parishes of Whittington and Sylattin, and justice of peace for this county.—Mr. R. Barnet, of Grinshill.

WORCESTERSHIRE.

The hops, in what is called the Worcester-plantation, extending through the counties of Worcestershire, Shropshire, Herefordshire, and even into some of the Welsh counties, are generally good, healthy, and free from mould, and more abundant than has been witnessed for many years. The crops of fruit, likewise, both for cyder and perry, are equally fine.

At the Hop-market, at Worcester, September 7, only two or three lots remained unsold of about 145 pockets of new hops. General prices 90s. to 100s.; a few at 80s. and 105s. per cwt.—all handsome, but none quite ripe—will be extremely good when they are so.

The hops, in what is called the Farnham district, both as to quality and quantity, exceed the average of any other plantation in the kingdom. Although they gather their hops perfectly free from leaves, yet so abundant is the crop, that the pickers have agreed to take 2d. per bushel for picking them.

At the late Anniversary Meeting of the Governors of Worcester Infirmary, the collection for the benefit of the charity amounted to 102l. 19s 6d.

Married.] J. Allcock Lowe, esq. of Stourport, to Miss C. Carlow, late of Bristol.—Mr. H. Raymond, of Worcester, to Miss Beeston, of Bromsgrove.—Mr. Parkes, to Miss Noke, both of Stourbridge.—Mr. M. Jones, of Worcester, to Miss E. Sanders, of Bromsgrove.

Died.] At Worcester, aged 72, Mr. T. Poole, senior.—S. Amphlett, esq. of Omberiley.

Mr Locke, farmer, of Kempsey, near Worcester. He went out in the morning to course, in company with another gentleman, in perfect health, when he suddenly dropped down in the field without uttering a word, and instantly expired.

HEREFORDSHIRE.

There has lately appeared in the Hereford Journal an advertisement, purporting, that as various opinions have been expressed at the Agricultural Meetings, &c. on the comparative merit of the several breeds of cattle, encouraged in different districts of the kingdom, Mr. Mason, of Chilton, near Durham, declares himself to be desirous, that if the prevailing opinion of this county, in favour of the short-horned breed, be erroneous, the error may be corrected, and therefore, as a motive for others to bring their breeds to the test, he proposes to shew the next produce of five cows, now in his possession, at the time when that produce shall be three years old, against the next produce of any five other cows, now the property of any one man in Great Britain, on a wager of 100 guineas per cow.

At the late boat-race at Hereford, August 27, which afforded very particular satisfaction to a great concourse of spectators, as the beautiful reach of the Wye, from the bridge to Belmont, is admirably adapted for purposes of this kind, the silver cup was won by Mr. T. Downes, beating four others in a rowing-match so well contested, that the second and third boats were close astern of the winner. The colours were won by Mr. R. Parchas, beating two others. On the following day the silver cup was adjudged to Mr. G. Bird, and the colours to Mr. Price. A considerable subscription was made by the nobility and gentry present, in order to render this amusement annual, at the time of the races.

It is in contemplation to form a new road from the present Bredwardine and Whitney turnpike road, to the bridge erecting over the river Wye, near Whitney; also to widen part of the road on the Whitney line, and to erect a stone arch at Pontvaine, &c. all in this county.

Married.] The Rev. W. Parsons, vicar of Stretton Grandsome, to Miss Poole, of Homend.

In London, R. Harrison, esq. of the 7th Dragoon Guards, to Miss James, late of Moor Court, near Kington.—Mr. B. Wainwright, land-surveyor, of Hereford, to Miss Wainwright, of Exton, near Bewdley.—The Rev. Mr. Thickens, of Ross, to Miss Carleis, of Eccles Green.

Died.] At Ross, J. Holder, esq.—Mrs. Eckley, wife of R. Eckley, esq. of Credenhill.—The Rev. J. Symonds, rector of Dinedor.—Miss Hoskyns, daughter of Sir Hungerford Hoskyns, bart. of Harewood.—In his 70th year, J. Freeman, esq. of Gains.

OXFORDSHIRE.

Application is intended to be made to Parliament, for an act for erecting a bridge, at or or near Culham-wharf, in this county, to extend a cross the river Thames, into the parish of Sutton Courtney, in the county of Berks.

Married.] S. P. Newell, esq. of the Oxfordshire Militia, to Miss Sergeant, of Winbourne, Dorset.

Mr. C. Cox, jun. of Oxford, to Miss M. Minchin, of Northmore.—Mr. Jones, brewer, of Lambourne, Berks, to Miss Richings, of Oxford.

Died.] At Oxford, in her 43d year, Mrs. Cooke, wife of Mr. Cooke, bookseller.—Aged 57, Mrs. C. Rusbridge, wife of Mr. E. Rusbridge, shoemaker.

At Henley-upon-Thames, in an advanced age, Mr. G. Haye, many years butler to the Freeman family, at Fawley-court.

At Holywell, in her 71st year, Mrs E. Wallington, sister of the late Mr. R. Wallington, of Oxford.

At Northleigh, in his 44th year, Mr. R. Green.

At Clifton, near Bristol, aged 25, Miss M. E. Whiting, milliner, of Oxford.

BERKSHIRE.

Married.] Mr. Mathews, of Standford Dingley, to Miss Kidgley, of Bradfield.

At Reading, the Rev. Mr. Jeary, to Miss S. Tudor.—C. Dixon, esq of Savage Gardens, to Miss H. Wilder, daughter of the Rev. Dr. Wilder, of Purley Hall.

Mr. J. Butterfield, to Miss Poulton, both of Maidenhead.—Mr. Grigg, of Newbury, to Miss Fussell, of Winchester, Hants.

Died.] At Reading, Mrs. Lamden, wife of Mr. Lamden, baker.—Mrs. Staples, wife of Mr. Staples, poulterer.—Mr. Osmond, collector of the excise.

At Abingdon, aged 74, W. Bowles, esq.

Mrs. Perfect, only daughter of the late Sir Thomas Hayward, of Carswell.

At Farnham, aged 91, Mrs. J. Mayne, a maiden-lady.

At Windsor, in his apartments in the Queens'-mews, Mr. G. Harding, many years body-coachman to her Majesty.

At his house in Sunning Hill, in his 74th year, the Hon. John Yorke, fourth son of Philip Earl of Hardwicke, Chancellor of Great Britain.

In her 73d year, Mrs. Griffith, relict of C. Griffith, esq. of Padworth House, formerly M P. for Berkshire; she was a lady peculiarly distinguished for the virtues of a good heart, and her loss will be feelingly regretted by the numerous objects of her unremitting bounty.

BUCKINGHAMSHIRE.

Preparations are making, agreeably to a late act of Parliament, for paving, watering, lighting and otherwise improving the streets, lanes, and other public passages and places, within the parish of Stony Stratford, and for removing obstructions, annoyances, &c. therein; also for repairing the rampart-road or causeway, leading from the town to the bridge over the river Ouse, near thereto, and for repairing the said bridge.

Died.] At Thames Bank, near Great Marlow, Mrs. Winford.—Miss B. A. Hicks, of Bradenham House.

At Great Marlow, aged 85, the Rev. J. Cleobury, vicar of that parish and of West Woburn almost fifty years, and justice of peace for this county.—Mrs. M. Grignion, late of Chelsea.

BEDFORDSHIRE.

Married.] The Rev. T. Grut, of the Island of Guernsey, to Miss E. Martin, of Shafford, in this county.

NORTHAMPTONSHIRE.

Married.] At Daventry, the Rev. W. Benson, B. D. vicar of Ashby St. Ledgers, &c. to Miss Harrison.—The Rev. W. Lockwood Maydwell, of Geddington, to Miss A. Hodson, of Wellingboro'.

At Guilsboro', the Rev. J. Buckby, to Miss Wigley, eldest daughter of the late Dr. Wigley.—Mr. Sefsly, of Great Bowden, to Miss M. Nursey, of Sutton.—Mr. C. Heygate, surgeon, of West Haddon, to Miss Lovell, of Winwick-warren.—Mr. D. Hennels, of Kettering, to Miss Gale, of King's Ripton, Huntingdonshire.

In London, Mr. J. Clark, coachmaker, of Northampton, to Mrs. M. Berry.

Died.] At Northampton, after a lingering illness, and a well spent life of near 78 years, Mr. Alderman Sutton.—Mr. Stables.—Mr. W. Wykes, formerly a coach-proprietor.—Mrs. Eck.

Mr. J. Denton, member of a benefit society, held at the Swan-inn, from the fund of which he had received the sum of 104l. 17s.

At Thrapstone, in her 71st year, Mrs. Hooke, relict of the late Rev. T. Hooke, rector of Birkby, in Yorkshire.

Aged 24, after a few days illness, Mr. J. Goodman Maxwell, son of Mr. G. Maxwell, of Fletton, near Peterboro'.

At Finedon, Mr. W. Stanton, formerly of the Bell-inn.—Mr. Bowker, attorney, and coroner for the soke of Peterboro'.

At Marston Trussel, in her 22d year, Miss A. Bullivant, eldest daughter of the Rev. J. Bullivant, rector; a truly amiable and good young lady.

At Hollowell, aged 83, Mr. J. Hassock, more than fifty years master of the coach and horses public-house.

Mr. Higgins, of the Swan-inn, Newport Pagnell.

HUNTINGDONSHIRE.

Commissioners have been lately appointed for the inclosure of the parish of St. Ives.

Married.] S. Peacocke, esq. of Cavendish-square, London, to Miss Apreece, only daughter of Sir T. Hussey Apreece, of Washingley-hall, in this county.

Died.] At St Neots, in his 54th year, Mr. Halliley, an eminent surgeon and apothecary.—Aged 79, the Rev. G. Coulton, vicar and patron of Ab Kettleby, in Leicestershire.

CAMBRIDGESHIRE.

Married.] At Cambridge, the Rev. C. Goodwin, of St. John's College, to Miss Naylor, daughter of the Rev. C Naylor, formerly fellow of King's College.—Mr. Home, of Oundle, to Miss Aylmer, of Ely.

Died.] At Cambridge, in his 53d year, Mr. J. Hart, formerly master of the Rose-tavern.

In the West Indies, where he went to settle as a barrister, Mr W Mathews, of Pembroke-hall, Cambridge, and son of Mr. J. Mathews, bookseller, in the Strand, London.

Mrs Edwards, of Fordham.

Mr G. Heady, of Doddington, in the Isle of Ely.

On the 7th of June last, suddenly, on his estate at Barbadoes, Sir Francis Ford, bart. he was formerly a fellow-commoner of St. John's College, Cambridge.

NORFOLK.

Married.] Mr. J Fuller, farmer, to Miss Percival, both of Hale, near Swaffham.—Mr. Harbord, of Eye, to Miss J. Townshend, of New Buckenham.—The Rev. J. Lloyd, of Hildolvestone, to Miss Reeve, of Barney.

Mr. J. Payne, of Colchester, to. Miss F. Back.

Died.] At Norwich, ged 27, Mr. T. Plaford, late Midshipman on board the Ruby ship of war.—Aged 41, Mrs. Forster, widow.—Aged 70, Mr E. Amond, keeper of the county-jail.—In her 41st year, Mrs. R. Harvey, generally beloved and sincerely lamented, as a lady of an amiable mind, ingratiating manners, and a cheerful disposition, ever embellished and enlivened.

Aged 65, Mrs. Flackburn.

At Yarmouth, aged 75, Mrs. Symonds, butcher.

At Dulwich, in Surrey, G. Giles, esq. late Associate of the Norfolk Circuit.

At Somer's Town, St. Pancras, aged 66, Mrs. M. Bacon, relict of Mr. R. Bacon, of Holt.

Mr. J. Hull, of Wolverton.—Mrs. Cubitt, of Catfield.

At New Buckenham, aged 56, Mr. J. Rayner.—In an advanced age, Mrs. H. Winn, late of Holt.—Mrs. Martin, of Great Bradley.

At Saxmundham, Mr. T. Mayhew, attorney.

At Gatesend, Mr. S. Helsdon.—Aged 37, Mrs. T Branch, of Billingford, near Scole-inn.

At Diss, Mr. B. Parker, gardiner.

At East Dereham, Mr. Burgess, principal brewer in the office of Mr. W. Taylor.—Aged 64, Mrs. Raven.

SUFFOLK.

At the late sheep-fair, at Herringer, a turnip was produced, grown this season at Great Barton, which measured one yard, three inches in circumference, and weighed thirty-five pounds!

Married.] Rear-admiral Wilson, of Redgrave hall, in this county, to Miss C. Pollard, of Ewell, in Surrey.

At Lowestoft, the Rev. R. Parry of St. Giles's Norwich, to Mrs. Freeman, of that city.—The Rev. C. Eade, of Cotton, to Miss French, of Eye.

Died.] At Bury, Mr. Tickell, gunsmith.—Mr. C. Buxton, of the Bushel-inn.—Aged 84, Mrs. Brand, mother of Mr Brand, of the Queen's Head public-house.

At Fornham St. Genevieve, near Bury, aged 53, Mr. T. Cowsell.

At Melford, in his 89th year, Mr. J. Wink, sen.

At Troston, near Bury, where she had resided near twenty years, ANNE, the wife of CAPEL LOFFT, *Barrister at Law*, and daughter of Mr HENRY EMLYN, of WINDSOR, BERKS, *Architect*. She had been in her early youth an highly esteemed pupil of Mr. FERGUSON, the *Astronomer*, and celebrated *Mechanician*. She had a very correct and extensive knowledge, which she possessed without affectation. Pre-eminent in personal and intellectual endowments, with the greatest power to shine and please universally, she was content to be retired, beneficent, and unreservedly useful. She will long be remembered by her acquaintance, she will never be forgotten by her friends; and she will live in the remembrance of her poor and suffering neighbours, to whom she was the tenderest, most judicious, and honest friend: of her family in general, in the conduct of which she was considered fondest, mildest, and affectionately kind; and of her children (of whom she has left four, a *daughter*, and *three* sons) who have every motive to cherish the affection due to the memory of the most affectionate, amiable, and excellent mother. To the sufferings of all that is endowed with sensation, she was sensible, and attentive to avoid inflicting misery, and to promote comfort. She had seen great and continued difficulties for many years! By prudence and persevering attention, she had nearly surmounted these, and seemed to have a prospect of seeing her family established in ease and comfort, and of enjoying with them that serenity, which years of anxious attention had been spent to secure. This character of her is not the result of short observation—She was married *August* 20, 1778. She began, and with gratitude to Heaven, to think herself that her prospects were clearing. Her last year was, however, a year of uncommon trial. In the beginning of it, she was suddenly, under the call of duty and affection, hurried from her home to attend, as she did most tenderly, judiciously, and successfully, an apparently dying sister; and, at the same time she soothed the pains of a justly and highly esteemed friend, and softened to her the bed of death. She then not much, and her friends in no degree, apprehended how soon that lot was to be her own. She had enjoyed an excellent

cellent constitution, and an uniform state of health, which great simplicity of diet, evenness of temper, and activity, with regular exercise in the open air, and various employment, promised to continue, at least, to the full usual extent of life; yet this she was far from reaching. A most dangerous and afflictive complaint had been long and imperceptibly stealing on her constitution, which, though good, was delicate, as it generally is, where, with great force of mind, there is much sensibility. Suddenly this fatal complaint manifested itself by a most alarming attack on the system. The immediate danger, which was excessive, was obviated by the use of RUSPINI's STYPTIC, aided, it may be justly believed, by her own fortitude, and constant equanimity; and by the skill and attentive care of Dr. WHITE, of BURY, and Mr. BARKER, of IXWORTH. But the last stroke, although delayed, could not for more than some weeks be averted*. A most severe and excruciating illness she sustained, as long as the powers of nature would permit, with her habitually mild composure. Recollected to the last, her mind was occupied, as from the first of her life it had been, in thoughts and exertions of sympathy and beneficence; and her last hours were comparatively easy and even chearful. She was removed from this life by an almost imperceptible expiration, about a quarter before *eight* in the morning. That such a being was lent to society, especially to that portion of society to which she could be most useful, was no ordinary blessing; and, in *times like these*, however encouraging the prospects were which seemed to be opening to her family, who can say how far her removal now from this state of existence may have been an essential and necessary blessing to herself. Though we speak here of a female character, we may judge of this truth by considering others eminent in the public view; and the most private characters possessed of foresight and social feeling, have sufficient cause to think of impending ill. If our late admirable female HISTORIAN, if MARY WOLLSTONECRAFT, if Madame ROLAND, if of men who have adorned literature and science, and benefited mankind, a JEBB, a PRICE, and a WAKEFIELD, a ROUSSEAU, a MALESHERBES, were now living, we are sure they would have cause to suffer for themselves, their connections, their country, and human happiness in general; and we are far from sure that they could have lived to see these days of gloom and destruction, so baneful to private and public welfare, pass away. HEAVEN only knows, and alone can do, what is ever best; and when the wife, the amiable, and the useful, are taken away, it is often seen by events, that they have been mercifully withdrawn *from the evils to come.*

CAPEL LOFFT.

* From the 1st of *August.*

ESSEX.

At the Essex Agricultural Meeting, held at Chelmsford, Aug. 11, there was a general shew of stock evidently very much improved since the meeting of the last year. The ten prizes of the Society's, silver medals, for the best produced stock, were adjudged as follows:—1. To Mr. Wakefield, for the best cut stallion; 2. To Mr. Western, for the best bull; 3. To Mr Smith, for the best cow or heifer; 4. To Mr. Robinson, for the best Leicestershire or other ram; 5 To Lord Petre, for the best South Down ram; 6 To Mr. Boosey, for the best Leicestershire or other ewe; 7. To Mr. Western, for the best South Down ewe; 8. To Lord Petre, for the best fat ox; 9. To Mr. Robins, for the best wether of his age; and 10. To Mr. Knight, for the best boar.

KENT.

It is contemplation to make a road from Canterbury to the Isle of Thanet, either entirely a new one, or at least, to make a turnpike road from Canterbury to Sarr, and to divert, in some parts, the present line of road, and in other respects, so materially to widen and improve it, as to make it perfectly safe and convenient to travellers.

It is likewise intended to apply to Parliament, for an act for widening and improving the road that passes from Canterbury, through Longport, Littlebourn, Wingham, Ickham, Staple, Ash, and Woodnesborough, to the town and port of Sandwich, and for making the same a turnpike-road; also for making such new cuts or lines of road, in or through such of the parishes aforesaid, as may be necessary for the better improvement of the said road.

A few pockets of new hops were sold at Maidstone, August 29, at 5l. The quality of the new hops is good, and the colour very handsome—the crop is abundant. At Southwark, September 8, coloured bags were most in demand, which sold from 75s to 80s. current prices—pockets, 80s. and 95s. to 100s. —bags, 70s. to 84s

Married.] At Canterbury, Mr. R Dodd, baker, to Miss Carter —Mr T. Mourylian, grocer, to Miss S. Clayson.—Mr. W. Stanton, to Miss H. Baker, of Deal.

At St. George's church, Hanover-square, London, Mr. Smith, coal-merchant, to Miss Child, of Sittingbourn.

Mr. P. Ewes, purser, in the navy, to Miss Dehane, of Deal.—Captain Wilson, of the 22d regiment of foot, to Miss Wybourn, of Hull-place.—Mr J. Tappley, butcher, of Folkstone, to Miss H. Lamiden, of Rolvenden.—Mr. De Lasaux, attorney, of Ashford, to Miss F. Taylor, of Newhouse.

Captain Mulcaster, of the corps of Royal Engineers, to Miss M. Lucy Montresor, of Gore Hill.

At Margate, Mr. Hannah, of Great Surrey-street, London, to Miss Akenhead.

At

At Folkstone, Mr. J. Bateman, to Miss A. Clark.

W. White, esq. of Deal, to Miss Priestly, of Camberwell.

Died.] At Canterbury, Mrs. Hatton, wife of Mr. Hatton, keeper of the county jail.—Mrs. Holman.—Aged 17, Mr. W Ruck, late a midshipman in the navy.—Mrs. Teshire.—Mr. Fortune, bricklayer.—Aged 88, Mrs. Kirby, widow of the late Mr. Kirby, common-carrier.—Mr. W. Sladden.—Mrs. Miles, of the Fountain-inn.

At Maidstone, in his 70th year, Mr. J. Oliver, formerly of the Bull-inn.

At Ramsgate, Mrs. Elizabeth Gillespy, of Well-close square, London; she was an exemplary character, as an affectionate parent, a valuable friend, a kind and generous benefactress to the poor, and a real Christian: she lived beloved and respected by all who had the pleasure of her acquaintance, and died sincerely and justly lamented.

At West Malling, in an advanced age, Mrs. Miller, many years Mistress of the Ladies' Boarding-school there.

At Tenderden, Mrs. Avan.—Aged 54, Mrs. Payne, of Crundale House.

At Chalk, near Gravesend, Mr. Bass, Master of the White Hart-public-house.—Mrs. Bubb, victualler, of Upper Deal.

At East Farleigh, Mr. F. Long, hop-planter.

At Chatham, aged 81, W. Storey, esq.

At Margate, Major Beneact.—G. White, esq. late of Fetter-lane, London.

At Gillingham, in his 74th year, N. Thompson, esq. purser in the navy.

At Little Bourne, in his 70th year, Mr. Holness, a sincere friend, a chearful companion, and constant benefactor to the poor.

Suddenly, while playing a single match at cricket, Mr. Bates, of Egerton.

At Chart, near Sutton, Mr. G. Pettitt.

At Eltham, while sitting at his door, aged 81, Mr. J. Hambrook, shopkeeper.

At Dover, in his 68th year, Mr. H. Farley.—Mr. J. Polack.

SURREY.

Application is intended to be made to Parliament, in the next Session, for a bill for making and maintaining a navigable collateral cut or canal, from and out of the Basingstoke Canal, at or near Chilton Moor, in the parish of Purbright, in this county, to or near Bagshot Green, in the parish of Windlesham, in the same county; which cut or canal is intended to pass through the several parishes of Purbright, Cobham and Windlesham, all in the same county; and also for vesting further powers in the Company of Proprietors of the Basingstroke Canal, empowering them to make cuts, drains and other works, for better supplying the said canal with water, and for other purposes.

Married.] The Rev. J. Chandler, of Witley, in Surrey, to Miss M. Currie, of Burwood House, in the same county.

At Battersea, Mr. N. Clarkson, of Guildford, to Miss London, of Shalford, near the same place.

Died.] At Clapham Common, Mr. W. Leatham, merchant, of Basinghall-street.

SUSSEX.

At the late annual shew of sheep, at East Marden, near Chichester, the several prizes were adjudged as follows:

To Mr. Pinnix, for the best pen of six South Down ewes, a silver cup, value five guineas—To Mr. Brinstead, for the best pen six South Down ewes, two years old, a silver cup, value five guineas—To Mr. Souter, for the best pen of six South Down ewes, three years old, a silver cup, value five guineas—To Mr. Pinnix, for the best of three pens of ewes, a second cup of the same value—To Sir H. Featherstone, for the best South Down ram, one year old, a silver cup, value five guineas—To the Duke of Richmond, for the best South Down ram, two years old, a silver cup, value five guineas—To Mr. Pinnix, for the best South Down ram, three years old, a silver cup, value five guineas; and also to ditto, for the best of three prize rams, a silver cup, value five guineas.

The beautiful painted window, executed by Mr. Eggington, of Birmingham, and which cost the Duke of Norfolk 1200l. was opened at Arundel Castle, on the 13th of August last.

At the late anniversary shew of cattle and sheep, at Lewes, the Earl of Egremont, President of the Sussex Agricultural Society, presented the premium, a piece of plate, given by the Society, to Mr. Allfrey, for the best bull produced in the field. His Lordship afterwards presented a silver cup, value five guineas, the liberal offer of Mr. Ellman, of Glynde, to Mr. Peckham, of Charlston, for the best one year old South Down ram. Mr. Ellman at the same time informed the Meeting, that it was his intention to give a silver cup, of the value of ten guineas, every year, upon the same conditions as the one then disposed of.—At this shew, Sir Thomas Carr's stock made a distinguished figure; he exhibited nearly forescore oxen (twenty-two yoke of which were driven in one chain) and produced a considerable number of sheep. Mr. Ellman produced, for competion, one yoke of oxen, for which the judges awarded him a premium. The sweepstakes for the best pen of twelve South Down stock-ewes, were gained by the following subscribers:—Mr. Anger, of East Bourne, the best, six guineas—Mr. Scrase, of With Dean, the second best, five guineas—Mr Manshar, of Patcham, the third best, three guineas—C. Gilbert, esq. of East Bourne, the fourth best, two guineas—and Mr. Gorringe, of Kingston, the fifth best, one guinea. Among the two company present, were his Royal Highness the Prince of Wales, the Stadtholder, the Dukes of Richmond and Bedford, Lord Pelham and Lord Carrington, with a long train of the nobility, gentry and breeders from every part of the kingdom.

The Crescent, near the New Steine, at Brighton, is either completely finished or nearly so. It forms a row of 14 houses, each having two in front, and a paved court-yard for carriages inclosed in a brick-wall. For the accommodation of occasional residents, a subterraneous passage has been made to the sea shore, by which means those who wish to bathe, can avoid the inconvenience of walking to the town.

Application is intended to be made to Parliament, in the ensuing Session, for a bill to make a turnpike-road from a place called Stone-street Hatch, in the parish of Ockley, in Surrey, through the several parishes of Ockley, Wootton and Abinger, in the said county: and through the several parishes of Rudgwick, Warnham and Slinford, in this county, to a place called Dedisham-park-corner, in the parish of Slinford, in the road leading from Horsham, to Pulboro', Petworth and Arundel.

Died.] At Bognor, J. Farhill, esq. of Mortimer-street, Cavendish-square, London.

At Landport, near Lewes, Mr. J. Tourle, a capital farmer, worth between 2 and 300,000l.

Mr. J. Atall, a respectable yeoman, of Ditchling, near Lewes.

Mrs. Lambert, wife of Mr. Lambert, publican, at Ripe; she was suddenly taken with a bleeding in one of her legs and bled to death, before any assistance could be afforded her.

At Hastings, Mrs. Scott, wife of J. Scott, esq. of Beaufort-buildings, in the Strand.

HAMPSHIRE.

Married.] Captain R. W. Otway, of the royal navy, to Miss Holloway, daughter of Rear admiral Holloway, of Portsmouth.

At Winchester, Captain Ludgate, of the 4th regiment of foot, to Miss King, of St. Cross.—Mr. J Grigg, grocer, of Newbury, to Miss A. Fussel.

At Bishop's Waltham, G. Skottowe, esq. to Miss Robinson, daughter of Captain Robinson, of the royal navy.

At Alverstoke, T. Stapleton, esq. of the 60th regiment of foot, to Miss M'Killop.

At Stoneham, the seat of Hans Sloane, esq.—J. Jekyll, esq. M. P. to Miss Sloane.

At Millbrook,— Edwards, esq. to Miss Innes.

At Corhampton, Mr. Cowdery, of Exton, to Miss Aylward.

At Bishop'stoke, Mr. Hutchins, blacksmith, aged 82, to Mrs. Payne, widow, aged 34.

W. Bryen, esq. of Brook's-green, Hammersmith, to Miss S. Wiggins, of Southampton.—Mr. T. Kerlley, to Miss Frost, both of Mitcheldever.

Died.] At Southampton, Mrs. Barnouin, relict of the late Rev. Mr. Barnouin, minister of the French Protestant Church in this town.—In child-bed, Mrs Paul, wife of Mr. Paul, miller.—Madame Reboul, wife of Dr. Reboul.

At Portsmouth, Mr. Riboleau, late a landing-waiter at this port.

At Northam, Mr. Blackman, wharfinger.

At West Bourney, Miss M. Tizard, formerly of the Black Bear-inn, Havant.

At Medstead, Miss M. C. S. Lovell.

Mr. Knight, a young man of the wharf-mill, near Winchester. He was there for the purpose of learning to be a miller, and while drawing up a sack of flour, by means of a wheel, a man in a neighbouring garden caught his attention, during which his shirt-sleeve got entangled with the rope, drew him round the wheel, and instantly killed him. He called for help the moment he found himself entangled, but though assistance was near at hand, it was too late. There was no appearance of any bruise about his body.

Mr. J. Burrell, jun. of Hilsea.

In the 17th year of his age, at Gosport, Mr. James Edward Dean, junior, eldest son of J. E. Dean, esq. He was a youth of a fine manly figure, and most admirable talents; had made considerable progress in the classics, and in the study of physic and surgery, in which department, he (although so young) held an appointment, which he filled with unremitted attention, and the greatest success; he is greatly lamented, and has left behind him an excellent character, although his family are too deeply affected by their loss to make public mention of it, one who has marked with surprise and pleasure his growing excellence, cannot withhold this small tribute to his worth.

" *By strangers honor'd, and by strangers mourn'd.*

SOMERSETSHIRE.

The Rev. J. New, in a letter to the editors of Mr. Farley's Bristol Journal, attempts to account for the decrease in the number of inhabitants in the interior parts of the city of Bristol, by representing that within the last seventy years many hundred houses have been destroyed, either for erecting new streets, or large buildings. Many populous lanes and courts were pulled down to make room for the Exchange, and High-street-market; many for the new bridge, and the opening to it; many in Marsh-street; the whole of Fisher-lane and the old Fish-market; St. Stephen's-lane; several houses at the head of the quay, and even a church to make Clare-street, and St. Stephen's-street; to say nothing of the houses in Narrow Wine-street, to make Union-street, and the new Fish-market, or of those in Quay-lane, Hallier's-lane, &c. to Broad Mead and many other parts of the city; amounting altogether, to several hundreds. To the objection that new houses

houses and even new streets have been built in the room of those pulled down, he replies, "surely, but not near so many. Most of the new houses occupy the ground of double the number of old ones; neither are the new ones so fully inhabited, and where many well inhabited ones formerly stood, there are nothing now but warehouses. About the Exchange, three-fourths of the rooms are let to attornies and brokers, for their offices. Besides, many, very many tradesmen now occupy two houses; one only to dwell in, the other as a warehouse; which was not the case formerly. Having thus sufficiently accounted for the decreased population of the city, Mr. New gives it as his opinion, (of which he is thoroughly convinced), that the parishes in the suburbs will more than make up the deficiency, and prove that the population will not fall short of 100,000. Mr. New further adds, having been indulged by the respective incumbents with the examination of their registers, that the parishes of St. James, St. Michael, and St. Augustine, had considerably increased in population between the years 1770 and 1780; and several new streets have been built since 1780, and are well inhabited, in St. Michael's and St. Augustine's, to say nothing of St Paul's or St. James's. The number of persons then in St. James's he estimated at 15 or 16000, and not less in St. Augustine's. Mr. New proceeds to insert the following state of his own parish, St. Philip's, the greatest part of which is out of the liberties of the city, as procured from the proper officers, adding, that just twenty years ago, he took almost the same steps to ascertain the population of his parish, as have been now enjoined upon every parish in the kingdom by parliament. He went from house to house) and from room to room, (where there were more than one family in a house, and took the number of houses and inhabitants, distinguishing the males from the females, and the void houses from the inhabited ones. In 1781, he found 1529 inhabited houses, and 9850 inhabitants. In 1801, 1720 inhabited houses, and 10761 inhabitants, an increase of 191 houses and 911 inhabitants, notwithstanding 8 or 10 houses have been pulled down in the in-parish, and that the out parish has furnished the navy and army with several hundred men this war.

It appears from a report of the Committee of the Bristol Society for the Relief and Discharge of Persons confined for Small Debts, lately published, that the Society has liberated, in the course of the last year, seven disconsolate debtors, whose petitions came well recommended, and that those forlorn objects had seven wives and twenty-one children to deplore and participate of their calamities; and they have, also, in particular cases of absolute distress, administered relief to several other prisoners, whose indigence and urgent necessities rendered them proper objects of the charity; and that the whole sum which has been advanced for these beneficial purposes, including all charges, amounted to no more than forty seven pound, eight shillings, and eleven pence. It appears, likewise, that in the course of a little more than twenty-seven years, no less than 605 debtors have been emancipated by this charity, out of the gloomy recesses of a dreary jail, who had 438 wives, and 1266 children to look up to and depend on them, not so much for the comforts as even the common necessaries of life; and that it has also, in the mean time, afforded merciful relief, so as to alleviate the distresses, of a great number of other objects, and who during their confinement, were reduced to the most indigent and deplorable condition; and that the whole amount advanced in this laudable labour of love, has not exceeded 2957l. 18s. 1½d.

The new Assize-hall at Bridgewater has just been compleated. The two courts are commodious, spacious and airy, extremely well adapted for the accommodation of the judges, counsel, witnesses and auditors. No place in the kingdom can now boast of a superior hall for the administration of justice, and it certainly does credit to the architect who planned it, and reflects honour on the county, and particularly so on the town of Bridgwater.

Married.] At Bath, Sir Marcus Somerville, bart. M. P. for the county of Meath, to Miss Meredith, daughter of Sir Richard Gorges Meredith, bart.—Mr. Smith, apothecary, to Miss C. Walsh.—Mr. C. Banbury, grocer, to Miss Davis.

Mr. Chamberlain, to Miss Crane, both of Walcott.

J. A. Lowe, esq. of Stourport, Worcestershire, to Miss C. Barlow, late of Bristol.

At Swimbridge, the Rev. N. Dyer, to Miss E. Nott, of Torrdown House, near Barnstaple.

At Bristol, Mr. T. Haynes, of the Customs, to Miss Ridler.

At Clifton church, near Bristol, Mr. William Roe, of Blandford, Dorset, to Miss Eliza Banister, second daughter of Mr. John Banister, Broad Mead, Bristol.

Died. At Bath, aged 27, Mr. T. Jelly, attorney.—P. Walsh, esq.

At her lodgings in this city, the lady of J. Butler, esq. of Caerleon, Monmouthshire. Her loss will be severely felt by her indigent neighbours, all of whom occasionally experienced the effects of her beneficence, and many of whom were wholly indebted to her for support.

The lady of Dr. Smith.—Mr. Barrett, butcher—J. Roberts, esq. of Christ's Hospital, London.

At Bristol, Mr. Charles Harford, merchant.

In Henrietta-street, Bath, Miss Mary Kiddell,

dell, much beloved and regretted. Her sweet and amiable temper, mild and gentle manners, and an accomplished and elegant mind, eminently qualified her for the station she so honorably filled as an instructress of youth. Her heart was feelingly alive to every religious sentiment. Strict honour and integrity governed all her conduct; and she was never more happy than when contributing to the happiness of others. She endured a lingering and most painful illness with great fortitude. Her resignation was exemplary. In the firm hope of a Christian, and in perfect serenity of mind, she breathed her last. Never did a purer soul ascend to heaven. To her family and friends her death is an irreparable loss. In the happiness of the writer of this affectionate memoir, it has left a chasm, which time can never fill.

DORSETSHIRE.

Married.] At Corton, Mr. Clarke, to Miss Feaver.—Mr. W. Spooner, jun. printer, of Sherborne, to Miss E. Spurway, of Sert, near Bridport.

Died.] At Poole, in his 46th year, Mr. Jacob Rumsey, a quaker; of considerable mental endowments, and much devoted to scientific and literary pursuits. A lingering and painful illness had been gradually debilitating his frame, and drawing him towards 'the house appointed for all living;' but, under pungent corporeal sufferings, he manifested the greatest composure, and contemplated the certain approaches of death, with a fortitude and resignation truly exemplary.

At Sherborne, Mr. S. Williams, attorney.

At Dadbrook, near Collumpton, W. Sydenham, esq. uncle to the present General Sydenham.

The Rev. W. Hawkins, vicar of Whitchurch, in this county, formerly of Pembroke College, Oxford, and professor of poetry in that university.

At Winborne, in her 29th year, Mrs. A. Hanham, wife of the Rev. J. Hanham.

At Bruton, aged 59, Mrs. Agnew, wife of Lieut. Agnew.

At Grampound, aged 64, Mrs. S. Moore, widow, a person of most exemplary and amiable manners.

DEVONSHIRE.

On Monday, August 17, the silver-cup given annually by Lord Viscount Courtenay, was sailed for, on the River Exe, in front of Powderham Castle; sixteen boats were entered, but the successful candidate was one belonging to Mr. Dyer, of Plymouth, master of La Nymphe frigate, who received the elegant silver-cup, value twenty-five guineas, from the fair hands of the Hon. Miss Courtenay. The second prize of five guineas, and the third prize of three guineas, were likewise won by Plymouth boats; the fourth prize of two guineas was won by a Lympstone boat. The boats started by a signal-gun, at about 11 o'clock, and returned to the goal about one. His Lordship's yatchs were dressed in their colours; a number of pleasure-boats crowded the river, and (the day being remarkably fine) a large assemblage of company attended, forming altogether a most pleasing prospect, highly gratifying to every spectator.

At the late meeting of the East Devon Agricultural Society, at Southernhay, 24 premiums, consisting of three of 5 guineas, six of 3 guineas, ten of 2 guineas, one of 1 guinea and a half, one of 1 pound 8 shillings, and three of 1 guinea, were adjudged and distributed to the successful candidates respectively, for the longest service in husbandry, and bringing up the greatest number of children without parish assistance; and also for the best bull, the best heifer, ram, shew of ewes, heaviest entire fleece of wool from a ram, the best ditto from a ewe, the best sheep shearer, and for the second and third best respectively, &c.

At a late meeting of the South Devon Agricultural Society, at Ivy bridge, three premiums of 5 guineas, three of 2 guineas, two of 1 guinea, and one of 10s 6d. were adjudged to the successful candidates respectively, for the best ram, the best hog, or two-toothed ditto, and for the best bull; also for the best boar, the best ram's fleece, and the best sheep shearer; also for the second best ram's fleece, the second best sheep shearer, and the third best ditto.

An asylum, to be supported by voluntary subscription, was opened, on the first of June last, for the reception of lunatic patients, of the four western counties, at Bowhill house, near Exeter. On that occasion, the treasurer received a benefaction of 100 guineas, for that long wanted and most laudable institution, from S. Milford, Esq. of Exeter.

Since the opening of the Exeter Lying-in charity, in May last, forty-one poor women have received the benefits of that truly laudable institution.

Married.] At Kenton, Mr. Beard, to Miss Bartlett, of Teignmouth.—Captain Bartlett, of Teignmouth, to Miss Beard. J. Bolton, Esq. of Exmouth, to Miss F. Stoodly, of Exeter.

At Plymouth, Mr. T. Twynham, merchant, to Miss Garland, of Stoke.—G. Follet, esq. of Exeter, to Miss A. M. Milford, second daughter of the late S. Milford, esq. banker.—The Rev. S. Woolmer, of Plymouth, to Miss Gray, eldest daughter of Mr Gray, surgeon, of Kingsland, near Plymouth.—Mr. Payne, druggist, to Miss E. Baron.

At Tiverton, Mr. Armitage, merchant, to Miss Hayne.

Died.] At Exeter, in an advanced age, W. Nutt, esq. formerly captain in the army.—In an advanced age, the Rev. Mr. Brereton.—Mrs. Townshend, formerly of Southampton.—Mrs. Turner, wife of Mr. Turner, master of a mathematical academy.

At Plymouth, aged nearly 80, Mr. S. Brooking.

At Okehampton, in his 79th year, Mr. H. Luxmore, surgeon, eminent in his profession, interesting and instructive as a companion, and exceeded by few in the practice of Christian morality, and every social duty.

At Dawlish, Mrs. Maunsell.

At Great Torrington, J. Mallet, esq.

At Heavytree, aged 21, J. Hamilton, esq. son to W. Hamilton, esq. of Blackheath; a young man of great expectations, on whom his parents and friends had formed their fondest hopes.

At Warminster, Mrs. Smith, relict of the late T. Smith, esq. of Heytesbury.

Almost suddenly, in the prime of life, the Rev. J. Arundel, rector of Cheriton, Fitzpayne, and Lifton.

CORNWALL.

Died.] At Liskeard, leaving a widow and young family, Mr. J. Austin, woollen manufacturer.

At Fowey, Miss Austin.

WALES.

Application is intended to be made to Parliament in the next session, for a Bill for making and maintaining a navigable canal from Spitty, in the parish of Llanelly, to or near the town of Llandovery, in the same county, which canal is proposed to pass through the several parishes of Llanelly, Llongennech, Llanedy, Llandebye, Llandingar, &c. all in the county of Carmarthen.

Lately was carried from Bersham Ironworks, near Wrexham, to the Glass-works, near St. Helen's, Lancaster, a large iron-plate, of 18 tons, 11 cwt. upon a carriage constructed for the purpose, and drawn by 12 horses. This amazing weight is supposed to be the first of the kind that was ever carried over land in England.

Application is intended to be made to Parliament, in the ensuing session, for an Act for building a bridge across the Streights of Menai, from the county of Carnarvon to the opposite shore in the county of Anglesea, at or near Porthaethwy-ferry, at the Swelly Rocks.

A similar application is intended to be made for an Act for building a bridge and embankment across the ferry at Conway, in the county of Carnarvon, from or near Conway Castle, in the parish of Conway, to the opposite shore, in the parish of Llanross, in the said county.

There is now growing on the estate of Arthur L. Baker, esq. of Glyn Ciriog, near Chirk Castle, Denbighshire, an oak-tree that measures the following uncommon dimensions: length to the crown 23 feet; circumference at bottom, two feet from the ground, 51; ditto, in the middle, 32; making a total of no less than 1472 cubical feet, which, at 5s. the foot, the common trade-price, amounts to 368l.

The Wrexham Agricultural Society have offered a number of premiums for the ensuing year, consisting of four silver medals, one premium of 7 guineas, three of 5 guineas or a silver cup, two of five guineas, four of 3 guineas, one of 2 guineas and a pair of buckskin breeches, three of 2 guineas, and ten of 1 guinea respectively, for laying down the greatest quantity of water meadow, not less than 5 acres, making the best reservoir for the reception of dung water, raising the best crop of turnips, thoroughly cleaned from weeds and thinned by hoeing, and for cultivating the greatest breadth of potatoes, not less than 4 acres, in rows not above 3 feet asunder, the cleaning and earthing of the intervals, to be performed with the plough; also for the greatest number of stocks of bees, greatest quantity of grass seed, the best cart stallion, the best Chapman's stallion, the best fleece of wool, erecting the best stone dry wall, the best ploughing, &c.

Married.] At Llangadwalladyr, in the Isle of Anglesea, A. E. Fuller, esq. of Ashdown House, Sussex, to Miss Meyrick, of Bodorgan, Anglesea.—J. N. Myers, esq. of Cadoxton-place, Glamorganshire, to Miss M. Hill, of Plymouth Lodge.

Died.] Mr. Jones, of Dolydd, near Carnarvon.—Mrs. Wynne, wife of the Rev. T. Wynne, of Furnace, near Conway.—Mr. J. Lawrence, hosier, of Builth.—Miss Marment, of Pyle, Glamorganshire.

At Milford, Pembrokeshire, aged 71, Mrs. Abigail Starbuck, a Quaker.

SCOTLAND.

At Leith, on May 14, the foundation-stone of the new and extensive Wet Docks was laid by Robert Dundas, of Melville, esq. Deputy Grand Master of the Craft of Free and Accepted Masons in Scotland, in absence of the Grand Master, the Right Hon. Charles Earl of Dalkeith. The procession consisted of the Lord Provost, Magistrates, and Council of the city of Edinburgh, with the Magistrates of Leith, in their robes, preceded by the usual insignia of office. Next followed the Grand Lodge of Scotland, the brethren of the different Lodges in and near the city, the Master, Wardens, and brethren of the Trinity House, Leith, &c. &c. attended with several excellent bands of music, and by a large guard of militia, &c. The procession closed by a great number of the most respectable merchants and inhabitants of Edinburgh, the whole forming a very grand and pleasing spectacle.

For many years past the trade of Leith has been greatly on the increase, and it must afford high satisfaction to every friend of the country to contemplate the honourable and successful exertions of our merchants, who have embarked large capitals in extensive commerce, thus adding opulence to the metropolis of Scotland, and placing her in a commercial point of view, far more respectable

ble and eminent than ever was the case before. By the improvement of the harbour, the ships from Hull, and the other northern ports of England, bounded by the Baltic, will find very great and excellent accommodation by rendezvousing at Leith. Indeed the whole of the Baltic trade, whether of England or Scotland, will be materially benefited. The shipping engaged in the West India trade will also be greatly accommodated, as they will be enabled to come into the harbour without unloading part of their cargo, as is now the case, which is attended with much trouble and expence. The plan of that able engineer, Mr. Rennie, has been adopted through the whole of this undertaking, which will eminently benefit the country at large, as it is intended to render the harbour convenient for the admission of even large ships of his Majesty's navy.

The foundation of the building for the Bank of Scotland was lately laid in Bank-street, Edingburgh, by a Committee of the Directors.

At the late annual shew of rams bred by W. Robertson, esq. of Ladykirk, in Berwickshire, which was numerously attended by the gentlemen and principal breeders of the adjoining counties, Mr. Robertson produced, to the entire satisfaction of the company, the best rams unquestionably that ever were witnessed on the North side of the Tweed, and perhaps inferior to none on the other. The best part of them were quickly let for the season, to gentlemen of acknowledged skill in the science of breeding, at from 20 to 150 guineas each. The novel mode that Mr. Robertson took this year to let his sheep, viz. by public auction, evinced his desire effectually to do away all manner of concealment or mystery, which, however unjust, gave rise to reports inimical to the cause that it was intended to promote.

The workmen have lately begun to build again on the east front of the New College of Edinburgh. The foundation was laid in 1789.

Married.] At Strabane, Col. R. Anstruther, of the Loyal Tay Fancibles, to Miss Nairne, daughter of Lieutenant-col. Nairne, of the Breadalbane Fencibles.

Died.] At Fetternier, Miss T. Leslie, 3d daughter of J. Leslie, esq. of Balquhain.

Lately near Rothbury, where he had resided many years, in his 83d year, Mr. Alexander Hume. He suffered the same fate as many other gentlemen who joined in and survived the rebellion of 1745; he afterwards to the end of his life, supported himself by breaking dogs. He was remarkable for the stoutness of his person, the intrepidity and independency of his spirit, the strength of his understanding, the acuteness of his remarks on men and things, and the general excentricity of his life and character. He died, as he wished, alone, and as if he had fallen asleep, in his chair.

[Bequests of the late Mr. Cushnie, of Aberdeen, (mentioned in vol 11. p. 473):—To the Society of Ship-masters and Seamen of Aberdeen, for behoof of their Poor, 500l.—To said Society, for behoof of the poor White Fishers of Footdee, 200l.—To the Guildry of Aberdeen, for their Poor, 500l.—To the Managers of the Infirmary of Aberdeen, 300l.—To said Managers for behoof of the Lunatic Hospital, 500l.—To said Managers for behoof of the two Dispensaries, 200l. each, 400l.—To the Managers of the Poor's Hospital 500l.—To said Managers for behoof of the Fund for providing Coals for the Necessitous Poor, 400l.—To said Managers for behoof of Sunday Schools, 400l.—To the Trade's Hospital of Aberdeen, 200l.—To the Narrow Wynd Society of Aberdeen, 300l.—To the Shiprow Society in Aberdeen, 200l.—To the Porters' Society of Aberdeen, 100l.—To Mr. Thain's School, 200l.—To the Public Kitchen, 100l.—To the Poor of Old Aberdeen, 200l.—To the Master of Kirkwork, of Aberdeen, 200l.—And to his Executors, in trust for the Managers of any Fund to be established in Aberdeen, for the support of decayed Women Servants, in Aberdeen, of unexceptionable character for fidelity and honesty, who shall have resided there fifteen years or upwards, and are not under sixty years of age, unless sooner incapacitated to earn their livelihood from bodily infirmities, 50l.]

DEATHS ABROAD.

At Ostend, on the 25th of April, of a dropsy, in his 58th year, Mr. Wm. Brooke. He was a native of Worcester, and in the early part of his life, a merchant in Crutched Friars. For the last sixteen or eighteen years, he had resided in America, from which country he went to France, on account of an American vessel in which he had some share, having been condemned in the French court of Admiralty.

At Harbour Grace, in the island of Newfoundland, Mrs. Garland and her daughter; the former at the extraordinary age of 118 years, and the latter 86. The elder lady was mother to C. Garland, esq. the present collector of the customs at Harbour Grace. She had been deprived of sight some years, but retained all her other faculties to the last.

At Mentz, on May 28, W. Pottgeisser, esq. late of Leeds.

On the 23d of March, on board the Andromache frigate, of the wounds he received on the preceding night, in attempting to board and cut out some vessels from a Port in Cuba, Mr. G. Winchester, midshipman, second son of Major Winchester, formerly of Exeter, but now barrack-master at Hounslow.

ERRATA.—*Owing to an Oversight of the Printer,* "LXXX Psalm," *for* "LXXXIX Psalm," *is put at line 6, col. 2, p. 220. As the error destroys the meaning of this interesting Paper, the Reader is requested to correct it with his pen.*

In the Table, p. 90, for "Northumberland with Durham," *read only* "Durham."

MONTHLY COMMERCIAL REPORT.

IN the year 1665, Sir W. Petty stated the shipping of England at 500,000 tons, worth 6l. a ton, or, in all 3,000,000l. sterling. About the year 1750, the merchant-shipping belonging to the single port of London, amounted to 600,000 tons: and this, though above one-third, could be scarce so much as one-half of the total shipping belonging to these kingdoms. But in the MONTHLY SHIPPING LIST—a publication which throws much new light on the state of the maritime commerce of the British empire—we have data upon which we can safely estimate the whole tonnage of the ships of all sorts, in all conditions, and in all modes of employment, which now belong to British subjects, at not less than 4,000,000 of tons, worth at least 4 ,000,000l. of our present money; and yielding to the owners, a return of 10 per cent, per annum, beside affording subsistence and wages to the seamen by whom the vessels are navigated. The same List appears to indicate, that most of the ships now in the British trade are not old, crazy vessels, but of the first class, and built within the last twenty or rather within the last ten or twelve years; a proof, if such were necessary, that the commercial navigation of Britain, was never more flourishing than at present. A nation, not mistress of the sea, would necessarily lose her commercial navigation in the midst of such a war. But, we engross more of the carrying trade of Europe at this than at any former time.

The subject of the EAST INDIA SHIPPING still engages much discussion. It is of even greater importance than those whose thoughts it chiefly occupies seem to be well aware. The plan of the Court of Directors, if it could be made permanently effective, is the most consistent that could be proposed with the interests of the company, and even of Great Britain at large. But it cannot be made permanently effective to the desirable extent. Should it be persisted in, the carrying trade between Europe and India, will be, in time, entirely transferred to other nations.

The danger in which we not many months since found ourselves, of being deprived of the usual supplies of iron and other metals from the Baltic, has suggested to the land-holders in many parts of these kingdoms, the necessity of A MINERAL SURVEY of their respective estates; and if possible, by a common national undertaking, of the whole British isles. It is believed, that such a survey will render us much more independent of foreign countries than we now are, for the materials of the most essential utility in the arts, on which our strength and prosperity depend.—The greatness of that country stands on a very insecure foundation which does not contain within itself the raw materials of its staple and most necessary arts.

Nothing can be of greater importance to the political and commercial greatness of any nation, than to have a large foreign trade in BOOKS and STATIONARY goods. Unhappily, this branch of the trade of Great Britain is utterly ruined by the enormous duties upon paper, &c. The diffusion of our language, literature, manners, and opinions, and of the partiality which these would every where excite in our favour as a nation, is hence entirely checked. New advantages towards universality are conferred by it on the languages of France and Germany. The Americans are reduced to print our books for themselves. A branch of trade of infinite importance to this country is absolutely lopped from the trunk of British commerce.

On the Continent, British merchants and British manufactures are still superior to almost all competition in the markets. But it is believed that the late sales in Germany, &c. were at prices which would not repay the prime cost with any reasonable profit to the manufacturers. So high, indeed, are the wages for labour in England, and such the dissolute luxury of the poor when they are not starving, that, if it were not for the frequency of those inventions which abbreviate labour, and perfect its manipulations, among us; we should have been, long since, utterly unable to stand our ground in any foreign market, in which the same sort of goods as we bring are offered to sale by other manufacturers. It is, therefore, of the utmost importance, that patent-rights should be freely granted and carefully protected. Effects highly injurious to the manufacturing prosperity of this country, may perhaps ensue from the slighting manner in which patent-rights have been from *high authority* spoken of, in some late trials in the courts of law.

Iron-rail-ways are *found* an improvement in the highest degree advantageous in canals. They begin to be preferred continually more and more, wherever there are steep declivities to be surmounted in the line of a canal. By extension of canals, it appears that the number of *cart* and *waggon horses* to be sustained, begins, in proportion to the quantity of goods now transferred from place to place, to be sensibly diminished.

The *Cottons* of the West India Isles have recently fallen in price, in the London market. There has been a rise, however, in the prices of the cottons of Greece, Georgia, and the late Dutch Settlements in South America.

Sugars do not just now fall in price; though, we should expect, that the abundance of the present harvest, and the advantages with which its produce has been gathered in, might tend to lower the price of both melasses and coarse sugars, by affording grain to be put to some of the uses in which those matters were substituted for it.

Grain does not yet fall in price, in proportion to the expectations of the country. The price of wheat and barley rose last week in the London markets.

Baltic goods have not had lately any very considerable fluctuation in price.

Spirituous liquors are rising in price; though, about 7000 gallons of brandy were, last week, imported from Hamburgh, Guernsey, and France. Very large quantities of coffee, cotton, and wine, were also entered, last week.

The

The ceſſation of the *bounty* on *corn*, &c. on the firſt of October, muſt, no doubt, tend to keep up its market-price.

Conſiderable ſales by auction, chiefly of Weſt India and European goods have taken place in London, ſince the 20th of September.

1,366 cheſts of Indigo, at from 5s. 7d. to 10s. 11d. a lib. on credit for two months were ſold on the 24th of September, by the Eaſt India Company. The price of Eaſt India Indigo, of courſe, riſes in the market.

The præmia of inſurance are, in all times, a heavy burden upon trade. In war, they are peculiarly burthenſome—Yet, it is impoſſible now to contemplate the tables of the rates of inſurance, at the principal ports of Great Britain, without being aſtoniſhed, not that the inſurance is ſo high, but that it ſhould be ſo moderate.

The contention reſpecting the COUNTRY BANKS, and the competition between them and the BANK OF ENGLAND is ſtill eagerly continued. It is clear, that for the convenience of ſo great a trade as that of Great Britain, there ought to be as well country-banks as one great national one. But, nothing can be more evident, than that the legiſlature ought to eſtabliſh certain proportions between the Bank-notes, the coin, and the whole moving property of the kingdom; and that the proprietors of country-banks ought, as well as the Bank of England, to be obliged to give to the public and even to the ſtate, full ſecurity for their ſolvency. It would be a check againſt forgeries, and alſo againſt the undue iſſue of country-bank-notes, if they were all to be regiſtered and ſigned by ſome exiſting public officer in each county-town, with whom a ſecurity might be lodged for the amount iſſued.

MONTHLY AGRICULTURAL REPORT.

THE preſent ſeaſon has ſhewn all the commonly received prognoſtics of abundance, and a general crop of all the fruits of the earth—*throughout the ſummer alternate warm ſhowers and dry weather; a profuſion of nuts, acorns, hips, haws, ſloes, and beech-maſt*—the ſame ſigns are ſuppoſed to indicate the ſeverity of the approaching winter. By the laſt accounts from the Continent, the crops ſeem every where to be equally abundant, as if, by natural conſequence, the late univerſal ſcarcity was actually reverſed. The aſpect ſeems flattering in the higheſt degree to this country, where the firſt neceſſaries have too long been at a moſt exorbitant rate; but a crop of wheat upon the ground, or even in the early period of threſhing, has often diſappointed the moſt experienced practical men. We ſhall be able to ſpeak more poſitively of the yield of this year's wheat, both in point of quantity, and in the quality of the manufactured article, two or three months hence. The wheat has been generally well harveſted throughout South Britain; in the North, it has been, in ſome degree damaged by the rains, and by the defect of drying winds. There will be a conſiderable quantity of ſmutty wheat in the North, and in the counties on the ſouthern coaſt, in conſequence of a blight caught towards the end of July and the beginning of Auguſt, from miſts and ſhowers, accompanied with cold night winds. It clearly appears now, by accounts from all quarters, that the ſtock of old Engliſh wheat is fairly exhauſted, nor is the quantity of ſuperfine foreign, on hand, at all too abundant, compared with the demand for grinding with the new Engliſh; of ordinary foreign, unfit for the Engliſh bread-manufactory, the quantity (as is uſual in all importations) is immenſe. Under the preſent happy appearances of univerſal plenty, peace only is wanted to bring the neceſſaries of life to that eaſy and comfortable rate to the lower and middle claſſes, of which they ſtand in ſuch preſſing need: we are warranted, nevertheleſs, to expect a further conſiderable reduction of prices. Never was there in Britain ſo widely extended a growth of wheat and potatoes in any former year.

Throughout Cornwall, Devon, Somerſet, Wilts, Berks, and all the ſouth-weſt to the eaſtern coaſt, all crops are moſt abundant; in the weſt, the barley-crop particularly great. Same accounts from Wales, including hops and fruit.

From Hereford to Glouceſter, Oxford, and throughout all the middle counties, to the Fens and Lincolnſhire, we have the moſt flattering accounts of every ſpecies of produce. In Yorkſhire, all the crops of corn and fruit, great and well got in: farther to the north, the oats are, in many diſtricts, diſcoloured, although they are plump, and weigh well; and the barley is ſtained and coarſe. The average price of corn, &c. for England and Wales, from the returns received in the week ending Sept. 19, was, for wheat, 88s. 10d.; rye, 54s. 8d.; barley, 49s. 9d.; and oats, 30s.

Turnips look well in the beſt counties, but they are ſaid not to apple well in the north: conſidering the vaſt ſpread of potatoes this year (by ſome aſſerted to be even fifty times greater than any preceding) the crop of turnips cannot be expected ſo extenſive as uſual; the potatoes, however, will be found a noble ſubſtitute, by thoſe who have conveniences to ſteam or bake them, ſhould the ſeaſon prove rigorous. Of rape and cole, and even of tares, as cattle-feed, we have heard but little, and wiſh to hear more. Hay is ſaid to be a particular good crop, and of fine quality in the north. Of artificial graſſes, no material account has reached us.—Hay, at St. James's Market, on the 19th of Sept. fetched from 3l. to 5l. 16s.; ſtraw, 1l. 10s. to 1l. 16s. 6d. At Whitechapel Market, it fetched from 4l. to 5l. 16s.; clover, from 6l. 6s. to 7l.; ſtraw, 1l. 8s. to 1l. 16s.

Of

Of Potatoes, the quality is said to be generally good this year, and no where better than in Herefordshire; in some parts, the northern particularly, they have been affected by the curl, a disease from obstructed circulation, obviously occasioned by the same misty and blighting weather, which affected the wheat in July and August.

In Worcestershire, and in all the fruit counties, the trees absolutely bend under the weight of the crop: it is to be hoped this great abundance will not encourage the too free use of sour harsh cyder among the lower classes, so productive of the cholic in the cyder-counties. Wall-fruit seems to be the smallest of the fruit-crops.

Hops a general great crop; and, in the best districts, the quality of the pockets very fine. In Kent, Surry, and Sussex, the speculators are fairly caught, with nearly the whole of last year's stock on hand. Old bags, three to four guineas per cwt.; Pockets four to five guineas, the same which, some months ago, fetched 22l. 10s.!

Live-stock, both fat and lean, at an immense price, and the latter not to be obtained in quantities equal to the feed on the ground, a plain proof that we have sadly anticipated our stores, and neglected breeding; an improvident system, which, if persevered in, will have very serious consequences. Breeding-sows are at the enormous price of five to seven guineas each; three guineas to three guineas and a half for such as formerly were sold at eighteen shillings to twenty shillings each. Good horses have been all the spring and summer excessively scarce and dear, and yet there seems rather a less than the usual attention to increase the breed, notwithstanding the prospect of a general demand at the return of peace.

In Smithfield Market, on the 21st of Sept. beef fetched from 4s. 6d. to 5s. 4d.; mutton, 5s. 4d. to 6s. 8d.; veal, 4s. 8d. to 6s. 4d.; pork, 6s. 4d. to 7s.; lamb, 5s. 4d. to 6s 6d. In Newgate and Leadenhall Markets, beef fetched from 4s. to 4s. 8d.; mutton, 4s. 10d. to 5s 10d.; veal, 4s. to 6s.; pork, 6s. 4d. to 7s.; lamb, 4s. 8d. to 5s. 8d.

There is a considerable quantity of wheat well got into the ground, in the forwardest counties; and in Essex and Suffolk, the drill-husbandry seems getting by degrees into fashion.

METEOROLOGICAL REPORT.

Observations on the State of the Weather, from the 24th of August, to the 24th of Sept. inclusive, 1801, two miles N. W. of St. Paul's.

Barometer.	*Thermometer.*
Highest 30. 12. Sept. 15 & 16, Wind S. E.	Highest 76°. Aug. 29 & 29 Wind variable.
Lowest 29. 2. Sept. 4. Wind S. W.	Lowest 50°. Sept. 24, Wind N. W.
Greatest variation in 24 hours. } 4.4 tenths of an inch { Between the mornings of the 17th and 18th of Sept. the mercury fell from 29.85 to 29.44	Greatest variation in 24 hours. } 13°. { Between the mornings of the 31st of August and the 1st of September, the Thermometer fell from 66° to 53°.

The quantity of rain fallen since our last report is equal to 1.77 inches of depth.

During the last month, the changes in the atmosphere, with respect to its density, have been more considerable than usual: it has frequently happened, that in the course of twelve hours the mercury in the barometer has varied from two to three-tenths. In consequence of the great depression noticed above, we experienced a very heavy storm in the evening of the 18th instant, after which the barometer began immediately to rise.

The variations in the heat of the atmosphere, have not been very great; two days only, as we have remarked, has the thermometer stood at summer-heat; and, on two other days, September 22 and 24, the greatest heat was 55°. From the 14th to the 18th instant, the weather was, for the season, unusually warm, during which, even in the night, the glass was scarcely lower than 60°.

Since our last report we have had 18 days without rain, and the wind has been easterly 16 days.

THE
MONTHLY MAGAZINE.

No. 79. NOVEMBER 1, 1801. [No. 4, of Vol. 12.

ORIGINAL COMMUNICATIONS.

To the Editor of the Monthly Magazine.

SIR,

VOCAL-MUSIC is likely to form so prominent a feature in the polite amusements of the present winter, especially in those of the theatre, in London, that, perhaps, the following observations on an art so pregnant with rational delight, and cherished and cultivated by every civilized country, will not be uninteresting to a considerable part of the readers of your widely-circulated Miscellany.

There are, I allow, other provinces of the musical science, which are not only more generally practised, but which also afford employment to a much greater number of professors, than that of singing; but certainly no one is so universally attractive, and, at the same time, so difficult of acquisition, as that of vocal-performance, and in the pursuit of which the practitioner is so liable to fall into erroneous practice and obvious imperfection.

In instrumental-performances, though unmeaning flights and tortured modulation, falsities of expression and misplaced *fortes* and *pianos*, may too frequently wound a nice and judicious ear, yet, provided the notes are truly and clearly given, the melody is preserved, and, at least, the harmony of the composition faithfully rendered; and, though the execution should fail in *time* or *style*, yet, if the performer possess the least delicacy of ear, it will be in *tune*: the instrument will be true to the mechanical operation of the finger, and give, with a corresponding exactness, all the sounds within its compass. But in *singing*, in the employment of that natural instrument, the *voice*, the practitioner is continually liable to a defect the least sufferable of any—that of being *out of tune*, by which both melody and harmony are injured, expression destroyed, and, to a cultivated ear, absolute pain substituted for that pleasure which fine singing is so particularly calculated to produce.

Some masters have carried this idea so far as to assert, that the accomplishment of singing, however alluring to the novice, should never even be attempted, but with the greatest scrupulosity and caution; and that, before the inclination to vocal-performance be too freely indulged, the taste and feeling of the candidate for praise in this department of the harmonic science should be consulted, and the powers of discrimination in the auditory faculty be scrutinized and ascertained.

Certainly this first and finest effort of the science merits too much deference and respect to be lightly and inconsiderately attempted; the qualification, at least, of a *good ear* seems indispensable to success in its practice: taste, feeling, and a fine voice must not be too rigorously insisted upon; they are attributes which Heaven has not bestowed on the many; but, whenever they happily combine, then it is that the lovers of fine vocal-music are treated with such performers as Billington, Storace, Mara, Banti, Dussek, Parke, Braham, Harrison, and Bartleman; and that the most charming effects of instrumental-performance yield to the fascinating powers of the voice. In a word, it is then that melody, uniting itself with sentiment, passion, and eloquence, at once enchants the ear, and captivates the soul.

We, however, must allow, that there is another description of vocal-performers, whose merit is all their own; who, by the aid of perseverance, both in study and practice, execute much with little voice, and express more than, perhaps, they are capable of feeling; and to such singers must be given all the praise due to acquired powers; powers which, when confined to what is called *part-singing*, as in quartetts, trios, duetts, catches, and glees, are sometimes productive of very charming and impressive effects. Singers of this cast, by practising together, and learning to blend their tones, and to cover, by mutual accommodation, each others natural defects, have often proved how high a degree of excellence may be attained even without the aid of fine voices or exquisite sensations.

Though all the nations of Europe at present encourage and cultivate the vocal-art, still to the Italians will every nation of true taste give the palm in all the principal qualities of fine performance. Indeed, while they not only seem to possess some exclusive and natural advantages, their language, it is almost superfluous to observe, is peculiarly adapted to musical expression: it is so melodized by its numerous vowels, as at once to open the lungs, smooth the passages of sound, and give that superiority of effect only produced by the natives of Italy, or those who by a long residence in that country have acquired its language and its taste.

The Italians, I would wish to notice, have within these few years acquired a manner or style of singing, called by them *tempo-rubato*, or a stealing, or taking away the time from some notes, and giving it to others; which contrivance, in the hands of a proficient, is capable of adding much beauty to the general effect: but nothing is more dangerous than this practice, when not controuled by the most correct judgment; it then tempts the performer into all the variety of false ornament, and betrays the juvenile practitioner into the worst errors of inverted taste.

Indeed, neither this nor any other extemporary embellishment should be hastily attempted; progressive advances in this, as in every other refined art will ever prove the shortest road to success;—a maxim, of the verity of which the practice of every great singer is a proof: the march of excellence is sure, but it is also slow; and the rare and superior beauties of performance should by no means be the *immediate* object of early practice.

From what has already been said, it will then appear that genius, taste, a discriminating ear, good voice, and considerable perseverance, with gradual advances in practice, are requisites, without which the fine and accomplished singer can never be formed: I might also add, that it is equally indispensable that this practice should commence early in life; nature is then unfixed, and the *glottis*, *larynx*, and other fine parts, on the perfection and flexibility of which the tones and volatility of the voice so greatly depend, will gradually form themselves to the necessary movements and vibrations.

It is, however, still proper to observe that the practitioner, in the earlier stages of life, should be particularly guarded against all straining, or violent efforts, since the very circumstances which render juvenile practice so necessary, expose the voice, weak and unconfirmed as it yet is, to future coarseness, debility, and confinement of compass. To this particular the Italians are uniformly attentive. The voice is nursed by them with the nicest care and most solicitous tenderness: the master, leading it gently on from stage to stage, just gives it the exercise suited to its growing strength, and constantly aims at improving its power and volubility, without endangering its future sweetness and extent.

While the judgment is strengthening, and the taste improving, the young pupils are initiated in *sight-singing*, and made acquainted with all the first elements of their science; the progress of their information keeps pace with that of their practice, and every exercise is read before it is sung. It is only when pupils are instructed on this regular and systematic plan that they arrive at that proficiency which they ought always to have in view, and which, indeed, can alone qualify them for teachers. It is only to the vocal artists thus trained that the various and secret tracks of certain improvements are developed; and only these ever acquire in perfection that first of all musical requisites, *expression*; a qualification that forms the very soul of music, as well as of the other arts: indeed, of so much consequence to good singing is a just and powerful expression, that no other excellencies can compensate for its absence, or produce in any degree that refined pleasure and intellectual gratification which a polished audience chiefly expects and values.

With respect to the various styles of vocal performance, nature has both pointed out and provided for them, by the diversity she has exhibited in the different *tones* and *scales* of the human voice. The *tones* are indefinite, but the *scales* are reckoned by musicians to be six in number, the *bass*, the *baritone*, the *tenor*, the *counter-tenor*, the *counter alto*, or *mezzo soprano*, and the *soprano*, or *treble*. To some of these may be added the *feigned* voice, the constant resource of ordinary natural voices, and very rarely managed with that skill by which alone it can be rendered agreeable. The transition from the *natural* to the *feigned* voice, and *vice versa*, is seldom conducted with that ease and smoothness which should render it imperceptible: the last note of the one and the first of the other should so far consist of a similarity of tone as perfectly to conceal the change. By the aid of *feigned* notes, judiciously employed, it often happens, that a voice of confined compass assumes many of the advantages of a more extended scale: but I must also observe that feigned notes are only properly admissible under the management of thorough and accomplished performers, and that only such performers should venture on its adoption.

To these remarks, sir, many more of equal importance to those who are in a course of vocal study and practice might be be added; but to avoid prolixity, I shall close my letter with a remark or two, on another requisite in fine singing of scarcely less consequence than that of *expression*, and on which, indeed, expression in a great measure seems to depend—I mean *articulation*.

Sense and sound, when united, accomplish all the effects of music: it is then that we understand what we hear, and that while the auditory organ is delighted, the mind is employed and gratified: the poetry and music lend reciprocally their aid, and we become sensible of impressions not to be derived from either of these divine arts alone. The necessity of an early and unremitted attention to this great requisite, without which the expression must be faint and imperfect, will therefore, I trust, be as manifest to every one as is the too general neglect of its practice: a neglect which cannot be too much deprecated, and which cannot fail to render every other vocal acquisition vain and ineffectual. I am, Sir,

Vauxhall Road, Your's, &c.
Oct. 20, 1801. T. BUSBY.

To the Editor of the Monthly Magazine.

SIR,

I SHALL be happy to receive the opinion of any of your learned Correspondents upon the following passage in Lucian's Dialogue between Terpsio and Pluto. In the Amsterdam edition of Benedict, 1687, page 271, it runs thus:

Η τὸ πλουταῖον ἐιδέναι ἐχρῆν, πότε ἀ τεθνήξεται τῶν γερόντων ἔκαςος, ἵνα μὴ μάτην ἂν ἐνίους Ε'ΘΕΡΑ'ΠΕΥΟΝ.

I wish to be informed, whether the ο in the last word be not an error of the press, and whether it ought not to have been printed with an ω instead; ἐθεράπευον, thus becoming the third person plural of the imperfect tense; the conjunction ἵνα frequently preceding the indicative, as well as subjunctive and optative, moods; and Zeunius upon Vigerus observes (de conjunctione ὡς, cum adjunctis particulis, p. 557, edit. Lipsiæ, 1788), that "sæpissime construitur cum *imperfecto*. Nec hoc mirum videri debet, cum et idem tempus aliis particulis, quæ vel conjunctivum vel optativum poscunt, subinde jungi soleat; quare probabile videtur, Græcos, et in primis Atticos, per imperfectum non modò indicativum, sed et optativum conjunctivumque expressisse." Sic Plato. Symp. cap. x. Χρῆν δὲ καὶ νόμον εἶναι, μὴ ἐρᾷν παίδων, ἵνα μὴ ἐις ἄδηλον πολλὴ σπουδὴ 'ΑΝΗΛΙ'ΣΚΕΤΟ.

Dem. Phil. i. p. 47. Οὐ γὰρ ἐχρῆν ἐπάρχυς παρ' ἡμῶν ἄρχοντας οἰκείυς εἶναι, ἵν' Η'Ν ὡς ἀληθῶς τῆς πόλεως ἡ δύναμις.

Id. pro Phorm. p. 958. ἵνα ταῦτα ὡς εὐσχημονέςατα ΕΦΑΙ'ΝΕΤΟ.

A learned friend, whose assistance I sought for the solution of my doubt, proposed to read ἵνα μὴ μάτην ἂν ἐνίυς ᾖ θεραπεύων, thus converting the ε into η, rendering it the subjunctive of εἰμί, and making θεραπεύων a participle, analogous to the frequent use of the substantive-verb with the participle instead of the other moods, as ὅτι ΕΙΗ Νικόδημον ΑΠΕΚΤΟΝΩΣ (Because he had killed Nicodemus). Χάρις χάριν Ε'ΣΤΙ'Ν ἡ ΤΙΚΤΟΥΣΑ ἀεί. Sophocl. (One favour always begets another). Ου ΣΙΩΠΗΣΑΣ ΕΣΗ; Sophocl. (Will you not hold your tongue?) Port Royal Grammar, second edition, 1759, p. 328. Annotation.

Fifth Mile-stone,
Highgate, I am,
Sept. 13, 1801. Sir, your's, &c.
SAMUEL WESLEY.

P. S. If either ἐθεράπευον or ᾖ θεραπεύων be right, it still seems necessary to substitute τινὶς in the former case, and τὶς, or the like, in the latter, as a nominative understood: but I humbly submit the whole to the sentence τῦ ἰθυδικῦ.

To the Editor of the Monthly Magazine.

SIR,

I Have just perused, with no common degree of satisfaction, a work containing some preliminary observations on certain medals and gems bearing inscriptions in the Pahlavi or ancient Persic characters. In this interesting publication, which proceeds from the pen of that learned Orientalist, and accomplished scholar, Sir William Ouseley, some remarks on a gold-coin of Baharam the 5th are concluded in the following candid terms: "I cannot, however, proceed to the next section, without remarking, that a gold-medal of the Sassanidæ is in itself a numismatick treasure of uncommon value; because, according to Procopius, 'it was not lawful for the Persian Kings, or any other monarch of the Barbarians, to stamp their images on pieces of gold, whatever quantities of that metal they might possess; since, money of such a description was not used in the commercial dealings even of the Barbarians themselves.' The reader must determine, whether the discovery of a single medal should invalidate the evidence of Procopius. I know not of any other exception to the general rule; and even this may perhaps have been stricken as a proof-piece, and never intended for general circulation," p. 10, 11. On the above, I would beg leave to observe, that, if this medal do not entirely invalidate the testimony of Procopius, it serves, at least, to shew how little regard was paid by the barbarous sovereigns who, at that time, were gradually shaking off the Roman yoke, to the haughty mandates of the Emperor of Constantinople. Procopius had indeed, a little before, hinted at something like a permission on the part of Justinian to the French Kings to coin money from the gold-mines in Gaul, not with the image and superscription of the Roman Emperor, as had been the custom, but with their own images; it is very probable, however, that the victorious Franks would assume this privilege without much regard to the Emperor's pleasure. Much about this period also, the Visi-Gothic Kings of Spain were striking gold money with their own portraits (if such rude features may be called so); though it certainly does not appear that any of the Gothic Kings in Italy had ever assumed the like privilege of striking *gold-money*. The general veracity of Procopius, as an historian, is not, I believe, impeachable; and the curious information which he has given on the usual practice of putting the effigies of the Roman Emperors on the coin struck in Gaul, throws some light on the multitudes of Roman coins bearing the names of the mints of Arles and Lyons, and perhaps other places in that province of the empire. Many really Barbaric coins likewise, carrying the rude imitation of a Roman mintage, with illegible letters, are also thus accounted for; and these may have been fabricated in remote and obscure parts, where the currency of Roman money would be essential, but where regard to workmanship would be altogether unnecessary. D.

Oct. 8, 1801.

To the Editor of the Monthly Magazine.

SIR,

AUDI *alteram partem* has been an old and approved maxim. I adopt it as a sort of text for what I am going to say relative to a very undeserved expression made use of in your last Magazine by a *Pedestrian Traveller*. He says he visited the grounds of Wardour, *because they were untaxed*.

Now, if he had given himself a moment's consideration respecting the situation of those who, without any benefit to themselves, or from any obligations to the public, allow their houses and grounds to be shewn to tourists, he would not perhaps have hazarded such an injurious slur on them.

You are perhaps ignorant of the curse of having a fine improved place near to any large manufacturing town. I feel it, and from that cause may have been sore at reading such an undeserved expression. My house and grounds are open at all times to the curious; but a small gratuity is always expected to the housekeeper and gardener; and this I have allowed because it would keep off the multitude. However, such serious consequences have happened, on Sundays in particular, that I shall be forced to sell my place, or shut my doors. Why, Sir, I have had my servants ill-treated by drunken workmen, and ladies insulted, in so much, that in the cool of the evenings they dare not enjoy the pleasures of my walks. My case is not singular; for I have a friend who has a very beautiful place at a much greater distance than I am at from the metropolis. His fortune is moderate, but his place so beautiful as to attract crowds of admirers.' The servants are ordered to accept never more than five shillings, let the company be ever so numerous; and yet this sum, moderate as it may appear, has not made him escape censures, alas how undeserved! for, during six months of the year, his servants are more occupied with shewing strangers his house and walks than with their own business.

I really think when such sacrifices are made to the public, that the public ought to be more grateful for them.

Sept. 1801. I am, Sir,

Your's, &c. A. Z.

To the Editor of the Monthly Magazine.

SIR,

IN the last Number of your Magazine, one of your Correspondents expresses a conviction that the Bank-directors have not merited the blame imputed to them by Mr. Allardyce, and undertakes to suggest to that gentleman the ground of his mistake, without shewing what this mistake is, or that he has fallen into *any error* on the subject. It is not because private bankers make a greater profit that Mr. Allardyce contends the dividend to the Bank-proprietors should be increased, but because he shews from the most authentic information respecting the Bank, which has been made public, that the income of the Company is fully adequate to a considerable increase of the dividend. In the

first

first address to the proprietors, the different sources of the Bank's income are enumerated, and upon a moderate estimate of the produce of such branches as are not precisely known, the total amounts to 1,435,104l.; from this sum is to be deducted 814,968l. for the dividend on the Bank capital, and there remains 620,136l. a sum much greater than all the expences of the institution, including the income-tax, can possibly amount to, and consequently there must be a very considerable annual surplus, which the proprietors, if they think proper, have an undoubted right to require should be applied in increasing their dividend. Your Correspondent does not deny that there exists such an annual surplus; he does not deny the right of the proprietors to such an increase of dividend as the surplus would afford; but he brings forward a singular statement to shew that the whole disposeable capital of the Bank does not exceed 2,500,000l.; If this is really the case, how is it possible for them to make the usual advance of 2,750,000l. on the annual taxes, besides very considerable temporary advances on exchequer-bills, or even to take in the omnium of a large loan in addition to their mercantile-discounts.

To the interest of this disposeable capital of 2,500,000l. your Correspondent adds, "profits stated above 1,150,000l." and thus makes the total income of the Bank 1,275,000l. I cannot discover the least traces of the sum of 1,150,000l. in any other part of the letter, which certainly contains no explanation how this sum arises; such an account is surely very improperly set in opposition to the distinct and intelligible statement of Mr. Allardyce.

The sum paid by the Bank for income-tax is stated at 127,500l.; but, if it is properly computed, it will be found that it cannot exceed 50,000l.; I have good reason to believe that it is somewhat below this sum.

We are told, that "probably one-third part of the capital originally subscribed by the Bank-proprietors, would be sufficient to carry on their business to its present extent." The capital that has been subscribed by the Bank Proprietors is 11,642,400l. consequently the Company have two-thirds of this sum, or 7,761,600l. more than they have occasion for; but the next paragraph informs us, that the only real efficient capital which the Bank possesses is the hoarded surplus of their income; and, that if this accumulation were to be divided among the proprietors, their annual dividend would be diminished, and the business of the Company could not be conducted with facility or security.

In 1799, the Bank divided 1,164,240l. loyalty five per cents. among the proprietors, and in the present year a similar division has been made of 582,120l. navy five per cents. If the Company prefer this mode to an increase of the regular dividend, it is not liable to any material objection; but that the profits of the institution considerably exceed the present dividend of seven per cent. and that the proprietors have a right to require a participation of such profits, has been fully shewn by Mr. Allardyce, and certainly has not been disproved by your Correspondent.

Oct. 12, 1801. J. J. G.

To the Editor of the Monthly Magazine

SIR,

I Shall be much obliged to any of your Correspondents to inform me, through the medium of your Magazine, who was the author of a curious and very entertaining book, published by Dodsley in the year 1751, intitled "The Life and Adventures of Peter Wilkins, a Cornish Man, &c." said to be written "by R. S. a Passenger in the Hector." with such other particulars of his life and writings as may be thought generally interesting.

Oct. 5, 1801. I am, Sir,

Your's, &c.

CURIOSUS.

For the Monthly Magazine.

Ought a SPIRIT *of* ENQUIRY *to be encouraged among the* COMMON PEOPLE?

IN my opinion, the most unpropitious title that a paper can make choice of, under the genius of the present day, is that of the Enquirer. With a great majority of literary men, enquiry is at present a term, if not altogether synonimous with, at least that savours of, innovation; and nothing therefore can be more unpopular among the aristocracy of the learned, so closely allied with the persons and principles of the political aristocracy, as any title symptomatic of that inquietude, which wishes to agitate the established order of things, either in the literary or political world. Guarded as political-enquiry is from vulgar inspection, by silence and mystery, somewhat like a locked-up chamber in an ancient castle, which, as the report goes among us menials, is haunted by the spirit of our fathers in arms, the perturbed spirit of the British Constitution,

tion, there is, even among the other apartments, though not closed with such dreadful secrecy, a dispiriting gloom reigning through the whole mansion of mind, which tends to repress enquiry, and chills curiosity into silence.

At first view, it might be supposed that the spirit of enquiry being so completely laid at rest in one department of knowledge, the search after unknown truth would be invigorated in other branches; but experience proves an emulative principle to be, in every art and science, the true excitement of excellence, and nothing deadens this so much as a restraint on the liberty of speaking our thoughts and laying open our sentiments. A principle may exercise a tyranny as well as a person, and the *ipse dixit* of Aristotle was as despotic and mortal to the mind, as those reigns of terror, where all the freedom left was a choice in death. "*Liberum ei mortis arbitrium permisit.*"

The truth is, that, even among the learned world, enquiry becomes less popular, when it is not only discouraged, but dreaded, among the vulgar. "Keep henceforth (said one of the tyrants of Athens to Socrates); keep at a proper distance from the carpenters, smiths, and shoemakers, and let us no more have your examples from among them." When this maxim of government is put into action, learned men, who in general are timid men, adopt an obedience to the rule, and a fear of innovation seems to spread through every region of the mind. "*Populare nunc nihil tam est, quam odium popularium.*"

I have a strong suspicion, that, when the priesthood wished to secure to themselves the choicest fruit in the garden, they contrived a terrible tale about the mortality of the Tree of Knowledge, of which the alphabet may be called the leaves; and the Pagan priesthood, with a similar wish of making Paradise a privileged place, spread a similar report of the Dragon which guarded the golden apples of the Garden of the Hesperides.

> Aureaque Hesperidum servans fulgentia mala,
> Asper, acerba tuens, immani corpore serpens
> Arboris amplexus stirpem.

This was the doctrine of those who wished, in the pride of philosophy, to cover knowledge with religious mystery, the better to secrete it from the bulk of mankind; and the seditious spirit of research and discovery is at present equally discountenanced by the ministers of the state and of the church, not from the pride of philosophy, but the interest of their respective orders.

In Ireland, for example, the general diffusion of knowledge and civility has been effectually repulsed by the Act of Union, which has locked up the printing press in that country. The progress of improvement depended upon cheap editions of the best publications which issued from the Irish press; and a lucrative trade was carried on by a large exportation of such editions, which was made to the United States of America; but, from the first of July, this branch of business will be annihilated by the establishment of copy-right. No *new* work will ever be printed in Ireland; for what author would be so absurd as to print his performance in Dublin rather than in London. In London, books are printed in so expensive a manner, that literature will be soon as effectually secluded from the common people as before the art of printing was invented, when works were laboriously written on vellum, and reposited in monasteries, or chained down in college-libraries.

It was a happy revolution (similar to the one that diminished the power, by dividing the property, of the proud feudal Barons), which reduced to a portable and popular size the German folio, and the Scotch quarto, the haughty aristocracy of literature, that built their systems (as the chieftains did their castles), entrenched in terms of art, and rendered inaccessible to the vulgar understanding. But the price of publications, as they at present issue forth, with every embellishment that can recommend them to the eye of the reader, has operated as a counter-revolution in the commonwealth of letters, and again introduced the misfortune of a manuscript age.

America will vindicate the genuine character of the PRESS, its publicity: the public will, its guide; the public good, its end. The consequence of the abolition of printing in Ireland, will be the speedy establishment of an American press, which may supply this part of Europe with cheap publications, at least until the Imperial Legislature thinks proper to prohibit an importation of such a nature. The legislature of the state of New Hampshire has passed thirty acts, of which fifteen were for incorporating library-societies in different towns of that state;—so little is it thought that a general passion for literature and study forms, on that continent, any obstacle to the speed of the plough, or the progress of commerce. In

4 Ireland

Ireland, the provincial-government is directing roads to be made into some of the mountainous and savage districts of the island; but, as for any performance of promises to cultivate or civilize by education the long-neglected waste of the public mind—O! if knowledge be the wing wherewith men fly to heaven, with what ostrich-wings have the rulers of this country been furnished!

They have degraded the character of the press by methods unknown in any other nation. Instead of the public prints being, as they ought to be, a palæstra for the exercise of literary talent, and the wrestle of rival minds, they are turned into a sickly pestilential pool, which extinguishes every spark of literature, and the great instrument of freedom is immersed in the very cloaca of the city. I know not how any dignified government can give countenance and sanction to such papers, except under the same pretence that the Popes are said to give their licence to brothels, and an Emperor drew a tax from ordure.

As the Maratism of politics poisoned the virtue of the Parisian Revolution; so it is the contagious effluvia of corrupted minds, such as penned the History of the late Irish rebellion, which may be called the Maratism of loyalty, and which prepares us for the extinction of the press, by polluting it with the virus of personal scandal. Habit indeed may, in some measure, fortify us from such infection, and (after washing our hands) we may take up, without harm, some of the journals of the day; but, notwithstanding, the fair and free character of the Irish press is injured, just as the town of Philadelphia suffers from the dirt of the docks, and the filth of the common sewers. The style of the public-papers has its influence upon the manners of the country, and is again influenced by those manners. They copy that tone of conversation too common among men of high station, which mixes a coarse contempt of decency with the blackguardism of the bar, and banishes from the lesser intercourses of life that gentlemanship which is equally the duty of democrat and aristocrat. I know no character so complete and consistent as a person uniting the principles of republicanism with the manners of refined aristocracy.

I have ever liked the principles better than the persons of democrats, their political maxims better than their private and personal manners;—and were I to judge of the doctrine *merely* from the disciples—of the mind from the manners, which are nothing else than mind at the surface, I should be led to conclude that the extremes of political character are apt to assimilate, and that democracy is for the most part nothing but aristocracy in a shabby coat. I see the same insufferable pride and fatal self-confidence in both parties, and I say with the immortal Montesquieu, "As distant as heaven is from the earth, so is the true spirit of equality from that of extreme equality." O sacred names of Liberty, Justice, our Country, Concord, Peace!—I see them written on the standard of Democracy; but in the manners of the men that march under these banners, I find aristocratic self-sufficiency—aristocratic and exclusive party-spirit—aristocratic demeanour to menials—aristocratic neglect, not to say contempt, of the houshold virtues, which, if not essential to the grand public virtues, are at least their most amiable accompaniment, and perhaps their best and surest guarantee.

There is a ferociousness of spirit among the great vulgar as well as the small, which equally actuates the loyalist and the revolutionist, which has much more of personal vengeance in its nature, than any public feeling, and which arising from a partial view of things, both as to the causes and the remedies of national evils, is to be mitigated not by the preamble of an Act of Parliament, but by an encouragement to the spirit of inquiry, which would insensibly tame the violence of our passions by enabling us to see things as they really are. We want the means of exciting *great* passions. We have lost our country. It is the ascendancy of little personal passions which are the effect of bigotry in the common people, of a domineering habit in the upper classes, and of gross ignorance in both, fostered by a partiality in the legislature, and a strong aversion in the Catholic clergy to yield up to their laity the free exercise and enlarged cultivation of their own reason; it is to these causes we are to attribute rebellious dispositions, and the barbarities that were, will be, and must be, consequent upon inveterate party and religious animosities. Education is the harp of Orpheus, which gradually mollifies the furiousness of uncivilized nature, and tames the tigers of the human breast. If the priests take and keep possession of the reason of mankind, I say they are responsible for the fatal effects of their passions. I will allow that the sacerdotal influence in early stages of society

society may be a necessary supplement to the defects of law and order, and if we are to be always brutes and savages, a hierarchy, or a control like that of the Jesuits in Paraguay, is the most desirable kind of government: but it is impossible in the present situation of the world to incarcerate a whole people. Were I to ask whether roads and canals be useful in a country, a smile would be the answer to the question: but it is, it seems, a serious question in the eyes of church and state, whether the common people should receive the knowledge of reading, writing, and arithmetic, which, like high roads, and internal navigation in the cultivation of the soil, serve to create and communicate social inclinations—to bring capacities into action—and to reclaim the savage nature into an immediate and marketable value. Were it the disposition of government to grant as much money as is annually voted to maintain the beggars of the metropolis, in order to make a proper establishment of parochial schools throughout Ireland, and particularly in the south and west, even this would at least soften and civilize the rising generation; and whenever I see the smallest progress made in any system of national education, common both to catholic and protestant, I shall then begin to think this Legislative Union of the two countries not made merely for military and financial purposes, but for the love of the people, the union of the different orders of the state, the prospects of peace, and the prevention of rebellion.

To the Editor of the Monthly Magazine.

SIR,

DR. HAGER's derivation of the word pyramid, in p. 185, of your last Number, is too elaborate to flash conviction on his readers. It would be very unsatisfactory to deduce an Egyptian word from Greek radicals, as Dr. Hager has observed of *pur*, fire; and *puros*, wheat: but is there any greater satisfaction in seeking a name for one of the wonders of Egypt, either in Arabia, Syria, or Chaldea?

Dr. Hager rejects the derivation of pyramid from *piromi*, on account of the iota, without considering the careless mode in which all Greek writers express in their characters the words of other nations. Thus, according to their manner of spelling, Khorou, the Persian monarch, (Cyrus) is Kóurǝs; Ardshir is Artaxerxes; Baal is Belus; Addir-dag is Atergatis; Ashur is Assyria; Ashdod is Azotus; Japha is Joppè; Hephra is Apries.

It cannot be doubted that the word Pharaoh, or, as some express it in our letters, Peroeh, of Josephus has the same designation as the Pirôm of Herodotus, or Peirom of Synesius. Josephus (Ant. Jud. viii. 6.) says "The title of Pharaoh was applied to the kings of Egypt from Menes to the time of Solomon, but not long afterward." According to Herodotus, (Euterpe) there were in a spacious temple at Thebes "colossal statues of the mortal* princes of Egypt, and their cotemporary high-priests; and that the priests informed him, "each of these colossal figures was a Pirômis, descended from a Pyrômis, to the number of 341." The bishop of Cyrene (Treatise on Providence) observes, "the father of Osiris and Typhon was at the same time a king, a priest, and a philosopher. The Egyptian histories also rank him among the gods: for the Egyptians are disposed to believe that many divinities reigned in succession before their country was governed by men, and before their kings were reckoned in a genealogical series by Peirom after Peirom." Synesius, in declining this word, makes the genitive case of it Peiromidos.

It is now generally understood that the pyramids were royal burying-places and monuments: would it not therefore be better, without paying much attention to the Grecian mode of writing foreign words, to pursue the general analogy, according to which the names of many antient cities, temples, and monuments, are derived from their founders; and rest satisfied that those immense structures, the pyramids, were so denominated as being the works of the old Egyptian kings who were called Pharaoh's, Piromis or Piromides? If it be asked what is the meaning of the word *Pirom*, Herodotus informs us that in the Egyptian language it expresses "dignity and worth."

Bloomsbury square, W.
Oct. 20, 1801.

P. S. The Greek word *Obeliskos* literally signifies "like a spit," and so clearly marks the thing to which it is applied, that we need not surely go farther in search of a derivation. Should Dr. Hager still insist upon it that Bel is the radical of *obelos*, and that Belus taught his friends the use of the spit, perhaps neither you, nor I, Mr. Editor, will make an objection; but think ourselves obliged to the old sage for his invention.

---

* Herod. and Diod. Sicul. ii. c. 3. give the statement made by the Egyptian hierophants, that their country was governed for 18000 years by gods and heroes, before any man became their king.

To the Editor of the Monthly Magazine.

SIR,

MR. WALKER has, I think, clearly proved Thomson's obligations to the *Sophonisba* of Trissino, *Hist. Mem. on Ital. Trag. Append. n.* (*i*). Had it fallen within that gentleman's plan, he might have also shewn his obligations to Æschylus and Seneca. In his *Agamemnon*, he is abundantly indebted to both, particularly to the latter, whom he has servilely copied. His Egistus is as fatiguingly tedious as the Egistus of Seneca; but the ravings of his Cassandra do not exhibit any of those marks of divine inspiration, which, in the noble tragedy of Æschylus, occasionally raise the lovely prophetess above humanity. Instead of the fine, but irrelevant, description of a storm in Seneca's tragedy, Thomson has given us a description equally beautiful, and equally misplaced, of a desert island. Is it then to be wondered at, that this tragedy struggled with difficulty through the first night?

But, if Thomson had obligations to the continental stages, the stage of modern Italy is not less obliged to him. *Vide Hist. Mem. on Ital. Trag. p.* 270, *note* (*u*). The tragedy of *Zelinda*, which gained the laurel-crown in Parma, 1772, is said to be a close imitation of *Tancred and Sigismunda*.

Having mentioned the laurel-crown, permit me to ask, whether the newly created King of Etruria be the Spanish Prince who instituted that noble mode of encouraging the exertions of the Italian Tragic-Muse?

If the tragedy of *Valsei, ossia l'Eroe Scozzese*, merits the praise bestowed on it in the work alluded to above, p. 270, 271, is it not extraordinary, that it has not found a translator amongst some of the men of genius who now adorn Scotland.

Can any of your Correspondents inform me, who was the author of an *Essay on the Life and Character of Petrarch*, which appeared in 1784? Or, what was the fate of Huggin's Translation of *Dante*? What was his motive for destroying the printed copies of his translation of Ariosto?

Perth, Sept. 4, 1801. Z. R.

To the Editor of the Monthly Magazine.

SIR,

ON reading, the other day, Professor Richardson's very elegant and ingenious *Essay on the Character of Lear*, I was surprised to find, in the account of the assassination of Alessandro de' Medici, some extraordinary misrepresentations of historic facts, which could only be occasioned by the learned Professor's writing from memory. In order to afford Mr. Richardson an opportunity of correcting those errors in a future edition of his Essay, I shall take the liberty to state the facts to which I allude. "Lorenzo de' Medici wished to enjoy pre-eminence; but his *brother* Alexander, the reigning Prince, &c." Now Lorenzo, or Lorenzino de' Medici was the son of Pietro Francisco dè Medici and Maria Salviati; and Alexander was the supposed natural son of Lorenzo Duke of Urbino; they could not therefore be brothers—*Vide Mem. of the House of Medici, vol. ii. p.* 176 *and* 413. Yet our elegant Essayist falls again into the same error. Having mentioned Lorenzino's motive for the assassination, he proceeds, "Thus prompted, and thus unguarded, he perpetrates the death of his *brother*." He then adds, in a strain of glowing eloquence, "He feels his blood streaming; hears him groaning in the agonies of death; beholds him convulsed in the pangs of departing life: a new set of feelings arise; the delicate accomplished courtier, who could meditate atrocious injury, cannot, without being ashamed, witness the bloody object; he remains motionless; irresolute, appalled at the deed; and, in this state of amazement, neither prosecutes his design, *nor thinks of escaping*. Thus, without struggle or opposition, *he is seized, and punished* as he deserves." Now let us hear the Historian. "No sooner was the deed done (says Dr. Robertson) than, standing astonished, and struck with horror at its atrocity he forgot in a moment all the motives which induced him to commit it; and, instead of rousing the people to recover their liberty, by publishing the death of the tyrant:—instead of taking any step towards opening his own way to the dignity now vacant, he locked the door of the apartment, and, like a man bereaved of reason and presence of mind, fled, with the utmost precipitation, out of the Florentine territories." *Reign of Ch. V. vol. ii. p.* 94. Instead of immediately meeting the punishment he deserved, it was nearly ten years after Alexander's murder, that he was assassinated, in his turn, at Venice, by two of the late Duke's guards. *Hist. of the House of Medici, vol. ii. p.* 410. Mr. Richardson has, I am sure, too much liberality of mind to expect I should offer an apology for the liberty I am taking with him: I shall therefore only add,

add, that I am a warm admirer of his critical powers, and

A LOVER OF HISTORIC TRUTH.

London, Sept. 6, 1801.

To the Editor of the Monthly Magazine.

SIR,

ON the western side of the island of Zante are two springs of bitumen, distant from each other about two hundred paces at most. They seem to take their rise eastward, and they communicate with the sea by the west. The mouths of these springs are nearly round, the larger being about twenty feet in diameter, the lesser between ten and twelve. Within is seen constantly boiling a perfectly liquid bitumen, of very strong odor. The surface of the bitumen is covered by a foot-depth of water, whose color at the spring-head nearly resembles that of coffee-liquor viewed in the sun. The water appears dormant, notwithstanding the boiling of the bitumen: and both the one and the other constantly remain cold, even in the hottest weather. That boiling increases in the summer, and is particularly remarkable during earthquakes. These two springs are considered as one of the causes why those convulsions of nature have not always produced such ravages in the island as there was good reason to apprehend. It is remarked, that the shocks are ever much more violent in this spot than in any other part of the country. If a person stamps with his foot on the ground near them, he feels the earth tremble to a considerable distance on every side. Frequently people hear from the springs a very loud subterraneous murmur, which sometimes continues during whole days.

There appears reason to believe, as several enlightened travellers have supposed, that the whole of this tract is actually undermined, and that these springs once formed a lake which was bounded by the circumjacent mountains, and which may have been gradually filled up with the soil thrown down from the eminences by the shocks of successive earthquakes. This opinion seems to derive support from a passage of Herodotus*, who says, "I saw at Zacynthes† a lake from which bitumen issued in abundance. There are several of the kind: but the largest is seventy feet in circumference. The inhabitants fasten myrtle-branches to long poles, which they use to extract the bitumen. It has a strong smell, and is superior in quality to that of Persia. The islanders dig a pit, into which they conduct the bitumen; and when they have collected a sufficient quantity, they put it into vessels. Whatever falls into this lake, passes under ground, and is afterward seen floating on the sea at the distance of four stadia."

In effect, nobody has ever been able to find any bottom to those springs; and every thing thrown into them, that was capable of swimming, has always been found afterward floating at sea. About the month of April they begin to fill with bitumen, so as even to overflow. It is then that the peasants collect it; in doing which, they pursue nearly the same process as their ancestors in the time of Herodotus. Instead of poles and myrtle-branches, they more conveniently use buckets. To the pit destined for the reception of the bitumen, they add a small channel to drain off the water, which runs down to the sea. After this, the bitumen is put into kegs or skins, each containing about a hundred and fifty pounds weight.

The water taken from these springs is limpid: that of the greater is very salt, and retains a strong scent of the bitumen: the water of the lesser is sweet, and has very little smell. It is used by the neighbouring peasants as a medicine, which often proves efficacious against the fevers to which they are subject. It facilitates digestion, and purges without fatiguing the frame. Employed in venereal complaints, it promotes copious urine and abundant perspiration. It dries up and cicatrises internal sores which are the consequence of that distemper. It has also been successfully used for the scurvy by English mariners visiting the isle in quest of the Corinth raisin. The Greeks use it for their common drink, even when in perfect health.

The Zantiots employ the bitumen from those springs, mixed with an equal quantity of tar, in the building and repairing of their barques. The bitumen, when dried in the sun, is extremely binding and tenacious. A convincing proof of this appears on the very spot where it is collected: the stones that form the circuit of the pit into which the peasants pour it, are so strongly cemented together by the bitumen dropped on them, that they may more easily be broken than separated. Such, no doubt, was the nature of the bitumen employed as a cement in the construction of the celebrated walls of Babylon.

For

* Melpom.

† The ancient name of Zante.

To the Editor of the Monthly Magazine.

SIR,

"SEE," said the Mother of the Gracchi, to a Roman lady—she happened to be a lady of high distinction, of a patrician family: so indeed was Cornelia, but she had married a plebeian—The lady had called on Cornelia for the single purpose of dazzling her eyes, with the display of a diamond-necklace, which she had that morning received from her husband.—She was the childless wife of the Edile Lucretius Vespillo. Cornelia, at that time, had two boys. The necklace was now disclosed. Cornelia requested her guest to wait a while. The boys were sent for. They entered without bowing their heads—they ran to their mother—Tiberius took her by the hand; Caius clasped his arms around her neck. She pressed him to her heart: and, "See! (said the mother of the Gracchi) These are my jewels; this is my necklace." The lady put her's in the casket, and, with a sort of smile, hastily took leave. Cornelia remained at home.

Happy, or hapless, mother! which shall I call thee? Daughter of Scipio the first Africanus, and mother-in-law of Scipio the second Africanus, and better than both, as the first wish of thy heart is to be called mother of the Gracchi! But, of thy twelve children, nine have died in infancy, or early youth; and of those remaining, Tiberius shall be the buckler of thy people, and thy Caius, now caressing thee, shall be the sword of the people —in vain—for the people will, in the last extremity, desert them. They shall be murdered by Romans—their mangled bodies shall float upon the Tiber. Hapless mother! I was about to say—but thy awful magnanimity, thy matron dignity, repress me. I still see thee happy; and when thou hearest of the sanctuaries in which thy darling sons were slain, I see thee exclaiming, with elevated arms— "They were tombs worthy of the Gracchi!"

For what were these men slain? They were slain for attempting to preserve the genuine spirit of the constitution, and for wishing to make the happiness of the mass of the people a foundation for the safety of the state. Rome was split into two parties; parties which divide the world at this moment—the rich and the poor. All other distinctions are nominal: this alone is real. Strange as it ought to sound, the people were obliged to act as a party, and the commonwealth was a monopoly. The rich, by various means, got possession of the lands destined by the constitution and the law for the support of the poor, and purchased by the sweat of blood. They were not only dispossessed of their property, but they were not even suffered to cultivate as labourers the ground they had held as proprietors. Slaves were preferred to citizens—aliens to natives.

Tiberius, one of the jewels of Cornelia, had then attained to manhood: and a man he was most pure in private life; ripe in the powers of his mind; fixed in the purposes of his heart; adorned with every virtue which nature in her bounty, and education in her care, could pour down on the head of humanity. "Antistia (said the president of the senate, on entering his house) I have just now promised our daughter Claudia in marriage."—"Why in such haste (said the alarmed mother) have you promised her to Tiberius Gracchus!" This young man had just returned from the siege of Numantia, where the great Scipio (accursed be such greatness!) had, with the help of 60,000 men, cooped-up and starved 4000 brave men, only for refusing to be slaves; for fighting in defence of their wives, their children, and their liberty; which in despair of maintaining, they set fire to their own houses, and every living creature dying by famine, fire, or the sword, left the victor of Numantia nothing to triumph over but a name. Scipio felt as a Roman—Tiberius as a man "Joyless triumph," said he to himself, "that can boast only of battles. He has acquired a name for destroying men who would die rather than be slaves. Be it my better ambition to emancipate slaves who wish to be men!"

He had crossed Hetruria. He had seen the fields without other husbandmen and labourers than aliens and slaves; with no affection for the republic; with no interest in its preservation; with no encouragement to have children; without means of educating them. He returned to Rome. He ascended the rostrum.

"The wild beasts of Italy," said he (he began in the high tone of strenuous liberty) "the wild beasts have, at least, the shelter of the den and the cave. The people who have exposed their lives in your defence are allowed nothing but the light and air. These are the gifts of the gods: on earth they have nothing. They wander up-and-down with their wives and little ones, without the comfort and consolation of a home. Our generals mock the soldiery. They exhort them before battle to fight for their sepulchres, and houshold-gods. Where are *they*? among all this

Pp 2 number

number of Romans, who has a domestic-altar? Who, at this hour, possesses the burial-place of his fathers? They live, they fight, they die, to maintain you and yours in superfluities that satiate; in luxuries that sicken; and the Roman people are styled Conquerors of the Globe, in which they have not a single foot of ground, except that which they stand on in the day of battle.

"I wish to revive those regulations, which may, at one stroke, destroy indigence and ambition—on the one part, the power of corrupting, on the other, the inclination to be corrupted. I wish to crush the heads of that monstrous aristocracy, which, sooner or later, will conduct us to monarchical despotism. It is an equalized distribution of lands which raises a nation to power, and gives strength to its armies. Every individual has then an interest in the defence of his country. The avarice of some, and the profusion of others, have made our country the property of a few. Our soldiers are therefore few. Our citizens are few. The slaves, and artificers of luxury to the new proprietors occupy the whole: a cowardly and abject population, corrupted by a luxurious city, corrupted by the arts they profess; without any country; with little to keep, and little to lose. I do not wish to make the poor rich, but to strengthen the republic by an increase of useful members. I wish not an equality, but an equability of property, that the laws should not complot with the wealthy against the weak, but should tend, in an opposite direction, to counterbalance inordinate wealth, to promote the circulation of happiness through the whole community; to put a staff into the hand of indigence, which may support it under the burthen. If property be in itself power, why add to it the power of government? A republic for the rich! A country for the edile, the questor, the knights, the senators, the consuls! Liberty for the civil mercenary! for as such I account these fingering artists, and these hireling labourers of the land. The milk of our common mother is bitter in their mouths. We are become aliens in our own country. He who has not a portion of land can scarcely be said to have a country. Sweet is the possession of the least spot of cultivable ground. Sweet to say: There is a fixed fortune for my family. I planted those trees; I trained up those vines. There, in that hallowed spot is the burial place of my fathers; there shall I one day repose by their side. He it is, the cultivator of his own ground, who is tyed to his country by the heart-strings, who is always willing as able to defend it, and who alone can maintain you all in pecuniary opulence, by the superfluity of his solid and substantial wealth. Those miserable artisans, those heart-broken hirelings, are men, and as such I pity them; their fate I deplore; but Romans I cannot call them. Their morals are to sell themselves to the highest bidder. Their health is poisoned by confinement, or excessive and irregular labour. Their happiness is precarious and fortuitous. Their touch contaminates, and their suffrage is infamy.

"I demand the enforcement of the Licinian law, limiting to five hundred acres the proprietor of the conquered lands. I demand this for the sake of the rich as well as the poor; for the honour, stability, and true interest of the republic; and (why should I conceal it?) for my own glory. Octavius, my colleague and friend, you are a wealthy man. You are a proprietor of these lands, and you therefore resist my purpose. Will you accept of my personal fortune (would it were on this account larger) as a compensation for what you may lose by the execution of the law? Believe me, you travel by a clandestine road to power. I wish to travel the high road with my equals. Virtue is the strength, as well as glory, of manhood. It is the conquering and unconquerable genius of the Roman Republic."

The faction of the rich behaved like the wife of Vespillo. Calumny began to distil her poison (for such is the lot of those who dare be singularly good). "'Tis envy of Scipio;" said one: "'Tis his mother's ambition," said another. "He is a disturber of the public *peace*," said Nasica. "He is seditious (whispered Cicero); for he has rebelled from the party of the senate."—Cicero, that fine genius! that common soul! always agitated about himself, and who would save the republic, that he might boast of the action. "Let us assassinate his character!" said those of high distinction. "Let us assassinate himself!" cried their hirelings. He carried a dagger under his robe, but the shining point was exposed to view, and seemed to say—Let me die in honourable defence, not by the treachery of an assassin.

He persevered in the cause of patriotism with unabating ardour. He got a law passed for lessening the number of years that soldiers were obliged to serve; another law for establishing the last appeal to the people; another law for dividing the judicial power between the knights and the senate,

senate, which before was judge in its own cause. In fine, he desired the tribuneship a second year, to ratify these laws, and put them in action.

On the day of election he was about to repair to the capitol. Unlucky omens were reported. He had embarked in the cause of his country. Cornelia trembled, and was silent. He hastened to the assembly. The people burst into shouts of applause. One of his friends rushed through the crowd—"The senators have conspired to murder you"—"Then gird up your gowns, and stand on your defence as well as unarmed men can."—"People (cries he) your defenders are in danger. This head is in danger"—and he touched it with his hand. The people fled. "He demands a crown," said an informer, and hurried with the news to the senate. Nasica, a great land-holder, and proprietor of men, fuming with wrath, cries, "Let those who regard the republic, and the public-peace, follow me." The senate, their clients, and slaves, armed with clubs, ran furiously to the capitol. They broke through the pusillanimous populace (they were not a people), slew three hundred, and murdered Tiberius.

The senate of Rome first spilled the blood of the Roman people—first had recourse to arms and slaughter, and assassinated, before the Temple of Jupiter, a magistrate whom the law had declared sacred and inviolable. The dead body of Tiberius Gracchus was thrown into the Tiber. The people beheld it. The wife of the Edile Lucretius Vespillo passed by—"Lo! (she said) one of the jewels of Cornelia."

Cornelia had still another—it was Caius.

F. G.

For the Monthly Magazine.

SKETCH *of a* JOURNEY *from* COPENHAGEN *to* HAMBURG, &c.

(*Concluded from page* 203.)

THE *free** imperial city of *Hamburg* is divided into the Old and the New Town; the situation of the former is on low ground, but that of the latter is rather elevated. The fortifications, which envelope the city, are good; but the works are not what an engineer would call very strong: there are generally one hundred cannon, of large calibre, mounted; these are fine brass pieces, and, with about four hundred more in the arsenal, would, with a well-disciplined garrison, make a formidable defence against an enemy; but, for obvious reasons, there would be great danger in admitting a *well-disciplined garrison* into Hamburg, and, without it, nothing effectual could be done. The ramparts, which are planted with rows of trees, are very broad, and have good roads for carriages and foot-passengers, where any person is at liberty to ride or walk; they extend round the city, and are in circumference about five miles. The number of gates* is six; they are called as follow: 1st. The *Altona-thor*, so called because it leads to that town, from which it is distant about one mile and a half; the *Dam-thor*; the *Diech-*(Ang. Dyke) *thor*, and the *Stein-thor*, each of which leads to different parts of the country; these are the principal gates: the remaining two are smaller ones, of little consequence: they are called the *Brock-*(Ang. Brook) *thor*, which is scarcely ever used but in the winter, when sledges are in use; and the *Sand thor*, by which the masters, &c. of vessels lying in the harbour go out in the evening to their ships.

This city, situated chiefly on the river Elbe, and partly on the Alster and the Bille, is seventy miles from the sea. The Old Town is interlected by canals, over which there are a great number of bridges. Many of the streets are broad and handsome: the best are the *Admiralty strasse* (i. e. street), the *Neuenwall strasse*, the *Rödings markt*, and the *Grossen bliechen*. The *Rödings-markt* is a broad street; it has a canal in the middle, with cranes fixed on each side, for the purpose of landing the goods, which are brought up in small craft from the ships lying in the harbour; by which means the goods are landed at the merchant's door, which is very convenient in a place where so much trade is carried on as in Hamburg. The description of the *Rödings markt* will serve for that of most of the large streets in the Old Town. The houses of the principal inhabitants are built of brick; they are six or seven stories high, and very large, but not commodious, a principal part of them being occupied by halls and staircases. They are sometimes furnished in an elegant style, but not frequently; for, though the furniture is always costly, yet little taste is generally shewn in the selec-

* Is it not a Solecism to call that city *free*, the freedom of which is liable, at any time, to be violated with impunity by its neighbours on either side?

* Dutch *Thörer*, singular *Thor*, pronounced *Dore*.

tion

tion and appropriation of it. Trees are planted in the large streets; for the Hamburgers, like the Dutch, are fond of the *rus in urbe*; still the latter have the advantage, as their houses are painted light green, or other colours pleasing to the eye, which give them a light and airy appearance, beside which, they keep them perfectly clean and neat on the outside, which is not always the case in this city. The inhabitants of the Old Town are subject to one inconvenience in the winter, when the wind blows strong from the westward; at that time, their cellars (warehouses under ground) are often filled with water, which does great damage to the goods contained in them. On this occasion, if it happens in the night, the inhabitants are warned of the overflow of the river by the firing of cannon, at which signal, those who sleep in the cellars make their escape, else many would be drowned in their beds, which has frequently happened. The pavement is of small flint-stones, which are very disagreeable to the foot-passenger; and, there being no distinction between the foot-path and the carriage-road, the unfortunate pedestrian is subject to many interruptions, and, what is worse, is often in danger of being seriously hurt: if he be not lucky enough to press himself behind one of the small stone-posts, with which the fronts of the houses are *ornamented*, he will stand a chance of being much annoyed, as the coachmen drive through the streets with great impetuosity, and make a point, if possible, of distressing every person on foot.

None of the churches, or other public buildings, in this city, are sufficiently striking with respect to their architecture, or their inside ornaments, to demand a particular description. The church called the Grossen St. Michel (*Ang.* Great St. Michael), is the handsomest; its steeple is very high, and it is built in an airy situation, on high ground, in the New Town: besides this, St. Peter's, St. Catherine's, St. Nicholas's, St. James's, and the Dome Church, are all handsome buildings. In other parts of Germany, the Dome Church is the cathedral, but here it belongs to the Hanoverians; in it a fair is held every year about Christmas. Neither the Calvinists, nor the Roman Catholics, are allowed churches, nor are the Jews permitted to have a synagogue, no religion being tolerated by the government but Lutheranism. The English are indeed allowed a meeting-house, which is called the English house: the want of a church, or place of worship, would be no obstacle to their residing at Hamburg, as they appear to be sufficiently aware that they "cannot serve both God and Mammon;" they would therefore content themselves with knowing that they have at least *one* object of worship, and that the *one* which is productive of the most personal advantage to themselves. The Senate-house, the Bank, and the Exchange, are situated near each other, almost in the centre of the city; the two former are of ancient-architecture; the latter is partly covered by a range of warehouses, under which the merchants crowd together in wet-weather. But the building most worthy the attention of the man of benevolence is the Orphan-house: this is a spacious square brick-building, situated in the *Admiralty-strasse*, in the New Town; by this public institution, which appears to be extremely well conducted, a great number of orphans of both sexes are educated and provided for, and, when of a proper age, put out to trade or service. There are about six hundred children constantly resident in this house.

This city has two theatres, the one German, the other French; they are both well attended, and the performances are above mediocrity; on the latter stage, *Madame Chevalier* is the principal actress.

The number of hotels, taverns, coffee-houses, and *restorateurs*, is great. Strangers, whose stay is intended to be but short, are better accommodated at a hotel, than at private lodgings; but then the expence, as in other large cities, is in proportion*. The coffee-houses are numerously attended by the merchants about noon, who at this time generally take a cup of coffee, a glass of liquor, or *ein snaps*†, and smoke a pipe till 'change-time, which is at two o'clock. These houses have generally one or two billiard-tables, as the Germans and French are very fond of this game: but

* One piece of advice it may be necessary to give the *unexperienced* English traveller (though we seldom meet with an English traveller, who will himself answer to this description): that is, never to go to any tavern, hotel, or coffee-house, in a foreign country, which is kept by one of his own countrymen; should he not feel himself inclined to take my advice *à priori*, he will find perhaps, *to his cost*, that even experience itself may, sometimes, *be bought too dear.*

† This is a vulgarism for a glass of French brandy, better elucidated by referring to a significant expression of the lower class of people in London, who call a glass of gin *a flash of lightning.*

few respectable merchants are seen at them in the middle of the day.

Besides the usual walk on the ramparts, there is the *Jun fern Steig* (Ang. the Young Maidens' Walk), which is planted with trees, and on one side has a handsome row of houses; it is situated nearly at one extremity of the city, on a fine piece of water, called the Inner Alster, which is here very broad, and forms a reservoir: this walk runs up towards that part of the ramparts in which is the *Dam-thor*; the English call it the Ladies-walk. It is very much frequented by the younger part of the *beau-monde*, and is, in fine weather, really a pleasant *promenade*. There are several tea-drinking houses in the neighbourhood of the city, which are resorted to in summer every Sunday evening, by the trades-people and their families; dancing is allowed at these houses, and this amusement is the principal one of this class of people: I wish it were in my power to say, that the amusements of the higher classes are as innocent—but of these I shall presently have occasion to speak.

The markets in Hamburg are well supplied with butcher's meat, poultry, butter, eggs, and vegetables, and in summer with fish, which, particularly turbot, may then be bought very cheap. Beef and mutton are nearly as good as in England, but veal and pork are very inferior; meat is sold by the pound, which is about seventeen ounces English (100 Hamburg pounds weighing 107 English pounds nearly). The price of meat, and of provisions in general, except fish, was always high; but since this has been so much the resort of the emigrants from France, every article of this kind has become exorbitantly dear. The bread, both white and brown, or rather black, is unadulterated; the Germans almost without exception prefer the latter; the white bread is mostly eaten by the French and English. Fruit is not plentiful, except strawberries and cherries; the apples used here are scarce, this fruit being chiefly imported from France. In Altona, all the necessaries of life are much cheaper than they are here.

This city is not particularly distinguished for its manufactories, except for that of refined sugar, in which the Hamburgers certainly excel: there are a great number of sugar-houses, and the sugar-bakers' journeymen are estimated at seven or eight thousand. There are several breweries; the beer is light and good for present use, but it will not keep.

The great commerce of this city is so well known that it needs no description, I shall therefore only make a remark on the character of those through whose hands it passes. The minds of every class of men, and of almost every individual of the different classes, from the burgomaster to the lowest barrow-man, seem to be absorbed in *gain*. The old maxim of "*Get money*" &c. appears here to be completely exemplified, and the proviso of "Get it honestly, *if you can*," is seldom brought to their recollection; for the association of their ideas is such, that it generally leads them to the *end*, without allowing them to be very scrupulous about the *means* by which it may be attained. In fact, (as has been well observed), "body and soul, muscles and heart, are equally shrivelled up by a thirst of gain, and the character of the *man* seems to be completely lost in that of the *Hamburger**."

If my information be correct, the executive and legislative government of this city is composed of a prætor, four burgomasters, four syndics, twenty-four burghers, and four secretaries, but the latter are only recorders of the acts of government. All the offices, except that of the prætor, are for life: he is chosen yearly; his office is nearly similar to that of the Lord Mayor of London. Of the twenty-four burghers or senators, twelve are graduates, and twelve are merchants—Dutch *Kaufmanns*; this title, which would be treated with the greatest contempt only twenty miles from Hamburg, is here one of the highest that a man can have†.

The inhabitants are reckoned at 140,000, but this number fluctuates; before the French Revolution, it did not exceed 100,000: since that period, crowds of emigrants have fixed their abode here, and the commerce of the city has been extended to an unparalleled degree. One cause which operates in favour of the population of Hamburg is the ease with which a foreigner may be made a burgher:

* See Mary Wollstonecraft's admirable "Letters written during a short Residence in Sweden, Norway, and Denmark."

† In Germany, and in the northern parts of the Continent, every man, whatever his situation may be, has a title prefixed to his name, the respectable appellation of *gentleman*, so much used (and sometimes so much abused) in England, is here unknown. Every man is here the *Baron* ———, the *Professeur* ———, the *Agent* ———, the *Kaufmann* ———, the *Advocat* ———, &c. &c. and if his title be not known, S. T. (*Salva Titula*) is prefixed to the address of a letter, &c. This latter mode is chiefly used in Denmark and Sweden.

for

for this purpose, it is only requisite to appear at the Senate-house on a public day, and then take the oaths to the city; a person then becomes a citizen of Hamburg without any further trouble, except that of paying the fees, which amount to about 200 current marks (i. e. 15l. sterling). It is absolutely necessary that a person who intends to trade should become a citizen, as he cannot carry on any business in his own name (except for a short time) till he be such. On a burgher's quitting Hamburg, he is obliged to leave one-tenth of his property in the city. Great numbers of adventurers, both Scotch and English, are daily made burghers of this city; and it is not being too severe to say, that, with some few exceptions, they do little credit to the countries which claim their nativity. Hamburg swarms with Jews, particularly the New Town; in the Old Town, their residence is generally in or about the *Drinkwall strasse* and the *Altenwall-strasse*. The character generally attributed to the Jews in other countries, that of low cunning, is not particularly confined to this race of people here—I doubt whether most of the Hamburgers do not possess every characteristic attributed (often erroneously) to the persecuted Jew, without having, like him, the plea of necessity to urge in their excuse, and without his inoffensiveness of manners to palliate their conduct.

The police of this city is good; and a robbery attended with any atrocities is seldom heard of. The system of *espionage* is here carried to a great extent; but, on this subject, perhaps the less that is said the better! Four newspapers are published daily, the principal of which are the *Hamburg Correspondenten*, and the *Gazette d'Hamburg*; but none of them, except the former, can be depended on for authenticity of intelligence. There is a public-library here, called the *Harmonie*, on an extensive scale; but literature meets with little encouragement. I had almost forgot to mention, as it is so common that it does not strike the attention of a person accustomed to German manners, that high and low, rich and poor, in every city, town, and village, are always smoking: the pipe is hardly ever out of their mouth, except when they are asleep; they sometimes smoke in bed at night, and often before they rise in the morning.

Next to commerce, the delight of the Hamburgers, particularly of the higher classes, is in grand entertainments, which continue a long time, and at which they make an ostentatious display of wealth and luxury: at these times, card-playing is always introduced: *l'ombre* and whist are the games generally played, at which they bet high, and often large sums of money are lost and won; in this they are imitated by the middling class of merchants, who, in all that is licentious, tread close at the heels of those above them. Since the French have been here, *rouge et noir* tables and pharo banks have shewn themselves; but these species of gambling are discountenanced by the magistrates. The manners of the emigrants here, many of whom are of the *ci-devant* French *noblesse*, are a striking contrast to those of the money-getting Hamburger. To conclude, in Hamburg there is as much sensuality, as much gross debauchery, and as small a portion of *true happiness*, as is to be found in any part of the world. Let the philosopher speculate upon this, my province is only to describe the effects which are produced by wealth, on men of uncultivated minds and uncontrolled desires.

If it is thought that I have been harsh in the above Sketch of the Hamburgers, I beg it may be recollected, that I disclaim all *personality* in my narrative; that I have spoken *generally*; and, that I believe, in the city of Hamburg there will be found many exceptions to the characters which I have delineated.

After crossing the Elbe, you arrive at Haarburg, a small town in Hanover. The journey to Cuxhaven is performed in a coach or an open carriage, according to the inclination of the traveller*—the distance is seventy miles—and for a coach and two horses the expence is about 30 specie dollars (i. e. 7l. 10s. sterling). The time taken in travelling (if the traveller does not sleep at an inn on the road) is, in summer, about eighteen hours; in that season of the year, the roads are not very bad, though sandy.

Ritsbuttle (Dutch *Ritzenbüttel*) is a small town, containing about two hundred houses; it is half a mile from Cuxhaven; it has a castle, which is garrisoned by Hanoverians. The port of Cuxhaven at present belongs to the English. The road for foot-passengers, from Ritzbuttle to Cuxhaven, is on a causeway, raised about eight feet from the carriage-road; being

* I am informed that there are now stage-waggons established on this road, which were very much wanted; the charge of travelling in them is moderate. In summer, they are twenty four hours on the journey, and in winter nearly three days, as the roads at that season are almost impassable.

made

made of clay, it is, in wet-weather, dirty and slippery beyond description. The road for carriages is a very bad one. Half way between Ritzbuttle and Cuxhaven is the Commodore's house; it is a neat cottage, painted white, and the pleasantest-looking house that we had seen for some time. The port of *Cuxhaven* has only two or three little hovels, and a windmill, near it, and hardly a tree is to be seen. The passengers, who go by the packets, reside, during their stay on shore, at Ritzbuttle; the best accommodations there, for those who do not regard the expence, is at the English tavern, which is kept by a civil man, of the name of Miles: he may be recollected by some Englishmen, as he was formerly a waiter at Mays's Tavern*, near the Planket in Ostend. The wind being foul, we resided a few days at a small house kept by a shopkeeper in the town, where our expences were moderate. The packets usually leave Cuxhaven on Thursdays and Sundays; the expence of an order to be received on board is 12s. 6d. The order is obtained from the agent of the English packets, resident at Ritzbuttle. The passage on board the packet cost four guineas for each person. Having a fair wind, on the 16th of May, 1796, we bade adieu to the Continent, and in forty hours landed at Yarmouth.

And now, Mr. Editor, it only remains for me to thank you for the space which you have allowed me to take up in your Magazine, and to assure you that I feel myself much obliged by your indulgence. I should be happy, if, from the few materials in my possession, I could have rendered this *Sketch* more interesting; but, such as it is, it will give me much gratification, if it should be the means of conveying a small portion of information and entertainment to your readers. I am, Sir,

Hackney, Your's, &c.
Sept. 6, 1801. ROBERT STEVENS.

To the Editor of the Monthly Magazine.

SIR,

THE following facts appear of so singular and almost incredible a nature, that I think necessary to apprise the reader that they are extracted from the "*Voyage Historique, Littéraire, et Pittoresque, dans les Iles et Possessions ci-devant Vénetiennes du Levant.*" After having barely added that the scene of the phenomena here described is the isle of Cephalonia, I proceed to the narrative.

"I was (says the author) at the country-seat of one of the chiefs of the isle, and drank every morning a glass of goat's milk. The Greek who supplied me with that beverage had accustomed a goat to come into my apartment, where she suffered herself to be milked in return for a few handfuls of Corinth raisins which I gave her.

"One day, I accidently perceived that the teeth of the goat were all of a very beautiful yellow hue, inclining to the color of gold. I immediately opened the animal's mouth, and rubbed her teeth: but the rubbing only rendered them more brilliant. This discovery was to me extremely interesting: and I would certainly not have exchanged my goat for the famed Amalthæa, although the latter had the honor of giving milk to the Master of the Thunder. I made my host acquainted with my adventure, expressing to him the great pleasure it had given to me. He replied that my goat was not the only one remarkable for gilded teeth: and he proved the truth of his assertion by conducting me to an inclosed meadow where I saw above two hundred of those animals, which all exhibited the same phænomenon. They were much fatter than any I had seen in other parts of the isle, and yielded milk in greater abundance, and of superior quality.

"A very sensible and enlightened physician, with whom I discoursed of these facts, showed me, by way of answer, a gold ring, of which one part appeared to me to be silver; observing to me that the white color was only a wash, but so strong that the most violent friction was incapable of diminishing it. He told me, that, returning once from Santa-Maura to Cephalonia, he cast anchor on the coast of a rocky uninhabited islet, about eleven or twelve leagues distant from the latter of those two islands; that, having landed, he amused himself by collecting plants on the rock, and filled a handkerchief with them. After his return to the barque, which unfortunately was not at his sole disposal, and when he was already advanced on his voyage, he was extremely astonished to observe that the gold ring which he wore on his finger appeared almost entirely silver. He rubbed it, but to no purpose. This trans-

---

* I am sorry to remark, that this house at Ostend was the only solitary instance which I have met with on the Continent of an inn kept by one of my own countrymen, where no imposition was practised. I was at Ostend in the year 1791, and again in 1793 and 1794, and I invariably found that Mays would rather lose money himself than impose upon his customers: yet this man was a *smuggler.*

transmutation powerfully excited his curiosity. Attributing it to the virtue of some of the plants growing on that islet, he immediately began to rub another gold ring with each of those which he had gathered; but he had the mortification to find himself destitute of the particular plant which had produced so wonderful an effect. He earnestly wished to return to the islet, and made the proposal to his fellow-passengers and to the skipper: but they, stupid ignorant beings who felt no curiosity for the wonders of nature, refused to comply with his wishes."

Such, Mr. Editor, is the account given by a writer who does not, in other parts of his work, appear to deal in romance, and who resided many years in the Greek islands in a public character. That many of your readers will treat the whole as a fable, I have not a doubt. For my own part, I do not profess implicitly to believe it: yet, when I consider how various and unaccountable the wonders of nature, I should deem it presumption to condemn the story as false, merely because it surpasses my comprehension. At all events—whether the mischievous plant can ever again be discovered which deteriorates gold to silver—I suppose the truth or falsity of the other circumstance may easily be ascertained by some of our Levant-traders, who may, upon enquiry, learn whether the isle of Cephalonia really does contain goats with gilded teeth; and, if it does, whether they be a particular race of goats which enjoy that distinction by hereditary descent, or whether any common white-toothed goat, after having fed during a certain period in a particular pasture, has the color of its teeth changed to a golden hue.

Nov. 26. I am, Sir, yours, &c.

W. W.

For the Monthly Magazine.

DESULTORY COMMENTS *on* MASON'S SUPPLEMENT *to* JOHNSON'S DICTIONARY.

(*Continued from Page 101.*)

DACTYLE.

THIS way of spelling is adopted by Johnson; but it is more usual to omit the final *e*, and to write *dactyl*, which better accords with pronunciation. It would have been convenient for the memory, if all our names of poetic feet had themselves been examples of the feet designated. In this case, we must have written Pyrric, Iamb, Trochy, Tribrachys, Anapæst, Dactylus, Spondee, Molossole, &c.

Dado.—Dado signifies *a die* in Italian. It is therefore (1) a *square* compartment in wainscotting, and (2) any compartment, whether square or oblong. Mr. Mason defines it "the plain part of a side of a room between the base and a cornice." My carpenter says it is never applied to "the plain part of a side of a room" above the wainscotting and below the cornish, unless the wall be divided into pannels; but that it is applied to "the plain part of a side of a room" above the foot-board, and below the cornish of the wainscotting. It seems then applicable only to framed spaces.

Death-practised.—A compound word, which ought to mean *practised in death*, and might suit a bad physician, a good general, or an old carronade. The use of it by Shakespeare was an abuse, even in Shakespeare's time, when *practise* meant *mal-practice*.

Decanter.—This every-day word does mean, as Mr. Mason observes, "a glass vessel for holding decanted liquor:" it is, however, an anomalous word. *Decanter* ought to signify *he who decants*; as *giver*, he who gives; *skinker*, he who pours out; *drinker*, he who drinks: it ought to be nearly synonimous with butler.

And how should the recipient of decanted liquor have been called? In order to ascertain this point, recourse must be had to the technical Latin of those alchemists or chemists, out of whose writings the word has slidden into use. I have read many a page of Lord Bacon in order to find it, but in vain. I cannot read Van Helmont and Paracelsus. Was it perhaps *decantatorium*? If so, it would be better to write *decantor*, or *decantory*.

Decard.—An anomalous word properly superseded by *discard*: the like may be said of *decrown*, which is superseded by *discrown*.

Defoul.—A hybrid coinage of Spenser's, neither English, nor of any other language: perhaps it is a mere error of the printer, and the poet wrote *yfouled*, the old past participle formed with the augment.

Defray.

Here, in this bottle, said the sorry maid,
I put the tears of my contrition,
Till to the brim I have it full *defrayed*.

In this passage of the Fairy Queen (b. vi. c. 8. st. 24.) says Mr. Mason, *to defray* means *to fill up*, which is a Gallicism. Why not call it an impurity, a blunder? Gallicisms may be worthy of imitation. There is no instance in French of the verb *defrayer* having any such signification. According to Menage, its etymon

etymon is *fredum*, which, in the laws of the Lombards, signifies the fine imposed for sedition. Seditious persons were often abetted by men of consequence, who paid the fine for them. Such employers were said *defredare, to fine for* their underlings. Hence *to defray* always signifies to bear the charges of another.

Dilatante.—One would attribute to the printer this symptom of illiterature, were not the word arranged before *Dilatability*. Read *Dilettante*.

Disbowel.—This word, being regularly compounded of *dis* and *bowel*, is certainly good English, and signifies, if one may repeat Mr. Mason's somewhat coarse definition, "to gut." Spenser compares Rome to

A great oak dry and dead.
Yet clad with reliques of some trophies old,
That half *disbowel'd* lies above the ground,
Showing her wreathed roots.

It is become the more necessary to remind English writers of the existence and legitimacy of this word, as Mr. Burke has vitiously employed in its stead the word *embowel*, which is regularly compounded of *in* and *bowel*, and signifies just the reverse; as *to embowel sausage-meat*. To *disbowel* is to take out bowels; to *embowel* is to put into bowels; and to *disembowel* is to take out that which has been put into bowels.

Mr. Burke writes thus in his Reflections:

"In England we have not yet been completely *embowelled* of our natural entrails."

He was probably misled by the carelessness of Dr. Johnson, who defines *embowel* "to eviscerate;" in consequence of misunderstanding three out of the four authorities adduced in his own Dictionary.

Spenser understood and used the word aright:

He, with his dreadful instrument of ire,
Thought sure have pounded him to powder soft,
Or deep *embowel'd* in the earth entire.

where the meaning is "put into the bowels of the earth."

In like manner the word is used by Shakespeare:

Imbowell'd will I see thee by and by;
Till then in blood by noble Percy lie.

where the meaning is "put into the bowels of the earth," "buried;" and certainly not, as Johnson supposes, "exenterated:" Of such brutality Prince Henry was incapable.

In like manner, the word is used by Milton:

The roar
Embowell'd with outrageous noise the air,
And all her entrails tore.

where the noise is metaphorically described as introducing itself *into* the bowels of the air, and tearing them.

The passage from Philips is quaint and unclear: he talks of—"minerals that th' embowell'd earth displays"—meaning, apparently, "minerals which within its bowels the earth displays." The other passage from Shakespeare I know not where to seek: if it occurred in Richard II. or Henry VIII. and related to the Lollards, or the Protestants, one might with propriety say,

The schools,
Embowell'd of *their* doctrine, have left off
The wholesome lore.

meaning the schools, or universities, "which have received into their bowels the new doctrines." And thus every one of Dr. Johnson's cases would be a precedent against his definition.

Disputable.—Disputable signifies *able to be disputed, controvertible*: it is vitiously used for *disputatious* in the adduced passage from As You Like It. Dictionaries cannot be worse employed than in preserving authorities for the abuse of words, without any accompanying asterisk of reprobation. The use of *distrain* for *constrain* by Fairfax, or of *distroubled* for *troubled* by Spenser, is no less exceptionable.

Dizzard.—Once it was very common to form personal substantives descriptive of character by adding the syllable *ard*, which probably comes from the Mœso-Gothic *bairta*, heart. Thus, from wise, *wisard*; dote, *dotard*; drunk, *drunkard*; slug, *sluggard*; dull, *dullard*. This word is of the same class, and is formed from *dizzy*; it means therefore one *dizzy of heart*, or, as we now say, giddy-headed.

Dolphinet.—A dolphinet is a small dolphin; if the female be smaller than the male in this class of animals, the passage from Spenser is sufficiently justifiable.

Duette.—Why not adopt the usual spelling *duet*. *Duette* is of no language, neither Italian, nor French, nor English.

Earne.—Why should this *spell* (as school-children say, and, I think, rightly, for *mode of spelling*) be authorized? It is likely to be mistaken for the verb *earn*, "to gain by labor." It is far less usual than *yearn*. And it is less analogous than

 yearn;

yearn; for the cognate-words, in other Gothic dialects, begin with *g* aspirate, which in English is mostly softened (as in the participal augment *yclad, yclept*, &c.) into *y*. Such allied or kin words are in Ottfried, *gerno*; in Tatian, *gernilibo*, willingly; in Icelandish, *girn*; Swedish, *gerna*; Mœso-Gothic, *gairnan*; Anglo-Saxon, *geornian*; Danish, *giären*; Low-Dutch, *gheren*, to desire, &c. all perhaps from some patriarchial word, signifying, like the Friesish *gere*, the side.

Dr. Johnson ignorantly gives, as the etymon of *yearn*, the Anglo-Saxon *earnan*, which means *to ear*, *to shoot in ears*, *to bear spikes*: and belongs to a different family.

Effierced.—A word evidently formed by the same rule of analogy as, to *abase*, to *ascertain*, and others quoted already in the article *Abear*; which ought therefore to be written *affierced*.

Electral.—The adjectives *electric*, *electral*, and *electrical* have all been used by writers of education: are they in purity, as in meaning, equivalent?

The termination *ic* derives from the Greek ικος, as μοναρχης, monarch, μοναρχικος, monarchic; κωμος, fun, κωμικος, comic: the termination *al* derives from the Latin *alis*, as *æquare*, to level, *æqualis*, equal; *navis*, a ship, *navalis* naval: but the termination *ical* is a hybrid coalescence of the Greek and Latin formative syllables, a mongrel affix peculiar to English language. If then (as was observed at the word *Antiguggler*) the spirit of our language does not favour the breed of mule words; it would follow, that, where the radical substantive or etymon is Greek, the inflection of the derived adjective should be in *ic*; and where the etymon is Latin, in *al*: but that, to words of low and ludicrous signification, an affix *ical*, somewhat barbarous and illiterate in its very composition, would best be adapted; as *whimsical*, *finical*, *pedantical*, *satirical*.

As the old word *electre*, amber, may come from the Greek, or from the Latin, the adjectives *electric* or *electral* are alike proper. Would it not be worth while to revive the use of this substantive, which Lord Bacon long ago employed, as the name of that fluid which occasions all electric phænomena?

Embarquement.—This substantive is a regular derivative of the verb *to embark* or *imbark*, and can only signify (1) *the state of being on shipboard*, (2) *any thing put on shipboard, a cargo*, in which last sense it apparently occurs in Coriolanus. Mr. Mason confounds the word with *embargo*.

Enchase.—Mr. Mason proposes, as a fifth sense of the word *enchase*, "to delineate:" he then quotes these two lines of Spenser:

My ragged rimes are all too rude and base
Her heavenly lineaments for to enchase.

Here the word obviously means "to inshrine," *thecâ condere*, which is its primitive meaning. So in French: *Enchasser une relique dans une chasse d'argent*; to enchase a relique in a silver shrine: *Enchasser une fenetre dans son chassis*; to frame a window in a sash: *Enchasser une pierre dans de l'or*; to set a stone in gold.

Endoss.—There is an habitual neglect of precision in the definitions of Mr. Mason: this word does not mean "to mark *by incision*," but "to mark *on the back*:" and also *to put on one's back*. Its etymon is the French *dos*, the back.

Il s'habille en berger, *endosse* un hoqueton.
LAFONTAINE.

Chariots, or elephants *endossed* with towers.
MILTON.

Exorable.—Mr. Mason has discovered in an obscure corner an authority for this word: do such words require to be authorized? We are in the familiar use of *inexorable*, *unweildy*, *indestructible*, *uncontestible*, surely we may infer the legitimacy of *exorable*, *wieldy*, *destructible*, *contestable*: privatives imply the existence of the integral word.

(To be continued.)

For the Monthly Magazine.

ACCOUNT *of an* ANCIENT MONUMENT *at* VIENNE.

CIT. SCHNEIDER, Professor of Design at Vienne, has lately read to the Lyceum of Grenoble a Dissertation on the Cenotaph in the former city, called the Spire (*le Plan de l'Aiguille*), in which he enters into an exact description of its construction, according to the principles of architecture, and accompanies these details with a number of conjectures; which may serve to shew on what occasion this monument was erected; conjectures, he observes, which carry with them the greater air of probability, as they will be found to be supported by the usage of the Romans, and by general history. The singular structure of this monument attracts the curiosity of travellers; but no one, there is reason to think, has hitherto discovered its precise destination nor its architecture. It would appear, according to many designs and memoirs which the Professor

Professor has met with, to be a shapeless mass, without taste or without art; but he proves the contrary by his description alone, and by the simple and natural reflections resulting therefrom, which develope the merit of this fragment of antiquity. This monument occupies but little space; it only comprehends seventeen feet eight inches square, not including the fore part of the pedestals of the angular columns, which take up thirteen inches six lines (a line is the twelfth part of an inch), without their bases; and which further extend four inches six lines square (*en carré*), in all, twenty feet, eight inches square. Its height, to the upper part of the entablature, is twenty-two feet; and the pyramid, with its base, is nearly fifty feet; which gives in all seventy-two feet in elevation, although there wants about twelve feet in proceeding from the progressive proportions observed in its tapering, from its base to the apex, to form the point or needle. The thickness of the walls which form the body of the pyramid, is two feet, seven inches; consequently its interior space is twelve feet, six inches at the base. The angular columns by which this monument is flanked, are about twenty-two inches in diameter; their height is fourteen feet nine inches, including the bases and chapiters, which would only make seven diametres and a half, or fifteen modules, which are the proportions of the columns between the Doric and Ionic. These columns are engaged by quarters (*du quart*), in the construction make a part of it, and sustain the whole monument. Doubtless the Corinthian proportions would have been too feeble to accomplish this object. They lessen gradually to the top, as almost all the ancient columns do, and sufficiently fill the eye in the *ensemble*. The bases are Attic, and have never been completed; one of the four is still rough and unpolished, which has given cause to certain ignorant persons to call this a monument of the bad ages and Gothic. The proportions of the chapiters are Corinthian. Although they are not as yet sculptured, it is easy to see that they have been prepared for chapiters of that order, and will not agree with any other. VITRUVIUS only assigns them two modules, and these have something more; although to the eye they appear too low, they would, no doubt, appear more elevated, if the sculpture were finished. Four arcades in the four fronts reveal a very bold cieling (*plafond*), made of basket-work (*par encorbeillement*); the stones of the architecture appear supported by the four key-stones of the arcades, and covered by the stones of the frieze and cornice, formed of two beds of stones, laid by bound masonry on each other. These and other proportions indicated by Citizen Schneider shew clearly that this monument is Corinthian, and of good taste. The inclination of the pyramids is so well combined, that all the weight rests on the centre of the pedestals of the columns; so that the columns serve for buttresses, and uphold the whole fabric. The totality of this structure is seated on a massive base of free stone, of a quality similar to those employed in the rest of the work, cramped horizontally with iron, and cemented with lead; so that the whole is bound together, and forms only a single body. (This may serve to prove the durability of iron in monuments, and consequently justify the use made of that metal by the celebrated modern architect, the late M. Soufflot, in the construction of the famous church of St. Geneviève at Paris). The whole monument is only composed of thirty-four rows of stones, of which the pyramid has twenty-three, including the base. Neither lime nor cement has been employed in it; the stones are so well joined, that the finest blade could not be insinuated between two, and indeed it would be difficult to find the junctures in many places. This is a method of perfection in handycraft work, in which the moderns have never yet approached the Romans. There are in the base some stones so big that some pass from one arcade to the other, and make part of the two walls and of the columns, and sometimes even of the pedestals. All these precautions of solidity, the figure of the monument, its regular order, the quality of the materials, which are selected stones, an antique species of marble, susceptible of the finest polish; its arcades, all its parts, in a word, announce that it is a public monument which has never been finished; even the surface of the facings has not been smoothed over in any part, nor even the columns; which would induce a presumption, that they would accord better with the Corinthian order. The *ensemble* of the monument is beautiful; it breathes an air of grandeur, and inspires a veneration, which well characterizes the antique. Different opinions have prevailed relative to the origin and subject of this monument. Some pretend, that it is the tomb of VENERIUS, founder of Vienne; others say it was the military stone of the city, serving for a decoration to the middle of its ancient precinct; while CHORIER, in his Antiquities of Vienne, pretends that it is the cenotaph of AUGUSTUS,

GUSTUS. In regard to its denomination, the antiquary Chorier is right, having discovered the true qualification of the pyramid, and is only mistaken as to the name of the prince who was the object of it. The other conjectures are fabulous. Citizen Schneider proceeds to observe, that he found it necessary to penetrate into the centre of the pyramid, in order to find out its interior construction more perfectly, and to ascertain the form and object of the pyramid. This operation, he adds, might be performed without damaging or degrading the monument. He communicated his project to Monsieur the Intendant of the province, in the presence of Messieurs the Mayor and *Eschevins*, in the month of October, 1776, who appeared to applaud it unanimously. He had scarcely, however, set his hand to the work, before he experienced opposition, founded on false alarms, and which betrayed more of inquietude than of science. These obstacles long suspended his labour, which consisted in taking away, by means of pincers, one of the stones of the body of the pyramid to discover if it was hollow, as he had always suspected, and in that case, to penetrate into it, examine it, and describe its interior structure. Being cited before the municipal body, he tranquillized Messieurs the Magistrates as to the fate of the monument; and having, after some time, resumed his researches, under the protection of Monsieur the Intendant, he at length opened the desired passage. He found nothing above the cieling (where there was a heap of earth and dust, which the rain had filtrated through in the course of time) but an empty space of about six feet square, and which grows narrower to the top, following the form of the pyramid, that is to say, as far as the sixteenth row of stones; the rest is massive as far as the apex; the stones are of bound masonry, and are rough and unpolished within. After having thus dissipated his doubts, it was easy for him to shut the momentaneous aperture he had made in the pyramid, by substituting another stone in the place; but it was thought preferable, he says, to place there an iron door, by favour of which they are enabled to introduce the curious who would verify his observations. Lastly, to see whether it contained any subterraneous vault which served for a tomb, he pierced and sounded the middle, and, perpendicular with the cieling, the massive on which the whole structure is established; he then dug up the earth which surrounded it, and, after having examined the foundation through its whole interior and exterior *pourtour*, as far as was possible, he found no index which might lead to a presumption, that it incloses any subterranean or void space destined to receive a coffin. In effect, says the Professor, it did not accord with the religion of the Romans thus to expose the remains of the persons whom they honoured with the apotheosis, to be trampled under feet; and the sarcophagus, if there had been one in the monument, would have had its place in the void part of the pyramid, and would have reposed on the cieling; or else, after other examples, the ashes, deposited in an urn, would have been placed on the pinnacle or top part of the pyramid. It is then, says the Professor, a real cenotaph. It remains to determine, to the honour of whom it was erected. It could not be to Augustus, because no author mentions it; and besides, that Emperor had already at Vienne a celebrated temple elevated to his memory, as the Professor has especially established, in his description of the *de la Vie*; and the usage of the Romans was not to multiply those sorts of honours in the same place for the same person. After all the researches here detailed, Citizen Schneider, at length, had recourse to ancient history. He proceeds to say, that he has remarked no great personage who has better deserved to be honoured and immortalized by a similar monument, than ALEXANDER SEVERUS. In effect, according to the report of Lampridius, in his *History of the Emperors*, he was a just and amiable prince, a lover and favourer of the arts and sciences, and one who made it his whole business to secure the happiness of the people, who had surnamed him, it seems, Severus, because of his rigour in military discipline. A model and protector of virtue, this prince highly approved of the Christian morality, and never ceased that fundamental maxim of all morality—*Do unto others as you would they should do unto you.* He caused this fine maxim to be engraved in his palace, and on the public edifices. His moderation and his modesty, which equalled his merit and courage, made him refuse all the vain and fastidious titles with which the senate would decorate him, accustomed to adulation under the preceding reigns. But all the great qualities of Alexander could not save him from the most fatal destiny. In the flower of his age, in the midst of his triumphs, beloved by his subjects, honoured by his enemies, he fell, assassinated in his tent by a cruel monster, whilst he was

reposing

reposing at noon in the environs of Mentz, at Schilingen, in the year 235 of the Christian æra, at the age of twenty-six years and some months, after having reigned thirteen years complete. The death of Alexander Severus caused a universal grief (says Lampridius, and after him Crevier, *Ancient History*) at Rome, and throughout the whole empire, as the mildness and equity of his government had rendered him extremely popular. He was bitterly lamented; in short, made a god of. Lastly, the historians add, that a cenotaph was erected for him in Gaul, and that his body, taken to the capital (Rome), was inclosed in a magnificent tomb, and the highest honours paid to it. A religious solemnity and festivals were instituted to his honour, which were still observed at the time when Lampridius wrote. We are not acquainted, says Citizen Schneider, with any cenotaph in Gaul, but that of Vienne, excepting that of Drusus, erected near the Rhine, at Mentz, of which history makes a particular mention. Hence arises a principal and strong presumption that this cenotaph is that of Alexander Severus, of which Lampridius speaks; although he does not cite the city, he says, in Gaul. Vienne was the principal city of it, the capital, and one of the most considerable places of war, as, says Citizen Schneider, I have already shewn. It scarcely admits of a doubt, and is, on the other hand, very natural to think, that Vienne would have the honour of immortalizing a prince so generally regretted as Alexander Severus. Thus, says Citizen Schneider, from a variety of causes, great cities striving to imitate Rome (and Vienne, it seems, justly merited the title of beautiful and second Rome), an *ensemble* of facts, circumstances, and conjectures, a sort of probable certainty is formed, which authorises us to conclude that our monument is the cenotaph of Alexander Severus, respectable for its antiquity, and much more as it is the cenotaph of the first protector of the Christians; and indeed it was under his reign that the first church was raised in which worship was publicly rendered to Jesus Christ. Although he made profession of Paganism, we are informed that he had a secret inclination for Christianity, which his mother, Mamea, a Christian born, had inspired him with. Things soon changed their face under the reign of Maximin, the murderer and successor of Alexander Severus, but a tyrant as much hated and detested as his predecessor was beloved. Maximin, doubtless, with a view to conceal his crime and conciliate the people, at first affected respect for the memory of Alexander, and even feigned to approve of the funeral honours which had been decreed to him. But not being able to conceal his ferocious character long, he soon manifested contrary sentiments, by banishing from the court and army all the friends of the young and virtuous Alexander, among whom were a great number of Christians, who were violently persecuted, and their churches pulled down. Civil wars and other revolutions rendered the reign of Maximin very stormy. This universal disorder was doubtless one of the principal causes which prevented our monument from being terminated and brought to perfection.—The Professor then proceeds to investigate and explain why this sort of monuments had a pyramidal form. The pyramid is a well-known symbol of immortality, as we learn by its etymology from the Greek word πυρ, which signifies *fire* or *flame*. Another reason and motive of this construction is, that its form is more solid and more durable than any other—on this account, the Kings of Egypt adopted it for their famous tombs, known by the names of the Pyramids of Egypt. In effect, this figure of a building resists better the injuries of time; the rain-water runs from it more easily, and cannot lodge on it; the four corners are exposed to the four cardinal points, so that the four principal winds cannot strike it at right angles. The Greeks have preserved for their funeral monuments the pyramidal figure, which they had received from the Egyptians, as the Romans learned it from the Greeks. We have retained it from both these nations, and preserved it in our mausolea. The Greeks and Romans endeavoured to bring these monuments to perfection, and to render them more agreeable to the eye, by giving them a lighter and bolder construction. For this purpose, they elevated them, some by means of a pedestal, and some were placed on an entire body of architecture, which served for a basis. Of the latter kind is the cenotaph of Vienne. Nevertheless this novelty of method did not at all injure the solidity, as our monument demonstrates. The four angles in it are opposed to the four cardinal points, in imitation of the pyramids of Egypt, which, in all probability, has greatly contributed to its preservation. Father Montfaucon makes mention likewise of this monument (in his book, intitled *Antiquities explained*), after Spon. On the article of Tombs, he gives a design in which our cenotaph is not at all discernible. These are his words:—"I conceive that we ought

ought to take for a mausoleum the pyramid which is near Vienne, sustained by four pillars, adorned with four columns that support a vault of eighteen feet elevation; on the vault rises a pyramid of from twenty-five to thirty feet; the whole may stand from forty to fifty feet high." This description, continues the Professor, is doubtless made at random, for here are neither pillars nor vault in the body of the architecture that supports the pyramid; and Montfaucon is mistaken by twenty-four feet in the whole height,—he forgets the entablature, and supposes, in his design, elliptic arches, which were never yet seen in antique monuments. It is surprising, that both Spon and Montfaucon should have been so negligent in verifying so fine a fragment of antiquity; and Spon especially, who was some time at Vienne. But probably he spoke or wrote of it when he was no longer in the country. The Professor terminates these observations by some general reflections on the object and principal utility of this sort of works.

To the Editor of the Monthly Magazine.

SIR,

THE question which will principally engage the attention of those who feel themselves interested in the subjects of Mr. Godwin's late pamphlet, is whether he has successfully combated the objections advanced against his theory by the author of the much-applauded Essay on Population. It appears to me, that Mr. Godwin has most lamentably failed in the defence of his favourite positions. He would have merited well of mankind had he succeeded; for there is no benevolent mind which would not rejoice in the belief, that all moral evil might, and will, be rooted from the face of the earth.

I proceed to state my reasons for asserting that Mr. Godwin has not defended the practicability of his speculation against the obstacles arising from a too-extended population. To obviate the evils that would spring from this source, we find two expedients suggested; but, at the same time, rejected: one, the exposing of infants; the other, a certain method of preventing their appearance in the world. Now, if it were not intended to advise the substituting of these checks on population in lieu of those which at present exist, it is difficult to account for the introduction of such unpleasant subjects in the pamphlet before us. Besides, the writer has mentioned no others which carry in them any appearance of efficacy at all adequate to the end in view. I must therefore suppose, that Mr. Godwin designed to *recommend* the above-named expedients: and the question to be decided will then be, Are these expedients (what they are expressly said to be) "better than vice and misery?"

I am striving, Mr. Editor, to treat this subject with as much coolness as if it were merely an abstract question, unconnected with the best feelings of the heart: and have already expunged twenty harsh epithets, which the very mention of the above practices had forced from my pen. But the matter may be safely entrusted to the calm decisions of the reasoning faculty.

What could be Mr. Godwin's opinions respecting the nature of vice and misery—where the perspicacity and benevolent bias of the author of Political Justice—when he was recommending, as substitutes for vice, the most shocking and revolting crimes? If it be vicious to invade the liberty, rights, or property of another—a too-frequent vice of poverty—is it less so to take away his life? If it be miserable, as Mr. Godwin remarks, "to have the body maimed and distorted by disease—to live under the shelter of a hovel or a garret—to exhibit to every spectator the wretchedness of penury, and the meagreness of a shattered frame"—is it less miserable to stifle and subdue a parent's yearnings towards his helpless new-born—to inflict, or cause to be inflicted, the stroke of death on the engaging little-one, that from the moment of quickening has excited your tenderest hopes and fears, and is become, as well on its own account as on the mother's, writhed and twisted round your heart by ten thousand sacred bonds of sympathy and love? Who can ask these questions, and not be pitied for his ignorance? Are they not then vice and misery which Mr. Godwin recommends as checks on increasing population? Nor are the vice and misery inferior in extent to what result from the present subsisting checks. I presume it is not necessary to go into detail to prove that bodily sufferings are more easily endured than mental anguish—or, that the man who is doomed to penury and distress in outward circumstances, yet keeps alive an affectionate heart, full of good-will to his family and friends, has a more honourable and valuable character than his, who, though possessed of fortune's choicest gifts, is yet unadorned by the charms and graces of affection. Nor can it be needful to shew,

before

before it is controverted, that the *worst* vices of poverty are not *so bad* as barbarity and hardness of heart—as the loss of that principle within, on which hangs every thing valuable in the poor man's character; but which is indeed an ample moral recompence for every mischief to which he may be goaded by the circumstances that must take place in the best-regulated society. If then the *pains* of poverty are not so great to the tender mind, as the pains of a custom, happily most repugnant to the native feelings of the heart; we gain nothing in point of *happiness* by the expedient proposed. And if the *vices* of poverty are not so debasing, unnatural, nor pregnant with such baneful consequences to society, as the vice of habitual murder, as the cold unfeeling sacrifice of innocence and parental affection on the bloody altar of state expedience—we do not gain much, I conceive, in point of *virtue*. In the words then of Mr. Godwin, we may say, "there is nothing very seducing or agreeable in the appearance" of these substitutes. But, he adds, "I hope no such expedients will be necessary to be resorted to in any state of society which shall ever be introduced in this or the surrounding countries."—"I have not introduced these particulars as seeming to me necessary to the solution of the difficulty proposed." By what other methods then is the difficulty to be removed? 1st. By the future possible discoveries of the human mind. 2d. By allowing every marriage to produce only two or three, or, at most, four, children.—But Mr. Godwin has not discovered, or rather not disclosed, any scheme for limiting the number of children to a marriage so that they shall not exceed the number four. He has therefore either left the difficulty as he found it, or must be supposed to refer us to one of the expedients considered above: now both of these he has rejected; lastly, he resorts to the existing checks on population, in despair of finding substitutes; and asserts, that in the improved state of society, to which he anxiously looks forward, the prudential considerations which form the principal restraints at present, will have greater weight, and more general effect than they have in the times we live in. But he has not supported this assertion, by replying to the powerful arguments of his opponent against this hypothesis, derived from a consideration of the nature of man, and the past history of his kind in connection with this subject.

To sum up the whole: It seems then that Mr. Godwin has proposed expedients* for stemming the tide of population, which strike as revolting on the heart as they appear injudicious to the head—or, he has furnished means perfectly inadequate to the end—or, he has referred the solution of the difficulty to the acuter intellects which future times may perchance bring forth.

I wish, in conclusion, to offer to the consideration of those who take an interest in these speculations, the following problem: 'What would be the improvement in the moral condition of man, were he sublimed to the utmost pitch of intellectual excellence, yet deprived of those pleasures which are the primary source of the parental, filial, and conjugal affections, and are the chief support of all the endearing charities of domestic life?' I propose this question, because it is obvious that Mr. Godwin's scheme, when perfected, will include the downfall of family-empire, and the annihilation of fire-side enjoyments. Hitherto I had always considered that chapter in the Political Justice, which treats of the omnipotence of intellect, and its sublime inventions, as an amusing speculation not necessarily connected with the leading objects of Mr. Godwin's inquiries, and as such have always defended it: but the serious defence of it, conducted in so pertinacious a style, which is now set up, removes all doubts from my mind of its being the darling child of an over-fond parent, whose anxiety for its safety never slumbers, and whose exertions to support it are never-ceasing. Your's, &c.

Shrewsbury, Sept. 14, 1801. W.

For the Monthly Magazine.

A PEDESTRIAN EXCURSION *through* ENGLAND *and* WALES, *during the* SUMMER *of* 1797.

(*Continued from Page 200.*)

BATH has been too often described to need any particular notice here: and, if it had not been so, it is a subject much too copious to be introduced in these brief and hasty sketches. Even a general criticism on the style and arrangement of the objects that rise in succession upon the ob-

* I have considered these two expedients under one view: because, until Mr. Godwin can produce better evidence for the safety and innocence of the medicines which he recommends, than "I am told they are innoxious," the prevailing prejudices will continue to be felt. There cannot be much difference in their moral effects.

servant eye in a walk through this city of palaces, would fill more columns than, in a periodical work, can be afforded to the topographical survey of a county. Suffice it to say, we were delighted—we were fascinated—we exclaimed in a rapture—This only is worthy of being called a city!—all that we have seen before were but congregations of pig sties! We had intended to have passed through Bath post-speed, as through a place of vulgar note (for what were its splendours to us!) and to have hastened to the main point of our destination, and we had made our arrangements accordingly. But what signified arrangements? We had eyes, and they were masters of us. Our habiliments, however, were somewhat out of harmony with the scenery around us; they bore the evident marks of pedestrian toil; while every thing we beheld was stamped with the character of equipage and elegance. We determined therefore to repair to Bristol, whither our portmanteau had been sent from London to wait for our arrival, and then return to see the city of Bath, when we ourselves might be not quite unfit to be seen. Accordingly on

Monday 10, we took a morning-walk to Bristol by the upper-road; whence, between the second and third mile-stones, we enjoyed a pleasant expansive view of the course of the Avon, the surrounding country, and the city to which we were directing our march,

Bristol. At this place (where we arrived about 2 o'clock) we had each of us some friends, with some of whom, after dinner, we took a ramble to the fine rocks of St. Vincent's, with the alternate beauty and rough sublimity of which, diversified as they are in many places by the luxuriant cloathing of woods and coppice, we were very considerably interested. Hence, also, we commanded some very fine views of the surrounding country; and pursued with our eye the winding course of the river that flows at the bottom of this precipitous chasm, till it empties itself into that fine estuary, the Bristol channel. One thing, however, seemed necessary for the perfection of this scene: it was clearness and transparency of water. "Though deep, yet clear; though gentle, yet not dull;" can never be applied, even by hyperbole itself, to the Bath Avon. On the contrary, all the way that we had traced it, its waters, in appearance, were mere liquified mud. To the margin of these waters, however, we scrambled down, that we might enjoy the upward as well as the downward gaze. Here again we experienced sensations of delight, the objects that excited which (as they also are familiar to the tourist) I must not pause to describe. For the same reason I pass over with a hasty dash of my pen, the Wells, the Mall, the shops, and the fine buildings—"tier o'er tier, high-piled from earth to heaven!" that rose upon our view. Upon these, however, we could not but observe the very evident marks of the arresting hand of war—whose trumpets and whose cannon, though not *heard* in our island, were yet felt through our else growing neighbourhoods; and which here (as at Clifton, as Bristol, at Bath) with a sort of silent earthquake had shaken many an unfinished street and edifice into premature ruin, and rendered the taste of the architect, and the labour of the builder, of no avail.

On our return from this excursion, we found ourselves trapped into a very large party; with whom we kept it up, as it is called, till half past twelve o'clock—sad hours for pedestrian hunters of the picturesque and sentimental!

Tuesday 11. Be it known, however, to the credit of our temperance, that, after a sound and refreshing sleep, we rose at half past seven without any head-ach, and, separating to our distinct breakfast-parties, united again at between ten and eleven, in a ramble of observation, with some of our new acquaintance, about the town.

Our attention of course was commanded, in no secondary degree, by the church of St. Mary Radcliff. This is indeed the finest object in the city of Bristol. The architecture is in the fine florid Normo-Gothic style, lofty and light, yet majestic and solid. The aisles are beautiful—the proportions are good. It is indeed one of those buildings, the sight of which compels me to lament, that this style of architecture should ever be laid aside; till, recollecting what tame and incongruous specimens have, in these our days, been produced even by *the most celebrated doers* in this way, I became reconciled to the change, and content that our modern church-builders should shew their bad taste and bungling execution on the models (how poorly imitated) of Greece and Rome, and exclaim, in the enthusiasm of my devotion—Spare! spare the sacrilegious mockery! Let the ghost of departed Gothic-architecture sleep undisturbed—uninsulted by *such* imitations—unprophaned by *such* comparisons!

These were not the only reflections suggested by our survey of this noble, but time-

time-shattered, edifice. We remembered, Chatterton—his Rowley, and his fatal cup—his premature genius, and his premature fate! We recollected also some later instances—less tragical indeed—but not less eloquent to presageful conclusion. We recollected, that whenever genius has sought for patronage in the second city of this great commercial nation, it has sought in vain. And perhaps to the observant moralist and calculator on existing appearances it may be evident, that it is something more than fancy that traces, in the traits of character connected with this neglect of genius, the fore-doomed decay of the trade and opulence of Bristol; while Liverpool, from characteristics the very reverse, is rising, with incalculable rapidity, to a precedence that appears inevitable.

The Tower of St. Stephen's—the fragment of the Cathedral—the New-bridge—the Quay (on which, at that time, were scarcely any vessels, except a few West Indiamen and Americans recentlyarrived), and another visit to St. Vincent's Rocks, and the extensive scenery of Durdham-Down, occupied our time till dinner, when a pleasant family-party, and an interesting conversation on subjects of literature and science, at Dr. ———'s, prepared my mind to enjoy with full zest the beauties of an evening-prospect of Bristol from Brandon-hill.

The evening was devoted to a chearful supper at the Rummer; and it commenced with auspices highly flattering. The spirits flowed without the necessity of stimulating excess—Hilarity hovered over the board, and that sort of free-thinking and free-speaking, in which the most opposite opinions chime together without discord, gave wings to the happy hour. But suddenly all was blasted. The fire-bell jarred its horrible peals in our ears; and all was panic and apprehension. All flew to the scene of disaster. Fortunately the hour was too early for life to be endangered; and the flames, though very furious at first, were extinguished before their ravages had spread to any thing like the extent that was expected. The company returned to the place of meeting. They endeavoured to resume their vivacity, but in vain. The genii who preside over the social banquet, had fled: they refused our libations—our invocation was rejected—our efforts at mirth only increased the general tedium. We kept it up till one o'clock, in the hope that we should be merry; and retired, at last, to our beds, dissatisfied that we had not been so.

Wednesday 12. Having enjoyed a social (almost a public) breakfast, to which some fine passages from "Lucan's Pharsalia" and "Southey's Joan of Arc" furnished a sort of poetical grace, we proceeded to complete our perambulation about the town. Of the objects that now attracted our attention, I select only that expensive pile of grotesque absurdity—the new church of St. Paul, in Portland-square. The Gothic front that presented itself as we approached, inspired me with a sort of hope, that we were going, for once at least, to contemplate a decent modern imitation of that fine, but obsolete, style of sacerdotal building. But, what was our surprise! when, instead of the long-drawn aisles—the *high-peaked* roof, and the comparatively narrow body, that harmonises so finely in the architecture of our ancestors, and give space for that sublime perspective that at once fascinates the eye, and awes the mind to devotion, we perceived our Gothic-spire to be flanked with a short, squab, square, flat-roofed, box, of a body that gave us more the idea (only that it lacked dimensions) of a modern music room, than an ancient church. With these proportions correspond the back-front, which is in the Grecian style: but the windows again are Gothic. The inside is equally pie-balled with the out; the pillars, the arched-roof, the decorations of the galleries, &c. being all in fine Attic-style; while the part assigned to the communion-service is Gothic, with a Gothic-arch behind the altar, blended with an Attic-termination, apparently copied from that of St. Stephen's, Walbrook, in the metropolis.

Appearances so incongruous must necessarily have originated in some latent cause out of the customary routine: for, certain it is, that the parts and proportions (disproportions, I should say) of the church of St. Paul, Portland-square, Bristol, did not come together by accident; and equally certain it is, that no architect, capable of projecting those parts respectively, could have been mad enough, or stupid enough, to have devised so heterogeneous a combination. The mystery, however, was soon explained. Two rival architects had been employed by two rival church-wardens, and each had produced his plan in the parochial conclave. Each of the patrons was inflexible in the support of his particular *protegé*; and each of the patrons had his party inflexible in the support of his superior sciences and the vestry, thus equally divided, was in danger of open rupture and civil-war; to avoid the horrors of which, it was agreed that a compromise should take place between the Athenians and the Goths, and plenipotentiaries were appointed by both parties to arrange the mutual concessions that should be made. From this negociation originated, perhaps, the most complete solecism in architecture, that is any where to be found, even in this land of whims and oddities. To crown the anecdote, economy next stepped in, and, without any attention to breadth or proportion, cut off a part of the intended length of the building, which is now found not to be nearly large enough for the audience it was intended to contain.

After dining with a family-party, we returned to Bath, in the afternoon, by a return-post-chaise; but not till I had yielded my promise, to the entreaties of some friends, to repeat my visit before I quitted that side of the country.

Having spent two more days in contemplating the beautiful buildings, and still more beautiful females, of the city of Bath, and in social reciprocations with a small circle of friends; on

Saturday 15, my companion took his farewel of me, directing his course homeward in the Southampton stage; and shortly after I took my farewell of Bath, thenceforward to pursue my way with solitary step—far from each endearing intercourse—seeking from without for the happiness that was not within, and exclaiming, every time that the smoke of the lone cottage from some sequestered dingle chanced to rise upon my view—"When—when shall I be the peaceful lord of such a mansion, and repose me again in obscurity!"

(To be continued.)

To the Editor of the Monthly Magazine.

SIR,

YOUR Correspondent (p. 100. of the present Volume) objects to the word *Corival*, and would expunge it from the English language; because, "as the word *rival* includes the idea of competition, the *co* is redundant." I beg leave to dissent from so general a conclusion, grounded upon such partial reasoning. All that can fairly be inferred from the argument here adduced is, that *co-rival* ought not to be admitted into composition where nothing but the simple rivalry of individual against individual is meant to be described. But surely there are instances in which the prefix *co* not only would not be expletive; but where it would be highly expressive and comprehensive:—for example, *the suitors of Penelope* might very properly be called the *co-rivals* of Ulysses; and any one of them, spoken of separately, might very properly, in reference to the association or combination that existed among them, be called, in this sense, a *co-rival*. The same rule may be applied to any of those instances in which combinations and associations are formed to rival any trader, or set or description of traders: as the New Flour Company (for example) may be called the co-rivals of the fair independent trader in that article. I wish it may not ultimately indeed cease to be an illustration in point; and by the extinction of all rivalry, place the necessary article of bread in the same situation in which the luxury of tea has so long (and, for the East India Company, so happily) remained.

SARPI.

Sept. 22, 1801.

For the Monthly Magazine.

DESCRIPTION *of the* ISLES *of* FERRO, TRANSLATED *from* LE NORD LITERAIRE, &c.

THE little isles of Ferro, Fero, or Feroen, situated between Norway and Iceland, are but very little known, and undoubtedly merit to be more so; their present state may furnish matter to an interesting and curious description, if undertaken by a skilful hand. This has been lately executed by the Rev. Mr. Landt, who from the year 1791 to 1798 has officiated as minister in these islands, and has just published in Danish, under the title of an Essay, a description of them, accompanied with engravings, plans, memoirs, &c. relative to his work. The author, who is an accurate and well-informed observer, has travelled the whole country, to collect all the rare objects of natural history which it offered; these, it appears, he has sent to the Society of Natural History at Copenhagen.

The islands of Ferro are situated between 61° 15′ and 62° 21′ of north latitude; they have Norway to the east, at about 168 leagues distance; at the S. W. lie the islands of Shetland, distant about 99 leagues; on the S. lies Ireland; on the W. Greenland; and on the N. W. Iceland. Seventeen of these islands are inhabited and the three others are desart; they extend from S. to N. about 30 leagues and about 20 from W. to E.

The aspect which they present, is that of a groupe of rocks, elevated, steep, and almost contiguous, most of them in form of a pyramid, or like truncated cones, proceeding from the bosom of the sea. The

The principal of these rocks, is about 400 toises in height; the crust of earth which covers them, is no where more than four feet in thickness, and is generally about a foot and a half. The naturalist discovers here the most certain indexes of antient volcanic explosions;—they had not escaped the discerning eye of the learned Captain Born, to whom we are indebted for a geological description of the different strata, which here form the promontories, as likewise for a plan of these islands, with geographical charts, the whole inserted in the Memoirs of the Society of Natural History at Copenhagen.

The isles of Ferro are watered by many brooks or streams, which are generally crossed by fording; there are few lakes; the largest is not more than four leagues in circumference; it abounds in salmon trout. Some springs of hot water are found; the best known is that of *Warmakielde*; the author, on examining it towards the latter end of the month of November found its water luke-warm, like milk just taken from the cow.

There are often seen perched on the peaks and extremities of the rocks, innumerable flocks of aquatic birds, drawn up, as it were, rank and file; they make their nests in the clefts above the precipices, and are so little accustomed to be disturbed, that numbers of them may be killed by the dischage of a single musket, without causing the others to stir.

One of these isles contains only a single habitation, and it is only in summer, that the curate can go to visit it. Even to enter it, one is obliged to be raised up by the help of a machine, which likewise serves to descend by; the rock is so abrupt, that the islanders cannot use a boat, and they cannot quit their island, without the assistance of their neighbours who come in search of them.

It was only at the commencement of the century just elapsed, that coal-mines were discovered in the southern part of these islands. The government had caused many trials to be made of these coals; but it was only in 1777 that those trials were judged to be of sufficient interest and consequence. A commissary named *ad hoc* determined that the quarry was about 12,000 feet in length, by a medium width of 4000, and that the height of the combustible matter was five feet, so that it promised an immense profit to the state for centuries to come; but the difficulty of working it appeared so great, that the labour was abandoned. The celebrated professor Kratzenstein, of Copenhagen, analysed the coals, and found them to produce a heat more ardent and of a longer duration than those of England, but that they were less easy to kindle; he, likewise, found them proper for all sorts of uses. A trial of them has been likewise made in Scotland, and they are now acknowledged to be of a superior quality. One of the principal reasons which induced the relinquishment of an enterprize likely to be so lucrative, was the difficulty and the expence of freight, from a country so remote from others, in which, moreover, wood and turf are every day getting dearer. Among other measures suggested to remove this obstacle, it has been proposed, and the idea does not appear destitute of foundation, to send there, to load with coal, such vessels as, having been employed in the whale-fishery, might have made an unprofitable voyage. The necessary permission for this purpose would be easily granted, and there is no doubt but the coal might be had at a very moderate price. The author of this account takes some pains to shew all the advantages which Denmark might derive from this useful production. It likewise appears, that a particular society, not long ago established at Copenhagen, has undertaken the importation of this coal, which it proposes to do on a large scale. It must be granted, however, that a sufficient degree of zeal has not yet been attached to the business, or, at least, government has taken no part in it, and bestowed no particular attention upon it.

It is a circumstance very favourable to the exportation of the productions of the country, and, at the same time, very singular, that, notwithstanding the situation of these islands, in the centre of the north, their harbours are never frozen, so that the entrance to them is always free, and the navigation is not at all interrupted during the winter. It excites astonishment in the author that the vessels sent to the whale-fishery, do not pass the winter in the port known by the name of Vestmanhavn, from whence they might repair very easily to their destination in the first days of spring; the coast is, in general, good; vessels have nothing to fear from rocks or shallows, and it offers many good havens.

It has been remarked, that the measles and the small-pox only attack the inhabitants when brought there by strangers: but in that case, they makes ravages as terrible

terrible as the most frightful plague; they have now been exempt, however, 70 years from the small-pox.

The temperature is neither very hot in summer, nor very cold in winter; it has been already remarked that the sea never freezes on the coasts. The air is reckoned to be nebulous, moist, and unhealthful; in fact, mists are very frequent, but they are not unhealthful, not being fetid, and the inhabitants feel no inconvenience from them; besides, they are not so gross as to conceal the sight of the houses, as some pretend. The winds, which get ingulphed between the rocks, blow sometimes with such violence, that they detach large fragments from them, dash others to pieces, and become so impetuous, that persons on horseback, when they hear the whistling across the rocks, are obliged to dismount, to avoid being overset; even persons on foot throw themselves on their face, to avoid a more dangerous downfall. The wind not seldom announces its approach by a crack, which is heard through the whole house, and which precedes it by some seconds;—but when the hurricane arrives, it has already spent so much of its force, that the building is not damaged; at other times, there comes on the back of it a second blast, which, with fresh impetuosity, shakes the house, pierces beneath the flooring, and tears it up, or, at least, makes the chair or bed tremble, whereon the inmate reposes.

The most violent winds are those which, passing across and over the rocks, are reflected from them with redoubled violence; and which, meeting opposite winds, acquire a considerable concentration, and thus struggle as it were in the plains; they sometimes come on so suddenly that an instant before the tempest a person might walk in the open air with a candle in his hand, without extinguishing it. Thunder is not frequent; but when it does take place, the continued roar with which it causes the rocks to resound, is really tremendous.

An opinion not a little singular prevails among the inhabitants of these islands, that the sun rises higher, at present, than it did formerly; in some places the form and the height of the rocks conceal the view of that luminary, during some months of the winter; there it is known exactly, what day it is to appear again:—in 1789 it was seen at *Qualvig*, two days sooner than it was expected. "Some old men, (adds the author,) have assured me, that certain sides of the rocks, which in their youth were but slightly illumined by the sun, are now much more so."

The culture of corn is comparatively trifling here, by reason of the excessive labours which it requires in a country so mountainous, and where besides it would be necessary to devote so much care and application in the spring, which is precisely the season when the fishery calls for a general attention and employs all hands. Gardening must naturally be very little exercised in a country where the soil is so ungrateful. Among the vegetables which thrive here, we must reckon potatoes, the cultivation of which is rapidly increasing; radishes and turnips thrive equally well. It is not so with trees; of course there is no wood. The author made a number of trials on different plants of fruit-trees, but without success; cherry-trees, although they put forth abundance of flowers, drop the fruit, before it grows to half its size; many wild trees, likewise, perished at the first appearance of the winter.

The principal, or we may even say, only riches of the inhabitants, consist in their flocks of sheep; and, provided these prosper, they give themselves little trouble about their bad harvests, or unsuccessful fisheries; their sheep serve them for food and furnish them with cloathing, and a medium of exchange for the commodities of life, which are not very numerous with them. The sheep are never folded, neither in summer nor winter. When this last season is not very rude, those animals maintain themselves in tolerable condition, by making holes in the snow to browze on the grass which is preserved underneath; but if the winter is long and rigorous, they often perish. The snow, which covers the fields, obliges them to make for the rocks next the sea, as being always less loaded with snow; but sometimes, not being able to keep their footing on the ice, they slide down headlong into the sea; or else, wandering along the brink, they are drawn into the sea with the *avalanche*, often to the number of 50 or even 100; or, lastly, they get enveloped by the snow in the midst of the rock: in this last case, sometimes they keep themselves for six or seven weeks on the little grass which they find under the snow. Here and there a sort of stables have been provided, where they are penned up together to keep themselves warm. If from the rigour of the season, they should be left there too long; at the end of some weeks, hunger impels them to eat one another's skins.

The chace of marine birds, which make their nests in the mountains, is,

likewise

likewise, very advantageous. When they are found apart in places almost inaccessible, they are sometimes so tame, that they may be taken with the hand; and if they are wild, nets are laid for them; and the method which these islanders employ to catch them is alike curious and dangerous. Two men, armed with staves of four fathoms in length, furnished with branches forming a net or snare, tye themselves together with a cord of from eight to ten fathoms, and by means of a plank adapted to the end of the staves, one of them, placing it under the seat of the other, raises it till it meets a solid point of support on some projection of the rock; then the latter assists his comrade to rise by help of the rope; this operation is repeated from precipice to precipice, till the adventurers have gained the summit of the rock, or, at least, the crevice which serves for an asylum to the birds. Instances have been known of one of these bravoes happening to slip, when, dragging along the other, both are tumbled down headlong.

Some rocks are of so sharp and steep a cut, that they cannot climb them by help of the staves or poles; in this case they endeavour to ascend them another way; when arrived at them, six men tie a seventh to a cord, which they keep hold of, and thus make it carefully descend into the different cavities which the flank of the rock presents, to catch the birds that have lodged there. By a second cord the latter gives the signal when he wishes to stop or to be lifted up. This chace usually takes place at the approach of night and in calm weather. One man can take in a night many hundreds of birds. It is sometimes necessary to tie another cord to the extremity of that which supports the fowler and to fix it on a boat placed on the sea; by this means they can give him a flight or range of 20 fathoms which enables him to penetrate every where. It is easy to conceive what must be the address and the courage of these persons; let it be supposed only, as it often happens, that the man in passing over a large piece of rock, happens to detach it from the mass, and he is inevitably crushed under it.

The fishery here was, in ancient times, an object of the greatest importance; at present, the fish are no longer in such abundance, and the moment is perhaps come, when it would be advantageous to sacrifice this branch of industry to agriculture.

The whale fishery offers a curious spectacle. The whale, which is found here at stated periods, is of a small species, but is met with in companies of 100, and even 1000. They are commonly discovered in open sea by the fishers: as soon as they are perceived, the fisherman gives a preconcerted signal to the other boats, which collect and drive those enormous animals before them, by repeatedly hurling large pebbles behind them. When this manœuvre is perceived on the coast, messengers are immediately dispatched to spread abroad the agreeable news. One party throw themselves into the boats to assist the fishers, others wait on the shore; bread, meat, &c. are brought; acclamations of joy are heard, and, being repeated from rock to rock, often precede the arrival of the messenger.

Sometimes the whales themselves are driven like a tame flock; at other times they escape; a fresh chace is then commenced, and by oars and pebbles successively hurled at them, they are forced to turn towards the shore; which often causes a painful labour of many days and nights, and, to augment the misfortune, sometimes without success. When they have been able to push the whales into some gulph or creek, it will be requisite, in dark weather, to surround it with a semicircle of boats, that they may not escape in the night. In the day-time, fires are kindled on the coast, that the smoke may conceal the sight of land, and likewise because it has been observed, that the whale steers for the coast where the full moon appears, when that luminary is sinking on the horizon.

But soon the combat commences; the boats break the semicircle, and dart into the midst of the whales; the seamen armed with a kind of long pikes, display all their address to wound as many whales as possible, and above all try to direct their blows towards the tail of the animal; but they take great care not to strike them when they are too near; in such a case they would not fail to overset and even break the boats.

When the attack is thus commenced, the troop of whales spring forwards towards the land, impelling an immense volume of water before them, with which they precipitate themselves on the coast, where many remain dry.

Now is the time for those who had remained on the shore in concealment to shew themselves; they now run up and throw themselves on the whales, to wound them

them in the neck with long knives; an adroit champion with two stabs will pierce the whale to the bone, who, in his agitations and struggles to disembarrass himself, finishes by twisting his own neck.

The fishermen lay hold of this opportunity to drag it further off, to dispatch it with less trouble: but they take great care not to strike it in the eyes, the pain of which would cause it to brandish its tail very vigorously, as it has a singular strength in that part, and might wound the operators very dangerously with it.

The sea is reddened with the blood of these fishes to a considerable extent; but, what is astonishing, no sooner do those that have escaped being wounded gain the open sea, than they return to the field of battle, yet covered with the blood of their comrades, where death awaits them.

Great advantage is made by the acquisition of this species of whale; the natives eat it with pleasure, while it is fresh; and certain morsels of it are in much request with foreigners; the flesh found under the fat has almost the taste of beef; what is not eaten fresh, is cut into long slices and dried. The fat serves to make oil with, or it is salted and eat like meat; it will keep for many years.

Independently of these whales, of the smaller species, sometimes the larger whale is found in the circumjacent seas. The fishery of this is much more easy. They approach it in a boat, and tickle its back with an oar, which it supports patiently. While it complacently submits to this sport, a seaman thrusts into his spout-hole a woollen glove, which deprives it of the faculty of being able to plunge; he next pierces it in a part full of fat, and ties a cord to it, with which they are enabled to drag it towards the shore, where they make it fast. The animal seems amused with this manœuvre, which is to become so fatal to him; but he is soon assailed with a multitude of boats, from which they dart their harpoons on him, till he loses blood. The combat then becomes dangerous for the fishermen, from the terrible strokes of the tail which it gives when it feels itself wounded.

Neither the fat nor the flesh of this sort of whale is eaten. It has been found, that when the fat was eaten, there exhaled through the pores a fetid sweat, which tinged the wearing apparel yellow. A property so singular seems worthy to fix the attention of physicians, and to be the object of some experiments;—as does, likewise, another observation, which doubtless will not appear indifferent, that many women in the flower of their age experience here, without any apparent cause, a compleat suppression of their *menses*, and often without any inconvenience.

We are not to expect to find a considerable commerce in a country which is totally destitute of manufactures and where agriculture and the fishery can never become objects of importance. The exportation is reduced to some trifling articles, such as stockings, flannel waistcoats, suet, fish, fish-oil, quills, skins and butter; it is carried on, provisorily, by a monopoly, which the government has reserved to itself, not to enrich the fiscal purse at the expence of these islanders, but to supply their ever-urgent wants, without being obliged to make too considerable sacrifices.

The inhabitants of these islands, the population of which does not exceed 5000 souls, are, in general, well-made; they have fair complexions, and the sun seldom impairs their whiteness. No faces are seen among them, which offer those hideous marks which the small-pox leaves, and which are so common elsewhere. A great number of them have white hair. They are not deficient in understanding, which may be, doubtless, attributed to the little confinement and constraint which they experience, and to the extreme liberty which they enjoy in infancy. They are phlegmatic, but nevertheless sympathizing, beneficent, and hospitable. Nothing is more rare than quarrels among them; they carry *politesse* in conversation so far, that in addressing a discourse to any one, they entitle him *Vålsigvaur*, that is to say, 'The blessed.' They are upright and frugal, and are scarcely ever seen to be intoxicated with brandy, although they are very fond of that liquor. We may, perhaps, reproach them with a blind attachment to antient usages, and with a singular tendency to credulity, and to superstitious practices. Even envy is no stranger to them.

As there is no school, and the parents themselves are the instructors of their children, it may be easily conceived that knowledge here must be very backward. They are fond, however, of reading. Many know how to write; and in general they can calculate very well, without either pen or pencil. The frequent nocturnal fisheries, and their residing among the rocks, have taught them so well to know the stars, that they can usually indicate the hour by the rising of those stars.

They

They do not divide the day into hours like ours, but into hours three times longer, without however being very exact in that respect; the hours of night are indicated agreeably to the position of the stars. Skilful players at chess are every where found among them; but instrumental music is perfectly unknown, and they only dance to the sound of the voice.

For the Monthly Magazine.

A SKETCH *of* VIENNA, *and of the* MANNERS *of its* INHABITANTS.

VIENNA has been so long the capital of the Empire, that it seems to possess some claim to the highest rank among the cities of Europe. It has so much encreased in dimensions of late years, that, including its vast suburbs, it has not unaptly been compared to a swallow with the wings of an eagle. In 1796 the city itself was computed to contain 1397 houses, and the suburbs 5102, besides a considerable space reserved for building. The suburbs likewise are adorned with a great number of spacious gardens, and many of the buildings occupy a large extent of ground.

From the latitude of Vienna, which is nearly the same as that of Orleans, it would be supposed that the temperature of the air was in general very high; but this metropolis is surrounded with lofty hills and mountains that collect much ice and snow in winter, the retreat of which, in spring, is very tardy. Hence it is that the intense summer-heats last only a couple of months, and in winter the cold is often very severe.

The heat too is much moderated by very frequent and often keen winds which prevail here, greatly to the inconvenience of of the refugee Milanese, and other Italians, who have taken up their abode in this city. The inhabitants of Vienna, like their neighbours, the Hungarians and Poles, use warm clothing, and wrap themselves up in their pelisses on the first appearance of cold weather; besides using the German custom of warming their houses with stoves, which are always of a size amply sufficient for the climate.

The number of those who fall victims to pulmonic diseases in Vienna, is remarkably large. All great cities, it is true, are unfavourable for the consumptive, but nowhere does this disease appear so fatal, notwithstanding all the efforts of the medical art, which is cultivated with more care, and practised with more skill here, than perhaps in any other part of Germany.

The small-pox too is often very fatal here. In 1795 it carried off 1098 persons. The inoculation for the cow-pox has, however, been lately introduced, which may prove of essential benefit.

Vienna has the advantage of being divided by the Danube, but this is purchased by some inconveniences; for, when the river is suddenly swelled by the melting of the snows from the hills, it inundates a part of the suburbs, often to a considerable height. It is then that the excellence of the police is peculiarly distinguished: it is not easy to conceive greater precautions, and more admirable methods than are here employed, for the preservation and relief of the families exposed to the effects of this calamity.

It would be imagined that advantage would be taken of possessing so fine a river, to form numerous parties of pleasure to sail beside its beautiful banks; but this amusement is not at all suited to the taste of the inhabitants. They possess, however, the important advantage of an easy navigation for goods and provisions of every kind.

Vienna is one of the least beautiful of all the capitals of Europe. There is very little to strike the stranger's eye; the streets are crooked, and very irregular, with but little appearance of any plan or order. Near the centre of the town is the singular sight of a bridge thrown across a deep low street, which admits of carriages passing over, whilst the usual thoroughfare is going on in the street below; resembling the canals in England, which are often thrown over navigable rivers.

There is but one street in Vienna that can properly be called magnificent, and this is a continued line of splendid houses and palaces. It is called the *Nobles'-street*. The suburbs are constructed on a better plan, and would be very elegant, if the houses were larger, and richer in architectural ornaments. The greater part of the streets are wide, level and regular, but they are chiefly inhabited by manufacturers and workmen of various trades.

The whole of the population of Vienna, in 1795, was computed at 231,105 inhabitants, of whom 1231 were ecclesiastics, 3253 nobility, 4256 public functionaries and persons living upon their private fortune, and 7333 citizens belonging to the corporation.

Among the establishments for the relief of the sick, must be first mentioned the Great

Great Hofpital, the direction of which is entrusted to the celebrated Frank. In 1796 it received 11,860 patients. A pathological Mufeum is contained within its walls.

Another inftitution is the hofpital for lying-in-women. In the year abovementioned it received 1904 women, of whom 111 died.

The Lunatic Hofpital contained in 1796, 261 infane perfons, 156 of whom were males, and 105 females. The following year 190 patients were received, and 122 went out. The principal remedy ufed in the houfe is abftinence and a ftrict regimen; and no one is admitted without bringing with him an account of the previous treatment to which the patient has been expofed.

There is, befides, a military hofpital, feveral charities which are attended to by the different religious orders, and an hofpital for Jews, which laft is diftinguifhed for neatnefs and excellent management.

Vienna may likewife pride itfelf on an inftitution peculiar in its kind, and of fingular utility, founded by Leopold. By this, the fuburbs of the town are divided into eight diftricts, each of which has its phyfician, its furgeon, and its midwife, all paid by government, whofe office it is to vifit the poor at their own houfes. Thefe practitioners, in 1795, had the care of 19,820 patients, of whom 464 died, and 623 were fent to the hofpital. This inftitution has been found fo beneficial, that on the fucceeding year to its eftablifhment it was extended to the whole city.

One more inftitution we muft mention, which is fomewhat fimilar to the former; it is for difeafed children under ten years of age. In 1795 it had the care of 1935 patients, of whom only 113 died.

Among the various regulations for the public health, one deferves to be mentioned, which was ordained in 1796. It is, that no new-built houfe may be inhabited, before the phyfician of the diftrict has examined whether the walls are fufficiently dry. This marks a degree of vigilance and attention in the health-police, almoft carried to excefs.

The price of provifions in Vienna is almoft inconceivably low. Hungary furnifhes meat, corn, and wine in abundance; Auftria fupplies plenty of wood by the navigation of the Danube; and there are about 150 large gardens for table-vegetables around the fuburbs of the town, which are cultivated with fkill and attention, and with the advantage of plenty of water. By thefe means, all kinds of legumes are always cheap and abundant, though the gardeners are in very eafy circumftances. Their labourers are chiefly inhabitants of the Styrian mountains, who come regularly every fpring to Vienna for employment. As the articles of the firft neceffity, bread, wine, meat, and vegetables are plentiful, the wages of workmen are low; and as the country likewife furnifhes itfelf with the principal materials for the moft neceffary manufactures, there are few things, except foreign productions, which require much expence. The police pays particular attention to the fupply of provifion, and often infpects the markets, and the weights and meafures of the dealers.

In private fociety the number of polite circles is fo great, that the coffee-houfes are not much frequented. The taverns, however, are much more fo, and there is no town in which there is a greater proportion of taverns and public-houfes. The coffee-houfes are very good, but the eating-houfes not fo comfortable. The greateft hofpitality reigns among the inhabitants of Vienna, for, independently of a number of houfes where an open table is kept, a ftranger will find many houfes where he may come at all hours of the day, and take part in the converfation, and the refrefhments which are liberally handed about.

The ftreets of Vienna are remarkably quiet and orderly, fo that as early as ten o'clock at night every thing is filent. It is the cuftom, indeed, for a lodger when he returns home later than that hour, to pay a fmall fee to the porter of the houfe, for every houfe has one. If in the evening after ten o'clock you walk in any part of the fuburbs, the ftillnefs of the ftreets is truly ftriking; fcarcely any-body but the watch is ftirring, and yet the people of Vienna are not very early rifers, and in this refpect the difference between this city and Naples is highly remarkable.

There is a coffee-houfe in the fuburb of Leopoldftad, called the *Greek Coffee-houfe*, which is worthy the ftranger's notice. It is fituated between the Danube and the ftreet through which all the carriages pafs to the promenade of the *Prater*, and is almoft entirely frequented by Greeks (who are very numerous at Vienna), fo that a perfon hearing their language and feeing their drefs, might imagine himfelf in the midft of Greece.

It muft be acknowledged to the praife of Government and private perfons, that much pains have been conftantly taken to prevent common begging. The Orphan Houfe, in 1797, contained 1479 of thefe unfortunate

unfortunate children, and there is an establishment for providing for old people, and fathers of families who cannot earn their subsistence. Still, however, there are beggars, and this part of police is not brought to such perfection as at Hamburg, and some few other towns on the Continent.

The people of Vienna are industrious, though by no means equal, in this respect, to the English. The town and suburbs contain a great variety of manufactures, particularly in silk. In no place is embroidery more encouraged, though these articles have lost much of their demand from the pressing necessities of the war; and both workmen are scarce, and the raw materials, especially the Italian silk, are become very dear. The people of Vienna likewise excel in manufactures of steel, carriages of all sorts, silk ribbands, harness, saddles, &c. There are, however, very few manufactured articles exported, but only raw materials.

The Academy of Arts is divided into seven classes, each of which has its own Professor. There is one for objects relative to manufacture, another for historical painting, for taking views from rural scenery, for sculpture, for architecture, for sculpture on metal, and for engraving on copper. Each class contains a large number of scholars. The Professor for painting rural scenery, makes a weekly excursion during the summer into the country around the town, along with his scholars, to exercise them in their art. Many of these Professors have attained considerable celebrity. The Gallery of Painting of the Prince of Lichtenstein, and the Belvedere, are very magnificent.

The art of ornamental gardening has, of late years, made very great progress; so that it would be difficult to find any where, except in England, so many gardens laid out in excellent taste, as in the neighbourhood of this capital.

In a country, where the memory of a Gluck and a Mozart is so much cherished, and which possesses a Haydn, and so many other eminent composers, music cannot fail to be highly cultivated. A taste for this fine art pervades every class of people. There are a number of circles where a concert never fails to form part of the evening's amusement. Indeed a stranger is often fatigued with the many hours that are devoted to this entertainment.

The German theatre at Vienna has always enjoyed a great reputation, and has long been the best in Germany. The Italian comic operas are also in general very well performed. Almost every one of the suburbs has its theatre. The taste which the people of Vienna have for *ballets* has been formed by the pains taken at the principal theatre to engage capital dancers, so that the public are not to be satisfied except by great excellence in this kind of performance.

Literature does not flourish here. It is neither the capital of the Empire, nor any part of the south of Germany, that can entitle the Germans to the appellation of a learned nation. Petersburg and Rome excepted, there is no town, perhaps, in which the list of prohibited books is so large as at Vienna.

The town, however, contains a large university, and a splendid collection of manuscripts and works, all purely literary or scientific. There are, it is true, several eminent men who may dispute the palm of learning with any in Europe; but the privileges of science are very difficult to obtain here, the examinations being very numerous, and full of that kind of argumentation which is quite foreign to genuine science. Very few journals are read in Vienna, and they are rarely to be met with in public places; and books of science are very difficult to be obtained.

In such an order of things, which is doubtless kept up from system, nothing great can be expected in literature or the arts. Every bud of genius is destroyed in the birth, and no encouragement is given to rising talents.

It is remarkable, however, that modern Greek is much cultivated here. It employs, at present, three presses; and there are Greeks who translate into their own language a variety of German, Italian, and French works. They likewise publish Greek almanacks and gazettes.

Whether it is from a partiality to the English, or a dislike to the French, we know not, but it is now more than ever the custom for the nobility and gentry to teach their children English; so that it is not uncommon to see young ladies going to mass with the prayer-book in use among the English Catholics.

We may here observe that an Englishman, whatever be his condition, enjoys, from long custom, the privilege of being presented to court by the resident minister from his country, and consequently an access to the first circles, which has often given rise to very singular and entertaining adventures.

Besides the university, there are a number of large schools, where every thing relating to commerce is taught at a very moderate rate. In general, however, the

 business

business of education is much behind-hand with the improvements of the present age.

The people of Vienna are in general honest and simple in their manners. Now and then one may remark a kind of studied politeness, and a kind of affectation of loading with titles and compliments, which forms a considerable contrast with the natural frankness and even roughness of manners. This may be attributed to the influence of the court, and the vast number of diplomatic agents in this capital, where every German Prince has some affairs to carry on.

The strongest passion of the inhabitants of Vienna seems to be for good cheer. If they do not always take the most delicate food, they at least eat very largely, and drink in proportion.

The traveller coming from Venice or Milan will find here some little admixture of Italian customs. Chocolate, for example, which the Italians are so fond of, and which is little used in the North, is much in vogue here: so are certain vegetables, such as brocoli, and the like. The Italian language is also much spoken here.

The people of Vienna have so long been reproached with the badness of their language, that in general they have come (at least the well-educated among them) to speak their native tongue very correctly, and perhaps with more purity than in most other parts of Germany, though still they may be distinguished by a peculiar accent.

The women are handsome, and mild in their manners, and often preserve their beauty very long. They love dress and luxurious living; their minds do not want cultivation, but the books that they read are very few. Music is what they attend to the most assiduously.

No where are there so many amusements going on as in this town. Besides a great number of houses of public entertainment, where eating, drinking, and dancing, are constantly going on, the people take their part in the diversions which seem reserved for the higher classes.

The greatest happiness which the inhabitants of Vienna can enjoy, has been, at all times, a good table, and with it two or three choice friends. The latter, however, it is now difficult to find, for the people of Vienna are of late become very little communicative, reserved, and mistrustful. They love to frequent public places, and hear and see with interest what is going on, but they do not like to be observed. Formerly they took pleasure in hearing from strangers what was passing in the world, now they only read the news, or pick it up as they can; they used to be fond of adopting new opinions, now they have their system, from which they seldom depart. This change in the conduct of the people of Vienna is partly owing to the revolutionary events which have taken place on every side, which attach the people still more to the enjoyments which they find at home; and partly to the vigilant eye which the government keeps over all the public opinions and conversations, which renders the people timid and suspicious.

Among the crimes committed in this capital, theft is by far the commonest, and the extent to which it is carried is truly alarming. Every workman in gold and silver is constantly trembling for the security of his property. There are pick-pockets, house-breakers, thieves who steal the linen from the house-tops and garrets, horse and carriage stealers, and those who take the bodies from church-yards for the use of the surgeons. There are, besides, highwaymen, who imitate the politeness of those that are so common in England.

Some of the lower class of citizens and servants still retain the use of bonnets richly embroidered with gold; and these, too, sometimes become the plunder of street-robbers.

On going out of the city, the stranger is struck with the beauty and magnificence of the numerous houses, parks, and gardens, which crowd its environs. Among these he will distinguish the imperial residences of Laxenbourg and Schöonbrunnen; the Belvidere, particularly celebrated for its noble collection of pictures, and embellished with the spoils of the churches of Brabant, under Joseph; the majestic palace of Gallizinberg, the magnificent Dornbach, the extensive establishment of Marshal de Lascy, and especially the Augarten and the Prater.

The Emperor Joseph opened the Augarten to the public. The first entrance presents a magnificent garden, but entirely the creature of art. It is formed of long straight shady walks, impenetrable to the sun, full of nightingales, and the favourite promenade of all the pretty women. At the principal entrance is a large building, converted into a splendid eating-house. It is composed of large galleries, beautifully decorated, in which the business of good cheer is going on from morning to night, either to large or small parties.

Before this building is a circle surrounded with large chesnut-trees, under which are tables for serving tea, coffee, ices, &c.

A fine

A fine raised terrace surrounds the lower part of the garden, beneath which the Danube is seen running in a gentle current. From hence the eye wanders with delight to a fine picturesque chain of mountains in the distance; and nearer, to fine woods and country villas, beautiful meadows, and numerous hamlets and villages; and just before the eyes is the thick and gloomy forest of the Brigit. This forest, which is about a league in extent, is divided through its whole length by the Danube, the banks of which offer a delicious walk, and the stream is here peaceful and slow. At the entrance of the forest are small houses, where refreshments are sold. On feast-days and holidays the forest is full of people, and then every cottage is the scene of mirth and good cheer, besides numerous parties under trees, in the adjoining meadows, or on the banks of the river.

On crossing the river to the opposite forest, the scene is quite changed. Here the scenery is wild and solitary. The Danube now becomes a sea, and spreads itself majestically into several branches, forming, by its divisions, large islands, some of which are thick woods, others only sprinkled with beautiful groves, and others rich meadows. Here the stag bounds along the thickets, whilst the nightingale and other singing birds enchant the ear of the traveller. At the end of this fine forest the Danube is lost to the view.

The cottages are small buildings, of a single story, well built, and white-washed without, whilst within the appearance of health and plenty sits on the countenance of the inhabitants.

The magnificent garden of Augarten, however, is much neglected by the inhabitants, who prefer the *Prater*, especially those who keep carriages and splendid equipages. A little beyond the town you arrive at the *Prater*, by a fine avenue, a league in length, which runs through a forest. This forest, however, appears a large village, for houses and cottages are scattered throughout. There are houses for refreshment in the Turkish, Chinese, Italian, and English, taste, besides rooms for billiards and other amusements, all painted and decorated with great elegance. The inhabitants of this forest are neither woodmen nor shepherds, but are sellers of coffee and lemonade, confectioners, keep eating-houses, or else are musicians, dancers, shew sleight of hand tricks, and a number of similar employments. Here is a particular privileged part of the wood, in which princes and citizens, monks and soldiers, all that is high or low in rank, all that is pretty or homely among the women walk together without restraint or distinction. In the evening it is the mall for all the pretty women, whilst all the houses around are so many temples of good cheer, which are constantly crowded. Genteel company, indeed, generally satisfy themselves with ices, or coffee and cream, but before and after the promenade they require something more substantial. This is the place too for rope dancers, dealers in various toys and curiosities, so that in truth the whole wood seems an enchanted palace of pleasures. Whilst the walkers are thus amusing themselves, the large avenue is crowded with splendid equipages (which are extremely numerous in Vienna); and carriages of every description, coaches, cabriolets, light elegant whiskeys, drawn by Barbs, English or Spanish horses, glance rapidly along, so that the whole road is in motion as far as the Danube, which terminates the course.

The *Prater* is the place in which magnificent fire-works are often exhibited. From hence, too, the aëronaut Blanchard ascended in his balloon; and in short, this is the spot in which all out-door spectacles are given, which are very numerous in this large capital.

Nothing, however, equals the pleasure, in a fine day, of dining under some tree on the banks of the Danube, regaled with charming music that attracts the stags and deer, who come and eat bread out of the hand.

These are enjoyments which render Vienna so attractive, and which are possessed by few other capitals in Europe.

For the Monthly Magazine.

PARTICULARS *relative to the* NEW PLANET, *discovered on the first* DAY *of this* CENTURY.

THE celebrated Astronomer M. von Zach, had communicated to Dr. Olbers, of Bremen, M. Piazzi's observations of the 1st and 23d of January; and on the 30th of May received from him a calculation of new elements of the planet's orbit. These elements, however, could not be determined with any great exactness, as the observations are only twenty-two days distant from one-another, and are only given in minutes. Dr. Olbers found, however, from all the data then known, the Diameter of the orbit 2,947465 —Longitude of the ascending node, 2ˢ 21° 55′ 10″—Inclination of the orbit, 7° 54′ 38″—Heliocentric longitude on the 1st of January, 1801, 2ˢ 7° 40′ 36″—Sidereal Revolution, 1841,24 days =

5,04096 years—Diurnal heliocentric motion, 11′ 43,″87—Annual motion, 71° 24′ 57,″6—With these elements it would have been difficult to calculate beforehand the course of the planet, so as to be able to find it again on its re-appearing in the morning in August, if it be not at first sight distinguishable from a star of the 8th magnitude; "for, probably, (says Dr. Olbers) it has a considerable eccentricity. In opposition it may, perhaps, increase in luminousness, so as to equal a star of the 6th magnitude. I have little doubt that it will be found in La Lande's Catalogue."

On the 16th of May Professor Bode writes to M. von Zach, "That it gave him great pleasure to find, that M. von Zach agreed with him in opinion respecting the Piazzian comet, and that Oriani and Piazzi himself incline towards the same opinion.—How often (continues he) have I wished that I might live to witness this discovery—I have been several times laughed at by others about my ideas of the harmonic progression in the distances of the planets.********** Adopting 2,75 for the distance, I find the heliocentric difference of longitude, betwixt the 1st and 23d of January very well corresponding with the observations; the planet goes to its node, which I placed in ♉: its inclination must exceed 6°; and this I think was one of the causes why it was not sooner discovered."

Till towards the end of May M. von Zach received no farther accounts relative to this star. He had communicated to his friends the Parisian astronomers the observations and elements calculated: and, not doubting that La Lande, to whom Piazzi had sent the first account of the discovery of the comet, had likewise been made acquainted with the subsequent observations and conjectures, he requested him to send to him an account of all the particulars that had come to his knowledge relative to the new planet.

But to his no small surprise he received, in the beginning of June, several letters from Paris; one from the Senator La Place, dated the 25th of May; from La Lande and Burckhard, of the 26th of May; from De Lambre, of the 24th of May; from Méchain, of the 26th of May; from Henry, of the 28th of May; in which none of these *six* astronomers, who had communicated several important observations and new discoveries, writes even a single syllable about the new planet! Méchain only makes mention of *Piazzi's* comet;—from which it appears, that so late as the end of May they knew nothing of the conjecture of its being a planet; although the astronomers in Germany had been made acquainted therewith by Professor Bode already in the month of March.—Méchain in his letter to M. von Zach, of the 26th of May, merely says, "Have you seen the comet, which the journals announce to have been discovered at Palermo last January? No one here has yet found it. Our astronomers have not discovered any since that of the month of December, 1799. I sometimes look out for them; but without success."

On the 10th of June, M. von Zach received another letter from Professor Bode, in which he says, "Piazzi's first letter I received on the 20th of March, and on the next post-day, the 23d, I answered it. But he did not wait for my reply; and—conceive my joy and at the same time my vexation!—I received a second letter from Piazzi, in which I found only the following few words relative to the newly-discovered planet: 'I wrote to you in January, informing you that I had discovered a comet in Taurus, which comet I continued to observe till the 11th of February, when I was attacked by a dangerous disease, from which I have not entirely recovered. As soon as the state of my health will permit, I shall calculate elements for it, and send them to you. In the mean time I have communicated my observations to M. La Lande.'—It is remarkable that he still calls the star *a comet*, as in his *first letter*."

On the 18th of June, M. von Zach received a letter from Dr. Burckhardt, in Paris, from which we learn the following particulars: La Lande had received Piazzi's observation on the 31st of May, when *Dr.* Burckhardt immediately began to calculate its orbit. Two days later they received Von Zach's and Oriani's investigations, which gave them cause to hope that the supposed comet would prove to be a planet. Dr. Burckhardt had already found that the arc described by it was not considerable. The small geocentric and heliocentric motion of the comet gave him a great deal of trouble in calculating its orbit. He had first chosen for this purpose the observations of the 14th, 21st, and 28th of January: but from this circumstance found himself under the necessity of selecting the observations most distant in time from one-another, viz. those of the 1st and 21st of January, and of the 11th of February. During these 42 days the geocentric longitude of the comet varied only 3°, and the heliocentric longitude only $10\frac{1}{2}$°. On attempting to correct, by La Place's methods, the parabola found by his method,

he

he discovered that nothing in this respect could be effected by the conditional equations. He then tried La Place's method of approximation, but with as little success: the unavoidable errors of observation having too great an influence on the differences of the geocentric longitudes and latitudes. He now proved eight hypotheses by means of La Place's method of correction, but without approximating nearer to the truth. He then calculated the following orbit which agrees with the three observations to within ± 2½ minutes:

Diameter of the orbit, 2,74.—Epoch, 1801, 2ˢ 8° 16′ 20″.—Ascending Node, 2ˢ 10° 15′.—Inclination of the orbit, 11° 21′.—Period of revolution, 4½ years.

However various the trials that had been made; yet, as it did not thence follow, that it was impossible to find a parabola for these observations, he determined to apply a method, which had often proved successful, when all other methods of interpolation failed.***** Putting the logarithm of the distance from the sun equal 0,378, the smallest error was ±8′; then putting the logarithm of the distance 0,378, the smallest error was ±4. It was therefore necessary still more to diminish the distance; and after 20 hypotheses he found the following parabola:

Place of the ascending node, 2ˢ 20° 50′.—Inclination of the orbit, 9° 41′.—Place of the perihelium, 4ˢ 8° 38′ 25″.—Smallest distance from the sun, 2,21883, its log. 0,3461250.—Logarithm of the diurnal motion, 9,4409408.—Time of the passage through the perihelium, 1801, 30th June, 19h. 1′.

Dr. Burckhardt is of opinion, that there is no other parabola that more nearly agrees with these three observations. The errors in the longitude are on the 14th and 28th of January—1′ 47″ and + 38. But Piazzi had not mentioned any thing respecting the accuracy with which he was able to observe the comet.

On the 21st of June M. von Zach received the promised continuation of Dr. Burckhardt's researches. He had calculated an ellipsis for the comet, although the arc it had run through was too small for us to expect great accuracy, but he thought he should thereby facilitate the finding of the star.

Place of the ascending node, 2ˢ 20° 58′ 30″.—Inclination of the path, 10° 47′ 0″.—Place of the aphelium, 2ˢ 8° 59′ 37″.—Time of the passage through the aphelium, January, 1801, 1,3328.—Excentricity, 0,0364.—Logarithm of half the great axis, 0,4106586.—Period of sidereal circumvolution, 4,13 years.

This ellipsis represents, within a few seconds, the longitudes and latitudes of five observations. It would have been easy to obtain a greater degree of accuracy, but he thought it quite superfluous, as the arc run through is so small." The above ellipsis gave Dr. Burckhardt the following

Places of the Planet discovered by PIAZZI.

1801.		*Medium Time.*		*Geocentr. Long.*		*Geocentr. Lat.*	
20th June	-	13h	4′	101°	45′	30°	26′ N.
17th July	-	1	43	113	3	4	6
12th August	-	10	54	124	21	4	51
7th September	-	16	19	135	28	5	41
12th ———	-	22	—	137	40	5	52
18th ———	-	3	—	139	50	6	3
23d ———	-	8	—	141	58	6	15
28th ———	-	13	—	144	5	6	27
3d October	-	17	41	146	9	6	40
8th ———	-	22	—	148	12	6	53
14th ———	-	3	—	150	12	7	8
19th ———	-	7	—	152	11	7	22
24th ———	-	11	—	154	8	7	37
29th ———	-	14	45	156	3	7	53
3d November	-	18	—	157	56	8	9
8th ———	-	22	—	159	48	8	26

It was to be expected, that there would be various opinions respecting the name that should be given to the new planet.—A Correspondent of the Allg. Liter. Anzeig. No. 72, proposes the name of *Vulcan*. He thinks it would not be improper

proper to assign to the god who fabricated the arms of Achilles a place in the heavens, near the God of War—to the husband of Venus a place near her paramour. Nor could Vulcan murmur that it was so late before this honour was done him, and a planet of so small luminosity called after his name, since he himself, on account of his unfortunate lameness, is not very swift-of-foot, or stately in his appearance. Vulcan too, he says, being the son of Jupiter, is one of the family, and in this respect, likewise, had a well-founded claim to the honor intended him.

Professor Reimarus, of Hamburg, is of opinion that it should be called *Cupid.* It being an established custom to name the planets after the deities of antiquity; there is, he thinks, sufficient reason for adopting that of Cupid, for he would be the nearest (reckoning downwards from Venus) to Mars, the lover of Venus.—Others think, that the name of Cupid would therefore, be proper, because it conveys an idea of blindness; for the new planet has the appearance of a star of only the 8th magnitude, and cannot be seen by the unassisted eyes of man. But on this point, if the right of the newly-discovered star to be admitted among the number of the planets be confirmed, the plurality of voices, or perhaps only accident, will decide. It is, likewise, possible, that, as it happened with respect to Uranus, there will be no general agreement among astronomers. In Italy it will, perhaps, retain the name of *Ferdinandeum Sidus*, in France that of *Planète Piazzi*, till time and circumstances shall have otherwise decided.

It has long been customary to express the order of the planets in Latin verses, that they might the more easily be committed to memory; as for instance, in the old well-known distich:—

Saturni atque Jovis sidus, Mars, Sol, Venus alma,
Mercurius, claudit ultima Luna chorum.

When Herschell discovered the new planet beyond Saturn, Poinsinet Desivry wished to have it named after Cybele, the wife of Saturn; and gave us the order of the seven planets in the following verses:—

Ambit Solem Hermes, Venus hunc, mox Terra, Diana,
Mars sequitur. Pergit Rex Jupiter. Hunc Saturnus;
Omnes hos orbes amplectitur alma Cubelle.

A friend of M. von Zach expresses the order of the now *eight* planets, in the following lines:—

Mercurius primus; *Venus* altera; *Terra* deinde;
Mars posthac; quintam sedem sibi vindicat *Hera:*
Jupiter hanc ultra est. Sequitur *Saturnus*; at illum
Uranus egreditur, non ausim dicere summus.

Or,

Mercurius Solem comitatur proximus. Illum
Insequitur *Venus*, hanc *Tellus*, *Luná* comitante;
Mars posthac; Martem prohibet Jovis esse sequacem.
Hera latens frustra, et melioribus obvia vitris.
Saturnum extrema proavi statione locabant,
Nos aliter. Supremam cœli nunc *Uranus* arcem
Usurpat, pœnas ausi fortasse daturus.

MEMOIRS OF EMINENT PERSONS.

MEMOIRS *of* PRINCE PIGNATELLI, *late* VICEROY *of* NAPLES.

FRANCIS PIGNATELLI, of the Princes of Strongoli, was born about the year 1730, from an illustrious family, whose origin is certainly prior to the foundation of the monarchy of the two Sicilies, and probably derived from some of the Lombard Lords in the principality of Benevento. If we may give credit to the ancient and uncontradicted tradition, the name of this family was undoubtedly derived from the Italian word *Pignattelio*, a small pipkin, and adopted by the founder of the family, since he penetrated victoriously into the entrenched camp of the Greek Emperor, and into the very tent of the general of the army. He went out of the apartment with three pipkins in his hand, shewing them to his soldiers as a proof of a complete victory. This accords, at least, with the coat of arms of the eldest branch of the family. It represents three small pipkins in a triangular figure, with the following line under them, if we recollect rightly:

Quas rapuit Graecis ollas Landolphus fe.

Prince Francis early in his youth entered the army; and he began his career with such unfavourable auspices that nobody could foresee he would one day be raised to the pinnacle of dignity in the kingdom. Being an inferior officer, and hardly

hardly twenty years of age, he received a challenge from an able and gallant officer, Count Pilaſtrelli. His friends conſidered the riſk of his life to be imminent, as he was a young man juſt entered into the world, and his antagoniſt acknowledged to be one of the beſt ſwordſmen in the army. This inequality, however, was the ſafety of the Prince, and the deſtruction of his antagoniſt. Count Pilaſtrelli, according to every report, too ſenſible of his own ſuperiority, treated the young man with great contempt in the fight, inſomuch that he neglected the uſe of his weapon on a neceſſary guard, and ſeemed to deſpiſe the leſſons taught in the fencing-ſchool. This inſulting preſumption proved fatal to him: he lay open to a thruſt which his adverſary did not fail to make at him, and that ſo promptly, that he had not time to parry it —Prince Pignatelli's ſword paſſed through his body, and left him dead on the ſpot. The Prince was, in conſequence of the duel, degraded from his rank, and ſent to the Caſtle of St. Elmo, where he remained confined for ſeveral years. Reflection on the committed homicide, with its conſequent repentance, added to regret for the fruſtration of his hopes and ambition, together with the effects of a long confinement, produced in him that religious turn of mind, which has been ſo conſpicuous in the ſubſequent part of his life.

Juſtice obliges us to ſtate, to the greateſt honour of the Italians, that, although ſlaughters, murders, and aſſaſſinations are more frequently perpetrated in their country than any where elſe, there is, perhaps, no people in Europe, who theoretically have more abhorrence than they have to taking a man's life. A perſon, who has happened to kill a man, even in the moſt gallant and honourable way, inſpires a diſlike in all people, gives embarraſſment by his preſence, and very ſeldom can gain admittance into ſocieties of cordial friends. The moſt unaccountable point in this national habitude is that the very ſame individuals who are ready to own, that, in ſome part of their lives, and on ſome ſtrange occurrences, they were in danger of committing ſimilar exceſſes, are diſturbed upon ſuch occaſions, and uneaſy at the converſation of others, who have been more unfortunate than they. This is, perhaps, the contraſt which nature has put in the temper of the Italians between delicacy of ſenſibility, and violence of paſſions. But, be it as it may, it was neceſſary to notice it here for the purpoſe of ſtating, that, owing to that unfortunate event, Prince Pignatelli, even when he was delivered from priſon, and re-admitted into the army, ſpent upwards of fifteen of the beſt years of his life in the greateſt obſcurity, and in the utmoſt inſignificancy. He was preferred by degrees to the rank of lieutenant, captain, and lieutenant-colonel, by very ſlow ſteps; nor was any more notice taken of him than of the leaſt officer in the royal ſervice.

His greateſt ſtrides towards the eminent dignities began about the year 1770. His Sicilian Majeſty, at that time in the bloom of his youth, was extremely fond of military parade and exerciſes. He projected, among other things, the erection of a new regiment, which ſhould be compoſed only of young gentlemen and noblemen from the two kingdoms. They were to be from fifteen to twenty-five years of age, ſupported by monthly appointments from their families, beſides the large wages of the court, and brought up in ſciences and tactics, in one large college, or rather quarters, in the capital. They were to be conſidered as the ſole candidates for any vacant place of officer in the inferior regiments, to live in their corps under the command of none who ſhould not be a nobleman, and intitled to the peculiar honour of attending his Majeſty in all public ceremonies, and in his country-ſeats and diverſions. Whether M. Pignatelli was the firſt to give ſome hints of this new eſtabliſhment to the King, or he found himſelf occaſionally in the way, it is more than we know: this is certain, that he was appointed director of the college, and commander of the new raiſed regiment, to which the name was given of *Battaglione*, *Brigata*, and ſometimes of *Cadetti*.

The purpoſes of his Majeſty were exceedingly well anſwered by the young gentlemen of the *Battaglione*, with reſpect to the military ſhew—A body of about 1500 young men, finely equipped, rivalling each other in elegance and martial air, the greateſt part of them tall, ſtout, and handſome, and officered by individuals of the firſt nobility in the kingdom, made ſuch a ſhining figure in the royal and religious ceremonies as to overjoy the natives, and to aſtoniſh and charm every foreigner. But no worſe eſtabliſhment was ever ſeen for the purpoſe of promoting morals and ſciences! Theſe *Cadetti* ſoon proved the moſt ignorant and vicious body of young men in the kingdom. They were as wicked towards each other within their quarters, as towards all the people of the town. Cheats, violences, injuries, inſults, gaming, clandeſtine marriages, elopements, ſtabbing, and murders, became almoſt their exclu-

five

five department; and their profligacy of every kind had actually become so defamed and proverbial, as to deter every honest man from putting his children in the army. His Majesty avowed more than once, that he had been strangely disappointed, and could not help remonstrating to M. Pignatelli on the subject. The commander excused himself on the age and condition of the young people, which rendered them incorrigible and disrespectful to their superiors. The ultimate consequence was the suppression of such a scandalous body! and M. Pignatelli, however unsuccessful might have been his exertions in the command of the *Battaglione*, carried on through them his great object of having frequent opportunities of seeing and ingratiating himself with his majesty. From that time, he has always possessed a considerable favour at court.

The public opinion, with respect to the morals and abilities of M. Pignatelli, whilst commander of the *Cadetti*, was not decidedly in his favour. His great activity, supported by the affection of the court (which is a great prepossession under an absolute monarchy) enabled him to acquire, among the bulk of the people, some degree of reputation for talents and military knowledge. Those, however, who could judge for themselves, were able to appreciate him in his just value. He was considered by the latter as a man of no abilities, of many intrigues, and of an insatiable ambition. The writer of this article was, when in Naples, assured by a clergyman of great respectability, who had been the spiritual director in the college, that no particular establishment in that place was well projected or executed, and that the wickedness of the young people there was, in a great measure, occasioned by a defect of administration. Many Neapolitan officers also gave him a disadvantageous character. But what most unquestionably betrayed the narrow mind, and the insufficiency of M. Pignatelli in this station, was an order solicited by him from the court, purporting that all the officers in the *Battaglione* should be chosen thenceforward from the nobility of the metropolis, excluding all the provincial *noblesse*. This was certainly a disgraceful blunder, as no man is so totally unacquainted with the history of the two Sicilies as not to know that Naples became the metropolis of the kingdom under Charles I. and that the body of the Neapolitan nobility in that city was formed by Charles II. towards the close of the thirteenth century; whereas, Sicily, Apulia, and Calabria, having been the theatre of all the civil revolutions in the middle ages, and the occasional residence of the founders of the monarchy, as well as of the overthrown dynasties, prior to the house of Anjou, possessed a nobility who had a claim to be the descendants of the Lombards, of the Normans, and the Greeks! This subjected him to the most humiliating animadversions from the provincial nobility, and to plenty of pamphlets and lampoons from every quarter. Two stanzas of a very fine sonnet are still in remembrance, which we shall here insert for the pleasure of such readers as are acquainted with the Italian language:

> Un provinciale il bel dispaccio ha letto,
> Uscito, poco fa, pe'l Battaglione,
> Ed il medesmo appena scorso, ha detto:
> Quel santo direttor quanto è c—g—one!
>
> Cede Napoli al regno, a suo dispetto,
> Di nobiltà vetusta al paragone:
> E gente è là di tal condizione,
> Che i *seggi* in *seggio* tien, con buon rispetto.

M. Pignatelli being aware that the body of *Cadetti*, of which he was director, was not likely to last long, and having no prospect of continuing in the favour of the court by that means, he sought for others. From the year 1775 to 1780, he projected several public and private buildings for the service of the court and the state; the most capital of which was the *Magazine*, erected on the sea-shore, beyond Magdalen's Bridge, in Naples, intended as a warehouse for the city, as well as for a repository of naval and military stores. The building is immense, and second to none in Naples, but to the *General Hospital!* It is, however, so disproportioned in length, height, and breadth, as to disgust a man of taste at the very first view. This disproportion is so conspicuous, even in the doors, windows, and apartments, as to give to the building no character at all; and were an informed traveller to judge of it only by the style or the appearance, he would be at a loss to guess whether it is a palace, a court of justice, an hospital, a warehouse, or a jail! The inside is, if possible, more defective: no regular distribution of rooms, no easy communication between the several apartments, no part perfectly connected with each other, and, what is more shocking, the whole intersected with long and narrow galleries, or *corridores*, which would be scarcely tolerated in a convent of Capuchins! The view of such *corridores* is so gloomy and uncomfortable, that the noted scurrilous philosopher, the Abbé Galiani, could

4

could justly affirm that, *when he wanted to set his mind on religious meditations, he would take a walk either under the grotto of Puzzuoli, or under the galleries of Pignatelli's warehouse.*

During these transactions, Prince Pignatelli was preferred, by degrees, to the ranks of brigadier and field-marshal; and the latter was his condition in the beginning of the year 1783, when the ever-memorable earthquake took place in Calabria. He was sent there as a vicegerent and representative of his Majesty to relieve the distressed province, and took with him some officers belonging to the impure remnants of the body of the *Battaglione*, who were intended as his agents in the several districts. Were the Neapolitan nation at large more informed than it is; or, at least, were it less careless of the public prosperity, this very moment would have enabled it to appreciate M. Pignatelli's just value. The officers under his command in Calabria rendered themselves guilty of the greatest enormities, both from ignorance and wickedness. Violences and depredations were so widely and systematically committed, that the poor Calabrese considered the mission of M. Pignatelli as a greater calamity to their unfortunate country than the dreadful earthquake which had lately desolated it! He himself was guilty of no rapacity, nor of any intentional oppressions; however, he was of a despotic and ambitious temper; and, on the other side, destitute both of law and history. He occasioned, from such disqualifications, as many distresses, at least, as his inferior agents from their calculated crimes. The court being sensible that he might commit some errors for want of legal knowledge, gave him an assessor taken from the body of magistracy. This election fell on M. Vanvitelli, chief of the provincial tribunal of Catanzaro, one of the best magistrates in the kingdom, if not from extensive learning, from clearness of conception, assiduity of labour, sobriety of manners, and love of justice. He proved, indeed, a temporary check to despotic presumption. But the vicegerent was too powerful not to get rid of him. A few months after his appointment, he represented to the court his great abilities and signal services, and solicited for him, as a reward, a preferment in the supreme courts of justice in the metropolis; stating, at the same time, that he had met with, among the inferior assessors of his agents, a *very eminent civilian*, whom he designed to be his successor. The court fell into the snare. M. Vanvitelli was soon promoted to the metropolis, and Mr. Zurlo was appointed his successor in the assessorship of the vicegerent. This Zurlo was a young man who had never been at the bar; he was a native of a small village in the neighbourhood of *Campo Basso*, and of an obscure extraction. He had been brought to Naples in order to study the law, but he never so much as took the trouble of reading the elements of it. He was noted for indolence and idleness to such a degree as to prefer poverty and distress to any thing like labour. He was, on the other hand, ambitious, cunning, investigating, intriguing, and assumed airs of importance by conversing with literary men, to whose society he was indebted for a superficial, unconnected, and desultory information, ten times more dangerous than ignorance. In the course of his excursions, he met with an officer of the name of Micherou, more ignorant than himself, and, happily for him, less malicious. With this officer, he repaired to Calabria, and by this means he was noticed by M. Pignatelli! This was *the eminent civilian!*

One of the projects now upon the carpet for the regeneration of Calabria, was the suppression of all convents fallen a prey to the earthquake! This was certainly an exorbitant measure, as it implied the confiscation of their estates, which had been held until then by as good titles as any secular proprietory. The Prince was zealous for the interest of the treasury whilst he feared to give any offence to the Holy See. He prevailed on the court to suppress the convents, with the approbation of his Holiness, and he set off himself for Rome, as an extraordinary ambassador, for the purpose. This was one of the most remarkable absurdities and contradictions lately exhibited by the government of Naples! Whilst the active platoon of lawyers and canonists, under the protection of the minister for ecclesiastical affairs, were struggling for the support of the royal prerogatives upon the ecclesiastical discipline in the kingdom, and so many fatal blows had already been given by their Philippics to the court of Rome, a vicegerent of his Majesty, with the approbation of the minister of war, goes to Rome, acknowledges the authority of the Holy See as paramount to the royal jurisdiction, and gives of course an implicit disavowal to his colleagues in the government! On the other hand, the appointment of M. Zurlo to the assessorship fully answered the purpose! He was the meanest and most devoted flatterer of the vicegerent; whatever the latter was doing, he approved!

 He

He made it his sole study how to indulge his master in every act of ambition and despotism; and, at last, he was rewarded for his meanness, by being promoted to the supreme magistracy of the metropolis! These two things rendered M. Pignatelli utterly odious to the Neapolitan lawyers. They considered him as a man who betrayed the rights of his sovereign, in going to Rome, and asking from the Pope the permission of exercising one of the innate prerogatives of the crown for which they were actually struggling, and who had defiled the sanctuary of laws, by introducing into it such an unworthy man as M. Zurlo, who, in the happier days of their profession, would not have been a serjeant at mace! The gentlemen of the bar were perhaps wrong in the former of their complaints, as it was better to bring about a violent ecclesiastical reform, with the consent of the chief of the church, obtained in a gentlemanlike way, than to expose it to murmurs of one side, and to chicanery of the other. In the latter, however, they were altogether right; for it was shocking and scandalous that a young man under thirty, who had never been able to write an *affidavit*, should be suddenly raised to the highest juridical dignities in the kingdom!

In the year 1784, M. Pignatelli was sent as extraordinary ambassador to Spain, for the purpose of trying to restore the good understanding betwen the two courts, then suspended by family dissention. At his return, he was preferred to the rank of lieutenant general; in the year 1787, he was appointed President of the Military tribunal; in 1790 Commander of the Citadal of St. Elmo; and, in the year 1795, Extraordinary Civil and Military Governor of the City of Naples. We presume that he had occupied no other places before his late appointment as a Viceroy of the Kingdom at the time of the French aggression.

"*The revolution* (says Mallet du Pan very properly) *has reduced the statesmen and rulers of Europe to their just standard. It has proved that the world was in general governed by routine.* Had not the French attacked the kingdom of Naples, M. Pignatelli would, in all probability, have preserved his reputation among the common people, and his insufficiency would still have remained a secret with the well-informed persons in the Two Sicilies. That extraordinary event has rendered him contemptible to all Europe. Intrusted by his sovereign with the defence of the kingdom to the last extremity, and receiving express instructions that, in case every defence proved ineffectual, he should retire with the troops towards Calabria, he made bold to violate the commands of his master, to conclude an armistice, and to deliver to the enemy several unconquered provinces, and the strong place of Capua, the only bulwark of the metropolis! And to what? To the French, who were become another name for intrigue, perfidiousness, and treachery! The devastation of Naples was the result of the armistice! The writer remarked, in the answer of his Sicilian Majesty to the Viceroy Pignatelli, a sentence which opened to him a large field for reflection—*You may imagine* (said his Majesty) *how I am incensed against your perfidious advisers!*—This sentence made him suspect that the Prince was still under the counsel and direction of his favourite magistrate Zurlo, imbued perhaps with Jacobinical principles, and that this impudent adviser was the person alluded to in his Majesty's subsequent proclamation to his subjects. Time will unravel this secret. The Prince is now confined, by the King's order, in the Tower of Girgenti, and most likely he will be brought to a trial.

Francis Pignatelli is about seventy years of age, tall and stout, dark complexion, of a forbidding look, and a screaming tone of voice. He married, some years ago, the young Duchess of Maddaloni, who had been divorced from her first husband. This lady being heir of an immense fortune, he is likely to become as rich as any other individual of his illustrious family.

ORIGINAL LETTERS.

A COPY *of an* ORIGINAL LETTER *from* DR. HALLEY, *to* MR. FLAMSTEAD, *afterwards* ASTRONOMER-ROYAL.

SIR, *Oxford, March 10, 167⅞.*

"THE veneration I have for all who think astronomy deserves their care, and are not dismaid at the laborious and chargeable trouble of making celestial observations, was the chief motive which induced me to give you the trouble of these lines, which I thought I might with the more confidence do, considering how free and communicative a genius you expressed in your satisfactory answer to the request of of my very good friend, Mr. Charles Bouchar; yet, I dare not promiſe to myſelf the like favour from you on any other grounds than that I am a true honourer of your worth, and a well-willer to aſtronomy and all its followers. You may perhaps have expected that Mr. Bouchar ſhould have returned you thanks for the great trouble he put you to by his l're; he doubtleſs would have done it, had not his occaſions called him, ſoon after the receipt of your's, to take a voiage to Jamaica, where he will not neglect to make what obſervations he can, but eſpecially thoſe of Mercury, for which that horizon will be moſt convenient. Since his departure, I have been wholly deſtitute of a coadjutor in my ſtudies; yet, whenſoever the heavens favour us with ſerenity, I omit not to make what obſervations I may of the planets, being reaſonably well provided with inſtruments in which I can confide to one minute without error, by means of the teleſcopicall ſights, and a ſkrew for the ſubdiviſion; by my quadrant, ſo furniſhed, I have obſerved ♄ and ♃ to differ conſiderably from Hecker's Ephemeris, which makes ♄ at leaſt 20′ in conſequence to his viſible or true place, but ♃ about 8′ in antecedens; nor doth Street's Caroline Tables repreſent ♄ much better, for in the Obſervations of Hevelius, Aug. $\frac{18}{28}$ 1670, Philos. Trans. Num. 65. Pa. 2089, ♄ was ſeen $10^s\ 5^\circ\ 15'\ 25''$ à 1 ✱ ♈, with ſouth lat. $1^\circ\ 54'\ 11''$, but by the Caroline Tables ♄ was in $10^s\ 5^\circ\ 32'\ 32''$; diff. $17'\ 7''$, in the ſame lat. preciſely: and, according to Hecker's Ephemeris, he was in $4^\circ\ 11'$ of ♓ lat. auſtr. $1^\circ\ 53'$;-19+obſer.—whence ſo great differences ſhould ariſe is hard to conjecture; however, future obſervation will declare, whether it be the fault of his eccentricity or middle motion: if you have obſerved any thing of the like nature in ♄, I beg you would communicate it. Your obſervations of ♃, publiſhed in Philos. Trans, Num. 82, make ♃ 13′ in conſeq. to Hecker's Ephem. and thoſe Num. 87. diff. 8′, the ſame way, agreeing with mine preciſely;—♂ I find little fault with; yet, about his oppoſition to the ſun, he was near upon 5′ in conſeq. to Hecker's place. If you are pleaſed to ſend me any of thoſe moſt accurate obſervations you do daily make, whereby I may confirme mine, I ſhall ever own it as a ſignal obligation, and ſhall endeavour to return my gratitude by making any obſervation you ſhall deſire me. I requeſt that you would ſend me Caſſini's Suppoſition of the Hight of the Atmoſphere, and the Horizontall Refraction, and what other hypotheſis he hath of the Doctrine of Refraction, and whether experiment hath been made to confirm thoſe quantities; to me it ſeems to vary from any certain rule, and to be ſubject to the accidents of the heat and cold, which may conſiderably alter the denſity and altitude of the ſphear of air, and conſequently alter the refractions made in it, which ſeems to be confirmed by comparing the refractions of the ſunn with thoſe of the fixt ſtars obſerved by Tycho, where the ſlower decreaſe of the ſunn's refractions argues a greater hight of the atmoſphere, as if the preſence of the ſunn did elevate the air, which if ſo, the afternoon refractions would be greater than the morning's, and theſe uncertainties will make the place of ☿ dubious to 2′ or 3′ in moſt obſervations that can be made in our climate.

The late eclipſe of the moon, Jan. 1, I obſerved at London, with Mr. Street, as followeth:—The preciſe beginning we ſaw not, by reaſon we had not fitted our inſtruments ſoon enough, truſting too much to the calculation, but $\frac{2}{3}$ of a digt. were eclipſed when the upper limb of the ☽ was $11^\circ\ 39'$ high at $5^h\ 30^m\frac{1}{2}$; the immerſion was, when Pollux was high, $27^\circ\ 15'$ a $6^h\ 25^m\frac{1}{4}$, emerſion at Pollux $41^\circ\ 35'$, $7^h\ 58^m$;—The juſt end, when the ☽ lower limb was $42^\circ\ 30'$ high, time $9^h\ 0^m\frac{1}{3}$, whence the middle may be $7^h\ 12^m$, i. e. 8′ too ſoon for the calculation of Mr. Stevenſon. During the time of totall darkneſs, the moon covered a ſtarr of the 6 mag. viz. 29 of ♊, the immerſion was 15° or 16° from the nadir toward the weſt, when Pollux was $33^\circ\ 5'$ high, $7^h\ 3^m\frac{1}{3}$; but the emerſion was 75° from the nadir toward the weſt, alt. Pollux $37^\circ\ 45'$—$7^h\ 42^m\ 20''$;—what you or your friends have obſerved of this eclipſe, I entreat you to ſend me.—One thing more I thought fit to ſignifie to you, that is, that the 13th and 20th of ♓ are erroneouſly placed in Ticho's Catalogue, the 13th is there in $14^\circ\ 19'$ of ♈. $0^\circ\ 57'\frac{1}{2}$ lat. bor. but its diſtance from Ala Pegaſi is $16^\circ\ 36'\ 30''$, and from Cinguli Andromedæ $28^\circ\ 4'\ 15''$; whence I computed his place in ♈ $14^\circ\ 19'\frac{1}{4}$, with ſouth lat. $0^\circ\ 11'\ 50''$,—and the 20th is in $22^\circ\ 12'$ ♈ with $1^\circ\ 38'\frac{1}{2}$ bor. lat. but by his diſtance from Lucida ♈ is $15^\circ\ 15'\ 5''$, and from Os Ceti $19^\circ\ 44'\ 45''$ I computed its place in $22^\circ\ 11'\ 17''$ cum lat. aus. $1^\circ\ 40'\ 40''$;—moreover, I am fully ſatisfied that cor ♍ is at leaſt 5′ in antecedence to his Tichonic place, which is confirmed by Ticho's own obſervations, who, 5th Februarii mane name obs. (1584) the distance of cor ♍ from (*here the name of the star is not legible*)....♍ 45° 51¼, and my observation was 45° 50′ 55″, the same to sense, whereas Ticho's data require the distance to be 56° 57′—The appulse of the moon to ♂ (22 March instant) I intend diligently to observe, and hope you will doe the like. I beleive that about 9 P. M. her northern horn will goe near to cover him, which, if it doe, I will note the time of the immersion and emersion, otherwise the time of the right line with the Horns. I desire you would send me the like observations made with you, whereto I shall subjoin my own, if the heavens favour us. These, Sir, as a specimen of my astronomical endeavours, I send you, being ambitious of the honour of being known to you, of which, if you shall deem me worthy, I shall account myself exceedingly happy in the enjoyment of the acquaintance of so illustrious and deserving a person as yourself. I am, Sir,

Your's and Urania's most humble
Servant, though unknown,
Queen's Coll. Oxon. EDM. HALLEY."

LETTER II.
Dr. Halley to Dr. Wallis.

"REVEREND SIR,

I fear I have too long trespassed upon your goodness, in not returning you Mr. Newton's Letters, with which you were pleased to furnish me to my great satisfaction; for therein I find what I most wanted in the doctrine of series, viz. the method of reverting them, whereby the whole is rendered compleat, and there are very few problems that yeild not to this process. Since my last, I have been considering the construction of the Nauticall Chart, commonly called Mercator's, designing a discourse upon that subject in the Philos. Trans. and by help of a discovery I have made of a rule to find the intervall of meridionall parts, answering to any differences of latitudes given, I have solved all the possible cases except one, which, without an infinite series of series, I fear, will hardly be resolved, and 'tis this—" A ship sails from a certain given latitude (suppose of 50 deg.) 500 leagues, and in that course has made 20 leagues of longitude, I demand the course on which she saild, it being only known that it is between the west and south?"—I know this is of no sort of use, because this case does not occur in navigation, but without it the science cannot be esteemed perfect.

Your's, &c.
E. HALLEY."

This letter is not dated, but the time when it was written may be very nearly ascertained, as Newton's Letters, containing his discoveries on the method of Series, Fluxions, &c. were circulated among his literary friends, and pretty generally known, before 1676. The method of reverting series, which Halley here speaks of, is contained in Newton's tract, intitled "*De Analysi per Equationes numero Terminorum Infinitas*," which was communicated to Dr. Barrow, and by him sent to Mr. Collins, July 31, 1669—See Collins's *Commercium Epistolicum* (4to edit.), page 3 & seq.—Raphson's Hist. of Fluxions, page 92, 95.—And Professor Stewart's Comment on the Tract above-mentioned, page

The "Discourse," which Dr. Halley here speaks of, was published in No. 219. of Phil. Trans.—See Motte's Abridgment, vol. i. page 665; and the "case" or problem he mentions was first resolved by Israel Lyons of Cambridge.

ORIGINAL POETRY.

AD UMBRAM GILBERTI WAKEFIELD
ELEGIA.

TE quoque subripuit nobis Libitina severa
Nostratis critici gloria prima chori!
Subripuit flenti sponsæ, sobolique tenellæ;
Flentibus agnatis, omnibus atque bonis.
Quæ tua sors!—Vixdum lætis reparatus amicis,
E tristi exilio carceribusque cavis;
En! subito traheris torvi ad vestibula Ditis,
A queis nemo redit—nemo redire potest.
Scilicet, insipiens, sapiens, probus, improbus æque,
Obscurus proavis, nobilitate tumens;
Plebs, princeps, pannis squalens et murice fulgens;
Pauperie oppressus, divitiis que valens:
Serius aut citius metam properamus ad unam,
Quicunque hanc auram haurimus ætheream!
Sed quem non doleat, cernentem vivere vitam
Longævam stolidos, criminibusque graves:
Dum

Dum pius, innocuus, doctus, vernantibus annis,
Ceu rosa florescens tabe peresa, jacet?
Ast tibi, quantumvis fuerit brevis orbita vitæ,
Nec fama abfuerat, nec bene partus honos:
Vixisti, Wakefield! et longos vivet in annos
Pectoribus nostris lucida imago tui.
Interea ad campos felices dirige gressus;
Rura beatorum ac elysiumque pete.
Nam te non Erebus speret retinere barathro;
Nec piceas biberis tu Phlegetontis aquas.
Non etenim hirsuto tua nunc sub judice lis est:
Arbiter est justus, Gnossius ille, Minos.
Hunc, placido vultu, gratas effundere voces
Audire has videor: "Vir bone! mitte metus!
"Novimus et qui sis, Wakefield! quantasque tulisti
"Noxas—hæc Hermes omnia nos docuit.
"Sed quicquid terris fit vestris, fasve nefasve,
"Justitiæ lex hic inviolata manet.
"Nil hic vel tituli valeant, nec dura potestas:
"Hic VIRTUS, VIRTUS semper, et una, valet.
"Perge igitur quovis, et quasvis elige sedes:
"Colles, convalles—omnia aperta patent.
"Si Sophiæ lubeat claris te jungere alumnis,
"En Tibi Pherecydes, Atticus atque senex!
"Hos prope Pythagoras, Thales, doctusque Epicurus;
"Magnus Aristoteles, major et ipse Plato.
"Nec desunt Latiæ notissima nomina gentis;
"Tullius insignis, Brutus, uterque Cato:
"Plinius, et Seneca, ac Marcus cognomine Divus,
"Cui nomen virtus, non diadema, dedit.
"Hos inter vestras Baconus, Lockius, atque
"Newto, Britannorum gloria, fama, decus!
"Quod si oratorum tenearis dulce loquentûm
"Flexanimis verbis, lenibus atque sonis;
"Æolidis liceat niveas haurire loquelas;
"Nestoris et liquido melle fluente favis
"Dulcius eloquium—Periclis retonantia dicta,
"Queis Hellas toties territa, quassa, fuit!
"Vim Demostheneam miraberis—et Ciceronis
"Aurea verborum copia grata fluet
"Auriculis avidis—Cum illis, simul, et tuus, olim,
"Sedes non imas Foxius ipse premet.
"Sin mavis tete sacris sociare poëtis,
"In vita studio deliciisque tuis;
"Linus, et Hesiodus, Moschus, divinus Homerus,
"Pindarus altivolans, mellifluusque Bion,
"Æschylus, et grandis Sophocles, castique cothurni
"Princeps Euripides—ista vireta colunt.
"Illic et Siculus jucunda idyllia cantat;
"Ludit et argutis Teia Musa jocis.
"Illic Virgilius, Flaccusque, et Lusor Amorum,
"*Ingenio periit qui miser ipse suo.*
"Illic sublimis spectabilis umbra Lucretî,
"Magnificè scriptis jam decorata tuis.
"Illic Miltonus, Popius, Drydenus, et ille
"Naturæ potuit qui reserare sinus
"Shakspērius—secus ac Cowperus, flebilis iste,
"Orco quem ante diem bilis acerba dedit!
"Hos—illos—istos adeas: Nam nulla cupido
"Visendi heroas te capit—ipse scio:
"Sunt generis vani, ac inflati pectora fastu;
"Semper gestantes triste supercilium."
Sic fatus, tacuit—Cum tu, Gilberte, vicissim,
Solvere sis visus talibus ora modis:
"Si mihi permissum est optatâ sidere sede,
"Sit cum philosophis sæpe sedile meum:
"Philosophis, inquam, veris; minimèque Sophistis!
"Isthæc mî semper turba odiosa fuit.
"Rhetoribus rarò jungar: nam garrula gens est,
"Vendere quæ fumum vanaque verba solet:
"Qualia multiloquus suevit depromere Pittus!
"Qualia spumoso Wyndhamus ore vomit!
"Sæpius ast inter sim claros nomine vates;
"Cumque illis liceat fundere molle melos:
"Inter sim vates—vates mea pectora suavi
"Carmine lætificent, blandisonisque modis.
"Nil mihi cum vestris heroibus—Arma gerebant
"Impia mente inopi, sanguineaque manu!
"Sacram LIBERTATEM sternentes cuspide Martis,
"Cudebant miseris non toleranda juga.
"Ah! procul, ah! semper procul a me estote profani.
"Nemo tyrannorum proximus esto mihi!"
Optanda optasti, Wakefield!—O! sors mihi tandem
Sit similis—tecum et carmina sacra canam:
Carmina sacra canam, chordas et pectine pulsem,
Indoctâ quamvis ac trepidante manu,
Carmina sacra canam, faveat modo Musa canenti
Suavis Terpsichore, suavior aut Erato:
Me nam delectant dulces ante omnia Musæ;
Musa mihi cunctis est medicina malis.
Harum colloquiis blandis, Gilberte, fruaris;
Atque his-cum liceat fundere molle melos.
Neo ventura dies distat qua, stamine vitæ
Truncato, celeri te pede, Amice, sequar.
Morbificus languor jam fessos occupat artus.
Paulatim emorior—Sed satis—Umbra, vale!

Londini, Prid. Non. Octobr. 1801. MUSÆUS JUNIOR.

SONNET

SONNET *to* CATHERINE:—*On meeting her, for the first Time, in a Boat on the River Thames.*

THO' lovely Catherine! whilst we plough'd the tide,
I seem'd but conscious of the scenes around,
(The sunny lawns, and slopes with shade embrown'd)
And to depict them with my pencil try'd;
Oft, with stolen glances I thy beauties spy'd.
Tho' blushing fear my lips in fetters bound,
I listened to thy voice, and caught each sound;
Tho' to an envied other it reply'd.
Would that my hand to paint thy lovely face
Had dared; my lips my passion to explain!
Yet, since I ne'er may see thee more, to trace
The scenes I pencil'd in thy sight again;
To hope thine eyes these artless lines may grace,
Will give some solace to my hopeless pain.
May 14, 1801. D. S. Y.

The CONDEMNED SAILOR.

By FANNY HOLCROFT.

'TWAS mine to watch the dreary night,
The threat'ning storm to brave;
'Twas mine to view the morning light,
"And hail myself a slave."

But now sweet sleep shall not deny
A respite to my grief:
"My former wrongs I now defy;"
Oh death, thou bring'st relief!

I hail thy sad yet welcome shore,
Where mis'ry finds repose;
Where coward-boys shall strike no more
Who struck his country's foes.

My indignant soul, by wrongs inflam'd,
Receiv'd a mortal wound:
A boy my veteran-locks defam'd!
I fell'd him to the ground.

Nor could the captain's wrathful eye
The burst of passion quell:—
Tyrant, behold your minion lie;
Thrust by this arm to hell!

Now bind these limbs; the scars efface,
By honour proudly worn:
Nor chains, nor whips, can brand him base,
Whose wrongs are nobly borne.

PART *of an* INSCRIPTION *designed for a* GARDEN.

THOU who shalt mark this spot with pensive eye,
Where mem'ry claims affection's frequent sigh!
Whate'er the intrusted talent, wouldst thou raise
From gifts divine the Giver's holy praise?
The Christian's hope eternal wouldst thou feel,
The patriot's energy, the martyr's zeal?
And, scorning tyrant-pow'r, delighted prove
Each social blessing, each domestic love?
Then linger here, to rouse the sacred flame,
And teach these echoes Wakefield's honour'd name:—
But wouldst thou, heedless of the destin'd hour,
Inglorious dream in pleasure's fairy-bow'r?
Or does ambition prompt thy vain desires,
Lur'd by each magic form the world admires?
Haste, ere these hallow'd scenes dissolve the spell!
Yet, first to virtue bid a long farewell!
W. F. Oct. 15. J. T. R.

SONNET *to* LOUISA:—*On being informed that her Miniature was in the Exhibition, without its being distinguished by the Author from any other Portrait in the same Frame.*

BELOV'D Louisa! fairest of thy land!
(The truth, tho' haply to my loss, I own)
Not e'en to me thy charms pourtray'd were known.
Was it that absence wore thee from my mind?
Ah! no; how oft, upon my couch reclin'd,
Thine airy form in midnight dreams has shone;
How oft, escaping from the world, alone,
Thee, in my noon-tide musings, thee I find.
Was it that art's bold pencil try'd in vain
To paint thy charms that nature claims with pride?
Ah! from whichever cause mine eyes complain,
To know thy semblance 'twas to them deny'd;
Would that these charms 'twere theirs to see again;
Thus to be able rightly to decide!
May 14, 1801. D. S. Y.

The SWEET-BRIAR; *written in* AUGUST, 1798, *at* KESWICK, *in* CUMBERLAND.

AS late along the flowery side
Of Derwent's murmuring stream I stray'd,
A rosy sweet-briar-bush I spy'd,
Full blooming in the sunny glade.

Its blossoms glow'd with crimson dye,
As o'er the glassy wave they spread,
And on the gales that sported by
Their delicate perfume was shed.

This

This day, returning to the spot,
To view the bush so richly blown,
With tearful eye I marked its lot;
For all the crimson bloom was gone.

"Now far away thy blossoms glide,
"Along the stream that laves thy feet—
"Ah! cruel was yon faithless tide,
"To rob thee of thy flowers so sweet!

"Thy fate demands a pitying tear;
"Yet why, sweet mourner, thus complain?
"For smiling spring shall soon appear,
"To swell thy ruby buds again.

"Like thee the artless maiden smiles,
"Adorn'd with beauty's mildest grace;
"Till robb'd by man's insidious wiles,
"The virgin bloom forsakes her face."

But when *to her* shall spring appear,
Soft beauty's germ again to break?—
Not all the roses of the year
Can animate her faded cheek.

Ye wintry winds! O, freeze the wave!
That caused yon rosy sweet-briar's doom;
And O! ye lightnings, blast the slave,
That dares despoil a virgin's bloom!

Liverpool.

PROCEEDINGS OF LEARNED SOCIETIES.

NATIONAL INSTITUTE OF FRANCE.

(Continuation of the Sitting in Messidor, Year 9)

ILLUSTRATIONS *relative to a* POINT *of* HISTORY *of the* TRIGONOMETRICAL TABLES.—*The* TRIGONOMETRICAL TABLES *of* BORDA, *published by* DELAMBRE.

THESE Tables are purely logarithmical. The decimal division of the circle for which they were constructed, is, doubtless, more commodious than the sexagesimal-division. These signs, composed each of thirty degrees, which divide the circumference into twelve parts, while each degree is sub-divided into sixty minutes, and the minute into sixty seconds, is too remote from the simple and uniform process of the arithmetical system, which proceeds invariably by tens, not to occasion frequently very serious inconveniences in practice. They had been acutely observed, near two centuries ago, by BRIGGS, who, with a view to remedy them, without too openly shocking the received system, had proposed to banish, at least, the minutes and the seconds, which he replaced by tenths and hundredths of a degree. The tables which he composed to accredit his mitigated system, and which have appeared, since his death, through the cares of Gellibrand, were so exact and complete, and the new logarithms which he employed in them, gave to his work such a superiority over all that had appeared till then, that he would infallibly have introduced the happy change which he proposed, if Vlacq, printing at the same time his *Artificial Trigonometry*, in which the logarithms of Briggs were adapted to the ancient division of the circle, and tables 3; six-times larger than those of Briggs, had not furnished astronomers with a specious pretext to adhere to their ancient routine.

The French geometers and astronomers, in proposing a total change in the division of the circle, had, in like manner, to struggle with the tables of Vlacq, become still more commodious in the editions of Gardiner and of Callet. They were obliged to give to their new tables three or four-times less extent than those of Vlacq. In both these points they have succeeded. The first part included a considerable augmentation of volumes; but this inconvenience could not retard Citizen Prony, appointed to raise a monument which was to surpass all that had been executed or even conceived of the greatest in this kind. Borda wanted tables more for use (*plus usuelles*); it was requisite, therefore, that in respect of extent they should come near to those of Briggs, and then he found himself under the size of Vlacq, Gardiner and Callet. He made it his study, therefore, to bring himself to their level, and he succeeded very skilfully.

These little registers of the proportional parts, so commodious, which accompany the logarithms of the numbers, could not, as yet, have place in the tables of the sinuses and tangents. Borda is the first, and the only one hitherto, who introduced them into his. He kept an account of the inequality of the differences; he has, moreover, re-established the secants, long suppressed by Vlacq and all his editors; and such are the means by which he has been able to compensate for the smaller size of his tables, that their use is, at least, as expeditious and as exact as that of the sexagesimal tables, the most commodious and the most generally known.

Different causes have retarded the publication of this work, the manuscript of which was finished in 1792. The scrupulous accuracy which the author would bestow on every part, the bad state of his health, the difficult circumstances under which he had begun the impression, the resolution he took to cancel and to begin again a considerable part of the edition, which he had not been able to superintend properly himself, and in which he had found some faults of little importance in respect of truth, but yet pretty numerous; these causes deprived him of the satisfaction of compleating a work he had very much at heart, and for which he had made great sacrifices. The preface found in his papers was incompleat. The part which remained to be done would, doubtless, have been the newest and the most interesting. What he has left of it contains scarcely any thing but a syllabus of the theory of logarithms, after Euler, and the usages of his tables. We find in them, however, a new and very expeditious formula to calculate the logarithms of numbers. He had said nothing of the construction of his tables of sines. The editor has endeavoured to supply what was wanting in this introduction; he has given new formulæ, and both sure and expeditious processes to construct, verify, or extend all the tables which compose this collection. He has compared these tables with all those of the same kind which he could procure, in print or manuscript, and has spared neither labour nor care to insure the correction of this work, the typographical execution of which does honour to the printing-office of the Republic.

Citizen LALANDE has read a Memoir on the longitude of Florence, the position of which was remarkably uncertain. From the new observations he has received from Chevalier CICCOLINI, and which he has recently calculated, he finds the difference of the meridians of Paris and Florence, to be 35′ 40″.

Citizen Lalande has read another Memoir on the secular motion of Venus. He has discovered by the last inferior conjunction of this planet, that the epoch of the longitude is exact, as well as the equation of the orbit, and that there remains nothing to be changed, in this respect, in the last Tables. In these calculations, Cit. Lalande has kept an account of the perturbations that Venus experiences from the action of Jupiter and from that of the earth, according to the formulæ which he himself gave in the Memoirs of the Academy of Sciences.

NEW GALVANIC EXPERIMENTS.

Citizens FOURCROY, VAUQUELIN and THENARD, who are occupied in the management of these experiments, have been lately recompensed for their labours by the discovery of one of the most curious and the most important facts which have a relation to this order of phenomena.

It was already known that by multiplying the discs which compose the pile, the force of the commotions and the rapidity of the decomposition of the water was augmented; they wished, however, to see what would be the result if the surface of each disc were augmented; they, consequently, composed a pile with plates of a foot square. The commotions and the decomposition remained the same as with a similar number of small discs; but the combustion of the metallic wires operated on the spot, with much force, and, by plunging them into *oxygene gas*, they were seen to flame with a very lively *éclat*, while small plates, however great the number of them may be, produce no such effect. Thus combustion follows a law relative to the surface of the plates, while the other phenomena have reference only to their number.

GEOLOGY.

On the Eruption of Vesuvius, in the Year 2,

One of the most important points to determine in the history of Volcanoes is, the degree of heat necessary to give fluidity to lavas: "Is it a fire of fusion similar to that which produces glass; or is this fluidity owing to some other cause?" This question has long occupied the attention of Citizen DOLOMIEU, who had already entertained some doubts (on considering many of the substances contained in the lava, and which remained untouched in it, although very fusible in themselves) with respect to the great heat which is commonly attributed to these volcanic mines. The eruption of Vesuvius, in the year 2, furnished him with the means of ascertaining this degree of heat, so to speak, as with a thermometer; he made it his business to trace the effects of the lavas on the substances which it had inveloped, and principally on metals.

He found, after this examination, that volcanic heat does not surpass that which is capable of melting silver, and that it is less than would be requisite for melting copper. The metals susceptible of being oxydated in a heat less than what would be necessary to melt them, have been so, even in the centre of the most voluminous masses; lead has been converted into a tessulary *galena* with large faces, glass into porcelain of Reaumur, &c. Citizen Dolomieu has

has laid before the Class the objects extracted by him from under the lava, and which establish the facts here presented, in an incontestible manner.

METEOROLOGY.

Agreement between the Variations of the Atmosphere in a large extent of Country.

We noticed in the last Quarterly Sitting, the efforts that Citizen LAMARCK has made to determine whether the variations of the atmosphere are marked by any thing periodical. He has since been employed on a no less important object, to know whether they extend to great distances. In fact, he has plainly discerned, that without this condition, all the means resorted to, to predict them, could only serve for a given place; and that a particular labour would be requisite for every district. To proceed in order, he at first attached himself to only one species of variations—that of the gravity of the air marked by the barometer; the following is the method which he employed to render his results more striking. He traced on a paper twenty-six parallel lines representing the space in which the barometrical variations are commonly limited in our climates. Other lines, perpendicular to the former, represent the days, and by marking on each the heights observed, he traces a curved line which represents the progress of the mercury.

Having then traced such a line, agreeably to the observations which he has himself made at Paris; a second, agreeably to those of Citizen PICTET, Associate Member of the Institute at Geneva; and a third, agreeably to those of Citizen THULIS, another Associate of the Institute at Marseilles, he found that these lines ascend and descend generally together, and scarcely differ but in respect to the height of the place of observation, or only as to the extent of the variations, but not as to their direction.

He found in the Memoirs of the Academy for 1708, a note of MARALDI, which indicates the same concordance between the heights of the barometer observed at Paris and at Zurich. This valuable remark had neither been repealed nor confirmed by any one since.

ON BELEMNITES.

We give this name to fossils in form of a lengthened cone, of a weaver's shuttle, or sometimes of a spindle, which appear to be kernels of unknown shells; they are pretty abundant in certain orders of mountains, and especially in marble, and other calcareous stones, which contain cornua, ammonia and other fossils, the living analogies of which have not yet been discovered.

Citizen SAGE, who had described many new species of them, in one of the last numbers of the *Journal de Physique*, has lately communicated some to the Class, which he had not seen before, and which form an interesting addition to this part of the progress of our knowledge.

Programma of the Prizes proposed by the National Institute of Science and Arts, at the Public Sitting, the 15th Vendemiaire, in the 10th Year.

CLASS OF MATHEMATICS AND PHYSICS.

Subject of the Prize of Chemistry.

The Class of Mathematics and Physics had, in the year 8, proposed for the subject of a prize which the Institute would determine on the 15th Vendemiaire, in the 10th year, the following:

To point out the earthy substances and the proper process for making a kind of pottery, capable of bearing a sudden transition from heat to cold, and which will be within the ability of persons of all classes.

At the end of this notice, the programma adds,

"The art of fabricating the more valuable pottery, known by the name of *porcelain*, has arisen to such perfection in the Republic, as to leave scarcely any thing to be desired; but the case is different with the species of pottery which is in common use: this kind of ware is very far from that state of improvement and perfection so necessary to supply the wants of the great body of citizens. Meantime, some of the neighbouring nations, who cannot manufacture *porcelain* equal to ours, make a pottery much superior to that made in France. The Institute, therefore, require the candidates to examine the composition of these potteries, to discover the earths which have been used in their composition, or point out such artificial mixtures as will supply their places; the manner in which these earths should be treated to give them the necessary qualities; the art of baking; the degree of heat, and the form necessary for the furnace; but, above all, a method of glazing them without the oxydes of any injurious metal."

The Class has received only one Memoir on this subject; accompanied by many samples of pottery and of the earths of which they have been made. The Memoir is written with perspicuity and method, contains the acknowledged principles of philosophy and chemistry, and the details which are employed to explain them shew a long and attentive practice of the art of pottery, joined to much knowledge of the theory; but the patterns which accompany the Memoir do not meet the ideas pointed out by the Class. Consequently, the distribution of the prize is postponed to the 15th Vendemiare, in the 11th year; the Class strongly recommending to the candidates to apply themselves with particular attention to the fabrication.

This double prize, of the value of two gold kilograms (about 6800 livres) will be bestowed in the meeting of the 15th Vendemiaire, in the 11th year. Papers will not be received after the 1st of Messidor, in the 10th year.

CLASS OF LITERATURE AND FINE ARTS.

Grammatical Prize.

Eloge of Cæsar Cheneau Dumersais.

The prize to be a gold medal, weighing five hecto-grammes, and will be determined at the public sitting, on the 15th Vendemiare, in the 11th year of the Republic. The papers must be delivered before the 1st of Messidor. The Members and Associates of the Institution, alone, are excluded from being candidates.

Prize in Antiquities:

The same Class proposed, in the year 8, as a subject for a prize:

What are the studies that form, and the knowledge which characterizes, the antiquary? What are the advantages arising to social order from their studies.

Considering the importance of the subject, the Class has judged proper to extend the time for delivering the Memoirs, to the 15th Vendemiaire, in the 11th year.

The prize is a gold medal, of the weight of five hecto-grammes, and will be determined in the public sitting of the 15th Nivose following—Members and Associates of the Institute are alone excluded as candidates.

General conditions, with which candidates for prizes must comply, on whatever subject they treat.

No Memoir sent in must have the name of the author, but only a sentence or device; the candidate may, if he pleases, annex to or accompany in with a note, sealed, which, besides the device or sentence, shall contain his name and address. This note shall not be opened, unless the Memoirs shall obtain the prize.

The Memoirs must be sent free to the Institute, or they may be addressed to one of the Secretaries of the proper Class, at Paris. In the latter case the Secretary will give a receipt.

The candidates are informed that the Institute cannot return either the memoirs, drawings, or machines which shall be sent in for the prizes; but the authors shall always have the privilege of copying the memoirs or drawing; or they may have the machines, on delivering drawings of them.

The Committee of the Treasury of the Institute will deliver the golden medals to the person who shall bring a certificate; and when there shall be no certificate, they will be delivered only to the author himself, or the bearer of his procuration.

Prize determined at the Public Sitting, the 15th Vendemiare, in the 10th year.

In the Public Sitting of the 15th Vendemiaire, of the 9th year, the Class of Literature and Fine Arts proposed, as the subjects of the prize of Poetry,

The Foundation of the Republic; an ode, poem, discourse in verse, or epistle.

Twelve pieces, in verse, have been sent in.

The Class decreed the prize to the Ode marked No. I. with this motto, '*Jam nova progenies cœlo demittitur alto*,' the author of which is Citizen Masson, author of the *Helvetians*, Secretary-general of the Department of the Rhine and Moselle.

Names of the Artists who, in the Judgment of the National Institute of Science and Arts, have gained the grand Prizes for Painting, Sculpture and Architecture, of the Year 9.

PAINTING.

The subject was "The arrival of the Ambassadors of Agamemnon at the Tent of Achilles, sent by that Prince to appease the Anger of the Son of Peleus."

This embassy was composed of Phœnix, the friend of Jupiter, of the great Ajax, and the divine Ulysses. They arrive at the quarters of the Thessalians and tent of Achilles, who is amusing himself by playing on a lyre, of admirable workmanship, and which he had taken when he plundered the city of Aetion; he was singing the glorious exploits of the heroes. Patroclus, alone, sat opposite to him in profound silence, waiting until he had ceased singing: Ulysses entered first; the other ambassadors respectfully wait a few steps distant from the son of the gods. Achilles, surprized at the visit, rises precipitately, his lyre still in his hands; Patroclus, who soon perceived them, rises also. Achilles gives them a very good reception and speaks to them in these terms: "Be welcome; you are certainly my friends; and that convinces me that the Greeks must be pressed by extreme necessity, since they send the greatest personages of the army, and those whom I esteem the most."

In concluding these words, he causes them to advance into the tent.

First prize, to John Augustin Ingres, born at Montauban, aged 20 years, a pupil of Citizen David.

Second prize, Jules Antony Vauthier, born at Paris, aged 27 years, a pupil of Citizen Regnault.

SCULPTURE.

The subject: "Gracchus quitting his House to repair to the public Place: Licinia, his Spouse, bathed in Tears, throws herself on her Knees, holding her Child, and endeavours to stop him. Gracchus gently withdraws himself from her arms, and walks, in profound silence, surrounded by his friends. She follows, endeavouring to hold him by his robe, falls down on the pavement, and remains there motionless."

I. First

I. First prize, to Joseph Charles Marin, a native of Paris, aged 37 years, a pupil of Citizen Claudion.

II. To Dominic Aimé Milhomme, born at Valenciennes, aged 35 years, pupil of Alegrin.

Second prize, to Joseph Alvarez, a native of Cordova, in Andalusia, aged 27, a pensioner of the King of Spain, and pupil of Citizen Dejeux.

ARCHITECTURE.

The subject of this prize, was "A Forum or Public Place, dedicated to Peace, and decorated with a triumphal arch to the glory of the French armies, and with two palaces;" one for the Minister of War, the other for the Minister for Foreign Affairs.

First prize, Auguste Pierre Sainte Marie Famin, of Paris, aged 24, pupil of Citizen Percier.

Second prize, Jean Baptiste Dideban, of Paris, aged 20, pupil of Citizens Vaudoyer and Percier.

The pupils who gain the first prize, will be sent to the French Academy of Fine Arts, at Rome, there to continue their studies at the charge of the Republic.

REVIEW OF NEW MUSICAL PUBLICATIONS.

Five Songs from the celebrated Opera of Artaxerxes, with all the Variations and Graces introduced by Mrs. Billington, at the Theatres Royal Drury-lane and Covent-garden. To which is added, a Piano-forte Accompaniment, newly arranged from the original Score, by Dr. Busby. 4s. *Rolfe.*

THIS collection consists of "Adieu thou lovely Youth"—"If o'er the cruel Tyrant, Love"—"Monster, away"—"Let not Rage thy Bosom firing"—and, "The Soldier tir'd of War's Alarms."

The novel as well as arduous task of committing to memory, and rendering permanent, the fleeting and evanescent sounds of extemporaneous embellishment, particularly excited our curiosity and attention, and we were not a little surprized to find on *paper*, all those beautiful *apogiatures, semi-tones, turns,* and *rapid flights,* which we had heard before, but which we thought, like the transient scintillations of a *feu d'artifice,* had been lost in air.

Admirers as we profess ourselves to be of the sweet and modest simplicity of Arne's native and original text, yet we cannot but highly commend many of these elegant and characteristic, though exotic, ornaments; and we are glad to find that we were deceived in supposing them too intricate and fleeting for scientific retention.

Among the most striking of these extempore beauties are, those in "Let not Rage,"—and in "The Soldier tir'd:"—In the variations in the repetition of the last division of the latter air, the voice rising by sixths instead of thirds, produces a fine relief, and bespeaks much theoretical knowledge, as well as a glowing and inventive imagination in the performer.

Dr. Busby, by giving permanency to these rare examples of high and finished execution, has furnished, to vocal practitioners a kind of *guida melodia.* Indeed, so perfectly calculated is it to improve and fix the general taste, that we hope he will oblige the musical world with similar publications from the *Duenna,* and other operas in which Mrs. Billington may hereafter appear.

The Review; or, Wags of Windsor: A Comic Opera, performed at the Theatre Royal Haymarket. The Words by George Colman, Esq. The Music composed by Dr. Arnold. 8s. *Caulfield.*

We find in the *Review* much of that easy pleasant style of composition by which Dr. Arnold's productions are generally distinguished. In the overture, consisting of three movements, we meet with a *gavolto,* written for the bassoon and hautboy, alternately, the style of which is simple, natural, and perfectly suited to the characters of those instruments. Among the airs, the most prominently pleasing are, "The poor little Gypsey," the plaintive melody of which is so engaging and persuasive, as to oblige us to attend to "The lesson she gives in her strain."—And, "Will my Love contented be," a cheerful pleasing little composition. The duo and chorus "When the Lark in Æther singing;" the glee "Bacchus and Apollo," the marches, and the finale also, contribute to the general good character of the piece, and merit our honourable notice.

Three Union Sonatas for the Piano-forte, with an Accompaniment for a Violin and Violoncello Obligato, in which are introduced several National Airs peculiar to each Country, composed by Sig. Rampini. 8s. *Lavenu.*

These sonatas, in which are introduced Dr. Arne's charming little air of "Sweetest of of pretty Maids," Harry Carey's "Sally of our Alley,"—"O the Roast Beef of Old England,"—"Come haste to the Wedding," and other old favourites, English, Irish, and Scotch, are written in a style much above that of the common productions of the day. All the introductory movements are conceived with taste and spirit, and by their gay and florid character frequently remind us of those of Bach, Abel, and Giordani. The national melodies are judiciously introduced, and the variations are constructed with ingenuity.

"Constancy," written by Peter Pindar, Esq. Composed by William Birch. 1s. Preston.

The melody of this canzonet, to which Mr. Birch has given a piano-forte accompaniment, is composed in an expressive style, and perfectly accords with the cast and sentiment of the words. The modulation, from the original key to its fifth, at the words "When thy beauty begins to depart," is particularly pleasing; and the closing the air by an ascent to the E in the fourth space, has a good effect. The introductory and intermediate symphonies we must not omit to notice; they are both tasteful and appropriate.

Notturno Quintetto, for the Harp, Two Violins, a Tenor, a Violoncello, composed and dedicated to the Countess of Shaftesbury, by Viscount De Marin. 7s. 6d. Clementi and Co.

This Notturno, which consists of an introduction and three succeeding movements, possesses considerable claims to our commendations. The passages are, for the most part, conceived with taste and spirit, and the accompaniments are so adjusted as to evince no slight knowledge in orchestral composition. The last movement, or *casaque*, arranged as a rondo, is both elegant and animated in its *motivo*, and forms a most agreeable close to the piece.

Number I, of The Bee, being a Selection of the most esteemed Vocal Productions, consisting of Songs, Duetts, and Glees, including the Compositions of Haydn, Mozart, Dr. Arne, Mr. Michael Arne, Jackson; Shield, Hook, &c. &c. adapted for the Piano-forte, Violin, or German flute. 1s. 6d. Longman.

This little work is printed in the same size, and on a similar plan, with the *Caledonian Museum*, and is intended to be comprized in twelve Numbers. The engraving is neat and correct; and of the contents the public will be enabled to judge, by being informed that they consist of "The Inconstant," (the melody from Mozart) "The Mansion of Peace," by Webbe, "The Morn in Saffron drest," by Paxton, "The Kiss," (the melody from Scultz) and "The Fair Thief," (the melody from Mozart.)

The celebrated Canon "Non Nobis Domine," adapted as a Fugue for four Voices (Treble, Counter-tenor, Tenor, and Bass) with two Violins, a Tenor, and a Bass, for the Accompaniments, and an Introduction, composed and calculated for a Grand Orchestra, by Joseph Diettenhofer. 3s. Preston.

Mr. Diettenhofer has displayed great depth of science in this publication. His introduction is elaborate and masterly, and evinces a familiar knowledge of the first secrets of *part* composition. We do not commit ourselves in saying, that Mr. Diettenhofer's additional matter is by no means unworthy of its intermixture with that of the great Bird, and that, performed by a full and able band, it would produce a striking and noble effect.

A Duetto, for two Performers on one Piano-forte, composed and dedicated to the Margravine of Anspach by John Jay. 5s. Goulding, Phipps, and D'Almaine.

Of this duetto we cannot speak in very high terms. The passages are not conceived with much spirit or taste, nor are the parts adjusted with that skill requisite to the producing the best effects in compositions of this kind. Here and there, however, we discover traits of talent, and have no doubt but that, by the aid of application and experience, Mr. Jay will become a very respectable composer.

Two Trios, selected from the Works of Mozart, arranged for the Harp, with Accompaniments for a Violin and Violoncello, by Viscount de Marin. 8s. Clementi and Co.

It is sufficient to say of these trios, that they contain a proper variety of movements; that some of the passages are graceful, and others brilliant, and that, in a word, they are every way worthy of their great author. Viscount de Marin, by his judicious arrangement, has rendered them excellent exercises for the instrument for which they are here intended, and the accompaniments are calculated to greatly heighten the general effect.

Number II, of the Caledonian Museum; or, the Beauties of Scottish Harmony, intended to form a select Collection of the most esteemed Songs for the Piano-forte, Violin, and German-flute. 1s. 6d. Longman.

In the present Number of this amusing, useful little publication, we find "Peggy I must

I must love thee"—"Lochaber"—"I'll never leave"—"Gilderoy"—"Tweed-side"—"Auld lang syne"—and "Johnny Fa." The neatness, clearness, and accuracy of the printing keep pace with our commendation of the first Number, and augur well of the future parts of the work.

"*When I beheld thy blue Eyes shine,*" *a Canzonet, with an Accompaniment, for two Performers on one Piano forte, adapted for three hands; composed by Joseph Kemp, Exeter, and inscribed to Miss Mary and Miss Emily Veale.* 1s. *Clementi and Co.*

The melody of this little song is by no means destitute of merit; nor is the accompaniment adjusted without meaning and effect; but the accent is not always just, nor is the bass the best that might have been chosen.

"*Human Life in a Mirror,*" *a Glee, for four Voices, composed by J. Marsh:* 1s. *Goulding, Phipps, and D'Almaine.*

Mr. Marsh has acquitted himself with much success in this glee. The sense of the words is forcibly conveyed, some *points* are well sustained by the responsive parts, and the harmony in general is sound and correct.

NEW PATENTS LATELY ENROLLED.

MR. ZACHARIAH BARRAT'S PATENT *for a* MILL *that is portable, and may be wrought by* WIND, WATER, *or* HORSES.

THE peculiarities of this mill are, that it is smaller or greater in size at the pleasure of the mechanist; runs upon castors; employs a crown-wheel, which, by three notched orbits, one still at some distance within another, gives motion to the mill-shaft, and is fitted by a slight alteration in the machinery, such as any workman may easily conceive, to be moved either by sails, horses, or water. It may be fitted up with sufficient convenience at the gable-end of a barn. In other respects, its machinery is not essentially different from that of a common mill.

MR. SPENCER'S (*of Duffield in Derbyshire*) PATENT *for a new* METHOD *of making* HORSE-SHOE NAILS.

In this method of making horse-shoe nails, Mr. Spencer provides *two rolls*; one which has longitudinal impressions to correspond to those parts of the iron-plate to be applied to it, which are to be thickened for the heads of the intended nails; the other, perfectly plain.

He then applies a plate of iron between these rolls, under a pressure, and in a heat, by which the parts for the heads of the nails may be thickened in the hollows of the roll which was so prepared.

The plate, after suffering this pressure, is cut, at the middle, between every two of the thickened parts, into pieces of a breadth equal to the length of two nails.

These pieces are then successively applied upon a bed with a punch, and subjected to the operation of a screw-press or any other adequate power. A piece consisting of two nails joined by the heads at its middle, is thus cut off.

This piece, consisting of two nails, is then applied upon another bed fitted with a separater. They are by the action of the separater, under a screw-press or other power, divided into single nails.

It is in the use of the rolls to make the impressions, and of the punches to press out the nails, that the peculiarity of this invention consists.

Being employed upon a matter of such extensive common utility; and affording a very great saving in time; it may be considered as an invention of very great value to the public.

MR. BENJAMIN HAWKINS'S (*of Red Lion-street, Clerkenwell, Middlesex, London*) PATENT *for a new* FLOATING MILL, *to be worked by Tides or Currents of Water, for grinding all sorts of grain, &c.*

Mr. HAWKINS'S contrivance *moors* the hulks of suitable vessels, or floats like those floating-baths which we see on the Thames, in situations in which any thing attached to them, shall be exposed to the force of a tide or current. It then erects the outer wheels and other exterior machinery of the proposed mill, on the out-side of the vessel or hulk, just as these are erected on the out-side of the walls of mills on land. The interior machinery of the mill, is, of course, within the vessel. The work of grinding is performed, with the greatest convenience and ease, under the action of the tide or current.

It is obvious, that there are, on the coasts

coasts, and in the rivers of Great Britain, many situations, in which, in a variety of easily supposable circumstances, the use of such mills might be, with great advantages, adopted.

In long voyages, grain more preservable than biscuit might be rather taken among the sea-stores, and with it, the machinery of such a mill as Mr. Hawkins's; which the carpenter could easily set up, occasionally, in a suitable boat, to furnish fresh flour, bread, &c. for the ship's crew.

MR. EDWARD WALKER'S (*of Rathbone-place, Mary-le-bonne, Middlesex*) PATENT *for a* PORTABLE STOVE, *or* KITCHEN, *for dressing Victuals.*

Mr. WALKER's portable kitchen is a construction of cast or wrought iron, in a square or oblong-square form. It has, at the middle of its front, a fire-place, with an ash-pit beneath, and for the conveyance of the smoke, a funnel above. A door shuts up the fire, while the kitchen is in use. In a closet on one side of the fire, is a convenience for roasting meat, consisting of two spits, with racks, &c. On the opposite side of the fire is another closet, for baking. The cover or top of this apparatus may be used as a broiling plate, or may sustain a pot or kettle for boiling. The whole apparatus is close on all sides. At each end is a door for the admission and removal of the bread and meat to be baked or roasted. The spits are turned by a smoke-jack which is fixed in the funnel.

For camps, barracks, hunting excursions, and every occasion in which meat is not to be had otherwise than cold or dressed in the open air, or in huts dirty to loathsomeness, the use of such a kitchen as this must be highly eligible. Pity but it could be made of lighter materials, so as to be more easily portable in travelling. It would be exceedingly serviceable to persons journeying through Spain or Portugal, or in the wilds of America.

MR. THOMAS GERMAN'S PATENT *for a new Method of* EFFECTING *the* ROTATORY MOVEMENT *of* WHEELED CARRIAGES.

Mr. GERMAN's contrivance consists simply in the *adaptation of castors moving round sledges* to perform for all wheeled carriages, those movements which are effected by their present wheels. He took the hint of the invention from considering the motions of vessels on the particles of water over which they float. He is yet to give corrections and elucidations of the specification of his patent, after examining which, we shall be enabled further to gratify public curiosity respecting a contrivance so ingenious.

Extracts from the Port-folio of a Man of Letters.

DR. YOUNG.

THE following are extracts from letters to Dr. Birch, by the curate and executor of Dr. Young. Although not very important, they give some notices of his domestic life, which merit preservation, and shew that a poet is not always the most prudent master. Some particulars throw a favourable light on the character of his son, who probably was not that gay and dissipated Lothario whom his father addressed; and indeed nothing is more common and unjust than applying in *toto* to individuals, characters employed by a poet or novelist. The narrative of some of the last moments of Young is authentic and interesting.

To Doctor Birch.

"SIR, *Wellwyn, Sept.* 4, 1762.

My ancient gentleman here is still full of trouble, which moves my concern, though it moves only the secret laughter of many; and some untoward surmises in disfavour of him and his household. The loss of a very large sum of money is talked of, whereof this village and neighbourhood is full. Some disbelieve; others say it is no wonder, where about eighteen or more servants are sometimes taken and dismissed in the course of a year. The gentleman himself is allowed by all to be far more harmless and easy in his family, than some one else who hath too much the lead in it. This, among many others, was one reason for my late motion to quit.

"JOHN JONES, his Curate."

"*Wellwyn, April* 2, 1765.

As soon as I got home, I enquired after Dr. Young, and found that he had gone through very great pains since the time when I had left him, and the pains return pretty frequently. Dr. Cotton, of St. Albans, and Dr. Yates, of Hertford, meet at

 his

his house every day on consultation. Opiates are frequently administered to him, I suppose to render him the less sensible of his pain. His intellects, I am told, are still clear; though what effect the frequent use of opiates may by degrees have upon him, I know not. I am pretty much of his son's sentiments as to this, viz. that those ingredients, if for some time longer continued, may have an ill-effect upon the brain. Having mentioned this young gentleman, I would acquaint you next, that he came hither this morning, having been sent for, as I am told, by the direction of Mrs. Hallows. Indeed she intimated to me as much herself. And, if this be so, I must say, that it is one of the most prudent acts she ever did, or could have done, in such a case as this, as it may prove a means of preventing much confusion after the death of the Doctor. I have had some little discourse with the son: he seems much affected, and I believe really is so. He earnestly wishes his father might be pleased to ask after him; for, you must know, he has not yet done this, nor is, in my opinion, like to do it; and it has been said farther, that, upon a late application made to him on the behalf of his son, he desired that no more might be said to him about it. Mrs. H. has fitted up a suitable apartment in the house for Mr. Young, where I suppose he will continue till some farther event. I heartily wish the ancient man's heart may grow tender towards his son; though, knowing him so well, I can scarce hope to hear such desirable news."

"*Wellwyn, April* 13, 1765.

I have now the pleasure to acquaint you, that the late Dr. Young, though he had for many years kept his son at a distance from him, yet has now at last left him all his possessions, after the payment of certain legacies; so that the young gentleman, who bears a fair character, and behaves well, as far as I can hear or see, will, I hope, soon enjoy, and make a prudent use of, a very handsome fortune. The father on his death-bed, and since my return from London, was applied to in the tenderest manner by one of his physicians, and by another person, to admit the son into his presence, make submission, intreat forgiveness, and obtain his blessing. As to an interview with his son, he intimated that he chose to decline it, as his spirits were then low and his nerves weak. With regard to the next particular, he said, *I heartily forgive him*; and, upon mention of the last, he gently lifted up his hand, and, letting it gently fall, pronounced these words—*God bless him!* After about a fortnight's illness, and enduring excessive pains, he expired, a little before 11 of the clock at night of Good Friday last, the 5th instant, and was decently buried yesterday, about 6 in the afternoon, in the chancel of this church, close by the remains of his lady, under the communion table; the clergy, who are the trustees of his charity-school, and one or two more, attending the funeral; the last office of interment being performed by me.

I know it will give you pleasure to be farther informed, that he was pleased to make respectful mention of me in his will, expressing his satisfaction in my care of his parish, bequeathing to me a handsome legacy, and appointing me to be one of his executors, next after his sister's son (a clergyman of Hampshire), who this morning set out for London, to prove the will at Doctors' Commons, so that, much according to my wishes, I shall have little or nothing to do in respect of executorship. J. JONES.

JOHN LAW.

This once celebrated personage, since the happy arrival of General Lauriston in this country, has once more become an object of curiosity. His history is instructive, yet little is to be found relating to him in our Biographical Dictionaries.

He was the author of the most considerable revolution that ever the finances of a nation experienced: France in one week appeared to enjoy incalculable millions, while in the following she was buried in bankruptcy.

Law was the son of an advocate at Edinburgh, and born in 1688. In London, he became enamoured of the sister of a lord (whose name I cannot discover). This lord, not approving of her marriage with an adventurer, challenged Law, and fell in the duel. Law immediately escaped into Holland, and was tried, convicted, and outlawed in England. Perhaps it was in Holland he acquired that turn of mind which pleases itself with immense calculations; he became an adept in the mysteries of exchanges and re-exchanges. From thence he proceeded to Venice and other cities, studying the nature of their banks. In 1709, he was at Paris the same speculative genius he had hitherto been.

At the close of the reign of Louis XIV. the French finances were in great disorder; and, having obtained an audience of that monarch, the bankrupt-king was much delighted by his projects. Law offered to pay the national debt by establishing a company whose paper was to be received with all possible confidence, and who were to make immense profits by their commercial

cial transactions. The minister Desmarest, to get rid of Law, threatened him, by one of his emissaries, with the Bastile. Law quitted Paris, and was a wanderer through Italy. He addressed himself to the King of Sardinia, who refused our adventurer's assistance, declaring, that he was not powerful enough to ruin himself!

At the death of Louis XIV. the Duke of Orleans was regent. Law ventured again to Paris, and found the regent more docile. The Duke indeed was placed in a most trying situation; the finances were all confusion, and no hope was offered by any one to settle them. The Duke lent his ear at first reluctantly to Law, convinced what consequences must follow such ideal wealth as that in which our adventurer dealt. In despair, the numerical-quack was called in to relieve, by his powerful remedy, the disorder which no one would attempt to cure.

Law commenced with a most brilliant perspective. He established his bank, was chosen director of the East India Company, and soon gave his scheme that vital credit which produced real specie; for, in that distracted time, every one buried or otherwise concealed his valuables; but, when the illusion of Law began to operate, every coffer was opened, while the proprietors of estates preferred his *paper* to the possession of their *lands*. All Europe seemed delighted, Law acquired millions in a morning, and even the Regent himself was duped, and felicitated himself on his possession of so great an alchymist.

Law was honoured with nobility, and created Count of Tankerville; as for marquisates, he purchased them at his will. Edinburgh, his native city, humbly presented him with her freedom, in which appear these remarkable expressions: "The corporation of Edinburgh presents its freedom to John Law, Count of Tankerville, &c. &c. &c. a most accomplished gentleman; the first of all bankers in Europe; the fortunate inventor of sources of commerce in all parts of the remote world; and who has so well deserved of his nation." From a Scotchman (says Voltaire) he became, by naturalization, a Frenchman; from a Protestant, a Catholic; from an adventurer, a prince; and from a banker, a minister of state.

While Law was undergoing these metamorphoses himself, he was performing the same droll exhibition in all kinds of individuals. Fortunes were made in a month, and stock-jobbing was seen even in the narrowest alleys at Paris. Singular anecdotes are recorded of those days.—A coachman gave warning to his master, who begged, at least that he would provide him with another as good as himself. Whip replied:—"I have hired two this morning; take your choice, and I will have the other."—A footman also set up his chariot, but going to it, he got up behind, till he was reminded by his own servant of his mistake.—An old beggar, who had a remarkable hunch on his back, haunted the *Rue Quincampoix*, which was the crowded resort of all stock-jobbers: he acquired a good fortune by lending it out for five minutes as a desk!

Law himself was adored; the proudest courtiers were humble reptiles before this mighty man; dukes and duchesses patiently waited in his anti-chamber; and Mrs. Law, a haughty beauty, when a duchess was announced, exclaimed, "Still more duchesses! there is no animal so tiresome as a duchess!" In the curious Memoirs of the Duchess of Orleans, a singular fact is recorded:—One morning, when Law was surrounded by a body of princesses, he was going to retire. They enquired the occasion. He gave one, in which they ought to have been silent; but, on the contrary, they said, "Oh! if it is nothing but that, let them bring here a *chaise percée* for Mr. Law!" When the young king was at play, and the stakes were too high even for his Majesty, he refused to cover them all; young Law (the son of our adventurer) cried out, "If his Majesty will not cover, I will." The King's governor frowned on the boy of millions, who, perceiving his error, threw himself at the King's feet.

The infatuation ran through all classes, and even the French Academy solicited for the honour of Law becoming their associate, the only *calculator* they ever admitted into their body.

But at length the evil hour looked dark and darker; the immense machine became so complicated, that even the head of Law began to turn with its rapid revolutions. In 1719, he created credit, but in May, 1720, uncounted millions disappeared in air. Nothing was seen but paper and bankruptcy every where. Law was considered as the sole origin of the public misfortune: no one taxed his own credulity. They broke his carriages, destroyed his houses, and sought the arithmetician to tear him to pieces. He escaped from Paris in disguise, and long wandered in Europe incognito. After some years, he found a hiding-place in Venice, where he lived poor, obscure, yet still calculating. Montesquieu, who saw him there, says, "He is is still the same man; his mind ever busied in financial schemes; his head is full of figures, of agios, and of banks. His fortune is very small, yet he loves to game high." Indeed of all his more than princely revenues, he only saved, as a wreck, a large white diamond, which, when he had no money, he used to pawn.

Voltaire saw his widow at Brussels. She was then as humiliated, as miserable, and as obscure, as she was triumphant and haughty at Paris. Such revolutions are not the least useful objects in history.

MACHIAVEL.

THE PRINCE of this profound observer of human nature is a work, which being diabolical in its principles, it has ingeniously been imagined, that the author meant it as an ironical work, like Swift's Advice to Servants, where you are very minutely informed how to do those things which ought not to be done, but which the writer was aware were constantly practised.

Some of his maxims are these: "When a man resolves to injure another, he should do it in such a manner as to cut off all possibility of revenge; if the injury is slight, he is able to return it; but, if it is done to the purpose, it is not in his power.

The Prince who would keep possession of a new acquisition, must, in the first place, take care to extinguish the whole family of the last reigning Prince.

The Prince who contributes to the advancement of another causes his own diminution of power.

When Cæsar Borgia inveigled, by reconcilement, several dukes, and strangled them as soon as they entered his palace, Machiavel says, that this evinced a great politician, and is worthy of imitation.

He says, that in the fable of Achilles educated by the Centaur Chiron we are to understand that a great Prince ought to be half man and half beast, and make the lion and the fox his pattern."

GIANTS.

Sir Walter Rawleigh's History of the World abounds with very eloquent passages. Writing on the GIANTS of antiquity, he gives the whole a very pleasing turn.

"It is certain that the AGE of TIME hath brought forth stranger and more incredible things than the INFANCY. For we have now GREATER GIANTS for vice and injustice, than the world had in those days for bodily strength; for cottages and houses of clay and timber, we have raised palaces of stone: we carve them, we paint them, and adorn them with gold, insomuch as men are *rather known by their houses*, than their houses by them. We are fallen from two dishes to two hundred; from water to wine and drunkenness; from the covering of our bodies with the skins of beasts, not only to silk and gold, but to the very *skins of men*. TIME will take REVENGE of the excess we bring forth!"

VARIETIES, LITERARY AND PHILOSOPHICAL.

Including Notices of Works in Hand, Domestic and Foreign.

**** Authentic Communications for this Article will always be thankfully received.*

LITERATURE may be said already to feel the return of Peace. Orders for books from the country and for foreign markets are given with less reserve, and various projects have been revived which had previously been suspended. In short, we have reason to suppose, that, in spite of oppressive duties, the present will be a busy winter, as well among the publishers as the retailers, and the readers and purchasers of books.

The complete edition of the British Poets, which had been abandoned on account of the high price of paper, has been resumed in consequence of the peace, and will be published with all convenient speed.

A History of the War, from the commencement of Hostilities between France and Austria, till the Peace with Great Britain, has been undertaken by Mr. ALEXANDER STEPHENS, and will make its appearance early in the ensuing spring, in two volumes, quarto, accompanied by maps and other suitable embellishments.

Dr. MAVOR has undertaken to edit a Popular View of Universal History, from the Creation of the World, till the Peace of London in 1801, to be completed in about twenty-five small volumes. The ignorance of the bulk of the English nation upon subjects of General History, may, in a great measure, be ascribed to the deficiency of our literature in popular

 histories.

histories. This intended work, by Dr. Mavor, will therefore be highly acceptable to the numerous persons to whom the great Universal History, in 66 volumes, 8vo. is either too expensive or too voluminous.

Mr. BERESFORD intends to publish a Translation of the interesting work of Kotzebue's, which he calls *an Account of the most remarkable Year of his Life*. He has been favoured by the author with the use of the original manuscript.

A novel will make its appearance, in a few days, from the pen of Miss PLUMPTRE, which, on account of the *ugliness* of her heroine, she entitles *Something New*.

The Memoirs of Mrs. INCHBALD may be expected to make their appearance in the course of the winter.

Some of the manuscripts of the late Rev. NEWCOME CAPPE are now in the press, and will be published early in the winter, together with the Memoirs of his Life, by Mrs. CAPPE. Among other Dissertations are the following: an Introduction to the Proem of St. John's Gospel, with a Paraphrase, Notes and Reflections. A Dissertation on the Scripture-meaning of the Terms, Kingdom of Heaven, of God, and of Christ. An Introduction to, and Paraphrase on the Discourse of Christ with Nicodemus.—A Dissertation, in two Parts, of the 11th of Philippians, 5—13, Christ in the Form of God; and a Paraphrase of the 5th and 6th Chapters of John's Gospel.

Dr. GARNETT having fitted up an elegant and commodious lecture-room, in Great Marlborough-street, intends, we understand, to begin his Lectures on Natural Philosophy and Chemistry immediately. The Introductory Lecture will be delivered on the 2d of November, at eight o'clock in the evening. The Lectures on Experimental Philosophy will be delivered every Monday and Friday, at the same hour; and those on Chemistry every Tuesday and Thursday, at one o'clock, P.M. The Medical Lectures will not commence till January, 1802.

A Course of Clinical Lectures on the Diseases and Operations of Surgery, will be delivered this winter, by Mr. BLAIR, of Great Russel-street. This Course will possess the obvious advantage, that the surgical practice of two considerable dispensaries will be open to the inspection of all the gentlemen who attend the Lectures.

Dr. BARRETT's splendid publication of the Ancient Manuscript of St. Matthew's Gospel, in the library of Trinity-college, Dublin, is expected in London in a few days. The learned and indefatigable editor described this valuable manuscript, near fifteen years since, in the first volume of the Transactions of the Royal Irish Academy; this notice of it attracted much attention from the learned in Great Britain, and on the Continent; particularly, as, of the 64 leaves of which the manuscript consists, 59 supply parts wanting in the Codex Alexandrinus. The Provost and Fellows of Trinity-College caused the *fac simile*, which Dr. Barrett had made, to be engraved at their own expence, and munificently presented him with the plates for publication. The work is beautifully printed, at the University-press, in royal 4to. and is the most splendid book ever printed in Ireland. In the first Part of the Prolegomena, the Doctor describes the Manuscripts, and enters largely into the subject of their antiquity. The second Part is a Dissertation on the Discrepancies in the Genealogies of St. Matthew and St. Luke, which are elaborately discussed.—After the Prolegomena, follow the 64 plates, in *fac-simile*, opposite to each of which is printed its contents in modern Greek characters, and at the foot of the page the *Variæ Lectiones*, some of which are curious and important.

Mrs. MACKIE, of Southampton, has in the press *A New Translation of Madame de Sevigné's Letters to her Daughter*, compressed into two small octavo volumes, and preserving every beauty, anecdote, and incident of the original, with the addition of several interesting Letters never before translated. The work will be embellished with engravings from genuine originals of Madame de Sevigné and her daughter.

The Rev. EDWARD DAVIES, Curate of Olveston, Gloucestershire, solicits the patronage of his friends and the public, in order to *enable him* to publish *An Essay on the first Introduction of the Art of Writing into the West of Europe, more especially into the British Islands; and another on the Nature and Origin of the Celtic Dialects.*

The Translation of CUVIER's Comparative Anatomy, which we have already noticed, will be published in the course of the ensuing month. It is translated by Mr. ROSS, and revised by Mr. MACARTNEY, Lecturer on Comparative Anatomy and Physiology in St. Bartholomew's Hospital.

Dr. TYTLER of the Cape of Good Hope, advertises the loss of some valuable manuscripts of the *Punics of Caius Silius Italicus*,

Italicus, in seventeen Books; translated into Ryme-verse by himself, and written by his own hand upon two hundred sheets of quarto. At the same time were stolen a packet of *Miscellanies*, some part prose; written on the same sort of paper and by the same hand: among which was one piece in the French language, in the hand-writing of the Earl of BUCHAN.

In January a First Number will make its appearance of the Costume of Turkey, Asiatic, as well as European; also including that of the Greek Islands of the Archipelago: in a series of coloured Engravings, illustrative of the singular and diversified Manners, Customs, and Dresses of those interesting Nations. Faithfully copied from drawings, taken on the spot, by OCTAVIAN DALVIMART, with Descriptions in English and French. It will be published by MILLER, who has acquired so much credit by his elegant work on the Costume and Punishments of China.

The Rev. COOPER WILLYAMS will speedily publish in quarto, A Voyage up the Mediterranean, in his Majesty's Ship the Swiftsure, one of the squadron under the command of Admiral NELSON. Several Views on the shores of Egypt and Syria, from drawings made by the author, on the spot, will be given to elucidate the description. The events attending the re-capture of Naples, and some Memoirs of the Court of Sicily, at Palermo, will be related: also some new light will probably be thrown on the cause of the horrible butcheries and disgraceful proscriptions which followed the re-capture.

It has been the misfortune of the proprietors of the new edition of Calmet's Dictionary, to find that the materials of paper bleached with the muriatic acid produce an article wholly useless. Signatures Z, A a, and B b of the fine paper copies in the third part of the Supplement have been printed on this over-bleached paper; and the consequence is, that the leaves fall to pieces by their own weight, and if squeezed in the hand crumble to powder. This kind of paper may be discovered by its acid taste when applied to the tongue; it is otherwise not to be detected till it is wet down for printing. The proprietors of Calmet will gladly exchange the three sheets printed on this kind of paper.

Sir W. OUSELY, after having published his learned Observations on the *Pehlavi* Medals of Dr. HUNTER's Museum, is now preparing moveable types to express the true and ancient *Pehlavi* character for his Treatise on the *Numismatick and Miscellaneous Antiquities of Persia*, to be published in the beginning of next year.

Mr. TILLOCH, the editor of the *Philosophical Magazine*, has published an Account of the Origin and Progress of *Stereotype Printing* in England, in which he bears so great a part. By this account it appears, that the *English Stereotype* is much anterior to DIDOT's invention in France, and has been practised by *Mr. Tilloch* himself for twenty years and upwards.

Citizen CHAPTAL, the French Minister of the Interior, has given orders to have the Babylonian inscriptions at Paris copied for Dr. HAGER, of this metropolis. As soon as *Dr. Hager* has received them, he intends to join them as an appendix to his Dissertation *on the newly-discovered Babylonian Inscriptions*, now printing.

The Abbé DELILLE, advantageously known for his Poem on the *Gardens*, has been engaged by the booksellers of *London* to translate *Milton's Paradise Lost* into French verse, for which he is to receive the sum of 1000l.

The Duke of *Brunswic-Oels* has ordered a monument to be erected to the late *M. Kästner*, the celebrated German mathematician, in the library of the university of *Gottingen*, with an inscription composed by the Duke himself. The bust of Kästner, with which this monument is decorated, is of *Carrara marble*.

The Academy of Sciences at Berlin has lately granted prizes for two memoirs concerning the question of the *Origin of Human Knowledge*: the first has been given to *M. Ben-david*, of Berlin; the second to *M. Degerando*, Professor of Philosophy at Paris.

The King of Prussia has bought for 80,000 rix dollars the library of the late *M. Forster*, Professor at *Halle*, with which the royal library at Berlin is to be enriched.

The new university for the provinces of *Finland*, *Esthland*, *Livonia*, and *Courland*, in Russia, will be established at *Dorpat*.

The royal cabinet of Natural History at *Madrid*, has been lately enriched by the return of the botanists, Don HIPPOLYTO RUIZ, and Don JOSEPH PAVON, from South America, with above fifty boxes filled with minerals, quadrupeds, birds, fishes, insects, shells, American monuments, seeds of different plants, barks, roots, gums, and balsams celebrated for their usefulness and medical virtue.

M. HAMMER, one of the gentlemen educated

educated in the Oriental Academy at *Vienna*, and at present employed in the Emperor's service at the Legation of Constantinople, has undertaken a literary excursion into *Asia-minor*, and chiefly in the province of *Troas*.

The celebrated FONTANA (formerly director of the Grand-duke's collection of natural history at *Florence*) who had retired to *Milan*, is returned to his former residence at *Florence*, where he is making very curious experiments on the *sensitive faculty* of *vegetables*, which experiments will soon be published.

By a decree of the Consuls of the French Republic, of the 3d of *Fructidor*, the *National Library* is to be removed from its present place (*Rue Vivierre*) into the *Louvre*, or the great palace joining the *Thuilleries*. In consequence of this decree, the private lodgers of that quarter are obliged to leave their apartments before the first of the next month (*Frimaire*). From that day, no fire of any kind will be permitted to be lighted in the whole circumference of the *Louvre*. The library will be completely established there during the course of the 11th year.

The Minister of the Interior has just published a *Programma*, in order to excite the artists to render their machines for working wool more perfect. To this end, after having ordered the machines hitherto known to be described and engraved, he has propose a first prize of 40,000 livres to the artist, who, before the 1st of *Messidor*, shall have constructed his machines of a degree of excellence the most advantageous to commerce; and a second prize of 20,000 livres, for the artist who shall have deserved the second best. The sentence of the jury will be proclaimed on the 1st of *Fructidor*, of the year 10; and in the same year the machines, which have received the premium, will be publicly exposed among other productions of French industry.

The Society of Sciences and Arts in the department of the *Gironde* is about to encourage plantations of trees in the cemeteries round the towns, and on the highways.

The King of Spain has lately given orders, that, through his whole kingdom, only one kind of weights and measures shall be used.

The Botanical Garden of *Madrid*, whose director at present is the Abbé CAVANILLES, has lately obtained a new organization. Its space is to be enlarged, so as to receive the *quinquina*, the *balm-tree*, the *sagou*, the *coco*, and other palm-trees. These precious plants were first transplanted from their native soil to the *Canary islands*, and thence to *Andalusia*, the most southern province of Spain. By this successive transplantation, they are accustomed to the climate of the capital, *Madrid*. It is to M. CEVALLOS, Minister of State, that Spain is indebted for its progress in natural history, and particularly in botany. His taste for plants has been communicated to a number of Spanish pupils. They sedulously frequent the lessons of *M. Cavanilles*, the only professor of that science at *Madrid*.

M. KANT, the German philosopher of *Königsberg*, has been elected an honorary member of the *Academia Italiana*, established at *Sienna* in the year 1799. The Count VARGAS, in his letter directed to him, says, among other things, that the Italian Academy has proposed particularly to make known his sublime philosophy in Italy.

Captain BAUDIN, on his voyage of discovery, left the *Isle de France* the 24th of April last, and was to that time safely prosecuting the objects of his voyage.

The celebrated German composer, HAYDN, is about to publish a new musical performance, under the title of "*The Last Judgment*."

The same gentleman has lately received the gold medal, coined on purpose, from the Musical Society of the *Théatre des Arts* at *Paris*, as a token of their high esteem for his talents displayed in the oratorio of "*The Creation*."

At *Vienna* there has been established a *Panorama* after the English fashion, in which *London*, from the point of the *Albion-mills*, is represented. At *Copenhagen* another Panorama will be erected, to exhibit the last naval battle in the *Sound*. M. LORENZEN, the aulic-painter, has just finished his great picture, in which the battle of the 2d of April is to be exhibited.

The King of Spain has ordered, that, in the capital of each province a Professorship of *Chemistry* and *Botany* shall be established.

A new Translation of Ossian's Poems, in poetical-prose, by SCHRÖDER has lately been published in Germany.

The celebrated artist, *M. Abramson*, at Berlin, has struck a medal on the accession of the present Emperor of Russia. One side represents the image of the Emperor in uniform, with an inscription in German: *Alexander I. Sovereign of all the Russias*; on the reverse is impressed a young Hercules, who, instead of the club, holds a rudder in his hand, embracing the

Goddess of Wisdom, whose shield is inscribed with the name of the late Empress Catherine II. in allusion to the first ukase of the Emperor, in which he declares to follow the principles of government adopted by that sovereign. The inscription is in German, *Strength* and *Wisdom*; underneath is engraved *d. 12 März*, 1801, the day when the Emperor came to the throne.

The French Minister of the Interior has lately issued a decree respecting the restoration of the famous groupe of *Laocoon*, which was formerly attempted by MICH. ANGELO, who however found his work not satisfactory. All statuaries are now invited to communicate models of arms for the three figures of the groupe to be examined by a committee, who will adjudge the prize to that model which is found worthy of the whole, and the artist whose work it is will be engaged by government to undertake the restoration, for which he is to receive the sum of 10,000 franks. For the first accessit 2000, and for the second 1200 franks are appointed.

It is reported that the bookseller FAUCHE, at Paris, has obtained the exclusive privilege of importing French books into the Russian empire, after he had presented his Majesty with a plan drawn up for that purpose.

There has been lately established at Paris a *Bureau de Legislation Etrangère*; or, an Office for Foreign Legislation; in which every law, civil, criminal, military, marine, or those respecting police and trade, of all European nations, are to be translated into the French language. The persons employed in this institution are the following: for the Flemish, P. H. MARRON, known by the share he has in the *Magazin Encyclopédique*; for the Italian, BOLDONI and PODOLERI: for the German, LAMEY and WINKLER, the last of whom has translated several German papers for the *Magazin Encyclopédique*. The directors of the institution are LA MIERRE, sworn translator of the northern and southern languages, and author of many translations from the English; and BROSSELARD, known by his translation of *Cicero de Officiis*, the second edition of which was printed last year.

Citizen DUVIVIER, at Paris, has struck a medal of eighteen lines in diameter, in memory of the well-known Abbé DE L'EPEE, late instructor of the deaf and dumb. As the image bears a striking likeness to the deceased, the minister of the interior has thought proper to distribute this medal in future as a prize in the Institution for the Deaf and Dumb. The inscription is *Charles de l'Epée, né à Versailles An 1712, mort à Paris en 1789*; on the reverse is read, *Au gemé Inventeur de l'Art d'instruire les Sourds Muets dans les Sciences et les Arts.*

Another medal has been lately struck at Paris on the Peace of Luneville, which is thought to be one of the best that has appeared during the Revolution. On one side is impressed the head of the Chief-consul, with the inscription, *Bonaparte Premier Consul de la Republique Française*; on the reverse, an upright standing figure, holding in one hand an olive branch, in the other a cornucopia, with the inscription, *La Paix de Luneville.*

The celebrated Dr. HUFELAND has published an address to the physicians of Germany respecting the Cow-pox; in which he earnestly solicits their attention to the following important queries:—"Is the Vaccine-inoculation a sure Preventive against the Small-pox; and, if it does not always secure against the small-pox, under what circumstances is it not found to be a Preventive?"—"Does the Poison imparted by the Vaccine-inoculation produce any mischievous change or degradation in the organization, from which evil effects might be apprehended, after having recovered from the disease itself?"—In order to bring into one point of view all the experience relative to these points, so that satisfactory results may thence be drawn, Dr. Hufeland invites all those who have practised the vaccine-inoculation in Germany, to inform him as concisely and distinctly as possible how many subjects they had inoculated—On how many they had afterwards tried the effects of inoculation with the small-pox?—Whether any of these latter had been infected with the small-pox; and, in such cases, what was the state of the matter with which the patient was inoculated, and what the symptoms of the disease that was the consequence of the inoculation?—Whether dangerous or fatal accidents had occurred in the cow-pox?—Whether any diseases, or even sickliness, have afterwards followed, which seemed to have a connexion with the cow-pox?—Whether the disease be found on the cows in various places, and the accidental infection of men, and the thereby effected security from the small-pox, had been there observed?—All the reports sent to him Dr. Hufeland means to publish in his Journal, which, as it is read by almost every physi-

cian

cian in Germany, he thinks a very proper receptacle for the documents necessary towards a final decision of this important controversy. Mr. Hufeland concludes his address, by requesting his colleagues to be on their guard against prejudice or partiality in their investigations and reports; for, says he, "it is not the interests of the vaccine inoculation, but the good of mankind and truth, that is our object; and therefore unsuccessful experiments are as important and interesting to us as those which have been attended with success."

An analysis has lately been made by VAUQUELIN of the *sour water of the starch-makers*, a liquor produced in great quantity during the maceration of the wheat in this manufactory, and which has hitherto been thrown away as useless. It is of a turbid milky-white colour, of a slightly acid and spirituous odour, and a sour and somewhat putrescent taste. By being passed through a filtering paper, it becomes clear and colourless. Twelve thousand parts of unfiltered *sour water* were distilled in a copper alembic; the first five hundred that came over contained nearly all the spirit, which, being rectified, yielded 30 parts of a pure inflammable alcohol, but of an unpleasant flavour: the remaining 11,500 parts being distilled off clear, were found to have a strong acid taste, and dissolved readily 288 parts of litharge; this solution being evaporated, and set to crystallize, afforded 384 parts of acetite of lead (sugar of lead). By further analysis, the other component parts of the *sour-water* were obtained, from which it appears to consist of acetous acid, ammonia, phosphat of lime, animal matter, and alcohol. In an economical point of view, all the ingredients, except the first and last, may be neglected, and the method of making the most profit out of it will be to distil the liquor, reserving the first runnings for rectification, and making sugar of lead of the remainder. From these data, 120 gallons of the *sour-water* should yield about three pints of alcohol (rectified spirit), and thirty-two pounds and a half of acetite of lead (sugar of lead).

The use of fumigations as an antidote to putrid-air has been examined into with much care by MORVEAU: he inclosed a quantity of infected air in a jar, and kept it in contact with perfumes of various kinds; this being afterwards washed, the putrid smell remained as strong as at first: no better success attended the alcoholic solutions of myrrh, benzoin, &c. the weak acids, such as vinegar, &c. the pyraligneous acid had no effect; neither had concentrated sulphuric acid any: sulphureous acid in part took away the bad smell; but the nitric, muriatic, and especially the oxymuriatic acid, instantaneously destroyed every trace of the fœtor. Air highly charged with the effluvia of putrid flesh exhibited neither acid nor alkaline properties, and the cause of this loathsome smell is, at present at least, beyond the power of chemical analysis.

The flexible sand-stone of Brazil is well known to all mineralogists, and M. FLEURIAU DE BELLEVUE, of Rochelle, has succeeded in giving this quality of flexibility to Carara marble; thin slips of which being exposed in a sand-bath to a certain temperature become so far weakened in their power of cohesion as to be very sensibly flexible.

A singular discovery has lately been made in Spain. In digging the foundation for a bridge, the workmen met with six small eggs, which, upon examination, bore a near resemblance to those of patridges; their colour is a yellowish white: they effervesce with nitric-acid. One of them being divided with the saw, the yolk was found flattened, and reduced to a line in thickness, and the whole of the rest of the cavity was filled with beautiful crystals of prismatic calcareous spar.

Much doubt has of late existed among chemists about the sebacic acid; some maintaining it to be nothing but acetous acid, while others consider it as possessed of peculiar properties. A paper of Citizen THENARD, presented to the *Société Philomathique*, contains several important researches into the nature of this substance. Sebacic-acid may be obtained by distilling animal-fat with a naked fire, and washing the product in warm water, which, when evaporated, deposits the acid which it had dissolved in needle-shaped crystals; or, the water holding the acid in solution, may be saturated with potash; if to this acetite of lead is added, a copious precipitate falls down, which is sebat of lead, and this being decomposed by sulphuric acid affords pure sebacic acid. This salt has a slightly acid taste, is without smell, is much more soluble in hot than in cold water, from which, by gentle evaporation, it may be obtained in the form of large brilliant plates: it precipitates and decomposes acetite and nitrat of lead, nitrat of silver, and acetite and nitrat of mercury; with potash it forms a permanent, soluble, insipid, salt; it does not render turbid

turbid the water of lime, barytes, or strontian. If the produce of the distillation of fat is washed in water, and this water saturated with potash, there is produced a saline mass, which, when heated in a retort with sulphuric acid, yields vapours of acetous acid; hence originates the error of those who imagined the sebacic and acetous acids to be the same.

Since the abolition of the game-laws in France, not only every species of game, but even the commoner birds, have almost been exterminated in several parts of that country. To prevent the entire depopulation of the woods and fields, some regulations have lately been adopted in some of the departments, of which the following proclamation of C. BOUQUEAU, Prefect of the Rhine and Moselle, is an example. It runs thus—"Whereas there has been for several years so great a destruction of game and birds of every kind, that the forests are quite deserted; and it becomes necessary to take as many precautions to prevent the entire extermination of useful and innocent animals, as it was in the feudal times to destroy the noxious beasts:—the Prefect, conformably with several laws and decrees which exist, but have not been put in force, forbids hunting in those seasons and places in which it would be prejudicial to the public and private territories, to the fruits of the earth, and the re-production of useful animals." The destruction of wild animals has perhaps been too much recommended in France. Those, at least, which form a part of the food of man, such as the hare, should not be wantonly destroyed, as they are now, by every youngster who can fire a gun, and who does not scruple to kill the female big with young. Still less should those animals be molested which render essential services to man by removing various nuisances and noxious insects, such as the swallow, the crow, and a number of other birds; and the lover of nature will plead for those which are entirely innoxious, and enliven the country with their songs, as the linnet, the goldfinch, and the nightingale. The following fact may serve to shew that very essential service is done to man by some animals which he has proscribed as noxious. Some years ago, a Prussian nobleman revived on his territories an ancient law, which imposed on the peasants an annual tribute of a certain number of sparrows' heads and crows' feet. As his design was well-intended, he required this tribute to be paid in kind. Soon the crows no longer dared to follow the ploughshare, and the whole race of sparrows appeared to be exterminated in several villages. It was not long before the inhabitants felt the inconvenience of this practice. Caterpillars of every kind devoured the leaves of the trees, and all the garden vegetables, for several years successively. The clergyman of the place attributed this to the destruction of the birds; and the nobleman, who was soon convinced of the same, abolished the tribute, and even brought back sparrows into some of the villages from which they had been entirely exterminated. Another fact of the same kind will serve to confirm the above observations concerning the vast utility of many species of birds. In the year 1798, the forests of Saxony and Brandenburgh were attacked with a general mortality. The greater part of the trees, especially the firs and different kinds of pine, whose bitter and aromatic branches are rarely the prey of insects, died as if struck at their roots with some secret malady. It was not here, as too often happens, that the foliage alone was devoured by caterpillars, but these trees perished without shewing any external sign of disease. This calamity became so general that the regency of Saxony sent naturalists and skilful foresters to find out the cause. They soon found it in the unusual multiplication of one of the *lepidoptera* insects, which, whilst a worm, insinuated itself within the tree, and fed upon the wood. Whenever any bough of fir or pine was broken, this detestable insect was found within it, which had often hollowed it out to the very bark. From the report of the naturalists and most experienced foresters, it seemed highly probable that the extraordinary increase of this insect was owing to the entire disappearance of some species of woodpeckers and titmice, which had not for some years been seen in the forests. The above insect, in its larva-state, was a large, white, soft-bodied, caterpillar, with twelve rings, and a hard and corneous head, furnished with very strong jaws, extremely proper for gnawing wood. On the breast it had two tubercles, and beneath its body short and fleshy legs. It turned into a moth of remarkable size and beauty.

LIST OF NEW PUBLICATIONS IN OCTOBER.

ANTIQUITIES.

Grecian Antiquities; or, An Account of the Public and Private Life of the Greeks, relating to their Government, Laws, Naval and Military Officers, Religion, Games, Marriages, Funerals, Food, Drefs, Mufic, Painting, Public Buildings, &c. chiefly defigned to explain Words in the Greek Claffics, according to the Rites and Cuftoms to which they refer. To which is added, A Chronology of Remarkable Events in the Grecian Hiftory. By the Rev. Thomas Harwood, 8vo. 9s. boards. Cadell and Davies.

BIOGRAPHY.

Public Characters of 1801-2; being a new Volume of Biographical Memoirs of Eminent Living Perfons, faithfully and impartially drawn from authentic Sources, 8vo. 10s. 6d. boards. Phillips.

COMMERCIAL.

Commercial and Notarial Precedents, confifting of all the moft approved Forms which are required in Tranfactions of Bufinefs; including the whole Practice of Notary and Conveyancer, as far as regards Trade and Commerce; and intended for the Ufe of Merchants, their Clerks and Agents, at Home and Abroad; to which is added, An Abftract of Commercial Law, exhibiting the Subftance of all the Acts of Parliament relating to Trade and Commerce, and which are neceffary to be known or confulted by a Man of Bufinefs: By Jofhua Montifiore, Attorney and Notary Public in the City of London, 4to. 1l. 1s. boards. Phillips.

The United Monthly Shipping Lift, containing correct Defcriptions and the prefent Situation of the Merchant Veffels of Great Britain and Ireland, embracing, among other Intelligence, the Tonnage, Captain or Commander, Owner or Broker, and Age and Condition of every Veffel, Corrected to the 1ft of November, 1801, 2s. Steele and Phillips.

DRAMA.

Euripidis Medea, ad Fidem Manufcriptorum emendata, et brevibus Notis, Emendationum potiffimum Rationes reddentibus, inftructa. In Ufum ftudiofæ Juventutis. Edidit Ricardus Parfon, A. M. 3s. 6d. Wilkie.

Remarks on the Character of Richard the Third, as performed by Cooke and Kemble, 2s. 6d. Parfons and Son.

Holiday Time; or, The School Boy's Frolic, a Farce, as performed at the Theatre Royal Norwich: By Francis Latham, 1s. 6d. Longman and Rees.

EDUCATION.

Poetry for Children, confifting of fuch Pieces as may be committed to Memory at an early age: By Mifs Aikin, 2s. 6d. Phillips.

Mentor; or, The Moral Conductor of Youth from the Academy to Manhood, adapted to the Level of Youthful Underftanding; to which is annexed, An Effay on the Utility of Mathematical Learning, defigned as an Incitement to Youth to the Study of it during their leifure hours: By David Morrice, Author of the Art of Teaching, &c. 7s. boards. Rivingtons.

The Little Hermitage, with other Tales, Plates, 2s. 6d. Phillips.

The Juvenile Plutarch; or, Lives of celebrated and extraordinary Children: Plates, 2s. 6d. Phillips.

Vifits to the Menagerie and Botanical Garden, 2 vols. Plates, 4s. Phillips.

LAW.

The Laws refpecting Travellers and Travelling, comprifing all the Cafes and Statutes relative to that Subject, including the Ufing of hired Horfes, Robbery, Accidents, Obftructions, &c. upon the Road, and Land and Water-carriage in general; alfo the Laws relating to Innkeepers, 8vo. 3s. fewed. Clarke and Son.

Precedents of Warrants, Convictions and other Proceedings before Juftices of the Peace, chiefly original, and not containing any that are in Burn's Juftice; to which this Publication is offered as a Supplement: Interfperfed with Notes, References to Cafes, and Obfervations, by Richard Williams, Efq. Barrifter at Law, 8vo. 10s. 6d. boards. Pheney.

MILITARY.

Confiderations of the Reafons that exift for reviving the Ufe of the Pike and Long Bow, with the Exercife of the fame, by Richard Ofwald Mafon, Efq. 5s. 6d. Egerton.

MEDICAL.

The Principles of Surgery, (vol. 1,) as they relate to Wounds, Ulcers, and Fiftulas, Aneurifms and wounded Arteries, Fractures of the Limbs, and the Duties of the Military and Hofpital Surgeon: By John Bell, Surgeon, Royal 4to. illuftrated by Engravings, accurately coloured from Nature, 4l. 4s. boards. Cadell and Davies.

Obfervations on the Marfh Remittent Fever, more particularly in regard to its Appearance and Return every Autumn, after the Inundation from the Sea, on the firft of January, 1795, and the five fucceeding Years, at Lynn, and its Environs. Alfo, on The Water-canker, or Cancer Aquaticus of Van Swieten, with fome Remarks on the Leprofy; by the late Robert Hamilton, M. D. of King's Lynn, F. R. S. Edinburgh, &c. with Memoirs of the Author's Life, 8vo. 4s. fewed. Mawman.

First Lines of Phyfiology, by Albert Von Haller; tranflated from the third Latin Edition, with a Tranflation of the Index, printed under the Inspection of Dr. William Cullen, 8vo. 10s. 6d. boards. Murray and Highley.

New Progress of Surgery in France, or Phenomena in the Animal Kingdom, published by Command of the French Government, translated from the French of Imbert Delonnes, M. D. by T. Chavernac, Surgeon, embellished with curious Plates by W. Nutter, 4s. Kay.

A Short Account of the Island of Madeira, with Instructions to those who resort thither for the Recovery of their health, by Joseph Adams, M. D. Physician in the Island, 1s. Longman and Rees.

Elements of Chemistry, by J. Murray, Lecturer on Chemistry, &c. 2 vols. 8vo. 12s. boards. Longman and Rees.

An Introduction to the Studies of the Animal Economy, translated from the French of Cuvier, by John Allen, Surgeon, Edinburgh, 2s. Longman and Rees.

MISCELLANIES.

Dodsley's Annual Register, vol. 42, for the Year 1800, 10s. 6d. boards. Otridge, and other Proprietors.

The Speech of the Hon. Charles James Fox, on the Restoration of Peace; to which is added, An Hymn to Peace; with the Proceedings at the Shakespear Tavern, on Saturday, October 10, 1801, being the Anniversary of Mr. Fox's first Election for Westminster, 1s. Jordan.

Senilities; or, Solitary Amusements, in Prose and Verse, with a cursory Disquisition on the future Condition of the Sexes, by the Editor of The Spiritual Quixotte, Crown 8vo. 6s. boards. Longman and Rees.

The New Annual Register for the Year 1801; to which is prefixed, The History of Knowledge, Learning, and Taste, in Great Britain, during the Reign of Charles II. 14s. boards. Robinsons.

A Narrative, founded on a Series of Events which took place in the Island of St. Marcou, by James Gomm, Esq. late Commander of the Tickler Gun-vessel, 1s. Steele.

New Joe Miller, vol. 2, and last, 3s. sewed. Ridgway.

Letters from Eliza to Yorick, transmitted from a Gentleman in Bombay, and now first published, small 8vo. 3s. unbound. Ginger.

NOVELS.

Atala; or, The Amours of Two Indians in the Wilds of America, with Frontispiece, 12mo. 4s. boards. Didier and Tebbett.

Letitia; or, The Castle without a Spectre, by Mrs. Hunter, of Norwich, 4 vols. 12mo. 1l. 1s. boards. Longman and Rees.

The Spinster's Tale, in which is introduced Landbridge Fort, a Romance, by Ann Wingrove, of Bath, 3 vols. 10s. 6d. sewed. Dutton.

Ariel; or, The Invisible Monitor, 4 vols. 12mo. 18s. sewed. Lane.

The Mysterious Husband, by the Author of the Mysterious Wife, 4 vols. 12mo. 18s. sewed. Lane.

The Welshman, A Romance, by William Earle, jun. Author of Natural Faults, a Comedy, &c. 4 vols. 12mo. 16s. sewed. Earle and Hamet.

POETRY.

Jacobinism, a Poem, 4to. 3s. 6d. Nicol.

POLITICAL.

Political Recollections relative to Egypt, containing Observations on its Government under the Mamelucks, its Geographical Position, its Resources, its relative Importance to England and France, and its Dangers to England in the Possession of France; with a Narrative of the British Campaign in the Spring of 1801, by George Baldwin, Esq. late King's Consul in Egypt, and attached to the Commander in Chief during the above Campaign, 6s. boards. Cadell and Davies.

The Preliminary Articles of Peace, as ratified between Great Britain and France, with Observations, &c. 6d. H. D. Symonds.

Reflections on the Preliminaries of Peace between Great Britain and the French Republic, by Benjamin Flower, 4d.—3s. 6d. per dozen—or a guinea per hundred. Crosby and Letterman.

The immediate Causes, and remote Consequences, of the Peace, considered, 1s. Thurgood.

TRAVELS.

Travels in Greece and Turkey, undertaken by Order of Louis XVI, and with the Authority of the Ottoman Court, by C. S. Sonnini, 4to. with Plates, 2l. 12s. 6d. boards. Longman and Rees.

THEOLOGY.

A Sermon preached at Knaresborough, for the Benefit of the Sunday Schools, Aug. 16, 1801, by the Rev. Samuel Clapham, 1s. Rivingtons.

A New Version of the Psalms of David, by Joseph Cottle, Fool's-cap 8vo. 4s. boards. Longman and Rees.

The Church of England vindicated from Misrepresentation, shewing her genuine Doctrines as contained in the Articles, Liturgy, and Homilies, with a particular Reference to "The Elements of Christian Theology, by the Bishop of Lincoln:" By a Presbyter of the Church of England, 8vo. 3s. Mawman.

An Essay on Religion, pointing out the Beauty and Excellence of the Christian Doctrine, and the Necessity of an early Attention to it, addressed to Young Persons, by John Fullager, 6d. Rivingtons.

Scripture Biography, containing the Lives, Actions, and Characters of the most important Personages of the Old and New Testament, interspersed with Moral and Practical Observations, by the Rev. John Watkins, L. L. D. 5s. Phillips.

Practical Lectures on the proper Lessons in the Old Testament, by F. T. Travell, A. M. 5s. Rivingtons.

A Layman's Account of his Faith and Practice, as a Member of the Episcopal Church in Scotland; to which are added, Forms of Prayer for assisting the Devotion of private Christians, with a Letter from the Rev.

Charles Daubeny, on the Subject of Ecclesiastical Unity, 12mo. 2s. 6d. boards.
Rivingtons.

The Importance of Religion to the Military Life; A Sermon, preached September 6, 1801, at the Garrison Service, in the Church of St. Peter's Port, Guernsey, by Thomas Brock, A. M. 1s. 6d. Rivingtons.

Discourses on the Scriptural Doctrines of Atonement and Sacrifice, with additional Remarks on the Arguments advanced and the Mode of reasoning employed by the Opponents of those Doctrines, as held by the Established Church; and some Strictures on Mr. Belsham's Review of Mr. Wilberforce's Treatise; by the Rev. William Magee, D.D. 8vo. 9s. boards Cadell and Davies.

New French Books, just imported by J. Deboffe, Gerrard-street, Soho.

Bibliothéque Françoise, a French Monthly Review, conducted by the following celebrated French writers, viz.—Berthollet, Desmarais, Labillardiere, Laffus, Lacroix, Teiffier, Langles, Laporte Dutheil, Leblond, Emanuel, Toulongeon, Valmont Bomare, Molé, Villeterque, Legouvé, (all Members of the French National Institute); Fortia, D'Urban, Delamalle, Paul Urtery, Chardon Larochette, Maton, Beufflers, Segur l'armé, &c.—Mesdames Beaufort, d'Hibuet, Poul, Henriette Bourdie, Viot, Louise St. Leon, Helêne Maria Williams, Legroing, Lamaironneuve, &c. Subscription 1l. 11s. 6d. per ann.

Histoire Naturelle des Minéraux, par Patrin, 5 vols. 18mo. coloured plates; this work accompanies a new and handsomely printed Edition of Buffon (including a History of the Fish tribe) by Cartel.

Les Chevaliers des 7 Montagnes; ou, Aventures arrivées dans le 13me Siècle, 3 vols. 9s.

Du Commerce Maritime, et de son Influence sur la Richesse et la Force des Etats, par Auduin, 2 vols, 8vo. 9s.

Daudin, Histoire Naturelle des Quadrupédes, et des Ovipares, the 1st and 2d liv. 4to. fine paper, coloured plates, 10s. 6d.

Ditto, common paper, 7s. 6d.

De la Fièvre en général, de la Rage, de la Fièvre Jaune, et de la Peste, par Reich, 2s. 6d.

Des Causes des Révolutions, et de leurs Effets, par Blanc de Volx, 2 vols. 12s.

Dictionnaire Portatif de Prononciation Espagnol-François et François-Espagnol, par Cormon, 2 vols, 12s.

Essais Historiques sur la Révolution de France, avec des Notes, par Beaulieu, 2 vols. 14s.

Essai sur l'Art de rendre les Révolutions utiles, 2 vols 8vo. 12s.

Choix d'Œuvres Dramatiques de Goldoni, François et Italien, 3 vols. 18s.

Histoire des Pêches, des Decouvertes, et des Etablissemens des Hollandois dans les Mers du Nord, 3 vols. 1l. 7s.

Histoire du Directoire Exécutif de la République Françoise, depuis son Installation jusqu'à sa Chûte, 2 vols. 14s.

Histoire Universelle, en Style Lapidaire, par Anquetil, 8vo. fine paper, 12s.

Homère et Alexandre, Poeme, par Lemercier, 4s.

Precis Historique de la Révolution Françoise, par Lairetelie, pendant l'Assemblée Legislative; servant de Suite à l'Histoire de la Révolution, par Rabaut de St. Etienne; fine paper, proof plates, 8s.

Ditto, common paper, 4s. 6d.

Cours de Littérature, par Laharpe, vol. 11, and 12, in 3 vols. 8vo. 18s.

Ditto, vols. 11 to 14, 12mo. 14s.

Promenade d'un François en Grande Britagne, Irlande, Suède, et Norvége, accompagnée des Causes de la Révolution Françoise, par M. Latoenaye, 5 vols. 1l. 5s.

Lettres de la Vendée, écrites en Fructidor, An 3, jusqu'à Nivose, An 4, 2 vols. 6s.

Nouveau Dictionnaire de Santé, d'Education, Physique, et Morale, par Macquart, 2 vols. 15s.

Cours Diplomatique; ou, Tableau des Relations Extérieures des Puissances de l'Europe, par Martens, vols. 1 and 2, 8vo. 1l 4s.

Médicine du Voyageur, par Duptanil, 3 vols. 18s.

Mémoires sur la Vie et les Ecrits de Saussure, 3s.

De l'Influence attribuée aux Philosophes, aux Francs-Maçons, et aux Illuminés sur la Révolution Françoise, par Mounier, 6s.

Essai sur le Hauchiment, par O'Reilly, 8vo. 7s. 6d.

Palmira, Romance, par Madame Amande R***, 4 vols. 14s.

Politiques de tous les Cabinets de l'Europe, par Segur, l'aîné, 3 vols. 18s.

By C. Geisweiller, Parliament street.

Knauer Selectus Instrumentorum Chirurgicorum, folio, Vindob, 1801, cum 25 tab.

Lefebure über den Schwarzen Staar, 1801, 5s. sheets.

Traité de l'Innoculation Vaccinne, par Ballhorn et Séromeyer, avec fig. 1801, 6s. 6d. sewed.

Adelungs Wörterbuch der Hochdeutschen Mundart, 4ter. und letzter Band, 1801, 1l. 18s. 6d.

Schillers Macbeth eingerichtet für das Hoftheater zu Weimar, 1801, 5s. 6d. sewed, f. p.

Schillers Maria Stuart, 1801, 6s. 6d. sewed, f. p.

Schillers Geschichte des Abfalls der Vereinigten Niederlande von der Spanischen Regierung, neu bearbeitet, 2 vols, 1801, 16s. sewed.

Translations of German Poems, German and English, 1801, 6s. 6d.

Archenholtz, Geschichte Gustavus Wasa 1801, 2 vols, 1l, 1s. sewed, f. p.

Cramer

Cramer, Der Polter Abend, 2 vols. 12s. sewed.

Cramer, das Harfen Mædchen, 8s. 6d. sewed.

Freymaurer Lieder zum Logen Gebrauch, 2 vols. 8s. sewed.

Huber, Erzæhlungen, 1801, 7s. 6d. sewed.

La Roche, Schönes Bild der Resignation, 2 vols. 1801, 12s.

Kotzebue, Die Kluge Frau im Walde, 3s. 6d. sewed.

Marianens Reise und Schicksale, 1801, 5s. 6d. sewed.

Reise von Wien nach Venedig, 1800, 8s. sewed.

Reise von Wien nach Madrid, 5s. 6d. sewed.

Theodor König der Korsen, 3 vols. 1801, 15s. sewed.

Iflands Dramatische Werke, 15ter, Band.

Schlegel— Shakspeare übersetzt von, 7 vols. 1801, 2l. 16s. sheets.

MONTHLY RETROSPECT OF THE FINE ARTS.

(*Communications and the Loan of all new Prints are requested.*)

The Assault and Taking of Seringapatam, on the 4th of May, 1799. Dedicated by permission to his Majesty, by Anthony Cardon and L. Schiavonetti. Painted by H. Singleton, and engraved by A. Cardon.

TAKEN altogether, this is a singularly lively and bright print, but in such a subject we expected to have seen a greater number of figures. The action seems desultory, and impresses the spectator with the idea of a flying skirmish, rather than the regular and formidable attack of a powerful army on a strongly fortified city. It is admirably engraved in the chalk manner. The contrast between the Eastern and European soldiers is well understood, and accurately described.

The Body of Tippoo Sultaun recognised by his Family. Dedicated to the Hon. the India Company. Painted by R. K. Porter. Engraved by L. Schiavonetti. Published by L. Schiavonetti, No. 12, Michael's Place, Brompton; and Anthony Carden, No. 31, Clipstone-street, Fitzroy-square. Price of this, and the preceding print, to which it is intended to be a companion, 4l. 4s.

This is a very good design; the figure of Tippoo is simple and interesting, and the group which surrounds him, is disposed in an easy and natural style. Considering how much our East India transactions have lately engaged the attention of the public, there is every reason to think that these two prints, from their subjects, as well as from their intrinsic merit, will excite a general interest.

The Woodman. Painted by S. Drummond. Engraved and published by W. Barnard, Fitzroy-square.

The Shepherd—companion print. Printed by G. Morland. Engraved and published by W. Barnard. Price of the pair, 3l. 3s. in colours.

The first of these designs does great credit to the taste and talents of Mr. Drummond; it is a simple, and well-chosen copy of nature. The head is well imagined, and the minutiæ of dress marked with a judicious accuracy, which we have seldom seen attended to, except in Barker's Woodman, from which it has the additional merit of being totally different. He has taken nature, and nature only, for his model; and whoever does so, will assuredly produce originality; while the vapid copier of a copy will give a feeble *shadow of a shade*, which, like a translation from a translation, will retain little of the spirit of the original. It adds another leaf to the laurel of Drummond, that the companion-print, by so exact an imitator of nature as Morland, representing a *Shepherd-boy*, is a very inferior design. It is a common-place attitude, and has not, in any part of it, that sweet simplicity, and rustic ease, which we generally find in the delineations of this artist. The truth is, we have here what is, perhaps, the best design Drummond ever made, contrasted with one of the worst of Morland's. These, also, are sold in colours, a gaudy fashion, which we are sorry to see prevail so much; but our modern artists, in making their prints so *fine*, act on somewhat the same principle as the painter, who, because he could not design *a hand*, gave his figure a pair of *point lace ruffles*.

Landing of William III. at Torbay, on the 4th of November, 1668, in Company with the Dukes of Schomberg, Leeds, &c. Painted by James Northcote, Esq. Engraved by James Parker, R. A. Published by John Harris.

The hero, William, in complete armour, with five other figures, are here exhibited on a platform. On the ground beneath them are a number of heads and bodies of gentlemen, mariners, trumpeters and horses. On the same platform with the monarch, and placed in the right-hand corner,

corner, is a bishop, holding a book inscribed *The Holy Bible*; and near him a flag, on which is written, ***For the Protestant religion, and the liberty of England.*** In the back ground is part of a ship, boats landing troops, &c. &c. and on a hill in the distance are an immense crowd of spectators, shouting welcome to their great deliverer. There are parts of this print that are good, but it does not form a *whole*, and the platform is confused, so as to appear like a great table. It would have had a better effect if the plate had been broader, for the heads of the figures come too near the top of the print. It is well engraved in line.

You Can't Spell! You Can't Write!—companion prints. Painted by W. M[illegible]. Engraved by R. Cooper. Published by Testolini, 73, Cornhill. Price 1l. 11s. 6d.

These are very pretty designs of the School of Bartolozzi, and most admirably engraved.

Miscellaneous British Scenery.

No I. Plate 1st, View of Oakhampton Castle, Devon. No. II. Ivy Bridge, Devon. No. III. View of Berry Pomeroy Castle, Devon. No. IV. View near Oakhampton, Devon. From designs by Mr. Walmesley. Price 4l. 4s. the set.

Of Mr. Walmesley's designs we have spoken in a former Retrospect. The four preceding prints are in a similar style, distinguished by a good taste, and, we dare say, accurate representations of the places delineated: They are very well engraved in *acqua tint*, two of them by Hassell, and two by Cartwright.

Bonaparte. Painted by Northcote. Engraved by S. W. Reynolds. Published by W. Jeffries, Clapham-road, October 15th, 1801. Price, in colours, 3l. 3s. plain, 1l. 11s. 6d.

It is designed in a grand style, but the horse has a more than accidental resemblance to some of those painted by Rubens; and we have previously seen one of the same prancing family, in the picture of the Triumphal Entry of Henry IV. in the Shakespeare Gallery. The head of Bonaparte borders upon the caricature; the design, though spirited, is not conceived with much originality, yet it is, altogether, a splendid and rich-looking plate, and admirably engraved. The plain impressions have a very superior effect to those that are coloured.

The Holy Family. Painted by R. Westall, R.A. Engraved by S. W. Reynolds. Dedicated to the Countess of Rosslyn, and published by Jeffries. Price, in colours, 3l. 3s.

This design is conceived with the usual delicacy of Westall's delineations: the figure of the Virgin is simple, elegant, and singularly beautiful; and the surrounding scenery enchanting. They are sold only in colours.

Fox-hunting. The Check. Designed by G. Morland. Engraved and published by E. Bell, No. 45, Islington-road, near Sadler's Wells. Going into Cover. The same painter and engraver.

The two first prints of this series were published some time ago, and noticed in a former Retrospect. Both of these, especially the first, are designed and engraved in a very good style. The horses, dogs and figures are spirited and natural; and in that of *the Check*, particularly, the sky is light and airy, the fore-ground rich, and the foliage of the old tree, &c. superior to any thing we have often seen in a mezzotinto.

A few copies of *Shakespeare's Seven Ages*, designed by Stothard, and engraved by Bromley, and published by Symonds, in Paternoster-row, are now taken off in colours, which have an effect nearly equal to the original drawings, price, 3l.

The very capital plate, engraved by Bromley, from Loutherbourg's *Valenciennes*, is printing with all the expedition of which so large and capital a print will admit, and will be ready for delivery to the subscribers, &c. in the early part of the winter. From the very superior style in which it is designed and engraved, this print will hold a very high class in the arts; and from there being twenty-eight portraits, will be a valuable addition to the cabinets of those who wish to possess portraits of the great characters of their own day. A list of their names will be given in a future Retrospect.

Considering the splendour with which the apartments of the nobility and gentry of this country are furnished, it has often been thought singular, that we should never have had any good book of designs of furniture, and the interior decorations of houses. Such a work enables the gentleman and the artisan to understand each other, and will be extremely useful to each, and such a work Ackerman, of the Strand, has just published. It is printed by *Dulau*, both in French and English, and contains about thirty engravings of the most superb and elegant decorations, with which the various apartments of a capital mansion can be furnished. The title is, *Designs for Architects, Upholsterers, Cabinet-makers, &c. such as Breakfast, Dining and Drawing-*

ing-rooms, Bed-chambers, Bath, Library, Boudoir, Hall, Stair-case, &c. &c. The price is 1l. 11s. 6d. and it is printed on superfine wove paper, elephant quarto.

Independent of portraits on canvas and portraits on copper, there has lately arisen another species of portraits, on which *a Retrospect of the Arts* should not be wholly silent. They are shewn in a room totally dark, but illuminate themselves, are seen floating in the air, varying their appearance, diminishing in their size as they recede from the eye, and at length *vanishing into air—into thin air*. We allude to the Exhibition which M. De Phillipstal every evening displays at the Lyceum, in the Strand, and which he denominates *the Phantasmogoria*. This very singular *spectrology* has been already exhibited in Dresden, Paris, and other principal cities of Europe; and the proprietor professes it to be one of his objects to unmask artful impostors, and open the eyes of such persons as still retain a belief in ghosts, enchantments, conjurations, &c. The different figures are, in part, made up of portraits of distinguished characters; among them are Queen Elizabeth, Mary Queen of Scots, Cromwell, Voltaire, Louis XVI. Admiral Nelson, and a variety of other distinguished personages. These freely originate in the air, and unfold themselves under various forms and sizes. Some from a star-like point of fire; others from an ascending cloud or vapour; and, what is extremely singular, change their figures and assume other forms while floating before the eye.

The friends of the late Mr. Wakefield will be happy to learn that a very striking and characteristic portrait of him was painted by Mr. Artaud, of Great Marlborough-street, a very short time previous to his death. The portrait is now in the hands of Mrs. Macklin, at the Poets' Gallery, Fleet-street, who has engaged an artist of great respectability to make an engraving from it, which will be finished soon after Christmas. Those who may wish to have early impressions, will do well to send their names to Mrs. Macklin, who promises to deliver the impressions in the order in which they may be subscribed for.

LIST OF DISEASES IN LONDON.

Account of Diseases in an Eastern District of London, from the 20th of September to the 20th of October, 1801.

ACUTE DISEASES.

	No. of Cases.
Typhus	22
Peripneumonia	2
Dysenteria	15
Rheumatismus Acutus	2

CHRONIC DISEASES.

Peripneumonia Notha	4
Phthisis Pulmonalis	2
Tussis	10
Tussis et Dyspnœa	7
Pleurodyne	3
Hepatitis Chronica	1
Hydrothorax	2
Anasarca	3
Ascites	1
Diarrhœa	10
Hæmorrhois	4
Tenesmus	6
Amenorrhœa	3
Menorrhagia	5
Leucorrhœa	4
Hypochondriasis	1
Vertigo	3
Paralysis	1
Vomitus	4
Prolapsus Vaginæ	1
Herpes	5
Rheumatismus Chronicus	15

PUERPERAL DISEASES.

Low Puerperal Fever	3
Menorrhagia Lochialis	1
Mastodynia	3
Dysuria	1

INFANTILE DISEASES.

Febris Mesenterica	1
Herpes	4
Tinea Capitis	2
Diarrhœa	12

The fever, which has long prevailed, and the influence of which has been so extensively diffused, still continues. The symptoms attending it are very similar to those which have lately been described. Those violent affections of the brain, which have formed so important a characteristic of the disease for a considerable time, are less frequent; and, at present, diseases of the stomach and bowels seem to be more common attendants upon this fever. This occurs under various forms and in different degrees. A moderate diarrhœa, occurring at an early stage of the disease, has generally proved salutary, and has frequently afforded a pretty just prognosis

prognosis of a favourable termination of the disease: but when at a more advanced period evacuations from the bowels have increased, have assumed a dark appearance, and have exhaled a fœtid odour, they must be viewed as symptomatic of disease and danger, rather than as affording the hope of any critical relief. It by no means, however, follows from hence, that such evacuations are to be checked, whilst the presence of this offensive matter is an indication of disease; the removal of it may prove the means of relief, and therefore to correct and discharge what is so offensive to the intestines and to the constitution, is surely a more rational practice than to detain it.

Besides these affections of the bowels, which may be considered as symptomatic, there have been others which have constituted the original disease. A large number of Dysenteries have lately occurred, and some of them have proved very obstinate.

This disease, as it is well-known, usually occurs at this season of the year, and as a diarrhœa frequently prevails at the same time, owing, probably, in some instances, to a larger quantity of fruit being eaten, these diseases are too often confounded. The patient complains of pain in his bowels accompanied with a large number of stools; and before any medical assistance is requested, every domestic medicine, calculated to stop a purging, is administered: but when the quantity and kind of discharge from the intestines are examined, it proves, that, though the inclination to have a stool has been very frequent, the discharge has been very small, and this consisting rather of mucus, or mucous-blood, than of fæces. A considerable degree of fever usually accompanies this disease; and the frequent inclination to go to stool, and the tenesmus which succeeds it, are a source of constant uneasiness. This disease is to be traced to a spasmodic stricture in the course of the large intestines, by which fæces are detained; and, consequently, the cure must be attempted by relaxing the spasm, and evacuating the fœces. Opium may be administered as an antispasmodic, but its exhibition should be immediately succeeded by that of a brisk cathartic. In the treatment of most of the cases referred to in the list, *pulv. opii comp.* from ten to fifteen grains, was preferred to any other opiate; and *cryst. tart.* from two to four drams, with six or eight grains of scammony, generally answered the purpose of discharging a considerable quantity of fæces, which was followed by an abatement of the most urgent symptoms.

STATE OF PUBLIC AFFAIRS,

In October, 1801.

FRANCE.

THE Ratification of the Preliminaries of Peace has, it appears, diffused an equal joy throughout both nations. In consequence of this event, the Consuls of the French Republic have decreed, that on Nov. 9, a festival shall be celebrated in all the extent of the republic. On the 4th of October, the members of the Conservative Senate proceeded to the palace of the government, to congratulate the Consuls on the signing of the preliminaries. Kellermann, the President, expressed the sentiments of the senate; and the First Consul answered, that the news of an event which had so much influence on the happiness of the French people, had with reason excited the joy of the Conservative Senate, which had constantly shewn itself the protector of liberal and pacific ideas.

The peace between France and Great Britain has been followed by a peace with all other nations. France has ratified her treaty with Russia, and this has also been celebrated at Paris. She has moreover concluded a peace with Portugal, against whom indeed she could no longer have any cause of complaint; and another with the Turkish Empire.

We learn from Corfu, August the 8th, that, instead of a well-regulated republic, they had the most complete anarchy. The inhabitants of the country had revolted against those of the city, and both the one and the other were upon their guard against the vengeance of the Turks since the sanguinary quarrel of the 27th of May. As to the other isles, the following is the intelligence we received from them. Cerigo has declared itself independent. Zante has hoisted the English colours. Santa Maria is threatened with an invasion by Ali Pacha of Janina. Cephalia is at the mercy of the two factions, who destroy it.

By a letter from General Watrin to Citizen Belleville, commercial commissary of the

the French in Etruria, intelligence was received that Admiral Warren's squadron, consisting of seven ships of the line, three frigates, and two brigs, landed, in the beginning of September, about 3000 men to the right of the French camp at Porto Ferrajo. After an obstinate engagement of six hours, the French compelled them to re-imbark, with the loss of 1200 men killed, drowned, and wounded: the French made two hundred prisoners, and several officers, whom the General says he purposed sending shortly to Leghorn. The French batteries dismasted a frigate, which escaped from the circumstance of being towed by twenty boats. Seven gunboats were sunk, and three taken by the French soldiers, who boarded them by swimming. The action covered with glory the troops of the republic, who being sick, and destitute of every thing, required all their courage to fight an enemy at least double their number, and supported by the tremendous fire of their vessels. The English disembarked at several points. A thousand men, covered with three ships of the line, also attacked Marciana; but the brave garrison, joined by a few of the inhabitants and some Poles, compelled them to retreat with loss.

Treaty of Peace between the French Republic and the Kingdom of Portugal.

The First Consul of the French Republic, in the name of the French People, and his Royal Highness the Prince Regent of the kingdom of Portugal and of Algarva, equally animated with a desire of re-establishing the connections of Commerce and Amity which subsisted between the two States before the present war, have resolved to conclude a Treaty of Peace by the mediation of his Most Catholic Majesty, and for this purpose have named as their Plenipotentiaries, viz.—The First Consul of the French Republic, in the name of the French People, Citizen Lucien Bonaparte; and his Royal Highness the Prince Regent of the kingdom of Portugal and of Algarva, his Excellency Cyprian Bibeiro Freire, Commander of the Order of Christ, Member of his Royal Highness's Council, and Minister Plenipotentiary to his Most Catholic Majesty; which Plenipotentiaries, after exchanging their reciprocal powers, have agreed upon the following articles:—

Art. I. There shall in future and for ever be a peace, amity, and good understanding, between the French Republic and the kingdom of Portugal, all hostilities shall cease by land as well as by sea, dating from the exchange of the Ratification of the present Treaty, viz. in 15 days for Europe, and the seas which wash its coasts, and those of Africa on this side of the equator; 40 days after the said exchange for the countries and seas of Africa and America, beyond the equator; and three months after, for the countries and seas situated to the West of Cape Horn, and to the East of the Cape of Good Hope. All prizes made after each of these periods in the seas to which they apply, shall be respectively restored. The prisoners of war shall be given up on both sides, and the political relations between the two Powers shall be re-established on the same footing as before the war.

II. All the ports and harbours of Portugal, in Europe, shall be immediately shut, and shall remain so till Peace between France and England, to all English ships of war and merchantmen; and the same ports and harbours shall be open to all ships of war or merchantmen belonging to France or its Allies.

In regard to the ports and harbours of Portugal, in the other parts of the world, the present article shall be obligatory, according to the terms above fixed for the cessation of hostilities.

III. Portugal engages not to furnish, during the course of the present war, to the enemies of the French Republic and its Allies, any aid in troops, ships, arms, warlike ammunition, provisions, or money, under whatever name or denomination. Every anterior act, engagement, or convention, which may be contrary to the present article, shall be revoked, and shall be considered as null and void.

IV. The limits between the two Guianas, the French and Portuguese, shall be determined in future by the river Carapanatuba, which empties itself into the Amazon, at about one-third of a degree of the equator above Fort Macapa. These limits shall follow the course of the river to its source, whence they shall proceed towards the great chain of mountains which divides the waters; they shall follow the inflections of that chain to the point where it approaches nearest the Rio-Blanco, towards about two degrees one-third north of the equator.

The Indians of the two Guianas, who, in the course of the war, may have been taken from their habitations, shall be respectively restored.

The citizens or subjects of the two powers, who may find themselves comprehended in the new determined limits, may reciprocally retire into the possessions of their respective States: they shall have power also to dispose of their property, moveable and immoveable, during the space of two years, dating from the exchange of the Ratifications of the present Treaty.

V. There shall be negotiated between the two Powers a Treaty of Commerce and Navigation, which shall definitively fix the commercial relations between France and Portugal. In the mean time it is agreed—

1st. That the communications shall be re-established immediately after the exchange of the

the Ratifications, and that the agencies and commissariats of commerce shall be put in possession of the rights, immunities, and prerogatives, which they enjoyed before the war.

2d. That the citizens and subjects of the two Powers, shall equally and respectively enjoy, in the States of both, all the rights which are enjoyed by the subjects of the most favoured nations.

3d. That the articles of trade and commerce, the produce of the soil or manufactories of each of the two States shall be reciprocally admitted without restriction, and without their being subjected to any duty which shall not bear equally upon analogous articles imported by other nations.

4th. That French cloths may be immediately introduced into Portugal, on the footing of the most favoured merchandizes.

5th. All stipulations in regard to commerce, inserted in preceding treaties, and not contrary to the present treaty, shall be provisionally until the conclusion of the Definitive Treaty.

VI. The Ratifications of the present Treaty of Peace shall be exchanged at Madrid, within the term of twenty days at most.

Done, in Duplicate, at Madrid, the 7th Vendemiaire, year 10 of the French Republic—(29th Sept. 1801.)

(Signed) LUCIEN BONAPARTE.
CYPRIANI RIBEIRO FREIRE.

Treaty of Peace between the French Republic and His Majesty the Emperor of all the Russias.

The First Consul of the French Republic, in the name of the French people, and his Majesty, the Emperor of all the Russias, animated with a desire of re-establishing the relations and good understanding which existed between the two governments before the war, and of putting an end to the evils with which Europe is afflicted, have named as Plenipotentiaries for this purpose, viz.—the First Consul of the French Republic, in the name of the French people, Citizen Charles Maurice Talleyrand, Minister of Foreign Relations; and his Majesty the Emperor of all the Russias, the Sieur Arcadi, Count de Marcoff, a Member of his Privy Council, and Knight of the Order of St. Alexander Newski, and Grand Cross of that of St. Wladimir of the first class, who, after a verification and exchange of their credentials, agreed on the following articles:—

I. There shall in future be peace and good understanding between the French Republic, and his Majesty the Emperor of all the Russias.

II. In consequence, no hostility shall be committed between the two States, dating from the day of the exchange of the ratifications of the present Treaty; and neither of the Contracting Parties shall furnish to the enemies of the other, either external or internal, any assistance or contingent, in men or money, under any denomination whatever.

III. The two Contracting Parties being desirous, as much as in them lies, to contribute to the tranquillity of the respective governments, mutually promise not to suffer any of their subjects to maintain any correspondence whatever, either directly or indirectly, with the internal enemies of the present governments of the two states, to propagate in them principles contrary to their respective constitutions, or foment troubles; and in consequence of this agreement, every subject of either of the two powers, who, while residing in the states of the other, shall attempt any thing against their safety, shall be immediately removed from the said country, and transported beyond the frontiers, without power of claiming in any case the protection of his government.

IV. In regard to the re-establishment of the respective legations, and the ceremonial to be followed between the two governments, it is agreed, that the usage which existed before the present war shall be adhered to.

V. The two Contracting Parties, until the formation of a new Treaty of Commerce, agree to re-establish the commercial relations between the two Countries on the footing on which they were before the war, so far as can be done, and consistent with the modifications which time and circumstances may have introduced, and which have given rise to new regulations.

VI. The present Treaty is declared common to the Batavian Republic.

VII. The present treaty shall be ratified, and the ratification exchanged within fifty days, or sooner, if possible.

In faith of which we, the undersigned, by virtue of our full powers, have signed the said treaty, and have affixed to it our seals.

Done at Paris, the 16th Vendemiaire, 10th year of the French Republic, (October 8, 1801.) (Signed)

CH. MAU. TALLEYRAND.
COUNT DE MARCOFF.

Preliminary Articles of Peace between the French Republic and the Ottoman Porte.

The First Consul of the French Republic, in the name of the French people, and the Sublime Ottoman Porte, being desirous to put an end to the war which divides the two countries, and to re-establish the ancient relations which united them, have nominated, with this intention, for Ministers Plenipotentiary, to wit: The First Consul of the French Republic, in the name of the French people, Citizen Charles Maurice Talleyrand, Minister for Foreign Affairs; and the Sublime Ottoman Porte, its *ci-devant* Basch-Muhassebe and Ambassador Esseyd Ali Effendi, who, after having exchanged their full powers, have agreed upon the following Preliminary Articles:

ART.

ART. I. There shall be peace and friendship between the French Republic and the Sublime Ottoman Porte; in consequence of which, hostilities shall cease between the two powers, from the date of the exchange of the ratifications of the present Preliminary Articles. Immediately after the said exchange, the entire province of Egypt shall be evacuated by the French army, and restored to the Sublime Ottoman Porte, the territories and possessions of which shall be maintained in their integrity, such as they were before the present war.

It is understood, that, after the evacuation, the concessions which may be made in Egypt to other powers, on the part of the Sublime Porte, shall be common to the French.

II The French Republic acknowledges the Constitution of the Republic of the Seven Islands and Ex-Venetian Territories, situated upon the Continent. It guarantees the maintenance of that Constitution. The Sublime Porte acknowledges, and accepts for that purpose, the guarantee of the French Republic, as well as that of Russia.

III. Definitive arrangements shall be made between the French Republic and the Sublime Ottoman Porte, relative to the goods and effects of their respective citizens and subjects confiscated or sequestered during the war. The political and commercial agents and prisoners of war, of every rank, shall be set at liberty immediately after the ratification of the present Preliminary Articles.

IV. The Treaties which existed before the present war between France and the Sublime Ottoman Porte shall be renewed in the entire. In consequence of this renewal, the French Republic shall enjoy, in the whole extent of the state of His Highness, the rights of commerce and navigation which it formerly enjoyed, and which may hereafter be enjoyed, by the most favoured nations.

The ratifications shall be exchanged at Paris in the space of twenty-four days.

Done at Paris the 9th of October, in the 10th year of the French Republic, or the 1st of the month Gemasy-ul-ahir, 1216 of the Hegira.

(Signed) CH. MAU. TALLEYRAND.
ESSEYD ALI EFFENDI.

GERMANY.

Citizen Bacher, the French minister at Ratisbon, delivered, we find, on the 4th instant, the following extract from his last dispatches: "As it is fit that at Ratisbon there should be no uncertainty with respect to the particular views of the French government, the Chief Consul gives me now the commission to declare to the members of the Diet, in the most determined manner, that the French government is astonished at the delay of the execution of the 7th article of the treaty of Luneville; and that it considers it as a duty to demand of the Diet to declare itself definitively, in what manner the indemnities of the Princes who have suffered are to be adjusted."

The directorial-body returned for answer, that the affair had hitherto been carried forward with as much dispatch as the forms of the Diet, and the constitution of the Empire, permitted.

The Diet of Ratisbon has at length, it is said, drawn up, and dispatched to Vienna, its conclusum. Bohemia, Brandenburg, Bavaria, Wirtemberg, the Grand Master of the Teutonic Order, and Cassel, are to treat in concert with the French government, and submit the result of their operations to his Imperial Majesty and the Empire, to be ratified. The deputation are to have full powers, but are to observe the restrictive clause by which the deputation of the Empire at the congress of Rastadt gave, in their note of the 4th of April, 1798, their adherence to the principle of indemnities. In this note, the deputation "consented to the indemnities then demanded, by the mode of secularizations for the losses sustained on the left bank of the Rhine, and that new negociations should be entered into upon the subject, in such a manner, however, as to proceed in it with all the precaution and restriction which are essentially necessary for the maintenance of the Germanic Empire in all its relations, as well as for the establishment and security of the well-being of the states, members, and subjects of the Empire."

Circumstances however have materially changed since the breaking up of the congress of Rastadt, and the measure of indemnities and secularizations will probably be a more sweeping one than it would have been at that time; for Tuscany had not then been wrested from the Grand-duke.

It will be seen, that, though the affair is nominally entrusted to a deputation of eight members, yet, that in reality it will be settled between Austria, Prussia, and France; and, as those three powers have already, it is believed, agreed upon a plan, the deliberations of the deputation will be soon at an end.

BATAVIAN REPUBLIC.

The plan of the new constitution is already printed, and consists of 108 articles. The Executive-directory is to be abolished, and in its stead a State-directory instituted, to consist of twelve persons, one to go out yearly. There is to be a legislative-body, consisting of thirty-five members. The territory of the republic is to be divided into eight departments, whose boundaries are to be the same with those of the old provinces.

The allowance of the members of the legislative body is to be 4000 florins. They are to meet twice during the year, and are to sit from the 15th of April to the 1st of June, and from the 15th of October to the 15th of December. On any emergency it will be competent for them to assemble as often as necessary, and the government is to have the power of convoking them.

Military force, in these concerns, has not been employed, nor has General Augereau, nor the Minister of the French Republic, had the smallest concern in them.

TURKEY.

The Brunn Gazette says, the insurrection in Belgrade is only a part of a very extensive plan, as the flames of sedition broke out at the same time at Constantinople, at Adrianople, Philipoli, Nissa, and other places, where the inhabitants rose upon the magistrates, and, dividing into parties, fought furiously with each other. Civil war appears likely to become general throughout European Turkey. The commandant of Nissa was obliged to fly. The Pacha of Belgrade, before the late commotions there, was much esteemed at Constantinople, and appointed Seraskier by the Porte.

GREAT BRITAIN.

Amidst the universal apprehension of all parties, that the desirable and glorious event of Peace was as improbable as at any period during the war, and that the negociation for the attainment of it was abruptly broken off, the Preliminaries for a Peace between Great Britain and France were suddenly and unexpectedly signed on Thursday evening, the first day of October, between Lord Hawkesbury and M. Otto; and confirmed by the arrival of the agreeable ratification of the Preliminary Articles from the Chief Consul of France on Saturday the 10th day of October.

The following is a copy of the Preliminary Articles; the Definitive Treaty is to be settled at Amiens, in France, whither Plenipotentiaries are at this time repairing.

Preliminary Articles of Peace between the French Republic and his Britannic Majesty, signed at London, October 1, 1801.

The Chief Consul of the French Republic, in the name of the French people, and his Majesty the King of the United Kingdom of Great Britain and Ireland, animated by an equal desire to put an end to the calamities of a destructive war, and to re-establish union and good understanding between the two nations, have nominated for this purpose, that is to say—The Chief Consul of the French Republic, in the name of the French people, Citizen Louis William Otto, Commissary for the exchange of French prisoners in England, and his Britannic Majesty the Sieur Robert Banks Jenkinson, Lord Hawkesbury, Member of the Privy Council of his Britannic Majesty, and his Principal Secretary of State for Foreign Affairs; who, after having formally communicated to each other their full powers, have agreed upon the following Preliminary Articles:

ART. I. As soon as the Preliminaries shall be signed and ratified, sincere amity shall be re-established between the French Republic and his Britannic Majesty, by sea and by land, in all parts of the world. On this account, and that all hostilities may immediately cease between the two powers, and between them and their allies respectively, orders shall be transmitted to the forces by sea and land with the greatest celerity, each of the Contracting Parties engaging to give the necessary passports and facilities to accelerate the said orders, and to insure the execution of them. It is farther agreed, that every conquest which shall be made by either of the Contracting Parties upon the other, or any of its Allies, after the ratification of the present Preliminaries, shall be considered as null, and faithfully comprised in the restitutions to be made after the ratification of the definitive Treaty.

II. His Britannic Majesty shall restore to the French Republic and its Allies, that is to say, to his Catholic Majesty and the Batavian Republic, all the possessions and colonies occupied or conquered by the English forces during the course of the present war, with the exception of the Island of Trinidad, and the Dutch possessions in the Island of Ceylon, of which Islands and possessions his Britannic Majesty retains the full and entire sovereignty.

III. The port of the Cape of Good Hope shall be open to the commerce and navigation of the two Contracting Parties, who shall enjoy the same advantages.

IV. The Island of Malta, with its dependencies, shall be evacuated by the English troops, and restored to the Order of St. John of Jerusalem.

To insure the absolute independence of this Island of both the Contracting Parties, it shall be placed under the guarantee and protection of a third Power, to be named by the definitive Treaty.

V. Egypt shall be restored to the Sublime Porte, the territories and possessions of which shall be maintained in their integrity such as they were before the present war.

VI. The territories and possessions of Her Most Faithful Majesty shall likewise be maintained in their integrity.

VII.

VII. The French troops ſhall evacuate the Kingdom of Naples, and the Roman States. The Engliſh forces ſhall likewiſe evacuate Porto Ferrajo, and generally all the Ports and Iſlands which they ſhall be found to occupy in the Mediterranean or in the Adriatic.

VIII. The Republic of the Seven Iſles ſhall be recognized by the French Republic.

IX. The evacuations, ceſſions, and reſtitutions, ſtipulated by the preſent Preliminary Articles, ſhall be executed for Europe in one month, for the Continent and Seas of America and Africa in three months, for the Continent and Seas of Aſia in ſix months after the ratification of the Definitive Treaty.

X. The priſoners of war, on both ſides, immediately after the exchange of the ratifications of the Definitive Treaty, ſhall be returned in a body, and without ranſom, on paying on the one ſide and the other the private debts which they ſhall have contracted.

Diſcuſſions having ariſen with regard to the expence of the maintenance of the priſoners of war, the Contracting Parties reſerve the deciſion of this queſtion till the Definitive Treaty, when it ſhall be ſettled agreeably to the Law of Nations and principles conſecrated by uſage.

XI. To prevent all the ſubjects of complaint and conteſt which might ariſe with regard to the prizes made at ſea after the ſignature of the Preliminary Articles, it is reciprocally agreed that the ſhips and goods which may be taken in the Channel or in the North Seas, after twelve days from the exchange of the ratifications of the preſent Preliminary Articles, ſhall, on both ſides, be reſtored; that the period ſhall be one month from the Channel and the North Seas to the Canary Iſlands incluſively, whether in the Ocean or the Mediterranean; two months from the ſaid Canary Iſlands to the Equator; and, finally, five months in all other parts of the globe, without any exception or any more particular diſtinction with regard either to time or place.

XII. All ſequeſtrations laid on either ſide upon the funds, revenues, or debts of what kind ſoever, belonging to one of the Contracting Powers, or to its citizens or ſubjects, ſhall be taken off immediately after the ſigning of the Definitive Treaty.

The deciſion of all ſuits between individuals of the two nations for debts, property, effects, or dues, which, agreeably to received uſages, and to the law of nations, may be brought at the concluſion of Peace, ſhall be referred to the competent tribunals, and in this caſe juſtice ſhall be adminiſtered ſpeedily and ſubſtantially in the countries where the ſuits ſhall be commenced reſpectively. It is agreed that immediately after the ratification of the Definitive Treaty, the preſent articles ſhall be applied by the Contracting Parties to the reſpective Allies, and to the individuals of their nations, under the condition of a juſt reciprocity.

XIII. With regard to the Fiſheries on the Coaſt of Newfoundland, and the adjacent Iſlands, and in the Gulph of St. Lawrence, the two Powers have agreed to place them on the ſame footing on which they ſtood before the preſent war, reſerving to themſelves power, by the Definitive Treaty, to form regulations which ſhall appear juſt, and reciprocally uſeful to place the fiſhery of the two nations on the footing beſt calculated to maintain peace.

XIV. In all the inſtances of reſtitution agreed upon by the preſent Treaty, the fortifications ſhall be delivered up in the ſtate in which they are at the ſignature of the preſent Treaty; and all the works which may have been erected ſince the occupation of the different places, ſhall remain untouched.

It is agreed, moreover, that in all the inſtances of ceſſion ſtipulated in the preſent Treaty, there ſhall be allowed to the inhabitants, of what condition or nation ſoever they may be, a term of three years, to be reckoned from the notification of the Definitive Treaty of Peace, to diſpoſe of their property, acquired and poſſeſſed, whether before or ſince the preſent war; during which term of three years they ſhall be at liberty freely to exerciſe their religion, and to enjoy their property.

The ſame power is granted in the countries reſtored to all thoſe who have made any ſettlements there during the period when theſe countries were in the poſſeſſion of Great Britain.

As to the other inhabitants of the countries reſtored or ceded, it is agreed that no one of them ſhall be proſecuted, moleſted, or diſturbed, in his perſon or his property, under any pretext, on account of his conduct or political opinions, or on account of his attachment to either of the two powers, or for any other reaſon, unleſs for debts contracted to individuals, or acts poſterior to the Definitive Treaty.

XV. The preſent Preliminary Articles ſhall be ratified, and the ratifications exchanged, at London, within the term of fourteen days at the lateſt; and immediately after their ratification, Plenipotentiaries ſhall be named on both ſides, who ſhall repair to Amiens, to proceed with the formation of a Definitive Treaty, in concert with the Allies of the Contracting Parties.

In witneſs whereof we the underſigned Plenipotentiaries of the Chief Conſul of the French Republic, and of his Britannic Majeſty, in virtue of our reſpective full powers, have ſigned the preſent Preliminary Articles, and thereunto ſet our ſeals.

Done at London the Ninth Vendemiaire, Year Ten of the French Republic, the Firſt Day of October, One Thouſand Eight Hundred and One.

(Signed) OTTO. HAWKESBURY.

We ſhall now make a few obſervations both upon the baſis itſelf, and the mode in which the treaty was finally acceded to. It

It is said that a new *conclusum*, from which ministers were determined not to deviate in an iota, was dispatched to the Chief Consul about ten days before the signing of the Preliminaries, and that very few of the Cabinet had any expectation of his assenting to the new arrangement proposed, while several were even against any additional attempt whatever; but that, contrary to the general expectation of the Cabinet, Bonaparte returned the scheme on Wednesday, the 30th of September, fully empowering M. Otto to carry it, on his part, into execution. The only change proposed in the project above referred to, was the equal abandonment of Egypt on both sides, instead of its being retained by either; and it is said, the Cabinet were determined to accede to Bonaparte's answer, be it what it might, even prior to its arrival. The dreadful deficiency of the treasury—the extreme difficulty of coercing the people into new taxes—the immediate want of an immense sum of money—and the prospect of a very formidable opposition on the ensuing meeting of Parliament, all concurred in determining the cabinet upon the procuration of a Peace, even upon their antagonist's own terms, prior to the commencement of the Parliamentary Session. So much then for the manner in which this most desirable treaty has been concluded.

Respecting the terms proposed as its preliminary basis; it has been confidently affirmed, that it is the very project of Bonaparte himself, scarcely softened in any respect by all the remonstrances that for six weeks had been almost daily urged upon the subject. It is certainly calculated to gratify him in the utmost scope of his ambition; and though not humiliating to the English character, it humiliates and disgraces the character of those Ministers who wantonly and needlessly plunged the nation into the war.

We shall advert but to two causes for which the war was commenced, and has been persevered in. It was opened declaratively for the preservation of the established order of Europe, generally, and of our own Constitution individually. The established order of Europe has nevertheless been totally subverted, and the British Constitution more injured by those Ministers, both by corruption and open force, than it will probably be ever able to recover under the guidance of the most virtuous and patriotic administration. These Quixotic and romantic views, however, were in a few years relinquished, and the more gross and tangible source of contest—that of territory—was then acknowledged. The British Ministry, whose nerves were so finely attempered, as to tremble at the remotest view of political injustice and turpitude, joined in the general scramble after additional acres, and conceived, on a new principle of arithmetic, that they should hereby acquire immortal glory to themselves, and amply remunerate the people for having doubled the national debt! Three hundred millions have been expended—half a million of British lives have been sacrificed—and what now is the extent of territory that is to console us for this prodigious loss? A Spice Island in the East, and a Sugar Island in the West Indies! neither of which, by the way, will diminish the price of these articles at home one farthing in the pound. Futile is it to boast of our having obtained and secured the integrity of Portugal. The French indeed may make a boast of this; but the declaration is absurd on our part; for, by the present treaty, we have compelled ourselves to re-surrender Madeira, the only portion of the Portuguese territories which had been wrested from the hands of its Government; and as to the integrity of Naples, it was settled long ago by the humane interference of the emperor of Russia, and required no kind of assistance from the projects of a British Minister. The treaty, in fact, abandons every thing for which the late Ministry pretended they were contending.—It abandons the Stadtholder, Sardinia, and the whole house of Bourbon to an inexorable fate; and sanctions the dethronement of the Grand Duke of Tuscany: for the *people* of this country, nevertheless, the present Treaty is an event of the utmost exultation, and it ought to be received with transport and gratitude, although against the talents and conduct of the late Ministry it is the severest sarcasm that can possibly be directed!

If the peace be *necessary*, the war *was not*, for it has gained not an individual object for which it contended, while it is impossible to calculate the innumerable evils it has occasioned. These reflections do not certainly make against the present Ministers, but against their predecessors in office, WHO OWE A STRICT ACCOUNT TO THEIR COUNTRY FOR THEIR GROSS MISCONDUCT. The present Ministers found the country in a most perilous situation. It was their business to make peace upon the best terms they could; and every thing considered, better could not be

expected;

been expected; indeed, we have given up nothing, which on sound principles of policy we ought to have retained. We remember the silly exclamation of one of those *pseudo*-statesmen to whom we allude, "that the Minister who should give up the Cape of Good Hope deserved to lose his head." The Cape is given up, and we do not hesitate to affirm that it is better for this country that it should be a free port, than remain exclusively in our hands: In short, the present men had to make up for all the blunders of their predecessors—but that was a task above the powers of man!—They have great merit in making such terms as they have, and the PEACE, as a PEACE, is a GOOD ONE.

On no occasion has the joy of the nation been more universally or more fervently and unequivocally expressed. It would fill our Magazine, were we to attempt to detail the particular instances of celebration. Every city, village, and cottage was illuminated during several successive evenings, and the people were every where almost delirious in their extacy on being relieved from the most mischievous, unmeaning, and useless war into which a nation was ever plunged.

ALPHABETICAL LIST *of* BANKRUPTCIES *and* DIVIDENDS *announced between the 20th of Sept. and the 20th of Oct. extracted from the London Gazettes.*

BANKRUPTCIES.

(The Solicitors' Names are between Parentheses)

AUBER, Peter, East place, Lambeth. (Pearce and Dixon, Paternoster row)
Ashdowne, Robert, late of the Cliffe, near Lewes, mercer. (Milditch, 55, High Holborn)
Alnade, Samuel, late of Blossom's street, Spitalfields, cooper. (Speck, Back street, St. John's, Southwark)
Andrews, John, King street, Bloomsbury, bridle-cutter. (Newman, Aldermanbury)
Bairstow, Mathew, Thornhill, and Thornton, Yorkshire, corn-miller. (Lambert, Hatton garden)
Britten, Joseph, Birmingham, jeweller. (Savage and Spike, Temple)
Bate, Edw. Westbromwich, Staffordshire, timber-merchant. (Lee and Tottie, Birmingham)
Bride, Edw. Duke street, Artillery ground, dyer. (Noy and Templer, Mincing lane)
Betley, George, Liverpool, vinegar-maker. (Clements, Liverpool)
Beal, George, Great Surry street, Christ Church, cheesemonger. (Spearing, 19, Walbrook)
Bodin, James, Hockly, Warwick, shopkeeper. (John Lilly Parker, Stafford)
Bently, Charles, and John Dale, Norwich, warehousemen. (John Stewart, Norwich)
Bird, Sarah, Manchester, linen-draper. (Holland, King street, Manchester)
Browne, Robert, Adam's court, Broad street, merchant. (Palmer and Tomlinson, Warnford court)
Bowker, George, and James Chapman, Manchester, corn-dealers. (Ellis, Cursitor street)
Cartwright, Abel, late of Isarlaston, Staffordshire, baker. (Chrees, Wightwick, and Chrees, Wolverhampton)
Crossley, John, Manchester, cotton-manufacturer. (Wright and Reynolds, Temple)
Carter, Daniel, jun. Great Bromley, Essex, shopkeeper. (Naylors, Great Newport street)
Dennis, Joseph, formerly of Leadenhall market, late of Wild street, Lincoln's inn fields, broker. (Harvey, Cursitor street)
Dean, Joseph, Strand, laceman. (Lloyd, Clifford's inn)
Davidson, John, senior, Wm Davidson, and John Davidson, jun. Halifax, dyers. (Wiglesworth, Gray's inn)
Dobson, Thomas, Kendal, merchant, partner with George Dobson, of Philadelphia. (Johnson, Ely place, and Duckworth and Chippindale, Manchester)
Dimmock, Moses, Winchester, bookseller. (Davies, Ely place)
Dakeyne, Daniel, senior and junior, and Thomas and Joseph Dakeyne, all now or late of Darleydale, Derbyshire, bankers and cotton-spinners)
Davis, Humphry, Bear inn, Welchpool, Montgomery, innkeeper. (R. Griffiths, Lincoln's inn)
Eccles, Thomas and Barnard, Thomas Holbrook, Watling street, warehousemen. (Walton, Girdlers' hall)
Gower, John, Piccadilly, draper. (J and R. Willis, Warnford court)
Greenaway, Mary and Francis, Calne, Wilts, collar-makers. (J. and R. Willis, Warnford court)
Gulley, James, Frome Selwood, Somerset, innholder. (Tarrant, Chancery lane)
Hart, Jacob, Old Compton street, Soho, jeweller. (Jacobs, Mansfield street)
Harmer, John, Stroud, Gloucestershire, clothier and shopkeeper. (Warren, Stroud)
Harris, Moses, Wiewiley, Middlesex, coal-merchant. (Walters, 195, Shadwell)
Hodges, Thomas, Puntington, Sussex, timber-merchant. (Dally, Chichester)
Hopwood, David, late of Union street, St. Mary-le-bone, grocer. (Johnson, Southampton court, Queen square)
Higginbotham, Jonathan, Blackburn, cotton-spinner. (Ellis, Cursitor street)
Harrop, William, Salford, manufacturer. (Ellis, Cursitor street)
Hendy, Christopher, Falmouth, mariner. (Carpenter and Guy, King's Arms yard)
Haigh, Samuel, Manchester, merchant. (Ellis, Cursitor street)
Jones, John, late of Birmingham, draper. (Field, Friday street)
Irwin, John, late of Aldgate High street, innkeeper. (Walter, 185, Shadwell)
Last, John, Brighton, builder. (Robinson and Crawford, Craven buildings, Old street)
Lawson, William, formerly of New Inn, and afterwards of Great St. Helens, and late of Park place, Islington, money-scrivener. (Lloyd, 11, Cullum street)
Lewis, Samuel, Southampton, victualler. (Nicholls, Southampton)
Milner, Jos. Haymarket, baker. (Pearce and Dixon, Paternoster row)
Mottram, Thomas, late of Atherstone, Warwickshire, woolcomber and grocer. (Tebbut, Staple's inn)
Middleton, William, Liverpool, merchant. (Windle, Bartlett's buildings)
M'Minn, George and Alexander, Liverpool, merchants. (G. and J. Crump, Liverpool)
Macklin, John, Cheapside, stationer. (Mangnall, Warwick square)
Matson, George, Farleton, parish of Melling, Lancashire, horse-dealer. (Baldwin and Dowbeggin, Lancaster)
Owen, Robert, and William Marale, Houndsditch, coppersmiths. (Thomas, Fen court, Fenchurch street)
Onion, Francis, junior, Croydon, miller. (Carter, Staple's inn)
Porter, Richard, junior, Derby, grocer. (Chilton, Exchequer Office, Lincoln's inn)
Paget, William, junior, Wombourn, Staffordshire, miller. (Constable, Symond's inn)
Pollard, James, Essex street, Strand, taylor. (Pinero, Charles street, Cavendish square)
Robert, Richard, William Fulford, and B. Henbury, Great Russell street, Bloomsbury, shoemakers. (Warrant, Arundel street)
Redhead, Robert, Mark lane, wine and brandy-merchant. (Scott and Landon, St. Mildred's court)
Smith, Edward Shepherd, and John Stanley, Liverpool, merchants. (Battye, Chancery lane)
Simonds, William, Market street, St. James's, grocer. (Lewis, Chancery lane)
Smith, Parmenter, Budge row, wholesale draper. (J. and R. Willis, Warnford court)
Thomas, Richard King, Evesham, mercer. (Bousfield, Bouverie street)
Tandy, Joseph, Great Mary-le-bone street, glass-seller. (Pearce and Dixon, Paternoster row)
Thacker, Anthony, Upwell, Isle of Ely. (Miller, Carey street)
Vaughan, Charles, Liverpool, wholesale grocer. (Lace and Hassall, Liverpool)
Webb, John, Spond street, Coventry, dyer; under the firm of John Webb and Son. (Parnel, Spitalfields)
Williams, William and Edward Evans, Poultry, linen-drapers. (Thomas, Fen court, Fenchurch street)
West, William, and Thomas Hughes, Paternoster row, booksellers. (Abbott, Rolls yard, Chancery lane)
Whitehead, John, Marfleet, Yorkshire, contractor. (Ellis, Cursitor street)

DIVI-

DIVIDENDS ANNOUNCED.

Adams, Thomas, Upton-upon-Severn, grocer, Dec. 3
Anfield, John, Newcastle, linen-draper, Nov. 24
Bulter, Wm. [illegible], tavern-keeper, Oct. 14
Burford, W. Finsbury square, Blackwell-hall-factor, Nov. 14
Biffin, R. and J. Bristol, sugar-bakers, Nov. 2
Bridges, F. Haymarket, boot and shoemaker, Nov. 27
Borgnis, J. Great Marlborough street, printseller, Oct. 24
Bell, William, Bath, coachmaster, Oct. 26
Blunt, William, Swindon, dealer, Oct. 24
Bohart, G. Hoskinson, Woodstock, mercer, Oct. 31
Birchall, John, late of Worcester, dealer in salt, Nov. 2
Barrett, George, Clifton, shopkeeper, Nov. 9
Bayly, John, Alnwick, bookseller, Nov. 20, final
Boult, Gerard James, Pimlico, malt and confector, Nov. 14
Barker, William, Samuel Field, and Abraham———, Leeds, woolstaplers, Nov. 2
Crafts, R. Holt, innkeeper, Oct. 18, final
Cavenaugh, John, Portsea, shopkeeper, Oct. 27
Cruft, James, Zachary Bayly, senior and junior, Nathaniel Bayly, Robert Gutch, and Thomas Cruft, late of Bath, bankers, Oct. 31
Corlis, Thomas and John, Grimsby, grocers, Oct. 30
Carson, Robert, Clifton, Dykes, drover, Nov. 4
Clark, John, Pancras lane, taylor, Nov. 26
Chatterton, Thomas, and Edward Wells, Brenchley, hat-manufacturers, Nov. 13
Cumper, James, St. Pancras, near Chichester, linen-draper, Nov. 16
Denton, R. Liverpool, linen-draper, Oct. 16
Ditchfield, James, Newgate street, victualler, Nov. 24
Derwin, William, late of the Haymarket, hackneyman, Nov. 10
Eldon, John, Liverpool, merchant, Oct. 13
Edwards, John Pully, and William Purl, both lately of Red Lion street, Southwark, contractors, Nov. 14
Fisher, Joseph, Pollington, Yorkshire, seedsman, Oct. 31, final
Goodrich, Lemuel, Leicester, baker, Nov. 2
Gillman, John, Great Yarmouth, linen-draper, Nov. 10
Gazeley, J. T. Great Queen street, Lincoln's Inn fields, merchant, Nov. 24
Bailey, T. Kingston, Hull, dealer, Oct. 31
Hewitt, J. Guildford, Surrey, carpenter, Oct. 20
Harrison, Thomas and Arthur, and John Kinder, late of Croydon, jointly and separately, callicoprinters, Nov. 5
Hobson, Joseph, Thurstonland, tanner, Nov. 6
Hawkins, Robert, Kingston, Hull, cabinet-maker, Oct. 27
Harries, J. D. Cardigan, shopkeeper, Oct. 27
Holroyd, Henry, Greenwich, hoop-bender, Nov. 7
Hylton, William, Robertsbridge, shopkeeper, Nov. 28
Harding, William, and Francis Mellers, Derby, mercers, Nov. 7
Herilnck, John, C. Julius Hutchinson, and William Playfair, Cornhill, bankers, Dec. 12
Ibbet, J. Crown street, Finsbury square, shoemaker, Oct. 17
Jones, Rice, Lower street, Islington, victualler, Nov. 14
Jones, John, Wigmore street, coach-maker, Nov. 5
Irlam, John, Shap, Westmorland, Oct. 31
Kempster, John, junior, South Merston, corn-dealer, Nov. 2
Lowe, H. Liverpool, hardwareman, Oct. 19
Longstaff, Simon, Sunderland, ship-owner, Nov. 7, final
Lea, Richard, Sherston, Magna, baker, Nov. 9
Mathewman, Joseph, Sheffield, merchant, Oct. 31, final
Mickliss, William, Erifworth, grocer, Oct. 28
Mason, Richard, Birmingham, grocer, Nov. 4
Mammatt, Moses, Birmingham, grocer, Nov. 5
Manion, Thomas, Tokenhouse yard, merchant and insurer, Nov. 14
Neale, Edward, Grantham, mercer, Nov. 3
Owen, Evan, Alnwick, Anglesey, shopkeeper, Dec. 4
Poole, John, E. and Thomas Shrigley, Burslem, potters, Oct. 14
Parvis, F. Chester-le-street, miller, Oct. 17
Paul, Thomas, North Shields, butcher, Oct. 28, final
Paul, John, Winchester, hardwareman, Nov. 4
Parker, Benjamin, Birmingham, scrivener, Nov. 3
Pugh, E. and James Davis, Old Fish street, chemists, Nov. 12
Pollard, William, Wakefield, grocer, Nov. 9
Panton, Thomas, West Smithfield, woollen-draper, Nov. 13
Richardson, Norburn, Hecklington, farmer, Oct. 30, final
Reimer, Henry, Catherine court, Tower hill, merchant, Nov. 25
Sherwood, J. Birmingham, saddler, Nov. 4, final
Stone, William, Bristol, grocer, Nov. 2
Smith, Edward, Birmingham, hat-manufacturer, Nov. 8
Smith, F. Grosvenor street, taylor, Oct. 17
Stone, J. S. James street, Westminster, oilman, Nov. 7
Smethurst, James, Oldham, innkeeper, Nov. 7
Scudamore, Richard, Red Lion street, Holborn, taylor, Nov. 21
Segary, John, Northampton, gun-maker, Oct. 30
Savage, William, Holborn, grocer, Nov. 10
Sainty, Philip, Brightlingsea, ship-builder, Nov. 9, final
Tanner, William, Paddington, smith and farrier, Oct. 17
Terry, J. and William Richards, Birmingham, button and buckle-makers, Oct. 26
Tite, John, Loughton, farmer, Oct. 21
Thornborrow, Henry, Little Bolton, cotton-manufacturer, Oct. 30
Tweddell, J. Liverpool, Nov. 6
Tipping, Ebenez. Liverpool, soap-boiler, Nov. 23
Veville, Thos. Leadenhall market, Nov. 12
Willats, Fred. Brewer street, cheesemonger, Nov. 5
Wilkinson, Wm. and Thos. Chapman (jointly and separately) late of Jewry street, and of the Coal Exchange, coal-factors, Nov. 7, final
Walford, J. Pall Mall, haberdasher, Nov. 3
Walker, Wm. Monkgate, York, ink-maker, Nov. 2, final
Wright, Geo. and Jos. late of Leeds, flax-spinners, Nov. 4
Whittington, Wm. Bradford, Wilts, clothier, Nov. 9
Walford, John, Red Lion square, apothecary, Nov. 28

INCIDENTS, MARRIAGES AND DEATHS IN AND NEAR LONDON.

With Biographical Memoirs of distinguished Characters recently deceased.

The corporation of the Trinity-house, London, have lately ordered a survey to be taken of a shoal (either newly discovered or not generally known) lying S. W. from the Floating Light upon the Well, on the coast of Norfolk; the survey, though a cursory one, is sufficiently accurate to ascertain nearly its situation.—The marks and bearings are as follow: the Dudgeon Light vessel, N. E. about six miles; Blackney church, S. half W.; Cromer Light S. by E. half E.; and Holkham church S. W. half W. The north end is nearest the light; the south end has about three fathoms at low neap tide, but at low spring tide, not more than 14 feet; it is very narrow, and ranges nearly N. and S. in length about three miles. This shoal lies far within the common track, but as colliers, &c. keep near the land, for fear of the enemy, they frequently fall in amongst these shoals.

The two celebrated grape-vines of Hampton-court and Valentines, in Essex, have been astonishingly productive this year, the former having yielded one ton six hundred and fifty pounds, and the latter one ton two hundred and twenty seven pounds. For one year's crop of the last mentioned vine, the late Mr. Weltje, about 15 years ago, gave the sum of 400 guineas!

Application is intended to be made to Parliament in the next session, for an act for enlarging the market-place of Smithfield, in the city of London; for purchasing such houses and land, in the parish of St. Sepulchre, as may be wanted for that purpose, and for the better regulation of the market.

We are sorry to mention the loss of his Majesty's frigate Lowestoffe, of 32 guns, Captain Plampin; also, according to report, six sail of the homeward-bound West Indiamen, part of her convoy. They were lost soon after they left Jamaica, on one of the Heneagas, a small island of the Bahamas. The crews were, however, happily saved by the Acasto frigate, Captain Fellows.

La Determinee frigate of 24 guns, Capt. Searle captured

captured at the latter end of July, off Alexandria, a French corvette with a valuable cargo, and 10,000l. in specie, destined for the payment of General Menou's troops. This event is communicated in letters from La Determinée, dated the 26th of July.

On Tuesday, (being Michaelmas-day,) the election of the Lord Mayor for the ensuing year took place at Guildhall. The several aldermen, in rotation, being put up, alderman Newman had an universal show of hands of the livery in his favour, and Sir John Eamer, had such a number that he and alderman Newman was returned to the Court of Aldermen for their selection, and that Court thought proper to declare the election to be in favour of Sir John Eamer, who thereupon made a speech, in which he said, he would make no promises, but called the gentlemen of the livery to witness his affection to the best of sovereigns and attachment to the constitution, and reminded them of his merits as a man of business, a magistrate, and a *soldier*.

At the Shakespeare Tavern, on the 10th of October, a numerous meeting was held, of the friends of Mr. Fox, to celebrate the anniversary of his election for Westminster. The wonderful coincidence in the anniversary of the first election of this patriotic friend of Peace and Liberty, and the Ratification of that peace he had so ardently, but unsuccessfully, endeavoured first to preserve, and afterwards to restore to his country, attracted an unusual assemblage to this joyous meeting. After dinner, Mr. Fox drank—"Success to the Preliminaries of Peace." The health of Mr Fox, being drank with unbounded and enthusiastic applause, he arose and expressed himself to the following purport:—"Gentlemen, it is now twenty-one years since you first did me the honour to elect me as your Representative in Parliament. We were then engaged in a war against the freedom of the human race, and having, as I flattered myself you had done, given me credit for opposing with all the powers I was able, that diabolical war, and the detestable views that produced it, you elected me as an abettor of your general principles, rather than on account of any intrinsic merit of my own. At that time, however, I was comparatively but little known to you; we have since been better acquainted; a war of a similar description has since been excited; and the political sentiments which induced me to oppose the former, have compelled me, with all the powers of which I am possessed, year after year, to resist this second aggression against the general liberties of mankind. A frequent appeal to your principles has rendered me well acquainted with them; I know that in general you, as well as myself, objected to this war, and I exerted all the efforts of which I was possessed to put an end to it. I saw that it involved the very basis of our own free constitution, as well as that which the Republic of France had voluntarily, determined to accept: its very commencement declared, that mankind should have a monarchy, whether they wished for a monarchy or not; and *that* a monarchy, with respect to the nation then resisting so detestable a doctrine, the worst and most tyrannical under heaven; for, let us not deceive ourselves, the increased gentleness in the manners of mankind at large, and particularly in those of the people to whom I now advert—the augmented diffusion of knowledge, and the superior cunning of diplomatic science, had certainly, even long before this period, rendered the tyranny of this constitution less prominent, and consequently more tolerable, than that of perhaps several other constitutions within the precincts of Europe—but I scruple not to assert, that in itself it was the most despotic and detestable constitution under the sun. The war, however, was commenced for the express purpose of compelling this immense body of people to submit, against their consents, to this iniquitous Government. The Ministry of this country were determined that they should have a king, whether they would or not; and, sanctioned by what I knew to be the opinion of the inhabitants of this city, I felt myself bound, as I ever shall do, to resist so tyrannical an effort, and to hope and pray that the general rights of mankind would be triumphant over every part of the globe, whenever called in question. With this view I opposed the conduct of the Ministers, as long as I thought my own individual opposition could be of any avail; and I then withdrew, from a consciousness of my own inability, but not without its having been since supported by far greater talents and abilities than those to which I have any pretension."

After congratulating the country upon obtaining Peace, as to the terms he should, not he said, critically enquire into them; and he hoped they would not very scrupulously be enquired into by any man. The mere possession of an island or two in the West Indies, or a province in the Mediterranean ought not to be put in competition with the duration of the evils of war for a single month. He acknowledged that he opposed the late Ministry till he thought opposition was useless. He concluded with saying, that the conditions were glorious for the French Republic; it must be confessed that they are, and there is not a Briton who ought not honestly to rejoice that such is the fact. The people of France resisted as they ought to do, and as our own ancestors heretofore had done, the whole combination of powers who would have imposed upon them a constitution contrary to their own will—their's was the cause of liberty—the cause of mankind at large.

Married.] At Tottenham, N. Harden, esq. to Miss H. Meeke.

Mr. Sparrow, to Miss Higginbotham, both of King-street, Westminster.

At St. George's church, Hendon, Mr. C. Townley, engraver to the King of Prussia, to Miss M. Durham, of Doctor's-commons.

Mr. Langhorn of Clapham, to Miss Box, of Doctor's-commons.

Mr. T. Follett, of the Salopian coffee-house, Charing Cross, to Miss A. Stevenson, of the same place.

P. Benezech, esq. of Beaufort-buildings, to Mrs. M'Lachire, widow, of Oxford-street, Marybone.

At Aldersgate church, Mr. J. Smith, grocer, to Miss M. Eyre.

At Marybone church, E. Hillard, esq. of Cowley-house, Middlesex, to Mrs. Colborne, of Shriding-green, Bucks.

Captain R. Lowe, of the Fifeshire Fencibles, to Miss Manners, daughter of the Hon. Mr. Manners, of Lambeth.

Mr. Clement, of Wotton, to Miss Hardisty, of Bedford Court, Covent-garden.

Mr. W. Blackhall, to Miss E. Hewson, both of Basinghall-street.

By special licence, at Earl Fauconberg's, T. Wynn, esq. nephew to Lord Newborough, to the Right Honorable Lady C. Bellayse, eldest daughter of the Earl of Fauconberg.

At Ampthill, Bedfordshire, the Hon. G. Brown, lieutenant in the 13th light dragoons, to Miss M. Colston, youngest daughter of the late Reverend A Colston, of Filkins-hall, Oxfordshire.

Mr. W. Wood, soap-manufacturer, of Bishopsgate-street, to Mrs. Taylor, of Maryland-point, Stratford, Essex.

At St. George's Wapping, Richard Ellis, esq. of Church-alley, Abchurch-lane, Lombard-street, to Miss Mary Spence, of Wapping. An agreeable young lady, with every accomplishment to make the married state happy.

Mr. Clarke, junior, of Upper Belgrave-place, Chelsea, to Miss Nalder, of Cheapside.

Mr. J. C. Lowe, of Pentonville, to Miss S. Howell, of Monmouth.

Captain Byron, of the navy, to Miss Sykes, of Arundel-street.

Mr. B. Barfoot, of the Curtain-road, Moorfields, to Miss R. Harris, of Harwich.

Mr. T. Jefferies, of Spitalfields, to Miss Anderson, of King-street, Westminster.

The Rev. R. Durnford, of Sandleford, Berks, to Miss Mount, of Merton, Surrey.

At Christ Church, Surrey, Mr. St. Jones, of Friday-street, to Miss M. Ligley, of Great Surrey-street.

At Marybone Church, ——— Brisac, esq. to Miss Farquharson, of Harley-street.

Mr. Bolton, of Great Queen-street, Westminster, to the only daughter of the late J. Carlton, esq. of the navy.

The Rev. Sir J. Head, bart. of Marybone, to Miss Walker, of Russel-place.

Died.] In his 89th year, the Rev. O. Manning, B. D. Vicar of Godalming in Surrey. This gentleman, when a student at the University of Oxford, fell sick of the small-pox and was supposed to die of it; in consequence of which he was laid out. His affectionate father, having left the room, returned to take a last view of the youth, and looking steadfastly on the countenance, thought he perceived something uncommon, and fancied he saw signs of life. The more he looked, the more he was convinced. He accordingly ordered proper means to be used with the body, and the young man was restored to life, and in a short time to perfect health. He has since had several children, and about sixty years have been added to his life.

In her 66th year, Mrs. Morris, of Knightsbridge, widow of the gallant Captain Morris, who was killed at the attack of Charlestown, in the beginning of the American war.

In her 25th year, Mrs. Smith, wife of Mr. R. P. Smith, of Whitechapel-road.

T. Hammond, esq. clerk in the Tellers-office, Exchequer, and for many years deputy agent to the Out-pensioners of Chelsea Hospital.

At Clapham Common, Mr. W. Leatham, merchant, of Basinghall-street.

At Dulwich, aged 72, Mrs. Flint, of London-bridge.

At Chelsea, Mrs. S. Holder, widow of Mr. R. Holder, late of Innholders-hall, London.

Mrs. E. Charlesworth, of Cornhill, who for many years kept a childbed-linen-warehouse there.

Mr. Davenport, one of the assistant pages to the Queen.

Mrs. Calvert, wife of Mr. Calvert, of the Stamp-office.

At Brompton Villa, Sir J. Gresham, bart. the last male-heir of that ancient family.

At Greenwich, Mr. T. Shipman, grocer, a very old inhabitant of that place.

At his son's house, in New Bond-street, aged 69, Mr. T. Stewart.

At Edmonton, Mrs. H. Wilson; this lady was taken suddenly ill with a pain in her head, went to lay down, and continued, to all appearance, in a comfortable sleep, till two days following, when she expired without a sigh.

At Sir Vere Hunt's, bart. Whitehall, J. Hamilton Lane, esq. of Lane's-park, county of Tipperary.

In Berwick-street, S. James's, aged 64, Mr. W. Brown.

Mrs. Wimperis, of St. John's-square, Clerkenwell.

At Richmond, Surrey, in his 68th year, R. Darell, esq. of Sackville-street, Deputy Governor of the South Sea Company.

In Hertford-street, Park-lane, aged 80, of a cancer in her mouth, the Right Hon. the Countess of Holderness.

In Bridge-street, Mrs. Letsom, widow of the late Dr. J. M. Letsom, and daughter of W. Nanson, esq.

PROVINCIAL

PROVINCIAL OCCURRENCES.

WITH ALL THE MARRIAGES AND DEATHS,

Arranged geographically, or in the Order of the Counties, from North to South.

**** Authentic Communications for this Department are always very thankfully received.*

NORTHUMBERLAND AND DURHAM.

The Infirmary in Newcastle is, at length, about to receive those considerable additions and repairs it has so long wanted:—a more complete separation of the sick-wards, a thorough ventilation, and the introduction of water by pipes to every apartment, are among the leading projected improvements. An additional wing is also intended to be built, the foundation stone of which, including a plate with an appropriate inscription, was laid on the 23d of September, by Sir M. W. Ridley, bart. one of the Vice Presidents of the charity, who delivered a neat, occasional speech, expressed in the most feeling manner, in the presence of a great number of subscribers, well-wishers, spectators, &c.

The Agricultural Society for the county of Durham, at their meetings lately held at Darlington and Durham, adjudged and paid the following rewards:—to Mr. R. Chipchase, of Chester-le-street, five guineas for the best tup; to G. Baker, esq. of Elemore, five guineas for the best shearing tup, both kept in Chester ward; to Mr. M. Hutton, of East Shaws, five guineas for the best cow; to Mr. C. Colling, of Ketton, five guineas for the best shearing tup; to Mr. W. Gascoigne, of Middleton-one-row, two guineas, fo bringing his tup to Darlington; all kept in Darlington and Stockton-wards. Also to W. Bruce, a cottager of Redworth, for having maintained, educated and placed in service, nine legitimate children without assistance from his parish, four guineas; to J. Sanderson, cottager, of Wolviston, for having maintained six legitimate children, &c. &c. two guineas; to George Wilkin, of Kibblesworth, for continuing 37 years in one place of service (husbandry) four guineas; and to Jane Brancepeth for continuing 22 years in one place of service (management of a dairy) four guineas.

A Lobster was lately caught near the town of North Berwick, which weighed between six and seven lbs. avoirdupoize. The extreme joint of the claw measured nine inches in length, and, at the thickest part, 10 inches in circumference!

Married.] Mr. T. Sheffield, of the Land-tax-office, Durham, to Miss Sparrow, of Sunderland.—Mr. G. Henderson, traveller to Messrs. Starforth and Son, to Miss Robinson, all of Durham.—The Rev. C. Isham, rector of Polbrook, Northamptonshire, to Mrs. Bradford, second daughter of the late Reverend G. Johnson, vicar of Norton.

Mr. J. Fenwick, ship owner, to Miss E. Frank, both of North Shields.

At Sunderland, Captain C. Sharp, to Miss Brass.

At Newcastle, Mr. A. Sillick, currier, to Miss Kell.

At Long Benton, Mr. J. Sanderson, to Miss Lumsden.—Mr. J. Jopling, to Miss Allison, both of Gateshead.

Died.] At Monk Wearmouth, Mr. Wake, senior.—Mr. Gowland, smith.

At Stockton, at an advanced age, Mr. S. Wheelwright.

At Barnsley, in Yorkshire, Mr. Hepper, hosier, father of Mr. J. Hepper, hosier, in Newcastle.

At Sunderland, Mr. M. Stephenson, sadler.—Mrs. Cassop, wife of Mr. Cassop, ship-owner.—Mr. J. Punshon, anchorsmith.—Suddenly, Mr. J. Hardcastle, attorney.—Aged upwards of 90, Mr. J. Galley, fitter.—Miss Richardson, youngest daughter of W. Richardson, esq. of Hauxley.—Aged 19, Miss Fenwick, daughter of N. Fenwick, esq. of Lemington.

At Port Royal, Island of Jamaica, Mr. W. Smith, formerly of Newcastle.

At Wolsington, Miss D. Bell, second daughter of M. Bell, esq.

At Chester-le-street, Mrs. Colling.

In the Manor Chare, aged 74, Mr. R. Bell.—Aged 50, Mr. S. Smith, of Bushblades, near Durham.

Mr. J. Emmerson, a young man of Birtley; he had been advertised several weeks, as missing, and was lately found dead in Leeburnhold Gill.

At Apple-cross, in Scotland, T. Mackenzie, esq. father of Mr. Mackenzie of Durham.

CUMBERLAND AND WESTMORELAND.

Application is intended to be made to Parliament, in the next session, to obtain an act for making a new road, to extend from Beatock, in the parish of Kirkpatrick Juxta, Dumfriesshire, North Britain, to the city of Carlisle, in Cumberland; and also for making and erecting a bridge across the river Sark, betwixt the present bridge and a place called Allison's Bank; and, likewise, another bridge across the river Esk, near to a place called Gariftown; which said road and bridges are proposed to extend and pass through the several parishes of Kirkpatrick Juxta, Johnston, Applegarth, Lochmaben, Dalton, Cummertrees, Annan and Gretna, all in the county of Dumfries, in North Britain; and also through the several parishes of Kirk Andrews-upon-Esk, Rockliff,

liff, and Stanwix, and the extra parochial hamlet of Kingmoor, all in the county of Cumberland.

A mushroom was lately taken upon Underbarrow Common, near Kendal, which measured twenty-seven inches in circumference, and eight inches in diameter, and weighed fourteen ounces avoirdupois-weight. Both nuts and mushrooms have been, indeed, very abundant through the whole county of Westmorland.

The depth of rain which fell in Carlisle last month, was 4,804 parts of an inch. Greatest height of the barometer, 30.32: least ditto, 29.48. Greatest height of the thermometer, 71°: least ditto, 35°.

A newspaper has, within these few weeks past, been established in the Isle of Man, from one of the later numbers of which, we copy the following paragraph: "We are happy to state that the harvest through this island promises greater plenty than has been known in any former year!"

It is well worthy of remark, that the manure arising from the streets of the city of Carlisle, which, about twenty years ago, was considered of so little value that a person used to receive the annual reward of a new cart, for the trouble of taking it away, has been lately let for upwards of 100l. for the ensuing year.

A field belonging to Mr. John Wright, of Longtown, in Cumberland, has produced, this season, two very productive crops of barley. The first crop was reaped on the 25th of July, and the second, (which grew from the old root) on the 15th of September.

As a further instance of the extraordinary mildness of the season, and the vegetating tendency of the weather, the Cumberland papers mention a second crop of strawberries as growing, at this time, in the garden of John Sanderson, esq. of Plumpton. They are in different stages of growth; some in full blossom, some just forming, and others perfectly formed and verging to maturity.

Married.] At Whitehaven, Mr R Greggs, to Miss S. Trimble.—Mr. Postlethwayte, to Miss Rochford.—Mr. J. Irvine, widower, to Mrs. M. Wilkinson, widow.—Mr. W. Chambers, widower, of Aglionby, to Mrs. E. Potts, widow.

At Harrington, Mr. J. Kay, master of the ship Eagle, to Miss Plaskett, of Dissington.—Mr. J. Lawson, to Miss D. Simpson.

At Workington, Mr. J. Donald, to Mrs. Rickerby.

At Kendal, Mr. W. Elleray, tanner, to Miss A. Wilson, of the Black Swan inn.—Mr. J. Baynes, plumber, &c. to Miss A. Tate, innkeeper.—Mr. T. Brinnan, linen-manufacturer, to Miss Smith, mantua-maker.

At the Quaker's meeting-house, Mr. Ebenezer Bowman, farmer, of Oak Oak, near Buxton, Derbyshire, to Miss Ann Stewardson, daughter of G. Stewardson, linen-draper, of Kendal.

At Gretna Green, Mr. Graham, of Stoney Flatts, to Miss Warwick, of Burnside, in Kirklinton

Died.] At Carlisle, at an advanced age, Mrs. J. Weightman, wife of Mr. W. Weightman, taylor.—Aged 62, Mrs. M. Batey, a maiden-lady.—Mr. T. Pulletts, a private in the 3d regiment of dragoons.—Aged 48, Mr. C. Kallan, weaver.—In his 22d year, Mr. J. Borriskill, attorney.—Mrs. M. Armstrong.—Aged 95, Mrs. Priestman, school-mistress.

At Whitehaven, in his 56th year, Mr. N. Thompson, merchant.

In his 51st year, Mr. W. Perry, iron facturer; esteemed through life, for his industry, spirit and probity, in an extensive line of business, and regretted in his death, as a truly valuable member of society.

Aged 63, Mr. J. Martin.—Aged 63, Mr. J. M'Farlin, shoe-maker.

At Kendal, in an advanced age, Mrs. Wilson, wife of Mr. T. Wilson, formerly an alderman of the burgh.—Mr. B. Sinkinson, fish-hook-maker.

At Workington, aged 65, Mrs. Thompson, relict of the late Capt. Adam Thompson, of the ship Love.

At Cockermouth, aged 33, Mr. W. White, in the service of Mr. A. Robinson, carrier between Whitehaven and Carlisle.—Aged 96, Mr. Plasket.

At Beck-mills, near Kendal, in the prime of life, Mr J. Holme, miller.

At Cleator, Miss Forster.

Lately, in the West Indies, Mr. C. Skelton, lieutenant on board the sloop of war Calypso, and son of the late A. J. Skelton, esq. of Whitehaven.

At Cumrenton, near Brampton, in an advanced age, Mr. J. Bowstead, father of Mr. T. Bowstead, tanner, of Carlisle.

At Fredericksburg, in Virginia, Mr. D. Blair, merchant, formerly of Whitehaven.

At Rowscale, in the parish of Greystoke, in his 83d year, Mr. J Wilson, a Quaker.

At Morland, in Westmorland, in his 62d year, Mr. J. Thompson, a Quaker; much respected by a numerous acquaintance, for his innocent life and conduct.

At the Rev. Mr. T. Williamson's, New Cavendish-street, London, aged 69, Mrs I. Huddlestone, one of the daughters of the late W. Huddlestone, esq. of Millom Castle, in Cumberland.

At Catcoats, near Carlisle, aged 87, Mrs. I. Topping.

YORKSHIRE.

Application is intended to be made to Parliament, in the ensuing session, for an Act for making a New Wet Dock at the port of Hull, to extend from the town to the Long Jetty, westward,

westward, within the lordship of Myton, in Trinity parish.

By the plan proposed last year, for making a Wet Dock, to extend round the town of Hull to the Humber, the Dock-Company were to give 30 shares, which, at 1000l each share, makes 30,000l.; the waste-ground not less than 10,000l. more; the annual expence attending the undertaking, would have been about 2000l. per annum, which, at 20 years purchase, is 40,000l.; so that, according to that scheme, the Dock Company would be sinking 80,000l; whereas, according to a plan at present in agitation, the New Dock may be made for about half the money, in much less time. A general wish has been, indeed, expressed, that a coalition for this purpose should take place between the Corporation of the town and the Dock Company, which would put a friendly period to all that contention that seems to agitate the public mind; under this union the works might be immediately begun, and that without the intervention of parliamentary authority.

Proposals are in general circulation for publishing, by subscription, a Plan of the Town of Kingston-upon-Hull, including the garrison or adjoining forts, the parishes of Sculcoates and Drypool, and the principal part of the lordship of Myton. To be executed on the same large scale as the plans of London and Liverpool, i. e three chains, or 66 yards, to an inch. It is intended to distinguish, accurately, the different parishes and wards, and likewise every yard, garden, passage, entry, staith, and even the number and form of every house. To be finished and ready to be delivered to the subscribers in the year 1803.—Price to subscribers two guineas.

Married.] Mr. Wilkinson, surveyor of taxes, late of Ackworth, to Miss Humphrey, of Fulford, late of York.—Mr. Lindley, of Bubworth House, near Ferrybridge, to Miss A. Warren, of Empingham.

At Barnsley, Mr. J. Hindle, linen-merchant, to Miss Whitworth, daughter of Mr. Whitworth, sadler.—The Rev. W. Lax, F. R. S. Lowndes Prof. of Astronomy in the university of Cambridge, to Miss Cradock, of Hartforth, in this county.

At Hull, Mr. H. Lee, grocer, to Miss M. Ryder.—Mr. G. Glen, tallow-chandler, of Sculcoates, to Miss M. Stephenson, niece to the late Mr. Stephenson, cornfactor.—Mr. T. M. Rickhard, merchant, to Miss Leigh, daughter of R. Lee, esq. collector of excise.—Mr. E. Chimley, miller, of Sculcoates, to Miss C. Shephard.—Mr. W. Roberts, hardwareman, to Miss Nuttell, daughter of Mr. J. Nuttell, hatmaker.—Mr. T. Staniland, spirit-merchant, of Thorne (late of Hull) to Miss A. Fleming, daughter of the Rev. J. Fleming, rector of Thornton, near Skeptow, in Craven.

At Acklam, Mr. J. West, Methodist local preacher, aged 70, to Mrs. J. Harrison, aged 44.—Mr. J. Steer, farmer, of Hansworth, to Miss S. Lomas, of Attercliffe Forge.—Mr. J. Cooper, draper, of Sheffield, to Miss E. Martin, daughter of Mr. T. Martin, merchant, of London.—Mr. Allott, of Wakefield, to Miss Hodson, of Middleton hall.

T. Midgley, esq. of Cookridge-hall, near Leeds, to Miss Bulmer, of Middleham.

Mr. J. Littlewood, of Gainsboro', to Miss S. Gilderdale, of Thorne.

Captain Schonswar, of the East York regiment of Militia, to Miss L. Smith, of Willerby, second daughter of the late J. Smith, esq. of Hull.—Mr. W. Calvert, master of the ship Barneveldt, in the London-trade, to Mrs. Wallis, widow of the late Mr. W. Wallis, of Hull.

At St. Anne's, Aldersgate, in London, Mr. J. Crossley, formerly of Hull, to Miss Slate, of Noble-street, London.

Mr. W. Ware, merchant, of London, to Miss Wetherall, of Hutton, near Thirsk.

Died.] At York, in her 73d year, Lady Anderson, relict of Sir Edmund Anderson, bart. formerly of Kilnwick Piercy.—In her 71st year, Mrs. Calvert, widow.—Aged 53, Mr. Francis Mason, a Baptist-preacher, and founder of the Baptist Society in this city.—Aged 58, C. Benson, esq.—At his lodgings in this city, where he had come for medical assistance, aged 58, Mr. J. Nicholson, cloth-manufacturer, of Wass, near Easingwould.—Aged 74, Mrs. Dunnington, sister to Mr. Dunnington, of Thorganby, near this city.—In her 82d year, Mrs. M. M. Wynn, sister of the late C. Wynn, esq. of Acton-hall, in this county.—Mrs. Garencieres, wife of Mr. Alderman Garencieres.

At Hull, aged 44, Mrs. E. Gibson, wife of Mr. Gibson, ship-builder.—Aged 53, Mr. W. Drew, master shoemaker.—Aged 49, Mrs. Rogers, wife of Mr. H. Rogers, tobacconist.—Miss A. E. Read, daughter of Col. Read, of the Northumberland Militia.

At Leeds, Mr. J. Scott, corn dealer.

At Sheffield, Mr. Knutton, merchant.—Mr. Harrison, of Holliscroft.—Mrs. Hodgkinson, of the Queen's Head-inn.

At Beverley, aged 21, of the gout in his stomach, J. Sutton, esq. eldest son of Sir R. Sutton, bart. of Norwood Park, in Nottinghamshire.—Aged 74, Mr. W. Brown, butcher.

At Settle, while drinking tea at the house of a friend, the Rev. R. Williams, A. M. formerly of Christ College, Cambridge, and incumbent of two benefices in Kent.

At Calverley, Mr. R. Clayton, merchant, late of Leeds.

At Scarboro', Mr. W. Kirkby, late master of the ship Advice, belonging to Hull.

At Doncaster, aged 63, J. Cowlry, esq.—Aged 47, Mr. Campbell, musician, who, about six weeks ago, buried three of his children within the space of seven days.

Aged 42, Mr. Daniel, steward to the corporation.

At Howden, aged 77, Mr. J. Whitaker.

In

In his 77th year, Mr. C. Wilſon, of Rawmarſh, near Rotherham.

In London, Mrs. Rhodes, wife of A. Rhodes, eſq. of Acacia Cott, near Leeds.

At Hambleton, near Selby, Miſs Richardſon, a young lady univerſally lamented.

At Bilham, at an advanced age, Mr. Porter, late of Pigburn, near Doncaſter.

At Wilton, aged 64, Mrs. Acklom, relict of J. Acklom, eſq.

At Settrington, Mrs. Gilbert, wife of the Rev. R. Gilbert.

Aged 21, Mr. T. Stickney, of Summergangs, near Hull.

At Briſtol, after a ſhort indiſpoſition, for which the waters of that place had been tried without effect, aged 60, Sir Chriſtopher Sykes, of Sledmire, near Malton, bart, L.L.D. and juſtice of peace for the Eaſt Riding. His death is generally and juſtly lamented, as he was an indulgent huſband, a tender father, a ſincere friend, an impartial magiſtrate, a good man, a liberal benefactor to the poor, and, on the whole, a bright ornament to ſociety. Few men have, perhaps, exiſted, whoſe taſte has more ſtrongly improved his country's beauties, or whoſe memory will live longer in the works they have left behind them. What, in ſome parts of England, have been called "ornaments and decorations," ſink to nothing, when the large ſcale of his improvements are conſidered, which extended themſelves, in various directions, over a ſurface of near 100 miles. The exact order, too, in which they were preſerved, is not leſs remarkable than their formation. Of his own labours he was unſparing. He generally roſe at an earlier hour than the labourers of the country, and had frequently rode 20 miles before thoſe, who think themſelves active, have riſen from their beds. Every plan of amending the ſtate of the country, whether by drainage or incloſure, by building or navigation, found in him an active friend and zealous ſupporter. In fine, he was, in every ſenſe of the word—*an enlightened country gentleman.*—By ſome, perhaps, it may have been thought that he was too attentive to the accumulation of riches. But to no paltry purpoſe were they applied, nor confined within his own coffers. The large demands for money, which his eſtabliſhments, his numerous buildings, his various plantations, and a never-ceaſing ſeries of new works, continued to make, required, indeed, no ſmall foreſight to provide that, which ſo much beneficence freely paid away. He who converts a *barren land* into a ſtate of *decorated agriculture*, and who changes the whole face and figure of a country, cannot do it at little coſt. In ſhort, Sir C. Sykes has left behind him, in his works, a memorial that will grow with time itſelf. Whoever paſſes over the Wolds of Yorkſhire, where this gentleman had property, and recalling to his mind what they formerly were, now ſees what they are, will have cauſe to remember the name of Sykes, who has truly realized the antient inſcription—"*Si quæras monumentum, circumſpice*"—"If you aſk for his monument, look around you." May the example operate upon others, and while the numbers of thoſe who *live to do miſchief*, and of thoſe who *live to do nothing*, are conſidered, HE who lived to do a GREAT PUBLIC GOOD, may well be ſelected for grateful remembrance. Sir Chriſtopher is ſucceeded in the title by his eldeſt ſon, Mark Sykes, eſq. of Setterington, high-ſheriff for this county, in 1795.

Mrs. Biſhop, of Salter-lane, near Sheffield.

Suddenly, Mr. J. Knowles, merchant, of Gomerſall, near Leeds. He had been at Leeds-market on the preceding day, apparently, in perfect health.

LANCASHIRE.

The eſtabliſhment of union corn-mills, at Mancheſter, will be ready for work about the beginning of the enſuing month. The avowed purpoſe of this undertaking is to ſerve the ſubſcribers, and the public at large, by reſtoring the corn-market, and enabling individuals of all deſcriptions as well as bakers and retailers of flour, to have their corn ground as may be moſt ſuitable for their own uſe, and likewiſe to preſerve it pure and unadulterated. The ſituation of theſe mills on the bank of the Rochdale Canal, will greatly facilitate the conveyance of grain from Liverpool and from the Duke of Bridgewater's, Staffordſhire, Yorkſhire, Derbyſhire, Peak Foreſt, Huddersfield, &c. canals; there is little doubt but the farmers will have a quick and regular ſale for their corn, at fair and more ſettled prices than by depending on the corn-dealers for the diſpoſal of their ſtocks. Private families may ſend ſingle loads, exempted from the charge of carriage, and half-loads will be received from the middle and lower claſſes of people. The price of grinding, is fixed at 1s. 6d. per load, excluſive of carriage.

Of the various extraordinary productions which have marked the preſent year, as wonderfully abounding in inſtances of prolific vegetation, the following, which is aſſuredly a fact, and, as ſuch, is vouched for by the Editor of the Mancheſter Chronicle, muſt certainly be eſteemed as one of the moſt ſingular. In the ground of Mr. J. Royle, publican, at Withington, in the neighbourhood of Mancheſter, there is, (or lately was) a ſingle potatoe, which meaſures, in the circumference of ſpace it takes up, twenty feet!

There is at preſent living in the townſhip of Over Darwin, near Blackburn, a winder of twiſt, named Mr. James Morice, who, on the 9th of July laſt had attained the age of 102 years; the twiſt which he winds he uſually carries home, from whence he can walk to Preſton, (a diſtance of 14 miles) and back again any day.

A new theatre is to be erected by ſubſcription, at Preſton, in a ſtile of capacious elegance, correſponding with the other improvements

ments daily making in that flourishing town. It is expected that it will be completed for the reception of company, by August next, when the famous mart or guild merchant, held there every 20th year, will be celebrated with the usual festivity. This mart will be the 29th since the first institution, in the 2d year of the reign of King Edward the Third, in the year 1329. Upwards of 1500l. have been already subscribed towards the expence of building the fabric, the execution of the internal part of which is to be under the direction of Mr. Stanton, whose architectural abilities have been long known and admired. The intended new theatre is to be erected on the South side of Fishergate, near the Toll Bars.

In consequence of defects in the original plan of the Lunatic Hospital, at Manchester, and other imperfections in the institution, it is proposed to convert the present hospital into a Fever-ward, and to erect a NEW LUNATIC HOSPITAL, upon an *improved plan*, thoroughly adequate for correcting the existing evils, near the town, yet at a convenient distance from it. The original plan is acknowledged to be ill adapted to the present modes of treating insane persons, and the faculty have, moreover, declared their opinion, that it cannot be altered, so as to accomplish their views, for the benefit of their patients. It appears, likewise, that numbers of incurable patients have been admitted into the present Lunatic Hospital, from other places of confinement, while patients, whose cases were proper objects of practice, have been excluded. To the above suggestion it may not be unseasonable to add the following: the experience of five years has proved that febrile contagion is not communicated from a Fever-ward to neighbouring buildings. No person in the present Lunatic Hospital has been seized with a fever since the House of Recovery was opened. Should the intended plan be effected, a distinct part of the rooms in front of the Lunatic Hospital will be appropriated to the nurses, as there would be sufficient remaining room for the patients. The necessity for establishing a large Fever-ward on the Infirmary-grounds is generally admitted; by the proposed plan, an excellent Fever-ward and an improved Lunatic Hospital will be obtained, for the expence which a sufficient Fever-ward alone would cost. A new Lunatic Hospital, with the proposed improvements, may be erected for about 6 or 7000l, while the alterations necessary to convert the Lunatic Hospital into a Fever-ward, would be very speedily executed, and at a comparatively trifling expence.

Application is intended to be made to Parliament, in the ensuing session, for an act for making a turnpike-road, from or near Worsley, in the parish of Eccles, through Worsley, Barton upon Irwell, and the hamlets of Dumplington, Croft, and Loftock, all in the parish of Eccles, to the township of Stretford, in the parish of Manchester, all in this county, there to join and communicate with the turnpike-road, leading from Manchester to the town of Altringham, in the county of Chester. A similar application is intended, to obtain an act for inclosing, &c. the several moors, commons, &c. within the manor and parish of Rochdale.

Married.] At Lancaster, Mr. J. Woodburn, druggist, to Miss Gerrard.

At the Quakers' Meeting-house, Mr. W. Tessimond, to Miss M. Jepson.—Mr. R. Gibson, ironmonger, to Miss Atkinson.

At Liverpool, Mr. Jones, attorney, to Miss Thomas.—Captain G. Louthian, of the ship Barratt, to Miss S. Allcock.—T. Fenwick, esq. of Burrow-hall, in this county, to Miss Samms, of Margaret-street, Cavendish-square.—P. Ormerod, esq. of Rossgrove, to Miss Morris, of Burnley.—Mr. T. Smith, tanner, of Maudsley, to Miss B. Hatton, of Parbold.—Mr J. Okill, jun. of Liverpool, to Mrs. M. Orme, of Ormskirk.

At Manchester, Mr. W. Thompson, of Newark upon Trent, to Miss A. M. Worsley.—Mr. C. Bedford, of Wigan, to Miss Greendy, grand daughter of R. Kenyon, esq. of Highfield, near Wigan.

Died.] At Liverpool, Miss M. Powell, second daughter of the late Mr. J. Powell, merchant.—Aged 70, Mrs. Bayley, widow of the late Mr. Bayley, manufacturer, of Macclesfield.—Aged 61, Capt. J. Joy.

At Manchester, Mr. J. Heywood, manufacturer of small wares.—Mrs Dockwrag.—Miss Seddons, daughter of Mr. Seddons, attorney.

At Lancaster, Mr. H. Bell, silversmith.—Mr. Stirrup, liquor-merchant.—Mr. W. Mashiver.—T. Harris, M. D. alderman, much respected as a gentleman of great abilities.

In the prime of life, Mr. E. Burnett, linen-merchant.

At Ulverstone, Mr. T. Brockbanck, senior, grocer.—Captain William Shaw, of Urswick.

At Blackburn, Mrs. W. Wood, of the Dun Horse Inn.—Mr. Thomas Sharpless, attorney.

At Old Harbour, Jamaica, aged 37, Capt. R. Croasdell, of Liverpool.

At Prescott, aged 65, Mrs. Hatton, and in July last, at St. Vincents', West Indies, Mr. T. Hatton, her son. It is remarkable that five of the family have died within 13 months.

At Preston, Mr. W. Wilkinson. He had complained some days before of a pain in his left side, and in passing along the street, dropped down and instantly expired.

Mr. R. Holden, nailer.

Aged 71, Mr. J. Foster, of Elliot-hill.—Miss E. Andrew, of Green Mount, near Manchester.

At the Isle of Man, Mr. J. Lees, merchant, late of Halifax.

Mr. J. Hoskinson, of Holland-house, near Preston

Preston. His death was occasioned by a fall from a cart, by which he was so much hurt that he expired in a few minutes.

At Sephton, the Rev. R. Rothwell, rector.

At Marsden Chapel, near Colne, aged 78, Mr. J. Burrows, and on the same day, aged 78, his wife, Mrs. M. Burrows, and on the preceding evening, their grand-daughter, Jane Burrows.

Mr. J. Eccles, butcher, of Skerton, near Lancaster.

At St. Kitts, aged 35, Mr. J. Tyson, merchant.

Lately, in London, Mr. J. Brown, surgeon, of Liverpool.

At Ashton-under-Line, Mr. J. Ogden, spindle-maker.

At Grenada, West Indies, Mr. J. Bond, formerly of Lancaster. Mr. T. Bingley, one of the agents of the Warrington Cotton-Twist-Company.

At Demarara, Mr. J. C. Dawson, late of Manchester, and a captain in Colonel Silvester's battalion of Manchester and Salford Volunteers. This gentleman possessed an excellent understanding, an amiable disposition, an elegant deportment, and uncommon suavity of manners. Having visited a great part of Europe, he had successfully engrafted the brilliancy of foreign manners on the sterling worth of English character.

At North Meols, Mr. L. Hall, near 50 years schoolmaster and parish-clerk of that place.

At Poulton, in the Filde, Mr. Brown, formerly of Liverpool.

At Runcorn, Mr. J. Cooke, tin-plate-worker, of Manchester.—In her 65th year, Mrs. Graham, of Ardwick.

At Haton-hall, near Lancaster, R. Bradshaw, esq.

At his house, at Edge-hill, near Liverpool, aged 49, Mr. Richard Lowndes, of the Custom-house, where he had executed for upwards of 30 years an office of more labour than profit, and of more trust than honour, without having had the good fortune to arrive at any of those stations which are the fair rewards of industry, integrity, and superior understanding. The moderation of his desires, and the prudent economy of his private life, prevented him from feeling the want of promotion as a disappointment, and he rather chose to preserve with firmness his own liberal, though unobtrusive opinions, than to join as an advocate for a war which has impoverished and disgraced his country, and of which he only just lived to see the termination. His leisure hours have been devoted to literary studies and particularly to that of the best authors in our own language, in which he was a critic of uncommon accuracy, and an assertor of the purity of the true old English stile in opposition to the elisions and intrusions of some modern writers. In the year 1788, he married Susanna, the only surviving daughter of the late eminent Dr. Matthew Dobson, formerly of Liverpool, afterwards of Bath, and of the late Mrs. Dobson, well known in the literary world as translator of the Life of Petrarch. He survived her about two years, and has left several children by her.

CHESHIRE.

Married.] J. Boydell, esq. of the Rossett, in Denbighshire, to Miss Parker, of Chester.

At Kilken, Mr. R. Owen, grocer, of Mould, to Miss James, of Maes-y-Groes, Flintshire.

Mr. R. Sutton, attorney, of Macclesfield, to Miss H. Faulkner, of Stafford.

J. Harrison, esq. jun. of Cheadle, in this county, to Miss Jesson, of Wolverhampton.

Mr C. Bagnall, eldest son of C. Bagnall, esq. of Shelton, Staffordshire, to Miss F. Tolver, of Chester.

Mr. W. Caldwell, attorney, to Miss Billington, milliner, both of Frodsham.—The Rev. Mr. Warner, of Bath, to Miss A. Pearson, of Tettenhall.

Died.] At Chester, — Townshend, esq.

On the 13th of Sept. last, on his passage from the Baltic, Lieutenant J. Wilbraham, of the armed ship Sally, son of Mr. J. Wilbraham, of Chester.

At Nantwich, Mr. Martin, sen. much respected as a man of unblemished character.

At Frodsham, Mr. J. Urmson.

At Norley, Mrs. E. Hall, aunt to G. Whitley, esq. of Chester.

At Parkgate, Mrs. Townshend, wife of T. Townshend, of Chester.—Mrs. Roberts, of Tyn-y-Caia, near Ruthin, Denbighshire.

At his lodgings in London, aged 23, Mr. D. Hughes, surgeon, son of the late D. Hughes, esq. of Abergely; a young man of promising abilities.

DERBYSHIRE.

It is in contemplation to apply to Parliament for a turnpike-road to pass from Afreton through Ripley, and to join the Mansfield turnpike-road at Little Chester.

Married.] At Croxall, Mr. M. Webb, of Donkhill Pitts, to Miss Top.—Mr. H. Webb, of Swinford, in Worcestershire, to Miss E. Simpkins, of Eardingale.

At Derby, Mr. Wallis, to Miss Yates.—Mr. R. Jackson, to Miss Ward, both of Belper.

At Chelmorton, near Buxton, Mr. S. Britain, butcher, of Sheffield, to Miss A. Swan, daughter of Mr. T. Swan, cheese-factor, of Kingsterndale.—The Rev. J. Sidney, vicar of Ilkeston, to Miss Knighton, of Cotmanhay.

Died.] At a very advanced age, Mr. S. Mellor, of Itheridgehay.

At Wingfield Manor, Miss F. L. Halton, second daughter of W. Halton, esq.

At Streatham, near London, in her 48th year, Mrs Harding, wife of Mr. Harding, of Pall Mall, London, and sister to Mr. Ashby, of Egginton, in this county.—Also, at the same

same place, aged 22, Miss Lowe, niece of Mrs. Harding, and daughter of Mr. Lowe, of Egginton.

NOTTINGHAMSHIRE.

Married.] At Nottingham, Mr. Green, hosier, to Miss Howard, eldest daughter of Mr. J. Howard, maltster.—Mr. Fothergill, of York, to Miss R. Bott, dentist.—Mr. Brommitt, gun-smith, to Miss Beardsall.

At Southwell, Mr. Stead, of London, to Miss Falkner.

Died.] At Nottingham, Miss Swan, eldest daughter of Mr. E. Swan, grocer; a young lady greatly esteemed for her abilities, and equally admired for the excellency of her disposition.

LINCOLNSHIRE.

A new turnpike-road is intended to be made from the parish of Scartho, through the several intermediate parishes, to the town of Louth, all in this county.

The late collection at Lincoln Cathedral, for the benefit of the County Hospital, amounted to 85l. 16s. 6d.—exceeding the last year's collection more than 30l!

It is a very remarkable fact, that a single barley-corn, of the present year's growth, sown at Welbourn, near Grantham, has produced 208 straws, bearing 5,545 grains of corn!

There was lately growing (on Thursday, October 1,) in the garden of Captain Elmhirst, at Bag-Enderley, near Spilsby, an apple tree with full-blown blossoms upon it, and, at the same time, the tree bears a very large quantity of of exceeding fine fruit.

Lately was slaughtered a fat heifer belonging to Mr. R. Onyan, of Billinghay, near Sleaford, and upon her being opened, an entire calf was taken from her, with two complete heads, two livers, and six legs (three before and three behind); in other respects she was formed naturally.

Married.] Mr. J. Brown, of Butterwick, to Miss B. Ellis, of Flixborough.

At Goxhill, near Barrow, Mr. R. Woodale, farmer, to Miss S. Fulstow.—Mr. Whaley, of Wyvel, to Miss Emenson, of Barrowby, near Grantham.—Mr. Meadows, carpenter, of Stamford, to Miss Thorp, of Hykeham, near Lincoln.

At Louth, Mr. J. Healey, tanner, to Miss Taylor.—Mr. Pooley, of Upwood, in Huntingdonshire, to Miss Bromhead, of Duddington, near Stamford.

Died. At Lincoln, at the Saracen's Head-inn, aged 45, Mr. W. Motteram, factor, late of Birmingham.—Mr. J. Hare, peruke-maker, and one of the vergers belonging to the cathedral.

At Boston, Mrs. Kyme.

At Stamford, Mr. G. Parnham, youngest son of Mr. Parnham, saddler.—Aged 71, Mr. J. Crowson, shop-keeper.—Aged 92, Mrs Barker, widow.—Aged 85, Mrs. Edwards, mother of S. Edwards, esq.

At Louth, aged 91, Mrs. Gostolow.—Mrs. Chambers, widow of the late Mr. R. Chambers, baker.

Aged 35, Miss Godley, of Bicker, near Boston.—Mrs. Sneath, of Castle Bytham.

At Stamford Baron, aged 71, Mr. Cummins, grocer.—Advanced in years, Mrs. E. Hurton, publican, of Washingborough, near Lincoln.—Aged 75, Mr. C. Partridge, schoolmaster, of Carlton, near Lincoln.

At Benniworth, near Wragby, aged 98, Mr. J. Babington.—Aged 66, Mr. J. Bartholomew, of Bardney, near Lincoln, in consequence of a mortification, to stop which his leg was amputated about three weeks before.

In London, advanced in years, P. Renouard, esq. late of Stamford, and formerly justice of peace for the Soke of Peterborough.

At Sleaford, aged 53, Mrs. A. Goodyear.

At Surinam, of the yellow-fever, aged 25, Mr. W. Bennett, of the ship Louisa Henrietta, of London, youngest brother to Mr. C. Bennett, of Lincoln.

In the West Indies, Captain J. Hunt, son of the Rev. Mr. Hunt, rector of St. George's parish, Stamford.

Aged 56, Mrs. A. Carwell, of Ryal, near Stamford.

LEICESTERSHIRE.

At Leicester, lately, the collection for the benefit of the Leicestershire Infirmary and Lunatic Asylum, amounted to 69l. to which may be added, a donation of 10l. from Mr. Macready, manager of the theatre, and several other smaller benefactions.

Married.] Mr. J. Nutt, wine and brandy-merchant, of Leicester, to Miss Lloyd, of Coventry.

At Leicester, Mr. R. Kinton, ironmonger, &c. to Miss Harrison.

Died.] At Leicester, of a decline, Mrs. Peet, wife of Mr. Peet, taylor.—Mr. Bruce, surveyor, of the Ashby-road.

At Lutterworth, Mrs. Buzzard, wife of Mr. Buzzard, surgeon.—Of a decline, Mr. J. Reynolds, eldest son of the Rev. Mr. Reynolds, of Great Bowden, a young gentleman of engaging manners and amiable disposition.

At Claybrooke Hall, aged 20, deeply regretted, Miss Dicey, eldest daughter of T. Dicey, esq. an amiable young lady, possessed of fervent piety, with very superior intellectual accomplishments.

STAFFORDSHIRE.

Married.] J. Harrison, jun. esq. of Rolleston, to Miss Jesson, of Wolverhampton.

At Stafford, Mr. R. Sutton, attorney, of Macclesfield, to Miss H. Faulkner.

At Burslem, Mr. Bell, of Gaston, near Liverpool, to Miss Robinson.

At Wolverhampton, Mr. J. Ash, to Miss J. Greaham.

Died.] At Burton-upon-Trent, in his 18th

18th year, Mr J. Davenport, seventh son of the late Rev. S. Davenport, of Horsley, Derbyshire

At Uttoxeter, aged 74, Mr. S. Shaw.

At Walcot, Mr. J. Dyer, a blind man, who had resided 45 years in the parish, and supported himself by his own labour, having never received any parochial aid.

At Wolverhampton, aged 93, Mrs. E. Tildesley, late of the Bull's Head public-house, Willenhall.

Lately, in London, T. Fowler, esq. M.D. formerly of Stafford, and many years physician to the General Infirmary.—In her 13th year, Miss Child, only daughter of Rear-Admiral Child, of Newcastle under-Line.

WARWICKSHIRE.

Married.] At Birmingham, Mr. E. Dugmore, japanner, to Mrs. Butler.—Mr. J. W. Crompton, to Miss Webster.

At Shiffnall, Mr. F. Halley, builder, to Miss S. Cherrington.

At Aston, Mr. J. Wynn, of Islington-wharf, to Miss M Palmer, of Deritend.

At Dudley, Mr. J. Baker, of Old Hill, to Miss A. Wilkes.

Mr. J. Cox, junior, plane-maker, to Miss Wallins, both of Deritend.

At Rugeley, Mr. R. Waddams, hat-maker, to Miss M. Nixon.—Mr. J. Flynd, gimblet-maker, of Deritend, to Miss S. Satterthwaite, of Kenilworth.—The Rev Mr. Walford, Dissenting minister, of Yarmouth, to Miss H. Vernon, of Pailton, in this county.

At Dunchurch, Ensign Moore, of the Warwickshire Militia, to Miss A. Worth.—Mr. W. Wood, of Southam, in this county, to Miss Partridge, of the Pump-house, near Bromsgrove.—Mr. Pattishall, publican, to Mrs. M. Sharp, both of Coventry.

Died.] At Birmingham, Mrs. Adcock—Mr. C. Constantine, bellows-maker.—Mrs. Hill, wife of Mr. Hill, plater.—Aged 21, Mr. W. Humphreys, eldest son of Mrs. Humphreys, button-maker.—Mr. W. Vickers, of the Chain-inn.—Mrs. Williams.—Suddenly, Mr. C. Spozzi, dancing-master.—Mr. Simmons.—Mr. Pegg, formerly an eminent silkman, of Coventry.

Mr. R. Farmer, of Stoneleigh.

At Priors Marston, Mrs. Packwood, widow.

At Solehull, aged 20, Mr. C. Green.

At Tamworth, Mr. H Woodcock, of the Post-office.

At Deritend, Mr. J. Cottrell, file-maker.

Mr. M. Fitter; he went to bed apparently in good health, and was found dead the next morning.—Mrs. Hopper, of the Five Ways-house, Birmingham.

Miss Campion, of Leamington, near Warwick.

SHROPSHIRE.

Application is intended to be made to Parliament, in the ensuing session, to obtain an act for erecting a bridge across the river Severn, at a place called Hempton's Load, in the parish of Chelmarsh, to the opposite shore, in the parish of Quatt, and for making a turnpike-road from or near Billingsley, to communicate with the Dudley and Wolverhampton turnpike-roads; which said road is intended to pass through the several parishes of Billingsley, Chelmarsh, Quatt and Alveley, all in this county, and through the parishes of Bobbington and Envilie, in the county of Stafford.

The following may be stated, among many others, as a striking instance of the astonishing produce of wheat, this harvest: a gentleman in the neighbourhood of Bridgenorth, having observed a root of wheat to have vegetated and nurtured twenty strong stems, with a large ear to each; curiosity led him to gather and preserve the same, and on rubbing the grains thereout, they amounted to no less a number than nine hundred and sixty-eight! A truly grand production from one single seed.

The collection at Shrewsbury, September 18, for the benefit of that valuable establishment, the Salop Infirmary, amounted to the handsome sum of 147l. 8s. 2d.

Married.] Mr. T. Higginson, of Rorrington, to Miss Bowdler, of Meadow Town—C. Scale, esq. of Coton Hall, in this county, to Miss H. Griffiths, of Birmingham Heath, near Birmingham.

At Broseley, Mr. A. Pugh, of Coalport, to Miss H. Lloyd.—Mr. Vernon, of Bellahill, to Miss Marshall, of Hadleigh.

Mr. Pyle, coal merchant, of Bath, to Miss S. Perry, of Shrewsbury.

Died.] At Shrewsbury, R. Jeffreys, esq.—Mr. Bowdler, working cutler, an industrious, honest man—Aged 97, Mrs. Allen, relict of the late Rev. Mr. Allen.—Mrs. Ball.—Mrs. Perrett.

At Mawley Hall, after a residence of thirty-five years, as chaplain to the late and present Sir Walter Blount, barts. the Rev. R. Gibson.

On the 8th of July last, in his 33d year, on board the Leviathan ship of war, in the West Indies, Mr. J. Nelson, son of Mr. Nelson, marble-mason, of Shrewsbury.

Mrs. Yarrington, widow, of Milsom.—Also, within half an hour afterwards, her brother-in-law, Mr. W. Yarrington, an eminent hop-merchant, of Worcester; distinguished by his benevolent zeal and strict integrity in the public charitable committees of that city, as well as in many important private trusts.

At Oswestry, Mrs. Lloyd, relict of the Rev. S. Lloyd, formerly rector of Llanymyneck.—Mrs. Jones, wife of L. Jones, esq.

In Feb. last, in the East Indies, Capt. J. George, son of the late Mr. George, of Meeltown, in this county.

At Ludlow, Mrs. Bigg, wife of Mr. Bigg, seedsman, of Shrewsbury.—In an advanced age, Mrs. Baugh.

Mr.

Mr. Basnett, of Wem.—Mr. Gough, farmer, of Acton Reynold.

At Upton, Mr. C. Lloyd.

At Oxon, aged 84, W. Spearman, esq.—Mrs. Trustram, of Whettall, near Wellington.—Miss Roberts, of Stanwardine.

WORCESTERSHIRE.

Married.] At Worcester, Mr. Cooke, to Mrs. Kitchen, of Henwick, near Worcester.—W. Sanders, esq. of Worcester, to Miss L. O'Toole, youngest daughter of Col. O'Toole, of Newtown, in Wexford, Ireland.

At Bromsgrove, Mr. Wood, to Miss Partridge.

At the Quaker's meeting-house, Bristol, Mr. T. Newman, jun. of Worcester, to Miss L. Fry, of Castle-street, Bristol.

Died.] At Wilden, near Kidderminster, J. Pratt, gent.

Mrs. Howell, wife of Mr. Howell, of Benhall Farm, Kempsey, near Worcester.—Mrs. Stinton, of Cotheridge.—Mr. Shelton, of Partridge, near Worcester.

At Malvern, aged 78, Mr. T. Woodyat.

In Sansom-fields, Miss A. Newman, schoolmistress, and a Quaker.

At Borafton, near Tenbury, in his 69th year, Mr. T. Knowles; for many years master of the Swan-inn, at Tenbury Bridge, but had retired from business. He was a kind master to his servants a bountiful donor to the poor, and of great urbanity and attention in business.

HEREFORDSHIRE AND MONMOUTHSHIRE

Hereford Music-meeting—This meeting was really uncommonly elegant. So much company had not been known in the city for some years; and the style of elegant simplicity that prevailed in the dresses of the females gave a finishing grace to the accumulated attractions of this musical-jubilee.

Application is intended to be made to Parliament in the ensuing session, for an act for making and maintaining a turnpike-road from the town and parish of Newent, in Gloucestershire, to the city of Hereford, passing through the several parishes of Newent and Pountley, in Gloucestershire; and the several parishes of Linton and Upton Bishop, in this county: with an additional branch intended to pass from Newent, to a place called the Lea Line, in Gloucestershire, through the several parishes of Newent, Longhope, and the hamlet of Newland, and the parish of Aston Ingham, in this county; and another branch to pass from Witnymore and Aston's Croose, to join the last-mentioned road leading to the Lea Line.

Married.] At Hereford, Mr. P. Farren, to Miss Perry, both of the Hereford theatre.—Mr. Wainwright, land-surveyor, of Hereford, to Miss Wainwright, of Over Areley, Staffordshire.

At Monmouth, Mr. Davies, carpenter, to Miss Williams.—Mr. I. Billinge, aged 82, Mrs. Ashford, aged 73; being the bridegroom's fourth wife, and the bride's third husband.

Mr. Thomas, post-master, of Neath, Glamorganshire, to Miss Proctor, of Effinghall, in this county.

Died.] At Monmouth, H. Phillips, esq. many years member of the corporation.

At Hereford, in his 55th year, Mr. J. Meredith, hair-dresser.

Mrs. Treaherne, of Lugwardine, near Hereford.

At Eardisley, aged 76, Mrs. Palmer.

At Kingston, in his 68th year, Mr. P. Turner, of the Royal Oak inn.

WALES.

Married.] At the Quakers' Meeting-house, in Neath, Glamorganshire, Mr. G. Boone, wine-merchant, of Birmingham, to Miss M. Rees.—Mr. J. Evans, draper, of Swansea, to Miss Thomas, of Rhyd-Saison, Caermarthenshire.

At Machynleth, Montgomeryshire, Mr. M. Davies, of Aberystwith, to Miss M. Davies.

At Swansea, Mr T. Williams, tanner, to Miss Spencer, daughter of Mr. Spencer, paper manufacturer.—Mr. S. Broom, wool-factor, of Kidderminster, to Miss Nevil, of Swansea.

Died.] At Wrexham, Miss S. Ratcliffe; formerly of Borras Hall, near Gresford.—Aged 84, the Rev. D Williams, of Llanvairfechan, of which parish he was rector 52 years. He was religious without ostentation; an affectionate relation, a sincere friend, a kind neighbour, and his whole life was uniformly virtuous.

Mr. T. Parry, timber-merchant, of Flint. While bathing his children in the river Dee, he was alarmed by the cries of his eldest daughter, who had got out of her depth, he rushed into the water with a part of his cloaths on, and brought her safely to shore, but instantly fell down and expired.

At Swansea, in his 20th year, Mr. C. Evans, of Bath, son of the late Mr. Evans, the celebrated performer on the harp.—Mr. W. Williams, ironmonger.

At Laugharne, Carmarthenshire, Miss M. Laugharne, daughter of captain J Laugharne, of the Royal Navy.

At Manason, Montgomeryshire, aged 82, Mr. C. Evans, formerly mercer and flannel-draper in Berriew.—Mrs. C. Kemp, wife of the Rev. W. Kemp.

At the Hay, Breconshire, aged 74, of a paralytic stroke, Mrs. Watkins, wife of J. Watkins, esq.—Also in his 22d year, J. Williams, esq.

At Mould, Denbighshire, Mrs. Lloyd, relict of the late H Lloyd, esq. of Hafodunos.

In the prime of life, Mr. T. Owen, of Mathraval Hangynog, Montgomeryshire.

On a farm of Lord Penrhyn's, near Chapel Curig, in Carnarvonshire, Mr. Owen, aged 104.

At

At Machynleth, Mrs. Edwards, of Guildsfield, relict of the Rev. Dr. Edwards, rector of Machynleth.

GLOUCESTERSHIRE.

Application is intended to be made to Parliament, to obtain an act for making a turnpike-road, from the present turnpike-road which leads from Rodborough, to Caincross, in the parish of Stonehouse, to join the turnpike-road which leads from Cirencester, to Stroud, at or near the seventh mile-stone from Cirencester, (and to pass through the lower end of the town of Stroud, to Bowbridge and Brimscombe, along the valley of Chalford, and through or near Cowcombe) with a branch from such intended road, at or near a stream called Painswick Water, to join the present road which leads from Stroud, to Caincross, at or near a place called Stratfords, both in the parishes of Stroud and Painswick.

An application is also intended to be made to Parliament, for taking down the bridge, called the Westgate Bridge, in the parishes of St. Nicholas and St. Mary-de-Lode, in the city of Gloucester, and for building a new bridge across the river Severn, in the said parishes, at or near the place where the said Westgate Bridge now stands, and for making proper roads and avenues to and from the same.

A similar application is also intended, for making a navigable canal from the town of Cheltenham, to the river Avon, at or near the town of Tewkesbury, to pass through the several parishes or townships of Cheltenham, Swindon, Uckington, Elmstone Hardwicke, Elmstone Tredington, and Tewkesbury, all in this county.

At a late meeting at Bristol, of the gentlemen, natives of this county, M. H. Beach, esq. President, the sum of 170l. 5s. 6d. (including the liberal benefactions of absentees) was contributed for the laudable purpose of apprenticing poor boys, sons of natives of the county, and for relieving, in the hour of child-birth, poor women, natives, or the wives of natives of the county.

Married.] At Gloucester, the Rev. Mr. Cornell, aged 69, to Miss Pervis, aged 25.

T. Bold, esq. of Brecknock, to Miss Baily, of Hambrook, in this county.

At Bognor, H. Howard, esq. of Thornborough, and M. P. for the city of Gloucester, to Miss Long.

Died.] At Gloucester, Mrs. Ellis, widow of Mr. G. Ellis, late an eminent ironmonger. —Miss E. Palmer, second daughter of the late Rev. Mr. Palmer, rector of St. Michael's. —Miss Boughton, daughter of the late Mr. Boughton, currier.

At Kington, Mr. Bartlett, an opulent farmer.

In her 22d year, Miss P. Beard, fifth daughter of the late Mr. Beard, of Beards Mill, in the parish of Leonard Stanley.

At Tewkesbury, the Rev. J. Robinson.

At Winchcomb, Mr. J. Baylis, formerly of Pegglesworth.—In his 24th year, Mr. T. Cornhill, bookbinder, late of Great Chapel-street, Westminster.

At Berkeley, Mrs. Hale, mother of Mr. Hale, tanner, of Gloucester.

At Barnwood, near Gloucester, Mr. W. P. H. Mainwaring, youngest son of the late C. H. Mainwaring, esq.—Mr. C. Adkins, of Weston-upon-Avon; a man of exemplary piety and charity.

At Cheltenham, T. Velley, esq. lieut. colonel of the Oxfordshire militia. He had, for many years past, made the city of Bath his principal residence.

At Newent, in his 71st year, M. Paul, esq. formerly of Burstock, Dorsetshire.

Miss S. Buckle, 2d daughter of Mr. Buckle, of Uckington.

At the Hill House, Grimley, in his 76th year, Mrs. Bedford, relict of the late W. Bedford, esq. formerly of Worcester.

OXFORDSHIRE.

A most horrible example of a crime almost new to human nature lately occurred at Woodstock.—A woman appears deliberately to have destroyed her three children, and afterwards herself, in the lake belonging to Blenheim park!!!—The circumstances which attended so unprecedented an act of parricide will be anxiously enquired into by readers of sensibility; and we shall endeavour therefore, as briefly as possible, to satisfy a curiosity so natural.—This woman's name was Watts. Her husband was a hard working day-labourer at Barton, about six miles north of Woodstock. They had been married nearly thirty years, and had had nineteen children; nine of whom had died in their infancy; the others were grown up and married. During various pregnancies she had evinced a disposition to be very low-spirited, and had three or four times left her husband's house, and rambled and concealed herself in the fields; excepting on these occasions, her conduct was regular, industrious, and affectionate to her family. No indigent persons could have a better character in their parish during a great number of years, than had this industrious couple. In February last, being at that time about five months gone in her 20th pregnancy, she had some dispute with her husband about the expenditure of a guinea. After some loose and passionate declarations that she would destroy herself, she availed herself of the absence of her husband, and of her son who resided at home, both of whom were gone to their daily labour, and absconded from her cottage, accompanied by her eldest girl about eleven, a boy about eight, and another boy about four. Whatever might have been her original intentions on leaving her own house, it appears that she left a small bundle, containing a change of cloaths for her children, at the house of an acquaintance at Wotton, near Woodstock, directing that it should be sent back to her

 husband,

husband, and afterwards entering Blenheim park, spent part of the afternoon in the vicinity of the Great Bridge. On this spot she was observed, late in the day, quieting to sleep her youngest child; and from that time this unhappy family were not seen any more till they were found drowned, under the small arch of the bridge, at its north-west corner, near the spot called Rosamond's Well. The solid architecture and the magnitude of the walls of this bridge render it impossible that they could have fallen into the water by any common accident, and no doubt existed in the minds of the Coroner's Jury, nor has since arisen in consequence of the fullest inquiries, but that this wretched woman was induced, in a fit of phrenzy, to throw her three children over the bridge into the water, and then to let herself drop upon them! This shocking incident is supposed to have happened on Thursday-evening, the 26th of February; and on the Sunday-morning following, the body of the mother was discovered, and shortly after those of the children, all close together, nearly one upon the other. More lovely children were never seen, and every reader can conceive the horror excited by the spectacle of a mother and her three infants laid dead beside each other under such circumstances. The agony of her husband, deprived so suddenly of his wife and children, was excessive; and nothing could exceed that of the Coroner's Jury, who, after finding a verdict of insanity upon the mother, pronounced, upon satisfactory evidence, that each of the children died by the hands of its parent!—The intelligent reader will endeavour to account for the motives which could prompt the commission of so horrid a deed.—At Woodstock those who knew the woman, hope that the melancholy result was solely occasioned by some unaccountable accident; others ascribe it to deliberation, occasioned by a mistrust that her children might be ill-used or deserted if they survived her; and others conceive that she was under the influence of a temporary insanity, arising from her husband's threatening language—from her pregnancy—and from her fears relative to the future destination of her children. Whatever may have been the cause of this dreadful act, it deserves record as a new trait in the history of human nature, and as an example of the indulgence of passion, which occasioned a well-disposed mind to commit a diabolical deed, at which it would previously have shuddered!

Married.] At Oxford, T. Appletree, esq. of Hook Norton, to Miss R. Hopkins, youngest daughter of — Hopkins, esq. of Sibford Ferris.—Mr. J. Wintor, of Stoke, to Miss A. Viret, of Wheatfield.—Mr. J. Slatter, glazier, o Oxford, to Miss Rogers, of Draycott.

Died.] At Oxford, aged 63, Mrs. Hownam, wife of R. Hownam, butler, of Christ Church.—Aged 51, Mr. M. Dorich, victualler.—Aged 55, Mr. E. Ward, many years proprietor of the stage-waggons from this city to London.

At St. Mary's Hall, aged 73, the Rev. T. Nowell, D.D. 37 years Principal of that Society, and Professor of Modern History in the University.

In her 72d year, Mrs. M. Burrows, widow.—Mrs. M. Slatter, wife of Mr. R. Slatter, printer and bookseller.

BERKSHIRE.

It has long been a matter of surprise, that, in a town like Reading, surrounded by two rivers, no establishment had as yet taken place, for the benevolent purposes of the Humane Society: a plan, however, is now in agitation and likely to be adopted for that laudable design; which, aided by the liberal subscription of the public, will, no doubt, be carried into effect.

Married.] At Donnington, G. Blackshaw, esq. to Miss Brummell.

At Aldershot, near Farnham, J. Taylor, esq. of the Custom House, to Miss Newnham, of Aldershot Lodge.

Died.] At Uffington, aged 93, Mr. Garrard.—Miss Girdler, only sister of J. S. Girdler, of Hare Hatch.

At Clewer, near Windsor, Mrs. Peers, relict of C. Peers, esq. of Chilton Lodge, Oxon.

BEDFORDSHIRE.

At a general meeting of the subscribers to the intended Infirmary, held at the Session's-house, Bedford, Sept. 10, his Grace the Duke of Bedford in the chair, a report was read by Mr. Whitbread, chairman, purporting that the committee, in pursuance of the directions of the last general meeting, had taken every means in their power to diffuse a knowledge of the proposed undertaking, having advertised in the different London and Provincial Papers, and caused upwards of 1000 circular letters to be distributed to the different landed proprietors, principal occupiers and clergy of the county, &c. &c. but that the success of the applications has not altogether corresponded hitherto with the zeal of the committee, or the noble ardour of the original and great benefactor. Still, however, many liberal contributions have been received, and a fund has been created, sufficient to justify the committee in laying before the meeting, a plan and estimate for a building; which, although not upon a scale so extensive as they might have wished, is of a size not unworthy the purpose for which it is intended, and such as will be highly beneficial to the county. The report proceeds to state, that the treasurer has delivered in a list of donations and subscriptions, by which it appears, that the donations up to the present time amount to the sum of 1917l. 4s. Of annual subscriptions to the sum of 297l. 3s. exclusive of the benefaction of the late Mr. Whitbread. A plan has likewise been laid before the committee, for the intended building, by Mr. Wing, architecture chitect, of Bedford, to hold 33 in-patients, so well calculated for the purpose, that the committee do not hesitate to recommend it to the adoption of the meeting. Mr. Wing has been indefatigable in his enquiries as to the construction of the several infirmaries of the best repute; and the plan recommended appears to the committee, to combine the excellencies, and to obviate the defects of those already built. Mr. Wing has further proposed to the committee, to contract for the building, to be finished by the first of June, 1803, for the sum of 5800l. Mr. Whitbread has proposed to the committee to furnish to the treasurer the funds necessary for the payment of quarterly instalments of 500l. each (the first instalment to be made at Christmas next) out of the legacy of his father, till the whole of the 4000l. the sum appropriated for the building shall be exhausted; to which the committee have agreed. The report likewise states, that the committee have fixed upon a spot of ground for the building, south-west of the town of Bedford, in a close, called Thomas's close, so eligible, that they have not hesitated to treat with the Duke of Bedford (to whom the ground belongs) for the purchase of three acres, so much being deemed necessary for the building and its appendages, garden, airing-ground, &c. and that no part of the present season might be lost, they have ventured to order the making of a large quantity of bricks. It appears that the expences incurred for printing, &c. amount to 52l. 8s. 5d. and the treasurer has in hand the sum of 276l. 17s. The amount of donations, added to the sum appropriated to the building by the late Mr. Whitbread, appears adequate to the expence; but besides the building, there are many articles of immediate and necessary expence to be provided, before patients can be received, the most obvious of which are the furniture, stores and medical apparatus, which will take up large sums; in the event of any excess above the whole sum required, it will be added to the fund established for the permanent endowment of the hospital. At the above meeting, the report, and the plan of the building proposed by the committee, were unanimously adopted, and a permanent committee, consisting of the Duke of Bedford, Lord John Russel, Mr. Osborn, Mr. Pym, Mr. Higgins, Mr. Whitbread, and Dr. Yeats, was appointed, with full powers to contract for the building, draw upon the Treasurer for the discharge of necessary expences, &c &c.

NORTHAMPTONSHIRE.

It appears that in the management of that noble charity, the General Infirmary, at Northampton, intended for the reception and relief of the sick and lame poor, of all counties, 37,427 persons have been relieved since the original foundation of the Old County Hospital, in 1744. The collection lately made at the church doors, Northampton, amounted to 101l. 8s. 7d.

Married.] At Banbury, Mr. W. Turnbull, mercer, to Miss S. Mosley, daughter of Mr. Mosley, timber-merchant.—Mr. Myers, attorney, of Daventry, to Mrs. Humphreys, widow of the late Rev. Mr. Humphreys, late of the same place.

Died.] At Kingsthorpe, near Northampton, W. J. Lockwood, esq.—In her 74th year, Mrs. Wildgoose, of Daventry.

Mrs. J. Farrer, relict of the Rev. R. Farrer, rector of Ashley; a lady of exemplary charity and Christian piety.

Miss S. Berrill, youngest daughter of Mr. J. Berrill, farmer, &c. of Yardley, Hastings.

At Kettering, Mrs. Dash, wife of Mr. Dash, bookseller.

CAMBRIDGESHIRE.

Married.] B. Muntague, esq. barrister, of Gray's-inn, London, and formerly of Christ's-college, Cambridge, to Miss Rush, eldest daughter of Sir William B. Rush, knt. of Roydon.

Mr. R. Rogers, printer, of Newmarket, to Miss A. Wilson, milliner, late of Bury.—Mr. Smooth, of Carlton, to Miss R. Wakefield, of Great Chesterford Park.—Mr. Palmer, whitesmith, of Ely, to Mrs. Palmer, widow, of Cherryhinton.

At Stoke, near Clare, J. T. Hervey Elwes, esq. to Miss Payne.

At Newmarket, Mr. Day, of the Half-moon-inn, to Miss Jackling.

At Lambeth, the Rev. A. Jobson, M.A. late of Trinity-college, Cambridge, and Minister of March, in the Isle of Ely, to Mrs. Budd, of Prince's-place.

Died.] At Cambridge, in his 46th year, Mr. W. Palmer, apothecary.—In her 80th year, Mrs. M. Sharp, mother of Mr. T. Sharp, peruke maker.

Aged 33, Mr. J. Wells, bricklayer. He was well known to the gentlemen of the University, as a remarkably fine skaiter.

NORFOLK.

A two-shear wether, belonging to Mr. Moneyhill, of Waterden, on being lately killed, was found to weigh ninety-four pounds, and the bone weighed only four pounds and a half: the proportion of meat to bone being nearly *as twenty to one.* This proportion should be more generally attended to, in order to shew the fair results of such experiments.

Married.] At Lynn, Mr. S. Filbey, to Miss Locket.

At Swaffham, the Rev. W. Taylor, rector of Earl Soneham, in Suffolk, to Miss Rolfe, daughter of the late Rev. R. Rolfe, rector of Hilboro', in this county.

ESSEX.

A curious circumstance occurred lately near Saffron Walden, which was witnessed by several spectators. A vast number of swifts and swallows had assembled in the air, apparently for the purpose of taking their departure to another climate, when a battle ensued, in which several of them were killed. One gentleman picked up seven which had perished in the conflict. None others of the feathered tribe mingled in the fight, which did not end

until

until the combatants were wrapped in darkness.

Married.] Mr. J. Wilkin, of Tiptree, to Miss Woodward, of Feering.

Mr. J. Copland, attorney, to Miss E. Bigg, third daughter of Mr. E. Bigg, farmer, of Benson, in Oxfordshire.

After a courtship of three days, and a widowhood of about three months, Mr. J. Bowtell, basket-maker, of Braintree, to Mrs. Wilder, of Bocking.

Mr. J. Beadle, jun. of Dengy-farm, Witham, to Miss Spackman, of Fairsted.—Mr. J. Pavitt, jun. of Clavering, to Miss Hawkes, of Berden-hall.

At Writtle, the Rev. S. Bennett, jun. A.M. chaplain to the garrison in Chelmsford, to Miss M. A. Craneis.—Mr. Kennington, of the Angel-inn, Edmonton, Middlesex, to Mrs. Johnson, widow of the late Mr. Johnson, artist, of Chelmsford.—Mr. J. Cardy, grocer, of the Borough, London, to Miss Vial, of Writtle.—Mr. J. Gilson, surgeon, of Chelmsford, to Miss A. Snell, second daughter of Mr. Snell, of Bocking-hall.

H. D. Bland, esq. of the East India House, to Miss R. Cope, of Rochford.

Died.] At Colchester, aged 80, Mrs. M. Purvis, widow.—Mr N. Tills, surgeon. Miss Fenning.

In his 86th year, Mr. S Finch, grocer, of Stisted.

Mr. T. Pettitt, master of the Bell-inn, Ingatestone.

At Great Dunmow, suddenly, Mr. W. Johns, tanner; much esteemed by all ranks of persons as a man of an upright character, and a sincere friend to the poor.

At Maldon, Mrs. Hall, widow of the late Mr. M. Hall, timber-merchant, &c.

At Langford Parsonage, the Rev. Mr. Phillips, vicar of Terling, and one of the deputy-lieutenants and a justice of the peace for this county.—Mr. Kiddy, of the Hoy-inn, at Heybridge, near Malden.

In her 52d year, Mrs. Raven, of Kelvedon.

The Rev. N. Salter, rector of East Donyland, in this county, and of Westore, in Suffolk.

At Halsted, in his 56th year, Mr. J. Crump, farmer; much respected and lamented by all who knew him, particularly by the indigent poor.

At Southend, Mrs. Jay, of Wood Walton, in the county of Huntingdon.

At Stratford-le-Bow, the Rev. A. H. Eccles, many years rector of the parish of St. Mary, and formerly fellow of Brazen Nose College, Oxford.

On the 20th of October, died, at Fox-hall, Upminster, Mrs. Charlotte Lovewell, wife of Mr. John Lovewell, of Wood-street, London.

KENT.

The New Cattle-market of Canterbury was opened there for the reception of stock, on Saturday, October 10. It is not yet finished, but when completed will be without exaggeration, in point of extent and accommodation, inferior to none in the kingdom. It occupies the entire space from St George's to Riding-gate; the various pens for the accommodation of the cattle are judiciously disposed; there is also a very extended ride to shew the horses, with foot-paths for spectators railed off, so as to preclude any possibility of danger. The principal entrance, which fronts Dover-street, comprises a handsome elevation, the toll-house on one side, and a correspondent building on the opposite, for buyer and seller, on the front of which are placed tables enumerating the tolls and penalties. From this principal entrance to St. George's-street, is a brick-wall, coped with stone, and surmounted with an elegant iron-railing, giving a very light and airy appearance, and shewing, at one view, the whole extent of the market; the lower part, beyond the toll house is railed off, by a neat oak-fence. Much credit is due to the corporation and citizens, who have spared no expence in carrying into execution so desirable an acquisition to the trade of Canterbury.

The late collections at Margate, for the benefit of the Sea-bathing Infirmary, amounted to 195l. 17s. 6d. A subscription has been lately opened there for the purchase of land surrounding the Infirmary, to be added to the ground now in possession of the charity: considerable sums have likewise been subscribed for this purpose.

The Pavilion, which the volunteers of Kent have erected in Mote Park, as a tribute of respect to Lord Romney, is a circular building, surrounded by columns, and covered with a dome: it is built after the models of the Temple of the Sibyls, at Tivoli, near Rome, and the Temple of Minerva, at Athens.

Married.] At Tenterden, Mr. Wilson, linen-draper, of London, to Miss Coucher.

At Ainsford, Mr. G. Rule, of the Inner Temple, London, to Miss Jeffery.

At Tunbridge, P. Nouaille, esq. of Greatness, Kent, to Miss A. Woodgate, second daughter of W. Woodgate, esq. of Summer Hill, in the same county.

At Whitstable, Mr. J. Smith, farmer, of Clapham-hill, to Miss J. Reynolds.

At Chatham, Mr. W. Hemsley, to Mrs. Seyer, a widow lady, of Rainham.—Also, Mr. T. Saunders, maltster, to Miss F. Norwood, of Rainham.—Mr. B. Hobday, of Whitstable, to Miss E Fordred, of Canterbury.—Mr. J. Tut, of Cheriton, to Miss S. Peters, of Folkstone.

At Canterbury, Mr. R. Ruglys, linen-draper, to Miss Hobday.

At Maidstone, Mr. T. Pine, schoolmaster, to Miss Alchin.

Died.] At Wrotham, Mr. C. Bishop, attorney.

At the Court Lodge, at Mersham, aged 81, J. Markett, esq.

At

At Hawkhurst, T. Redford, esq. deputy-receiver of the land-tax for this county.

At Loose, aged 13, Miss M. Thomas, daughter of Mr. T. Thomas, taylor and draper.

At Plaistow, Mrs. Ommaney, of Bloomsbury-square, London.

At Greenwich, T. M. Maddox, esq.

At Margate, Mrs. Spencer, widow, late of Shepperton, Middlesex.

At Ramsgate, Mrs. Roebuck, widow of Ebenezer Roebuck, esq. late supercargo at Canton. Grief for the loss of a darling and only son, a youth of the most promising disposition, who perished by shipwreck, on the coast of North America, destroyed the health of this amiable person, and finally brought her to an untimely grave.

At Canterbury, aged 31, Mrs. Lepine, wife of Mr. C. Lepine, cabinet-maker.

At Rochester, Mr. W. Penn, ironmonger.—The Rev. E. Rice, head-master of the King's School, in this city, and vicar of Hoo.—In an advanced age, Mr. R. Fauchon, farmer.

At Maidstone, A. Carter, M. D.

SURREY.

Application is intended to be made to Parliament in the next session, for a bill for extending the Surrey iron rail-way, and for making and maintaining an inclined plane or railway, with proper works and conveniencies for the passage of waggons, carts, and other carriages, &c. from or near a place called Pitlake-meadow, in the town and parish of Croydon, through the several parishes of Croydon, Beddington, Coulsdon, Chipted, Gatton, Mestham, Ryegate, Buckland, Beachworth, Dorking, Wotton, Abinger, Ockley, Capel, and Newdigate, all in this county; and also through the several parishes of Rusper, Rudgwick, Warnham, Horsham, Slinfold, Itchinfield, Billinghurst, and Wisborough-green, to or near to a place called New Bridge, in the said parish of Wisborough-green, all in the county of Sussex; and also for making and maintaining a dock or bason, with cuts, locks, and other works, for the passage of boats, barges, and other vessels, from the termination of the said intended inclined plane or rail-way into the Arundel navigation, at or near a place called New Bridge, in the parish of Wilborough-green aforesaid; and also a collateral branch from the said inclined plane or railway, from or near the village of Mestham, into and through the several parishes of Mestham, Nutfield, Bletchingley, Godstone, Hourne, and Burstow, all in this county; and also into and through the several parishes of Worth, East Grinstead, West Hoathley, Horstead, Keynes, and Ardingley, to or near to Linfield, all in the county of Sussex; and also for making and maintaining a dock or bason, with cuts, locks, and other works, for the passage of boats, barges and other vessels, from the termination of the said inclined plane or railway, into the river Ouse navigation, at or near Linfield.

Application is likewise intended to be made to Parliament, to obtain an act for making and maintaining a rail-road, from near the river Thames, in the parish of Sunbury in the county of Middlesex, to or near the town of Leatherhead, in this county; which rail-road is intended to pass through the following parishes and townships, viz. West Moulsey, Walton-upon-Thames, Cobham, Stoke D'Abernon, Little Bookham, Great Bookham, and Fetcham, all in this county; with a necessary cut and bason for the accommodation of the said rail-road in the parish of West Moulsey.

SUSSEX.

A correspondent of the Lewes Journal complains, that, while the commissioners sit in their easy chairs, the harbour at Newhaven (which, from its easterly direction, is so very indifferent that vessels of any consequence cannot approach it with a westerly wind) might have been opened straight to sea, at a very little expence, the last spring or equinoctial tides.

The Duke of Norfolk is still pursuing his extensive plan of improvements at Arundel Castle; the expence already incurred is supposed to fall little short of 150,000l.

Married.] The Rev. W. Delves, vicar of Ashburnham, to Miss Eyles, Frant.—Mr. J. Hitchins, of Hall-farm, Hoxtead, to Miss Hardwick, of Lewes.

Mr. W. Hodson, of Riverhead, in Kent, to Miss Farncomb, of West Bletchington.

In the Isle of Anglesea, A. E. Fuller, esq. of Ashdown House, in this county, grandson of the late Lord Heathfield, to Miss Meyrick, daughter of O. P. Meyrick, esq.

In London, Brigadier-general John Murray, to Miss M. Pasco, late of Montreal, and daughter of the late Mr. E. Pasco, of Chichester.

Major Newberry, of the 23d light dragoons, son of F. Newberry, esq. of Heathfield-park, in this county, to Miss A. Wooldridge, of Londonderry, Ireland.

Died.] At Battle, in Sussex, Sept. 7, suddenly, Mrs E. Vidler, sen. aged 81; at the time of her death, her natural offspring had been 12 children, 83 grand-children, 31 great-grand-children—total 126; of whom were living 6 children, 46 grand-children, and 22 great-grand-children—total 74.

On Monday, Sept. 28, at Lewes, in Sussex, Mr. Richard Peters Rickman, merchant.

HAMPSHIRE.

Married.] At Southampton, E. D'Anfossy, esq. to Mrs. Sherlock, relict of the late Col. Sherlock.

Mr. J. Cull, of Wareham, Dorset, to Miss Clarke, of Newport, in the Isle of Wight.

At Newport, Isle of Wight, R. Bullen, esq. of the 2d regt. of North British dragoons, to to Miss J. Sutherland, youngest daughter of the late Capt. Sutherland.

At Aldershott, J. Taylor, esq. of the Custom-house, to Miss Newnham, of Aldershott.

Died.] At Winchester, Mr. W. Gauntlett.

At Shirley Cottage, near Southampton, Mrs. Maskelyne; a truly good woman, whose loss will long be mourned by all her surviving friends.

In her 78th year, Mrs. E. Prince, of Abington, widow, and sister to Sir C. Saxton, bart. commissioner at Portsmouth.

Mr. J. Withers, farmer, of Plaitford, in the New Forest.

At Medstead, Master E. Grœme, son of C. Grœme, esq. of Kilmiston; his death was occasioned by inadvertently eating of the herb called *deadly-night-shade!*

At Lymington, the Rev. J. Bromfield, rector of Market Weston, in Suffolk.

WILTSHIRE.

Married.] At Salisbury, Mr. Bolster, of the Catharine-wheel-inn, to Miss Martin.

Mr. W. H. Awdry, of Chippenham, brother to A. Awdry, esq. of Seend, to Miss Hill, daughter of Doctor Hill, of Devizes.

In London, G. W. Osbourne, esq. of Bath, to Miss Hodgson, of Downton.

At Sopworth, Lieut. F. Frome, to Miss Shute.

At Sutton Waldron, Mr. J. Kearsley, butcher, of Iwerneminster, to Miss Miles.

Died.] At Bath, the Rev. T. Pollocke, D.D. rector of Grittleton.

At Lyncham, in his 90th year, Mr. J. Large; he had been father of thirteen children, nine of whom are now living, with fifty-eight grand-children, and forty-four great-grand-children, altogether one hundred and one, exclusive of those who have been united to the family by marriage, which are twenty-five, being in the whole number one hundred and thirty-six persons.

SOMERSETSHIRE.

Married.] At Bath, Mr. R. Jones, linen-draper, to Miss C. Green.

N.B. The marriage inserted in a former number, of Dr. Crossman and Miss Hannah More, copied from a provincial paper, proves to be an idle or malicious fabrication.

Died.] At Bristol, Mr. O'Brien, well-known throughout the kingdom under the appellation of the Irish Giant—he was no less than eight feet six inches in height.

DORSETSHIRE.

Married.] At Stoke Fleming, J. H. Southcote, jun. to Miss Netherton.

Died.] At Dorchester, Col. J. Grant, of the 46th regt. of foot.

The Rev. C. Moss, A. B. of Wadham-college, Oxford, vicar of Whitchurch. Canonicorum in this county, &c.

At Blandford, R. Pulteney, M.D. F.R.S.

In the West Indies, of the yellow-fever, Mr. N. Bristed, son of the Rev. N. Bristed, vicar of Sherborn.

DEVONSHIRE.

Married.] At Tiverton, Mr. D. Gould, of Ottery St. Mary, to Miss How, of Honiton.—Mr. Trist, to Miss Walker.—W. Nation, esq. banker, to Mrs. Walker, widow of the late R. Walker, woollen-draper, all of Exeter.

Died.] At Exeter, Miss Adams, daughter of Mr. J. Adams, jeweller.—Mr. W. Martin, shoemaker.

In her 65th year, of a paralytic seizure, Mrs. E. Locker, wife of the Rev. J. Locker, vicar of Kepton, and great-grand-daughter of the truly apostolical Doctor Wilson, bishop of Sodor and Man.

Mrs. Williams, sister of the late S. Newberry, B. D. Fellow of Exeter-college, Oxford.

*** SCOTLAND, IRELAND, *and* DEATHS ABROAD, *are deferred till our Next for want of Room.*

MONTHLY COMMERCIAL REPORT.

THE ratification of the preliminary conditions of a TREATY OF PEACE with FRANCE, and the consequent suspension of hostilities between the two nations, have in the course of October, materially altered both the state and the prospects of British trade.

The first effect of the news of this event, was to produce a rise in the price of stocks. That took place to a considerable amount, the moment this news was known on 'Change. A secrecy respecting the progress of the negotiation, such as has rarely been, in similar circumstances, so effectually maintained—had baffled all the guesses and enquiries of the gamblers in 'Change Alley. And fictitious engagements to an immense extent had been made for the deliverance of stock on a day subsequent to that of the news of the treaty, at prices not greater than it was likely that stocks would be then really sold at, if there were still a prospect of future years of war. Those gentlemen who were to pay the differences upon engagements, were, therefore, confounded at the sudden alteration. They naturally tried every expedient to renew the anxiety and doubt of the public, and if possible, to depress the prices of the stocks against their day of settlement. Their stratagems had small success. With some slight fluctuation, the prices of stock have continued to rise or to maintain with steadiness the high pitch they had gained. On the 23d of September, the 3 per cent consols were at 59 5-8ths: On Friday, the 23d of October, the same 3 per cent consols were at 69 7-8ths. The further progress and ultimate terms of the treaty; the discussions which it may excite in Parliament—the quantity of the sum wanted for the public service of the ensuing year—and the mode which shall be adopted in funding the floating debt; are the events and circumstances by which the next fluctuations in the prices of stock will be chiefly influenced. There is little reason to fear, that, as some persons pretend, they will be much depressed by the withdrawing of the property of Foreigners now invested in them. No other public funds in Europe can stand in competition with them for stability: and if much be withdrawn; a good deal, even from France, and certainly from some other parts of the continent, will, on the other hand, be now placed in them. Not to speak of that property which will be immediately thus disposed of by British subjects.

Government had announced to the merchants, that, in consequence of the suspension of hostilities, the convoy duty should immediately cease. It must have been the meaning of the ministers, that the duty should cease as soon as the suspension could actually take effect in the different seas. Many of the merchants, however, are said to have understood that it was to cease from the day of the final ratification of the preliminaries. From this misunderstanding have ensued a number of troublesome enquiries, remonstrances, and demands at the Custom-house; and a good deal of dissatisfaction on the part of the merchants.

The rates of *Insurance* have, however, universally fallen, except where they are regulated by circumstances independent of the war, or the preliminaries of peace. The insurance to American parts, for American ships, is the same as it was a month since; the insurance on voyages to the North Seas and the Baltic, is now higher, on account of the greater danger of winter navigation; and for voyages on seas where the suspension of hostilities is not known to have been yet published, the insurance must be still the same as formerly. In all other cases the reduction has taken place. The insurance, for instance, to Malaga and places adjacent, for a voyage from the Thames was, on the 25th of September, from 10 to 12 per cent.; it was, on the 23d of October, only 1½ per cent.

As the course of mercantile correspondence between London and most places again opens; the *Ratio of Exchange* with almost every mart or capital is now much less against us than it was a month since. On the 25th of September the Exchange with Hamburg was at 2½ months usance, 31 f. g. 6 st. per pound sterling; it was, on the 23d of October, at 2 months usance, 32 f. g. and 6 st. per pound sterling. The abundance of the harvest diminishing the exportation of money for grain, and the late large transmission of British goods and West India Produce to the Baltic, &c. have contributed, as well as the cessation of hostilities, and the approach of general peace, to accomplish this favourable alteration in the course of Exchange.

The price of *Silver Bullion* has also decreased, as the course of our trade with the countries from which it is supplied, has become more free and secure. New Dollars were sold, on the 25th of September, at 5s. and 10d. an ounce; they were, on the 23d of October, at 5s. and 9d. per ounce.

The chief *Imports* into the port of London, since the preliminaries of peace were signed, have been in brandy, coffee, cotton, Swedish herrings, isinglass, nuts, oils, hides and skins, sugars, Russian wheat, wines from Portugal, Spain, Madeira, France, and Germany, and Spanish and African wool. Of isinglass, not less than 20,000lbs. were last week imported. The importation of cotton was nearly 1,450,000lb. More than 50,000 gallons of French and Spanish brandy were brought in. Among the other imports were nearly 2000 cwt. of rags for paper, from Germany and Holland. We have heard of large importations of eggs and fowls into Dover from France, but cannot speak of them with certainty. Among last week's imports into the Thames, we have observed some beans, butter and pork from France. From our African colony of Sienna Leone, were entered, last week, 14 cwt. of dry ginger and a single deer-skin.

Sugars, teas, cottons, woollens, instruments of art, and utensils of elegant domestic accommodation, to a large amount, were last month shipped in the Thames, for *Exportation* to the Elbe, the Ems, and the Weser, and to the ports in the Baltic and the North Seas. Large quantities of linens, pottery, iron work, cabinet work, implements of husbandry, with cotton stuffs, and woollens, were also, during October, shipped for America and the West India Isles. Glass now goes to a great value from this country to Russia. Our exports to the Mediterranean begin to increase.

Ministers expect *Passports* from the French Government, for the admission of British goods, in British bottoms, into the French ports, during the course of the negociation. They will, in return, no doubt, transmit to France, similar passports for the provisionary admission of French ships into the ports of Britain. These passports will, on both sides of the channel, be delivered to the merchants desiring to profit by them. This will be the first renewal of direct mercantile intercourse between France and Britain.

It is not so much the actual quantity of provisions bought, as the manner in which it is bought, that in such a country as this, affects the level of the markets. The same quantity purchased in half a dozen great contracts, contributes much more to raise the prices than if it were bought only in 50,000 small portions. Hence the *Cessation* of the *Contracts* with *Government* for the supply of the army and navy, has already occasioned a prodigious fall in the prices of most of the necessaries of subsistence. The price of bacon fell, in one day, from 1s. 6d. to 10d per lb. The prices of other articles of provisions have been diminished in similar proportion. *Wheat* and *Rye* were, on the 25th of September, each 20s. a quarter higher in the London market than on the 23d of October.

Wood ashes, affording potash for the manufacture of soft soap, for bleaching in its simple state, &c. have for this last month continued stationary in price. *Ashes of Barilla* and *sea-weeds*, for soap, glass, &c. have fallen in price; because those of this year's burning have now come into the market.

Russia goods have not recently fallen in their market-price; for very no large importa-

tions

tions of those articles which are chiefly wanted from that country can arrive sooner than next spring. But the cessation of the equipments for the royal navy, in the mean time, cannot fail to lessen the prices of hemp, cordage, ship-timber, &c.

The prices of *Cotton*, *Sugars*, and West India *Coffee*, continue for the present, at the same rates in the London Market, to which they had risen above a month since. Had it not been for the peace, both sugar and cotton must of late have fallen in price. *Molasses* are lower; as grain will again be freely used in the distilleries,—and more copiously than of late in the breweries. Fine *West India Coffee* is now at 7l. 5s. per cwt. *Mocha Coffee* at only 5l. 15s. per cwt.

Teas remain at the September prices. *Spirits* of all sorts are lower. *Tar* is also lower in price: and so is *Tobacco*.

The *manufacturers of Fire Arms, Swords, Bayonets, Gunpowder, Shot* and *Balls*, &c. in London and its vicinity, at Birmingham, at Sheffield, and in other places throughout these kingdoms, cannot but, for the moment, find themselves somewhat at a loss by the cessation of their usual orders. But, the demand of arms and toys for export to distant regions,—the use of metallic utensils and implements in agriculture and the other arts at home,—and the invention of new fancy-works of metal,—will, soon, in peace, more than restore that activity of business which they enjoyed during the war.

Bristol, *Liverpool* and *Glasgow* already find the state and prospects of their trade, sensibly improved by the effects of the Preliminary Treaty. The woollen-manufacturers in the western, the middle, and the northern counties, begin to find their labours equally animated by the increase of orders, and the diminution in the prices of provisions. *Manchester*, and all the seats of the cotton-manufacture, northward to Dundee, on the one side of the isle and *the Banks of the Leven*, on the other, had begun to feel a revival of industry from the restitution of peace in the Baltic. They feel it much more in consequence of the pacification with France.

Around the whole coast of Scotland, the fisheries, especially of *Herrings*, have afforded prodigious returns of wealth, during the present year. The herring-fishery in the Frith of Forth is just beginning to be in its greatest activity. Fishermen from all parts of Scotland resort thither, to take a share in it. We have good authority for affirming, that the gross product of the Forth herring fishery alone will be little less than 300,000l.

A thriving manufacture of coarse and light woollen stuffs, has for some time existed at *Galashields*, in the South-east of Scotland. Its prosperity is, at this time, in a way of rapid advancement.

The manufacture of *stockings*, in *Aberdeenshire*, and the other northern counties of Scotland, even to the extremity of the Shetland Isles, is now thriving, and is likely to be much advanced by the effects of peace. It is surprising that the exquisitely fine wool of Shetland should not be tried as well as the Spanish, in some of our lighter and more elegant fabrics, in the English woollen manufacture.

Great efforts of manufacturing, naval, and agricultural improvements are now made at the maritime town of *Thurso*, in Caithness.

The *Irish Board of Trustees* are now zealous in their exertions to connect the *Shannon* with the *Liffy*, by a system of inland navigation. Permission has been given, in Ireland, again to use grain in the distilleries. The Exchange between London and Dublin is at par.

America will sensibly feel the pacification between France and Britain. Much British property will be withdrawn from the American carrying trade. And that trade will in various other ways be unfavourably affected by the peace. The Americans at Charlestown in South Carolina, at New York, Boston, and Philadelphia, are much dissatisfied with the impositions on their trade by the agents at Hamburg and other continental parts.

The French *Tiers Consolidé* is at 59 ¾.

MONTHLY AGRICULTURAL REPORT.

THE season in the southern parts of the kingdom, has still, on the whole, continued favourable for preparing the land and putting in the wheat, much of which has now been sown; but in the more northern districts of the island it has not been so favourable, therefore a great part of the business of wheat-seeding is still to be performed.

On threshing out the different crops of grain, though they, in general, turn out extremely good, in some places, especially in the north, the produce has been found coarser than usual, particularly wheats and barleys.

The cessation of hostilities and other causes, have now had a very great effect in lessening the prices of all sorts of grain, especially in the country markets.

Average price of England and Wales, October 17, wheat, 77s. 2d.; rye, 48s. 3d.; barley, 46s 6d.; oats, 26s. 10d.; beans, 46s. 11d.; peas, 48s. 3d.

The state of vegetation has continued such as was scarcely ever remembered at this period of the autumn, and both the natural and artificial grasses are unusually abundant; but the prices of fat stock still keep high. Lean stock is, however, everywhere lower; in some of the northern parts of the kingdom so much so, we are informed, as fifteen or twenty per cent.

In Smithfield Market, October 26th, beef fetched from 4s. 4d. to 5s.; mutton, 5s. to 6s.; veal,

veal, 4s. to 6s.; pork, 5s. to 6s. 6d. In Newgate and Leadenhall Markets, beef yielded from 3s. 8d. to 4s. 4d.; mutton, 4s. to 5s. 4d.; veal, 3s 4d. to 5s. 4d.; pork, 5s. to 6s.

In the hay districts, much of the manure has been already put upon the wet, moor, poachy grounds, and also upon the drier ones, in cases where the injudicious practice of manuring them, at this season, is had recouse to.

In St. James's Market, October 24th, hay fetched from 3l. to 5l 10s.; straw, 1l. 11s. 6d. to 1l. 19s. In Whitechapel Market, hay sold at from 4l. 4s. to 5l. 5s.; clover, 5l. 5s. to 6l. 6s.; straw, 1l. 6s. to 1l. 12s.

METEOROLOGICAL REPORT.

Observations on the State of the Weather, from the 24th of Sept. to the 24th of October inclusive, 1801, two miles N. W. of St. Paul's.

Barometer.			*Thermometer.*		
Highest 30.03. Oct. 13 & 24, Wind W.			Highest 70°. Sept. 29 & 30. Wind S. W.		
Lowest 28. 8. Oct. 18. Wind N. W.			Lowest 34°. Oct. 22. Wind N. W.		
Greatest variation in 24 hours.	5 tenths of an inch	Between the mornings of the 17th and 18th of Oct. the mercury fell from 29.5 to 29.	Greatest variation in 24 hours.	17°.	At nine in the evening of the 30th of Sept. the mercury stood at 60°: at the same hour on next day it was no higher than 43°.

The quantity of rain fallen since our last Report, is equal to 1.99 inches of depth.

Although the variations in the barometer have been very frequent during the last month, yet those, which we need notice, are 1. a small depression of the mercury, previously to one of the most violent storms of thunder, lightning and rain, we ever witnessed, on the evening of the tenth, between the hours of nine and eleven. The lightning, on this occasion, was not only much more vivid than common, but the colour of it was of an unusual and highly brilliant blue tint. 2. In the morning of the 17th, the mercury stood at 29.5, at noon, the next day, it had fallen to 28.8, or seven-tenths of an inch; such a depression in so short a period does not often occur, and, in less than six hours after, it has risen three-tenths, viz. to 29.1.

The changes, from heat to cold, and back-again, have also been considerable; the thermometer has several times marked the difference of from ten to fourteen degrees, in the course of twenty-four hours. Early in the morning of the 22d inst. it must have been as low as the freezing point, as there was ice of a considerable thickness; and at eight o'clock the mercury was no higher than 34°. At no time has the thermometer been at *temperate*, since the 18th of the present month.

There have been thirteen days without rain; and, during the month, the wind has not blown from the East more than four days. It has come chiefly from the West.

TO CORRESPONDENTS.

We have received a Letter containing Strictures on a Paper inserted in our last Number, on a supposed Dirge of Jeremiah, and we are called upon to shew our impartiality by admitting it. We printed that paper merely as a piece of literary criticism, on a topic which appeared to us fairly open to such discussions; but the answerer begins with virtually arraigning our judgment or intentions, by calling the piece an "Attempt to insult the Holy Scriptures," and representing it as what "Ought to be resented with indignation by every man who believes that he has a soul to be saved." He will pardon us if we tell him, that this is not a spirit which can recommend any thing to our Miscellany. We are ready to give admission to any sober and judicious reply to any opinion maintained by our Literary Correspondents; but we must decline becoming the vehicle of controversial rancour.

THE
MONTHLY MAGAZINE.

No. 80. DECEMBER 1, 1801. [No.5, of Vol.12.

ORIGINAL COMMUNICATIONS.

To the Editor of the Monthly Magazine.

SIR,

THE newspapers have informed us, that a certain Lord, in his speech on the peace, asserted "that he was sure it was a peace in which every Jacobin in the kingdom would *rejoice*." The term *Jacobin* has been used in so indefinite a manner during our late party contests, that it is impossible for me to be certain who were the persons intended by his Lordship; nor, moreover, do I feel any great confidence in a broad assertion made upon guess, and proceeding from an individual of that class which stands too much apart from the mass of society to form any accurate judgment of its opinions. Men constantly surrounded by sycophants and dependants will ever view the world through a deceptive medium, and will find their own prejudices reflected back in every information which they receive. It is not improbable that *Jacobin* in his Lordship's idea may comprize all those who place government upon the basis of public consent, or who maintain the principles which distinguished the *Old Whigs*. That these, as good citizens, universally rejoice in a peace which has rescued their country from intolerable evils, and has freed it from the disgrace of supporting a cause in diametrical opposition to that which was once its own, I can well believe. But, if *Jacobin* be understood in its sole proper sense, of a minority which aimed at altering the constitution of the country by force, and with the aid of a foreign power, I would venture to affirm, that, with the exception of those who profited by the war, and of the small number of unconverted fanatical crusaders, the Jacobins are the only persons who are hostile to the peace. In fact, no circumstance could so completely overthrow all their hopes, as that which put a period to all further causes of domestic distress and discontent, and disarmed the power from whose victories they expected the consummation of their daring projects. I suppose it cannot be doubted, that the remnant of Jacobinical rebels in Ireland must be thrown into utter despair by the returning friendship between this country and France.

Having thus corrected his Lordship's assertion respecting Jacobins, I shall add a few observations upon what I suppose to be the sentiments of the Whigs, or temperate friends to liberty, on the state in which the peace will have left the affairs of Europe; whence the degree of their present *rejoicing* may be estimated.

That they are unequivocally glad of the failure of all attempts to force its ancient despotism upon France, I cannot in the least question. If Lord Chatham could "rejoice that America had resisted" the coercion of her parent state, they who are proud of adopting the same liberal principles with him, may well rejoice in the successful resistance of any other country to the interference of strangers in its domestic concerns. They lamented the fall of Poland beneath the iron yoke of foreign force, and they must triumph in the noble assertion of independence by a stronger and more energetic people. But they will scarcely join in the satisfaction expressed by another member of the British legislature, that the exterior independence of France has been purchased by the loss (at least the suspension) of her internal freedom, and that she is, in some measure, degraded to the rank of those powers which were leagued against her. They will remark with sad and boding reflection, that France has yet *every thing to do*, in order to establish her claim to the rank of a free nation; that her boasted name of republic is as little deserved by her, as by those wretched satellites of her power, to which she dictates constitutions with such insolent authority; and that her morals and manners are far remote (and perhaps becoming still more remote) from those upon which alone stable liberty can be founded. Further, they will fear that the suspicion and disgrace under which the principles of freedom have so long laboured, will have materially injured its cause in the rest of Europe, and will have supplied the advocates for power with fresh weapons in their unceasing warfare against it. An *Old Whig*, too, can scarcely view without hereditary uneasiness the vast accession of dominion to a nation, which seems to have retained all its dangerous fondness for martial glory, and which, if administered by an able military government, may exert energies

energies inconceivable under the splendid weakness of a corrupt monarchy.

Under the impression of these feelings, I believe that many of those whom the noble Lord meant to stigmatize as rejoicers in a peace apparently humiliating to their country, while their windows were blazing at the command of a half-starved populace, sat retired in pensive thought, balancing the obvious and present good against disappointed expectations and melancholy forebodings. Your's, &c. N. N.

To the Editor of the Monthly Magazine.

SIR,

WHILST I express obligations which I am sure your readers will feel with me in common to the author of the Comments on Mr. Mason's Supplement to Johnson's Dictionary, I must beg leave to differ with him in the construction of the word *embowel*, which he has given in p. 299. Mr. Burke and Dr. Johnson are accused of a total misconception of this word, when they interpret it to mean *eviscerated*; and really, until I re-considered the passages adduced by the learned commentator in opposition to this construction, as well as some others, I was inclined to adopt his opinion. Let us, however, try the question by an examination of the following passages from Shakespeare:

"Embowel'd will I see thee by and by."

HEN. IV. Part 1. Act 5. Sc. 4.

Here the commentator's negative argument against Dr. Johnson's construction is, that the prince would not be guilty of such brutality, as to see Falstaff eviscerated. But surely there would have been nothing barbarous in causing the *usual practice* to be adopted previously to the embalming of a dead body, which is, I think, all that the prince means. When Falstaff rises, he exclaims, "If thou embowel me to day, I'll give you leave to *powder me*, and eat me, to-morrow;" evidently alluding to the above practice of evisceration and subsequent preparation of a dead body by *powdering*; that is, strewing aromatics, &c. over it for preservation. If the body were *put into the bowels of the earth*, as the commentator contends, Falstaff's "eat me to morrow," would be manifestly an absurd expression.

The next passage that I shall produce is what the commentator admits he knows not where to seek; and I think if he had found it, and considered the context, he would not have quoted it. It is in *All's Well that Ends Well*, Act 1. Sc. the last.

————how shall they credit
A poor unlearned virgin, when the schools
Embowel'd of their doctrine, have left off
The danger to itself?

Helen had undertaken to cure the king's malady; and the countess, in the above speech, expresses her doubts of Helen's capacity, *when the schools of medicine, exhausted of all the learning they had been able to collect on the occasion, had left the disease to itself.*

The last quotation with which I shall trouble you is the following:

The wretched, bloody, and usurping boar
Swills your warm blood like wash, and makes
his trough
In your *embowel'd* bosoms.

RICH. III. Act 5. Sc. 2.

I shall only remark on this extremely obvious passage, that the trough could not well have been made in a bosom (here poetically put for body) wherein the bowels remained.

Whether the word have been "viciously employed," it is not my object in this place to inquire: but in shewing, as I hope I have done, that neither Mr. Burke nor Dr. Johnson have misunderstood the sense in which it was used by Shakespeare; I am extremely willing to admit, with the ingenious commentator, that Spenser's *disbowel'd* is a word of far more apposite application to the sense of *eviscerated**. D.

Nov. 7, 1801.

To the Editor of the Monthly Magazine.

SIR,

I Have lately been well informed that the Poems of Ossian, in the Gaelic tongue, with a new Latin version, in addition to the celebrated English one, are now printing in a very splendid manner, agreeably to the will of the late James Macpherson, Esq. That such an edition will be valuable and curious in several respects, there can be little room to doubt; but more especially in having the dispute respecting the authenticity of those productions settled to the satisfaction of the public.

It is not unlikely but that the result of the industry and research of the editor will be some disappointment to each of the parties, who originally entered into the contest, as well the zealous defenders of the bard of other times, as those whose preju-

* We have received another Letter on this subject, which supports the same meaning of the word by similar arguments.

dice

dice would bar a dispassionate appeal to the tribunal of truth:—*There will be adduced indisputable proofs of the existence of traditionary remains, in the form of ancient tales and songs, containing the ground-work or materials; and wherein may be recognized, but in a detached order, the leading incidents and characters of Macpherson's epic. But the union and combination of them into that regular whole in which they appear, I suspect will turn out to be the work of a modern band.*

Highly gratifying it would be to me that more might be proved of the legitimacy of the Muse of Ossian, than is here anticipated, as well for the honour of the Gaelic minstrels, as for the character of him whose veracity has become so questionable, however it may extenuate his fame as a poet.' Yet, to expect any thing further is nearly hopeless, when all the circumstances are duly considered; and particularly that total want of old writings, which prevails in the Highlands. Why there should exist no such books, is to me a very surprising fact, on taking a retrospect of the state of literature amongst the ancient Welsh; who have bequeathed many hundreds, nay even a few thousands, of manuscripts to their descendants: but they have little appreciated the gift; as it may be safely asserted, that a number, equal to what now remains, has perished through neglect within the last two hundred years: but I am happy in being enabled to say, in justice to the zeal of a few individuals, some atonement is now making, by the publication of a Welsh Archaiology, two volumes of which are already before the world.

Out of the first volume of the abovementioned Archaiology, page 168, I take the liberty, Mr. Editor, of presenting you with a production, which may excite in you considerable surprise, and, being of such a tendency, it is of consequence to prevent every idea of imposition. In order to do so, I beg leave to mention, that there are several copies of it in old manuscripts, and particularly in the *Hengwrt* Library*, the title of which piece is given by *Lluyd*, in page 258 of his *Archaeologia Britannica*, in describing the contents of the manuscripts of that collection. What I lay before you is an Elegy by *Taliesin*, the subject of which is not one of his patrons, no, not even one of his countrymen; but is wholly Irish; yes, is to be found among the heroes of Ossian!

* The seat of Gr. Howell Vaughan, esq. in Merionethshire.

Marwnad Coroi mab Dairi, à gant Taliesin.

Dy fynon lydan, dyleinw açes;
Dyzaw, dyhebgyr dybris, dyorys:
Marwnad Coroi a'm cyfroes!
Oer deni gwr garw ei anwydau!
A oez mwy ei zrwg nis mawr giglau:
Mab Dairi dalai lyw ar vor dehau;
Dathyl oez ei glôd cyn noi adnau!

Dy fynon lydan, dyleinw nonau;
Dyzaw, dyhebgyr, dybrys dybrau:
Marwnad Coroi a'm cyfroes!

Dy fynon lydan, dyleinw dyllyr;
Dy saeth dyçyrç draeth, dwg dybyr
Gwr à oresgyn mawr ei varanres,
A wedi Mynaw, myned trevyz,
Aethant wy fres fraw wyonyz.

Tra vu vuzygre vore zygrawr,
Hwedlau a'm gwyzir o wir hyd lawr:
Cyvranc Coroi â Cyçwlyn,
Lliaws eu tervysg am eu tervyn;
Tarzai pen amwern gwerin goezwyn!

Caer y sy gulwyz, ni gwyz, ni gryn;
Gwyn ei vyd yr enaid ai harobryn!

The Elegy of Coroi, son of Dairi, sung by Taliesin.

Thy ample fountain, it overflows the plain; it comes, it dispenseth with a course, it hurrieth onward: with the death-cry of *Coroi* it hath disturbed me! Gloomy the dissolution of a man of rough passions! None greater in deed of ruin hath been often heard of than him: the son of *Dairi* was wont to hold the helm on the *sea of the south*; splendid was his fame, ere he was laid in earth!

Thy ample fountain, it overflows the bounds; it comes, it dispenseth, it hasteneth woes: the death-cry of *Coroi* hath disturbed me!

Thy ample fountain, it overflows the spreading sand; thy arrow doth approach the shore, it bringeth woe! A man pursuing conquest with a squadron of mighty front, who, passing the *Isle of Man*, approaching of towns, penetrated the fresh rippling streams.

While the course of victory, through the morn, heaped carnage, to me rumours were revealed down from air: the conflict of *Coroi* with *Cuchullin*, who urged the frequent tumult round their borders; the yawning slough rising to end the toil-enjoying multitude.

A secure refuge existeth, ruled by love, which shall not fall, shall not be moved; happy is the soul that shall it inherit!

That a Welsh bard of the sixth century should mention *Cuchullin*, is a proof of his being a great character in his time: but it seems that he was of uncommon celebrity; for, which is very remarkable, I find him again sung of by *Llawzen*, about the year 1440. This poet addresses an ode to his patron, wherein he compares him to several personages of high fame; and

and, amongſt others he ſpeaks thus of *Cuchullin*:

Nid av o'th blâs, diveth blaid,
Oni ranwyv a'r enaid.
Un vezwl â Cyçwlyn,
Diorr wyv, wyd benadur yn:
Un urzas, i'th blâs a'th blwyv;
Un nôd Cyçwlyn ydwyv.

I will not go from thy court of unfailing protection, until I part with life. With a mind like *Cuchullin*, certain I am, thou art to be our chief; the ſame honour in thy court and ſociety, the ſame rank with *Cuchullin* I enjoy.

Conceiving, Mr. Editor, that the above extracts may be evidence of conſiderable importance to produce at the bar of the public, when a final deciſion ſhall be pronounced on the Poems of Oſſian, I ſend them to be inſerted in the Monthly Magazine, that they may obtain the conſideration which they merit. I remain, &c.

Nov. 10, 1801. MEIRION.

To the Editor of the Monthly Magazine.

SIR,

IT may amuſe thoſe of your readers who are fond of critical learning, to ſee what *has* been ſaid, and *may* be ſaid, upon a hemiſtich of Virgil, which the ordinary ſcholar paſſes over without embarraſſment or obſervation:

Æn. lib. ii. v. 619.—*Eripe, nate, fugam.*

The ſenſe is clear, but the expreſſion dubious.

Heyne, a man in whom learning, judgement, taſte, and candour, are united in a very extraordinary degree, conſiders *eripe* as a poetical ſubſtitute for *rape*. Scioppius conjectures *fuga*, as did alſo your humble ſervant; and this may perhaps be defended by Æn. v. 741.

Æneas, quo deinde ruis? quo *proripis?* inquit.

Heinſius on Val. Flac. l. ii. 247, defends *eripe fugam* from *iter eripere* in Frontinus. Burmann reads *arripe fugam*, a phraſe, which, in the judgment of Heyne, requires confirmation as much as that for which it is ſubſtituted. This confirmation, however, is at hand from Claud. Rutil. Itiner. lib. i. v. 165.

His dictis *iter arripimus*; comitantur amici.

Oudendorp agrees with Burmann. Jo. Schrader, with his uſual acuteneſs and elegance, reads *I rape*. Mr. Wakefield, the laſt, but not the leaſt, in this honourable groupe, in one of his lectures on the ſecond book of the Eneid, which I had the felicity of attending, propoſed, with the ſpirit which characteriſed every thing he did, *En! rape*, appealing to the well-known paſſage in the Georgics, *En, age, ſegnes rumpe moras*.

Eligat Lector. Equidem cum Wakefieldio ſentio.

Cheſhunt, I am, Sir, your's, &c.
Nov. 14, 1801. E. COGAN.

To the Editor of the Monthly Magazine.

SIR,

I AM much pleaſed with the title of a paper in your Magazine for October, viz. WALKS BY THE FIRE SIDE; and as no part of your publication is expreſsly appropriated to ſuch deſultory diſcuſſions as WALKS BY THE FIRE-SIDE will very properly admit of,—*ſmall-talk*, if I may ſo term it, *of the pen*, rather than elaborate details or minute reſearches,—I ſhall beg leave, occaſionally, to join the author of the ſaid paper in ſtretching acroſs his parlour: in the preſumption that, like his great, periodical predeceſſors, the writers of the Spectator, Tatler, and Guardian, he can have no objection to ſuch my company; ſeeing my hints, if even they are bad, may ſerve to draw forth ſomething better from himſelf. From this he will eaſily gather that my pretenſions are not lofty. Whatever of philological acumen or philoſophical preciſion is neceſſary, in our WALKS, I will leave to their original projector. A random-ſhot in the way of *common-ſenſe* is all I ſhall aſpire to; and if, thus humbly gifted, I may not rank as the ſpouſe and participator of his cares and honours, he will allow, I hope, that I ſhall be no deſpicable handmaid.

My exordium thus made, the reader will pleaſe to conſider me as juſt returned from my bookſeller's ſhop, where I had been turning over the moſt celebrated publications of the laſt thirteen years, to THE FIRE-SIDE; and, after a few impetuous ſtrides, and, in the abſence of mind or non-perceptibility to ordinary objects which *intenſe thinking* occaſions, having run againſt and overſet the maid and coal-pan, the vagrant cogitations labouring in my pericranium at length break forth as follows:

What an immenſe advantage *he*-authors poſſeſs over *ſhe*-authors, in their title-pages! Had *books* formed any part of the enjoyments and pleaſures of the primeval Eden, it might prove a copious ſubject of reſearch to the antiquary, whether Adam had not been the firſt diſpenſer of honorary titles; and, in his tyrannical intentions effectually to ſubjugate not only his own "better-half," but the "better-halfs" of all ſucceeding poſterities, had denied to woman-kind every academic

academic distinction! One cannot glance into the first page of an *he*-author (I am sorry the disuse of the word *authoress* obliges me to have recourse to such ugly compounds), but R. A's, and B. A's, and M. A's, and M. D's, and F. R. S's, and A. S. S's*, and L. L. D's, and God knows how many consequential letters besides, meet the eye at every fresh volume; or, where none of these are tugged in, ESQ. seems now to be as prescriptive a part of the title-page as the name of the publisher or printer: whilst all of wisdom and genius that, from the remotest ages to our own times, was ever written by WOMEN, has, Quaker-like, been ushered into the world as the production of plain Elizabeth this, or simple Mary the other!

Now without entering into that field of disputation, *the equality of the sexes*, the observation on the disadvantages which female writers labour under, in their title-pages, leads me naturally enough to conclude, that women are unjustly treated in those respects. A dereliction from the paths of virtue has been known to procure them titles of nobility, but who ever heard of any letter in the alphabet, R. A. excepted, being honorarily attached to the names of those who have shone pre-eminent for virtue and talents?

It might seem invidious or I would roundly assert, that 90 out of a hundred who bear off "their blushing honours" from our Universities, would find it difficult to establish claims to intellectual excellence with a Barbauld, a P. Wakefield, a Cowley, a C. Smith, &c. &c.;—that Hannah More and Mrs. West can furnish as solid pretentions to lawn sleeves and mitres as many upon the episcopal bench; and that Mrs. Piozzi, for all her literary wings are now in the moult, through "Retrospection," has yet enough of the old woman and the unqualified aristocrat about her, to capacitate her, with the help of Latin and Greek, for some professorships. But I repeat it might be esteemed invidious, if I were roundly to assert such an hypothesis; therefore the above gentle hint must suffice.

I shall now beg leave to change my ground towards those who maintain, that women were created for nobler purposes than making puddings and pies, and providing linen for their families; and conceding, for the sake of peace, that such is the grand *desideratum* of female existence, still I must conclude, that women are unjustly treated. No honorary appellation belongs to superiority in the arts of pudding and pie-making but a transitory remark, "it's very good!" gulped down with the very mouthful of it which pleased the palate! No other praise attends cleanliness of linen, but the private and humble testimony of time and the washer-woman!

Moreover be it known, that in the College or Academic Institution for the due honouring of Female Excellence, which I hope some person wiser than myself, will, for the credit of their age and country, shortly propose to the learned world, I shall have no objection to there being "degrees" for pudding and pie-making, as well as every other feminine art. On the contrary, I shall have as much pleasure and pride in seeing my wife and daughters add to their signatures S. P. P. (Supreme in puddings and pies) as any of his Majesty's liege subjects whatsoever. W.

* Vide Colman's Doctor Pangloss.

To the Editor of the Monthly Magazine.

SIR,

IF the following singular circumstance comes into your plan, it is at your service for your Miscellany.

No. 9, Harley-street, Your's, &c.
July, 1801. J. C.

LUSUS NATURÆ.

"NOTHING more surprised me, or entertained my fancy more, than when, on a fine warm, serene summer's day, the Kookoernan, or the islands that lie four leagues west of Good Hope, presented a quite different form than what they have naturally. We not only saw them far greater, as through a magnifying perspective glass, and plainly descried all the stones, and the furrows filled with ice, as if we stood close by, but when that had lasted a while, they all looked as if they were but one contiguous land, and represented a wood or tall cut hedge. Then the scene shifts, and shows the appearance of all sorts of curious figures, as ships with sails, streamers and flags, antique elevated castles, with decayed turrets, storks nests, and a hundred such things, which at length retire aloft or distant, and then vanish. At such times the air is quite serene and clear, but yet compress'd with subtile vapours, as it is in very hot weather; and, according to my opinion, when these vapours are ranged at a proper distance between the eye and the islands, the object appears much larger, as it would through a convex glass; and commonly, a couple of hours afterwards, a gentle west wind, and a visible mist, follows, which puts an end to this lusus naturæ."

CRANTZ's *Hist. of Greenland*, I. 49.

DEAR CRANCH, *Modbury, 25 Feb.* 1801.

I OUGHT certainly before now to have replied to your's of the 27th December, containing the curious account of the effects of terrestrial refraction, in Greenland, by an author whose name in English is, it seems, the same

ſame as your's. The appearances are undoubtedly of the ſame nature with thoſe which have been obſerved from our laurel-mount; but more remarkable in their degree, as well as more frequent, on account of the different conſtitution of the atmoſphere in Greenland, and probably the greater diſtance of the objects obſerved, &c. The whole ſeems eaſy to be accounted for on optical principles; and may be illuſtrated by comparing the qualities of the atmoſphere with thoſe of glaſs. The opticians, I apprehend, find it difficult to procure glaſs free from *veins*; which are parts of its ſubſtance of a different degree of denſity (and conſequently of refractive power) from the reſt. The whole maſs, however, being equally *tranſparent*, the veins are undiſcernible by a common eye; but the irregularity which they occaſion in the refraction of the rays is a material impediment to the perfection of refracting teleſcopes. Juſt ſo the atmoſphere, being ſubject to continual changes, and having vapours and fluids of different qualities and conſiſtences always riſing or gathering in different parts, may ſometimes have in it what may be called *veins*, of a greater denſity than the reſt of it's general ſubſtance. If then any ſuch *vein*, of a *globular*, or *convex* form, and ſufficiently tranſparent, preſents itſelf ſuitably between the eye and a diſtant object, that object will appear magnified and *brought nearer*; and if the vein be of a *priſmatical* form, the object will appear *ſhifted from it's place, without being magnified*, &c. Appearances of this kind are, I believe, only ſeen in calm ſtill weather; and ſuch alone is favourable to the undiſturbed collection of theſe heterogeneous maſſes of aërial fluid. They will not, however, remain long in the ſame form and ſituation; but will (eſpecially on being rarified by the heat of the riſing ſun, or agitated by a wind) begin to diſſolve and diſſipate into the ſurrounding rarer atmoſphere, till an equilibrium take place. This accounts for the gradual variation, and final diſappearance, of the phenomena: and, that rain ſhould uſually follow ſoon after a ſolution of this kind, ſeems very probable, and appears to be conſiſtent with experience. JOHN ANDREWS.

To the Editor of the Monthly Magazine.

SIR,

IN common, I am perſuaded, with many other of your readers, I was much diſappointed at not finding in your laſt Number, the further account you had ſolicited of the late ingenious Mr. Bage. When I firſt read his admirable "Hermſprong," I naturally felt deſirous of learning ſome particulars of its anonymous author; and your late brief but impreſſive annunciation of his death has made me truly anxious for a ſpirited ſketch of his character. Permit me therefore, Mr. Editor, to join you in the intreaty, that ſome one of his ſurviving friends would favour you with ſuch a communication, as an act of juſtice to his memory and of gratification to the world.

Malton, Your's, &c.
November 9, 1801. W. W.

To the Editor of the Monthly Magazine.

SIR,

I HAVE read with pleaſure and improvement your Correſpondent, W. N's Account of Portſmouth, &c.—in which he ſhews a laudable deſire to defend his town's people againſt the character which I have given them, in my Sketch of a Journey from Copenhagen to Hamburg. I viſited Portſmouth ſeveral times before the war, and what I wrote was in conſequence of actual obſervation; how far a nine year's war may have improved the morals of the lower claſſes, and with them their cleanlineſs of dreſs, and decorum of manners, I will not preſume to determine. But, Sir, when I was in Portſmouth, there were two places of infamous notoriety, called the *Back of the Point* and the *Sally-Port*, the enormities nightly committed in which were connived at by the police: I ſhould have thought this circumſtance ſufficient to have produced amongſt the lower claſſes debauchery, with its conſtant attendants, poverty, filth, and wretchedneſs; and indeed this appeared to me to be the caſe; but I am extremely glad to learn from W. N's Account, that the war, which has in other places been ſo diſaſtrous in its conſequences, has not affected the morals of the lower claſſes of Portſmouth, and that *they* have eſcaped the contagion of the above-mentioned ſink-holes of proſtitution, of robbery, and of murder.

Hackney, Yours, &c.
November 5, 1801. R. STEVENS.

To the Editor of the Monthly Magazine.

SIR,

I AM ſorry to remark, that your Correſpondent who furniſhed the Account of the State of Manners, &c. at Vienna, which I read in your laſt number, has apparently fallen into a very glaring error reſpecting the population of that city.

He firſt informs us, that in the year 1796, the city contained 1397 houſes and the ſuburbs 5102, amounting jointly to 6499 and afterwards that in 1795 the inhabitants were computed at 231,105

This

This statement gives nearly 36 persons to each house. If it be correct, the houses in Vienna must be on a very different construction and much more fully inhabited than those in this kingdom; our author would therefore have done well had he remarked a circumstance which would form to us a very distinguishing peculiarity. But I am more disposed to think there is an arithmetical error in his computation; and the above may serve to remind your correspondent that some explanation on the subject is due from him.

Liverpool 12, 1801. P. P

To the Editor of the Monthly Magazine.

SIR, *Nov.* 10, 1801.

I FIND that a misrepresentation of *Mr. Godwin's Reply to Dr. Parr*, has crept into your last month's Magazine. I therefore request your immediate insertion of the following letter from that gentleman, addressed to a friend, which seems, to me, to contain the only proper answer that can be given to such aspersions.

"DEAR SIR, *Aug.* 29, 1801.

"I thank you most sincerely for the kindness of your letter. Human creatures living in the circle of their intimates and friends are too apt to remain in ignorance of the comments and constructions which may be made of what they say and do, in the world at large. I entertain a great horror of this ignorance. I do not love to be deceived, and to spend my days in a scene of delusions and chimera. I feel it as an act of unequivocal friendship, that you have communicated to me a fact in which I must hold myself interested, though you deemed the communication to be ungracious.

"Good God! and so you heard me gravely represented in a large company yesterday, as an advocate of infanticide! I have been so much accustomed to be the object of misrepresentation in all its forms, that I did not think I could be surprised with any thing of that sort. The advocates of those abuses and that oppression against which I have declared myself, have chosen it as their favourite revenge to distort every word I have ever written, and every proposition I have ever maintained. But there is a malignity in this accusation, which, I confess, exceeds all my former calculations of human perverseness.

"They build the accusation, it seems, upon a few pages in my Reply to Dr. Parr, &c. where I am considering the hypotheses of the author of the Essay on Population. They eagerly confound two things so utterly dissimilar, as hypothetical reasoning upon a state of society never yet realised, and the sentiments and feelings which I, and every one whom it is possible for me to love or respect, must carry with us into the society and the transactions in which we are personally engaged. Because I have spoken of a certain practice prevailing in distant ages and countries, which I deprecate, and respecting which I aver my persuasion, that in no improved state of society will it ever be necessary to have recourse to it, they represent me as the recommender and admirer of this practice, as a man who is eager to persuade every woman who, under unfortunate and opprobious circumstances, becomes a mother, to be the murderer of her own child.

"Really, my friend, I am somewhat at a loss whether to laugh at the impudence of this accusation, or to be indignant at the brutal atrocity and outrageous sentiment of persecution it argues in the man who uttered it. I see that there is a settled and systematical plan in certain persons, to render me an object of aversion and horror to my fellow-men: they think that when they have done this, they will have sufficiently overthrown my arguments. Their project excites in me no terror. As the attack is a personal one, it is only by a retrospect to my individual self that it can be answered.

"My character is sufficiently known to you and the friends in whose habitual intercourse I live. Am I a man likely to be inattentive to the feelings, the pleasures, or the interests of those about me? Do I dwell in that sublime and impassive sphere of philosophy, that should teach me to look down with contempt on the little individual concerns of the meanest creature I behold? To come immediately to the point in question, am I, or am I not, a lover of children? My own domestic scene is planned and conducted solely with a view to the improvement and gratification of children. Does my character, as a father, merit reprehension? Are not my children my favourite companions and most chosen friends?

In this sense the charge is too ridiculous. How can such men as the calumniator you describe, be confident or weak enough to flatter themselves that, by their obscure and reptile efforts, they can change the character of a man in the apprehension of his contemporaries, into the reverse of all that it is? What man of a sober and decent mind will credit such accusations, without first endeavouring to seek out the truth? What man of a sober

4 and

and decent mind, having, in the flightest degree, investigated my temper and habits, will suffer so execrable a supposition, as that I should be the advocate of an unnatural disposition, the inciter and persuader of acts of horrible enormity, to pass unbranded by his condemnation? Let then these men go on in their despicable task of misrepresentation and calumny.—Let them endeavour to exhibit me as the advocate of every thing cruel, assassinating and inhuman. You and I, my friend, I firmly persuade myself, shall live to see whether their malignant artifices, or the simple and unalterable truth, shall prove triumphant.

For the Monthly Magazine.

EXTRACT *of* A LETTER *from* A GENTLEMAN *on a* TOUR *through* GREECE.

"FROM Venice we proceeded on board a Sclavonian ship to Cattaro, and along the whole of the Adriatic coast, casting anchor, as it is usual with these coasting vessels, in almost every harbour. We thus spent a whole month before we arrived at Corfu, where we were received with the greatest distinction by the senate of that little republic, and were treated with respect by all parties, notwithstanding the violent fermentation then existing among the people, who insisted on the nobility's being deprived of their titles and privileges. Five Russian and three Turkish ships were lying in the road; the latter we frequently visited, and found here, and indeed throughout our whole journey thro' Greece, the Turks most obligingly polite and willing to render us every service in their power. At present, indeed, every Englishman is looked upon by them as a kind of demi-god. From Corfu we went in a boat to St. Mauro, where a house and a guard of honour had been prepared for us by order of the senate of Corfu. In Nicopolis we found the Pacha extremely polite and friendly, and we still carry on an epistolary correspondence with him. We took a view of the celebrated Leucadian Rock, and by measuring its height with the eye easily convinced ourselves, that whoever takes a leap from it, will be freed for ever from the cares that imbitter life. From Nicopolis we proceeded to Ithaca, where we lodged in the house of Dr. Zaro, a physician. Ithaca is truly a wretched country; but has five or six excellent anchorage-places. Thence we went to Patrass, [*Naupactus*] where all the remains of ancient monuments and edifices have long ago been either burnt to lime, or used in building modern houses. We were treated with the greatest politeness by the Turkish Governor, and conducted to the two castles, which should defend the bay of Corinth, but we saw no other ammunition except stones, which were laid in heaps near the quite unserviceable cannon. Though they were daily expecting a visit from the French, no preparations were making to give them a proper reception. At Delphi, whither we journeyed from Patrass, we saw, besides some old walls and the romantic rocks of Parnassus, nothing except the bath of the Pythia, which is in a good state of preservation. At Thebes there are some remains of gates, but no other antiquities. The Aga invited us every day to his garden, and furnished us with horses, sheep and rice, without accepting any thing in return. From Thebes we proceeded to Athens: this part of our journey was extremely fatiguing. The country, just before we descended into the plain of Athens, has a very picturesque appearance. The beauties of the city and citadel are so numerous that they are beyond my power to describe. The Temple of Jupiter Olympus, raised on pillars 16 feet in height, and the Temple of Minerva, in the castle, excite astonishment in the admiring spectator. Here too we daily receive proofs that this is the auspicious moment for Englishmen to travel in Greece: the respect shewn us by the Turks is boundless. But the climate is, at this season of the year, extremely disagreeable. Of the 24 hours there are at most two, during which we can venture to take a walk, early in the morning, at five, and about seven o'clock in the evening.

"Lord Elgin has sent hither from Constantinople, several artists, who are now employed in examining the Temple of Theseus, in the citadel. Since our arrival, they have dug up almost all the relievos and figures, which once ornamented the friezes of the Temple of Minerva. As they have just met with some broken-off horses-feet, we are in hopes that they will find the celebrated horses belonging to the chariot of Minerva, which the antients ascribed to Phidias or Praxiteles. These, all inscriptions, and other interesting remains of antiquity which can be removed, are carefully packed up, and sent to England. Here they would only be thrown into the lime-kiln. Every thing is good here except the climate, whose indescribable heat obliges us to be almost the whole day in the bath; and except the wine. That which grows here is not drinkable, and from the islands none can be procured. But every thing, however, is very cheap. How flourishing a country might this become!"

Th

To the Editor of the Monthly Magazine.

SIR,

TO impart instruction to the deaf and dumb, and, by rendering them capable of mental improvement, to rescue them from the most humiliating and melancholy degradation, is one of the noblest efforts of human ingenuity. The task indeed is arduous, and was long deemed impracticable. Credulity itself could hardly be persuaded, that a person born deaf could be taught, not only to read and write, but also to communicate with others by the medium of oral language. Experience, however, has incontestably proved the fact; and we may behold some of those, whom Nature, as if in a malignant mood, would have excluded from the rank of human beings, enlarging the sphere of human knowledge, and asserting their claim to literary honours. A phenomenon so extraordinary naturally excites amazement.

Accustomed to observe, that those who are born deaf are likewise dumb, we are prompted to infer, that between the sense of hearing and the power of speech there subsists an inseparable or necessary connection. The conclusion however is precipitate and erroneous. An infant may possess the sense of hearing, and the organs of speech, in full perfection, and yet, if secluded from society, would never speak; as, on the contrary, where the sense of hearing is denied, the use of articulate language may be acquired. For as certain conformations of the organs are the chief requisites for the production of articulate sounds, and as these conformations may be rendered objects of sight; so articulation may be learned without the sense of hearing. It is likewise observable, that as there subsists no natural connection between the visible sign and the sound which it denotes, so the association between audible signs and the objects which they signify, is purely arbitrary. Hence the interchange of sentiment may be effected without audible signs, or alphabetical symbols.

The perfection to which the Abbé de l'Epée has carried the art of *dactylology* and *methodical designation*, were it not amply authenticated, would exceed belief. The most abstruse ideas he could correctly communicate; and his pupils, with a promptitude and accuracy truly wonderful, could transcribe from a book or letter, without seeing it, any passage not involving technical terms, merely by the medium of methodical signs exhibited by the Abbé.

The first attempt to teach the deaf and dumb was made by one Peter Ponce, a Benedictine Monk, who lived near the end of the sixteenth century. After him, this art was considerably improved by the labours of Bonet, Amman, Wallis*, Holder, and a few others.

These, however, must yield the palm to the illustrious Abbé de l'Epée, whose eminent success in his arduous office, combined with that pure and singular benevolence with which he discharged it, have justly immortalized his name, and entitled him to rank among the highest benefactors of the human kind.

In this country, the art of instructing the deaf and dumb has been cultivated by Mr. Braidwood with considerable success. This gentleman's plan of education differs, I understand, from that which was adopted by the venerable Abbé. The latter began with the communication of ideas, associating them with appropriate visible signs; the former adopts the common elementary mode of instruction, commencing with alphabetical characters, as denoting certain conformations of the organs. Of the success accompanying this mode of instruction, the writer had this season, during a short stay at Margate, the most ample evidence in the pupils of Mrs. J. Braidwood, who, with her sons, superintends a most respectable seminary at Hackney for teaching the deaf and dumb.

To one of her pupils I proposed in writing the following questions, the answers to which he wrote with surprising promptitude, and, for his years, with wonderful neatness:

What is your name?—*Thomas Pooley.*

How old are you?—*I am eight years old.*

Where were you born?—*I was born in Dublin.*

What is Grammar?—*Grammar is a collection of rules for speaking or writing any language correctly.*

How long have you been at school?—*Two years.*

How many months are there in a year?—*There are twelve months in a year.*

How many weeks are there in a year?—*There are fifty-two weeks in a year.*

* Wallis relates a curious instance of a deaf woman, who could hear distinctly if a drum were beaten in the room with her; and informs us, that when she was married, her husband hired a drummer for a servant, that, by the help of the drum, he might be able to converse with her.

Where is your school?—*At Hackney.*

Who teaches you?—*Mrs. Braidwood and her sons.*

What is the sum of five and seven?—*Five and seven is twelve.*

I then desired him to name the parts of speech, and to write 23 in letters, which he did with great readiness. I likewise prescribed to him two questions in arithmetic, one in *addition*, the other in *subtraction*, which he solved very correctly. To a young girl, who had been a pupil of Mrs. Braidwood about eighteen months, I proposed the question—What is my name? pronouncing the words as articulately as possible. She answered distinctly—*Doctor Crombie.*

I had also the pleasure of seeing a letter to Mrs. Braidwood, from a gentleman, who was born deaf and dumb, of which it is but justice to say, that its grammatical accuracy forms by much the least part of its merit. This gentleman, though deaf, understands the oral language of others, and converses, I am informed, with surprising facility. He transacts the business of two departments in a respectable public office under government, and has already appeared before the public as an author.

I may say with truth, that I never received a higher gratification than in examining these young pupils of Mrs. Braidwood; and, if these observations will furnish amusement to your readers, and serve to render this useful seminary more generally known, the intention of the writer will be fully answered.

Highgate, Oct. 2. A. C.

For the Monthly Magazine.

ACCOUNT *of* ASBY, *in the* COUNTY *of* WESTMORELAND.

ASBY, or, as it was formerly written and pronounced, Ashby, and, still more anciently, Askeby, is said to have derived its name from an ancient family called Askeby, that once possessed the whole, or principal part, of this parish, and which flourished in the reign of Henry II. but has been long extinct. This parish lies in the Barony of Westmoreland, and Diocese of Carlisle; is four miles south from Appleby; and situated, as nearly as has been ascertained, in 54° 35′ 30″ of northern latitude, and in 2° 33′ of western longitude from Greenwich. It is bounded on the east by the parishes of Ormside, Warcop, Musgrave, Kirkby-stephen, and Crosby-garret; on the south, by the parishes of Crosby-garret and Ravenstonedale; on the west, by the parishes of Orton and Crosby Ravensworth; and on the north, by the parishes of Crosby Ravensworth and St. Lawrence, Appleby.

The whole extent of Asby may probably be about four miles in diameter. A great part is mountainous, although the hills are of no very considerable height above the rest of the parish. The following are deemed the highest, and their altitude is taken from the level of the sea: Gathorne-linglow, 1538 feet; Castle-folds, 1700 feet; and Oxenburgh, 1620 feet in height. This parish is beautifully diversified with hill and dale; and Asby-scar forms a ridge of almost solid rock, extending about two miles from north to south, and four miles from east to west. From this ridge, which is near the southern extremity of the parish, the ground declines gently, with many beautiful swellings, to the village of Great Asby.

The soil is mostly upon a limestone; but in some situations a sandy loam, and clayey earth, may be observed; and, in the village of Great Asby, the soil is a loamy gravel. In some parts of this district, the soil is tolerably deep and fertile; but in others it is more shallow, and yields lighter crops. Much of the arable land is sloping, but not steep. All the different strata uniformly verge to the north and north-west.

The climate is more dry and healthy, than in some of the more western parishes of this county. The air indeed varies considerably, as it does in every other situation where the surface is unequal. It is frequently mild and temperate in the internal and northern parts of the parish, when the air is sharp and severe in its southern and more elevated points. Chronical diseases are however very rare. Sudden cold and heat, or violent exercise, will sometimes occasion fevers; but destructive epidemical distempers are almost wholly unknown. Inoculation for the small-pox has been practised by the people in general for many years, and has proved almost always successful in preventing the fatal effects of that disease. Although there be few instances of remarkable longevity, yet there are persons now alive, who are considerably above 80; many survive the age of 90; and, in the year 1781, died a woman at the advanced age of 101.

As

As the justest notions relative to the climate of this district may doubtless be formed from the following abridgment of a register, kept for eight years (from January 1, 1791; to January 1, 1799), by Mr. William Fairer, of this parish, at a place situated 1150 feet above the level of the sea, it is thought proper to insert it here.

TABLE.

Years.	Barometer.			Thermometer.			Weather.					Lightning.	Thunder.
	G. H.	L. H.	M. H.	G. H.	L. H.	M. H.	Wet.	Fine.	Snow.	Hail	Frost.		
1791 -	29.744	27.925	28.991	77	23	44.1	232	124	37	12	71	29	23
1792 -	29.755	28.115	28.904	74	10	44.1	249	64	49	10	70	25	16
1793 -	29.665	27.915	29.008	77	23	45.2	235	92	65	9	94	16	7
1794 -	29.744	28.395	28.991	77	23	44.1	232	124	37	12	71	13	10
1795 -	29.865	27.945	29.032	70	11	56.5	206	121	50	10	58	24	10
1796 -	29.857	27.905	29.070	70	5.75	43.2	214	129	47	17	101	18	14
1797 -	29.778	28.028	29.005	73	18.75	42	248	93	48	22	69	55	43
1798 -	29.956	27.971	29.010	73.5	13	43.6	218	118	47	22	87	17	14

The three first columns contain the mean and extreme height of the barometer; the three next, the mean and extreme height of the thermometer; the five following, the number of wet and fine days, together with those that were accompanied with snow and hail, and that were frosty; and the two last, the number of days on which were lightning and thunder. The barometer was marked every day, at nine o'clock in the morning, and at three in the afternoon; and the thermometer at the same hours; insomuch that columns third and sixth, express the mean height between the extremes throughout the year.

In the years 1687 and 1696, the inhabited houses were 87 at each period; and, allowing six persons upon an average for every house (a number perhaps pretty near the truth), the population in those years will amount to 522. By an exact numeration, made January 1, 1748, there were found to be 72 families, and the whole amount of persons was 361, of whom 178 were males, and 183 females. In 1777, the number of families, according to Dr. Burn, was 72. By an exact numeration, taken December 13, 1787, the inhabited houses amounted to 65, and the number of people to 588, of whom 188 were males, and 200 females. The inhabited houses, in 1796, were 65, which, computed at the rate of six persons for every house, will leave a population of 390. By another numeration, made in June, 1798, there were found to be 72 families, consisting of 171 males, and 168 females, and amounting in all to 339 persons.

The following is a copy of the report relative to the population in the present year: 66 inhabited houses, 70 families, three uninhabited houses; 169 males, 188 females; 118 employed in agriculture, 13 in trades, 226 of other classes—total 357.

	Males.		*Fem.*
Under 2 years of age	6	-	16
From 2 to 5 ———	12	-	16
—— 5 — 10 ———	20	-	18
—— 10 — 20 ———	32	-	30
—— 20 — 30 ———	29	-	31
—— 30 — 40 ———	17	-	25
—— 40 — 50 ———	18	-	12
—— 50 — 60 ———	11	-	14
—— 60 — 70 ———	12	-	22
—— 70 — 80 ———	10	-	2
—— 80 — 90 ———	2	-	2

There is one clergyman, who is the rector of the parish, and schoolmaster; but there is no surgeon nor attorney. There are also four weavers, three shoemakers, two carpenters, three blacksmiths, and one taylor.

According to the report, therefore, respecting the present population, it appears, that there are, upon an average, 5 1/10 persons to every family. And, from considering the different accounts that have been given of the population at different times, from 1687 to the present year, it would seem that, in the course of 113 years, the decrease in the number of inhabitants has amounted to 165 persons in the whole, and that the annual reduction, upon an average, has been 1.46. The decrease in the population may very probably have been occasioned by the extension of farming, by which some very small farms, each perhaps competent to the maintenance and support of a family, have been consolidated into larger ones. This cause appears to have operated more particularly in the higher parts of the parish, where the ground is chiefly in pasture, and where the number of inhabitants is evidently very few. He who occupies a farm larger than the rest of his neighbours will, no doubt, be enabled to afford more rent for his land, than what *many* families can possibly pay for the same extent of ground. But the consolidation of farms, as it tends greatly to diminish the population of a country, and to render many dependent for support on the bounty and caprice of others, who might otherwise perhaps have earned for themselves a decent subsistence, will, in length of time, prove injurious to the value of property in general.

Another cause of depopulation may probably be the modern improvements in agriculture. Formerly it was thought necessary to have four horses for every plough, and that a person should drive them. At present, two horses are deemed fully adequate to the purpose, and they are so trained as to plough equally well without a driver. It is possible also that the same might be instanced in several other departments of husbandry.

The following is an abstract of the parish-register, and exhibits the number of baptisms, burials, and marriages, distinguishing males from females, with the annual average of each, for every ten years, from 1657 to 1797, inclusive and exclusive, and from thence to the commencement of the year 1801.

Years.	Baptisms.			Burials.			Marriages.	Annual Average.		
	M.	*F.*	*Total*	*M.*	*F.*	*Total*		*Bap.*	*Bur.*	*Mar.*
From 1657 to 1667	61	56	117	34	39	73	27	11.7	7.3	2.7
—— 1667 — 1677	52	60	112	46	43	89	43	11.2	8.9	4.3
—— 1677 — 1687	48	30	78	37	46	83	28	7.8	8.3	2.8
—— 1687 — 1697	43	48	91	41	39	80	15	9.1	8	1.5
—— 1697 — 1707	47	49	96	41	48	89	25	9.6	8.9	2.5
—— 1707 — 1717	35	30	65	38	39	74	14	6.5	7.4	1.4
—— 1717 — 1727	37	28	65	39	35	74	20	6.5	7.4	2
—— 1727 — 1737	65	55	120	34	30	64	51	12	6.4	5.1
—— 1737 — 1747	45	51	96	23	35	58	24	9.6	5.8	2.4
—— 1747 — 1757	42	33	75	28	23	51	30	7.5	5.1	3
—— 1757 — 1767	61	40	101	43	23	66	39	10.1	6.6	3.9
—— 1767 — 1777	62	79	141	42	38	80	30	14.1	8	3
—— 1777 — 1787	55	50	105	33	46	79	21	10.5	7.9	2.1
—— 1787 — 1797	37	42	79	24	38	62	22	7.9	6.2	2.2
—— 1797 — 1801	19	21	40	9	13	22	9	10	5.5	2.25

It

It has been computed, that the population in some parishes is in the proportion of twenty-six persons for one birth. But, according to the above table, which, as the register bears every appearance of having been kept with care and regularity, may possibly be considered as pretty exact, we must, in order to arrive at the real population, suppose a much greater number of persons for every birth. For instance, in 1748, the number of people amounted to 361; whereas, that of births for the same year was only nine. And, to make up the population for the years 1787 and 1796, we must reckon at least 60 or 70 persons for one birth. It has also been computed, that the burials are in the proportion of 36 persons living for one dying annually. But, according to the above extracts, the number of deaths, upon an average, is in the proportion of one to 60 or 70; and, in the year 1800, the deaths were in the proportion of one to 119. All this perhaps tends to demonstrate, that from the parochial records of baptisms and burials no certain conclusions or data can be drawn, on which to found the *precise* population of a country.

On the supposition that this parish contains 16 square miles in superficial extent, it necessarily follows, that there are in the whole 10,240 acres; and, allowing 6,800 acres for roads, commons, and waste ground, there will remain 3440 acres of inclosed and cultivated land. The rate of land is from 7s. to 3l. *per* acre, according to the quality of it; but the average rate is probably about 14s. *per* acre. Now 3440 acres, at 14s. an acre, will amount to 2408l. which is about the present yearly rental. The ancient and supposed valuation, according to the book of rates, by which the land-tax and other assessments are collected, is not more than 50l. 4s. for the whole, *per annum.* The property of the parish is divided amongst thirty-six persons, some of whom do not reside in it; and the number of tenants amounts to twenty-eight. The value of the largest estate on which any of the proprietors reside, does not exceed 80l. a year, and that of the smallest may be 5l. The estates may be classed in value as under;

Estates.	*Acres.*	£.
1	700	250 *per annum.*
1	336	180
1	180	130
1	136	80
1	130	80
7	that are above	60
16	———	40
13	———	20
19	———	10
13	———	5

The greatest part of the land here is in pasture, and the quantity of corn grown in the parish will not perhaps serve the inhabitants more than nine months in the year. There are only five farmers that grow more than what is sufficient for their own use; many sow none at all; and most of the small farmers not a quantity adequate to the consumption of their own families. The ground, however, which is arable and in tillage seems to be as well cultivated as any land in the neighbourhood. It yields all the ordinary kinds of grain sown in England. Oats, pease, beans, and barley, have been raised from time immemorial; and, what may appear very singular, though not on that account the less true, it is evident from some ancient and authentic records preserved in the parish that the tithe of barley in the year 1703 amounted to more than the whole quantity of this species of grain produced at the present time. It is, however, only of late years, that wheat, potatoes, clover, and rye grass, have been introduced; the last of which the farmers here have not been able to cultivate so successfully as is reported to be done in some other districts; and, in fact, every kind of artificial grasses, clover alone excepted, has been found greatly to injure and impoverish the land. Rape is a crop, which, though very lately introduced, has already obtained much repute; and the success with which it has been cultivated, seems to have excited the intention of many to attempt it in future. The different kinds of grain, &c. with the number of acres of each, together with the average value, at a very moderate rate, are as follow;

Grain,

Grain, &c.	*Acres.*	*Produce per Acre.*	*Price per Boll.*	*Total Value.*
				£. s. d.
Oats - -	206	30 Bolls	6s. od.	1854 0 0
Wheat - -	28	12 ——	15s od.	252 0 0
Peans and beans	3	10 ——	8s. od.	12 0 0
Barley - -	4	10 ——	10s. od.	20 0 0
Potatoes - -	20	150 ——	4s. od.	600 0 0
Turnips and Rape	30		2l. *per* acre.	60 0 0
Hay - -	1103	300 Stone	4d. *per* ſtone.	5515 0 0
Paſture - -	2022		16s. *per* acre.	1617 12 0
Fallow - -	24			0 0 0
	3440			9930 12 0

Great quantities of potatoes are annually raiſed: a conſiderable proportion of them is uſed for food by the inhabitants; many are given to the horſes and cows, or uſed by the farmers in fattening pigs, which is juſtly conſidered a very lucrative article of rural attention; and thoſe that are not neceſſary for purpoſes of internal conſumption, are ſent to market. Though it muſt be confeſſed, that potatoes require much labour and attention, and a great deal of manure, in the cultivation of them; yet they not only in general produce a plentiful and lucrative return, but leave the land in ſo excellent a condition, that the farmers, as ſoon as the potatoes are taken out of the ground, ſow it with wheat, and have frequently very good crops. An inſtance of which in this pariſh the writer of this article was not long ſince an eye-witneſs of; where he obſerved that ſome ground, on which potatoes had been planted the laſt year, yielded during the preſent ſummer one of the beſt crops of wheat, for the quantity of the land, that he ever remembers to have ſeen grown in Weſtmoreland. Wheat is alſo ſown after fallow. On account, however, of the great autumnal-rains that fall here, and the alternate froſts and thaws in the ſpring, the produce of a crop of wheat muſt at all times be rendered ſomewhat precarious. The ſpecies of grain that chiefly employs the care of the huſbandman, and which moſt liberally repays him for his time and attention, undoubtedly is oats; and it is highly probable, from conſidering the nature both of the ſeaſons and the ſoil, that this will ſtill remain the ſtaple commodity of Weſtmoreland*. The land on which oats are ſown, is ſometimes ploughed in Auguſt or September, and undergoes no other operation previous to the ſowing in the ſpring. This however is a mode of cultivation, which, though found to anſwer very well, has been practiſed only a few years, and is not yet univerſally adopted. The moſt generally received method, and that which has been uſed for the greateſt length of time, is to plough the ground immediately preceding the ſowing.

(To be continued).

To the Editor of the Monthly Magazine.

SIR,

YOUR Pedeſtrian Touriſt through England and Wales, in the ſummer of 1797, has given, in your laſt Number, ſuch a vague deſcription of Frome, in Somerſetſhire, and its neighbourhood, that it would have been as well had he remained a *ſtranger* to that part of his excurſions. His information, whether acquired on the ſpot, or borrowed from the fertility of his own mind, is ſuch, that there is no one acquainted with the town and neighbourhood, who would not feel a want of truth in the diction of his pen.

His morning ramble was to *Vallis* or *Valois* bottom, or, as he informs us, "the *Vales* bottom," in which the powers of his deſcriptive genius are exerted in diſplaying its beauties; and, "tracing this dingle upwards towards its abrupt termination or boundary," he was ſhewn a

* But were all the heaths, commons, and hills in this county, which are now ſuffered to lie waſte and neglected, appropriated to the moſt beneficial purpoſes of which they are capable, the nature of the country would be greatly changed, and every kind of grain be probably raiſed, with the ſame facility as in other parts of England. And the Biſhop of Landaff has ſhewn the probability of planting with ſucceſs the higheſt mountains in Weſtmoreland.

very

very curious and mysterious spring, that flows outward to the river (that runs near it) for one half of the year, and inward from the river during the other half; and this change always taking place on Old Midsummer day:" whatever were the reports he had gleaned of this phenomenon from the "pallid and miserable-looking old women and children" that he met with at the factories, it is *ridiculous* and *absurd*:—true, it is a curious spring; but not for its "disrespect to the act of parliament that altered the style of Midsummer-day, without effecting any compliance with its usual custom of changing its current at Old Midsummer;" it is remarkable only for its clearness and never-failing stream.

From this, he rambles back to "Vales Farm-house," formerly the manor-house, where still are the ruins of a Roman Catholic chapel. This admits of some doubt, as we find in it a large (and I suppose once comfortable) fire-place. It appears more likely to have been a large hall, which oft had cheerly rung with many a burst of laughter; and where mirth, in lively mood, had driven sorrow to the shades in the vale beneath.

"Having explored this dale to its upper extremity," he returned to contemplate its sinuous appendages towards *Elm*; and passing, I fear, too hastily, over its romantic beauties, and slightly noticing rocks, water, and ruined buildings, he visits again the town of Frome, where he speaks of its factories. Among other objects worthy of his observation was the large cask, which is not at the sign of the *Bell*, as he writes, but at the *Spread Eagle*:—for the information of his readers, he might have said, it contains 170 hogsheads. He appears more interested in describing the meeting-houses than the church, which only is "*spacious and neat*:" no town in the west of England has a more beautiful church than Frome.

"After dinner, he walked to *Longleat*, in Wiltshire," about four miles from Frome. It is (and perhaps was at that time) unfortunate, that after a hearty meal, the senses are grown too dull and tasteless for any interest of the mind; every object has inconsistencies; and, instead of cool judgment, an hasty improper decision satisfies the understanding.—"A heavy, dull, and tasteless incumbrance," are terms in which he describes the mansion of Longleat; the park, is but "so so;" and the canal, "a nasty stagnant pool." He had almost rebuked himself for this tempest of exclamation, by reflecting, that a great personage (the King, I believe) had thought this place "a very fine thing." Perhaps my conjectures might be grounded on substantial foundations, if I suppose that this tourist speaks in these or similar terms of every nobleman's house he meets with; and that, *living in an age of reason*, these habitations of the rich are to him *eye-sores*.

Correctness, Mr. Editor, in local description is of no small importance: and it is with regret that I feel the necessity of thus addressing you, as the Editor of the Monthly Magazine, with the above observations. With every deference to the author of these excursions now before us, I would much rather we had no ramblers at all, than such whose information is so opposite to the necessary rules of descriptive writing. As a lover of the sciences, I consider this as one, not of the least indifference; and, knowing your work to be open to every party, I consider myself at liberty to beg an insertion of this paper.

Frome, Oct. 16, 1801.

To the Editor of the Monthly Magazine.

SIR,

IN the Encyclopædia Britannica, the Eudiometer of Guyton de Morveau is strongly recommended. In that instrument, the purity of the atmospheric air is ascertained by means of sulphuret of potash, which is said to possess the property of absorbing oxygen. I have made use of an eudiometer constructed on this principle; but, though the directions given in the Supplement to the Encyclopædia Britannica, under the article Eudiometer, were exactly attended to, no absorption of oxygen whatever took place. The sulphuret of potash was the best I could procure, and was hot when put into the retort; I have repeatedly tried the experiment, and uniformly failed of success in every instance. If any of your readers have succeeded better than myself, I should be obliged to them to inform me, through the medium of your interesting publication, whether they adopted any precautions not mentioned in the Encyclopædia, or whether they can account for my want of success. I should not have troubled you with these inquiries, if I had not known that others, as well as myself, have failed in their attempts to perform this experiment, whom you will oblige by inserting this letter, as well as

Your's, &c.

A.

For

For the Monthly Magazine.

DESCRIPTION *of all the* DEPARTMENTS *of the* FRENCH REPUBLIC, *including those in the* CONQUERED COUNTRIES.

(*Continued from Page* 494, *of Vol.* XI.)

Department of La Creuse.

THIS department is one of the three formed of La Marche, Le Doran, and the Upper and Lower Limosin. It is bounded on the north by the departments of Allier, Cher, and Indre; on the east, by those of Allier and Puy de Dome; on the south, by those of Correze and Vienne; and on the west, by that of Upper Vienne. Its superficies is about 1,135,332 square acres, or 579455 hectares; its population about 225,373 individuals. It is divided into four communal districts.

Department of Dordogne.—This department is one of those formed of the *ci-devant* Perigord. It is bounded on the north by the departments of Upper Vienne and Charente; on the east, by those of Correze and Lot; on the south, by those of Lot, Lot and Garonne, and Gironde; and on the west, by those of Gironde, Lower Charente, and Charente. Its superficies is about 1,759,997 square acres, or 898,274 hectares; its population consists of about 441,380 individuals. It is divided into five communal districts.

Department of Doubs.—This department makes a part of Franche Comté, which comprizes three. It is bounded on the north by the departments of Upper Rhine and Upper Saone; on the east and south, by Switzerland; and on the west, by the department of Jura, and a part of that of Upper Saone. Its superficies is about 1,040,381 square acres, or 530,993 hectares; its population is about 216,578 individuals. It is divided into four communal districts.

Department of Dreme.—This department is one of the three formed of Dauphiné. It is bounded on the north by the department of Isere; on the east, by the Saine and that of Upper Alps; on the south, by the departments of Lower Alps and Vaucluse; and on the west, by that of Ardeche, which is separated from it throughout its whole length by the Rhone. Its superficies is about 1,324,327 square acres, or 675,915 hectares; its population is about 232,619 individuals. It is divided into four communal districts.

Department of the Dyle.—This department is one of the nine formed of part of Hainault, and of the *ci-devant* Austrian Flanders, Brabant, country of Liege, &c. It is bounded on the north by the department of Lower Meuse, the Two Nethes, and that of the Scheldt; on the east, by those of the two Nethes and Ourthe; on the south, by this last, those of Sambre and Meuse, and Jemappes; and on the west, by those of Jemappes and the Scheldt. Its superficies is about 671,756 square acres, or 342,848 hectares; its population is about 396,789 individuals. It is divided into three communal districts.

Department of the Scheldt.—This department is one of the nine formed of Hainault, and the *ci devant* Austrian Flanders, Brabant, country of Liege. It is bounded on the north by the German Ocean and the Batavian Republic; on the east, by the department of the Two Nethes and that of the Dyle; on the south, by this last and those of Jemappes and of Lys, which last likewise bounds it on the west. Its superficies is about 565,986 square acres, or 288,870 hectares; its population is about 578,550 individuals. It is divided into four communal districts.

Department of Eure.—This is one of the five departments formed of Normandy and the northern part of Perche. It is bounded on the north by the department of Lower Seine; on the east, by that of the Seine and Oise; on the south, by those of Eure and Loir and of Sarthe; and on the west, by Calvados. Its superficies is about 1,221,206 square acres, or 623,283 hectares; its population is about 405,705 individuals. It is divided into five communal districts.

Department of Eure and Loir.—This department is formed of the *ci devant* country of Chartrain. It is bounded on the north by the departments of Seine and Oise and of Eure; on the east, by those of Seine and Oise and Loiret; on the south, by this last, and those of Loir and Cher and of Sarthe: and, lastly, on the west, by those of Orne and of Eure. Its superficies is about 1,191,904 square acres, or 607,915 hectares; its population is about 257,986 individuals. It is divided into four communal districts.

Department of Finisterre.—This is one of the five departments formed of Brittany. It is bounded on the north by the ocean; on the east, by the departments of the Coasts of the North and of Morbihan; and on the south and west, by the ocean. Its superficies is about 1,358,554 square acres, or 693,324 hectares; its population is about 442,782 individuals. It is divided into five communal districts.

Department of the Forests.—This department is one of the nine formed of part of Hainault, and the *ci-devant* Austrian Flanders, Brabant, and the country of Liege, and the duchy of Luxemburg. It is bounded on the north by the departments of the Ourthe, of the Sambre and Meuse, and of the Rhine and Moselle; on the east; by this last and that of Sarre; on the south by those of the Moselle, the Meuse, and the Ardennes; this last, with that of the Sambre and Meuse, bounds it on the west. Its superficies is about 1,353,952 square acres, or 691,035 hectares; its population is about 194,011 individuals. It is divided into four communal districts.

Department of Gard.—This department is one of those formed of Languedoc. It is bounded on the north by the departments of Ardeche and Lozere; on the east, by the departments of Vaucluse and Mouths of the Rhone; on the south, by this last, the Mediterranean, and the department of Herault, which, with part of Aveyron, bounds it likewise on the west. Its superficies is about 1,175,044 square acres, or 599,723 hectares; its population is about 309,802 individuals. It is divided into four communal districts.

Department of Upper Garonne.—This department is one of the seven formed of Languedoc, Comminge, &c. It is bounded on the north by the departments of Tarn, Lot, Lot and Garonne, and Gers; on the east, by the departments of Tarn, Aude, and Arriege; on the south, by the departments of Arriege, the Pyrenees, and the departments of Upper Pyrenees, which, with that of Gers, bounds it on the west. Its superficies is about 1,481,083 square acres, or 755,921 hectares; its population is about 404,936 individuals. It is divided into five communal districts.

Department of Gers.—One of the four departments formed of Guienne. It is bounded on the north by the department of Lot and Garonne, and part of that of Landes; on the east, by the department of Upper Garonne; on the south, by the departments of Upper Garonne and Upper Pyrenees; and on the west, by the departments of Lower Pyrenees and Landes. Its superficies is about 1,312,926 square acres, or 670,096 hectares; its population is about 288,555 individuals. It is divided into five communal districts.

Department of Gironde.—This is one of the four formed of Guienne. It is bounded on the north by the department of Lower Charente; on the east, by the departments of Dordogne and Lot and Garonne; on the south, by that of Landes; and on the west, by the ocean. Its superficies is about 2,121,055 square acres, or 1,082,551 hectares; its population is about 557,558 individuals. It is divided into six communal districts.

Department of Golo.—This department is one of the two formed of the Island of Corsica. It is bounded on the north and east by the Mediterranean; on the south, by the department of Liamone; and on the west, by the Mediterranean. Its superficies is about 1,017,472 square acres, or 519,301 hectares; its population is about 157,874 individuals. It is divided into three communal districts.

Department of Herault.—This department is one of those formed of Languedoc. It is bounded on the north by the departments of Gard and of Aveyron; on the east, by the department of Gard and the Mediterranean, which likewise washes it on the south; and on the west, by those of Aude and Tarn. Its superficies is about 1,236,198 square acres, or 630,935 hectares; its population is about 273,452 individuals. It is divided into four communal districts.

Department of Ille and Vilaine.—This is one of the five departments formed of Brittany. It is bounded on the north by the ocean, and the department of the Channel; on the east, by the department of Mayenne; on the south, by the department of Lower Loire; and on the west, by the departments of the Coasts of the North and Morbihan. Its superficies is about 1,336,205 square acres, or 681,977 hectares; its population is about 511,840 individuals. It is divided into six communal districts.

Department of Indre.—This department is the second of the two composed of Berry. It is bounded on the north by the departments of Cher, Loir and Cher, and Indre and Loire; on the east, by that of Cher; on the south, by those of Creuse, Upper Vienne, and Vienne; and on the west, by that of Vienne, and that of Indre and Loire. Its superficies is about 1,347,536 square acres, or 687,760 hectares; its population is about 216,882 individuals. It is divided into four communal districts.

Department of Indre and Loire.—This department is formed of Touraine. It is bounded on the north by the department of Loire and Cher and of Sarthe; on the east, by those of Loire and Cher and of Indre; on the south, by those of Indre and Vienne; and on the west, by that of Mayenne and Loire. Its superficies is about 1,220,799

1,220,799 square acres, or 623,076 hectares; its population is about 264,935 individuals. It is divided into three communal districts.

Department of Isere.—This department is one of the three formed of Dauphiny. It is bounded on the north by the departments of Ain and of Rhone; on the east, by those of Mont Blanc and the Upper Alps; on the south, those of the Upper Alps and of Drome; this last, together with those of the Loir and of the Rhone, bounds it on the west. Its superficies is about 1,648,230 square acres, or 841,230 hectares; its population about 430,106 individuals. It is divided into four communal districts.

Department of Jemappes.—This department is one of the nine formed of part of Hainault, and of the *ci-devant* Austrian Flanders. It is bounded on the north by the departments of Dyle, the Scheld, and the Lys; on the east, by those of Dyle, the Sambre and Meuse, and the Ardennes; on the south, by those of Ardennes and of the North; and on the west, by this last, joined with that of the Lys. Its superficies is about 737,990 square acres, or 376,658 hectares; its population is about 408,668 individuals. It is divided into three communal districts.

(*To be continued.*)

To the Editor of the Monthly Magazine.

SIR,

THE fashionable outcry of the present day against farmers (a body of men entitled to the gratitude, rather than the reproach, of their country) calls to my recollection an adage as common as it is wise —"Place the saddle on the right horse."

The facility with which superficial observers may fall into this popular mistake, is a kind of apology for *them*; but that men capable of deducing events from their causes, should suffer themselves to be equally guilty of error, by joining the former in abusing the *supposed* authors of an evil too generally felt, is surely unworthy of them, and calls forth our just disapprobation.

To place the subject in a clear light, and guard against false conclusions, it may be necessary to define what is understood to be the duty of a farmer. As connected with the landholder, he agrees to pay him a certain annual rent, for a specified portion of land; and it generally happens, that he stipulates to farm it in a particular way:—now, if he honestly fulfils these engagements, he has discharged his duties as a tenant. With regard to those which he owes to himself, he may be viewed in the same light with the merchant, who turns his talents and his capital to the best possible advantage.

In his relation to the public, the farmer certainly has an important part to act, and stands upon very delicate ground; from furnishing the necessaries of life, he is placed immediately in contact with the consumers of them: so that if any difficulty arise in procuring the usual supplies, he, being the most obvious, is too generally accounted the only, cause of the evil, when, in reality, others, perhaps still more important, may be discovered by the judicious and candid observer.

The most prominent of these seems in truth to be the landholder, excepting in cases where farmers have obtained their leases ten or twelve years ago, when land was not of half its present value, but which are now daily expiring to be renewed upon the abominable and ruinous principle of secret proposals.

The proprietor having the power does not fail to use it to his own advantage; he or his agent, understanding what the land is capable producing, takes good care that its rental shall keep pace with the times; for it is evident that when farms are offered to the public through the medium of *proposals*, a spirit of competition is excited among the candidates, which, while it compels them to hold out terms so nearly approaching to the amount of the probable produce of the farms, as hardly to leave themselves a scanty maintenance, doubles, or even triples, the rent-roll of the landholder.

So hazardous indeed is it become for tenants to engage farms at the present advanced rate, that some landholders, at once with a view to keep up the price of land to the highest possible pitch, and guard against their own loss through the failure of their farmers, have even stipulated to reduce their rents, in case the value of produce should be diminished in the markets. I now leave to the decision of impartial men, whether the farmer or landholder has the greatest share in creating the high price of provisions, exclusive of the actual scarcity which has, for some time back, prevailed.

But it may be said, that the eagerness with which land is sought after is the cause of the rise in the rent of farms; and indeed, as it must be admitted, that competition will be in proportion to the number of competitors, it may be asked, whence their preternatural increase?

Now, in order to solve this question, I with diffidence submit my opinion, that the practice of throwing a number of small farms into *one* upon a large scale, under the management of a single individual, instead of several, is the true cause, both of the scarcity of land, and the eagerness with which it is sought after.

I shall now make a few animadversions upon the practice of letting farms by secret proposals. If it be true that a spirited competition among farmers has tended to raise the rent of land above its real value; and if landholders, finding it to their immediate advantage, do continue to avail themselves of *that* circumstance, then the following consequences appear inevitable:—We must either shut our ports against foreign grain, whenever its more moderate price would reduce that of our own, or farmers must *force*, and ultimately injure, the land, in order to produce crops equal to their overstrained rents, or submit to immediate ruin, should extensive importation be permitted. In the former case, the price of labour increasing with that of the necessaries of life, must fall upon our manufactures, and produce incalculable mischief. But I cease to trace any farther the consequences of this alarming system, generated surely in the brain of some desperate spendthrift, at a moment when pressed for immediate supplies to satisfy his clamorous creditors. Let the landholders, who alone can remedy the evil, apply their sanative influence ere it be too late; but, at all events, let us not blame the farmers, who, as well as the rest of the community, are suffering under the pressure of a calamity they have not the power of removing. AN OBSERVER.

To the Editor of the Monthly Magazine.

SIR,

I Stand engaged to your readers to attempt an explanation of the manner and degree in which the restriction upon the Bank of England from making payments in specie may have been detrimental to the nation. This engagement, with your permission, I will now perform.

But first I wish to observe, that I did not intend to intimate, in my former paper, that this measure was wholly produced by the motives which I then ventured to assign. Under all the circumstances that existed when the suspension of cash-payments took place, the measure might have been warranted by something like necessity. The Bank might doubtless have obtained gold and silver sufficient to answer any demands made upon it, if the floating-debt due from government could have been reduced as much as the case required. Government, however, was not able, it seems, to make immediately any material repayments, and thence the Bank *might* have been placed in the situation of a person who has lent more than he possesses or can borrow, and whose debtor at the same time cannot assist him. But the sagacity of the Bank-directors, and of the members of government, must, I think, have foreseen, that if the measure in question succeeded, it would produce the advantages to their respective concerns and to the mercantile interest, which have resulted from it; and such a consideration would have the force of a strong motive to the adoption of a proceeding which, as Mr. Allardyce shews, could very probably have been avoided.

Much argument, and more declamation, has been employed to stigmatize the measure of suspending cash payments at the Bank. I imagine, that, when fairly considered, it will be found to have produced effects of a mixed kind. In my opinion, the evil preponderates; but on subjects that must obviously partake of uncertainty, I dare not draw very positive general conclusions. If my ability qualifies me for executing my task, every one shall be furnished with the means of judging for himself.

Dr. Adam Smith has clearly shewn that the precious metals used as money are a dead stock; and that a well-secured paper-currency may be *substituted for them* with great advantage. By means of such a paper-currency, a proportionable quantity of cash might, and would be, converted into an active capital, and thus employed in maintaining productive labour, and improving the national wealth. The notes of the Bank of England are, beyond dispute, well secured, and therefore the nation is benefited by the *single* circumstance of their being *substituted for gold and silver* to a greater extent than formerly.

It is obvious, that by the suspension of payments in specie, the disposeable fund of the Bank was augmented in a greater degree than its issue of notes. If those notes were exchangeable for cash, a quantity of the latter article must be held in reserve proportioned to the probable demand, and certainly much beyond the amount which the Bank is now *under the necessity* of keeping. Cash kept for such purposes would be dead stock, and the interest upon it consequently lost.

Dr. A. Smith has well observed, that it is

is the interest of all banks to proportion their paper-circulation and discounts to the fair demand, and to the circumstances of a country. If a bank issue paper exceeding the wants of those among whom it is to circulate, the surplus will speedily and continually return for payment upon that bank, which must, to answer their demand, keep a quantity of cash beyond the usual proportion. But bankers have not always been sensible of this truth; and the necessity of making good their engagements in cash seems proper to remind them of it. Indeed, with few private bankers could the power be safely entrusted of issuing notes not payable when due in substantial value. The privilege granted to the Bank of England has been exercised in a manner which justifies the confidence reposed in its directors. Yet, I have scarcely any doubt, that the circulation is overstocked with paper. It may be said, that the issue of bank-notes above 1l. and 2l. value is very little increased, and that those of 1l. and 2l. only supply the place of so much cash withdrawn from circulation. Let it, however, be considered, that from other quarters a great addition has been made to the paper-currency. The number of country bankers has apparently been every year increasing; and, as they likewise have issued notes for small sums, is it not to be presumed, that generally the amount issued by each house has been larger than formerly? It is impossible with the data that are now accessible to form any accurate calculations upon this subject, but, I am persuaded, that the present amount of country bank notes very much exceeds their amount in 1797. Private bankers stand in the same predicament now as formerly. They must discharge their engagements with cash, or with Bank of England notes, which they must purchase generally with substantial property. If, therefore, those bankers overstock the circulation, they suffer for their misconduct. But the temptation to issue an excess of paper has been great, and, I imagine, that many have thus injured both themselves and the public. They can at least safely supply the circulation of the country around them to its full extent, and by that means exclude from thence a quantity of Bank of England notes. Country-bankers, besides, extend their discounts in proportion as they augment the issue of their paper, and London-bankers discount more or less freely, according to the liberality with which the Bank of England treats them.

Notwithstanding the opinion of some very respectable men, I conceive that the Bank may be too liberal in its assistance to the commercial world. It cannot investigate the history of every bill that it discounts. Unavoidably therefore it happens, that many of those bills do not represent property. The money besides, which it advances, is not always employed advantageously to the country. By purchasing commodities, not to transport them to other places where they are more wanted, nor to break them out into small quantities for public accommodation, nor to perform any manufacturing operations upon them, but to hold them till a profit can be obtained, by selling them to some other dealer; by this kind of trade, I say, no public advantage is likely to be gained. Very little labour is thus employed, and consequently very little real value is added to the commodities. In some cases, that is to say, when such a trade answers, the consumers will pay for articles that are the subjects of it a very advanced price, which will include the profits of all these middle dealers. Often, however, that line of business must produce disappointment and ruin to the parties engaged in it, besides embarrassment and distress to others connected with them. A number of persons are always to be found prone to speculation—during war, perhaps, they are particularly numerous—and when much money is to be borrowed, they will generally obtain a share. Those articles which are of the most necessary and extensive consumption, and which can with facility and safety be kept for some time, are the only profitable subjects of this traffic. When it is known that the quantity of corn in a country is not equal to the ordinary consumption of its inhabitants—when, from the dearness of other provisions, that consumption is likely to be increased—and when there is no prospect, that, by a speedy importation, the supply would be brought to equal the demand; then speculators may engage in the corn-trade with every chance of success. A small deficiency in the market always occasions a more than proportionate advance in the price of this indispensable commodity. The trade of speculators, indeed, can only *completely* succeed, while the prices continue in general to advance; and, as that cannot be the case for any very long space of time, they must take care to get out of the concern before the tide sets against them. The public will judge whether such a trade has, during these last few years, been extensively carried on at Mark-lane, and in other places. In my opinion, it it has, and to it I ascribe much of the acknowledged *excess* in the price of corn. I consider that the Bank by its liberal discounts has unintentionally supported this trade. I think, that if the Bank had continued its cash-payments, the assistance given to that traffic (as also to the forestalling of butter, cheese, and some other articles, which has lately been a practice in trade) *must* have been much less. In this point of view, therefore, it appears to me, that the suspension of those payments has been materially detrimental to the nation. I might besides remark, that although an increase of capital *employed in trade* has a tendency to reduce the rate of profit, yet it undoubtedly will cause an advance in the price of commodities, while the quantity of those commodities remains nearly the same.

It has been observed, that the multiplication of the circulating medium enhances the prices of commodities, because a person will pay more money for an article when he has more to pay. As a general truth, nothing can be more clear and certain than this. But surely it must be very incorrect to apply the observation to the present state of things, and thereby alone to account for the advance that has taken place in the price of commodities. A paper-currency has that effect when it is called for by the real wealth of the society. When that wealth is not generally increased, the excess of paper that is emitted in the form of loans to merchants and bankers, will only circulate among that description of persons. It does not add to the fund destined for consumption, and therefore it *can* only operate as capital to enhance in some degree the wholesale price of articles.

The nation may be obliged to the Bank for the extraordinary assistance which the suspension of its cash-payments enabled it to afford to government. But, in my opinion, the benefit derived to the public revenue cannot be great, as upon our present scale of expence and revenue it appears that two or three millions additional might, *almost* at any time, have been funded without difficulty or hazard; and thus, upon nearly the same terms, other creditors might have been found for the excess of government's debt to the Bank of England.

It seems, from this view of the case (which I judge to be a fair one), that, upon the whole, the suspension of cash-payments at the Bank has not been so injurious as *some* have supposed.

A person is not injured by being obliged to receive, instead of cash, paper which represents its real value, and which is every where taken for its expressed value in the purchase of goods. The Bank has assuredly given more assistance than it otherwise could have given to useful trade, to manufactures, and to plans of national improvement. But, at the same time, it has, in about the same proportion, supported a trade that has been, and always must be, prejudicial. By the increase of apparent capital to which it has given birth, the value of commodities in general has likewise been advanced. When cash is issued, the public are, in a great measure, secured from a paper circulation much too abundant. I conclude then that evil preponderates in the consequences of the measure which I have discussed; but I am of opinion, that this *balance* of *actual* evil is not *very* great. J. N. HUNT.

Sept. 7, 1801.

P. S. I am sorry, that the few observations which I ventured to lay before the public, through the medium of your Magazine, were not intelligible to your Correspondent J. J. G. The statement in figures of the Bank concerns is indeed sufficiently obscure, in consequence of a very material omission, which candour would, I think, have suspected, and for the correction of which I refer to the continuation of that paper. I certainly do not deny, that since the suspension of its payments in cash, the Bank of England could divide more than seven per cent. or that the proprietors have a *right* to demand a division of the whole profits, and even of the sum accumulated. But I imagined, that I had made it plainly apparent, that the continuance of the present large amount of profits is very precarious, as a considerable reduction *must* take place when payments in specie are resumed. And with respect to the sum accumulated, I observed, that it was the only efficient capital possessed by the Bank, and therefore that it would be highly *impolitic* to divide that sum among the proprietors. It peculiarly excites my regret to find that I have incurred the animadversions of a writer to whom the readers of your Magazine are much indebted, either because I have expressed myself unintelligibly, or because my remarks have not been favoured with an attentive perusal. At present, I cannot consider your Correspondent's Letter as a reply to any other part of mine, than my conjectural statement of the income-tax paid by the Bank, which is not a very material article, and the *probable* amount of which can only be estimated by a reference to the Income-tax act. Those who read my paper attentively will perceive, if they did not before know, that the eleven millions forming the nominal and original capital of the Bank, have been lent,

lent as a permanent loan to government, for which three per cent. is paid, and no part of which can consequently be employed as a banking-capital. J. N. HUNT.

Nov. 3, 1801.

To the Editor of the Monthly Magazine.

SIR,

WHEN an error finds its way into a celebrated work, in very extensive circulation, it ought not to pass unnoticed, particularly by those whom it concerns; I have therefore to request the favour of a place in your valuable publication, to rectify an error in the Supplement to the Encyclopædia Britannica, under the word Reflector. It is there mentioned, that "Mr. Thomas Smith, tin-plate-worker, Edinburgh, seems to have conceived the idea of illuminating light-houses by means of lamps and reflectors, instead of coal-fires, without knowing that something of the same kind had been long used in France; he has therefore all the merit of an inventor, and what he *invented*, he has carried to a high degree of perfection."

The writer of this article has certainly been misinformed, for reflectors, such as he describes, were invented by me; they were also made, and fixed up, under my direction, in a light-house on the coast of Norfolk, in the year 1779. And, in the year 1787, at the request of the trustees appointed by act of parliament for erecting four light-houses on the northern parts of Great Britain, I instructed the abovementioned Mr. Thomas Smith, in this method of constructing light houses.

Should the learned editor of the Encyclopædia Britannica be inclined to make inquiry concerning the truth of what I have here advanced, the following may be of use to him, being a copy of a letter which I received on this business from the then Lord Provost of Edinburgh.

Lynn Regis, I am, Sir, your's, &c.
Oct. 29, 1801. EZEKIEL WALKER.

To Ezekiel Walker, Esq. Lynn Regis.

SIR,

IN consequence of your letters and opinion, the trustees appointed by act of parliament for erecting four light-houses on the Northern parts of Great Britain have resolved to have them constructed and lighted agreeable to your principles, explained in part by the different letters received from you on that subject.

The places most proper for these lights are of difficult access (one of them at present almost inaccessible); the trustees therefore imagine you would not choose to go there yourself, and have agreed with Thomas Smith, tin-plate-worker, in this place, to be instructed by you, who will set off for Lynn Regis so soon as you inform of your being there, and of its being convenient to you; and the premium mentioned in your letter of the 11th of October will either be remitted by a bill on London, or paid here to your order.

There will be sent by Mr. Smith a description of the height and situation of the ground whereon the different light-houses are to be erected, in order to shew from what number of the points of the compass the lights will require to be seen, and also the necessary height of the building.

I am directed by the trustees to give you their sincere thanks for the attention and information you have already given to this business, of great importance to navigators; and they hope, by your assistance, that the lights, when constructed, will give general satisfaction, and they are anxious to have the whole finished during the ensuing summer.

Edinburgh, I am, Sir, your's, &c.
Jan. 22, 1787. JOHN GRIEVE.

Please to direct for me,
Lord Provost of Edinburgh.

For the Monthly Magazine.

DESULTORY COMMENTS *on* MASON'S SUPPLEMENT *to* JOHNSON'S DICTIONARY.

(Continued from page 300 of our last Number.)

FLECKER.

THE existence of this word rests solely, says Mr. Mason, on a misquotation of Johnson's from Romeo and Juliet. —Surely not. The word *fleck*, a *spot*, is common to most of the Gothic dialects, to the Swedish, the German, and the Icelandish. Hence the verb *to fleck, to spot*, used by Dryden:

Fleck'd in her face, and with disordered hair.

From *to fleck* is formed the frequentative *to flecker*; by the same rule of analogy as from *to chat, chatter*; *beat, batter*; *spit, sputter*; *flit, flutter*; *fly* (A.S. *fligan*), *flicker*; *mould, moulder*; *gleam, glimmer*; *wave, waver*. *To flecker* therefore means *to spot frequently*; and *fleckered* is synonymous with *many-spotted*. It is still in vulgar use, and is especially applied to dappled cattle. The sign of the *fleckered* bull represents a white animal mottled with black spots. Yon *fleckered* dog is a Romeranian. Our poets say, "the *speckled* snake;" but the German poets, "*Die bunt-gefleckte haut der Schlange*," The snake with *gaily fleckered* skin.—*Fleckered* describes larger spots than *speckled*, and *speckled* larger spots than *freckled*; but *pied*,

pied, or *pie-bald*, describes larger spots than *fleckered*.

There are many frequentative verbs in *er*, of which the immediate etymon is become obsolete; such are *to glitter* from *glede, a live coal*; *to linger* from *long*, unless *to lounge* be the intermediate verb; *to clatter, stammer, simmer, smatter, loiter*, &c. *To bicker* seems also to be a verb of this class, deriving from *beak*: if so, it means *to strike at often with the beak*, and was originally applied to the quarrelling and fighting of birds: it answers to the French *becqueter*. Milton has thus employed the word with picturesque propriety;

> And from about him fierce effusion roll'd
> Of smoke, and *bickering* flame, and sparkles dire.

Dr. Johnson's strange derivation of *bicker* from the Welsh does not account for the presence of the *k*: such consonants may be dropped in process of time, but are never inserted.

It is not peculiar to the English language to form frequentatives in this manner: the other Gothic dialects do the same. German; *flattern, klettern, poltern, schmettern*: Hollandish; *stammeren, schitteren, klapperen*: Swedish; *fladdra, klettra*: Anglo-Saxon; *flicerian*, &c.

Flotsam.—Lawyers affect archaisms of language, as of dress: of this kind are *flotsam, jetsam*, and, as they might with equal propriety say, *ligsam*. Why not spell *floatsome, jetsome, ligsome*? for these words were formed originally with the same affix, as *irksome, lightsome, toilsome, tiresome, buxome*, &c.

From a Gothic root answering to the German *saame, seed*, comes the Anglo-Saxon *samnian, to gather, samnung, assembly, samodh, together*, and the inseparable preposition *sam*, corresponding to the Latin *con*, and English *with*, and serving both for a prefix and an affix. Thus, *sam-biran, fellow-hireling*; *sam-mæle, messmates*; *sam radhe, alike-counselled*; *sam-wiste, matrimony (consciousness)*; *lang-sam, longsome*; *bocksam, buxome*; *balsam, wholesome*; *eorksam, irksome*, &c. in all of which words, *sam* may be translated by *with*: as, hired *with* another, eating *with* another, counselled *with* another, knowing *with* another; and again, *with* longness, *with* bending, *with* healing, *with* irke. This formative syllable *sam*, whence the modern *some*, is probably the imperative mood of *samnian, to gather*: (as *with* is of *withan, to join with osier-twigs*, from *withe, an osier*:) and requires an objective case.

This being admitted, it follows that the English formative syllable *some* can with propriety be united only to substantives, or to verbs in the substantive or infinitive mood. And consequently that such adjectives as *longsome, wholesome, lonesome*, &c. ought to be exchanged for *lengthsome, healsome, lonely*, &c. *long, whole, lone*, not being substantive etymons. But from the infinitives, *to float*; *yetan, to sink*; and *ligan, to lie*; it seems allowable to deduce *floatsome, jetsome*, and *ligsome*.

Fluxive.—There are many adjectives in *ive*, as *communicative, conducive, expressive*, and they are mostly formed from infinitives of Latin origin, as *to communicate, to conduce, to express*. In signification they nearly bear to the participles present of such infinitives the relation of habituality to actuality: habitually communicating, habitually conducing, habitually expressing. The Latin affix *ivus* is probably from *ire*, whose primitive meaning is *to flow*: *Euphrates ibat jam mollior*: motion in consequence of inclination, *proneness* is therefore the radical idea associated with the formative syllable *ive*. The most precise definition of *communicative*, &c. would consequently be *prone to communicate*, &c.

To flux is a technical term of the metallurgists, and means, to melt by immingling a substance which increases fusibility. Such substance is called a *flux*. *Fluxive* therefore is an epithet adapted for borax, which *fluxes* tin; or for lead, which *fluxes* glass; but not, as in Ben Jonson, for arguments, or for liquor spilt on a table.

Sportive, talkative, and some other hybrid words formed by this affix, are still freely used by writers; but they are not sufficiently numerous to justify a wanton annexation of the syllable *ive* to verbs of Saxon descent.

Fly-flap.—This compound, although employed by Congreve, is anomalous. We say, *chuck farthing, fear-nought, get-penny, hold fast, pick tooth, save-all, scare-crow, steel-feast, tel-tale, turn-coat, wag-tail*, &c. We are accustomed therefore to construe the incipient word as a verb, and the concluding word as a substantive: so that *fly-flap* suggests the idea of one who avoids flaps, or a pick-pocket. We ought then to say, *flap-fly* or *fly flapper*.

Form.—Mr. Mason justly observes, that this word is pronounced with the o long, when it means "the seat of a hare," or "a long bench." Why not in these

cases

cases spell *forme?* *Former* again stands both for "he who forms," and for the comparative of *fore.* Why not in the last case employ *foremore*, which is the regular comparative? To use *formest* for *foremost* would not be more anomalous, than to use *former* for *foremore*: in the common antithesis, "former and latter," both the adjectives are impurely inflected.

Freak.—It may be doubted, whether this word ought not to be spelled *freck*, as it seems to be the etymon of the frequentative verb *freckle*, and of the adjective *freckly*. The common substantive *freckle* is probably a corruption of the diminutive *frecklet*.

For the Monthly Magazine.

STATE *of* ARTS, MANNERS, *&c. in* EDINBURGH *and* LEITH.

ALLOW me to add the capital of Scotland to those towns and cities of which the present state has been, with so much valuable information, illustrated in the Monthly Magazine.

The Anglo-Saxons of Northumberland, as early as the sixth century, established a permanent military station on the rock on which the Castle of Edinburgh still stands. For some centuries following, here was no town but what stood within the immediate precincts of the castle. It was not till long after the Scots and Picts from the north and north west of the Forth had subdued the southern country, nearly to the present border of England, that the Scottish Kings began to reside, for a part of the year, at Edinburgh;—as well as at Dunfermline, Stirling, and Linlithgow. David the First founded the monastery of the Holy rood, at about a mile's distance south-east from the site of the castle; and, from that time, the vicinity of a religious community to a military strong-hold began to give rise to the existence of a town between them, that was to become, at length, considerable. The first buildings of the town, which extended beyond the precincts of the castle, were framed chiefly of wood; were covered on the roof with turf, straw, heath and ferns; and lay in an irregular line along the ridge which runs from the Castle-hill to that which is still called the Abbey. As the inhabitants became more numerous, the streets and lanes were extended on the south, on the west, and on the south-east of the High-street; and the Grassmarket, the Canongate, the Cowgate, were gradually filled with buildings. The acclivity which rises southward from the Cowgate, was more loosely occupied by religious houses, and the residences of some of the nobility, and other attendants on the court. The walls comprehended the High street, the Cowgate, and the southern elevation to a small distance beyond where the buildings of the college and the infirmary at present stand. From the æra of the institution of the Court of Session, and its permanent local establishment in Edinburgh, this town may be considered as having properly become, and not before, the capital of the kingdom. It was greatly enlarged and improved during the reign of James the Sixth (the First of England). The accession of the line of the Scottish Kings to the English throne, instead of interrupting the prosperity of Edinburgh as a metropolis, seems rather to have advanced it. Edinburgh became, henceforth, the permanent seat of Government for Scotland, and the centre of correspondence for all the rest of the kingdom with the Court in England. Besides, the institution of the college by King James, and that of the High School, were such events as could not but advantageously influence the growth of the city. Even during the civil wars and the usurpation of Cromwell, Edinburgh, though, perhaps, not another town in Scotland, still continued to thrive. After the Restoration, many new and lofty edifices were built in it; and it began to experience a liveliness of trade to which it had been hitherto a stranger. That trade was greatly enlivened in consequence of the Revolution. From the æra of the Revolution to that of the Union, the buildings and the wealth of Edinburgh appear to have been very much enlarged. By the immediate consequences of the Union, the prosperity of the Scottish capital was, for a while, interrupted. It was not effectually renewed till after the rebellion of 1745 was suppressed. From that period till the accession of George the Third, many bold projects were conceived for the improvement and extension of this city, and some progress was even made in their execution. But, it was not till after the peace of 1763, that the old *edifices* began to be generally renovated, and the city to be extended to the north and the south over more than twice that compass of ground which it had so long irregularly covered. Till the commencement of the American war, the spirit of building continued to prevail here. During the misfortunes of that war, it languished. It was revived upon the return of peace.

From

From that æra till the renewal of war, the public and private buildings of Edinburgh, and the streets, roads, and bridges belonging to it, were extended and improved still more rapidly than at any former time. Even within these last ten years, the afflictions which the war has imposed on the whole country, have not had power to interrupt the extension of this town, especially towards the north. Now, since peace is once more restored, it may be expected, that no town in the empire will more signally benefit by the consequences of so desireable an event.

Edinburgh, of which I have thus briefly deduced the rise and progress, is situate in 2° 55′ of long. W. from the meridian of Greenwich, and in 55° 52′ of N. lat. It may be about six miles in circumference, and spreads over three oblong hills or elevated ridges; covering, likewise, more or less closely, the intermediate declivities, and rising irregularly up the sides of two or three insulated heights in which the lower elevations, more or less, abruptly terminate. Its prospect toward the north-east and the south-east, is into the Frith of Forth, and to the German Ocean. To the north and north-west, a wide view opens across the Forth at its greatest expansion, and over the section of a vast amphitheatre to where the horizon is bounded by the Grampian Mountains. Immediately to the west and the south-west, the adjacent country rises into hills of considerable though not astonishing elevation, which confine the range of the eye within narrow bounds. Southward extends a beautiful territory, of an irregular but rich and cultivated surface, alternately rising and subsiding towards the banks of the Esk, the ruins of Roslin, the town of Dalkeith, and the fine maritime village of Inveresk. Arthur-Seat, Salisbury-Craggs, and Caltonhill protect the town, to the east, from those chilling winds from the sea, to which it is, by its situation, exceedingly exposed; and present, in their columnar stratification, their volcanic aspect, their insulated height, and their air of desolate barrenness, a striking contrast to the refinement, art, and cultivation which are eminently conspicuous all around them. The Castle-hill and several other contiguous heights are of a similar aspect and stratification. The surface of the whole territory is varied and unequal to a degree such as is rarely to be seen even in other parts of this isle. The climate would be mild and genial in proportion to the latitude, were it not for the winds from the east and north-east which, in spring and summer, perpetually blast vegetation, and to an almost inconceivable degree afflict the human health. The same eastern exposure renders Edinburgh and its neighbourhood also subject to sudden and most severe storms in winter. It is too much excluded by the interior hills, at all times of the year, from the soft and cheering breezes of the west. Its vicinity to the sea, the shelving inequalities of the surface, the lightness of the soil on a bottom of lime-stone, granite, and trapp or basalt, render the town and the surrounding territory subject, in summer, often to an intensity of heat that is sufficient to ripen, in the open air, the fruits of much more southern latitudes; and that would be scarcely tolerable in the thin brick-buildings of London, or, indeed, in any others than the cool and somewhat gloomy stone-edifices which we here inhabit. It is confessed by all travellers who have skill in the beauty and grandeur of landscapes, that scarce another spot in Europe affords within not more than an equal range of horizon so great a diversity of views, and those so admirable equally in the three different classes of the sublime, the picturesque, and the beautiful.

Considered in regard merely to its streets and buildings, Edinburgh may vie with most great towns in Europe. It consists of three parts;—the New Town, its most northern division; the Old Town, comprehending the High-street, Canongate, Cowgate, and other parts within the circuit of the walls; and the Southern Suburbs, including George's-square, Nicolson's park, &c. &c. The Castle at the one end and the palace of Holy-rood-house at the other, may be considered as belonging to the Old Town.

The New Town, for the uniform beauty of the buildings, the spaciousness of the streets and squares, the unity of its plan, its advantages of cleanliness, air, and water, and, above all, that charming *rus in urbe* which it enjoys in Queen's-street, York-place, St. Andrew's square, and Charlotte's-square, is certainly the finest assemblage of streets and buildings in the world. James's-square, however, protects it but partially from the east winds; and by its exposure, and by the width, the straightness, and the regularity of its streets, it is subject to the violence of the winds blowing from the east, the north-east, and the north, even to such a degree as to be, in all seasons, an uncomfortable and even dangerous residence to the valetudinarian. The greater part of its buildings,

buildings, too, like the Inns of Court in London, contain a number of houses or stories, one over another, and occupied by separate families, under one roof; an arrangement much less convenient in several respects, and especially less favourable to cleanliness, and to the easy supply of water, than where each building is, from top to bottom, destined to serve only as one house and for a single family.

The High street, about a mile in length, from the Castle-hill to the Abbey, forms the principal part of the Old Town. Its width and the loftiness of its edifices on both sides, give it, to the mind especially of an unprejudiced stranger from England, an aspect of dignity and ancient grandeur scarce to be equalled by the effect of any other street in Great Britain. The houses are built of stone, and covered on the roofs with slates. The walls are uncommonly strong. Each house resembles the keep of an ancient castle. In front, these dwellings rise almost every where to the height of five or six stories. But, as the fore-ground is the summit of the ridge—the back-ground, but the steep descent of its sides;—some of the same buildings which appear in front only five or six stories high, are, on the opposite side, not less in height, than nine, ten, or eleven stories. Lateral *wynds* or streets, at right angles with the High-street, descend, on the north-side, to the brink of that which was, forty years since, the *North Loch*; on the south-side, to the Cowgate. These wynds are exceedingly narrow and inconvenient. Their houses are lofty, in many instances ruinous, tenanted chiefly by the poor, and on the ground and in the upper-stories by the most wretched part of these. The *Cross* in the midst of the High street, was once a curious Gothic monumental structure, but exists now only in a coarse Mosaic work in the pavement. Contiguous to it, on the north side, is the *Royal Exchange*, a small square of not inconvenient buildings, with a piazza, which was, about the middle of the last century, erected to favour the business meetings of the merchants. The buildings of the *Parliament-square*, almost a century and a half older than those of the Royal Exchange, stand nearly opposite, on the south side of the Cross. They consist of the *Parliament house*, a spacious edifice, in the different apartments of which, the Courts of Justice have their seats—of several churches—of a banking-house, belonging to Forbes, Hunter and Co.—and of shops with chambers above, occupied by goldsmiths, booksellers, lawyers, &c. The Canongate, properly a suburb, and in old times the court-end of the town, contains a number of good old houses and gardens which were once occupied by the chief nobility and gentry of the kingdom. The Palace of Holyrood-house is a venerable and spacious quadrangular edifice, not unworthy of the Kings for whose residence it was destined. James the Seventh, when Duke of York, was the last sovereign of these kingdoms who resided in this palace. His grandson, the Pretender Charles, held here, for a few days, his mimic-court, in the year 1745. It was lately, for some time, the asylum of the head of the exiled Royal Family of France. Several of the Scottish nobility have, by the King's favour, apartments in Holyrood-house. The Castle is strong by its natural situation, and by the fortifications which it comprehends. Considerable quantities of military stores of all sorts are deposited in it. Even in time of peace, a battalion or two of troops usually lie in its garrison; and the Lieutenant-governor is almost constantly resident. The declivity between the street named the Cowgate, and the ancient southern limits of the town, is occupied by lateral streets, by some new squares, by one or two insulated mansions, by the High School, the Infirmary, the College, and one or two other public buildings. Westward is the Grass-market, in which hay, straw, grain, sheep, horses, cows, and oxen have long been exposed to public sale;—Heriot's Hospital, a noble charitable foundation, of which the revenues have not been perverted from the just, original purposes;—and, in the midst of an extensive burying-ground, that venerable religious structure, the Grey Friar's-church. Many of the old buildings in this part of Edinburgh are continually in a state of dilapidation and renewal. The old castellated structure gives place still more and more to a lighter, cleanlier, and more commodious plan of building.—But, perhaps another century may elapse ere the Old Town of Edinburgh shall be, in all its parts, completely accommodated to the modern methods of living and of trading industry. It was when every town was, as it were, but the enlarged *bas-cour* of a castle, when people crowded within the walls for protection against hostility, that, in order to afford dwellings to as numerous a population as might be, the fashion of raising houses like those at Edinburgh began. It was continued here, from use, and on account of the advantage which was found in sharing the privileges of burgesses.

The

The Southern Suburbs are much less regular in arrangement, than the opposite New Town. The access to them is principally by Bridge-street, composed of the North Bridge that passes across the evacuated bason of the North Loch, and the South Bridge which, in the same line of direction, covers the Cowgate. At its northern extremity, this street has directly in front the Register-office, one of the most beautiful and useful edifices in Scotland. On the sides of the South Bridge, and at one end of the North Bridge, are a number of very rich and elegant shops. The College and the Infirmary stand opposite to one-another, at the southern end of Bridge street. The street terminates, at this end, in that which is named Nicolson's-street; and the two together, viewed in their common line of direction, have an admirably fine effect to the eye. Westward, by the Parliament-square and the Lawn-market, a similar line of communication by bridges begins to be opened. There has been, for many years, a rude communication between the New and the Old Town, by an *earthen mound*.—To perfect this branch of the improvements of Edinburgh, the cross-streets should, in general, be made twice or thrice as spacious, and not above one third as numerous as they are at present; and all the lower parts of the declivities should be abandoned to the use of gardens, warehouses and manufactories. It would be a pleasant and salutary thing, if a living stream *of fresh* water might be conducted, in a clear channel, along that which is now the middle of the street of the Cowgate.

The Southern Suburbs, thus communicating with the Old and New Town, consist of Lauriston, Watson's Hospital, George's-square, Park-place, Buccleugh-place, Bristol-street, Potter-row, Nicholson's-street, Richmond, Pleasance, and Cross-causeway, &c. &c. George's-square is one of the most elegant and agreeable places of residence in either this or any other town or city I have seen. Park-place is likewise occupied, as is also a part of Nicholson's-street, by genteel families. The rest of these suburbs are, in great part, inhabited by labourers, inferior tradesmen and students. The houses of the poorer people in general, even in the modern-built parts of Edinburgh, have not at all the lightness and chearful cleanliness of the snug brick-houses which are reared for dwellings to persons of the same class in London and its vicinity.

(To be continued.)

To the Editor of the Monthly Magazine.

SIR,

THE following remarks, the result of practical knowledge and accurate observation, may demonstrate the cause of the late scarcity, and of the absurdity of supposing that the price of corn has been kept up by farmers, millers, mealmen, &c.

1st. The unfavourableness of the seasons for several years past has doubtlessly contributed to the scarcity; for in the last *nine* years, the produce of the land has not exceeded that of *seven* in the nine preceding years. This may more fully appear, by the following observations on the state of the seasons and crops, from the year 1792 to the present time.

1792 was exceedingly rainy from the beginning, continuing through the harvest until April 1793. The land, in many places, did not produce half a crop, and much of that was damaged. A great quantity of land could not be sown to wheat in the autumn.

1793. January, February and March wet; nearly one-third of the land, in many places, could not be sown to Lent grain, and much of that sown produced but little, through the unfavourable seed-time and the drought in the summer; but a great quantity of land was sown to wheat in the autumn.

1794. March was again exceedingly wet, so that a considerable quantity of the land intended for Lent corn could not be sown, and a great deal of that which was sown produced but little. The peas and vetches were almost totally destroyed by the blight or blast, in the latter end of May. Part of the summer was dry, and the wheat looked well until near the harvest, but yielded little more than one-third of the quantity expected.

1795. A severe winter and great floods; very rainy in March and during the hay-harvest; some frosts in June did considerable damage. Wheat was at a very high price, the old stock being nearly exhausted by the time of harvest. The crops of corn were pretty good and harvested well, but the autumn being very dry, the quantity of wheat sown was considerably less than usual.

1796. A cold and dry spring; the crops of corn were in most places good and harvested well, and the autumn was a good seed-time for wheat.

1797. The winter was mild and wet; a great quantity of wheat was destroyed by the wire-worm, &c. Rainy in the spring and in the latter part of the summer, whereby the grain was damaged, and it was also very light.

1798. A cold and backward spring, but a favourable seed-time. Of wheat, beans, peas, barley and oats, there was a tolerable crop, which was harvested well, except the late crops, which were much damaged by the rainy weather. A great quantity of land could not be sown to wheat, through the abundance of rain, which continued the whole of the autumn, and much of the wheat sown in wet land rotted.

1799. A very wet winter, spring, summer and autumn, so that full one third of the land could not be sown to grain at all; a good deal of that which was sown produced but little, and much was damaged by the wetness of the harvest, as also was most of the hay. A vast deal of land could not be sown to wheat in the autumn, and of that sown much perished, through the wetness of the season and badness of the seed. Severe frosts set in early, by which the wheat in the ground was injured.

1800. A wet winter and spring until the middle of May, so that in some districts half the land intended for Lent corn could not be sown in season, and that which was sown late, came to little. The latter end of May and beginning of June was a fine growing season, but the summer afterwards was very hot and dry. The crops of corn were very light, except peas, but of those the quantity sown was very small, owing to the wet winter and spring. A very great scarcity in autumn; but an unusual quantity of land sown to wheat, the season being very favourable until the end of the year.

An old adage says, "that a bushel of March dust is worth a king's ransom;" and every one experienced in agriculture knows that rainy weather at seed time as well as at harvest is very prejudicial to the produce of grain in this kingdom. In such seasons, the greatest part of the arable-land cannot be ploughed to any advantage, and if grain is sown where the land is very wet, it seldom produces more than half a crop; but in many districts a fourth part of the land cannot be sown at all in rainy seasons. The vale-lands, which in fruitful years are the most productive, are most affected by unfavourable seasons.

2dly. The many false paragraphs published in the newspapers respecting the crops of grain in this kingdom, have contributed not a little to the high price; and the consequences of them have been severely felt, not only in the discontent and inclination to rioting that appeared amongst the people, and which, in some measure, may be attributed to those paragraphs; but we are informed by the Americans, that, had it not been for such misstatements as appeared in most of the papers announcing the very great abundance of the crops in the kingdom, the exportation of corn and flour from their country to ours would have been very great, four months sooner than it was, whereby wheat would have been prevented from rising to the enormous price which it did. The printers of newspapers should, therefore, be especially careful to have their information from experienced men, and not from those who, travelling, perhaps, through a great part of the kingdom, form a judgment by looking at the corn as they ride along; for it is impossible to ascertain the state of the crops, by viewing the fields in riding from place to place. The farmers themselves are frequently deceived for want of more narrowly inspecting their corn, and often much disappointed in the cast or yield when it comes to be threshed.

3dly. The war was, in some measure, a cause of the scarcity; for, in a general peace, corn might be imported from any part of Europe or America, at a much less expence, and therefore rendered cheaper. The demand for foreign service, expeditions, sea-stores, &c. would also be lessened. Beef, pork, cheese, butter, &c. are dearer, in time of war, from the same causes. With respect to the great fluctuations in the markets, they are not at all to be wondered at, if we reflect, that when corn is at a very high price, very few who are concerned therein keep much stock by them; and if the market happens to fall, they will not buy, until that which they have is nearly exhausted; but being at length forced to purchase, the market takes a turn, upon which they all eagerly purchase, and the commodity, of course, is advanced in price.

The importation of corn and flour has certainly been very great; but when it is considered, that the consumption of corn in this kingdom amounts to, at least, 150,000 quarters per week; the quantity imported will appear comparatively trifling.

As to the opinion, that farmers, &c. keep up the price of corn by unfair means, it is contrary to common sense; for is it reasonable to suppose that many hundred thousand men, dispersed all over the kingdom, can combine together so as to keep up the price of a commodity; if so, why do do they not the same at all times. Besides, the farmer knows it is contrary to his interest to have corn dear, which will occasion an advance in his rent, a certain and constant disadvantage, whilst a high price for corn is only a contingent advantage. Neither can millers, mealmen, &c. enhance the price by monopoly, for corn and flour are articles which will soon damage, and sometimes will be almost spoiled by keeping them a few weeks. J. S.

For the Monthly Magazine.

REMARKS *on the* CALMUCS, *their* MANNERS, *and* CUSTOMS*.

Sarepta, July, 1793.

I Had lately the pleasure to attend the Russian councillor of state, M. Pallas, and his family, on a visit to a Calmuc Prince; and I flatter myself that a description of the horde, and of the manner in which we were entertained by the Prince's family, will prove acceptable to you.

The Calmucs belong to those nomadical peoples who in the plains and deserts on the Volga and the Ural (Yaik) live a truly patriarchal life, in separate hordes, under the government of their chiefs; drawing their subsistence entirely from their herds and flocks, and remaining only so long in one place as they can find pasture for them. The horde of the above-mentioned Prince was now encamped near the German colony Sarepta, our present place of residence.

The choice of the day on which, in consequence of an invitation from the Prince, we were to visit the Calmuc camp was left to M. Pallas; and he appointed Friday, being their day of rest, like our Sunday, so that we might have an opportunity of assisting at the public worship of their gods. We were unacquainted with the Calmuc language; but M. Hammell, master of police at Sarepta, who had lived several years among the Calmucs, was so obliging as to accompany us, and undertake the office of interpreter.

It was in the middle of June, in the most delightful season of the year, that we made this excursion. The weather was very favourable, the air pure and serene, and the sun arose in full splendour, announcing a fine summers-day.

Our road led through the German village *Schönbrunn*, which is distant two versts from Sarepta, and derives its name from a spring, the water of which is conducted in pipes to the latter place. Having passed the agreeable wood *Tschapurnick*, which lies near Schönbrunn, and belongs to the colonists, we found ourselves in an extensive barren desert, and, after travelling eight versts more, arrived at the tract of country where we were to meet with the horde. We soon reached an eminence, commanding a full view of a broad valley, in which stood their camp, in scattered clusters of tents, and which was hitherto hidden from us by the hills over which we had passed. The rays of the sun had added fresh lustre to the soft verdure of the fruitful plain, through which a small rivulet glided with gentle meanders. Innumerable herds of camels, horses, sheep, and horned cattle, were feeding on the downs, the limits of which our eye could not reach; and various groups of men were busily employed in their various occupations. The newness and uncommonness of the scene before us made an impression which it is impossible to describe. We stood a considerable time on the eminence, absorbed in the contemplation of the fine prospect before us, and gave ourselves up to our feelings, while our eager eyes wandered over the various objects that presented themselves to our view.

As soon as we were observed by the Calmucs, the Prince, a young man about sixteen or seventeen years of age, and of rather a rude appearance, came on horseback to meet us, accompanied by several of his court retinue. His dress consisted of a coat of light-blue cloth, ornamented with gold tassels, and reaching down as low as the knee; the sleeves were slit up; and his under garment was of the same length. He wore yellow boots, and a sabre at his side, and on his head a little flat yellow cap, with a black border. His hair plaited into a cue on the crown of the head. His attendants had very little in their dress to distinguish it from that of the common Calmucs. When they had approached near enough, the Prince dismounted to bid us welcome; and, having informed us of the indisposition of his mother, accompanied us down into the valley, to the encampment of the horde.

A little before we reached it, a wooden cross, which was stuck in the ground, attracted my attention. It was about two feet high; and red, white, and blue twisted yarn was drawn from the upper point to the two sides of the cross-beams, and thence again down towards the upright one, so as to form an oblique-standing quadrangle.

* From the Letter of a gentleman residing at Sarepta, to his friend in Germany.

quadrangle. At the ends of the cross-beam hung tassels of the same three-coloured yarn. Having inquired the use of this cross, I was told, that it had been placed there by the priests on account of the sickness of the Prince's mother, and as a means towards effecting her speedy recovery. It seemed strange to me, that these Heathen priests should have chosen for this purpose a cross, the symbol of Christianity.

Our arrival, which was a before-unseen phenomenon to the horde, attracted the attention of all. Men and youths left their herds, and the women, who were engaged in making butter, in weaving felt, sewing, and other domestic employments, came running out of their tents, with their children, to view the strangers.

The whole behaviour and appearance of these people evinced a great rudeness and want of civilization. Many of the men were half naked, and even boys of ten years of age flocked around us in the same state as they had come out of the hands of Nature. The women and girls must, however, be excepted from this general charge of unbecoming nudity, though it must be owned, that their cloaths were not remarkably clean or neat.

The boys who had from their infancy been destined for the priesthood, had their heads close-shaven: but the others, for the most part, wore in the plaits of their hair small bells, which jingled at every motion of the body. Almost every one, men, boys, women, and young girls, even children from three to four years of age, had tobacco-pipes in their mouths; which, joined to the nakedness, brown mulatto-colour, and characteristic broad Calmuc faces, gave the children a truly ridiculous, and even ape-like, appearance. The strange sight of these naked boys and half-naked men was quite new and unexpected to us, especially to the ladies of our party, who, blushing with shame and confusion, knew not whither to turn, that less offensive objects might meet their eyes.

At last, accompanied by a great crowd, we arrived at the huts, or *kibitks* (as they are called), of the horde. They were all made of brown felt, had a very dirty and sneaky appearance; and the flesh and hides, which were hung on them to dry, rendered them still more disgusting. Two only, which stood conspicuous in the middle of the others, were distinguished by their superior size, and by their colour, being of white felt; and we learned that one of them was the habitation of the prince, and the other the temple of their gods.—Having observed small wooden wind-mill-wings fixed at the entrance of the brown felt huts, I inquired for what purpose they were put there, and was told, that they were *praying-machines*, on which the owner of the hut causes certain prayers to be written by the priests, that they may be turned round by the wind, and he thereby be freed from the trouble of repeating them himself. The priests have likewise a very commodious method of expediting their prayers: when they have a number of petitions to offer up for the people, they for this purpose make use of a cylindrical wooden-box, into which they throw the written prayers; and having placed it perpendicularly on a stick, they sit down beside it, pull it backwards and forwards with a string, gravely smoaking their pipes while performing the ceremony; for, according to their doctrine, in order to render prayer efficacious, it is only necessary that it be put in motion; and it is a matter of indifference, whether this be done by means of the lips, of a wind-mill, or of a cylindrical box.

Adjoining to the Prince's kibitk stood another, likewise somewhat larger than the others, which served for a kitchen. Although the Prince's kibitk was distinguished from the other felt-huts by its external appearance, and by its much larger size, yet the entrance to it was so low, that we could not go in without stooping: but we found the interior of it very roomy, and ornamented in a singular manner.

The middle of the ground was covered with a variegated carpet, and the other parts with fresh-mown grass. Round about the sides stood or hung a number of chests with iron-cramps, leather-bottles, saddles, guns, bows, arrows, and other warlike instruments. Opposite to the entrance of the kibitk lay the princess on a low sopha, over which hung festoons of yellow silk. She appeared to be about fifty years of age, had an orange-coloured silk dress, and on her head a Calmuc cap, likewise of a yellow colour (which is held sacred among the Calmucs) with a black border and her hair hung down over her shoulders in two long plaits.

The sister of the young prince, a girl of about fifteen or sixteen years of age, of a pleasing physiognomy, and who, for a Calmucket, might be deemed a beauty, met us at the entrance of the tent, and welcomed the ladies of our party. She wore a wide dress of green silk, and had

a red

a red tuft on the crown of her yellow cap. Her hair was formed into many small plaits.

As we approached the mother of the Prince, she raised herself up a little from her sopha, bid us welcome by a nod of her head, and made us take our places near her; some of the chests being pushed forward to the right of the Princess, to serve as seats for the ladies.

The crowd of people, who had followed us, remained on the outside of the kibitk. Besides the Prince and his family, several other persons of both sexes, belonging to the court-retinue, were with us in the tent. The Princess opened the conversation by inquiring our names, age, condition, and the like.

In the mean time, a leather flask, full of spirits, and a small set of China cups and saucers, in a small wooden chest, probably the most precious furniture the Princess was possessed of, was brought out. Some of the spirituous liquor, which the Calmucs distill from sour mare's milk, was poured into one of the saucers, and handed to the company. Most of our party refused this singular liquor. I endeavoured, from curiosity, to drink a little of it, but could not reconcile myself to the taste of it; I could, however, perceive that, if, drunken in large quantities, it must be very intoxicating. M. Police-master Hammel, however, who by a long residence among these people had become accustomed to their manner of life, took a hearty draught of this welcoming potation.

M. Pallas then, in order to treat the company with something more palatable, had some of the wheaten bread and wine, which we had brought with us for breakfast, fetched from the carriage, and presented to the Princess, to the Prince, and to his sister. As the Calmucs cultivate no corn, the bread was a great rarity to them, and they devoured it with much appetite. The Prince and young Princess gave a part of what they had received from M. Pallas to those standing nearest them, and these again divided it with their neighbours, so that each received only a small morsel. In the same manner they proceeded with the wine, which the priests especially seemed very much to relish; the Prince being the only one of the company who refused it. But his mother, who, in handing about the wine, had been forgotten, requested us herself to give her some. All the Calmucs present then received from the priests out of round brass bottles, which they constantly carry about with them hanging on the left side of their girdles, a few drops of holy water, with which they purified their mouths, and then spit it out again.

We could not help remarking the unmannerly behaviour of the priests and the attendants of the court, who, even in the presence of the Prince and his family, were not ashamed to commit indecencies which, in countries only a little civilized, we should hardly pardon in the lowest vulgar; for some of those standing behind us shocked our ears with the pretty loud explosions of their overcharged stomachs.

About nine o'clock, we went with the Prince, and the crowd of people who had remained on the outside of his tent, to the *kibitk* which was fitted up to serve for a temple. Like that of the Prince, it was made of white felt, and perfectly resembled it in size and shape. Opposite to the entrance, there stood, in the back-ground, on an altar about three feet high, seven cups full of water, and above them the principal divinities were hung up, being painted in a variety of ridiculous forms, with divers glaring colours, on parchment. Round the sides of the tent hung the other pretty numerous pictures of their gods, consisting only of black outlines drawn on parchment. The ground was covered with carpets. Eight priests performed the service. Their long wide garments were made of orange-coloured nankin; from their right shoulders to the left thigh they wore red belts, fastened to a girdle of the same colour, whence depended the little brass bottle for holding holy water. Their close-shaven heads were covered with yellow, flat, round hats; and their boots were of yellow Morocco leather.

The laics, who take no part in the divine service, but leave the whole to be performed by the priests, who compose almost a fourth part of the nation, remained on the outside of the kibitk, and lifted up the felt, that they might have a view of the whole. The eight priests having seated themselves, with their legs crossed, in two rows from the altar towards the door, two of them began the service with wooden pipes, on which they for some time preluded in horrid dissonance; the whole then joined in a chant, which perfectly corresponded with the preceding music. The chorus being finished, the two priests again began their cat's music, and two others joined in the concert on two horns, with wide mouths, and four yards long; and two others had small

 drums

drums, fastened to a stick, which they beat with an instrument made of iron-wire, having a wooden handle at the lower end, and at the upper a leather knob. The remaining two of the officiating priests, at the same time, with various ridiculous grimaces, clapped their hands, and, in conjunction with the two kettle-drummers, chaunted with great vociferation. The penetrating squeaking noise of the two small pipes, the loud droning of the horns, the incessant drumming and clapping of hands, and the harsh voices of the priests, formed a most abominable concert, such as might be expected from a band of Furies; and we were heartily glad when it was finished. They then murmured forth a few prayers in unison, with which the service concluded; when we again returned to the tent of the Prince. Here a large, not very clean, vessel full of Calmuc tea awaited us. They prepare their tea with milk, butter, and salt, and it looked like milk-coffee. Some of this liquor was offered to us in a large wooden-bowl; but we declined partaking of it, alleging as an excuse, that we were not accustomed to drink hot liquors at that time of the day.

The priests then mixed in the conversation, representing to us the state of the horde, and complaining of the encroachments of the new Russian colonies, which were so numerous, that the neighbouring Calmucs began to be in want of pasture for their flocks and herds.

It being now time for us to return home, we took leave of the Prince's family. His mother recommended her children to M. Pallas, adding, that she herself was too far advanced in years to be able to enjoy the benefit of his protection. The Prince and his suite accompanied us a part of the way, and we arrived in safety at Sarepta, without repenting that we had made this excursion to visit the chief of a nomadical horde of Calmucs.

MEMOIRS OF EMINENT PERSONS.

MEMOIRS OF GALIANI.

FERDINAND GALIANI was born in Naples about the year 1720. He was descended of a noble family, his father being a Marquis, and his uncle a benedictine monk, and afterwards promoted to the dignities of Archbishop and Great Almoner to the King. The Archbishop was a man of superior talents, celebrated for his prudent conduct (being that of a nice neutrality) during the memorable struggles between *Sacerdotium* and *Imperium*, and entitled to unfading honours in the History of the two Sicilies, for having been the chief author and promoter of the famous concordate of 1741, which happily terminated the jurisdictional disputes between the court of Naples and the Holy See.

To the high preferments and care of this uncle Galiani was indebted for a liberal education, and for the high character he afterwards attained in Italian literature. By an ancient law of the kingdom of Naples, the Great Almoner of the King, is *ipso facto* constituted superintendant of the university, and exercises a considerable share of authority and some jurisdiction over its professors and students. It was therefore no wonder that a person in such a situation should be courted by the first literary men; and still less so, that the education of the nephews of *Monsignor Galiani* should be assigned to tutors of eminent abilities.

If the testimonies of the instructors of young Galiani may be implicitly credited, he displayed very early an extraordinary genius in every line of study. According to their reports, at the age of sixteen, he had mastered the Latin and Greek languages, and was equally acquainted with classical literature, the mathematics, philosophy, and with the civil and canon law.

At the age of twenty, about the year 1740, he made his entrance on the stage of literature, by publishing a ludicrous work, which evinced the turn of his genius for wit and humour. It was a prevailing custom at that time in Naples (as well as in other cities of Italy), on the decease of any great or eminent person, to make a large collection of songs, sonnets, epigrams, elegies, and inscriptions, in praise of the real or reputed talents and virtues of the deceased. This nonsense had grown so much into fashion, that Counsellor *di Gennaro*, and Canon Mazzochi, the former one of the most illustrious civilians, the latter deemed the greatest antiquarian of the age, both allowed to be men of polite and elegant taste as Latin writers, and perhaps

perhaps inferior to none since the revival of ancient literature, were the most active in employing their pens on similar subjects, prostituting their valuable talents in these whimsical exertions. The abuse called loudly for reformation, and nothing could have better answered the purpose than a *jeu d'esprit* calculated to cover it with ridicule. Galiani, catching the opportunity of the death of a famous public executioner, named *Jannaccone*, spotted a droll funereal collection of prose and verse in his praise, in which the manner and style of the respective anthors, accustomed to that sort of compositions, were ingeniously personated and burlesqued. Moliere, by his happy comedy, *Les Femmes Savantes*, cured the mania of his countrywomen for the study of classical literature, and the Mesdames Daciers, after its appearance, were no more to be found in France. Galiani, however, was not so fortunate in curing the folly of his countrymen for funeral collections. To the disgrace of the Italian nation, this absurd custom continued to prevail many years afterwards; and so late as the year 1783, on the death of the Princess of Roccella, an insignificant woman, in every sense of the word excepting one, we witnessed a profusion of compositions in the same strain, by the best Italian poets, including the respectable Bettinelli, in a volume too, printed on large superfine paper; and, to complete the farce, with the inimitable types of BODONI!

Much about the same time, Galiani had an opportunity, in another work, of producing another specimen of his humour. Pope Benedict XIV. had applied to his uncle, the Great Almoner, to procure him a complete collection of the various materials which compose Mount Vesuvius. This Prelate intrusted the commission to his nephew, who actually undertook to make the collection, accompanying each article with a short philosophical comment. Soon after, he addressed them in a box to the Pontiff, with an humorous inscription to the whole—*Si filius Dei es, fac ut* LAPIDES *isti* PANES *fiant*.—The turn of this motto was easily apprehended by the Pope, who was himself one of the wittiest men of his age, and it could not fail to procure Galiani what he hinted at. He accordingly received soon afterwards a rich abbey, worth four thousand ducats (nearly seven hundred pounds) per annum. It is a desirable condition for men of letters when they have to deal with sovereigns like Benedict XIV.! But how seldom do we find, in the chronological tables of princes, men like him, whose virtues reflected honour on the diadem, and would have been an ornament to any church!

These exertions, however, were of inferior moment, compared with the history of the human mind. Galiani soon afterwards displayed his abilities in a philosophical line: and we find him, about the year 1745, publishing his well-known political tract, *Trattato della Moneta* (a Treatise on Money). This was unanimously pronounced in Italy an original and capital publication. The important science of political-economy was then, as it were, in its infancy; in England, indeed, a few hints had been suggested on the subject by Mr. Locke, and other writers; and some fewer in France, by Melon and Tutot; no one consequently will dispute the palm of originality with M. Galiani.

It was this work which firmly established his reputation in the world. He was now appointed secretary to the Neapolitan ambassador in Paris, where he soon exhibited other specimens of his philosophical abilities, by publishing an *Essay on the Commerce of Corn*. This new work was very favourably received in France, where some of their philosophers were candidly wont to say: *Le petit Italien est en cela plus instruit que nous.*—By the word *petit*, they alluded to the diminutive stature of the author.

It was not long before he was recalled to Naples, where he was appointed a counsellor in the tribunal of commerce, an office of magistracy not incompatible with the order of a clergyman. He retained this place during the remainder of his life; and as it required much time and application to perform its duties, M. Galiani after this was not so active in literary exertions as he had been heretofore. In 1779, he published a work *on the Origin of the Neapolitan Dialect*. This performance was thought not to bear an accurate correspondence to the title. Galiani might have thrown much light upon this branch of Italian philology, as well as on the civil vicissitudes of a nation whose misfortune it has been to be so frequently conquered or governed by foreign powers. His work was judged superficial and unsatisfactory by those who wished that the interesting questions involved in the subject should have been profoundly and freely canvassed. In the year 1780, he published a treatise on the *Armed Neutrality*, which he dedicated to the late Empress Catherine of Russia. This work, on a question entirely new and complicated in the system of public law of Europe, fell likewise

considerably

considerably short of the expectation of those who had been before highly prepossessed in favour of the author.

M. Galiani died in 1789, having nearly attained the 70th year of his age. He was very short in stature, extremely vivacious, remarkable for an uncommon share of wit and humour, which frequently became satirical, and for seasonable *bons mots*, and smart repartees, in familiar conversation. He was highly admired by their Sicilian Majesties, and kept a constant correspondence with many European princes, and especially with the Landgrave of Hesse Cassel. The late Empress of Russia did him the honour to place his portrait in the Imperial Gallery at Petersburg, by the side of Voltaire's. On account of his well known wit and vivacity, the late Mr. Gibbon used to call him—*That Laughing Philosopher, the Abbé Galiani.*

Truth and impartiality oblige us, however, to remark here, that the literary fame of M. Galiani has been very much contested since his death. If some latent anecdotes recently brought to light are to be credited, by the influence of his birth, dignity, and power, he borrowed his best works from other persons. It is believed by very great numbers of the Italians, that his witty collection of songs in honour of the deceased executioner Jannacone, was really the production of M. Carcani, an eminent literary character of that time; that his *Treatise on Money* should be ascribed to M. Intieri, a Florentine economist; his Essay on the Commerce of Corn, to the illustrious Diderot; and, lastly, his History of the Italian Dialect, to M. Meola, a learned man in Naples, who lived in great poverty and distress. It may be further observed, that such as have intimately conversed with M. Galiani shrewdly suspected some artifices of this kind, even during his life-time. For, setting apart his witty and humorous sallies, and reducing his method of discoursing and arguing to the scale of sensible and rational ideas, he frequently betrayed deficiency which indicated a narrow mind and superficial information. When, moreover, we call to mind the high encomiums bestowed on his genius yet adolescent, by the Professors of the university, and other eminent literary characters, who may well be thought caterers for the patronage of the Great Almoner, his uncle; we cannot help recollecting, at the same time, the brilliant pleasantry of Voltaire on the celebrated Paschal—*At twelve, he was an inventor of new theorems; at thirty, he was a mediocre geometer.*

BIOGRAPHICAL ACCOUNT *of the late* MAJOR-GENERAL GREENE, *of the* AMERICAN ARMY.

NATHANIEL GREENE, was born in the town of Warwick, and county of Kent, in the state of Rhode-Island, in or about the year 1741; and was the second son of a respectable person of the same name, who was descended from some of the first settlers of that fertile country. His father was extensively concerned in very lucrative iron-works, which he left to his children at his death, prior to the American war.

Nathaniel was endowed with an uncommon degree of penetration and judgment, which, with a benevolent mind and affable deportment, acquired him numerous and respectable friends; in consequence of which, he was, at a very early period of life, chosen a Member of the Legislature of the (*then*) Colony of Rhode Island. The manner in which he acquitted this trust, which was to the entire satisfaction of his constituents, procured him a permanent interest, and ensured him a seat in the Legislature, till, and at, the period of opposition to Great Britain.

After the commencement of hostilities at Lexington and Concord, the spirit of resistance became general throughout the colonies; and Rhode Island was not deficient in her contributions. She raised three regiments of militia, the command of which was conferred on Mr. Greene, who was nominated Brigadier-general; and he resigned the pacific principles of Quakerism, in which he had been bred, to take upon him a military command.

He led these troops to Cambridge, and there beheld three times as many troops as the English had supposed equal to a total conquest of the whole country, under the necessity of evacuating the city of Boston, where they had first landed!

The General's merit and abilities were soon noticed by the discriminating eye of General Washington; who reposed in him the utmost confidence, and paid a particular deference to his advice and opinion, on all occasions of doubt and difficulty. This circumstance had its accustomed tendency to excite jealousy in the breasts of officers of older standing and higher rank, who used some degree of industry to supplant him with the Commander in Chief. His worth was, however, too well known, and he himself too much esteemed by General Washington, to be easily supplanted by his adversaries. In a short

short time after this, he was appointed Major-general by the Congress*.

Towards the close of 1776 he was present at the surprise of the Hessian troops at Trenton, in New Jersey; and, at the beginning of the next year, he served at the battle of Prince Town. In both of these actions he highly distinguished himself, and gave great satisfaction to General Washington and his country. At the battle of German Town, he commanded the left wing of the army, and his utmost endeavours were exerted to retrieve the misfortunes of that day; on that occasion, he received the applause of the officers and troops, as well as the approbation of the Commander in Chief.

In March 1778 he was appointed Quartermaster-general, which office he accepted under a stipulation that his rank in the army should not be affected by it, and that he should retain his right to command in time of action according to his station and seniority. This privilege was accordingly exercised by him, for he commanded the right wing of the army at the battle of Monmouth.

About the middle of the same year an attack was concerted, in conjunction with the French fleet, on the British garrison at Newport, Rhode Island. General Sullivan was appointed to lead the troops, and General Greene served under him. This affair proved unsuccessful; for the French Admiral having sailed out of the harbour to engage Lord Howe's fleet, his squadron was dispersed by a storm, and the Americans were obliged to raise the siege. General Greene on this occasion, also, acquired much credit, by the skill displayed by him in drawing off the army in safety.

The schemes of the British Commanders to effect something decisive in the New England States being now rendered abortive, and there being little hopes of better success in that quarter, they determined to make the southern colonies the scene of action, as they appeared to be not only less capable of defence, but promised more advantage to the invaders. An armament was accordingly equipped at New York; the army embarked there, on the 26th of December, 1779, and landed on the 11th of February, 1780, about thirty miles from *Charlestown*, in South Carolina; which, after a brave defence, was surrendered to Sir Henry Clinton, on the 12th of May.

A series of ill-successes followed this event, and the American arms in South Carolina, were, in general, unsuccessful. Such was the situation of affairs when General Washington appointed General Greene to command the Southern army, which Lord Cornwallis had nearly *annihilated*. He arrived at Charlotte, in Mecklenburgh county, in North Carolina, accompanied by General Morgan, who had already distinguished himself in the Southern States, and also acquired great reputation during the expedition against General Burgoyne. He found the forces which he was to command reduced to a small number, both by defeats and by desertion. The total returns were but nine hundred and seventy continentals, and thirteen hundred militia. Their provisions, forage, and military stores, were in a still worse state than even the troops themselves. The men were without pay and almost naked; nor were supplies of cloathing to be procured nearer than two hundred miles. He had, in the midst of all these inconveniences, to oppose a respectable and victorious body of veteran troops; but he, at the same time, enjoyed the good fortune to behold numerous bodies of men, who had hitherto remained neutral, driven to his assistance by the mistaken zeal of the royalists, which compelled large numbers to an active defence of their persons and property.

The ravages committed by individuals professing to be royalists, and following Lord Cornwallis for the sake of plunder and depredation, rather than from any motive of good will, or principle of attachment to the cause, soon gave offence to his Lordship; and answered, negatively, a good purpose to General Greene. The prudent measures taken by the latter, for, repairing every injury which the army had recently sustained, as well as for conciliating the good will of the inhabitants by acts of humanity, justice, and kindness, soon brought together a considerable body of adherents to the revolution; yet it must be confessed that they were far inferior to the British party. Among these he regained the active services of many distinguished and enterprizing inhabitants of wealth and influence, who had either remained in a state of inertness, from their dread of the superiority of the British forces; or, whose apprehensions, joined to their ignorance of what had been achieved in another quarter, had induced them to give up the contest as a point decidedly unfavourable to the cause of America.

The General, having thus reinforced the southern army with all the strength which could be collected together by the friends of the revolution, immediately detached General Morgan to the western extremities

* August 26th 1776.

ties of the state, to protect those who were well disposed to the revolution from the ravages of the disaffected.

This force, which was the first which had appeared there on the part of America for a considerable time, inspired the friends of her cause with renovated ardour; and such numbers flocked around Morgan's standard, that Lord Cornwallis thought it proper to send Colonel (now General) Tarleton to dislodge him from the station he had taken. That officer, with every advantage which could be derived from a successful reputation, is said to have put himself at the head of a thousand regular troops, with two field-pieces. On the 17th of January, 1781, at a place called the *Cow Pens*, he came up with General Morgan, whose force was inferior in point of numbers; and in addition to this, only one-third of his troops consisted of continental soldiers: the remainder consisted of undisciplined militia. An engagement took place immediately, and the Americans proved victorious.

This success on the part of General Greene entirely disconcerted the plans of Lord Cornwallis; who could have had no idea of such an enemy in South Carolina, which seemed to be completely conquered. He had, indeed, made the necessary arrangements for carrying his operations into the Northern States, where he was flattered with the prospect of similar successes. Disappointed, however, in these operations, he now found it necessary to postpone his design, and march speedily after General Morgan, in hopes of not only recovering the prisoners, but of revenging the losses sustained by Col. Tarleton. The rapid movements of the Americans once more eluded his efforts; and General Greene actually found means to effect a junction of the two divisions of his little army, on the 7th of February: but it was yet too weak to resist Lord Cornwallis, and he found it necessary to make a retrograde movement; which the vigilance of his Lordship was not able to prevent.

The American Commander having conducted his army in safety into Virginia, and received some reinforcements there, with the promise of still more effectual aid, soon returned into North Carolina with the hopes of being able to act offensively. He even encamped in the vicinity of his enemy, and conducted his enterprizes with such ability and promptitude, that, during three weeks that he lay near to Lord Cornwallis, that officer was unable to reap any advantage from his superiority; on the contrary, he found himself cut off from those succours which the royal party were disposed to afford him.

About the beginning of March General Greene effected a junction with a continental regiment, and two considerable bodies of Virginia and North Carolina Militia. He then determined on attacking the British army without loss of time; "being persuaded," as he declared in his subsequent dispatches, "that if he was successful it would prove ruinous to the enemy; but, if otherwise, it would be only a partial evil to himself."

On the 14th he arrived at Guildford Court House, from which place the British army was only twelve miles distant. His forces consisted of about four thousand five hundred men, of whom near two-thirds were North Carolina and Virginia Militia. The British were about two thousand four hundred, all regular troops, and the greater part were inured to discipline and service in expeditions under an able commander, who, on the morning of the 15th, being apprised of the enemy's intention, marched to meet him.

The engagement commenced at half an hour past one o'clock by a brisk cannonade; after which the British advanced in three columns, and attacked the North Carolina Militia, which gave way, and could not be rallied by its officers. This disaster decided the fate of the day, although the Virginia Militia, which composed the second line, behaved with great gallantry; for they fought with great bravery, and several times returned to the charge after being repeatedly broken and disordered, after they had kept up a heavy fire for a long time. At length, however, they were driven back on the third line; and the action becoming general, severe, and bloody, terminated in favour of British discipline against American numbers. This conflict lasted an hour and a half; and was ended by General Greene's ordering a retreat, when he perceived the enemy were on the point of surrounding his troops.

The loss sustained by Lord Cornwallis's army was stated at 532, including killed, wounded and missing; among whom were several officers of rank and importance.

Such trifling disasters as these, when compared with the more ripened science of slaughter at the present day, may perhaps appear trivial: but they were, on this occasion, decisive in their consequence, for, in three days after, Lord Cornwallis in his turn was impelled to a retrograde movement, and retreated from the scene of his victory to Wilmington, which is more than two hundred miles distant from the field

field of battle, leaving behind him many of his troops, who were desperately wounded.

General Greene now formed the resolution of expelling the British entirely from South Carolina; and he some time afterwards returned thither for that purpose. His first object was to gain possession of Camden, where Lord Rawdon (now the Earl of Moira) was posted with about nine hundred men. This place, rendered strong by the united efforts of nature and art, was covered by a creek and a river on the south and east sides; and as securely defended by redoubts on the north and west. It seemed, therefore, to be too formidable a post to be carried by storm, with the small force which the American General then commanded, consisting chiefly of about seven hundred regulars. He therefore encamped at about a mile from the town, in order to prevent supplies from being carried thither on one hand, and to take advantage of any favourable circumstance on the other.

Lord Rawdon's situation was now rendered peculiarly distressing. He had detached Colonel Watson for the protection of the eastern frontiers, and recalled him on receiving intelligence of Gen. Greene's intentions; but this officer was so closely watched by General Marien, that it was impracticable for him to join Lord Rawdon. His Lordship's supplies were also very uncertain; and, should General Greene's reinforcements arrive, he might probably be compelled to surrender. He, therefore, armed every person who could use a gun, and attacked General Greene in his camp, which was obstinately defended, and for some time victory seemed to declare in favour of the American arms. Lieutenant-colonel, now General (*William*) Washington, who commanded the cavalry, had, at one time, not less than two hundred of Lord Rawdon's men prisoners; but, in consequence of the misconduct of an American officer, General Greene was compelled to retreat, having lost, in this action, about two hundred killed, wounded and prisoners. Lord Rawdon stated his loss at two hundred and fifty-eight.

This affair produced a similar result to the battle of Guildford: Lord Cornwallis was successful in that action, but retreated two hundred miles, and abandoned, for a time, his grand object of marching northward. In the latter case, Lord Rawdon enjoyed the honour of the field, but was shortly after reduced to the necessity of quitting his post, and leaving behind him several sick and wounded.

The evacuation of Camden, and the vigilance of General Greene and his army, gave a new face to the affairs of South Carolina, where the British influence declined with as much rapidity as it had formerly been established. The numerous forts which the English had garrisoned fell, one after another, into the hands of the Americans. Orangeburgh, Motte, Watson, George Town, Granby, and all the rest (Fort Ninety-six excepted) were surrendered; and a considerable number of prisoners, with artillery and military stores, were found in them.

On the 22d of May General Greene commenced his operations before *Ninety six*, with the main body of his little army. The siege was carried on for some time with considerable spirit, and the place, on the other hand, was defended with great courage. At length the works were so far reduced that the place must have infallibly surrendered, if the arrival of three regiments from Europe, which landed at Charlestown, had not enabled Lord Rawdon to march to the relief of so important a post.

The superiority of the British forces now preponderated once more, and offered only to General Greene the alternative of either raising the siege, or attacking the place by storm, before the arrival of the expected reinforcements. He attempted the latter, and was repulsed with the loss of one hundred and fifty men, after which he retreated over Saluda river.

This active and vigilant officer did not however despond. It was in vain that his friends wished to persuade him to retire to Virginia, for he boldly replied—"I will recover the country, or die in the attempt."

His plan seems to have been, at this period, to avoid any decisive engagement until the British force should become divided; nothing, therefore, but a few immaterial skirmishes took place for some time.

On the 9th of September however he assembled two thousand men, and proceeded to attack the British, under command of Colonel Stewart, who were posted at the Eutaw Springs in South Carolina.

As the Americans advanced to the attack, they fell in with some of the reconnoitring-parties of the English, about two or three miles in front of the main-body; these, being closely pursued, were driven back, and the action soon became general. The militia however were forced at length to give way, but were well supported by the second line; and during the hottest part of the engagement, General Greene ordered the Maryland and Virginia

Conti-

Continentals to charge with the bayonet, which decided the day, for theſe troops ruſhed on with ſuch impetuoſity, that the Britiſh lines being ſoon broken and diſordered, the troops were cloſely purſued, and about five hundred taken priſoners.

The Engliſh, however, made a ſecond ſtand, in a poſition favoured by impenetrable encloſures and a piqueted garden; and Lieutenant Colonel Waſhington, after having made every effort to diſlodge them, was wounded and taken priſoner. Four ſix-pounders were brought forward to play upon them, but theſe alſo fell into their hands; and it being found impracticable to acquire any further advantage, the Americans retired, leaving a piquet on the field of action.

The Congreſs honoured Greneral Greene with a Britiſh ſtandard, and a gold medal, emblematical of this ſucceſsful affair, "*for his wiſe, deciſive, and magnanimous conduct in the action at the Eutaw Springs, in which, with a force inferior in number to that of the enemy, he obtained a moſt ſignal victory.*"

The battle of Eutaw, although rather equivocal in point of actual ſucceſs, yet effected ſo material a change in the affairs of South Carolina, that the Britiſh troops afterwards confined themſelves chiefly to the town of Charleſtown, being content with a few foraging and depredatory excurſions, in which little more than ſkirmiſhing occurred.

In this ſituation of affairs the American ſoldiers endured great and extraordinary hardſhips, in conſequence of being deprived of many neceſſaries and comforts; and a plot was at length hatched to deliver up their victorious General to his adverſaries: happily for the cauſe of America, there were only twelve perſons concerned in it, and the deſign, equally deſperate and atrocious, was providentially diſcovered.

The ſurrender of Lord Cornwallis's army, at the ſiege of York, in Virginia, (where General Waſhington commanded in perſon) had, at length, convinced the Britiſh Miniſtry of the impracticability of ſubjugating the United States, and they diſcontinued offenſive operations. It had been reported, from the beginning of 1782, that Charleſtown was to be evacuated; and it was officially announced for the ſeventh of Auguſt, but did not take place till the ſeventeenth of December.

The period having at laſt arrived, when Great Britain thought proper to acknowledge the Independence of the United States; the officers of the army, after eſtabliſhing the Society of Cincinnatus, retired to plough their paternal fields. Among the reſt, General Greene was now at liberty to return to his native country, where he diſplayed the ſame equanimity and good conduct as a citizen which he had evinced during his military career, in the courſe of which the two Carolinas were reſcued from invaſion, and the grand ſtruggle, in a great meaſure, decided.

While the General was abſent from Rhode-Iſland, political animoſities had riſen to a conſiderable height among his countrymen; and, on his return, he exerted himſelf, ſucceſsfully, in reſtoring harmony and quiet. In October, 1785, he embarked on board a veſſel for Georgia, to viſit his eſtate in that part of America. While employed there, on his domeſtic affairs, he happened to walk out in the month of June, in the extreme heat of an exceſſive hot day, and being taken ſuddenly ill, died on the 19th of the ſame month, in the year 1796.

On receiving the account of this melancholy event, the inhabitants of Savannah expreſſed the moſt poignant grief and concern. The ſtores and ſhops were immediately ſhut up, and the ſhipping in the harbour diſplayed their colours half-maſt high. The body was carried to the capital of the province, and interred on the 20th of the ſame month, in a public manner, being attended by the Society of the Cincinnati, the militia, citizens, &c.

General Greene left behind him a widow and five children, the eldeſt of whom was about eleven years old at the time of his father's death.

On Tueſday, the 12th of Auguſt following, the United States, in Congreſs aſſembled, came to the following reſolution:—

Resolved—That a Monument be erected to the Memory of Nathaniel Greene, Eſquire, at the Seat of Federal Government, with the following Inſcription:—

Sacred to the Memory of
Nathaniel Greene, Esquire,
Who departed this Life
On the Nineteenth of June,
M,DCC,LXXXVI.
Late Major General
In the Service of the United States,
and
Commander of their Army
in the
Southern Department.
The United States, in Congress
assembled,
In Honour of his
Patriotism, Valour, and Ability,
have erected this Monument.

ORI-

ORIGINAL POETRY.

To the Editor of the Monthly Magazine.

SIR,

THE charge is too generally urged against farmers, that they are reluctant to acknowledge the supplies of Providence to have been *abundant*, with *whatever liberality* those supplies may have been bestowed. Inclosed you have a copy of verses, which I drew up to read to my own labourers at their harvest-supper, after lodging fifty acres of wheat safely in the barn. The lines have no other merit than as breathing a different spirit from what the agricultural interest are too generally charged with. Having the pen in my hand, I have likewise added a few lines on the intended inclosure of Enfield-chace, by which my own situation will particularly suffer, my premises, for nearly a mile, being benefited by the ornamental shade and shelter of the woods. Though a decided friend to inclosures, I may be allowed to lament the consequent devastations of the axe, while I acknowledge the political necessity of the measure, and am, Sir, your's, &c.

A. WILKINSON, M.D.

White-webb Farm,
Enfield-chace, Oct. 22, 1801.

BLOW joyfully the winding horn
Among the rising ricks of corn;
Lo! the last waggon's come!
The wheat and barley now are stor'd,
Enough to fill the winter hoard—
So shout the harvest home!

We've risen with the earliest light,
And work'd till evening clos'd in night
The loaded field to clear;
What wheat before our sickles fell!
What oats! what barley! few can tell,
So thick they rose in ear!

No falling rain, no cloudy skies,
No lightning flashing in our eyes,
No workmen at a stand:
Thanks to a liberal Providence,
That does with kindest hand dispense
His blessings thro' the land.

No corn by the fierce tempest laid,
No mildew blasts the sick'ning blade,
No blight shrinks up the ear.
The *poor man* pray'd—his voice was heard:
God, ever faithful to his word,
With plenty crowns the year!

He does both hay and corn prepare,
For man and beast are still his care,
And want is known no more;
Let joy be felt and heard around,
Let hill and valley swell the sound,
His bounty feeds the poor!

Let not the *rich* the *poor* disdain,
Nor think our little labours vain,
'Tis these their food prepare;
But while with liberal kindness fed,
Should any honest poor want bread,
Oh! make their wants your care.

VERSES *on the intended* INCLOSURE *of* ENFIELD-CHACE.

ADIEU to the woodlands, their shelter and shade,
Where the nightingale's music enlivens the glade!
Adieu to the greensward, so lively and gay,
With daisies and cowslips, with vi'lets and May!
Adieu to the woodlands, where oft I have rov'd,
And sweetly convers'd with the friend that I lov'd!
Adieu to the woodlands—my fav'rite retreat
From noise and from dust, from wind and from heat!

Adieu to the woodlands, that give to the poor
The faggot that warms, and the bough at the door!
May the axe slip aside from the barbarous stroke,
And the saw in the contest be shiver'd and broke!

Adieu to the wood-pigeon's heart-moving strain!
No more shall I hear the ring-dove complain;
From ploughs and from harrows she rapidly flies,
The brown dusty clods have no charms in her eyes.

Adieu to the woodlands, where sportive and gay,
The cattle, light-bounding, so frolicksome play!
Adieu to the woodlands, the pride of the place!
May the hand that despoils them be mark'd with disgrace!

THE RETURN.

AGAIN I see thee, cliffs and rocky shore,
Ye rough opponents of th' Atlantic wave;
Delighted hear the dashing waters roar,
While 'gainst my native land the billows rave.

Once

Once more, lov'd isle, thy verdant turf I tread,
With transport, absence only can bestow—
Joy in the breeze that winnows round my head—
Such joy, alone, returning pilgrims know.

And those grey mists, which up yon mountains steal,
And mix their wavy summits with the sky—
Rise they, slow curling, from the peaceful vale
Where I was born—where yet I hope to die?

And shall I meet, in that elm-shaded home,
Upon the green, beside the murmuring brook
(Blest solace, after such a weary roam)
A parent's welcome, not a stranger's look?

Shall I behold the fond, the ardent gaze,
'Ere to a mother's bosom closely prest,
Immingle tears, and join the faltering praise
For this sweet moment unto Heav'n addrest?

Ah Hope! still dress thee in those grateful smiles,
By which the weary wanderer thou dost cheer;
Divine consoler amidst all my toils,
Bliss-picturing Hope, ah! be not now severe!

Still wear thy visions that enlivening form
(Hostile to stern Despair, joy-withering fiend)
That bids the seaman struggle with the storm,
And midst the danger arms the valiant mind.

But if I'm doom'd the bitterest pangs to feel,
O'er the low tomb of those I love to mourn;
To find my home an alien's face reveal,
And all my favourite haunts defac'd, forlorn;

Then to some spot I'll glide unseen away,
Where I was wont in happy hours to lie,
Yield up my aching heart to sorrow's sway,
Then far to distant climes for ever fly.

Ye gloomy thoughts, be gone; my friends still live;
Still do my native groves remain the same;
Still shall affection, blest, her blessings give,
And all my sufferings vanish as a dream.

Again the clover-border'd paths I'll tread,
That near the river's side meand'ring run;
Inhale the fragrance which the meadows spread,
While scatter'd oaks exclude the noon-day sun.

And while I view the stream's clear glassy face,
O'er which yon herb-clad rocks their shadows throw,
I'll think of Neptune's wrath, and angry seas,
When from their murky clouds the tempests blow.

Or, stretch'd beneath the shade, in listless ease,
While harmless humming insects round me play,
Mem'ry her phantoms shall begin to raise
Of toils endur'd, and war's confus'd affray;

Till, starting from the tumult of the fight,
No longer hostile images annoy;
But pastoral objects greet my raptur'd sight,
And scenes of rural peace and tranquil joy.

Thus shall my hours advance on golden wing,
Amidst the bliss by home and nature given,
Sweet as the opening beauties of the spring,
Smooth as the summer clouds beneath the vault of heaven.

SONNET.

HAIL, bright-ey'd Goddess of the cheerful mien,
With rosy lip, and halcyon look serene,
Divine Hygeia! touch my favourite swain
With thy pure wand, and give him health again.
O pour salubrious streams thro' ev'ry vein
To chase disease, and all her baleful train;
Again his rapture-beaming eye shall roll,
Inspire delight, and cheer my drooping soul.

Thus to his woes, who holds in magic-chain
My captive heart, in sympathy I turn:
With sick'ning anguish doubly feel his pain,
And seem in fancy bending o'er his urn;
But when again restored to rest,
No pains his frame annoy,
The faithful magnet in my breast,
Tho' trembling, points to joy.
Can dull Indifference, with leaden eye,
Impart, O Sympathy, a bliss like thine?
To her for ever lost the mutual sigh
Which misery can to happiness refine.
Then hail, sweet Sympathy! thou cherish'd guest,
Who giv'st an edge to Grief, to Joy a zest;
From me, I know, thou never wilt depart,
But make thy warm abode within my heart.

To the QUEEN *of* PRUSSIA, *on her* BIRTH-DAY.

WHILE titled suppliants throng the glitt'ring scene
To hail the day that gave the world a Queen,
Shall regal beauty deign to lend an ear,
Nor scorn a bard uncourtly and sincere?—

Wha

Who sees, undazzled, scepter'd pomp display'd,
Yet bows to worth that shames all borrow'd aid;
To worth that shines untarnish'd on a throne,
In fair LOUISA's bright example shewn!
O, form'd alike to grace the courtly scene,
Or smile the sweetest on the village-green,
To charm alike the heart, the eye, the ear,
And claim the palm, though all around were fair;—
Amid the varied incense of the day,
Accept the tribute of an honest lay;
Nor deem the praise it bears, though warm it flows,
An elogy that Flattery's breath bestows:—
For know, while such desert shall grace the theme,
That Praise for Truth is but another name.

Berlin, B. BERESFORD.
March 10, 1801.

Extracts from the Port-folio of a Man of Letters.

ORIGINAL HENRIAD.

GIULIO CESARE MALMIGNATI was born in the Venetian territory, at Lendinara, a corporation town on the Adige, in the last quarter of the 16th century.

At Trevigi was printed his first poetical work, *Chlorindo*, a Pastoral Tragedy, which was so popular as to be reprinted in 1618, and again in 1630.

Probably he studied at Padova; for some complimentary verses of his on the Departure of Maximo Valerio, *Capitano di Padova*, are comprehended in a Collection of Poems, printed there in 1619.

In 1620 he published, again at Trevigi, a Tragedy called *Ordaura*, of which a second edition appeared at Venice, in 1630.

And in 1623, at Venice, and printed by Marco Guarisco, appeared *l'Enrico, o la Francia conquistada*, an epic Poem on the same events, which Voltaire afterwards chose for the subject of his Henriad. This poem is written in *octave rime*, and consists of twenty two cantos. It is printed in Italic letters on four hundred and eighty-two duodecimo pages, and is ushered in by a dedicatory epistle to Louis XIII. King of France.

More fancy is displayed or indulged by this Poet than by Voltaire. Angels, Incubusses, Saints jostle in his song. In the sixth canto, Henry is conveyed to heaven in a fiery car, and beholds the destined mansions of all the Christian princes. In the sixteen canto, Merlin (it is no anachronism surely, thus to preserve the lives of the more than mortal) accompanies Armilla into an enchanted palace, where they see in painting the future ornaments of Italy, among whom the Poet, not very modestly, reckons himself.

Fur cinque stanze adorne e scure quante
Ornarle puo quaggiu l'arte o l'ingegno,
Ne pone alcun nel ricco suol le piante,
Ch'anco non dia di maraviglia il segno.
Qui appar tra gli altri fregi, e fra le tante
Bellezze, di pittor l'opra e'l disegno;
Gli heroi che fur d'Italia i rai lucenti
Serbansi illesi a secoli vegnenti.—

Vide Merlin ch'esser dovea chi l'armi
Cantasse, e'l Franco re con l'ampio acquisto;
Ch'al dolce suon di bellicosi carmi
Trarria d'Italia e Francia il popol misto;
E ch'esser quel dovea GIULIO.—'

In the twenty-second canto, an apparition of Saint Louis invites and induces Henry to embrace the religion of Rome; and thus the epopœa concludes.

In the enumeration of his works, which takes place in the sixteenth canto, Malmignati mentions, besides the *Ordaura*, *il Thisi*, *l'Iride*, *la diva Caterina*, and *Rime Diverse*. It does not appear that these have been printed.

Another epic Poem, entitled *l'Enrico, o Bisantio Acquistato*, appeared at Venice, in 1635, which consists of twenty-seven cantos. It seems to have obscured, by resemblance of title, the Poem of Malmignati, which escapes the notice both of Crescimbeni and Tiraboschi.

EMBLEMATIC PLANTS.

The Parisian Minister of the Interior lately requested the Professors of the Museum of Natural History, to indicate two trees to be consecrated to science and to literature. The Professors (Citizens Desfontaines and Thouin) pointed out the cedar of Lebanum for science, and the oriental plane for literature.

These emblematic plants may be, and probably are, well-chosen; but it would facilitate the general reception of such hieroglyphs, which to the allegoric sculptor may be very convenient, if the trains of idea were revealed which have led to the selection. The myrtle of love, the palm of religion, the laurel of victory, the oak of liberty, the olive of peace, the ivy of criticism, the mimosa of sensibility, are not all equally characteristic of the abstractions

abstractions with which they are become associated.

SUPPOSED IMITATION.

A French critic ascribes Pope's famous simile, "So pleased at first the towering Alps we try, &c." to the following passage from the Fourth Book of the Anti-Lucretius.

Ac veluti medio jam fessus monte viator,
Saxosum per iter postquam ereptavit, in altâ
Tandem rupe sedens vultum sudore madentem
Tergit, et ascensu labefactos recreat artus:
Tum rigidas cautes et quæ juga vincit anhelans
Cernere amat, relegitque oculis vestigia lætis:
Surgit mox, avidus summum exsuperare cacumen,
Quique viæ superest labor, hunc animosior implet.

LA BRUYERE.

The Text of Theophrastus, with many additional Fragments derived from a Vatican Manuscript, accompanied by a French Version of the whole, has been published at Paris, by Dr. Coray, a Greek: and the Parisians begin to perceive, that Bruyere's is a very inaccurate translation. It may possibly be discovered shortly, that his Imitations are maukish and vague, that as a characterizer he is inferior to our Butler, and that his celebrity, however great at home, is one of those French reputations, which, when weighed in the European scale, is almost unperceivable.

WIGS.

Some years ago we had to read the Pogonology. Caxons have now succeeded to beards, and a similar work appears, entitled *Eloge des Perruques par le Docteur Akerlio.* This book is ascribed to Deguerle, the translater of Petronius: it deserves, for micrology of erudition, a place in the Transactions of the Society of Antiquaries; and for frothiness of eloquence, to be studied by puffers and auctioneers.

BROTHELS *invented by* SOLON.

Nicandre raconte dans le troisième livre des Choses remarquables de Colophon, que le legislateur Solon a été le premier qui ait bâti un temple à *Venus Pandémos.* Philemon (Athenée liv XIII. p. 569) loue beaucoup la sage indulgence que Solon a temoigné par cette loi pour la foiblesse humaine: "Solon tu as vraiment été le bienfaiteur du genre humain! car on dit que c'est toi qui as le premier pensé à une chose bien avantageuse au peuple, ou plûtôt au salut public. Oui, c'est avec raison que je dis ceci, lorsque je considere nôtre ville pleine de jeunes gens d'un temperament bouillant, et qui, en consequence, se porteroient a des exces punissables. C'est pourquoi tu as acheté des femmes, et les as placées dans des lieux, où, pourvues de tout ce qui leur est necessaire, elles deviennent communes à tous ceux qui en veulent."

SEXUAL SYSTEM.

The author of the *Connubia Florum,* a Latin Poem, first printed in 1727, and written by D. Delacroix, ascribes to Vaillant, author of *Botanicon Parisiense,* the invention of the sexual system.

At sibi stravit
Intactum Vallantius iter, qua callidus arte
Dirigat in flores etiam sua tela Cupido,
Vidit, et herbarum detexit primus amores.

There are passages in this Poem which the author of the Botanic Garden might have embellished and employed.

MERCIER'S OPINION *of* VOLTAIRE.

"Voltaire," says the author of the New Picture of Paris, "has been our grand corrupter: he flattered every king and every vice of his age. He knew not how to strike at superstition without mortally wounding morality; unlike Hercules, who transfixed the Centaur without hurting the beautiful Dejanira. He saw nothing in the Theodicea of Leibnitz but a subject for his Candide, that mischievous production, which attacks the consolatory doctrine of a Providence. With his eternal Sardonic smile he has bequeathed us a shameful pyrrhonism and a cruel levity, which makes us glide alike over virtues and crimes. The writings of the author of the Pucelle and Republican manners are incompatible.

RALPH CUDWORTH'S WORKS.

In the Life prefixed to Birch's Edition of Cudworth's Intellectual System, it is stated, that the still unpublished Manuscripts of this great author consist of one thousand folio pages. Surely the profound though discontinued learning, the perspicuous though quaint precision, the all-clasping though overwhelming information, and the useful though mystical tendency of his writings, entitle them all to publication, and would secure, in these days of architectonic metaphysicians, a sufficiently extensive sale. The Disquisitions on Natural Justice, on the Hedonic Philosophy, on the Controversy of Liberty and Necessity, and the Answer to Hobbes's Reflections (to say nothing of the theological pamphlets) cannot but retain a high degree of interest.

THREE

THREE-WHEELED CARRIAGES.

"Along the Belgic frontier," says Professor Bygge, "three-wheeled carts are used by the farmers instead of four-wheeled ones. They are made of all sizes, for one, two and four horses, who will draw in them as large a load as two, four or six horses in a four-wheeled cart. They are more easily turned, incur less friction, and ought to be generally preferred."

PLASTER-CASTS.

"To Lysistratus," says Pliny, "the world is indebted for the invention of plaster-casts. *Hominis autem gypso e facie ipsa primus omnium expressit, ceraque in eam formam gypsi infusa emendare instituit Lysistratus Sicyonius, frater Lysippi.* (XXXV. 12). This Lysistratus flourished in the time of Alexander the Great: all the busts of an earlier date are consequently not copied from modellings; but must be likenesses comparatively imperfect. Let us not attempt to study physiognomy in the pretended heads of Homer and of Plato.

IMPROVEMENT *of the* ÆOLIAN HARP.

The anemo-chord was invented by John James Schnell, who was born in 1740, at Wahingen, in the Duchy of Wurtemberg. He was bound apprentice to a cabinet-maker, and in 1760 let himself as journeyman to an organ-maker, at Rothenburg, named Geisinger. Thence he removed into Holland, and was a distinguished workman under Van Dilken. In 1777 he went to Paris and set up for himself. He obtained splendid patronage, and became musical instrument-maker to the Countess of Artois. The sounding of a harp hung by accident in a breezy passage on his premises suggested the idea of that instrument, which, in 1789, he first exposed to sale by the name *anemo-chorde.*

WAX-WORK.

Leopold, while Grand-duke of Tuscany, caused to be made, under the direction of Fontana, and exhibited in the Palace Torreggiano, at Florence, a series of anatomical sculptures in coloured wax, which have long amused the curious traveller and instructed the medical student. In 1775 eight rooms, in 1794 twenty rooms were filled with these imitations, which represent in every possible detail, and in each successive stage of denudation, the organs of sense and reproduction, the muscular, the vascular, the nervous, and the boney system. They imitate equally well the form, and more exactly the colouring of nature than injected preparations; and they have been employed to perpetuate many transient phænomena of disease, of which no other art could have made so lively a record.

Cupids of wax are mentioned by Anacreon. Saints of wax were common in the middle ages. For portraiture in wax Andrea del Verrocchio was famous, in the fifteenth century. But the first application of *ceroplastic* to anatomical science, is due to Cajetano Julio Zumbo of Syracuse, born in 1656. Ercole Lelli, of Bologna, assisted by Manzollini and his wife, made the first public collection of wax-modellings systematically adapted to the instruction of surgeons and artists.

PROCEEDINGS OF LEARNED SOCIETIES.

NATIONAL INSTITUTE OF FRANCE.

CONTINUATION *of the* THIRD QUARTERLY SITTING *of the* CLASS *of* MATHEMATICAL *and* PHYSICAL SCIENCES, YEAR 9.

ZOOLOGY.—*On the* MONOCLE FLEA.

UNDER the vulgar name of water-flea, (*puce d'eau*) is commonly known a small crustaceous animal, very abundant in still waters, and which has sometimes given rise to reports of its raining blood, because in the spring the eggs with which it is loaded give it a red colour, and the waters where they are found in numbers, have really then the appearance of being dyed with blood.

The most skilful naturalists, Swammerdamm, De Geer, Schæffer, and Otto-Frederick Muller, have successively studied it; but nature is inexhaustible, even in its smallest productions; and Citizen JURINE, associate-member of the Institute, at Geneva, has further discovered, with respect to this single insect, a multitude of curious facts which had escaped those learned men. Although this insect is but two or three millimeters in length, in its largest state, Citizen Jurine, on a minute inspection, has observed in it two compound eyes, so near together, that many have taken them for a single one; two short mandibles without indentations; a particular organ, which he calls the valves or sucker fucker of the mandibles, and which conveys the food between them; two small articulated barbles, which, in the male, resemble harpoons, and which induced Muller to think, though wrongly, that they were the sexual organs; two branching antennæ; five pair of feet, extremely complicated, and which produce a retrograde current in the water behind them—a current which causes the moleculæ, on which the insect lives, to move towards the extremities of those feet, from whence they re-impel them towards the mouth, by a very singular mechanism; the first of these pair is the longest, and is armed with two crotchets, or hooked claws, in the male; there is, lastly, a very mobile tail, terminated by two spinous flat excrescences.

Citizen Jurine does not confine himself to these exterior parts. As the insect is transparent, he has been able to describe the interior. Near the intestinal canal are two species of cœcum, which appear to shed a dissolving liquor; the heart, situated towards the back, is contracted about 200 times in a minute. The ovaries, in number two, contain a greenish matter, which they cause to pass successively into the matrix, where it is formed into distinct eggs, which are hatched there. This matrix can contain, at once, 18 young ones.

Citizen Jurine enters with much detail into the history of this insect. The male is smaller, by half, than the female. When about to copulate, he darts upon her, seizes her with the long fibres of his fore-claws, clasps her with his harpoons, and draws his tail towards the shell of the female, who flies off, at first, with rapidity; but the male still adhering, she, at length, conforms her position to his. The copulation does not last above an instant. The eggs are nine or ten days hatching in winter, and two or three only in summer. The young *pulex* only differs from the adult, by more length in the point which terminates their shell. Muller has, improperly, made a species of them (*daphnia longispina.*) In summer these monocles mew or cast their skin, eight times in nineteen days; the ovaries only appear after the third time. In winter, there sometimes pass eight or ten days between two moultings. The first laying of eggs produces four or five young ones; the others go on augmenting to about eighteen. Their fecundity is sometimes stopped by a singular malady, the symptom of which is a blackish spot, somewhat resembling a saddle, placed on the back. Citizen Jurine conceives this spot to proceed from the displacing of the matter of the eggs.

Lastly, the most singular fact of all those discovered by Citizen Jurine, is, that a female, which has received the male, transmits the impregnating influence to her female descendants, so that they all lay eggs, without being obliged to copulate, to the sixth generation, after which they perish in mewing. Another species has carried this influence of one single copulation to the fifth generation: the vermin called vine-fretters (*les pucerons*) have, as is well known, furnished similar observations to Bonnet. These generations without copulation are less abundant, and succeed each other less rapidly, than those in which the males have borne a part.

BOTANY.

Descriptions of New Plants, or such as are little known, in the Garden of Citizen CELS, *by Citizen* VENTENAT.

This work is one of the finest which has appeared on the descriptive part of botany, and it reflects equal credit on the two members of the Class who have contributed to it: Citizen Cels, by his zeal in procuring, from all parts of the world, the seeds and plants discovered in them, and by his skill in making them come to maturity; and Citizen Ventenat, for the elegance and accuracy of his descriptions—for the botanic erudition which he displays—for the justness with which he assimilates the new genera and the new species, lately discovered, of those which were before arranged in system; and, lastly, by the curious observations which he makes on their properties. The plates, engraved from the designs of an artist, whom it is sufficient to name, Citizen Redouté, designer to the Class, are such as may be expected from the skilful engravers who have charge of them; that is to say, that if some works executed by the same persons be excepted, such as the *Flora Atlantica* of Citizen Desfontaines, no book of the kind presents any so highly finished. Four numbers have already appeared, containing each ten plants.

Notice of the History of the Oaks of America.

We owe the same tribute of eulogium to the work of Citizen MICHAUX, on the oaks of America. It is a fact, singular enough, that the oak genus, of which we have so few species in Europe, should be so diversified, under the same latitude, in the new continent. The history of these numerous species is so much the more interesting, as they may be, doubtless, for the

the most part, transplanted into our climates; and no one was better qualified to make us acquainted with them than Citizen Michaux, who has observed them in their natal soil, and who has cultivated many of them himself, in the establishment which he superintended in the United States.

TECHNOLOGY.

A new Method of bleaching Household Linen.

We gave an account, eighteen months ago, of the process recommended by Citizen Chaptal to bleach cotton, which consists in impregnating it with an alkaline lye, and exposing it, in that condition, to the vapour of boiling water. We have since made mention, after the same learned man, of the success which his process had obtained, and of the improvements made upon it in Ireland, where the public papers had carried the accounts of it; at Paris, in the manufacture of Citizen Bawens; and in many similar establishments, which this manufacturer has formed, in partnership with another distinguished artist, Citizen Bourlier, in different parts of France, simple machines have been contrived to turn the stuffs in the apparatus, and to present them on all sides to the vapour. It has been found, that linen requires only a weak lye; but that, to bleach it completely, the action of the lye should operate alternately with that of the atmospherical air; and, at length, they have been enabled to produce, in two or three days, a perfect whiteness on the coarsest linens, and for a price less, by half, than that of ordinary bleaching.

Citizen Chaptal, wishing to carry as far as possible the utility of his process, has made an experimental use of it for the washing of linen. Trials have been made on some hundred pair of sheets taken from the Hotel Dieu, at Paris, and selected from among the dirtiest; and it is allowed that they have been perfectly washed in two days, at seven tenths only of the ordinary expence. Another advantage attends it, that from their not being submitted to batting, or the other operations of washer-women, they are much less worn away, and the extreme heat to which they are exposed, must totally destroy in them every contagious principle.

Improvements in the Art of making Paper.

Citizen SEGUIN, who has been employed, for five years past, in the art of making paper, has obtained for his first results the means of performing in some hours what before required a process of several months; he has, at length, succeeded so far as to substitute straw for rags, in this manufacture; and he has presented to the Class a number of specimens of paper formed with this substance. This paper is not yet as white as that made with well-sorted rags: but Citizen Seguin remarks, that this imperfection is owing to the little care taken in making it, and not to the nature of the first materials; and that in its present condition it may very well suffice for counting-house-writings, law-writings, and all printing of a common nature.

The author has not, as yet, communicated his process.

NOTICE *of the* LABOURS *of the* CLASS *of* MORAL *and* POLITICAL SCIENCES, *during the* THIRD QUARTERLY SITTING *of the* YEAR 9, *by* CITIZEN LEVESQUE, SECRETARY.

Citizen ANQUETIL, in a Memoir on the Merovingian Franks, and the manners of the Franks, has presented the picture of the principal political, military, and religious events, which occupy, in the French history, a period of 147 years, from Clovis to Pepin. The former Prince, by force of arms, by a subtle policy, by perfidy and assassinations, acquired an extensive empire in Gaul. Seconded by the ferocious valour of a handful of Franks, he was more powerfully so by the pious intrigues of the Catholic bishops. Those prelates preferred an idolatrous conqueror to those Christian kings who did not think like them on the mysterious subject of the Trinity. They preached to the people disobedience to the Arian Princes of Gaul; and by their means, and by his own seasonable conversion, he successfully established his fortune. But although Clovis acted with consummate prudence, in various respects, Citizen Anquetil shews that he did not employ the most proper means to secure the duration of his empire. The powerful dominion of which he was the founder, was considered by him as a patrimony to be divided between his four sons; he parcelled it out, and bequeathed them four feeble sovereignties. Forty years after, partly by good fortune and partly by successful villainy, Clotaire, the youngest of his sons, regained the entire empire—but he followed the example of his father. To this sinister policy may be traced the imbecility of the Merovingian race, who became, in fact, the slaves of the first officer of their palace, and, at length, saw one of those officers, the

the fortunate Pepin, found a vast empire on the ruins of their dominion.

Whilst, in an advanced age, Citizen Anquetil is, in this manner, reposing from the historical labours to which he owes his reputation, Citizen BOUCHAUD, that Nestor of literature, whom sixteen complete lustrums, and three years additional, cannot wean from the studies which have constituted the charm of his life, has read to the Class three Memoirs, all of which indicate a very extensive erudition and indefatigable research.

1. *A Second Memoir on the Authority and Use of Inscriptions, in the Laws affecting the private Life of the Romans, and in their Pontifical Law, till the Period in which they embraced Christianity.*

2. *A Memoir on the Perpetual Edict*, divided into three parts.—It appears from the first that this edict was compiled by order of the Emperor Adrian, and was intended to be referred to as a perpetual law in the tribunals of Rome. The second part contains some particulars of the life, the knowledge, and the writings of the lawyer Salvius Julianus, to whom the execution of this labour was entrusted. In the third, the author investigates the authority which the perpetual edict had acquired, explains the order and materials, and, lastly, treats of the different commentaries and lawyers relative to this edict, from which it appears that, in general, they adopted the order which Julianus followed.

3. *A Memoir on the Moral Writings of Cicero.*—The author admits that the morality of Cicero is sound; but he observes, that the ideas of the philosophical orator, taken collectively, do not form a regular system, and that the passages which contain those ideas, lose much of their force, for want of coherence and arrangement. It may be further objected to the principles of Cicero, that he is sometimes at variance with himself;—the cause of this inconsistency may be traced, perhaps, to the state of human knowledge at that period. There was no truth which had not been called in question by certain philosophers, which some had not even absolutely rejected, and which had not been obscured by the sophisms of the rhetoricians. Truths which appeared inconvenient were attacked, denied, and ridiculed. Some writers defended them, merely to display their wit, and did not convince, because they were not convinced themselves. In fine, every thing was uncertain, every thing was a subject of dispute, and Cicero appears, sometimes, a sceptic, like the other philosophers. We are often at a loss to understand whether he speaks of the opinions of his time, as a simple historian, or whether he proposes his own thoughts to the reader. Moral principles presented with so much dubiety by the author, can have but little influence on the reader.

Citizen LEGRAND-LALEU, an associate-member, has read a *First Memoir on the ancient Administration of Criminal Justice in France.*

Another associate-member, Citizen KOCH, has transmitted to the Class the *Notice of a Manuscript Code of Rachion, Bishop of Strasbourg*, written in the year 787, and now deposited in the central library of the department of the Lower Rhine.

Citizen POIRIER has made *some Observations on this Notice*, which he has communicated to the Class.

UNIVERSITY OF GÖTTINGEN.

In the public hospital some alterations took place in 1800. The Regency of Hanover assigned to Professor ARNEMANN two beds for his chirurgical clinical lecture, and eight beds to Professor WARDENBURG, for his medico-chirurgical clinical lecture. Since the union of the City Sick-house with the Academical Hospital, the whole has been fitted up, so as to contain twenty-one beds. Professor STROMEYER, who had been sixteen years physician to the hospital, and who, by his skill and attention, had deserved well of the Institution, has requested permission from the Government to resign that laborious office, which has been graciously granted, and Professor Wardenburg appointed to succeed him. Professor Arnemann has published further accounts of the state and happy progress of the *Clinicum* founded by him, and continued under his direction—(1) State of the clinico-chirurgical Institute at Göttingen, by J. Arnemann, 4to. Gött. 1800—(2) Ninth Report relative to the Chirurgico-clinical Institute at Göttingen, 4to. 1800.—In it he gives a review of the diseases of the last half-year; and we learn, that the number of patients amounted to 101, whom the author has classed according to the diseases with which they were afflicted—i. Diseases of the eye, 61—ii. Defect of hearing, 2—iii. Cancer of the lips, 4—iv. Swelling of the neck—v. Deformity of the back, 1—vi. Rupture, 1—vii. Dropsical rupture, 1—viii. Preternatural excrescences, 3—ix. Varicose ulcers, 1—x. Glandular tumours, 1—xi. Cancerous sores, 1—xii. Ulcers in the leg, 1—xiii. Fistula, 1—xiv. Chronical inflammation,

2—xv.

1—xv. Swelling of the joints, 1—xvi. Broken bones, 1—xvii. Chronical eruption, 6—xviii. Scaling off of the skin, 1—xix. Consumption, 1—xx. Retention of urine, 1—xxi. Ulcers and degeneration of the penis, 1—Several operations to remove cataracts; and likewise the rare, important, and successful operation of amputating the penis.

SOCIETY *of the* SCIENCES *at* GÖTTINGEN.

On the 1st of November, 1800, the Society celebrated its institution-day. Forty-nine years had now elapsed since it was first formed. Professor HEYNE read a Discourse on the occasion; and the subjects of which it treated were various:—A. The History of the Society; of which an extract is published in the *Götting. Anzeig. von gel. Sachen*—B. An Account of the Prize-dissertations received, and of the new Prize-questions for the following year:—I. No treatise had been received in answer to the mathematical prize-question, the object of which was "*Definire, accuratius quam adhuc factum sit, theoriam motus vaporum.*"—The economical question, for the best answer to which a prize of 12 ducats had been offered, related to the most efficacious means of promoting horticulture, or the cultivation of garden-plants, in the villages. Fifteen treatises were sent in; and the Society adjudged the prize to No. 15, the author of which is M. J. F. von Rotbergiil.—II. New prize-questions for the following year:—For November, 1801, the following historical prize-question: "Desiderat Societas, ut magnus dissensus, quo in historia veteris regni Persici a scriptoribus Graecis et Latinis discedunt Orientales, sub criticum examen vocetur, et quidem ita, ut, missis antiquissimis et fabulosis regibus, in aetate historica post Alexandrum M. h. e. regum Graecorum, Parthorum s. Arsacidarum et Sassanidarum, versetur disputatio."—(2) For November, 1802, the physical prize-question of 1799, which was not then satisfactorily answered, is again proposed, viz. "Quaeritur, in quibusnam insectorum et vermium ordinibus respirationis functio et effectus primarius, qui vulgo processus phlogistici, combusturae certo respectu comparandi, nomine venit, observationibus et experimentis demonstrari possit?"—(3) For November, 1803, a new prize-question: "Cupit R. Societas I. experimentis exquisitis, et calculo illis innixo, sollicite investigari, quomodo corpora ex diversis materiis, sed ejusdem figurae et voluminis (optime forsan sphaerae diametri unius circiter pollicis) sub eodem aëris statu, eadem luminis intensitate, eadem temperie initiali, &c. sensim per singula minuta temporis observationis in lumine solari calefiant; II. Ad quem gradum temperiei corpus quodlibet adhibitum, in fine observationis, h. e. cessante caloris incremento, perventum esset, vel directa observatione (quod praecipue cupimus), vel saltem ex lege observata increscentis caloris erui."—The authors of the best dissertations will receive prizes of 20 ducats.—(4) Economical prize-questions:—(*a*) For July, 1801: The most accurate and complete Natural History of the insects, which are called earth-fleas (chrysomelae), and the most effectual remedy to prevent the damage which they occasion.—(*b*) For November, 1801: The clearest and best founded instructions how to find fossile-coal, &c.—(*c*) For June, 1802: The best physical and economical description of some considerable district of the Elector of Hanover's dominions in Germany.—The prize is 20 ducats.——III. A learned dissertation, the object of which was to shew, from the ancient historians, what effects had been produced by the sudden influx of gold and silver into a country. Professor Heyne takes his examples principally from the history of the Lydians, Persians, Macedonians, and Romans. A copious extract from this dissertation is inserted in the *Gött. Anz.* 1800, p. 1921-36.—At the same meeting was read a Treatise by M. von Köhler, of Petersburg, containing learned researches relative to the Sarda, the Onyx, and the Sardonyx, of the Ancients. For an extract from this treatise, see *Gött. Anzeig.* 1800, p. 1929.—In the November-meeting, Professor Wildt laid before the Society a Critical History of the Air-pump. There will follow the description of an air-pump constructed by himself, and which is, in some measure, the result of the foregoing critical investigations, as the author has endeavoured to unite in his air-pump all the advantages he had discovered in preceding ones. An extract of Prof. Wildt's treatise is inserted in the *Gött. Anz.* 1800, p. 1035.—On the 6th of December Professor Buhle read a dissertation "De librorum Aristotelis, qui vulgo in deperditis numerantur, ad libros ejusdem superstites ratione." The author examines all the existing lists of Aristotle's works, and endeavours to remove the great confusion and alterations of the titles, in order to obtain a more certain and complete view of the whole scientific cycle of Aristotle. He shows that it is owing to the multiplicity of the titles, that many of the works of Aristotle, which still exist, are thought to be lost.—An extract from this treatise is inserted in the *Götting. Anzeig.* 1800, No. 207, p. 2037. In the meeting on the 27th of December, Mr. Court counsellor Wrisberg read "Observationum Anatomico-neurologicarum de Nervis Viscerum Abdominalium Partic. III. de Nervis Hepaticis et Splenicis.—An extract from this dissertation may be seen in the *Götting. Anzeig. von gel. Sachen*, 1801; No. 9, p. 81-88.

THE MINERALOGICAL SOCIETY OF JENA.

On the 2nd of last March this Society held their second public meeting for this year. The objects which occupied the attention of the members present, were the following prælections:—(1) The Director of the Society, Mr. Professor LENZ, opened the meeting with a treatise on the Belemnites, in which he discussed the opinions of lithologists relative to this subject; and at the same time laid before the Society the supposed originals from the animal kingdom.—(2) Mr PANZER read a Dissertation on Crystallizations, written and sent to the Society by Mr. Mihatik, of Eperies.—(3) Mr. SCHWABE, librarian to the Society, and keeper of their Museum, read a Report on the present state of the Library and Museum, and gave notice, that in future they would be open twice a week for the use of the public.—The Society has lately published the first part of their Transactions. The Museum, in which their meetings are held, is very rich, particularly in Hungarian gold-ores and minerals.

REVIEW OF NEW MUSICAL PUBLICATIONS.

Musical Game-tables and Apparatus for facilitating the Acquisition of the Elementary Principles of the Harmonic Science. Invented, and dedicated to the Princess Charlotte, by Anne Young. 7l. 7s. *Preston.*

THESE TABLES and APPARATUS, the ingenuity and utility of which demand our highest commendation, are of too diverse and elaborate a construction to admit of our entering into a minute description of their parts; and, indeed, the pamphlet of the Inventress, which may be had separately, renders such a detail from us unnecessary.

It will be sufficient for us to say, that the contrivance consists of a box, composed of two equal pieces, or frames, united by hinges, like backgammon-tables, and a numerous variety of characters, chiefly formed of ivory, representing those used in music, and so corresponding in their construction with the figures and apertures of the tables, that by the help of dice and dice-boxes a kind of *musical game* may be played, highly pleasant and diverting, and at the same time pregnant with scientific instruction.

The style and fashion of the whole apparatus, the idea of which has, we learn, been realized at an expence little short of eleven hundred pounds, is elegant and beautiful, and does much honour to Miss Young's taste: but her great praise consists in the happy facility she has produced of attaining all the leading rudiments of the science, and so shortening the road to musical knowledge, that more may now be acquired in one week than could be learnt in six months before the invention of her *Tables*. We recommend this singular and valuable novelty to the attention of all practitioners and teachers: the progress of the former will, by its assistance, be greatly accelerated, and the labour of the latter considerably eased.

The Songs sung by Mrs. Billington in the celebrated Opera of the Duenna, with all the Graces, Variations, and Embellishments, introduced by her at the Theatres Royal Drury Lane and Covent Garden, with an Accompaniment for the Piano-forte, newly arranged by Dr. Busby. 4s. 6d. *Rolfe.*

We are glad to find that the sale of the Airs of *Mandane*, in ARTAXERXES, as ornamented by Mrs. Billington, has been such as to induce Dr. Busby also to favour the public with the embellishments given by that exquisite performer to the songs of Clara, in the revived and justly-admired opera of the DUENNA.

The idea of transmitting to paper the fleeting and evanescent notes of extemporaneous decoration, is as new as it is happy, and while it gratifies the curiosity of the vocal proficient, also produces the most improving subjects of study for the young and emulous practitioner.

We have, as far as our recollection would permit, compared the variations in these songs with those given by Mrs. Billington,

lington, and must say, that we are not a little astonished at their nicety and faithfulness. Of the arduousness of the task of giving permanency to such rapid and transient sounds we are well aware. Only profound science, the most acute ear, and an uncommon power of retention, could execute such an undertaking.

Clementi's Introduction to the Art of Playing on the Piano-forte; containing the Elements of Music, Preliminary Notions on Fingering, with Examples, and fifty fingered Lessons in the Major and Minor Keys, mostly in use with Composers of the first Rank. 10s. *Clementi and Co.*

However we may be delighted with the efforts of men of real genius, we are, perhaps, never more indebted to their labours than when they stoop to the humble but amiable task of throwing new light on the tracks of science, and of giving, by their super or arrangement and address, an ease and smoothness to the progress of the pupil, at once alluring and encouraging.

Mr. Clementi's present work amply intitles him to the commendation implied by this remark, and places him high among the public promoters of improvement in the art of playing the piano-forte.

We not only agree with this great master, that "to produce the BEST EFFECT by the EASIEST MEANS, is the true basis of good fingering," but are inclined to extend his rule to every art whatever, and do not scruple to assert, that he has, by the just and luminous order of his precepts, and the excellence and pertinency of his examples, so clearly demonstrated the *easiest means* of producing the *best effect*, that to read his work is to acquire the knowledge sought for; and to practise by its rules is to ensure that free and graceful execution which alone can bring that knowledge into effective operation.

A Duett, for two Performers on one Piano-forte, composed by A. Betts. 4s. *Goulding, Phipps, and D'Almaine.*

This duett is comprized in four movements, the first of which, by its time and style, forms an excellent introduction to the latter three.

The second movement is characterized by a glowing cast of fancy, and the third is both neat and graceful in the turn of its passages. The subject of the succeeding rondo, though not remarkably original, is pleasant and animated. The *two parts* are, generally speaking, skilfully blended, and produce an effect which evinces a familiar knowledge of the character and powers of the instrument for which the composition is written.

The Peace of 1801, a new Emblematical Sonata for the Piano-forte or Harp, interspersed with several celebrated Airs, appropriate to this great Occasion, composed by Handel, Arne, and Hook. 2s. 6d. *Riley.*

This little *occasional* compilation contains, among other things, "The Soldier Tir'd of War's Alarms," from *Artaxerxes*, and "O Lovely Peace!" from *Judas Maccabeus*. The other parts of the work consist of well chosen materials, and the whole forms an *analagous* and improving exercise for the piano-forte. The *instrumental cast* given by the Editor to Dr. Arne's celebrated bravura is a bold licence, but certainly does credit to his fancy, and, with piano-forte performers, will add to the value of the publication.

Three Pieces, arranged for the Piano-forte, composed by W. A. Mozart. 4s. *Longman.*

We do not profess ourselves to be friends to *book-making* in general: but when a compilation is of a nature to induce application and promote improvement, we deem it intitled to our recommendation. The three present pieces are so many pleasing rondos. They are selected with judgment, and adjusted for the piano-forte in a style which cannot but render their practice profitable to the young pupil.

"I'm a Jolly Roving Tar," a favourite Song, composed by Wm. Reeve. 1s. *Goulding, Phipps, and D'Almaine.*

The only praise we can give this song is, that the vulgarity of the melody corresponds with the subject of the words. From the burthen "Fish away, that's your play," our musical readers will be enabled to judge of the style of the whole.

"The Banks of the Nore," a Pathetic Ballad; the Subject of the Words taken from an Idea, by the Author of the Worlds. The Music composed by Theodore Smith. 1s. *Goulding, Phipps, and D'Almaine.*

This gentleman, who long since acquired so much reputation by his excellent piano-forte duetts, has done himself much honour by his present little effort. The style of the melody is strikingly consonant with the general sentiment of the words, and the expression, with some few exceptions, is just and forcible. The two last bars but one of the symphony we must, however, remark, would have been better omitted, as not sufficiently of a colour with the previous part; and at the words "Ah, happy Girl!" the notes, to express the

the exultation of the poetry should have been in an ascending direction.

Three Solos for the German-flute, in which are introduced three Scotch Airs, with an Accompaniment for the Violoncello (ad libitum); composed and dedicated to the late Mr. Norris, by the late F. Linley. 4s. *Riley.*

These solos are written with considerable taste, and the passages, for the most part, are well disposed for the execution of the flute. The subject of the *rondo* in the first solo is lively and pleasing, though it certainly consists of little more than an ingenious alteration of the introductory bars in the first movement. The effect of the *tout-ensemble* is truly engaging, and reflects much credit on the talents of the deceased author.

VARIETIES, LITERARY AND PHILOSOPHICAL.

Including Notices of Works in Hand, Domestic and Foreign.

*** *Authentic Communications for this Article will always be thankfully received.*

THE first number of Dr. BEDDOES' popular *Essays on Health* makes its appearance on the first of December. It is intitled An Essay on Personal Prudence, and on Prejudices respecting Health, addressed to Heads of Families, inhabitants of the British Isles. There can be no doubt but these essays will meet with the attention which the importance of their subject, and the popularity of their author deserve.

Besides the republication of *Johnson's Poets*, which is projected by the proprietors of that selection, another republication is intended of the same work, to be edited by Dr. AIKIN and embellished by the engravings of Mr. HEATH. This edition is designed to be more *select* and at the same time more *extensive*, than that superintended by Dr. Johnson; and it is proposed to unite the most beautiful specimen of typography, with that degree of perfection in the arts of design, which now exists in this country. The first six volumes, comprizing the Works of Spenser, will be ready for delivery in January.

Mr. FELL, whose Tour in Batavia has been so favourably received by the public, will speedily publish an account of a Tour to Paris, containing full and comprehensive directions to Englishmen who visit that city, with an account of all the objects deserving of notice. Such a vade-mecum cannot fail to be of the highest service, at a moment when so many thousand persons in England are prompted by interest or curiosity to visit the metropolis of France, many of whom, without a guide of this kind, would sustain much inconvenience, or become the dupes of artifice and fraud.

Dr. RUSSELL will speedily publish a second volume of his magnificent work on the East Indian Snakes; and he has in forwardness a work on the same scale relative to the Fishes of the Indian Seas.

Mr. KITSON will speedily publish his long expected edition of some Ancient Dramas,

Dr. HAGAR, in consequence of the high opinion entertained of his "Keys to the Chinese Language," lately published at the expence of a bookseller in London, has been appointed by the French government to superintend in Paris the publication of a Chinese Dictionary. The appointment is no less honourable to Dr. Hagar, than to the liberal and enlightened character of the French government, which has properly appreciated the national honour attendant upon the production of so desirable a work. Dr. Hagar is placed upon the same respectable establishment as the learned Oriental Professors, LANGLES and DE SACY, and all the expences of the work are to be defrayed by the republican government. We cannot dissemble our regret, that the total want of a single Mæcenas among the race of contemporary English nobility*, and the operation of a spirit wholly mercenary and commercial in the East India Company, should have been the occasion of this literary Honour being transferred from Great Britain to France.

Dr. BARCLAY has undertaken an important work on Anatomical Nomenclature, which it is expected will soon make its appearance. In this work, the language of anatomy, at present so vague and indefinite, and often ludicrous and absurd, will be new-modelled and established

* It is honourable to Prince Augustus Frederic, who knew Dr. Hagar in Italy, that, before his departure to Portugal, he took considerable pains to procure subscriptions towards defraying the expences of this Dictionary; and, in the true spirit of an English Prince, he declared, that not a single particle of glory ought to be lost to his country. The East India Company subscribed a nominal 100 guineas towards a work which could not be published with less than seven years' labour, and at an expence of 5000 guineas!

on

on fixed and rational principles;—an improvement which will greatly facilitate the study of this important branch of medical science.

Dr. NESBITT will publish in January a comprehensive work, intitled the Edinburgh School of Medicine, forming an introduction to his other works.

Dr. T. THOMSON, of Edinburgh, has in the press, and will publish in January or February next, a work on Chemistry, in four vols. The intended publication will be enriched with all the discoveries in this interesting science which have been made, either in this country or on the Continent, down to the present period; and will be improved by the experience and assiduous application of the author, who, for several years, has been engaged in chemical studies, both as a public teacher, and an experimentalist.

The Society for Promoting Christian Knowledge have taken such cognizance of Mr. MOSELEY's Memoir on the Practicability of circulating a Translation of the Scriptures through the Chinese Empire, as affords a prospect of his plan being adopted in such degree as may be consistent with the political relations of the two empires. The Bishops of Durham and London have given it their countenance.

The Cambridge University Calendar, by B. C. RAWORTH, A. B. of Trinity Hall, is announced for publication in January next, with considerable additions and improvements.

The Rev. H.C.MASON, of Bermondsey, is preparing for the press a new and uniform edition of the works of his father, the late W. Mason. The works are to be completed in about forty weekly numbers, making four handsome vols. in 8vo. The first number will be published about the middle of November, in which will be given an elegant portrait of the author.

A volume, in octavo, intitled Oriental Customs; or, an Illustration of the Sacred Scriptures by the Application of the Customs and Manners of the Eastern Nations, and especially of the Jews, by the Rev. SAMUEL BURDER, of St. Alban's, is nearly completed, and will be published the first week in January.

A Topographical History of Cleveland, in the North Riding of the County of York, is in forwardness for the press. This district abounds in curiosities both of nature and art. It will be published in a splendid form, and be ornamented with a great variety of elegant engravings, and likewise an accurate Map of the district. The author is the Rev. JOHN GRAVES, of Yarm, in Yorkshire.

Mr. BLAINE, author of a work intitled The Anatomy of a Horse, has in the press a System of Veterinary Medicine, illustrated with proofs.

Several Lives of BONAPARTE have been announced in France, Germany, and England, probably all of them intitled to an equal degree of respect. The public is already in possession of all the facts connected with the private History of this extraordinary man, and the mingling of these with public incidents and documents can at present serve no other purpose than to enrich the book-makers. It is not till some years after the death of a public character that such memoirs of him can be expected as will completely satisfy curiosity.

The usual Courses of Philosophical and Medical Lectures, in the University of Edinburgh, have commenced. In addition to the latter, Dr. MONRO, jun. now associated with his father in the anatomical-chair, has announced his intention of fitting up rooms in which students will be accommodated with the important advantages of dissection, to be superintended by himself, and the ingenious Mr. FYFFE.

Dr. BARCLAY has commenced his Winter-course of Lectures at Edinburgh, in which he gives a full and comprehensive view of what is known of the anatomical structure and functions of the human body, explained and illustrated by a numerous detail of facts and observations drawn from comparative anatomy.

The Clinical Lectures or Surgical Cases of patients in the Royal Infirmary at Edinburgh, will be delivered this session by Mr. RUSSELL, and Mr. JOHN THOMSON, surgeons.

Mr. JOHN BELL, the Teacher of Anatomy at Edinburgh, is soon to resume his annual labours on that subject. His brother, Mr. CHARLES BELL, has begun a Course of Lectures on Midwifery.

The following has been lately announced as the Chinese method of rendering cloth water-proof: to one ounce of white-wax, melted, add one quart of spirits of turpentine; when thoroughly mixed and cold, dip the cloth into the liquid and hang it up to drain until it is thoroughly dry. By this method, the most open muslin as well as the strongest cloths, will be rendered impenetrable to the heaviest rain, without the composition even filling up the pores of the finest lawn, or changing, in the least, the most brilliant colours.

The people of London, who ran with so much eagerness to see a foreigner get into a quart-bottle, have, during the present month, been attracted in crowds to see an exhibition of optical images at the Lyceum, in the Strand. These ghosts and spectres, as they are called, are the simple production of a common magic-lantern, the objects from which are thrown upon the farther side of a transparent screen, which is hung between the lantern and the audience. When the lantern is brought nearer the screen, the object is diminished in size, and appears to retire; when taken farther off, the object is encreased in size, and appears to approach the spectator. The exhibitor who deserves the praise of great ingenuity, would however do himself more credit as a philosopher, and as a detector of imposture, if he were to bring forward his apparatus after his exhibition, and explain to the ignorant part of his audience that the illusion arises simply from the application of a magic lantern.

The following is an account of the curious experiments for lifting ships in dock to put in a new keel, which was lately tried for the first time on the Canopus, of 84 guns, in Plymouth Dock, by Mr. SIBBINS, the builder's first assistant. By means of wedges driven against the blocks on each side of the keel, and the use of the catapulta or battering ram applied to them, the blocks are forced out much easier, and with less danger. Fewer shores are required to support the ship, which also strains less, and hangs, as it were, in slings: by this simple operation, forty men, in twelve hours, can perform as much work as used to take, on the old principle, three hundred men three days; although some ships, in the old method of knocking out the blocks under the keel, have settled from eight to ten inches, the Canopus only settled one quarter of an inch, by this new method. A numerous concourse of artists and others attended to see the experiment tried on the Canopus, and were perfectly satisfied with its usefulness and simplicity.

Beech-nuts are not only excellent food for pigs, but they are now known to yield an oil fit for all ordinary purposes. Major MARSAC, who occupies the house at Caversham, formerly belonging to Lord CADOGAN, lately sold the beech nuts on his estate for 50l. to a person at Reading, for the purpose of extracting oil from them.

By the accounts of the *General Missionary Society*, published at their anniversary meeting in June last, it appears that the subscriptions, donations and collections for the last year, amounted to 1781l. 10s. 3d.; that the Directors purchased during the year, 2800l. four per cents. and 1000l. three per cents.; and that their present fund consists of 16,000l. three per cents.; 9037l. four per cents.; 3300l. new five per cents.; 1000l. old five per cents. and 500l. in an Exchequer-bill. These modern missionaries do not seem to emulate the poverty of the apostles!

An Englishman has lately obtained leave to establish a paper-manufactory in Portugal, by which it is likely he will make immense profits. He manufactures the paper from the delicate white skin of the aloe, which grows wild in that country, in a prodigious abundance. The paper is of a beautiful texture, and extremely white, and he can sell it at half the expence that imported paper is bought here. The paper is of a quality superior to any at present manufactured in this country.

Early in May next will be published, by Mr. W. SHEARDOWN, a new Map of the *Country round Doncaster*, extending from east to west 60 miles, by 40 miles north and south: the scale two miles to an inch.

Travellers in the Levant.—Letters from Vienna contradict the reports that were circulated last summer about M. VON HAMMER, an Hungarian, who studied in the Oriental Academy at Vienna, and was afterwards with the Imperial Ambassador at Constantinople. It had been said by some, that he had been drowned: Mr. KEITH, indeed, private-secretary to Sir SIDNEY SMITH, thus lost his life at the entrance of the Nile: but luckily Mr. Hammer was not on board the ship. Equally false is the report, that the Capitan Pacha had caused him to be beheaded at Rosetta. M. Hammer has made some literary discoveries in Paphos, and in a library at Rosetta, where he found a complete manuscript copy of the Arabian Tales, or Thousand and One Nights. KLARKE has lately been three weeks in Troas, and his observations very much agree with those of Hammer.

It has long been the opinion of many learned men, that the Fables usually ascribed to Esop probably belong to the Abyssinian Fabulist Lokmann.—A German Correspondent informs us, that in Germany, a person of the greatest credibility at present asserts, that he had seen in Syria a manuscript, with the superscription, "Lokmann's Works," which contained, besides the Fables, Proverbs, Maxims, and Moral Doctrines, and was divided into sections, in one of which he found the Fables hitherto ascribed to Esop.

The

The most interesting literary *morceau* which has appeared in Germany during the present year, is KOTZEBUE's Narrative of his Adventures in Russia, and his Extraordinary Exile into Siberia. It is intitled "*The most Wonderful Year of my Life*;" and a translation may confidently be expected to appear in England.

The French artist TOUREL, and the Austrian Major SCHWARZ, who now resides at Vienna with Count VON FRIESS, and is worthy, on account of his extensive knowledge, and the amiableness of his manners, to be the companion of a man, who in himself and others sets more value on the endowments of the mind, than the possession of millions, have been making important researches at Athens. Some fears, however, are entertained of the safety of Tourel. An English traveller, of the name of TWEDDEL, has been murdered by his Greek servant, and buried by his countrymen in an ancient Temple of Theseus. Professor CARLYSLE has received his papers.

Citizen ANDRE MICHAUX, thinking he could not render a greater service to his country than by transporting thither the useful plants which grow in analogous climates, first visited Syria, Babylonia, and Persia. He found, among the natural productions of these countries, a multitude of kitchen garden plants, ornamental plants, and others for fodder, cultivated amongst Europeans, and he brought from thence new riches. On his return, in 1785, he set out for North America. He established two gardens, one near New York, the other near Charlestown, to raise there the plants which he might collect. He afterwards traversed North America for eleven years together, from the Bahama Isles and the Cape of Florida, to Hudson's Bay, that is to say, from the 27th to the 58th degree, or in a space of 750 leagues. He did not make this tour along the coasts; he penetrated into the country more than 400 leagues from east to west; he lived with the savages, whose affections he gained, whose cares he repaid, and who assisted him in his researches. During this interval, he sent to France many chests of seeds, and a great number of shoots of trees, most of which are now cultivated through all Europe. Among these trees were distinguished an ilicium, the aromatic fruit of which will serve the same purposes as that known by the name of the stellated *anis* of China (*anis etoilé de la Chine*); a larch tree, the wood of which is used in building; a new neighbouring kind of quinquina, and which will perhaps supply its place; and, lastly, many magnolia, a pavia, a rhododendron, an acacia, which already are the ornaments of our gardens. On his return, Citizen André Michaux was employed in putting his collections in order, and in drawing up an abridged Relation of his Voyage, and giving an History of the Plants of America. Government having nominated him to form a part in the expedition of Captain BAUDIN, he has left to his son, who had accompanied him in one of his journies, the care of superintending the printing of his manuscripts. The History of the Oaks of America was in the press at the time of his departure, and has been lately published. It is written in French; the botanical phrases only are in Latin. It contains twenty species, and a number of remarkable varieties; arranged in methodical order, according to the form of the leaves and the annual or biennial fructification; and characterised in a sure and invariable manner. All these species have been designed in their different states, by Citizen REDOUTE, whose talents are well known to painters and naturalists; and elegantly engraved by Citizens SELLIER and PLEE; making in the whole thirty six plates. At every species, Citizen Michaux has carefully marked the manner of cultivating it, the soil which suits it, the uses to be drawn from it, and the districts of France where it would be advantageous to naturalize it. Among these species are some absolutely unknown; to others are annexed new and interesting observations. The following article on the maritime oak or green oak of Carolina, may give an idea of the observations which accompany the description of divers species.—"This tree grows from Lower Virginia to Florida, and the Mississippi, along the coasts, on the isles and the tracts exposed to the stormy winds of the ocean. The lower countries of North America are lands of a new formation. The surface of the soil is a sandy layer, on a very deep mass of argill. The maritime oaks here acquire a rapid growth, because the fibrous roots with which they are provided in their adolescent state find in a moveable sand the facility of spreading in all directions. In proportion as they arrive at adult age, the principal roots reach the clayey bottom, where they imbibe a nourishment which supports their vigour for many centuries, and renders them capable of resisting the impetuosity of the winds, and of supporting the heat of the sun. From Virginia to the extremity of Florida, the traveller often perceives this isolated tree, preserving

ing all its vigour, in a soil where others cannot exist. It is never damaged by animals. In the plantations situated in the lower part of the two Carolinas, the proprietors keep it to serve for shelter to the cattle. Its tufted foliage is impenetrable to the rays of the sun, and the umbrage of a single tree often covers a space of more than thirty toises. Its fruit (in abundance) is less sour than that of the other species. We are told that the savages obtain from it an oil which they mix with their food. It wood is of an excellent quality. In the North of the United States, it is employed with the greatest advantage in the construction of ships, which last for a long time. The soil of Lower Carolina and of Georgia being of the same nature as that of the *landes* of Bourdeaux, the maritime oak is worthy to fix the attention of the French and Spanish Governments. It offers a means of giving a value to the lands which border on the Mediterranean and the ocean. In the introduction, Citizen André Michaud makes a number of curious remarks on oaks in general, on their uses and their culture, and on the knowledge which the ancients had of them. This work excites a lively desire to see the Flora of America.

According to the observations made by the Academician KRAFFT, the city of St. Petersburgh, on an average of ten years, has annually 97 bright days, 104 of rain, 72 of snow, and 93 unsettled. There are every year from 12 to 67 storms, which, sometimes, when they proceed from the west, occasion inundations. From an experience of more than sixty years, the ice of the river Neva never breaks up before the 25th of March, and never later than the 27th of April; the earliest time of its freezing is the 20th of October, and the latest the 1st of December.

M. ZINCK, the Co-regent of Hesse Homburg, has invented an instrument of music, to which he has given the name of *Harmonica Celestina*. This instrument is in the shape of a spinnet, or small harpsichord, with three rows of keys. As he has only used it in public to execute some pieces of music, the German journalists do not give any details respecting its interior mechanism. He draws from it the sound of the organ, the flute, the piano-forte, of several bowed instruments, and of that called the harmonica. He can derive these sounds either singly or collectively, at pleasure. The purchaser of this instrument, which we are assured is capable of one hundred changes, is the Empress of Germany.

Citizen LALANDE has addressed the following note to the Editor of the *Moniteur*: —"The astrologers alarmed Europe, in the year 1186, by announcing a *conjunction of all the planets*, which was to occasion very extraordinary ravages. I mentioned the circumstance in the Preface to my Astronomy, but was anxious to ascertain whether this rare and singular phenomenon actually took place in the course of that year. Citizen FLANGERGUES, an Associate member of the National Institute, and a zealous astronomer, took the trouble to make the requisite calculations, and the result certainly was, that on the 15th of September, A. D. 1186, all the planets were comprehended within from six signs to six signs, ten degrees, of longitude. This, however, *was not an exact conjunction*; but perhaps many thousand years may elapse before they again so nearly approximate each other."

The Prince Royal of Denmark has lately established a Board of Longitude, at the University of Copenhagen, the chief employment of which will be to calculate Ephemerides in a nautical almanack, as likewise the moon's distances from the planets, Venus, Mars, Jupiter, and Saturn, and thereby to increase and render less difficult the methods for finding the longitude at sea. This commission is to consist of Professor BYGGS, of an extraordinary professor of astronomy, and two adjuncts. The director of the commission must annually deliver a distinctly written copy of the Ephemerides calculated by them, together with the moon's distances from the above planets, to the director of the depôt of sea-charts, who is to superintend the printing and publishing of them.

Four years ago, an Academy of Architecture was instituted at Berlin, in which one hundred students learn the higher branches of the science; and for the purpose of initiating youths in the first principles thereof, and preparing them for admission into the Academy, provincial schools of architecture, and the arts therewith connected, have been erected at Breslau, Magdeburg, Halle, and Königsberg, and are to be erected in several other towns of the Prussian dominions. In these schools, pure and mixed mathematics, geometry, the economical and higher branches of architecture, the forming relievoes in clay, &c. are taught gratis; and artists and handicraftsmen connected with architecture are instructed in a variety of useful knowledge, necessary towards

perfectionating

perfectionating their trades and professions. The teachers are nominated by a committee of the academy at Berlin. The pupils are taught drawing in the drawing-schools already established at a former period.

A person at Paris has discovered a kind of ink, which cannot be effaced by oxygenated muriatic acid, nor by any reactive chemical preparation.

Citizen LANGLES has lately printed in Paris, a Notice on the History of GENGISKAN, extracted from a Persian manuscript, which gives a new proof of the talents and the enlarged views of that conqueror, who was likewise a legislator. The curious reader will see here a pretty long and very interesting extract from the code which he published, and which is printed in the work here announced, in its original language, with the Persian characters in the possession of the National Printing office. This Persian *morceau* contains thirteen pages, and is larger than any similar fragment printed in France for more than a century past.

In another notice by Citizen LANGLES, on a Latin-Chinese-Mantchou Dictionary, in manuscript, the reader will further see a model of the Mantchoux characters, the first which have been engraved in Europe, and so much the more valuable as the Mantchoux language may perfectly supply in Europe the knowledge of the Chinese. In fact, the Emperors of the Mantchou race, who have governed China for 150 years past, have not ceased during that period to cause to be translated into their maternal tongue all the good works which exist in China. KAM HI, the second of that dynasty, established for this very purpose a *Tribunal of Translators*, which even subsists to this day. In expectation that the peace may finally re-establish the relations which formerly existed between Citizen Langles himself and the Missionaries in China, he informs us that there is already a collection of 200 Mantchou works, both original and translated from the Chinese, that have been accumulating for 150 years past in the National Library; and that it is his intention to profit by the Continuation of the *Notices and Extracts*, to make these works known to the public. These Notices and Extracts, taken from the manuscripts of the National Library and other libraries are published, from time to time, by the National Institute of France, and are intended to form a sequel to the Notices and Extracts formerly read to the Committee established in the *ci-devant* Academy of Inscriptions and Belles Lettres. Before the revolution the manuscripts of all kinds, contained in what is now call'd the National Library, amounted to more than 80,000; but this valuable *depôt* having been since enriched with the manuscripts that have come from Belgium and Italy, and with all those, which formerly making a part of other public or private collections, have been thought worthy to enter into this, it is now more complete than ever in its *ensemble*, and more rich in rare, valuable and well preserved works, so that no other existing collection in Europe can now be compared with it. The above work is intitled Notices and Extracts, and is the fifth volume of a collection, designed in its progress, to execute an immense and difficult undertaking, viz. by smaller or larger extracts, to spread the knowledge of such an immense quantity of valuable works, which, however well preserved now, must necessarily, in time, undergo the common law of returning to dust.*

The Museum Gallery of Antiques at Paris, has been open since the 18th of Brumaire last. On the three last days of each *decade*, the entrance is public; the other days are reserved for the artists that go there to perfect themselves in the study of design. What interest, what resources will they not henceforth find, in this collection of the finest remains of antiquity!—a collection such as could never have been met with at Rome, where they were, for the

* It was the Academy of Inscriptions and Belles Lettres, that in 1785 conceived the idea of this great and commendable undertaking. It nominated for this purpose eight commissaries, and moreover invited all its members to concur in it; the Academy further addressed a general invitation to all the *literati* of France, to make known the manuscripts contained in public or private *depôts* where they had access. The first volume of the *Notices and Extracts* appeared in 1787; the second in 1789, and the third in the following year. The printing of the fourth volume had been begun in 1791, but circumstances, and, above all, the suppression of the Academy, which was decreed in 1793, retarded its publication, and it was only lately carried into effect. After the storms of the revolution, on the revival of sciences and letters, the National Institute was charged by a formal law to *continue the notices of the manuscripts*; and it has accordingly, in every point, followed the plan of the Academy, and the fifth volume, already announced, is the fruit of this new labour; it contains 43 Extracts or Notices of Arabic, Persian, Turkish, Tartar, Mantchou, Greek, Latin, and French Manuscripts, with some anecdotical pieces.

the most part, scattered in different Museums. The Gallery contains, in all, more than a hundred and eighty objects, and is divided into a number of saloons, each of which has a particular character. The Museum of Antiques, the vestibule of which is not yet finished, and which is only now entered by a lateral door, near the stair-case of the Museum of Painting, is composed of ten contiguous saloons, connected together by the perfect accordance of their adjustments. The first of these saloons is that of the Seasons. It derives its name from the cieling which crowns it, and whose paintings, executed almost under the reign of Louis XIII. by ROMANELLI, an Italian painter, in high fame for the grace of his compositions and the sweetness of his pencil, represent the four Seasons. Here, it is thought, should be assembled the antique statues of the rural divinities, and those relative to the different epochs of the year. The cielings of the three following saloons, viz. that of Illustrious Men; that of the Romans, whose paintings offer many traits of history of that people; and that of the Laocoon, of which this admirable groupe makes the principal ornament, have been painted by the same artist. The gildings with which the dome is enriched, contrast, in a striking manner, with the noble simplicity of the constructions which sustain the upper architecture; and if they do not offer any violent—any disagreeable opposition, it is because the skilful architect (Citizen RAYMOND) who has directed all these labours, has known how to replace adroitly, in some parts of the new decoration, a very small number of rich details, which unite the whole and form an harmonious *ensemble*. To prevent a return to the paintings which decorate the cieling of the Gallery, it is proper to observe here, that a painting executed on a wall which it was necessary to pull down, in order to enlarge the Hall of Laocoon, has been transported elsewhere without any injury, and in one entire piece, with the masonry which served to support it. This painting is, at present, above the niche where this groupe is seen, and many toises from the place which it formerly occupied. The success of this delicate and hazardous undertaking, does honour to the artist to whom it was intrusted. In the Saloon or Hall of Laocoon, many frescoes have been destroyed, either by time or by humidity; the same spaces have been again occupied by new compositions; these last have been painted in oil. The Minister of Interior has chosen for this purpose, some of the artists who, in the last public *concours*, had obtained prizes of encouragement. A cieling and two vertical paintings have been executed by Citizens HENNEQUIN, PEYRON and LETHIER; they represent allegorical subjects. Citizens PRUDHOM and GUERIN have painted groupes of infants in two spaces of a circular form, making part of the dome. These different paintings, the authors of which are justly held in estimation, have been finished with as much success as could be expected from artists distinguished by their talents, but little accustomed to the painful and wearisome posture, which they were obliged to submit to, during the term of their labour. Citizen Raymond, Member of the National Institute, and Architect of the National Palace of Sciences and of Arts, has designed and superintended all the labours which have been carried on in the Saloons which compose the Gallery of Antiques; as likewise the new dispositions, decorations and embellishments. It is wrongfully therefore that some persons have pretended that he only executed the plans of HUBERT, his predecessor. It is undeniable, that those plans were not even communicated to Citizen Raymond.

LIST OF NEW PUBLICATIONS IN NOVEMBER.

ANTIQUITIES.

A Dissertation on the newly discovered Babylonian Inscriptions; illustrated with Copper-plates, and an Inscription found on a Fragment of Jasper, printed from the Stone itself, by permission of the Hon. Directors of the East India Company. By Joseph Hager, D. D. 1l. 1s. boards. Richardsons.

The Archaiology of Wales, for preserving the Contents of ancient Manuscripts; the two *first* Volumes, which contain a Collection of the Poetry of the British Bards to the beginning of the Fourteenth Century; and various Historical Documents and Chronicles to the end of the same Period. Royal 8vo. 2l 2s. boards. Longman and Rees.

BIOGRAPHY.

The Juvenile Plutarch, or Lives of Celebrated and Extraordinary Children. 2s. 6d. Phillips.

An

An Account of the Life and Writings of William Robertson, D. D. By Dugald Stewart, F.R.S. 4to. and 8vo. Cadell.

DRAMA.

Mary Stewart, Queen of Scots, an historical Drama. 4s. sewed. Longman and Rees.

Kemble and Cooke; or, A Critical Review of a Pamphlet, entitled, "Remarks on the Character of Richard the Third, as played by Cooke and Kemble." With other Remarks on the Performances of these two Gentlemen. 1s. 6d. Westley.

The Philanthropist, a Play. With an introductory Address attendant upon the Blessings of Civilization, demonstrated by the Establishment of the Royal Humane Society. By J. Jones, Navy Surgeon. Dedicated by permission to Dr. Hawes. 1s. 6d. Mawman.

EDUCATION.

The Little Hermitage, with other Tales. Plates 2s. 6d. Phillips.

Visits to the Menagerie and Botanical Garden, 2 vols. Plates. 4s. Phillips.

The English Spelling-Book, accompanied by a progressive Series of easy and familiar Lessons, intended as an Introduction to the first Elements of the English Language. By William Mavor, L. L. D. 1s. 6d. Phillips.

Arithmetical Questions, on a New Plan, intended to answer the double Purpose of Arithmetical Instruction and Miscellaneous Information. By W. Butler. 3d edition, 5s. 6d. Mawman.

HISTORY.

Dodsley's Annual Register (Vol. 42) for the Year 1800. 10s. 6d. boards. Otridge, and other Proprietors.

LAW.

Commercial and Notarial Precedents, consisting of the most approved Forms, special and common, which are required in Business. With an Appendix, containing the Principles of Law relative to Bills of Exchange, Insurance and Shipping. By Joshua Montifiore, Attorney and Notary Public. 4to. 1l. 5s. boards. Phillips.

Reports of Cases determined in the Courts of Common Pleas and Exchequer, in Hilary and Easter Terms, 1801. By John B. Bosanquet and C. Puller, Esqrs. Barristers at Law. Volume II Part IV. 7s. 6d. Butterworth.

The Law of Bills of Exchange, Promissory Notes, Bank and Bankers' Notes, Drafts, and Checks; containing all the Statutes, Customs of Merchants, and Decisions at Law and Equity on those Subjects, to Trinity Term, 1801. Including a Case in July, 1801, when essential Information occurred respecting Country Banks. Together with the Stamp-duty on the respective Sums to the latest Act By Edward Manning, Esq. 8vo. 3s sewed. Stratford.

Reports of Cases determined in the Court of King's Bench, in Trinity Term, 1801. With the Indexes, completing the First Volume of a new Series, in royal octavo. By E. H. East, Esq. Volume I. Part IV. 7s. Butterworth.

An Abstract of the Cause just arbitrated, (and the Award given in Favour of the Defendant) between the Birmingham, and Birmingham and Fazeley Canal Navigation Company, and John Pinkerton as Defendant. The Evidence of Mr. John Houghton, Clerk of the Company, is given at full length. With Observations. 10s. 6d. boards. Johnson.

MEDICAL.

A Treatise on the Cow-pox, containing a History of Vaccine Inoculation, and an Account of the Publications on that Subject. By John Ring, Surgeon. Part I. 8s. Johnson.

Hygëia, a series of Essays on Health; on a plan entirely popular. By Thomas Beddoes, M. D. No. I. (to be completed in 12 or 16 monthly numbers) 2s. Phillips.

MATHEMATICS.

The Gentleman's Mathematical Companion for the Year 1802; containing Answers to the last Year's Enigmas, &c. and new Rebusses, &c. for the next Year. With some curious Papers from the Transactions of the Royal Society. (To be continued annually) 1s. 6d. Symonds.

MISCELLANIES.

Various Thoughts. By W. Burdon, M. A. 3s. Clarke.

The Supplement to Hogarth Restored, engraved by Cook, containing Henry the Eighth and Anna Bullen, &c. No. I. (to be completed in Six Numbers, with the last of which Descriptions of the Plates, and a List of the Subscribers will be given) 10s. 6d. Robinsons.

Hints for Increasing the Splendour of Illumination with security and convenience; and Remarks for the Prevention of Tumult and Disorder: adapted to the Illuminations expected to take Place on the Proclamation of Peace. 1s. Jordan.

An Accurate and Impartial Account of the Apprehension, Trial and Execution of Sir W. E. Crosbie, Bart. Published in Justice to his Memory by his Family. 3s. Hatchard.

The Art of Cookery Refined, in which Attention has been paid to Economy as well as to please the Palate; forming at once a complete Guide for the Family of the Nobleman, of the Tradesman, and for the Professor at a Tavern. By John Mollard, Cook, One of the Proprietors of Freemasons' Tavern, Great Queen-str. With Plates. 10s. 6d. Nunn.

NOVELS.

Something New; or, Adventures at Campbell House. By Anne Plumptre, 3 vols. 15s. boards. Longman and Rees.

Literary Leisure; or, The Recreations of Solomon Saunter, Esq. 2 vols. 8vo. 12s. bds. Lane.

Welch Legends, consisting of Oral Traditions from the Æra of the Bards of Ancient Britain, and now first printed in English. With plates. No I. (to be continued monthly) 1s. 6d. Earl and Hemet

The Mysterious Friendship; a Tale, in 2 vols. Price 8s. sewed. Earle and Hemet.

St. Margaret's Cave; or, the Nun's Story; a Romance, by Mrs. E. Helme, in 4 vols. Price 1l. 1s. in boards. Earle and Hemet.

NAVAL.

The History of the Rise and Progress of the Naval Power of Great Britain; with important Notices relative to the French Marine, and Observations on the Navigation Act. Illustrated with Notes, translated from the *original* French, by Thos. Evanson White. 8vo. 7s 6d. Jordan.

An Authentic Narrative of the Proceedings of the Squadron under the Command of Sir James Saumarez. 1s. Egerton.

POLITICAL.

Thoughts upon the Preliminary Articles of Peace. By a Kentish Clergyman. 1s 6d. Faulder.

A Vindication of the Convention lately concluded between Great Britain and Russia. 3s. Wright.

A Collection of Facts and Observations relative to the Peace with Bonaparte; including M. Cobbet's Letters to Lord Hawkesbury. With an Appendix, containing the Conventions, Treaties, and Dispatches connected with the Subject. With Extracts from Speeches in Parliament respecting Bonaparte, and Peace with France. By William Cobbett. Cobbett and Morgan.

A Review of the Principles on which the Clergy are excluded from Sitting in the House of Commons. 1s 6d. Reynolds.

An Address to the Inhabitants of Great Britain and Ireland on the Termination of the War with France. By the Rev. T. Robinson, A. M. 8vo. 1s. 12mo. 4d. Rivingtons.

Reflections on the Conclusion of the War. By John Bowles, Esq. 2s. 6d. Rivingtons.

POLITICAL ECONOMY.

Statistical Account of the Population and Cultivation, Produce and Consumption of England and Wales. With Observations and Hints for the Prevention of a future Scarcity. By Benjamin Pitts Capper. 8vo. 4s. sewed. Kearsley.

Facts, explanatory of the Instrumental Cause of the High Price of Provisions. By Thomas Butcher, late Clerk of the Drystores at the Victualling-office, Deptford. 1s. 6d. Scott.

POETRY.

The Dawn of Peace, an Ode; and Amphion; or, the Force of Concord, Regulation and Peace, an Ode. By Thomas Noble. 4to. 2s. 6d sewed. Ginger.

Poetry for Children, consisting of such Pieces as may be committed to Memory at an early Age. By Miss Aikin. 2s. 6d half-bound. Phillips.

The Conjunction of Jupiter and Venus on the 29th of September, 1801, a happy Prelude to a Peace. Mercury's Apology for the Curate's Blunder, &c. By the Rev. J. Black. 1s. Robinsons.

TRAVELS.

Travels in the Ottoman Empire, Egypt and Persia, undertaken by Order of the Republican Government of France. By G. A. Oliver, Member of the National Institute, &c. Illustrated by Engravings, and a Map of Greece, the Archipelago, &c. Translated from the French. Volume I. 4to. with an Atlas. 2l. 12s. 6d. boards. Longman and Rees.

TOPOGRAPHY.

The Reading Guide and Berkshire Directory for 1802; concluding with a short Description of the County. 8d. sewed in col. paper. Rusher, Reading;—Crosby, London.

THEOLOGY.

An Introduction to Christianity, designed to preserve young People from Irreligion and Vice. By Joseph Sutcliffe. 12mo. 2s. 6d. boards. Butterworth.

A Blow at the Root of Infidelity; or, the Agreement of Nature and Scripture in Testimony of a Triune God, a Sermon. By the Rev. John Chamberlain, Bath. 8vo. 1s. Mawman.

Dr. Watts's First Catechisms and Prayers for Children. Rusher's edition, in coloured paper, 2d. or 14s. per hundred. Crosby.

Sir Richard Hill's Present for Your Neighbour. Rusher's edition, in blue paper 3d. or 20s. per hundred. Crosby.

VETERINARY ART.

Veterinary Pathology; or, a Treatise on the Cause and Progress of the Diseases of Horses, together with the most approved Methods of Prevention and Cure. To which are added short Observations on Bleeding, Firing, Roweling, Fomentations, and Poultices; and an Appendix, or Veterinary Dispensatory, containing the most approved Prescriptions for the different Diseases of the Horse. The whole intended as a Guide and Companion to the Gentleman, Veterinarian and Farrier. By William Ryding, Veterinary Surgeon in the 18th regt. of light dragoons. 8vo. 5s. boards. Mawman.

Latin Books imported and sold by J. Bein, No. 31, South-street, Soho.

Dindorfii, J. J. Novum Lexicon Linguæ Hebraicæ Commentario in Libros Veteris Testamenti, 1 vol. 8vo. Lipsiæ, 1801, 1l. 2s.

Hermanni, God. de Emendanda Ratione Græcæ Grammaticæ, 1 vol. 8vo. Lipsiæ, 1801, 12s.

Juvenalis Satyræ XVI. 2 vols. 8vo. 1801, 18s.

Meisneri, J. H. Nova Veteris Testamenti Clavis, 2 vols. 8vo. Lipsiæ, 1800, 1l. 2s.

Trochassii, G. Opera omnia Phisiologica et Pathologica, 3 vols. 8vo. Viennæ, 1800, 1l. 10s.

Storchii, F. A. Chrestomathia Græca, Quedlinburg, 1801, 6s. 9d.

Schleussneri Lexicon in Novum Testamentum, 1 vol. 8vo. Lipsiæ, 1801, 1l. 1s.

Testamentum Novum, Græc. et Lat. cum Tab. Æneis 29. ex recens. Mathæi Riga 1788; 8vo. 3l. 10s.

Cornu-

German Books.

Abicht, J. H. Phyfiologifche Anthropologie, 1 B. 8°. Erlangen, 1801, 6s.

Efchenburg's, J. J. Handbuch der Klaffifchen Litteratur, 8°. Berlin, 1801, 11s

Hug, Leon, Erfindung der Buchftabenfchrift, 4°. Ulm, 1801, 6s.

Lippold's Natur und Künftler Lexicon, Weimar, 1801, 8°. 1 vol. 1l. 4s.

Paul, Jean, Heimliches Klaglied der jetzigen Männer, 8°. Bremen, 1801, 4s.

Vernunft Katechifmus, Deutfch und Französifch, 8°. Leipzig, 1801, 3s. 6d.

Wallenrodt, Frau von, Karl Moor und feine Genoffen, 8°. Hamburg, 1801, 6s.

Kotzebue, neue Schaufpiele, 7ter band.

Göthes neüe Schriften, 7ter band.

DICTIONARIES.

Campe, J. H. Deutfches Wörterbuch, als Fortfetzung zu Adelungs, 4°. Braunfchweig, 1801, 1l. 6s.

Adelung's Grammatifch-Kritifches Wörterbuch der Hochdeutfchen Mundart, 4ter band. 4°. complet. Leipzig, 1801, 6l. 12s.

NEW PATENTS LATELY ENROLLED.

MR. HOLEMBERG'S PATENT *for* LOCKS *or* FASTENINGS *for* GENERAL USE, *on a new and improved* CONSTRUCTION.

THIS invention prepares locks of the fame exterior form as thofe which are in common ufe. Internally it ufes an *orbicular bolt* inftead of a rectilineal one. An infide tumbler ferves to increafe the fecurity of this bolt. It is double-faftened by a fpring flat bolt. The whole ftructure of the lock is moft ingenioufly fimple; and, after careful infpection, we are inclined to give it that preference to other locks, which the inventor claims for it.

MR. CHABANNES' PATENT *for a* MACHINE *for* SEPARATING COALS, *and a* COMPOSITION *for making* SMALL COALS *into* CAKES *or* BALLS *to be ufed for* FUEL.

Mr. CHABANNES ufes a grating of wood or metal, having bars, of which the mutual diftances muft not be fmaller than a quarter of an inch, nor larger than an inch and a half. On this grating, he difcharges the coals, in the mixture of fmall and great, in which they are bought in the Pool. The great coals are detained above the grating, the fmall pafs through it; and it is thus the feparation is effected.

The fmall coals he then mingles in a wooden veffel, with a fmall proportion of earth, clay, cow-dung, tar, pitch, broken glafs, fulphur, faw-duft, oil-cakes, tar, wood, or any other combuftible matter. A fufficient quantity of water is ufed in preparing the mixture; and it is ground with a wheel, fo that it becomes of one confiftency. Out of this veffel, it is conveyed by pipes or otherwife into pits or holes of any dimenfions. Thefe pits are lined, every where but at the centre, with bricks united by a cement. At the centre is a drain or water-courfe paffing under the pit, and covered only with uncemented bricks, amongft which the water may run eafily off from the compofition. The compofition thus cleared from the water, is, while yet foft, moulded into brick-cakes or balls. Thefe are put on a frame, to dry; when dry, they may be ufed as fuel.

MR. GODFREY'S PATENT *for a* TAMBORINE, TABOR, *or* DRUM *and* PIPE, *to be annexed to a* BARREL-ORGAN, *&c. and for the* CONSTRUCTION *of fuch* BARREL-ORGAN, *or other* MUSICAL INSTRUMENT.

Mr. GODFREY in this invention, made nearly twelve years fince, prepares the frame of his tamborine, tabor, or drum, of any variety of the common forms of thefe inftruments, of the ufual materials; with heads or covers of parchment, vellum, leather, &c. in two or more parts, and with a ftraining-frame to be put within the inftrument. He unites the frames by fcrews and nuts, or by pins, wires, and other faftenings.

He next prepares a barrel-organ, or other mufical inftrument, of the common ftructure in all refpects, but that it poffeffes likewife the following additions: pins on the barrel, by means of which a hammer or drum-ftick may beat according to the time of the tunes fet on the barrel; a key in the key-frame, to touch thofe pins; ftaples in and upon the barrel, to make the hammer or drum-ftick beat to time; and a key in the key-frame of the organ, to touch and take the ftaples in playing.

When the tamborine and the organ are thus both prepared, he adds to the organ, a bar or piece of wood or brafs, which reaches between its two ends, his at one end a joint or hinge by which it is fastened to the organ, and rests at the other on the case or frame of the organ, or on a draw-stop or key. Upon this bar in the organ, he fastens the tamborine.

Within the organ, he puts a frame to sustain the hammer, or drum-stick; a spring is annexed to the hammer; and there is a wire, rod, or slip of wood, extending from the end of the hammer to the key in the key-frame.

In the frame or case of the organ, he puts a stop; to this stop he annexes a string or wire, which passes across the organ to the hammer or drum-stick. To the hammer or drum-stick that wire is fastened, and the movements of the wire from the stop make that to strike or be silent at pleasure.

A lever hung in the frame of the organ-case, makes the hammer or drum-stick to beat time. A wire or rod is put to connect it with the key in the key-frame, which comes upon the staples in the barrel.

With the tamborine, he also affixes to the organ, one or more upright pipes, which, by a key in the barrel, may be played at pleasure.

The tamborine, tabor, or drum, may be put within the organ, either by hanging it an-edge or by laying it horizontally. It may be hung or fixed in the frame at one side or end of the organ; and with proper variations, the tamborine, tabor, or drum, may be in like manner added to several other musical instruments.

MONTHLY RETROSPECT OF THE FINE ARTS.

(*Communications and the Loan of all new Prints are requested.*)

Terror or Fright. Tranquillity. Crying. Laughter. Invented and modelled by George Stubbs. G. Townley Stubbs, sculpt. Price 6s. each, or four for a Guinea.

HOGARTH, in his Analysis of Beauty, speaking of the fine winding forms of which the human body is composed, and which, by their varied situations with each other, become more intricately pleasing, and form a continued waving of winding forms from one into the other, introduces a drawing of a muscular leg and thigh, which shews the serpentine forms and varied situation of the muscles, as they appear when the skin is taken off. This was drawn from a plaster of Paris cast of nature, the original of which was prepared for the mould by Cowper, the famous anatomist. In this figure, he observes, that as the skin is taken off, the parts are too distinctly traced by the eye for that intricate delicacy which is necessary to constitute perfect beauty.

The same objection will apply to Mr. Stubbs's Views of the Passions, which appear to be in part built on the basis of Le Brun, and have for their object to shew to the tyro the exact form and combination of the muscles, without any attempt to deviate into grace. So far, we think, they may be very useful to the student, as correctness of outline should unquestionably be the leading object; and though heads, thus stripped, being coloured according to nature, *as it would appear if covered with skin*, gives them a most grotesque appearance; yet, as we wish every artist to be well grounded in every separate branch of his profession, we again repeat, they may be a very useful study. This system may certainly be carried too far; as we remember an itinerant portrait-painter, who some years since was resident in Suffolk, made it his constant practice to begin with painting the bones of the head and shoulders, hands, &c. he afterwards inserted the muscles; and finished, by covering his portrait with skin and colour; and this, he insisted upon it, was the process of nature, and ought therefore to be the practice of painters!

Solicitude. Sympathy. Contempt. Singleton pinx. G. T. Stubbs sculpt.

Reverie. Enquiry. Portia. Nerissa. W. F. Wellings inv. G. T. Stubbs sculpt.

The same price as the preceding article, and built in some degree on the same system, but not quite equal in either conception or execution. *Sympathy* is, we think, superior to any of the others.

A View of Porto St. Giovani. E. Edwards, R. A. pinxit. F. Jukes, Aqua-tinta sculpt. Published by Jukes, Howland-street, May 29, 1801. Price 1l. 1s.

There may be those to whom this view is interesting; but, considered as a print, it is not marked with any very singular beauty, either in the design or engraving.

The

The Deaf and Dumb Alphabet; humbly inscribed to Sir John Leicester, Bart. Painted by J. Northcote, R. A. and engraved by W. S. Annis. Published by Jeffreys, Clapham-road, price 15s. in Colours.

This is an interesting and pleasing little figure, extremely well imagined, holding up her hands, and talking by signs.

The Goddess of Wisdom. Shelley pinxit.—Vide Akenside's Pleasures of the Imagination.—Caroline Watson sculpt. Published by Molteno, Pall-mall.

This is a pretty half-length figure, *neatly* drawn, and exquisitely engraved.

Political Dreaming.—Visions of Peace.—Perspective of Horrors. Gilray inv. et sculpt. Published by Humphreys, St. James's-street, Price 3s. 6d.

Of Mr. Gilray's multifarious and many-coloured productions it is not easy to speak in higher terms than they deserve. For incident, character, and combination, they very happily seize on the floating subjects of the day, and he treats them in a manner which we think no other artist, except our late unrivalled Hogarth, has been capable. We sometimes lament that such talents should be so much confined to politics; but whatever is the ruling and leading folly is the proper object of satire. The spirit of his etchings would illuminate any subject that they touched upon, and the rapidity with which they are etched is manifested in every line. To describe the variety of characters and combinations introduced into this *three-titled* print is impossible. Mr. Windham's horrible dream, and the little brood scampering to the cheese-parings and candle-ends, are admirably marked.

Preliminaries of Peace; or, John Bull and his little Friends marching to Paris. The same Artist and Publisher as the preceding.

Though this print has a considerable portion of wit and whim, it is not equal to that which precedes it.

Edward Jenner, M. D. F. R. S. Painted, engraved, and published, by J. R. Smith, King-street, Covent-garden.

Correctly drawn, and well engraved; and, as we have been informed by those who know the original, a good likeness.

Constance, Arthur, and Salisbury. R. Westall, R. A. del. S. W. Reynolds, sculpt. Published by J. R. Smith.

The taste, talent and accuracy of character, which Westall displays in his historical drawings, we have had frequent occasion to notice; this delineation is worthy of the artist, and, as far as we remember it, the print is a fair copy.

John Philpot Curran, Esq. Painted by T. Lawrence, R. A. principal Painter to his Majesty. Engraved by J. R. Smith, Engraver to His Royal Highness the Prince of Wales. Price 10s. 6d.

We sometimes meet with a face peculiarly formed for the painter's giving a striking likeness of it, and where, if the artist attends to the lines, he produces a picture of the mind—Such is the head of Mr. Curran. It is one of those countenances on which God and Nature have set the broad seal of independent thinking and speaking, without regard to the opinion of those he addresses, or perhaps rather better disposed to *oppose* than agree with his hearers in any proposition that is advanced. It is a very spirited and fine engraving, and decides itself to be a strong resemblance of the original.

The Right Hon. Lord St. Vincent, First Lord of the Admiralty, and one of His Majesty's Privy Council. Painted by Kernan. Engraved and published by Mr. Barnard, Fitzroy-square.

We have not happened to see the gallant Admiral since he, many years ago, two or three time sat for his portrait to Gilbert Stuart, the American, and, from the portraits then painted, this is very different; the veteran is now marked much more than we could wish with the characters of age. It must be the earnest wish of every friend to Great Britain, that he may long—very long—retain his health and spirits; and to have the resemblance of such a man at the *later*, as well as the *earlier*, period of his life, must be a gratification to every naval character in the country.

The Right Hon. Lord Viscount Macartney, K. B. S. de Koster pinxit. C. Townley, Engraver to his Majesty and the Prince of Wales, and Member of the Academies of Berlin and Florence, sculpt.

This painting is dressed in the robes of the order of the garter, the spurs, &c. In air and manner it carries clear marks of being a portraiture painted by a foreign artist. Mr. Townley has engraved it extremely well.

Right Hon. Robert Banks Lord Hawkesbury. Painted by T. Lawrence, R. A. Engraved and published by John Young, Engraver to the Prince of Wales, No. 58, Charlotte-street.

This portrait may at the present period become popular: whether it does or not, it is extremely well painted, and admirably engraved.

Vice-admiral Lord Viscount Nelson, Duke of Bronte, &c. Painted by John Rising. Engraved by John Young.

If the merit of all our artists were appreciated according to their abilities, Mr. Rising would rank higher than many of those whose effrontery has raised them to a higher scale. This is a very strong resemblance of the Hero of the Nile, extremely well drawn; and Mr. Young has engraved it in a very masterly style.

The Right Hon. Sir W. Fawcett, K. B.—Sir J. Reynolds pinxit. Engraved and published by J. Ward, Engraver to the Prince of Wales, Newman-street.

This was one of the President's finest portraits, and we were much gratified to find it brought under the burin of Mr. Ward, who has done perfect justice to the original.

The Sportsman's Repast. The Enamoured Sportsman. Painted, engraved, and published by J. R. Smith, King-street, Covent Garden.

These two prints are somewhat in the manner of Morland; but, though equally *rustic*, they are not so vulgar nature as that artist sometimes delineates. In both composition and execution, *the Repast* is the superior print.

He would be a Soldier. Painted by Shee. Engraved by Nugent.

To this pleasing little figure the painter has given a good deal of character, and a natural easy air; and the engraver has well preserved the spirit of the original.

Price four Guineas in Boards, a Selection of Twelve Heads from the Last Judgment of Michael Angelo, of the same Size as in the Fresco-pictures, being Fac-similes of Drawings made in Rome, in 1797, by R. Duppa, Author of the Account of the Subversion of the Papal Government.

The work, which is rendered more ornamental and complete by a vignette title-page from the Inferno of Dante, and a small print of the Last Judgment by Bartolozzi, is also accompanied by letter-press, briefly explanatory of the picture, and the leading principles of Michael Angelo as a painter; and the engravings are intended to illustrate those principles. Proof sets seven guineas.

Printed for the author, No. 7, Weymouth-street, Portland-place; Robinsons, Paternoster-row; and Edwards, Pall-mall.

Iron Bridge over the Thames.

This very curious print is now delivered to subscribers at two guineas each, at Mr. Taylor's, Holborn; Mr. Ackermann's, Strand, &c. The view is taken from the Surry end of the present London Bridge. The plate is four feet long, and two feet wide, and besides the new bridge, comprehends the principal objects of the Cities of London and Westminster, from Bow Church to Whitehall; also the proposed wharfs and terraces on each side of the river; engraved by two artists whose talents are well known to the public. The bridge by Mr. Lowry, and the other parts by Mr. Malton.

Mr. Bryan of Pall-mall, having had permission to attend Mr. Robit's famous collection of pictures at Paris, has purchased the celebrated *chefs d'œuvre* of Morillio, representing the Good Shepherd, and St. John with the Lamb; together with other distinguished objects in that celebrated assemblage; and they are now added to his other collection, and exhibiting for sale by private contract, at his Gallery, No. 88, Pall-mall, and at the Great-room, No. 118, near Carleton-house. Admission to both rooms, half a-crown.

ACCOUNT OF DISEASES IN LONDON, *from Oct 20, to Nov. 20.*

Admitted under the Care of the Physicians of the Finsbury Dispensary.

	No. of Cases.		
ASTHENIA	11	Ascites, and Anasarca	19
Hœmoptysis	5	Febris intermittens	[illegible]
Dysenteria	13	Hysteria	[illegible]
Diarrhœa	18	Angina	4
Typhus	9	Cynanche Trachealis	2
Catarrhus	42	Dyspnœa	10
Vermes	7	Scorbutus	3
Amenorrhœa	12	Scabies	6
Menorrhagia	5	Scarlatina	2
Rheumatismus	7	Tussis	12
Epilepsia	2	Paralysis	13

Diarrhoeas

Diarrhoeas and Dysenteries have prevailed in an unusual degree during the last two or three months; but nothing worthy of remark has occurred either in the symptoms of these diseases, or in the mode of treating them. Typhus has likewise been widely propagated, but has by no means shewn that alarming virulence and malignity which committed such frightful ravages for a considerable period previous to the publication of the last report from the Finsbury Dispensary. It is to be hoped, from the already ameliorated and still ameliorating condition of the poor, that this fever will long continue more innocent, as well as contracted in its influence.

A large proportion of the diseases inserted in the above catalogue were gradually induced by habits of spirituous intemperance. Punishment, in some cases, treads instantly on the heels of transgression; in others, with more tardy, although equally certain, steps, it pursues the commission of moral irregularity.

During the course of a long-protracted career of intemperance, the malignant power of alkohol, slow and insidious in its operation, is gnawing incessantly at the root, and often, without spoiling the bloom, or seeming to impair the vigour of the frame, is silently hastening the period of its inevitable destruction.

In connection with this remark it may not appear unseasonable to suggest an objection against the too general employment of *Tinctures* in cases of disease. They have a direct tendency to destroy the powers of digestion, and to induce the future necessity of artificial stimulation.

Tinctures are *medical drams*—the habitual use of them can be regarded only as a more *specious* and *decorous* mode of debauchery. A lady of fashion and delicacy may in this way most effectually ruin her health, without in the slightest degree impairing her reputation. She may quell the qualms of the stomach, without the inconvenience of inducing any qualms of conscience.

However, it should be remarked, that there are instances in which stimuli may be useful in deducting from the operation of causes still more injurious and more rapidly fatal in their effects.

When, for instance, pain, either corporeal or mental, has arrived at a certain pitch, wine, brandy, or laudanum, although they should always with caution, may sometimes with propriety be prescribed; as, by affording temporary relief, they spare, for a time at least, the wear and tear that is occasioned by too acute and violent emotion. Such aseasonable use of them may perhaps, upon the whole, be regarded as a *saving* to the constitution. Likewise it is a thing that cannot too deeply be impressed upon the mind of the medical practitioner, that whenever a patient expresses an excessively violent appetite, which, from his never having experienced it before, appears clearly to have been *created* by the disease, it ought universally to be regarded as indicating what is subservient to his cure.

As in the lower animals, which are constitutionally deficient in reason, instinct supplies its place; so during the time that the mental power in man is in some measure impaired by disease, Nature uniformly provides him also with a *temporary* instinct, still more sure in its dictate than the reasoning faculty.

Owing to a neglect, as there was every reason to suppose, of this important medical maxim, the reporter has recently lost a young patient, whose character gave to her life an almost incalculable value. Her youth made her death more deeply sorrowful and affecting.

The pale and yellow leaf may fall in autumn unnoticed upon the ground, but it is not without sensation that we regard the vernal flower torn up by the roots or its early blossom withered by the blast.

A person, for some time past, has been under the care of the Dispensary, who, from a morbid visceral affection, has, for upwards of four years, been liable, with short intervals, to fits of the most excessive agony.

The manner in which this poor creature speaks of his excruciating feelings excites horror, without giving any reason to doubt the fidelity and rigid accuracy of his representation.

No limit can be assigned to the possible exacerbation of suffering.—As, by the application of a certain force, all the matter of this vast globe might be compressed within the compass of a nutshell; so it is not out of the reach of possibility that the sensations of a thousand years may in some cases be condensed even into the space of a single instant.

In a report published about two years ago, the case of a young woman * was mentioned,

* Mr. Bartlett, the apothecary of the Finsbury Dispensary, from having repeatedly attended the patient, would, if required, be able to give a more satisfactory and particular account of this very curious and singular case.

mentioned, who had been confined to her bed for nearly twelve years, in a state of apparent insensibility; she has not indeed lost the power of feeling altogether, although she seems to have almost entirely lost the power of expressing it; the presence of the medical attendant seems to excite an ineffectual struggle for utterance—still she remains in the same melancholy condition. Her mind is as it were kept in a *state of preservation* by being for so long a time *locked up* from the agency of external objects. It is not *time* that destroys life, it is *sensation*. Every single impression that is made upon the body or the mind takes something from the original fund of vitality. Other circumstances being the same, the less a person feels the longer will he live. The disease of this patient was first occasioned by a fall upon her head, that produced a pressure, probably an effusion, upon the brain.

Medicine in such a case as this can be of no avail; the only chance of recovery would arise from the performance of a painful and dangerous surgical operation. —Her countenance is evidently phthisical; —a physiognomy that is in general, especially in females, more than commonly interesting and attractive.

The qualities which it is delightful to contemplate it is not always desirable to possess! Those exquisite charms that are felt by lovers, and are celebrated by poets, and the splendor of that genius which in man dazzles and delights, both touch alike on the confine of disease. Beauty is allied to phthisis—wit is almost contiguous to insanity. J. R.

STATE OF PUBLIC AFFAIRS,
In November, 1801.

FRANCE.

THE peace has undoubtedly been not less popular in France than in England: of this an unequivocal proof is the favourable reception given to an English minister. Lord Cornwallis was conducted to Boulogne from Calais by Ferrand, General of Brigade, commanding on the coast of the department of Calais, at the head of a numerous escort. His excellency invited Ferrand to supper at Boulogne. His lordship slept one night at Amiens, at the house taken for him during his residence at the Congress. About two posts from Paris, Lord Cornwallis was met by Mr. Merry, with whom he entered Paris in his chariot and four. The other carriages followed, escorted by one hundred and fifty of the finest hussars in the French service. The Parisians had previous notice of his arrival, and the streets were lined with people.

The French fête in honour of the peace took place on the 9th of November at Paris, with all the brilliancy that was to be expected. On the Pont Neuf was raised a magnificent triumphal arch. Opposite to the port of St. Nicholas was a temple dedicated to Commerce, and built on boats tied together and boarded over. Fire-works were let off from boats placed by the side of this temple. The arches on the Pont Neuf were covered with circular frames, loaded with variegated lamps. The elegant baths of Vigier added to this illumination a picturesque effect. Farther on appeared the Altar of the Invalids, at the gate of which had been raised a triumphal arch, decorated with antique crowns. From the basement was hung a globe, bespangled with stars; and a frame, placed above the key-stone of the arch, exhibited in letters of fire, of prodigious dimension, the name of *Bonaparte*. Four Pyramids were displayed along the front.—Near the *Place de Concorde* an immense Theatre was constructed, on which was elevated the Temple of Peace, the same which was raised on the 14th of July, on one of the squares of the interior of the *Champs Elysées*. It was supported by ninety-four columns of the Ionic order, disposed in a right angle of ten to sixteen. Two other temples, on a smaller scale, were erected beside that of Peace. On both sides of the grand alley of the Thuilleries were raised arcades, with their sub-basements. The octagonal bason was illuminated in all its circumference.

On the morning of the fête an appropriate proclamation was issued by the Chief Consul.

From Berlin it was reported about the beginning of November, that, in consequence of the restoration of Peace betwixt Great Britain and France, the motives which led to the possession of Hanover no longer existing, his Majesty had agreed immediately to evacuate that electorate. In consequence of this resolution, orders were to be forwarded without delay to the commander of the Prussian troops to with-

draw

draw from the Hanoverian territories. According to the same accounts, the Courts of London and Berlin were likely to enter on negociations for the removal of every difference which might for the present exist.

SWITZERLAND.

The discussions on the new Constitution of Switzerland commenced at Berne on the 29th of September; and the following articles were accepted by a majority of 60 voices against 16:—

First, the integrity of Helvetia is a fundamental article of the Helvetic Constitution. Second, the Helvetic Republic forms only one State, its territory is divided into Cantons. Third, there is one right of Helvetic Citizenship; there are no political rights of citizens relative to distinct cantons.

The question relative to the cession of the territories of the Valais was likewise discussed, and after a long debate it was resolved by 34 voices against 7—"That the whole canton of Valais should appertain to Helvetia, and not be ceded unless France should take possession of it by force."

On the 31st of September the Diet came to the following resolution:—"The supreme power shall be exercised by a Diet and a Senate, in the name of the Helvetic people." The Paris papers, however, to the 4th of November assert, that the Helvetic Diet has been dissolved just after it had completed the Constitution, and appointed the members to the Senate. All its proceedings have been declared null, and the old Legislative Body, taking the reins of government into their hands, have appointed a Provisional Executive Government, and restored the Constitution agreed to in May last.

Accounts from Berne state that the antient Swiss cantons, Uri, Schweitz, and Underwalden, have sent a deputation to Paris, to conjure the First Consul, by the names of Tell and Winelreld, to protect them in their antient constitution, under which alone they can enjoy tranquillity and happiness. The accounts from the same place of the 7th of November state, that the greater part of the members of the Diet have returned to their homes. The public tranquillity has not any where been disturbed. The Helvetic troops have already quitted the small cantons. They are on their return to Lucerne. The Helvetic Senate is constituted, and Dolder is appointed president.

BATAVIAN REPUBLIC.

The Batavian Council of Regency have elected the new Legislative Body, almost all of whom belonged to the former Legislation. They are to proceed immediately to the organization of the inferior departments of the government. This change of constitution continues to be received with complete apathy.

WEST INDIES.

Citizen Vincent, chief of brigade, and director of the corps of Engineers at St. Domingo, arrived at Paris in the beginning of October. He was the bearer of many letters from Toussaint L'Ouverture, and an official copy of the constitution that was transmitted for the approbation of the parent country. This plan was within a few days to be submitted to the consideration of the Council of State. Citizen Vincent gives the most satisfactory details of the state of cultivation in the colony.

EGYPT.

Official accounts came from Egypt on the 14th of November, with the final account of the conquest of that country, which, although from the event of peace, not so interesting as they would formerly have been, will be read with satisfaction, as the termination of an expedition, which, however disgraceful to the late ministers, from the unnecessary and dishonorable rupture of the treaty of El-Arish, has been honorable to the British arms.

GREAT BRITAIN.

The Parliament commenced its Session on Thursday, the 29th of November, and the King was sufficiently recovered to attend its opening in person. The import of the Speech from the Throne was nearly as follows:—His Majesty had the satisfaction to inform the Parliament, that the important Negotiations in which he was engaged at the close of the last Session were brought to a favourable conclusion. The differences with the Northern Powers have been adjusted by a Convention with the Emperor of Russia, to which the kings of Denmark and Sweden had expressed their readiness to accede. The essential rights for which this country contended were hereby secured: Preliminaries of Peace had also been ratified between him and the French Republic; and he trusted that this important Arrangement, whilst it manifested the justice and moderation of his views, would also be found conducive to the interests of this country, and honorable to the British character. He then addressed the gentlemen of the House of Commons and said, he had directed such estimates to be prepared for the various demands of the public service, as appeared to him to be best adapted to to the situation in which the country was now placed. It was painful to him to reflect, that provision could not be made for defraying the expences which must unavoidably be continued for different parts of the world, and for maintaining an adequate peace establishment, without large additional supplies.

He finally addressed himself to both Houses of Parliament and said, "I cannot sufficiently describe the gratification and comfort I derive from the relief which the bounty of Divine Providence has afforded to my people, by the abundant produce of the late harvest. In contemplating the situation of the country at this important conjuncture, it is impossible for me to refrain from expressing the deep sense I entertain of the temper and fortitude which have been manifested by all descriptions of my faithful subjects, under the various and complicated difficulties with which they have had to contend." After paying the politest compliments to his forces both by sea and land, he concluded with wishing "That his people may experience the reward they have so well merited, in a full enjoyment of the blessings of peace—in a progressive increase of the national commerce, credit, and resources, and above all, in the undisturbed possession of their religion, laws, and liberties, under the safeguard and protection of that Constitution, which it has been the great object of all our efforts to preserve, and which it is our most sacred duty to transmit unimpaired to our descendants."

Lorh Bolton, in the House of Lords, moved the address, which contained no material deviation from the speech. Lord Lifford seconded the address, which he had no doubt would meet their lordship's unanimous consent. He contrasted the happy and flourishing situation of this country at this moment with that in which it was when they last met.

The Duke of Bedford gave the address his hearty concurrence—he all along wished for peace, and now that it was made, he received it with the most cordial satisfaction. He could not, however, agree with the noble lords who had spoken as to the fitness of the time. There hardly had been a period during the war in which it would not have been at least as fit and as practicable. In this however, no blame was attached to the *present* ministers, who had negotiated and effected a peace with all the alacrity in their power. He hoped now that with peace, the Constitution of which the people had been so long deprived, would be restored to them, and a due attention paid to their rights and liberties.

On the next day copies of the Convention between his Britannic Majesty and the Emperor of Russia, signed at St. Petersburgh the 17th of June last, and of the Preliminary Articles of Peace between his Britannic Majesty and the French Republic were laid upon the table.

Lord Pelham gave notice, that he would on Tuesday move, that the Preliminaries of Peace, with the Republic of France be taken into consideration, and his lordship moved, that the lords be summoned for that day.

Mr. Vansittart, in the House of Commons on the 2d of November, rose and observed that from the abundance of the late harvest, and other circumstances, it appeared unnecessary to continue the restrictions on distilling. He therefore moved that a committee be appointed to consider of the expediency of discontinuing the late Acts of Parliament respecting the importation of foreign starch, the distillation of home spirit from melasses only, and the prohibition of distilling the same from corn. Ordered.

The order of the day being read in the House of Lords on November the 3d, Lord Romney, after a pertinent speech, moved, "That an humble address be presented to his Majesty, to thank him for his gracious condescension in ordering a copy of the Preliminaries of Peace to be laid before them," &c. Lord Limerick seconded the motion.

Earl Spencer regretted that he felt himself obliged to deliver sentiments in opposition to the two noble lords who moved and seconded the address; and he particularly regretted feeling himself called upon to oppose a government, composed of men with whom he had so long acted, and with some of whom it had been the pride of his life to maintain the strongest friendship. Peace, abstractedly, was doubtless a blessing; a safe and honourable peace was the end of every legitimate war—had that now been obtained? No; we had sacrificed every thing. In every part of the world we had ceded to France or her allies the conquests our fleets and armies had gallantly atchieved. The integrity of the dominions of the Porte, it was true, had been preserved, but this had been the result of the glorious campaign in Egypt. The integrity of the dominions of Portugal was also in the Preliminaries stated to be preserved, but we find this in fact to be the integrity of a part. The important province of Olivenza was to be ceded.

Our faithful ally the Prince of Orange was not even named in the treaty. In vain did we look for the objects of the war—*indemnity* for the past and security for the future.—The only indemnity was the settlements of Ceylon and Trinidad; certainly altogether inadequate. In India we had, by the gallantry and enterprise of our armies, reduced Tippoo Saib, and extinguished the danger of the enemy. But look at this treaty. By ceding the Cape of Good Hope and part of Cochin, you give an opening again to the coast of Malabar, while in South America by the treaty with Portugal the enemy was to have a military post at the mouth of the River of Amazons, which would be fatal to our possessions in the east. We had surrendered the valuable island of Martinique. In the Mediterranean we had surrendered every thing. In short, in a peace so unequal, he could only see a short truce. By such a peace the French had been able to give eclat to those dangerous principles upon which he and the other noble lords had been ridiculed. It was said that it was the interest of France to preserve peace; how do we know that? Who can see what will be the interest of an usurper?

The Duke of Clarence expressed his entire approbation of the peace, as safe, honorable and becoming.

Lord Pelham entered into a detailed justification of the terms of peace, and a comparison between it and the *projet* given in by the late ministers in 1797.

Lord Grenville said it would have covered his heart with joy had the *great* objects for which we had been struggling, and to which the best part of *his life* had been devoted, been obtained. His lordship then described the situation of France and Great Britain at the time of peace being signed. We were in a situation of the highest prosperity. In the West Indies we had every thing except St. Domingo. In the East we had an absolute dominion France, on the other hand, had attained inordinate power on the continent of Europe; but the British conquests in the other parts of the world were surely such as to enable us to command equivalents for the sacrifices we made. His lordship then followed nearly the arguments of Earl Spencer.

Lord Grenville was followed by the Lord Chancellor, Lord Rawdon, Lord Warwick, Lord Mulgrave, the Bishop of London, the Bishop of Rochester (who, though a Minister of the Gospel of Peace, voted against the peace) and Earl Fitzwilliam.

After this Lord St. Vincent rose to take notice of an expression which had fallen from a noble lord for whom he had the highest respect and esteem. That noble lord (Earl Spencer) had said that the Preliminaries on the table were attended with circumstances of humiliation and disgrace to this country. His lordship denied that any thing like either attached to them. The preliminaries he was convinced, were equally honorable and advantageous to this country; and the share he had the honour to have had in advising their being acceded to, he should ever consider as the pride of his life.

Lord Nelson rose to speak a few words respecting a point, in regard to which no one of their lordships could, perhaps, speak with more information than himself. With regard to Malta, that island, when the noble earl sent him down the Mediterranean, was in the hands of the French, and on his return from the battle of Aboukir he thought it his first object to blockade it, because he deemed it an invaluable piece of service during the then state of affairs in Egypt, to rescue it from the hands of the French. In any other point of view, he could assure their lordships, that Malta was of no sort of consequence to this country; it lay at two great a distance from Toulon, to serve as a station to watch the fleets of the French that put to sea from that port.

The Marquis of Buckingham expressed the pain he felt at being obliged not to give a silent vote, but at that late hour to have occasion to rise. He lamented sincerely that he could not give his consent to the Preliminaries on the table, because he thought them highly humiliating and disgraceful to this country.

The Earl of Carnarvon assigned his reasons for not concurring in the motion for approving the Preliminaries. His lordship declared he should vote against the motion.

The question being then put from the woolsack, the house divided—Contents 94. Proxies 20. Non-contents 10. Proxies 0.

In the House of Commons, on the same day, Sir Edmund Hartop moved, and Mr. Leigh seconded, an address to his Majesty.

Lord Hawkesbury, after some prefatory remarks, expatiated on the benefits resulting to the nation from the restoration of peace. He then went more particularly into the subject, calling the attention of the House to the peculiar circumstances under which his Majesty's Ministers had brought about the treaty. The government of the French Republic had been so changed, that Jacobinism was no longer talked of, and every thing at present was so ordered in that country, as to give a rational ground to expect permanency and stability to whatever engagements they might enter into. The terms of the treaty were both honourable to our allies and safe to the country. The great object of the war was to prevent the introduction of the pernicious principles that were then prevalent in France; these principles being now materially changed, the necessity of continuing the contest no longer remained. In this struggle, however, two coalitions had totally failed, and incalculable blood and treasure had been expended. England, deserted by Austria, Russia, and Prussia, and left to combat with the whole world, had concluded a treaty of peace both honourable and safe. At the same time he was by no means of opinion that France could have injured this country. In the situation in which things were, being unable to save Europe entire, as it was before the revolution, was it not better we should, by entering into terms with France, secure what we could? His Lordship then took a view of the comparative state of France and England, and the advantages which must result to our commerce by the cession of Ceylon and Trinidad, and concluded by saying, that a reconciliation had been happily effected, and he prayed to God it might be for the country's good.

Mr. T. Grenville rose to oppose the terms of peace, and in doing so he would not lull the people into a false repose, nor be deterred from speaking his sentiments, however unpopular they might be; but would plainly and explicitly declare, that by the treaty he considered this country entirely ruined!!! The system of vigour long carried on by this nation, but now fatally laid aside, was the only way to secure our independence as a nation. With respect to this being an honourable peace, a slight view of its terms would clearly prove the reverse. He then took a view of the terms of the treaty, and concluded with saying, let the peace be carried into execution—let the cession be completed, and he would ask what chance England had that she would not, within eighteen months, again be plunged into war, after she had laid up her ships, and discharged her army and navy, when France might seize on her military posts, and, combining with the maritime powers of the North, sweep her seas before she could get a ship afloat.

Lord Castlereagh then rose, and defended the preliminaries against the attacks of the last speaker. He maintained that the terms were both safe and honourable, and that had we continued the war, we probably should not, at the end of several years, have been able to procure better.

Lord Temple followed on the opposite side, and condemned the peace in the most unqualified terms. He asked Lord Hawkesbury how he, who had boasted that he would dictate a peace at the point of the bayonet, could sign, in the capital of his own country, such a disgraceful capitulation?

Mr. Banks highly approved of the preliminaries, and after eloquently supporting his opinion, concluded by giving the Address his hearty support.

Mr. Pitt said, that since the coalition of the Continental powers was dissolved, the question of peace or war had become only a question of terms. Whatever might be our wishes, nothing remained for us but to obtain just and honourable conditions for ourselves and the few allies that remained to us. By the preliminaries now submitted to the consideration of the House, we had not gained every thing, but the difference between the terms we had obtained and those we had a right to expect, was not to be compared with the evils resulting from the continuance of the contest. We did not materially want an extension of territory, but, retaining those parts of our conquests unattached to our ancient possessions, our grand object was to add fresh security to our maritime strength and commercial greatness. In the East and West Indies we had got all we had a right to expect, and any acquisitions in the Mediterranean were comparatively of less consequence. He confessed he was sorry we did not retain Malta, and still more so that that place was not more particularly specified in the treaty; but if we were to give it up, he did not know we could better dispose of it. Mr. Pitt then went into a long defence of the preliminaries; and with regard to the Consular Government, he said he wished to banish all harsh language, all acrimonious epithets, all irritating allusions. It would be hypocrisy in him to deny, that all his opinions with regard to personal merits and demerits had undergone a change, but if a laudable line of conduct be in future pursued by the First Consul, he was afraid it would be dictated by interest more than principle. He had no difficulty in saying, that though he never considered the restoration of Monarchy in France as a *sine qua non*, he thought it would have been a happy

happy thing for France and all Europe, and he thought so still. He sought not to disguise from all the world his regret at the disappointment of his hopes. Happy would he have been to have put together the fragments of a venerable edifice so cruelly scattered. We had, however, succeeded in the demolition of Jacobinism; at least we see it stripped of the delusive colour, which gave it its chief power of distinction. Mr. Pitt then enumerated the advantages we had gained in the Union with Ireland, by our naval and military reputation, and the consolidation of our Indian Empire; and after predicting to the country, if it was true to itself, a long train of prosperity and happiness, concluded by giving his hearty assent to the motion.

Mr. Fox said he never in his life gave a vote more cordially than he did in favour of the treaty of peace. It was an honourable peace; if it was not glorious it was no wonder; no peace could be glorious unless founded on a glorious war, which was by no means an epithet that could be given to the late one. If Ministers could, without risk, have obtained better terms, they were certainly blameable in not doing so; but was this the case? No. In continuing the war we incurred a certain expence, and every day our situation was rendered worse. Ceylon and Trinidad were both valuable acquisitions. The situation in which the Cape was placed in the preliminaries was better for this country than if we ourselves retained it; we should have all the advantages without the expence.* The loss of Malta was rather to be regretted. The Ministers had acted with dignity in acceding to a peace, while they were still able to carry on the war. Let the gentlemen consider not merely the financial loss, the lives sacrificed, but the misery to which, for two years, the people of this country had been reduced. The fall in the price of the necessaries of life since the peace, unexpected as it was, had shown the effect which the war had in enhancing the price of every article of consumption. Some regretted that the peace was glorious to France. If peace could be glorious to the French Republic without being dishonourable to this country, it would not give him any concern that it should be so. The object of the war was the restoration of the accursed House of Bourbon, and to him it was a recommendation of the peace that this object had failed. Had that project succeeded, it must have been attended with the most fatal effects to the general liberties of mankind. To the people of this country it must have been attended by the most deplorable consequences. It was true that Egypt had been recovered by the unexampled gallantry of our troops, but who was so fond of military glory as to wish to purchase it without necessity? Egypt might have been our's by the capitulation of El-Arish. But it was said at that moment that we were to *pause!* We did pause, and the pause cost us seventy-three millions of money, besides the lives of thousands. The noble Lord said, that the danger of French principles were extinct, and that we had only to dread the power of the Republic. Undoubtedly no man felt more strongly than he did the misfortune to England and Europe, from the unsatisfactory state of the Continent; but it was not the peace, but the war, that had produced so fatal an aggrandizement. It was the measures of the Right Hon. Gentleman (Mr. Pitt) which had excited an irresistible spirit in France—a spirit of proud independence. All men were fired with devotion to their country, and the thoughts of independence inspired an energy which nothing could subdue. With respect to the future, he was of opinion, that to enjoy the blessings of peace small establishments were necessary. It was in commercial resources that we were to counterbalance the aggrandizement of France. The French Revolution was calculated to divert men's attentions more eagerly to the question of liberty. But was that to be opposed by the sword? Mr. Fox then made some remarks on the Government of France, and commented, with some severity, on the observations of Lord Castlereagh, who had said, that Ireland had been treated with a delicate hand: Mr. Fox contended, that the conflagrations, whippings, &c. in the year 1797, deserved a very different character. He concluded by saying, that if the common law was restored in the room of martial-law, in Ireland; if the Habeas Corpus Act was put in force, he should rejoice.

Lord Folkstone said a few words; and Mr. Windham rose and said, he still retained his former opinions. The question was then put and carried without a division.

The Chancellor of the Exchequer on the next day moved the order of the day for the House to go into a Committee of Supply. The House went into a Committee,

* This our readers will recollect was exactly our own sentiment.

mittee, and Sir William Elliot moved, that 130,000 men be granted for the sea-service for three months, commencing on the 3d of January, 1802, and ending on the 3d of April; in which number was included 30,000 marines. That 740,000l. be granted for victualling the same, at the rate of 1l. 18s. per man per month, for the same period. That 721,500l. be granted for wages for the same at the rate of 1l. 17s. per man per month, for the same period. That 240,604l. be granted for the ordinaries of the navy for the same period. That 97,500l. be granted for the ordinaries of the service for the same period, at the rate of 5l. per month per man. That 1,180,000l. be granted for the same period, for wear and tear, at the rate of 3l. per month per man."—Agreed to. The Chairman then asked leave report progress and sit again.—Agreed to.

Sir William Hartop brought up the Report of the Committee on the Address.

Mr. Windham said, he had not departed from those opinions which it was well known he held in opposition to the treaty: all he heard on the subject only tended to root them more strongly in his mind. The result of the debate of last night was, that we were in the power of France; that France had the power, but we hoped not the will, to crush us; that we were in the paw of the lion, but he not being hungry, did not tear us to pieces, and we were happy to see him turn about and lie down. This was the real state of the case, and he was sorry to find it so.

Doctor Lawrence said, he had entertained a hope that the dangers of the peace would be farther removed from us; but this hope vanished when he saw the Marquis Cornwallis sent, bound hand and foot, to Amiens. He would not hesitate to assert, that no treaty had ever been made that was not infinitely preferable to those articles in question. The Chancellor of the Exchequer, the Secretary at War, and several other members spoke in strong terms of approbation of the peace. After which the report was agreed to without a division.

Both Houses, on the 6th of November, went in state to St. James's, and presented Addresses on the preliminaries of peace, to which his Majesty returned gracious answers. The House of Lords adjourned till Tuesday; the House of Commons to Monday.

On the 10th of November Lord Hobart, after a speech highly complimentary to General Hutchinson and his army, moved "That the Thanks of the House be given to Lieutenant General Sir John Hely Hutchinson, K. B. for his eminent services in Egypt."

Lord Nelson, Lord Pelham, and the Duke of Clarence, successively spoke in favour of the motion, delivering the highest eulogiums on General Hutchinson and his troops. The motion was then put and carried unanimously.

The important debate which occupied the attention of the House on the 13th of November was upon the subject of the Northern Convention. Like the preliminaries with France, it is a compromise with which every one may be pleased, but of which no man can be proud. A war with the Northern Powers is itself an evil of such extreme magnitude, and so truly to be deprecated, and more especially if brought upon ourselves by a too rigid adherence to demands, in themselves questionable, if not in several instances impolitic and unjust, that any Convention which prevents such a calamity must be heartily approved by every friend to the peace and happiness of mankind. By this Convention we have secured enough for every proper purpose of marine advantage and dignity, but it has by no means secured to this nation all the haughty and pre-eminent terms which were at first contended for, and is obviously formed upon the basis of the treaty of the Armed Neutrality, which was drawn up in express opposition to the interests of this country.

In the course of the debate Lord Grenville expressed his disapprobation of some of the leading articles of the Convention, which he contended were injurious to the maritime and commercial interests of this country, inasmuch as we had renounced several important points, which he asserted, by the law of nations, we had a right to maintain. Some of the stipulations in the Convention were loosely and vaguely worded, so as to require explanation or amendment. This he hoped Ministers would do, now that the communication with all the parts of the Continent was completely open. The Lord Chancellor, Lord Holland, Lord Mulgrave, and Lord Nelson, all spoke in favour of the Address, and the question was carried without a division.

In the House of Commons Lord Temple wished to know, whether the Courts of Denmark and Sweden had agreed to the Convention. Lord Hawkesbury replied, that he had a communication with the Ambassadors of those Courts, who assured him that their respective Sovereigns were

were ready to give their concurrence, which he expected hourly. Mr. Grey was of opinion that Ministers had acted judiciously, in the state matters were in, to make a compromise rather than carry the business farther; but he thought it rather unparliamentary to call for unqualified approbation, without any official documents from Sweden and Denmark. The favourable termination of the business he attributed to the death of the Emperor Paul. He concluded by saying, that notwithstanding the observations he made, it was not his intention to oppose the Address.

Lord Temple and Lord Hawkesbury severally spoke, the former against, the latter in favour of the Convention. Lord Glenbervie, Sir W. Scott, Mr. Sturges, and Mr. Newbold, were in favour of the Address, as well as Mr. Erskine, who said, he placed the fullest confidence in the measures of the present Government. Mr. Tierney was in favour of the Address. He approved of the measures of his Majesty's Ministers, and said, this was a golden gleam of that happiness we were encouraged to expect from the restoration of peace. The question was, after a long debate, carried without a division.

Mr. Vansittart, on Saturday, the 14th of November, brought up the report of the Committee of Supply. The several resolutions were read and agreed to.

Mr. Tierney moved for leave to bring in a Bill to repeal an Act passed in the last Session of Parliament, rendering it penal for bakers to sell, or expose to sale, bread that had not been baked twenty-four hours. He observed, that the Bill had been brought in to answer a temporary purpose, arising from the scarcity of corn, which now, by the bounty of Providence, in sending us a plentiful harvest, no longer existed. The Act had a fortnight to run, but it would nevertheless be a considerable relief to a number of industrious and honest bakers, who might have infringed its provisions under the idea that the cause had ceased, if it was immediately repealed: he wished, therefore, that it should have a retrospective operation from last Monday. The Secretary at War said, he was too well convinced of the motives of the Hon. Gentleman to doubt the propriety of adopting a measure he recommended; but he wished to suggest, whether, as rights of actions might have already accrued, it would not be unjust towards those who had commenced them to give the Bill a retrospective operation. He thought it would be better if the Bill took effect from the day of giving the notice.

Mr. Tierney said, he would wish to consult with his friends upon the subject. —Leave was given to bring in the Bill. The Revenue Bills on the Table were forwarded in their respective stages.

The House resolved itself into a Committee of Ways and Means on the 16th of November, Mr. Bragge in the Chair. The Chancellor of the Exchequer said, the House had determined, for wise and prudent reasons, to continue for three months our naval and military establishments the same as they were during the preceding year. It was therefore become necessary to provide the ways and means for carrying into effect the intentions and vote of Parliament.

In the Supply the following sums were voted:—

	£.
Army	2,382,625
Navy	3,562,000
Ordnance	400,000
Miscellaneous Services	200,000
Army of Ireland and Ordnance	610,000
Making in the whole near 7,000,000	

The Land and Malt produced 2,750,000l. for the purpose of meeting part of the demand.

In providing the Ways and Means there were three modes that offered themselves to his consideration. First, an issue of Exchequer Bills to be superadded to those already outstanding. Secondly, that of a short loan. And thirdly, to fund the Exchequer Bills now afloat. The second consideration he rejected, because was aware that two loans in the same year operated to the injury of the public funds, as the payments clashed continually, and would consequently occasion their depression. The outstanding Exchequer Bills amounted to 8,500,000l. of these 2,300,000l. were held by the Bank, and the remainder were in the hands of private individuals.

On the 11th of November the terms agreed upon between the Chancellor of the Exchequer and the Committee appointed to wait upon him that day, for settling the terms of funding 8,500,000l. of Exchequer Bills, were as follow, viz.

For each 100l. of principal, the holders are to receive the undermentioned sums of stock, which are estimated at the following prices:—

£.		£.	s.	d.
25	Consols at 68¾	17	1	10½
25	Reduced at 67¾	16	16	10½
25	New 5 per Cents. at 99	24	15	0
50	Four per Cents. at 84¾	42	7	6
0 1 9	Long Annuities at 19⅛	1	14	4
		£.102	15	7

The

The proprietors are to have the option of subscribing 50l. additional for every 100l. bill to be applied to redeeming the sum of about 2,300,000l. bills held by the Bank of England.

The bills to be carried to the Exchequer on or before the 24th of November, and the interest to be calculated to the day, and paid in money.

The deposit of 25l. per cent. on the additional 50l. for each 100l. Exchequer bill, to be paid at the time of leaving the bills for payment, 25l. per cent on the 18th of December, and the remaining 50l. per cent. on the 15th of January. Such is the bargain that Mr. Addington has made. He has funded the bills on terms which bear an interest of 4l. 16s. 9d. The new stock of all kinds created is 10,625,000l. And the long annuity for 59 years will be 7,437l. 10s. The interest due upon the bills is to be paid in money when they are delivered into the Exchequer; and the dividends on the new funded stock are to be paid at the respective periods of the several stocks. The house adjourned until next day.

Monday the 9th of November being Lord Mayor's day, was celebrated with unusual magnificence. Sir John Eamer, notwithstanding "these piping times of peace," thought it his duty as a soldier, to revive the custom of exhibiting a man in armour; and to improve on ancient custom, three others in armour accompanied him on foot. A dragoon undertook to be the champion, and he was fitted with the armour of William the Conqueror from the Tower. Sir John's corps likewise attended to do him honour. The dinner was sumptuous, and had every justice done to it by the numerous guests. The late Lord Mayor was received by the people with just and well-earned marks of affection. They took the horses from his carriage at Blackfriar's-bridge, and drew him to Guildhall. They paid the same mark of respect to his independent and popular predecessor, alderman Combe, whose horses they also took out, and drew him in state to the hall.

Citizen Otto and Mr. Addington were received with the most rapturous bursts of applause. Neither Mr. Pitt, Mr. Windham, Lord Grenville, nor Mr. Dundas attended to experience the reception which their conduct deserves.

Alphabetical List *of* Bankruptcies *and* Dividends *announced between the 20th of Oct. and the 20th of Nov. extracted from the London Gazettes.*

BANKRUPTCIES.

(The Solicitors' Names are between Parentheses)

AITKIN, James, Castle street, Leicester fields, print seller. (Hill, Rood lane)
Atfield, John, late of Red Lion street, Clerkenwell. (Yother, Rane Savage, Old Broad street)
Atherton, Robert, Latchford, Chester, tanner. (Hilton, Manchester)
Andrews, George, Holybourne, Hants, tanner. (Drew, Bermondsey street)
Allen, Theodore, Bath, fishmonger. (Becker, Clement's inn)
Bromwich, Joseph Haines, Birmingham, factor. (Whateley, Birmingham)
Binney, George, Mile-end, ship-owner. (Wawr, Mark lane)
Buchanan, John, Woolwich, pork butcher. (Owen and Battle, Bartlet's buildings)
Brock, John, jun. Wapping street, slopseller. (Wagener and Weil, Red Lion street, Wapping)
Bitter, Richard, Tetbury, and John Ireland, Culkerton, Wiltshire, corn dealers. (Pitt, Cirencester)
Blair, John, Lowman street, Ratcliff cross, mariner. (Sind, Prescott street)
Barnes, John, Bolton, cotton manufacturer. (Windle, Bartlet's buildings)
Cawthorn, George, British Library (late Bell), Strand, London, bookseller. (Thomas Lamb, Harper street, Red Lion square)
Craig, James, Lime street, merchant. (Leigh, Bridge street, Blackfriars)
Coalman, Abraham Hart, Leman street, merchant. (Wilson and Annesley, Finsbury square)
Cheyney, John, Oxford street, linen draper. (T. and T. Reeves, Angel court, Throgmorton street)
Cumming, John, Deptford, butcher. (Jones, Nag's Head court, Grace Church street)
Cobham, Elijah, Liverpool, merchant. (Ellames, Liverpool)
Crakes, John, White Horse lane, Stepney, coal merchant. (Harper, Cannon row, Westminster)
Deighton, John, Piccadilly, bookseller. (Wright and Bovill, Chancery lane)
Dwyer, James, Bristol, hatter. (Blandford and Sweet, Inner Temple)
Elft, William, Fleet street, warehouseman. (Kibblewhite, Gray's inn place)
Evans, Richard, City road, Middlesex, umbrella maker. (Swann and Wilkington, Ford street)
Evans, John, late of Wolverhampton, now of Liverpool, hardwareman. (Windle, Bartlet's buildings)
Furnell, James, Kentroad, fellmonger. (Drew, Bermondsey street)
Hodgson, Thomas, Liverpool, broker. (Edward Foulkes, Manchester)
Heachan, John, Liverpool, dealer in muslin. (Pennington, Liverpool)
Halliday, William, Watling street, warehouseman. (Palmer and Tomlinson, Warnford court)
Hefford, Joseph, Curtain road, Shoreditch, taylor. (Walton, Great Charter lane)
Humphreys, Evan, Temple street, Bristol, victualler, &c. (C. Meldin, Bristol)
Harvey, W. Liverpool, woollen draper. (Freeleton, Liverpool)
Henderson, Robert, Oxford street, fishmonger. (Orrell, Windley street)
James, Robert, Lydstone, Penryn, dealer. (George Chapman George, Penryn)
Jeayes, John, Aldersgate street, merchant. (Hall, Red Lion court, Fleet street)
Jead, William, Lamb street, Spital fields, baker. (Crosby, Dyer's buildings)
Kind, Peter, and William Smith, Southampton, linen drapers. (Leigh, New Bridge street)
King, George, Frome-Selwood, Somerset, cabinet maker. (Walthew, Lower Seymour street)
Leigh, Thomas, Foxdenton, Lancaster, dealer. (Low and Halsted, Manchester)
Ludley, William, Petworth, shopkeeper. (Pearce and Dixon, Paternoster row)
Miller, James, Hammersmith, wheelwright. (Williams, Bartlet's buildings)
Mitchell, Henry, Gosport, rope maker. (Lewis Young, Gosport)
Middleton, William, J. H. Pemberton, and George Felton, Liverpool, merchants. (Statham and Keen, Liverpool.
Mallalieu, George, Salford, cotton manufacturer. (Lowe and Halsted, Manchester)
Marshall, John, Little Russell street, Bermondsey, tanner. (Lee, Tanfield court, Temple)

Meycock,

Meyerick, James, Broad street, St. Giles's, haberdasher. (Weightman, Castle street, Holborn)
M'Carty, John, Liverpool, merchant. (Windle, Bartlet's buildings)
Newton, John, Manchester, check manufacturer. (G. and W. Nabb, Manchester)
Newton, J[illegible] by Lonsdale, Westmoreland, liquor merchant. ([illegible])
Nathan, [illegible], Houndsditch. (Lewell, Little Grov[illegible], Mayfair)
Ogden, James, [illegible] cotton spinner. (J. [illegible], Manchester)
Ort[illegible], Fred. [illegible] street, mathematical [illegible] maker. (Palmer, Doughty street, Foundling Hospital)
Pe[illegible], John Holland, Liverpool, merchant. (Ward, D[illegible] and Greaves, Covent garden)
Pheasant, Edward, Grantham, dealer. (Concanen, Coleman street)
Palmer, Mark, Monkwearmouth-shore, Durham, sail maker. (Nawn, Mark lane)
Quantril, Wm. William street, Shoreditch, carpenter. (Moore, Jauncey's court, Fleet street)
Rowlands, Edward, Coalbrooke dale, Salop, barge owner. (Morris, Newport)
Rookham, Ant. Bedminster, Somerset, baker. (B. and O. Smith, Bristol)
Rawley, Joseph, Chancery lane, boot and shoe maker. (Newcomb, Vine street, Piccadilly)
Ross, Henry, now or late of Liverpool, Co-partner with William Ross, of Washington, North Carolina. (Peter Maines, Liverpool)
Serle, John, Shepton Mallet, Somerset, clothier. (Henry Davis, Bristol)
Scott, John, and Francis Roach, Castle street, Leicester fields, linen drapers. (Parry, [illegible])
Shynn, Benjamin, late of [illegible], Essex, shopkeeper. (Henry Francis, [illegible] Office, Guildhall)
Strong, Edward, and William Hardy, Liverpool, anchorsmiths, &c. (George Rowe, Liverpool)
Shuttleworth, James, Manchester, cotton manufacturer. (Ellis, Cursitor street)
Serres, John Thomas, Wimpole street, bookseller. (Placer, Charles street, Cavendish square)
Simmonds, John, Canterbury, linen draper. (Brown, Little Friday street)
Stentaford, John, Plymouth Dock, shopkeeper. (Dutten and Anstice, Temple)
Tinson, Thomas, Fenchurch street, wine merchant. (Pulleus, Fore street)
Tayler, Joseph, and J. B. Marsh, Wigmore street, linen drapers. (Willett and A[illegible]ley, Finsbury square)
Tayler, Thomas, Birmingham, draper. (Smart, Staple's inn)
Tickens, John George, Queen row, Bethnal green, merchant. (Wybourn, Craig's court)
Tripp, John, Bristol, salesman. (Jenkins and James, New inn)
Tomlinson, John, Salford, Lancaster, weft and warp dealer (Hurd, Furnival's inn)
Tomkinson, Richard and John, and Daniel Fred. Bollcke, Liverpool, merchants. (Jerreis, Winsley street, Oxford street)
Tilstone, John, Newcastle, Staffordshire, hat manufacturer. (Poole, Newcastle)
Virtue, Timothy, Hammersmith, carpenter. (Hamilton, Berwick street)
Varley, Ingram, Wigan, shopkeeper. (Gaskell, Wigan)
Wall, Edward, Shrewsbury, innkeeper. (Bolfer, Kirby street)
Wallis, Joel, Tiverton, Somerset, baker. (J. Moon, Keynsham, Bristol)
Yeoman, William, Theobald's road, tallow chandler. (Pearce and Dixon, Paternoster row)

DIVIDENDS ANNOUNCED.

Auriol, Peter James, Devonshire square merchant, Dec. 5
Ayres, John, Old Broad street, broker, Dec. 12
Ansell, George, White Cross alley, watch spring maker, Dec. 8
Alderton, John, Robertsbridge, Sussex, dealer, Dec. 5.
Bennett, R. S. Houndsditch, hatter and hosier, Dec. 17
Bayley, William, Wakefield, ironmonger, Dec. 1
Butler, William, Holborn, tavern keeper, Nov. 21
Barry, John, Orchard street, Portman square, haberdasher, Nov. 28
Bartlet, James, Frome-Selwood, clothier, Dec. 14
Brydges, Theo. Colchester, innkeeper, Nov. 30
Bonnington, John, City road, umbrella maker, Dec. 19
Betts, William, William Peter Betts, and George Vestiar, Lambeth and Cheam, bocking manufacturers, December 1
Cooper, Thomas, Jun. Liverpool, horse dealer, Nov. 16
Curtis, J. Warwick street, Golden square, harness maker, Nov. 17
Collins, Robert, Jun. late of Union court, but now of Queen street, Lincoln's inn fields, Dec. 19 (final)
Churchill, William, Yeovilton, Somersetshire, maltster, Dec. 3
Cockett, Thomas, Peckham, baker, Dec. 8
Chauvet, Lewis, and Peter Turquand, Old Jewry, merchants, Dec. 17
Davies, William, Bartholomew close, linen draper, Dec. 5
Danson, George, Lancaster merchant, Nov. 27
Davies, John, Liverpool, dealer, Nov. 19
Denne, William, Canterbury, draper, Nov. 30
Elbridge, Charles, Cheltenham, victualler, Dec. 21
Fishwick, William, Whittle in the Woods, Lancaster, Nov. 25
Fugill, Joseph, Bristol, woollen draper, Nov. 23
Forch, [illegible], Abingdon street, wine merchant, Dec. 5
Foster, Christopher, Poultry, bookseller, Nov. 4
Fir[illegible], John, [illegible] Lambeth [illegible], Dec. 8
Gr[illegible], William, Wickham market, linen draper, Nov. 7
Ga[illegible], John, late of Whitechapel, [illegible], scrivener, Nov. 24
Gregory, Matthew and Thomas, [illegible] Arms yard, merchants, separate estate, Dec. 1, joint estate, Dec. 8 (final)
Ginger, Richard, Queenhithe, salter, Dec. 5
G[illegible], Daniel, [illegible], shopkeeper, Nov. 28
Gearing, William, Water lane, timber [illegible], Dec. 15
Grove, John, late of Liverpool, mariner, Dec. 8
Goldsmith, Richard, New Bond street, embroiderer, Dec. 5
Hatfield, Joseph, Crown court, Broad street, merchant, Nov. 21
Hathaway, Thomas, Cheltenham, linen draper, Dec. 12
Ho[illegible], Solomon, Doncaster, leather dresser, Dec. 1
Hughes, John, Silver street, Falcon square, victualler, Nov. 17
Haynes, Thomas, Duke street, Westminster, haberdasher, Nov. 28
Haywood, F. and George Palfreyman, Manchester, calico printers, Dec. 11
Hopping, James, Southwark, hatter, Dec. 19
Hendy, Christopher, Falmouth, mariner, Dec. 12
Hazlewood, Joseph Thomas, Bridgnorth, grocer, Dec. 10 (final)
Ireland, Samuel, St. Clement Danes, merchant, Nov. 28
Jackson, Ralph, Market Weighton, shopkeeper, Nov. 26
Jackson, N. [illegible], and George Bartlet, Gerard street, ironmongers, Dec. 15
King, William, Birmingham, factor, Dec. 4
Kemble, Samuel, and Walter Spens, Norfolk street, merchants, Dec. 1
Knight, Susannah, Aldersgate street, cork cutter, Dec. 5
Lomax, John, Liverpool, woollen draper, Nov. 16
Lloyd, Jam[illegible], Audley, [illegible], Dec. 21
Lindegren, Charles, Mincing lane, and Andrew Lindegren, Jun. Portsmouth, merchants, Dec. [illegible] (final)
Merrit, Nicholas, Newcastle upon Ouse, dealer, Nov. 27
Mainwaring, Charles, Manchester, [illegible] maker, Nov. 10
Mewburn, Philip, Newcastle, [illegible] merchant, Dec. 15
Milnes, Richard, late of Crowcroft, Pasbury, maltster, Dec. 3 (final)
Morgan, William, Portsmouth, mercer, Dec. 15
Manton, Thomas, Tokenhouse yard, merchant, Nov. 24
Norris, Thomas, Jun. Lincoln's Inn fields, cabinet maker, Dec. 5
Nicnol, Morgan, St. Martin's le Grand, pawn broker, Dec. 9
Orlord, Edward, Bristol, brewer, Dec. 5 (final)
Phillips, D. Oxford street, stable keeper, Nov. 28
Pawley, Richard, Beverley, Yorkshire, dealer, Nov. 21
Parker, Richard, Little Argyle street, ironmonger, &c. Nov. 21
Phelps, James, Bristol, innkeeper, Nov. 24
Pitman, John, Worcester, coach proprietor, Dec. 8 (final)
Perry, George, Long Acre, coach maker, Dec. 5
Pa[illegible], Charles, Croydon, taylor, Dec. 17
Parkes (otherwise Leazerhouse), John, Birmingham, gunmaker, Dec. 9
Reid, W. Stockport, draper, Dec. 9
Reilly, James, and James Collins, Mead's court, taylors, Dec. 19
Roberts, John, Pontefract, druggist, Dec. 14
Roberson, William, Gerard street, [illegible], Dec. 8
Rennie, George, St. Olave's, coal merchant, Dec. 5
Street, Thomas, Park lane, [illegible] baker, Dec. 5
St[illegible], Edward, Jun. [illegible] flaxdresser, Dec. 5
Simpson, Thomas, Oxford street, Goldsmith, Nov. 28
Scott, James, [illegible], Essex, lime burner, &c. Dec. 5
Stone, John Sykes, James street, Westminster, chapman, Dec. 5
Schofield, Richard, Batley, maltster, Dec. 19
Storr, William, Queen street, Cheapside, merchant, December 10
Smith, Thompson, Lambeth, potter, Dec. 2
Stratram, [illegible], Tiverton, chemist, Dec. 5
Stonebrewer, William, and William Davies, Manchester, fustian manufacturers, Dec. 15
Sm[illegible], James, Oldham, innkeeper, Dec. 8
T[illegible], George, [illegible], miller, Dec. 8
Taff[illegible], Charles, Cal[illegible] street, merchant, Dec. 19
V[illegible] [illegible], currier, Dec. 1
W[illegible], F. and C. Gardner, Carey street, [illegible], Dec. 5
Walker, Thomas, Green street, Oxford street, carpenter, Dec. 1
Wh[illegible], James, Pudding lane, merchant, Dec. 5
Wilkinson, William, and Thomas Chesman, Jewry street, coal [illegible], Dec. 5
Walker, Thomas and Richard, Manchester, merchants, Dec. 8
Winter, Thomas Wilson, Kingston, Hull, upholsterer, Dec. 2
W[illegible], Stephen, [illegible], Dec. 5
Watson, William, [illegible] street, silk mercer, Dec. 19 (final)
Wood, Robert, Blackburn, fustian manufacturer, Dec. 15
Wilson, Henry and Samuel, [illegible], Dec. 15
Williams, [illegible], Manchester, umbrella manufacturer, Dec. 7
Woolgar, William, Minories, brazier, Dec. 19
Wooley, John, Rumford, [illegible], Dec. 19
Yates, T. Stockport, and [illegible] Lowes, late of [illegible]chester, muslin manufacturers, Dec. [illegible]
Yates, Edward John, Bishopsgate street, drug merchant, Nov. 21
Yates, William, Little Guildford street, Dec. 5

INCIDENTS, MARRIAGES AND DEATHS IN AND NEAR LONDON.

With Biographical Memoirs of distinguished Characters recently deceased.

The number of British ships entered and cleared in British ports, in the year 1782, was 11,615, tonnage 1,123,000; in 1800, ships 22,364, tonnage 2,825,000—Increase in nineteen years, ships 10,379, tonnage 1,702,000.

"A curious and singular fact worthy the attention and inspection of the naturalist:— A sow belonging to Mr. Thomas Grace, of the Borough-road, Southwark, within the last week, had a litter of nine pigs, and an animal resembling, in every respect, an elephant !!!" —— *Whitehall Evening Post, Nov. 3.*

Melon Society.—The late anniversary took place at the George, Chiswick, when about three hundred gardeners and nurserymen attended. Soon after dinner, the several gardeners produced their melons, many of which were of an excellent quality. Mr. Phillips, of Richmond was the umpire. Mr. Whitman, of the Duke of Northumberland's, Sion-house, was allowed to have produced the finest; Mr. White, of Richmond, had the next. To the former was voted a silver cup, and to the latter a silver punch-ladle. Notwithstanding these decisions, the landlord of the Pack-horse, Turnham-green, was seemingly the favourite, as the best judges present not only bestowed many encomiums on his melons, but devoured them very greedily, fearful lest he should offer them by way of competition.

Married.] At Marybone, Sir John Murray, bart. of Stanhope-street, to Miss Callander, eldest daughter of Adam Callander, esq. of New Cavendish-street, Portland-place.

At Broome-house, Shooter's Hill, the seat of Sir Hyde Parker, J. Restal, esq. of Stratford, Green,-Essex, to Mrs. Roche, only daughter of W. Osborne, esq.

Dr. Nevinson, of Somerset-street, Portman-square, to Mrs. Moody, of Coopersale, Essex.

Mr. R. Nunn, of Friday-street, to Miss C. Wilmot, of Tottenham.

Mr. J. Le Prince, of Ringwood, Hants, to Miss Francillon, of Pentonville.

At Walton upon Thames, H. Goldney, esq. to Mrs. Hitches.

J. Ferguson, esq. to Miss Bloxam, daughter of Sir Matthew Bloxam, M.P.

The Rev. H. Okes, esq. A. B. of Corpus Christi College, Cambridge, to Miss P. Bulby, of Kingston upon Thames.

F. C. Wingrave, esq. of the excise-office, to Miss Dawson, of Albion-street, Blackfriars.

J. Cripps, esq. of Cirencester, to Miss Harrison, of Clapham Common.

Mr. R. Lee, of Bernard-street, Brunswick-square, to Miss Prowting, of Chawton, Hants.

H. Hartwell, esq. to Mrs. Elrington, of York-street.

At Christ Church, Newgate-street, Mr. E. Goddard, brandy-merchant, to Miss C. Campbell, eldest daughter of the late W. Campbell, esq. distiller, of Dock-head.

Mr. W. Russell, of London-street, Fitzroy-square, to Mrs. Clarke, relict of G. Clarke, esq. of Sevenoaks.

At Marybone, W. Glen Johnstone, esq. to Miss H. M. H. Richardson, sister of Sir G. Richardson, bart. of the sixty-fourth regiment.

Also, L. Vassall, esq. to Miss S. Fitch.

Mr. Whitford, of Broad-street Buildings, to Miss H. Wells, of Westminster.

At Mortlake, R. Melville, esq. of Amsterdam, to Miss E. Skurray, of Wakefield.

Mr. Dent, bookseller, Coventry-street, to Mrs. Hurford, widow of the late Henry Hurford, esq.

At St. George's, Bloomsbury, Mr. Jeremiah Sinderby, of Brook's-market, Holborn, to Miss Poate, of King-street, Bloomsbury, and of New Town, Hants, and niece of Capt. Colnett, of the navy.

J. Grant, esq. wholesale linen-draper, of Cheapside, to Miss Smith, eldest daughter of R. Smith, esq. wholesale grocer, of Aldersgate-street.

Lieutenant Lloyd, of the train of artillery, to Miss Campbell, fourth daughter of R. Campbell, esq. of Blackheath.

Mr. W. F. Gardner, merchant, of Crutched friars, to Miss Englehart, daughter of J. D. Englehart, esq. of Kew.

Mr. Richardson, of Islington, to Mrs. Hayes, of St. Clement's, Strand.

At Pimlico, Mr. Knight, to Miss M. White.

Mr. Lane, of South-street, Manchester-square, to Miss A. Townson, of Threadneedle-street.

In Marybone, J. F. Steadman, esq. of Bread-street-hill, to Miss Greening.

H. W. Mortimer, esq. of Fleet street, to Miss Ritchie, of Otley.

F. Perkins, esq. of Park-street, Southwark, to Miss Sanders, of Camberwell.

Mr. W. H. Houghton, of the navy-office, to Miss S. A. Kidington, of Great Portland-street.

J. S. Walton, esq. to Mrs. C. C. Diemar, widow of the late Rev. Dr. Diemar, of Calcutta.

At Bishopsgate Church, Mr. J. Ebenezer Saunders, fish-factor, to Miss S. Gondge, of Norton Falgate.

At St. Margaret's Church, Westminster,

G. Ellis,

G. Ellis, esq. M. P. to Miss Parker, daughter of Admiral Sir Peter Parker, bart.

J. Macmaster, esq. of Doughty-street, Guildford-street, to Miss Roberts, of Southampton-buildings, Holborn.

The Rev. J. Myers, rector of Walton on the Hill, Surry, to Miss Woodman, of Ewell.

At Martin's, in the Fields, the Rev. T. Baker, of Crowhurst, in Sussex, to Miss A. Gledstanes, daughter of Col. Gledstanes.

Died.] Mr. F. Brazier, of Shadwell.

At Islington, in her 81st year, Mrs. F. Barker, widow.

Mrs. Avery, wife of Mr. Avery, organ-builder, Queen-square, Westminster.

Mrs. C. Lovewell, of Wood-street.

In Southampton-street, Strand, Mrs. Cameron, wife of J. Cameron, esq. of the East *India* Company's service.

At Burwood, in Surry, in her 76th year, Mrs. Currie.

Mr. T. Higgs, one of the cashiers of the Bank of England.

Miss L. Mackie, of Marden-hill, Herts.

In his 39th year, P. Stanhope, esq.

Mrs. Claridge, of Potter's Bar, near Hatfield, Herts.

Mrs. Sims, of Newington-place, Surry.

Mr. Oddie, of the Bear-yard, Lincoln's-inn-fields.

At Ockham, in Surrey, in her 23d year, Miss N. Bonsey.

G. Crowe, esq. late of Shotton.

At Hackney, in her 80th year, Mrs Corneck.

In Harley street, Cavendish-square, two months after the death of his wife and infant son, the Hon. John Cochrane.

Mrs. Millikin of Norfolk-street, Strand.

At Highgate, in his 80th year, T. Isherwood, esq.

At Hayes, near Uxbridge, on his road to London, P. Drinkwater, esq. of Manchester.

At Harrow, the Rev. B. Escott, M. A.

Mr. J. Woodcock, fourteen years assisting-clerk to W. Rix, esq. late town-clerk of London.

Aged 80, J. Crosier, esq. of Ickenham, in Middlesex.

At Epsom, Mrs. A. Cook.

At Hendon, G. Harvey, esq.

In his 72d year, J. Farmer, esq of Cumberland-place, Marybone; this gentleman has bequeathed a large personal property to the Society for Maintaining and Educating poor Orphans of Clergymen till of Age to put Apprentice.

S. Thurston Adey, esq. M. P. for Higham Ferrers.

At Upper East Hayes, in his 69th year, Dr. W. Lowdor, late lecturer on midwifery at St. Saviour's, Southwark.

On Highbury-terrace, in his 77th year, Mr. E. Jackson, of Grace Church-street.

Mrs. A. Davison, of Tyndale-place, Islington.

In Chancery-lane, Mr. J Hodgson, attorney.

Mr. R Kaye, of High-street, Bloomsbury.

At Windsor, Mr. Wright, one of the Queen's pages.

In her 86th year, at her son's house, in Rosamond street, Mrs. M. Biggs.

At Bish-court, Surry, in his 83d year J. Ewart, esq.

At Guildford, Captain Hayes, of the 15th light dragoons.

In Bond-street, Captain P. Scott, of the Bengal military establishment.

At Brompton, J. Fearnside, esq. of the Exchequer.

In Charter House-square, in his 87th year, the Rev. A. Natt, A. M.

Mrs. Downes, of Upper Ranelagh-street, Pimlico.

Mrs. D. Young, of Lincoln's-inn.

At Putney, in his 93d year, P. Stapel, esq. formerly an eminent Dutch merchant.

Lately, in Brewer-street, Mrs. Philips, late of Abbey-green.

PROVINCIAL OCCURRENCES.

WITH ALL THE MARRIAGES AND DEATHS,

Arranged geographically, or in the Order of the Counties, from North to South.

*** *Authentic Communications for this Department are always very thankfully received.*

NORTHUMBERLAND AND DURHAM.

A correspondent of the Newcastle Advertiser recommends to the conservators of the river Tyne, and the commissioners for the improvement of Tyne-bridge, certain alterations which he thinks necessary to be made, for the safety and convenience of those who pass under the bridge. Tyne-bridge, in its present state, is composed of 9 arches, and from the massy size of its pillars, so much of the water-way is taken up, that at the distance of about 30 yards above bridge, and nearly in the middle of the river, two sands cast up, one of which appears before low water, the other is not quite so soon visible; to clear the navigation of which two sands, he further recommends the consolidating of the five and six arches into one, which he thinks would be about 144 feet span, and this one likewise to be of cast iron; its rise so high

high as to admit a keel to sail through it, at high water in spring tides. To the enquiry, how the height of the cast iron is to be overcome on the upper side, this correspondent answers, that the design of the present improvements (an act of parliament having been lately obtained for the widening and improving Tyne bridge, as noticed in a former number) obliges the conservators to give it more rise, so that a little more than what is now intended, will effectually accomplish this design. It may be further objected, that this rise running so near the south end of the bridge, may not look so well to the eye; but when objects of such great consideration are obtained by it to the trade, as that of the keels sailing through it or under it when the wind admits, at all times of tide, independantly of many other improvements to the trade and navigation, these considerations, he judges, will finally remove every objection that may be made against it. But these are not the only instances in which the navigation will be thereby benefited; for in winter, when the river has been frozen any length of time, and the weather is changeable, it will, he presumes, be more certain to break up these first, on account of the passage being more open, there, than many other places, by the openings of the present main arch, and that of cast iron, which will be a certain means of directing the ice from the shipping at the quay, and thereby preventing all that damage which is so frequently happening at those seasons. Another good which will attend it, is, that when ships are warping in or out from the quay, the keel or other craft navigation, will be chiefly on the south side of the river, so that, under such circumstances, there will be a greater certainty of keeping clear of each other; thereby preventing much damage and loss of time; and lastly when the below-bridge coal is nearly exhausted, this part of the navigation will then be found more useful, not only to the proprietors of those large and extensive fields of untouched coal on both sides of the river Tyne, but to those of the Darwent likewise, which will, most assuredly, be brought down either by canal navigation, inclined planes, or railways, to the river, above bridge. As an additional number of keels will then pass this way, and most probably a new kind, that of canal bridges; this, which will be still a greater increase, will, by this plan, be effectually provided for. The above suggestions, if attended to, would not only provide for the improvement of Tyne bridge, but likewise for that of the river Tyne and the navigation in general, and in all probability would prevent the further consideration of any alteration or improvement to be made at any future period.

An agricultural society was formed lately at Barnard Castle, (October 7), consisting, wholly or chiefly, of practical farmers, and improvers of ground; it is proposed to confine the attention of the members to improve and advance the husbandry of the county, lying, in general, within a circumference of 10 or 12 miles distant from the town of Barnard Castle.

Married.] At Coitness, G. Callender, jun. esq. of Craigforth, major in the Rifle corps, to Miss E. Compton Erskine, eldest daughter of the Hon. H. Erskine, advocate.—Mr. E. Heron, butcher, in Morpeth, to Miss Richardson, of Acklington.—Mr. J. F. Stanfield, manager, to Miss M. F. Kell, both of the Morpeth theatre.—Mr. P. Hardcastle, of Stockton upon Tees, to Miss Wailes, of Hearl.—Mr. J. Foggin, jun. carpenter, to Miss J. Pettigrew, both of Gateshead.

At Kirk Merrington, Mr. J. Liddell, wine merchant, in Durham, to Mrs. Hewit, relict of Mr. Hewit, late of the Durham bank.—Mr. J. Walton, merchant, in Stanhope, to Miss Rippon, of Durham.—Mr. B. Woodman, tanner, of Morpeth, to Miss Wilson, of Ulgham.

At Newcastle, Mr. T. Winship, roper, in partnership with Messrs. Hood, and Co. to Miss A. Fothergill, daughter of the late Capt. G. Fothergill.

At Morpeth, Mr. Burrell, son of P. G. Burrell, esq. of Alnwick, to Miss C. Sanderson, daughter of the Rev. Mr. Sanderson.

At Durham, Mr. Parker, an eminent stationer in Cambridge, to Miss S. Hayes, daughter of the Rev. T. Hayes, of Durham Cathedral.

At Marybone, London, Mr. J. Tate, of Cornhill, London, to Miss Robson, of Greenhill, Belford, Northumberland.

At Whickham, Mr. H. Greenbank, officer of Excise, to Miss C. Collingwood, daughter of Mr. W. Collingwood, innkeeper, of Smalwell.

At Sunderland, Mr. W. Arlot, watch maker, to Miss Dobson, daughter of Mr. Dobson, ship-owner.—Mr. J. Proctor, bleacher, of Elswick, to Miss P. Walton, of Newcastle.—Mr. C. Burton, tallow chandler, of Blyth, to Miss M. Garvey, of Morpeth.

At Whitburn, Mr. G. Chambers, grazier, &c. to Miss Brown.—Mr. T. Fox, brewer of Stockton, to Miss E. Trewhitt.

Died.] At Durham, aged 66, Mrs. Nicholson, widow of the late Mr. G. Nicholson, architect.—At an advanced age, Mrs. Pew, mother-in-law to Mr. Richardson, cabinet maker.—Mr. R. Lambton, hair dresser.

At Newcastle, at the house of his son-in-law, Mr. Marley, linen draper, Mr. Spencer, sen. formerly of Leeds.—Suddenly Mr. J. Weir, whip-maker.—In the prime of life, of a decline, Mr. T. Henderson, woollen draper, much respected by all his friends and acquaintance, and likewise by the corps of Newcastle volunteers, of which he was a member, who have resolved to erect a mural monument in Gateshead church, as a testimony of their regard for him.

Suddenly Mr. T. Emerson, of Staples inn, London.—Mr. R. Hodgson, son of the late Mr. Hodgson, an eminent founder.—Aged 47, Miss M. Smith, daughter of the late Dr. Smith.

Smith.—Mrs. Brumell.—Aged 66, Mrs. S. Bell.—Mrs. M. Strologer.—Mr. T. Mood, joiner &c.—Aged 84, Mrs. Drummond, relict of the late Mr. A. Drummond, mason.—Mr. T. Arthur, butcher.—Aged 56, R. Huntley, esq. Mr. T. Mason, butcher.

At Stockton, Mrs. Forster, wife of Mr. Forster, itinerant preacher in the methodist connection.

At Sunderland, Mr. J. Downey, an eminent attorney.—Mr. G. Hogg, dyer.

At North Shields, aged 46, Mr. J Millie, ironmonger; universally respected as a very worthy man, and an ingenious mechanic.

At South Shields, Mrs. A. Smart.—Captain T. Todd, of Yarmouth.

Aged 50, Mr. S. Smith, of Bushblaties, near Durham.

At his seat at Arthington, in his 75th year, T. Arthington, esq high sheriff for Yorkshire, in 1767.—Aged 48, Mr. J Graham, formerly agent to J. Thornhill, esq. of Sunderland.—Miss Orde, daughter of Lieut. Col. Orde, of Holliwell, near Durham.—Also Mrs. Thompson, nurse in Col Orde's family.

At Chimney Mills, near Newcastle, in her 65th year, Mrs. E. Pentland, relict of the late Mr. J. Pentland, miller.—Mrs. Graydon, wife of Mr. Graydon, miller, at Southwick.

At the Windmill Hills, Mr. M. Mills, many years an eminent flour-dealer on the old Tyne bridge, and afterwards on the Battle Bank, Gateshead.

At the Leases, near Newcastle, Miss Smith, daughter of the late Mr W. Smith, surgeon, &c.

CUMBERLAND AND WESTMORELAND.

Among the numerous instances of very extraordinary productiveness of the late season, are the following, taken from the Cumberland Packet, of October 20.

A pear was lately pulled in the garden of Mr. Routledge, of Shaddongate, near Carlisle, which weighed 11 ounces, 11 drams, and measured 11 inches in circumference. The tree on which it grew is only three years old.

Lately a common field pea, in the garden of Mr. J. Ostle, of Newtown, in Abbey Holm, which had taken root there accidentally, produced 404 pods, containing 2213 peas! It had only a single stalk or stem, for several inches above the ground.

A cabbage was lately cut upon the estate of G. Sadler, esq. of Dean Scales, in the parish of Deane, which weighed 41 pounds, and measured 5 feet 15 inches in the circumference!

An apple was lately plucked from a tree, of the Patagonian kind, in the orchard of Mr. J. Hunter, of Millom, Cumberland, which measured 15 inches in circumference, and weighed upwards of a pound!

A new and commodious butchers' market has been lately opened at Carlisle.

Married.] At Whitehaven, the Rev. Mr. Grice, rector of Drigg and Irton, to Miss Hogg, daughter of the late Mr. Hogg, merchant, of Whitehaven.—Mr. W. Hoatham, grocer of Sheffield, to Miss M. Sutton, of Scotby, near Carlisle.—Mr. Ant. Sharp, grocer, of Kendal, to Miss Wharton, of Orton, in Westmoreland

At Brampton, Mr. J. Armstrong, to Miss M. Highmoors.

At Kirk Andrews upon Esk, Mr. A. Batey, to Miss J. Coulthard, of Beck.

At Hutton, Mr. J. Brown, of Hornsby Gate, to Miss M. Bell, of Thomas Close.—Also, Mr. J. Ousby, of Fort Putnam, near Greystoke, to Miss O. Cameron.—The Rev. Mr. Sanderson, of Ponsonby, to Miss Fell, daughter of the late Captain Fell, of Parton.

At Carlisle, Mr. R. Asbridge, brewer, of Parton, to Miss D. Littledale, of the cottage, Morresby.—J. Beck, Esq. to Miss S. Gill.

At Workington, Mr. T. Cragg, merchant, to Miss Brough.

At Bolton, near Lancaster, E. Pennington, esq. of Kendal, Colonel in the East India company's service, to Miss Sparling.

At Lancaster, Mr. Turner, bookseller, to Miss Clarkson, of Brackenthwaite, near Burton, in Kendal.

Mr. R. Coulston, to Miss J Bourtholme, both of Wornell Fell, in Sebergham Parish.

At Harrington, Mr. T. Skerry, ship-carpenter, to Miss N. Sproat, both of Lowca.

At Orton, near Kendal, Mr. A. Sharp, grocer, to Miss Wharton.—Mr. W. Garnett, aged 66, to Miss Phillipson, aged 22, both of Crosthwaite, in Westmoreland. It is remarkable, that the bridegroom weighs twenty-one stone, and his bride only seven!

Died.] At Carlisle, Mr. J. Sewell On leaving the Guildhall in a dark night, he unfortunately missed his way to the stairs, walked out of a window three stories high, and was killed on the spot.

R. Lodge. esq —Aged 37, Mrs. E. Hutton, wife of Mr. W. Hutton, hatter.—Aged 54, Mrs. M. Jackson, widow.—Aged 27, Mr. J. How, weaver.—Mr. W. Smith, sen. staymaker,

At Kendal, Mr B Linkinson, fish-hook-maker.—In an advanced age, J. Lambert, esq. of Watsfield, near Kendal.—Mr. T. Benson, merchant, of Liverpool, and a quaker.—Aged 91, Mrs. Moser.

At Whitehaven, aged 94, Mr. R. Sanderson.—In her 41st year, Mrs. Hodgson, wife of Capt. J. Hodgson.

Mr. T. Barnfather, of Garthside, near Brampton.

At the house of his son-in-law, J. Hetherington, esq. of the Intack, near Brampton.—In an advanced age, Mr. Smith.

At Parton, in his 32d year, Mr. J. Gibson, principal clerk in the 'compting house of the Old Brewery company, Whitehaven. It is a circumstance very singular, and equally creditable to all parties, that the grand-father of the deceased, his father, his uncle, his elder brother, and himself, have, for upwards of 60 years past, lived and died in the employ

of

of that house; successively filling places of considerable trust, and severally discharging the duties thereof with integrity and fidelity. The deceased was, in every respect, highly estimable to his friends and to society.

At Harrington, Mrs. Stockdale.

In Jamaica, in the prime of life, Mr. J. Tyson, son of Mr. N. Tyson, merchant, in Kendal.

At Workington, aged 65, Mrs. Piele.—In the prime of life, Miss M. Sherrington.—In his 51st year, Mr J. Hodgson, sen. merchant. —Aged 21, Mr. J Fearon, son of Mr. J. Fearon, ship owner.

YORKSHIRE.

An elegant engraving will, in the course of a few months, be published, of the beautiful monument erected in Trinity Church, in Hull, to the memory of that highly respected and much regretted Christian minister, the Rev. Joseph Milner, M. A. who was upwards of 30 years master of the free grammar school in the above town, and successively lecturer and vicar of the said church. We mention this circumstance, because we believe it will afford peculiar pleasure to the inhabitants of Hull in general, and, likewise, to his numerous pupils in various parts of this kingdom and on the continent, at whose expence the monument, which was the last work of the celebrated sculptor, Bacon, was erected.

Married.] Mr. J. Richardson, corn miller, to Miss A. Freeman, both of South Owram, near Halifax.—Mr. W. Crowther, corn-miller, to Miss S. Walton, both of Norland, near Halifax.—Mr. W. Maude, of Otley, to Miss Robinson, of Lombard street, London.—Mr. J. Hill, merchant, of Leeds, to Miss Hepworth, of Pomfret.—Mr. S. Jones, of Friday street, London, to Miss M. Lilley, late of Wakefield.—Mr. J. Petch, attorney, of Kirby Moorside, to Miss H. Cooke, youngest daughter of the late A. Cooke, esq. of Hart Hall, near Whitby.

At Doncaster, Mr. Jarman, to Miss M. M. Errington, both of the Theatre Royal.—Mr. J. Swale, attorney of Settle, to Miss Hogarth, of Kendal.—Mr. R. Blezzard, merchant of Leeds, to Miss S. Blezzard, youngest daughter of the late Mr. J Blezzard, of Guiseley.—Mr. Mirfin, mercer, &c. of Sheffield, to Miss Flower, of Worksop.

At Hull, S. Gee, jun esq. to Miss Moore, daughter of the late J. Moore, esq. merchant. —Mr. T. Harrison, of Sigglesthorne, in Holderness, to Miss M. Westoby.

At Wakefield, W. Groom, esq. of Lincoln's inn, London, to Miss A. Maude, of Lethley, near Otley.—Mr. J. W. Neale, to Miss F. Maude.—Mr. W. Cass, of Thirsk, to Miss Cowen, of Sutton-under-Whitstone Cliff.—Mr. Poynton, of Wakefield, to Mrs. Standage, of Dewsbury.

At Leeds, Mr. R. Myers, to Miss Edgcumbe, of Wakefield.—Mr. C. Morris, to Miss M. Sharp.—Mr. R. Hicks, of Hippax, to Miss M. Brown.

At Northallerton, Mr. Hirst, attorney, to Miss Walton.

Mr. G. Lockwood, woolstapler, of Honley, near Huddersfield, to Mrs. H. Dickinson, of North Owram, near Halifax.

At Halifax, Mr. J. Hiley, to Miss M. Clapham.

Died.] At Hull, suddenly, Capt. J. Brown, master of the ship Manchester, and late of Stockton upon Tees. He had walked out with a friend to view the illumination; returned home, and expired almost immediately.

In his 80th year, greatly respected, Mr. J. Picard, formerly a wine-merchant of Nottingham.—Aged 49, Mrs. E. Atkinson, widow of the late Mr. Atkinson, bookbinder, and daughter of Mr. Martin, shopkeeper.—Aged 32, Mr. D. Walker, hair dresser.—Mrs. Hartley, wife of Mr. Hartley, dancing master.

At Leeds, Mrs. Soper, wife of Mr. Soper, surgeon.—Mr. J. Heath, of the Horse and Groom public house.—Mr. Haist, merchant. —Far advanced in years, Mr. D. Rider, formerly an eminent clothier.—Mr. C. Wrigglesworth, butcher.—Mr. B. Kaye, mercer, and a quaker.

At Halifax, after a very short illness, Mrs. Norris, wife of Mr W. Norris, jun.—In her 60th year, Mrs. Schorey, wife of Mr. Schorey, of the White Swan inn.—Mrs Ogden, wife of Mr. J. Ogden, worsted manufacturer.

C. Steer, esq. of Birstall, near Halifax.—J. Armitage, esq. of Kettlethorp, near Wakefield.

At Knaresborough, suddenly, aged 77, Mrs. A. Archdale.

Mrs. Sylvester, relict of the late E. Sylvester, esq. of Bramhope, near Otley.—Mrs. Shepley, wife of the Rev. W. Shepley, of Horsforth, near Leeds.—Mr T. Bass, of the Rose and Crown public house, Barnard Castle.

At Patrington, aged 74, Mrs. Sayle, widow of the late Mr. E. Sayle, farmer, of Hedham.

At Woodhall, near Selby, Mrs. M. E. Graham.

At Thorpe, near Market Weighton, aged 66, Mr. A. Adamson, farmer and grazier; of a sincerely upright and charitable disposition.

At Sutton on the forest, in his 82d year, the Rev. H Goodricke, Prebendary of Grindall, in York cathedral, rector of Hunsingore, and vicar of Aldborough, both in this county. He was younger brother of the late Sir John Goodricke, bart. of Ribstone.

Mrs. M. E. Graham, of Woodhall, a maiden lady. She has left the bulk of a large fortune to the sons of two servants that had lived with her for several years.—Aged 24, Mr. R. Kirkby, 2d son of Mr. Kirkby of Mowthorpe.

At Howden, in her 21st year, Miss E. Clayburn.—Mr. J Whiteley, worsted manufacturer, of Stainland, near Halifax.—Mr. J. Sutcliffe,

Sutcliffe, worsted manufacturer, of Holdsworth, near Halifax.

At Bradford, aged 86, Mrs. Rawson, relict of the late J. Rawson, esq. She was a lineal descendant of Archbishop Sterne, and cousin to the celebrated author of Tristram Shandy, &c.

Mrs. Baldwyn, wife of the Rev. E. Baldwyn, head master of the free-grammar school. Mr. J. Atkinson, of the Bishop Blaze public house.—In his 76th year, Mr. J. Maude, tobacconist.—Mr. W. Fryer, of the Bowling Green inn, near Bradford.

At Doncaster, Mr. Lister, grocer.

LANCASHIRE.

There is now living and exhibiting, at Liverpool, a most singular and, indeed, uncommon animal, hitherto undescribed by any naturalist; it approaches in its form, nearest to the land tortoise, but has a tail exactly like a crocodile, and is extremely fierce.

The following is an accurate statement of the shipping belonging to the ports of Lancaster and Ulverstone, within the last 12 months, made up to the present time. The total number of vessels has been, 158, producing upwards of 25,625 tons, and navigated by 2332 men; of these vessels, 68 were employed in the foreign and 90 in the coasting trade. During the above period, these ports have been deprived, by capture, wreck, and transfer to other ports, of 44 vessels of 5255 tons burden, and containing upwards of 628 men; the exact number, therefore, is 114, of 16,370 tons and 1710 men; of which 76 vessels, of 13,996 tons and 1605 men belong to Lancaster, and 38 ditto of 2374 tons, and 105 men to Ulverstone. Total 114 vessels, 16,370 tons, and 1710 men.

Married.] Mr. J. Conway, merchant, of Liverpool, to Miss Christie, eldest daughter of J Christie, esq. of Pall Mall, London.—Mr. L. Burgel, merchant, of Liverpool, to Miss Mansergh, of West Hall, near Kirkby Lonsdale.—Mr. R. Ashur, of Maghull, to Miss M. Winstanley, of Aughton.

At Liverpool, Capt. Boyd, to Miss Hill.—Mr. J. Taylor, to Miss S. Brownbill, of West Derby.

At Hemel Hempstead, Herts, Mr. J. Leigh, merchant, of Liverpool, to Miss Hilton, of Bury House.—Mr. T. Griffith, draper, to Miss D. Medley, youngest daughter of the late Rev. S. Medley.—Captain M. Humble, to Miss A Johnson.

At Manchester, Mr. Smallpage, druggist, to Miss Browne.—Mr. F. Dixon, to Miss M. Bond.—Mr. J. Walker, to Miss A. Howard.—N. A. Schaufthen, ensign in the Cheshire militia, to Miss Stewart.—Mr. G. Nelson, of Liverpool, to Miss L. Fairclough; also Mr. J Barker, of Norwich, to Miss S. Fairclough, both daughters of Mr. H. Fairclough, of Liverpool.—J. N. Brown, esq. Lieut. of the 14th light dragoons, to Miss S. Fawcett, of Manchester.—Mr. M. Browme, of Manchester, to Miss C. Walker, of Gorton.—Mr. T. Bell, of Garstang, to Miss E. Robinson, of Burslem.

Died.] At Lancaster, aged 2K, Miss J. Bowes, daughter of the late J. Bowes, esq. and alderman.—Mrs. Wilson, relict of the Rev. D. Wilson, and daughter of the late Mr. Wilson, of Liveley Hall, near Blackburn.

At Liverpool, aged 15, master J. Graham.—Mr. Watkinson, brush-maker.—Aged about 23, Mr. J. Kerr, jun. ship chandler.—Mrs. Allen, widow.—Suddenly Mr. J. Knight, late glass-manufacturer; and in two or three weeks after, in her 20th year, Miss Knight, niece to the above Mr. Knight, and daughter of Mr. G. Knight.—Mrs. Williamson.—H. Lake, esq. formerly of Wavertree.—Aged 70, Mr. D. M'Lean, much respected as a truly honest man.—Aged 24, Mrs. R. Richardson, wife of Mr. J. Richardson, merchant, late of Glasgow.—Mrs Morrison.—In his 22d year, the Rev. P. Aikin, Baptist Minister; alike eminent for the endowments of the scholar, the piety of the Christian, and the fidelity of the minister.

Mr. P. Robinson.—Mr. T. Ellison, who had been 45 years employed in the tool manufactory of Mr. J. Wyke, originally, and now of Mr. S. Green.—Aged 53, Mr. J. Kerr, warehouse-keeper of Excise.—Aged 74, Mrs. Swift.—Aged 42, Mrs. Bradley, wife of Mr. Bradley, dock-master.—In her 57th year, Mrs. Speers, widow of the late Capt A. Speers.—Miss E. Whitfield, daughter of Mr. Whitfield, cooper.—Aged 16, Miss E. Jump.—Mr. James, tobacconist.

CHESHIRE.

Henry Rice for uttering a forged bank note, Aaron Gee, for stealing calico in a bleaching ground, Thomas Gibson for burglary, Edward Dearon for burglary, and Benjamin Bebbington for horse stealing, received sentence of death. The three first were ordered for execution on the 3d of October. The two last were reprieved.

Married.] At Chester, Mr. T. Tyas, jun. of Liverpool, to Miss Jones, of Huntingdon Hall.—Mr. E. Roberts, to Miss M Drury.

In London, E. V. Townshend, esq. of Chester, to Miss C. A. Du Pré, daughter of the late J. Du Pré, esq. of Portland Place.

At Totteridge, Herts, J. L. Panter, esq. of Muswell Hill, Middlesex, to Miss S. Downes, youngest daughter of the late P. Downes, esq. of Shrigley.—Mr. S. Lowe, of Whitchurch, to Miss Murray, of Park Gate.—The Rev. P. Halsted, rector of Grappenhall, to Miss Leigh, of Booths, near Knutsford.

Mr. J. Harrison, of Aldford, to Miss Colley, of Churton Heath.—Mr. R. Roberts, jun. of Milford place, to Miss Williams, of Mold.—Mr C. Ferguson, printer, of Liverpool, to Miss A. Morris, of Chester.

At Neston, Mr. J. Parry, to Miss Bloore, of Leighton Hall.—J. Cotter, esq. of London, to Mrs. Price, relict of the late Rev. Mr. J. Price, of Broughton, near Chester.

Died.]

Died.] At Chester, Mrs. Leet, late of the Yacht inn.—Mr Haultier, drawing master. Mrs. Griffith, wife of Mr. Griffith, box book keeper to the theatre.—Mr. Parsonage, of the Roebuck public house.

At Nantwich, suddenly, Mr. T. Steel, stay and corset maker. His loss will be deplorably and distressfully felt by a widow and eight children, mostly small, who had nothing to depend upon but his earnings.

At Nantwich, Miss Hall.

Suddenly in the prime of life, Mr. J. Egerton, of Tattenhall.

DERBYSHIRE.

Married.] At Ashover, Mr. Colmore, to Miss Milnes.

At Derby, Mr. T. Morris, cabinet maker in St. Paul's Church Yard, London, to Miss, Handford.

Died.] At Derby, aged 80, Mrs. Broughton.—In her 31st year, Mrs. Edwards, wife of Mr. W. Edwards, watch-maker.—Aged 77, Mrs. Vickers, relict of Mr. E. Vickers, hosier.

At Rushton, near Chapel in Le Frith, very suddenly, aged 75, Mr. S. Needham.

At Buxton, C. Steer, esq. of Birstall, near Leeds.—The Hon. Capt. Hamilton Lindsay, brother to the Earl of Crawford.

At Blackwall, Mr. J. Breward.

NOTTINGHAMSHIRE.

It is in contemplation to erect a stone bridge over the river Trent, at Gunthorpe Ford, and likewise to raise a flood-road on the South side of the river, to Bridgford Lane End, and a flood road on the North side, to the village of Gunthorpe, with sufficient arches in the said roads.

Married.] The Reverend J. Sidney, vicar of Ilkeston, to Miss Knighton, of Cotmanby.

At Banbury, Mr. Hase, sailer, to Miss Walker.

At Lenton, near Nottingham, Mr. J. Musson, to Miss M. Harpham, of the Stragglers hotel.

At Worksop, Mr. J. Wilson, attorney, to Miss Wright, daughter of the late Mr. Wright, of Wombwell, in Yorkshire.

At Nottingham, Mr. S. Roberts, fellmonger, to Miss Barber, daughter of Mr. Barber, grocer.

At Newark, Mr. Moorhouse, surgeon, of Sheffield, to Miss Cramper.

Died.] At Nottingham, T. Boot, esq.—Mrs. Porter.—In her 97th year, Mrs. Hall, widow.—In her 63d year, Mrs Collinshaw, a maiden lady, sister to Captain Collinshaw, of the Nottinghamshire militia.—Mrs. Savage, wife of Mr. Savage, cooper.—Mrs. Bigsby.—Mr. Taylor, frame-smith.—Mrs. Watts, of Coddington, near Newark.

At Banbury, Mr. W. Shirley, wholesale grocer.

At Thoresby Park, to the inexpressible grief of the family, the Honorable Evelyn Pierrepoint, eldest son of Lord Viscount Newark, one of the knights of the Shire for this county, and a captain in the Nottinghamshire regiment of Militia.

At Claypole, near Newark, Miss E. Cooke, youngest daughter of Mr. S. Cooke.

LINCOLNSHIRE.

Application is intended to be made to Parliament in the ensuing session, for an Act for building a bridge over the river Witham, in the borough of Boston, at or near the place where the present bridge crosses the said river, and for powers to purchase houses, lands, &c. for making convenient ways and passages to the said intended bridge; as also for enlarging the Jail of the said borough, and for building a new Jail there; for powers to purchase houses, lands, &c. for that purpose; also for supplying the town of Boston with water; for improving and enlarging the Market-cross, and for improving and regulating the fairs or marts, and markets, within the said borough; and for stopping up common ways or streets in the said borough, which are of no public utility.

A new turnpike-road is intended to be made from Spittlegate, in Grantham-parish, to Bridge-end, in Horbling-parish, to pass thro' the several parishes of Spittlegate, Somerby, Welby, Ropsley, Owsby, Hador, Braceby, Haceby, Dembleby, Scot Willoughby, Newton, Osbournby, Threckingham, Spanby, Horbling, and Swaton, all in this county; with a power to extend the same, if thought adviseable, to Corby (from Spittlegate) thro' the several parishes of Somerby, Boothby Pagnell, Bitchfield, and Burton Coggles, all in this county. It is likewise intended to apply to Parliament for leave to make a turnpike-road from the point where the Barton-street-road intersects the turnpike-road in the parish of Laceby, to a certain place called Hollow-gate-head, in the parish of Louth, through the several parishes of Laceby, Irby, Beelsby, Barnoldby le-Beck, Hatcliffe, Ashby-cum-Fenby, East Ravendale, Hawerby, North Thoresby, Beelby, Ludborough, Utterby, Fotherby, Brackenbury, and Louth, all in this county.

The commissioners for improving the outfall of the river Welland, have lately come to a determination to make a new river, or cut, from the Shepherd's Hole, in the parish of Surfleet, across the salt marshes, to Fossdyke inn, being in length about two miles one furlong, the bottom thereof to be 50 feet feet, and each side to batter two feet for every foot in depth; the forelands on the north side to be 30 feet, and on the south side 50 feet wide; the south bank to be 60 feet wide at its base, 30 feet wide at the top, and 11 feet in perpendicular height.

There is now in the possession of Mr. Pindard, of Donington, a beautiful white heifer, which has, every year, since its birth, had a succession of upwards of 30 horny protuberances stretched along the ridge of the back, some of them from 6 to 8 inches in length, which,

which, in the spring, with the change of coat, are regularly supplanted and shed. From the misery which the animal is subject to, in having their horns injured and broken off, the owner has humanely resolved to kill it.

Married.] Mr. Allen, jun. to Mrs. Wharry, both of Casterton Magna, near Stamford.—Mr. Phillips, mercer, &c. of Wragby, to Miss M. Hairby.—Mr. J. Fretwell, grocer, of Gainsborough, to Miss Dewdney, of Exeter.—Mr. Thorpe, farmer, of Witchley Warren, to Miss E. Ullet, of Stow, near Gretford.

At Lincoln, Mr. R. Featherby, ironmonger, to Mrs Wood.

At Marybone Church, London, Mr. J. Hildred, attorney, of Bolton, to Miss M. Hardy, late of Grantham.

At Bourn, Mr. Beaumont, surgeon, of Gravesend, to Miss Olbourn; eldest daughter of Mr. R. Olbourn.—The Rev. Mr. Brown, of Dunsby, to Miss F. Wright, of Fulbeck.

Died.] Aged 66, Mr. J. Fowler, late of Goltho, near Wragby.

At Lincoln, in the prime of life, Mrs. Wright, wife of Mr. W. Wright, joiner, &c. —Aged 30, Mr. W. Tilleard, late musician in Messrs. Roberts and Franklin's company of comedians.—Aged 25, Mr. N. Simpson, late common carrier from Lincoln to Gainsboro'.

At Cockerington, near Louth, Mr. Coverdale, of London.

In Manchester Buildings, Westminster, Mrs. Cooper, wife of Dr. Cooper, of Bath Easton Villa, and late of Stamford.—Mrs. Dickins, of South Witham.

At Louth, far advanced in years, Mrs. Taylor, widow.

At Barton, while on a visit, aged 17, Miss Hesleden, daughter of T. Hesleden, esq. of Ferritz, in Yorkshire. She was in good health as usual, until late in the afternoon of the preceding day.

At Marton, near Gainsborough, in the prime of life, Mr. T. Stow, butcher.

At Gainsborough, aged 77, Mr. W. Wright, bookseller. Mrs. West, wife of Mr. J. West mariner. Mrs. Watson, wife of Mr. Watson, inn keeper.

LEICESTER.

Married.] At Collington, Mr. T. Castledine, of Mounterel, to Miss Gilbert.—The Rev. Dr Hardy, rector of Loughborough, to Miss M. Smear, third daughter of the Rev. C. Smear, rector of Frottenden, Suffolk. —Mr J. Pufter, of Sapcote, to Miss Haines, of Gilmorton.

At Leicester, Mr. Bruce, coach proprietor, to Mrs. Gibbs.

At Sapcote, Mr. J. Wood, to Miss M. Moore.

At Ansty, Mr. Beaumont, hosier, to Miss S. Johnson.—Mr. H. Yates, of Brailsford, in Derbyshire, to Miss Etton, of Oakthorpe, in this county.

Died.] At Leicester, at his brother's house, Mr. J. Peach, son of Mr. Alderman Peach, of Bristol.

At the Trinity Hospital, in his 102d year, Alice Gilbert.

At Blandford, Dorset, R. Pulteney, M. D. F.R.S. an eminent physician and naturalist, formerly of Leicester.—Mr. H. Henton, an opulent farmer, of the Redale.—Suddenly, of an apoplectic fit, aged 70, W. Clare, gent. of Ibstock.

STAFFORDSHIRE.

At Wolverhampton, Mr. J. Smith, to Miss E. Adshead.—Mr. J. Smith, of Lower Penn, to Miss S. Neachols, of the Heath.—Mr. T. Perks, butcher, to Miss M. Roden. —Mr. W. Barrs, of Birmingham, to Miss Cooke, of Morton, in this county.—J. Smith, esq. of Great Fenton, justice of the peace for this county, to Miss E. Turner, of Lane End. —Mr. G. Shaw, grocer, of Stone, to Miss Hammond, of Eccleshall.—Mr. J. Ironmonger, of Wolverhampton, to Miss Bunn, daughter of Mr. Bunn, flax dresser, of Worcester.

Died.] At Litchfield, aged 28, Mr. T. Godwin, hair dresser.

At Newcastle-under-line, Mrs. Blunt, wife of the Rev. Mr. Blunt.

At Wolverhampton, Mrs. Olarenshaw.—Mrs. Prettie, wife of Mr. R. Prettie, attorney.—Mrs. Robins, wife of Mr. Robins, butcher.

WARWICKSHIRE.

Married.] Mr J. M. Gutch, son of the Rev. J. Gutch, registrary of the university of Oxford, to Miss M. Wheeler, of Birmingham.—Mr. G. Bellamy, of Birmingham, to Miss A. Crowdry, of Glamorganshire.

At Harborne, Mr. Bennison, of Smethwick, to Mrs. A. Parkes.—Mr. Wiggan, druggist, &c. of Bilston, to Miss Hateley, second daughter of Mr. J. Hateley, coal master, of Ettingsall.—Mr. W. E. Johnson, only son of Mr. D. Johnson, of the Portway House, to Miss S. Warren, of London.

At Birmingham, Mr. T. Barber, jeweller, of London, to Miss Kendrick, eldest daughter of Mr. J. Kendrick, of Digbeth.—Mr. W. M. Steel, to Miss Carr.—The Rev. J. Kennedy, curate of Kimcote, Leicestershire, to Mrs. Storace, of Summer's Hill.—Mr. J. King, merchant, to Miss A. Snape.—Mr. T. Heathcote, to Miss E. Ewer.—Mr. T. Rastin, to Miss P. Wright.

Died.] At Birmingham, Mrs. Norris, widow of the late G. Norris, esq. of Droitwich, in Worcestershire.—Mrs. Cooper, formerly of the Red Cow public house, in the Horse Fair.—Mr. J. Wright, of the Coach and Horses public house.—Mr. Jefferies, shagreen case maker.—Mr. J. Allen, for upwards of 20 years, master of a respectable academy in Dale End.

At his house in this town, Mr. Gibbs, of

Cubbington, near Warwick.—Mr. Kimberley, writing master of King Edward's School in this town.—Mrs. Barnet, wife of Mr. P. Barnet, saw plate maker.—Mrs. Taylor, wife of Mr. W. Taylor of the Crown public house.—Far advanced in years, Mr. D. Davies, wire worker.—Mr. Sheldon, pincer maker.—Mr. W. Cooper.—Mrs. Harris, wife of Mr. Harris mercer.—Mr. J. Meridith, factor.—Aged 87, Mrs. M Fullelove, a maiden lady.

At Stratford upon Avon, aged 70, Mr. W. Sandland, a traveller in the haberdashery line.

SHROPSHIRE.

Married.] Mr. Beaman, of Westcot, to Miss S. Clarke, of Church Pulverbatch.

At Shrewsbury, Mr. W. Brundon, hair dresser, to Mrs Bailey.—Mr. W. Jones, of Shrewsbury, to Miss Scoltocke, of Kenrock, near Shrewsbury.

At Whitchurch, Mr. Lowe, attorney, to Miss Massey.

At Bridgnorth, T. Herd, esq. of the Custom-house, London, to Mrs. Guest, widow.—Mr. J. Harris, of Hales Owen, to Miss Darby, of Green Hall, near that place.

At Clapham, Surrey, Mr. Neal, builder, to Miss A Daires, of Emstrey, near Shrewsbury.—Mr. Pea, confectioner, of Wem, to Miss Derrett, of Shrewsbury; also Mr. Evans, taylor, of Shrewsbury, to Miss Pea, near the former place.

Died.] At Shrewsbury, Mrs. M. Clarke.—Suddenly, Mrs. Cartwright, widow of the late Mr. Cartwright, apothecary.—Miss Baxter, the last surviving of five sisters, who have all died of a decline.—Mrs. Leighton, wife of the Rev. F. Leighton.

At Oswestry, in his 18th year, Mr. J. Dovaston, son of Mr. Dovaston, attorney of Llanymynech; respected and lamented as a pattern of duty and obedience to his parents, and in other respects, a youth of great promise.—Mr. F. Howells, of Walton.

At Bridgenorth, Mr. G. Carter, many years landlord of the Upper Fox inn.—Mr. C. Prince, sen. of Wem.

At Quatford, near Bridgenorth, Mr. W. Lowe, many years landlord of the Tumbling Sailors inn.

At Lampeter, in his 75th year, Mr. R. Owen.

GLOUCESTERSHIRE.

Mr. W. Lawrence, a medical gentleman of Cirencester, in a letter to the printer of the Gloucester Herald, dated November 15, among other arguments and testimonies to refute an erroneous idea, entertained by some, that the vaccine disease yields a power of protection only for a limited time, produces an extraordinary instance, which lately occurred to him. He states the case as follows:—"A woman had *suffered the disease twenty one years ago*, fearing that time had worn out its power of shielding the constitution, submitted to repeated inoculations with active small-pox infection; and lived about a month in a house for the reception of those who labour under the small pox, where several had heavy burthens; these she constantly associated with, and breathed the infectious atmosphere of the place, without feeling the smallest effect."

Application will be made to Parliament in the ensuing session, for power to carry into effect a proposed rail-way, across the forest of Deane, from the river Wye to the Severn, on a plan of general benefit that shall connect the said rivers, and conciliate and combine all other collateral interests connected with the forests.

Married.] At Gloucester, Mr. J. Dovey, grocer, to Miss Gale.—Mr. W. Saunders, of Saul, to Miss H. Vick, eldest daughter of Mr. D. Vick, of Elmore, near Gloucester.—Mr. R. Mayo, to Miss H. Dangerfield, both of Slimbridge.

Died.] At Gloucester, Miss M. Stephens, daughter of D. Stephens, esq. of the 5th regiment of dragoon guards, quartered in this city.—Mr. P. Cooke, third son of Mr. J. Cooke, plasterer.—In his 82d year, Mr. D. Spencer, sen.—In her 25th year, Miss M. Goodyer, a young lady of a mild and benevolent disposition, and engaging manners, and much endeared to her relatives, by her dutiful and affectionate behaviour, as a daughter and a sister.

HEREFORDSHIRE.

Married.] At Hereford, M. T. Evans, attorney, to Miss Watkins, only daughter of the late Rev. T. Watkins, a prebendary of the cathedral, &c.—Mr. W. Tanner, of Hampton Court, to Miss Grubb, of Shobdon.

Died.] At Hereford, Mr. T. Price, many years a faithful servant in the family of Mr. Wainwright.

Mrs. Pember, wife of Mr. Pember, saddler.—Mrs. Prosser.

At Sydenham, near London, Miss Eliz. Price, second daughter of the late M. Price, esq. of Lincoln's inn fields.—In his 67th year, Mr. W. Wathen, of Dinedor-court, near Hereford. The warmth of his attachments, and his social, generous mind, and liberal disposition, endeared him to a numerous circle of friends.

OXFORDSHIRE.

Married.] Mr. J. Parker, bookseller, of Oxford, to Miss S. Hayes, youngest daughter of the Rev. Mr. Hayes, of the city of Durham.

At Banbury, Mr. J. Pain, to Mrs. Wykham, widow, of Swalcliff, in this county.

At Maddern, J. Eye, esq. to Miss Baynes, only daughter of C. Baynes, esq. of Penzance, in Cornwall.

Died.] At Oxford, aged 89, Mrs Betsworth.—The Reverend C. Blackstone, jun. fellow of Winchester College, Oxford, and only surviving son of the Rev. C. Blackstone, of the same College.

At Henley, Mr. A. Rowden.—The Rev. C. Wake, B D. Rector of Fenny Compton, and late fellow of Corpus Christi College, Oxford.—Aged about 60, Mr. W. Hacks, master of the Bear inn, Woodstock.

At

At Bampton, in a fit of apoplexy, aged 49, the Rev. W. Hawkins, sen. fellow of Pembroke College, Oxford, and Rector of St. Aldates, in that city.—In his 59th year, Mr. J Haines, of Whitchurch.—Mr. T. Stevens, of Nettlebed.

Aged 63, Mrs. Anthony, of Shipton house, near Abingdon, Berks, and daughter of C. Pleydell, esq. formerly of Northmoore, in this county.

At Kingston, in Jamaica, aged 21, Mr. J. Dury, second son of Mr. J. Dury, attorney, of Banbury.

[We must beg leave to contradict the paragraph copied from a late Oxford Journal, (which was in this particular imposed upon) respecting the marriage of Mr. J. Winter to Miss A. Viret, no such marriage having taken place.

NORTHAMPTONSHIRE.

Married.] At Finedon, Mr. J. Stanton, farmer, to Miss Berry, of Ashley, in this county.

Mr. Cope, surgeon, of Wellingborough, in this county, to Miss Sharp, of Fryar's Farm, Bedford.

The Rev. R. B. Hughes, of Riflingbury, to to Miss Jephcott, daughter of the late Rev. H. Jephcott, of Nether Heyford.

At Banbury, Mr. J. Pain, son of the late Alderman Pain, to Mrs. Wykham, widow of the late R. W. Wykham, esq. of Swalcliffe.

Mr. Smith, grazier, of Market Deeping, Lincolnshire, to Miss Goodale, of Carlton, in the county.

In London, Mr. Whiteman, to Miss Cole, both of Daventry.

Mr. R. B. Warwick, of Standground, to Mrs. Meadows, widow, of Peterborough.

Died.] At Peterborough, in an advanced age, the Rev. Mr. Bateman, vicar of Whaplode, Lincolnshire.

At Ounde, Mrs. Gregory, relict of the late Mr. Gregory, of Barnwell Mill.

At Daventry, Mr. Freeman, attorney.

At Dunstable, of a consumptive habit, Miss E Brown.

Mr. Gentle, farmer, of Hemington, near Oundle; he was apparently well and walked in his garden a few hours before he died.

Mrs. Bayley, widow, of Little Stukeley, Huntingdonshire, and grand-daughter to White Kenett, D. D. formerly bishop of Peterborough.—Mrs. Mortimer, widow, of Milton.

At Kingston, Jamaica, aged 21, Mr. J. Day, second son of Mr. J. Day, attorney, of Banbury.

At Bath, in her 69th year, Mrs. Hunt, widow of the late Rev. R. Hunt, rector of Stoke Doyle, in this county.

CAMBRIDGESHIRE.

Married.] Mr. J Johnson, junior, farmer, to Miss P. Sparrow, both of Chesterton.

In London, Mr. C. Johnston, of Cambridge, to Miss S. Johnson, of Bottlesham.—Mr. J. Nunnely, draper, of Kettering, to Miss Luccock, of Cambridge.—Mr. J. Rumbold, baker, of Margle Eon, to Miss Collett, eldest daughter of Mr. Collett, of Cambridge.

The Rev. Z. Stichall, of Wisbach, to Miss Burnham, eldest daughter of J. Burnham, esq of Buxton, in Norfolk.

Died.] At Cambridge, aged 70, J. Merrill, esq. alderman, and many years a respectable bookseller, but had lately retired from business.

In her 70th year, Mrs. Smith; a woman of real goodness of heart and a truly Christian disposition.

Mrs. Freeman, wife of Mr. T. Freeman, maltster, of Barrow.

NORFOLK.

Married.] At Catton, the Hon. G. Irby, eldest son of the Right Hon. Lord Boston, to Miss R. Ives Drake, daughter of W. Drake, esq. late Member for Amersham, in Buckinghamshire.

Mr. R. Chasteney, land-surveyor, of Norwich, to Miss J. Samson, of Sedgeford.—Mr. J. Gillings, surgeon, of London, to Miss George, of East Dereham.—Mr. B. Brown, wheelwright, of Swaffham, to Miss Castle, of Magdalen

Mr. R. Mann, merchant, of Bungay, to Miss Day, of Norwich —Mr. R. C. Harvey, of Alburgh, to Miss M. Blyth, of North Creak Abbey.

Mr. T. Wright, stationer, of Wisbeach, to Miss M. Taylor, only daughter of Mr. Taylor, wool-comber, of Norwich.

In London, Mr. W. G. Graham, of Norwich, to Miss M. Wingrove, of Bath.

At Sedgeford, —— Green, esq. to Miss Wethered, daughter of the Rev. Mr. Wethered.

The Rev. D. Lewes, of Thuruden, in Suffolk, to Miss A. M Leathe, eldest daughter of Mr. Leathe, surgeon, of Acle.

At Norwich, Mr. S. Linstead, butcher, to Miss Bellamy.—Mr. J. Smith, to Miss E. F. Rackham.—Mr. S. Dunham, cordwainer, to Miss A. Betts.—Mr. B. Norman, hempen-cloth-manufacturer, to Miss Freeman.—Mr. J. Knights, taylor, to Mrs. Jenkinson, widow.—Mr. E. Barnard, to Miss P. Chapman.—Mr. Robinson, hot presser, to Miss Woodcock.

At Ringsfield, near Beccles, Mr. R. Berry, farmer, to Miss Fox, eldest daughter of Mrs. Fox, of Worlingham.

Mr. T. Thompson, of Roydon, to Miss Cosher, of Lynn.—Mr. Rodwell, linen draper, of Lynn, to Miss Stanton, of Ling House.

Mr. D Lovelt, of Colton, to Miss Luck, of Honingham; also, Mr. T. Luck, farmer, of Honingham, to Miss S. Lovelt, of Colton.

Mr J. Mills, farmer, to Miss Gosling, both of Trowse Newton.

Died.] At Norwich, aged 45, Mr. E. Elden, manufacturer.—Aged 59, Mrs. Plaford, wife

wife of Mr. R. Plaford, patten-maker.—In her 63d year, Mrs. Hedgman, wife of Mr. R. Hedgman, carpenter.—Mr. J. Simpson, many years a driver of the Newmarket mail-coach.

Aged 23, Mr. P. Betts, eldest son of Mr. Betts, wheelwright, of Happisburgh.

At Lynn, while in his chair, getting his breakfast, Mr. R. Hamond.

At Yarmouth, aged 84, Mrs. M. Waller.

SUFFOLK.

On the 5th of Nov. last, at Bury, while a *mob of Christian savages* were indulging themselves in the inhuman amusement of baiting a bull, the poor animal (which was, by nature, perfectly gentle, but which had been privately baited in the morning and goaded with sharp instruments, in order to render him furious enough for public exhibition) although tied down with ropes, in his agony and rage, (baited as he was by dogs and gored by brutes in the shape of men) burst from his tethers, to the great terror of his tormentors, and the no small danger of the peaceable inhabitants of the place.—After this, the poor beast was doomed to be a victim of still greater barbarity, of fresh tortures inflicted: he was entangled again, with ropes, and horrible, monstrous to relate! his hoofs were cut off and he again baited, while he had to defend himself on his mangled, bleeding stumps! The magistrates of Bury have repeatedly tried to prevent such infernal, demoniacal proceedings, but the demons are sanctioned, it seems, by an act of Parliament.—Surely such an act is highly disgraceful to the period of the world we live in, to our country in general, and to the exalted character of the British nation.

ESSEX.

The Essex Agricultural Society, at their late anniversary meeting, October 9, resolved, in consideration of the high price of corn, and the great advantages arising from the dibbling and drilling of wheat and other corn, both with respect to the saving of the seed, and the improved mode of cultivation, to give a silver medal to the person, who, for the year 1801, dibbles in the greatest number of acres of wheat in proportion to the whole quantity of land sown with that grain, so that the same be not less than twenty acres. Also to give a silver medal to the person, who, for the crop of the year 1801, dibbles in the greatest number of acres of any other corn, in proportion to the whole quantity of land sown with such other corn except beans (being already generally dibbled), so that the same be not less than forty acres. Also to give a silver medal to the person, who, for the crop of the year 1801, drills in the greatest number of acres of wheat, in proportion to the whole quantity of land sown with that grain, so that the same be not less than twenty acres. Also to give a silver medal to the person, who, for the crop of the year 1801, drills in the greatest number of acres of any other corn, in proportion to the whole quantity of land sown with such other corn, so that the same be not less than forty acres. And that the successful candidates for the drilling premiums be allowed one guinea each for the drill-holder. At a previous meeting of the general committee, it was resolved to offer four premiums of five guineas each, to five labourers in husbandry, one guinea each, who shall have brought up the greatest number of children, &c. &c. to five men servants, who shall have received wages during the greatest number of years, &c. to five women servants, who shall have received wages, &c. and to five wives or widows of labourers, who shall have done the greatest number of days work in husbandry, between the 20th of September, 1800, and the 20th of September, 1801.

At the above meeting at Chelmsford, (of the Essex Agricultural Society,) Mr. Wakefield gained the medal for dibbling wheat, having dibbled 26 acres. Mr. Tweed was the successful candidate for drilling wheat, but waved his claim in favour of Mr. Ambrose; he received a prize, however, for drilling the greatest number of acres of other corn.—The candidates for drilling and dibbling wheat were very numerous. The Society have announced their intention to enlarge their subscriptions, for the special purpose of extending their premiums for stock.

Married.] Mr D. Lamprell, of Rettendon, to Miss Balls, of Runwell.

At Colchester, at the Quakers-meeting, Mr. J. De Horne, linen-draper, to Miss S. Bell.

Mr. Smith, surgeon, of Wevenhoe, to Miss A. Cock, of Bull's Bridge, Hempstead.

At Heybridge, near Malden, Mr. W. Wood, to Miss S. Barnard.—Mr. G. Parr, of Writtle, to Miss Leake, of Wealchall.—Mr. Parris, of Long Barns, Beauchamp Roothing, to Miss J. Elliston, of Quickbury, near Sawbridgeworth.

Died.] At Chelmsford, Mr. G. Wood, who formerly kept the Canteen, at the Old Barracks.—Mr. Packman, cabinet-maker and upholsterer.

At Colchester, Mr. Till, surgeon.—Mrs. Jacobs, widow.—Mrs. Anderson, wife of Mr. Anderson, linen-draper.

At Bassingbourn Hill, near Dunmow, his Grace Robert Fowler, D.D Archbishop of Dublin, and Primate of Ireland; he had been in the possession of the see about 21 years.

At Beccles, aged 20, Miss E. King. This young lady entertained a strong presentiment of her approaching dissolution, and mentioned it to her friends about two months before, although she was, at that time, in apparently good health, and continued so till the Wednesday preceding her death.

At Leigh, in his 20th year, Mr. E. Harridge, son of D. Harridge, esq. of Little Stambridge Hall.

At Swaffham, Miss J. Appleyard.

At

At Braintree, at the Wheat Sheaff, aged 63, Mrs. Hocker.

At Helvedon, fuddenly, aged 63, Mr. S. Harvey, a refpectable fchoolmafter.

At Riven Hall, in his 91ft year, Mr. J. Wood, farmer.

At Galleywood Common, Mr. P. Ruffle, fon of Mr. Ruffle.—Mr. Hammond, miller, of Galleywood Common.

Mr. C. Francis, fon of Mr. R. Francis, of Heybridge Hall, near Malden.—Mr Phillips, of Purleigh.—Mr. K. Jennings, butcher, of Great Wakering.

Aged 26, Mr. C. Francis, farmer, of Munden.

At Maldon, Mr. J. White, tanner. He was fuddenly feized, fhortly after his going to bed, with an apoplectic fit, which baffled every medical affiftance.

Mr. W. Thompfon, comptroller of the cuftoms.—Mrs. Bright, relict of the late Mr. Bright.

Mrs Smith, of Prittlewell.

At Leigh, Mr. W. Elliott, farmer.

At Witham, Mifs M. Church, niece to Mr. J. Scott, attorney.

Mr. J. Bell, corn-merchant; a man of an upright character.

Mr. S. Baker, of Thorrington Hall.

At Bocking, Mr. J. Englifh, formerly a confiderable baize-maker.

The Rev. J. Thorogood, Diffenting minifter; univerfally refpected for his learning, abilities, and piety.

Mrs. White, of Gold Hanger.

At Brentwood, in his 81ft year, E. Benfon, efq. a Bencher of the Middle Temple.

Mr. Barnard, of Heybridge-mill, near Malden.

KENT.

An Agricultural Society has been lately formed at Margate, for the exprefs purpofe of *growing Indian Corn*, and the members, and a number of other gentlemen, have each agreed to form a plantation of it. It appears that fome plants have been produced in that neighbourhood equal to what has been feen to grow in America or the Weft Indies. It is devoutly to be wifhed that this laudable purfuit may be extended, as the produce of this plant is well known to be very ufeful to fociety.

Married.] Mr. J. Bird, to Mifs E. Wood, both of Hearne.

At Waltham, Mr. R. Keeler, farmer, to Mifs M Sutton.—F. S. Pitcher, efq. of Cobham, to Mifs Hole, daughter of the Rev. T. Hole, of Georgham, Devon.—Mr. E. Strickland, grazier, of Appledore, to Mifs S. Huggett, of Canterbury.

In London, T. Collier, efq of Southfleet, to Mifs Snelling, of St. Mary Cray.

At Kingfnorth, Mr. J. Bingham, blackfmith, to Mifs S. Cafbey.

At Deptford, Mr. E. Alfton, to Mifs Gooch, of Swainftorp, Norfolk.—Mr. H. Elliott, to Mifs M. Furley, both of Ofpringe.

Mr. J. Saintclear, of Folkftone, to Mifs M. A. Sims, eldeft daughter of Mr. R. Sims, farmer, of Caple-le-Ferne.

At Greenwich, Lieutenant Lloyd, of the Artillery, to Mifs Campbell, fourth daughter of R. Campbell, efq. of Blackheath.—Mr. J. White, woollen-manufacturer, of Newgate-ftreet, London, to Mifs A. White, third daughter of Mr. White, of Hale Farm, St. Nicholas, in Thanet.—Lieut. G. Graymell, of the North Gloucefter regiment of Militia, to Mifs Frifby, of Sandwich.

At Folkftone, Mr. T. Caifter, grocer, to Mifs S. Graylon.

T. Mitchel, efq. of Dover, to Mifs S. A. Porter, of Canterbury.

At Canterbury, Mr. Sheaf, wool-comber.—Mr. Greaves.—Mr. T. Hayward, gardiner.

At Maidftone, Mrs. Sawer, widow.

At Rochefter, in an advanced age, Mrs. S. Rondeau.—Mr. W. Tanner, fon of Mr. Tanner, of the Red Cow public-houfe.—In an advanced age, Mrs. Drury

At Warehorn, Mr. W. Maylam.—Mrs. Spratt, wife of Mr. J. Spratt, paper-maker, at River.

At Whitftable, fuddenly, Mrs. Kemp, wife of Mr. Kemp, fenior.

Mrs. Mecrow, wife of Mr. Mecrow, carpenter, at Wingham.

At Wrotham, Mrs. E. Medhurft, a maiden lady, of Maidftone.

At Tiehurft, aged 33, Mr. J. Morphett, jun. of Tenterden.

At Tenterden, aged 61, Mrs. Carpenter, wife of Mr. T. Carpenter, taylor.

In her 20th year, Mifs C. Smith, of St. Dunftan's, near Canterbury.

At Exmouth, G. Frend, efq. of Kenton, Devon, eldeft fon of the late Mr. Alderman Frend, of Canterbury.

At Folkftone, Mr. E. Smith, attorney.

At Sandgate, Mr. T. Kirwin.

At Rofetta, in Egypt, in his 30th year, Captain W. Netherfole Long, of the 86th regiment, only fon of the late W. Long, efq. of Canterbury.

Mr. J. Hawker, boarder, of Dover Caftle.

At Bearfted, Mrs. Filmer.

SUSSEX.

Mr. Kennard, miller, of Lewes, has at prefent in his poffeffion a hog only eleven months old, whofe weight is between fifty and fixty ftone, which makes his increafe confiderably more than a ftone per week from the day he was farrowed!

Died.] At his houfe, in the Cliffe, near Lewes, aged 85, Mr. G. Verralt, fen. auctioneer; the deceafed has left behind him fix children, thirty-feven grand-children, and twelve great-grand-children; he has quitted the world with an unblemifhed reputation, having conducted himfelf, in every relation of life, as "God's nobleft work—an honeft man."

HAMPSHIRE.

Married.] At New Alresford, Mr. J. Holder,

den, surgeon, to Miss Shawford.—The Rev. W. Harrison, rector of Tadley and Overton, to Miss A. Nichols, daughter of Major Nichols, of the 45th regt. of foot.

Died.] At Winchester, Mrs. Bartholomew, wife of E. Bartholomew, esq.—At an advanced age, Mrs. Clark, widow, of Lymington.

WILTSHIRE.

At the anniversary meeting for the benefit of the Salisbury Infirmary, Sept. 23, the collection at the church doors for the benefit of the institution, amounted to sixty-nine pounds twelve shillings.

Married.] Mr. Smith, of Luggarshall, to Miss Mortimer, of Marlbro'.

At Corsley, after a courtship of 20 years, Mr. J. Eyre, to Miss E. Collins.—The Rev. J. W. Champneys, of Ogbourn, St. Georges, Wilts, to Miss M. Merriman, of Bath.—Mr. D. Jenkins, of Charter house, Hinton, to Mrs. Milson, widow of Mr. Milson, of Bradford.—Mr. H. Hancock, mealman, of Bath to Miss J. Simkins, of Stanton street, Barnard, in this county.—Mr. J. Offer, brush maker, of Bristol, to Miss J. Churchplate, of Malmsbury.—Mr. T. Merriman, town clerk of Marlborough, to Miss Clark, of Preshute house, near Marlborough.

At Warminster, Mr. J. Roles, grocer, to Miss F. Hinton.

At Salisbury, Mr. Young, butcher, to Miss Green.

Died.] At Salisbury, Mr. J. Goddard, eldest son of J. Goddard, esq.

At Devizes, Mr. W. Halcomb, sen. of the Bear-inn, in which he had honourably acquired a handsome fortune.

At Broughton, near Stockbridge, the Rev. J. Williams, many years curate of Downton.

At an advanced age, Mr. W. Batten, malster, of Quidhampton, near Salisbury.

SOMERSETSHIRE.

Married.] At Bath, Mr. Longdon, of George-street, Manchester-square, London, to Miss Smith.

G. Potter, esq. to Miss Gunning.—Mr. W. Bendale, corn-factor, to Miss Smith, only daughter of Mr. W. Smith, brewer.—Mr. King, apothecary, to Miss P. English, eldest daughter of Mr. English, auctioneer.—Mr. T. Newman, jun. glover, of Worcester, to Miss L. Fry, second daughter of Mr. R. Fry, woollen-draper, of Bristol.

The Rev. G. Barry, curate of Walcot, to Miss Squire, of Walcot-parade.

At Walcot Church, Mr. Mathias, at Messrs. Lintern's, music-sellers, to Miss Godwin, daughter of Mrs. Godwin, haberdasher.

Lieutenant Knott, of the second regiment of Somersetshire Militia, to Miss Clarke, eldest daughter of the late Mr. Clarke, merchant, of Bristol.

At Hatherley, Devon, B. Arthur, esq. to Miss M. Cross, daughter of the late Mr. W. Cross, of Bath.

Died.] At Bath, in the prime of life, and after the most acute sufferings during a lingering illness, the lady of Lord John Russel.

Mrs. Phillott, wife of the Rev. Archdeacon Phillott, rector of this city; a lady of whom it may be declared, without exaggerating her character, that she was pious, without ostentation; generous, without prodigality; mild and affable, without weakness; and affectionately indulgent, without transgressing those rules by which alone any charities can be exercised. It might be truly said of her, what Addison said of himself, and what will almost ever be the reward of Christian virtue—"See with what fortitude a Christian can die."

In her 70th year, Mrs. Hopkins, long known to the public as an actress at Drury-lane Theatre. She enjoyed a good state of health till a few months before she paid the common debt to nature.

At his lodgings in the Circus, after an illness of only a few hours, Major Boland.—Mrs. Smith, wife of R. Smith, esq.—Mrs. Byam.

At Bristol, Mrs. Whitney, wife of Mr. Whitney, apothecary.—Mrs. Beale, sister to Mrs. Ireland of Brislington.

Mr. C. A. Lawrence, son of Mr. Lawrence, of Cross-inn.

At Surinam, in his 27th year, Mr. J. Evans, son of Mr. J. Evans, of Clifton.

At Batcombe, aged 79, Mr. Boord, maltster (which business he had carried on upwards of sixty years), and father of Mr. Boord, attorney, of Bath.

Aged 76, the Rev. Mr. Turner, upwards of fifty years rector of Loxton.

At the Hotwells, in his 28th year, Lord Augustus Fitzroy, fourth son of the Duke of Grafton, post-captain in the navy, and late commander of the L'Oiseau ship of war.—The lady of E. Simeon, esq. M. P. for Reading.

At East Harptree, near 90 years of age, Mrs. Walker, a maiden lady.

The lady of Dr. Cooper, of Bath Easton Villa.

At Sandhill Park, near Taunton, Mr. T. Jennings; he was shortly to have been married to an amiable young woman to whom he has bequeathed all his property.

H. Edgell, esq. of Standerwick-court, justice of peace for this county; a gentleman universally esteemed in public and private life, and whose loss will be severely felt by the poor of his neighbourhood.

DORSET.

Married.] T. Bunn, esq. of Frome Selwood, to Miss Kelson, of Beckington.

Died.] At Hawkchurch, Mrs. Domett, mother of Capt. Domett, of the navy.—Mrs. Abbott, of Charlton Herethorne.—Mr. Nichols, of Cruxton.

At Cotham, the Rev. W. Topham, vicar of Shaftsbury.

Aged 63, the Rev. H. Sherive, L.L.D. of this

Hide House, near Bridport, and justice of the peace of this county.

DEVON.

The Commissioners of the Navy have lately made a survey of the whole of Cawsand Bay. They have it in comtemplation, by the advice of Mr. Penn, King's-pilot, at Cawsand, to construct a pier from Pinlee Point, to the S. E. part of the bay; which desirable object, if once obtained, will secure the bay completely against the E. S. E. gales, the only winds which can now affect it, and there can be moorings then laid down for forty men of war.

Married.] In London, Mr. J. Hyde, woollen-draper, of Exeter, to Miss Bidlake, of Totness.

Mr. Fretwell, grocer, of Gainsborough, to Miss Sweetland, youngest daughter of the late Mr. T. Sweetland, baker.

At Plymouth, Lieut. Clavell, of the Barfleur ship of war, to Miss C. Bully, 2d daughter of Mrs. Bully, wine-merchant.

At Georgeham, F. Pilcher, esq. to Miss Hole.

Mr. Bailey, attorney of North Petherton, to Miss S. Morle, of Williton.

Died.] At Dartmouth, at the house of his son, aged 65, Mr. Laurence Tremlett, merchant, late of Totness. He sustained through life, in all the domestic and social relations, as well as in the transactions of Commerce, the character of a good and upright man.

WALES.

Married.] At Forden, Montgomeryshire, Lieutenant-col. Cockburne, eldest son of Sir James Cockburne, bart. to the Hon. M. Devereux, eldest daughter of Lord Viscount Hereford.

At Haverford West, Mr. Duvan, to Miss Stokes.

At Prendergast, Pembrokeshire, W. Bowen, esq. late Major in the Haverford West Leyton, to Mrs. Morris, widow.—Mr. Lloyd, attorney, of Llanfair Carinion, to Miss Pugh, of Kerry, in Montgomeryshire.

At Abergavilly, Mr. J. Spurrell, auctioneer, of Carmarthen, to Miss M. A. Board.

At Lamphy, Pembrokeshire, W. Parry, esq. of Portclew, to Miss A. Kemm, second daughter of H. Kemm, esq. of North Downhouse.

At Llandovery, Mr. W. Price, surgeon, to Mrs. E. Jones.—R. W. Price, esq. of Rhiwlas, Merionethshire, to Miss F. Lloyd, second daughter of J. Lloyd, esq. of Berth, near Ruthin, and chief justice of the Carmarthen circuit.

At Aberin, in Carnarvonshire, Captain J. Crawley, of the navy, to Miss Roberts, daughter of the late Rev. G. Roberts, vicar.

Died.] Aged 81, Mrs. Kenrick, wife of J. Kenrick, esq. of Ruthen, Denbighshire.

At Carnarvon, M. Owen, esq. of Tygwin, Merionethshire.

In her 69th year, Mrs. Jones, relict of Mr. Jones, attorney, of Builth, Brecknockshire.

In Llandovery, Miss Phillips, sister of T. H. Phillips, esq. of Pontywall, Brecon.—Mrs. Mayne, wife of Mr. Mayne, wine-merchant, of High Wycombe, Bucks, and relict of the late N. Mayne, jun. esq. of Carmarthen.

At Lambstone, near Haverford West, aged 90, W. W. Bowen, esq.

At Haverfordwest, suddenly, W. Bland, esq.

At Carmarthen, Miss M. Oakley.

SCOTLAND.

A potatoe was lately dug out of the garden of Mr. Andrew Morris, in Abernethy, measuring in circumference 15 inches by 11½. It weighed 1lb. 12 oz. avoirdupois!

The workmen have lately begun again to build on the east front of the New College of Edinburgh. The foundation was laid in 1789, upon a large scale, conformably to an elegant plan by the late Mr. Adam, architect. The building continued to advance for several years, till the subscription fund was exhausted. The north-west corner was completely finished, and the north-east corner roofed in.

The new channel in the Frith of Forth, to the southward of the island of Inchkeith, has been lately bouyed up and rendered navigable by order of government, for the greater safety of ships of war entering the Frith. This passage, which is also found to be of the greatest utility to the trade of Leith, and the ports higher up the Frith, has greatly enhanced the grandeur and beauty of the highly interesting prospect it affords; by bringing the ships so much nearer the coast, and consequently so much more within the immediate view of Edinburgh and its environs.

A life boat, of a construction similar to that at Shields, has been lately built at Montrose.

Population of Berwickshire:—Males 14058, females 16033—Total 30291.

Population of the city of Glasgow.—Parishes of Inner High Church or North, 8059 persons—Outer High Church, or East, 5263—St. Andrew's ditto, or Middle, 4338—Blackfriars ditto, or South, 4901—Tron ditto, or South West, 6594—Ramshorn ditto, or North West, 7401—Wynd ditto, or West, 3799—St. Enoch, 6704—Barony parish comprehending the suburbs, North of the Clyde, 29431—Gorbals, comprehending Tradestown, Hutchiestown, &c. being the suburbs south of the city, 7559—Total 83769.

It is in contemplation, to erect a new county hall, with suitable offices, also a prison and bridewell, in the town of Perth: these, with several other improvements now in a state of forwardness, will tend greatly to augment the town. Plans are accurately prepared, and an act to empower their being put in execution, will, it is expected, pass next session, for a new dock and bason, where 30 vessels may unload at one time, and a fine broad

street

ſtreet will be thrown open to the road, and which is intended to join the bridge.

Married.] At Strabane, Colonel R. Anſtruther, of the Loyal Tay Fencibles, to Miſs Nairne, daughter of Lieut. Col. Nairne, of the Breadalbane Fencibles.

J. Robertſon, jun. eſq. merchant, of Glaſgow, to Miſs J. Grey, of Gartcraig.—Captain W. Erſkine, of the 16th regiment of foot, ſecond ſon of J. Erſkine, eſq. of Cakroſs, Perthſhire, to Miſs Myers, only daughter of Major General Myers.

At Dumfries, Mr. C. Paterſon, to Miſs J. Laurie.—Major Mc Murdoe, to Miſs Wilſon, daughter of the late Captain J. Wilſon, of the Queen's Ranger Dragoons.

At Edinburgh, W. Moxon, eſq. from Hull, to Miſs I. Williamſon, eldeſt daughter of J. Williamſon, eſq. of Polmont-houſe.—Mr. P. P. Sherill, merchant, to Miſs C. Stirling.—Mr. J. Crawford, of Paiſley, to Miſs M. Richmond, eldeſt daughter of Mr. Richmond, of the Nurſery, Leith-walk.

At Leith, A. Scott, eſq. purſer of the ſhip Iris, to Miſs P. Forbes, daughter of the Rev. W. Forbes, late miniſter of Fordown.

Mr. G. Yuille, merchant, in Glaſgow, to Miſs M. Buchanan, of Ardenconnel.

At Glaſgow, A. Bogle, eſq. of Kingſton, Jamaica, to Miſs M. Stirling.

At Gretna-green, Capt. Lloyd, of the Coldſtream Regiment of Guards, to Miſs Williams, of Pool, Montgomeryſhire.

At Scoure, Iſle of Mull, the Rev. Edmond M'Queen, miniſter of Barra, to Miſs I. M'Lean, ſecond daughter of Mr. C. M'Lean, of Scoure.

Lieut. Col. J. Purnett, late of the Eaſt India Company's ſervice, to Miſs M. Steele, youngeſt daughter of J. F. Steele, eſq. of Gadgirth, in Ayrſhire.

At Montroſe, T. Bruce, eſq. the younger, of Arnot, to Miſs Renny, eldeſt daughter of R. Renny, eſq. late of Borrowfield.

Died.] At Edinburgh, J. Mc Dowall, eſq. late of Woolnet.—Miſs A. Scott, daughter of the deceaſed W. Scott, eſq. writer to the ſignet.—A. Seton, eſq. ſon of the deceaſed Sir Henry Seton.—J. Baird, eſq. Deputy King's Remembrancer of the Exchequer.

Lady Elizabeth Kemp, wife of the Rev. Dr. Kemp, one of the miniſters of the city, and ſiſter to the Earl of Hopetoun.

The Reverend Dr. Charles Wilſon, Profeſſor of Church Hiſtory in the Univerſity of St. Andrews.

Major Robert Wallace, of the 17th regiment of foot, eldeſt ſon of A. Walpole, eſq. banker.

At Strabane, Miſs M. Somerville.

At Kincubbin, the Rev. Dr. Frazer.

In his 51ſt year, and 24th of his miniſtry, the Rev. J. Punton, miniſter of the Aſſociate Congregation of Hamilton. he expired ſuddenly, when on his way to Glaſgow.

At Carnſalloch, J. Hannay, eſq. of Torrs.

At Loſſie Barns, near Elgin, J. Walker, M. D.

At Old Meldrum, Dr. J. Gordon, a gentleman of eminent abilities in his profeſſion.

W. Glen, eſq. of Aſloſs, juſtice of peace for the county of Ayr.

At Falkirk, Mr. J. Bell, merchant.

At Wigton, in his 84th year, Mr. J. Martin, a Quaker, late of Kirkbride; with the character of a man of rigid integrity, habitual ſobriety, a vigorous underſtanding and independent mind.

At Kirkmichael, Ayrſhire, the Rev. J. Ramſay, miniſter of the goſpel.

At Fairgirth, near Dumfries, in his 71ſt year, J. Dixon, eſq. late of Whitehaven.

At Glaſgow, Mrs. Mc Dowall, wife of J. Mc Dowall, eſq. merchant.—The Rev. Dr. M. M'Culloch, miniſter of Bothwell.

At Dumfries, J. Mundell, eſq. ſurgeon.—Miſs Culton, of Auchnabony.

In his 90th year, Mr. F. Mitchell, writing maſter, and the oldeſt freeman of the Incorporation.

At the Manſe of Kirk Oſwald, in her 85th year, Mrs. M. Woodrow, wife of the Rev. Mr. Biggar, and daughter of the author of the Church Hiſtory of Scotland.

At Ellon Caſtle, in the county of Aberdeen, in his 80th year, the Right Hon. George Gordon, Earl of Aberdeen; he was made a colonel in 1762, a major-general in 1772, a lieutenant-general in 1777, and a general in 1793.

At Coates, near Edinburgh, aged 77, the Right Hon the counteſs dowager of Glencairne.

At Dundee, Captain A. Bower, of the 93d regiment of foot, ſecond ſon of A. Bower, eſq. of Kinnettles.—Mr. J. Grant, ſurgeon.

In Egypt, of the wounds he received in the battle of the 21ſt of March, Lieut. A. Donaldſon, of the 42d regiment, ſecond ſon of the deceaſed Lieut. Col. Donaldſon, of the 3d regiment of Fencibles.

At Dalkeith, Mr. J. Dick, tobacconiſt, and adjutant to the Dalkeith Volunteers. While on duty with the corps he was ſuddenly taken ill, and expired in a few moments.

At Fairley, Mr. A. Dunlop, ſon of the late Mr. A. Dunlop, Profeſſor of Hebrew in the Univerſity of Glaſgow.

At Thunderton, Lady Dowager Dunbar, of Northfield.

At Halhill, near Dunbar, Miſs J. Tate, daughter of Mr. W. Tate, late merchant in Glaſgow.

At Braehead, Miſs M. Houiſon.

At Perth, in his 85th year, Mr. Patrick Niſbett, ſurgeon to the Royal Artillery. He was above 60 years in that ſtation, and acted as a ſurgeon in the expedition to Carthagena, in 1739. He alſo attended the artillery in the battles of Dettingen and Fontenoy.

IRELAND.

IRELAND.

Confiderable progrefs has been already made in the line of military-road, which has been laid out in the county of Wicklow, and which is intended to interfect the great chain of fouthern mountains, in their utmoft length, in a direction nearly from north to fouth. This great national work, which will doubtlefs prove highly conducive to the improvement of that part of the kingdom, is likely to be very fpeedily completed.

There are now in the city of Dublin, about 6000 merchants, traders and fhopkeepers, of different denominations; of thefe there are 311 wholefale merchants, free of the 6 and 10 per cents, in the cuftom-houfe, as regulated by act of parliament. There are, likewife, 267 principal grocers and 120 bankers.

Married.] R. Lafcelles, efq. county of Downe, Ireland, to Mifs Hutchinfon, niece to lord Frankfort.

In Dublin, P. French, efq. aged 21, to Mifs Dennis, aged 46.—D. Reid, efq. of Canton, in China, to Mifs Bell.

J. Blake, efq. eldeft fon of Sir Walter Blake, of Mentol Caftle, in Galway, to Mifs Brice, of Kilrout Houfe, in Antrim, grand-daughter to Lord Ventry.

At Waterford, Edm. Cafhin, efq. to Mifs Moriffey, daughter of the late captain Moriffey.

The Hon. H. Blackwood, to Mifs Finlay, of Griffith, county of Meath.

At Limerick, S. S. Benwell, efq. of the 21ft regiment of light dragoons, to Mifs W. R. Lewin, daughter of the late J. R. Lewin, efq. of Port Fergus, in the county of Clare.

Died.] At Dublin, at his houfe in Kildare-ftreet, the Right Hon. Lord Roffmore. His lordfhip, the preceding day, had dined abroad in a felect company of friends, where he was diftinguifhed by his accuftomed chearfulnefs, and kind manners. In the evening he was at the drawing-room, at the Caftle, and remained till half after 11, when he retired, and on going to bed, was apparently in perfect health; about two o'clock he rang for his fervant, who, inftantly appearing, his lordfhip faid he was a little fick, and inftantly expired, without a groan.

In Dublin, in his 69th year, Mr. Thomas Mercer. To an uncommonly ftrong, clear and comprehenfive underftanding, this gentleman added a rectitude of heart, and an ardour of fentiment and affection, which imparted a peculiar energy to every thing he did or faid. He was the enlightened, warm and fteady friend, and affertor of the rights of man, on the broadeft bafis, civil, political and religious. His ample fortune, acquired in the Eaft, with unfullied integrity, by the laborious purfuits of commerce, was uniformly devoted to a well-regulated hofpitality, and acts of noble and generous kindnefs. Mr. Mercer was born at Newry, in the Province of Ulfter, and received fuch an education as fell to the general lot of merchant's fons at that day, in fmall commercial towns. He was fent to a grammar-fchool, where he learned but little of the Latin language, as might be expected when it is known that he was fent to an uncle, a merchant in Dublin, at the early age of thirteen, in whofe counting-houfe he remained a fhort time. From this fituation he removed to the houfe of another friend in Liverpool, under whofe protection he had a better profpect of making his way in the world, and fecuring that independence, which was the early object of his honeft policy and ambition. In this enterprizing mart he entered into a fea-faring life, which he purfued with fuch induftry, and every requifite quality of head and heart, that before the age of eighteen he was appointed Captain of a Weft Indian merchantman. In this ftation he remained for feveral years, fometimes in the employment of others, and fometimes trading on his own account between Europe, the Weft Indies and America. But finding that the moft precious part of his life was paffing away without any rational profpect of the object which he was anxious to obtain, he turned his views in 1767 to the Eaft, where he flattered himfelf that perfeverance and integrity would crown his wifhes with fuccefs: and from thence, after various viciffitudes, fome of which had nearly extinguifhed his moft flattering hopes, he returned in 1787 with a fortune of not lefs than fixty thoufand pounds. No man could love money lefs on its own account, or from any view to improper expenditure than Mr. Mercer. No confideration of this kind could engage him in the purfuit of it; becaufe, when obtained, it was the minifter of a truly generous fpirit. Ever ready to relieve the unfortunate, he had a peculiar pleafure in affifting thofe, efpecially young men, who poffeffed a difpofition congenial with his own, and aimed at independence by fkilful enterprize, but with fcanty means. His love of an independent fortune arofe from an independence of mind, which from an early period of life grew with his growth, and marked his character in a very peculiar manner. So ftrongly was he impreffed by thefe principles, that, when in India, he had the following beautiful paffage engraved on a folid plate of gold and hung up in the cabin of his fhip; and it ftill continues to hang over the chimney of his parlour.

> Hail! Independence; hail! Heav'n's next beft gift,
> To that of life, and an immortal foul;
> The life of life! that to the banquet high
> and fober meal, gives tafte.

While in India, Mr. Mercer formed an intimate friendfhip with Lord Macartney, then Governor of Madras, of whofe abilities and integrity he had a very high fenfe, and to whom he was enabled to do effential fervice in his contest with General Stuart, who was arrested by the late Sir George L. Staunton, his Lordship's Secretary, at the very instant the General seemed to meditate the same attack on his Lordship, which he had before effected on Lord Pigot. After Lord Macartney's and Mr. Mercer's return from India, a very regular and affectionate correspondence by letters subsisted between them; and in his Lordship's occasional visits to that country, the most friendly interviews and visits, during which a highly pleasing and unreserved communication of sentiment took place.—But, from his Lordship's frequent absence on foreign embassies, &c. and Mr. Mercer's declining health since his Lordship's return, their epistolary correspondence, in a great measure, ceased for some time past. Mr. Mercer's attachment to the cause of liberty was ardent. While absent in India he entered most warmly into the cause of America, and rejoiced exceedingly in her full emancipation from the unwarranted claims of Great Britain. Shortly after his return from India the French revolution commenced. Here his predominant principles and feelings were again called forth. Having been a witness in early life to the degrading system of oppression which pervaded France, he espoused her interests (as the interests of all mankind) with his whole heart, and to the last hour of his life, watched with solicitude every event connected with her freedom and independence. Having more than a common acquaintance with the late Mr. Edmund Burke, on his first marked disapprobation in the British Parliament of the proceedings of the National Convention, Mr. Mercer in a letter to him expressed his surprise, that from the course of Mr. Burke's past life he should declare the sentiments which he then uttered. This brought an answer from Mr. Burke in justification of them, which produced a long reply from Mr. Mercer, containing a discussion of the subject highly worthy of the public eye, and which will probably, at no distant period, entertain the readers of the Monthly Magazine. Mr. Mercer was distinguished by a peculiar clearness and precision of thought on every subject which occupied his mind: and no subject occupied it with any forcible impression, that was not intimately connected with the most important interests of mankind. Although his education was limited, this circumstance could not be discovered by his writing or conversation: as he possessed an acuteness and comprehension of mind, joined to an accuracy and force of expression, seldom equalled even by professed scholars. He drew from the powerful resources of his own mind what others are indebted for to much study and investigation: and in every expression of his sentiments the honest independence of his mind shone as the most conspicuous trait. He was an absolute stranger to that tameness of spirit which suppresses feelings under the impression of timidity, sometimes assuming the plausible name of moderation. Conscious of the rectitude of his sentiments, he uttered them with ingenuous freedom, unawed by power, even when power was uncontrouled, and suspicion but another word for guilt—and he spoke of men as he spoke of things—integrity commanded his esteem and respect wherever it appeared—the want of it called forth his reprobation, whether in public or private life. Men of strong intellects in other respects, and men of self-reputed abilities have often declared themselves the champions of infidelity; but Mr. Mercer was of a very different stamp. His mind could embrace nothing *without evidence* or *against evidence*. He was a truly enlightened and firm friend of revealed religion: but his views of the Christian scheme were most rational. He rejected with scorn all those doctrines, which the rash interpretations of men have ascribed to the gospel, without attempting to reconcile them to common sense and reason. In short, Mr. Mercer's religious sentiments were grounded on the soundest principles of reason. He was from conviction a dissenter from the church establishment, but he was so, on the most enlarged and liberal principles. He was a warm friend to the full emancipation of the Roman Catholics from every penal restraint and coercion. Under the influence of the same sentiment he entered with fervour into the case of Dr. Priestley, whose unchristian treatment, sanctioned apparently as it was, by some authority, will fix a stain on Great Britain, while science and religion find respect on the earth. Though not personally acquainted with the Doctor, nor an adopter of all his religious opinions, he admired his learning, candour, liberality and regard for true religion. Deeply concerned for the Doctor's loss of property (part of which no pecuniary compensation could repair) he conceived an idea, that Great Britain and Ireland contained one hundred persons, possessing an independence of mind and purse, which would incline and enable them, if publicly called on, to lay down one hundred pounds each, and, by constituting a fund of ten thousand pounds, do honour to themselves and the Doctor, by testifying their sympathy for his sufferings, and recording their testimony against the savage spirit which had destroyed his fortune, and would have destroyed his life, if it had fallen into the power of his persecutors. But when Mr. Mercer wrote with sanguine expectation to some friends in England on this subject, and found that there was no probability that it would be brought to the desired conclusion, he deemed himself bound to perform his part, and accordingly presented the Doctor by the hands of his brother with the sum of one hundred pounds. Mr. Mercer's bodily frame was corpulent; but for the last eighteen months of his life he found

found his size and strength decreasing, and latterly, he was subject to a spasmodic affection of the lungs, attended with swelling in the lower extremities which indicated a collection of water in the breast, and, whatever the proximate cause might be, ended in his dissolution; and though he deemed it his duty to take the aid of the best medical advice, he spoke with great composure of the improbability at his advanced period of life of keeping up a machine, which is at best frail, and liable to sudden changes. He viewed death, however, without dismay, and spoke of it with unconcern, though impressed with a deep sense of its awful consequences —But he accustomed himself to look beyond the grave with a steady faith in a future state of impartial retribution —And, as an habitual regard to it was the sure guide of his life, he found in it an effectual support and comfort under the approach of the last struggle which flesh is heir to. Most justly may it be said of him, in the expressive language of the immortal Poet:—
"The elements were so mixed in him, that Nature might stand up, and say to all the world,—"This was a man."

Mr. J. Turner, agent for transports; this gentleman, on the first night of the illuminations, was thrown from his horse, in consequence of the animal being frightened by a squib thrown at him: his death was occasioned by a fracture he received in the head from the fall.

Mr. R. Rogers.—Christopher O'Bryan esq. —Mrs. Lloyd, relict of the late R. Lloyd, esq. of Fourry Park, county of Longford.

At Cork, Mr. H. Wetherland.—W. Smith, esq. of Rollestown, county of Dublin.

Lately at Cleonate, county of Roscommon, P. Keller, esq.

At Limerick, aged 22, Mr. J. Watson, son to Mr. Andrew Watson.

At Mount Melick, aged 108 years, Mr. J. Kerwan, parish sexton; he retained the use of his faculties to the last.

At Carrick Maccross, in his 77th year, the Rev. Dr. O'Reilly, Catholic bishop of Clogher.

At Phillsboro', aged 82, suddenly, P. Wilson, esq. a respectable printer and bookseller.

At Londonderry, Lieutenant S. Goodson, of the royal navy.

At his seat at Hillsboro', the most noble Arthur Hill, Marquis of Downshire, Earl of Hillsboro', &c. and in England, Viscount Fairford and Baron Harwich; his death was occasioned by a severe attack of the gout in his stomach, which produced almost instant death. His Lordship was born Feb. 23, 1753, and succeeded his father, the late Marquis, October 13, 1793.

At Cheltenham, Gloucestershire, in his 72d year, the Right Honourable the Earl of Howth, Viscount St. Lawrence and Baron Howth, in the county of Dublin. His Lordship married a sister of the Earl of Kingston, in 1750. He is succeeded in his titles and estates by his eldest son, William Viscount St. Lawrence.

DEATHS ABROAD.

At Norkoping, in Sweden, John Henry Liden, a celebrated Swedish *literateur*. He presented to the university of Upsal, or rather to the students of East Gothland, who frequented it, nearly the whole of his library, consisting of about 6000 volumes, on condition of its being made public; he likewise endowed the University, with the interest of a capital of 1333 rix-dollars, for the acquisition of new works. His step-mother, Hedwig Sophia Liden, a woman replete with respectability, and who seemed to rival him in acts of beneficence, sunk a capital of 2777 rix-dollars, the interest of which was to serve as a salary to a librarian. He and his step-mother left a salary for an amanuensis, to be employed in the library of the University of Upsal, and the interest of a capital to form a purse of rix-dollars, every year, for two students not opulent, that should discover talents. Liden likewise gave the sum of 1000 rix-dollars to the Royal Academy of Stockholm, and a like sum to the Academy of Belles Lettres, History and Antiquities of the same city, of which he was a member. He also gave 500 rix-dollars to the library of the Academy of Abo, to purchase new books; and a like sum, with the profit of two works which he had printed at his own expence, to the library of Linkoping. He added a number of his own valuable books to the library of the Swedish Academy; as also to the library of the University of Lund, to that of Abo, and to the library of the Gymnasium of his own city. In 1791, on the death of his step-mother, he gave 200 rix-dollars* to the chest of the poor of the city of Linkoping. The king confirmed these different dispositions of Liden, and insured their duration. It would be difficult to enumerate all the beneficent gifts which he distributed in his life-time; which, however, did not amount to less than 11,622 rix-dollars; and he never let slip any opportunity of doing good. Liden languished under a complaint of the joints (a catastrophe so much the more deplorable for him, as before he was attacked with it, in 1776, he had only been ill twice in his life) twenty-one years, seventeen of which he passed without being able to quit his bed. As his pain and the obligation of remaining always bed-ridden, gave him no little uneasiness, to calm his mind in the moments of ill humour, he placed before his eyes, on his bed, the two words, *patience and meekness*. On the 1sth of April, 1793, he was seized with a cough which he considered as the precursor of a spring fever, under which he had laboured many years. At first, he paid no at-

* A Swedish rix-dollar is worth nearly six Francs of French money.

tention

tention to it. But he soon had to suffer from a pain in the side, which daily weakened him, but without diminishing any thing of his good humour. On the 22d of April, he dictated his will, which was a new proof of his beneficence, and expired on the 28th, retaining the perfect use of his senses to the moment of his departure. He died at Norkoping, where he resided all the latter part of his life, a town particularly endeared to him, in the house of a merchant called John Kuhlman, one of his dearest friends. As he never could be useful to his country, in the employ which had been entrusted to him, that of Adjunct in the Chair of History in the University of Lund, (where he was to read lectures of history in place of the celebrated Professor Sven Lagerbring, who had obtained a dispensation from the duties of his place, that he might have leisure to terminate his Grand History of Sweden,) he demanded to resign it, which he obtained in the most honourable manner, October 29, 1776, retaining the title of Professor. His bed was every day surrounded by the most interesting persons of both sexes, who found the greatest pleasure in his conversation, alike instructive and witty, and which made him forget, for a time, the state of suffering in which he was. The present king, while Hereditary Prince, the Duke of Sudermannland, the Duke of Ostrogothland, and many distinguished Lords of the Court of Sweden, went to visit him, and, in general, no traveller of distinction quitted Norkoping, without calling upon him and without admiring his imperturbable patience and good humour. When not engaged with visitors, he was employed in literary labours; he read, he dictated and published, many works during his malady. In the first years of his sufferings he kept up a very extensive correspondence with a number of learned foreigners. His solid erudition, joined to great refinement of understanding, rendered his society extremely agreeable; and his probity, his love for his country, his qualities and his virtues, secured him the general esteem of all his fellow citizens; this esteem exists to this day. He was a model of beneficence. His memory is still dear to a great number of distinguished learned men of Sweden, whom he supported in their youth, and was their counseller in their studies. He lived in a very œconomical manner, in order to have the pleasure of doing good to others.

In India, at Galipore, Lieutenant Colonel Pigott, of the 6th regiment of Native Cavalry.

At Ganjam, Lieutenant Colonel J. Patton, of the Bengal Artillery.—Lieutenant Colonel R. Frith, of the 1st Native Cavalry.—Captain A. Ormsby, of the 10th Native Infantry.

At Goa, Captain Robinson, of the 8th regiment.

At Amboyna, Captain Stratton, of the Vulcan ship of war.—Captain Mathews, paymaster of the troops at Amboyna.—Lieutenant Luskin, of the Virginia frigate.

In Egypt, Lieut. J. Macpherson, of the 2d battalion of the 1st regiment, eldest son of J. Macpherson, esq of Ardersier.

At Hydrabad, in India, on the 7th of December, 1800, Lieut. Col. Dalrymple, in the service of the East India Company, and son of the late Sir William Dalrymple, of Cousland.

At Calcutta, on the 29th of December last, aged 75, R. M'Farlane, esq.

At Mergentheim, July 26, Maximilian F. Xavier Joseph, Prince and Bishop of Munster, and Archbishop and Elector of Cologne. He was brother to the two last emperors, and likewise to the unfortunate Marie Antoinette, late Queen of France.

At New Providence, Lieutenant J. Taylor, of the royal navy, eldest son of the late P. Taylor, esq. of Whitehaven.

At Berlin, in her 24th year, Miss Brown, second daughter of Dr. Brown, physician to his Prussian Majesty.

At Tobago, Miss C. Bird, third daughter of the late T. Bird, esq. of that island.

At Madeira, on the 6th of May last, Mr. G. Murdoch, son of J. Murdoch, esq. merchant there.

At Malta, Lieut. Pacon, of the 35th regiment, formerly of Salisbury.

In Jamaica, of the yellow-fever, Major H. Jervis White, of the 83d regiment, and brother to Sir John Jervis White, bart.—

In America, W. Russell, esq. late of Birmingham, and formerly a magistrate of the counties of Warwick and Worcester.

Lately at an advanced age, the Russian Field-marshal, Prince Repnin.

On the 13th of April last, at Lusignan, in the colony of Demerara, South America, in his 25th year, Mr. K. F. Mackenzie Wilson, second son of Mr. Wilson, tide-surveyor of the port of Whitehaven.

At Lisbon, on the 19th of June, in his 72d year, Mr. T. Goodall, merchant, and formerly of Leeds.

Lately in his 7th year, of the small pox, the Prince of Beira, eldest son of the Prince of Brasil, regent of Portugal.

At Kingston, Jamaica, on the 26th of March last, of the yellow fever, Mr. J. Walker, of Edinburgh, assistant surgeon to the army in Jamaica.

At Canton, in January last, on his voyage from Madras to London, for the recovery of his health, aged 21, Lieutenant M. Hutchins, of the East India Company's service, only son of W. Hutchins, Esq. of Canonbury-place, Islington.

In the West Indies, Laune. Burton, esq. second son of T. Burton, esq. of Braconddale.

At Barbadoes, greatly lamented, Charles Smith,

Smith, esq. paymaster of the 47th regiment of foot, and formerly of the 14th ditto.

On the 18th of June last, at the Cape of Good Hope, in his 17th year, Mr. Nugent Heriot, a cadet in the India Company's service. This young gentleman was a passenger for Madras, on board the True Briton East Indiaman.

At Rosetta, in Egypt, in the month of July last, of a wound he received in the battle of the 13th of March, Lieutenant Colonel McDowall, of the 79th regiment.

On board the City of London, East Indiaman, on her homeward bound passage, aged 20, Mr. J. W. Dale, eldest son of Mr. Dale, of Hatton Garden.

In the East Indies, at Calcutta, Captain Joseph Stokoe, of the corps of engineers.

At Penang, Lieutenant Duham, of the Dædalus ship of war.—Ditto, Lieutenant Hayley, of the Braave.

At Sea, Lieutenant Gordon, of the 12th regiment.—Ditto Ensign Neil, of ditto.

In Egypt, Captain Perry, eldest son of Mr. J. Perry, late of Bath.

In his 46th year, Vice-admiral Lord Hugh Seymour, third brother to the Marquis of Hertford, and commander in chief on the Jamaica station; he had been attacked by the fever of that clime, about the middle of the summer, from which he had a temporary respite, but it returned, with increased violence, on the 1st of September, and on the 10th of that month, deprived the service of a gallant and meritorious commander, and society of an accomplished and estimable member. His Lordship was made post-captain in 1779, and commanded the Leviathan of 74 guns, in the memorable action of June 1, 1794, on which day, he captured the Sans Pareil of 98 guns, in which ship, on being promoted to the rank of Vice admiral, he hoisted his flag, in June, 1795, where it continued to fly till his death. He became shortly after one of the Lords of the Admiralty, but soon quitted that appointment for the command of the Leeward Island station, from whence, after the conquest of Surinam, he succeeded to the Commandership in Chief on the Jamaica station.

At Madras, G. A. Ram, esq. paymaster at Masulipatam.

On the 30th of August, on Sullivan's Island, in the vicinity of Charlestown, South Carolina, Mr. G. Tair, son of Mr. J. Tair, of the Excise-office, Glasgow.

On the 4th of July last, off the Cape of Good Hope, on board the ship Cornwallis, Lieutenant-colonel Walker, of the East India Company's service; this gentleman was on his return from Bengal, after an absence of thirty years.

On the 24th of February last, in the Cotiote Country, India, Lieutenant W. Monteath, of the 12th regiment, second battalion of native infantry, on the Madras establishment; this gentleman was the son of Mr. Walter Monteath, merchant, of Glasgow.

The following Statement and Distribution of the immense Naval and Military Force of Great Britain, during the last Month of the War Establishment, are entitled to the Attention of our Readers.

General Distribution of the British Army, Dec. 1, 1801.

	Regulars.		*Fencible Inf.*	*Militia.*	*Total Battalions.*	*Inv. Companies.*
	Cav.	*Inf.*				
England and Wales - -	23	25	3	74	125	40
North Britain - -	2	—	—	12	14	6
Ireland - - -	7	12	32	—	51	6
Jersey, Guernsey, &c. - -	—	4	2	—	6	20
Gibraltar - - -	—	5	4	—	9	—
Madeira - - -	—	1	—	—	*a*1	—
Minorca and Malta - -	—	11	—	—	11	—
Egypt - - -	3	26	1	—	30	—
Canada, Nova Scotia, &c. -	—	5	2	—	7	—
West Indies - - -	1	34	—	—	35	—
Cape of Good Hope, Goree, &c. -	1	8	—	—	9	—
East Indies - - -	4	18	—	—	*b*22	—
Total -	41	149	44	86	320*	72

(*a*) And Detachments.
(*b*) The Company's Troops exclusive.
* Exclusive of artillery and Engineers at home and abroad, independent companies, recruiting corps, volunteers, &c.

Distribution

Distribution of the British Naval Force, Nov. 1, 1801.

	Line.	Fifty's.	Frigates.	Sps.	Total.
In port and fitting - -	16	1	28	67	112
Guard-ships - - -	5	3	2	—	10
In the English and Irish Channel -	36	—	20	43	99
On the Downs, and North-sea Station	16	4	31	62	113
At the West India Islands, and on the Passage - - -	1	—	14	32	47
On the Jamaica Station - -	3	1	20	11	35
American and Newfoundland Stations	—	—	7	6	13
Cape of Good Hope, East Indies, and on the Passage - -	9	7	8	15	39
Africa, and on actual Service -	—	1	5	3	9
Spain and Portugal, without the Straits	14	—	10	4	28
In the Mediterranean - -	23	4	55	36	118
Hospital and Prison Ships - -	22	4	7	—	33
Total in Commission -	145	25	197	279	676
Receiving-ships - -	5	1	1	1	8
Serviceable and repairing for Service	6	—	3	1	10
In ordinary - - -	25	2	30	71	128
Building - - -	19	1	4	—	24
Total -	200	29	235	352	846

State of the Ordinary at each Port.

	Line.	Fifty's.	Frigates.	Sps.	Total.
Portsmouth - - -	13	1	9	19	42
Plymouth - - -	15	—	8	18	41
Chatham - - -	5	1	—	—	6
Sheerness - - -	3	—	10	27	40
River - - -	—	1	7	9	17
Total -	56	3	34	73	146

MONTHLY COMMERCIAL REPORT.

TRADE, in many of its branches, appears to be for the present moment in a sort of pause, between the particular state of activity in which it existed during the war, and those new channels of operation into which it must turn itself in consequence. Every great change in the state of trade tends, for the moment, to increase the number of bankruptcies beyond their ordinary proportion. Such an effect took place remarkably at the commencement of the war. It seems to take place at present, though in a smaller degree, in several parts of the island.

The *market value* of the different species of the *National Debts*, or in other words, the *price of Stocks*, was, on Monday, November 22, between two and three per cent. lower, for the consolidated 3 per cents. than on Thursday the 22d of October. Other stocks have fallen in a proportion nearly similar. Bank stock alone, in consequence of the secure responsibility of the Bank--- the great accumulation of its property, and the increase in the ratio of its dividends, &c. has, in the course of this last month, risen not less than 4½ per cent. There is no reason for supposing that the fall in the prices of other stocks is owing to any large sales of stock belonging to foreigners, for the purpose of transferring the value to other countries. The creation of new stock, by the funding of such a quantity of Exchequer-bills; the greater profits yielded by money in trade; the very inviting character of property in land; the demand of money for the instalments of the last loan; the expectation of a new one of not less than eighteen millions; and the uncertainty which must hang over money-dealing and other branches of trade, till the Definitive Treaty with France, and Commercial Treaties, on the basis of the general pacification, shall have been

been ultimately concluded. These causes alone are fully adequate to have produced that diminution in the prices of stock, which has happened in the progress of November.

The *Bank of England*, now that Government is likely to make fewer demands for their support, shew a disposition to accommodate trade with a liberality of discount upon bills of exchange, which cannot but command the warmest gratitude of the merchants, and promote in the most essential manner, the general interests of British commerce In justice to the conduct of the Directors, it ought to be known, that discounts for the purpose of monopolizing speculation, or to enable the holders of grain and other provisions to keep them unreasonably back from the market, have hitherto been, and wherever the intention can be suspected, still are, most rigorously refused. But, it has long been by the extent and the length of the credits they are enabled to give, that British merchants and British commodities have preserved the accustomed preferences in many foreign markets; and, it is by the credit they themselves find with the Bank of England, that they are enabled to give credits so necessary, abroad.

India Stock has had a fall of ½ per cent. within these few days. Yet, this can hardly be attributed to any diminution of its permanent value in consequence of the advantages relinquished to France and Holland by the peace. An half is sometimes better than the whole: and our Indian greatness is probably more secure, as having become less invidious, by the cessions we have consented to make. From the debate in the House of Commons on the night of the 25th of November we have the pleasure to learn, that the East India Company have at last agreed to comply so nearly with the plan for the opening of the carrying trade to India, which was suggested by the Marquis of Wellesley, as to resolve to give full scope to the transference of private property between India and this country by British-built ships and British seamen, if not by India-built vessels and Lascar sailors. It might be painful to the Directors to come to such a resolution: and, had this been possible, we should not have been greatly dissatisfied to see the Company preserve their monopoly of the navigation to India still in its pristine rigour; but the carrying trade with India must have otherwise been relinquished to Foreigners; —how much better to open its advantages to British merchants solely, and in general! The plan said to be adopted, is, in many respects, preferable to that of employing Lascars and India-built shipping. But, we would still earnestly exhort all concerned, to render the voyages as frequent and short, and the freightage as cheap, as possible: otherwise we shall, yet, undoubtedly, have the misfortune to see the trade to India, by the operation of a natural necessity, wrested from us.

The *Course of Exchange* is now open with the countries which were shut up against us by the war; and bills on almost every great capital and commercial emporium on the Continent, may be purchased in London. We observe, that the variation in the exchange with Hamburg, has been, in the progress of November, somewhat in favour of this country. Such a fact must, no doubt, be interpreted as implying, that the proportion of the money to be remitted from Hamburg to London is, in comparison with that due from London to Hamburg, greater now than it was a month ago. Our exportations to the Elbe appear, therefore, to increase. With Spain, the last variations in the rate of exchange have been favourable to us; as there must be considerable remittances to come for the purchase of British goods from Spain to this country. With Portugal and Italy, the turn of the exchange is against us; as our merchants now adventure freely in the purchase of the produce and manufactures of these countries; and remittances to our fleets and armies probably pass in that course. The exchange with Dublin is still more and more to the advantage of Ireland; affording, among other things, a clear proof that the Irish nation already derives important pecuniary benefits from the Union.

The danger of capture is no longer among the risks for security against which the *Insurance Premium* is paid. The rates of that premium have therefore fallen to the wonted medium in time of peace.

The prices of *Grain* do not continue to fall in proportion to the wishes and hopes of the consumers. This effect is understood to arise from the endeavours of the corn-dealers, and from the permission renewed by the Legislature, soon to use grain in the distilleries. Against the renewal of the distillery of spirits from grain, petitions have been prepared to be offered to the Legislature from Edinburgh, Glasgow, Aberdeen, and almost every other considerable town in Scotland. Equal alarm has been excited in England against the probable consequences of that renewal. To deny to the farmers the benefit of that market for grain which is created by the distilleries, might seem unreasonable; and yet, it were perhaps still more unreasonable to open that market, if the price of grain be already sufficiently advantageous to the farmer, and even too high to be easily afforded by the ordinary consumers. Upon these considerations, we should think, that a wiser temporary measure cannot be thought of, than that which the Legislature has adopted, of offering every encouragement to the use rather of melasses in the distillation of spirits, without absolutely prohibiting that of oats.

The exports of cotton yarn from Glasgow and Manchester to Germany continue to be very large. We would much rather that the yarn were made into cloth before exportation. Manchester begins again to find the wonted market of Leghorn open to its manufactures That of America and the West Indies is now freer than ever; and the exports to it, must, of course, be greatly augmented.

Sugars and some sorts of raw cotton have declined in price. Of cotton large quantities have, within these last ten days, entered the port of London.

The

The improvements of our internal trading intercourse, by canals and iron rail-ways, are advancing with extraordinary spirit and rapidity. The Grand Surry Canal, will, under the direction of Mr. Dodd, be very soon completed.

The coast-trade of Leith, Dundee, Inverness, and other towns on the north-east coast seems to be fast increasing.

The prices of wool rise, in consequence of the prospect which the peace affords of an increased sale of all sorts of woollen goods.

Hops.—This article has had a very brisk sale since the season commenced, as might be expected from the excessive high prices at which those of the two preceding growths had been kept up, caused by the most extensive and unexampled speculations ever known. The drop of price from 16l. 16s. and 17l. 17s per cwt. to 4l. and 5l. was such as to encourage brisk sales for new ones at these prices, which has again tended to advance the markets, and reward the planter, who, it were to be wished, may henceforward see his true interest, and not be misled by designing men. These *promoters of British commerce* seem not to have improved their fortunes by their immense stocks of old hops, which sold at a loss of 12l. 12s. per cwt. besides the loss of warehouse rent, weight, and interest of money. The market is now rather dull, and as the crop of this season is expected to produce 225,000 bags, they may still decline, unless speculations prevent it.

METEOROLOGICAL REPORT.

Observations on the State of the Weather, from the 24th of October to the 24th of November inclusive, 1801, two miles N. W. of St. Paul's.

Barometer.	*Thermometer.*
Highest 30. 1. Oct. 26 & 27, Wind N.	Highest 61°. Oct. 31. Wind W.
Lowest 28. 98. Nov. 4. Wind N. W.	Lowest 26°. Nov. 6. Wind N.
Greatest variation in 24 hours. 7-tenths of an inch. Between the evenings of the 4th and 5th of Nov. the mercury rose from 29.3 to 30.	Greatest variation in 24 hours. 19°. At eight in the morning of the 2d inst. the thermometer stood at 52°. and at the same hour on the 3d it was no higher than 33°.

The quantity of rain fallen since the last Report, is equal to 3.89 inches of depth.

The state of the atmosphere during last month, has been very variable. In several instances beside that which we have noticed above, has the mercury in the barometer risen and fallen from 4 to nearly 7-tenths in the course of twenty-four hours; these changes were, as might be expected, attended with stormy weather.

The variations with regard to the temperature of the atmosphere, have likewise been considerable. For some days at the end of October, and the two first of the present month, it was unusually close and warm; but the 5th and 6th were attended with very severe frost, on the former the mercury was 2° degrees below the freezing point, and on the latter it was as low as 26°, or 6° below the freezing point. On the 23d inst. the thermometer was at 28°.

There have been seventeen days without rain; the wind has blown from the east but nine days; as in the last month, it has been chiefly in the West.

*** *Persons who reside Abroad, and who wish to be supplied with this Work every Month, as published, may have it sent to them,* FREE OF POSTAGE, *to New York, Halifax, Quebec, and every Part of the West Indies, at Two Guineas per Annum, by Mr.* THORNHILL, *of the General Post Office, at No. 21, Sherborne-lane; to Hamburg, Lisbon, Gibraltar, or any Part of the Mediterranean, at Two Guineas per Annum, by Mr.* BISHOP, *of the General Post Office, at No. 22, Sherborne-lane; to the Cape of Good Hope, or any Part of the East Indies, at Thirty Shillings per Annum, by Mr.* GUY, *at the East India House; and to any Part of Ireland, at One Guinea and a Half per Annum, by Mr.* SMITH, *of the General Post Office, at No. 3, Sherborne-lane. It may also be had of all Persons who deal in Books, at these Places, and also in every Part of the World.*

THE
MONTHLY MAGAZINE.

No, 81. JANUARY 1, 1802. [No. 6, of Vol. 12.

ORIGINAL COMMUNICATIONS.

To the Editor of the Monthly Magazine.

SIR,

IN the Monthly Magazine for November last, page 345, after the relation of the destruction of various quadrupeds and birds in France, in consequence of the relaxation of the game-laws, it is observed, that Citizen Bouqueau, Prefect of the Rhine and Moselle, had issued a proclamation tending to check this general destruction of useful animals. Some reflections are added, I suppose by the Editor of the Magazine, to prove, that, by the extermination of birds in, or their desertion of, certain parts of the Continent, vegetation has materially suffered. In addition to these remarks, I transmit a few of my own, which have resulted from reading or conversation, and which I relate from memory.

Some years ago Lieutenant King, the early nautical companion of our circumnavigator, Cook, left his government of Norfolk Island,* to consult me on account of his health; and during my attendance he put into my hands his valuable MSS. in two folio volumes, containing an excellent account of the rise and progress of that infant establishment, which he lived to see matured, and the island itself become one of the most populous and productive in the world. Considerable extracts from these volumes have been inserted in Collin's Account of New South Wales.

I often intimated to the Governor the utility of printing the whole MSS. as affording a connected chain of judicious management, not only in cultivating the soil, but in reforming the mind, and reclaiming from vicious propensities the worst outcasts of society. In these views my friend appeared in the light of a modern Solon, in introducing gradually laws, regulations, restraints, and rewards, suited to the state of that community he presided over.

But to revert to the cultivation of the soil, he found by experience, that the island was periodically visited by a desolating insect, which consumed the tender corn and maize, and nearly produced a famine. After every other endeavour had failed, it occurred to him, that poultry would not only eat but fatten upon insects, penned his poultry upon the cultivated lands infested by insects, and thus gradually extirpated them; by degrees he increased his domestic stock of fowls to nearly 3000, and these, on a subsequent visit from the insects, soon cleared the soil; and it has since been preserved in the most productive condition.

Some modern writer, I think J. Weld, junior, mentions in his Travels in America, that the crops of corn suffer greatly for want of proper birds to destroy the insects which infest that continent, and proposes the transportation thither of our common crow, to effect this purpose—a bird that is deprecated here for its supposed injury to the corn, a portion of which it certainly eats, but which philosophy will sacrifice to it for the superior good it performs by destroying those insects which are capable of producing infinite mischief to the grain and tender blade. I think, however, Professor Barton enumerates our common crow among the birds indigenous to America. This reminds me here of an observation frequently made, although perhaps erroneously, that there are fewer insects after a hard frost in this country, and that it affords a prelude to a plentiful harvest. I can suppose, from chemical knowledge, that a frost may render the earth more nutritive to the seed committed to it, but not from the destruction of insects, which may even be preserved by the frost from the access of crows and other birds, whose food they partly constitute; and an intelligent farmer assures me, that the insects I allude to are most numerous after a severe frosty winter, as the birds are by the severity of the weather, and hardness of the soil, precluded from finding them.

I imagine that our small birds, that frequent our fruit-trees, do more good by destroying insects, than mischief to the buds or fruit. Buffon, who gives a pompous account of the salacious and impudent disposition of the sparrows, supposes, if I mistake not, that, to nurture one nest of

* Since his return to his former government he has been promoted to that of New South Wales.

of its young, about 4000 insects or caterpillars are devoted for their food.

I am, as an individual, so well satisfied with the visits of the feathered tribe on my small premises in the vicinity of London, as not only to discourage their destruction, but in severe weather, of frost or snow, to sprinkle corn in the walks for their preservation; and it might be suggested, from the numbers and varieties that frequent these premises, that they possess some medium of conveying to each other a sense of the security they enjoy. Some, indeed, that are rare in these parts of England, I frequently meet with. Without much water I have the king's-fisher. The diminutive and beautiful golden-headed wren is my denizen; the jay enlivens the trees, and creepers and wood-peckers climb their trunks.

Grovehill, J. C. LETTSOM.
December 9, 1801.

To the Editor of the Monthly Magazine.

SIR,

I WAITED, and earnestly wished, to see in your Magazine some memoirs of the late worthy Mr. Robert Bage. But none appearing after so urgent a solicitation, I think myself bound to pay a tribute to a departed friend whom I dearly loved, who stood one of the first in my esteem, whom I have known perhaps longer than any man living, and with whom I have lived in the closest friendship fifty years.

This uncommon but excellent man was born Feb. 29, 1728, at Darley, a hamlet in the parish of St. Alkmond's, Derby, where his father worked a paper-mill. Though he lived to the age of 73, he could not celebrate more than 18 birthdays.

His mother died soon after his birth, when his father removed to Derby, but kept the mill. He quickly married a second wife, and, as I resided in the same street, and near him, I well remember he buried her in 1732. He soon procured another, buried her, and ventured upon a fourth, who survived him.

Robert was put to school, so that I did not perfectly know him till 1735, when he was seven years old. He had made at that age such a progress in letters, that he was the wonder of the neighbourhood; he was then in the Latin tongue. My father often held him up to me for imitation, I being much bigger and older. I was then but little acquainted with him, for he moved in a sphere more elevated than I. At this time he was completely master of the manual-exercise, and I saw him instructing some young men. He afterwards was trained to his father's business.

In about 1751 he married a young lady, who possessed four accomplishments which seldom meet in one woman, fortune, beauty, good sense, and prudence; I might add a fifth, necessary for the peace of a family, good nature. I have reason to think he found more happiness in domestic life than is usually experienced. Having embraced the marriage state, he entered upon a paper-mill at Elford, four miles from Tamworth, which he conducted to the time of his death.

Some men's capacity opens at a late day, and some wither soon after the meridian of life, but Robert Bage's opened and shut with his existence. His enlivening sun shone with vigour during a long period of years. His talents, humanity, honour, and generosity, appeared, through the whole of his life, conspicuous to all who knew him. I could bring numberless incidents to establish every trait of his character: but as this would lead me into too wide a field, I shall confine myself to one or two proofs to each assertion. The *powers of his mind* were amazingly strong; these, in the early part of his life have already been noted. During my acquaintance with him he learnt music, and the French and Italian languages, without a master. Being inclined, in 1760, to learn the abstruse branches of mathematics, he applied to Thomas Hanson, a celebrated teacher, and spent a night in Birmingham once a week for instruction. As I was intimate with both, I sometimes attended, and before the scholar had been a month, I could easily perceive, though no adept myself, he was able to teach his master, nay, even set him fast. Perhaps part of this victory might arise from the easy fluency with which Mr. Bage delivered himself, while the master of figures was better formed for thinking than speaking.

His humanity will appear from his treatment of his servants, and even his horses, who all loved him, and whom he kept to old age.

Trade, which is thought to corrupt the mind, made no such impression upon his. Though he laid no stress upon Revelation, his dealings were stamped with rectitude; he remarked to me, "Fraud is beneath a man." He had no other love for money than to use it, or he might have left a much larger property than he did. In Feb. 1756, he asked me to spend the evening

evening with him. He proposed a connection (not a partnership) which I accepted, and which continued, with small variations, according to the mutations of time, till the day of his death. From that date, perhaps, I have paid him 500l. a year, upon the average, and always with *pleasure*, which proves this simple point, *I was treated with honour*. During this long course of 45 years he never gave me one cause of complaint. His *honour*, and peaceable temper, will farther appear from a remark he made while we travelled in a chaise from Wolsey bridge to Tamworth, in October 1795—he had then been in partnership with a person in another concern near 15 years—"that they never had one word of difference since they met."

His generous cast of mind will appear from two, among many, incidents. I accidentally remarked that, "I had seen a distant relation of his, who was out of employment."—"Give him, (says he) upon my account (though he did not know him) five shillings a week till he gets into work." When the rioters, in 1791, had cruelly destroyed my property to a large amount, and obliged me, with my family, to run away without a shilling, and none durst take us in, we drove, among other places, to the Castle at Tamworth. I asked the people of the inn if they knew me? "No."—"I have no money to pay my way, or property to pledge." Their looks fell. "I am known to Mr. Bage, of Elford, whom I will request to pay my bill." Their looks and my credit rose together. He cheerfully paid it, blamed me for not coming to his house, and I could never prevail upon him to accept a return.

With all these rich *talents* and rare endowments he was mild in the extreme; an enemy to no man, and, I believe, never had one himself.

His reason for becoming an author was singular, and such as would have driven another out of authorship. I shall state the cause, and deliver the result as given me by himself in the chaise above-mentioned. About the year 1765 he was induced to enter into partnership with three gentlemen in a wholesale iron-manufactory. The pursuit continued about 14 years, then dissolved, when it appeared he had lost a sum, which I have now forgotten, perhaps 1500l. Fearing the distress of mind would overcome him, he took up the pen to turn the stream of sorrow into that of amusement; a scheme worthy a philosopher. His first production was *Mount Heneth*, in 1781, which he sold for 30l. His succeeding works followed nearly upon the same terms. The public are in possession of his writings, and have given him an ample return of praise. Excellent as they are, yet, in my opinion, his private letters, of which I must have received more than a thousand, surpass them. They are replete with vivacity, witty turns, and fine humour, spontaneously springing, without effort, from the heart.

A sketch of this amiable man may be seen in *Hutton's History of Derby*, 1791, where he possesses a niche among the worthies of that place. I shall transcribe the passage.

"If we find a pleasure in drawing a valuable character which has *left* the stage, that pleasure must be double when we treat of those who still adorn it; because we revere both the *character* and the *man*. This, in the present case, is my pleasing task. The man I now delineate is a native of Derby, but left it at an early period. He amuses the world and himself with novel productions of a superior class, as Mount Heneth, Barham Downs, The Fair Syrian, James Wallace, &c. wherein is an excellent picture of life, a full display of character and sentiment. These have travelled to the continent, passed through the Frankfort-press, and appeared to the world in a German habit.

"Although fortune never made him conspicuous in the great world, she gave him what was preferable, affluence and content. In directing a paper-mill may be found that head which is able to direct empires; that judgment, which can decide in difficult cases; a penetration, which can fathom the human heart, and comprehend various systems of knowledge; a genius, which constitutes the companion for Newton in philosophy, for Handel in music, for Euclid in mathematics; a master of the living and dead languages, and all, like the wealth of a merchant who rises from nothing, acquired by himself. Nay, I should even rank him with that learned body, the physicians, if he were not defective in the art of killing.—That rectitude, which is rarely found, is here obscured from the public eye, but is a pearl of great price, and a credit to our species. Though a diminutive figure, yet one of the most amiable of men; and though barely a Christian, yet one of the best. I have known him fifty-six years; his friendship is an honour; I have long possessed it; to which I shall add another, by writing his name with my own. Should

he

he frown at this liberty, I will take twice as much: should he retort, I will take my revenge by drawing a complete character; for he has amply furnished me with materials."

This worthy man afterwards charged me with too strong a colouring. I told him in reply, I was not used to heap praise upon any man wholesale, therefore took every expression to pieces, and shewed him the firm foundation on which I built. He seemed satisfied, and returned a smile.

Four or five months prior to his death, he paid me a visit. I was secretly alarmed to observe his countenance changed, his constitution breaking, as if threatening a dissolution. When we parted, I took what I thought an everlasting farewel. As he went out of the house, he shook hands with my nephew (a boy of thirteen), and, with a smile, "Farewel, my dear lad, we shall meet again in heaven!" Though spoken in the jocular stile, it seemed to indicate a sensibility of his approaching end.

Still declining, and attended with feverish symptoms, but sensible to the last, he left the world September 1, 1801, after a life of seventy-three years, six months, and one day.

His person was of a smallish size, about five feet three inches, and of a spare habit, not robust, but his constitution good. He left an amiable widow to lament his loss, by whom he had three sons; one of them died a young man, an affliction he severely felt, the others are in genteel situations, and inherit a large portion of their father's talents. WILLIAM HUTTON.

Birmingham, Dec. 5, 1801.

To the Editor of the Monthly Magazine.

SIR,

I HAVE noticed in your Chronicle what you have extracted from the Bury paper, of the shameful treatment of a young tame BULL at BURY, on the 5th of November last.

The term BULL-BAITING, disgusting as it is, does not sufficiently characterize this outrage on humanity, good order, and the safety of a populous town.

But you go on "It seems they are sanctioned by an act of Parliament." Had you attended to my letter, I think you would, at least, have doubted of the truth of this supposition, with respect to sanction. An act of Parliament could not have sanctioned cruelty and injustice. It could, at most, only protect it from civil punishment. I know not of any such act of Parliament as protects *bull-baiting* at a stake. Until any one can shew such an act, I shall rely on the best information my reading and researches give me, that there is not such a disgrace to our Parliamentary Code. If such an act could be shewn, I am sure it ought to be repealed; and I trust that now it would be repealed. In the mean-time, I trust the idea that there is such an act—is to be added to the list of errors noticed by BARRINGTON.

But if bull-baiting at a stake were, unhappily and disgracefully to our law, protected by statute; driving a bull maddened by torture through the streets of a populous town would not come within the protection, and must be regarded as a shocking and most dangerous nuisance.

And I trust, were *death* to happen from it to any human being, that it could not on trial be ruled on other principles than those laid down by Sir MICHAEL FOSTER, in his Treatise on Homicide. That humane and very learned judge ruled it *manslaughter*, where death to a bye-stander happened at *cock-throwing*. And where the danger of human life is much more probable and immediate, and the act whence that danger results yet more cruel and unlawful, it is difficult to imagine how it could be less than MURTHER.

It has been wished, and was lately attempted and strangely frustrated, that there were an act of Parliament to prevent this horrid and exceedingly dangerous barbarity:—so injurious to the morals of youth; so incompatible with the comfort and safety of the peaceable and good; the young, the innocent, the infirm and helpless.

I own I am not for adding to the enormous and most rapidly accumulating mass of our *statute-laws* without necessity. I am for relying on the vigour of our COMMON LAW carefully considered and applied and duly enforced. Without any other aid, *bull-baiting* was suppressed at *Windsor*, when my father was recorder there. Another magistrate of that corporation, the late Mr. HATCH, suppressed *cock-throwing*. Both I believe effectually; for I have not heard that either has been revived.

And I have no doubt that, in BURY or elsewhere, if the magistracy will exert themselves by causing the offenders to be apprehended for a *breach* of the *public peace*, bull-baiting, and this yet more inhuman practice, will completely be done away without requiring the intervention of of Parliament. That it is an *indictable nuisance* I have already said; and I trust that if repeated, some of those who are annoyed, and who with their families are endangered by it, will indict it and thereby bring it under such legal censure and restraint as shall prevent its repetition, and convince the PUBLIC that *inhumanity* and PUBLIC MISCHIEFS, such as this, are effectually restrainable by the COMMON-LAW OF ENGLAND.

Troston, I remain, your's, &c.
Dec. 10, 1801. CAPEL LOFFT.

SOLAR SPOTS.

THESE have been, all the year nearly, uncommonly numerous and extensive, and still continue to be so. On the 9th they formed a curve-line south-west of the ⊙'s centre springing upward, and above 100,000 miles in extent. At the same time a cluster was entering south-eastward; then appearing like a large spot. Now the advancing cluster has resolved itself into a line of very detached spots, while the receding, which is now pretty near going off, appears, by the effect of the convexity of the sun, like a large spot with one or two faint smaller spots; the larger about $\frac{1}{24}$ of the sun's diameter, or about 33,000 miles. It seems as if the conjecture of some great astronomers were just; and that these spots do excite the action of the *solar atmosphere* to a greater intensity.

C. L.

To the Editor of the Monthly Magazine.

SIR,

THERE is an article in your last Magazine which I wish to correct, not only because it is untrue, but also because it is calculated to give uneasiness to the relations of my late very excellent and amiable friend John Tweddell. It is there stated, that an English traveller of the name of Tweddell had been murdered by his Greek servant at Athens. Mr. John Tweddell died at Athens, on the 25th of July, 1799, in the house of Logotheti, the English Agent in that place: but his death was occasioned by a fever, brought on probably by excessive fatigue in a journey to Thebes, from which he had just returned. A statement of the circumstances of his illness and death was drawn up and signed by a respectable physician who attended him, officially communicated to Mr. Smith, the British Minister at Constantinople, and by him forwarded to Mr. J. Tweddell's family in England. His servant, an Austrian, was, some time after, taken into the service of two English travellers, and I believe still continues with them. Professor Carlyle lived a considerable time in the house of Logotheti, on his return from Constantinople, and his testimony might be added to the above, were any further testimony necessary.

A schedule of Mr. J. Tweddell's manuscripts, drawings, and other effects was transmitted to Mr. Smith from Athens, signed by Logotheti, some of the municipal officers of the town, and by a French artist of the name of Prianin, who had been for some time employed by him. Most of the things of value, however, appear to have been stolen or lost in their passage from Athens to Constantinople: but what remained were, by the kindness and attention of Lord Elgin, Mr. Smith and Professor Carlyle, put on board the Lord Duncan armed ship, bound for England. This vessel was unfortunately afterwards sent to Egypt, but may now, I suppose, be soon expected in this country. Much must not therefore, I fear, be hoped from the extensive and valuable information, which my friend had collected during a residence of many months in Greece; and this is the more to be lamented, because, both from his knowledge of the modern as well as the ancient Greek language, and from his activity and perseverance, he was eminently qualified to illustrate the antiquities of that most interesting country.

Fortunately, when he set out from Constantinople to Greece, he left in the hands of Mr. Thornton (a respectable merchant in the former place), his Journal and other papers, relative to his travels through Germany, Switzerland, Poland, the Crimea, &c. so that we may still flatter ourselves that something may yet be preserved of the four years incessant labours of this learned and accomplished young man: and if so, I have no doubt, it will do credit to his own memory, and merit the attention of the public*. I am,

Gesmond Grove, Sir, your's, &c.
Dec. 6, 1801. JAMES LOSH.

To the Editor of the Monthly Magazine.

SIR,

AT length I have escaped from a lonely crowd, where idiot ceremony has almost

* The paragraph to which this letter refers, was translated from a German journal.

almost sickened me with *healths*, and palled a graceless meal, which began without a thought of thanks to God, and ended with a loud and general call for the Devil. He came, instinct with fire, amid an universal hubbub wild of soft piano pipes, and brazen throats, striving for mastery. "The Devil, the Devil!" Ithuriel once touched him lightly with his spear, but our fearless fair ones stick their trident forks deep in the grisly king, and then, with breath that whispers whence it stole its savoury spoil, transmit this type of Satan. The smug curate gives thanks, and then retails some paltry pun.

At length, I can shut my chamber-door in the world's face—I can stride across my room in proud independence—I can tread upon the servitudes of life as I tread on this carpet of chequered colours—I can describe my semicircle round one warm friend, my perennial fire. It is the sun of my system, and I am an avowed enemy to the anti-social conspiracy of a Rumford-grate. I should not have expected this attempt to extinguish the light of our terrestrial sun from a person who *has been* supposed one of the *illuminati*. Perhaps, however, he knows the proper times and places to conceal or to reveal his light, as well as heat. If *stirring the fire* be no longer the order of the day throughout Europe, let us at least be suffered to *snuff the candle*. The light of reason is now the only resource, the sole hope, of mankind.

I am struck with the account given by Fourcroy of the wonderful change wrought by the chemistry of nature in the bodies interred in the church-yard of the Innocents at Paris. They were changed into a material for giving *light*, and some successful experiments have been lately made in England for shortening the process by which dead bodies are changed into an excellent spermaceti. It gives me great pleasure to think, that William Pitt and Thomas Paine may, at some future time, mingle their light for the good of the rising generation. As the price of spermaceti will be reduced by the increase of quantity, the ex-minister may contribute to the illumination of some cobler's stall, while Common-sense is spreading its rays thro' the cabinets of princes.

This material metempsichosis (and light seems so much the soul of the world, that I may hazard the expression) cherishes my heart, which always grows cold on approaching the repository of the dead. The idea, like one of those perpetual lamps to be found burning in ancient sepul-, and which in reality is only the decomposition of the brain into a phosphoric light—the idea of this change seems to irradiate the gloom of the grave, and feeds the fancy with the hope of early resurrection into useful existence. It must indeed be observed, that this change or conversion is truly of the democratic kind, as it happens, at least in the natural process, to take place only where multitudes of bodies fill up one common cavity. The selfish aristocrat shudders at the dread equality of the tomb, and, in his triple coffin, seems to endeavour at a perpetual seclusion from the commonalty, maintaining even there his favourite principle of keeping mankind *in the dark*. But it is to be hoped, that, as the substance of the brain is especially disposed to this change into a fatty and inflammable matter, the great majority of the people will, at length, be permitted to lay their heads together, and that even Irishmen may be allowed to unite in peace, in the brotherhood of the grave. The despot may wish, as it were, to egotize himself for ages to come in the central chamber of a pyramid. The aristocrat may, in his mausoleum, still prove a drag on the great revolutionary wheel of useful existence: but the multitude will supply sufficient oil for the motion of that wheel, whose ceaseless rotation renovates the elements, while life, like the phœnix, springs from the ashes of dissolution.

Instead then of inscribing on the entrance of our cemeteries, "The place of eternal sleep," I should, on this discovery, substitute the words "*Fiat lux*." I think I see the Corresponding Society as rows of lamps, giving light to the streets of the metropolis; and, in this terrestrial resurrection, even Messieurs Wyndham and Wilberforce may turn out the incendiaries of the next generation. I have heard it said of late, that Charles Fox was in an eclipse. This expression put me in mind of the blunder which our almanack-makers are so frequently guilty of—"This year (say they) an eclipse of the sun *invisible*;" and, although the eclipse of Mr. Fox at present be, as I think, of this class, I believe any accidental deficiency of light that now takes place will be amply restored by his posthumous resplendence. He will burn like an Argand's lamp, the flame of which is always pure and clear, and never requires trimming.

Of light celestial, infinite is the variety from that which Milton addresses to that which Mammon worships.—"From that divine and incomparable greater light, which illumines all, delights all, from which all proceed, to which all must return, which

which can alone irradiate all our intellects;" from this holy light, of which the sun is the prototype, to the light of 45,000 stars, which *have been* counted, and of ninety comets, whose courses have been ascertained. Of light terrestrial, great is the variety, from the hallowed light of nature to the light of an *auto da fe*, or that of the funeral pile prepared for the self-devoted victim of superstition on the banks of the Ganges; from the pure light of Christianity (the best of commentaries on the law of nature) to all the gradation of lesser lights, which each sect calls the light of orthodoxy; from the light of philosophy, which illumines the understanding, and cherishes the adoration of the heart, to the light of modern methodism, if that can be called a *light*, which propagates the darkness of mystery, and perpetuates the blindness of ignorance, with a proud pretence to extraordinary piety, sets religion at variance with philosophy, and would dare to make the worship of God incompatible with the knowledge of his works.

There is a sort of piety grown into some degree of popularity, ostentatious in its humility, and proud in its self-abasement, which affects to discredit and despise all investigation into the nature of things—which pretends to see God *only*, who *can be* seen *only* in his creation, over which this false devotion would drop a curtain of darkness, and plunge the world of Newton and Franklin and Lavoisier into the ignorance of the middle ages. In the extreme of infatuation, it sits with the Indian faquir; and with eyes shut, and all the senses obstinately closed against any external impression, fondly and foolishly supposes, that self-annihilation is an absorbtion into the Divine Mind. In a degree somewhat less absurd, it becomes the apathy of the Turks, or the indolence of the Quietists, with whom the dogma of their devotion supplies the place of all knowledge, and supersedes all inquiry. The Turk cloaths himself with the raiment of the dead, and, when attacked by the plague, exclaims, "Such is the will of God!" Invention searches for the causes of things, and, having mounted to a higher link in the series of causes and effects (by which this universe is suspended, as with a golden chain from the throne of Heaven,) he not only commands a more extensive view of nature, but can act upon the surrounding elements with greater power, with a stronger purchase, and make them, as it were, the Ariels of his bidding, for use, or for pleasure. The first and final answer which the light of Methodism affords to any question concerning the phenomena of nature, or the uses of their different changes, ratifies and sanctifies ignorance and inaction by the name of God. The truer worship of God consists in the performance of our various duties, the assertion of our rights, the pursuit of knowledge, and the communication of happiness. When held in the light cast by such a worship, the light of Methodism is as a candle held in the mid-day sun. The flame becomes invisible.

If man be made after God's own image—if the divine similitude ever descended in glory upon the head of mortal, it is upon him who has conquered for his country liberty and peace; who in the tumult of battle can maintain a presence of mind, and, at the same time, a faculty of looking *before* and *after* far beyond that of other men; whose power of combination describes, as it were, a great circle, which includes and circumvents their plans, and descends in thunder and lightning from Mount Cenis, to blast at once their confidence and success; who consolidates victory, not by laws martial, but by the wise magnanimity of amnesty, and the conciliation of the most adverse parties to the common attachment of country, to the delight of seeing public glory in the forum, and feeling happiness at the fire-side; who, after a conflagration which threatened general dissolution of law and order, does not seek to build a golden palace for himself with the ruins of the ancient regime, but wishes to establish a civil code, which, like a new city built on the same *foundation*, and with the same *materials*, will be regular in its construction, plain to every passenger, nay, to every stranger (who must now lose his way at every turn in the crooked lanes and dirty *cul-de-sacs* of feudal laws and feudal constitutions), and will supply the accommodations of life to the lowest as well as the highest of the public family; in fine, a man who will gradually, *and not slowly, force* a revolution in other countries, not by the cannon and the bayonet, but by the irresistible influence of personal and national example; not by the invasion of rafts, and flat-bottomed boats, but by the constant contemplation, and consequent imitation (Oh Britain! Oh land of *Magna Charta*, and the Bill of Rights! that I must use the term *imitation*)! of a truly great

great and generous people, full of personal attachment to their chiefs, and yet fond of public freedom, loyal with liberty, enlightened by literature, frank in theire friendships, and enthusiastic in their desire to cement not only the profession, bu t th practice, of peace with a people like themselves. Yes, by the approximation and example of such a man and such a people—by their rapid prosperity abroad, and felicity at home—the British ministry, *whoever they may be*, and whether the ex-minister be again at their head or at their tail—the British ministry will, they *must*, every day, diverge more and farther from the politics of Pitt, and incline more and more to freedom and Charles Fox, whether that man takes a seat in the council-chamber, or sits quietly in his own.

Dec. 9, 1801. P.

To the Editor of the Monthly Magazine,

SIR,

I HAVE this afternoon seen in your Magazine for November, a Letter, signed by Mr. Samuel Wesley, in which is a quotation from Lucian's Dialogue between Terpsio and Pluto. The writer doubts whether ἐθεραπεύων be misprinted for ἐθεράπευον. Be so good to remove his doubt by assuring him, that it not only ought to be but actually is ἐθεράπευον in Benedict's edition of 1619, now lying before

A TRANSLATOR OF LUCIAN.

Dec. 15, 1801.

To the Editor of the Monthly Magazine.

SIR,

IT may be necessary for the instruction of your anonymous Correspondent, who so anxiously required the insertion of a letter from Mr. Godwin in your last Number, to observe that he has not used his friend in a friendly or even a decent manner. It was neither generous, nor handsome, nor yet tolerable, to make Mr. Godwin address an open antagonist in the same style in which he had with propriety resented the secret attacks of some malignant traducer. So defective in discernment himself, he should have returned the letter for revision to its author, who might have made its contents more applicable to the strictures of W. before he ventured to publish it as "the only proper answer." I cannot for a moment suppose, that the fair argumentative mind of the author of Political Justice, whose rare merit it is to have allowed the fullest weight to the objections of his antagonists, by the strong statement and minute examination which he has given of their opinions, could possibly have replied to what was *intended* for reasoning, by such indignant language as your Correspondent has copied, and misapplied.

I know not whether I ought to condescend so far, by way of rejoinder, as to observe that, if this well meaning friend wishes it to be understood that Mr. Godwin utterly abjured the horrid idea of infanticide on the 29th of August, 1801, most certainly my accusations would not attach, on the 20th of September, on the supposition that he continued in the same sentiments until that date. But then it appears that my charges were not brought against the Mr. Godwin of August or September, but against the Mr. Godwin of April or May, in one of which months, I believe, was published his Reply to Dr. Parr and others. Now this pamphlet most assuredly does not exhibit any such symptoms of horror against the exposing of infants, as we find manifested in the letter of August 29. Few, however, will forbear to rejoice that the writer's sentiments are altered, or that his pen expressed what was far from his heart.

Had the spirit of candour or modesty, or even the faculty of discrimination, graced the few lines that usher in Mr. Godwin's letter, no one would have suspected its being addressed to W. and the trouble of inserting this would have been spared to the Editor of the Monthly Magazine. W.

Shrewsbury,
December 9, 1801.

To the Editor of the Monthly Magazine.

SIR,

I Should be much obliged to any of your Correspondents, to inform me where I may find an account of the life and literary labours of Dr. Robert Simpson, of Glasgow; and whether there he any painting or engraved portrait of him.—Any information respecting this able geometrician would be acceptable to several who are admirers of his genius and writings, and to none more so than to

Yorkshire, Oct. 6. Your's, &c.
L. R.

To

To the Editor of the Monthly Magazine.

SIR,

EVERY investigation into the structure of the earth, every discovery in the sciences of fossiology and geologic chemistry, confirms the tradition of an universal Deluge; and every research into the customs, superstitions, and languages of different climates, induces us to believe that mankind originated from one common family, and were primarily possessed of one common tongue; thus conjointly establishing two most important facts in the Mosaic annals of the origin of mankind, and giving authenticity to all the rest. In the present paper, I shall confine myself to the latter consideration, leaving to Mr. Kirwan and M. Cuvier to demonstrate the prior position. The Mosaic writings not only inform us of the existence of these two events, but that, at a period of small descent from the flood, there was a general confusion of this primitive language, and a dispersion of mankind over the face of the whole earth. And whoever compares the different dialects of different nations, how widely soever they may be separated from each other, while he is astonished at the variation of tongues into which human speech is divided, will nevertheless perceive just enough of similarity in all of them, of radical elements which have lived through every change, and uniformly preserved an expression of the same ideas, to convince him that every existing language is derived from one common stock. There is no scholar, perhaps, who has laboured with so much toil, or with so much success, in this immense field of inquiry, as Mr. Bryant; and he has found a most able disciple, or rather coadjutor, in Mr. Allwood, whose "Literary Antiquities of Greece" exhibit an exuberant fund of historic research, and cannot but amuse, by the richness of their fancy, even where they depart from the sobriety of consecutive speculation. After taking a general survey of the dispersion of the human race, in consequence of the idolatry that soon succeeded to the event of the general Deluge, the elaborate volume of this latter gentleman is devoted to a consideration of the origin of the characters of the Greek alphabet, and the introduction of a system upon this subject with which I can by no means agree; and the object of the present paper is therefore to point out a few of the more prominent inaccuracies under which, in my own judgment, it appears to labour, and to offer another theory in its stead.

Before the general reader, however, can become duly qualified to determine between us, it will be necessary to lay before him the basis upon which we equally proceed; and which is deduced, for the most part, from that very valuable and recondite work, "The Analysis of Ancient Mythology." In doing this, I shall not stay to prove any thing, meaning to be as summary as possible, and referring your readers, for individual authorities, to Mr. Bryant himself.

According to this system, then, independently of the Mosaic records, the traditions and historic annals of all nations extend no higher than the universal Deluge. A disposition to revert to idolatry began once more to shew itself, among the descendants of Noah, very speedily after this event: emblems of the Creator were sought for among his works; the SUN began to be deified and worshipped, as the most glorious proof of divine power and beneficence; and the SERPENT, as the reptile, of all animated beings, supposed to be endowed with the largest portion of subtilty or wisdom; and perhaps, from the vibrating radiations of his scales, particularly when coiled up in the figure of a circle, as a beautiful type of the SUN himself. The ARK also was not neglected, in whose capacious womb the whole remnant of animated nature had safely reposed during the rage of the devouring flood; nor Noah, the constructor of the ark, the great patriarch of mankind; nor the element itself, which kindly sustained, and suffered it to float upon its bosom, while every creature around was overwhelmed by its violence. Hence, not only the SUN, and the SERPENT, became objects of religious adoration; but the ARK, and every thing connected with it, added largely to the idolatry of this early æra. Noah himself was regarded as a god; and, in consequence of being the common father of the human race, as the supreme god, or god the creator. The ark itself, from its having afforded life and protection in its nutritious womb, was generally worshipped as a female deity; and from the veneration paid to the element that supported this original father and mother of mankind proceeded that which was afterwards paid, and continues to be so still in some countries, to the ocean, to rivers, rivulets, and fountains; to the Nile, in Egypt; the Ganges, in India; the Yellow River, in China; and the Tiber, in Rome; and almost every spring and streamlet throughout Greece. The adoration paid to Noah was also paid to several of his immediate posterity, and particularly

ticularly to Ham, his son, and Chus, his grandson, whose progeny were chiefly concerned in erecting the Tower of Babel, and promoting those religious rites connected with this building, which induced the Almighty to disperse them by a confusion of tongues. Upon this miraculous event, the Ammonians and Cushites, or descendants of Ham or Chus, migrated in different colonies, from the plains of Shinaar to almost every point of the compass. We trace them by their very name, as well as religious rites, the worship of water, and of the sun, or fire, its representative on earth, in Persia, Thibet, Bootan, and China, as well as among the 'Scuthians, or Scythians, of Erythrea. But the largest or most adventurous band of this wandering race extended themselves towards Egypt, took possession of the country, and again migrated, some centuries afterwards, under different leaders, towards Phrygia, and over the whole region of Greece. The sun, in the Ammonian language, was denominated *an* or *on*; and its representative fire, *or*, or *ur*: hence the name of Ammon or Hammon, which is literally Ham-on, "Ham, the sun," the "resplendent and illustrious Ham:" hence the name of Hercules, the deity supremely adored over all Egypt, Ethiopia, and Syria, which is, in like manner, Ur-cal es, "the radiant hill of fire;" *cul* or *col*, meaning a hill or mountain, whence the Latin *collis*; and ēs or ees resplendent or excellent, whence the Greek ευ, "good or lovely." The pyramid was the form of the temple peculiarly dedicated to the adoration of fire or the sun; its figure, as has has been long observed by Ammianus Marcellinus, admirably delineates a flame of fire issuing from a broad basis, and terminating gradually in an apex; or, conversely, a pencil of rays streaming from every point of the solar disc, and perpetually increasing in its angles. Its name is derived, not, as has been generally believed, from the Egyptian ΠΙΡⲰⲘⲒ, or the Chaldaic [illegible], but the Babylonian radicals, pi-ur-am-ait, contracted into P'-ur-am-ait, "the glorious emanation of the supreme Ham," or "Ham, the sun." While the obelisk, which was a form of temple, dedicated to the divine rites of the serpent, is deduced from ob-el es-ca, "the illustrious dwelling of the serpent god;" *ob*, in the same language, meaning a serpent, whence the Per. [illegible] اوب (aub) the Coptic ϨΟϤ (hoph) the Greek οψ and οφις (ops and [illegible]s), terms significative of the same reptile; whence also Europa, Europe, Ur-oph, "the serpent of the sun," Sol Pytho; Cecrops, Ca-cur-ops, and with the use and contraction of the Attic dialect Ce-c'r-ops, the "dwelling or temple of the solar serpent," and a vast variety of similar derivatives. From the name of Noah, the founder of the ark, or primæval ship, and the mythic creator of all things, the Greeks, the Romans, and all the southern nations of modern Europe, derive their immediate term for a *ship* in general: thus, from Noah, Νεαυε, Ναυς (Noaus, Naus), Navis, Navire, Navio, Navigio; hence also Danäus (Da-näus, literally "the ship," from the prefixed use of the Chaldaic particle דא.) and the Danaïdæ, the people or subjects of Danäus. While most of the other languages of Europe, and particularly those of Gothic origin, derive their term for the same vehicle from the word *hip* or *hips*, which was another name attributed to it by the Ammonians themselves: it furnishes the English with *ship*, the Dutch with *schip*, and the German with *schiff*. From the Ammonian radical *hip*, the Greeks derived their (ιππος) *hippos* or horse; the water-carriage being merely converted into a land-carriage; *hippophaes*, and a great multitude of names both of persons and places: the Egyptians their ϨΙΠ (hip) or ibis, a water-fowl peculiar to that country, and sacred in consequence of its being a *water-fowl*; and the Ethiopians their ሀበ: (hybo) condensed dew, water. There were also many other radicals by which the ark was designated, and which have afforded to all languages terms immediately expressive of this machine, or of ideas connected with it. It was denominated mēn, and hence the Greek words, Μην, Μηνη (a month, the moon), the latter of which was probably so denominated, at first, in consequence of her crescent form, by which she was supposed to resemble the figure of the ark, and was worshiped as such by the best of arkite idolators; as, for the same reason, in consequence, I mean, of the crescent shape of their horns, the bull and heifer, the Osiris and Apis of Egypt, were advanced to similar religious honours. Hence also, Minos, Menu, Menestheus, and a variety of other proper names. From the name of Theb (תבה), it furnished an appellation for the country of the Thebais, and for several cities, which were denominated Thebes: from Erech, in the Hebrew ארך, another name applied to it, were obtained Αργος (Argus), Arcadia, ark, and arc, a term still in general use to express the

the segment of a circle, or the figure of the ark itself. It was possessed also of a multitude of additional appellations, upon which I cannot enter in the present paper: nor can I (for the subject would become too long for discussion) into that part of this ingenious system, which represents almost all the mythic deities of the Greeks, all their traditionary princes and heroes to be nothing more than different types of Noah, or Theuth as he was denominated by the Chaldeans, or of his descendants; or else mere Αυτοχθονες or Γηγενεις, deified hills or elevations, affording generic denominations alone to the different Ammonian tribes, who wandered from Egypt towards Attica. I cannot, however, quit this subject without observing, that here, at least, Mr. Bryant and Mr. Allwood seem to indulge themselves in a most unwarrantable display of fancy. Admitting that Erectheus was originally a mere term for Noah himself (Erech-Theus or Theuth of the Ark), it by no means follows, that there might not have been a chief of this very name, who led forth a colony of Hellenists from Egypt towards Greece, who gave them his own appellation of Erechtheïdæ, and was elected their king. Danäus and Cadmus are, in like manner, supposed to be different terms for Noah or Theuth, and consequently identified with Erectheus: but, allowing that these were all of them terms originally applied to this patriarch, it is more rational to suppose that there were many heroes and chiefs of these very names in different ages, whose histories tradition has intermixed; and that the wandering tribes who arrived in Greece, under the generic denominations of Danaïdæ and Cadmians, were expressly conducted by princes or rulers, from whose names such denominations were derived, than to conceive that no person but Noah himself, or the arkite deity, and his immediate votaries, are hereby referred to. Cecrops, in its original etymology, may be interpreted, "the temple or residence of the solar serpent:" but it does not follow, that no hero may ever have possessed such a name as well, and that it must necessarily, and in every instance, refer to some mountain or eminence dedicated to Ophite idolatry. In reality, such mountains themselves, instead of being nothing more than hills consecrated to the worship of some fabulous Γηγενης, or Titan, may, in many instances, have been the real tombs or barrows of celebrated and actual chiefs. We have immense sepulchres of this description existing at the present day, in almost every country of Europe; and that such did exist from the remotest antiquity, and of an equal magnitude, we know from the concurrent testimony of the most authentic historians—such were the tumuli, or sepulchral hills, erected on the plains of Troy, in honour of several of the Grecian heroes, who fell in the course of this obstinate controversy: tumuli, which Alexander visited with sentiments of religious awe, and which were traced, and even measured, with considerable accuracy, so late as the period of Dr. Chandler's Voyage to the Troad. Herodotus, however, gives us a very explicit account of a more immense barrow, or funeral mountain, still; it was the sepulchre of Halyattes, the father of Crœsus, who was interred in Lydia, and had a monument thrown over his remains, more stupendous, observes the Greek historian, than any thing of the kind, excepting the labours of the Egyptians and Babylonians. The circumference of this tumulus was six stadia and two plethra, which is more than three-quarters of an English mile.

If the etymological meaning of names be to be solely attended to, in the developement of the history of the persons to whom they appertain; there is just as much reason to deny the existence of Cain and Abel, as of Cadmus and Cecrops; the former implying, etymologically, a mere fountain (Ca'-ain "the place" or "dwelling of the spring"); and the latter referring to the Almighty himself (Ab-el, "God the Father or Creator"). Who is there, however, who does not instantaneously perceive, that both these appellations are figurative? that the former ought to have the interpretation of "the Permanent Fountain;" and the latter of "the Divine Progenitor?" The same degree of fancy, which could annihilate the Theban or the Trojan war, and reduce the histories of them to mere poetic fables, might as readily, a century or two hence, if the fact should not be protected by written and concurrent annals, represent the whole of the last expedition to Egypt as a fable; and pretend to reason upon the subject from the names of Menou and Abercrombie, who were the antagonist commanders; the former of which might, with much facility, be deduced from the Ammonian Mēn, whence we obtain our appellation for the *moon*; and the latter from the compound Ab-ur c'r-om-pi, in literal English, "the emanation of Ham, the glorious and creative sun." The whole, in few words, might be resolved into a solar eclipse:—The temporary power of the moon over the sun might be admi-

admirably delineated by the transient successes of the forces of Menou, the Deus Lunus, or Lunar God of the Babylonians, over those of Abercrombie, the Ham-on, or illustrious sun, of the same people; and the final triumph of the latter, and recovery of his wonted glory, by the eventual victory of the English troops, the splendour of whose fame immediately irradiated the whole country, and dispelled the dread darkness with which it was overpowered. Learning might liberally be made to contribute towards the elucidation of this mythic tradition, and not a few would be convinced by the arguments advanced in its favour.

Your readers must excuse the digression into which I have been undesignedly seduced. Having expatiated at large upon the system of which I have now given a brief statement, Mr. Allwood enters upon the subject of the origin of the Greek characters, which were principally, if not wholly, imported into Attica from Egypt. He selects seven letters from the entire alphabet, and apprehends, that, by a close attention to his explanation of these, his readers may be able for themselves to explain all the rest. The letters made choice of are Α. Β. Γ. Δ. Μ. Ρ. and Ω. Of these, he conceives the first to have originated from an instrumest consisting of two piles driven occasionally into the banks of the Nile, "so as to be inclined at an acute angle, and to be fastened to each other at the apex," in consequence of which, "the surface of the water would point out to an observer, both the height of the stream on any particular days, and the whole height to which it rose in any one year. This instrument (continues he) is no other than the Α of the Greeks:" and he imagines it presents an object of such importance to the country where it was used, that it seems to have been, in a peculiar manner, dedicated to the chief deity. Its name is derived from Al-phi, the oracular influence of this deity." Upon this interpretation, I shall make no other comment, than that we may allow it to be ingenious, but that it does not appear to be intitled to any other praise. The term beta, designated by Β, implies, in the Hebrew, a house or temple. It is thus written ב: Mr. Allwood supposes it to "present to our view the section of one of the abodes of mankind, in the early ages of artless simplicity;" and conceives, that the Β, the synonymous character of the Greeks or Cuthites, was formed from an improvement upon this building, suggested by an inundation of the Nile; in consequence of which, it was necessary to place the original tent or abode upon piles, giving us hereby a representation of such a figure as  "which may have been polished down by use into Β." With as little authority upon which to repose, there appears to me less ingenuity in this interpretation, than in the foregoing. "As to the form of the letter gamma Γ, observes Mr. Allwood, it perfectly well expresses the flexure of the knees in the posture of *sitting*:" its meaning is cham-ai, "the place of Cham," or Ham; and the deities of Egypt are "always represented in a *sitting* attitude, during the time that any offering is made to them." To my comprehension, the letter Γ represents any other attitude just as well as that of *sitting*; and I must leave it to your readers to find out the resemblance for themselves. The fourth letter or Δ (delta) is deduced from a supposition, that the Cushites, who subdued Egypt, drained that part of the Egyptian territory which is comprehended by this name, and accurately preserved the memory of this achievement, by the introduction of the present character, which represents the form of the country drained, into their alphabet. This is the most ingenious conjecture we have yet met with; but it labours under two difficulties: the first is, that it appears more consonant to history that this country was drained by the natives, than by their conquerors; and next, the character was most probably in existence prior to this mighty achievement by either party; the name of Delta Δ being, conversely, bestowed upon the region thus drained, in consequence of its resemblance to the pre-existent letter. The next character selected by Mr. Allwood is the Μ, denominated *mu* by the Greeks, the sound of which resembles, says he, the *lowing of cattle*, and its shape that of a bull or a cow. The latter, nevertherless, in my apprehension, just as much as the letter Γ, delineates the sitting-attitude of a deity. To explain this, however, we have a figure presented to us—a precaution which was highly necessary: and in this figure, the front column is supposed to represent the fore legs; the back, the hind legs; and the point of the central angle, the depth of the body of the animal: after which, by adding a head and tail, which even the figure itself shews plainly the letter does not describe, we obtain an emblem of the Osiris or Apis, the sacred bull or cow of the Egyptians. And here, indeed, Mr. Allwood appears to be most decidedly mistaken; for, in opposition to any conjectures of his own, and independently of the total want of all resemblace whatever,

we

we have the positive testimony of a variety of Greek historians, that the Α was the letter peculiarly appropriated to these deities. But what resemblance, it may be asked, is there between the Α, and the Egyptian bull or cow greater than between these and the Μ? or, what possible reason could the Egyptians have for dedicating it to their honour? A little attention will, I trust, explain these difficulties. The pyramidal letter Α was an emblem of the *breath* or *emanation* of fire: and the bull or cow was probably represented, like the chimæra, which was an animal of this very class, as *breathing* or *emaning* fire from its nostrils. We are at least well assured, that it was the head alone of these animals, and probably, like the crescent moon, from the circular figure of their horns, that was esteemed sacred, Αλφα, βοος κεφαλη, φοινικες, says Hesychius very justly—"It was the *head* of the ox that the Phœnicians called alpha." The ox's head and the letter Α are hereby, therefore, rendered convertible characters; and it is a curious fact to observe, how both of them are blended in the aleph, or corresponding letter of the Hebrew and Chaldaic alphabets, which occurs thus א, and seems to be a compound of the ox's horns, and a section of the pyramid: in the older Chaldean alphabets, however, the sacred horns alone are depicted, and they then appear crosswise, thus [illegible].

The character Π, corresponding with the Roman P, Mr. Allwood deduces from the Egyptian prefix ΠΙ; and "as the prefix (says he) is to the word before which it is placed, so was the original of the hieroglyphic Π, by which it is represented, to the structure to which it was the entrance; for it was no other than the portal of an Egyptian temple." The Ω he resolves, as it has generally been resolved, into a serpent coiled round in the figure of a circle; the two ends of the coil representing its head and tail, and the circle itself being complete in almost every remain of Egyptian antiquity. With this last import I perfectly agree, and shall not be found to disagree very largely with the former. Throughout the whole of these explanations there is, nevertheless, a want of general design: every conjecture is isolated, and detached from every other: there is less system than we have even a right to expect—though we have no reason to expect any thing of this kind in a state of complete harmony and perfection—and the individual interpretations are many of them extremely irrelevant and unsatisfactory. I shall proceed, therefore, to offer an hypothesis of a different kind, and, as I hope, of more general and pertinent application.

The Greek characters, then, I conceive, with Mr. Allwood, to have been almost, if not altogether, imported from Egypt; and my intention is to prove, that they are every one of them, without a single exception, sacred symbols; equally so, indeed, by figure as by name. The idolatry of the Egyptians, upon the system already detailed, divided itself into the three grand classes of the solar, arkite, and ophite worship—the adoration of the sun, of the ark, and of the serpent. Each had occasionally its exclusive votaries; but the generality of the people were attached to the whole, giving, perhaps, at different periods or on different occasions a preference to the one over the other: in consequence of which, we have a right to expect simple or uncompounded symbols of each individual idolatry, in some instances; and mixed or blended symbols of the whole, in others. The Greek hieroglyphics, then, are precisely of this description: they are all of them either solar, arkite, or ophite characters, or combinations of these various superstitions; or, in other words, they are either pyramidal, crescent, or obeliscal, or intermixtures of any two, or of the whole: the pyramid, as I have before observed, being the form of the temple peculiarly dedicated to the sun; the obelisk, that of the temple of the serpent; and the crescent, the exclusive symbol of arkite devotion. This being premised, it is obvious, that Α, Δ, Λ, are all solar hieroglyphics; the first representing a story or platform in the middle of the pyramidal temple, of which it was the immediate type; the second, a mere ground-floor, or platform at the base; and the third, an unexcavated pyramid, or with a chamber too small for notice. It has been generally conceived, that the Egyptian pyramids were not possessed of stories, but this is an undoubted mistake: for those of Sakkara, in the vicinity of Memphis, afford many examples of this kind of edifice; a fact long since noticed by M. Grobert, and now fully confirmed by the testimony of M. Ripaud, since his return with Bonaparte. In reality, the pyramids of Babylon were most of them of this description, particularly the Tower of Bel, which is specially noticed by Herodotus: the pagodas of Hindu and China, which are only variations of the Ammonian pyramid, uniformly present a similar appearance of distinct stories; and there is no reason to suppose, that a division of the structure into a variety of tiers was

evec

ever uncommon in any country into which the pyramid was introduced. It is also well ascertained, that, although these stupendous edifices appeared to a spectator on the ground, to converge to a point at their summits, yet, that, in reality, these summits constituted a platform for the conjoint purposes of sacrifice, divination, and astrology: such platforms were sometimes, moreover, thrown forth at different distances from the sides of the building, and gave a still nearer resemblance to the pagodas of the East.

Γ, Ε, Η, Ι, Π, Τ, are all ophite or serpent hieroglyphics; they are obelisks or columns, with platforms or stories; an appurtenance which the obelisk occasionally boasted, in common with the pyramid, in different parts of the buildings; excepting in the instance of Ι, which, like the pyramidal Λ, appears to be the emblem of a structure devoid of excavation; while the Η and Π are types of double obelisks, the former with a platform uniting the two columns in the centre, and the latter on the summit. Many of the Greek characters, I am well aware, were formerly expressed by figures that vary, in some degree, from those in present use: but such variations are not of any great consequence to the purpose before us; although I shall notice the change which has taken place in the Σ, as well as several others, when I advance to the interpretation of their names. Ζ, Σ, Χ, are again all of them pyramidal letters; the first is a section of a pyramid, with termini representing the divergescence of its angles; a design equally observable in the second; and the whole are admirably adapted to delineate the perpetual stream of different pencils of rays from the solar orb in every different and possible direction. Ν, Κ, Μ, are compound characters, and exhibit a combination of the solar pyramid, with one or more serpentine obelisks: the Ν, like the Ζ, possessing a mere section of the former. Β, Ρ, Φ, Ψ, are also double characters, but compounded of the obelisk and crescent; and are consequently both ophite and arkite; the first and third have a two-fold crescent or arc, the second and fourth one alone. Θ and Ο are pure solar hieroglyphics, in which a different taste is indulged from that which introduced the pyramids. The former may be supposed to be a large golden ball, with a table or platform in the centre, not dissimilar, perhaps, from that on the summit of the dome of St. Paul's Church. The Ξ is a character totally different from all the rest, for its different members are totally disjoined and unconnected. I have always regarded it in its present form as imperfect; I have long conceived that its central line was originally united to the two extremes by converse curvatures, thus S and that it was the archetype the Roman S, which in pronunciation exhibits most accurately the latter half of its powers: and I was extremely gratified in observing of late a copy of an old Greek alphabet in Le Clabart, in which it occurs exactly like the Roman S, its immediate offspring. In a great variety of other copies, the lines are also connected, though in a more zig zag direction still; from all which circumstances, as well as from the smaller or running ξ, which is a mere diminution of the capital, as it appears on many ancient inscriptions, there can be no doubt, that this was originally a serpentine hieroglyphic. The only remaining letters are the Τ and the Ω, both of which are also most obviously serpentine; the former representing the reptile pendulous from a tree, or raising himself from the ground, with his head and tail elevated above the rest of his body, which hangs down in the figure of a loop, as it occurs in the Georgian alphabet, or a loop contracted into a single line, as in the modern mode of writing the Greek; and the latter exhibiting him in a coil more complete still, and, at first, entirely so, with the head and tail peeping out, or forming tangents beyond the circular line. This sort of device, as Mr. Allwood has justly observed, is to be met with in almost every remain of Egyptian antiquity.

In many of the Greek alphabets several of these characters are totally suppressed, or are very differently imprinted; in others, on the contrary, we meet with one or two additional characters, and particularly with the F often written, as in the present instance, like the Roman, but more frequently, I believe, thus ϛ: in either case, it is easy to class the letter, as it will also be to arrange any other, whenever it be found to vary in its figure. I may not, perhaps, have arranged them altogether aright, in the present cursory survey; but I hope I have at least established this principle, that they are uniformly sacred symbols appertaining to the different systems of idolatry professed by their inventors. And as, I trust, I have proved this by their configuration, I now proceed to establish it by their names.

The word *alpha*, typified by the hieroglyphic Λ, is very generally known to imply "the breath, inspiration or oracle of God;" from the radicals al-phi. No character could be better calculated to express

press this idea than a pyramid, or ascending flame of fire. The letter B is denominated beta, (beth-ai), which is literally "the place of the temple;" or rather perhaps, "the temple of temples;" the Ammonian *ai* importing both a *place* and a *temple*. I have before observed, that in the Greek it is a compound character, equally dedicated to ophite and arkite worship: in the Persian, it retains nearly the same name (b'ai), and is an arkite or crescent character alone, thus ب. The letter Γ, denominated gamma or chamma (Cham-ai), is literally "the place or temple of Ham." Δ, pronounced delta, which is a contraction from Ad-el ait ai or 'D el-'t-ai, imports "the great temple of the supreme God:" such contractions are common to every language, and were peculiarly so among the Egyptians and Greeks: thus, the sacred heifer or apis, which was denominated Mnevis, was curtailed into Mneuis, and Ad-el ais ("the glory or radiance of the supreme God") into Adlas or Atlas. E, enunciated Epsilon, or rather Ipsilon (Ips-el-on) is "the glorious arkite god:" *hip*, *ip*, or *ips*, meaning, as I have before observed, the ark of the deluge. In its present form, it is an ophite character, and consequently does not altogether correspond to its name: in almost all the old inscriptions it is written, however, thus Є, and the modern Copts continue it in this manner to the present hour. Expressed in this manner, it becomes an arkite hieroglyphic, and is truly correct. Nevertheless, in consequence of the intermixture of these three different classifications of idolatry, and their mutual convertibility, there is no necessity that the name of every character should precisely correspond with its figure: there would then, indeed, be more of system than we have a right to expect. Z, the next letter in the order of the Greek alphabet, pronounced Zeta or Saita (Sait-ai), is literally "the place of olives." The olive-tree appears to have been sacred among the Ammonians from a very early period after the return of the Jōn or dove to the ark, with a branch of this tree in its beak: it was therefore peculiarly consecrated to Aphrodite, Venus, or Minerva, which are only so many names, as Herodotus himself admits, for the same deity, who was the mēn or ark under a female personification. The whole of the upper part of Egypt was denominated Zaït, or Saït, a name still applied to the southern side of the Nile by the Arabians, who call this country صعيد (Saied) and the people Saïtæ, "the region of olives." The olive was immediately dedicated to Minerva, or the Goddess of the Ark, Mēn-ur-ph-ai, "the place of the oracle of the glorious ark:" she was worshipped, according to Pausanias, under the title of Saitēs, at Pontinus; and the Athenians, who elected her for their patronimic goddess, are well known to have been called, like the Egyptians, Saitæ. The Z is obviously, therefore, an emblem of Minerva, the Goddess of the Ark or Olive. The letter which follows, H, is of general import, and, excepting by its hieroglyphic figure, not appropriated exclusively to ophite worship: it is pronounced Eta or Aita (Ait-ai) "the supreme temple" or "temple of the supreme god." Θ, Theta, originally, perhaps, Theuta, is (Theut-ai), "the temple of Theut," Theuth, or Noah, so denominated by the Chaldeans. I, Iota, is a mere contraction for Io-ait-ai, thus Io't-ai, and expresses "the supreme temple of Iö, or the dove who returned to the ark with the olive branch. From Io or Iön (Ιων), the Greeks derived the term Οινας (Oinas), and the Romans Venus, to whom the dove was peculiarly dedicated. Hence too the Ionians, votaries of the dove or the arkite idolatry, a name which is usually employed by the Arabian writers to express the Greeks at large يونان (Iounans). Iö was feigned to be the daughter of Inachus; which Mr. Bryant very ingeniously conjectures to have been only another term for Noachus or Noah: in the tradition, therefore, that Iö was given to the world by Inachus, we have a pure allegorical representation of the dove's having been entrusted abroad by Noah. The I is obviously, then, a character dedicated to arkite worship. By figure, it is an ophite hieroglyphic; but the ark is frequently represented under the symbol of the great mundane egg, floating on the surface of the mighty deep, and coiled around by the serpent for its protection. An image of this kind will be found in Vaillant's Coins of the Colonies, p. 136—147. The hieroglyphic of the obelisk to represent the Iota requires, therefore no comment. K, Kappa or Kabba (Ka ab-ai), contracted into K'-ab-ai, is "the temple or residence of the Sovereign Creator:" it is a term of general import; and, by its hieroglyphic, is equally appropriated to the sun and the serpent. Λ, Lambda, (El-am-pi-ad-ai, contracted into 'L-am-p'-'d ai), is literally "the place of the supreme oracle of the god Ham." M, Mu, originally Am-eus, and abreviated into 'M-eu,' is "Ham the Benevolent," or "the beneficent

ficent god." Ν, Nu, in like manner, is Ain-eus, contracted into 'N-eu', "the good or perfect fountain:" its hieroglyphic adds "of light" or life. Ξ Xi or Ksi, Yk'si or Ykus-ai, contracted into 'Ksi, is, in literal version, the "sovereign temple:" yk (ικ), according to Josephus, or ykus (ικυς), as it is written by Eusebius, being an Egyptian term, importing royalty, or supreme excellence; the radical, perhaps of the Ethiopic ለህቀ (lyhyk), 'to become perfect,' in opposition to ለሐመ (lyhym), "infirm, imperfect." Ο, Omicron, is Am, or, (as it is pronounced in many countries), Aum-ai-cur-on, curtailed into Aum-, or Om-ai-c'r-on, "the radiant and sovereign temple of Ham." It is a pure solar hieroglyphic; and is occasionally written, and particularly in an inscription on the pedestal of a well-known bust of Alexander the Great, □; a character which affords us an accurate representation of the square pyramid (πυραμις τετραγωνος), as it is termed by Strabo, which constituted the celebrated Tower of Bel; a quadrangular edifice, whose sides diverged indeed from a right line, but whose divergescence was imperceptible. The ο and □ are equally, therefore, characters expressive of solar idolatry, but only by different emblems. Π, Pi or Phi, is a mere aspirate; its meaning of course is "breath"—"inspiration"—"oracle:" and its device imports it to be "the oracle of Python," or "the serpent god:" it is from this aspirate the Latins derive their *spiro, aspiro.* Ρ, Rō, is perhaps Eröe (ερως), contracted into 'ro'; a Greek term, implying "a spring or fountain;" and which is here used κατ' εξοχην, for "*the* spring or fountain;"—the word also implies an *overflowing* or *flood*; and may perhaps be employed to express the *deluge* itself. It is a general expression, and, by its hieroglyphic, appertains equally to the ark and the serpent. Σ, Sigma, or Sykma, is probably As-yk-am-ai, abbreviated into 'S-yk-'m-ai, "the temple of Ham, the Radiant Prince," or "Lord of the Sun;" the element *as* or *ais*, importing light, or the sun himself, the source of light; and being apparently the radical of the Greek *eus* (ευς), excellent or perfect. Τ, *Tau*, originally Taut, is merely the Phœnician name for Noah, Theut, or Thoth; who, among this nation was called Taautes; as among the Celts he was denominated Teutates. Noah was not only the former, but the guide and protector, of the ark: the latter character is implied by the hieroglyphic itself, which is altogether ophite; and we may hence see how easily the arkite, solar, and serpentine idolatry convert into each other; for the serpent is sometimes the protector of the ark as well as Noah: Noah was Osiris; Osiris, Apollo; Apollo, the Sol Python. We have met with the same name, varied only a little in its enunciation, applied already to another character in the alphabet—I mean the Θ, Theta, or Theuta; but these instances are not uncommon, and the very next letter furnishes us with another example. Υ, Ypsilon, or Upsilon (Ips-el-on), is, as already observed under the hieroglyphic Ε, "the glorious arkite god:" the device is unlike the former, though each of them apply to the arkite serpent—the two names have a trifling variance in their enunciation for the mere purpose of discrimination. Φ, Phi; this, like the term Pi, is a mere aspirate; they are the same words, with a small variation alone in the mode of pronouncing them: their meaning, of course, is alike. Χ, Chi, or Ki, contracted from Yk-ai into 'K-ai, or 'K'-i: its interpretation, like that of Ξ, Xi or Ksi (for the words are the same), is "the sovereign temple." Ψ, Psi, is a mere abbreviation of Ips-ai into 'Ps-ai or 'Ps-i; the reader will readily perceive, therefore, that it imports "the residence or temple of the Ip, Hip, or Arkite God." Ω, Omega, or Omeka (Aum-yk-ai), explains itself, and is literally "the sovereign temple of the God Ham." This letter occupies the the last place in the alphabet, and is supposed to have been the last added to it; its power, in enunciation, is double the length of the former ο, or omicron; in consequence of which the Greeks made choice of the omicron to express whatever was small or diminutive, and the omega to express the contrary: hence the adjectives μικρος (micros, contracted from ομικρος, omicros), little, and μεγας (megas, contracted from ωμεγας, omegas) large or great.

It may perhaps be conceived by many of my readers, that the radicals here pretended to be given of the characters of the Greek alphabet, and their respective names, are so simple that they may be applied with equal ease to any other alphabet; but let those who may thus object to the key I have now ventured to offer, make a single attempt, and they will find themselves completely disappointed. In a few instances, perhaps, they may succeed with some difficulty; but, excepting in the example I have given of the Greek, and that of the Asiatic and Europepean languages, derived from the same source, I have never been able to succeed myself, though I have made many efforts for this purpose. The keys of the Hebrew, Chaldean, and generally of the Celtic, appear to be derived from sources very different; or, at least, there is such an intermixture of other symbols with those which designate the Greek, that no solution of the latter can be successfully applied to any of them: while the Gothic, Sclavonian, and most of the southern European alphabets, which are obviously either Greek or Roman derivations, not only retain the general character of the Greek elements, but as uniformly their names; excepting that, by way of abbreviation, they are, for the most part, curtailed of all but the first Greek syllable. It is curious to observe, that in the Celtic alphabets, and particularly the Welsh and Irish, the pyramidal figure appears to prevail, as though the sun, or his representative fire, had been regarded amongst these nations as the chief deity in the mythic hierarchy: a fact which history will perhaps very sufficiently establish. The same observation may be made with regard to the alphabet of Thibet; while those of Persia, Arabia, and particularly of the Birman Empire, are almost entirely crescent, combined occasionally with ophite characters, as though invented by sages who were chiefly attached to arkite idolatry. In the Birman alphabet, this indeed is peculiarly conspicuous; for several of the characters are perfect phases of the moon, who, as I have before observed, is a mere arkite symbol herself, represented as she appears in different periods of her menstrual revolution; the external and internal outline being equally preserved. There is a beautiful copy of this alphabet appended to Major Symes's very entertaining "Account of an Embassy to the Kingdom of Ava."

The length of this letter precludes me from prosecuting an inquiry closely connected with the antecedent observations: I mean, whether the different orders of architecture may not have originated from the same source as the characters of the Greek alphabet? Whether a superior attachment to the system of solar or fire-worship may not have produced the order of Gothic architecture, both in Europe and Asia; an order, whose very essence is that of the pyramid; and which, in its spires, its arches, its roofs, in every part of its design, is perpetually producing a pointed summit from an expanded base? And whether, in those countries in which little or nothing of this order is to be traced; where the obelisk, column, and circular arch are predominant, the idolatry of the sun or fire have not been nearly or altogether relinquished for that of the serpent and the ark, separately or conjointly; the former, in Oriental mythology, being the avowed protector of the latter? I cannot at present pursue these inquiries as they seem to deserve. But, as it is highly uncertain when I shall be able to resume this speculation, which I believe to be altogether novel, I cannot avoid adding, that so far as I have been able to make a cursory investigation into the architecture of different nations, it appears to be consistent with fact. The Goths or Cuths (Getæ) were certainly of Scythian (Scuthian) descent, and imported the pyrean idolatry with them into the whole of the north of Europe: the religion of the Druids was of the same description: and the general character of the pyramid not only exists wherever the Goths or Celts have had a footing, but so deeply did it establish, in the general mind, a taste for this species of architecture, that the pyramid was still suffered to prevail in all their religious edifices after their conversion to Christianity. Among the Oriental nations, this is not less obvious than in Europe: the Persians, Hindus, Thibetians, Chinese, have uniformly evinced a greater veneration for fire than for any other element; and their religious edifices are all of the Gothic or pyramidal order. The great temple at Pegue is of this precise description; and the image of Boodth, whose worship extends over the larger part of India, is generally ornamented with a conic or pyramidal cap. If we turn to Mexico and Peru, where the sun is adored not only as the supreme, but almost as the only, object of religious worship, we meet with nothing but pyramidal or Gothic architecture in the construction of the public temples. That of the sun and moon at Mexico is here peculiarly intitled to notice, and an elegant engraving of it may be seen in vol. iii. of Mr. Maurice's Indian Antiquities. Such, however, was not the chief or general devotion of Greece: the sun undoubtedly was worshipped by this idolatrous people as an individual deity in their sacred hierarchy; but he never rose higher than to a middle rank in the scale; and while the principles of arkite adoration were recognised by the deification of every ocean, river, and streamlet, the solar representation of fire appears to have been almost forgotten, or, at most, was but little resorted to. In this country then the order of of architecture ought to be as different as the order of religion; and while we meet with but few traces of the pyramid or spire, we have a right to expect a large prevalence of the very symbols that are presented to us: columns, typical of the protecting power of the ark, ornamented at their capitals with vignettes, the fruit and leaves of the vine first cultivated by its founder; united, where such union was necessary, with circular or crescent, instead of pointed arches; and crowned, instead of the spire, with the dome. The subject is interesting, but I can pursue it no farther: yet I hope to see it resumed by some person who may be better qualified to do it justice than myself.

JOHN MASON GOOD.

Caroline-place, Guildford-str.
Nov. 17, 1801.

To the Editor of the Monthly Magazine.

SIR,

IN a work of such magnitude as the rebuilding of London-bridge, every possible mode should be taken into consideration; and, among others, I have heard it frequently mentioned, rather as a thing to be wished, than as one capable of being put in practice, to have the intended bridge of one single arch.

Being in company, some time past, with a constructor of iron bridges, I urged this to him as a fair opportunity offered of immortalizing his name, by devising a method of accomplishing this arch of cast materials: but he candidly owned, that the elevation necessary to be given to such an arch would prove a great obstacle.

I then suggested to that original genius *Bean*, the smith of Bath-wick, that he would do well to propose his entire new principle, by means of which a great centre arch might be got with the most perfect security and durability. What he has done, I know not; but I have lately, I think, discovered in your Work a means by which it might be accomplished with the greatest ease. What I refer to is your account of Mr. Jordan's plan of taking off lateral pressure, by suspending bridges to a grand arch, and making a draw-bridge where the passage of masts is necessary; for here, where the old bridge exists as a scaffolding, an arch of any diameter may, with certainty and safety, be raised on its own stirrups, and the new bridge entirely completed before the old one is taken down. Neither would any draw-bridge be necessary; as, although his plan renders it possible to have a flat bridge of any length, yet, at the same time, it enables the artist to give the passage over any degree of curve that shall be suitable to the public, yet still without the smallest lateral pressure; and, in the hands of a man of genius, make such a bridge the admiration of the world.

As you have already published his principle in your Magazine, I shall only refer your readers and the public to the work itself; since it appears to me, that if a bridge of *one* arch be desired, this *great*, because *simple*, invention, is likely to be the one that must ultimately be adopted, I am, Sir, your's, &c.

C.

For the Monthly Magazine.

The NOBLE LETTER *of* BRUTUS *to* CICERO;—*dedicated to the* FIRST CONSUL *of* FRANCE.

"MARCUS BRUTUS *to* MARCUS TULLIUS CICERO.

ATTICUS sent me an extract of your Letter to Octavius. You have been so long my faithful friend, that I can receive little *new* pleasure in reading your expressions of regard for my general welfare, and solicitude for my personal safety. I am so accustomed to hear of what Cicero has said, or of what he has done, to serve my interest, or exalt my character, that such proofs of friendship have lost the freshness of novelty, and I am come to look on them as things of course, mere occurrences of the day: I am, on this account, the less able to bear the pain which this part of your letter has given me that relates to us and to our cause. When you express your gratitude to Octavius in such a fulsome detail of adulation, (I feel my cheeks redden while I write; the rank and station of a republican recoil at the idea—recommend our lives to *him!* —as well commend to him the daggers with which we stabbed his uncle)—When you are thus eager in paying homage, and in imploring clemency, do you not, as it were, mount the rostrum to declare, that it is vain for us to remove the masterdom, while you are resolved to keep the master; and is not Cicero transformed into a lictor, who lays down the fasces of the empire at the feet of a boy.

Recollect the words that you have written; and if you dare, deny that they pre-suppose, on the one part, the impotence of the slave; and, on the other, the self-sufficiency of the tyrant. "One request (you say) must be made, one supplication, that he will not use those two ill of whom

whom the Roman world think well; that he will save such respected citizens." What if he refuses to save us?—Shall we not be safe?—Our right hands have taught us how. Better indeed to perish than find safety through him. I do not think—no, by the Gods! by Virtue, the God within me, whom I choose to worship! I do not think that we of Rome have deserved so ill of Heaven, as to petition any inferior power for the safety of a single citizen, much *less* for the saviours of the world. I speak like a boaster: I should not do so, but to those who are as little acquainted with the measures of fear, as with the measures and limits of submission.

Can Cicero confess that Octavius is all-powerful, and yet be his flatterer and friend? Could Cicero bear to see Brutus reside in Rome; if, to reside in Rome, Brutus must intercede for passport and protection from this boy? Is this stripling to be made the subject of Cicero's panegyric for willing, for suffering the breath of life to remain in our nostrils, for graciously *conniving* at the life of a Roman? Is he conferring a favour, when, rather than suffer Antony to tyrannize over us, he, with all due humanity, may choose to play the tyrant himself? Were he the avenger of usurpation, not, as he is, the mere vicegerent of an usurper, would *you* be forced, at this time, to supplicate for men who have deserved of their country as we have done?

It was, in truth, a want of energy, a want of self-confidence, not confined to your breast, but diffused through the public mind, which instigated Cæsar to the wretched ambition of sovereignty; which, when he fell, stimulated Antony to make the dead body a footstool to raise himself above his equals; and which, at this moment, lifts up this young man to such an overweening height, that, with uplifted hands and upturned eyes, you must propitiate his mercy for us—the mercy of a scarce bearded youth, without which there can be no redemption. But, if some among us would, or if they *could*, remember they were Romans, bold as these have been to rob us of our rights, they should meet with others as bold to vindicate them; and, though the crown of Cæsar would sparkle in the eyes of Antony, the wounds of Cæsar would burst out in his memory, and quell the madness of his heart. You Cicero—you, who so illustriously avenged yourself on the enemies of your country, how can you bear, at one moment to recollect the deeds you have done, and in the next to approve of such men, and such measures; to debase yourself into such lowliness as to have even the *semblance* of approbation? From whence sprung your enmity to Antony? Was it from personal pique, or from the general good? You said, the latter. It was, you said, because he wanted to make *his* hand the sword of justice, and *his* heart the only fountain of mercy. It was because he wanted to dole out rights and liberties to the very men from whom he had begged his life. It was because the weal or woe of the empire was to hang, as it were, by a hair of his head; to be blessed when he was in good humour, and to totter when he frowned. You called aloud, To arms! Why? Was it that the Genius of Rome should rouze to vengeance; or, was it that Cicero might gratulate a successor? My eloquent friend turned sophist, to prove that it is good to serve, if we serve a good master! If any master could be good, we might fare well and fatten in the service of so good a master as Antony. What think you—would he deny to men, whose *patience* was his sole ground of safety, the sole pledge of assurance for his life? We might obtain every thing from his fears, except that, without which all is nothing,—liberty and honour. If we must talk of these things as if we were haggling in the market-place about a bargain, how much, pray you, would our apathy and acquiescence *come to* in the estimation of this boy, who seems to think, forsooth, he ought to succeed Cæsar in nature because he succeeds him in name? How much would he give us, if we were content to live in peace, to grow fat and sleek, and shining; to lay up trash in coffers, and to divert ourselves with counters and consular dignities? But Cæsar had then been sacrificed in vain—In vain had I lifted this arm on the living Cæsar, if the dead Cæsar is to be a god, and we his idolators; if his spirit be suffered to walk abroad, and migrate into other men. My sword ought, in this case, to have slept in its scabbard. May the gods blot out and annihilate every feeling of my soul, rather than the one which, at this moment, prompts me to declare—that, so far from suffering in this *second* Cæsar what I disdained to suffer from the *first*—that, if he who begot me had done as Cæsar did, I should have done as I did; nor should it have saved him, had he cried aloud—I am your father!—No, by Heaven, not he whom I call father shall violate the laws—shall trample upon our liberties with impunity, while I have a being. Is it possible, Cicero, you can suppose the state to be free, if the supporters of the state be obliged to skulk in holes and corners when his countenance lowers; or to come abroad at times, like reptiles, and sport in the sunshine of his favour? Not even Octavius, I tell you, my friend, *can* grant the prayer of your petition. You intercede for our safety; that is, you ask quarter for our lives.—Insurance for the lives of slaves! Who will insure the lives of those who have lost their liberty and stained their honour? But then you say, we may reside in Rome. Liberty, my friend, has nothing local in it: it is not confined to the bricks and mortar, the stone and marble of your capital. If I be free, I shall carry Rome along with me; and they are exiles *in* Rome, who can bear the contumelies, or the courtesies, of a tyrant. In Greece, that title was fatal even to the surviving family; but when this lad has insulted us, by adopting the very name of the late usurper, Cicero runs to recognize the name—gives the all-hail—falls on his knees for the safety of those who have served the state, and makes that state once more, not merely a nominal, but a real substantial slave—an abandoned, irredeemable slave, that kicks away the cap of liberty, and dances to the clank of his chains. If Cæsar himself, in the plenitude of his power, felt what could be done by one or two resolute men, shall we now crouch to the sovereignty of his *naked name?* Rome appears to me like a huge heavy ox, goaded on by a boy. The name of Cæsar serves Octavius by way of goad, and the great unwieldy animal moves along, unconscious of its strength, and patient of injury.

Never, therefore, from this hour commend my safety to this Cæsar of your's: never, if you love me, commend your own. You pay too high a price for a few years of frail and feverish life, if you purchase them with a single prostration at the feet of an equal. I should not wish that your enemies had it in their power to put such a vile construction on your prosecution of Antony, as to refer it to motives of personal fear, rather than to a regard for the common-weal; and I should be sorry to see them urge this petition of your's to Octavius as a proof that Cicero could contrive to bear tyranny, provided he had a tyrant *to his taste.* I do applaud the boy for the good you say he has done. If the *will-be* should resemble the *has-been*—if it appears that his aim is to level upstart ambition, not to put his own in its place, I shall applaud him more; but if, on this account, you dress him up in the attributes of sovereignty, with the prerogatives to pardon or to punish, you compliment him rather highly. I have no notion, Cicero, of handing over the common-weal to any person, by way of compliment. Cicero, the man who writes to you, not only will not pray for his life, but, as far as he can, will hold down those that offer to do so for him. I am determined to banish your servile city, satisfied, as I am, that wherever liberty is, there is Rome—there is my country; yet sometimes I shall sigh to think of those left behind, whom a fullness of years only renders more avaricious of life—a life drawn to the very *lees*—accounted more precious than honour, friendship, and fair fame. Happy in the home of my own heart, I shall think myself sufficiently rich in the debt of gratitude which the world owes, but has not paid, me: and I shall glory in being the disinterested creditor of mankind. I know nothing sweeter than the memory of virtuous actions; nothing greater than the stern self-sufficiency of freedom. As to what has been done, it has been well done; as to what there is to do, I know what I shall do. Sunk as your city is, I will not sink or succumb. I shall never be overruled by those who wish that others should over-rule them. I will try all things, hazard all things. What will I not do, what not suffer, to raise up my fallen country a second time, and crown her with freedom! As to what will be, if Fortune does as she ought to do, you shall all be happy. Let her do as she chooses, I shall be happy. O, my friend, how can this little life of our's be so happily filled up, as when our every thought and action, our every word and work, are dedicated to the salvation of our country?

Cicero, dear Cicero, again and again do I beseech, do I implore you to hold up your head, and wrestle with difficulties like a man. Do not despond; do not despair. As you cannot be what you choose, be what you ought. Keep watch, and be silent. Set your face and lift your voice against those measures, nor suffer a single poisonous precedent to insinuate itself, pregnant with future evil. The boldest and brightest actions of your life will fade in the memories of men, if the tenor of this life be not to the last uniform and consistent. The virtue that has done much lays on itself an obligation to do more; and the benefits we confer on our country are debts for which the greatest and best are must accountable. That the Consular Cicero should counteract

Antony with the same zeal with which the Consul Cicero crushed Catiline, is no subject of surprize, for it only preserves the unity of the piece: but if the same Cicero would direct the thunderbolt of his eloquence with such energy and success against others, his former fame would sink in comparison, and the last dazzling act of the illustrious drama would be crowned with the plaudits of remotest generations; and surely if ever one was fitted to be the guardian of the common-weal, and patron of the people, by the endowments of nature, by high reputation, and by the concurrent testimony of the world, that one is my friend.

A truce, then, with your paltry petitions, and memorialize me no longer. Rather retire in o the sacred recess of your own great heart as into that inmost apartment where are placed our altars, and houshold gods: there commune with the spirits of your ancestors—be rapt into the deeds of less degenerate days—call up your own heroic acts, and let them stand, as it were, embodied before you, nor dare to come out to the world, until you can shew this sentence beaming on your breast: —The people may, the people must, be free, if the leaders of the people be ready with head, and heart and hand, to write, to speak, to act, and to suffer, in their cause."

For the Monthly Magazine.

DESCRIPTION *of all the* DEPARTMENTS *of the* FRENCH REPUBLIC, *including those in the* CONQUERED COUNTRIES.

(*Continued from Page* 398, *of No.* 80.)

Department of Jura.

THIS department is one of the three formed of Franche Compté. It is bounded on the north by the departments of Doubs, of Upper Saone, and of Côté d'Or; on the east, by the departments of Doubs and the Swiss Cantons; on the south, by the departments of Leman and of Ain; and on the west, by those of Saone and Loire, and of Côté d'Or. Its superficies is about 986,246 square acres, or 403,364 hectares; its population 284,460 individuals. It is divided into four communal districts.

Department of Landes.—This is one of the four composed of Guienne. It is bounded on the north by the department of Gironde; on the east, by the departments of Lot and Garonne, and of Gers; on the south, by that of Lower Alps; and and on the west, by the ocean. Its superficies is about 1,764,425 square acres, or 900,534 hectares; its population 249,140 individuals. It is divided into three communal districts.

Department of Leman.—This department is formed of the territory of Geneva united to several cantons taken from the departments of Ain and of Mont Blanc. It is bounded on the north by the Leman Lake, Helvetia, and the department of Jura; on the east, by le Valais, Piedmont, and the department of Mont Blanc; on the west and on the south, by the departments of Ain and of Mont Blanc. Its superficies is about 550,000 square acres, or 280,000 hectares; its population is about 195,000 individuals. It is divided into three communal districts.

Department of Liamone.—This department is the second formed of the island of Corsica. It is bounded on the north by the department of Golo; on the east, on the south and on the west, by the Mediterranean. Its superficies is about 903,652 square acres, or 461,209 hectares; its population about 72,656 individuals. It is divided into three communal districts.

Department of Loir and Cher.—This department is one of those formed of Orleanois, Blaisois and le Pays Chartrain. It is bounded on the north by the departments of Loiret, of Eure and Loir, and of Sarthe; on the east, by those of Loiret and of Cher; on the south, by those of Cher, of Indre, and of Indre and Loire; and on the west, by this last, and that of Sarthe. Its superficies is about 1,181,692 square acres, or 603,161 hectares; its population about 205,749 individuals. It is divided into three communal districts.

Department of the Loire.—This department is taken from that of Rhone and Loire, which, by a decree of the 29th Brumaire, in the second year of the Republic, was divided into two, under the denominations of the Loire and of the Rhone. It is bounded on the north by the departments of the Rhone, of Saone and Loire, and of Allier; on the east, by those of Rhone and of Isere; on the south, by those of Ardeche and Upper Loire; and on the west, by those of Puy de Dome and of Allier. Its superficies is about 964,083 square acres, or 270,423 hectares; its population about 322,965 individuals. It is divided into three communal districts.

Department of Upper Loire.—This department is one of the three formed of Auvergne and le Velay. It is bounded on the north by the departments of the Loire and of Puy de Dome; on the east, by those of the Loire and of Ardeche; on on the south, by those of Ardeche and of Lozere; and on the west, by that of Cantal. Its superficies is about 985,246 square acres, or 502,854 hectares; its population is about 259,143 individuals. It is divided into three communal districts.

Department of Lower Loire.—This is one of the five departments formed of Brittany. It is bounded on the north by the department of Ille and Vilaine, and part of that of Mayenne; on the east, by the department of Mayenne and Loire; on the south, by the department of Vendée, and on the west, by the ocean. Its superficies is about 1,383,831 square acres, or 706,285 hectares; its population is about 451,366 individuals. It is divided into five communal districts.

Department of Loiret.—This department is one of those formed of Orleanois, Gatinois, &c. It is bounded on the north by the departments of Seine and Marne, of Seine and Oise, and of Eure and Loire; on the east, by that of Yonne; on the south, by those of Nievre, of Cher, and of Loir and Cher; and on the west, by this last, and that of Eure and Loir. Its superficies is about 1,322,909 square acres, or 675,191 hectares; its population is about 290,031 individuals. It is divided into four communal districts.

Department of Lot.—This department is formed of the *ci-devant* Quercy. It is bounded on the north by the department of Correze; on the east, by the departments of Cantal and of Aveyron; on the south, by those of Tarn and of Upper Garonne; and on the west, by those of Lot and Garonne, and of Dordogne. Its superficies is about 1,400,160 square acres, or 714,619 hectares; its population about 387,019 individuals. It is divided into four communal districts.

Department of Lot and Garonne.—This department is one of the four formed of Guienne, Agenois, &c. It is bounded on the north by the departments of Dordogne and of Gironde; on the east, by that of Lot; on the south, by those of Upper Garonne, and of Gers, and of Landes; and on the west, by this last, and that of Gironde. Its superficies is about 1,116,221 square acres, or 569,703 hectares; its population about 339,821 individuals. It is divided into four communal districts.

Department of Lozere.—This department derives its name from a mountain of the Cevennes, between Mendes and Usez; it is one of the seven formed of Languedoc, Gevaudan, &c. It is bounded on the north by the departments of Upper Loire and of Cantal; on the east, by those of Ardeche and of Gard; on the south, by those of Gard and of Aveyron; which last bounds it, also, on the west. Its superficies is about 997,661 square acres, or 509,543 hectares; its population about 132,502 individuals. It is divided into three communal districts.

Department of the Lys.—This department is one of the nine formed of part of Hainault and of Austrian Flanders, of Brabant, the county of Liege, the duchy of Luxembourg, &c. It is bounded on the north by the German Ocean and the department of the Scheld, which bounds it, also, on the east; on the south, by the departments of Jemappe; and from the north to the west, by this last, and the German Ocean. Its superficies is about 718,892 square acres, or 566,911 hectares; its population is about 459,142 individuals. It is divided into four communal districts.

Department of the Channel.—This is one of the five departments formed of Normandy, and the north part of Perche. It is bounded on the north by the Channel; on the east, by the Channel and the department of Calvados; on the south, by those of Mayenne, and of Ille and Vilaine; and on the west, by the ocean. Its superficies is about 1,323,932 square acres, or 675,713 hectares; its population is about 538,000 individuals. It is divided into five communal districts.

Department of Marne.—This department is one of the four formed of Champagne. It is bounded on the north by the departments of the Ardennes and of the Aisne; on the east, by those of the Meuse and of Upper Marne; on the south, by those of Upper Marne, of Aube, and of Seine and Marne; and on the west, by those of Seine and Marne, and of Aisne. Its superficies is about 1,607,169 square acres, or 820,273 hectares; its population about 291,484 individuals. It is divided into five communal districts.

Department of Upper Marne.—This department is one of the four formed of Champagne, Charleville, Sedan, &c. It is bounded on the north by the departments of the Meuse and of Marne; on the east, by those of the Vosges, and of Upper Saone, and of Cótè d'Or; on the west, by those of Côté d'Or and of Aube. Its superficies is about 1,240,580 square acres, or 633,172 hectares; its population

tion is about 222,585 individuals. It is divided into three communal districts.

Department of Mayenne.—This is one of the four formed of Maine and Anjou. It is bounded on the north by the departments of Orne and of the Channel; on the east, by that of Sarthe; on the south, by that of Mayenne and Loire; and on the west, by that of Lower Loire. Its superficies is about 1,016,614 square acres, or 518,863 hectares; its population is about 324,730 individuals. It is divided into three communal districts.

(To be continued.)

For the Monthly Magazine.

STATE OF ARTS, MANNERS, &c. IN EDINBURGH AND LEITH.

(Continued from Page 407 of No. 80.)

LEITH, the *Piræeus* of Edinburgh, has not been hitherto mentioned in this Account. It was once a royal burgh; but the rights of the sovereign over it were, more than two hundred years since, transferred, for a sum of money to the town of Edinburgh. It lies at the distance of about a mile east from Edinburgh, on the banks of a moderate stream which has also the name of Leith, at a small space between south and south-east from the southern bank of the Forth, and on the very eastern extremity of that bank, and on the very beach of the southern side of the Frith. It consists, as yet, chiefly of buildings of which a great part may be not less than two hundred years old, and which are placed in an awkward, inconvenient arrangement. The two principal of the old streets are the Kirkgate, in which the road from Edinborgh ends, and Shore-street which lies along the south-side of the harbour. The other streets run in various directions between these, and contiguous to them, for that which is named *South Leith.* There is on the north side of the river Leith, indeed, a good deal of irregular building, old and new, which has the name of *North Leith*, as forming the northern-division of the town. Beside the old parts of this town, it is now diffused southward around the skirts of a pleasant and extensive plain, Leith Links, in elegant and commodious houses with gardens, warehouses, &c. in which the principal merchants not living in Edinburgh have their residence. The harbour has been lately improved and enlarged. A draw-bridge over the river Leith affords a convenient passage between the north and the south parts of the town, without any straitening of the limits of the dock and harbour. On all sides, the buildings continue to be rapidly extended. On the bank of the Forth, North Leith is in a progress of being continued to join the fishing village of Newhaven, another dependency of the town of Edinburgh. On the two sides of the walk and carriage-road between Edinburgh and South Leith, is gradually formed a street of villas with gardens, establishments of manufacture, and other handsome and commodious dwelling-houses, which is likely to be very soon complete; and when complete will, probably, be one of the busiest and most interesting of all the streets which belong to these towns. On all sides, for the space of three or four miles round, the vicinity of Edinburgh and Leith is covered with villas, gardens, ornamented farms and hamlets, which, though they do not, in *summer*, equal the environs of London, in an aspect of sweet, rich, simple and graceful rustic beauty, have, however, a less naked and desolate appearance in *winter*.

The population of Edinburgh and Leith has been variously estimated. The latest enumerations do not raise it to the sum of 100,000 souls. But I certainly know those enumerations to have been made in circumstances which hindered them from swelling the estimate to its just amount. A part of the inhabitants of Edinburgh are migratory, and live but half the year in the town:—these should have been taken at half their real number, but were not at all reckoned. Most of the poorer families were alarmed for some new taxation to be imposed in proportion to their respective numbers; and therefore represented theirs as smaller than they, in truth, were. I do not then hesitate to state 105,000 as the probable present number of the inhabitants of Edinburgh and Leith, with the suburbs belonging to them, and the hamlets and villas which lie between them, and in their environs to the distance of a mile from the exterior streets on all sides. The proportion of those who exceed the age of sixty years, is less numerous here than in many other places in the interior parts of the isle, and on its western coast. The proportion of persons dying between the ages of five and threescore is very considerable. An extraordinary number between three-and-twenty and five-and-forty years; the men chiefly of the effects of venereal complaints and Bacchanalian excess;—the women by the diseases incident after child-birth. As this is a capital inviting many young people into it for education and employment, the proportion of persons in it between the ages of fifteen and forty is unusually

ally great. Young persons between eight, and twenty years of age generally enjoy good health here. For children between birth and seven or eight years of age, it appears from many instances within my knowledge to be a very insalutary situation. Neither small-pox nor measles is, here, exceedingly mortal. But, chincough, colds, putrid fevers, consumptions, &c. make extraordinary havock among children in infancy, and the latter even upwards to the ages of seventeen and five-and-twenty years. Rheumatism, much exasperated by the frequent prevalence of east winds, is extremely afflictive to almost all persons of all ranks, after the decline of life begins.

How is this large population of 105,000 souls sustained?

A part of them possess *lands* in the country, *money* in the public funds, or property in the East and West Indies, out of which capitals, or the annual produce from them, the expences of their living are defrayed. It is probably between 200,000l. and 300,000l. of the annual revenues of the inhabitants that comes thus in. In this estimate, I include only the incomes of persons living here upon their fortunes, and to their amusements; expressly excluding that of the students at the University, of which I shall afterwards more particularly speak. Many of the gentry of Scotland, whose fortunes will not bear the expence of yearly journies to and from London, and who yet like the society and amusements of a great town, chuse, of course, to spend here one half or two-thirds of the year. Many gentlemen's families come to Edinburgh for the purpose of uniting, in regard to the children, the benefits of a domestic with those of a public education. Many gentlemen advanced in years, after serving in the army, or making fortunes abroad in trade, come to pass the autumn of life in this city, rather than either in London or in remote rural retirement, on account of its advantages of society, quiet and agreeable accommodation, with all the luxuries of life and all the elegant amusements. It is common also for widow ladies with small but not incompetent jointures to retire to Edinburgh for the sake of society, as persons of the same class and rank in life are wont in England to retire to Bath. Such are they who live, in the Scottish capital, on independent incomes derived from other places.

A number also of the gentlemen's families in this town enjoy places under Government, the duties of which are to be here executed, and on the emoluments of which they live. The Commander in Chief of the forces for Scotland, the Lieutenant-governor of the Castle, the soldiers of the Castle, and of certain barracks erected since the beginning of the war, at a place named Jock's Lodge, at the south-east extremity of the town, expend a good deal of money in Edinburgh for their subsistence. The Judges and inferior officers of the Courts of Session and Exchequer; the Commissioners of the Boards of Excise and Customs, with the inferior persons serving in Edinburgh and Leith on these establishments; the officers belonging to the departments of the Lord Clerk Register, to the Stamp-office, the the Tax office, Post-office, and the Herald's Office; with a few who belong to the establishment of the Royal Household, and a few enjoying honorary or eleemosynary pensions from the Crown; may all be reckoned to defray the expences of their living here, out of the revenues they receive from Government, chiefly for the discharge of official duties. The whole sum thus contributed out of the common revenue of the state towards the support of persons resident in Edinburgh, cannot, I should think, be less than 100,000l. sterling. The exact amount I do not, at this moment, know. But it may be, without great difficulty, ascertained.

Another part of the inhabitants of this place subsist upon their incomes as *practitioners in the law*. These are, beside the judges already mentioned, advocates, writers to the signet, agents, solicitors before the inferior courts, apprentices and hired clerks, &c. These different classes of persons in the profession of the law may draw from the whole country, professionally, for their subsistence, a gross annual sum of perhaps 130,000l. sterling. Few or none derive, for a single individual, an yearly income from their business of more than 2000l. a year. The writers to the signet are those who gain the most.

The persons belonging to the University, the High School, and the other establishments for education, professors, masters, and students may have, in all, an income of about 100,000l. a year. Of this, about 60,000l. may consist of allowances by parents and others to the students from the country and from foreign parts. The number of the students is, at an average, about one thousand two hundred. No student can attend a session of between six and seven months at this University at a smaller expence than 20l. The medium

expence

expence for a session is 50l. Many students pass the whole year here; attending both the summer and the winter Courses of Lectures. The average allowances to gentlemen's sons attending this University may be from 100l. to 300l. sterling a year. The income of the professor of anatomy may be about 1200 guineas each session. The professor of chemistry may have fees to the amount of about 700 guineas each session. The professors of Latin, Greek and moral philosophy, three of the ablest, the most unwearied, and the most successful teachers in Europe, have, at an average, not more than 350 guineas each for their labours each session. The fees of the professor of logic may be of nearly the same annual amount.

Bankers, merchants, ship-masters, and shop-keepers compose a large proportion of the inhabitants of Edinburgh and Leith. I should suppose, that above 200,000l. sterling of the total yearly income of these places may be the produce of their business and industry. Here are two incorporated banking-companies, the *Old Bank* and the *Royal Bank of Scotland*, and several private banking-houses; the two most eminent of which are, that of Forbes, Hunter and Co. and that of Mansfield, Ramsay and Co. The merchants deal in corn, in wine, in timber, pitch, flax and hemp, in tea, sugar, rum and other West India produce, and in all the goods usually imported from the Baltic. The ship-masters sail from Leith, in the coast trade, in the Baltic-trade, in the North Seas and Greenland Fishery, as also in the West India and American trade. The merchants reside rather at Leith than in Edinburgh. The shipping and the sea-faring trade belonging to these places is considerable; and they have been much augmented since the completion of the canal which joins the Forth and Clyde has enabled the merchants of Glasgow to carry on by the way of Leith their commercial intercourse with the east coast of England, and with the ports of Germany and the Baltic. Lead and cast-iron in various useful forms are among the exports from Leith. Cotton yarn and stuffs have, of late, been also exported from it in large quantities. Pit-coal is exported from the Forth to places on the north-east coast. There has been, of late, a great exportation of herrings, herring-oil, and glass from this port. The shop-keepers are so numerous that, in the middle parts of the town, four-fifths of the houses have their lower stories occupied as shops. The business of a shop-keeper is, in Edinburgh, as a capital to which there is a concourse from all parts of the kingdom, more considerable than in any other town in the northern parts of the island. Many shop-keepers unite to a certain degree the character of importing merchants with that of retail-dealers, procuring, by large orders, from London, from Manchester, from Glasgow, &c. those goods which they are to sell out in small portions. Woollen-drapers, linen-drapers, mercers of silk and cotton goods, booksellers and stationers, jewellers and watch-makers, dealers in hard-wares or utensils of iron, tin, &c. grocers, glass men, &c. are some of the most considerable classes of shop-keepers in this town. It is not unfrequent for prudent and active men in this sort of business, to accumulate fortunes of from 5000l. to 25,000l. sterling. A capital of from 500l. to 2000l. is required to begin the business of a shop-keeper in a manner tolerably reputable. Fortunes of from 10,000l. to 60,000l. have been, in many instances, realized by merchants resident in Edinburgh. Some bankers have acquired property to the amount of from 200,000l. to 300,000l.

The *artisans and manufacturers* of Edinburgh and Leith, are also a very considerable body; and a large share of the income of the inhabitants of this place depends on their industry.

At Leith are some glass-manufactures in a very flourishing condition, which, beside supplying window-glass, bottles, drinking-glasses, &c. furnish these articles likewise for a large exportation by sea, and into all the surrounding interior country. Messrs. Biggar and some other gentlemen carry on here a considerable linen-manufacture. The manufacture of paper was carried on here, before the war, to considerable extent, and with great profit to the manufacturers. In the progress of the war, rags, which had been usually procured, for the greater part, by importations from Germany, became so excessively dear, the wages of the workmen so high, the consumption of printing-paper so small, and the duties on this commodity so enormous, that the manufacture has been in consequence greatly checked. There is reason to hope that, since peace is restored, it may soon flourish here infinitely more than in its best former prosperity. Ropes and canvas, especially the former, are made in large quantity at Leith. Utensils of cast-iron are made here, on Leith-walk, in large quantities, and with the greatest success. Some cotton-works have been established in the neighbourhood, the property of manufacturers living in Edinburgh. The business of building, though somewhat checked during the war, has still continued to employ during the war a number of master-builders and many working-masons. It must, almost immediately, begin to employ a great many more. House-carpenters and cabinet-makers are numerous; and the value of their industry certainly arises to a great annual amount. Brewers and distillers perform much business with considerable capitals in Edinburgh, Leith, and their environs. The ale and spirits here prepared, are exported in large quantities to London and various other places. Leather and shoes, both for the consumption of Edinburgh and for exportation, are made here; but there is an importation of leather and shoes from Yorkshire, from Russia, &c. One of the most elegant manufactures flourishing in this place, is that of coaches. The Scottish gentry and nobility have their carriages made chiefly in Edinburgh; and carriages built by the coach-makers of this place, are exported to Germany, Russia, &c. Bricks and tobacco-pipes of clay are manufactured here: but no spirited attempts have been made to introduce the manufacture of any of the finer sorts of earthen-ware. Hosiery of all sorts is manufactured in Edinburgh in great perfection, and with the greatest success. Clocks and watches are among the manufactures of this place: but I believe that the finer parts of the machinery are, for the most part, imported from London. The bakers are, of course, numerous in such a town as Edinburgh. They are reputed to make the best bread that is to be eaten in either Scotland or England.

The butchers are likewise numerous; though there be but one flesh-market, which stands contiguous to the North Bridge, for the use of the whole town of Edinburgh. Leith has, indeed, a flesh-market of its own. Fresh vegetables of all sorts, and in the greatest abundance, are sold in the passages leading into the Flesh-market, and in most other parts of the town. There is a Meal-market, not exceedingly commodious, where oat-meal, flour, butter, cheese, and grain are sold. Unless when extreme scarcity prevails, it is well supplied. In the Grass-market, hay, corn, sheep and horses are, on certain days, put to sale. Coffee-houses are not numerous; but here are many taverns and small public-houses. In Edinburgh, as in every other part of this country, the Scots live much less in these houses, than is common for the English. The hotels of Edinburgh are adapted to afford the most agreeable accommodation that is any where to be had for strangers of rank and fashion. The lodging-houses are numerous; and are, in general, kept by people more respectable and honest, than one should easily find elsewhere in that way of life. The inns are few and paultry. Chop-houses, tap-rooms and other similar places of resort for eating, are rare in Edinburgh. A very large annual sum is received in this town from the expenditure of merely passing visitants of one or a few days.

(To be concluded in our next.)

To the Editor of the Monthly Magazine.

SIR,

ALLOW me to propose, through the medium of your Magazine, a Topographical Table, by which the state of a place may, as I conceive, be determined with some accuracy, and which would admit of various useful comparisons. The sort of table that has occurred to me is the form used under the Population-act, with the addition of columns for the following heads, or such of them as may be chosen, with any others that may be thought proper—New Houses—Houses occupied by One Family—Houses assessed to the Window and House Duties—Inns and Alehouses—Churches and Chapels—Dissenters' Meeting Houses—Charitable Institutions—Persons assessed to the Duty on Four and Two Wheel Carriages (in separate divisions)—Persons assessed to the Tax for Male-Servants—Professional Men (enumerated in proper divisions)—Booksellers—Schools (subdivided)—Teachers of Arts indicative of opulence and luxury—Businesses of the same Class (distinguished by necessary divisions)—Manufactories (under specific heads). Tonnage of Shipping belonging to the Place (if a sea-port)—Yearly Imports and Exports on an Average—Rental—Account of Poor's Rates—Persons Assessed—Paupers (distinguishing their several kinds)—Amount of Assessed Taxes—Births and Deaths in a Year on an average—Agriculture, under such heads as may admit of numerical statement.

If this or some improved plan were to be adopted as a general measure, by authority, the real state of the country, and of each place in particular, would be ascertained, which I presume must be a great desideratum. Your's, &c.

Portsmouth, Oct. 8. W. N.

4 *For*

For the Monthly Magazine.

HISTORICAL STATEMENT *of the* GALVANIC DISCOVERY, *and of the* PUBLICATIONS *which have appeared on that* INTERESTING SUBJECT.

THE discovery of Mr. GALVANI is undoubtedly one of the most important that has ever been made in the ample field of natural philosophy, and, from the extensive views which it opens to the inquiries of naturalists, it seems to deserve their utmost attention. Although we may suppose the principal works on that interesting subject to be known to professional naturalists, yet it may not be improper to give an account of all the transactions on that most important phenomenon to the public at large, which, however, we purpose to be merely historical, because it would be unjust to criticise the more early theories and hypotheses relating to that object, guided by the late discoveries with which it has since been enlightened.

The first traces towards this discovery is found in the following book, where, however, it was overlooked, and soon buried in oblivion.

SULZER'*s Theorie der angenehmen und unangenehmen Empfindungen*—i. e. Theory of agreeable and disagreeable Sensations, translated from the French into German, under the direction of the author, with additional remarks in *Sammlung vermischter Schriften zur Beförderung der schönen Wissenschaften*—i. e. Collection of Miscellaneous Writings for the Improvement of *Belles-lettres* and of Fine Arts, Vol. 5, No. 1, Berlin, 1762, and also in *J. G. Sulzer's vermischte Schriften*—i. e. Miscellaneous Writings, Leipzic, 1773. "When two pieces of metal (says Mr. Sulzer), one of lead and the other of silver, are thus joined together, that their edges make one surface, a certain sensation will be produced on applying it to the tongue, which comes near to the taste of martial vitriol, whereas each piece by itself betrays not the least traces of that taste. It is not improbable (he continues) but that by the combination of the two metals, a solution of either of them may have been produced, in consequence of which, the dissolved particles penetrate into the tongue, or we may conjecture, that the combination of these metals occasions a trembling motion in their respective particles, which, exciting the nerves of the tongue, causes that particular sensation." This hint, however, seems to have been disregarded, till Galvani published the following work:—

Aloysii Galvani de viribus electricitatis in motu musculari commentarius, 1791, p. 58. 4to. Bologna, for the Institute of Sciences; which was soon followed by other publications relating to animal electricity, viz.

Lettera del Dottore Eusebio Valli sull' Elettricità Animale ad un suo amico, Pavia, 1792, p. 15, 4to.

Memoria su l'Elettricità Animale, inserite nell Giornale Fisico-medico del Sigr. Brugnatelli—i. e. Memoir on Animal Electricity, inserted in the Physical and Medical Journal of Mr. Brugnatelli, Pavia, 1792, p. 147-8.

A. Galvani Abhandlung über die Kräfte der thierischen Electricität auf die Bewegung der Muskeln, &c.—i. e. Treatise on the Effects of Animal Electricity on the Muscles, together with some Writings of Messrs. Valli, Carminati, and Volta, on the same subject, a translation, edited by Dr. J. Meyr, with 4 plates, 1793, p. 183, Prague, for Calve, 8vo.

Schriften über die thierische Electricität—i. e. Memoirs on Animal Electricity, by Dr. Alexander Volta, translated from the Italian by Dr. J. Meyer, 1793, p. 144, Prague, for Calve, 8vo.

The work of the celebrated Galvani is divided into four parts; the *first* of which treats of the effect of electricity, which is produced by art; the *second*, of the action of atmospherical electricity, the *third*, of the effect of what he calls animal electricity; and the *fourth*, contains some conjectures and conclusions. But he confesses, with an ingenuousness which always attends true merit, how much of his discovery is owing to accident, and he never dissembles the false conclusions to which he was misled by the first view of each new phenomenon.

Whilst Mr. Galvani was dissecting a frog on a table, whereon accidentally stood an electrical machine, one of his pupils happened to touch the *nervus cruralis* of the frog with the point of the dissecting-knife, upon which immediately the muscles of all the members were convulsively contracted. Another standing by thought to have observed, that this phenomenon took place when a spark was drawn from the conductor of the machine; an idea which was afterwards confirmed. For on touching the same nerve of another frog, and likewise pricking it, in order to assure himself, whether it was owing to his having accidentally wounded the nerve, without drawing a spark at the same time, not any motion ensued; but if the nerve was touched with the point of the knife at the time when he had ordered a spark to be taken from the machine, the same phenomenon appeared again. On repeating the experiment with the same knife, the motions were sometimes stronger, sometimes weaker, and sometimes disappeared entirely, which was found to arise from the manner in which he happened to hold the knife, because, when he held the handle, which was of bone, the animal remained motionless, but as soon as he touched the metallic part, the contractions were immediately produced. In order to determine whether this phenomenon did depend on the idioelectric nature of the dry bone, or on the conducting property of the metal, Mr. Galvani changed the knife for a clean glass tube, and for an iron cylinder, but the above phenomenon never appeared on applying the glass tube to the nerve, even when very strong sparks were drawn, whereas it was immediately produced by the least spark on applying the iron cylinder. Thus Mr. Galvani found it confirmed, that for producing the above phenomenon the contact of a conducting body with the nerve was requisite. When the iron cylinder was applied to the nerve, without being held by the hand of any body, the drawn spark occasioned no motion, whereas the contraction came on when, instead of the cylinder, he took a long iron wire, so that a certain length and extension of the conducting body seemed to be required for effecting the above phenomenon. These conducting bodies were called by Mr. Galvani nervous conductors. The experiment likewise succeeded at a distance, by very long insulated conductors, in animals prepared for that purpose, particularly when a conducting tube was hung at the feet of the frog, communicating with the floor; these conductors he distinguished by the name of muscular conductors.—After having made a great number of experiments in a different manner, viz. by interrupting the free course of electricity, by coating the nervous conductors to their ends, with an electric substance, and by applying negative electricity, the electrophor, &c. the effect of atmospherical electricity on muscular motion remained to be examined. To this end he raised a long and proper conductor, which was insulated, on the roof of a house, from which frogs, or the legs of warm-blooded animals, were hung by the nerves; another conductor being attached to their feet went into the water of a well. As soon as it began to lighten, the muscles were seized with violent and repeated contractions, which, like the lightning, preceded the thunder; these contractions did even ensue when no muscular conductor had been applied, and the nervous conductor was not insulated. They were even observed when the conductor was raised on lower places, and in gloomy weather. The experiments succeeded with dead animals as well as with living, but the mere lightning, without thunder, produced no movements.

These curious experiments happened to give rise to the proper Galvanic discovery. Mr. Galvani being curious to know what effect atmospherical electricity might have in quiet and clear weather, he suspended some frogs on metal hooks, fixed in the spine of the back, from the iron-rails of his garden, and he observed those contractions, not only when it lightened, but also in clear and quiet weather. At first he thought that the causes of these contractions might arise from changes in the electricity of the atmosphere, but upon a more minute examination he found, that on bending the hook with which the spinal-marrow was perforated, towards the iron-rails, in order to see whether muscular-motion might be thus produced, and whether any difference or change in the state of atmospherical electricity would manifest itself, he began to conceive, that the contractions did not relate to this state of the atmosphere. Having, however, only seen these contractions take place in open air, he was, notwithstanding, inclined to ascribe them to the atmospherical electricity, which running over into the animal, may there be accumulated, and he imagined, that hence it might be vehemently discharged at the contact of the hook with the iron rail, but he was soon undeceived. Having placed a frog upon an iron-plate in his room, he happened to press it against the plate with his dissecting forceps, whereon immediately the contractions took place. The experiment succeeded with all metals, but never on employing non conducting substances. Induced by these experiments, our author began to suspect the animal to possess an electricity of its own, a conjecture which appeared to him to be confirmed by the phenomena of a circulation from the nerves to the muscles, similar to that taking place in the Leyden phial. For on holding a frog that had been previously prepared for the experiment, by a hook fixed in the spine of the back, with one hand, so as to let the feet reach a small silver cup, and on touching the cup with the other hand, by means of a metallic body, the animal fell into violent convulsions. If one person

son held the prepared frog, while another touched the cup, no movements were excited, but they did immediately ensue when both took hold of another. If both laid hold of a glass tube, the contractions were likewise not excited, but they came on when they took an iron cylinder instead of the glass tube. The investigation of this subject was farther prosecuted by a series of experiments. He first placed a frog on an electric plate, and touched the animal sometimes with a conducting arch of iron, sometimes with an arch that was but for a part electrical, so that he brought one arm in contact with the copper-hook, which secured the animal, the other arm to the femoral muscles; the movements were produced in the first experiment, but in the other the animal remained motionless. Hence he concluded, that the motions proceeding on the iron plate had been owing to a similar arch represented by that plate. He likewise found, that different metals, joined together in a different manner, were the most efficient, but above all silver. The experiment succeeded under water quite as well as in open air. It surprised Mr. Galvani, that, if the hook fastened in the spinal marrow was touched, the water replacing the conducting arch would excite contractions in the animal, which did not ensue on the experiment being made under oil. Our author thought himself now entitled to assert, that there is in the animal a double electricity, opposite to one another, the one in the muscles, the other in the nerves, or both at the same time in either of them. In order to ascertain this circumstance, he coated the nerve or the spine of the back with tin-foil, by which he found the motions to be extremely increased. The contractions, however, proceeded less vigorously by coating the muscle. If a part of the nerve as well as of the muscle was coated with a non conducting substance, as silk, or pitch dissolved in oil, no contractions were excited, even on applying the conducting arch. Mr. Galvani also observed, that this animal electricity, as it was styled by him, opens itself an easy passage through some conducting solid bodies, whereas through others it passes with more difficulty; but the best conductor of this electricity is water, while oils destroy the phenomena of this matter. To the conducting property of water the author was inclined to ascribe the fact, that, having coated the spinal-marrow, and separated the lower extremities, he only observed contractions in the leg that was touched, which were, however, communicated to the other as soon as he had brought both in contact with each other. Mr. Galvani proves next, in the most convincing manner, that the contractions are nowise excited by mechanical stimuli, as was first supposed by others. He also observed the contractions to succeed less vigorously when the muscles were placed on a glass-panel, and the spinal-marrow on an electric plate; but they became stronger after having changed that situation: most violently, however, they were excited when the legs as well as the spinal-marrow were placed on coated glass-panels, particularly on giving them some electrical strokes. When the nerves were entirely separated from the surrounding parts, the contractions did considerably increase. The experiments succeeded equally well with warm-blooded and with cold-blooded animals. The contractions being diminished, were restored to their former vigour after a time of rest had been allowed.

We must acquiesce in mentioning only the conjectures and conclusions which the author has drawn from his discovery, without farther entering into the subtle arguments he has brought forth in support of his ideas. The conclusions he builds on the facts related by him are as follow:—Animals are endued with a peculiar electricity, to which he gives the appellation of *animal electricity*, and which he thinks to be contained in most animal parts, chiefly, however, manifesting itself in the muscles and nerves. It seems to be secerned in the brain from the blood, whence it is communicated through the nerves to the different parts of the body, but it appears to reside chiefly in the muscles. A muscular fibre is similar to a small Leyden phial, and the nerve represents the conductor of the phial, and consequently the whole muscular substance is to be considered as a number of Leyden phials. The external surface of the muscle possesses negative, the internal substance positive, electricity. The interior of nerves is composed of a matter capable of conducting electricity, while the exterior prevents, by the oily coating, its effusion and dispersion. Muscular motions proceed, when the electric fluid is conducted from the interior of the muscle into the nerve, whence it is brought back again to the muscle, either through the external fluid of the nerves or through the membranes and the adjacent parts, as it were through an arch, so that, according to the laws of equilibrium, the same quantity may be united in the negative electric part

part of the muscular fibre, which issued by means of the stimulus in the nerves from the positive electrical part. Dr. Eusebius Valli relates, in his Memoir on Animal Electricity, a series of thirty-two experiments, by which he particularly endeavours to determine the effects of tobacco and opium on Galvanism, but he found these substances, as well as other poisons, to have no action on the electrical principle; the gasses, however, do violently affect it.

Journal de Physique, T. XLI.—GREN's *Journal der Physik, T. VI.* In a letter of Mr. BOSSANO CARMINATI to Mr. Galvani, the following notice is given of the results of Mr. Volta's experiments:—"Prepared frogs, whose spinal-marrow, and part of the nerves, are coated with metallic plates, may be used as the most sensible electrometers.—The negative and not the positive electricity is seated in the nerves."—Mr. Volta describes the experiment from which he has drawn that conclusion in a letter to Dr. Boronio. "Not being able to trace the nature of this very weak electricity by means of the most sensible electrometer, I proceeded in another manner. I called to mind that two phials being brought in contact with each other by their synonymous electric surfaces, do not discharge themselves, which, however, is the case as soon as they touch each other with their opposite electrical points; and I thought it, therefore, not indifferent whether I applied the internal coating of a weakly charged phial to the muscle or to the nerve. On making a series of experiments according to this idea, I have frequently observed, that on applying the positive surface of a phial to the nerve, $\frac{5}{100}$ or $\frac{6}{100}$° of the electrometer did suffice for producing contractions in a frog, whereas hardly from $\frac{70}{100}$ to $\frac{10}{100}$° were sufficient for the same purpose, when the positive surface of the Leyden phial was brought in contact with the muscle, and the negative surface with the nerve. Thence we may conclude, that a negative electricity is imparted by nature to the nerve, and a positive electricity to the muscles." Mr. Galvani, in reply to this, writes in a letter addressed to Mr. Carminati, as follows:—"Might we not think it probable that, in the case where the head of the Leyden phial was brought in combination with the nerve, the convulsions might have entirely, or for the most part, been [illegible]g to the electrical matter having pe[illegible]ed from the internal coating of the phial into the nerve, and thence into the internal surface of the muscular fibre? For though, according to my hypothesis, a plus of electricity exists in the head of the phial as well as in the interior of the muscular substance, both electricities are most probably efficient in the same degree of force, and it is most likely, that the weak natural electricity of the nerves is overcome by the stronger efficient electricity. We may therefore assert, that a part of the positive electricity of the phial penetrates into the internal substance of the muscles, by means of the conducting substance of the nerves, where, being assimilated to their natural electricity, it occasions a discharge, which is not produced by a process of the animal machine, but effected by the Leyden phial in the hands of the experimentator.

(To be continued.)

For the Monthly Magazine.

INSTRUCTIONS *by the celebrated* ABBE BARTHELEMY, *to* M. HOUEL*, *respecting his* JOURNEY *to* NAPLES *and* SICILY.

IN the tour which you, Sir, are about to undertake through Sicily and Greece, you may have frequent opportunities of collecting medals for the King's Cabinet. It is on this account that I beg leave to subjoin some observations, which may assist you in making these purchases.

I suppose you at Naples.—I will pass over in silence the towns of Herculaneum, Pompeium, &c. where you will be guided by the superior knowledge of M. l'Abbé Galiani; M. Hamilton†, whom you will also meet at Naples, will assist you with any correct plans which he may have taken of the antiquities of Sicily.

If you should have a draughtsman with you, he might frequently visit the excavations of Pompeium, and either from memory, or without being perceived, make sketches of the street, and of some of the buildings which have been discovered.

I beg you will urge the eager expecta-tion

* This artist was at that time painter to the King; he published at his return, "A Picturesque Tour in the Islands of Sicily, Malta, and the Lipari, during the Years 1783, 84, 85, and 87, printed in 4 vols. *folio.* The plates are in aquatint, which fades very quickly, and greatly fatigues the sight when the impressions are half effaced.

† Sir William Hamilton, K. B.

tion which every one feels for the publication of the manuscripts found at Herculaneum. Of the original number, which consisted of from five to six hundred, two or three only have been unrolled*; the rest are shamefully neglected: and yet they are the most valuable of any discoveries which have already been made or can be expected. This negligence, which would have astonished the Goths, is the more incomprehensible, as Naples contains a sufficient number, both of idle Monks to unrol these manuscripts, and of learned men to decypher and publish them.

If you go to Rhegium by land, you will traverse the ancient country of the Lucani and the Brutii. If you should meet with any Greek medals, I beg you will take them, and you may give for them two or three times their weight, if they are of either gold or silver.

Those in bronze, with the word BPETTIΩN, were struck by the Brutii; those of the Lucani, ΛΟΥΚΑΝΩΝ, are more scarce.

I know of no antiquities at Reggio†; but silver medals are here to be met with, bearing the Greek name of the city, RECI (*Regi*), or RECINON (*Rheginon.*)

Messina contains few or no antiquities. The ancient silver medals with the name ΔANCLE‡, are rather scarce, and worth from ten to twelve times their weight.

M. le Baron de Riedezel mentions a cabinet of medals, which is in the possession of M. le Prince de Sperlinga: these collections are to be found in many towns in Sicily. If you meet with any I request you will inquire, without appearing too eager about them, whether the possessor is willing to dispose of them; what price he requires, and whether he will give a catalogue of the collection. In the event of his not chusing to sell them, it would be useful to have a catalogue, merely of the gold and silver medals of the different kings and towns of Sicily. If you cannot procure this catalogue, I shall be content with a general account of the principal medals of these kings and towns.

The towns of Miletium, Tindaria, Himera, and the Thermæ of Himera, which contains some warm-baths, formerly occupied the coast from Messina to Palermo. If you should land on this coast, and the peasants should offer you any medals, of any kind of metal, I beg you will take them, provided they are Greek.

Palermo—In this city you will see Doctor Tardia, to whom I lately sent some corrections and additions taken from a manuscript in the King's Library, for the new edition which he is preparing of the Ancient Constitutions of Sicily*. I have also sent to him a note of the medals which are deficient in the King's Cabinet. You will oblige me by taking charge of any which he may commit to your care. The Jesuits of Palermo had a succession of Sicilian medals. What is become of them?

Segesta—Baron de Riedezel, after having left Palermo, arrived at the Ruins of Segesta, which consist merely of the remains of a very ancient Temple of the Doric Order. M. Dorville has given a drawing of this Temple†, but he has not informed us of the dimensions of its various parts, as Desgodets has done of the Antiquities of Rome, and the English of those of Palmyra, of Balbec, and of Greece. Your draughtsman might dedicate a day to the taking the exact dimensions as well of the general outline as of the separate parts of this building.

In addition to these remains of antiquity, Fazello ‡ pretends, that there is in the town itself an old temple, at present consecrated to the Blessed Virgin.

Some medals of Segesta bear Greek inscriptions: these, when of silver, are worth

---

* These manuscripts, according to the custom of the ancients, were in large rolls, and though burnt by the lava which buried the famous city of Herculaneum, were yet, when discovered, not so completely destroyed but that, with very great care, they could be unrolled, and being placed on a light ground, the characters became legible.—(*Editor's Note.*)

† Jos. Morisano published, in 1770, ten inscriptions found in Rhegium, but they afford little information, and are not very ancient.

‡ This town bore the name of Zanell, before the Messenians, driven from Peloponnesus by the Lacedæmonians, established themselves there. M. Schiavo has published some inscriptions found in this city. In speaking of the Ancient Messina we should always say, in conformity with the Doric pronunciation, and with the orthography of the medals, *Messana.*

* Barthelemy sent also some extracts from Novarii, upon Sicily, respecting the history of that island, which the learned Caussin extracted at his request, and which have been printed in the "Recueil des écrivains Arabes," published at Palermo in 1790, by M. Gregorio.

† Sicula, tom. 1, page 54.

‡ De Rebus Siculis, lib. vii. page 142.

procuring

procuring for the double or triple of their weight, and for from five to six times their weight when they are of gold. The inscriptions should be nearly this, ΣΕΓΕΣΤΑΖΙΒ; sometimes it is deficient in some of the letters, sometimes they are reversed. These medals generally represent a head on one side, and a dog on the reverse.

Drepanum or *Trapani*—Some vestiges of antiquities are discoverable upon Mount Erix, six miles distant from Trapani, but they do not appear to be of any importance.

Phœnician Medals are found between Palermo and Agrigentum. As this coast was occupied by the Phœnicians for a considerable length of time, and since them by the Carthaginians, I am particularly anxious to procure antiquities of this description, as they are becoming very scarce. If chance should throw any of these medals into your hands, I beg you will take them, and at the same time inform yourself in what particular spot they have been found; but as it is possible that you may have some Arabic medals brought to you, which are of no importance to me, it is necessary I should inform you how to distinguish them.

1. The Arabic medals in gold and in silver are very thin and light. Those of the Phœnicians are thicker, and when they are of the size of a shilling, their thickness is nearly that of a half-crown-piece: the price is always nearly the same. Those of bronze have only one or two letters, and are of but little value; those of silver contain one, two, or three words, and are worth four or five times their weight. If you should meet with any of gold, having the same number of words, the price should be relatively the same.

2. The letters on the Arabic medals are joined, those on the Phœnician are separated.

3. I annex a plate of Phœnician medallions in silver, formerly struck in Sicily, which will serve as a specimen. Medals of this size are called medallions. If by chance you should meet with that of No. 3, pl. 1, which bears on the side representing Victory and the Horse the Greek word ΔΙΟΝΥΣΙΟΥ (*Dionusiou*) of *Dionysius*, King of Syracuse; I would wish you to give three or four Louis for it: the others are worth three or four times their weight.

Baron de Riedezel* mentions a small island, situated between Trapani and Marsanna, bearing at present the name Saint Pantaleon, which is said to be the ancient Motya, where, according to Thucydides, the Phœnicians *built a town*. I wish to be informed whether any Phœnician medals are found there, and of what kind they are.

Selinus—Twelve miles to the eastward of Mazara, are the Ruins of Selinus, where you will find the magnificent remains of the three temples of which Dorville has contented himself with giving the plans.* Your draughtsman might make some more accurate plans, containing the dimensions of the whole, and of the separate parts. These ruins richly deserve the attention of architects. Fazello mentions having seen three quarries in the neighbourhood, from which the stones have been taken, and where there are still to be seen columns half carved in the rock: one quarry is situated near the river, at two miles distance from the town; another four miles to the northward, in a place named *Bugilifer*; the third in a place called *Ramunura*, six miles to the westward. These quarries still retain the name of *Latomiæ*.

Silver medallions and medals are found at Selinus, with this inscription, ΣΕΛΙΝΟΝΤΙΟΝ (*Selinontion*) of the Selinontians.

Sciacca—In proceeding along the coast you will arrive at Sciacca, formerly Thermæ Selentinæ, on account of its containing various baths. Fazello† mentions one of these baths in the form of a cave, where are still to be seen the remains of the benches placed for the convenience of the bathers. He adds, that above these benches there are some letters, considerably effaced, which have not as yet been decyphered, and which are not in any known language. Perhaps they are Phœnician! Baron de Riedezel‡ says they are Greek characters: but this wants confirmation.

Agrigentum, or Girgenti—Here your draughtsman will have ample scope for exercising his talents, more especially if he understands architecture. I would recommend your taking the plates of the Ruins of Girgenti out of the "*Antichita Siciliana*, by Father Pancrace, a Theatin the first part of which was printed at Naples in 1751, but met with so little success that the author relinquished his intention of continuing the work. I do not know what is become of his other drawings.

* Voyage en Sicile et dans la Grande Grèce, page 23.

* Sicula, page 70, 71.

† De Reb. Sic. page 129.

‡ Voyage en Sicile, &c. page 30.

logs. Those, however, of Girgenti, although very imperfect, will be of some assistance to you, when you are on the spot, as will those also which you will find in Dorville's work *.

Baron de Riedezel † mentions an inscription to be seen in the Market-place, and "*which*," he says, "*is in a barbarous language*." It is in the Arabic or the Phœnician. If the account is true, of its having been taken from the Temple of Olympian Jupiter, the language is probably the Phœnician; and in that case I intreat you will make a correct copy of it; and if a cast from it can be procured and sent to me by some safe conveyance, I shall be highly gratified. Not only will the Bishop of Girgenti inform you respecting the language of this inscription, but the rules which I have already had occasion to mention will enable you to determine this point yourself. If the letters are joined, it is Arabic; if they are separated, and nearly resembling those on the medals, it is Phœnician.

"This Bishop of Girgenti," we are informed by Baron de Riedezel ‡ "has a collection of medals of the Roman Emperors." I am not anxious about these, but he proceeds—"Among the Greek medals are those of the ancient towns of Sicily, in silver, with a considerable number of Carthaginian medals in gold." These I should most particularly wish to obtain. If the Bishop is willing to dispose of them, they would undoubtedly be a valuable acquisition to the King's cabinet. First, the silver medals are worth four or five times their weight; those of gold, the same, provided they have Phœnician letters, and that they contain more than one of such letters; for if they represent merely a Horse or a Palm-tree, they are worth little more than their weight. If the Bishop is unwilling to part with these medals, I should wish to obtain an exact description of them, and most particularly of the Carthaginian medals of gold. In case he does not choose to dispose of these medals separate from the rest of the collection, I should wish to have an account of the whole, and to be informed what value he sets upon it.

Malta—If you should go to Malta from Girgenti, I request you will collect all the bronze medals which are frequently found there, and which contain these three letters ЬЬΦ. If they are in good preservation they are worth eight or ten-pence. Enquire whether they are found at Malta or at Goza.

You will find here the same Phœnician inscription on two Marble Altars, a cast of which I have got, and have decyphered. Le Chanoine Agio will inform you whether any Phœnician inscriptions have been lately discovered, and he will give you copies of all those which he has collected.

You may also address yourself to one of our foreign members, named M. de Ciantar, should he be still living, which I think doubtful, as it is now ten years since he has been heard of at the Academy.

Phintias and *Gela*—Beyond Agrigentum, and proceeding to the eastward, are Alicata, Terranova, &c. where Phintias, Gela, &c. formerly stood. Dorville has been as far as to the spot where Gela is supposed to have been situated, but has not discovered any remains. From thence he pursued his route by land. Baron de Riedezel went from Malta to Syracuse. I am ignorant whether any discoveries are to be expected in coasting from Girgenti to Syracuse.

Syracuse—I will not trouble you with any observations respecting this town: your draughsman will be able to judge for himself what antiquities will merit your attention, and of some of which you will find incorrect engravings in Dorville's work. You may give three or four times their weight for the medals which bear the name of ΣΥΡΑΚΟΣΙΩΝ (*Syracosiorum*), particularly those of gold and of silver. This instruction equally applies to those of the town of Leontium, near Catana*.

Catana—Prince Biscari has a fine succession of Sicilian medals. You cannot with any propriety ask him to part with them, but he may have some duplicates which he would perhaps be glad to exchange for those medals of which he is not possessed.

Taurominium—The antiquities of this town, as well as those of Catana, are to be found in Dorville's work, but always with the same defect, very inaccurate and unsatisfactory in the dimensions.

There do not appear to be many antiquities

* Sicula, page 97, 99, 107.
† Voyage en Sicile, &c. page 38.
‡ Voyage en Sicile, &c. page 56.

* Barthelemy, in that part of his Paleography which he has left in manuscript, has entered into equally curious and correct details relative to the Numismatical History of Syracuse, and all the ancient towns of Magna Græcia and Sicily.

tiquities remaining on the coast between Rhegium and Tarentum, although it was formerly entirely occupied by celebrated towns: but medals are to be found on this coast. For instance, you will probably meet with some medals of the Epizephyrian Locrians, in the neighbourhood of Gierani. These medals are silver, and of the size of a sixpence, but rather thicker. The generality of them represent the head of Jupiter on one side, and on the reverse an eagle holding a hare in its talons, with this word ΛΟΚΡΩΝ, the name of the people.

I should wish to be informed whether any medals have been found in this part of the country, of the same metal and of the same size, which, without the name of the Locrians, represent on one side the head of Minerva, and a winged horse on the other; the price of these is two or three times their weight.

Caulonia—Baron de Riedezel* places the ancient town of Caulonia on the spot where Squillaci now stands. According to M. Danville it was situated on this side. However, it is certain that Caulonian medals are found in the neighbourhood of Squillaci—they are of silver. The most ancient are large and thin; the others are in general smaller and thicker. They represent a stag, and a naked figure holding a branch, with this word ΚΑΥΛΟΝΙΑΤΑΝ, (*Kauloniatan*) either at full length or contracted. The figures on one side of the most ancient are indented. I give you a specimen of these medals.

Cape Collona; or, *The Promontory of Lacinium*—It was on this Promontory that the celebrated Temple of Juno Lacinia was built, of which Baron de Riedezel † informs us there are still very considerable remains.

It was in this Temple, according to Livy ‡, that Hannibal caused an Altar to be placed, with an inscription in the Greek and in the Punic languages, containing the detail of his exploits. I do not imagine that the Romans have been generous enough to spare this monument; however, I do most earnestly beg and intreat you to search both in the Temple and its environs. The discovery of this inscription would be of the utmost importance to the progress of Punic and Phœnician literature.

In this neighbourhood you may possibly meet with some medals of Crotona. They represent a tripod and an eagle, one or other sometimes indented, with this beginning of a word ΚΡΟΤ (*Krot*) or ΚΡΟ (*Kro*): price, two or three times their weight. They frequently bear the head of Apollo or of some other divinity.

Sometimes the name of Crotona is at full length; if you should meet with any of gold, they are worth two or three times their weight.

Sybaris—On the bay of Tarentum, near Corigliano, is situated the town of Sybaris, of which we have some silver medals, resembling those in the annexed drawing. I should be glad to procure some, whether they are precisely the same as those, or varying in the letters or in the size *.

Thurium—At a small distance from Sybaris stood Thurium. Here you will find silver medals, representing on one side the head of Pallas, and on the other a bull, with this word ΘΟΥΡΙΩΝ; price, about double their weight.

Siris and *Heraclea*—A little further on the coast are situated Siris and Heraclea, with some of whose silver medals we are acquainted. They are of the same value with those of Thurium. All the Greek medals which are found in this district are in general worth procuring; as are those which have one side indented. Those of Heraclea most commonly represent the head of Apollo or of Pallas, and the combat of Hercules with the Lion.

Metapontum—The medals of this town generally represent an ear of corn on one side, and a head of Mars or Ceres on the reverse. They are easily distinguished by the word ΜΕΤΑ.—Same price.

Tarentum—The silver medals of Tarentum are by no means scarce. They bear the word ΤΑΡΑΣ (*Taras*); they are worth double their weight. Those of gold have the word ΤΑΡΑΝΤΙΝΑΝ: they are more scarce; you may give for them two or three times their weight.

A great number of medals are to be met with, according to Riedezel †, at the village of Martanna, situated between Otranto and Brundusium. If they are Greek, I beg you will procure some, and be very exact respecting the places in which they have been found. Our German traveller informs us, that at Lecce, the Palmyri-family possess several medals. I have only to repeat my request. You must see whether those are Greek medals,

* Voyage en Sicile, page 184.
† Voyage en Sicile, page 186.
‡ Lib. xxviii. cap. 46.

* Vide Acad. des Insc. T. xxvi. page 546.
† Voyage en Sicile, page 219.

and

and whether the possessors are willing to part with them;—the price of those of god and silver is two or three times their weight.

Brundusium—Two of the inhabitants possess some medals—the same request—the same questions—the same price—the same offer for the duplicates, if you cannot obtain any others.

For the Monthly Magazine.

DEFENCE *of* FORESTALLING, &c.

[*Continued from page* 205.]

BEFORE I proceed to examples, I shall lay down three other maxims relating to the commerce in provisions, and add some previous and explanatory reasoning. These maxims, and those which you have inserted in your Magazine for September, will be opened by the same reasoning, and confirmed by the same examples.

1. No monopoly of any article of general use can be made but by the whole strength of the community; that is, by the interference of Government.

2. When undue quantities of any article of general use are kept back, the certain consequence to the public is, a lower average price, and to the hoarder loss*.

3. The average price of every thing is set, not by the seller, but always by the wants of the buyer, conjointly with the quantum of produce. The wants of the buyer regulate consumption; and the balance between consumption and produce is price.

The man who travels about the country, and buys of the farmers poultry to carry to market, is called a higler, and, it is agreed, does no harm. But, if the same man meets the same farmers on their way to market, and *then* buys their poultry, he is called a forestaller, and punished for preventing the farmers from going the whole way. If he is to be punished at all, it should be for not being more alert, and for suffering them to go so far. The good that he has done is but a part of the good that he might have done. He has saved but a part of the time of the farmers, when he might have saved the whole. The evil that he is accused of doing is, that he has raised the price of the poultry at the market: for, that the price must be higher in proportion to the profit made by the forestaller. The contrary is the truth. The forestaller can afford to sell the poultry for less than the farmers could have afforded if they had gone on to the market: for the forestaller, like the higler, has spent the time of one; the farmers must have wasted the time of more, perhaps of many more, than one. If the forestaller has sold the poultry at the same price as, or even at a higher price than, that at which the farmers would have sold them, the public, in the first case is, in the second case may be, ultimately benefited; because, whatever abridges the farmer's labour, is an advantage to the public. The price of any produce is, other circumstances being the same, in proportion to the time consumed in producing it. Each individual farmer valued the time saved, at more than the difference between the sum at which he sold to the forestaller, and the sum at which he might have sold at the market. But what reason is there for supposing that the farmer would have sold at the market for less than the forestaller? None, but that he is in haste to return home. Yet the foes to forestalling will hardly allow, that they wish to make provisions cheap by distressing the farmer in point of *time*.

A small farmer must make up his rent soon after Michaelmas, and is obliged to sell all, or an undue quantity, of his corn. The corn-dealer buys it, 1st at the farmer's house, though this is not penal, unless, in the opinion of the interpreters of the common law, he should happen to buy too much; yet it raises an outcry, and is not pardoned like buying poultry 2dly, or in the way to market, which is forestalling; 3dly, or in the market, and, if he sells any part of it again on the same day, it is regrating, and regarded by many as the most enormous crime of all. He may sell what he bought yesterday, and keep what he has now bought till to-morrow, but must not sell the identical corn. What difference this can make to the consumer has, I believe, never been explained. The good, however, that the corn-dealer has done to the farmer is this: he has saved the whole, or half, or some part, of his time; and, what is in this case of more consequence, he has assisted him with his capital. It will be said, that, in the case of the farmer being arrived at the market, he would have had the same price from the

*By *undue* I mean a greater quantity than would be kept back, if equal quantities were brought forward throughout the year. If, for example, the consumption of any country be 365 in the year, and less than one per day be brought forward, an undue quantity is kept back.

the mealman, or the consumer, that he had from the middleman. Put what many will think the worst case, and suppose that the farmer has received a higher price from the regrater, than he would have received if the regrater had not been present—"The farmer is certainly benefited; but does not the public suffer in proportion?" I answer, is it the object of the foes to withholding corn, to make corn cheap by distressing the farmer in consequence of his want of *capital?* It was his want of capital that made him bring forward his corn prematurely. If he had had capital, he would have done the same harm or good to the public as the regrater, who now stands exactly in his place. The regrater will keep the corn till there is a demand for it; beginning to sell to-day, if the demand should begin to-day. The advantage to him will be thus trading on his own capital; and the advantage to the public is, that the supply will be forthcoming, not when a small farmer wants money, but when the consumers want and demand a supply. The market will be supplied regularly, instead of being liable to those distressing variations which, by sometimes inducing habits of profusion, make want at other times to be more severely felt. The farmer, in the mean time, is employing his newly acquired capital, and his *labour*, which he could not otherwise have employed, in benefiting the public by a fresh produce. The small farmer, now that he is assisted by the corn-dealer, is doing the same as the rich farmer, who has his corn still in his barn. The rich farmer is, at least for a time, both farmer and corn-dealer. The small farmer and the corn-dealer together have a capital equal only to the capital of the rich farmer, and are, therefore, to the public, but one.

And it makes no difference if goods pass through many hands. The profit which each successive buyer, in his turn becoming a seller, makes, *on the whole* (for the profit is by no means certain and regular), is the profit to which he is intitled for his *labour, information, time, capital,* and *care*. And he benefits the public by supplying the capital that flows back to the original producer, and saving *his* labour and time. If A sells to B, and B to C, and so on to Z, the existence of the fact is a proof that the next purchaser could furnish some of the above improvements, which the purchaser immediately before him could not. And, in proportion as those improvements are more abundantly and regularly supplied by and through every improver to the producer, in that proportion is the advantage to the public. MISORHETOR.

For the Monthly Magazine.

ACCOUNT *of a* DESCENT *into the* CRATER *of* MOUNT VESUVIUS, *by Eight* FRENCHMEN, *on the Night between the 18th and 19th of July,* 1801*.

TO ascend to the summit of Mount Vesuvius, which is elevated 3600 feet above the level of the sea, is an enterprise of great difficulty, as it is necessary for nearly half the height to climb an exceedingly steep declivity up to the knees in ashes. Some philosophical men of eminence, however, as Spallanzani, Dolomieu, Dr. Moore, &c. have overcome all these difficulties. Sir William Hamilton, who caused a great many views of Vesuvius to be designed during his long residence in Naples, ascended to the summit of it sixty-two times; but no one, at least since the eruption in 1779, ever ventured to descend into the crater of this volcano, not even Sir William Hamilton, who considered it under so many points of view, and who visited it so many times. It was reserved for eight Frenchmen to hazard this dangerous enterprise, and to succeed in it completely, notwithstanding the timidity of their guides, the impossibility which the Neapolitans attached to it, and the instances they mentioned of rash travellers, who had lost their lives in the attempt, and been swallowed up by the volcano.

To be able to appreciate the danger of this enterprise, it will be necessary to have a correct idea of the form and position of Vesuvius, and of the matters which it throws up. This volcano has the form of a truncated cone, and a part of its base, which is altogether three leagues in circumference, is washed by the Mediterranean; its mouth, or upper base, which is a little inclined to the axis, is 5722 feet in circumference. The earth, from the base to half the height, consists of vegetable mould mixed with lava and stones which have not been attacked by the fire, tufas, pumice, and calcareous stones, different in their nature and colour, according to the different degrees of impression which have been made on them by the fire.

* This article first appeared in the Journal de Physique, and we have adopted this translation from the last Philosophical Magazine.

The

The half of the height next the summit is composed chiefly of pure ashes, but coarser than our common ashes. Till the present time, there have been twenty-four eruptions recorded in history. The first took place in the year 79 after the Christian æra: by these eruptions, volcanic matters have been successively accumulated, but by that of 1779 the situation of the crater and of the aperture was entirely changed. The focus or crater is now sunk 200 feet below the upper edges of the mouth of the volcano.

To arrive at the crater, and to observe the numerous spiracles, long crevices, and fires which issue from them in several places, and also the variegated and still smoking matters of which the crater is composed, it was necessary to pass over this space of 200 feet.

The inner sides of the volcano are nearly perpendicular, or exceedingly steep, and composed of ashes, lava, and large calcareous stones; but these lava and stones, as they form no connection with the ashes, cannot serve as any point of support; and when any one is so imprudent as to adhere to this kind of rock, the least motion, the least displacement of any part, makes the whole crumble to pieces. Besides, from the summit of Vesuvius to the crater, the declivity, being exceedingly rapid, cannot be traversed but on all fours, and suffering yourself to glide down amidst a torrent of ashes and lava. But the most dangerous obstacles are those awful excavations, which cannot be passed over without great trouble and difficulty.

Disregarding the terror with which the Neapolitans endeavoured to inspire us, after having received their adieus, as if our separation had been likely to be eternal, we set out in a carriage, at half after eleven at night, on the 18th of July, from the hotel of the French Ambassador, fourteen in number, furnished with ropes and other articles which we supposed might be necessary, and all in a state of the highest spirits, which never forsook us, even at times of the most imminent danger. We arrived about midnight at the foot of Vesuvius; and, having quitted our carriage mounted well-experienced mules, and proceeding one after the other, with Adjutant Dampierre at our head, amidst the thick darkness of night, reached half way to the steep summit of the mountain. We had a numerous body of guides, and their lighted torches gave to our expedition a mysterious and solemn air, which formed a striking contrast with the mirth and gaiety of the company.

When we had ascended about half way, we were obliged to alight, and to clamber up the steepest and most difficult part of Vesuvius, wading through the ashes up to the knees, till, exhausted with fatigue, and covered with sweat, we reached the summit at half past two in the morning.

The first thing that struck us, as soon as the morning began to dawn, was a most magnificent spectacle—a superb view of the city and port of Naples, the beautiful hills which surround them, and the vast extent of the sea by which they are washed. After walking round part of the aperture of the volcano, that we might choose the most commodious place for descending, Adjutant Dampierre and C. Wickar first descended, without any accident, at the determined point. When they had got about a third of the way, they were suddenly stopped by an excavation of fifty feet, which it was necessary to pass. As they found that it was impossible to obtain any fixed point of support on ashes so moveable, and being convinced that the friction of ropes would have soon destroyed both the point of support and the neighbouring masses to a great distance, they resolved to return. Besides, while deliberating on the means of descending, some stones rolling down from the summit occasioned a general agitation wherever they passed: Adjutant Dampierre found the ground on which he stood shake beneath his feet; and he had scarcely quitted it, calling out to C. Wickar to follow him, when it disappeared. Soon after, indeed, the whole place where they had stood, and all the neighbouring small eminences, crumbled down successively, in the course of half an hour, and were precipitated to the bottom of the crater with an awful noise.

Before we renounced our enterprise to return to Naples, dejected on account of not having succeeded, we once more walked round the mouth of the crater, and at last discovered a long declivity, pretty smooth, though very steep, which conducted to the focus. Without examining the precipices, which it might be necessary to pass before it could be reached, C. Debeer, the ambassador's secretary, accompanied by a Lazzaroni, set out first to attempt the passage. When they had got half-way, amidst a torrent of ashes, which the impression of their feet made to roll down along with them, they found means to fix themselves on the edge of a precipice, twelve

twelve feet in height, which it was neceſſary to paſs before they could reach the lower declivity. The Lazzaroni, frightened, refuſed to proceed; but, being promiſed a double ducat, avarice got the better of his timidity; he ſpeedily made the ſign of the croſs over his whole body, and, having invoked the Madonna and St. Anthony of Padua, threw himſelf, along with C. Debeer, to the bottom of the firſt precipice: ſoon after, they arrived at another, but being of leſs height, it was paſſed with more eaſe. At length, amidſt a continual torrent of falling lava, aſhes, and ſtones, they arrived at the bottom of the crater, and ſtretched out their arms to us, ſending forth ſhouts of joy, which we returned with the utmoſt ſatisfaction and enthuſiaſm.

C. Houdouart, engineer, immediately followed C. Debeer, and, after encountering the ſame difficulties, and paſſing dangerous precipices, joined him at the bottom of the crater. Being there both convinced of the almoſt inſurmountable difficulty of aſcending, they threw themſelves into each other's arms, like two friends reduced to the neceſſity of terminating their lives together in a deſert iſland without any hopes of eſcaping from it.

They then began, but with cautious ſteps, to walk round this immenſe furnace, which ſtill ſmokes in ſeveral places. The intrepid Wickar, who was very deſirous to participate in their fate, called out to them to ſend ſome one to aſſiſt him in paſſing the two cliffs; but ſeeing no one coming, and growing impatient, he ruſhed forward, and rolled down towards them, amidſt a torrent of ſtones, aſhes, and volcanic matters. Adjutant Dampierre, C. Bagneris, phyſician to the army, Freſſinet and Andras, French travellers, and Moulin, inſpector of poſts, ſoon followed, and arrived at the crater, after having incurred the ſame dangers.

Wickar immediately ſat down on a heap of ſcoriæ, and, with that ſuperiority of talents for which he is diſtinguiſhed, ſketched out in profile, with a perfect reſemblance, the portraits of the eight Frenchmen who had deſcended. Each then formed a ſmall collection of the different volcanic matters which appeared to be new or curious, and endeavoured to make a few obſervations.

Had we been allowed to depend on ſucceſs, had we not been retarded in our preparations by our timid guides, and if ſome of us, having only juſt arrived at Naples, had not been ſtraitened in point of time, our deſcent would certainly have been much more uſeful, and the reſults more ſatisfactory. However, though ill furniſhed with means, the following are the obſervations we were enabled to make.

Reaumur's thermometer, the only inſtrument we poſſeſſed, ſtood at 12 degrees on the ſummit of Veſuvius: the air was cold, and ſomewhat moiſt: in the crater, the quickſilver roſe to 16 degrees, and we experienced the mildeſt temperature.

The ſurface of this place, which, when ſeen by the naked eye, looking down from above, appeared entirely ſmooth, exhibited, when we were at the bottom, nothing but a vaſt extent of aſperities. We were conſtantly obliged to paſs over lava exceedingly porous, in general pretty hard, but which, in ſome places, and particularly thoſe where we entered, was ſtill ſoft, and yielded under our feet. The ſpectacle which ſtruck us moſt was the numerous ſpiracles, which, either at the bottom of the crater, or the interior ſides of the mountain, ſuffer the vapours to eſcape. When we arrived at the crater, we were deſirous to aſcertain whether theſe vapours were of a noxious quality: we walked through them, and inſpired them ſeveral times, but felt no inconvenience from them. The thermometer, placed in one of theſe ſpiracles, indicated 54 degrees, in another it roſe only to 22. In all theſe experiments, our inſtrument was covered with a humid matter, which was ſoon diſſipated in the open air, without leaving any traces.

In traverſing the ſurface of the crater, we perceived a focus, half covered by a large maſs of pumice-ſtone, and which, from its whole circumference, emitted a ſtrong heat. The thermometer, placed at firſt at the entrance of it, and then immerſed to as great a depth as the nature of the ground and the heat would admit, never roſe higher than 22 degrees. This ſingularity ſurpriſed us, but we were not able to explain it.

The volcanic productions which we obſerved in the whole crater were lava, exceedingly porous, and which the fire in certain places had reduced to ſcoriæ. It was of a dark brown colour, and ſometimes reddiſh, but it is rare to find any white. The ſubſtances neareſt the ſpiracles are all covered or impregnated with ſulphur. This mineral is found very often in a ſtate of oxygenation. It is ſometimes white, and ſometimes of a yellowiſh colour, and the ſharp and pungent impreſſion it leaves on the tongue ſufficiently

ently indicates the ſtate in which it is. The burning focus, of which we have ſpoken, produces the ſame reſults. Some baſaltic lava is alſo found, but in ſmall quantity; one ſpecimen only, of a conſiderable weight and beautiful poliſh, attracted our attention.

On the north ſide of the crater there are two large fiſſures, one of which is twenty feet in depth, and the other about fifteen. They are ſhaped like an inverted cone. The matter with which they are covered is entirely ſimilar to that on the reſt of the ſurface. They emit neither ſmoke nor heat; yet ſome ſulphureous productions plainly ſhew, that the fire in theſe places has not long been extinct.

When we had finiſhed theſe few obſervations, it was neceſſary that we ſhould think of returning. The deſcent is far leſs laborious than the aſcent; for it is difficult to climb eminences where the points of ſupport are ſo moveable. Beſides, people cannot aſcend but one at a time in ſucceſſion, after long intervals, for fear of burying under a torrent of volcanic matters thoſe who follow, as the foot, when moved, diſplaces the aſhes, &c. to the diſtance of thirty feet round.

When we arrived at the two precipices, we were obliged to aſcend by mounting on the ſhoulders of a man placed at the bottom, and laying hold of a ſtick held by another at the top, and to reſt our feet no where but in a very gentle manner. At length, by prudence and caution, we reached the ſummit of Veſuvius without any accident, but exhauſted with fatigue, and ſo covered with aſhes and ſmoke, as to be ſcarcely diſtinguiſhable. Our ſix companions, who had not deſcended into the crater, were overjoyed when they ſaw us again, and ſupplied us with ſome refreſhments, of which we had great need.

When one grand difficulty is ſurmounted, inferior ones are overlooked, as of little importance. In leſs than twenty-five minutes, we again deſcended, having confirmed, after examining various ſtones, this obſervation, that Veſuvius is the only known volcano which throws up from its bowels primordial ſubſtances, without being altered by the fire, and ſuch as are found at preſent in banks and veins.

At half after eight in the morning we arrived at Portici, the inhabitants of which were much ſurpriſed to ſee us return all ſafe. Their delicious fruits, and their excellent wine, called *lacryma Chriſti*, ſoon made us forget our fatigue, and we then proceeded to Naples, which we reached in ſafety.

The reſult of this excurſion, which was only an experiment, can be of no further uſe than to ſhew the poſſibility of reaching the crater, and to open the way to it to philoſophers, naturaliſts, and chemiſts, who, by exploring this immenſe furnace of nature at their leiſure, will find a variety of matters, which will afford an ample field for the application of their chemical knowledge, and may enable them to make diſcoveries intereſting to the arts and the ſciences.

The names of the eight Frenchmen, in the order in which they deſcended, are as follow: Debeer, ſecretary to the Ambaſſador Alquier; Hodouart, chief engineer of bridges and cauſeways, attached to the army of Italy; Wickar, painter; Dampierre, adjutant-commandant; Bagneris, phyſician to the army of obſervation; Freſſinet and Andras, French travellers; and Moulin, inſpector of poſts.

To the Editor of the Monthly Magazine.

SIR,

IN Number 79, page 339, among the excerpts from the Port-folio of a Man of Letters, are inſerted ſome ſketches of the Life of the celebrated John Law, projector of the Miſſiſippi ſyſtem. Had this Man of Letters been, as every Man of Letters ſhould be, acquainted with the recent publications on the ſubject upon which he writes, he might have avoided ſeveral notable errors which occur in that article. A Biographical Account of Law, with a particular Detail of his famous Financial Projects, was publiſhed in 1791, by Mr. John Wood, of Edinburgh. In the New Annual Regiſter for that year, this piece is ſtyled "an intereſting and pleaſing piece of biography, which contains ample matter to gratify the curioſity of the reader." In the Critical Review for April, 1792, it is mentioned in ſimilar terms, and copious extracts are inſerted reſpecting the Miſſiſſippi ſyſtem; and in the Analytical Review for January, 1792, an Abſtract of the Life of Law from this publication is given, the work itſelf being particularly taken notice of, as "one that has a variety of claims on the curioſity of the public." This Biographical Sketch was ſoon afterwards inſerted, in an inlarged and improved form, in a ſubſequent work by the ſame author, "The Antient and Modern State of the Pariſh of Cramond," publiſhed in 1794, by Meſſrs. Whites, Fleetſtreet, in one volume, quarto, a work characteriſed in the Critical Review for October that year, as "one of the moſt exact and

and elegant topographical works ever published." The second part of it consists entirely of biographical and genealogical collections respecting the most considerable families and individuals connected with that district: among these is the celebrated John Law, whose family estate of Lauriston, in that parish, is still possessed by his descendants. A beautiful engraving of the old Castle of Lauriston is inserted in that work, and the Biographical Account of Mr. Law is rendered interesting from the various details relative to his life, as well as his unfortunate financial projects, collected not only from a number of scarce publications, but from authentic pieces in manuscript, in particular from copious materials furnished by his nephew, John Law de Lauriston, Governor of Pondicherry, and Marechal de Camp, father of General Lauriston.

From the details in this publication, I can take it upon me to correct a few of the errors of the Man of Letters. Law was the son, not of an advocate, but of a goldsmith or banker, in Edinburgh. He was born, not in 1688, but in April 1671. His duel was not with a Lord, but with Mr. Edward Wilson, a son of the house of Keythorpe in Leicestershire, who fell in the contest, as is particularly mentioned in the accurate and indefatigable Nicholl's History of that County, lately published. In the Anecdote from the Letters of Madame the Regent's Mother, *the Chaise Percée* is a circumstance not to be found in the original. Law's scheme, rash and unfortunate as it proved, appears to have been overturned more through the caballings, envy, and ignorance of the Regent, and some of his creatures, than, from the want of solidity in the system itself: at least, there is reason to think, that had it not been for a most foolish arrêt, issued upon some weak and groundless apprehensions of the Regent, particularly detailed in the above work, the system, if conducted agreeably to the ideas of the original projector, might probably have gone on, till, the first madness of the people having subsided, it would gradually have settled into something like a solid system of public credit. Even ending as it did, there seems reason, from what is justly stated in this account, to doubt whether, upon the whole, the remote benefits attending it did not more than counterbalance its immediate evils.

The publication I have mentioned, "The Account of the Parish of Cramond," contains also a number of interesting details, respecting the transactions of John Law de Lauriston, Marechal de Camp, and Governor of Pondicherry, during his long residence in India, from communications by himself. The eldest son of this distinguished officer failed, in 1785, in the unfortunate voyage of discovery under M. de la Pérouse; he was a lieutenant on board the Astrolabe, the commander of which, the Vicomte de l'Angle, was his intimate friend. In the Voyage of De la Pérouse, lately published, the talents, zeal, and merit of M. de Lauriston are honourably mentioned, and the skill in astronomy of that accomplished young man is particularly praised. "The death of M. de l'Angle (says Pérouse) will not make any change on board the Astrolabe, as to the astronomical observations. For near a year, M. de Lauriston, who is a young officer of the first merit, has had the sole care of them. For accuracy he may perhaps dispute the prize with our professed astronomers." This letter was dated at Botany Bay, the 7th of February, 1788; shortly after which, M. de la Pérouse's squadron left New Holland, and was never more heard of: consequently the next brother of M. de Lauriston became the head of the family, on the death of his father in 1796 or 1797; and this brother is General Lauriston, the bearer of the Ratification of the Preliminaries of Peace, who is now the proprietor of the estate and Castle of Lauriston, situated four miles to the north-west of Edinburgh. HIMENES.

Nov. 14, 1801.

ORIGINAL POETRY.

To the Editor of the Monthly Magazine.

SIR,

THE following exquisite little Poem, written soon after the year 1418, is extracted from Glass's History of the Canaries. It certainly affords a very interesting specimen of the simple pathos of the poetry of the ruder ages; a pathos, whose effects on the soul all the refined arts of more polished times have been unable to imitate: and which has caused it to remain in Palma, until the present period, a favourite national air.

It was occasioned by the death of Guillen Peraza, a young man of a bold and enterprising spirit, who was, at the time of his decease, Governor of the Canary Islands, and who

who perished in an attempt to reduce the before-mentioned Palma to the power of Spain.

In order to understand the second stanza, which partakes something of the pun, it will be necessary to premise, that "*Palma*" signifies a palm-tree, which, like the laurel, is rather emblematic of triumph and joy, than mourning; therefore, says the poet:—"*Thou art no palm; thou art a cypress, a bramble.*"

ORIGINAL SPANISH.

LLORAD las damas,
Assi dios os vala,
Guillen Peraza;
Quido, en la Palma,
La flor marchita
De la su cara.

No eres Palma;
Eres retaina:
Eres cypres
De triste rama:
Eres desdicha
Desdicha mala.

Tus campos rompan
Tristes volcanos,
No vean plazeres
Sino pesares.
Cubran tus flores
Las arenales.

Guillen Peraza!
Guillen Peraza!
Do esta tu escudo?
Do esta tu lanza?
Todo do acaba
La mala adauza!

IMITATED or PARAPHRASED.

Lament, oh ye fair, for Peraza is dead,
Lament, as ye hope that th'Almighty will save;
For in Palma the lily his manly front fled,
And the flow'rs were transferr'd from his cheek to his grave*.

Oh Island, no Palma art thou—but a thorn!
A funeral cypress, productive of ill:
No fruitage is seen on thy branches forlorn,
But misfortune and evil there vegetate still.

May the dismal volcano burst hot from thy hills,
And pleasure's sweet reign be usurp'd by despair;
May the sands of the desert alight on thy rills,
And thy flow'rets all die 'neath the parch'd western air.

Peraza! Peraza! oh where is thy shield?
Where the lance which thou hurledst thy foe-men among?
Alas, they lie useless upon the sad field!
Where thy rashness, thy zeal, laid thee lifeless along.

Nottingham. H. K. WHITE.

* As this is called a paraphrase, and not a translation, the reader will not be surprised if he find no vestige of this last line, and one or two others, in the original. So much difficulty attaches to giving a close version in English, and indeed such apparent impossibility of retaining its native spirit therein, that the author did not attempt it.

A FAREWELL to ENGLAND.—*By Miss Shackleton, Daughter of the learned Quaker, Abraham Shackleton, of Ballitore, in Ireland, the well-known Tutor to the late celebrated Mr. Burke.*

TO Britain's isle a long farewell!
Where plenty smiles and pleasures dwell;
Farewell, ye woods, all waving wide,
Ye vales attir'd in summer's pride,
Ye towers, which proudly rise in air,
Ye cots, so cleanly and so fair.
Now Cambria's rocky wilds appear,
Her mountains rude, and vallies drear,
While solemn midnight rules the sky,
And darkness veils the dangers nigh,
Save when the sullen gleams display
The rocky steep beside our way;
While the full torrent's hollow roar
Sounds sadly on the sandy shore,
And fancy dreads in every shade
The midnight robber's murd'ring blade.
And now we view the ocean wide,
And now the swelling surge we ride:—
Loud roars the wind, the billows heave,
Swift bounds the bark from wave to wave,
Oppress'd with sickness, pale we lie,
And wish for land—the land is nigh;
Hibernia's welcome isle appears,
Returning health our spirits cheers.
There, seated in her beauteous bay,
Eblana's towers their pride display;
But there tumultuous Folly raves,
And high her torch dire Discord waves;
Then—haste me to my native plain,
Where all the peaceful Pleasures reign.
Once more my longing eye devours
Her silent stream, and modest bowers;
Once more the welcome dear I prove
Of friends, whom, as myself, I love;
Once more confess, where'er I roam,
No place I find so dear as home.
Oh Thou! whose kind paternal hand
Preserves by sea, protects by land,
Grant us sweet peace—'tis thine alone—
To a tumultuous world unknown;
That—whether warring winds engage,
Or restless human passions rage—
A sacred refuge we may find,
The temple of a quiet mind.

AUTUMNAL VERSES, 1801.

LO! radiant Summer takes her flight,
And speeds to southern climes afar;
While streaming floods of lingering light
Float backward from her burnish'd car.

Her breath still warms the tepid breeze,
The fields her sprightly livery wear,
And Winter hesitates to seize
The sceptre of a year so fair.

Bright daughter of the Sun, adieu!
On whom descends his kindliest smile;
No more thy glorious form we view,
But still thy gifts rejoice our isle.

For see commission'd Autumn stand
With *Plenty*'s overflowing horn,
And scatter round with lavish hand
Rich fruits and life-sustaining corn.

But, hark! new sounds of rapture steal
Obscurely on the list'ning ear:
Now loud they grow: now louder peal
In full-ton'd accents soft and clear.

Oh, 'tis the voice of *Peace*! behold
Her steps pursue the warning sound;
And, as her heavenly charms unfold,
Unwonted glory beams around.

Contending hosts, in mute surprise,
Drop from their grasp the brandish'd blade,
Forget the fray, and turn their eyes,
Transported, on th'angelic maid.

Hail, lovely stranger! long-lost guest!
And dost thou greet us once again?
Oh! let us ever, ever rest
Beneath thy meek and holy reign!

Auspicious æra, dawn sublime,
Commencement of a golden day!
See in the longdrawn rear of time
Bright ages in august array.

The freeborn Briton shall embrace
The Gaul, who also dar'd be free;
And the wide world, compos'd in peace,
Shall learn the sweets of amity.

Worcester, Oct. 13, 1801. TREBOR.

For the Monthly Magazine.

WAKEFIELD is dead! See sacred Science, mourn,
Like her own Aikin, bending o'er his urn;
While every muse, by his fair daughter led,
In precious tears embalms th'illustrious dead;
While generous youths, enwrap'd in classic lore,
The Master Genius of the song deplore;
Here, tott'ring age essays with trembling tongue,
Fault'ring, to mingle in the tuneful throng,
And cast his feeble, last, expiring strain
On Friendship's altar, soon to blaze again.
Thus age and wisdom, youth and beauty join,
T' anticipate a sentence more divine.
Who would not thus, like Wakefield, wish to die,
Secure of fame and immortality! P. D.

Hackney, Oct. 1801.

SONNET, *written at the* CLOSE *of* EVE.

'TIS eve, 'tis solemn eve!—Still, pensive Thought
Sits in his robe of twilight sadly grey,
Musing o'er shadows by his dark eye caught,
The dimm'd and dying majesty of day!
Lorn murmurs tremble thro' the mournful trees,
Mute Philomel her leafy couch has found;
And Melancholy's music in the breeze
Whispers a note of soothing sadness round.
And now, as night her darker mantle draws,
The groves more low and deeply sullen wave;
Save when, as solemn comes a dreary pause,
'Tis stillness all;—the stillness of the grave!
The grave!—Ah, yet her absence I deplore,
Whose morn, and day, and eve, are now no more!

J. H. L. HUNT.

MEMOIRS OF EMINENT PERSONS.

A NOTICE *relative to the* LIFE *of* POISSONIER, *read at the* COLLEGE *of* FRANCE, *29th Brumaire, sixth Year, by* JEROME LALANDE.

PETER ISAAC POISSONIER, Doctor-regent of the Faculty of Medicine of Paris, Member of the late Academy of Sciences, Senior-member of the College of France, &c. was born at Dijon, on the 5th of July, 1720. He at first engaged in pharmacy, but being soon induced to visit the capital, whither he was led by his talents and his zeal, he studied medicine, and was received a licentiate, August 11th, 1744. His theses of 1743 and 1744, on the following subjects, announce the first objects of his labours;

"Do monsters originally exist, or are they produced by accident?"

"Ought the bark to be applied in diseases of the breast?"

"Is the lateral operation for the stone, the best?"

In 1749 he published a Continuation of the Course of Surgery, dictated to the Schools of Medicine, by Col de Villars, Vols. V. and VI. containing a Treatise on Fractures and Luxations.

Dubois, Professor of Medicine, having quitted the College of France in 1744, on purpose to retire to St. Lô, the place of his nativity, he was succeeded by Poissonier, who pronounced his initiatory Discourse, February 10th, 1746: he after-

ward

wards went through a Course of Chemistry, which was well attended and proved extremely useful; for at that period there was not any thing of this kind in any of the public establishments of Paris.

In 1757 and 1758 we find him acting as first physician of the French army, then composed of one hundred thousand men, and also consulting physician to the king.

In the course of the latter year he was sent to Petersburgh: the ostensible object of this mission, was his professional attendance on the Empress Elizabeth, whose health was supposed to be in a declining state; but it has been whispered, that the real one was certain political negociations with which he was entrusted. During his stay in Russia, General Montalembert, another academician, resided there also, with the view of procuring the adoption of such a plan for the next campaign as might prove serviceable to the interests of France, and of also accompanying Marshal Soltikoff, who commanded a body of eighty thousand Russians during the years 1759 and 1760. Poissonier remained there during two years, and gave an account in the History of the Academy for 1760, of the celebrated experiment relative to the congelation of mercury, at which he assisted.

On his return he was nominated a Counsellor of State, a distinction at that time granted to persons in his situation in extraordinary cases only.

In 1764 he was appointed inspector-general of medicine, surgery and pharmacy, in the sea ports and colonies of France. From that moment he had the entire superintendence of all such as occupied those situations; and I have often had occasion to remark the care and impartiality displayed by him in that capacity: he occupied this place until 1791.

In 1765 he was appointed an associate of the Academy of Sciences, an honour only bestowed on those who possessed a great reputation, and being attached to the church, to the court, to the armies, or to the parliament, and in consequence of their other avocations, were unable to devote all their time to a participation in our labours.

But the circumstance that reflects most celebrity on Poissonier, is the famous experiment undertaken by him in 1763, in order to extract the salt from sea-water. On this occasion he caused an alembic to be formed on such a construction as not to be affected by the motion of a ship under sail, and he added six ounces of *marine alkali* to every barrel of brine, in order to subdue the acrimony of the sea-water. Hales and Appleby had employed the *lapis infernalis* for the same purpose; but the result demonstrated the superiority of his method. Beaumé, the most celebrated pharmacopœist in France, who has given a detailed account of this experiment in his Chemistry, published in 1773 (Tom. III.) has also presented his readers with a plate of the apparatus employed; and Macquer has added a note on it in Bomare's Dictionary. Poissonier, during the operation, employed the fire of the cook-room of the vessel, so that a great saving resulted in the article of fuel; and in 1765, on board a ship belonging to the French East India Company, the crew were amply supplied with water produced in this manner during a whole month, without being under the necessity of recurring to what they had got in the hold. More than eighty experiments were made, and all of them succeeded completely. Citizen Bougainville asserts that, during his famous voyage round the world, he was indebted for the health of his crew to the water produced by means of this machine; and I am assured, that with a single barrel of coals six or seven of fresh-water may be obtained; which enables a commander to have always plenty of room on board, as the water always occupies the greater part of the vessel during long voyages.

Courcelles, naval physician at Brest, assures me, that one of the large alembics will expend in twenty-four hours 200 pounds weight of coals, and produce 600 of fresh water during the same period: still a greater saving will be obtained by continuing the distillation. The Minister Choiseul, on hearing of the experiment, was so struck with its importance, that he settled a pension of 12,000 livres on Poissonier.

This same physician had collected a curious cabinet of natural history, foreign curiosities, models, and machines of all sorts. His place procured him a numerous acquaintance, and enabled him to receive a variety of presents, which a learned man could accept of without blushing. It would be highly proper for the Government to purchase them.

Poissonier having quitted his professor's chair in 1777, was succeeded in 1778 by the younger Raulin; the latter, who died in 1795, has been replaced by

Citizen Corvisard, whose success is known to every one.

Poissonier still continued, however, to preside here as senior member, in consequence of a resolution of the 11th of January, 1778: he did less honour to that situation by a noble and commanding aspect, than by the dignity of his orations, the elegance of his manners, and the consideration he enjoyed in the estimation of the world. We have all heard him speak, at the periods of our re-assembling during twenty years, in a manner that did honour both to the society and its chief. He died on the 29th of Fructidor, 6th year, (September 15th, 1798) at the age of 78, in consequence of an abcess that had been too suddenly closed. He espoused Mary-Catharine Martinon who, as well as himself, was a native of Dijon, in 1753; this lady was indebted to him for an important place, having been appointed nurse to the Duke of Burgundy through his interest. He lost her in 1783: her merit and talents rendered this loss extremely afflicting to her husband.

In 1788 he married Jeanne Molay de Revroi, who was so attached to him, that she died suddenly of sensibility, uneasiness and fatigue, two months before Citizen Poissonier, while assisting by the side of is bed, during his last illness.

He has left behind him an only son, who obtained the rank of Advocate-general of the Parliament of Burgundy, which presupposes talents, and who succeeded Citizen Guyton Morveau, whose reputation as a chemist has surpassed that which he had obtained as an orator, lawyer and legislator. The Citizen Sue, Secretary to the Society of Medicine, will soon render a more suitable homage to the memory of our illustrious President.

TRANSLATION *of a* LETTER *from* SIGNOR A. J. CAVANILLES, *relative to* MUNOZ, *the* SPANISH HISTORIAN.

Madrid, Nov. 22d, 1799.

I HAVE just received your packet with an inclosure for Munoz, who alas! is no more. A fit of apoplexy, on the 19'h July, 1799, snatched this learned man, whose loss I shall ever deplore, from the career of letters.

He was born in the year 1745, at Museros, a village rather more than a league distant from Valentia, and he completed his studies in the University of that city. Always superior to the young men of his own age, he was their model, and not unfrequently their director in the different departments of *belles lettres*, philosophy and theology. It was he who overturned the idol of the Peripateticks, and substituted in its place good taste, the discoveries of the moderns, a sound logic, a real knowledge of nature, and, in short, a sure method of making a rapid progress in the sciences.

At the age of twenty-two years he drew up the Prefaces to the Rhetoric of P. Luis de Granada, and the Logic of Vernei, in which he displayed an astonishing degree of erudition acquired by him in consequence of the study of those authors who were the reformers of letters in the 15th and 16th centuries.

Invited afterwards by the Government to fill the place of principal Cosmographer of the Indies, he made himself acquainted with the various branches of this employment, which he filled with distinction until the moment that the Minister Galvez appointed him to draw up the History of America. That he might execute this task with honour to himself, during a period of five years, he visited and consulted the archives of Simancas, Seville, Cadiz, Lisbon, &c. and thus obtained admission to sources of information unknown, and even prohibited to those who had preceded him in the same career. The fruits of his zeal consisted of one hundred and thirty volumes of inedited papers, such as original letters from Columbus, Pizarro and Ximenes; a correspondence precious in respect to America, so far as its history both natural and political is concerned. It was on such solid foundations that he commenced his labours, the first volume of which has already been seen by the public; and the second, accompanied with justificatory papers, will soon make its appearance. Previously to his death he had completed the two first books of Vol. I. and the third was nearly finished; indeed, he was employed on it the day preceding his death, until two o'clock in the afternoon.

Munoz was the best husband, the most tender father, the most faithful and most constant of friends. I write you these particulars concerning him, without observing any order or ceremony, as they are merely intended to announce the, perhaps, irreparable loss of my learned friend. I shall transmit you his eulogium which is now preparing, and request you to render it public. A. J. CAVANILLES.

ORIGINAL

ORIGINAL LETTERS.

COPY *of a* LETTER *from the* REV. MR. ROBINSON, *of* CAMBRIDGE, *to* MR. MARSOM, *of* LONDON, *dated* CHESTERTON, WEDNESDAY, MAY 7, 1788.

I Accept with gratitude both the pamphlets you were so complaisant as to send me, and I thank Mr. Taylor for this additional proof of his esteem.

Eleven years ago, I published a Preface to the third volume of a Translation of Saurin's Sermons on the Doctrine of Christian Liberty, and in page 7 I said, "Mere mental errors, if they be not entirely innocent in the account of the Supreme Governor of Mankind, cannot be, however, objects of blame and punishment among men." *Error* is mistake; *mental* error is mistake of the mind; *mere* mental error is such a mistake of the mind as doth not affect the heart and life. This harmless position exposed me to many censures, and by a certain class of men my name hath been cast out as evil; ever since they have thought it a duty to preach and print against me, and to treat me with personal insults. About a year ago, I heard by a gentleman of Queen's College, that Sykes had published the same sentiment, and, since that, I saw, in Dr. Disney's Life of Sykes, an account of it. Ever since I have endeavoured to procure the book, but never could till the week your's arrived. Three days before, I had seen it in a Lynn catalogue, and I instantly wrote and procured it, but it was the first edition. Next day, a fellow of Trinity College found a second edition, in the College-library, and lent it me. Then came your's, the last and best edition, for which I most sincerely thank you. People are so thoughtless as to exclaim—"If this be allowed, the doors of our churches will be thrown wide open to all erroneous persons." I deny the fact, for I can easier find professors of a speculative system, than men of a holy life, and unholy professors are the most grievous Hereticks. Who is to judge of error, you or I; you for me, or I for you, or each for himself? There is no safe ground of action, except the leaving of every individual to judge for himself, and account to his master. My thanks are due most sincerely for your own performance*: I have read it with the most glowing affection for the author. I love a man who thinks for himself, think what he will. I honour the virtue of every one who dares to be free, and to shake off the petty tyranny of ecclesiastics, who bind the grievous burdens of tyrannical systems upon the consciences of another man's disciples—disciples whom they neither created, nor redeemed, nor are appointed to judge. My soul, come not thou into their intolerant assembly!

As to personality in God, a trinity of persons, I think it the most absurd of all absurdities; and, in my opinion, a man who hath brought himself to believe the popular doctrine of the trinity, hath done all his work; for, after that, there can be nothing hard, nothing inevident, the more unintelligible, the more credible; and, as this serves the purpose of producing implicit faith in pretended guides, priests will always try to keep it in credit. The Bible reads easy, if we consider God *one*; Jesus, the *Son* of God; and the Holy Ghost, the *Influence* of God. But this would spoil trade, the Scriptures would become plain and easy, and a learned priesthood would be unnecessary to make out and unfold that hard science Christianity to us poor blind creatures. Verily, my friend, priestcraft is at the bottom of all this burlesque upon religion, for such I account the grimace of one man's pretending to take care of another man's soul. The direct end of all their schemes is to cheat people into a disuse of their own understandings, and to pitch their eyes, and place their affections, upon a frail, and often a wicked, proxy.

I am sorry, I had not the pleasure of knowing you when I was in London; at present I have no immediate business there, and if I had, my stay would be short, not because I have not innumerable friends there whom I esteem, but because my present avocation is here—here I am, far from the din of unprofitable disputes about words and phrases. Here I enjoy a daily intercourse with men of the first literature, and the most amiable dispositions, sincere disciples of Jesus, who, thanks to Divine Goodness, are in this university studying the Holy Scriptures, and devoting their fine talents to the service of truth. Here too is a church of divers sentiments, but of uniform goodness, who enjoy Christian liberty, without assuming authority over one another. Here I weed my garden, plough the silver-stream with my two-oar

* The writer refers, in this place, to a Tract on the Impersonality of the Holy Ghost, written and published by Mr. Marsom.

two-oar boat, read, scribble, contemplate, and fill my soul with ideas of the Great Supreme, and with the joyful prospect of of a blessed immortality. Here the blossoms of my flowers and fruits regale my scent; the lark compliments me when I rise; the cuckow attunes the morning breeze; the owl sings me to sleep; and, if I wake in the night, the nightingale, beneath my window, lulls me to rest again:—

"These are thy works, Parent of Good."

Here also my distant friends visit me.—The last fortnight, my house has been filled with company from Oxford, Abingdon, London, &c. and, in their absence, I converse with the dead in the vast libraries of this university. O, how good is God to me, and I, with all these advantages, how unprofitable to him! Best of Beings—my Father and my God! Thy perfections are the base of my hopes: in Thee I live, in Thee I move, in Thee I have my being! to Thee, to Thee *alone*, be all the glory!

Believe me, my friend, your introduction elevates my soul. It lifts religion off the sand of authority, and places it on the rock of revelation: it makes the understanding free as the eye. Go on and prosper. Bring received opinions to the crucible. Take off the dross of human authority, antiquity, universality, and the rest, and reserve for public use the pure gold of revealed truth. Truth can never suffer by trial; and doctrines that shrink from examination and severe criticism, betray their origin.

If ever it lies in your way, I should be happy to see you at Chesterton; and when you see my friend Taylor, do me the favor to assure him of my most undisguised esteem.

When your's came, I was just reading the prose works of the divine Milton—one of the first of men. I am never tired of him. Are you acquainted with his Areopagitica, for the Liberty of unlimited Printing?—

"This is true liberty, when free-born men,
Having to advise the public, may speak free."

Pardon the length of this. I do not often offend in this way. Without ceremony, farewell.

Ever your's.
R. ROBINSON.

A COPY *of an* ORIGINAL LETTER *from* WILLIAM MOLYNEAUX, ESQ. *to* DR. EDMUND HALLEY.

Chester, Monday, Oct. 6th, 1690.

MY EVER HONOUR'D FRIEND,

I AM extreamly happy in your friendship and correspondence, and I should think myself the more so, could I make returns suitable to your kindness. The care and trouble you take about my trifles is a favour and act of friendship I shall never be able sufficiently to esteem; and I find you are so extraordinary accurate in your corrections, that you leave nothing for a review. I perceive you approve of the alteration I propose in page 21. I desire you wou'd move a little therein, and as soon as the printer has alter'd, according to the form I sent you in mine of Sept.—I desire that quarter of a sheet may be sent me: the last sheet I receiv'd is the sheet P: 'tis now a fortnight since I receiv'd any; I fear some are miscarried, but perhaps the post that comes in here this evening may bring the continuation.

I have your's of the 30th of September: what you therein offer is most admirably curious, which makes me the more concern'd at the miscarriage of your former; I entreat you to repair this loss, by recollecting what you then writ, and sending it to me; and, at the same time, be pleas'd to add an example or two, to illustrate what you gave me in your last.

I have promised Mr. Tooke a copy of my book, in Latin, to bestow on some foreign bookseller, if it be worth their pains to publish it in that language. I shall then crave your leave to insert your ingenious thoughts on this subject, asserting them, with all imaginable gratitude, to their own learned author.

The designe of my English edition is chiefly to propagate this part of the mathematicks (hitherto untouch'd) in our own language to those that are not masters of the Latin, as also to render it as plain and intelligible as I cou'd to the capacity of ordinary geometers; for I acknowledge my abilitys reach no others; so that to *such* your profound speculations concerning this affair would be lost. But I know there are some deep mathematicians plain English-men, and therefore, if, for their sakes, and to grace my poor work, you would add where you please, thereto, any of your own ingenious thoughts in this subject, I should acknowledge the obligation infinite. And because your own inventions of this kind are so far more excellent than mine, and surpass them so far in in the geometrical construction and calculus, I should approve of your adding them as an Appendix; your name would then grace my work infinitely, and you would therein be kind above measure to Mr. Tooke, who undertakes the work, and would hereby secure its sale. Pray, dear Sir, let me intreat this favour from you, and I do assure you, I'll make it my perpetual indeavour to return the obligation. If your next letter give me any hopes of this request, I shall be the most rejoyc'd man in the world; but, if you are silent therein, I shall be the most dejected, as thinking you look on my work as not deserving the ornaments you could give it.

I am your most humble servant,

WILL. MOLYNEAUX.

P. S. We have no news from Ireland, but expect it every hour. I am credibly informed, that all the Irish horse want shoes, and also their foot, insomuch, that a pair of shoes are sold in Limerick at 40s. (brass), a bottle of wine 12s. and a pot of ale 3s.—'tis certain their wants are very pressing.

Mr. Molyneaux, the writer of the above letter, is perhaps better known as the friend and correspondent of Mr. John Locke than as a mathematician. In 1689, among great numbers of other Protestants, he withdrew from the disturbances in his native country (Ireland), owing to the severity of Tyrconnel's government; and, after a short stay at London, settled, with his family, at Chester: here he employed himself in arranging the materials he had some time before prepared for his Treatise on Dioptrics, in which he was assisted by Flamstead. In August, 1690, he went to London to put it to the press, where the sheets were revised by Dr. Halley, who, at the author's request (as appears by the above letter) gave leave for printing, in the Appendix, his celebrated Theorem for finding the Foci of Optic-glasses. The book was published in 1692, in quarto, under the title of *Dioptrica Nova*;—a Treatise of Dioptrics, in two parts, wherein the various effects and appearances of spherical glasses, both convex and concave, single and combined, in telescopes and microscopes, together with their usefulness in several concerns of human life, are explained.

He called it "*Dioptrica Nova*," because it was almost wholly new, very little being borrowed from other writers, and because it was the first book published on that subject in the English language.

It does not contain any of the more curious speculations in optics, that being foreign to his design, but several of the most generally useful propositions are demonstrated in a clear and easy manner. The second part is very entertaining, especially in the history which he gives of the several optical instruments, and the discoveries made by them. In the dedication of the work (which was addressed to the Royal Society), he takes notice, among the improvements that had then recently been made in philosophy, of the advances that had also been made in logic, "by the incomparable John Locke, in his Essay on Human Understanding." This drew a letter of thanks from Mr. Locke, that soon grew into an intimate friendship, and a mutual correspondence subsisted between them till the time of Mr. Molyneux's death, which happened October 11, 1698.

Besides the work above-mentioned, he was author of

1. "*Sciothericum Telescopicum*," containing the description and use of a telescopic-dial, Dublin, 1686.—See Philos. Trans No. 184.

2. "The Case of Ireland stated, in Relation to its being bound by Acts of Parliament made in England." In this work, he was greatly assisted by Mr. Locke.

The following papers in the Philos. Trans. were also written by him.

1. Why four Convex-glasses in a Telescope shew Objects erect, No. 53.
2. Description of Lough Neagh, in Ireland, No. 158.
3. On the Connaught Worm, No. 168.
4. Description of a New Hygrometer, No. 172.
5. On the Cause of Winds, and the Change of Weather, &c. No. 177.
6. Why Bodies dissolved swim in Menstrua specifically lighter than themselves, No. 181.
7. On the Tides, No. 184.
8. Observations of Eclipses, No. 164,—185.
9. Why Celestial Objects appear greatest near the horizon, No. 187.
10. On the Errors of Surveyors, arising from the Variation of the Magnetic-needle, No. 230.

F. R. S.

ERRATUM.—In Halley's Letter to Flamstead, page 326, lines second and third, of the Magazine for November, read "*the distance of cor ♍ from spica ♍ 45° 51' ¼",*" &c.

ORIGINAL LETTER *of the late* SIR GEORGE SAVILE.

MADAM, *Rufford, Jan.* 27, 1757.

THE interfering in the private concerns of a family seems, in general, very much to want an apology. I have no other to make for doing it, than a persuasion that I am doing right, and a belief that what I am about to say may be of service to one, whom, I doubt not, you retain a real affection for, notwithstanding one capital breach of duty.

You easily guess, I mean your daughter at Egmonton.

The small rent I have a demand on her

3 husband

husband for has been in arrear some time. I thought it right to inquire into the cause of it, and, from the best intelligence I can get from those whom I have conversed with, I have reason to believe it impossible in the nature of things it should be otherwise. For I find it is not the practice of farmers on such a rent to keep a maid, and for this good reason, that the profits won't support one. Your daughter, therefore, must keep a maid, and the rent not be paid; or she must work herself at all the drudgery (without exception) of the farm, which, by all accounts indeed, she is willing enough to do; but neither do I believe that she is able, nor indeed can I persuade myself a mother wou'd desire it, her health being already, to appearance, impair'd.

I have been told, that it has been put in their power to mend themselves, by the husband's signing some instrument, the purport of which was to prevent his relations from ever being benefited by your money. If I have been rightly informed in this, nothing can be more reasonable. But I do assure you, you may venture to do something for them at present, nay, if it should be so put into your heart, even to fix a small annual income upon them, without the least hazard of his relations having any benefit from the overflowings.

I am informed he is so ignorant and obstinate, he will not sign this or any thing else. I beg you to consider how long she has been receiving the punishment due to *her* fault, and say, if you wish her now to begin to suffer for *his*. I entreat you to remember, she is your daughter, and turn it in your own mind, if it can be of an ill example to show some mercy, some charity, yea, to give alms to a distress'd child. Consider, for a moment, the difficulty she labours under between her two duties. I cou'd not but perceive it, and observe the hesitation with which she mentioned her husband's faults, and her silence regarding you, except in expressions of respect and gratitude for what you have done; nor did she, as I expected, desire my interfering in the case, so that if I have done wrong, I have no excuse to plead, but must rely on your candour in the case. The obvious way of accounting for my medling is that I am interested: and if you can think that is my motive, tho' concern'd that you should, I shall not set about to justify myself.

I have been already too long, to add to your trouble any farther, than assuring you, that I am, with more meaning than the words commonly imply, Madam,

Your faithful, humble servant,

G. SAVILE.

Extracts from the Port-Folio of a Man of Letters.

BRUNET LATIN *to* GUIDE CAVELCANT, DITEOR GREIGNOR, (*a celebrated* POET) *at* FLORENCE.

A MESSENGER going from hence with dispatches to our Holy Father the Pope, on the business of Holy Church, (*sainte yglise*); hath afforded me an opportunity of conveying a letter to you.

If you ask me, why I that am an Italian write to you, who are an Italian likewise, in the Romance, according to the idiom of France; [*en Romans selonc le Patois de France*]; I reply that I have two reasons for it, besides that it is equally familiar to you; the one, that it is constantly spoken here in the Court of London; the other, because the Romance language is the most delectable tongue I know, and assimilates best with all others. [*Porce que la parleure est plus delitable & plus comune atoz lenguages.*]

You will expect from me some particulars of the state of learning in England, and more especially of poetry. For the present I can just acquaint you, that at Oxford and Cambridge there are some who understand Greek, but their number is very small indeed. There are very few Greek books to be found in the English monasteries, as I am informed. A short time since, a Greek book was found on board a ship taken in the Mare Egeum, which was brought to Court, and has been interpreted by a learned monk of Westminster. It appears to be a Collection of Fables, the composition of a Phrygian slave named Esopus, who, after receiving great honours for his wisdom and integrity, was despitefully thrown from a steep rock at Delphos. Another learned monk has put many of these Fables into English rhyme. These monks are not of the class that indulge their carnal appetites like many great clerks of these times. [*Qui amoient que deliter luer chaitive charroigne com sont les grans cl's de cest tems.*]

I send

I send you one of these Fables by way of specimen of English poetry. As you are versed in the languages of Northern Europe, you will be at no great difficulty to understand it. I shall only observe that the pious and learned monk has made Esopus speak like a Christian in the application; but such is the nature of these Apologues, that they may be suited with morals at the pleasure of the interpreter.

Alle that will of Wysdam lere,
Herkeneth to me and ze schal here,
Appelogue in Greke y writ,
Esopus, Phrygius witnesset hit;
Esopus, he, for sothe, in Greke
Mad Fysch, and Bestes and Fowl to speke,
Who lyk un to grete Clerkes do preche,
Men that bin unroyse to teche.

Pryvily by nyght had Vulpes stole
With inne a Garner thorug litil hole;
Mete grek flore had thar bin sette,
The fals Thef eaten with oute let:
Agen could he nougt that weye passe,
The Schrewe with Mete so fyllid was;
Moche sorowe thanne was he, and creyen;
Allas, Allas! for glotonye schal y deyen.

Glotonye and Covetys I zow telle,
Draweth most Mannys soule to helle;
Lecherye is a nother schame,
That bryngs a man in wyked fame;
But Covetys hath ende no dele,
Ther fore it is lykenid to a whele.

In holy wryt it is sette,
That Lecherye is the Devels net;
And combre women that bin nougt good,
Both evel is to lered and lewed.

The wyly glotones they will not fyn,
Ere they ben dronken with ale or wyn;
They cryeth and the swereth as they were wood
By goddys soule and goddys blode.

He is wyse that hevene may wynne,
That kepeth hym from dedly synne.
Now, of this Fable y have maykid an ende,
Goddys blysse schal he have his lyfe that wil mende.

Brunetto Latini, of Florence, is said to have been the restorer of learning in Italy, and the friend and patron of Dante, Boccace and Petrarch. Villani, a Florentine, who has written the Lives of his Illustrious Fellow-Citizens, says, he was *gran Filosofo, ed sommo Maestro di Rettorica*; and he adds, *dittatore del nostro comune*, a magistrate of great account. Brunetto Latini was driven out of Italy by the faction of the Ghibelins (the Emperor's party), being a staunch Guelphite, in favour of the Pope. He sought refuge in France, from whence it appears that he came over to England with Richard, Earl of Cornwall, King of the Romans, who was the brother of our Henry the Third. He died in 1295.

Guido Cavalcanti is stiled *poeta gregio*. He was a native of Florence, born in 1290, and died in 1300.

Lered and *lewed*; the learned and unlearned. The *Leudes*, according to the feudal system, were the lowest kind of vassals, solely for the purpose of tilling the Lord's soil. These may well be supposed the most unlettered part of the kingdom; hence they are set in opposition to the *lered*, the *clergy*, *clerks*, or such as were ABLE TO READ AND WRITE.

JUDICIAL COMBAT.

In the dark ages of mankind, the ordeal, and trial by battle, took their rise; and seem to have been serious and religious calls to Heaven for judgment, in cases where the parties appear unwilling to submit themselves to the decision of the judges of the land. History tells us, trial by battle obtained so late as the reign of Charles the First; though the appeals were not suffered to terminate in combats, as the grand assize had been long before invented to remedy the inconvenience and uncertainty of them. In real actions, however, it still remained in the defendant's, that is to say, the tenant's power, to choose either method of trial as he thought best. Accordingly, we find an instance in the beginning of the reign of Elizabeth of issue joined by battle, which, as the custom was by that time much discouraged, was put off by repeated adjournments, until the parties came to an agreement; when, as Dyer reports, judgment was given upon failure of one of the parties to appear on the day appointed for combat. The last instance of judicial combat to be found in the History of France, was the famous one in 1547, between M. Jarnac and M. de la Chastaignerie.

I find trial by battle to have been regulated in the manner which here follows, in the possessions belonging to the Crown of England in France, during the thirteenth century. The account here set down is taken, and literally translated from a manuscript, composed in the French of that time, and written (according to its date) in the year 1344.

"When battle takes place, it is to be in this manner:—If the plaintiff declares and

and names sureties in his action [*Si la plainte avoct et nomet garenties en sa demande*], and the defendant defends himself against the plaintiff and his sureties in the action; then the plaintiff shall say openly in court, "I am ready to maintain by battle that what I demand is just and right, and here is my pledge." Thereupon he shall deliver to the judge of the court [*en la mayn dau feignor de la cort*] his pledge, a hood, glove, or other thing; [*son gage, chaperon, ou ganz, ou ov autres chozes.*] Then the defendant shall say, "I defend myself against the plaintiff and his sureties, and here is my pledge."

"Hereupon there shall be levied of the goods of the defendant, as much as shall pay all his debts. [*totes ses deptes.*] After which the plaintiff shall take of the defendant's effects a moiety, with which he shall provide two champions; [*Et apres aura la plainte sa meite dau remaignant daus moubles de son awersaire et querra a son propre cost dous champions.*] (But it is to be understood that the defendant may find his own champion, in which case there is to be no levy made on his goods.) [*Mas sachez que ceu est en election et en chois de laversaire de bailler a la plainte la meite de ses moebles ou de querre son champion.*] If two champions be provided by the plaintiff; the defendant shall make his choice of one according to his liking, which champion is to fight in his cause. The party whose champion is overcome is to pay sixty shillings to the King, and one penny for the ground.

"Trial of battle in real and personal actions [*por heritages, por deptes et per autres itaus chozes*] is always made by champions, never by the parties themselves, [*cors a cors*] (body to body) unless otherwise agreed by plaintiff and defendant.

"But in cases of treason [*traison*], murder [*murtre*], theft [*larroncin*], forgery or coining false money, or using false measures or weights, [*faussete faussenerie est espleiter fausse monoye, ou fasses mesures, ou faire vers autre fauffete por luy decevre de son cors ou de sa choze.*] or the like high crimes, the battle is personal, body to body, and never to be made by champions. [*Bataille ne se fait par champions ainz se fait cors a cors.*]

"The defendant has the advantage of chusing his weapons or manner of fighting, and the judges of the court are to name the day and hour. [*Li apelez ha tant davantage quil deviset la forme de la bataille & li sires de la cort assigne le jor & lou terme.*] If the defendant refuse to defend himself at the time appointed for the battle, he is to be adjudged guilty.

"Before the combat begins, the parties are to make oath before the judge upon the Holy Evangelists. The plaintiff is first to swear in these words, "So help me God and the Holy Gospels, as I now make just appeal [*leiau appeau*] against him," naming the defendant. And then the defendant maketh oath, and says, "So help me God and the Holy Gospels, as I make a just defence [*loyau deffense*] in that which I defend against him," naming the plaintiff. After this they are to enter the field of battle and engage each other;—the plaintiff as making the appeal is to attack the defendant first; and during the combat no person whatever present is to interfere betwixt the combatants, by speech or action, without permission of the judge, under the penalty of fine or corporal punishment at the mercy of the judge.

"And if either of the combatants refuse to fight, by yielding to his antagonist, or flying from out the lists, he shall be adjudged convicted, or as failing in the proof of his appeal. [*Est repris convaincuz.*]

"When the battle is carried on by champions, and plaintiff and defendant, being come into the field, shall agree upon the ground of complaint, before the champions begin to fight, the champions shall make a display of their skill for the diversion of the people present. [*Si la bataille est de champions et aloure quil serant en champ, hom en fait paiz avant quil se combattent, li champion deyvent mostrer les coups lo Roy, cest a dire quil deivent au maynz mostrer treys de lor estremies* (to skirmish three time, or make three skirmishes) *por la gent solacer.*]

The GEOGRAPHY *of* PYTHEAS.

The following passage is found in an ancient geographer, Pytheas of Marseilles —"In the proximity of Great Britain, on the north side, distant about six days' sail, there appears neither land, nor water, nor air; but these three elements confounded, form a substance which cements in its composition all the parts of the world. Neither vessels, nor persons on foot, can break through this impenetrable obstacle."* This passage has been treated as a ridiculous fable by the Abbé de Longchamp, and other learned men, particularly by the Benedictine Monks who published the *Literary History of France.* The substance, however, alluded to in the above passage is unquestionably that immense mass of eternal ice, which environs the poles of the earth, and which the boldest navigators could never yet pass. What Cook and Lemaire have demonstrably proved in our days, that there is no passage across the northern ices, appears to have been known even; in the time of Pytheas and the learned Benedictines have unjustly derided a man, who appeared to them to relate a fabulous tale, which is now known to be a very interesting and well-established fact. The works of the ancient authors, and especially of Herodotus and of Pliny the naturalist, contain a number of things apparently fabulous, and which yet perhaps will be demonstrated in the sequel as natural truths.

MISTAKES *in* COMPLIMENTING.

It is customary in China, on being introduced to any one, to ask a set of complimentary questions respecting their family, &c. A missionary, attending to the *etiquette* more than the person, one day put an eunuch out of countenance by asking him, how many children he had? On the other hand, a Mandarin once asked a Capuchin friar, how many wives he had? —and as he used the same word by which an ecclesiastical cure is denoted, the father innocently answered, three!

A NICE DISTINCTION.

Father Navarette, a missionary, observes, that the Bonzes in China have found out the method of granting plenary indulgences, and bulls for the dead, some of which they sell as high as 50 ducats. On which he sagaciously remarks, that the Devil still persists in his original design of appearing as like God as he can.

An INSTANCE *of* REGARD *to* VERACITY.

The Chinese annals relate, that a young prince once diverting himself in the garden with his pages in the presence of his preceptor, said to one of his pages in sport, "I make you king of such a place."—"What is your highness doing?" said the preceptor hastily. "I was only in jest," replied the prince. "Sir," said the preceptor, "the word of a prince should never be jest: you have made the boy a king and he must be so—your word cannot be recalled." The nomination was accordingly confirmed.

COOL PERSEVERANCE.

A Chinese Prime minister presented a Memorial to the Emperor on a subject he did not like. The Emperor disregarded it. The Minister repeated it three days successively. The Emperor at length in a rage tore it in pieces. The Minister coolly gathered up the fragments, and, pasting them together, presented it a fourth time. This proof of his patience and perseverance had such an effect on the Emperor, that he took the matter into consideration and complied with the request.

CALM FORTITUDE.

An Emperor of China proposed making a progress through part of his dominions. One of his counsellors opposed it, as at that time improper. The Emperor in heat drew his sabre and cried, "Pass the order for my journey this instant, or I will strike off your head." The officer without the least emotion took off his Manarin's cap and robe, and, kneeling down with his neck extended, said, "Your Majesty may strike, for I cannot comply with what I know to be contrary to the good of the empire." The Emperor checked himself and gave up his journey.

A RECEIPT *for* FAMILY-PEACE.

An Emperor of China, making a progress, discovered a family in which the master with his wives, children, grandchildren, daughters-in-law, and servants, all lived in perfect peace and harmony. The Emperor admiring this, inquired of the old man what means he employed to preserve quiet among such a number of persons. The man, taking out a pencil, wrote only these three words:—*Patience, patience, patience.*

A TRAGICAL INCIDENT.

At an Indian wedding in the Philippine Islands, the bride retired from the company in order to go down to the river and wash her feet. As she was thus employed, an alligator seized her. Her shrieks brought the people to the place, who saw her between the monster's teeth, and just drawn under water. The bridegroom instantly plunged after with his dagger in his hand and pursued the ravisher. After a desperate conflict he made him deliver up his prey, and swam to shore with the body of his dead wife in his arms.

SPANISH HIGH-SPIRIT.

Don Sabiniano, a Spaniard, being a prisoner in a dungeon at Lisbon, soon after the revolt of the Duke of Braganza, afterwards King John of Portugal, was told by the corregidor that the King was passing by, and that it would be a proper occasion to petition for release; instead of which, he shut his window in the King's face. For this affront his window was bricked up, and all access of light debarred.

PROCEEDINGS OF LEARNED SOCIETIES.

NATIONAL INSTITUTE OF FRANCE.

CONTINUATION *of the* THIRD QUARTERLY SITTING *of the* CLASS *of* MATHEMATICAL *and* PHYSICAL SCIENCES, YEAR 9.

CITIZEN KOCH has sent a *Memoir on a Literary Society, which appears to have been established at Strasburg, towards the end of the fifteenth and at the beginning of the sixteenth centuries.* The author observes, that letters from their earliest revival were favourably received in Alsace, and especially at Strasburg. This city held the first rank among the free cities of the Empire; and the inhabitants, who lived in ease and freedom, possessed that urbanity and independent spirit which are acceptable to the Muses.

Strasburg was in a manner the cradle of the art of printing, and by this invention the improvement of the human mind advanced with a celerity which it had not known before. By this means, facts, thoughts, opinions, the productions of genius, discoveries of every kind, are transported, like articles of commerce, over all parts of the globe where the art of reading is known. Guttemburg, the author of this new art, removed his establishment to Mentz; but he left industrious pupils in Strasburg. A literary society was at the same time formed there, an institution which, it may be asserted, was unknown to the ancients. As our learned societies are favourable to the progress of the human mind, so those establishments among the ancients which bore some resemblance to them, such as the Academia of Plato, the Lyceum of Aristotle, the Portico of Zeno, and the Gardens of Epicurus, were often contrary to it. In our societies each member has his own opinions, his own principles, his own views, and his own thoughts, all which may be considered as his peculiar property. Every new discovery is graciously received; every truth is admitted; every opinion may be presented without incurring displeasure, although what one of the members thinks is frequently that which his neighbour does not think; thence discussions take place, in which good faith predominates. But the ancient societies were merely schools, where the master preserved an ascendancy, and that even when he was no more; all sentiments were formed by his; his doctrine was the doctrine of all; his opinions were sacred dogmas, and it was a kind of sacrilege to submit them to examination. No new progress was therefore to be expected while the school lasted; it produced nothing but commentaries on the doctrine of the master. The truth which one school professed was only received into another, to undergo a sentence of reprobation. And lastly, each school piqued itself less on having reason, than on maintaining a usurpation by its principles over the rights of reason. In one they believed that there was no vacuum in nature; in another, that there was; in one, that God was of a spherical figure; in another, that he was perfectly flat *. Such however was not the school of Strasburg. Its founder was James Wimpheling, who was well seconded by some zealous partizans of reviving letters, who justly deserved to take a place with him. Here they entered into a critical examination of ancient and modern works, as being thereby qualified to decide which of them should first obtain the honour of printing. A still more fortunate result of these conferences, was to collect and concentrate in one focus the different parts of human knowledge, which, till then, isolated and without mutual correspondence, had been the subjects of separate instruction. And, above all, it is to the labours of the Society of Strasburg that we may attribute the astonishing success of the religious revolution in that city, in the beginning of the sixteenth century. It might be thought on a superficial view, that the human mind has little to congratulate itself on the superiority which the opinions of a Saxon monk obtained over those of the doctors of Rome, or that certain theological tenets were substituted for other theological tenets;—and that these novelties brought on fresh causes of persecution: but the truth is, that the reformation of Luther, followed by that of Calvin and many others, gave an acuteness to the reasoning faculty, and a happy audacity to explore that which men hitherto had been only accustomed to revere; and, in short, to grant nothing to authority when it is not in strict accordance with reason. Lastly, the combat of metaphysical ques-

* According to Zeno, God was perfectly round; according to Epicurus, the Gods were of a flat figure, not to be crushed by the various worlds or systems.

tions

tions has produced a philosophical spirit, which is likewise the spirit of liberty; and still further, the most friendly to order and the most averse to licentiousness. It may be ignorant—it oftens deems it glorious to doubt—but it never wanders out of the right-way, without ceasing to be itself.

One of the most honourable functions of the Man of Letters is to celebrate the memory of deceased men of merit, so as to excite an emulation to imitate their talents and virtues. Citizen DELISLE DE SALES has discharged his duty, in reading to the Class *the Life of the late Veron Forbonnais, an Associate Member*, and *the Literary Life of General Montalembert*, two men truly citizens, who devoted their whole lives to what they considered advantageous to their country.

Forbonnais was one of the first men who called the attention of the French to the different subjects of political economy. He wrote on the Finances, because he saw, with a virtuous grief, riches designed to reproduce riches snatched from the hands of the labourer, and the poor man, already succumbing under the weight of his burthen, obliged to bear likewise the fardle of the wealthy man. He wished to simplify the imposts, to render them less vexatious; he wanted even to reduce them to unity; a specious project, but which would cause the impost to fall too heavily on some, whilst others would but slightly feel it, and which would moreover fail to attain the object of the author, who established it as a principle, that the strength of an empire consists in taxing only superfluities. And how is it possible by one single method to come at the superfluity of so many persons who possess much, and whose selfish spirit is ever devising arguments to persuade themselves that they have not even necessaries? Forbonnais wrote on commerce, on the marine, on money, on agriculture, on legislation, and on diplomacy. He embraced in his mind the whole sphere of public utility. He everywhere discovers a sagacious intellect, a spirit animated with the desire of doing good. His *chefs-d'œuvres* are his *Elements of Commerce*, and his *Dissertation on the French Finances*. He has left a great number of manuscript pieces. When he had a part in the public Administration, he was just, severe and incorruptible; in private life, he was prudent, humane and beneficent.

Citizen de Sales in his *Life of Montalembert* connects with some anecdotes but little known relative to the life of that general, the history of his incessant controversy with the Corps of Engineers respecting his system of the defensive art, as likewise an analytical synopsis of the eleven volumes, in quarto, of his *Perpendicular Fortification*.

Some nations among the antients have had, at certain periods, very formidable navies, and were then called by metaphor, sovereigns of the sea; but without ever extending the idea so far as to suppose that the vast extent of the ocean could be the particular domain of one nation. This was reserved for the moderns; it appears to have been first adopted by the Portuguese, who wanted to expel the Dutch from the Indies, and has been since seized with avidity by the English. It produced a dispute near two centuries ago, of which Citizen CHAMPAGNE has collected the details, in his *Analysis and Exposition of the Treatise of Grotius*, intitled, *Mare Liberum*, or *the Freedom of the Seas*; and of the Treatise of Selden, intitled, *Mare Clausum*, or *the Dominion of the Seas, in Reply to that of Grotius.* These writers both employed their pens to defend the cause of their respective countries; but the pen was too feeble an instrument to terminate such a controversy. Grotius, in spite of numberless quotations, which injure the force of his arguments, proves the liberty of the seas by the laws of nature, and by the right which every nation has of carrying on commerce with another, without being obliged to submit to the arbitrary laws of a third, which can only make such for itself. Grotius, who was a Hollander, generously defended the rights of his country. Selden, an Englishman, entered into the lists with Grotius, by order of the Cabinet of London, and to serve the ambition of that Government; a government then atrocious in its mode of vindication, which employed the intrigues of its Minister at the Hague, to endanger the life of Grotius, and to involve that respectable man in the calamitous affair of Barnevelt. Grotius did not happily defend even a good cause, as he employed his vast erudition in supporting himself by authorities, when he should only have acknowledged that of reason. Selden defended a bad cause ill, precisely because it was bad, and that he could only resort to means of defence more or less ridiculous. He asserts that the sea may as well become a property as vacant lands, coasts, rivers and mountains; he seems to forget that all these may be included within the limits of a dominion, and that the ocean, far from being shut up,

com

comprehends and includes every thing. He calls Great Britain *the Island of the Ocean,* and pretends that reciprocally, the sea is the *Ocean of the Island.* He plunges his readers and himself in the night of past ages, and, holding them there in darkness, shews that Great Britain has exercised, at all times, her empire over the four seas which make part of her domain, by the same title as she holds her territory. He fixes the limits of the British seas, advancing them on the north no further than Greenland; and without rigorously bounding them on the side of America. He has also the condescension to leave to the nations, whose coasts are opposite to those of Great Britain, the property of their harbours and of their ports, and still further that of their rivers as far as to their *embouchures.*

The work of Grotius is useless, because it proves what has no need of proof. That of Selden is absurd. The ocean will be always free, by right; but, by a too long lethargy of the maritime powers, right may, at length, give way to force; and we may see the ocean become, at least for a time, the usurped domain of an island which is hardly to be discovered on its vast extent.

Citizen LEVESQUE has read a *third Memoir on the Construction of the Republic of Athens.* This Memoir relates to the *Tribunals of that Republic.* The number of judges at Athens was six thousand, and that of the citizens never surpassed twenty-one thousand. It should seem that this excessive number of judges, who were chosen out of the indigent class, must frequently prove injurious to justice; that a tribunal of a thousand or of fifteen hundred judges resembles too much the assembly of the people, of which history has handed down to us many unjust judgments, and that it must be, like the people, susceptible of credulity, of passion, of blind ignorance, of prejudice, of distrust, of fickleness and of facility of letting itself be carried along by the insidious eloquence of the orators. The author further indicates other vices which he thinks he has discovered in those tribunals. The result of his three Memoirs is, that if the Republic of Athens shone with the greatest lustre in letters and in arts, we must not thence conclude that every thing else was perfect, the constitution, legislation and the judicial forms. He dares to think, that in all these respects we have the ascendant over her, and over all the Republics of Greece. The reason is, that in these points we can only approach to perfection by a long experience. But the Republics of Greece would not acquire any, because a sort of superstition kept them scrupulously attached to the first essays of their infancy. We have in one assemblage both their experience and that of the Romans, and that of the long ages which have preceded us. Time produces every thing, but by a slow process, good constitutions, good laws and good judiciary forms; it matures human reason which perfects every thing, but this it effects slowly, as it does all the rest, and will never perhaps terminate this great work.

Works composed by Members of the Class, printed and deposited in the Library, during the last Quarterly Sitting.

An Abridgment of Universal History, during the First Ten Ages of the Vulgar Æra, by Citizen MENTELLE.

Observations on the present System of Public Instruction, by Citizen DESTUIT TRACY, an associate-member.

The History of France, since the Revolution of 1789, Volume I. in quarto, by Citizen TOULONGEON.

The Ruins of Port Royal, by Citizen GREGOIRE.

BRANDENBURG ECONOMICAL SOCIETY at POTSDAM.

This Society had offered a prize of 20 rix-dollars for the invention of a cheap and simple oil-press for the use of farmers. Five models of such machines were sent in, and the prize was adjudged to that invented by Mr. MAY, referendary to the Board of Trade and Manufactures in Berlin.—In the meeting of the 7th of May M. von Rochow, canon of the cathedral church, proposed a prize of five *Fredericsd'or* to the rural economist, who shall make known to the Society a certain remedy against the hunger-flower (*Draba verna L.*).—On the 7th of May the Society held their general meeting; M. VON VOSS being President. The following papers were read. 1. A treatise by M. von Rochow on the indispensability of arithmetic in rural economy.—2. On the degenerating of potatoes; by Pastor Stockmar of South Prussia.—3. On the improving of potatoes, by raising plants from the seed; by Dr. Keyselitz of Pless.—4. On the best method of employing fuel in heating ovens; with drawings and a model; by Professor Klaproth.—5. On the hindrances to the abolition of commons; by an unknown Correspondent.—6. On a proposal for supplying the want for hop-poles;

poles; by M. Hubert of Zoffen. A short account of the contents of the following treatises was given:—How to promote the speedy growth of oak-trees; by the Rev. Mr. Germershausen.—On the means of preventing the ravages occasioned by caterpillars; by Baron von Rusenberg of Dresden.—On the means of removing the dearth of wood; by M. Braumiller, merchant in Berlin.—An account of the inoculation of the sheep-pox; by Baron von Lauer of Plauen.—On a method of preparing syrup of turnep; by Privy-counsellor von Werdeck.—On the use of the seed of the *geranium gruinum* as a hygrometer; by the Rev. Mr. Lademann of Uhsleben.—On the sparing of wood; and on the effect of the light of the sun on the vegetation of plants; by R. Lindenthal of Küstrin.—Economical observations, by M. Henschke.—On the mode of instruction in the schools in town and country; by the Rev. Mr. Schlemüller.—Plan for establishing a company to insure the stock and crops of farmers; by Mr. Inspector Schäfer of Lohburg.—On the pressing of oil from seeds growing in the Margraviate of Brandenburg.—On the dividing of the pasturage-lands; by M. Fischer of Crailsheim, &c.—Models were likewise exhibited of a sawing-machine; of a plough; of a stove for cooking, so constructed as to save fuel; of a farm house, whose gable-sides are covered with straw or reeds; of a potatoe machine; and a drawing of a wood-saving stove for warming rooms.

ACADEMY *of* SCIENCES *at* BERLIN.

The public assembly of the Academy, held on the 3d of August 1801, for the purpose of celebrating the King's birthday, was opened by the perpetual Secretary, M. MERIAN, with an appropriate oration. The Secretary then read a report, from which it appeared, that in answer to the prize-question proposed by the Physical Class, viz. "On the influence of electricity on fermentation," only one treatise had been received, which had not been deemed deserving of the prize:—but that the Philosophical Class had adjudged the prize to be equally divided between the authors of two of the treatises received on the subject proposed by them, viz. "On the origin of human knowledge." The first had the following motto from Homer: ἀχλὺν δ᾽ἄϐ᾽ὀφθαλμῶν ἕλον, &c.; and the other, the following from Locke: "*l'Experience est le fondement de toutes nos connoissances.*" On opening the sealed billets, it appeared, that Mr. Lazarus Bendavid was the author of the first; and of the second, Joseph Maria Degerando, Member of the Council of Arts and Professor of Ethics in Paris. The *accessit* was adjudged to a treatise with the motto Δος μοι που στω. Mr. Merian at the same time gave notice, that the same Class proposed the following question for the new prize of 50 ducats for the year 1803: "How far the moral value of an action may be taken into consideration in the enacting of a penal law, and in the application thereof."—Mr. Merian then read the elogy of the late Minister of State, Count von Fichtenstein.—Professor Walter, senior, read a treatise on the question: "How is a child nourished while it remains inclosed in the womb?" and Privy-counsellor Ancillon a Dissertation on the Metaphysics of the Greeks. Mr. Privy-counsellor Ermann closed the meeting by reading A genealogical Account of all the Imperial, Royal, and Sovereign-princely Personages who in the last century were descended in a direct line from Queen *Sophia Charlotte* and her only son Frederic William I.

ACADEMY *of the* ARTS *at* VIENNA.

The prizes which are given by the Royal Imperial Academy of the Arts in Vienna, the large ones every two years, and the small ones every year, were distributed to the most deserving candidates in April 1801. The large prizes consist of medals; the first of a gold medal of the value of twenty-four ducats; and the second of a silver medal, with an addition of money, the whole worth eight ducats. The person who receives the first prize, leaves the prize-painting in the possession of the Academy; but the piece which obtains the second prize is returned to the artist. The smaller prizes consist of money, the most considerable of them seldom exceeding twenty-five florins. The subjects proposed for 1800 were:—In historical painting, "Adam shewing to Eve the murdered Abel," from Gesner's Poem. The two prizes were adjudged to Joseph Redel, and Frederic Matthæi of Dresden.—In landscape-painting, "A rocky tract of country, with a waterfall." J. Giebele, and Francis Jaschke obtained the prizes.——In statuary, "Homer, blind, and led by a boy. Joseph Geiger, and Elias Hütter obtained the prize.—In architecture, "A church." A. A. Ortner, and J. Neurohr obtained the prizes.

VARIETIES, LITERARY AND PHILOSOPHICAL.

Including Notices of Works in Hand, Domestic and Foreign.

*** *Authentic Communications for this Article will always be thankfully received.*

M. VON KOTZEBUE's work, entitled "*The most remarkable Year of my Life*, containing an account of his banishment and journey into the distant regions of Siberia, and of his other wonderful and romantic adventures in Russia, has been translated into English, from his own manuscript, by Mr. BERESFORD, at Berlin, and will make its appearance in London in the course of January. Those who have read it describe it as one of the most interesting works that has appeared for some years past. Since the beginning of October, M. von Kotzebue has resided at Weimar, and has been writing an extensive drama, the subject of which is taken from the Crusades. The new theatre at Berlin is, on the 1st of January, 1802, to be opened with this piece, by order of the King of Prussia, who is very partial to Kotzebue's plays.

Mr. BOWYER, of Pall-mall, intends to publish ten numbers, each containing four Views in Egypt, from the collection of Sir ROBERT AINSLIE, taken during his Embassy to Constantinople by LUIGI MAYER. The subjects are, Views of Alexandria, Aboukir, Rosetta, and Grand Cairo; of the Palace of Mourad Bey; of different parts of the Banks of the Nile; external and internal Views of the Pyramids; Pompey's Pillar; Obelisks, Catacombs, Sepulchres, Mosques, Villages, Arabian Fairs, Balls, &c. The Views will be accompanied with brief historical, and archaiological observations, and incidental illustrations of the manners and customs of the natives. Mr. Bowyer has also purchased the Manuscript written by the Athenian Reveley, of his observations made in his tour through Egypt upon the different objects of antiquity, particularly their exact measurement, &c. which will render the History accompanying these Views the most authentic ever published; and it is intended that Mr. Reveley's account shall never appear but in this work.

Mr. THOMAS TAYLOR's long-expected Translation of the entire Works of Plato is printing rapidly at the expence of the Duke of Norfolk, and will probably make its appearance in the course of the spring, in ten handsome volumes, quarto.

The matchless edition of Shakespeare published by the BOYDELLS' at length approaches to a conclusion, and only one Number remains to be delivered. This work will long continue a monument of glory to its publishers, and to the age which patronized it.

We congratulate the public on the prospect, that Stereotype-printing will soon be introduced into this metropolis, under the patronage and direction of a nobleman who has long deserved well of his country for his attention to the useful arts. The adoption of this invention, and the probable reduction of the ruinous and oppressive duty upon paper, will again reduce the price of books to their former standard.

A splendid work is announced to be published in quarterly numbers, intitled "*Scotia Depicta*; or, the Antiquities, Public Buildings, Castles, Noblemen and Gentlemen's Seats, Cities, Towns, and Picturesque Scenery, of Scotland illustrated; in a Series of finished etchings, by Mr. FITTLER, from accurate Drawings made on the spot by JOHN CLAUDE NATTES, from 1797 to 1800; the whole accompanied with Descriptions, antiquarian, historical, and picturesque."

The Rev. Mr. FIELD, of Warwick, proposes to publish, in the course of the present month, a second edition, with corrections and considerable additions, of his Introduction to the Use of the Globes. A much greater number and variety of problems, and a larger collection of examples for practice, are given, than are usually to be found in works of a similar nature. It is accompanied also with a series of questions for examination.

Mr. MILLAR, in Bond-street, who has published the Costume of China with so much applause, announces the first number of the Costume of Turkey, both Asiatic and European; including that of the Greek Islands of the Archipelago; in a Series of coloured Engravings, illustrative of the singular and diversified Manners, Customs, and Dresses of those interesting Nations; faithfully copied from Drawings, taken on the Spot, by OCTAVIAN DALVIMART, with Descriptions in English and French. The work will consist of eight numbers, each number containing seven and sometimes eight plates, coloured after the exact manner of the original drawings: the size will be imperial 4to, and the price

price of each number will be one guinea.

The same bookseller proposes to publish, under the patronage of the Right Hon. Lord Somerville, a magnificent edition, in imperial quarto, of the Chase, Field-sports, and Hobbinol of WILLIAM SOMERVILLE, Esq. with a new Life of the Author, by Dr. SOMERVILLE; superbly embellished with Engravings of various sorts, by Bartolozzi, Heath, Fittler, Byrne, Anker Smith, Neagle, Armstrong, &c. Among others will be given a portrait of the author, from an original picture, never engraved, and now in the possession of Lord Somerville; twelve curious paintings, illustrative of the Hobbinol, originally executed for the author, and now in his Lordship's possession: also portraits of the most eminent sportsmen of the author's time, as well as those most celebrated of the present day.

The Booksellers and Printers of London have resolved at a general meeting, to petition Parliament for a repeal of the late oppressive and impolitic duty on paper; and it is to be hoped their brethren, in every county throughout the kingdom, will follow their example, and omit no means of influencing Members of Parliament to support their reasonable application.

Messrs. GAMEAU and Co. will publish in January, a Poem, in eight books, intitled "Science Revived; or, the Vision of Alfred."

Mr. HUNT has in hand a tragedy intitled, "The Earl of Surrey," which will shortly be presented to the managers of Drury lane Theatre.

The Rev. E. FORSTER, F. A. S. announces a History of the County of Suffolk, which is not to exceed three volumes quarto. It is to be printed in the first stile of elegance, and to be enriched with engravings from drawings of the first artists, by Bartolozzi, Byrne, Heath, Fittler, &c.

A new Classical Dictionary of Ancient Geography, on a more extensive scale than any former publication, is now ready for the press, and is intended to be published during the winter.

Mr. DUPPA is publishing in a very splendid manner a selection of heads from the best fresco paintings of Raphael, accompanied with critical observations. He contrasts this with his former work, from the last judgement of Michael Angelo, and illustrates by the comparison the difference of feeling in their art, and the respective merits of those powerful and contemporary rivals.

Dr. GARNETT, whose Lectures on Experimental Philosophy and Chemistry have been very numerously attended, has issued a Prospectus for the following Courses:—1. A Course on *Chemistry*, comprehending all the modern discoveries in that science, with its application to the different arts and manufactures; particularly pharmacy, medicine, and agriculture. This course will consist of about forty lectures, two of which will be delivered every week, viz. on Tuesday and Thursday, at 8 o'clock in the evening. The first Lecture will be on Tuesday, January 19.—2. A Course of Lectures on *Zoonomia*; or, the Laws of Animal Life; in which a popular view of the animal economy will be given, and of the laws by which its different functions are regulated, with the methods of preventing and curing diseases. The object of the lecturer will be to render this course interesting, not only to medical students, but to all who think the study of the human frame a subject worthy their inquiry. This Course will consist of not less than fifteen Lectures, one of which will be delivered every Wednesday evening, at 8 o'clock. The first Lecture will be on Wednesday, January 20.

Messrs. A. and C. R. AIKIN will begin an evening Course of Lectures on various Chemical Manufactures, and the Outlines of Chemistry, on the 1st of March next. The Lectures will be given every Monday and Wednesday evening, in a commodious room at the Aldersgate-street Dispensary, with the use of which the lecturers have been favoured by the governors of that institution.

Dr. OSBORN's and Dr. CLARKE's Lectures on Midwifery, and the Diseases of Women and Children, will be given as usual, at the house of Dr. Clarke, New Burlington-street. The first of the two spring-courses will begin on Monday, January 24, 1802, at half past ten in the morning, and the lectures will be given at that hour every day for the convenience of students attending the hospitals.

Mr. J. THELWALL is delivering at Leeds, Sheffield, &c. a Course of five Lectures, on the Science and Practice of Elocution, which he illustrates by various readings and recitals in prose and verse.

There has lately arrived in the port of London, consigned from the Presidency of Fort St. George, a bale of *ulue nar*, a new article in the commercial world. It possesses the quality of hemp, and is said to be of very long duration in use. It is sent home for the express purpose of being manufactured and tried, as a specimen to ascertain how far it is likely to be of importance to this country.

Mr. BERESFORD, of Berlin, has announced for speedy publication in that city, a Dramatic Library; or, a Collection of the best English Plays. Indeed, in consequence of the impolitic duty, all the best English authors are now printed in various cities in France and Germany, and sold one hundred per cent. cheaper than the copy exported from England.

It is not perhaps generally known, that what is called gilt leather, owes its yellow appearance to a covering of tinfoil, lackered over with yellow varnish: this however is literally the fact, and hence gilt leather by long wearing becomes of a silvery white colour. The same method is employed to make various articles of brass to resemble gold, and to give certain pieces of iron furniture, the appearance of brass. To prepare the yellow varnish, dissolve, separately, two ounces of pure gum lac in forty-eight ounces of spirit of wine, and one ounce of dragon's-blood in the same quantity of spirit; then mix the solutions and add three grains of yellow wood, digest the mixture twelve hours in a gentle heat, then filter the liquor through blotting paper, and keep it in a clear glass bottle well stopped. If a paler varnish is required, the yellow wood may be omitted.

An improvement in the preparation of Pulvis Antimonialis has been communicated to the Royal Society by Mr. CHENEVIX. This medicine was originally introduced into the pharmacopœia as a substitute for Dr. JAMES's powder, but is more active in its operation and liable to considerable variation in the proportion of its constituent parts; Mr. Chenevix has therefore proposed another substitute not exposed to these objections. It is prepared as follows: Take equal parts of phosphat of lime and powder of algaroth, and dissolve the mixture in the least possible quantity of muriatic acid; then add some caustic ammonia to distilled water, and drop gradually into this the muriatic solution, a copious white precipitate will be produced, which when washed and dried, is ready for use. This medicine has been already exhibited by some eminent practitioners, and appears to have all the properties of the Pulvis Antimonialis but in a much less concentrated form, so that it may be given in doses of less than eight grains without occasioning vomiting.

M. KIRCHNER, M. D. of Würth on the Mayne, promises to make public a newly-discovered secret of nature!—a something, which, without being costly, "possesses tinging powers, is fire-proof, the only true alkahest, and universal-medicine, which contains the first principle of all wisdom, and fully explains the half solved enigma, in which the proper application of this alkahest to base metals lies hidden. For disclosing this notable, and in its kind unique arcanum, he modestly desires only 700 guineas!

The Elector of Bavaria has given a commission to the Court-councillor KLEINSCHROD, of Würtzburg, to compose for his electoral dominions a new Code of Penal Laws.

At the close of the year 1800, there were 751 students at the University of Halle; viz. 49 nobles, and 702 of the *tiers-état*. Of these 324 studied divinity, 372 jurisprudence, and 55 medicine—of the whole number only 91 were foreigners.

CHARDON-LA-ROCHETTE has undertaken a journey into the southern departments of France, in order to preserve and collect the monuments and works of art of every kind, which have luckily escaped the Vandalism of the Revolution.

At the Sitting of the National Institute of the 5th Messidor, year 9, citizen SICARD was elected to the place of the Section of Grammar, vacant by the death of citizen de Wailly, by a majority of 216 voices: citizen FONTANES had 208, and citizen THIEBAULT 158.

A useful experiment has been lately made at Rambouillet, (on the Merinos flock naturalized in France) which proves, contrary to vulgar prejudices, and even the opinion of a great number of naturalists, that the wool of sheep does not fall off or degenerate by letting it acquire more than one year's growth. Some two year fleeces have produced precisely double, in respect of weight, to that of one year; and the longest wool of the double quantity was equally fine in quality. Thus a two-shear Merinos has produced more than 16 pounds of a wool which sold for three francs the pound, like that of the one-year fleeces.

The Society of Medicine of Bourdeaux has just proposed a prize of the value of 300 francs, to the person that shall present, with order, regularity and method, the *Doctrine of Hippocrates*, or a *display of the Hippocratic Art of Medicine*. The prize will be distributed in the public sitting of Fructidor, year 10. The Memoirs will be received till the 1st. Thermidor of the same year, and should be directed, free of postage, to the Secretary-general of the Society.

A French translation of Wieland's Aristippus will shortly be published by POUGENS. Two other translations of the same work are announced.

CHARDON-LA-ROCHETTE, is preparing a complete edition of the celebrated Vatican Codex of the Anthology, with a Commentary, in seven vols.

CHAUSSARD has lately printed at Paris, a *Histoire des Courtisannes Grecques*, which he announces as a Continuation of the Voyages of Anacharsis and of Antenor ! ! !

Mr. AKERBLAD, a Swedish gentleman who belonged to the Swedish embassy at Constantinople, and thereby had an opportunity to make a literary tour in several parts of the Levant, is now diligently employed in examining the treasures in the National Library at Paris, especially the numerous Coptic manuscripts.

A circumstantial account of all the manuscripts in the National Library at Paris is now printing. A part thereof will appear in the 6th, and the remainder in the 7th volume of the *Notices des Manuscrits de la Bibliotheque Nationale*; so that the curiosity of those will soon be gratified, who wish to become acquainted with the contents of the treasures with which that rich collection has been augmented. A catalogue has been long ago prepared for the use of those who visit the National Library to collate or consult manuscripts for literary purposes: and every thing is there accessible.

In the Dukedom of Mecklenburg-Strelitz, an institution has been formed, by order of the Duke, for the instruction of future school-masters. Of several plans proposed for this purpose, the preference was given to that of *Pastor F. L. Reinbold*, of Woldegt: and a commission given him to establish the school at Michaelmas 1801, in his place of residence, himself being appointed Director thereof.

The prize subjects, viz. "Achillès in Scyros" and "Achilles combating with the River-gods", proposed by GÖTHE in the Propyläen (a journal published by him) vol. III. No. 2, page 163, produced an interesting and instructive exhibition at Weimar. The productions of those who contended for the prizes, were hung in the exterior hall; and in the second the spectators found a select and well arranged collection of drawings and paintings by ancient and modern masters. A whole series of drawings and paintings by Nahl of Cassel, in particular, attracted the attention of the connoisseur; as likewise several sketches and two well-finished heads, after Rafaelle's Transfiguration, by Tick of Berlin; Portraits by Bury; paintings in oil by Kolbe of Dusseldorf; two portrait-busts by Dannecker; a relievo by Wolf of Cassel; and some works of the ancient masters, among which are a Rubens and a Vandyke of extraordinary beauty. The happiest consequences are expected to follow in the reviving of the true spirit of the art, from such an exhibition, under the fostering guidance of so competent a judge, whom Germany is proud to boast of, as the first of her poets and connoisseurs, and on whose decisions neither the jealous zeal of rival schools nor little by-views will have any influence.

The lioness of the Menagerie at Paris, mother of the three young lions, has lately whelped two females; this is her third gestation. She suckles them with the same care, and always appears gentle and caressing to the keeper. The three young ones are well; the one that was castrated is grown very surly; it is kept in a separate den; the two others are very gentle.

Citizen ANTOINE ALEXIS CADET DE VAUX has lately addressed a letter to the Minister of the Interior, in which he communicates a cheap and efficacious process, to destroy, and above all to prevent, the mephitism with which walls are penetrated, wherever a number of people are, whether in a state of health or sickness. Walls under such circumstances, become insensibly impregnated with infectious exhalations, which they re-exhale, wherever there is an atmospherical motion; in fact there is both an aspiration and a respiration. Currents of air, when admitted, sweep and cleanse the atmosphere; but they do not carry away the miasmata concealed in the porosity of the walls, and which retain the infectious humidity of the perspiration of bodies, which gradually condenses on their surface. In the southern climates, and particularly in Italy, where the pulmonary phthisis acquires a character of energy which renders it very communicative, experience has proved, that not only the whole wardrobe should be burnt, all the moveable effects placed in contact with the phthisis, but likewise, that the superficial coating of walls and of floors should be done away, to prevent the contagion which they conceal and re-exhale. Citizen Cadet de Vaux is of opinion, that quicklime may be substituted for this purpose and become a sufficient a sufficient precaution, as being a powerful de-mephitisator. The most infected vans and sieves lose their smell when mixed with the whiting or size of lime. Citizen Cadet de Vaux makes mention of having brought a putrified carcase to such a state, as to be entirely free from odour, which he had been formerly authorized by an arret of parliament to exhume. This mephitism, he says, is so inherent, that even time cannot dissipate it; witness the *Donjeon* at Vincennes, when it ceased to be a prison of state, under the ministry of Malesherbes—the persons who had been prisoners in it, were, among a multitude of others, curious to see it, and they found again the same scent which had struck them on first entering it; the doors and windows however had been removed, and the elevation of the Donjeon exposed it to the free action of the air. Workshops, factories, infirmaries, hospitals, prisons, &c. have an atmosphere peculiar to them—this atmosphere is fatal, or often becomes the germ of epidemical, and sometimes pestilential, disorders, such as nictiopy, the hospital and prison fever, &c. &c. Plants deprived of air languish and fade, and by consequence much more animals, whose lungs consume so large a mass of it. Citizen GUYTON MORVEAU has discovered a method of purifying air, that contains in it the principle of epidemical or fatal disorders, by the help of muriatic gas, and especially of muriatic gas oxygenated. He purges these atmospheres, and deprives them of their miasmata, which he confines or rather destroys. But this salutary means of purifying the air cannot act so efficaciously on walls which conceal deeply, in the porosity of the stone, the miasmata with which they are infected; but the active power of lime produces this effect. Citizen Cadet de Vaux states the result of one of his experiments; being willing to try the effect of lime as a means of demephitisation, he removed from a wall a thickness of nine lines (a French measure containing the 12th part of an inch)* before he arrived at the coating or layer not yet affected. The other portion of the same wall, reserved for an experiment of comparison, was completely demephitised, in the same thickness, by three successive applications of common white wash clean water and quick lime. But lime enters white-washing, and may become the principal substance of it, by substituting it for Spanish white. This substitution is more œconomical, considering the cheap price of lime: a toise of this white-washing, will only come to five *centimes*; as to the workmanship, hands will not be wanting in houses or so large establishments, where every thing ought to be for œconomy. To destroy the mephitism of walls in asylums of indigence and misfortune, is some consideration; but to prevent the evil, not to have to remedy it, is no less an object; but white washing with lime as the principal ingredient answers this purpose, by preventing walls from being impregnated with infectious miasmata. To the objection for what purpose is the addition of the milk and the oil? the answer is, that lime has no adherence on walls, that no body or substance can be given to the layer; and lastly that the lightest rubbing with a simple pencil-brush rubs it off, and leaves the wall naked, whence it happens that the contact of walls so whitened stains the cloaths. The cheesy part of the milk, the addition of oil, which makes a soapy body with lime, form on the contrary, after the evaporation of the humidity, a dense, coherent layer, susceptible of a body; it is a sort of varnished plaster, which overcomes the porosity of stone, of plaster, of brick, and of wood, and the dust of which may be removed, without leaving the white-washed part naked. This wash has another advantage, namely, that of checking the nitrification of walls, which the painting of them in water-colours accelerates. In fact, glue is an animal substance, of which azote is one of the principal ingredients, but the decomposition of glue leaves the azote at liberty, which is likewise one of the constituent principles of nitric acid, and consigns it to the oxygen with which it forms this acid. White-washing forming no azote, there is one aliment less in the nitrification; it is not because the cheesy part does not also contain azote, but as it is not decomposed, this principle is not at liberty to contract another union. Moreover, this wash closes up the pores of the stone and is interposed between the walls and the nitrifying action. Citizen Cadet de Vaux concludes his letter by observing, that he has submitted his theory and experiments to the two principal French chymists, Citizens

* The author adds in a note, that in a glass bottle having exposed, to a moderate heat the dust removed from a wall, he can judge by the smell, whether it is or is not polluted. He has, he says, seen stones more than a foot and a half thick tinged with mephitic particles through their whole dimensions; and particularly in the privy of the *Hôtel des Invalides, and des Célestins*, he has noticed the remarkable circumstance of the stone which formed the interior being totally destroyed.

FOURCROY and DEYEAUX; and that, supported by their authority, he can now recommend, especially for the use of hospitals, his process of resinous white-washing (substituting, however, lime for Spanish white), as the most efficacious and œconomical means, to destroy and to prevent the mephitisation of walls; the introduction of it, he adds, will procure him the sweet satisfaction of having deserved well of humanity and of domestic œconomy.

FOURCROY, VAUQUELIN, and THENARD, being engaged in making Galvanic experiments, have been rewarded by the discovery of one of the most important and remarkable facts relating to that phenomenon. Though it is known, that by multiplying the plates of Volta's column, the force of the strokes as well as the quickness of the decomposition of water is considerably increased, yet it remained to be examined, what effect might be produced by increasing the surface of the plate. To this end the above chemists constructed a column of plates, the surface of each of which was one square foot: the strokes as well as the decomposition of water were the same as from an equal number of smaller plates, but the combustion of metallic wires proceeded immediately with great violence, particularly in oxygen-gas, which phenomenon was not produced by a number of smaller plates.

Mr. BLIFENER of Berlin, musician to the King of Prussia, has discovered a certain cypher applicable as notes in music, which though in itself very simple, easy and plain, is unintelligible to all who are not acquainted with the secret. It consists of a musical alphabet of five figures, which may be learned in half an hour even by those who do not understand music, and with the assistance of which a person may learn to play mechanically on any instrument, in the short space of five hours. By means of the same cypher, persons are likewise enabled to express words or ideas in any language, to do which we now make use of the 24 letters. The inventor offers to communicate his secret by letters to all, who wish to instruct themselves, for a reward of one Louis-d'or, under the condition that it is not published again.

It is known, that wood, on being burnt, yields one-sixth of its weight of coal and five-sixths of smoke, containing a considerable proportion of inflammable air, which is commonly wasted without use. For employing it to the purpose of heating and illuminating the room at the same time, an apparatus has been discovered by Citizen LEBON, engineer of bridges and roads, which he calls *thermolamp*, consisting of a box or vessel, in which the double advantage of heating and illuminating is united. The smoke rising out of it, freed from all vapours and soot, may be conducted through the smallest tubes, which may easily be concealed in the plaster of the walls or ceiling. They may be made of oiled silk, but the orifice must consist of metal to prevent the burning of the silk when the air takes fire at the contact with the atmospherical air. By this apparatus chimneys become quite needless, as the flame may be conducted in a moment from one apartment to another, without leaving either soot, ashes, or coals. The fire thus produced wants no particular care to be kept up, and has besides the advantage that its pure light may be formed into flowers, festoons, &c. or it may be made to emit its light from above in the purest brightness. The author of this curious discovery, who announced it to the National Institute in the year 7, is preparing for publication a full account of its nature and composition.

The King of Prussia has allotted a general fund for the schools of the arts. From this fund the salaries of the teachers in the provincial schools are to be paid, and all necessary drawings, busts and models purchased. In several cities of the Prussian monarchy, as for instance, in Frankfort on the Oder, and in several towns of South-Prussia, schools of the arts are to be erected, after the plan of that instituted at Magdeburg, in 1798. In this latter there are two teachers with salaries, Professor BREYSIG and the painter FÜSSLE. The Conductor, COSTENOBLE, instructs the pupils in architecture and geometrical drawing. The theoretical part of drawing and perspective is taught by Professor BREYSIGIN, an extraordinary lecture. Three afternoons and one forenoon every week are besides allotted to giving instruction.

The art of bleaching has derived considerable improvements from modern chemistry, a great share of which is due to Citizen CHAPTAL, now Minister of the Interior in the French Republic. A bleaching-manufactory has lately been established at Passy, by Citizen BAWENS, under the direction of Chaptal, where, on a visit of the Chief Consul, about 2000 yards of cotton cloth were bleached by one simple operation. Preparations are now made for bleaching linen in the same way. It was BERTHOLLET who first employed the oxygenated muriatic acid in bleaching cloth, but afterwards the acid was combined with fixed alkalis, and earths and an an oxymyriat in ſolid form obtained, of which the lye is prepared. Another ſubſtance however, that may be employed for that purpoſe, is the ſulphurated lime, or the liver of lime, which, beſides its acting ſtill more on the fibre of flax, has the advantage of being leſs expenſive than potaſh, and may be applied cold. Citizen Chaptal ſucceeded in employing vapours of oxygenated muriatic acid, for bleaching cotton, flax, and hemp, and invented the inſtruments with which that operation is performed at the manufactory of Citizen Bawens, and through means of which, 2000 or 3000 yards of cotton cloth are bleached in a day. Old engravings and books of a high value can be revived in a ſimilar manner, and the worſt ſort of rags prepared for very good paper. This method of bleaching is likewiſe of great uſe in cleanſing the linen of an hoſpital, which is ſtained with different morbid matters, and of which it is not freed by the moſt careful waſhing. A full account of the whole proceſs is to be found in the work of Citizen Chaptal, publiſhed by Citizen O'Reilly: *Eſſai ſur le Blanchement, avec la Deſcription de la Nouvelle Methode de blanchir d'après les Procédés du Citoyen Chaptal, et ſon Application aux Arts, Paris, 1801, with 14 engravings.*

A building is about to be erected at Paris, deſtined for the Conſervatory of Muſic, the groundſtone of which was laid by Citizen Chaptal, Miniſter of the Interior, on the 5th of Auguſt laſt. The muſical library conſiſts of more than 5000 manuſcripts of foreign muſic, the greateſt part of which were collected by Bonaparte, in the year 1797, in Italy. The number of pieces of French muſic is nearly the ſame.

Throughout the whole Ruſſian empire the bookſelling-trade is again as free and unreſtricted as under the reign of the Empreſs Catherine. It has been calculated, that ſince the death of Paul, 200,000 rubles-worth of German books only have been imported into Ruſſia. The Courlanders, Livonians, and Eſthonians are again permitted to ſtudy at the German Univerſities. At that of Jena alone, above 60 ſtudents arrived laſt autumn from Ruſſia.

In the margraviate of Baden, a law was publiſhed on the 18th of June, by which it was ordered, that in future no circulating library ſhould be eſtabliſhed without previouſly obtaining a licence from the magiſtrate; and that ſtrict inquiry ſhould be made relative to the character and qualifications of the perſon who forms ſuch an inſtitution.

It having been found, that the number of printers in Prague had increaſed beyond due proportion, it was ordered by an Imperial Edict, dated the 14th of April, that not only agreeably to the regulation of the 18th of May, 1793 the number of printing offices in the country-parts ſhould not be increaſed, but that in Prague too, it ſhould be ſo limited, that when two offices were relinquiſhed, only one ſhould be allowed to be eſtabliſhed in their ſtead, until the number of them ſhall be ſo far reduced, that every printer may be able to ſupport himſelf, and pay taxes to Government by profits ariſing from the printing of ſuch books as are publiſhed by the permiſſion of the licenſers.

Dr. Hildebrand, Profeſſor of Medicine at Lemberg, has been trying ſugar of lead as a remedy in pulmonic conſumption. Of 17 patients, whom he had under his care, he ſtates, that four were completely cured: but in the others, the ſuppuration of the lungs had already proceeded too far, as appeared on opening them after their death. The ſugar of lead is given, according to circumſtances, mixed with opium.

LIST OF NEW PUBLICATIONS IN DECEMBER.

ANTIQUITIES.

Munumenta Antiqua; or, Obſervations on Ancient Caſtles, on the Progreſs of Architecture in Great Britain, and on the correſponding Changes in Manners, Laws, and Cuſtoms. By Edward King, Eſq. vol. 2, 3l. 13s. 6d. Nicol.

ASTRONOMY.

A Treatiſe on Aſtronomy, in which the Elements of the Science are deduced in a natural order, demonſtrated on mathematical Principles, and explained by an application to the various Phenomena. By Olinthus Gregory, large volume, 8vo. with Plates, 13s. Kearſley.

COMMERCE.

Obſervations on the Reports of the Directors of the Eaſt India Company reſpecting the Trade between India and Europe. To which is added, An Appendix, containing the Papers referred to in the Work. By Thomas Henchman, Eſq. 10. 6d. Wright.

The

DRAMA.

The Thespian Dictionary; or, Dramatic Biography of the Eighteenth Century, containing Sketches of the Lives, Productions, &c. of all the principal Managers, Dramatists, Composers, Commentators, and Actors, in the United Kingdom, interspersed with Anecdotes, &c. Embellished with Portraits, 9s. 6d. boards. Hurst.

Alfonso, King of Castile, a Tragedy, by M. G. Lewis, Esq. 2s. 6d. Bell.

EDUCATION.

Hints for a Plan of General National Education, and a *Legislative* Revision of the present System, as it respects every Class of Children. By David Morrice, Author of the Art of Teaching, &c. 1s. Rivingtons.

A Defence of Public Education, in Answer to a Charge in a Discourse preached at St. Paul's by the Bishop of Meath, on the Anniversary Meeting of the Charity Children. By William Vincent, D. D. 1s. 6d. Cadell and Davies.

The Dog of Knowledge; or, Memoirs of Bob, the Little Terrier. By the Author of Dick, the Little Poney, 2s. 6d. Harris.

Select Amusements in Philosophy and Mathematics, proper for exercising the Minds of Youth. Translated from the French of M. L. Despiau, large volume, 12mo. 5s. 6d. boards. Kearsley.

The Way to Speak Well made Easy for Youth; with a short Dictionary; and an English, French, Italian, and German Vocabulary. *Book the First*, consisting of Words of one Syllable only, 3s. Cadell and Davies.

HISTORY.

A Universal History, Ancient and Modern, comprehending a General View of the Transactions of every Nation, Kingdom, and Empire on the Globe, from the earliest Accounts of Time to the General Peace in 1801. By William Mavor, L. L. D. Vicar of Hurley, &c. Volume the *First*, (A Volume to be published on the First Day of every Month, till the Nine Volumes of the Ancient Part, and Sixteen Volumes of the Modern Part, in the whole Twenty-five Volumes, are completed) printed in the same Size and Type as the Collection of Voyages and Travels edited by Dr. Mavor, 3s. 6d. sewed. Or, on fine Paper, corresponding in Size with the new Editions of the British Poets and Classics now in the Press, 5s. Phillips.

LAW.

The New Law List. To which are added, The London Agents to the Country Attornies, Tables of Sheriffs and Agents, List of Bankers, Mail Coaches, Newspapers, Army and Navy Agents, Law and Public Offices, Circuits of the Judges, &c. 3s. 6d. Clarke and Sons.

An Analysis of the Law on the Abandonment of Ships and Freight, as it relates to the Effects of the late Russian Embargo on British Ships, and to the subsequent Liberation of the Ships from the Embargo; wherein the Subject is also discussed on Principles of Policy and Equity. By Ailtroppe Stovin, 1s. 6d. Butterworth.

Compendium of the Law of Evidence. By Thomas Peake, Barrister, 8vo. 6s bds. Brooke and Rider.

Elements of Conveyancing. With An Essay on the Rise, Progress, and Present State of that Science; and Remarks on the Study and Practice, Part I. and II. 8vo. 10s. boards. Clarke and Sons.

Addenda to the Fourth Edition of the Bankrupt Laws, containing the Determinations to the end of the Year 1800. By Wm. Cooke, of Lincoln's-inn, Esq. 8vo. 5s. bds. Brooke and Rider.

Supplement to Viner's Abridgement of the Determinations in the Courts of Law and Equity. 8vo. 13s. Brooke and Rider.

MISCELLANIES.

The January Fashions of London and Paris, containing thirteen beautifully coloured Figures of Ladies in the actually prevailing and most favourite Dresses of the Month, intended for the Use of Milliners, &c. and of Ladies of Quality, and of private Families residing in the Country. To be continued Monthly, 1s. 6d. Phillips.

Recreations in Mathematics and Natural Philosophy, first composed by M. Ozanum, lately greatly enlarged by M. Montucla, and now translated into English, and improved with many Additions and Observations, by Charles Hutton, L.L.D. Part 1, (to be continued Monthly till completed, in 16 Parts) 4s. Kearsley.

The Song Smith; or, Rigmarole Repository: Written by C. Dibdin, jun. containing many Songs never before published, 2s. Symonds.

The Detector of Quackery; or, Analyzer of Medical, Philosophical, Political, Dramatic, and Literary Imposture. By John Corry, 12mo. 4s. bds. Ridgway.

Dividends of immense Value! And, My Claim on others; evidenced by indisputable Authority. By Miss Robertson, of Blackheath. Badcock.

Miss Sharpe's Letter to the Congregation-meeting at White-row, Spitalfields, 6d. Badcock.

An Essay; or, Practical Inquiry concerning the Hanging and Fastening of Gates and Wickets.

Wickets. By Thomas N. Parker, Esq. 2s. Lackington, Allen, and Co.

A New Oriental Register, and East India Directory for 1802. By John Mathieson and Alexander Way Mason, of the Secretary's Office, East India House, 4s. sewed. Blacks and Parry.

Specimens of Literary Resemblance in the Works of Pope, Gray, and other celebrated Writers, with Critical Observations. By Samuel

Samuel Cerdmore, D.D. 4s. fewed. Wilkie.

The Works of James Harris, Esq. With an Account of his Life and Character. By his Son, the Earl of Malmsbury, 2 vols large 4to. with Portrait, and other Engravings, 3l. 13s. 6d. boards. Wingrave.

Rural Sports, by W. B. Daniel. Embellished with Engraving, vol. 1, 2l. 12s. 6d White.

The Force of Contrast; or, Quotations accompanied with Remarks, submitted to the Consideration of all those who have interested themselves in the Blagdon Controversy, 6d. Cadell and Davies.

A correct and authentic Representation of all the British Provincial Copper Coins and Tokens that have been issued subsequent to the Year 1787, on fifty-five Copper-plates Quarto; to which is annexed a very copious Index, wherein is given the Names of the Die-sinkers, the Manufacturers, the Proprietors, the Quantity manufactured, and other Information, whereby any Person may distinguish the Difference between the genuine Coins and Tokens, and what were manufactured for Sale, or are spurious; great Care having been taken to insert all the genuine Pieces that were made either as Coins or Tokens, and no other, 2l. 2s. Seely.

Imposture Exposed, in a few brief Remarks on the Irreligiousness, Profaneness, Indelicacy, Virulence, and Vulgarity, of certain Persons who style themselves Anti-jacobin Reviewers. By Josiah Hard, Esq. 6d. Hurst.

Materials for Thinking, No. 1, price 1s. (To be continued Monthly). By William Burdon, A. M. Hurst.

This Publication is intended to form a Series of Essays on the most important Subjects connected with the Happiness and the Interests of Civil Society. As the Miseries of Mankind arise principally from those Evils which are imbibed by early Prejudice, the Errors of Habit, of Education, and of superficial Thinking, these Strictures are composed with a View of combating such secret Enemies, of correcting their baneful Tendency, and of contributing to the Comfort of Social Life and the Welfare of Man.

MEDICAL.

Cases of Phthisis Pulmonalis successfully treated upon the Tonic Plan; with Observations. By Charles Pears, F M.L. &c. 2s. 6d. Murray and Highley.

Medical and Physical Memoirs, containing, among other Subjects, a particular Enquiry into the Nature of the pestilential Epidemics of the United States. By Charles Caldwell, M. D. 8vo 8s. boards. Wynne and Scholey.

Experiments and Observations on the Mineral Waters of Hampstead and Kilburn. By John Bliss, Surgeon, 2s. Phillips.

New Inventions and Directions for Ruptured Persons. By W. H. T. Esq. With a Recommendatory Letter from William Blair, A. M. Surgeon, 2d. Edition, with Additions, 2s. Hurst.

Observations on the Opinion of Dr Langslow, that Extravasation is the general Cause of Apoplexy. By William Crowfoot. Robinsons.

Medicinæ Praxeos Compendium Symptomata, Causas, Diagnosin, Prognosin, et Medendi Rationem exhibens. Auctore E. G. Clarke, M. D. 5s. 6d Ogle.

Account of the Plan for the Improvement and Extension of the Infirmary at Newcastle. Walker, Newcastle.

The Modern Practice of Physic; which points out the improved Method of treating the Diseases of all Climates; and shews how every Species of Contagion is to be avoided and suppressed. By Robert Thomas, M. D. 2 vols. 8vo. 17s. boards. Murray and Highley.

Historical Surgery; or, The Progress of the Science of Medicine on Inflammation, Mortification, and Gun-shot Wounds. By John Hunt, 4to. 1l. 1s bds. Rivingtons.

Practical Observations on the Gonorrhoea Virulenta, and a new Mode of treating that Disease. By Robert Barker, 2s. 6d. Rivingtons.

A Treatise on the New Discovered Dropsy, in the Membranes of the Brain, and Watery Head of Children, proving that it may be cured. To which are added, Observations on Errors in Nursing, &c. By William Rowley, M. D. 2s. Murray and Highley.

The Anatomist's Vade Mecum, the Fourth Edition, revised and enlarged. By Robert Hooper, M. D. 12mo. 7s. bds. Murray and Highley.

NOVELS.

Justina. By Mrs. Ventum, Author of Selina, &c. 4 vols. 18s. Badcock.

Introspection; or, a Peep at Real Characters. By the Widow of the late Rev. J. Mathews, Rector of Newick, 4 vols. 15s. fewed. Carpenters.

Zelomer, a Romance, translated from the French of Morel De Vinde, by Thomas Noble, 12mo. 4s. fewed. Ginger.

The Scottish Legend; or, The Isle of St. Clothair, A Romance. By T. J. Horsley Curteis, 4 vols. 12mo. 18s. fewed. Lane.

Helen of Glenross, 4 vols. 12mo. 16s. bds. Robinsons.

St. Margaret's Cave; or, The Nuns' Story, an Ancient Legend. By Eliz. Helme, 4 vols. 12mo. 20s. fewed. Earl and Hemet.

The Peasant of Ardenne Forest. By Mrs. Parsons, 4 vols. 12mo. 20s. fewed. Hurst.

POETRY.

The Methodist, a Poem, 1s. Button & Son.

Peace, a Poem. By Thomas Dermody, 4to. 1s. 6d. Hatchard.

A Parnassian Shop opened in the Pindaric Style. By Peter Quince, Esq. 12mo. 5s. Wynne and Scholey.

The School for Satire; or, A Collection of Modern Satirical Poems, written during the present Reign, 8vo. 10s. 6d. boards. Jacques and Co.

Bread;

Bread; or, The Poor, with Notes and Illustrations. By Mr. Pratt, 4to. 7s. Longman and Rees.

Lines on the Death of Sir Ralph Abercromby. By the Author of the Conspiracy of Gowrie, 4to. 1s. Bell.

La Bagatella; or, Delineations of Home Scenery, a Descriptive Poem; with Notes Critical and Historical. By William Fox, jun. 8vo. 7s. 6d. boards. Conder.

POLITICAL.

The Speech of the Right Hon. William Windham, delivered in Parliament November 4, 1801, on the Report of an Address approving of the Preliminaries of Peace. Cobbet and Morgan.

Three Words to Mr. Pitt on the War and on the Peace, 2s. 6d. Ridgway.

Profusion of Paper-money, not Deficiency in Harvests, Taxation, nor Speculation, the principal Cause of the Sufferings of the People; with Observations on the Report of the Committee of Parliament to inquire into the High Price of Provisions, &c. By a Banker, 1s. Jordan.

Letters from the Dead; or, Epistles from the Statesmen of former Days to those of the present Hour, 1s. Stockdale.

THEOLOGY.

Sermons, by the Rev. George Patrick, L L B. To which are prefixed, Memoirs of his Life; with a Portrait, 8vo. 9s. boards. Williams.

An Essay on the Divine Authority of the New Testament. By David Bogue, 3s. 6d. boards. Seeley.

Sermons on Evangelical and Practical Subjects, designed chiefly for the Use of Families. By Samuel Lowel, 8vo. 7. 6d. boards. Ogle.

Religion without Cant; or, A Preservative against Lukewarmness and Intolerance, Fanaticism, Superstition, and Impiety. By Robert Fellowes, A. M. 8vo. 9s. boards. White.

Introduction to the New Testament. By John David Michaelis; translated from the fourth Edition of the German, and considerably augmented with Notes, and a Dissertation on the Origin and Composition of the three first Gospels. By Herbert Marsh, B.D. The second Part, which completes the Work, 8vo. 3 vols. 1l 1s. boards. Rivingtons.

A Thanksgiving for Plenty, and a Warning against Avarice; a Sermon preached at Lichfield, Sept. 20, 1801. By Robert Nares, Archdeacon of Stafford, &c. 1s. Rivingtons.

Nonconformist's Memorial, vol. 1. with ten Portraits, 8vo. 9s 6d. boards. Button and Son.

An Essay on the Sign of the Prophet Jonah, intended to remove the Deistical Objection concerning the Time of our Saviour's Burial. By attempting to prove, that the Prediction relates to the Duration of his Ministry upon Earth. By Isaac James; with a Letter on Rev. xxii. 6-21, intended to shew, that it was not Jesus Christ who forbade John to worship him 1s. 6d. Button and Son.

VOYAGES.

A Voyage round the World in the Years 1790, 91, and 92, by Etienne Marchand; with an Historical Introduction, and illustrated by Charts, &c. Translated from the French by C. P. Claret Fleurieu, 2 vols. 4to. with an Atlas separate, 3l. 13s 6d. boards. Longman and Rees.

Voyages from Montreal, on the River St. Lawrence, through the Continent of North America, to the Frozen and Pacific Oceans, in the Years 1789 and 1793; with an Account of the Rise, Progress, and present State of the Fur-trade in that Country. By Alexander Mackenzie, Esq. with Maps, 4to. 1l. 11s. 6d. boards. Cadell and Davies.

Imported by Earle and Hemet, No. 47, Albemarle-street, Piccadilly.

De l'Art de rendre les Revolutions Utiles, 2 tom.

Revolution de France, par Beaulieu, 2 tom.

Collection d'Ana, 10 tom.

Mémoires de Louis XVI, 6 tom.

Annuaire de l'Instruction Publique pour l'An X.

Bréviaire des Graces pour l'An X.

Histoire du Général Moreau.

Les Trois Ages des Colonies, 3 tom.

C'est cela, ou Questions Parisiennes.

Histoire d'un Chien.

Rouge et Noir.

Costume des Anciens Peuples, 4 tom. 4to.

Costumes civiles actuels de tous les Peuples, 4 tom.

Voyages dans les 89 Départemens.

Romans et Pièces de Théatre, Nouveautés, &c. &c.

New German Books imported by H. Escher, Gerard-street.

Handbuch der Spannichen Sprache, 13s.

Jördens Entimologie, 1 band. 4°. mit gemalten Kupfern, 3l. 3s.

Torkels Geschichte der Musik, 2ter. band. 2l. 8s.

Wildenows Kraüter-Runde, 12s.

Meiners Geschichte von Göttingen, 9s.

Reuss, Mineralogische und Bergmännische Bemerckungen, 18s.

Briefe über Italien, 1ster band. 5s. 6d.

Archenholz, Gustav. Wasa, 2 band. 1l. 1s.

Lichtenberg's auserlesene Schriften, mit Kupfern, 10s.

Kotzebues neue Schauspiele, 7ter band. 10s.

Hedwig, Species Muscorum frondosorum, 4to. with coloured plates, 6l. 6s.

Ocellus Lucanus, 9s.

Ciceronis Orationes, 1 vol. 8vo. vellum-paper, 1l. 10s.

Hermann de emendanda ratione Græcæ Grammaticæ, pars 1, 8vo. 12s.

Vita Hemsterhuisii et Rhunckenii, 5s.

Wittenbach, Vita Rhunckenii, 10s. 6d.

German Books imported by C. Geiſsweiler.

Küttner's Reiſe durch Deutſchland, Dænemark, Schweden, Norwegen, und einen Theil von Italien, in den Jahren 1797, 1798, und 1799, 4 vols 8vo. c. p. 3l. 1801.

Sitten, Gebræuche, und Kleidung der Ruſſen in St. Peterſburg, 1ſt and 2d Nos. 4to. pr. No. 4s. 1801.

Moral in Fabeln und Beyſpielen für die Jugend, 2 vols. cuts, 9s. ſewed.

Vieths Phyſikaliſcher Kinder-Freund, 4 vols. 16s. ſewed.

Schäſſerſpiele, cuts, 9s.

Die doppelte Urſuliner Nonne, 5s.

Geſänge aus Lafontaines Werken, mit Clavierbegleitung, 3s.

Aria aus dem Donauweibgen, 6d.

Der Blauiſche Grund bey Dreſden, mit Hinſicht auf Naturgeſchichte, &c. von Becker, with 25 cuts, 4°. c. l. 3l. 3s.

Rerum Auſtriacarum Scriptores qui lucem publicam hactenus non viderunt, et alia Monumenta Diplomatica nondum edita. ed. A. Rauch, 3 vols. 4to. 2l. 5s.

Scriptores Rerum Tranſilvanarum, cura et opera Societatis Philohiſtorum Tranſilv. 2 vols. 4to. 1l. 5s. Cibinii, 1800.

Titi Livii Operum Omnium Volumen III. ed. Doering, 9s. ſewed, 1801.

Ariſtophanis Nubes cum Scholiis ed. Erneſtius Hermannus, 9s. ſewed.

Theocrits Idyllia, ex rec. Valkenaerii, 3s.

New French Books juſt imported by J. Deboffe, Bookſeller, Gerard ſtreet, Soho.

Annuaire de la Republique Françaiſe, par le Bureau des Longitudes, pour l'An IX. Par. An VIII. in 18mo. 1s. 3s.

Carnot de la Corrélation des Figures de Geométrie. Par. 1801, 8vo. fig. br. 7s.

Clairault, Elemens d'Algebre 6th. Edition, par 1801, 2 vols. 8vo. fig. br. 14s.

Dictionnaire de la Fable par Noel. Par. 1801, 2 vol. gr. 8vo. br. 18s.

Elemens de Legiſlation Naturelle, à l'Uſage de l'Ecole centrale du Panthéon, par Perrault. Par. 1801, 8vo. br. 7s. 6d.

Eſſai de Statiſque, par Mourque. Par. An IX. 8vo. br. 4s.

Eſſais ſur la Ligne droite et les Courbes du ſecond Degré, par François. Par. 1801, 8vo. fig. br. 4s.

Fantin Deſodourds, Hiſtoire Philoſophique de la Revolution de France depuis la première Aſſemblée des Notables juſqu'à la Paix de 1801. Par. 1801, 9 vols. 8vo. br. 2l. 14s.

Gallitzin, Recueil de Noms, &c. appropriés en Mineralogie, ſuivi d'un Tableau Mithologique, Brunſwick, 1801, 4to. br. 12s.

Genlis, Nouvelles Heures, à l'Uſage des Enfans. Par 1801, in 18mo. br. 2s. 6d.

Haüy, Traité de Mineralogie, publié par le Conſeil des Mines. Par. 1801, 4 vols. 8vo. avec Atlas, 2l. 2s.

Hiſtoire de la Revolution de France de 1789, par Toulongeon, avec Cartes et Plans. Par. 1801, 2 vols. 8vo. br. 15s.

Ditto——— 2 vols. 8vo. velium, 18s.

Ditto——— 1 vol. 4to. ———, 18s.

Ditto——— 1 vol. 4to. ———, 1l. 16s.

L'Homme ſingulier, ou Emille dans le Monde, par Aug. Lafontaine. Par. 1801, 2 vols. in 12mo. br. 6s.

Inſtitutions de Médicine, ou Expoſé Théorique et Pratique de cette Science, par Petit Radel. Par. An IX 2 vols. 8vo. br. 15s.

Journal de Médicine, Chirurgie, Pharmacie, &c. par Corviſart, Leroux, &c. Par. An IX. in 12mo. br. les 12 prem. cah. 1l. 1s.

Lacroix, Conſtitution des Principaux Etats de l'Europe et des Etats Unis de l'Amerique, tom. 6e. Par. 1801, 8vo. br. 6s.

Lexicologie Latine et Françoiſe, par Butet, Par 1801, 2 vols 8vo. br. avec la Lexicographie, 10s. 6d.

Lulus et Cydippe, ou les Voiſins dans l'Arcadie, par An IX. 2 vols. in 18mo. br. 4s.

NEW PATENTS LATELY ENROLLED.

MR. WAKEFIELD'S *for an* IMPROVEMENT *in the* REFINING *of* SUGAR.

ON the ſecond of June 1801, Mr. Wakefield of Northwich, in Cheſhire, recorded the ſpecification of a Patent which he has obtained for the application of mechanical preſſure to the refining of ſugar.

To be ſubjected to this preſſure, the ſugar, ſtill ſoft and full of impurities, is put into any veſſel or covering which is porous and will yield to compreſſion.

The veſſel or covering may be of any capacity; and you may, at pleaſure, ſubject a ſmaller or a greater quantity of ſugar to the proceſs at once.

The ſugar, in the proper veſſel or cover, is then to be ſubjected to a weight which acts by rollers, a ſcrew or a wedge, "with the help of a ſteam engine," the action of a mill, or any other means of applying great force.

The ſugar being, though ſoft, in great part cryſtallized; only the impurities, and that part of the ſugar which is enveloped in the impurities, remain in a moiſt and ſomewhat gelatinous ſolution: hence the cryſtals of the ſugar will endure the preſſure; while the impurities, with ſome uncryſtallized ſaccharine matter, will paſs out by the holes or pores of the cover or veſſel in which the maſs is incloſed.

The ſugar thus once preſſed may be

again boiled, and farther refined by the accuſtomed chemical methods. The preſſure may after that be repeated. And the chemical and mechanical proceſſes may be thus alternately employed till the ſugar be refined to the deſired purity.

The impure ſugar or melaſſes extruded by the preſſure, may be either ſeparately uſed in diſtillation, or may be added to the more impure ſolutions of ſaccharine matter which are yet in an earlier ſtage of chemical refinement.

This improvement, the reader will obſerve, is the ſame with the preſſure applied in making cheeſe. Has it not been adopted in the manufacture of ſalt?

It ſeems to us an improvement of no ſmall value in the refining of ſugar; and ſo much the more valuable for its extreme ſimplicity.

MR. BOWDEN'S PATENT *for a* MACHINE *for beating* COTTON.

MR. ANTHONY BOWDEN, of Mellor, in the pariſh of Gloſſop, Derbyſhire, recorded on the firſt of July 1801, the ſpecification in a Letter Patent which he has obtained to ſecure to him for the uſual time the excluſive benefit of a machine that he has contrived to abbreviate the labour of beating cotton.

This machine has at the middle of its frame a flake or bed of cordage, on which the cotton which is to be beaten and cleaned, muſt be depoſited. That flake or bed is during the operation kept in continual movement, by the turning of certain rollers upon which it immediately reſts.

Over the cotton diſpoſed upon the flake, riſe arms from acroſs frame at the bottom. Theſe arms work in moveable iron ſlides. Rails fixed to the arms give the requiſite motions, and are themſelves moved by cranks. At the tops of the arms are fixed wooden rollers. Theſe rollers communicate their motion to axles in iron frames. The axles have each a ſocket fixed to it. In thoſe ſockets are by means of hoops and ſcrews placed beating-ſticks, by the action of which the cotton on the flake is beaten and cleaned. Leathern-ſtraps, ſprings, and ſlides regulate the movements of the rods.

An axle with ten cranks, derives its own motion from the impulſe given to the pulley at one end of it; and by its revolutions produces all the other movements of the machine.

The merit of this invention, conſiſts preciſely in its giving a new diſtribution of mechanical power, fitted to perform an operation in the preparing of cotton for manufacture, which has been hitherto done by unabbreviated human labour. Its principle is the very ſame on which the other improved machinery of the cotton-works is conſtructed.

In its uſe *two-thirds of the number* of labourers, and theſe the weakeſt inſtead of the ſtrongeſt,—children inſtead of women in the full ſtrength,—will execute the ſame quantity of work, which the *whole* could do in the former methods of beating and cleaning cotton.

REVIEW OF NEW MUSICAL PUBLICATIONS.

Volume I. of Clementi's Selection of Practical Harmony for the Organ or Piano forte, containing Voluntaries, Fugues, Canons and other Ingenious Pieces by the moſt eminent Compoſers. To which is prefixed an Epitome of Counterpoint by the Editor. 1l. 1s. Clementi and Co.

MR. CLEMENTI who, as we underſtand, has had the plan of the preſent work a conſiderable time in contemplation, ſtrongly claims the thanks of practitioners of keyed-inſtruments in general, but more eſpecially thoſe of the organ, for the clear and maſterly ſtyle in which he has written and edited the firſt volume of ſo requiſite and uſeful a publication.

With his *Epitome of Counterpoint* we have been particularly gratified. The precepts are ſhort and pertinent, and the examples ſelected with great judgment. In ſix pages only is comprized all the neceſſary intelligence reſpecting *ſimple*, *florid* and *double counterpoint*, exemplified in *Canto Fermo*, and exhibited in two, three and four parts. From his explication of the five different kinds of *double counterpoint*, the ſtudent in harmony may derive much valuable information; and the body of *contrapuntic* compoſition by which it is ſucceeded cannot fail to elucidate his doctrine, and confirm his rules to the ſatisfaction of the moſt ordinary mind.

The exemplars (which are compleat movements) occupy no leſs than one hundred and thirty-nine pages of the volume, are ſelected from the great productions of Handel, Agoſtini, Eberlin, Kirnberger,

Martini, Mozart, the Bachs, Haydn and several other classical composers, and at once manifest a highly cultivated taste, great practical experience, and an extensive acquaintance with the works of the great German musicians.

The Harmony of Jerusalem, being a Collection of of One Hundred and Six Psalms and Hymns in Score. Harmonized by John Alcock, Doctor in Music. 8s. *Clementi and Co.*

The melodies of these Psalms and Hymns are by Alcock, Brown, Calah, Flackton, Handel, Harrington, Heighington, Hewitt, Jackson, Madan, Marsh, Mather, Riley, Selby, Simmis, and other masters of respectability; and the whole are selected by Francis Roome, bookseller in Derby. The work occupies one hundred and twenty pages, and the lovers of church music will find in them many excellent specimens of what is called "the good old psalmody." Every piece is harmonized for favourites (*soprano, alto, tenor* and *bass*) which will give an additional value to the volumes with chapel and country choristers.

Fair Aurora, prithee stay," and "For Thee I Live, my Dearest." Two favourite Duets in the Opera of Artaxerxes, with all the Variations, Graces and Embellishments introduced by Mrs. Billington and Mrs. Mountain, at the Theatre Royal, Drury Lane. With an Accompaniment for the Piano-forte, newly arranged from the Original Score by Dr. Busby. 2s. *Longman.*

To those who are ambitious to sing with real taste and elegance, these duets will prove a valuable acquisition. Example, as well in music as in other polite arts, frequently accomplishes more than precept, and a more direct mode of instruction was never adopted than that of presenting to the *eye* those refined and transient evolutions of sounds with which every one is delighted, but which only the most acute and cultivated can retain.

An Anthem of Thanksgiving for Peace. Composed by Thomas Wright. 2s. *Goulding, Phipps and D'Almaine.*

This occasional Anthem comprizes four choruses, a semi-chorus, and three verse-movements. Of the composition in general we cannot speak in high terms. Mr. Wright, in aiming at a familiar simplicity, has degenerated into meanness. The *parts* are not always adjusted in a way that bespeaks much knowledge in *combination*; nor does the melody bear any marks of a strong or original fancy. In a word, the *motivo* is insipid, and the harmony inartificial.

"*Survey, my Laura, yonder Rose.*" *A Canzonet, with an Accompaniment for the Piano-forte. Composed and dedicated to Miss Cruden, by John Ross, of Aberdeen.* 1s. *Preston.*

This canzonet is characterized by a delicacy of expression, and easy gentility of manner. The melody throughout flows with a smoothness which indicates a familiar acquaintance with the true style of ballad composition, and the accompaniment is greatly calculated to heighten and improve the general effect.

The favourite Air of the Blue Bell of Scotland, with Variations for the Harp or Piano-forte, by T. Robinson, of Dublin. 1s. 6d. *Goulding, Phipps and D'Almaine.*

We have not for a long time seen any *variations* which adhere more strictly to the *thema* than those which Mr. Robinson has given to this popular little ballad. They are eight in number, and form a gradual climax of execution. The passages are for the chief part well disposed for the hand, and admirably calculated to improve the juvenile practitioner.

Farewell to Glenowen. A Glee for Three Voices, and the Piano-forte. Composed by J. Pratt. 2s. 6d. *Preston.*

This glee, the words of which are from the pen of the late Mrs. Robinson, exhibits striking traits of fancy and improveable talent. The melody is in many instances both novel and pleasing; and the *parts* are put together in a style which, if it does not argue mature judgment or profound science, evinces a respectable degree of harmonical knowledge, and proves that Mr. Pratt (who we understand is organist of King's College, and St. Mary's Church, Cambridge) may, with a little further study and experience, become a composer of deserved estimation.

Overture to Harlequin Amulet. Composed and adapted for the Piano-forte, by Thomas Shaw. 2s. *Caulfield.*

We have perused this overture with considerable pleasure. The construction of the first or introductory movements evinces considerable science, and the second is animated and original. The unexpected assumption of the *majore* towards the close of the second movement is striking in its effect, and the concluding *rondo* comprizes an attractive subject, relieved by well-fancied and judicious digressions. We must however beg to remind the ingenious author, that in passing from the twelfth to the thirteenth bar, an evolution between the notes of the upper and under parts

parts has escaped him, which is not sanctioned by the strict *laws* of harmonic progression.

"Sweetly Blooms the Opening Rose." A favourite Song, with an Accompaniment for the Piano-forte. Composed by Schultz. 1s. Rolfe.

The merit of this little ballad consists in a flowing sweetness of melody. The passages rise naturally out of each other; and if the effect of the whole is not that of novelty, it at least delights the ear, and exhibits much taste as well as art, in *disposition.*

Quartetto for Two Violins, a Tenor and Bass. Composed by Joseph Diettenhofer. 3s. Riley.

This Quartetto contains four movements:—The first movement is in common-time of four crotchets, *allegro con spirito*, and is bold, well contrasted and scientific: the second is in three crotchets, *adagio*, and is conceived in a finished style: the third is in six quavers, *allegro molto*, and furnishes by the playfulness of its subject an excellent introduction to the regular and well-wrought fugue with which the composition concludes.

Dr. Arnold, we understand, is about to publish a new, revised and corrected edition of the Works of Handel, dedicated to his Majesty. The mode of publication will not be precisely the same with that adopted in his former edition of this great composer. One volume in boards, containing a whole oratorio, or an equal proportion of the other works, will be issued in the first week of every month, from the time of commencement (February next) until the completion of the undertaking.

The lovers of familiar and tasteful vocal music will hear with pleasure, that Mr. Ross, of Aberdeen, has in the press a New Collection of Songs (fifteen in number) chiefly in the Scottish Style, with Accompaniments for the Piano-forte, Violin, or German flute. The poetry is by Burns and Rannie. The work is to be dedicated to Dr. Busby.

For the new musical piece of Haydn, intitled the Seasons, which is now publishing in Germany with the English and German text, Mr. Escher, German bookseller, in Gerard-street, Soho, takes subscriptions at 18s. a copy adapted to the harpsichord, and at 2l. 2s. a copy in score.

ACCOUNT OF DISEASES IN LONDON, *from Nov 20, to Dec. 20.*

Admitted under the Care of the Physicians of the Finsbury Dispensary.

RHEUMATISMUS	23
Catarrhus	53
Dyspnœa	17
Asthenia	12
Hæmoptysis	3
Dysenteria	5
Diarrhœa	7
Typhus	9
Vermes	15
Amenorrhœa	19
Menorrhagia	10
Epilepsia	4
Ascites & Anasarca	13
Febris intermittens	2
Hysteria	17
Angina	9
Cynanche Trachealis	1
Scabies	13
Scarlatina	1
Paralysis	3
Erysipelas	7
Cynanche	16

Previous to the publication of the last report for November, diarrhœas and dysenterias were already beginning to decline, as well in virulence as in extent: a very few cases of these diseases have occurred for the last month or six weeks. The typhoid fever has only in three instances during that time fallen under the observation of the reporter; and in those instances the symptoms were mild, and in a short time yielded to a very simple mode of treatment.

The present season of the year is more especially characterised by the epidemic prevalence of rheumatism and catarrh: complaints which, although seldom attended with immediate danger, are always inconvenient and distressing, especially where they induce the necessity of confinement, and take away the power of labour from those whose livelihood depends upon active occupation, and a constant, or at least occasional, exposure to the unwholesome influence of a cold and damp atmosphere.

Rheumatism is more widely extended, and much aggravated in the degree and nature of its symptoms, amongst the poorer classes of the community, in consequence of their being so frequently unable to procure sufficient external protection or internal support against the severity and trying changes of the weather. From their extreme

treme indigence, many of them cannot even afford a small fire; and those who can, seldom inhabit apartments that are so accommodated and contrived as to exclude the constant intrusion of the wintry blast, or to preclude the danger of being occasionally deluged by the showers of a stormy season. These shivering wretches may often be seen sitting with their knees almost in contact with the grate, whilst other parts of their body are attacked by a stream of cold or damp air from an aperture in some shattered window in the room. After being informed of such circumstances as these, the reader will not be surprised, that, at this time of the year, rheumatism is so *popular* a disorder. It is worthy of remark, that, amongst the emaciated and half-famished poor of the metropolis, even in cases of what would vulgarly be denominated acute rheumatism, such stimulating corroborants as *bark* and *steel* have been successful, after the ineffectual administration of other remedies. But this mode of treatment would seldom be judiciously applied to the rheumatic affections of the luxurious and plethoric. In such cases, gentle diaphoretics, such as guaiacum, combinations of opium and ipecacuanha, or of laudanum with antimonial wine; fomentations, frictions, or blisters applied to the parts more especially affected, and the use, for a time, of those mild and gentle aperients that may counteract the tendency to costiveness, which confinement, and a long continuance in the recumbent posture, so generally induce, may be considered as constituting the most essential and material part of medical practice in this disease.

In addition, however, to this, it may be proper to remark, that, not only as one of the most effectual preservatives against the attack, but also as one of the most likely mean after the attack, of deducting from the danger, or abridging the continuance, of the disease, a *complete armour* of flannel, or other warm cloathing, from head to foot, ought to be recommended, during the winter months, to those who are constitutionally inclined, or from their way of life are more than commonly exposed, to rheumatic or catarrhal affections.

In rheumatism, bleeding has been very generally had recourse to by medical practitioners; but not a single instance has ever fallen under the eye of the reporter in which copious venesection did not do evident injury; and, in many instances, he has been a witness to its almost immediately fatal operation. Bleeding is apt to convert what is called acute rheumatism into chronic, a state of the disease that is more tedious and more difficult of cure, and, when cured, seldom fails to leave behind it a loss of strength, which never, in future life, can be completely restored.

Bleeding may, in these cases, induce a temporary alleviation of violent pain, but it is only by inducing that universal debility of the powers of the system, which deducts, in a proportionate degree, from the particular power of sensation.

Local inflammation, so far from being, as is generally supposed, an argument for it, constitutes, in a majority of instances, one of the most urgent objections against the application of the lancet. Local inflammation implies a partial accumulation of that excitement which ought to be equally distributed over the whole frame. The frame in general, therefore, must be, in such cases, impoverished, and of course will be less able to bear any artificial or extraordinary evacuation.

In a report from the Finsbury Dispensary, which was published about fifteen months ago, an instance of habitual melancholy was mentioned as remarkable, in consequence of its having immediately succeeded, and of its having of course apparently been occasioned by, the sudden deprivation of sight.

At the present, there is a case under the care of the reporter of a different nature, in which affliction of mind, arising from a congregation of unfortunate circumstances, produced, at first, sensations of giddiness and dimness, and, in no long time afterwards, an almost entire loss of sight, that has now continued for a considerable period. As the moral cause of the disease still operates, it is not likely that any essential or permanent advantage should be derived from pharmaceutical assistance; although the tonics and stimulants that have been both locally and generally applied, have decidedly shewn a certain degree of salutary efficacy.

This, although rather a curious case, can by no means appear incredible, or at all difficult of explanation. Mental impressions, we know, act upon the nervous system in general, but especially upon that part of it which is more immediately instrumental to the function of vision. The appearance of the eye is in general a faithful index of the state of the mind. The eye seems to be equally acted upon by all the passions, whether of a pleasurable or a painful nature. It cannot then appear impossible, that, in some instances, especially in those where there happens originally

ginally

ginally to exist any ocular debility or defect, that highly excited, or long protracted, emotion should act so violently as to impair the structure, and altogether to destroy the capacity, of that organ.

The reporter has recently perused a letter from a poor French emigrant, in which he gives an account of his case, and complains of so great a degree of opthalmic weakness, "that he was unable to shed even one tear for all that he had left behind him." This, no doubt, arose from the many tears he had already shed. Still he retained his regrets, but he was no longer able to give a similar demonstration of them. The *heart* is not *so* soon exhausted as the *eye*.

Milton and Homer, the two most divine geniuses, if we except Shakespeare, that ever "lighted upon this orb," may, it is not improbable, have owed the deprivation of their physical, in a great measure, to the extraordinary strength and vivacity of their intellectual vision*. J. R.

Dec. 25.

---

* The lines of Gray alluding to the latter of these bards, although highly poetical, ought not, perhaps, to be considered as inconsistent with the principles of medical philosophy.

The azure throne, the sapphire blaze,
Where angels tremble as they gaze,
He saw; and dazzled, with excessive light,
Clos'd his eyes in endless night.

MONTHLY RETROSPECT OF THE FINE ARTS.

(Communications and the Loan of all new Prints are requested.)

BOYDELL's magnificent edition of Shakespeare is now nearly completed; every number, except the last, is delivered, and the last will be ready in a few months. This great work, which may unquestionably be considered as a national honour, has, in the sum that has been expended on it, taken the lead of any book that ever was published in any country. Indeed a fourth part of the expence would have startled the merchant of any other nation except England. It has, on the whole, been conducted in a manner highly honourable to the proprietors, and, notwithstanding any imitations that may follow, must always preserve its original superiority.

The Right Hon. Thomas Wallace, M. P. Theophilus Clark, pinxt. Charles Turner, sculpt. Published for Cribb. Holborn.

This is a good portrait, well engraved.

Samuel Whitbread, Esq. M.P. Hoppner, pinxt. S W. Reynolds, sculpt. Published October 10, 1801, by Reynolds, 47, Poland-street.

That a portrait painted by Hoppner, and engraved by Reynolds, should be superior to the common class, we may fairly expect, and in this point our expectations are realized. In painting and engraving it is in a superior style.

The Right Hon. George John Spencer, Lord Spencer, &c. J. S. Copley, pinxt. R. Dunkarton, sculpt. Published by J. S. Copley, George-street, Hanover-square. Price 1l. 01.

The Right Hon. Henry Addington, Speaker of the House of Commons. The same Painter, Engraver, Publisher, and Price.

This pair of prints are painted in Mr. Copley's usual style, and derive some consequence from the offices that have been, and are, held by the originals, to whom they in air and manner have a striking resemblance.

Sir R. Abercrombie. Hoppner, pinxt. F. Bartolozzi, sculpt. Published by Jeffries, Clapham-road, Jan. 1, 1802.

It is somewhat to the credit of our country that the portraits of eminent and distinguished characters are morally certain of being received with popular eagerness, and, if tolerably executed, to meet with a rapid sale. Prints of many of our eminent Generals and Admirals have been multiplied two and three times over, and with success.

Sappho. Painted by R. Westall. R. A. Engraved by E. Scriven, Historical Engraver to Her Royal Highness the Princess of Wales, to whom this Print is, with Permission, dedicated. Published Jan. 1, 1802, by Clay and Scriven, No. 18, Ludgate-hill.

St. Cecilia. Engraved by H. R. Cook, late Pupil of R. Thew, from a Picture painted by Westall, dedicated to the Princess of Wales, and published for Clay and Scriven. Price 12s. each. Proof Impressions 21s. each. In Colours 2l. 12s. the Pair.

The two very pleasing pictures from which these prints were engraved, were exhi-

exhibited at the Royal Academy, and must be in the recollection of many of our readers. They are drawn in such a style, and engraved with so much effect, and of such a size as has been long wanted for furniture prints, and we would recommend to the publishers to go on with a series of the same dimensions from subjects of a similar description. Designs of equal merit, engraved by Mr. Scriven in the manner of these two, *must succeed.*

With respect to the St. Cecilia, to tread the ground that has been previously walked over by Sir Joshua Reynolds is very dangerous: his St. Cecilia, being the portrait of so beautiful a group as Mrs. Sheridan and the two Miss Linleys, was a fascinating and popular picture, and the print was very well engraved. The face of Westall's figure is exquisitely fine; it has all the divinity of the character, and is calculated to *raise a seraph to the skies, or draw an angel down.* The rest of the figure is not quite so striking.

The figure of the Sappho, which is the companion-print, is superior. It is graceful, spirited, and original. In these prints of single characters, we have often wished that part of the space which is allotted to the dedication might be appropriated to a few lines from the poet, describing the point of time, or some leading circumstances in the history of the heroine. Sappho, in Pope's imitation of Ovid, describes her own person in the following lines:—

"To me, what Nature has in charms denied,
Is well by Wit's more lasting flames supplied:
Tho' short my stature, yet my name extends
To heaven itself and earth's remotest ends:
Brown as I am—an Ethiopian dame
Inspir'd young Perseus with a generous flame."

Some such inscription under prints of a similar description would surely be interesting to the admirers of English poetry, and pleasing to the admirers of English engravings.

Lady Elizabeth Gray, imploring of Edward IV. the Restitution of her Husband's Lands. R. Westall, pinxt. J. R. Smith, sculpt. Published the 3d of October, 1801, by Smith, King-street, Covent-garden. Price 1l. 1s.

An engraving by W. W. Ryland was some years ago engraved from this story from a drawing by Angelica Kauffmann; but Westall has treated the subject in a different and more historical manner, and Mr. Smith's engraving does ample justice to the original.

Joanna, Mother of the Emperor Charles V. watching over the Dead Body of her Husband. R. Westall, pinxt. W. Ward, sculpt. Published by Ward, Newman-street, October 3, 1801. Price 1l. 1s.

This print is the same size as that which precedes it: from its being published on the same day, and at the same price, it is, we suppose, intended for a companion.

Many of our readers must recollect the very fine picture from which it is engraved, being several years ago exhibited at the Royal Academy: the face was considered as one of the finest that ever was painted; the drapery was rather metallic. In the print the spirit of the face is preserved, and the drapery is soft and picturesque.

Mr. Desenfans has just published Anecdotes of Painters, and Remarks, in a descriptive Catalogue of pictures bought for his late Majesty the King of Poland, which will be exhibited and sold by private contract, by a Committee at No. 3, Berners-street, Oxford street, in February next. These two volumes contain a number of curious and whimsical anecdotes, some of which bear no small resemblance to the legends of the Saints recorded in the Roman Kalendar.

Mr. W. R. Daniel has published the first vol. of his Rural Sports, price 2l. 2s. It is embellished with neat and spirited engravings, from designs by Stubbs, Gilpin, Reinagle, Chilon, Elmer, &c. and to country gentlemen must be an interesting and useful work.

We in a former Retrospect noticed Mr. J. T. Smith's engravings from the paintings, ornaments, and other decorations discovered in the House of Commons. These, with a variety of original particulars relative to the ancient state of Westminster, with a history of painting and Gothic architecture, by John Sidney Hawkins, esq. F. A. S. is now publishing by subscription, and we are happy to find the subscription so liberally encouraged, and to see that it is already honoured with the names of many of the most distinguished characters in the science of which it treats. The paintings and specimens of the engravings are to be seen at Mr. Smith's, No. 20, Great-Portland-street, Oxford-street, where subscriptions for the work are received.

Mr. Bromley's admirable engraving of the Siege of Valenciennes, is now published, and the manner in which it is executed amply compensates for the time the subscribers have waited. It is one of the finest prints that has been engraved in this country. We promised a list of the portraits: those which follow are the principal:—.

Prince Frederick of Orange, Colonel Moncrief, Marquis of Huntley, Hereditary Prince of Orange, Prince Ernest, Field Marshal Freytag, Sir James Murray, Colonel Hulse, Prince Adolphus, Major General Lake, General Count Walmoden, Duke of York, Lieut. Colonel St. Leger, Prince Hohenloe, Major General Abercrombie, Archduke Charles, Ensign Tolkmache, Lieut. Colonel Doyle, Major Congreve, Colonel Leigh, General Count Feraris, Lieut. Thornton, General Count Clairfait, Prince Frederick of Wirtemberg, Major General Wankheim, Prince Saxe Cobourg.

Shakespeare's Seven Ages, engraved by Bromley, from designs by Stothart, are now publishing in colours, and have a very good effect of light and shade.

Messrs. Boydell have published the same series of subjects from designs by Smirke, but our remarks on them must be postponed to next month.

STATE OF PUBLIC AFFAIRS,
In December, 1801.

FRANCE.

SEVERAL Treaties concluded by the Chief Consul have been submitted to the consideration of the Legislative Body, who appear to have approved of the whole. It has chosen a Committee to examine into the schedule of the national code, lately communicated; but this Committee has inauspiciously rejected the first chapter altogether, as ill arranged, incoherent, and dissatisfactory.

The Valais, it is said, will be speedily united to France, in exchange for which Switzerland is to receive the Frikthal. If, as it is reported, England and Russia concur in offering Malta to the Pope, France can start no objection; the Ecclesiastical States are at this hour, and must continue to be, under the absolute controul of this Republic; consequently Malta may even then be regarded as her own.

The pacific Congress have at length assembled at Amiens, and commenced their important discussions: a variety of messages have been interchanged between the British Cabinet and Lord Cornwallis, and several points have been already started, concerning which, as may naturally be supposed, a difference of opinion has been manifested between the Plenipotentiaries. Among these, one of the most important relative to our own country is, an adjustment of the claims of British subjects to property of different kinds in France, so as to produce an equal advantage, or something like an equality, to property possessed by Frenchmen in Great Britain. Between their claimants of the two nations, the war has produced an immense difference in their situation, and a difference which it will be found extremely difficult to reconcile upon any terms. While in Great Britain property of every description has been progressively advancing in value, the very reverse has taken place in France: multitudes of houses, estates, and manufactories, appertaining to English families, have passed into other hands, or been totally destroyed, without compensation of any kind; while immense quantities of assignats, in many cases locked up in private drawers, or suddenly seized by some of the earlier factions of the Revolution, though they were at that time of considerable value, will be now, upon their restoration, found devoid of all value whatever. These British sufferers have certainly a strong claim upon the protection of the British Government, and if not provided for by the Convention at Amiens, should assuredly be recompensed at home.

The first part of the civil code we already intimated has been presented to the Legislature by three Counsellors of State, one of whom, Portalis, made a long and able preliminary speech, in which he developed the plan and division of the civil code; the fundamental principles of the legislation of persons; the rights of parents, and the duties of children; the principles of religion and civil institutions; punishments and penalties; marriages and divorces; children born in marriage and out; and the basis of property in general. The sacredness of marriage is declared, and divorces allowed only under particular and very singular circumstances. The last part of the code, which relates to property, is not yet completed, and is not to be submitted to the Legislature this session. The first plan of civil law, which relates to the promulgation, effects, and application of laws in general, has been laid before the Legislative Body and the Tribunate, and was discussed on the 14th of December.

The Legislative Body has presented an address of congratulation to the Consuls. The answer returned to it by the Chief Consul contains nothing remarkable.

Every class of religion is, moreover, to be equally protected and provided for, out of a general impost for this purpose, in proportion to the number of which the respective churches consist, and of course in proportion to what they may be supposed to have contributed, and the quantity of clerical duty for which they may have occasion.

General Menou, previous to his departure from Egypt, has sent to his brother, the Mayor of Boulai, a letter of the following purport:—"The fortune of war has turned against us; attacked by 40,000 English, Osmanlis, and Sepoys of India, on the land side; by upwards of 300 ships of war on the sea; a prey to hunger, thirst, and diseases, of all kinds; having no longer the necessary medical remedies for the hospitals; unable to reckon more than 1800 men under arms, and almost all having the scurvy; having eaten all the horses, asses, and camels, which were in Alexandria, we were obliged to capitulate, after we had fought with desperation. Eighty pieces of cannon, mortars, or howitzers, by land, and upwards of 2000 other pieces by sea, battered us, and would have reduced us to ashes; the siege, or the blockade, lasted six months. If we have fallen under the greatest force the English ever collected in an expedition by sea, we have at least preserved our honour. I shall not (says General Menou) bring back to France a single soldier that has not been wounded; several have more than fifteen wounds."

The Moniteur, of the 1st of November, contains the following notice:—The public are informed, that the reciprocal correspondence between the French Republic and England is re-established, from the 1st Frimaire (22d Nov.) Letters for England are to be sent off every day, but particularly on Tuesdays and Saturdays, from Paris for Calais, whence they are to be forwarded to Dover. Letters and packets are to be franked from the office of the place whence they are sent to Calais. Those which are not so, are laid aside, conformably to the regulations made."

The French Government have at length published the account transmitted to them by General Menou of the surrender of Alexandria. The Articles of Capitulation are preceded by an account of the proceedings of the Council of War, convoked by the French General previously to the surrender. The Council recommended the Capitulation; and it discovers *twenty-one* reasons for this, as honourable to the army as any testimonials they have received. The fall of Cairo is much blamed, as unexpected and extraordinary, and Gen. Menou himself adds, as unnecessary.

The sittings of the Legislative Body have been dedicated to harangues on the different Treaties of Peace concluded by the Republic. In the sitting of the 29th of October, Fleurieu presented that concluded between France and Russia; and Defermont on the following day presented that between Portugal and France. A speech from both these Members, enlarging on the advantages of those Treaties, was all the proceedings which took place on the occasion. It is well known, that the Negociation for a Peace had commenced prior to the entrance of a Spanish army into Portugal, and it now appears obvious, from this celebrated political *Notice*, that the Court of Spain was prompted to this attack in consequence of the discussion which had actually occurred between the Negociating Powers, and the refusal of the English Cabinet to surrender the Island of Trinidad. Portugal seems to have been regarded, and with too much justice, throughout the whole of the Continent, as a mere British Colony; and Spain was stimulated, in consequence, to make an attack upon Portugal, in order to recover the Island of Trinidad, by means of the provinces she might capture from Portugal, and the indemnification she could hereby offer to England for the restoration of this colony. It is also intimated in the State of the French Republic, which the First Consul has presented to the Legislative Body, that the French Government was not altogether satisfied with the abrupt Peace concluded at Bajadoz, and that it has, in consequence, acceded, as far as relates to itself, to the cession of Trinidad to the English; while it strenuously resisted a similar cession of the Cape of Good Hope, and insisted upon its restoration to Batavia.

Charles Augustus Lequier de la Neuville, Bishop of Arqs, has given in his resignation to the Holy Father, and transmitted a copy of it to the Archbishop of Corinth, with the following letter:—

"I have the honour to address your Excellency a copy of the resignation of my See, which, without delaying a single post,

I transmitted to Cardinal Casoni the moment he communicated to me the brief of his Holiness.

"I did not hesitate a moment to sacrifice myself, when I learnt that this painful sacrifice was necessary to the peace of the country and the triumph of religion. May she rise, not only upon the wreck of all my dearest interests and all my temporal advantages, but upon my very ashes, if I can benefit her by becoming a victim. May my fellow-countrymen return to concord, to the faith, and to true morality. These shall be the sole desire of my life, and I shall die happy if I see them accomplished."

With the same readiness and the same spirit their respective resignations have been sent to the Pope by Louis Rene Edouard, Prince of Rohan and Cardinal Bishop of Strasburgh; the Archbishop of Auch; the Bishop of Levaur; the Bishop of Venice; the Bishop of Rochelle; and the Bishop of Blois.

EAST INDIES.

A letter from Bombay of the 2d of March says, "On Wednesday the brother of Rajah Petumber departed this life, and, shocking to relate, with the corpse, which was burnt on Thursday morning, between eleven and twelve, at Cossinaut Baboo's Gaut, two fine young women, wives of the deceased, were also committed to the flames."

Advices have been received from Madras of two very severe actions having been fought in the Tinavelly country (in the Carnatic) between the Company's forces under Col. M'Cauley, and some native insurgents. In the first attack, which was made with a very inferior force, the Company's troops were repulsed with considerable loss, no fewer than 19 officers having (as it is said) been killed and wounded. In the last attack our troops were successful, and completely routed the insurgents.

Some arrangements of a political nature are said to be making at Surat. The Nabob has already signed a new Treaty, in consequence of which he has been solemnly placed on the Musnud by his Excellency Governor Duncan. The Nabob is firmly attached to our Government in consequence of this Treaty.

The Court of Directors of the East India Company have lately extended the indulgence of private trade to the Commander and Officers of their regular ships; so that the Commander is permitted to invest on board his ship to the extent of 56 tons out and home; the Officers likewise occupy a certain proportion of tonnage free of freight.

The last dispatches received from Sir Home Popham are dated from Cossire Bay, in the Red Sea, where his flag was flying on board his Majesty's ship the Romney, of 50 guns; Sir Home Popham and the squadron under his command were in May last in the harbour of Jeddah, in the Red Sea, where he received many very rich presents from the Chiefs in the neighbourhood.

GREAT BRITAIN.

We are sorry to state, that a disobedient and mutinous spirit has again discovered itself in the British navy, and has, in a greater or less degree, pervaded every part of the Channel fleet, though it has only broken out into overt acts of resistance in that department of it stationed in Bantry Bay, under the command of Admiral Mitchell. The Cabinet has been long apprised of a considerable degree of dissatisfaction, which, from some cause or other (for the whole is yet wrapt up in no small portion of mystery) has been displayed, not only by the mariners, but by many of the inferior officers appointed to this station; and on this account the fleet has been frittered into different divisions, to prevent the accustomed facility of communication. The immediate cause of resistance in the fleet under Admiral Mitchell, was an order from Government for this squadron to sail forthwith to the West Indies. The mutineering petty officers and sailors, however, now that the war has terminated, and left them no hopes of a splendid booty in a quarter towards which they would readily have advanced before, refused to weigh anchor, and insisted upon remaining at home. It is with real satisfaction we are enabled to inform our readers, that by the prudence of the Admiralty and the spirited conduct of Admiral Mitchell himself, and the officers who acted in concert with him, the mutiny is now completely quelled, and the ringleaders have been secured, and are to take their trials immediately.

The following is a Sketch of the principal Business of the Imperial Parliament, since our last Number.

On the motion of Mr. Vansittart, the 25th of November, the estimates relative to different articles of the public service, presented on the 17th of the present month, were ordered to be referred to a Committee of Supply.

 On

On the next day Mr. Bagwell rose to make some observations with regard to the poor of Ireland. Their situation, in many places, he described to be most deplorable. He had often seen them under hedges, and in the nitches of bridges, lying naked and dying for want. It was therefore his intention, after the recess, to propose a bill, which would have for its object to empower the grand juries, or justices of the peace, to erect houses in different parishes for the reception of the sick and indigent.

Mr. Corry stated, that this subject had engaged the most serious consideration of the Lord Lieutenant and the Government of Ireland; already a plan for relieving the sick and indigent in the city of Dublin was matured; and he had no doubt that the same benevolent attention would be extended to every part of the kingdom. Mr. Corry was therefore of opinion, that his Hon. Friend ought not to bring forward any measure of this kind, except in concert with the Irish Government.

The bill respecting the badging of the poor, was read a second time on the 25th of November, and committed for the 27th of the same month.

Mr. Newbolt on the 27th of November moved the order of the day, for the second reading of the above bill.—Read a second time and committed. The bill was ordered to be printed, and to be read a third time on the 30th of November.

On the 2d of December the Poor Badging Bill was read a third time and passed.

Irish army estimates.—The Secretary at War observed, that the House had already voted the principal army estimates for the service of Ireland for three months, ending the 24th of March. He should now proceed to move the remainder, the first of which was a sum of 46,660l. English money, for extra forage for cavalry for three months.

Mr. Corry moved a large sum for the miscellaneous services for Ireland. Mr. Robson objected to voting so large a sum of money out of the public treasury, for a service entirely of a private nature. He did not see why Parliament was to provide for the cleaning, paving, and lighting the streets of Dublin, any more than those of London. Upon which Lord Glenbervie rose to explain the Act of Union, as it referred to the resolution now before the Committee. The seventh article, after particularly enumerating certain charities, agricultural premiums, &c. concluded with saying, "and such other services shall be provided for by the Imperial Parliament." The word "such" had an extensive meaning, and was intended to include many services not specifically mentioned, among which were those now before the Committee.

The Committee then proceeded to vote a large sum of money for various charities in or near Dublin.

The House having resumed, the report was ordered to be received on the morrow, and the Committee appointed to sit again on Wednesday.

The Committee on the Bread Bill being resumed on the 2d of December, Mr. Alderman Curtis moved, that the clause he had submitted to the House, on the previous discussion, relative to the weekly returns of the sale of flour, meal, grain, &c. do stand part of the bill, which was agreed to. Mr. Alderman Curtis then followed up his motion with a variety of clauses, the most interesting of which were the following, viz. A clause for putting the allowance to bakers, on account of the additional salt duties, on its original footing, by repealing the act which granted them four-pence on every sack of flour, and substituting in its stead the former allowance of five-pence on every quarter of wheat.

Mr. Bragge proposed a verbal amendment, which was adopted. Mr. Alderman Curtis then proposed a clause for continuing the act in force from the 1st of January 1802, till the 1st of January 1803; but, after some remarks from Mr. Vansittart, consented to withdraw it, in order to make room for another clause, calculated to accelerate the abrogation of the assize, by enacting, that the said bill may be altered, amended, or repealed, at any time during the present session of Parliament that the House may think proper. This latter clause was agreed to; and the bill, on the motion of Mr. Alderman Curtis, ordered to be printed, and the report to be taken into further consideration on Monday next.

On the 8th of December, the Sheriffs of London presented a petition from the Lord Mayor, Aldermen, and Commons, in Common Council assembled, against the act of the 2d of the present reign, regulating the sale of fish in the London Market; it prayed that the said act of the 2d of the present reign be repealed. On the motion of Alderman Curtis, the petition was ordered to be referred to a Committee.

On the 8th of December the Sheriffs of London

London presented a petition from the corporation of the city, setting forth the great abundance of the late harvest, the present high price of bread, the exemplary patience of the poor under the scarcity of last year, and the cruelty of reducing them to want amidst plenty; and that measures had been taken to ascertain, through the medium of the clergy, the quantity of grain in the country, so as to enable Government to know before-hand when a real scarcity might be apprehended, and to provide, by importation or otherwise, accordingly; but that, from many places, there were no returns, and from others, the returns were defective and fallacious (hear! hear!). The petition then stated, that it would be expedient to have the quantity of grain completely ascertained; and concluded with praying, that something might be done to attain that purpose.—Ordered to be laid on the table.

On the 14th of December Mr. Burton moved that the petitions on the table, praying to continue in force the act for prohibiting the distilleries from working, be taken into consideration.—Ordered.

He then moved, that the act to which they alluded should be read, which was accordingly done, *pro forma*. Mr. Burton said, in conformity to the petition presented by him from his constituents, he now rose for the purpose of moving for leave to bring in a bill for continuing the act just read at the table, in force for some time to be limited. Mr. Burton said that the price of barley particularly had risen from three to four shillings the quarter. Probably gentlemen might argue that the stock of corn, at this time of the year, was not as great as during former years, in consequence of the corn of the country being nearly exhausted before the commencement of the harvest; but this argument was not tenable; the abundance of the produce of the vegetable and animal kingdoms the last year was unexampled, and in fairness the rise was attributable to the cause set forth in the petitions. It might be said, the remedy proposed would not meet the whole of the evil; but if it met it even in part, it was worthy the consideration and the adoption of the House. It was calculated and inserted in the Report of the Committee on the high price of provisions, that the quantity of barley consumed in the distilleries was equal to about 250,000 or 300,000 quarters of wheat. And here he wished to call the attention of the House to the fact, that in Cornwall, Devonshire, and the northern and other parts of England, the working people preferred bread made from barley-meal to that manufactured from wheat, which they considered as more nutritious.

In speaking of the immoderate use of ardent spirits he observed, from the discontinuance of their use, it was well known that the convicts of Botany Bay were much improved in morals, and many women who were barren became fruitful. He then moved for leave to bring in his bill. Mr. Peters seconded the motion. Mr. Dent also spoke against opening the distilleries. He had no doubt before Monday next, that several petitions would be presented similar to those on the table. Mr. William Smith spoke in favour of the distilleries. After some conversation the House divided. For the Minister's motion for the previous question 82. Against it 20. Majority 62.

By this decision Mr. Addington has completely carried his point, and consequently the distillers will be permitted to work grain from the first of January next. By this measure Mr. Addington shews a decided opposition to the system of the late Ministry; and he is assuredly actuated in no small degree by a wish to ameliorate the exhausted state of the treasury; but the grand motive that stimulates him appears to be, his being convinced of the propriety of leaving trade of every kind to take care of itself, from a thorough persuasion of the truth of the doctrine, that there will always be a sufficientcy of competition in the market to prevent the public from becoming injured.

The following are the diplomatic arrangements concluded upon, and which will take place in the course of the spring: —Lord Whitworth, to go as Ambassador to Paris, as soon as the Definitive Treaty is signed; Mr. Liston, Ambassador to the Hague, and Lord Henry Stuart (son of the Marquis of Bute) Secretary of Legation; Mr. Wickham, Minister Plenipotentiary to the Court of Petersburgh; Lord Robert Fitzgerald, Minister Plenipotentiary to the Court of Stockholm. The Embassy to Madrid is not settled.

Mr. Addington, it is said, has explained to several of the Members of the Whig Party, the grounds upon which he hopes for the independent support of those gentlemen. Among other things, he proposes to repeal all those acts which the termination of the war renders no longer necessary, and promises a moderate peace establishment.

ALPHA-

ALPHABETICAL LIST of BANKRUPTCIES and DIVIDENDS announced between the 20th of Nov. and the 20th of Dec. extracted from the London Gazette.

BANKRUPTCIES.

The Solicitors Names are between Parentheses.

AINSLEY, J. Newcastle, woollen draper (Bainbridge Newcastle.

Arthur, G. Shipley mill, Northumberland, miller (Dunn and Tesdale, Threadneedle street.

Avery, J. Queen square, Westminster, organ builder (Mills, Parliament street.

Beresford, S. Yeaton Baschurch, Salop, miller (Pullens, [illegible] street.

Brown, W. and J. Y. Jermyn street, shoemakers (Allen, Frith street.

Bourk, M. formerly of Rosemary lane, slopseller, late of New square, London (Jackson, Temple.

Barker, J. Upper Thames street, grocer (Rigge and Merryfield, Cowry street.

Beresford, R. Alfreton, Derbyshire, hosier (Ross and [illegible], Bolwell court.

Buckland, L. Kensington, haberdasher (Smith and Tilson, St. Paul's Churchyard.

Baily, J. late of the Walthamstow East Indiaman, and late of Bouverie street, Whitefriars, mariner (Delil, Brown's buildings.

Berthune, D. N. Bancroft row, Mile End, sugar grinder (Birkett, Basing lane.

Brookins, G. F. Swan Mead, Bermondsey, leather dresser (Rippon, Bermondsey street.

Bargrave, W. Abingdon, miller, &c. (H. Maddock, Lincoln's inn.

Brown, D. James street, Covent garden, victualler (Sherwood, Hart street, Bloomsbury.

Bulkin, W. Plymouth Dock, linen draper (Williams, Sion College.

Coulthard, J. Bucklersbury, warehouseman (Jackson, Walbrook.

Croydon, E. Stourbridge, baker and maltster (Strong, [illegible] and Strong, Lincoln's inn.

Cooper, W. Pancras lane, warehouseman (Shepherd & Adlington, Gray's inn.

Chamberlin, P. Norwich, linen draper (Bygrave, Norwich.

Coulson, T. Fenchurch street, cheesemonger (Robinson and Crawford, Craven buildings, City Road.

Cameron, D. Aldersgate street, jeweller (Knoblewhite, Gray's inn place.

Chivers, W. Newgate street, upholder (Devies, Lothbury.

Calvert, S. Liverpool, dealer (Price and Williams, Lincoln's inn.

Child, R. Walcot, Somerset, carpenter (Holloway, Chancery lane.

Cheetle, A. E. D. Lancaster, merchant (Sharpe and Eccles, Manchester.

Clayton, J. Sergeberrow, Worcester, mealman (Edmunds, Exchequer Office, Lincoln's inn.

Castro, T. Old Gravel lane, St. George in the East, baker (Jones, Whitefriars Wharf.

Clegg, C. Mill row, parish of Rochdale, Lancaster, woollen manufacturer (Harvey, Gray's inn.

Dyson, W. M. Almondbury, Yorkshire, drysalter and grocer (Battye, Chancery lane.

Davis, J. late of Fulwood's rents, Holborn, victualler (Abbot, Rolls yard, Chancery lane.

Dorell, E. and A. Whiting, Long Acre, coachmakers (Windus, Old Broad street.

Dawson, J. Manchester, dealer (Ellis, Cursitor street.

Dearcs, H. late of New York, now of Liverpool, merchant (Milne, Temple.

Dunnicliff, J. Leicester, grocer (Mitchell, Union court, Broad street.

Drinkwater, F. and T. Dakeyne, (Darley dale, Derby, under the firm of P. Drinkwater and Co. cornfactors (Hay and Ramshaw, Manchester.

Evans, J. Wapping, linen draper (Hall, 25, Poultry.

Edwards, J. Bensington, Oxon. miller (Price and Williams, Lincoln's inn.

Evatt, J. Bird lane, glassman (Atcheson, Ely place.

Fisher, R. Bedford street, Covent garden, tailor (Clarkson, Essex street.

Furlow, J. and T. W. Warnford court, London, merchants (Fryer, Temple.

Finlayson, J. Liverpool, merchant, partner with W. Finlayson, under the firm of J. and W. Finlayson, and Co. (Lace and Hassall, Liverpool.

Fryer, G. Red Lion street, Clerkenwell, merchant (Jopson, Lincoln's inn.

Fisher, F. Chepstow, currier (Price and Williams, Lincoln's inn.

Figgins, J. Trowbridge, carpenter (French and Williams, Castle street, Holborn.

Grange, R. York place, Portman square, miller (Latkow, Wardrobe place.

Glover, G. Dean street, Soho, grocer (Scott, Old City Chambers.

Hollands, S. Thomas street, Southwark, merchant and ship owner (Carter and Sheffield, Princes street.

Heaton, G. jun. Leeds, merchant (Battye, Chancery lane.

Hayman, T. Old City Chambers, merchant (Towse, Fishmongers hall.

Hughes, R. Charles street, Covent garden, woollen draper (Swaine and Waddington, Fore street.

Hawksey, W. Liverpool, merchant (Blackstock, Temple.

Hodgkin, D. Liverpool, brush maker (Cooper and Lowe, Southampton buildings.

Hindswell, J. Cawcliffe, parish of Huddersfield, Yorkshire corn dealer (Sykes, New inn.

Henderson, J. Long Acre, ironmonger (Eastman and Pringle, Ely place.

Harris, J. Newton St. Cyres, Devon, miller (Darke, Princes street, Bedford row.

Husledon, G. Liverpool, bookseller (Windle, Bartlett's buildings.

Holt, C. Leather lane, warehouseman (Abbot, Rolls yard, Chancery lane.

Houldsworth, A. and H. Grosvenor, Basinghall street, warehousemen (Battye, Chancery lane.

James, S. Cross street, St. Andrew, Holborn, hardwareman (Kibblewhite, Gray's inn place.

King, J. M. Liverpool, coffeehouse keeper (Blackstock, Temple.

Little, R. L. A. and T. W. all of Southwell, Nottinghamshire, woollen drapers and mercers (N. Milne, Hare court, Temple.

Lawton, J. Montague street, Spitalfields, chair maker, (Robinson and Crawford, Craven buildings, Old street.

Liddel, G. Newcastle upon Tyne, merchant (Atkinson, Chancery lane.

Muller, D. Fleet market, grocer (Pearce and Dixon, Paternoster row.

Morley, J. Walcot, Somerset, victualler (Shepherd and Adlington, Gray's inn.

Maynan, D. Batley Carr, Dewsbury, clothier (Sykes, New inn.

Masters, W. sen. and jun. Greenwich, distillers and wine merchants (Barrow and Forbes, Basinghall street.

Martin, A. and T. Panton street, cabinet makers (Hodgson, Charles street, St. James's square.

Merriman, G. Stockport, dealer (Young, Castle street.

Medley, E. Parliament street, scrivener (Maddocks, New square, Lincoln's inn.

Mouls, John, Hampstead, corn chandler (Seward, Princes street, Rotherhithe.

Mann, T. Howard street, Strand, dealer (Evans, Bury court, St. Mary Axe.

Marriott, C. Manchester, merchant (Milne, Temple.

Mitchell, J. Long Acre, cheesemonger (Mitchell, Union court, Broad street.

Marsh, J. [illegible] Thames, shipwright (Palmer and Tomlinson, Warnford court.

Madden, J. Page's walk, Bermondsey, victualler (Holloway and Windus, Southampton buildings.

Noble, Isaac, Penrith, ironmonger and grocer (Wordsworth, Staples inn.

Noble, N. Beemer, parish of Greystoke, Cumberland, dealer in butter (Lowndes, Red Lion square.

Newton, W. Exeter, druggist (Bal[illegible] and Anstice, Temple.

Norman, J. F. Bristol, baker (Gibbet, Lincoln's inn.

Offner, J. F. Kingsland road, brewer (Taylor, Old street.

Penny, B. jun. St. John's, Wapping, ship chandler (Hedley, Warren's square, Wapping.

Richardson, J. Carlisle, grocer (Pearson and Son, Temple.

Ross, C. St. Ann's, Westminster, cheesemonger (Fielder and Burgoyne, Duke street, Manchester square.

Robinson, T. Fulshaw, Chesher, cornfactor (Wright and Reynolds, Temple.

Rodd, T. Gerard street, jeweller (Parker, Palmer, and Cuppage, Essex street.

Rawlins, W. Gracechurch street, grocer (Figes, Norfolk street.

Rogers, R. C. Monmouth, dealer (Bowcher, Bath.

Satwarn, T. Dorset square, Cannon row, broker (Merishall, Millbank street.

Smart, W. Vigo lane, carpenter (Simpson, King's Bench walk.

Solomon, L. St. Martin's le Grand, merchant (Lihel, Catharine court, Seething lane.

Stephens, W. Exeter, fuller, (Drew and Lo[illegible]ham, New inn.

Sproston, J. Liverpool, merchant (Blackstock, Temple.

Smee, J. Newington place, Surry, potter (Palmer and Tomlinson, Warnford Court.

Schultze, W. and F. Unger, Little Britain, merchants. (R. S. Taylor, Gray's inn.

Stone, J. Mersey street, Liverpool, victualler (Windle, Bartlett's buildings.

Tonge, C. Liverpool, merchant (Sharpe and Eccles, Manchester.

Tomkins, E. and R. Deretend, Birmingham, plated inkstand makers (Lowe, Ravenhurst.

Waite, J. Paternoster row, bookseller (Eaton, Birchin lane.

Whiting, A. Long Acre, coach maker (Barnes, Soho square.

Wigful, T. King's Lynn, iron founder (Goodwin, King's Lynn.

Weldon, J. Lawrence lane, warehouseman (Cruickshank, Basinghall street.

Young, A. Bristol, cornfactor (Lewis and James, Gray's inn.

DIVIDENDS.

DIVIDENDS ANNOUNCED.

Ashburner, J. Bolton le Moor, cotton spinner, Dec. 24.
Attaud, S. Jan. Pinner, shopkeeper, Dec. 21.
Agur W. Whitechapel road, Bethnal green, whitesmith, Jan. 19.
Andrews, T. Hackney road, brewer, Jan. 12.
Alder, J. St. John's street, Clerkenwell, cabinet maker, Jan. 12.
Boonham, S. Atherstone, carrier, Dec. 12.
Barrett, W. Cheapside, linen draper, Dec. 19.
Bradley, A. Ashburne, and T. Marshal, of Birdsgrove, cotton spinners, separate estate of A. Bradley, Dec. 22, final.
Bond, J. Brittingsea, Essex, butcher, Dec. 28.
Bayne, W. Pateley bridge, York, inn keeper Dec. 28.
Barnes, T. Fleet street, stationer, Jan. 26.
Calvert, N. merchant, as partner with F. Simpson, of St. Christopher, Dec. 17.
Covenay, E. St. Mary at Hill, victualler, Dec. 22.
Cook, J. Royal Oak yard, Bermondsey street, tanner, Dec. 15.
Clutterbuck, P. York street, Westminster, brewer, Jan. 5
Carver, T. Retford, baker, Jan. 5.
Chauvet, L. and P. Turquand, Old Jewry, merchants, Jan. 9.
Dry, H. Uxbridge, liquor merchant, &c. Jan. 26.
Dickens, P. Bristol, soap boiler, Jan. 4.
Delaney, W. Liverpool, linen draper, Jan. 4.
Dodgson, P. Liverpool, linen draper, Jan. 8.
Elkins, W. Oxford street, bookseller, Dec. 19.
Eadon, M. Manchester, merchant, Dec. 24.
Emmett, J. Bush lane, merchant, Jan. 22.
Easthope, W. Bridgenorth, barge owner, Dec. 18.
Ewins, W. and W. James, Birmingham, composition ornament manufacturers, Jan. 8.
Eldershaw, J. Derby, dealer, Jan. 12.
Fozard J. Jun. Park lane, Piccadilly, stable keeper, separate estate, Dec. 19.
Finlay, A. Castle street, Oxford road, linen draper, Dec. 19.
Fletcher, G. Knightsbridge, hackney and stable keeper, Dec. 29.
Firth, J. of the Washway, Lambeth, dealer, Jan. 23.
Greaves, J. Royal Exchange, insurance broker, Dec. 15, final.
Gilbertson, R. Manchester, manufacturer, Dec. 21.
Greenwood, J. and T. H. Mason, Leeds, grocers and tobacconists, Dec. 21.
Gwinnett, G. Bristol, cornfactor, Dec. 21.
Glover, G. Paternoster row, warehouseman, Jan. 26.
Glover, J. Kensington, stone mason, Jan. 16.
Gell, W. S. St. Ive's, shopkeeper, Jan. 12.
Gregory, C. Elstow, baker, Jan. 12.
Gearing, W. Water lane, Fleet street, innholder, Dec. 22
Haycock, R. Wells, Norfolk, merchant, Dec. 15.
Hyland, R. Robertsbridge, grocer, Feb. 6.
Haigh, J. Low Whitley, factor, Dec. 16.
Harrison, J. Paternoster row, bookseller, Dec. 19.
Higson J. and T. Tasker, Liverpool, linen drapers, Dec. 25
Hodgson, G. Chester, soapboiler, &c. Jan. 12.
Herries, C. and J. Hellor, London, merchants, Jan. 26.
Holmes, J. Newbold upon Avon, lime merchant, Jan. 9
Hallewood, J. T. Bridgenorth, grocer, Jan. 23, final.
Ireland, S. St. Clement Danes, merchant, Feb. 6.
Jones, T. Charlton, parish of Toddington, Bedford, timber merchant, Dec. 19.
Kemble, T. and W. Spens, Norfolk street, Strand, merchants, Jan. 2.
Leigh, P. and J. and of J.'s estate separately, Dec. 28.
Lascelles, R. South Audley street, taylor, Dec. 19.
Maillard, J. J. Lime street, merchant, Dec. 17.
Masterman, J. Bucklersbury, warehouseman, Dec. 19.
Millar T. and J. Hulme, Manchester, dealers in wet, Dec. 29.
Marshall, J. and J. Longcake, Workington, mercers, &c. Dec. 29.
Mudhat, J. Cromer, merchant, Feb. 6.
Menton, T. Tokenhouse yard, merchant, Dec. 13.
Owen, W. Holywell Flintshire, grocer and linendraper, Jan. 9
Phipps, J. Bristol, innkeeper, Dec. 22
Parry, T. Birmingham, haberdasher, Dec. 15
Popple, W. Kingston Hull, brewer, Dec. 16
Price, T. Holywell, Flintshire, innkeeper, Jan. 19
Paine, C. Croydon, taylor, Jan. 12
Perry, R. and T. Andrews, George Brewhouse, Hackney, Jan. 12
Roberts, W. Rochester, grocer, Dec. 19
Richardson, R. partner with E. Strickland, Corporation row, merchant, &c. Dec. 15
Reynolds, J. late of Chesthunt, now of Newington Butts, brewer, Dec. 19
Reider, J. C. London House Yard, bookseller, Jan. 5
Senois, J. (wife of J. Senois) Fore street, shopkeeper, Dec. 15
Sutton, N. Walworth, victualler Dec. 22
Stevenson, J. Chandos street, Covent Garden, woollen draper, Dec. 19
Shepperson, W. Oxford street, grocer, Jan. 18
St. Gulliver, H. Richmond, Surrey, stablekeeper, Dec. 26
Scott, J. Stratford, Essex, lime-burner, &c. Dec. 9
Sommervail, J. Liverpool, merchant, Jan. 23
Skone, W. Bristol, grocer, Jan. 7
Smith, T. Tunstall, potter, Feb. 1, final.
Spier, T. Gloucester, mercer, Jan. 21
Staples, R. T. St. Ives, draper, Jan. 11
Towsey, G. Litcomb Regis, Berks, miller, Jan. 5
Taylor, W. B. Wolverhampton, japanner, Jan. 11
Underhill, G. Abbey Foregate, Shrewsbury, horse dealer, Jan. 19
Wilson, R. Bread street, merchant, Dec. 19
Wright, T. Eddington, Bucks, coach master, Dec. 19
Waldo, J. Birmingham and Bristol, in England, and of Boston, America, merchants, separate estate, Jan. 20
Wetherherd, C. Liverpool, merchant, Dec. 22
Whettal, W. and J. Poole, inn keepers, Jan. 11
Worthington, M. Norwich, linen draper, Jan. 26
Williamson, R. Wood street, Druggist, Jan. 22
Winter, E. Long Acre, dealer
Wallworth, J. Manchester, inn keeper, Jan. 25.

MARRIAGES AND DEATHS IN AND NEAR LONDON.

With Biographical Memoirs of distinguished Characters recently deceased.

Married.] At Burnham, near Windsor, Dr. Sewell, of Doctor's Commons, to Mrs. Stedman, widow, of Chigwell.

Mr. C. Cheyne, jun. of Pentonville, to Miss Winchester, of the Strand.

Lord Francis Spencer, second son of the Duke of Marlboro', to Lady Frances Fitzroy, fifth daughter of the Duke of Grafton.

J. Jortin, esq. of Lincoln's Inn, to Miss S. Bearpacket, of Wotton under Edge, Gloucestershire.

Mr. W. A. Slade, attorney, of Blenheim-street, New Bond-street, to Miss A. Fryer, of Old Cavendish-street.

At Twickenham, H. W. Espinasse, esq. major in the 4th regiment of infantry, to the Hon. Mrs. Petre, relict of the Hon. G. W. Petre, brother of the present Lord Petre.

At St. Paul's, Covent Garden, R. Rhode, esq. to Miss Sotheby, of York-street, Covent Garden.

At Kensington, Mr. Wright, merchant, to Miss M. Raybould, second daughter of W. Raybould, esq. of Brompton.

Died.] At his house, in Paradise Row, Hammersmith, in his 81st year, Mr. H. Barton, formerly an eminent cabinet-maker in Portsmouth-street, Lincoln's Inn Fields.

Aged 66, Mr. J. Sandell, silk-dyer, of Wych-street.

At his house, in Bedford-square, A. Willock, esq.

At Hackney, aged 73, Mrs. Alvarez, wife of J. J. Alvarez, esq.

At his house, near Hammersmith, Mr. W. Vernon, sen.

Mr. Pealy, attorney, of Cursitor-street.

At his house in Fitzroy-square, P. Douglas,

las, esq. many years in the service of the East India Company.

At Valenciennes, M. Francis de Liuat, late of Cheshunt, Herts.

Mrs. Sills, widow, of Upper Thames-street.

W. Fletcher, esq. of Welbeck-street.

At Hornsey, Mr. W. Lens, of the Three Per Cent. Reduced Office, Bank.

Mr. J. Yallowley, of Chiswell-street.

At Finchley, Miss S. Jordan, youngest daughter of the late Mr. E. Jordan.

Miss Carr, daughter of W. Carr, esq. of Hammersmith.

At his house in Lime-street, W. Hamilton, esq. of Blackheath.

At Chelsea, Mr. T. Pemberton.

In Upper Berkeley-street, Portman-square, G. Redhead, esq. of the island of Antigua; sincerely regretted by all who knew him as a man of the most humane and benevolent heart.

The Rev. T. Chamberlayne, vice-provost of Eaton, and rector of Worplesdon, in Surrey.

In Kensington, Mr. G. Egenoffe, son of the late Mr. Egenoffe, of New Lisle-street, Leicester-square.

In Highbury Place, Mr. W. Grey.

At her house in Grosvenor-square, the Marchioness of Antrim.

At Harleyford Place, Kennington, aged 74, Mr. Russell.

Suddenly, of an apoplectic fit, Lieut. Col. Forster, of the corps of marines.

At her house on Sion Hill, in her 57th year, Mrs. Porter, widow.

Sir John Parnell, bart. M. P. for Queen's County, Ireland; he had but the day before removed with his family from Sloane-street, to Clifford-street, London. He breakfasted as usual, and appeared to be in perfect health: immediately after breakfast he went into his room, where he was seized with an apoplectic fit, dropped down, and expired in less than half an hour. He has left two daughters, and three sons, the eldest of whom succeeds to the title. Sir John has always been considered as a very able politician, and was a distant relation of the poet Parnell. He was many years chancellor of the exchequer in Ireland, from which office he was removed by the Marquis Cornwallis, for his determined opposition to the question of the Union. Sir John had attended his duty in the House of Commons on the preceding day.

At her apartments, in Queen-street, Westminster, the celebrated Mrs. Crawford, once a bright ornament of the British stage. She was the daughter of a medical gentleman at Bath, and was first married to an obscure player named Dancer, and, on his death, her personal beauty, and theatrical talents, attracted the attention of the elegant and silver-tongued Barry, the rival of Garrick, under whose protection she played till his wife died, when she became Mrs. Barry. On his death, she was left the first female performer in the metropolis, and acquired a handsome independence, when she suffered her eye to be caught by the person of Mr. Crawford, a briefless Irish barrister, young enough to be her son, who squandered her fortune, the produce of her talents, broke her spirit, and at last died a martyr to his own dissipation, leaving her in straitened circumstances, and she was at last nearly reduced to a state of poverty.

At Chelsea, in his 73d year, the Right Hon. Joseph Leeson, Earl of Miltown, Viscount Russborough, in Ireland; he is succeeded by his brother, the Hon. Brice Leeson.

Aged 90, the Right Hon. Lord Kensington, M. P. for Haverfordwest.

Mr. J. Battishill, organist of Christ's Church, Newgate-street, and of St. Clement's Church, East Cheap, and well known to the musical cognoscenti for his extraordinary genius, and profound science.

In James-street, Westminster, aged 81, Mrs. J. Jackson, the last surviving issue of J. Jackson, esq. formerly of Chatham, who was the nephew and heir of the celebrated Samuel Pepys, esq. to whose genius and knowledge in the administration of naval affairs, may be ascribed the perfection of the system of naval regulation, established before the Revolution, in the year 1688, and still in force, and whose rare and truly valuable collection of books, known by the name of Pepy's Library, was, some years ago, presented to Magdalen College, in the University of Cambridge, by Mr. Jackson.

ERRATUM.—At page 203, No. 81, through some mistake, a part of the conjectural Statement of the Bank of England's concerns was omitted. That part of the statement explained that the profit of 1,150,000l. arose from the interest paid by Government upon its permanent debt to the Bank, from the interest received upon the amount of Bank-notes in circulation, and from the allowance made by Government for managing the public-funds, deducting from the aggregate amount of these sums the expence of conducting the business of the Bank.

PROVINCIAL

PROVINCIAL OCCURRENCES.

WITH ALL THE MARRIAGES AND DEATHS,

Arranged geographically, or in the Order of the Counties, from North to South.

*** *Authentic Communications for this Department are always very thankfully received.*

NORTHUMBERLAND AND DURHAM.

The following instances may be adduced as a proof, that the highest degree of improvement in the carcase of that valuable animal the sheep, without a deterioration of its fleece, is actually attainable:—A wether, bred and fed by J. Davison, esq. of Lanton (whose leading object, in the improvement of his stock, has been the latter, with a due regard, however, to the former), when lately killed, was allowed by all who viewed it, to have been the fattest animal that they had ever seen!

Annual account of the state of the Charitable Institution for the Relief of the Sick and Lame Poor, at Bamborough Castle, from October 17, 1800, to October 17, 1801.

Left upon the books	60
Out-patients admitted	1046
In-patients	76
	1182

Of these last, discharged.

Cured	958
Relieved	121
Sent to Newcastle Infirmary	3
Dead	26
Remaining upon the books	74
	1182

Exclusive of 38 poor women delivered at their own houses by Mr. Herriott, man-midwife to the Institution.

Married.] At Newcastle, Mr. Blundell, to Mrs. Austin.—Mr. W. Armstrong, merchant, to Miss A. Potter.

In London, Mr. R. White, of Norton, in the county of Durham, to Miss Richardson, of Durham.

Also, Mr. White, another son of the same gentleman, to Miss M. Smith, late of Stockton.

The Rev. J. Jones, of Sand Hutton, to Miss P. Pickersgill, of Ainderby House, Leming-lane.

At Norton, Mr. J. Hixon, to Miss White.—Mr. W. Redhead, jun. merchant, of Newcastle, to Miss M. Metcalfe, of North Shields.

At Durham, Mr. W. Thompson, to Miss Dunn.—Mr. J. G. Hopper, mason, to Miss E. Balmer.

Mr. J. Makepeace, to Miss M. Elliott, both of Langley Mill.—Mr. E. Shaftoe, brewer, in Durham, to Miss Hodgson, of Primrose, near Gainsford.—T. Thompson, esq. of Boughtrig, to Miss S. Robson, second daughter of the late J. Robson, esq. of Samieston.

Died.] At Newcastle, aged 89, Mr. J. Davenport, formerly a flax-dresser.—Aged 41, Mr. J. Coleman.—In his 46th year, Mr. W. S. Lake, attorney.—Mrs. Brown, wife of Mr. R. Brown, upholsterer.—Mrs. A. Wilson, widow of the Rev. W. Wilson, late curate of Falstone, in Northumberland.—Mr. T. Brown, master of the ship Halcyon.—Mr. J. Rogerson, a local preacher in the Methodist connection; respected and beloved by a numerous acquaintance as an intelligent preacher, a lover of candour, and of rational piety; and of great liberality of sentiment, which led him to an impartial and sedulous inquiry into theological truth.

At Sunderland, Mrs. Mounsey, a lady of pleasing manners, and a truly amiable disposition.

Mrs. Burn.

Mrs. B. Sinclair, a seller of old cloaths for near twenty years.

At North Shields, aged 24, Mr. S. Aydon, ironmonger.

At the Low Glasses, near Newcastle, aged near 70, Mr. G. Cram, shipbuilder.

At Broomhill, near Warkworth, Mr. T. Clark.

At Edinburgh, Mrs. Wilkie, relict of the late J. Wilkie, esq. of Foulden, near Berwick upon Tweed.

At Tynemouth, Mrs. Middleton.

The Rev. Mr. Weston, a prebendary of Durham, and rector of Therfield, in Hertfordshire.

At Woosten, near Stockton, aged 73, Mr. H. Scott, potter, late of Newbottle.

At Windlestone, Mr. H. Thompson, upwards of thirty years steward to Sir John Eden, bart.—Aged 60, Mr. Brown, horse-dealer, &c. of Old Brough, near Darlington.

At Shepherton, near Alnwick, Mrs. Ker, relict of the late W. Ker, esq. of Littledean.

In his 52d year, Mr. J. White, of Fugar House, near Wickham; his death was occasioned by a coal-waggon going over his body, his foot having unfortunately slipped, as he was crossing the way.

At Walthamstow, Essex, Miss Robinson, eldest daughter of the late Rev. Is. Robinson, of North Shields.

At Hexham, Mr. J. Dickinson, father of Mr. R. Dickinson, bookseller.

At Bishop Auckland, Mr. R. Sivers, formerly an officer of excise.

CUMBERLAND AND WESTMORELAND.

There is at present living at Hilhead, in the parish of Bewcastle, a widow woman in her 100th year, who is gaining that, which to a person of her age must be equally unexpected and acceptable, viz. a set of new teeth! She is also casting her hair. The new hair is of a whitish colour, and remarkably soft, resembling, in every respect, that of a child. She is still able to walk about, and do a little business in the house.—*From the Carlisle Journal, Dec. 5*

This year, a single stalk of hemp, which accidentally took root in the garden of Mr. J. Moore, of Great Orton, grew to the surprising height of eight feet, and measured six inches in circumference at the ground! It has been since dressed and varnished by order of Mr. Moore, and now forms an extremely handsome walking-stick.

During the last season, one grain of wheat, at Mr. Rushton's, of Little Broughton, near Cockermouth, shot up in forty stalks, which produced exactly 1662 grains of as fine full-grown corn as ever was reaped!

It appears that sixpence per month is collected from the seamen employed on board the ships and vessels belonging to Whitehaven, and the neighbouring outports of Harrington, Workington, and Maryport (within its limit; under the appointment of fifteen trustees (consisting of owners, masters, commanders, &c.), and which is applied for the relief and support of such seamen respectively, when maimed or disabled, and the widows and children of such as may be killed, slain, or drowned (in the merchants' service). The above regulation took place by virtue of an act of parliament, which passed for the purpose, in the twentieth year of the reign of his present Majesty.

Married.] Mr. H. Tyson, to Miss S. Blair, both of Wath.

At Whitehaven, Mr. J. Southward, of Arlecdon, to Miss Humes.—Mr. J. Brocklebank, rope-maker, to Miss Macdonald.—Mr. M. Nicholson, ship-carpenter, to Miss N. Hodgson.—Mr. J. Macgrey, ship-carpenter, of Workington, to Miss J. Bayley.—Mr. J. Jenkinson, ship-carpenter, of Harrington, to Miss S. Stephenson—Mr. J. Huddleston, cooper, to Miss E. Graham.

Mr. J. Mawson, jun. to Miss H. Alcock, both of Sandwith.—Mr. D. Walker, of the Ginns, to Miss S. Fidler, of Mirehouse.

The Rev. J. Fenton, of Newcastle, Staffordshire, and vicar of Sorpenhow, Cumberland, to Miss Livingstone, daughter of the late Sir Alexander Livingstone, of Westquarter House, Stirlingshire.

At Workington, W. Ormanby, esq of Dtig, to Miss Tye, only daughter of Mr. J. Tye, one of the apparators of the consistory court of Chester.—Mr. B. Durring, to Mrs. Wilson, innkeeper,—Mr. W. Clapperton, to Miss Hutton.

At Kendal, Mr. W. Bradshaw, cornfactor, to Mrs. Barrow, of Booth, near Kendal.

In the East Indies, in March last, J. Pattinson, esq. of Melmerby Hall, Cumberland, to Miss Harris, daughter of — Harris, esq. a free merchant.

Mr. Hobson, of Bedburn, near Witton-le-Wear, to Miss Hodgson, of Brough, in Westmoreland.

At Haverstram, Westmoreland, Mr. E. Fisher, to Miss Hairsnape.

At Brampton, Mr. J. Armstrong, to Miss M. Highmoors.

At Carlisle, Mr. J. Twentyman, manufacturer, to Miss M. Gibbon, daughter of Mr. J. Gibbon, mercer and draper.

Mr. J. Harrison, of Kentmeer, in Westmoreland, to Miss E. Johnson, of Lindale, in Lancashire.

Died.] At Carlisle, aged 17, Miss M. Pattinson Yeats.—Aged 29, Mr. J. Halton, eldest son of Mr. W. Halton.—Advanced in years, Mrs. Harington.—In her 82d year, Mrs. Warwick, sen. widow, formerly of Snow-hill, London.

Mrs. Hodgson, wife of Mr. J. Hodgson, merchant, of Coleman-street, London, and of Rockliff, in Cumberland.

At Whitehaven, in the prime of life, Mr. J. Pearson, cabinet-maker.

At Maryport, in the prime of life, Mrs. M. Taylor, wife of Mr. J. Taylor, master of the ship Isabella.

At Kendal, Mrs. Hutchinson, wife of Captain Hutchinson, of the Bengal Artillery, and daughter of Mr. Lambert, attorney, of Alnwick, Northumberland.—In the prime of life, Mr. J. Marr, spirit-merchant.—Aged 57, Mrs. E Preston.—In an advanced, Mr. R. Speight, cooper.

At Egremont, Mr. B. Towerson, tanner. —In the prime of life, Mr. J. Affleck.

At Upton, in Caldbeck, in an advanced age, Mr. J. Scott.—In the prime of life, Miss D. Jack.

At Dissington, near Whitehaven, aged 86, Mr. B. Kendall.—Mr. T. Branfather, of Garthside, near Brampton.

At the Intack, near Brompton, Mr. Smith.

At Houghton, near Carlisle, aged 88, Mr. W. Patrickson.

In London, W. Tweddle, esq. late of Carlisle.

At Dumfries, Mrs. Crosbie, wife of Mr. J. Crosbie, merchant, late of Whitehaven.

In the prime of life, Miss E. Crow, of Cartmel Fell.—Mr. R. Sill, late of Kendal, father of Mr. J. Sill, broker, of Liverpool.

In Jemaica, in the prime of life, Mr. J. Tyson, son of Mr. N. Tyson, merchant, of Kendal.

At Low Mill, near Egremont, Mr. W. Hayton, rope-maker.

At Duston, near Appleby, aged 78, the Rev. W. Kilner, rector, &c. and resident-minister of the parish upwards of half a century.

tury; sincerely regretted by his flock as a happy man, full of good deeds, as well as years. He has descended to the grave, accompanied with the blessings of both rich and poor, with the just and pious hope of all who knew and felt his worth, that his works have followed him, and will meet their due reward.

At High Ireby, Mr. R. Grainger, son of Mr. J. Grainger.

At Stainburn, near Workington, in the prime of life, Miss Thompson.

YORKSHIRE.

A carrot of the following extraordinary dimensions was taken up on the 3d of November last, in the garden of Mr. J. Roddick, of Richmond, viz. twenty inches and a half in length, and seventeen inches in circumference: it weighed six pounds, five ounces!

It appears that a fever of a very contagious nature exists, at present, in different quarters of the town of Leeds, and which has, in many instances, proved fatal, owing to the confined and unventilated apartments of those families where it usually takes place. Although the autumn of last year near doubled the present, in general mortality, yet the deaths by fever are increased; and the mortality by fever for the last month, is about one half more than the corresponding month of 1800. As examples of its highly infectious nature in the close and noisome dwellings of the poor, and of the impracticability of applying proper remedies, the following facts are inserted, from information collected by the gentlemen of the faculty in Leeds. In a family, consisting of thirteen individuals, five of them were infected within the first four days, and four more have since been attacked. The other case is still more deplorable:—Two forlorn beds, without linen, and covered only with rags, contained six adult persons; the fever, attacking one by one, soon spread through the whole, and the dead and the dying lay stretched on the same miserable bed; yet, such was the fatal perverseness of the relatives who attended them, that although wine and medicines were at their command, they could not be prevailed upon to give either, and for two days they received neither food nor medicine. The consequence was that the father and mother of the family both sunk under such accumulated wretchedness. Facts, such as these, clearly shew the inefficacy of any measures short of actual and timely removal from the place of infection. By timely removing the first who sickens, the rest escape infection; and, instead of wasting their time and strength in watching amidst infection and disease, are profitably employed in procuring their own subsistence, and preserving a numerous family from the parish. The object of this merciful care being removed to a comfortable house, where the resources of art can be employed for his benefit, and removed at a period when those resources can be applied with effect, is cheered with the prospect of a speedy return to his family. Urged by these considerations, a numerous meeting has been lately held in Leeds, Mr. Mayor in the chair, to devise the best means of establishing a HOUSE OF RECOVERY, in the case of fever patients, and to procure a proper building for that purpose. The committee appointed by the meeting have accordingly found a house in Ebenezer-street, which they have adopted as a temporary situation; and they have likewise come to a determination, that a subscription be immediately entered into for the purchasing a piece of ground in the town, and for erecting a House of Recovery for the reception of the sick in contagious fevers. In Manchester, by an institution of a similar kind, the number of fever-patients were reduced, the first year from 2880 to 1759, and there was a decrease of 400 burials within the same period. In one district, immediately in the vicinity of the fever-ward, the fevers were reduced from 400, the average number of fevers previously to opening the fever-ward, to twenty-six, in the first year. In Chester, fever-wards were established within the infirmary so early as 1783, and though one ward is situated within thirteen yards of the fever-patients, with whom it communicates on the same floor, by a passage and doors frequently left open, yet, during a period of eighteen years, it has never been once suspected that the patients, in other parts of the house, have caught any infection from the fever wards, by any contamination of the atmosphere, nor from any transgression of the rules of prevention. Some dwelling houses are placed at but a little distance from the fever-wards, and Stanley-place, inhabited by very genteel families, is not far distant. These facts prove undeniably, that a House of Recovery is by no means detrimental to a neighbourhood in which it is situated. In Chester, so salutary have been its effects for eighteen years, that in the spring of 1795, when a very fatal epidemic raged in Manchester, Liverpool, and other neighbouring towns, only two cases of fever occurred in the Chester fever-ward, and not one in the rest of the town. An institution pregnant with so much good, will, no doubt, meet every due encouragement;—liberal support, and patronage from the rich, who must here feel the motive of self-preservation, added to that of humanity, to induce them to support measures for the extermination of a disease, which by many unavoidable circumstances, and unforeseen events, may be unhappily introduced into their own families,—and cheerful and grateful acceptance on the part of the poor.

On the 18th of November last, a venerable oak, standing in the park of John Elliott, esq. of Elliott House, near Rippon, was struck with lightning, and literally shivered o pieces; the trunk, which measured twenty-seven feet in circumference, was torn into several distinct pieces, and many of the largest branches were thrown to a considerable distance: two deer, supposed to have been browzing under it, were also struck dead; the side of one of them appeared much scorched, as if by the application of an hexagonal instrument. It is a curious circumstance, and well worthy of remembrance, that this tree, which was considered by Mr. Arthur Young, who visited it some years ago, to be one of the largest, as well as oldest, in the county, appears from records still preserved in Elliott house, to have been coeval with the mansion itself, which was erected by Tiberius Elliott, esq. high-sheriff for Yorkshire, in the 38th year of the reign of King Henry VI. from whom the present possessor is lineally descended.

A piece of water, at Thornville Royal, in this county, which for several years had been ordered to be filled up, and for which purpose, logs of wood, roots of trees, rubbish, &c. had been thrown into it, lately being found useful, was ordered to be cleared. It was almost choaked up with weeds and mud, so that little water remained, and it was not conceived that any fish, except possibly a few large eels would be found in it, yet about 200 brace of tench of all sizes, and as many perch, were found, about ten brace of which weighed from three to four pound each. After the pond was thought to be quite free, under some roots there seemed to be some animal, which was conceived to be an otter; the place was surrounded, and on opening an entrance among the roots, a tench was found of most extraordinary form, having literally assumed the shape of the hole in which he had for many years been confined. His form was an irregular semicircle; his length from fork to eye was two feet, nine inches; his circumference, to almost the tail, was two feet, two inches; his weight eleven pounds, nine ounces, and a quarter: his colour was also singular, as his belly was the colour of vermillion. This extraordinary fish, after having been shewn to a sculptor, who has taken a model of it, and to a number of gentlemen, was carefully put into a pond, but either from confinement, or age, or bulk, it only floated, and with difficulty, at last, swam gently away. It is now alive and well.

A correspondent of the York Herald, in a Letter to the Editor, dated December 11. observes, that the solar spots, at present, exceed in number any that he has seen for a considerable time. The principal are past the sun's centre westward, and form a striking curve, extending one-eighth of the sun's diameter, or in a line of about 100,000 miles. A spot, he adds, is entering on the eastern side of the sun, which is also clustered. Altitude of the sun, at the time of observation, fourteen degrees; and latitude, by former observation, fifty-two degrees, eighteen minutes nearly.

Married.] Mr. Cattley, raft-merchant of York, to Miss Cattley, of Leeds.

Mr. H. W. Mortimer, gun-maker, of Fleet-street, London, to Miss Ritchie, of Otley; a lady for many years, esteemed and beloved by a numerous acquaintance, for her amiable disposition and deep piety.

Mr. J. Firth, merchant, of Birstall, to Mrs. Tinsdale, innkeeper, of Leeds.—Mr. J. Butler, of Kirkstall Forge, to Mrs. Maud, of Bingley.—Mr. J. Burnell, tobacconist, of York, to Miss M. Haliday.—Mr. A. Houghton, grocer, of Huddersfield, to Miss S. Fisher, daughter of Mr. Fisher, nurseryman, of Doncaster.

At Wakefield, Captain Norcott, of the 37th regiment of foot, to Miss E. Noble.—Mr. J. Pearson, cornfactor, of Hull, to Miss A. Johnson, of Kirkella.

At Hull, Mr. R. Swann, surgeon, to Miss Hall, daughter of F. Hall, esq.

Mr. W. Ilott, of Bardsey, to Miss S. Waddington, of Rigton, both near Leeds.—W. Vavasour, esq. of Weston Hall, to Miss S. Cook, of Swinton, near Doncaster.—Mr. J. Johnson, of Leeds, to Miss Moyser, of Fulford, near York.

At Thornhill, Mr. J. Law, cardmaker, to Miss Stocks, of Whitley.

At Leeds, Mr. W. Smith, butcher, to Miss M. Rishforth.—Mr. T. Hampshire, auctioneer, to Miss L. Carnett.—Mr. Barstow, merchant, to Miss Benson.—Mr. E. Bell, cloth-dresser, to Miss M. Farrah.

At Bradford, Mr. J. Gambles, linen-draper, to Miss Greenwood.

Mr. R. Ashworth, of Wadsworth, to Miss M. Sutcliffe, of Hepstontall, near Halifax.—Mr. A. Gibson, jun. to Miss H. Ogden, both of Hepstonstall.

In August last, in the Island of Trinidad, Lieutenant Shapter, of the 57th regiment of foot, to Miss H. Harrison, late of Knaresborough.

J. S. Walton, esq. of Northallerton, to Mrs. C. C. Diemer, widow of the late Rev. Dr. Diemer, of Calcutta, in Bengal.

Mr. J. Priestley, of Ovendon, to Miss Child, of Threapcroft, near Halifax.—Mr. R. Stephenson, grocer, of Beverley, to Miss Brocklebank, of Cottingham.

At Whitby, Captain Wilson, in the sea-service, to Miss E. Shimmings, of the Hare and Hounds tavern.

Mr. Parker, cotton-spinner, of Gargrave, to Miss C. Holdforth, of Leeds.—Mr. J. Smith, of Leeds, to Miss Alderson, of Birkin, near Pomfret.—Mr. Pontey, of Huddersfield, to Mrs. Pearson, of York.—Mr. T. Smith, tea-dealer, of Leeds, to Miss Clark, daughter of the late Mr. Clark, jeweller, of York.—Mr. J. Nixon, of Bassford, Nottinghamshire, to Miss Paley, of Leeds.—Mr. B. Kitson, to Mrs. Mortimer, both of Wrose, near Bradford.—Mr. J. Whitaker,

Whitaker, painter, of Huddersfield, to Miss S. Clapham, of Holdbeck.—Mr. Laverack, jun. of Hull, to Miss Dyas, of Tadcaster.—The Rev. G. Morris, of Croxton, in Lincolnshire, to Miss Hall, of Hull.—Mr. J. Pickhard, of Doncaster, to Miss E. Myers, of Leeds.—Mr. H. Breary, eldest son of C. Breary, esq. of Middlethorpe, near York, to Miss Benson, eldest daughter of Mr. J. Benson, attorney, of Thorne.—Mr. E. Peck, bookseller, of York, to Miss Ward, of Willerby, near Scarboro'.—Mr. J. Booth, of Leathley, to Mrs. Foster, of Otley.—Mr. T. Bromhead, of Birmingham, to Miss A. Glossop, of Stumperlow Hall, near Sheffield.

Died.] At York, in an advanced age, Mrs. Wormald, widow.—Mrs. Taite, wife of Mr. Taite, spirit-merchant.—Aged 85, Mrs. Gledhill.

Mrs. E. Yarborough, the last of the Campsmount branch of that ancient and respectable family.

Aged 60, Mr. J. Bland, druggist.—Mrs. Hopps, of the Pack-horse inn.

At Leeds, Mr. W. Blanchard, gardiner.—Mr. N. Booth, common-brewer.—Mr. Hutchinson, of the Willow-tree public-house.—Mrs. Skelton, wife of Mr. J. Skelton, attorney.—Mr. R. Wear, joiner.—Mrs. P. Ogle.—Mr. J. Chadwick, woolstapler.—Mr. W. Walton, many years book-keeper to the King's Arms coach office.—Very suddenly, Master Dixon, only son of Mr. J. Dixon, china-man.

At Hull, in his 26th year, of a decline, T. Horner, esq. A. M. of Trinity College, Cambridge; a young gentleman of very promising abilities; he lately gave one hundred pounds for the benefit of the Hull General Infirmary.

Mrs. R. Bonfield.—Mr. T. Lyon, publican.—J. Green, esq. an elder brother of the Trinity House.—Aged 77, Mrs. Cockshutt, wife of Mr. T. Cockshutt.

At Halifax, Mrs. Walsh, wife of Mr. R. Walsh, cardmaker.—Mrs. Heyland, sen.—Mrs. Hoyland.—Mr. W. Walker, worsted-manufacturer.—Mr. J. Lister, cardmaker.—Mr. R. Bolland, son of Mr. J. Bolland.—Miss Edwards, daughter of Mr. Edwards, attorney.

At Huddersfield, in his 80th year, Mr. T. Riley.

At Rippon, aged 32, Mrs. Fairgray, of the Unicorn inn.

At Skipton, Mr. W. Morrill, horse-doctor; very eminent in his profession.

Mr. G. Atkinson, upwards of forty years common carrier between this town and Lancaster.

At Bradford, Mrs. Barker, wife of Mr. J. Barker, woolstapler, and formerly of Baildon.—Mrs. Crossley, widow.—Mr. H. Linforth.

At Wakefield, Mr. King, a commissioner of excise.

At Selby, aged 89, Mr. R. Waite, of Loftsome, in the East Riding.

At Knaresboro', aged 48, Mrs. Simpson, wife of Mr. Simpson, surgeon.

At Whitby, aged 67, Mrs. M. Smithie, a Quaker.

In his 80th year, Mr. G. Cusworth, of Dirtcar, near Wakefield.

Aged 63, J. Ramsey, esq. of Elvington, near York.

At Rawcliff, near Snaith, aged 70, Mrs. Borthwick, a liberal benefactress to the poor of that place.

Mr. J. Blundell, of Ravenfield, near Rotherham.

At Scorton, near Richmond, Mr. W. Arrowsmith.

At Aldbord, in the North Riding, suddenly, Mr. J. Brown, grazier; highly distinguished for possessing a superior breed of cattle.

The Rev. F. Cleator, minister of Stainton and Thornaby, in Cleveland; much respected as a diligent and affectionate pastor, and a respectable and consistent friend.

Mr. R. Jefferson, one of the owners of the contract-vessels in the trade between York and London.

Aged 97, J. Day, esq. of Day Ash, near Harrowgate.

Aged 69, Mr Carr, of the Fox and Grapes inn, on Bramham Moor, near Leeds.—Mrs. Thompson, of Woodhouse-hill.—Mr. A. Marshall, of Horsforth.—Mrs. Hemington, mother of the Rev. M. Hemington, vicar of Thorp Arch, near Wetherby.

Lately, at Demarary, in the West Indies, of the yellow fever, Mr. R. Barr, joiner, &c. of Leeds.

In his 55th year, J. Redmayne, esq. of Yarlsher, near Ingleton.

In his 78th year, C. Ingleby, esq. of Austwick, near Settle, father of J. Ingleby, esq. of Lawkland-hall.

Lately, in America, in the prime of life, of the yellow fever, Captain Roper, brother to Mr. F. Roper, merchant, of Leeds.

Mr. W. Preston, of Room.—Aged 91, Mr. J. Carter, of Lightcliffe, near Halifax.—Mrs. Battle, widow of the late W. Battle, esq. of Welton.—Mr. Musgrave, farmer, of Halecoates, near Tickhill.

In his 66th year, Mr. Lumb, for forty years, parish-clerk and schoolmaster of Swillington, near Leeds; he had seventeen children by one wife.

Mr. Milthorp, of Arthington.

In the island of Malta, on the 11th of August last, Colonel Maccalaster, of the 35th regiment of foot, a gentleman well known in the neighbourhood of Halifax.

Mrs. Bingley, of Leathley, near Otley.

LANCASHIRE.

Married.] E. Garforth, esq. lieut. col. of the East York Militia, to Miss C. Asheton, youngest daughter of the late Rev. R. Asheton, D. D. warden of the collegiate church in in Manchester, &c.—F. Colquhoun, esq, of London, to Miss J. Hanson, of Manchester.

At Manchester, Mr. R. Bleasby, to Miss Tate.—Mr. J. Mallalieu, of Manchester, to Miss S. Hampson, of Hulme—Mr. J. Poulson, to Miss Lawrinson.—Mr. G. Scott, to Miss E. Rowbottom.—Mr. Dobson, surgeon, of Poulton, to Miss Miller, of Kirkham.

At Liverpool, Mr. Murrow, to Mrs. Dean. —Mr. J. Campbell, to Miss Codling—Mr. W. Rigby, brazier, to Miss E. Smith.—Mr. J. Porter, jun. to Miss Wilson.—Mr. H. Kirkham, shipwright, to Mrs. Newall, widow of the late Mr. Newall, stone-mason.—Mr. C. Dugdale, miller, to Miss A. Owen.—Mr. J. Williams, law-stationer, to Miss A. Pemberton.—Mr. J. Jones, mast-maker, of Mann's Island, Nova Scotia, to Miss M. Potts, of Walton.—Mr. G. Green, jun. merchant, to Miss J. Clark.—Captain Martin, to Miss A. Marsden.

At Preston, the Rev. Mr. Harris, incumbent curate of St. George's chapel, to Miss E. Lodge.

At Bolton, Mr. W. Appleton, manufacturer, to Miss Mellor.

At Wavertree, Mr. G. Anderton, to Miss M. Hodgson.—J. Hoyle, jun. esq. of Haslingdon, to Miss Brandwood.—Mr. Clarke, brewer, of Ormskirk, to Miss Forshaw, of Lathom.—Mr. T. Sellars, to Miss E. Taylor, both of Ashton-under-Line.

In the Isle of Man, J. Nelson, esq. to Miss Allen, daughter of T. Allen, esq. member of the House of Keys.

Died.] At Liverpool, aged 20, Mr. J. Jump, brother to Miss Jump, lately deceased, a young man of an amiable disposition and respectable mental accomplishments.

Mrs. Scott, widow.—Mrs. Barry.—Aged 22, after a life spent in innocence and virtue, and sincerely regretted, Miss M. Marrow. —Mrs Brownrigg.—Mrs Eyres, wife of Mr. T. Eyres, wheelwright.—Mr. J. Phillips, of the foundry.—Aged 82, Mrs. Grayson, widow.—Aged 92, Mrs. A. Davis.—Mr. W. Nelson, watchmaker.—Suddenly, after a few hours illness, aged 26, Mrs. Bullock.—In her 38th year, Mrs Green, wife of Mr. W. Green, landing waiter.—Aged 61, Mrs. Green, wife of Mr. J. Green.—Aged 77, Mrs. M. Tyndall, mother of Mrs. J. Wilson.—Suddenly, Mr. W. Tennant.

Aged 31, Mr. J. Barry, merchant. His young family, lately deprived of an affectionate mother, have now, in addition to their loss, to lament that of a beloved father.

In her 68th year, Mrs. Medley, relict of the late Rev. Samuel Medley.

Mrs. Asheton, mistress of a large and respectable school; universally respected in the more pleasing walks of social intercourse, for her habitual exercise of charity and benevolence.

At Manchester, Mr. J. Poole, merchant. —Mr. E. Bowden.

C. Alexander, esq of Edgehill, near Liverpool.—The Rev. F. Burton, curate of Poulton, near Lancaster.

At Kirkdale, near Liverpool, in her 19th year, Miss Crossley, eldest daughter of Mr. C. Crossley, late of the White Bull Inn, Warrington; a young lady whose talents and disposition promised fair to render her useful and amiable, through life. Her death was unfortunately occasioned by the following circumstance; being greatly fatigued by the business of the preceding day, she had set down to her sewing late in the evening, when falling asleep, her cloaths caught fire; every possible effort to extinguish the flames was ineffectual. She languished till the evening of the following day.

At Warrington, Miss M. Fairbrother.—Miss Birchill, of the Post-office.—Mr. J. Oddie, of Colne.

At Preston, G. Hornby, esq. one of the deputy-lieutenants for this county, and a constant and most liberal benefactor to the numerous poor in Preston. His nephew, the Rev. Mr. Hornby, rector of Winwick, and brother in law to the Earl of Derby, succeeds to most of his large estates. Mr Hornby, besides other bequests, has left to his upper servant, who was brought up in his service, one hundred pounds a year; to each of his other servants, a year's wages; and to 12 poor widows and widowers, who had, for a considerable time, been his weekly pensioners, at 2s. 6d. each, he has extended his benevolence, by leaving a sum adequate to their former weekly allowance, to be continued to be paid to them in the same manner during their natural lives, and to be continued in succession, to the same number of deserving persons for ever.

H. Walshman, esq. attorney, and alderman of this borough.—Aged 87, Mrs. Sill, mother of Mr. T. Sill, linen-draper.—In the prime of life, of a decline, Mr. J. Smith, printer.

In her 80th year, Mrs. E. Byrom, of Kersall; a lady who uniformly supported through life, a truly Christian character.

At Peeltoun, Isle of Man, in his 66th year, the Rev. H. Corlett, 42 years vicar of Kirk German; highly esteemed for his abilities and learning, and for the faithful and exemplary discharge of the duties of his sacred function. Mr. Corlett was one of the translators of the Manks' Bible (supposed to be the most consonant to the original of any edited translation whatever) and at the request of the Rev. Dr. Wilson, Prebendary of Westminster, &c. he also translated into the Manks' language, a selection of Sermons from the works of Bishop Wilson; the execution of which has been greatly admired by proficients in the Celtic language and its various

rious branches, Mr. Corlett was, undoubtedly, one of the chief ornaments of the Manks' church, adding to respectable talents, all the virtues and graces which distinguish and adorn the Christian Minister; and though living in a remote situation, his character was well known to many persons in this kingdom, eminent for their learning and piety.

T. Baron, esq. of Kousden, near Blackburn; highly respected as a gentleman of the most amiable manners.

In London, aged 29, Captain T. Waring, of the ship Princess Royal of that port, and son of Mr. L. Waring, of Liverpool; much lamented as a very worthy young man.

Aged 56, at Manchester, Mr. John Kay, attorney at law: a man of amiable manners, sound judgment, and most benevolent disposition. He was truly an ornament to his profession: the duties of which he discharged with the strictest integrity. Born and educated among the Dissenters, he was a steady friend to religious liberty. Firmly attached to the principles which produced the glorious revolution, and placed the illustrious House of Hanover on the throne of these realms; he was a determined advocate of constitutional freedom, which he ceased not, on every proper occasion, to defend against the subtle movers of sedition, or the misguided zealots of arbitrary power. A stranger to artifice or dissimulation, he made no scruple to avow his sentiments, at a time, when (unfortunately for his country) they were no longer popular. Yet so deeply was a sense of his worth engraven on the minds of all who knew him, that his language left behind it no trace of animosity on the minds of those whom his arguments failed to convince. For, in the warmth of disputation he never violated the rules of charity or decorum; and was ever ready to allow to others the privilege of individual judgment, which he claimed for himself. Gifted with a nice sense of honor, he was perhaps quick in resentment; but his enmity was momentary, and soon gave way to that serenity of temper, which no man ever possessed in a superior degree to himself. In friendship he was constant and sincere: equally ready to promote the happiness, or to participate in the distress, of those who shared his esteem. With devout acquiescence in the dispensations of divine Providence, and with pious confidence in the promises of the Gospel, he endured with resignation, a lingering illness, and contemplated the approach of death without dismay.

CHESHIRE.

Married.] Mr. R. S. Comberbatch, of Ruyton, to Miss Glover, of Ruyton Park.

At Liverpool, Mr J Brooks, to Miss A. Jones, of Newton, near Frodsham, in this county.

Died.] At Chester, of a severe paralytic stroke, Mr. Taylor, basket-maker.—Mr. Edwards, grocer, and alderman of this corporation.—Miss Adamson, milliner.

Mrs. Ankers, widow, of Boughton, near Chester.

At his house, in Upper Harley-street, London, aged 55, J. H. Smith Barry, esq. of Belmont, in this county.

DERBYSHIRE.

Married.] At Matlock, the Rev. G. Sanders, of Wollaton, near Nottingham, to Miss C. Eaton, daughter of Mr. Eaton, of Bonsall.—Mr. J N. James, hosier, of Nottingham, to Miss Goodale, of Rowsley, near Bakewell, in this county.—Mr. H. Woodcock, of Worksop Manor, to Miss S. Foster, of Brampton, in this county.—Mr W. Milward, attorney, of Chesterfield, to Miss S. Briggs, of Sheffield.—Mr. Wheeldon, to Miss Parker, both of Osmaston, near Derby.

Died.] At Derby, aged 34, Mrs. Clough, wife of Mr. G. Clough, grocer.

At the Park-houses, near North Wingfield, in his 71st year, Mr. E. Wilson.—Mr. J. Barker, of Stone Gravels, near Chesterfield; he fell suddenly to the ground and died, as it is supposed, of an apoplectic fit.

At Norton, aged 95, Mr. S. Deakin.—F. Beresford, esq. of Ashburne.

LINCOLNSHIRE.

An application is intended to be made to Parliament in the present session, for an inclosure of the open lands and commons within the parish of Coningsby, in this county.

Married.] At Gainsborough, Mr. T. Ashford, farmer, to Mrs. Ryley.

Mr. T. Lawrence, of Hacconby, to Miss Carter, of Dunsby.—Mr. Clark, of Moulton, to Miss Bellamy, of Gedney.

In London, Mr. T. Hyde, of Deeping Gate, to Miss Douthwaite, of Grantham; also, Mr. Sharwood, of Charter House-square, brother to Mrs. Clay, of Stamford, to Miss M. Kennedy, of Bunhill-row.

Mr. Edwards, watch-maker, &c. of Louth, to Miss Lyton, of Grantham.

Died.] At Boston, T. S. Brotherton, gent.

At Stamford, Mrs. Hodges, baker.—Aged 81, Mrs. Salter, widow; formerly many years mistress of a public-house. Six grand-daughters attended the funeral and held up the pall.

At Spalding, Mrs. Doughty, wife of Mr. Doughty, grocer, &c.

At Grantham, Mr. R. Taylor, publican.

Mrs. Stanger, of Ketton, near Stamford. She was apparently as well as usual, until attacked by spasms in her stomach, which unfortunately terminated her existence before she could be put to bed.

At Gainsborough, Mr. S. Turner, many years deputy overseer of the parish.

Aged 55, Mr. W. Toynbee, farmer, of Coleby, near Lincoln.

At

At Sleaford, aged 49, Mrs. Booth.—Aged 51, Mr. R. Toyne, farmer, of South Carlton, near Lincoln.

At Louth, aged 93, Mrs. E. Robinson, widow.—Aged 83, Mr. W. Gibbons.—Mr. Nidd, grazier, of Gedney Marsh.

Mr. T. Rogerson, farmer, of Couleeby; as he was riding to Louth fair, in apparent health, he suddenly fell from his horse and expired instantly.

At Ketton, near Stamford, aged 70, the Right Hon. Lady Elizabeth Noel, sister to the late Earl of Gainsborough. Her Ladyship resided in Bath for several years past, and was on a visit to her sisters in Rutland, when seized with the gout in her stomach which terminated her life.

Mr. Woodward, farmer, of Whitewater, near Stamford; he was taken suddenly ill with such excruciating pain, as deprived him of the power of speech, and he expired almost instantaneously. He had attended Stamford market on the preceding day, in his usual state of health.

At Marton, near Gainsborough, Mr. G. Foettit, bricklayer.

At Raithby, near Louth, aged 70, Mr. W. Stack.

At Fenton, near Gainsborough, Mr. Bridekirk, shoemaker; he was apparently very well in health the preceding day.

At Huttoft in the Marsh, near Alford, in his 102d year, Mr. J. Stephenson, farmer; his death was occasioned by a fall which brought on a mortification in his back. He had lived more than sixty years upon the same farm and enjoyed an uninterrupted good health during his life.

In her 22d year, Miss A. Lammyman, of Gedney.

LEICESTERSHIRE.

Married.] At Leicester, Mr. W. Harrison, to Miss Johnson, daughter of the late Mr. Alderman Johnson.

At Melton Mowbray, Mr. J. Hinde, currier, to Mrs. Dexter; by this marriage the bridegroom has obtained his 5th wife, and the bride her 3d husband.

Died.] Mrs. Abbot, of Wigstone.—Mr. Sergeant, grocer, of Holworth.

At Bath, Mrs. Mary Potter, sister of C. Neville, esq. of Holt, in this county; a lady not more distinguished for those splendid accomplishments which enrich and adorn society, than for uniform piety and benevolence; ever attentive to the calls of distress, she practically evinced the purity of her faith, by "visiting the fatherless, the orphan, and the widow, in their tribulation."

STAFFORDSHIRE.

Married.] At Walsall, Mr. Curtis, to Mrs. Davies. — R. Congreve, esq. of Iscod Park, Flintshire, to Miss Birch, eldest daughter of G. Birch, esq. of Hampstead Hall, in this county.

Mr. Lucar, of Leek, to Mrs. Gaunt, of Manchester.

Died.] At Litchfield, aged 85, Mrs. Hubbard.—Aged 75, Mr. J. Smallwood, shoemaker.

At Clonmell, in Ireland, aged 18, Mr. W. Barnett, son of Mr. Barnett, of the Crown-and-Horse-shoe public-house, Stafford.

At Newcastle-under-Lyne, Mr. T. Lloyd, attorney.

Aged 23, at Mr. Miller's, of Donstall, in this county, Mr. W. Phillips, of Brockton, Shropshire.

At Walsall, Mr. J. Burns, watch-maker.

Of an apoplexy, Mr. T. Foxall, surgeon; justly regretted as a good neighbour, an affectionate parent, and a truly honest man.

Mr. J. Watson, maltster, &c. of the Foregn, near Walsall.

At his seat, near Walsall, Mr. H. Whateley, attorney.

WARWICKSHIRE.

Married.] At Warwick, J. Greaves, esq. of St. Albans, to Miss M. Whitehead, second daughter of J. Whitehead, esq. of Barford.

At Rowley, Mr. J. Cutler, to Miss E. Evans.

Mr. C. Cross, of Birmingham, to Miss Reynolds, of Handsworth.—Mr. J. Burberry, of Kenilworth Chase, to Miss Jackson, of Wroxhall.

Died.] At Birmingham, Mr. J. Johnson, of the Green Man public-house.—Mr. T. Fleck, butcher.—Mr. S. Ashmore, youngest son of Mr. J. Ashmore.—Mr. T. Smallwood, cabinet-maker.—Mrs. Cherry, wife of Mr. J. Cherry, currier.—Suddenly, Mrs. Kempson.—Mr. T. Brown, of the Rising Sun public-house.—In her 47th year, Mrs. Holt, wife of Mr. Holt, brush-maker.—Aged 80, Mr. C. Elston, formerly a file-maker.

At Warwick, Mrs. Cattell, relict of the late Mr. J. Cattell, farmer.

At Coventry, Mrs. Owen, wife of Mr. G. Owen, attorney, of London.—Mr. Phillips, malster.

At King's Norton, aged 87, Mr. T. Reynolds.

At Rugeley, aged 83, Mrs. Hitchcock, widow of the late Mr. Hitchcock, grocer, &c.—Suddenly, Mr. T. Harding, steward to H. Legge, esq. of Astoon Hall, near Birmingham.

At New Orleans, in North America, in his 24th year, Mr. T. Heely, son of the late Mr. T. Oughton Heely, of Birmingham.

In London, Miss P. Aaron, daughter of Mr. Aaron, pencil-maker.

W. Homer, gent. of Bilston.—Mr. Pridmore, of Ansley, near Coventry.

At the Slade, near Rugeley, aged 10? years in April last, Mr. J. Milner.—Mr. T. Hunt, of the George-inn, in Solihull.

At

At More Green, near Birmingham, aged 56, Mrs. Turner, wife of W. Turner, esq. of Litchfield.

SHROPSHIRE.

Married.] At Shrewsbury, Mr. T. Ball, to Mrs. Norton.—Mr. J. Hulme, umbrella-maker, to Miss Derrett.

Mr. F. Blagdon, of Charing Cross, London, to Miss Edwards, of Oswestry.

Mr. R. Oakley, of Cotton Hill, to Miss Bennett, of the Crown-inn, Shrewsbury.—J. Walford, esq. of Pattingham, to Miss Wright, of Hatton Grange.

At Middle, Mr W. Wilkes, taylor, to Miss M. Griffiths.—Mr. T. Jones, weaver, to Miss M. Taylor.—Mr. H. Williams, wheelwright, to Miss H. Richards.—Mr. T. Williams, of Yeaton Hall, to Miss M. Parton, of Croesmere.

Mr Howell, tinplate-worker, of Whitchurch, to Miss Jones, sister to Mr. Jones, grocer.

W. Hanmer, esq. of Bicton, to Miss Austin, of Long.—The Rev. W. Pughe, curate of Talyllin, to Miss Owen, of Dolgoed.

Died.] At Shrewsbury, Master C. Oakley, youngest son of Sir Charles Oakley, bart.—On a visit in this town, after a few days illness, Miss Sambrook, of Westbury.—Miss E. Scoltock.

At St. Martin's, in this county, aged 101, Mrs. M. Davies

Mr. Brazenor, of Farley; sincerely lamented as a man of honesty and integrity which cannot be excelled.

Mrs. Urwick, of Shelton, near Shrewsbury; her life had for many years proved an ornament to the profession which she made of evangelical religion.

Miss Meredith, of Baschurch.—Mrs. Brag, wife of Mr. Brag, surgeon, &c. of Church Stretton.—In his 26th year, Mr. E. Thomas, of Llwynymaen, near Oswestry.

At Frankwell, aged 80, Mrs. J. Woodward, one of the resident widows at Mr. Millington's Hospital. The number of widows and widowers who have dwellings at this hospital is twelve, and the united ages of the eleven survivors with that of the deceased, make a total of nine hundred and sixteen years.

In the prime of life, Mr. R. Dawes, of Child's Ercall.—Mr. Poleston, of the Clive.—Mr. J. Morgan, of Measbury.—At a very advanced age, J. Gittins, gent. of Ruyton of the Eleven Towns.

At Ellesmere, Mr. R. James, of the White Hart-inn.

At Drayton, Mr. Redshaw, upholsterer.—Aged 23, Mr. W. Phillips, of Brockton.—Miss Vaughan, of Stanwardine.

HEREFORDSHIRE.

A new fair or great market has been lately established in Hereford, to be held annually, on the Wednesday after St. Andrew's-day, (between the Michaelmas and Candlemas fairs) for the sale of cattle, horses, sheep, pigs, hops, cheese, butter, and other commodities.

Married.] At Hereford, W. Higgins, esq. of Middlewood, to Miss Hancorn, sister of B. D. Dupps, esq. of Hollingbourn-place, Kent.

Mr. Preece, of Ross, to Miss C. Marsell, of Mitcheldean.—P. Jones, esq. of Sugwas, near Hereford, to Miss Roberts, of Ledbury.

Died.] At Hereford, Mrs. Hall, wife of Mr. Hall, coach painter.—Mrs. M. Martin.—In her 78th year, Mrs. Davies, wife of Mr. E. Davies, painter.

Mrs. E. Marsh, of Madeley; who had kept the Red Lion in that village, with great reputation, for upwards of 20 years.

At Homend, J. Poole, esq.; a gentleman whose strict integrity and profound knowledge of the law were universally allowed.

Mr. W. Merrick, auctioneer, of the Callow, near Hereford.

WORCESTERSHIRE.

Married.] At Bromsgrove, T. Phelps, esq. of Dublin, to Miss C. Lloyd, daughter of S. Lloyd, esq. of Birmingham.—Mr. Hadley, miller, of Leigh, to Miss Dunn, daughter of the late Mr. Dunn, surgeon, &c. of Worcester.—Mr. W. Long, of Worcester, to Miss Warren, of Severn Bank, near Worcester.

Mr. W. Webb, of Bromsgrove, to Mrs. Winter, of the Mouth of the Nile-inn, in Worcester.—Mr. J. Ironmonger, of Woolverhampton, to Miss Bann, daughter of Mr. Bann, flax-dresser, of Worcester.

Died.] At Worcester, in her 32d year, Mrs. Woodward, wife of Mr. T. Woodward, glover.

At White Lady Aston, Miss M. Roberts, 2d daughter of Mr. Roberts, senior; a young lady of great humanity, and proud to do every good office in her power.

Aged 92, Mrs. Iddins of Stourbridge.—Mrs. Haines, wife of Mr. J. Haines, of Cookhill.—Mrs Hodges, wife of Mr. Hodges, of Horsham.—At an advanced age, Mr. Powell, of Stoke Bliss.

At Droitwich, Mr. J. Lea, attorney, of Whittington, near Worcester; and four days after, Mrs. Lea, his mother. The various situations which this gentleman filed during life, form a memorable instance of the instability of human affairs.

At Alrick, aged 95, Mr. W. Walker, formerly a respectable farmer of Tunbridge; he enjoyed the use of his faculties to the last, and was able to walk to Worcester and back again without fatigue.

In her 89th year, Mrs Dowdeswell, of Chaceley; a lady, whose agreeable, easy, and chearful nature, gave an additional gratification to the hospitality that so uniformly characterized her residence.

GLOUCESTERSHIRE.

The Gloucestershire Society in London, have

have lately ordered at a general meeting, an encreafe of the premiums of the inftitution for the enfuing year of fifteen pounds; and the Committee have it likewife in contemplation to recommend to the Society, at the next anniverfary, a plan for affifting thofe young men who have been apprenticed by the Society with a fum of money, to be lent upon good fecurity, without intereft, to enable them to fet up in trade, upon the expiration of their indentures.

Preparations are making, agreeable to an act of Parliament lately paffed for dividing, allotting, inclofing, &c. the open and common fields within the tithing or hamlet of Cheltenham.

Married.] At Winterbourne, E. Brice, junior, efq. to Mifs Ford, both of Frenchag.

Mr. W. R. Wickham, of Sodbury, to Mifs Byam, of Wellefley Houfe, Wilts.—The Rev. D. Cooper, fellow of Worcefter College, Oxford, to Mifs Cooper, of Saintbury Ground, in this county.

At Frefhford, Mr. Grant, of Mitford, to Mifs H. Perkins.—Captain Jenkins, of the Monmouth and Brecon Militia, to Mifs —— of Fifhpond Houfe, in this county.

Died.] At Gloucefter, Mr. E. Quarrington, wine-merchant.—In her 11th year, Mifs Lenthal, only daughter of W. J. Lenthal, efq. of Broadwell.

Mr. Middleton, fon of the late Mr. Alderman Middleton.—Mrs. Hill, wife of Mr. Hill, late of the White Hart-inn.

Mr. M. Charlton, hatter and hofier; he carried on bufinefs for many years in this city, with the character (firmly eftablifhed) of a virtuous citizen and an upright man.

At Painfwick, aged 63, Mr. H. Jordan.—Mr. Millar, dyer, near Gloucefter.

Mr. Pope, a refpectable farmer, of Wotton-under-Edge. Returning home from Uley, he was unfortunately thrown from his horfe and fractured his fcull; which occafioned his death a day or two afterwards.

At Briftol, whither he had gone for the recovery of his health, T. P. Purnell, efq. of King's Hill, near Durfley, late lieut.-col. in the North Gloucefter Militia.

At Cheltenham, —— Moreau, efq. many years mafter of the ceremonies of that place.

At Prefton, aged 70, of the fmall-pox, which he caught accidentally.—Mr. Payne, farmer.

At Cirencefter, Mrs. Borton, wife of Mr. J. Borton, wine-merchant.

OXFORDSHIRE.

Married.] At Oxford, Mr. J. Blagrave, to Mifs M. Bellard, both of Abingdon.—Mr. Sims, to Mifs S. Wentworth.

Mr. R. French, to Mifs M. Wyton, both of Hook Norton.—Mr J. Preedy, of Dunftew, to Mifs Irons, of Eyden, in Northamptonfhire.

Died.] At Oxford, aged 55, Mrs. Curtis.—Mrs. Cofier, wife of Mr. Cofier, one of the city ferjeants.—Aged 78, Mr. V. Shortland, timber-merchant and alderman of the city.—Mr. G. Wilkins, watch-maker.—In her 20th year, Mifs J. Bartlett, eldeft daughter of Mr. J. Bartlett, manufacturer.

Lately, on his paffage home from the Jamaica ftation, Lieutenant M. Brookes, youngeft fon of the Rev. Dr. Brookes, of Shipton.—Aged 77, Mrs. A. Eaton, of Waterftock.

At Brill, Mrs. E. Elliott.

CAMBRIDGE.

Married.] J. D. Scully, efq. of Kilfeacle, in Ireland, and late of Trinity College, Cambridge, to Mifs Huddleftone, eldeft daughter of F. Huddleftone, efq. of Sawfton Hall, in this county.—Mr. C. Froft, of Newmarket, to Mifs Knights, eldeft daughter, of Mr. Knights, a reputable farmer at Ifleham.—Mr. Ruffel, of Downham, near Ely, to Mrs. Whiteley, of Ely.

Died.] At Cambridge, aged 78, Mr. S. Smith, peruke-maker.

At Wifbeach, Mr. J. Life, draper.

At Fordham, near Newmarket, Mr. H. Woollard, an opulent farmer.—In the prime of life, Mrs. Arber, wife of Mr J. Arber, lime-burner, &c. at Burwell.—Aged 46, Mr. J. Barwich, an opulent farmer at Haddenham, in the Ifle of Ely.—Mifs H. Battyl, eldeft daughter of Mr. T. Battyl, of Linton.

NORFOLK.

Married.] At Norwich, Mr. J. Symonds, carpenter, to Mifs Ingram.

Mr. W. Bell, to Mifs F. Dodd, both of Tiverfhall.—Mr. W. Arnold, mafter of the Trowel and Hammer public-houfe, to Mifs S. Dodd, daughter of the late Mr. C. Dodd, both of Shelf hanger.—Mr. W. Johnfon, of Redenhall, to Mifs B. Littell, of Norwich.

Died.] At Norwich, Mr. A. Kemp, butcher.—Aged 81, fuddenly, Mr. W. Webfter.

Aged 86, Mr J. Nafh; this venerable man has left behind him a progeny confifting of nine children, forty-five grand-children, and twenty-five great-grand-children.

Aged 81, Mrs. Kett, mother of H. Kett, efq.

Aged 24, Mr. Brown, breeches-maker; a very induftrious man, whofe family will feverely feel his lofs.

At Lynn, Mr. R. Dixon, farmer, &c.—Mr. D Stagg, fhoemaker.—Mr. J. Wefton, jun. a fheriff's officer.—Mrs. Smith, formerly of the Ferry-houfe.—Mifs Ruffel.

At Upwell, aged 57, Mr. W. Wells.—Aged 44, Mr. T. Snelling, farmer, at Moulton.

In the Weft Indies, L. Burton, efq. fecond fon of T. Burton, efq. of Braconda1e, near Norwich.

At Great Creffingham, in his 30th year, Mr. W. Browne.

At Holt, aged 75, Dr. Chambers, late of Dereham.

At

At Swaffham, aged 43, J. Woodward, esq. —Aged 43, E. Marcon, gent.

At Aylsham, Mrs. R. Pinkard.—In her 71st year, Mrs. Lovekin, relict of the late Rev. J. Lovekin, late rector of Colne Engain, Essex, and daughter of Mr. Hutchinson, late of Norwich.

At Stoke Holy-cross, aged 78, Mrs. E. Windett.—Mr. Alexander, farmer, of Loddon Englofs.

At Rodney-hall, in her 29th year, Miss Norris, eldest daughter of J. Norris, esq.—Aged 52, Mrs. S. Lock, of Hingham.

SUFFOLK.

The Earl of Bristol's new seat at Ickworth, in this county, will not be completed till the end of the approaching summer: the princely sum of 150,000l. has been already expended on this singular structure, and various monuments of taste have already arrived for its decoration, for which suits of apartments are constructing in a style of taste, elegance, and magnificence, that no private subject of this country has hitherto, it is said, been known to display!

Married.] Mr. Flude, of Ipswich, to Mrs. Durrant, of Sproughton.—Mr. T. Wright, merchant, of Ipswich, to Miss E. Pinchon, eldest daughter of Mr. W. Pinchon, farmer, &c. of Upminster, Essex.—Mr. F. Adams, plumber, &c. of Stowmarket, to Miss A. Mayston, late of Horney.—Mr. Y. Stammers, miller, to Miss Erith, both of Sudbury.—Mr. Coe, of the Park-farm, near Melford, to Mrs. Deresly, of Melford.

At Middletown, in North America, Mr. Collins, attorney, to Miss E. Watkinson, third daughter of Mr. S. Watkinson, late of Lavenham, in this county.

The Rev. M. Simpson, of Mickfield, and late of Caius College, Cambridge, to Miss Seaman, of Brockford.—Mr. Pollard, merchant, to Miss Harrison, both of Ipswich; and Mr. Cooper, farmer, of Dunkstone, to Miss E. Harrison, sister to the above.—Mr. J. Orbell, haberdasher, of Bury, to Miss D. Briggs, of Mildenhall.

Died.] At Bury, Mrs. Deck, wife of Mr. Deck, bookseller.—In her 38th year, after an illness of about two days, Mrs. Phillips, wife of the Rev. Dr. Phillips.

At Ipswich, in her 20th year, Miss C. Bond, second daughter of Mr. Bond, leather-seller.

Mrs. A. Norman; she distilled peppermint for her livelihood, but was supposed to be in a state of poverty. Having died suddenly, her cloaths were taken off, when there were found near 100 guineas sewed up in different parts, and property to the amount of 5 or 600l. more was found hid in different parts of the house.

At Rickinghall, aged 67, Mrs. Mills, widow, late of Fakin's Hall; a woman highly exemplary in the relative duties, as her charity was ever accordant with her piety and temporal ability.

At Coddenham, Mr Osborne, late of Ramsholt.

Also, in his 73d year, Mr. E. Jones, late an excise-officer; much regretted as a very intelligent and benevolent man, and a sincere friend.

At Southwold, in her 64th year, Mrs. Jermyn, wife of R. Jermyn, esq. collector of the customs.

At Stowmarket, suddenly, Mrs. Hildyard, wife of Mr. C. Hildyard, draper; this truly excellent woman was a most endearing companion to her relatives and acquaintance, a pious Christian, an affectionate wife, a tender mother, and a benevolent friend to the poor.

Suddenly, or rather without a moment's previous illness, Mr. J. Cornell, farmer, of Higham Green, near Kentford. After following his daily avocations, and smoking his pipe, he suddenly dropt the same from his mouth, fell to the ground, and instantaneously quitted the scene of human abode for a world of better hope.

Aged 66, Mr. P. Cutting, farmer, of Grundisburgh.—Aged 82, D. Guilt, esq. of Icklingham.—Mrs. Freeman, wife of Mr. Freeman, maltster, of Barrow.

At Beccles, in his 40th year, the celebrated Mr. James Bradnum, alias Lord Bradnum; a character well known on the turf, and more particularly at all the hackney-races in this county and Norfolk; indeed, sometimes, when he had been fortunate at home, he would make a dashing excursion to Ipswich or Newmarket. His death was occasioned by being thrown down, and held on the side of a cart, the wheel of which lacerated the flesh from the back-bone.

At Troston, at the house of her nephew, on Monday, Dec. 14, 1801, about two in the morning, after years of pain and infirmity, which had long confined her to her bed, but had not, till very near her death, overcome her spirits, Tho. Capell, the last surviving aunt of Capell Lofft, and daughter of Gamaliel Capell, formerly rector of Stanton All-saints, and Stanton St. John's, by Hester Maddocks, his wife. In her youth, she had been remarkable for the strength and activity of her mind, in a numerous and sensible family of her brothers and sisters. She was born Jan. 10, old style, 1718.

Aged 2., Mrs. Cooper, she was unfortunately taken ill after dinner, on the day of her marriage, and died about one o'clock next morning.

ESSEX.

Married.] Mr. J. Osbourn, to Miss R. Argent, both of Sible Hedingham.—Mr. E. Boltwood, to Miss A. Archer, both of Great Waltham.

Mr. W. Packman, of Aldgate High-street, London, to Miss Wood, of Heybridge, near Maldon.

Mr. Barnes, of the Swan public-house, to Miss Hardney, both of Colchester.—Mr. J. Ardley, miller, of Pentlow, to Miss Dorr, of of Stifted.—Mr. W. Hutley, farmer, of Bradwell, near Stiftead, to Miss Fairhead, of Bradwell Hall.

Died.] At Chelmsford, Captain Watts, of the regiment of Buckinghamshire Militia; greatly lamented as a very promising young man.

Mrs. Darby, relict of the late Mr. E. Darby, hatter, and latterly of Rochford.

At Colchester, Mr. Cole, baker.—In her 70th year, Mrs. Peartree, widow.

At Harwich, Mrs. Hobday.

At Castle Hedingham, in his 77th year, the Rev. B. Bridges, rector of Birdbrook, in this county, and justice of peace for the counties of Essex and Northampton.—Aged 47, Mrs. Walford, wife of Mr. T. Walford, wheelwright, of Braintree.

At Saffron Walden, aged 82, the Rev. R. Gaston.

At Rayleigh, Mr. Belsham, of the Crown public house.

Aged 79, Mr. Stock, of Warner's Farm, in Great Waltham.

At Calais, Mr. P. White, formerly of Ratsborough Farm, near Southminster, in this county.

At Great Waltham, Mr. S. Watkinson.

At Billericay, Mr. Coultas, master of the Crown inn.

At Halstead, aged 84, after a few hours' illness, Mrs. S. Wood, mother of Mr. E. Wood, ironmonger, of Chelmsford.—Mrs. Hogg, wife of Mr. Hogg, taylor, of Ingatestone.—In her 76th year, Mrs. Hawkes, wife of Mr. Hawkes, baker, of Newport.—In the prime of life, at St. Margaret's Farm, Little Burstead, Mr. F. French. His death, which is sincerely regretted by his relatives, and a small circle of acquaintance, was occasioned by an excessive inlargement of the glands, which resisted the efforts of the most eminent of the faculty. His patience and resignation under the severe affliction were exemplary in the highest degree.

KENT.

The Thames and Medway Canal has been lately completed from Gravesend as far as the parish of Denton. It stretches between the two rivers on one level, and has a culvert communicating with the Thames, in which the engineer has introduced a valve, by which to empty and fill the canal at pleasure.

Married.] At Canterbury, Mr. W. Smith, of Mrs. Baker's company of comedians, to Mrs. Cotesworth.

Mr. J. Temple, of Sandwich, to Miss E. Pott, of Word.

At Maidstone, Mr. T. Hills, baker, to Miss Beck, of Milgate.—W. Largent, esq. paymaster of the second or Queen's Regiment, to Miss S. Marshall, fourth daughter of J. Marshall, esq. late of Tenterden.

Mr. R. Goldridge, to Mrs. S. Rogers, both of Berstead.

At Dover, Mr. G. Friend, to Miss Fin.

At Kingsnorth, Mr. W. Pierce, gardener, to Mrs. M. Ham.

At Wingham, Mr. J. Hawkes, of Deal, to Miss Matson.—Mr. W. Kemp, to Miss Paine, both of Throwley.

At Littlebourne, Mr. J. Inges, to Miss Cooper.—Mr. J. Dyce, brasier, of Canterbury, to Miss Sweetlove, of Wingham.

Died.] At Maidstone, in his 79th year, W. Hawkins, esq.—In her 74th year, Mrs. Sawkins, widow, late of Lyminge.

At Canterbury, Mrs. F. Plater, widow.—Mr. B. Greenland, late mate of the Trelawney Planter West Indiaman.—Mrs. S. Stephenson, widow, of Whitstable.—Aged 86, Mrs. A. Tevelein.

At Deal, at the Signal-station, East Hill, Lieutenant J. Turner.—Mrs. Collard, wife of Mr. Collard, shoemaker.

At Tenterden, Mrs. Munn, widow.

Mrs. Hunt, of the boarding-school in Lynstead.—B. Blake, esq. of Westminster.—The Rev. J. H. Standen, rector of Milton.

At Rochester, aged 42, Mr. W. Stevens, formerly a butcher.

At New Romney, Mr. Masey, bricklayer, and likewise his son, aged about twenty; they were employed in sinking a well, when the bottom and sides fell in, and the sand instantaneously covered them both. All attempts made to recover them were in vain. The father was a sober, steady man, and an excellent workman.

HAMPSHIRE.

Married.] At Winchester, Mr. Allsop, silk-weaver, to Mrs. Tredgold.

At Lymington, Mr. Frampton, to Miss Jennings.

Sir Thomas Champney, bart. of Amport, to Miss Minchin, eldest daughter of the late H. Minchin, esq. of Soberton.

At Portsmouth, Captain Killet, of the marines, to Miss A. Cross.

The Rev. H. Atkins, of Odiam, in this county, to Miss H. Chandler, of Shapwick, near Chichester.

Died.] At Southampton, Mrs. Le Cras, widow of the late—Le Cras, esq. one of the commissioners of the navy.

B. Langton, esq. of whose character, after an observation of one who never bestowed undeserved praise, nothing need be said: Dr. Johnson, with a warm vehemence of affectionate regard, once exclaimed to Mr. Boswell, "The world does not bear a worthier man than Bennett Langton!"

WILTSHIRE.

The Wilts and Berks Canal is now completely navigable, from Semington to Chippenham, Calne, Dauntsey Park and Bowden Farm, near Wotton Basset; and there is now an uninterrupted communication by water, by the junction of the above with the Kennet and Avon Canal from those places to Bath, and from thence by the Avon to Bristol. The neighbourhood on the Line will, in consequence

sequence, be materially benefited, by obtaining a supply of excellent coal at a cheap rate, and the timber and other articles ready to be conveyed will create a very considerable trade immediately.

Married.] At Aldbourn, Mr. W. Smith, jun aged 19, to Mrs. Pizzy, a widow lady, aged upwards of 60, with a handsome fortune.—W. Higginson, esq. of Salisbury, to Mrs. Reading, relict of Mr. T. Reading, attorney.

Mr. T. Gale, of Tunbridge, to Miss Pike, of Great Bedwin, in this county.

Died.] At Ramsbury, suddenly, on his return from church, aged 83, Mr. J. Lewes.

SOMERSETSHIRE.

Married.] At Bristol, Mr. C. Morris, broker, to Miss E. Holloway.—Mr. W. Thomas, cabinet-maker, to Miss E Jones, of the Three Boars Heads public-house.

Mr. Luxton, ironmonger, of Bristol, to Miss Summerhags, of Broadwood Kelly, Devon.

At St. Elizabeth's, Jamaica, Mr. Chester, late druggist, of Bristol, to Mrs. Samuel, relict of W. Samuel, esq. of Richmond Hill, Jamaica.

At Bath, S. Senhouse, esq. to Miss M. Le Mesurier.—W. F. Count de l'Age de Labretolliere, to Miss S. Palmer, only daughter of J. Palmer, esq. of Alton Hall, Staffordshire.

Died.] At Bristol, Mr. Verry, land-surveyor: a man justly esteemed for his professional abilities, and no less highly valued and endeared to his acquaintance for his amiable disposition.

Aged 71, Mr. J. Hood, ironmonger.—Mrs. Lediard, wife of Mr. Lediard, drysalter.—Mr. W. Dyer, a respectable accomptant.

Mrs. Hagley; an amiable woman, possessed of an innate goodness of mind, joined to singular purity of heart, and extreme benevolence to the poor.

Mrs. A. Houston, widow of the late Mr. C. Houston, broker.—Mr. F. A. Brookman, youngest son of Mrs Brookman, confectioner.—Aged 70, Mr. R. Collins, formerly a maltster and brewer.—Mrs. Skone, mother of Mr. Skone, grocer.—Mr. Griffiths, plane-maker.—In the prime of life, Mr. J. Prothero, late assistant to Mr J. Evans.

At Bath, Mr. Andrews, cheesemonger.

DORSETSHIRE.

Addition to page 377.—Dr. PULTENEY, whose death was noticed in the Monthly Magazine for November, was born at Mountsorrel, in Leicestershire, in 1730, and known to the public as the author of "the General View of the Writings of Linnæus;" of "Historical and Biographical Sketches of the Progress of Botany in England;" and many other valuable pieces upon botanical and medical subjects. He first practised as a surgeon and apothecary at Leicester, and, upon obtaining the degree of Doctor of Physic in a way singularly honourable to himself at Edinburgh, he commenced practice as a physician at Blandford thirty-seven years since. Having accumulated a very large fortune, he has bequeathed a number of legacies amongst philosophical and medical institutions, and to several individuals respectable for their talents and attainments. To this brief account, we give place with pleasure to the following character of him communicated by a valuable correspondent:—

Dr. Pulteney's works in natural history were neither numerous, or of an unweildy magnitude; but they were the valuable result of laborious and long continued research, and evidenced a mind stimulated by an ardent passion for the pursuit of physical science, and that was, in an eminent degree, adapted, both by original genius and habitual activity, for promoting its diffusion and advancement amongst mankind. The conscientious, attentive, and cautious manner in which, during a long, useful, and highly reputable career, he discharged the important duties of a most awfully responsible profession, excited and permanently secured to him the confidence and regard of all who from their local residence, were so fortunate as to be within convenient reach of his medical assistance and advice. A young physician might have learned equally from the excellence of his precepts, and the purity of his example. The writer of this article regrets, now, alas! unavailingly regrets, opportunities he has neglected, of enjoying the converse, and of listening to the instructions, of so wise a monitor, and so faithful and invaluable a friend. Dr. Pulteney's uncommon merit was not restricted to the practice of physic, or to the prosecution of science; it shone equally conspicuous in every scene and department of his life. The most amiable, at least, if not the most splendid, part of his character was unfolded in social, and more especially in domestic and familiar intercourse. No person could be in his company without, for the time, being rendered not only the happier, but also the wiser, and the better for it. By the mild gaiety, and well regulated playfulness of his fancy, he amused and delighted; he instructed by the solidity of his judgment, and there was a commanding something in his presence and demeanour, which, even from the hearts of the most obdurately depraved, could not fail to extort at least a temporary veneration for virtue. That for so considerable a portion of his long life, a man of Dr. Pulteney's superior cast, should have existed in a state of almost complete exile from the intellectual world, and so long have submitted to the dreariness and *mental solitude* of an obscure provincial situation, must afford no small matter of wonder and of regret to those who are capable of appreciating the value of extraordinary talents, or or of enjoying the exercise and exhibition of them, in an improved and highly cultivated society. J. Reid.

CORNWALL.

A topographical description of this county lately published, mentions a steam-engine used for drawing off the water of the great tin-mine at Polgarth, which cost the sum of twenty thousand pounds. The quantity of coal requisite to keep this stupendous and wonderful engine in motion, is seventy-two bushels in twenty-four hours. It raises sixty-three gallons of water at every stroke, and performs fourteen of these motions every minute. The water thrown out upon the surface, runs off like a river, and according to the above calculation, must be upwards of nine hundred thousand gallons daily.

WALES.

Married.] In London, T. Waters, Esq. of Fountain Hall, Carmarthenshire, to Miss M. Ormond, of Trenewydd, Pembrokeshire.

Mr. L. Beynon, of St. Clear, Carmarthenshire, to Miss J. Stewart, of Swansea.—R. W. Price, esq. of Rhiwlas, Merionethshire, to Miss F. Lloyd, 2d daughter of J. Lloyd, esq. of Berth, near Builth, and chief justice of the Carmarthen circuit.

Died.] Mrs. Ewers, wife of the Rev. G. Ewers, of Haverfordwest.

At Upton Castle, Pembrokeshire, the Rev. T. Woods.

At Swansea, Captain J. Mills.

At Malta, Captain C. Hare, of Bathafarn Park, near Ruthin, and commander of the Madras ship of war.

At Ruthin, Mr. T. Turner, skinner and glover.—Mr. J. Paver, landlord of the Cross Foxes inn.

At Martinique, Mr. W. James, youngest son of Mr. J. James, of Dyffryn, Pembrokeshire.

SCOTLAND.

Of all the extraordinary, or rather immense, productions, which distinguished the late very fertile season, none can compare with those raised by Mr. W. Simpson, gardener, in the Abbey of Cambuskenneth, near Stirling, who produced a carrot eighteen inches in circumference, and thirty inches long; a potatoe which weighed three pounds, twelve ounces and a half; and an onion thirteen inches and a half in circumference!

IRELAND.

Married.] At Dublin, Mr. Powell, barrister, to the Countess Dowager of Alborough.—Mr. J. Grogan, of Dublin, to Miss Medlicott, of the county of Kildare.—Mr. J. Murphy, jun. of Callier, to Miss E. Murphy, of Cashel.

MONTHLY COMMERCIAL REPORT.

As the Definitive Treaty between Britain and France, has not yet been signed; and the conclusion of a Commercial Treaty between the two Countries, is perhaps still distant; no free trading intercourse between French and British ports has been, hitherto, opened. What sail from the one coast to the other, are either neutrals, subject to the regulations of the neutral trade, packets, or French or British merchant-ships under passports. French goods, therefore, have not yet begun to be poured, in excessive profusion, into our British markets. Nor have our merchants that direct access which they desire, to the markets of France.

Yet, in spite of every restraint or prohibition by the French Government, commodities of British manufacture continue to be used by the French people in general, in preference to all others. Our manufactures are still better accommodated than those of any other country, to the taste of the French, in fashion, as well as to their real convenience.

At the last great fairs in *Germany*, the sales of British goods were, again, prodigiously large, and at prices so low, that no Continental manufactures could keep the market in competition with them. These sales go, in great part, to the supply of France—of the more distant inland parts of Germany—of the frontier provinces of Turkey—of Poland, and even of the other parts of the dominions of Russia. But it is, undoubtedly, the carrying trade between France and Britain, by which the merchants who attend the Leipsic and Frankfort fairs are, for the present, chiefly enriched.

The trade to *Leghorn* is again brisk. A number of valuable cargoes have been lately shipped from London for that port. For our cottons, our woollens, our hard-ware, and our dried fish, that, and the other ports of Italy, now present highly convenient markets.

The prices of *Wool* are still high: and the manufacturers of woollen goods are now active in executing large orders. *Cottons*, almost of every sort are at higher prices than at the date of our last publication. Indigoes, and other *dye-stuffs*, have likewise risen in price. These circumstances bespeak a demand among the manufacturers; which could not arise, unless the last sales of manufactured goods had been favourable; and unless new orders to a large amount had been received.

The prices of *leather*, that staple article of British manufacture, have, within these five weeks, fallen somewhat lower. *Iron* is now considerably higher.

By some information of due authority which has been recently made public, we learn, that the *fur-trade* of the British Canadian Provinces, is now in a flourishing state. Its produce in the year 1798, consisted of 106,000 beaver skins, 2100 bear skins, 1500 fox skins, 4000 kitt fox skins, 4600 otter skins, 17000 musquash skins, 32000 marten skins, 1800 mink skins, 500 buffalo skins, a quantity of castoreum, 6000 lynx skins, 600 wolverine skins, 1650 fisher skins, 3800 wolf skins, 700 elk skins, 7500 deer skins, 1200 drelled deer skins. Of these furs, the greater part came to sale in London, in the year 1800. They are, directly or indirectly, paid for in the following goods of British manufacture; milled blankets; arms and ammunition; twist and carrot tobacco; Manchester goods; linens and coarse sheetings; thread, lines, and twine; common hardware

hardware; cutlery and ironmongery of different sorts; kettles of brass and copper, and sheet-iron; silk and cotton handkerchiefs; hats, shoes, and hose; calicoes and printed cottons, &c. The trade is in the hands of two Companies. The capital funded in it, may be about 150,000l. sterling. We understand, that the management of the fur-trade is subject in the port of London to embarrassments and restrictions, which render the direct exportation of the furs to China from the ports of the United States, much more eligible than the sending of them to sale in England. It is, therefore, most earnestly to be desired, that the British Government should, in one way or another, use, without delay, the fit means to hinder us from losing, by Anglo-American competition, a branch of our trade so truly valuable.

The final ratification of the recent Treaty between France and America was lately communicated from the Executive Government to the Legislative Body. By that communication we perceive, that the French and Americans mutually agree to treat one another's trading ships, when either of them shall be at war with a nation in peace with the other, agreeably to those claims of neutral rights upon which the late hostilities of the Powers of the North were excited against Great Britain.

Sugars of different sorts have, in the course of the last month, risen in price. The importers of sugar were not, indeed, gratified by the renewed prohibition of the distillery of spirits from grain: and, it would, no doubt, have been unreasonable to sacrifice the interests of our British cultivators to those of the planters in the West Indies. But sugar will still, in its coarsest forms, be consumed, in no small proportion, in the uses of the distillery. The exportation to the other parts of Europe will not, for the present year, be much hurt by French competition. And the immense consumption of this article among ourselves at home, is now becoming every day more considerable; so that we do not suppose that the present season can turn out very unfortunate for the proprietors of West India produce.

It is still exceedingly to be regretted, that the *Brewers* cannot be put in a situation in which they might be enabled to supply a *beer* so stout and wholesome to labouring men, as to supersede the use of gin. The beer even now in use, though better than that which was lately on sale, is far from possessing those qualities. The strength of our manufacturers, and the whole morals and industry of those on whose toil our commercial prosperity fundamentally depends, are so deeply interested in this matter, that it ought, in preference to most other objects of public economy, to fix the common national concern.

The late Chancellor of the Exchequer left paper, burthened with imposts so enormous, that not only the *extinction of English Literature*, but the ruin of our export-trade in *prints, books* and *stationary* appeared even then to be effects which could not but directly ensue. The exportation of stationary and English books to America, begins already to be transferred entirely from this country to Germany, Holland, and France. It begins to be more eligible to manufacture paper, and reprint English books even at Calcutta, than to take them by exportation from this Country. And it is now likely, that of all languages, the English will be in future the least known to foreign nations. And yet the book and paper trade, might be a capital branch of our commerce, and an inestimably powerful engine by which to extend our political influence.

MONTHLY AGRICULTURAL REPORT.

THE frost, during some part of the present month, has been extremely intense; but we do not believe that much injury has been done to the young wheats, either by it, or the gentle thaw that has succeeded. In general these crops look healthy and promising. The business of ploughing is at present, in most districts, as far advanced as is usual at this season; and on the wetter grass-lands, the hardness of the frost has afforded a good opportunity for casting out much manure. Grain is now somewhat on the advance, probably in a great measure from the distilleries being allowed to work again. Average price of corn in England and Wales to the week ending December 19. Wheat 74s. 10d. Rye 47s. 10d. Barley 44s. 1d. Oats 23s. 10d. Beans 44s. 6d. Pease 45s. 7d.

Potatoes, notwithstanding the very abundant crop of the last season, are likewise rising in price.

From the great scarcity of lean stock, although there has been, in most places, a very great supply of food for this period, is unusually high; and fat stock is of course dear. At Smithfield Market, Monday Dec. 28, beef sold from 4s. 4d. to 6s. mutton, 5s. to 6s. 6d. veal, 5s. to 6s. 6d. pork, 5s. 4d. to 7s. At Newgate and Leadenhall Markets, beef sold from 3s. 6d. to 5s. mutton, 4s. 6d. to 5s. 8d. veal, 4s. to 6s. 3d. pork, 5s. 4d to 7s.

Store hogs have likewise been sold at very high prices, both in the London and some of the Country markets; the price of pork is therefore high.

Turnips, in some of the more wet situations, have been greatly injured by the severity of the late frost, and consequently a great loss of useful food sustained. On the drier turnip soils, they have, however, received little or no injury.

Hops. This article has continued very dull, and now looks down in price. Notwithstanding the very deep speculations that have been made by some persons, who are determined to run all risks, although their losses have been very great indeed by what they held of the last and preceding years growth, we think it possible they may still decline considerably, for though the duty has been stated by the Newspapers to be 208,000l. we have no doubt it will amount to 230,000l. Bags are now from 78s. to 100s. per Cwt. Pockets, from 88s. to 108s. per Cwt.

Good hay has lately been rather looking up in price. At St. James's Market, Sat. Dec. 26, hay sold from 4l. to 5l. 8s. At Whitechapel Market, hay 4l. to 5l. 8s. clover, 5l. 10s. to 6l. 14s.

Straw

Straw, as is usual at this season, is high. At St. James's Market, Sat. Dec. 26, straw sold from 1l. 10s. to 2l. 2s. At Whitechapel Market, from 1l. 10s. to 1l. 16s.

The annual shew of prize cattle at Smithfield was remarkably well attended this year. The principal prizes were obtained by Mr. WESTCAR, for a Herefordshire ox; by Mr WATKINSON, of Woodhouse, Leicestershire, for a sheep of the new Leicester breed; and by Mr Helman for a sheep of the South Down breed. The Duke of Bedford obtained some premiums in several classes.

METEOROLOGICAL REPORT.

Observations on the State of the Weather, from the 24th of November to the 24th of December inclusive, 1801, two miles N. W. of St. Paul's.

Barometer.			*Thermometer.*		
Highest 29.98 Dec. 19 & 20, Wind W.			Highest 53°. Dec. 5. Wind W.		
Lowest 28.6. Dec. 9. Wind W.			Lowest 18°. Dec. 18. Wind W. by N.		
Greatest variation in 24 hours.	7-tenths of an inch	On the 8th inst. about noon the barometer stood at 29.3; the next day at the same hour it had fallen to 28.6, in the former case the thermometer stood at 40°, in the latter it was 50°.	Greatest variation in 24 hours.	26°.	Between 7 & 8 in the morning of the 4th inst. the thermometer was at 27°. at the same hour on the 5th it stood at 53°.

The quantity of rain fallen since the last report, is equal to 4.498 inches of depth.

We have, in our last two or three reports, marked the great and sudden variableness in the state of the atmosphere. The changes during the last month have been still more remarkable; some of the principal variations will be deserving of notice;—between the mornings of the 4th and 5th of December, the barometer fell six-tenths of an inch, consequently the pressure of the atmosphere upon the body of every common sized person was equal to about six hundred pounds weight greater on the former day, than on the latter. And when it is considered that during the same period the thermometer rose 26° viz. from 27 to 53, we might naturally expect that so sudden a change, both in the pressure and temperature of the atmosphere, would have a considerable effect upon the health and spirits of the animal frame.

In the evening of the 13th instant, between the hours of seven and half past nine, the *Aurora Borealis* was more brilliant and beautiful than we had witnessed for many years; at one part of the time, broad beams of light diverged from a point in the western horizon, over a great part of the visible hemisphere. At another period they put on the appearance of the arcs of a rainbow, only much broader, and extended from one side of the Heavens to the other, crossing the magnetic meridian at right angles.

The severity of the weather from the 12th to the 20th instant, was unusually great; in the morning of the 18th, just before sun-rise, the thermometer stood at 18° or 14 degrees below the freezing point. At the same time on the 20th it was as low as 19°, and at nine o'clock in the evening of that day it was as high as 39°. It is worth remarking that in the several severe frosts during the last month the wind was almost uniformly in the west, from which quarter it has chiefly blown since our last notice. It has been in the east but two days.

There have been twenty days without rain or snow. A considerable fall of snow happened on the 27th of November, some more fell on the 30th, and a little again on the 16th of the present month.

**** Persons who reside Abroad, and who wish to be supplied with this Work every Month, as published, may have it sent to them, FREE OF POSTAGE, to New York, Halifax, Quebec, and every Part of the West Indies, at Two Guineas per Annum, by Mr.* THORNHILL, *of the General Post Office, at No. 21, Sherborne-lane; to Hamburg, Lisbon, Gibraltar, or any Part of the Mediterranean, at Two Guineas per Annum, by Mr.* BISHOP, *of the General Post Office, at No. 22, Sherborne-lane; to the Cape of Good Hope, or any Part of the East Indies, at Thirty Shillings per Annum, by Mr.* GUY, *at the East India House; and to any Part of Ireland, at One Guinea and a Half per Annum, by Mr.* SMITH, *of the General Post Office, at No. 3, Sherborne-lane. It may also be had of all Persons who deal in Books, at those Places, and also in every Part of the World.*

SUPPLEMENTARY NUMBER

TO THE

MONTHLY MAGAZINE.

Vol. 12. No. 82.] JANUARY 20, 1802. [Price 1s. 6d.

HALF-YEARLY RETROSPECT OF DOMESTIC LITERATURE.

THANKS to the ſcarcity of rags, to the dearth of paper-ſtuff, to the exciſe on pulp, and to the law of libel! the maſs of publication begins to abate. Inſtead of provinces, only acres of ſheets have been ſullied; inſtead of a Thames, only a Tweed of ink has been let looſe; and the taſk of ſurvey, if it be flat enough to annoy, is not long enough to tire. If the Neckinger-mills become as efficient in withdrawing, as the price of publication is become in withholding, the ſuperfluities of literature; we ſhall be compelled ſoon to revert from the new to the good, to bring upon the parlour-table the claſſics of our forefathers, to view at length the inſide of volumes which the binder has labelled Addiſon and Richardſon, to learn our Anti-jacobiniſm in Berkeley, and our myſticiſm in Jeremy Taylor.

The form and order of retroſpection are of little moment: yet the fewer the ſubdiviſions into which the books are parcelled, the more conveniently can the heaps be arranged on the floor; and the leſs turning to and fro among Reviews will ſupply the reputed character of thoſe, which one wants the leiſure to ſlit open, or the will to read. A critical catalogue may be very equitable, if it only contains the criticiſms of others; and is perhaps moſt meritorious, when leaſt tinged with the perſonalities of autopſy. Readers are not to claim from the advertiſer of a Retroſpect, that he ſhould himſelf weigh every article he retales—it is enough to quote the avoirdupois of his invoice. Still leſs may they expect from his induſtry a complete liſt; which can as little extend to all the muſhrooms of literature, as to thoſe of vegetation.

CIVIL HISTORY, BIOGRAPHY, AND CHRONOLOGY.

"A View of the Origin and Conduct of the War with Tippoo Sultaun, by ALEXANDER BEATSON, 31s. 6d."

If there be any part of the map of the globe, on which the eye of an Engliſhman can repoſe with ſatisfaction—where the ſtateſmanſhip of miniſters has not flung away the acquirements of valour, or diſappointed the confidence of voluntary ſubmiſſion, it is on Hindoſtan. A vaſt diſtrict has there been added to Britiſh empire by the completed conqueſt of Myſore. To the eſſential intolerance of iſlamiſm has ſucceeded the unbigoted liberality of mercantile ſway; to the perſonal deſpotiſm of an iraſcible and cruel prince, the mild ſuperintendence of European gentlemen; to the intellectual twilights of printleſs literature, the radiations of the preſs of Calcutta. Under a ſecurer and more ſkilful government the whole ſurface of the country will embelliſh. Traffic will ſmooth his roads; induſtry widen his bazars; and agriculture collect in huger pools his hoards of irrigation.

The ſubſtance of the narrative may thus be condenſed. One Ripaud, captain of a French veſſel which touched at a port of the Myſore, by repreſenting the facility with which a large and efficient force of Europeans could be procured from the Mauritius, induced Tippoo to ſend deputies thither to treat for the hire of French ſoldiers. The Engliſh Governor-general thought it neceſſary to ſtrike a deciſive blow before ſuccours ſhould arrive. A negociation was opened with the Nizam, relative to the French army at Hyderabad, and leave was obtained to ſurround their camp. After this enterprize was ſucceſsfully executed, the Britiſh army, in concert with ſoldiers of the Nizam, marched forward to Seringapatam, where it was joined by troops from the oppoſite ſide of the peninſula. The ſiege was undertaken with a force of forty-five thouſand men; and the town eventually yielded to an aſſault, during which the Sultaun fell by a muſket-ball. His death

death terminated the conteſt; and his whole territory has been partitioned.

Mr. Beatſon's account of the acquiſition is what an original hiſtory ought to be, a clear orderly relation of facts, flanked with documents. It is compoſed in that regular book-maker's ſtyle, which the Scottiſh writers have introduced. The phraſeology is not idiomatic, as we talk, but European, like the thrice tranſlated columns of a newſpaper. The periods are ſmooth and ſimilar, as if cut out with a butter-ſtamp. The characters are drawn up with urbanity and numerus, and agreeably terminate in ſyllabic caſcades of humanity and moderation.

It may ſeem ſtrange to propoſe to a Burgeſs or a Southey a cotemporary event as a theme of epopœa; yet, it would be difficult to indicate any hiſtorical incident of equal importance—ſo glorious in its conduct—ſo neat in its ſolution—ſo dear to our patriotiſm—and ſo capable of mythologic decoration from local ſuperſtition, as the Conqueſt of Myſore.

"History of the Campaigns 1796—1799, 5 vol. 55s."

This tranſlation or compilation is drawn up with more apparent than real fairneſs, from authentic ſources of information, and will furniſh inſtruction to the officer, the hiſtorian, and the politician. The writer is ſteadily hoſtile to the French cauſe, but appears unſettled in his opinions of individuals; as, in the earlier volumes, Moreau is criticiſed with ſeverity, and in the later applauded without reſerve. The Dutch expedition is narrated with unſatisfactory civility. The political complection of the year has ſome influence on the direction of the author's blame and praiſe; yet his ability knows how to render plauſible his very dereliction of conſiſtency. It muſt be wiſhed he would reviſe and abridge the whole narrative, which ſubſequent publications enable him in places to correct.

"Summary of Univerſal Hiſtory, from the French of ANQUETIL, 9 vol. 72s."

To cleanſe the Augean ſtable of ancient chronology is not the proper office of an epitomator, nor has it been the object of M. Anquetil. He may obſerve, in the diſtribution of his matter, a more rational proportion than Boſſuet: he may narrate with more detail and intereſt than Millot; and he may bring out into new conſpicuity ſome hiſtorical periods, which are become important from their reſemblance to recent tranſactions: his geographical plan of arrangement may deſerve the praiſe of an amelioration; but he often repeats the fables of credulous antiquaries under the name of primæval hiſtory, and admits received miſrepreſentations, where he might have inveſtigated the ground-work. For him, Freret has in vain refuted the anachroniſm of Newton; for him, Volney in vain obſerved, that the ſon of Hyſtaſpes was the Darius of Daniel; nor does he detect the duplicity of Joſephus, in not recognizing the Nebuchadnezzar of Beroſus, and the Cyrus of Herodotus, as one and the ſame prince.

"Hiſtory of Helvetia, by F. H. NAYLOR, 2 vol. 16s."

Since their rebellion againſt Auſtria, the Switzers have been governed by the corporations of their large towns, each of which is ſovereign in its own diſtrict. A few of theſe corporations, like that of Zurich, were choſen *from without* by the burghers: theſe juriſdictions were called democratic cantons, and had in fact nearly the conſtitution of the City of London. Other corporations, and in far greater number, were choſen *from within*: on the deceaſe of one *ſixteener* or alderman, the remainder filled up the vacancy; theſe juriſdictions were called ariſtocratic cantons, and had in fact nearly the conſtitution of the borough of Great Yarmouth, where likewiſe a right of life and death veſts in the chief magiſtrate. Thoſe who have reſided in our cloſe boroughs will eaſily underſtand the manner in which, by intermarriages and partnerſhips in trade, a family-junto commonly obtain the excluſive management of ſuch a corporation, and diſtribute its privileges, honours, patronages, benefices, leaſes, and jobs, among their own relations and dependents. Into this ſtate, the government of the Swiſs cities has long ſince ſlidden. Wherever the public offices were ſufficiently important and reſpectable to be not beneath the notice of a man of intellect, parties grew up in theſe towns, and, in oppoſition to the domineering families, combinations of voters were formed, which often propoſed to extend the right of ſuffrage to all the educated claſſes, and moſtly became more popular than the ſelf-

self-elected oligarchy of magistrates. The instinct of office is every where alike. The Swiss aldermen gradually adopted an Anti-jacobin creed, gave the name of conspiracy to the pursuit of the most equitable reforms, and repeatedly stifled, especially at Bern, the complaints of the bold with the halter of the executioner. Thus arose, throughout Switzerland, what we should call a corporation-party, and a freeman's (or liveryman's) party. To the corporation-party, Mr. Planta's excellent work has a leaning; to the freeman's party, this shorter and convenient historical epitome. Mr. Naylor is a florid, an eloquent, an interesting writer; not a fagging, black-lettered, sedentary, charter-construing, record-gutting antiquary.

"LAING's History of Scotland, 2 vol. 12s."

This narrative extends from the union of the crowns of England and Scotland under James, to the union of the kingdoms under Anne. It fully accounts for the hostility which the family of Stuart experienced in the northern part of the island. Instead of being surprised that the Scottish nation threw off all allegiance to the sovereigns of that race, their cruelty, perfidy, and general misconduct, were such, that one rather wonders at the patience, long-suffering, and forbearance, exhibited by that injured people.

An Appendix to the second volume overthrows the authenticity of the English Ossian, a very small portion of which can have been derived from any pre-existing poems, and those of a far later date than the pretended æra of Fingal.

"Memoir of a Campaign with the Ottoman Army in Egypt, by I. P. MORIER, 4s."

Melancholy as it may be to compare the result with the effort of British valour in Syria and Egypt, it is still soothing. Although improvidence at home may have rendered the recent trophies piled at Acca, as useless as those of Richard Lion-heart, yet the narrative is attaching. The name of Sir Sidney Smith shall be pronounced with pride by the poet and the historian; if with a blush by cotemporary statesmen.

The condition of the Turkish army, according to the picture here drawn of it, seems to have fully justified Sir Sidney Smith in effecting the treaty of El-Arish, to which it is suggested Kleber would not have acceded but from hatred to Bonaparte. It is intimated, that while he was ignorant of the revolution which placed the latter at the head of the government in France, Kleber was sincere in the intention of evacuating Egypt; but that, as soon as he was made acquainted with that event, he disclosed a wish to violate his engagement, and was happy in having a pretext for releasing himself.

ECCLESIASTICAL HISTORY, THEOLOGY, METAPHYSICS, MORALITY, &c.

"Campbell's Lectures on Ecclesiastical History, 16s."

Except the political Annals of free states, Ecclesiastical History is the most interesting branch of record. Negligent of the destroying competitions of force, it is conversant, not with battalions of barbarians, but with combinations of educated men. It narrates conflicts of mind, it celebrates the victories or the defeats of reason, it investigates the ascent or descent of public morality, and embraces the universal progress of human culture. Events deserve and acquire majesty of importance in proportion as they busy a nobler agency. Siberian savages suffice to win trophies for an Attila, or a Suwarrow; it requires both knowledge and principle to inlist under the banners of a Calvin, or a Socini.

To the inherent interest of his subject, Dr. Campbell, in this instructive commentary, superadds what learning—what candour—can annex. His judicious work is peculiarly seasonable, when the claims of church authority, and the conquests of spiritual jurisdiction, are every where so rapidly progressive. May it contribute, by the liberal principles which it temperately attempts to revive, somewhat to interrupt, and for a while to defer, that relapse toward the servile credulity, and docile ignorance, of the dark ages, which seem likely a second time to attend the super-civilization, and to absorb the intellect, of Europe. Popery and despotism have re-conquered France; and the more accessible literature of the Continent is likely henceforward to promulgate the vindictive intolerance, and arbitrary policy, of Jesuitism. Yet alarms are still professed at the by-gone dangers of infidelity. Superstition of every fantastic kind is become a title to favour, not discouragement.

ragement. Prejudice apologizes to popism for the duration of its forgotten hatred. An affected apprehension of the judgments poured out on France yet drags into our churches the indolence of the great; week-day prayers are become a prelude to the breakfasts of our gentry; and men, apparently the most indifferent to futurity, lend the authority of their presence to assemblages for supererogatory devotion. A very numerous soldiery is regularly conducted to increase the pomp, and to imbibe the unction of the sabbath-lectures. Sunday-schools, the only places of education for most of the manufacturing poor, have been organized into classes of catechumens; writing and arithmetic are postponed to the definition of faith; and all chance of enabling the children to better their condition in life is wickedly sacrificed, in order to scatter among the multitude the thriving seeds of a pious, but extatically fanatical, spirit. Religious dilettanti, of every sex and age, reinforce the industry of the regular priesthood. Students of talent forsake the pleasures of youth and wealth to preach up a gloomy self-tormenting asceticism. Crowds of missioners contend for the holy task of carrying out the Gospel to the remotest east. Pietistical guilds have been instituted among devotees of every denomination. To hold more than the thirty-nine articles of faith is become the title to merit among our sects. Clergymen prefix their names to books of mysticism, not merely without the fear of ridicule, but with the expectation of preferment. Divination by means of the Scriptures is professed even in both parliaments. Petty pamphlets of the papists peep on us from every corner; their chapels multiply; their convents are re-peopling: even the Jesuits, whom their very pupils had suppressed, have here their seminary. Magazines of astrology are published monthly; almanacks indicating supposed planetary influences over the members of the human body, are printed in the very presence of one of our universities, and hung up in every house. Platonists write, and are read. Swedenborgians build magnificent temples. Manicheans tutor our very bishops. No garb, which credulity assumes, is now unwelcome: to be a Methodist, is to be comparatively rational. The classics of Paternoster-row supplant, in the libraries of priests, Lucretius and Cicero. Persons of unequivocal respectability have combined to prosecute the impugners of the faith, and have been supported by juries of the people. Plot-finders and heresy-ferrets multiply, and are patronized. We are in league to protest against the principles of Protestantism. In such a temper or distemper of the public mind, who does not perceive that reason is in danger, not faith; the press, and not the Gospel? Who does not feel, that it becomes the few residual friends of toleration and humanity to rally with closer union around the expiring flame of free inquiry, and, if possible, to shelter it from the rash gusts of popular fury, and that yet more formidable extinguishment by periodical pursuit and systematic suppression? Confederacies of another kind are assuming but too disastrous an aspect.

"Introduction to the New Testament, by John David Michaelis, translated by HERBERT MARSH, 21s."

Since Lardner, no theological work has appeared in England equally important with this. Michaelis, indeed, resembles Lardner by the undesigning fairness of his instruction, and the exhaustive completeness of his information; he has even greater resources of Oriental learning, and of modern travel-reading. Lardner delighted in historical, Michaelis in critical, illustration.

This translation is executed with an exactness, and annotated with an erudition, which will give to it, even in Germany, a value superior to the original. It is fit matter of congratulation to the country, at length, to possess such a work, so vernacularised. To religion and to learning a service has been rendered co-enduring with their influence: it is for ministers to discharge the national-debt of gratitude, by conferring a public and distinguishing recompence.

That the first edition of this work should be already out of print, is a good sign; may another more numerous impression shortly succeed, and as speedily be shelved. It is not a book to lend and borrow, but to have and hold as an everlasting possession.

"WRANGHAM's Thirteen Practical Sermons, 6s."

This learned and liberal writer knows how to interest, even when he epitomizes the writings of others; and it is

a task

a task much to be recommended to the clergy, to extract from ancient preachers of eminence the arguments and passages which have more than a temporary value. Beside the sermons from Doddridge, this volume contains the well-known and much-admired Rome is Fallen, and a Sermon concerning St. Peter, whose life is by no means well understood. It is probable that the Simon mentioned by Josephus (XIX. Ant. vii. 4) is the Peter of Acts; that he was imprisoned by the zeal of Herod, and released by the tolerance of Agrippa; and that the narrative contained in the twelfth chapter of Acts, is in fact the very anecdote of Josephus. If so, it throws light on the mode of narration adopted by the apostolic writers.

"Unjustifiableness of Cruelty to the Brute Creation, 1s."

This sermon merits diffusion, because it attacks a fault too common among the British vulgar.

"Sermon preached before the Manchester Volunteers, 2s."

Religion cannot be better employed than in enforcing the civic duties. The finest sermon of Massillon accompanied a consecration of colours. It might have been consulted—it has not been rivalled—by the author of this discourse.

"Dissertation on the Oriental Trinities, 14s."

It is surprising that this curious and ingenious work should have drawn no reply from the Unitarian writers. From the most early scriptures of the Jews, it is difficult to infer the doctrine of the unity; for they represent Jehovah rather as the exclusively rational, than as the exclusively real, God. About the time of the Babylonian captivity, monotheism becomes indeed the creed of their writers, and continues so until after the Macedonian conquest. Then a Platonism of opinion slides in, which may be traced in the Wisdom of Sirach, a book prior, and the Wisdom of Solomon, a book posterior, to the Christian æra. From this Wisdom of Solomon (which the Apostle James may be thought to have written, as it resembles in style his General Epistle), all the apostolic writers quote expressions; so that they appear to have derived from it those religious ideas and phrases which were afterwards supposed to assert the doctrine of the Trinity. By this book their phraseology ought to be explained. A creed more Platonical than the Priestleyan school of Unitarians have inferred from their imperfect and redundant canon, would likely result from an admission of the Wisdom, and a dismission of the Apocalypse. It is not improbable, that Plato and Sirach, and the Hindoos, all owe those opinions which they have in common to some Babylonian metaphysician.

"ROBERTS's Christianity Vindicated, 5s."

A sufficiently victorious reply to the wild positions concerning Christianity, which Volney has repeated from Dupuis. The answerers of the French Anti-christians would do well also to provide some convenient antidote to that "Examen des Apologistes de la Religion Chrétienne," which has been given to the public as a posthumous work of Freret. To the very early testimonies concerning Jesus Christ, ought surely to be added a passage of the Wisdom of Solomon, extending from the 12—20 verse of the second chapter: Gibbon, on the authority of Calmet, mistakenly attributes to this apocryphal work an antiquity prior to the Christian æra.

"HURDIS on the Nature of Psalm and Prophecy, 5s."

A learned, but mystical, commentary on the Psalms, which attributes to the early and the latter rain as much influence on inspiration, as Milton attributed to the vernal and autumnal equinox.

"CALMET's Dictionary of the Bible."

This very meritorious periodical publication continues to issue with regularity: it is, in some particulars, behind the present state of exegetic knowledge; but is, on that very account, the more convenient to men of letters. They can learn from it the reputed state of any biblical investigation, and thence perceive what remains for them to promulgate.

"DOBB's View of the great Predictions in the Sacred Writings, 6s."

A millenarian tract, worthy of Mr. Halhed.

"RICHARD's Bampton Lectures, 6s."

A perspicuous, praise-worthy, and specious vindication of the prophetic character of the Hebrew writers.

"HOUGHTON's Sermon for the Norfolk Hospital, 1s. 6d."

One of the most originally conceived, and pathetically written, sermons extant

extant in our own or any language. Like the Fast-sermon of Cappe, or the Militia-sermon of Walker, or the Omnipresence-sermon of Fawcett, it will be quoted by the future Priestleys, in their lectures on oratory and criticism, as a monument of the eloquence of the soul.

" GODWIN'S Strictures on Parr's Sermon, 2s. 6d."

For what reason can Mr. Godwin have thought it necessary to publish Strictures on a Sermon, in which he is not apparently noticed, and in the notes to which his writings are quoted with politeness? There is a want of that equanimity, which is supposed to characterise the philosopher, and which is the best support of his dignity, in thus wincing at every gall, and announcing now a concession, and now a reply. The Political Justice was probably as much over-valued at first, as it has been under-valued since. It was not immediately perceived, that many of the trains of argument pre-existed in Hartley, in Edwards, in Wallace, and in Hume; in Rousseau, Diderot, and Helvetius; and in Plato's Republic. It has lately been overlooked, that to have read and culled the syllogisms of such masters implies in Mr. Godwin no mean attainments of mind; and that although, like Bayle, he has re-stated sophisms, which, if received as irrefragable, would anarchize morality, he often proposes them with analogous scepticism, temper, and perspicuity. His publication was a tome of casuistry, which the Pascals of Anti-jacobinism have dissected into heinousness: it would have been more courteous, but less courtly, to reproach less, and to reply more. Mr. Godwin insufficiently distinguishes between personal and public duty, and, in his fits of voluntary transmigration, often makes his automaton reason as a citizen, a magistrate, or a statesman, when it ought to reason as a father, a brother, or a neighbour. If Fenelon and his valet are about to be executed, let the minister of the interior preferably recommend Fenelon to mercy, even if the valet be the minister's brother; but, if Fenelon and his valet fall into the Seine, let the minister preferably save his brother from drowning. In his public capacity, he is to consult the advantage of the country: in his private capacity, the tie of relationship. In the doctrine of promise and gratitude, Mr. Godwin has this way misled himself; his subject, however, is political, not individual, duty. That portion of his work, which has excited most outcry, is the theory of agamy, or of exempting matrimony from the notice of the magistrate. The plan is, no doubt, incompatible with inheritance, probably with the separation of property; it is ungrateful to the sex, whose age would be forsaken, and unfeelingly eradicatory of the domestic charities; yet, surely the individual, who offers it for discussion, and who is so little the fanatic of his system as to have married immediately after, does not deserve all that punishment of infamy which it is attempted to inflict. Plato, in the fifth book of his Republic, proposes this very system, with accompaniments of licence and of cruelty, to which Mr. Godwin invites not; yet bishops do not blush to quote Plato with attachment, and moralists have not shuddered to name him with applause. Plato addresses the beast in human nature: he tickles the humour at the expence of religion; he worships the courage at the expence of independence; he flatters the sensuality at the expence of morals; he absolves debauchery from the cares of parentality; and seduces intellect by the prospect of power. Mr. Godwin addresses only the reason, which is usually angered when it is not convinced.

Instead of adopting so apologetic a manner, Mr. Godwin, if he will reply at all, would do well to assume that higher tone to which his principled (if erroneously principled) character, and his disinterested independence, is entitled. Let him carry his attack into the camp of Anti-jacobinism, and bring the positions of his adversaries into the publicity which they want, and the moral indignation which they merit. The author of Strictures on Eyre's Charge is no contemptible analyst of the arguments of others. He may find among his numerous antagonists men, who have denied the greatest good to be the right object of action: men*, who have published satires on sensibility and philanthropy;—men who, because we are born selfish, acquire next an attachment to our kindred and neighbours, next a partiality

* The best satire since Dryden and Pope: its tendency will be regretted for ages to come.

for

for our country, and finally a regard for all mankind, have contended that the historical constitutes the moral order of our duties; and that we are bound to prefer our country to the whole, our family to the country, and ourself to our family. No wonder that the citizens of such a school squander on idle state and personal display what they ought to hoard for the dower of their daughters. No wonder that the statesmen of such a school build palaces, and pension cousins, while they fritter away the fortunes of Britain. As their creed is a digest of malevolence, so—but I mark the ghost of Gerrald planing over a sea-beat cove, pointing to the banksia-shaded hermitage of Palmer, and gibbering—" Beware !"

NATURAL HISTORY AND PHILOSOPHY; ZOOLOGY, MEDICINE, BOTANY, AGRICULTURE, CHEMISTRY, MATHEMATICS, &c.

" PARRY's Facts and Observations on Wool, 4s."

That Dr. Parry observes nature with the prepared eye of a physician and philosopher—that he knows, by a contrived and providential circumstancing of the subjects of his attention, to compress within a short time the experience which would naturally require a much longer period—and that his communications are consequently of great value to science, will readily be granted; yet, perhaps, it is allowable to regret, that he should lend the ornament of his celebrity to the support of a rustic and rusticating fashion for farmery, which becomes alarming to the national comfort, as well as dignity, which endears necessaries into luxuries, and travesties noblemen into cattle-jobbers, hog-feeders, and graziers of geese. Can the leisure of wealth devise no sublimer employment than what the most sordid motives would equally dictate? Must every landowner become the pupil of his steward, and the apprentice of his tenantry? Because Kien Long and his correspondent wisely speed the plough, must every subject have his share in the toil? The exile from court may do well to seek amusement in the country; but let the *involuntary* Cincinnatus beware, lest the part which he performs as a resource, should be mistaken for his natural destination. From such as aspire to offices of the state, some attention may be claimed to *human* merit (that is, the the flock with which they are to farm), some sharpness of discrimination in the detection of intellect, and in the allotment of its task; some forwardness of zeal to lead genius from its hovel, and to hoist excellence on the pedestal of distinction.

The utility of this sheep-breeding and wool-gathering, is but equivocal. For the success of manufactures depends much more on the cheapness, than on the refinement, of the raw material; because the more exquisite productions of the arts are consumed only by a comparatively innumerous public. The potters of England remove mountains, and turn them into plates and dishes for the million; while the porcelain-makers of Paris and Dresden are bepraised at the banquets of sovereigns, but saunter in ungaining idleness. It is therefore justly considered as symptomatic of commercial decline, when the arts of production are rather directed to the gratification of a curious luxury, than of a popular want; when they are exerted in rivalling the wool of Vicuna, or the shawls of Kashmire, and not in multiplying Norfolk fleeces, and Rochdale cloths. Of the late Mr. Bakewell, who introduced the rage for fancy-breeds of cattle, it was humourously observed—he had made mutton so fat that nobody could eat it, and so dear that nobody could buy it. What has happened to the carcase may happen to the fleece. By subdividing multifariously the sorts of wool to which the growers are to attend, the number of competitors in each line of shear will become very small, and will be able to impose on the clothier a monopoly-price for the clip. The fleeces of certain districts will acquire a Colchian reputation and a golden value, and will rival in price that tawny wool, which certain Argonauts smuggle for us from the coasts of Peru. But will not this dearth of top starve both the worsted and woollen-manufacture, and transfer to foreigners our staple-trade.

By a repeal of the laws against *owling*, and by the exportation of our best breeds of cattle to Canada, a greater competition of each growth might be obtained, which would likely conciliate the interests of commerce with the pursuits of the veterinary dilettanti.

" PRIESTLEY on the Doctrine of Phlogiston, 3s. 6d."

The system of chemical nomenclature, devised by Messrs. Lavoisier and Fourcroy,

Fourcroy, has a high degree of philological merit, and facilitates the orderly recollection of those substances with which their analysis is conversant. Yet some of their elements have been rashly named. *Hydrogen*, for instance, might, with equal propriety, designate any other constituent part of water, as oxygen, or latent heat. *Azote* might, with equal propriety, designate any other gaz, such as the carbonic, which extinguishes vitality. Such names should be changed. Common minds are very apt to confound words with things; to mistake philological precision for chemical truth; to consider the reception of the new nomenclature, as an admission of those doctrines which the inventers of the nomenclature happened to hold. Such prejudices are only worthy of sciolists. It may be hoped that the word *phlogiston*, which predicates nothing concerning the element designated but its presence in flame, will supersede the word *hydrogen* (water generater), which predicates concerning the element designated, perhaps a falsehood, and certainly a quality not exclusively peculiar to this substance. If, however, this exchange of a single term (which any algebraic *ex*, any undefining *atmé* might as yet represent) were made, the difference between Dr. Priestley and his antagonists would be so small, that a nitrous test could scarcely redden into visibility its gazeous evanescent subtlety.

"Horsley's Elementary Treatises on Mathematics, 8s. 6d."

If it be the intention of the University of Oxford, as we have heard, to introduce the study of mathematics into their system of education, it may now, with propriety and benefit to itself, testify its gratitude toward a learned and distinguished member, by employing the present treatise as a book of lecture and reference—a treatise, which, in the words of the preface, may be truly said to be plain enough for the learner, and adapted, at the same time, to the taste of the scholar.

"Comparative View of Cullen, Brown, and Darwin, by H. X. Baeta, 1s. 6d."

To the character and influence of our literature and language it is highly glorious, that the theories of our medical philosophers should be dividing the schools of Paris and Vienna into parties of Zoonomians and Anti-zoonomians; and that a native of Portugal should take a share of the controversy in an idiom to him so foreign. Dr. Baeta graduated at Edinburgh, and displays no common familiarity with our opinions and our tongue.

"Reich on Fever, translated by C. H. Parry, 3s. 6d."

The German author of this Dissertation professed to have discovered a cure for fever, which was purchased by the King of Prussia, and made public. It appears to be muriatic acid.

"Four Essays on Practical Mechanics, by T. Fenwick."

All these Essays have merit, particularly the fourth, on the simplification of machinery.

"Tatham's Historical Essay on Tobacco, 6s."

The chronological, natural, commercial, and political history of tobacco have all afforded to this writer an opportunity of curious and copious comment: but his information is so comprehensive as to be sometimes nugatory. He describes the method of *prizing*, or squeezing, by dint of mechanism, the article into its package, so as to reduce its bulk for stowage, and to exclude the air of fermentation. A little literary *prizing* would be of use to his volume, which, without the water-press of Bramah, might be condensed into much less space, and not incur the expulsion of useful and interesting details. The practice of smoaking the leaves of some plant is common to all countries troubled with mosquitoes; but the use of tobacco, as the herb of predilection, seems to have been familiar in China and Hindostan before the discovery of America, and to have been borrowed from the Europeans by the Floridans in preference to their own killiconik and sumach. Several productions, habits, and diseases, which the Portuguese brought from the East Indies, having become rife in Europe about the time of the discovery of America, were mistaken for American. The lues probably is a propagation of the Persian fire; and the segar, or cigarro, an imitation of the sharoot.

"New Observations on Thin Transparent Bodies, 2s. 6d."

This continuation of a well-conducted attack on the Newtonian philosophy of light and colours cannot but enfeeble the authority of the popular system. But as yet it substitutes nothing satisfactory. The theory of light

light respects its motion, and its colour. Concerning both, much remains to be ascertained. It is not known if reflected light moves with the same velocity as original light. Admitting that through empty space, or perfectly transparent substance, light travels in right lines; yet, as it is refracted in the neighbourhood of all bodies, and is made to swerve from its first path, probably with a diminished velocity, by the contiguity of every sort of matter—it may be suspected that a great deal of solar light, which rectilinearly would pass-by our earth, is, by the refracting principle, drawn within the limits of our atmosphere, made to alight on our globe, and habitually increases to our optics the apparent diameter of the sun. Colour is probably a merely chemical modification of the ray. The division into seven primary hues is wholly arbitrary, a result of reading Mallebranche, an imitation of the musical scale. The most luminous, no doubt therefore the most pure and unmixed, light is yellowish. By oxidation, probably, it becomes first green, then indigo, then dark and cold. By * phlogistication, probably, it becomes first yellow, then red, then dark and hot. Some chemists have told us that the lunar rays are septic, that they promote putrefaction, that they phlogisticate the atmosphere, and generate gazeous azotic fluids. It is more rational to suspect, at least of the sun's rays, that they are oxygenous; as the evaporation of water in the sunshine epurates the atmosphere; as house-paint, in which the lead has been revivified and blackened by foul vapours, recovers in the light its whiteness; and as bees-wax and linen undergo the same change, by sunning them in cool places, which they undergo from exposure to volatilized muriatic acid: they are bleached. Herschel has made it in some degree probable that there is an invisible as well as a visible radiation from the sun; and the laws of this calorique (or whatever it is to be called) may differ widely from those of its fellow-traveller. In velocity of motion it seems to be inferior; for the maximum of heat happens every day later by nearly two hours than the maximum of light. The fluid which occasions the luminous impressions is probably elastic; for if a beam of rays be admitted into a very dark room, the shadows are somewhat broader than if the rays continued parallel. It seems also detainable, like water, by an attraction of cohesion, on the surface of certain bodies immersed in it, for a sensible length of time. Thus the Bologna-stone, and the mimic compounds of lime and sulphur, when carried out of the sunshine, continue awhile luminous. In short, concerning light, we are much in the dark.

* *Hydrogen* is an absurd name: for water is not, like acid, a class of fluids in the formation of which this element is concerned; its very compoundness is still deniable. We already want to talk of oxygenous galvanism and hydrogenous galvanism; yet in the latter case water is not generated, but perhaps decomposed. What inconvenience is there in retaining the old word *phlogiston*, as the name of the element now called hydrogen?

Fine Literature and Arts, Philology, Criticism, Drama, Novels, &c.

"Thalaba, a Metrical Romance, by R. Southey, 14s."

To those who have been long accustomed to the swing of rime and the see-saw of couplets, the irregular verse, or measured prose, in which this very poetical poem is composed, will appear to have been adopted rather for the accommodation of the writer than of the reader—rather to elude the abecedary drudgery of spelling *ban, can, dan, fan,* &c. *bare, care, dare, fare,* &c. till the desiderated syllable arrives, than to invite from the second gate of the palace of pleasure a new charmer of the ear

> ———in our rude climes unknown,
> That on a leafy arbour sits alone,
> Strains his sweet throat, and waves his purple wings,
> And thus in human accents softly sings.
>
> Sir W. Jones's Works, IV. 437.

But those who delight in the narrative odes of Pindar, or the descriptive odes of Stolberg, will perceive that ages have sanctioned and nations have admired a similar structure of metre.

The fable or story of Thalaba is perhaps too marvellous: every incident is a miracle; every utensil, an amulet; every speech, a spell; every personage, a god; or rather a talismanic statue; of which destiny and magic overrule the movements, not human hopes and fears—not human desires and passions, which always must excite the vivid sympathy of men. It offers, however, scope beyond other metrical romances, for

for a splendid variety of description, which, as in Alexander's Feast, as in the Progress of Poesy, as in the Operas of Quinault, shifts, with the cameleon capriciousness of lyric inspiration, and with the versatile instantaneity of pantomime scenery, from the blasted wilderness, to caverns of flame; from bowers of paradise, to cities of jewelry; from deserts of snow, to aromatic isles; and from the crush of worlds, to the bliss of heaven. As in shuffling * tarocco-cards, figures, motley, new, and strange, causing palpitation, dance before the eye, and thwart the anxious grasp; so here portentous and alarming forms glare on the wonder, without enabling the spectator to form any guess about their approaching influence over the play, by any speculation of probability. Whatever loss of interest this poem may sustain, as a whole, by an apparent driftlessness of the events and characters, is compensated by the busy variety, the picturesque imagery, and striking originality of the parts, of which only a specimen can convey an idea.

All waste! no sign of life
But the track of the wolf and the bear!
No sound but the wild, wild wind
And the snow crunching under his feet!
Night is come; no moon, no stars,
Only the light of the snow!
But behold a fire in the cave of the hill
A heart-reviving fire;
And thither with strength renewed
Thalaba presses on.

He found a woman in the cave,
A solitary woman,
Who by the fire was spinning
And singing as she spun.
The pine boughs they blazed chearfully,
And her face was bright with the flame.
Her face was as a Damsel's face
And yet her hair was grey.
She bade him welcome with a smile
And still continued spinning
And singing as she spun.
The thread the Woman drew
Was finer than the silkworm's,
Was finer than the gossamer.
The song she sung was low and sweet
And Thalaba knew not the words.

He laid his bow before the hearth,
For the string was frozen stiff.
He took the quiver from his neck,
For the arrow plumes were iced.
Then as the chearful fire
Revived his languid limbs,

The adventurer asked for food.
The Woman answered him,
And still her speech was song,
" The She Bear she dwells near to me,
" And she hath cubs, one, two and three.
" She hunts the deer and brings him here,
" And then with her I make good cheer,
" And she to the chase is gone
" And she will be here anon."

She ceased from her work as she spake,
And when she had answered him,
Again her fingers twirled the thread
And again the Woman began
In low, sweet, tones to sing
The unintelligible song.

The thread she spun it gleamed like gold
In the light of the odorous fire,
And yet so wonderous thin,
That save when the light shone on it
It could not be seen by the eye.
The youth sat watching it,
And she beheld his wonder.
And then again she spake to him
And still her speech was song,
" Now twine it round thy hands I say,
" Now twine it round thy hands I pray,
" My thread is small, my thread is fine,
" But he must be
" A stronger than thee,
" Who can break this thread of mine!"

And up she raised her bright blue eyes
And sweetly she smiled on him,
And he conceived no ill.
And round and round his right hand,
And round and round his left,
He wound the thread so fine.
And then again the Woman spake,
And still her speech was song,
" Now thy strength, O Stranger, strain,
" Now then break the slender chain."

Thalaba strove, but the thread
Was woven by magic hands,
And in his cheek the flush of shame
Arose, commixt with fear.
She beheld and laughed at him,
And then again she sung,
" My thread is small, my thread is fine,
" But he must be
" A stronger than thee
" Who can break this thread of mine."

And up she raised her bright blue eyes
And fiercely she smiled on him,
" I thank thee, I thank thee, Hodeirah's Son!
" I thank thee for doing what can't be undone,
" For binding thyself in the chain I have spun!"
Then from his head she wrenched
A lock of his raven hair,
And cast it in the fire
And cried aloud as it burnt,
" Sister! Sister! hear my voice!
" Sister! Sister! come and rejoice,

The

* The Italians shuffle at tarocco their eighty cards the gay sides upwards.

"The web is spun,
"The prize is won,
"The work is done,
"For I have made captive Hodeirah's Son."

Borne in her magic car
The Sister Sorceress came,
Khawla, the fiercest of the Sorcerer brood.
She gazed upon the youth,
She bade him break the slender thread,
She laughed aloud for scorn,
She clapt her hands for joy.

O that Cesarotti, the translator of Bonaparte's classic, Ossian, would naturalize, in the country of Ariosto, and in his own exactly similar system of versification, these new fictions. Why should not the Simoorg of Ginnistan succeed to the Hippogryffon of chivalry; and an Arabian wildness of fancy, but which seldom shakes off the costume, or oversprings the range of Arabian idea, find admirers in the Castle of Otranto? Perhaps the Italian Thalaba will be sold at the Fair of Ancona to several of those Syrians, who there hold intercourse with Franks, and, like the merchants of the Court of Saladin, liberalize their leisure by studying the classics of the West, which are no longer confined to the remains of antiquity. Some youth, susceptive and industrious, who considers as the most precious jewel in the long bead-string of his pedigree the still-glistering name of one of the seven poets, may translate it into the language of the Koran, and suspend it on the gate-posts of the Temple of Mecca, for the pilgrims from every part of Arabia, while they loiter, to peruse. They will then compare the gloom of its fictions with those which darken the first book of the Shahnameh; where Eblis, the evil spirit, fastens to the shoulders of the tyrant Zohak serpents nourished with the blood of men (but too just an emblem of a warrior-prince); they will then weigh against each other the English and the Persian Bard, and admit that Southey can start a spirit as soon as Firdoosi.

"The Millennium, 3s."

This is a very pleasing poem, versified with ease, fluency, grace, euphony, copiousness, and variety, in the manner of Dryden; yet the author must not expect to delight the whole æra of which he is the harbinger, and to be saluted, in his own favourite language, with a *viva v. m. mil annos*. Temporary topics lose their interest with the times: the florist who cultivates only annuals has all his work to renew in the spring; and the satirist of fashionable folly can seldom publish in time to have the reputation of bringing down what was dead before his shot. Urbanity, which in a high degree characterizes this writer, is in all men an ornament, but least in a satirist. The knife of his good-natured irony is so far from cutting, that it is sometimes difficult to distinguish the back from the edge. As in the parody from Shenstone—

So gently he kick'd me down stairs
That I thought he was handing me up.

For instance, is the following passage intended as a puff or a quiz on Messrs. Beddoes and Jenner?—

O wise beyond repute! though every age,
Informed or rude, alike repute you sage,
Ye sons of Ægypt! in the world's first dawn
Who deemed the cow the goddess of the lawn,
Saw Heaven on her its choicest influence shower,
And founded altars to the *vaccine power*.—
Lo! at the distance of four thousand years
We catch the radiance of your sacred seers:
Apis and Isis now resume their sway,
And Britain hastes her homage first to pay.
See Beddoes, of the vaccine-church high-priest,
New temples rearing to the heavenly beast!
Daughters of Britain! ye whose weltered cheek
And labouring breath pulmonic ills bespeak,
Should medicine fail, here seek advice divine!
'Mid the sweet influence of celestial kine!
Here bring your beds, your flaccid frames repose,
And drink from cows the lily and the rose!
Ye spotless babes whose lips have never prest
Aught but the nectar of a mother's breast,
Now flushed with health, yet doom'd by loathsome ails
To lose, perchance, the bloom that still prevails,
Here be ye brought, and Jenner shall prepare,
From the foul dug, the pest to keep you fair—
Plant the vile antidote beneath your skin,
And pox without defy by pox within!

The notes display a profusion of learning which Sir W. Jones would have applauded: the author is polyglottic as the hydra, pantographic as Fry's letter-foundery; he would decypher, like Dr. Hager, the maker's name in arrow-head on a Babylonian brick-bat. If languages were diffluent, not confluent, and had not originally been as numerous as the primæval families, he would evolve, like Whiter, the elemental tongue. He quotes the ancient and modern languages of Bagdad, He-

 brew,

brew and Persian; the court-dialects of the Mahometan and Christian dynasties of Spain, Arabic and Spanish; Portuguese and Italian, German and French, to say nothing of those school-boy idioms, Greek and Latin, are to him no more difficile,

Than to a black-bird 'tis to whistle.

and he transcribes not merely with pedantry, but with selection: he is, however, less attentive to pertinence and to Greek, than the author of the Pursuits of Literature.

"Broomholme Priory, 6s."

It is honourable to the state of English culture, that an insignificant out-of-the-way market-town, like Holt, should issue from its printing-press a volume so elegant in its exterior and interior execution, as Broomholme Priory. The printer, the engraver, the poetess, have all surpassed any calculable expectation. How great a demand it implies for the arts of instruction that a press can subsist in such a village! How many must cultivate accomplishments of mind for any one to attain the excellence requisite—how many must attain the excellence for any one to determine on incurring the hazards of publication!—and shall the fair adventress have occasion to exclaim—

——forgive my erring quill;
A woman pleads, O Criticism be still;
Nor pluck the bandage from thy falcon's eye,
Where but a timid nestling learns to fly.

Let her flight proceed; she has already produced passages, which Harmony may love to repeat, and Tenderness to hear: but

"E'en copious Dryden wanted or forgot
The last and greatest art—the art to blot."

"Old Nick, a Satirical Story, 3 vols, 30s. 6d."

This is a very lively and a very original one; the literary old lady and the musical family are excellently drawn; yet the episodes and under-characters are more heeded than the main business and the heroes; and the roguishness of the author borders often on obscenity. There is a display of learning in the form of pedantry, quite to the purpose in Mrs. Pawlet, but sometimes improbable in other personages.

"The Father and Daughter, 5s."

The pleasures of melancholy are suited only to minds of uncommon susceptibility, to those who have a sympathetic taste for distress; and from such readers this tale of woe will meet with peculiar acceptance. It is replete with interest, and possesses pathos enough to affect the heart of the most callous reader. So tragic is the story and the catastrophe, that one is glad to seek consolation in disturbing the illusion of the narrative, in recollecting that it is not fact but fiction, and in rushing, like the remorseful, to incredulity for relief. The tendency of this novel is not merely harmless—it is moral. Some poems are appended.

"Letters of a Solitary Wanderer, by Mrs. SMITH, 13s. 6d."

Each of these three volumes contains a narrative, supposed to have been collected by the Solitary Wanderer: the tales are entertaining and interesting, and the composition has the habitual elegance of the authoress.

"Letitia, 4 vols. 21s."

This performance ought rather to have been entitled "The Three Letitias," for there are circumstantial memoirs of no less than three heroines of that name. The authoress possesses considerable merit as an observer of human life and manners; her discriminations are just and accurate, and there is a variety in her episodes which fatigues the attention while it shows a vigour of imagination.

"A Marvellous Pleasant Love-story, 12s."

The slang of polished life is caricatured with genteel humour in this marvellous pleasant love-story, which, though a little digressional, is more than a little entertaining.

"Amusing Conversations for Children, by the Abbé GAULTIER, 2s. 6d."

Prince Biribinker, says the fairy-tale, pittled orange-flower-water, and let off roses. A similar ambition to make every thing delightful characterizes the system of instruction of the Abbé Gaultier. Sometimes grammar is to be learned with a painting-brush, and the parts of speech distinguished by the prismatic colours: sometimes it is to be taught with a tee-totum, and substance is to be won with a substantive. Thus pleasure is to be the business, and acquirement the accident, of life.

GEOGRAPHY, TOPOGRAPHY, ANTIQUITIES, VOYAGES, TRAVELS LANGUAGES, &c.

"BARROW'S Travels in Southern Africa, 30s.

The

The idea of a perfect traveller comprizes, perhaps, more excellencies, natural and acquired, than Cicero exacts for his perfect orator. To a body which, like St. Francis, can wallow in the snow for amusement; bear wet, like a patient of Dr. Currie's, or, like Atabalipa, talk of roses while it roasts; which, like Mithridates, can swallow poisons in sport; banquet, like poor Tom, on nastiness; or fast a whole Lent in a desert; which is tolerant of vermin as Bellarmine; callous to contagion as a gaol-bird; fond of fatigue as Hercules; alert as Mercury, and so forth; must be superadded, the mind adapted by nature to observe, and instructed by education how much is recorded of the observable. In his memory, as in Noah's Ark, every living thing must be systematically arranged; every vegetable, as in the primitive island of Linnæus, must be present and ready to blossom; the swart fairies of the mine must have shown him through the calcareous, through the schistous layers down to the granite nucleus of the globe. All this he must know how to estimate, not in the scales of the naturalist, but of the cosmopolite; not inasmuch as it is rare in museums, and ill-depicted in Floras, but insmuch as it can be made a material of art, an article of commerce, a combiner of regions, an enricher of man. Such qualities Mr. Barrow realizes in a degree of which there are few examples, perhaps not one. He seems every where to have considered himself as the pioneer of the statesman; and although he loses no opportunity of adding to our knowledge of nature by a very careful survey of the land and its growth, yet he every where brings out, with predilection, the available circumstances of soil, irrigation, habitation, and produce, and seems only anxious to detect its eventual utility. His whole work tends to inspire a regret, that the Cape, hitherto so ill-governed, so unproductive, so little studied, should not have been preserved for the country which could alone have committed it to his sway, and have rendered the beneficence of his existence commensurate with the benevolence of his views. Let us hope that the mouth of the Orange-river, to the north of which the territories of the Hollanders no where extend, will still be thought worthy of colonization; and, like another Nile, become the waterer of a geometrical agricultural population.

"BYGGE's Travels in the French Republic, 6s."

The most satisfactory account of the instructional state of France, which has been obtained since the Revolution, is contained in these travels. It appears that the class of men who may be denominated civil engineers, are more carefully taught than in this country; that their bridge-builders study mathematics, learn the theory of pressure, attend lectures on conic sections under the name of stereotomy, and adapt themselves for employing public money with "useful magnificence." In England we have yet to learn, not the art of doing useful things, but of doing them grandly. Perhaps magnificence costs more than traffic can defray; if so, the trustees of our turnpikes act wisely, and the permanence of convenience is better consulted by its modesty than by its stateliness.

"Political Reflections relative to Egypt, by G. BALDWIN, 6s."

Before Saturn had invented manure, and Triptolemus the plough, Ægypt was the very place for agriculture to flourish. Accordingly we find the shepherd kings of Arabia selling the labour of their vassals to the Ægyptians to obtain corn during a cycle of dearth. But with every progress of surrounding nations, Ægypt has diminished in relative importance: her inhabitants are condemned, by natural causes, like the Arabians, to a stationary civilization, and are still the same barbarians whom the savages of antiquity admired. It is only by writing about obelisks and pyramids, and thus imbibing the childish wonder of the primæval world, that any modern nation can have been brought to covet the possession of such a strip of ooze; which is so ill situate for the transit of Oriental commerce, that under Trajan and the Antonines that traffic already passed through Palmyra and Antioch, and has only resumed, by fits, the Ægyptian-road, when Syria has been insecure through anarchy or war. If indeed it should be discovered, as the ancients testify, that the lake which absorbs the Joliba, overflows into the Nile; if the cataracts should be ascended by a stair-case of locks, and an inland navigation extended to Tombuctoo; if Alexandria is to import for the

the whole interior of Africa the muskets of Birmingham, and the dark-blue calicoes of Manchester, and to send the packages to be towed by hippopotamusses on to the negro-fairs of Houssa, Ægypt may more than resume the consequence she had under the Ptolemies. Mr. Baldwin, however, does not appear to found on such an expectation his estimate. His information is the result of long residence and natural sagacity; and it terminates in recommending the retention of Ægypt as a British colony. A very interesting narrative is given of Sir R. Abercrombie's campaign.

"Beauties of Wiltshire, 2 vols. 21s."

This splendid work does equal honour to the artist and the author: it is seldom that the same individual can employ with skill the pencil of the painter and of the enditer; like Gilpin, draw landscapes in acquatinta and in prose; or, like Angelo, immortalize in a sonnet and in a bust. The accounts of Stonehenge, of Salisbury Cathedral, and of Fonthill, are peculiarly interesting. Of the libraries of the gentlemen of Wiltshire these volumes will be a regular ornament.

"Grammar of the Malay Tongue, 7s. 6d."

Without pretending to decide whether the Malay language descends from that of Thibet, or of Arabia; or whether it be a sea-port jabber, formed in the Indian Ocean among sailors, by the mishmash of a hundred dialects, like the *lingua franca* of the Mediterranean, or the *norse* of the Baltic, it may be worth while to record one observation respecting it. The names of Mango Capac and of Oello, the founders of Peruvian civilization and of the race of Incas, are Malay, and signify *a man with an axe* and *a serpent*. Consequently neither the Welsh, as some English antiquaries pretend, nor the Icelanders, as some German antiquaries pretend, were the civilizers of Peru, but the Malays.

* STATISTICS AND JURISPRUDENCE.

"The Question as to the Admission of Catholics to Parliament considered, 3s."

If we inquire for the seats of practical tolerance, we shall find them to be trading towns. Venice set the example of alleviating the oppression of the Jews in Italy: Florence tolerated Antichristians; Genoa, Protestants. In Switzerland, in Holland, every variety of sect has been seen to live for ages in amicable contiguity, and to serve in concert the offices of magistracy. This is a natural consequence of the travel and intercourse of merchants; they perceive sincerity in the most opposite sects, and infer that what religion *can* do for the character it *may* do in any denomination. They experience the essential qualities of probity, fidelity, industry, hospitality, from Jew, Papist, Protestant, Deist, and no more ask what temple than what club he keeps.

But in all the feudal nations, in all the governments by country-gentlemen, a mighty stress has been laid on church-going. A son of the family preaches there perhaps; it is felt as an affront in the tenantry not to compliment him with a hearing. The pride of consequence is aroused against the independence of secession, and, as the chain of subordination is in a village very complete, the indiscipline of dissent is commonly got under. This principle, so learnt, is carried into the management of the state; and the inhabitants of towns, whose opinions the novelties of literature often metamorphose, are to be drilled into deference for the opinions of men whose rudeness has not yet ascended to curiosity about the opinions in discussion.

This was very much the real history of the persecutions of the Reformation. May no American historian fancy that any thing similar once prevailed in England; that by refusing to repeal the Test-act we almost irritated the Dissenters into becoming "a pernicious foreign faction;" and, by refusing to take off the restrictions on the Catholics, quite drove a multitude of Irishmen into connection with the public enemy. The desolation of the sister-island, the introduction of torture by flagellation into its jurisprudence, would be indeed an enormous price to pay for a question between a wafer and a crumb of bread.

But let the people, on their part, learn, that to no party has it ever answered to pursue its ends by foreign aid: a minority has no right to it, a majority

* The common expression, "political economy," signifying *city-house-law*, is a bull in language: it was borrowed from French writers; the Italians less inaccurately say *economia publica*.

majority no need of it. From Jeremiah the prophet to Sforza the Milanese, the importer of foreign force has been the misfortune of his country.

"ROBINSON's Collectanea Maritima."

This valuable periodical publication promises to fill a chasm in English literature.

"CONST's Laws relating to the Poor."

A judicious and to the magistrate almost essential tract.

"CLARKE's Survey of the Opulence of Great Britain, 5s."

The national debt of Great Britain is already so large, that its very amount is become an object of national vanity. It may be hoped, by funding the Income-tax and the Tythe; by converting the five-per-cents into three-per-cents, which would increase the nominal capital; and by new contrivances of expenditure; that the file of figures which represents our stock may yet considerably be prolonged; that we may shortly have to reckon our debt by *lacks* of millions, and bravely aspire to extend it to a crore. Such a consummation would, no doubt, give pleasure to this very encouraging writer, who thinks that taxes invigorate, and that the increasing price of most articles of consumption is a cause and a proof of unparalleled prosperity.

"BURCHELL's Observations on the Income-tax, 1s."

The Income-tax is assessed by a scale so unfair, and is levied with so questionable an equity, that some substitute should be contrived. The principle of the double, treble, and quadruple assessments, was much more just. A minister of finance may be compared to a common pump; he is the best who with fewest checks supplies the most reservoirs in the least time. Mr. Pitt, in this department of excellence, is unrivalled.

"Examination of the Sentence in the Case of the Swedish Convoy, by Professor SCHLEGEL, 4s."

Of this important publication two editions have appeared, the one translated by agents of the British Government, and printed for Wilson; the other translated under the author's inspection, and printed for Debrett. Of all tribunals the losers will complain. Suffice it, that the British courts of justice are of all others the least unjust. Comparatively speaking, they are no respecters of rank, little of wealth, seldom of party, and, in causes decided by jury, they arbitrate, without nationality, alien interests. It may, however, be questioned, whether, in those of our courts where the decision vests in the judge, sufficient provision has been made for habitual impartiality. Sir W. Scott is not immortal, nor has his spirit always animated his predecessors. Why not introduce, before the High Court of Admiralty, trial by mixt juries, half alien, half (to use the jargon of the law) natural-born. In this case, a decision hostile to the interests of foreigners could never become a just topic of complaint from foreign powers. Whereas now it will always seem reasonable to be jealous of a judge, apparently discretionary, and appointed by the English Sovereign.

A more important part of this pamphlet than what respects the Admiralty-sentence of the 11th of June, is a disquisition relative to international law, which has for its object to prove, that "*by right of nature* free ships make free goods:" and that all arrogation of a privilege of search, not reposing on express convention with the searched party, is usurpation, is despotism, is tyranny, and ought to be resisted (unless indemnity be made) by war.

This doctrine is more alarming to our military than to our commercial marine. If the right of search were withdrawn, midshipmen and admirals might have fewer prizes to partition: but the rates of freight and insurance on neutral bottoms would decrease, and, as ships are easily neutralized, trade would incur less change of path, during war, than now. It is curious to see claims reposing on general principles and abstract doctrines, patronized by the Court which collects the Sound-duties. On the grounds of prescription and convention only, can a levy so oppressive to universal commerce be defended.

"Remarks on Mr. Schlegel's Work, by A. CROKE, 4s."

This perspicuous, well-reasoned, and satisfactory answer to the foreign Professor, may suffice: yet in a question which depends much on authority, one desiderates, perhaps, more pedantry of quotation. The argument from the analogous usage in land-war might have been adduced: neutral buildings and fortresses may not only be searched, but

but occupied; neutral travellers and goods may not only be examined, but detained by belligerents. Maritime power has been used with a moderation which puts the Frederics and Bonapartes to the blush.

"Treatise on the Rights and Duties of Belligerents and Neutrals, by ROBERT WARD, 5s."

This work displays a command of library, well adapted for the refutation of a German Professor, and fills up the deficiency of Mr. Croke's less elaborate answer by a more exhaustive and minutious search into precedents. Yet Saint-Real (Science du Gouvernement, V. 471.) and some other decisively favourable authorities seem to have been overlooked.

By the Convention of Petersburg, of the 17th of June, this question has been settled nearly on the principles laid down in the admirable statesmanlike pamphlet of the Earl of Liverpool.

"Collection of Facts and Observations on the Peace, by W. COBBETT, 6s."

Various state-papers relative to the peace are here collected, and accompanied by eloquent culpatory diatribes. The publisher has been more known as a writer in America than in Europe; he has the reputation of talents strong by nature, not lithe by polish; and of a sincerity and zeal more intrepid than urbane. His resources of quotation and illustration may have increased in an European metropolis: it is, however, more likely that he has derived assistance from a higher hand. This seems, indeed, admitted—

——————————la temuta
Insegna anco nell' ombra e conosciuta.

Such writing must make a deep impression; but surely of a more turbulent kind than can be welcomed in a metropolis. May not the tremulous needle of alarm be undergoing a variation, and shortly point against the *ligue* instead of the *fronde*?

Some objections are thrown out against Mr. Fox (———*würdig von Ihm gekannt zu werden!) as if he wanted patriotism, because, instead of professing nationality, he proclaims cosmopolitism. The teachers of Anti-jacobinism lay mighty stress on the profession of an exclusive care for one's own country. It is a practice well adapted for demagogues, as it insures domestic popularity; but it unfits them for diplomatic intercourse, by exciting suspicion. He who employs a Jew (I crave pardon for using the word in its vulgar obnoxious acceptation) to drive a bargain for him, commonly misses his end: the antagonist takes for granted, that the agent will not agree unless he can over-reach, and hence rejects even an equitable proposal. The like is true of professing patriots. Mr. Fox has never blundered away the interests of his country, nor incurred continental mistrust, by a bigotted superstition for them. That he talks better than Demosthenes, every one knows; but he has that consummate statesmanship, which, if Macchiavelli had lived to observe it, would have convinced Macchiavelli of the expediency of virtue.

"Speech of the Right Hon. W. WINDHAM, delivered Nov. 4, 2s. 6d."

The speeches of this eminent orator, finely as they are composed, are probably adapted for yet greater effect in the senate than in the closet. That aquiline energy, piercingness, rapidity, which nature with no deceptious seal has stamped on his mien, must favour their efficacy. His early manner in speaking was classical, orderly, and syllogistic, but too unadorned for entertainment; it was acute and ingenious, almost to subtlety and paradox: his later and livelier manner abounds with Burkisms, with hodfuls of allusion to familiar national nature, daubed *al fresco* in freaks of humour, moulded into metaphors, or carved into comparisons, with marvellous plasticity. This harangue, as the subject demanded, partakes more of his original than of his acquired style, and employs them rather alternately than blended; for the arabesques of imagination do better in a running pattern than in patches.

In the life of nations, as in that of individuals, tides of opportunity arise, which if taken at the flood lead on to fortune, if neglected, to declension and to ruin. But with communities occasion is less momentary than with persons; so that the precipitancies of improvidence

* These words are from an Ode of Klopstock:—"I know (says the poet) what is great and beautiful in life; but the finest thing which the eye of a mortal can behold is the king bent on rendering happy—thou art *worthy by* HIM *to be known*."

providence may commonly be reformed by the wisdom of reflection. Nations change so slowly their relative power, that they have mostly leisure to revise even their apparently decisive determinations.

At the beginning of the late war (in which the French were strictly the aggressors; although to have recognized the upstart authorities would probably have prevented their acts of enmity), if the British nation had not been aroused by the declamations of Mr. Burke and the Anti-jacobins into a hostile mind against France, peace might have been successfully struggled for, after the taking of Valenciennes, while the Prussians were hesitating to secede from the coalition. At this moment again, if a hostile mind against France should be extensively avowed and proclaimed by the British people, ministers may easily be found, who would intercept the agreed handshake of reconciliation, and once more clench the fist of defial, and screw on the bayonet of carnage.

It is therefore of some consequence to the duration, or rather to the realization, of public tranquillity, that this speech, and other similar publications, should be received without plaudits, in silence, with at least an affected apathy, even if the mortifying sentences which they contain should strike home on the conviction and wound to the core. Compared with the possible peace of prior opportunities, the terms of the preliminaries may be mean and shabby; but, compared with the probable peace of future opportunity, be advantageous. Besides, the condescension of acceptance *is* incurred; let us keep the quiet to compensate the disgrace.

Incommoded as Great Britain already is by the multiplicity of her distant colonial possessions, many of which do not repay to her commerce the expence of protection and patronage, the cession of an island or two more or less in the European or Indian Archipelagos, can be of little moment. The resumption of Pondicherry was probably a point of honour with the French: it must have been fought for long, and paid for dear; and if obtained, like the gift of Canada, it would have lessened to the colonies the value of the mother-country. Two objections only against the peace can deserve to cost a pang. The one is an objection of immorality; the preliminaries dispose of territory belonging to neither of the contracting parties; this defect, not an unprecedented one, rests wholly with the peace-makers. The other is an objection of insecurity; no provision has been made to overthrow the French ascendancy in Holland, so that the Cape, and all the other settlements of the Hollanders, are likely to become eventually the means of aggrandizement to France: this defect results from the misconduct of the war; for the very important Dutch expedition failed partly from an unzealous tardiness of preparation, and partly from the servile choice of agency; the blame, therefore, should fall, no doubt, on the late Ministers.

Some pains are taken to prove, that a low war-establishment may not be more costly than a high peace-establishment. Is there no difference in the relative humanity? And what occasion for a high peace-establishment? If on grounds of internal security—it can only be necessary to an odious party—certainly not to ministers of popularity. Few soldiers would suffice to keep under those volunteers who may be for reviving the war. Meritorious officers, it is true, must not be dismissed with ingratitude: but are there no civil governorships, no donatives of land in Canada or the conquered countries, no remnants of sinecure patronage, appliable to their remuneration? Military labour, at best, is under-paid. It ought, perhaps, every where to be paid by a tontine, as the efficient principle of the service is to urge one another to the extreme risk: thus the veteran would always be opulent.

If on grounds of external security—it becomes necessary to ask, whether, in case of a soon ensuing war, the principles of the Anti-jacobins be those on which it could be conducted. Will a hacknied clamouring for order and religion abrade the popularity and weaken the energies of a French Government, orderly as an apprehensive garrison, and religious as a recent convert? Or for that purpose must unexpected sighs be heaved over the extinction of a liberal philosophy and of the emulous eloquence of representative liberty? If the Alpine frontier be alone mutable, will satires on democracy remind the Genevans that the limits of France extend beyond the bounds,

bounds which despotism had fitted to receive a conqueror with joy? Must not degraded mangled Switzerland be told, that independence is a blessing, and freedom a virtue? Must not D'Ivernois be invited to recollect the declamations of his youth, and to wake the mountain-echoes with tones of other times? In short, must not the Anti-gallicans seek fresh sophists to unteach all their lessons of the last decennium?

Statesmen ought never to be fanatics, for whatever creed they may profess to arm, and whatever war hoop they may provide to consociate their partisans, they ought equally to keep in view the greatness of their country. During the French Revolution one party arose, which consisted not of statesmen, which undertook to subdivide France into nine distinct federal republics, and thus to paralyze that empire for all purposes of offensive war and territorial encroachment. It was the interest of every foreign neighbour to support this party, the Girondist. And it was especially the interest of Great Britain, which in the progress of European partition can no where annex a share (except, perhaps, a mere feather—a feather of hoar-frost—Iceland) and therefore consults her own relative importance by checking that progress. The Girondist-party set so high a value on British recognition, that they indirectly offered, through the mouth of Condorcet, to cede Madagascar as the price of our guaranteeing the revolution, that is, of our propping their power. Those men and those societies in England, who, by their proposals and addresses of recognition, endeavoured to break for ministers the ice of unpopularity, and to blade the prow of the gondola of embassy, were proceeding extra-civically perhaps, but surely with sound patriotism. The prejudices of the Anti-jacobins prevented this critical recognition; and the opportunity returned not. The more exceptionable the men whom an enemy holds forth as his representatives, the more pleasure an intelligent malice would have taken in the recognition. Now they have recognized the superior of their King, whose dignity no prior recognition could have compromised, because not preceded by any assumption of parity.

But I am spinning out prate—without the leisure to splice its incoherence—to tinge it with ornamental colouring—to braid it into connection with the pamphlet to which it is attached—or to clip off its fag-ends—the imps of Faustus tug!

HALF-YEARLY RETROSPECT OF GERMAN LITERATURE.

TWO thousand seven hundred and sixty new works, or at least works which had been revived, re-moulded, or had assumed a new face, were, by 299 booksellers, advertised in the catalogue for the last Leipzig Easter-fair, as the produce of the preceding booksellers' year, from Easter, 1800, to the same period in 1801; for the Michaelmas Catalogue contains only the gleanings from the field of German literature, and the full sheafs are collected in that of the Easter-fair. But do they contain likewise full ears of corn? Never before, perhaps, was there more reason for asking this question, when, on the first slight examination, we cannot but observe, that, for ten stalks of wild oats and tares, it would be difficult to find *one* sound and full ear of wheat, which might be preserved in the granary of literature, or exported into foreign countries.

THEOLOGY.

That the invigorating breath of life which for the last twenty years has pervaded the school and church affairs of almost all the nations speaking the German language, still continues its animating influence; we find several indubitable proofs in the Catalogue for the last Easter-fair at Leipzig, and such as must prove very consolatory to the friends of gentle gradual reform.

The Criticism of the Sacred Records, on which so many works formerly appeared, would seem, if we might judge from the catalogue before us, to be almost entirely exhausted. Scarcely any thing worth mentioning appears, except a few gleanings which M. BIRCH, of Copenhagen, furnishes in his "Collection of Various Readings," to the diligent GRIESSBACH for his splendid edition of the New Testament.

Of

Of exegetical productions likewise, there was but a scanty after-harvest, which is carefully stored up in the periodical publications of Eichhorn, Henke, Augusti, and other intelligent collectors, the continuations of which were announced. On such foundations, the higher Dogmatism and Criticism courageously continue to build. The materials, however, are frequently twisted and warped in the most various directions, though proceeding from one parent stem. Thus from one *alma mater*, the University of Kiel, in Holstein, have come forth two widely differing productions, KLEUKERS "Encyclopädie der Theologischen Wissenschaften"—Encyclopædia of Theological Science (1 vol. Hamburg, Perthes) a work of the old stamp, and the frank and liberal-minded ECKERMANN's "Handbuch für die Glaubenslehre." Manual of Christian Doctrine.

We observe with pleasure, that less sense and nonsense had been printed relative to the liturgy, than in several preceding years. For towards bringing about a reformation of the liturgy more may be effected by the gradual and noiseless diffusion of opinion, than by the pompous announcement of new schemes, or by the thunder of eloquence hurled from the pulpit by fiery zealots: our readers will, however, hear with pleasure, that such men as Husnagel, of Frankfort on the Main, and Velthusen, of Stade, have not been silent on this interesting subject; and we hope that their temperate proposals of reform will be read by their countrymen with the attention which is due to their merit.

Very evident still is the influence of the new philosophy on all parts of theoretical and practical theology; sometimes, indeed, with a strong bias towards transcendental scholasticism. On the tendency of FICHTE's "Destination of Man," MNIOCH, of Königsberg, has published "Erläuterungs Variationen"—Illustrative Variations; and the Ex-benedictine SCHAD, of Jena, announces a *generally-comprehensible* View of the Theory of Religion founded on the System of Fichte—"Gemeinfassliche Darstellung der aus dem Fichteschen System hervorgehenden Religions Theorie," in 3 Parts; and an "Absolute Harmonie des Fichteschen Systems mit der Religion"—Absolute Harmony of Fichte's System with Religion, Erfurt, Hennig. This work is advantageously distinguished from similar publications by its more general intelligibility; and the theory of Religion, which is subjoined at the end, contains evident proofs that the author is a man who thinks for himself.

The prospect is still more cheering, when we view the unwearied, and in part successful, endeavours to give to these philosophemes a practical utility. Several of the Catholic states of Germany distinguish themselves so advantageously in this respect, that they might justly be proposed as examples worthy of imitation to some of their Protestant neighbours. Among others, Bavaria, in spite of a host of obscurants, and notwithstanding the internal and external calamities with which that country has lately been afflicted, still maintains an honourable place of distinction. The excellent noble-minded Mutchelle, of Munich, whose premature loss we have to lament, did not indeed live to see the publication of his Moral Divinity; but it is hoped, that enlightened theologians will not be wanting, who will adopt it as their text-book or guide in their lectures. Warmed by his zeal, and animated to good and virtuous resolves, a grateful generation will grave his name, not on marble or bronze, but on their hearts.

"Auch die Aufklärung hat ihre Gefahren"—Illumination too has its Danger. Under this title, the worthy M. SALAT, rector of Haberskirch, in Bavaria, has enlarged a pamphlet, formerly published by him, into a book, which attacks the worldling and the scoffer with their own weapons; and boldly discusses the necessity of adopting reforms in the Catholic part of South Germany, which the honest author of a pamphlet well worthy of perusal, entitled "Wie kann dem Katholischen Schwaben das Kriegs Ungemach zum grössten Vortheil für die Religion vergütet werden," only here and there ventured to hint at—How tender, and, at the same time, how forcible, are Salat's observations on the celibacy of the clergy.

The enlightened and eloquent M. FEDER, of Würzburg, has enriched the library of Roman Catholic preachers with a new collection. Who would not, then, when he sees such excellent productions issuing from the press, in the hitherto less enlightened part of Germany, willingly forget, that Kranzfelder, in Augsburg, again presents us with GALURA's "Newest Plan of Theological Studies;" the widow of Göbhard, in Bamberg, with GOFFINA's "Mess-buch Unterricht;" Instructions relative to the Mass; and another bookseller of Augsburg, with a

 "Liebes

"Liebes Flämmlein zu dem Heiligsten Herzen Jesu"—A Flammule of Love to the most Holy Heart of Jesus. Certain it is, that light daily more and more gains ground over darkness; and a small cloud before the sun does not constitute an eclipse. Such a cloud seems to have been raised up by a "Sermon on the Free Grace of God," preached on the feast of the Reformation by the chief clergyman in Saxony, a man held in the highest estimation on account of learning and zeal for the good cause, and distributed through all Saxony by order of the Ecclesiastical Council. It certainly was not the intention of the preacher, that an iron symbolical chain should be fabricated of a quickly-fleeting word, and the name of a just and tolerant prince be made use of for that purpose. Very hurtful and unwise, therefore, was the reforming zeal of some of his antagonists, who poured forth bitter invectives against him, and forced him to a new defence, as the champions who, without being called upon, undertook his cause fought with blunt and worn-out weapons. It were to be wished, that the controversy had gone no further than the publication of a Fast day Sermon, and of the "Vorlesungen über die Dogmatic, mit Litterarischen Zusätzen;" Lectures on Dogmatical Divinity, with Literary Additions, by IMM. BERGER, Sulzbach, 1801: and that the edict against Cannabich, a superintendent in Sandershausen, who published a sermon against Reinhardt's, and whose doctrines and writings were publicly stigmatised as of a pernicious tendency, did not give us cause to apprehend still severer fulminations of anathemas.

In Germany, too, a general complaint prevails of the emptiness of the churches during divine service, which may be partly owing to many of the ceremonies and dogmas being repugnant to the more enlightened spirit of the present times. On this subject, two pamphlets have appeared in Berlin. If the want of good pulpit-discourses be the cause of this striking decrease of church-going, it must at least be owned, that there is an abundance of excellent models for such as stand in need of them in the composition of their sermons. In turning over the pages of the Easter Catalogue, one is astonished at the number and copiousness of *materials* for preachers, which, from all quarters, are offered to the makers of sermons, and to those who wish to edify themselves by the perusal of such pious works. With pleasure, we here again behold the names of a Reinhard, a Ribbeck, a Hess, and a Tobler. Provision has been made in various ways for every class of readers. There is a Magazine for Country Parsons, who are overloaded with business; Journals for Preachers; Magazines for Sermons to be held at Funerals and Churchings of Women. A certain *Schulz* has established a Homiletical Magazine for the use of poor clergymen, whose spiritual must often give way to their temporal labours to obtain a sufficiency of the necessaries of life.

MEDICINE.

In this department of science, the greatest activity still continues to prevail. From the violent collision of old and new theories, war-enkindling sparks are daily struck out, and no where has the hereditary wisdom of the schools lost its authority more than in Germany. A hundred heads, and a hundred pens, are always in readiness to naturalize the discoveries made in other countries. Every separate branch of the science, and frequently every subdivision thereof, has had its peculiar treasurer, that is, physicians, who dedicated to it separate journals and repertories.

The "Uebersicht der Arzneikunde im Letztem Jahrhunderte," View of Medicine during the last Century," by KURT SPRENGEL, of Halle (Halle, Gebauer) will be received as a most acceptable present, even by those who are not initiated into the mysteries of the profession; as the interest which non-professional men and the public at large take in works treating of medical subjects daily increases, and, by a reciprocal action and re-action, partly calls forth a numerous host of popular treatises, and is partly thereby stimulated and increased. The above-mentioned "View of Medicine," written by an eminent German physician, whose "Geschichte der Medizin," History of Medicine, in 3 vols. has already passed through three editions, and from whom we are expecting considerable illustrations of the science of botany, is one of the most important works that were published at the last Easter-fair, and certainly deserves to appear in an English dress.

The many schools and sects into which medical practitioners in Germany were lately split, seem to be gradually disappearing, in proportion as a modified Brunonianism gains ground. See on this subject BURDACH's "Propedeutik zum Studium der gesammten Heilkunst," In-

 troduction

troduction to the Study of the whole Science of Medicine; MARTENS' "Paradoxes;" and, in some respects likewise, KLETTEN's "Beiträge zur Kritik der Neuesten Meinungen in der Medizin"—Contributions towards a Critique of the Newest Opinions in Medicine, No. I. Leipzig, Härtel.

The Medical School of Vienna again distinguishes itself by several productions in the spirit of the Brunonian System: M. FRANK, jun. is the editor of the "Wiener Gesundheits-taschenbuch," Vienna Pocket-book of Health, for 1801, and begins it with a Biographical Account of Dr. Brown. From the Vienna-press, the medical world likewise receives a Medical Archive of Austrian Physicians, and Transactions of the Josephine Society. OPPENHEIM has communicated Observations made in the Jewish Hospital at Vienna.

RÖSCHLAUB boldly continues his Magazine—the dreaded place of arms against all Anti-Brunonians—and has at length published his long-expected "Handbuch der Nosologie;" Manual of Nosology." A new edition is likewise announced of his Pathogony, which has received from Copenhagen interesting illustrations, together with a preface by the ever-ready preface-writer, Tode, in MENDEL's "Grundzügen der Neuen Theorie"—First Lines of of the New Theory.

The younger school of Göttingen daily more and more loudly raise their voices in favour of the new medical gospel. MATTHÆI has there published a "Handbuch der Erregungs-Theorie"—Manual of the Theory of Excitability—which certainly would not have been passed over in silence by Girtanner, whose premature death we have to lament as a great loss to medical criticism.

In the list of anatomical books published last Easter-fair, the names of Loder of Jena, and Sömmering of Frankfurt, again stand conspicuous. By the latter, we notice his long-expected "Icones Oculi Humani."

Beer, of Vienna, and Himly, of Brunswick, furnish some ophthalmological writings: the latter a work entitled "Ophthalmological Observations, No. I. Bremen, Wilmann.

For small but interesting treatises, we are indebted to Schweickkardt and Siebold; the former of whom has published a "Beschreibung einer Missgeburt," Description of a Monstrous Child (Tübingen, Cotta) and the latter, "Eine Praktische Dissertation über die Castration;" a Practical Treatise on Castration (Frankfurt, Varrentrapp.)

BLUMENBACH has given us an important Text-book on Comparative Anatomy; and with pleasure we find, that WEIDEMANN's "Archive for Zoology and Zootomy" is continued.

The smaller treatises in the department of Pathology and Therapeutics were again mostly polemical. According to Dr. Wickmanns of Hanover's Diagnostics, Sternberg has given us an examination of the nature of Dentition; and Dr. Rau, of Erlang, puts to the test Dr. Reich's remedy against the fever, which proved at least a golden tincture to the inventor; the King of Prussia having settled a pension of 400 dollars per annum on him for communicating his secret to the public. A small treatise has likewise been published at Gotha, on Dr. Hahnemann's remedy for the scarlet fever, which has been most severely attacked.

The diligent Dr. Struve, of Görlitz, has added to the stock of dietetical works by his "Wissenchaft des Lebens," Science of Life," which may be considered as a counterpart to HUFELAND's Art of Prolonging Life. A most important publication is the learned and acute Dr. ROOSE's, of Brunswick, "Buch über die Krankheiten der Gesunden;" on the Diseases of the Robust.

Whatever is newest and best in every department of science of medicine is, however, undoubtedly to be found dispersed through a number of collections and journals for the whole or separate parts of it. Indeed almost all the larger works on medicine are now published in parts and numbers. Arnemann, of Göttingen, Loder, of Jena, Mursinna, of Halle, regularly fill their Chirurgical Journals with important observations of their own and others; and Kausisch, of Breslau, gives us the spirit of all these journals in his "Geist und Kritik der Medizinisch-chirurgischen Journale." HUFELAND's Journal and Library seems to have undergone no other alteration by his transplantation to Berlin, except that it is now published by another bookseller. Starke, of Jena, and Osiander, of Göttingen, continue their "Archiv für die Geburtshülfe;" Archive for Midwifery. Horn, Formey, and Augustin publish Ephemerides, Archives, and Inventions. But the old, and justly esteemed, "Journal der Erfindungen, Theorien ur. s. w." is still carried on with vigour, and the tenth number of the second series had appeared at Easter. REIL's "Archiv der Physiologie,"

Physiologie," vol. 5; and the "Sammlung auserlesener Abhandlungen für Aerzte," Collection of Select Medical Treatises;" still maintain their reputation. Jugler and Rahn treat of Medical Police. A new separate Repository has likewise been established for Medical Geography.

TRIEFE, of Breslau, in his "Annalen der Brittischen Arzneykunde," Annals of Medicine in Britain; and SCHEELE, in his "Nordisches Archiv," make their countrymen acquainted with foreign medical literature. Provision has in particular been doubly and trebly made for detailing out the wisdom of the French medical schools.

VOGEL's, HILDEBRAND's, &c. "Almanacks of Health" are useful and acceptable presents for non-physicians. On the whole, the last Easter-fair produced six such Almanacks of Health.

The neglect of the study of the Latin tongue is observable in general, and particularly in medical works, which were formerly chiefly written in that universal language of the learned. We have here only to notice "Pandectæ Medicæ, s. Explicatio Rerum Medicarum in Instit. Digestis Novellis occurrentium."

Nor has the veterinary art been neglected. A capital work is the long expected "Handbuch der Vergleichenden Anatomie und Physiologie," Manual of Comparative Anatomy and Physiology, by Professor BLUMENBACH (Göttingen, Dietrich). Of the useful economico veterinary publication of Riem and Reuter, with drawings by Heine, the 5th number made its appearance (Voss, Leipzig); and ROHLWESS's "Magazin fur Thierarzneikunde," &c. Magazine for the Veterinary Art, and for the Results of Experience relative to the Diseases of Horses and Horned Cattle, of which three years have already appeared (Maurer. Berlin), comprehends the whole of the science, and proceeds without interruption.

On Galvanism, we find only one work announced, viz. PILGER's, of Giessen, "Versuch durch den Galvanismus die Wirkung verschiedener Gifte und Arzneimittel zu prüfen;" Attempt to prove by Means of Galvanism the Effect of various Poisons and Medicines (Giessen, Heyer).

In Germany too, the inoculation of the Cow-pox, or *Vaccination*, as the Germans name it, likewise employed the pens of a number of medical writers. The Easter-Catalogue swarms with treatises on this interesting subject, and with zealous calls to receive the new *Dea Salus*, whom the voice of Jenner has charmed forth from the cow-house. A number of excellent papers on the cow-pox have likewise been inserted in various periodical publications, as, for instance, in the "Reichs-Anzeiger," of which a leaf is published at Gotha every day, and which, being much read, quickly circulates generally interesting intelligence through all Germany; in the 33d number of the "Journal der Erfindungen für die Arznei-Wissenschaft," where there is a good History of Vaccination; and in the "Vienna Catechism of Health," in which Dr. Karros communicated his opinion to the public. Various Translations of Drs. Jenner's, Woodville's, and Aikin's publications have appeared. Dr. FAUST, author of a "Catechism of Health," a much esteemed book of instruction for the common people, even went so far as to celebrate an *Apis feast* in honour of the cow-pox. No good thing is ever improved without opposition: nor was it wanting here; Dr. MULLER, of Frankfort, has published a "Beweis," &c. or, a Proof that the Cow-pox have no Relation to the Natural Small-pox, and consequently cannot be considered as a Preventative against the latter. It may by some be deemed an interesting contribution towards medical geography, to be informed whence the voices of the physicians most loudly resounded in favour of the new practice of inoculation: Hamburg, Vienna, Schwerin, Brunswick, Leipzig, Breslau, Königsberg, Bückeburg, and Giessen; but, above all, Hanover and Berlin, honourably distinguished themselves. Drs. Himly, Wiedemann, and Roos, communicated their opinion in a joint publication; and Drs. Müller, Heffert, and Pilger, established a separate archive, exclusively appropriated to vaccine inoculation, "Archiv für die Kuhpocken-Impfung."

CHEMISTRY AND NATURAL HISTORY.

The names of all the celebrated German chemists again appear in the Leipzig catalogue for Easter-fair, except that of Göttling. Some of them come before the public with four productions, as, for instance, the learned Trommsdorf, of Erfurt. Besides his "Journal of Pharmacy for Physicians and Apothecaries," of which the 9th volume has already appeared, he has begun a "Allgemeine Chemische Bibliothek des XIX Jahrhunderts," General Chemical Library of the 19th Century, the first volume of which has been published by Henning, in Erfurt.

Three Translations of Fourcroy's Tables were announced; and his System, of which

which a great number of copies in the original French were sold at the fair, has even been enriched with additions by two German chemists, Dr. Veith and Dr. Wiedemann of Brunswick.

Wolf, Crell, and Scherer's periodical chemical publications go on as usual. The last-mentioned gentleman, in conjunction with the venerable Hermstädt, of Berlin, and with Wolf, has undertaken a "Physico-chemical, Metallurgical, Technological, and Pharmaceutical Library," from which something more than common may be expected.

SCHERER's "Grundiss der Chemie;" Elements of Chemistry, (Cotta, Tubingen,) contains a view of all the newest improvements in the science.

In metallurgic chemistry a capital work made its appearance, LAMPADIUS's "Handbuch des Hüttenwesens;" Manual of Metallurgy. M. Lampadius is Professor in the Metallurgic Academy at Freiberg, and of course has an opportunity of drawing his information from the fountain-head. His "Handbuch zur Chemischen Analyse der Mineral Körper;" Manual of the Chemical Analysis of Mineral Bodies (Freiberg, Kratz), contains much new and useful information. He is one of the most active promoters of the manufacture of sugar from turnips, and communicated the results of his experiments on that subject in a separate publication.

In Natural History, properly so called, the last Easter-fair produced few theoretical works of importance. We were happy to find, that there had appeared of BERTUCH's "Tafein der Allgemeinen Naturgeschichte," Tables of General Natural History, in all the three kingdoms, the first three numbers, which are drawn up with the greatest care, and with which Batsch's Elements go hand in hand. It is there attempted to give luminousness and order to a science, in which so many brightly illumined parts render the dark spots the more observable.

Three journals are exclusively dedicated to the study of botany by Schrader, Römer, and Usteri. The bookseller Raspe, of Nürnberg, has begun an "Allgemeines Botanisches Repertoriun"—General Botanical Repertory"—of which LANGSTEDT is the editor. The "Monography of the Astragalus," by PALLAS, advanced as far as the 7th number.

One of the most interesting productions of the fair was the long delayed "Species Muscorum Frondosorum, Leipzig, 8vo. Barth," by the late Professor HEDWIG, of Leipzig, whose cryptogamical researches first threw light on this part of botany. The present work comprehends all his researches, and the plates are executed with the greatest care.

Of the beautiful collection of rare plants at Herrenhausen, "Hortus Herrenhusanus, seu Plantæ Rariores quæ in Horto Regio Herrenhusano (one mile from Hanover) coluntur, fol. Wendeland has published the fourth number; and Count von Waldstein and Paul Kitaibel the 4-10th decades of rare Hungarian plants, (Plantæ Rariores Hungariæ Indigenæ descriptæ et Iconibus illustratæ, fol. Schaumburg, Vienna).

Sickler, a son of the celebrated pomologist of that name, and editor of the "Obstgärtner," Fruit gardener; (a journal, with cuts, of which twelve years (each year containing twelve numbers, and each number embellished with three copper-plates, representing various kinds of fruit) have already been published by the Industrie-comptoir at Weimar,) has given us a "Geschichte der Obstkultur von den ältesten Zeiten an"—History of the Cultivation of Fruit-trees from the earliest Times.

On the "Entomology and Helminthology of the Human Body," a new work, which recommends itself in particular by the beautiful execution and colouring of the copper-plates, has been begun by Fördens, a practising physician in Hof. The first part (4to. Grau, Hof,) has fifteen coloured plates.

SHOPP's "Tortoises," and Wolf's "Bugs," still continue to be published by Palm, in Erlang.

Fabricius, of Kiel, has given us a new "Systema Eleuteratorum," which will be an agreeable piece of intelligence to every entomologist; and Illiger, of Brunswick, has commenced a journal exclusively appropriated to Entomology:—"Magazin für die Insectenkunde," (Brunswick, Reichard.)

To the already known and established metallurgical and mineralogical journals, M. von Hoff has added a new Magazine for Mineralogy, Geognosy, and Mineralogical Geography, published by Roch, in Leipzig. In taking this retrospective view, we could not help admiring the enterprising spirit and perseverance of the German booksellers, who, in times so unfavourable, had undertaken, and carried on, such expensive works.

Geo

GEOGRAPHY, VOYAGES, AND TRAVELS.

Few important acquisitions have been made in geography, the knowledge of foreign countries and peoples, and mathematical geography, as far as relates to the scientific form.

Baron von Zach continues to diffuse, in his "Monatliche Correspondenz," &c. the newest intelligence relative to astronomy and geography, partly derived from an extensive correspondence with the most eminent astronomers and mathematicians of Europe. The "Geographical Ephemerides," published by Bertuch, likewise maintain their reputation. The extracts there given from the best and latest voyages and travels, and the copies of the newest maps, with a critical account of them, cannot fail to be very attractive.

In the geographical department, indeed, much cannot be expected till the final conclusion of a general peace. The lover of entertaining relations of travels, however, will find, among the productions of the Easter-fair, several works that will prove acceptable to him, as, for instance, ARNDT's "Bruchstücke einer Reise von Baireuth bis Wien;" Fragments of a Journey from Baireuth to Vienna, which has been published by Gräff, in Leipzig.

VON EGGER's (who belonged to the Danish Embassy at the Congress of Rastadt) "Reise durch das Südliche Deutschland, die Elsass, und Schweitz, in 1798—99;" Travels through the South of Germany, Alsace, and Switzerland, in 1798—99, Copenhagen, Storch—lays open the nefarious deeds of the French Directory.

The "Tagebuch über Rom," of FREDERICA BRUN, the poetess, 2 vol. Zurich, Orell, describes the state of Rome a short time preceding the irruption of the French Republicans.

KLEBE's "Reise auf beiden Ufern des Rheins;" Journey on both Banks of the Rhine, in the Autumn of 1800, Frankfort, Esslinger, gives an account of the state of the new departments of France, formed of provinces conquered from Germany on the left bank of that river.

In a publication, intitled "Kosmopolitische Wanderungen durch Preussen," &c. Cosmopolitical Wanderings through Prussia, Livonia, Courland, Silesia, and Galicia, 3 vol. Dantzig, Tröschel, we may acquire a more accurate knowledge of countries with which we are but imperfectly acquainted.

It is incomprehensible to us, how a Leipzig bookseller could have the effrontery to announce a third volume of *Taurinius*'s Travels. A certain *Röhrig* likewise seems willing to tread in the footsteps of the noted Damberger; for his book, "Schicksalen und Reisen durch Europa, von Holland nach Lissabon," &c. Adventures and Travels in Europe, from Holland to Lisbon, Italy, Africa, Asia, &c. bears in its very front the apocryphal mark of reprobation.

The "Travels through Upper Germany, the Mountainous Parts of Salzburg," &c. and "A Mineralogical Journey in the Harz," may be considered as a real gain to natural history.

SCHMIDT's "Reise durch einige Schwedische Provinzen bis zu den südlichen Wohnplätzen der Nomadischen Lappen," &c.—Travels through some Swedish Provinces, as far as the southern Dwelling-places of the Nomadical Laplanders, with beautiful Views, drawn from Nature by Gilberg—(Hamburg, Hoffman)—deserves to be particularly distinguished from the crowd of travels that were announced in the Easter-catalogue.

One of the most interesting productions of this kind, however, does not at all appear in the Catalogue; Göschen, the publisher, being too proud to insert in that list the select works of which he has the copyright. KÜTTNER, advantageously known to the German public by his earlier Travels through England, has given us a "Reise durch Deutschland," &c. Travels through Germany, Denmark, Sweden, Norway, and a Part of Italy, in the Years 1797—9, with cuts, 4 vols. which, whether we consider the form or the matter, may be esteemed as a real addition to the stock of German literature. Küttner, who made this journey as companion and conductor of a young Englishman, and had well qualified himself for the undertaking by a previous perusal of all the preceding sources of information, omits every thing which other travellers had already faithfully described. Notwithstanding this, the first volume contains an interesting view of Hamburg, and the third a faithful sketch of Vienna, totally contradictory to other celebrated tourists, and written with the genuine spirit of a Cosmopolite. Wherever any thing useful was to be seen, he describes it with the accuracy and perspicuity peculiar to him. For instance, in his account of the mines of Freiberg, he does not merely mention that amalgamation is used in the refining of the ore, but gives such a description of the whole process, that every cultivated reader,

reader, without being a miner or metallurgist, follows him with pleasure. The fourth volume gives an interesting account of Pola, with explanatory copper-plates.

Translations of all foreign books of travels are likewise published separately, or they appear; either translated at large, or abridged, in collections. Voss in Berlin, Heinsius in Gera, and the Industrie-comptoir at Weimar, publish such collections. Professor Sprengel, the celebrated statistician, is the editor of the collection which appears at Weimar. In the third part of that magazine, good abridgments are given of the works of the French travellers, Beaujour and St. Sauveur.

Besides Professor PAULUS's four volumes of the most remarkable Travels in the East, which may serve to illustrate the Bible, a new collection has been made by RINK, of Königsberg.

Among the topographical descriptions, MERKEL's Sketch of Hamburg, being the first part of his "Letters on the Hanse Towns," is particularly deserving of notice, and may be compared with MEYER's "Sketches of Hamburg," and the above-mentioned Account of that City in Küttner. With pleasure we observed the uninterrupted progress of the well-conducted "Hanseatic Magazine," by Professor SMID, of Bremen.

JURISPRUDENCE.

Positive customary law seems, if not in real life, at least in literature, to lose daily more and more of its long-established dominion; though we learn from the Catalogue, that it still has its own literary journals, repertories, and magazines; nor is the Roman law wholly neglected, as appears from the publications announced under the esteemed names of a Hofacker, a Glück, a Happel, &c. but here too, the philosophical tendency of the age has dislodged it from many a strongly entrenched point.

In KONOPACK "Ueber den Begriff und Zweck einer Rechts-encyclopädie;" in GERSTACKER's "Giltigkeit eines Oberften Rechts-begriff," &c. it is, on the one hand, endeavoured to establish and diffuse the most liberal principles; and, on the other, in THIBAULT's "Versuche über einzelne Theile der Theorie des Rechts," 2 vols. Jena, Manke; and, in other publications, we find the authors aiming to give a philosophical explication to the most intricate materials, and the liveliest activity in every thing that relates to what at present constitute the principal subjects of discussion, public and criminal jurisprudence. Here we again find the names of a Werner, Leyst, a Kamptz; but are surprised that FICHTE's "Geschlossener Handels Staat," which, even according to the judgment of Berlin statesmen, has many attackable points, had called forth only one refutation, by Hestermann.

Historical materials still continue to be furnished by HABERLEIN, of Helmstädt, in his "Staats archiv," of which the 22d number has been published by Cotta, in Tübingen. Each number contains single most important state-papers; as, for instance, in two of the latter numbers, two articles relative to Bavaria and Wirtemberg, in both which countries the states have shewn many signs of dissatisfaction with the government.

The venerable Klein, in conjunction with Kleinschrod and Konopack, continues his "Archiv des Kriminal Rechts," and furnishes examples and warnings to the systematicians. Indeed, from the publicity now given to law-proceedings in Prussia, and from the exposure of all the internal springs of action, there seems to exist there an earnest wish to introduce every possible reformation. How different in this respect from many of the other provinces in Germany, notwithstanding the best intentions of their rulers! as e. g. in Bavaria and in Saxony, where, for so many years, there has existed a commission instituted for the purpose of revising the laws.—In smaller treatises too, we may often discover the prevailing spirit of the age: such as the short, but with information abounding, Dissertation of the liberal-minded SONNENFELS of Vienna, "Ueber die Stimmen-mehrheit bei Kriminal Urtheilen;" on the Majority of Voices in the Decision of Criminal Processes.

HISTORY AND BIOGRAPHY.

The extensive field of history has been enriched in many detached parts, by small, interesting, and important contribution. But here, where the collecting and reviewing diligence of the Germans has established Magazines in almost every division and subdivision, we in vain look for an historical library, written in the spirit of a Gatterer, which would faithfully acquaint us with the clear profit that had arisen from these acquisitions. For WOLTMANN's journal, intitled "History and Politics," though, in other respects, abounding with matter of information, does not comprehend in its plan critical accounts of historical publications; and other historical journals are either exclusively appropriated to the history of the day, as the excellent Annals of POSSETT,

ARCHENHOLZ's Minerva, and the Genius of the Nineteenth Century; or confined to single provinces, as is the "Museum for the History of Saxony," by Professor WEISSE, of Leipzig. The grand historical drama of the present day, whose final act will hardly be received in Germany with general applause, put, at the beginning, numbers of rapid pens in motion; but, at last, the scenes succeeded one another so quickly, that even the most ready book-keepers gave up all hopes of being able to keep pace with the passing events. They are at last become sensible, that the storm must have gone by, before it is possible properly to appreciate the damages it has done, or the advantages that may result from it. Hence, on Bonaparte even, the last Easter-fair brought forth only two publications.

PAHL, author of a well-written "Geschichte des Französischen Revolutionskrieges;" History of the French Revolutionary War, 3 vols. Frankfort, Essling, has likewise given us an account of the short career of the Parthenopean Republic in his "Geschichte der Parthenopäischen Republik, Frankfort, Essling.

But Switzerland has undoubtedly furnished the greatest number of contributions towards the history of the present times. Among these, C. H. v. HALLER's "Geschichte der Wirkungen und Folgen des Oesterreich. Feldzugs in der Schweiz"—History of the Operations and Consequences of the Austrian Campaign in Switzerland—(Weimar, Gädicke) holds a distinguished rank. The author, who is a grandson of the immortal Haller, and now resides at Vienna, was himself employed in the negociations between the Canton of Bern, and the French Directory; but afterwards, unable to bear the domination of the insolent conquerors, left his country, to return again with the Archduke Charles; and consequently he almost every where speaks as an eye-witness. As he himself, however, wishes to have his work considered as a continuation of Mallet du Pan, it is probable that only one party will be satisfied with this account of the attempt to deliver Switzerland from the yoke of the French.

Von Junge has treated, in a work consisting of two thick volumes, of "The Political Relation of Switzerland to the Germanic Empire, from the Origin of the Helvetic Confederacy to the End of the Eighteenth Century." Two smaller works, "Helvetien zu Ende des XVIII. Jahrhunderts"—Helvetia at the Close of the Eighteenth Century; and "Ueber die Schweiz am Ende des XVIII. Jahrhunderts"—On Switzerland at the Close of the Eighteenth Century, seem to shew, by the different names which they give to the country of which they treat, that they are the productions of men of opposite parties. In the "Vermische Schriften," Miscellaneous Pieces, (4 vol. Copenhagen), of BONSTETTEN, who now lives at Copenhagen, in the bosom of friendship, we may likewise expect many interesting particulars relative to Switzerland.

Professor Tralles, of Bern, who was sent to Paris to assist at the synod there convened to deliberate on the propriety of adopting the new weights and measures, has given us an account of his mission in a treatise, "Ueber die Mittel, ein Allgemeines Maas und Gewicht in Helvetien einzuführen."

Gustavus Vasa, the founder of a new dynasty, and the establisher of Protestantism in Sweden, has found an historian worthy of him in M. VON ARCHENHOLZ, who has published a "Regierungs-Geschichte des Schwedischen Königs, Gustavus I." History of the Reign of Gustavus I. King of Sweden, 2 vols. Tubingen, Cotta. Besides the known sources of information, the author consulted the Dissertations of Befali, and had an opportunity of recurring for advice to a Gjöwell, a Fant, and a Nordenskiöld, Swedish resident in Hamburg. And although criticism may find something to blame in the too general views in the introduction, and in some other things; yet, in the sequel of the history, every reader will easily discern the hand of the master, who knows how to connect his scattered materials, to place every thing in most agreeable light, and to render Gustavus, the reformer and enlightener, dearer and dearer to us as he relates his repeated combats with the abettors of darkness.

In the biographical department of history, we observe with pleasure, that the Germans begin more and more boldly to contend for the palm of excellence with their neighbours, especially the English, whose appetite for biography, foreigners have remarked, is insatiable. One of the most interesting productions of this kind is the "Life of the President von Hippel, of Königsberg," derived chiefly from his own papers and confessions.

Of SCHLICHTEGROLL's "Necrology," an excellent national work, whose faults it is easier to blame, than to remove by something more finished and select, we have received the second volume of the eighth year, viz. 1797, in which a Life of of the Poet Gotter is particularly deserving of commendation.

According to the Catalogue, biographical monuments have been erected to the following men—to Deppisch, ecclesiastical councillor, and preacher at the Julius Hospital, in Würzburg, by his successor Förtsch; to Meierotto, consistorial councillor, and rector of the Calvinist gymnasium in Berlin, by his colleague, Professor Brun; to the meritorious Burgomaster Müller, of Leipzig, by an anonymous biographer; to Professor Büsch, of Hamburg, by Nölting; to Fasch, of Berlin, by Zeller; and to Lavater by Schulthess.

Professor Müller, of Schafhausen, has given us, in the fourth part of his "Selbstbekenntnisse," Memoirs of Christina, Queen of Sweden. Nor are self-biographers wanting. The long expected Life of Dittersdorf, chapel-master and opera-composer, is now in the hands of every man of curiosity; it is entitled "Carl von DITTERSDORF's Lebens Beschreibung; seinem Sohne in die Feder dictirt;" contains many interesting musical anecdotes, and well exposes the miseries of a court-life. THIESS, formerly professor of divinity in the university of Kiel, whence he was driven on account of the freedom with which he declared his opinions, has given an account of his fate and adventures in the "Geschichte meines Lebens: ein Fragment aus der Sitten und Gelehrten-geschichte des XVIII. Jahrhunders, vol. 1. Hamburg, Kratsch; and blind SACHSE, of Gera, has written a "History of his own Life and Sufferings."

Fülleborn, of Breslau, has begun a "Museum Teutscher Gelehrten, und berühmter Tonkünstler," in which he gives the portraits of celebrated musicians, and living German literati, with a short biographical account at the back of the portraits, in which the man is described chiefly from his works.

PHILOSOPHY.

There was a time, when Alchymy was called the queen and mistress of all earthy and heavenly wisdom, and when Turneiser and other German thesophists of the Paracelsian school sent year after year to the then flourishing fair of Frankfort their bales of the alone possible science. At the commencement of the nineteenth century another only possible science, Fichte's transcendental idealism, is again extolled as the queen and canon of all other sciences, and wanders in various forms and dresses to the great book-mart of Leipzig. Let us hope that it will be more productive than its predecessor of genuine gold, which will stand the test of the crucible.

Father Kant himself is now tolerated only by a few faithful adherents in the philosophical house-chapel. Rink brings once more from stuble-fields so often gleaned before a few almost empty ears. Pörschke has given us "Anthropologische Abhandlungen," intended as Commentaries on Kant's Anthropology;—and Rätze a "Critical Anthology," collected from Kant's writings. M. M. Rätze and Rink are professors in Königsberg, where Kant, in a very advanced age, now only vegetates physically.—Nor is Mellin, of Magdeburg, yet become tired of continuing his Marginal Notes.

But undoubtedly the philosophical work that most splendidly shines forth, is FICHTE's "Sonnenklarer Bericht an das grössere Publicum über das wahre Wesen der Neuesten Philosophie;" A Report, clear as the Sun, to the Public at large, relative to the True Principles of the Newest Philosophy." How will the irradiation affect poor Krug? who has continued his "Briefe über die Wissenschaftslehre," and even ventures to lay before the world the Plan of a New Organon. He might learn what awaits him from the castigation which Reinhold has received in Fichte's Answer to him. For those who have fallen back again into the old doctrines are there told, that such back-sliding cannot be accounted for, except by a total incapacity to comprehend Fichte's system. An impartial reader will however wish to examine likewise the documents produced by the other party, and, before he comes to a decision, peruse REINHOLD's "Beiträge zur leichtern Uebersicht des Zustandes der Philosophie." On the whole, the last Easter Catalogue, though we were surprised to find that Niethhammer and Fichte's Philosophical Journal is discontinued, shews that the newest Philosophy is zealously supported by many active partizans. Even the poet Mnioch, gives us Illustrative Variations on the Tendency of Fichte's Destination of Man.

Schad, of Jena, continues his View; and in another publication endeavours to prove, against Heusinger and other doubters, the "Complete Harmony of Fichte's System with Religion."

All this has given rise to a Lucianic piece of humour, entitled "The Last Judgment of Philosophy," by RUCKERT. But that this author is likewise capable of considering the subject in a serious point of view, appears from his "Realismus, oder Grundsätze einer durch aus Practischen Philosophie;" Realism, or Principles of a thoroughly Practical Philosophy (Leipzig, Göschen), which ought not to be overlooked by the Idealists of the newest schools.

To those who wish for an impartial, unprejudiced and luminous view of the new and newest philosophy, and of its sects and parties, from the days of Leibnitz to the present times, we may venture to recommend the "Uebersicht der neuern Philosophie," 2 vols. Hamburg, Bohn, by Professor SCHULZ, of Helmstadt, who here too has merited the praise which not even his opponents could refuse to his former productions.

The Catholic part of Germany continues to shew the most lively interest in the promotion of the critical philosophy. In Bamberg, Logics adapted to the Kantian System, have been published at Nüslein and Metz; and that very prolific writer G. F. Wenzel, of Vienna, who parades with no less than six new titles in the Easter Catalogue, has given us (besides the "Huarte," which he has retouched, and besides the "Goldener Schlüssel zum Menschlichen Herzen," The Golden Key to the Human Heart—and the "Diätetik der Menschlichen Seele;" Diætetics of the Human Soul); likewise a "Kanonik des Verstandes als Kommentar zu Kant's Logik," or Canon of Reason, being a Commentary to Kant's Logic. From all this one might easily be led to the false conclusion, that the thing is there a marketable, fashionable commodity.

The excellent Mutschelle, of Munich, continues, even after his justly lamented death, to instruct his countrymen by means of his *Moral Divinity*; and Salat, certainly the man best qualified to fill the deceased's place, shews by his latest publication, that in him philosophical illuminism is only the gentle flame of a light-diffusing taper, and not the glaring blaze of the incendiary's torch.

MEINER'S Ethics, 2 vols. Göttingen, is a good collection of materials for the history of philosophemes, which will perhaps be more frequently recurred to for information, than duly quoted and praised.

Though weeds and thistles thrive in many places with too luxuriant a growth; yet a glance at two divisions of the variously-cultivated field of literature before us, comforts and consoles the spectator. In the first place, ancient classical literature, the firmest foundation of all true culture of the mind, and the surest preservative against scholastic fooleries and jargon, still has a number of faithful admirers:—and secondly, every thing is every year rendered more and more practical and fitted for the common uses of life; rural economy, horticulture, forrestry, mechanics, and technology are improved by the results of scientific researches, which are divested of obscurity, and diffused in a hundred commodious vehicles of communication.—We now proceed to

PHILOLOGY.

The philology of our times is not content with merely collecting and comparing what had been said before, or with the often more shining than useful display of genius and learning in the emendation of the text. Founded on a philosophical anatomy of the component parts of language and on a more luminous grammar, she views antiquity from a higher point of observation, and with a bolder criticism examines into the validity of the claims of the remains of Greek and Roman culture, often more venerable on account of their age, than the excellence of their contents. Of this, the last Easter fair furnishes us with many examples.—The acute Herrmann, of Leipzig, shews the same powers of indagation, which he evinced in the development of the metres of the ancient Greek and Roman poets, likewise in the emendation of the Greek grammar: "HERMANNI de emendanda Ratione Grammaticæ Græcæ, libri I. & II. Accedunt Herodiani aliorumque Libelli nunc primum editi." 8vo. Leipzig, Fleischer. In this part the verbs only are treated of. Syntax and Prosody are to follow. Many new ideas are applied to the elucidation of his subject; and some before unpublished Greek grammarians are subjoined from manuscripts in Munich.

The polyhistor and critic of versatile talents, Schneider, of Frankfort on the Oder, who is at the same time employed, as one of the first naturalists of his country, on "Continuations of Bloch's Fishes," and "Lacepede's (by Bechstein much improved) Amphibia," and on a "Commentary on Vitruvius," has published the "Commentary to his Eclogæ Physicæ." In this commentary we meet with the most unlooked-for combinations of the newest discoveries in physics and natural history with those of the ancients. The Greek text fills the first volume, and the commentary the second. (Jena, Frommann.)

Schneider has likewise given us an excellent new edition of the "Memorabilia of Xenophon."

M. Wolfe,

M. Wolfe, of Halle, by a critical illustration of the four Orations of Cicero after his return from exile, has established by additional arguments Markland's doubts of their genuineness.

In a new edition of Juvenal, "Juvenalis Satiræ, varietate Lectionum, perpetuoque Commentario illustratæ" a GEORG. RUPERTI, 2 vols. Leipzig, Fritsch, 8vo. we find every thing collected that has in modern and ancient times been said and conjectured, to explain this very difficult poet. Ruperti, who is a disciple of Heyne, was furnished by him with much excellent auxiliary matter towards the execution of his design. More than 80 manuscripts, and all preceding editions, were collated.

The diligent Oberlin, of Strasburg, has finished a new edition of "Ernesti's Tacitus." The continuations of the edition of "Stobæus," by Heeren; of "Strabo," by Siebenkees and Tschukke; and of "Xenophon," by Weiske; may likewise be considered as important acquisitions to classical literature.

But, above all, the intelligence that a new volume of JACOBS's Commentary on the Greek Anthology; "Anthologia Græca, Tom. X. sive Commentarii voluminis II. Pars III." 8vo. Leipzig, Dyck, has appeared, will be received with pleasure by those who know with what treasures of critical learning it abounds. The same excellent philologer has given, in a late Number of Wieland's "Attic Museum," his countrymen a beautiful specimen of the manner in which Æschylus and Demosthenes ought to be translated. Some faithful and elegant translations of ancient writers have likewise appeared: of "Arrian," by Schulze; of the "Orator of Cicero," by Wolf, of Flensberg; of "Pliny's Letters," by Schäfer, of Anspach; and of the "First Part of Plato," by F. Schlegel, of Jena.

Nor was the Fair unproductive in good auxiliary philological books and lexicons, among which we may reckon FUNKE's "Real Schul-Lexicon," and STURZ's "Lexicon Xenophonteum, Tom. I. A—C." Of MANNERT's "Geography of the Greeks and Romans," the second division of Part VI. has been published, containing the Geography of Asia Minor. HERMANN, of Berlin, has given us "A Mythology of the Greeks, in 2 vols. with a Geographico-historical Introduction and Map," wherein the illustrative rays, which the Heynean school has diffused on mythology, are well concentrated.

Dornedden, of Göttingen, connects ancient mythology and art in new ingenious hypotheses in the following work: "Versuch einer neuen Theorie der Griechischen Kunst und Mythologie;" Göttingen, Dietrich.

"An Archæological Museum" is edited by BÖTTIGER, of Weimar, and MEYER, illustrated with well chosen plates: and the intelligent STIEGLITZ has given us a capital work on the architecture of the Greeks and Romans, viz. "Archäologie der Baukunst der Griechen und Römer," with the necessary explanatory plates. It is to consist of three vols. The first treats of the disposition of columns, and the internal decorations of the houses. There are a number of vignettes, in which specimens are given of ancient architecture, copied from medals.

In the "Acta Societatis Philologicæ," edited by BECK, of Leipzig, an account in the Latin language is given of the progress of philological science.

We shall close this account of classical publications with a work which for fine printing, correctness of the text, and the magnificence of its ornaments, is equalled by few. We allude to the splendid edition of HEYNE's "Virgil," in 6 vols. with 204 plates. The enterprizing and persevering publisher, Caspar Fritsch, bookseller in Leipzig, must be acknowledged to have thereby erected a fine monument to himself and his country.

Nor have the German philologers been neglectful of their own and other modern languages. We have the pleasure to announce to our readers the publication of the last volume of ADELUNG's "Wörterbuch der Hoch-Deutschen Mundart;" Dictionary of the High-German Dialect; Leipzig, Breitkopf. This monument of the learning and perseverance of one man will probably bid defiance to the fickle humour of innovation, and be generally received as the standard of the language. It consists of four large quarto volumes, each containing about 2000 closely printed columns. The whole has been re-moulded by the author, and enriched with innumerable additions. The second volume, which concludes the work, has likewise been published of CAMPEN's "Verteutschende Ergänzungen to Adelung," as likewise REINEWALD's "Hennebergisches and SCHÜTZEN's Holsteinisches Idiotikon;" or Vocabularies of the Provincial Dialects of Henneberg and Holstein.

Of chrestomathies, popular grammars, &c. the Catalogue announced a most abundant supply, adapted to every age, sex

sex, and condition: and under a separate head stand no less than 224 articles printed in foreign languages, among which we observe two editions of "Shakespeare," in English; and the French "Dictionnaire de l'Academie," with additions, in 4 vols. 4to.

The diligent Nemmich, of Hamburg, has added to his former useful labours a "Krankheits-Lexicon (Lexicon nosologicum polyglotton) in all the European Languages," 4to. Hamburg.

TECHNOLOGY, MECHANIC ARTS, FORESTRY.

The bookseller Roch, of Leipzig, publishes two well-conducted journals, and which contribute much to the popularization of useful inventions:—"Die ökonomische Hefte," and the "Journal für Fabrik und Handlung," which is well calculated to diffuse useful knowledge relative to manufactures and commerce. Almost every art and trade has found its peculiar writers and historiographers: the greatest activity in particular prevails in Germany, in applying the mathematical sciences to the improvement of the useful and mechanic arts, as appears from the numerous publications of Büsch, Brodhagen, Busse, &c. &c. Poppe, of Göttingen, has given us a well-executed History of the Art of Clock and Watchmaking—(Leipzig, Roch).

An excellent work "On the Application of Mechanics and Hydraulics to Architecture," with many plates, has been published at Berlin by Eytelwein, from whose connection with Gilly we still expect many mature fruits.

In most of the provinces of Germany a want of fuel begins to be felt, owing, in a great measure, to the ravages of a destructive caterpillar—to an adherence to long-established abuses in the pasturing of cattle, &c.—to the late requisitions of the French, and to the increased consumption in spite of the fuel-saving contrivances of Count Rumford. Accordingly a number of publications have appeared on the means of remedying these evils—on the proper management of the woods—and on the science of venery and forrestry in general; to teach which no less than nine academies have already been established by German Princes. Seckendorf still continues, in his "Forst Rügen," to excite the attention of his countrymen in the Electorate of Saxony to this important subject; and with the same view Franz has sent forth his "Freimüthige Gedanken über unsere heutige Forst und Landwirth-schaft," Leipzig, Fleischer. Von Witzleben, Director of a flourishing forrestrial Academy in Hesse, has given us a second edition of his useful work on the culture of forest-trees, "Beiträge zur Holz-Kultur." Von Vildungen continues his "Foresters' Calendar;" Professor Leonhardi, of Leipzig, his "Magazin für Jagt und Forstwesen," with coloured plates; and Gatterer and Moser their "Archiv für Forstwesen."

RURAL ECONOMY.

All the branches of rural economy have lately been much cultivated by many of the German noblemen and gentlemen. Happy will it be for that country, if, instead of wasting their time in hunting and in poring over regimental muster-rolls, the great landholders followed the example of M. von Teilitzsch, of Anspach, who has communicated to the public the results of his long experience and improvements in his "Œkonomisch-praktische Bemerkungen über den Ackerbau," (2 vols. Hof, Gran.);—of the patriotic Munchhausen of Saxony, who has given us an account of the manner in which he has abolished the oppressive feudal services on his estates, "Umständlicher Bericht von der auf dem Ritterguте Steinberg vorgenommenen Aufhebung der Frohndienste, Leipzig, Rabenhorst:"—or of M. von Richthofen, of Silesia, who has published a systematically arranged sketch of a theory of agriculture, "Systematisch-geordneter Entwurf der Ackerbau-Theorie," in 2 vols.

M. Riem, secretary to the Saxonian Economical Society in Dresden, has given us a new collection of papers relative to rural economy and the keeping of bees, "Eine neue Sammlung ökonomischer und Bienenschriften aufs Jahr 1801;"—and Gaudig, an excellent work, containing instructions in every branch of rural economy, founded on an experience of 30 years, "Auf dreissig-jährige Erfahrung sich gründender Unterricht der ganzen Landwirthscaft," (2 vols. Leipz. Rein.)

A number of other smaller pieces on rural economy, on police, &c. have appeared, which, though they should escape the attention of the 20 Reviews published in Germany, will no doubt at last be arranged in their proper places by the muster-master-general of the host of German authors, Dr. ERSCH, in his "Allgemeines Repertorium," which is to contain an alphabetically arranged list of all the works that have appeared in Germany and other countries. Three volumes in quarto, comprehending the years 1791—1795, have

have already been published at Weimar, in the "Industrie Comptoir;" and it is to be continued.

POETRY.

In the last Easter-fair there was a more than common dearth of poetical productions, which would have been still greater if some of the melodious songsters of the German Parnassus, such as Von Meyer, Müchler, Von Munchhausen, &c. had not chanted cradle-hymns to the new century.

Sophia Mereau, the lovely poetess of Jena, has collected the latest blossoms of her fancy in a Kalathiskos. Prändel and Von Wessenberg have likewise given us collections of their poems. Klamer Smidt describes in an elegy A Country-parsonage; and Gramberg, of Oldenburg, has formed Garlands of Romantic Tales.

The longest and most highly finished poetical production that appeared last Easter, is TIEDGE's "Urania," a lyrical didactic poem on the immortality of the soul, in six cantos.

But what no catalogue announced may be reckoned among the choicest fruits in the ever-blooming garden of the Muses: —we allude to the noble chanter's of Flora, VON DER LUTZE's "Hymn to Ceres," which Count Prosper von Sinzendorf, of Vienna, caused to be printed in a most tasteful manner with the stereotypes invented by him. The poet himself faded away like a tender flower; but to his hymn, one of the best that the German language possesses, we may confidently promise immortality.

Of the periodical collections, where poems and narratives, and essays in prose, stand amicably intermixed, BECKER's "Erhohlungen" still maintain a distinguished rank, for the entertaining variety and judicious selection of its contents.

NOVELS, ROMANCES, &c.

Under this head we counted no less than 261 titles: of these a very great majority is no doubt destined to supply the cheesemonger and grocer; here and there, however, a few illustrious names appear, which deserved to be ushered into public in better company.

The humorous JEAN PAUL has not only given us the continuation of his "Titan," but likewise reveals the secret threnody of the men of the present day," Das heimliche Klaglied der iezigen Männer." LAFONTAINE's "Landprediger" might, by a little more attention to brevity, have become a good counterpart to Goldsmith's Vicar of Wakefield. The "Pastor in Kartoffel-Feld," is another good novel of the same class, of which the title is, perhaps, the worst part.

F. Röchlitz has commenced a new series of modern tales, entitled "Familien-Leben," written with the tender sensibility peculiar to him. The comic poet Langbein has worked tales from the Thousand-and-One-Nights, and ancient popular stories, into a talisman against *ennui*, "Talisman gegen die Langeweile."

F. SCHLEGEL's "Florentin" might well be ashamed of his younger sister Lucinda, for the former novel, which, though written earlier, was published later than the notorious Lucinda, has nothing immoral in it, and abounds with many tender and happy passages.

Of tales in the Oriental style, the "Dya-Na-Sore," by MAIER, of Vienna, deserves to stand highest in the estimation of the reading public. The new edition which has been published in five elegantly printed volumes, by Schaumburg of Vienna, has been so remoulded, that it may be considered as a new production of a poet endowed with the greatest sensibility, and as the purest effusion of a true cosmopolite.

Among the historical romances, the "Romantische Biographie des Bertrand du Guesclin," by F. MAJER, of Weimar, particularly distinguishes itself by a faithful delineation of the manners and chivalric customs of the age in which Du Guesclin flourished. It may, indeed, be proposed as a model to those who would excel in that kind of composition; and we are happy to find that we may expect a Black Prince and a Maid of Orleans from the pen of the same author, whom his preparatory labours and researches so well qualify for the execution of such tasks.

An immense mixed multitude of giants, ghosts, necromancers, of wanton satyrs and love-sick maidens, of outlaws, robbers, and murderers, press around us: but who shall venture to penetrate into the crowd. We cannot help, however, admiring the inventive genius of the novel-scriblers, in coining strange and wondrous titles to draw the attention of the vulgar. Cramer, one of the most expeditious manufacturers of romances, who has already furnished above 50 volumes, does not yet seem to be exhausted: he has again given us a "Kix von Kaxberg," "Raserein der Liebe," and the like. But what seem to be most the order of the day are, the deeds and adventures of murderers, robbers, and captains of banditti; in imitation of the Glorioso, and Rinaldo Rinaldini, of Vulpius; the latter of which has even been translated

translated into English, although from its first appearance it excited disgust in every German of a cultivated mind. It would, indeed, be unjust to form an opinion of the taste of the nation from the quantity of such trash annually vended at the Leipzig Fair. No man of rank and education would soil his fingers therewith. But there exist among the lower orders above 400 circulating libraries, where the whole is eagerly received as a most delectable treat.

DRAMATIC PRODUCTIONS.

The most important of the 57 dramatic productions that appeared last Easter-fair is undoubtedly SCHILLER's "Maria Stuart." The same eminent tragic poet has given us a new elegant pocket-edition of his "Don Carlos," which he has entirely remoulded; and a metrical translation of "Macbeth," in which he has here and there attempted to improve Shakespeare.

Of KOTZEBUE's "Neue Schauspiele," the 5th and 6th volumes were published by Kummer, in Leipzig, containing among others "Die Klingsberge," one of his best comedies, and four other new plays.

Of the collection of IFFLAND's plays, the 13th volume has appeared. A number of inferior writers, such as Werthes, Kratter, Beck, Bilderbeck, &c. &c. likewise communicated their dramatic productions to the public. A certain Count of the Holy Roman Empire, Julius von Soden, ventured to give us, even after Kotzebue, a new drama, entitled "Menschenhass und Reue;" and Reinbeck sent to the Fair, all the way from Petersburg, his "Cossacs in Switzerland," which had been represented on the Petersburg Theatre. The Ex-jesuit, Tr. Xav. Jan, of Augsburg, has favoured us with the 5th volume of his plays, which he assures us are free from all "scandalous love-intrigues and marriages."

MICHAELMAS FAIR, 1801.

ACCORDING to the Leipzig Catalogue, 289 booksellers forwarded 1150 articles to the last Michaelmas Fair in that city; so that this after-crop of German literature would at first sight appear to be greater than the whole year's produce in England, which, if we may depend upon the accuracy of the lists that have been published, did not from Michaelmas 1800, to Michaelmas 1801, exceed 900 articles, including sermons and the smallest political pamphlets. But the Leipzig Catalogue is always a very uncertain and fallacious index of the real increase of the stock of books; and in particular that published at Michaelmas. Many a critical Achilles, who has fought his way through the crowds of the Easter Fair, might be tempted, at the sight of so many resuscitated book-titles, to exclaim with the son of Thetis (Il. xxi. 55.)

Ye mighty Gods! what wonders strike my view!
Is it in vain our conq'ring arms subdue?
Sure I shall see yon' heaps of Trojans kill'd
Rise from the shades, and brave me in the field!

For, besides the 106 new editions, actually bearing on their forehead the sign of regeneration (of which, however, more than one half, probably, have nothing new but the title-page) the intelligent observer easily discovers a large quantity of wares formerly rejected and condemned, but which are now again offered for sale under a new name. If we further deduct from the above sum total about 200 continuations, some of them only single numbers of magazines and journals; about 80 pocket books, almanacks, and similar annuals; moreover, a couple of hundreds of small pamphlets; and lastly, nearly 113 novels and romances, which were not inspired by genius but by hunger; there will remain but few articles which may be deemed a real acquisition to literature. In every branch, however, we observe some contributions and even complete works, which are deserving of attention.

THEOLOGY.

No where is it now so still and quiet as in the once so noisy and tumultuous fields of theology. The Göttingen Prize-dissertation on the opinions of the ancient Fathers relative to original sin, by HORN, scarcely attracts notice; for can any thing new on this subject be gleaned even from the patristic treasures of the University library of Göttingen?

Whilst PÖLITZ extracts the second part of the "Spirit of Reinhard" for the public at large; the venerable TELLER sends forth an explanatory epistle, in Latin, to Reinhard "de Finibus Gratiæ Divinæ," thus giving a hint to the numerous manufacturers of epistles, in what language even now such controversies ought to be carried on.

From the Gallo-Romano-Catholic Left Bank of the Rhine, we were favoured with Republican Devotions for every occurrence and condition in life.—The new organization of the Catholic Church in France gave rise to two epistles, one of which, published by Rein in Leipzig, it is pretended was translated from a Latin MS. written at Paris under Bonaparte's own

own eye; every curious particular relative to which we may expect to find in HENKE's copious "Religions-Annalen," which are still continued.

On the most proper method of teaching religion, Mr. NIEMEYER, of Halle, has published a "Lehrbuck für die obern Religionsklassen gelehrter Schulen," which supplies a long-felt pressing want, and in which animating zeal is joined to great comprehensibility and luminous order; such, indeed, as might be expected from the experience of the author, who, as director of the Pædagogium, in Halle, in which about 150 young gentlemen of the first families in Germany are educated, has for many years taken upon himself the charge of instructing the pupils in the principles of religion.

JURISPRUDENCE.

That, in the present violent collision of new and old times and doctrines, Jurisprudence too comes in for its share of attention, appears from the continuation of HUFELAND's "Beiträge zur Berichtigung und Erweiterung der positiven Rechtswissenschaft, (Jena, Stahl.) and from the rapid progress of the "Juridischer Archiv," which is supported by the contributions of a Danz, a Gmelin, and a Tafinger.

HABERLIN's "Staatsarchiv" continues to communicate important state-papers.

The bitter cup, which the Peace of Luneville prepared for many of the members of the Germanic Empire, has loosened the tongues of some, who otherwise would never have spoken. A Mr. Wagner, of Mentz, lays before the Holy Roman Empire only "Fifty Political Queries;" and from the same place have come forth "Free Thoughts on the Advantages and Disadvantages attending the Plan of Secularization." VOSS, known by his former publications on this subject, has given us another "Ueber die Schicksale der teutschen Staatsverfassung.

MEDICINE.

Here we still see a number of fiery champions under the Brunonian and Anti-Brunonian standard fiercely contending against one another. A particular account of these feuds may be found in the Medical Journals, edited by Dr. RÖSCHLAUB, in Würzburg, and by Dr. HUFELAND, of Berlin.

NAGELE has published, at Dusseldorf, a new Essay to render the Brunonian Pathogony and Theory of Excitability intelligible to Non-physicians: and on the other hand TRENKER, of Vienna, with his new Humoral Pathology, boldly enters the lists against whatever bears the name of Brunonian.

Dr. AUGUSTIN, of Berlin, gives us an account of the newest Galvanic experiments that came within his circle of observation. But what is still more deserving of attention, though not announced in the Catalogue, is a new Number of RITTER's "Contributions." M. Ritter now resides at Weimar, and is esteemed the most profound of all the German Galvanists.

FRORIEP, of Jena, has been reading Lectures on the ingenious Cranioscopy of Dr. Gall of Vienna. These lectures he has communicated to the public in his entirely remoulded "Darstellung der neuen auf Untersuchung der Verrichtungen des Gehirns gegründeten Theorie der Physiognomik des D. Gall in Wien."

It is with pleasure we announce the appearance of the second volume of the "Annales Instituti Medico clinici Wurceburgensis, J. N. THOMAN, Observat. illustravit," (Wirceb. Vid. Stahl, cum fig. 8.)

But in this department of science the *propaganda* of the vaccine inoculation have again most actively employed their pens. The order of the police, prohibiting the practice thereof in the suburbs, does not deter the patriotic Careno, of Vienna, from announcing, in German and French, popular treatises on the beneficent utility of the invention, nor from translating Dr. Jenner's Work into the classical language of Latium.—Dr. Herz, a Jewish physician in Berlin, had given great offence to all the friends and promoters of vaccination, by his "Epistle to Dohmeyer." His "Brutal inoculation," (for so he termed the cow-pox, and was of opinion, that human nature would by the prevalence of it become brutalized) could not fail to call forth the most violent opposition; and accordingly we find announced in the Catalogue no less than five polemical treatises against him. His entire refutation must be left to time, which brings every thing to maturity, unless, indeed, experience should confirm the opinion lately broached, that what are called the human-pox had a very brutal origin, viz. from the commixture of a disease of the cows with the miasma of a human fever. To those who wish to acquire accurate information relative to the progress of vaccination in Germany, the Collections published by Heffert and Pilger will be most acceptable.

NATURAL HISTORY.

Professor SCHNEIDER, of Frankfort on the

the Oder, has publiſhed a ſecond *faſciculus* of his "Hiſtoria Amphibiorum," (Jena, Frommann,) in which he has given us, in claſſical Latin, the natural hiſtory of the lizard, the crocodile, and of the ſerpent kind the boa, amphiſbæna, cæcilia, and ſome others, with that happy union of ancient and modern ſcience, in which he excels every other cotemporary naturaliſt. If we appreciate a work not according to its bulk, but according to the intrinſic value of its contents, this may be reckoned one of the moſt important that appeared laſt Michaelmas Fair.

JOANNIDES, a learned Greek, who ſtudied at Halle, has publiſhed a "Specimen Phyſiologiæ Mammarum Muliebrium," with notes by his preceptor and friend Reil, which authoriſes us to entertain the moſt ſanguine expectations from his future progreſs in the ſcience.

JÖRDENS, of Hof, has publiſhed the ſecond volume of his "Entomology and Helminthology of the Human Body," completing a ſplendid work, which, for the profoundneſs of the text, and the beauty of the plates, may boldly challenge a compariſon with the beſt works in that branch of ſcience. This laſt volume has ſeven coloured plates.

From G. FISCHER, profeſſor and librarian to the Central School at Mentz, and a pupil and friend of the celebrated Cuvier, we have received fragments on comparative anatomy and the phyſiology of animals and plants, "Naturhiſtoriſche Fragmente, mit beſonderer Rückſicht auf Anatomie und Phyſiology der Thiere und Gewächſe, (4to Varrentrapp), which are well worthy the attention of every naturaliſt.

To the venerable Dr. Brückmann, phyſician to the Duke of Brunſwick, we are indebted for a Diſſertation, which will be equally acceptable to the mineralogiſt and the antiquarian, containing obſervations and an analyſis on onyx and ſardonyx, and other ancient precious ſtones, uſed by the ancients for ſeals, &c. of which Dr. Brückmann has a very rich collection.

Towards geognoſy in general there are important contributions in VON BUCH's "Geognoſtiſche Beobachtungen auf Reiſen durch Deutſchland und Italien geſammelt." Geognoſtical Obſervations collected during a Journey through Germany and Italy, with a coloured map.

J. BECKMANNI "Lexicon Botanicum, exhibens Etymologiam, Orthographiam et Proſodiam omnium Nominum Botanicorum" (Götting. 8vo.) does great honour to the author, to whom we are already indebted for a number of curious and uſeful publications. Such an auxiliary book was indeed much wanted for thoſe amateurs who had not paſſed through the claſſical ſchools in their progreſs to the Temple of Botany.

Of Dr. ROSSIG's "Roſes," drawn and coloured from Nature, the firſt Number has made its appearance, and has been received with the approbation it merited.

Every botaniſt will hear with pleaſure, that continuations have appeared of two works of the celebrated THUNBERG—"Icones Plantarium Japonicarum, quas in Inſulis Japonicis collegit anno 1775-6, Upſaliæ, faſcic ii." and "Prodromus Plantarum Capenſium, Pars ii. Upſaliæ," both in folio.

The "Veterinariſche und ökonomiſche Mittheilungen von Rumpelts Reiſe durch Deutſchland, England, Frankreich, Holland, und die Schweitz," (Dreſden, Walther, 8vo.) ought not to be overlooked by thoſe who wiſh to be informed of the preſent ſtate of the veterinary art in Europe.

RURAL ECONOMY AND TECHNOLOGY.

Among the publications on rural economy, Baron von RICHTHOFEN's "Entwurf einer Ackerbau Theorie" is diſtinguiſhed by his giving us views of the ſubject peculiarly his own, and by the novelty of his theory.

STIEGLITZ has publiſhed the ſecond volume of his "Archæology of Architecture," which completes this important contribution towards the hiſtory of architecture.

WIEBEKING's "Allgemeine auf Geſchichte und Erfahrung gegründete Theoretiſch-praktiſche Waſſerbaukunſt,"—A general theoretical practical Hydrotechny, founded on Hiſtory and Experience—the 3d volume, with 17 copperplates, in 4to is publiſhed. It was not however inſerted in the Leipzig Catalogue, being ſold by the author himſelf. Having in the two former volumes treated of the forming of canals, of embankments, and other works on the ſea-ſhore, he completes in this the inſtructions relative to harbours. Mr. Wiebeking, who has travelled into many countries and ſpent half of his life in collecting materials, every where confirms his practical rules by examples. Thus, for inſtance, in the 5th ſection, we find diſtinct deſcriptions of all known light-houſes, and in the 6th, of the moſt important harbours, illuſtrated, where it was neceſſary, with copperplates.

BAHT-

BREITKOPF'S "Beiträge zu einer Geschichte der Schreibkunst," Contributions towards a History of the Art of Writing, as arranged and edited from the deceased's papers, by one of the most learned literators of Germany, M. Roch, of Leipzig, will be an acceptable present to every lover of diplomatics, and of the history of modern culture.

The speculating collector of antiques, M. von Murr, in Nürnberg, has begun "Gallery of the Hand-writings of celebrated Men," in which engraved *fac-similes* are to be given according to the order of time in which the writers flourished, and an illustrative commentary added. The first Number of these *Chirographa personarum illustrium* has been published in the "Industrie Comptoir," at Weimar, and is certainly a valuable present to libraries and book-collectors.

It is with pleasure we see announced the third and concluding volume of ROTH's "Versuch einer Geschichte des Nürnberger Handels"—History of the Trade of the City of Nurnberg; and a Complete Collection of Professor REINHARD's (of Erlang) Dissertation; "De Commerciorum in Franconia Initiis et Incrementis;" two excellent contributions towards the history of commerce and culture in Germany in the middle ages.

HISTORY AND BIOGRAPHY.

The last Michaelmas-fair has been rather unproductive of grand historical works: there were not however wanting interesting contributions and Sibyl's-leaves, which deserve to be collected and arranged by the intelligent historian.

GENZ "Von dem Politischen Zustande von Europa, vor und nach der Französischen Revolution"—On the Political State of Europe, before and after the French Revolution—which gives new currency to the specious sophisms of Mallet Du Pan, will be very acceptable to one class of readers. It is generally believed in Germany, that the author of this publication was pensioned by the British Government to write against France.

The "Geschichte der Emigranten Armee"—History of the Emigrant Army, seems to have flowed from a very different inkstand; indeed from the long mountebankish title page, one might be tempted to consider the whole to be a *Laukardian* production. A History of *France hors de France*, during the last eleven years, would certainly be a most interesting work, if written by a Malouet, a Mounier, or other historian animated with the same philosophical and cosmopolitical spirit; but such *sans-culotte* trash as the production before us, is not deserving of the name of history.

Of the memorable battle of Copenhagen, on the 2d of April last, several accounts have appeared, of which the "Gründonnersdag eller der 2te April, 1801," by Professor SANDER, of Copenhagen, is the most esteemed. Annexed to it, is a copper-plate with a plan of the engagement.

Leonhard Meister is supplying his countrymen with "A Helvetic History during the last 2000 Years, or from Cæsar to Bonaparte," of which the first volume has made its appearance at St. Gall.

Among the many continuations of historical works, JENISCH's "Universal Historischer Ueberblick des Menschengeschlechts;" Universal Historical View of the Human Race; particularly deserves to be noticed with praise.

Every investigator of history, who pays more regard to intrinsic worth, than to the dress in which it is cloathed, sees with pleasure the progress of VON ENGEL's "Geschichte des Ungarischen Reichs und seiner Nebenländer;" History of the Kingdom of Hungary and of the adjoining Provinces; which, with the original documents annexed to each volume, serves to illustrate many a dark spot in the history of the nations and tribes inhabiting the banks of the Danube. The Third Part, 4to. has just been published by Gebauer, in Halle.

The biographical department of history has been enriched by many new acquisitions. From the Pædagogical Press in Snepenthal, came forth "Denkwürdigkeiten aus dem Leben ausgezeichneter Deutschen des 18ten Jahrhunderts," a very good contribution towards German biography, and which may be very useful to foreigners likewise, who wish to become acquainted with the most eminent persons who flourished in Germany during the last century.

SCHELLE has given us a "Characteristic of Heydenreich;" and THIESS continues his "Autobiography."

The late celebrated Lavater's friends, in particular, seem emulously to contend with one another in placing in every point of view the character of that most remarkable man, and in transmitting to posterity every particular relative to him. Nüscheler and Tobler indeavour to free him from the suspicion of enthusiasm; whilst Stollberg's Epistle to him on his

Conversion, again revives that and many other previous suspicions. Haller too, has inserted in the "German Mercury," a paper in his favour, which has likewise appeared as a separate publication. But in preference to all these and other fragmentary essays, the copious "Lebensgeschichte Lavaters"—Life of Lavater—by J. G. GESSNER, of which the first volume has been published at Wintherthur, is deserving of attention. Mr. Gessner, Lavater's son-in-law, had access to the best sources of information; and it appears from the manner in which he has executed his task, that he both could and would speak the truth with the strictest impartiality.

One of the few very interesting productions of the last Michaelmas-fair must likewise be classed under the head of Autobiography: it is A. VON KOTZEBUE'S "Merkwürdigstes Jahr meines Lebens;" Most remarkable Year of his Life, 2 vols. 8vo. Berlin, Sander. What sudden vicissitudes of fortune and singular adventures did he experience within the short space of twelve months! If the dramatist could touch the tenderest strings of the sympathising heart by fictitious scenes and situations, how much more must we be affected by this true drama, where nothing was left for the fancy of the poet to add, and in which he himself was the chief actor! Such scenes as his wandering about for twenty four hours in the forests of Siberia, when he made an attempt to escape—his receiving the first intelligence of his liberation—his first interview with his wife and children at Petersburg—his first conversation with the Emperor Paul, who asked his forgiveness for the injustice he had done him, &c. would, even putting historical truth out of the question, ever remain interesting from the enrapturing vividness of the picture presented to our view.

GEOGRAPHY AND TRAVELS.

In this department, besides a few topographies, as for instance, ULMENSTEIN'S "History of the Imperial City of Wetzlar," the accounts of travels chiefly claim our attention: of these, the late Michaelmas-fair brought to light a few good ones, and several that are at least well meant. To the former class undoubtedly belong: the second volume of EBEL'S "Schilderung der Gebirgsvölker der Schweitzer;" Description of the Mountaineers of Switzerland; (Leipzig, Wolf) —the "Briefe über Italien;" Letters on Italy, by the author of Confidential Letters on France, the patriotic Polander WOYDA—and NERENST'S "Wanderungen durch Rügen," published by Kosegarten. The third and fourth volumes of the Prose-writings of the poetess FR. BRUN, likewise contain the interesting Journal of her Travels in Italy.

The "Fussreise durch Schweden;" Pedestrian Tour through Sweden; (Leipzig, Hartknoch)—the "Briefe eines Helvetiers auf einer Reise durch Thuringen und Hessen;" Letters of an Helvetian on a Tour through Hessia and Thuringia—and "Streifzüge durch Inner Oestreich bis Venedig;" Excursion through Inner Austria to Venice, with plates, (Vienna, Doll); will likewise be found entertaining, fire-side companions to employ an idle hour or two of a winter's evening.

The booksellers Hahn, in Hanover, have published STRACK'S "Mahlerische Reisen durch Westphalen;" Picturesque Tour through Westphalia. From the same author we have received likewise a collection of aquatinta copper-plates of the most beautiful views in Westphalia.

Of translations we shall only notice SUWAROKOFF'S "Reise durch die Krimm im Jahre, 1799"—Journey through the Crimea, in 1799: (Leipzig, Hartknoch)—translated from Russian into German by Richter, the elegant translator of Karamsin.

The universities constitute an important branch of literary history and statistics. Professor Meiners, who has for many years been collecting materials towards a History of the Universities, has at length published the first volume of an important work, "On the Constitution and Government of the German Universities," (Göttingen, Römer).—A very different branch of culture is treated of in LANGSTREDT'S "Denkschrift über die Evangelischen Missionsangelegenheiten;" On the Affairs of the Evangelical Missions, particularly in the East Indies; the greatest remarkability of the 18th century, as the title expresses it.

PHILOSOPHY.

The Schellingian transcendental philosophy received important contributions in the second number of the third volume of SCHELLING'S "Zeitschrift für Speculativ Physik." Those who may wish to become acquainted with the newest manifestoes, and other polemical papers that have passed between the contending philosophical parties in Germany, should consult the third number of REINHOLD'S "Beiträge zur Kenntniss des Zustandes

der

der Philosophie am Ende des 18 Jahrhunderts," in which, on the one side, a Paper against Fichte, by JACOBI, particularly distinguishes itself, and on the other HEGEL's "Difference between the Fichtian and Schellingian Systems of Philosophy." Every one had hitherto believed, and Fitche himself seemed to believe, that Schelling, of Jena, built his idealistical Temple of Nature on the foundation of Fichte's doctrine of science. But Schelling now brings from his native place to Jena a champion, by whom he announces to the astonished public how much even Fichte is beneath him. So rapidly does infallibility here pass away!

Of the diligent and learned MELLIN's "Encyclopädisches Wörterbuch," and "Marginalien," continuations have appeared, which will be very acceptable to every admirer of Kant's writings.

SCHULZ's "Kritik der Theoretischen Philosophie" (2 parts, Bohn, Hamburg) will probably give great offence to the zealous Kantians.

PHILOLOGY.

The second volume of the BUHLE's new edition of "Aratus," which we had been expecting for several years past, has at length made its appearance.

SCHAUBACH, of Meiningen, already advantageously known by his earlier labours on the subject, has published "Eine Geschichte der Griechischen Astronomie bis auf Eratosthenes."—History of Astronomy in Greece, down to the Time of Eratostenes, with plates and maps.

MATTHÆI of Wittenberg has given us a new edition, corrected by collating MSS. and several ancient versions, of "Nemesius de Natura Hominis (Gr. and Lat. Halæ, Gebauer). The works of this ancient Greek Father of the Church, in which, among other curious things, some think they find the discovery of the circulation of the blood, certainly deserved, in preference to many others, to be illustrated by the labours of the critic.

Of HEEREN's "Geschichte des Studiums der Klassischen Literatur"—History of the Study of Classical Literature, since the Revival of Letters—the second part has been published, comprising the flourishing period of Italy under the Medici, and shewing, that, even after Roscoe, it was possible to make many new and interesting discoveries on this subject, among the treasures of the Library of Wolfenbuttle.

Important, too, in a philological point of view, is the new edition of J. H. Voss's "Translation of Homer," in German verse in imitation of the ancient hexameter. Voss, the creator of this metre in the German language, has paid due attention to the objections made by critics against him, particularly with respect to quantity, and in its present improved state his translation is such as no other modern nation can boast of. A corrected map of the world, with explanations, and a plan of the house of Ulysses, are added to this edition.

An excellent contribution towards the philosophy of language in general, and the German in particular, is the seventh and last part of EBERHARD's "Allgemeine Deutsche Synonymik"—General Dictionary of German Synonymes—a work, which for completeness, and for nice discrimination of ideas, surpasses every similar production in any of the modern languages, and which ought to be studied by every one who wishes to make himself complete master of the treasures of the German idiom.

BELLES-LETTRES AND POETRY.

In the department of Belles lettres *one* production had excited the most eager expectation in the German public, which has been gratified in the "Kalendar for 1802," (Berlin, Unger). This pocket-book contains "The Maid of Orleans, a romantic Tragedy," by FR. SCHILLER. The adjective *romantic* is, in some measure, descriptive of this new kind of drama in which the supernatural is allied with the natural. When the heroine pays the debt of her sex, the spirit departs from her. This pure emanation of poetic genius, which will undoubtedly descend to future ages, cannot fail to produce the same powerful effect as it did on the Leipzig stage, wherever there is an actress capable of wearing with dignity the sacred armour of the Maid of Orleans.

The Michaelmas Catalogue likewise announces the publication of the third part of Wieland's Aristippus. Here the enchantress Lais no longer acts the principal part. With young Euphemisinus the poet roves through the delightful valleys of Thessaly. Higher objects here fetter the attention. The question so much agitated in our days, about the best constitution of Government, is well discussed in the analysis given of that most sublime, and yet in many respects absurd, political poem, "The Republic of Plato." Since the time when Platonizing table-companions encircled the great Lorenzo de' Medici, no one has penetrated so deeply into the spirit of Plato as this German Aristippus.

Besides

Besides the above, and some new editions of esteemed works, such as the "Sisters of Lesbos," by AMALIA VON IMMHOFF, and the poem "Siama and Galmory," which has been reprinted with most splendid decorations, at Leipzig, few other separate productions appeared in the department of fine literature. Indeed the finest flowrets that spring up on the German Parnassus are collected in the numerous pocket-books, calendars, and almanacks of the Muses, of which last autumn produced a greater supply than in any preceding year.—The "Taschenbuch für Damen"—Ladies' Pocket-book, published by Cotta in Tubingen, still maintains its pre-eminence over most of its competitors.—The "Taschenbuch für 1802," (published by Vieweg, of Brunswick, in five different sizes) disputes, however, the palm with it, and thereby increases the enjoyment of the tasteful part of the reading public. In this latter pocket-book Herder has inserted a paper in vindication of the chastity of Heloise against Pope's Letter from Eloisa to Abelard.—To the pocket-book published by Willman, in Hamburg, Romberg and Ridley furnished the decorations; nor will the reader look in it in vain for the names of a Göthe, a Schiller, a Halem, and of other celebrated German literati.—V. Halem sings his "Eleusina" in five cantos, in Unger's "Damen-kalendar;" Ladies-almanack.—Falk continues his Critique of the Spirit of the Times in his Satyrical Pocket-book.—The Pocket-book for Social Enjoyment contains poems and entertaining essays, which entitle it to a distinguished rank among its competitors, of which no less than thirteen appear at Leipzig. Indeed the appetite of the Germans for these Liliputian productions seems to be insatiable: every thing is compressed into the nut-shell size of an almanack: there are pocket books and almanacks for horticulturists, for horse jockeys, for freemasons, for travellers, for virtuosi, &c. &c. The bookseller Cotta, in Tubingen, gives us, in addition to his German one, a neat little French "Almanach des Dames, which Fragonard and Roger, of Paris, have decorated with plates, and Laharpe, Parny, Lebrun, Creuze, and others, embellished with fresh poetic flowrets.—Fleischer, of Leipzig, likewise announces a French "Almanach des Muses."

NOVELS, &c.

After the multitude of novels, romances, &c. with which at Easter the German public were gorged even to loathing, we little expected to see 113 such compositions announced in the Michaelmas bill-of-fare. Of these, perhaps, not above twenty are fit to make their appearance in good company. Among the better productions of this kind we may reckon "Henrietta Bellmann," a new family-picture, by LAFONTAINE, whose prolific pen has likewise furnished four almanacks with interesting little tales;—another volume of STILLING's "Scenen aus dem Geisterreiche," and MULLER's "Gustav Salden." An Englishman of the name of Lawrence has likewise favoured the Germans with a "Paradiese der Liebe," Paradise of Love, containing tales in the manner of Boccace.

Under the head of novels we are sorry to find some of the booksellers of Leipzig advertising books replete with the grossest obscenity, some under the veil of a decent title, and some announced with the most bare-faced effrontery. Surely the licensers might as usefully employ their authority in preventing the sale of such poison, tending to corrupt the morals of youth, as in suppressing pretended libels against church and state.

HALF-YEARLY RETROSPECT OF FRENCH LITERATURE.

HISTORY.

"HISTOIRE des Progrès et de la Chûte de l'Empire du Mysore," &ç. History of the Progress and Fall of the Mysore Empire, under the Reigns of Hyder Ally and Tippoo Saib, by J. MICHAUD, 2 vols. 8vo. Paris, 7 Fr.

The author dedicates the first chapter to the antiquities of India; but he omits the mention of Alexander and Porus, of Seleucus Nicanor, and a variety of other princes and generals, whose fate and history are intimately connected with that portion of the globe.

In Chap. II. he makes mention of Hyder Ally, and gives an account of the rise and progress of that celebrated warrior. On this occasion, he does not copy the errors contained in the first volume of "Revolutions d'Inde," which were falsely supposed to be written by Tippoo Saib: but he is greatly mistaken when he asserts, "that Hyder was the son of an officer of cavalry, belonging to the Mogul empire." The truth is, that his father was taken at Colar,

Colar, by a Mogul, who made a Mussulman of him; and, from being called Tille-Apa, he was known afterwards by the name of Chamcherkon.

Entering afterwards into the service of the Rajah of Bâlapour, he at length became a general of his army, and was killed at the siege of Sira. In 1757, when his son became Nabob, the body was disinterred, and carried to Colar, the place of his nativity, where his tomb is still to be seen.

The King of Mysore, being charmed with the military talents of Hyder, placed him at the head of a body of troops, and he was soon after influenced by his own ambition to aspire to the supreme power.

Canarao, the Vizier or Minister, having discovered his intentions; Hyder retired to the fortress of Bangalore, whence he soon after marched to Seringapatam, besieged the Rajah, took him prisoner, seized Canarao, and shut him up in an iron-cage at Bangalore, where he remained during two years. After this, the conqueror affected great moderation, secured the fidelity of his army by means of largesses, and became a considerable, and even a formidable, prince.

The author appears to have copied most of his facts and observations from books published in England.

" Tableau Historique et Statistique," &c. An historical and Statistical Description of the Russian Empire at the End of the Eighteenth Century, by M. HENRY STORCH, 2 vol. 8vo. with Charts and Prints, 15 Fr.

The French have not as yet attained any celebrity for their statistical accounts: but Chaptal, the Minister of the Interior or Home-department, has just formed a new establishment in his office, under the title of " Bureau de Statistique." In the mean time, they translate every thing on this subject published by other nations; and it must be allowed to have been carried to a greater degree of perfection in Germany than elsewhere.

The present work is not complete, the two first volumes only being as yet published; these are divided into three parts:

Part I. is occupied with an account of and enumeration of the inhabitants.

Part II. contains a description of the constitution of the state.

Part III. is dedicated to a detail of the administration.

In the first of these the author treats,

1st. Of the origin of the inhabitants of Russia.

2d. Of the physical or natural state of the country.

3d. Of the industry, commerce, and civil state of the natives.

4th. Of their moral state; or, in other words, their language, religion, education, arts and sciences, manners, and customs.

M. Storch asserts, that the annual increase of the inhabitants of this immense empire, may be fairly estimated at half a million of souls!

" Precis de l'Histoire Universelle," &c. A Summary of Universal History during the ten first Centuries of the Vulgar Æra; or, an Introduction to the Modern History of the different States of Europe, by ED. MENTELLE, Member of the National Institute of Paris, 1 vol. 8vo. with Maps.

An elementary work, to the advantage of being clear, ought to add that of being correct; this is all that can be fairly expected, for labours of this kind seldom experience either reputation or gratitude on the part of the public. It must be allowed, at the same time, that this little work possesses great merit; although, on the other hand, it is objectionable relative to certain principles of religion, which would render a translation utterly unfit for the perusal of our youth.

" Histoire de France depuis la Revolution de 1789," &c. History of France since the Revolution of 1789, written from contemporary Memoirs and Manuscripts collected in the Civil and Military Offices, by Citizen EMMANUEL TOULONGEON, formerly a military Man, Ex-constituent, Member of the National Institute of France, &c. Paris, vol. 1, in 4to. 15 Fr. 2 vol. 8vo. 12 Fr. The motto of

" Et quorum pars——"

sufficiently indicates, that the author has had some share in the transactions which he here relates. He divides his history into five different epochs. The first contains an account of the events that occurred posterior to the convocation of the States General, such as the royal session, the oath taken in the Tennis-court, the capture of the Bastille, &c.

The second commences with the organization of the national guard throughout the whole of France, and contains the details relative to the night of August the 4th, and the memorable 6th of October.

The third contains an account of the translation of the National Assembly to Paris, the disturbances in the southern departments, the federation of July 14, 1790, the revolt of the troops at Nancy, the troubles

troubles that occurred in the colonies, the oath to observe the civil constitution of the clergy, and the death of Mirabeau. This article closes with an account of the Society of Jacobins towards the middle of the year 1790.

In the fourth epoch, the author comprehends the flight of the King, his arrest at Varennes, the revision of the constitution, the proceedings of the first legislative assembly, the laws against emigration, and finally the declaration of war.

In the fifth, he traces the events of the war, from the sanction of the declaration of hostilities, until the retreat of the Prussian and Austrian armies. He also details the skirmish near Mons; the dismission of the King's guard; the establishment of a camp of 20,000 men near Paris; the proceedings of the 20th of June, and the 10th of August; the decree of accusation against La Fayette, and his departure; the nomination of Dumourier to the command of the armies; the massacres of the 2d and 3d of September; the invasion of the Germans; the battle, or rather the skirmish, of Valmi, &c. finally, the retreat of the combined forces.

This work is accompanied by several state papers, which the French usually term —*Pièces justificatives*,

"Tableau Historique, Topographique, et Moral," &c. Historical, Topographical, and Moral History of all the Nations inhabiting the four Quarters of the Globe, containing their Laws, Customs, and Usages, by A. M. Sané, sen. Paris, 2 vol. 8vo. 9 Fr.

A work of this kind of course requires immense labour, great discernment, and no small portion of philosophy; few are, however, more necessary, and none that ought to contain more matter within an equal space.

To do justice to the author, if he has not executed his work in such a manner as to evince great talents, he has, at least, exhibited no common share of industry, having laid the greater part of the historians, and all the modern travellers, under contribution. The annals of nations, their religious systems, their laws, their manners, their usages, the productions of nature, and those executed by human industry, are all classed with method and precision, in this useful compilation.

Citizen Sané has divided his work into four parts. From the Icelanders, he passes on to the Greeks of the Archipelago; from the Tartars, to the Arabians; from the Egyptians, to the Algerines; from the American Indians, to the natives of the Pelew Isles, and the other islanders of the South Seas. It must be owned, however, that the compiler has exhibited but little of the spirit of criticism; and it were to have been wished, that, like the author of "Anacharsis," he had pointed out, at the bottom of the page, the numerous sources whence he has extracted his materials.

"Histoire de Piémont, et des autres Etats du Roi de Sardaigne," &c. The History of Piedmont, and the other States of the King of Sardinia, by the Abbé Charles Denina, Counsellor of Legation to the King of Prussia, Member of the Academies of Sciences of Berlin, Rome, Naples, Florence, Padua, &c. translated from the Italian by Frederic Strass, 1 vol. 8vo.

The Abbé Denina, whose name is well known in the annals of modern literature, has only published an account of the first period of the history of Piedmont, the translation therefore comes down no lower than the dominion of the Lombards or Longobards. While employed in drawing up these memoirs, the house of Savoy received a violent shock, from which it is not likely soon to recover; the continuation, however, will be interesting, not only on account of the talents of the author, but the fate of Piedmont itself, and the alterations that have occurred in Italy, all of which he intends hereafter to detail.

NATURAL HISTORY AND BOTANY.

"Calendrier de Flore des Environs de Niort," &c. A Calendar of the Flora in the neighbourhood of Niort; or, the Time of Flowering, &c. of near eleven hundred Plants, described and classed methodically, Month by Month, according to the sexual System of the celebrated Linnæus; to which is prefixed, an Elementary Abridgment of Botany, by Dr. J. L. M. Guillemeau, jun. Author of the Natural History of the Rose, &c. 1 vol. 12mo. Paris.

This work is divided into two parts: in the first, we are presented with a general view of the universe; the elementary principles of botany; a dissertation on the mode of using the Calendar of the Flora of Niort, the climate of which is here described; the rules prescribed by Linnæus for making an herbal, and also a *floral clock* for Niort.

The second part contains the Calendar of Flora itself, divided into twelve months, each month presenting the series of plants then in flower. The French writers appear zealous to study and to quote famous poets, and Dr. Guillemeau, in conformity

with

to the usual custom, makes use of the following appropriate lines from Thomson, by way of motto:

"———The fall of kings,
The rage of nations, and the crush of states,
Move not the man, who, from the world escap'd,
In still retreats and flow'ry solitudes
To nature's voice attends, from month to month,
And day to day, thro' the revolving year."

"Essai sur l'Histoire Naturelle," &c. An Essay on the Natural History of the Quadrupeds of the Province of Paraguay, by Don Felix d'Azzara, Commodore in the Spanish Navy, &c. translated from the unprinted Manuscript of the Author, by M. L. E. MOREAU S. MERY, Counsellor of State, 2 vol. 8vo. Paris.

To such as study natural history, and are anxious to become acquainted with the productions of Spanish America, this work cannot fail to produce equal delight and instruction. Our limits will not permit us to enter into detail, but we cannot omit some mention of one of the noble quadrupeds to be found at the end of vol. 1. The city of Buenos Ayres, founded in 1535, having been abandoned with great precipitation; it was found impracticable to carry away all the Andalusian horses in the neighbourhood. On the return of the Spaniards, in 1580, they found they had multiplied to an astonishing degree, and their progeny is now almost innumerable, the race being extended as far as Patagonia. They are also to be seen to the north of the river of La Plata.

These horses move about in numerous herds, consisting frequently of ten thousand individuals. On perceiving their domestic brethren, they immediately run towards them, and engage them, by their caresses, to leave the protection of man, and become as wild and as free as themselves.

We are told that the Indians find means to render these horses tame, and eat their flesh: the Spaniards decline this; but, we are assured, that in those parts where wood is scarce, "they kill them in order to use their bones for the purpose of fire!"

"Flore Parisienne," &c. The Parisian Flora; or, a Description of the Characters of all the Plants which grow naturally in the Neighbourhood of Paris, distributed after the Manner adopted in the Garden of Plants of that City, with the Indication of their French, Latin, and vulgar Names, &c. &c. by L. B. F——, 1 vol. 8vo.

This work is somewhat on the plan of Curtis's Flora, which contains a list of the plants, &c. growing in the neighbourhood of London, although on a far different scale. It ought to be remarked, however, that the author hath not completely fulfilled his intentions, for this publication does not contain a complete list of the Parisian plants, many of which are omitted, while a number of those indigenous to different places are inserted. He has also introduced a barbarous vocabulary, and it is only by a second edition that errors of this kind can be corrected.

"Phenomènes d'Histoire Naturelle," &c. Phenomena of Natural History, containing an Account of the Gestation of Constantine, one of the Lionesses belonging to the Menagerie of the Garden of Plants; a Description of all the Quadrupeds under the Care of Citizen Felix Cassal, &c. intended for the Use of Strangers, and such as frequent the Museum of Natural History, by J. B. VIGNIER, a Man of Letters; a new Edition, corrected and augmented.

The author of this pamphlet is also the person to whom we are indebted for the work, entitled "l'Histoire d'Eléphans;" History of the Elephant, of which three editions have been published in succession. The style of the present publication is negligent, but the details which it contains cannot fail to prove interesting to the naturalist. Buffon, trusting to report, believed that the time occupied by the gestation of the lioness consisted of six months; but it appears, from the observations of E. J. B. Vignier, that it amounts only to one hundred and ten days.

"We perceive by the facts before us (says the author) that this celebrated naturalist is erroneous, when he asserts, after Gesner, that the Lioness brings forth in the spring, and produces only once in a year; the proof of the contrary is now evident: Constantine is at this present moment big for the third time; and it is only six months since, she was so before."

"Traité de la Physique Végétale des Bois," &c. A Treatise on the Natural History of Trees, and the principal Operations of the Forest, &c. to which is added the Proportions of Timber for the Marine, after the Manner of Decimals, by Citizen GOUBE, Conservator of the third Arrondissement, Paris, 1 vol. 8vo.

This work is divided into thirty-six chapters, in which the author treats:—

1. Of the anatomy; and
2. Of the maladies of trees.

3. Of the soil and climate most congenial to them.

4. Of the influence of these on the success of plantations.

5. Of the precautions required for the establishment of forests.

6. Of the restoration and melioration of the same.

7. Of the different species of forest-trees, such as the oak, the elm, &c.

8. Of the utility of barking trees previously to their being used.

9. Of the preception of causes that have contributed to the destruction of the forests. And,

10. On the means of remedying this evil.

The plan and style of this work are far superior to the knowledge displayed in it.

"Flore de Jeunes Personnes," &c. The Flora of Youth; or, Elementary Letters on Botany, 1 vol. 12mo.

The form of letters, in which this little work is drawn up, is calculated, perhaps, to give facility to the knowledge of botany by the youth of both sexes. The twelve engravings, which accompany it, represent the plants and the flowers, &c. so as to serve for models to the student. We have some reason to suppose, that this is not an original work, but merely a translation from our own language.

POLITICS.

"Politique de tous les Cabinets de l'Europe," &c. The Politics of all the Cabinets of Europe during the Reigns of Louis XV. and Louis XVI. containing authentic Memoirs relative to the Secret Correspondence of the Count de Broglio; a Work written for the express Purpose of exhibiting the Situation of the European Powers; drawn up under the Direction of the Count, and executed by M. FAVIER. Doubts relative to the Treaty of 1756, by the same. Several Memoirs, by the Count de Vergennes, M. Turgot, &c. published from Manuscripts found in the Cabinet of Louis XVI. second Edition, considerably augmented, with Notes and Commentaries, and also a Memoir on the Family Compact, by L. P. SEGUR the Elder, Ex-ambassador, 3 vol. 8vo. Paris.

It is well known that Louis XV. employed the Count de Broglio to carry on a secret correspondence wholly unknown, or meant at least to be so, to his ministers, and that Favier, a person of considerable talents, was employed to arrange the materials. Segur, now a man of letters, but invested with a high diplomatic situation during the existence of the monarchy, has here published the memoirs drawn up upon this occasion, and added a commentary of his own, which was indeed become necessary, in consequence of the important changes that Europe has so recently experienced. The Ex-ambassador contemplates nations, in respect to each other, as so many individuals scarcely emerged from a state of nature, possessing territorial property indeed, but governed by usage rather than by laws. He very properly considers petty states as those most interested in the maintenance of peace; their political activity, according to him, consists in nothing more than the conservation of their fragile existence; instead of disturbing the general order, they tremble at the least movement, and are attached to the powers most desirous to maintain it.

France being in possession of those limits seemingly assigned to her by nature; M. Segur thinks she neither possesses, nor ought to possess, any other ambition than that of obtaining tranquillity for herself and her allies. This pacific character, which it is the interest of her government now to adopt, must augment her consideration, and extend her influence to all the the states of the second order, such as Sweden, Switzerland, and Portugal, whose business it is, amidst the rivalship of great empires, to look to their preservation, rather than their increase. This being allowed, he proceeds to assert, that France is to look to five powers only for her friends and her enemies. Adopting the specious theory of the Count d'Aranda, according to which, the topographical position of states points out the system of alliances: France, according to him, ought to live on the most friendly terms with Spain and Russia, as this combination alone can oppose its united strength to the league of the only two Germanic sovereigns who could support the efforts of the cabinet of St. James's.

The editor has the insolence to assert, that, in consequence of the insulated situation of this country, Great Britain ought only to be considered as a secondary power; "one, that can never augment her influence, but by producing bloody wars on the Continent, and dividing the force of France, in order to prevent her from serving as a counterpoise to her own power, &c. a barrier to her ambition." He allows however that the English, in consequence of their wisdom, "have become models to the whole world, and that they would connect all the people of the earth by means of their commerce, were they but to introduce that justice in their

political

political relations, which characterizes their national institutions:"—"However (adds M. Segur), they are blinded by ambition and jealousy, and if in their own country they will not suffer a master, so on the ocean they will not admit even of rivals."

He concludes by asserting, that if the French Government follows up the pacific system adopted by it, with temper, boldness and constancy, "the English will either be constrained to restore peace to Europe, and liberty to the seas, or audaciously to declare themselves the adversaries of universal morality, and the enemies of all mankind—a rash undertaking, equally fatal to their reputation and security."

It may be necessary to remark here, that the author of this work, who had before attained considerable reputation by his "History of Frederick William of Prussia, &c." committed it to the press a considerable time before the signature of the preliminaries of peace between Great Britain and France.

VOYAGES AND TRAVELS.

"Voyage dans la Haute Pennsylvanie, &c." Travels through the Upper Part of Pennsylvania, and the State of New York, by an adopted Member of the Oneïda Nation, translated and published by the Author of the Letters of an American Farmer, 3 vols. 8vo. Paris.

This adopted member of the Oneïda nation is no other than the Count de Crevecœur, the father of Mrs. Otto, whose husband is at present Minister Plenipotentiary from France at the Court of St. James's. M. de Crevecœur lived for many years in the Back Settlements of America, in the situation of a farmer or planter; he has lately returned to Europe, and this work may be considered as the fruit of his experience. It is objectionable however in point of arrangement; and the mode he adopts of publishing the letters saved out of the wreck of a vessel that happened to be stranded, deprives the volumes now under consideration, of much of the interest they would otherwise possess.

We are however presented with a variety of anecdotes, &c. The author seems greatly attached to the Americans; more especially those who are removed at a distance from the maritime towns, where the demon of avarice seems to have taken complete possession of the minds of the people.

"Voyage en Grèce et en Turquie, fait par Ordre de Louis XVI &c." Travels through Greece and Turkey, undertaken by Order of Louis XVI. and with the Permission of the Ottoman Court, by C. S. SONINI, a Member of several literary and learned Societies in Europe, 2 vols. 8vo. with fine Plates and Maps, the latter coloured; price at Paris 21 fr. 50 cents. Twenty-five copies only are printed on vellum paper, at 36 fr.

The ancient philosophers of Greece, inflamed by their zeal for the melioration of government and the sciences, travelled among distant nations for the purpose of learning their manners, customs and laws. Pythagoras and Plato accordingly returned with an ample store of knowledge, highly useful to their countrymen; and we find even the Scythian Anacharsis visiting Greece, whither he was attracted by similar inducements. Notwithstanding the above exception, the inhabitants of polished states alone are desirous of travelling for information: barbarous tribes never dream of disturbing their monotonous repose by visiting any other climates than those in which they are fixed, as it were, by the hand of destiny.

Sonini, after having traversed Egypt, of which he has presented an interesting account to the public, was extremely desirous of visiting Greece; and on applying to the French Ministry, he obtained the permission of Louis XVI. for that purpose. His predecessors had been chiefly occupied in describing those ancient and precious remnants of the fine arts, which the ferocious Mussulmen had spared; but our present traveller was more intent on examining the moral and political state of the modern inhabitants. He compares the Ottoman Government to an immense and shapeless colossus, placed on a basis of clay, and ready to tumble down; while Greece, which is now crushed under the enormous weight, is preparing to take advantage of this event, and if not to resume her ancient position, at least to burst asunder her chains. "Whatever (says he), may be the novel and inevitable destiny of a people hitherto so celebrated, it is desirable to become acquainted with every thing concerning them, at the moment of their enfranchisement and regeneration, and to conceive a notion of those places which will be hereafter, as formerly, the theatre of memorable exploits."

Our learned traveller is anxious to describe the climate, soil, and productions of every region he has visited; and he is particularly attentive to the isles of the Egean Sea, among which he spent nearly two years. We are told that the leprosy is is very common in Candia, and learn, in opposition to the assertion of Savary, (Lettres sur la Grèce, Lett. XXIII.) that it attacks the rich as well as the poor. The dances of the Candiots exhibit great elegance and simplicity, and are as ancient as the days of Homer; they are accompanied by songs, of a slow and melancholy kind; their women are the least handsome of any of the neighbouring isles. The Spachlotes are the only Greeks who still preserve the warlike dance, called the *Pyrrhic*; their manners are accordingly savage, and they themselves are much inclined to violence.

"Voyage en Espagne, &c." Travels through Spain, during the Years 1797 and 1798, intended to serve as a Supplement to the Travels through Spain, by Citizen Bourgoing; written by CHRISTIAN AUGUSTUS FISCHER, and translated by CHARLES CRAMER, with an Appendix relative to the Manner of Travelling in Spain. Paris, 2 vols. 8vo. pr. 6 fr.

As this work has been translated by Professor C. F. Cramer, one of the most distinguished men of letters at present in Germany, that circumstance alone is sufficient to ensure it a favourable reception in the country where it is now published. The German traveller treats of the works of art, the manners, and the natural genius of the people; in short nothing is forgotten; but as the work is not extensive, it may be read with great utility after that of Bourgoing has been perused.

"Voyageur Curieux et Sentimental, &c." The Curious and Sentimental Traveller, by LOUIS D—. 2d edition.

This is written in imitation of Sterne, a mode in which it is difficult to succeed. It must be allowed, notwithstanding, that Chantilly and Ermenonville excite noble sensations, the Conqueror of Rocroy having lived at the one, and the author of Emilius at the other.

"Premier Voyage autour du Monde, &c." The First Voyage round the World, by the Chevalier Pigafetta, who served in the Squadron under Magellan, during the Years 1519, 1520, 1521 and 1522; to which is added, a Treatise on Navigation by the same Author, and a Biographical Memoir concerning Martin Behaim, with a Description of his Terrestrial Globe; ornamented with Charts and Plates, 1 vol. 8vo. Paris.

Anthony Pigafetta, of Vicenza, having embarked on board Magellan's ship, drew up a relation of the voyage, which he addressed to Philip Villers of Isle-Adam, Grand Master of Rhodes. On his return from this expedition, Pigafetta presented to Charles V. "not gold or silver (says he), but matters far more precious to his eyes. Among other objects of curiosity, I gave his Majesty a book written with my own hand, in which I kept a journal, day by day, of the various occurrences that took place during the expedition."

Of the work thus announced, which must have been highly valuable at that period, Ranusio published only an extract, and M. Amoretti, the editor, has been at great pains to discover the original, but in this he failed; he has however found in the Ambrosian Library at Milan a translation by the Chevalier de Forrêt, one of the brave defenders of the Isle of Rhodes.

Although the principal occurrences in Magellan's voyage are not unknown to the public, yet none of the particulars relative to the death of that great navigator can be considered as uninteresting. After mentioning that he was killed on the 27th of April, 1521, in an engagement with the inhabitants of the island of Zebu, Pigafetta expresses himself as follows:

"It was thus that our guide, our support, and our commander perished. When he fell, perceiving himself surrounded by the enemy, he turned several times towards us, with a view to discover if we should be able to save ourselves; and as none of us happened to be wounded, and we were equally unable either to succour or avenge our chief, we had the good fortune to retreat to our boats, which were about to depart. It is to our Captain then alone, we are indebted for our safety, because at the moment he was killed, all the islanders surrounded the spot where he fell. But the glory of Magellan (adds he) will survive his death, for he was adorned with all the virtues, and exhibited the most unshaken firmness, amidst the greatest adversity. While at sea, he made it a rule to experience the same privations as his crew. Better acquainted than any man of his age with nautical charts, he was likewise a proficient in the art of navigation, as is demonstrated by his having succeeded in sailing around the world, a project which no one before his time had dared to undertake."

The editor, who is keeper of the Ambrosian Library, here remarks, that Magellan had actually circumnavigated no mor than one half the globe, but, that Piga fetta with good reason pays him the abov com compliment, as the Portuguese were then well acquainted with the route from the Moluccas to Europe, by the Cape of Good Hope.

The biographical notice relative to the Chevalier Martin Behaim, a celebrated Portuguese navigator, with the description of his globe by M. de Murr, is also a very important document for the history of navigation; it is translated from the German, by Citizen Jansen, and serves by way of appendix to Pigafetta's relation. M. de Murr, in this learned dissertation, corrects many errors of Dr. Robertson relative to Martin Behaim; he proves that the latter possessed great merit, and assisted considerably in respect to the invention of the astrolabe; but he maintains at the same time, that Behaim had not conceived the idea of the discovery of a new world, when Columbus repaired to Lisbon, in order to propose his celebrated project. It may not be amiss again to repeat, that the description of Martin Behaim's terrestial globe is both curious and interesting.

"Voyage Pittoresque et Phisico-Economique dans le Jura, &c." A Picturesque and Physico-Economical Journey through the Department of Mount Jura, by J. M. LEQUINIO, Agent Forrester, 2 vols. 8vo. Paris.

These two volumes contain an interesting account of the department of Mount Jura, by a person well acquainted with its numerous hills, its scanty plains, and its various productions. Most of the inhabitants form themselves into little societies, &c. according to their proximity, for the purpose of making butter, cheese, &c. each member receiving his proportion, in the express ratio of his contributions. As the country abounds with ponds, we are told that the inhabitants are at great pains with them, and exhibit much ingenuity respecting "the breeding of carp and other fishes."

MISCELLANEOUS ARTICLES.

"De la Peinture, considérée dans ses Effets sur les Hommes en général, &c." On Painting, considered in the Relation of its Effects on Men in general, and its Influence on the Manners and the Government of Nations, by G. M. Raymond, Professor of History in the Central School of the Department of Mount Blanc, 1 vol. 8vo. Paris.

This subject is treated by Raymond under a variety of different aspects, both moral and political. In the first of these are necessarily included the deductions which every observer must make, in the immediate contemplation of the portraits of good men, and the representaion of good actions. The arts of imitation may also be used with great advantage for national purposes, such as the honouring of heroes and patriots, &c. The Professor remarks, that those productions are not the best which act most powerfully upon the multitude, and he is particularly anxious that mediocrity should never be rewarded, as in that case, the world would be "inundated" with the performances of inferior artists; on the contrary, excellence ought to be cherished, and to receive the most distinguished countenance and support.

Citizen Raymond asserts with much propriety, that every great effect of art should possess an imposing appearance; but he blames those who employ philosophical allegories, "as they do not inform the people of any thing."

"Des Causes Physiques et Morales qui ont influé, &c." On the Physical and Moral Causes which have influenced the Progress of Painting and Sculpture among the Greeks. A Discourse read before the Philotechnical Society, &c. by Citizen LE BARBIER, sen. Member of the former Academy of Painting, &c.

We learn from the preface, that this memoir is written by a man who is actuated by the desire of contributing to the progress of the fine arts, "which have already constituted, and shall until his last sigh, continue to constitute the supreme happiness of his life." While treating of the origin and progress of painting, sculpture, &c. Le Barbier divides his inquiry into two parts: in the first of which he treats of the physical, and in the second of the moral causes that have contributed to their perfection. He accordingly resolves the former of these into the influence of climate on the genius of nations; the fine forms and beauty of individuals; the nature of the aliments, which act so powerful on the temperament and conformation, &c. "The fine arts (says he) resemble plants, and demand a congenial climate—they will never be found to fructify either on the icy banks of the Neva, or the burning sands of Lybia." He remarks that, both Peter the Great, and Catharine II. made useless efforts to naturalize the arts of imitation in Russia; and he asks how it is possible to suppose that a nation hovering during three parts of the year over their stoves, and perceiving nothing but snow and icicles from their habitations, can conceive the least idea of smiling nature? Can they paint or describe the charms of the vernal season? "The festival of Flora (adds he) will never be

celebrated

celebrated on the borders of the Wolga, or the plains of Siberia, for the Goddess cannot there find a single rose, wherewith to adorn her garland!"

He advises those who wish to study and admire fine forms, to scale the Alps and penetrate into Italy, where, as they approach towards the south, they will behold the human profile assume a more marked and characteristic aspect, the nose and forehead approximate towards a right line, and the whole physiognomy exhibit a more noble, open, commanding, and characteristic appearance." But it is in Greece and the islands of the Archipelago that perfection is to be found: "It is in Greece alone, where man is created after the image of the gods, and where the statuaries and the painters will be able to form gods, resembling man."

This work of Cit. Le Barbier may be considered as a gallery of interesting pictures, in which we discover the purity of design, the delicate touch, and the exquisite colouring, that distinguish the hand of a great master.

"Tableau du Commerce de la Grèce, &c." A Description of the Commerce of Greece, estimated according to an average, from the Year 1787 to the Year 1797, by FELIX BEAUJOUR, Ex-consul in Greece, 2 vols. 8vo.

This interesting work is the result of the enquiries of the author among the best-informed merchants of Salonica, and it also contains such observations as his own respectable situation necessarily enabled him to make. In consequence of these sources of information, he has been enabled to collect every thing of essential importance relative to the commerce of modern Greece, and to estimate the advantages which the agriculture, the commerce, and the manufactures of France are likely to reap, in consequence of a connection with this part of the Archipelago. These various facts were annually arranged and inserted under their specific heads, after which it was the custom of the French Consul to transmit them home for the inspection of administration.

The first volume contains fifteen letters on the commodities fit for exportation from Greece, while the second gives an account of the amount of the importations from the several commercial nations of Europe.

England for a long time possessed nearly a monopoly of this trade: but France at length, by means of the port of Marseilles, not only entered into a competition, but in this particular instance obtained a superiority over her rival. Beaujour, who in consequence of his official situation may be supposed capable of deciding on a subject of this kind, asserts, that the profit reaped by France on the general balance of trade, formerly amounted to from thirty to thirty-six millions of livres.

The war with Great Britain and the Turks has nearly annihilated this, as well as every other branch of foreign commerce, but on the conclusion of peace, it is predicted by the Ex-consul, that the trade of the Republic will in a few years be equal to that of any other nation whatever.

"Discours sur la Vertu, &c." A Discourse on Virtue, recited before the Academy of Sciences and Belles Lettres, at Berlin, on January 25th 1797, by STANISLAUS BOUFFLERS, 2d edition, corrected and augmented.

This is a very fertile subject for declamation, and one which has engaged the attention of a multitude of writers, both ancient and modern. According to Cit. Boufflers, "all our virtues originate in compassion, and it is to the development of this faculty, partly physical, partly moral, that I assert," says he, "the whole system of virtue." Soon after this, he defines virtue, to be "a sincere disposition to do to others all the good in our power;" and this disposition, he maintains "to lie concealed at the bottom of the human heart, like gold in the entrails of the earth, until the labour of man has conferred beauty and value upon it."

"Physiologie Vegetale, contenant une Description des Organes, &c." Vegetable Physiology, containing a Description of the Organs of Plants, and an Exposition of the Phenomena produced by their Organization, by JOHN SENNEBIER, Associate-member of the Natural Institute, and also of several Academies and learned Societies, &c. 5 vols. 8vo. 2133 pages. Geneva. A new edition.

The learned and celebrated author of these volumes, has not only taken advantage of the discoveries of Spallanzani and Ingenhouz, but added new and important remarks on the nature and properties of vegetables, a subject which has long engaged his attention and excited his labours. While perusing this interesting work, we are charmed with the observations relative to the physiology of the vegetable word, and the curious and important investigations, not only of the two former men of science, but also of Coulomb,

lomb, Corti, Hedwig, and all those among the moderns who have directed their attention to the theory of vegetation, and the fructification of plants. Some indeed, have gone so far, as to wish in some measure to realize the suppositious dogmas of the ancient mythology; and Charles Bonnet in particular seems to have persuaded himself, that trees were not strangers to the sensations of joy and pain, and that in short they could actually feel pleasure, and suffer pain!

"Manuel Général pour les Arbitrages de Change, &c." A General Manual for the Regulation of Exchange, and a Variety of other Calculations necessary for Merchants, by Means of Logarithms, &c.

Until M. Gerhardt, of Berlin, brought logarithms into use, they were never, or, if at all, very rarely indeed, applied to the purposes of commerce; the present publication however is likely to render this mode still more popular, and thus facilitate the operations of the merchant and the trader.

This useful Manual contains, 1st, A table of logarithms of six cyphers.

2d, A collection of averages of exchange.

3d, A collection of the course of exchange for several years.

4th, The mode of employing logarithms.

And 5th, An alphabetical register for the purpose of easy reference.

"Mon Siécle; ou, les Trois Satires, &c." My Own Age; or, the Three Satires, accompanied by Notes, historical, critical and literary, by Louis Damin, a Member of several Literary Societies, 1 vol. 8vo.

To attack whatever is either ridiculous or vicious is the true object of satire, and France even at this period (Paris in particular) presents a variety of fair objects, at which the poet may take aim. The first of these satires is intitled "Les Portraits, &c." and is designed to expose those upstarts, who have risen suddenly without the influence of merit:

"Qui s'offrent à nos yeux, justement courroucés,
"Trainés par les chevaux que leur main a pansés."

Damin is anxious to attack another class of men, the *new generals*, who have obtained that rank, without possessing any claim on the score of reputation!

"De l'orguilleux Narbas, général inconnu,
"De bassesse en bassesse à ce rang parvenu."

On the other hand, he is particularly desirous to celebrate the heroes who have contributed to the glory of their country:

"Si de quelque génie Apollon t' a doté,
"Si d'un souffle divin tu te sens agité,
"Fils des Muses, bannis tout intérêt sordide,
"Qu' une plus noble ardeur et t'enflame, & te guide!
"De nos guerriers *vainqueurs* célèbre les exploits,
"Au son de leurs clairons, cours accorde ta voix."

The second satire is intitled "l'Intrigue & les Mœurs," and in this he contrasts the character and situation of the plunderer, with that of the republican soldier, the defender of his country.

The third is consecrated to the crimes that have occurred during the revolution, and the author concludes by a promise of still nobler efforts:

"J'irai!—de nos héros je chanterai la gloire;
"J'attacherai mon nom au char de la Victoire;
"Et mes vers, compagnons de leurs exploits heureux,
"Au temple de Memoire entreront avec eux."

"Traité des Moyens de disinfecter l'Air, &c." A Treatise on the Means of disinfecting the Air, so as to prevent and stop the Progress of Contagion, by L. B. Guyton Morveau, Member of the National Institute of France, and of several learned Societies, both Foreign and Domestic, &c. Paris.

To this work, which abounds with useful information, on a subject interesting to all nations, the author has prefixed the following appropriate motto from Virgil:

"Dira per incautum serpunt contagia vulgus."

For a long time past, the reputation of Citizen Guyton has been associated with that of Fourcroy, Lavoisier, Berthollet and Schiel. He was one of the first to adopt the pneumatic doctrine, which he has alike defended with his pen and aided by his experiments.

"Fêtes et Courtisanes de la Grèce, &c." Festivals and Courtisans of Greece; being a Supplement to the Travels of Anacharsis and Antenor, and containing,

1. The religious chronicle of the ancient Greeks, with a description of their public manners.

2. An account which some affect to term the *scandalous chronicle*, or a picture of their private manners; enriched with an Athenian

Athenian almanack; a description of the Greek dances, Anacreontic songs, &c. 4 vols. 8vo. Paris, 20 fr. common, and 40, vellum paper.

The learned author of this very elegant work has entered into a long and elaborate inquiry relative to the festivals of the ancient nations, particularly those of the Athenians, both religious and political. He illustrates his work by a variety of quotations both from the poets and historians of antiquity, and he insists that the institutions which he describes, are admirably calculated to excite and develope the sensibility of mankind.

It ought not however to be omitted, that there are certain parts of this publication, which Barthelemy would not have countenanced, although it be published as a Supplement to his "Anacharsis."

"Correspondence Littéraire, adressée à son Altesse Imperiale, &c." Literary Correspondence, addressed to his Imperial Highness the Grand-duke, at present Emperor of Russia, and to Count Andrew Schouwalow, Chamberlain to the Empress Catherine II. from 1774 to 1789, by JEAN FRANCOIS LAHARPE, 4 vols. 8vo. Paris, price 15 fr.

The author of the present work has long since distinguished himself by his literary labours, particularly his Course of Lectures at the Lyceum. On the present occasion, however, he has departed from the rule laid down by himself, which was to avoid giving offence to, or even mentioning living authors, when it could be avoided. Many of his contemporaries appear to consider this as a kind of *scandalous chronicle*, and upwards of twenty men of letters have had their feelings wounded by the publication. It has also been remarked, that Laharpe, while so ready to criticize the works of others, seems entirely to have forgotten all his own defects, which has occasioned some to exclaim with Lucretius:

> "O miseras hominum mentes! ô pectora cæca!"

Or with La Fontaine, they are eager to remark that

> ——— Le fabricateur souverain
> "Nous créa besaciers tous de même maniere,
> "Tant ceux du temps passé que du temps d'aujourd'ui:
> "Il fit pour nos défauts la poche derrière,
> "Et celle de devant pour les defauts d'autrui."

In fine this publication is considered as a kind of magic lanthern, in which the author exhibits both the dead and the living, in the most unnatural and distorted attitudes.

"Tableaux et Ordinaire de la Sainte Messe, &c." The Prints and Ordinary of the Holy Mass, preceded by Morning and Evening Prayers, and followed by the Seven Penitentiary Psalms, Verses, &c. Prayers of St. Bridget, 6 vols. 24mo.

This little book, which we merely notice to shew that the freedom of opinion is not entirely proscribed in France, is adorned with wooden cuts, and sold for 75 cents.

"De l'Excellence et de la Supériorité de la Femme, &c." Of the Excellence and Superiority of Women, translated from the Latin, 1 vol. 12mo.

Henry Cornelius Agrippa, the author, was born in 1486, and died at Lyons according to some in 1524, and according to others at Grenoble in 1535, in the hospital. The work in question was composed by him, with a view of flattering Margaret of Austria.

He asserts, that there is no difference between the soul of the female and that of the male; nay, he attempts to prove, that Eve was superior to Adam. He then enters into a disquisition on the beauty, modesty, cleanliness, &c. of the female sex, to which he attributes the principal share in generation. Nay, he asserts, that when woman was tempted, she was less culpable in the disobedience to the orders of the most High, that ensued, than man.—After this, he quotes Aristotle to prove, that all the good comes from the female, and all the evil from the male: without bad husbands there would never be bad wives, &c.; and he concludes with asserting, that woman was not intended to practise obedience.

"Les Nouvels Poids et Mesures, comparés aux Mesures et aux Poids Anciens, &c." The New, compared with the Old Weights and Measures; or, a Simple and Easy Method of reducing the Old to the New, and the New to the Old, &c. &c.

The title sufficiently announces the contents of this publication, which is chiefly intended as a *Vade Mecum* for the French merchants, traders, &c.

"Journal de Siége et Blocus de Malte, &c." A Journal of the Siege and Blockade of Malta, from the 16th Fructidor of the Year 6, the Epoch of the Revolt of the Maltese, until the 22d Fructidor of the

the Year 8, the Day of the Evacuation of the Fortresses by the French Garrison, by Citizen BOSREDON RANSIJAT, formerly a Commander, and President of the French Government at Malta, 1 vol. 8vo. Paris.

This military journal contains an account of all the material incidents relative to the siege, &c. of Malta. The author, who had refused to carry arms against his country, at the same time defends himself from the accusations of the Ex-Grand-Master Ferdinand Hompesch, and details the abuses that existed in the Order, &c.

"Mémoires Historiques de Marie Therese Louise de Carnigan, &c." Historical Memoirs of Maria Theresa Louisa de Carnigan, Princess of Lamballe, one of the principal Victims immolated during the 2d and 3d of September, 1792; published by Madame GUENARD, 4 vol. 12mo. price 6 fr. Paris.

Madame Guenard, the author of these Memoirs, has already acquired considerable reputation by her "Irma," an historical fiction calculated to please a numerous class of readers. On the present occasion, she has been at great pains to collect materials; and it must be allowed, that both the life and death of the Princess de Lamballe affords an admirable opportunity of drawing up the Memoirs of the latter end of the 18th century.

The French are perhaps the only nation that possesses good private memoirs; on the other hand, they have been wonderfully deficient in respect to historians.

"Notice Historique sur la Vie et les Ouvrages de J. B. Porta, &c." An Historical Notice relative to the Life and Works of J. B. Porta, a Neapolitan Gentlemen, by D***, 1 vol. 8vo.

It is well known that Porta held assemblies in his house, consisting of learned men and men of letters, who, in compliance with the prevailing fashion of a former age, were seriously employed about the mysteries, or rather chimeras, of magic. The Court of Rome soon prohibited their meetings, but the members acquired additional celebrity in consequence of the interdiction; Porta however, who was endowed with considerable talents by nature, consecrated the remainder of his life to the Muses, and composed many tragedies and comedies, which had considerable success. Here follows a catalogue of his works:

1. De Miraculis Rerum Naturalium, libri 4.
2. De Furtivis Literarum Notis, lib. 5.
3. Magia Naturalis, lib. 20.
4. Phytognomonica, lib. 7.
5. Pomarium.
6. De Humana Physiognomoniâ, lib. 6.
7. Villa, lib. 12.
8. De Refractione Optices, lib. 9.
9. Pneumatica, lib. 3.
10. Elementa Curvilinea.
11. De Cœlesti Physiognomonia, lib. 6.
12. Ars Reminiscendi.
13. De Distillatione, lib. 9.
14. De Munitione, lib. 3.
15. De Æris Transmutationibus, lib. 4.
16. Della Fisionomia dell' Uomo.
17. Della Chirofisionomia, lib. 2.

Theatrical Pieces in five acts, written in Italian prose.

1. Olimpia.
2. La Fantasca.
3. La Trapolaria.
4. La Sorella.
5. La Chiappinaria.

And 6. La Cintia.

"Origines Gauloises, &c." Gallick Origins, being those of the most Ancient People of Europe, drawn from their true Source, or discovered in the Language, Origin, and Antiquities of the Celtic Britons of Armorica, by Way of Supplement to the Ancient and Modern History of that People, and also of the French, by LA TOUR D'AUVERGNE-CORRET, First-grenadier of the French Republic; 3d edition, to which is prefixed, an Historical Notice relative to the Author. Hamburg and Paris, 1 vol. 8vo. price 4 fr. 50 cent.

La Tour d'Auvergne, after distinguishing himself as a brave and gallant soldier, endeavoured to acquire a still more permanent celebrity as an author. He accordingly chose the following motto:

> "Unius ætatis sunt res quæ fortiter fiunt; quæ verò pro patriâ scribuntur æternæ sunt."
>
> VEGET.

In consequence of being born in that part of France, the idiom of which he afterwards recurred to in the work now before us, the First-grenadier of the Republic has been enabled to make some figure as an etymologist. He died soon after the publication, and has been bewailed by all the Republican Muses.

"Traité des Telegraphes, &c." A Treatise on Telegraphs, and an Essay on a New Establishment of this Kind, by M. EDELCRANTZ, Counsellor of the Chancellery, and Private-secretary to the King of Sweden, Archivist of the various Orders belonging to his Majesty, and one of the Eighteen Members of the Swedish Academy; translated from the Swedish, by Hector B——, an Officer of the Royal Swedish Marine. Paris, 1 vol. 8vo.

This

This work, which is drawn up with great method, contains a history of the ancient telegraphs, and also indicates all the qualities necessary for a good telegraph. Besides this, it contains a variety of details relative to the introduction of the telegraphic art into France; a description of the French telegraphs; an exposition of the experiments made by M. Edelcranz, in order to introduce similar ones into Sweden, &c.

"Systeme des Connoissances Chimiques, &c." A System of Chymical Knowledge, with its Application to the Phenomena of Nature and Art, by A. F. FOURCROY, of the National Institute, Counsellor of State, Professor of Chemistry at the Museum of Natural History, the Polytechnical School, and the School of Medicine; a Member of the Societies of, &c. Paris. 11 vol. 8vo. price 50 fr. and 4 vols. 4to. price 72 fr.

This work, or, to speak more properly, this monument erected to chemical science by the celebrated Fourcroy, contains the history of its origin and its progress, as well as the principles and the details of those immense discoveries with which Europe became enriched towards the close of the eighteenth century. This eloquent writer has at length withdrawn the veil, and the archives of science have become the common treasure of the learned of all nations.

"Eloge Philosophique de Denys Diderot, &c." Philosophical Eloge of Diderot, by EUSEBIUS SALVERTE; read at the National Institute, on the 7th of last Thermidor, 1 vol. 8vo.

Eusebius Salverte states, that it is his intention to render homage to the talents and virtues of a philosopher who honoured and served his country, and who, persecuted during his life, has also been assailed by calumniators after he had ceased to exist. Of the numerous writings of Diderot, the author cites "La Vie de Seneque," as particularly deserving of praise, and possessing every thing, both in respect of matter and manner, appropriate to the subject. He considers him as profound in his "Pensées Philosophiques, et l'Interpretation de la Nature;" concise, elegant, and clear in his "Entretien d'un Philosophe;" a metaphysician superior even to Locke and Condillac in his "Lettres sur les Sourds et Muets;" possessed of taste in his "Lettres sur la Peinture;" brilliant in his "Religieuse," &c.

"Bibliographie Entomologique, &c." Entomological Bibliography; or, a Catalogue of the Works relative to Entomology and Insects, with critical Notes, and an Exposition of the various Methods, by CHARLES NODIER. Paris. 18mo.

Every one is acquainted with the excellent "Botanical Bibliography of M. Haller," and it is greatly to be wished, that every branch of human science should possess its particular bibliography, in which, following the ascending line, the rudiments of the science, and the works to be studied gradually, might be pointed out. A project of this kind was suggested to d'Alembert, and some progress made, but it was never carried into execution.

"Odes, traduites ou imitées d'Horace, &c." Odes, translated or imitated from Horace, by P. M. MIGER, 18mo.

The poetical essays contained in this little volume, appear to be the production of a man of some talents. The author has added to his translations, a fragment of his own, on the power of poetry, the first strophes of which are imitations of the seventh and eighth odes of the 4th book of Horace.

"La Paix avec l'Empereur, &c." Peace with the Emperor; or, the Treaty of Luneville, a Poem; to which is added, an Epistle to Virgil, on the Battle of Marengo; by CUBIERES, junior, Member of the Lyceum of Paris, of the Society of Arts and Sciences, and the Atheneum of of Lyons, &c. 12mo.

It is not the "Treaty of Luneville," but the actions that preceded the pacification, as well as the new prospects opened by it, that the poet considers as a fit subject for his Muse. To this little work is prefixed, an epistle which no friend to letters, to philosophy, and to taste will consider as despicable. The verses on the Peace are easy and flowing, and the Epistle to Virgil is accompanied by an Italian translation, by Povoleri, who has attained some degree of celebrity by his versification.

"L'Univers, Poeme en Prose, &c." The Universe, a Poem in Prose, and in Twelve Cantos, by P. C. V. BOISTE, Author of an Universal Dictionary of the French Language, 1 vol. 8vo. Paris. 7 fr.

The author tells us in his preface, that it is his intention to represent the universe, under four grand points of view, viz. its physical, moral, political, and religious aspect. The invocation to the Deity abounds with sublime and appropriate imagery, and the whole is accompanied with notes, and adorned with well executed prints. The frontispiece represents "The Eternal, dispersing chaos, after Raphael."

La

"Le Livre Singulier, &c." The Singular Book. Paris, 1 vol. 18mo.

The motto to this little volume, is the same as that worn by the Knights of the Garter; it contains 1. the reveries of an Englishman on seeing the dissection of the cranium of a fop, and the heart of a coquette; the laconic testament of an annuitant; the confession of a woman on her deathbed; the pleasant history of a man labouring under a suppositious malady; the epitaph of an hermaphrodite; description of the palace of Fortune; the art of avoiding to think, &c. &c.

BIOGRAPHY.

"Memoires de Le Kain, &c." Memoirs of Le Kain, published by his Son, 1 vol. 8vo.

Le Kain was an actor, who possessed great talents for the stage, and acquired wonderful celebrity; in short, he might have been termed the French Garrick. On the same day that Baron died, Le Kain was born, as if Nature had determined to restore to the theatre all it had been bereaved of on this occasion. Before the time of Baron, the French stage was far inferior to what it is at present; for the actors, who were fantastically clothed, sung, instead of declaiming, and recurred to the most extravagant and burlesque gestures, in order to attain applause; in short, they rather resembled *Merry-andrews* than Comedians. It was he who restored the empire of nature, and introduced theatrical grandeur; he entertained such an high opinion of his art, that he was accustomed to exclaim: "*Un bon comédien devroit avoir été élevé sur les genoux des princesses.*" (A good comedian should have been nursed upon the knees of princesses.)

Le Kain, the only actor who has ever been able to rival Baron, was gifted by nature with the same graces as his predecessor; but according to the opinion of an ingenious observer, "the one possessed that nobleness in his character which the other exhibited in his manners." Le Kain was the son of a goldsmith, and he himself for some time followed the same occupation; but a rage for celebrity tormented, and at length forced him to quit his shop. Nature however had refused him the external appearance of an hero, in the same manner that she had denied to the eloquent Athenian the first requisite of an orator; Le Kain was thick and clumsy, as Demosthenes was timid and incorrect: but art in both triumphed over nature.

A most unexpected accident brought together an actor and a poet, who seemed to be born for each other, for Le Kain was admirably adapted to do justice to the tragedies of Voltaire, and Voltaire the most capable of all the poets to give scope to the talents of the actor. Struck with the happy disposition of the young man, then not twenty years of age, the author of the "Henriade" took him home to his house, gave him lessons in his art, and at length introduced him to the French stage.

"De l'Homme d'Etat, considéré dans Alexandre Severe, &c." Of the Statesman, considered in the Character of Alexander Severus, and compared with the most Virtuous of the Roman Emperors, by Citizen DEMAISNIEUX, late Major of the German Infantry, &c. 8vo.

With the life of Alexander Severus, was extinguished the last spark of Roman virtue. Aurelian and Probus, having always been in the field and constantly engaged in wars, cannot be considered as models for the imitation of monarchs; as for Tacitus, he only held the bloody reins of empire during the short period of six months. Successor of the infamous Heliogabulus, Alexander Severus deserved to have lived during the times of Scipio and Paulus Æmilius.

This young Emperor, whose soul was so pure, and whose manners were so gentle, was but ill suited to a people who no longer possessed any thing Roman but the name. Cæsar, by addressing his soldiers with the appellation of "Quirites," instead of using the term "Commilitones," induced them to return to their duty; but in the time of Alexander Severus, such a conduct would have led to assassination, and not to obedience; so true it is, that it is difficult to conduct a degenerate nation by means of sage principles. A man, indeed, is almost tempted to despair of the destiny of empires, when he beholds a Maximin—a ferocious giant—triumphing over so many virtues, and preferred to one of the most sage and enlightened men that ever reigned over his fellow-creatures.

It must be acknowledged, notwithstanding the work written by Citizen Demaisnieux contains a variety of excellent ideas, that it is greatly to be regretted that his style is not always pure and correct, but it ought to be recollected on the other hand, that he has passed the greater part of his life under arms. He tells us, towards the end of his introduction, that his work has been seen by three crowned heads; having been read in 1774 to Catharine II.; in 1775 to Gustavus; and that it had not only been examined by Frederick II. but that several passages were communicated, by order of that Monarch, to the Academy of Sciences of Berlin.

NOVELS, ROMANCES, &c.

"Atala; ou, les Amours de deux Sauvages dans le Désert, &c." Atala; or, the Amours of two Savages in the Desert, by FRANCIS AUGUSTUS CHATEAUBRIAND, 1 vol. 18mo. Paris.

This little novel is not destitute of that kind of machinery which inspires interest, and, as we have savages, a hermit, and a desert, must be supposed to abound with new and romantic situations. The library of F. A. Chateaubriand has but little resemblance to that of the writers of a similar kind, as, according to his own account, it contains but two books; the Bible, and Homer.

"Orfeuil et Juliette, &c." Orfeuil and Juliette; or, an End to Delusion, by Mademoiselle ***, Author of Eugenio and Virginia, 3 vols. 12mo.

The passion for reading and writing romances and novels seems to be still stronger in France than in England; in short, the number already published is immense, and appears to be daily increasing. In respect to the present, it is acknowledged to be the best production of the fair author, to whom we are already indebted for the affecting "Adventures of Eugenio and Virginia." Orfeuil and Juliette, abounds with many affecting situations, and much sensibility is every where called forth; but we would advise translators to be on their guard, as novels calculated for the latitude of Paris, are not always suited to the meridian of London.

"Le Solitaire des Pyrénées, &c." The Solitary of the Pyrenees; or, Memoirs of the Life of D'Armaud, Marquis de Felcourt, 3 vols. 12mo.

The Marquis de Felcourt, an orphan, is educated along with his sister Amelia, by the Count D'Andreuil, his uncle and guardian. After receiving a brilliant rather than a solid education, he becomes a captain of dragoons, and contracts an intimate friendship with the Viscount de Montrosay, an officer of the same regiment. Felcourt having married a lady whose character was not approved of by his sister, his friend becomes enamoured of, and intrigues with her, which ends in the most direful catastrophe on the part of the two guilty lovers, and a life of seclusion on the part of the injured husband, who retires to the Pyrenean mountains, in order to spend the remainder of his days in solitude and affliction.

"William Hillnet; ou, la Nature and et l'Amour, &c." William Hillnet; or, Nature and Love, translated from the German of Miltenberg, by ADELINE D. C**, 3 vols. 18mo.

Lord Hillnet, the victim of the basest ingratitude, after being betrayed by his friends and abandoned by his wife, seeks for an asylum in one of his estates. He accordingly makes choice of a solitary valley, where he builds a house, to which he retires with his only son William, and an old domestic, called Thomas.

All the actions of this nobleman are characterized by a settled misanthropy, and he determines to educate his heir in the most complete ignorance of the customs of a world against which he has conceived the most rooted distaste. The infancy of William accordingly passes away in peace, but scarcely had he attained his fifteenth year, when he is induced by curiosity to pierce the valley, and have a peep at other objects than those he has hitherto been accustomed to. Become bold by success, he at length roams to a considerable distance, and arrives at a park, which he enters. As he approaches a noble mansion, he beholds women and children at a distance, and is so anxious to join them, that he wades through a canal, in order to effect his purpose.

Having accomplished this, he enters into conversation with a charming young lady, the daughter of the owner of the park, and, on his return, he exclaims—"O! my dear father, I have seen Fanny!"

Lord Hillnet, perceiving that his system of education was impracticable, carries his son to London, and, after a variety of adventures, he at length meets the lady who had gained his heart at Madras, who happens to have repaired thither with her husband. Afflicted at this circumstance, he travels over India, and at length consoles himself, for the loss of his Fanny, in the arms of Nahida, an Indian, possessing great beauty, &c.

The former part of this romance, although it be translated from the German, has evidently something English about it; the latter in part resembles the Indian Cottage (La Chaumière Indienne), of the celebrated St. Pierre; but it must be frankly confessed, that the situations are greatly exaggerated, and no one, who has lived either in Great Britain or India, can read this work without a certain degree of disgust.

"Elif

"Elise Duménil," &c. Eliza Duménil, by MARIA COMMARIEU MONTALEMBERT, 6 vols. 12mo. Price 9 Fr. Paris.

This novel contains an account of the travels and adventures of Alfred, his passion for Eliza, his misconduct on his return to Paris, in consequence of being carried to a gaming-house, &c. &c. The extreme severity of M. Duménil, the father of the heroine, is admirably contrasted with the feeble character of the Count de Borensac, the parent of the hero. The style of the work is in general easy, and even eloquent, but it at times exhibits certain defects, which the Parisian critics have not failed to notice, such as *c'est*, instead of *cela est*, &c.

"Romans Historiques, et Piéces diverses en Vers et en Prose," &c. Historical Romances, and a variety of Pieces, both in Prose and in Verse, by J. LABLEE, of the Athenæum of Lyons, Author of the Romances of Silvina, l'Accusta de Rapt, &c. &c. 1 vol. 12mo.

The greater part of these romances have appeared before, and already attracted the attention of persons of taste. The style is pleasing, and the poetry possesses that flexibility so much desired by dramatic musicians.

Among the prose works, the reader of sensibility will be pleased to select the Epistle from the Author to his Wife. It is followed by a letter of another kind; a letter containing a protest on the part of the author, against the introduction of his name into the "Dictionnaire des Athées," by SYLVAIN MARECHAL. He professes his belief in the Deity, and loudly and justly condemns the presumption of the editor.

"Amour et Galanterie," &c. Love and Gallantry, written after the Manner of Faublas, by B. DE S. V. Paris, 2 vols. 12mo.

This work is negligently composed, although it now and then exhibits portraits not very dissimilar to those that are to be met with in society.

"Angelina; ou, le Delire des Passions," &c. Angelina; or, the Delirium of the Passions, by P. F. B. of Lyons, Paris, 1 vol. 18mo.

This is a work conceived from, and addressed to, the passions. The following whimsical address is prefixed.

"O sombrous productions of the splenetic genius of the inhabitants of smoky foggy England; ye are but so many laughable fables, when compared with these recitals depicted by the pencil of truth! What a train of horrors! What a series of crimes! I am even ignorant if my pen will be able to retrace them."

"L'Enfant de Trente-six Peres," &c. The Child of Thirty-six Fathers, a Romance, serious, comic, and moral, by D. A. 3 vols. 12mo. Paris. 6 Fr.

The title of this work is rather calculated to mislead the reader, for we are here presented with scenes which are gay, without being indecent. Laurentini, the hero of the romance, born at Castelnaudary, is son of the beautiful Angelina. He is utterly ignorant, however, of his father; but, in consequence of a long search, and a variety of distressing scenes, he discovers Antonio to be the parent whom he was so desirous to become acquainted with. After this, every thing becomes easy, he espouses his dear Zelia, and is the happiest of mortals!

"Glorioso Demonio; ou, le Grand Diable," &c. Glorioso Demonio; or, the Great Devil; translated from the German of the Author of Rinaldo Rinaldini, 2 vol. 12mo. Paris.

This affects to be an historical romance and abounds with adventures and interesting situations, calculated to please a great number of readers. The hero, after exhibiting a number of generous actions, at length finds supreme felicity in the bosom of love and glory; in short, Glorioso founds hospitals in the name of his Miranda, and they are both adored by their numerous vassals.

"Les Horreurs de Destin," &c. The Horrors of Destiny; or, the Four Unfortunates, by CONSLADOZ, 2 vols. 12mo.

This is a romance of a very different kind; for the heroine, instead of becoming happy, perishes in the most cruel bondage.

"Lize; ou, les Hermites de Mont Blanc," &c. Lise; or, the Hermits of Mont Blanc, &c. by Madame G—— MORENCY, 1 vol. 12mo.

This may be considered as a continuation of the two novels, "Illyrine" and "Rosalina," of the same female author.

"Palme; ou, l'Ile de la Montagne," &c. Palma; or, the Isle of the Black Mountain, by J. A. GARDY, 1 vol. 18mo.

This contains a variety of adventures equally

equally strange and incredible, such indeed as can never occur but in a romance.

"Le Peruvien à Paris," &c. The Peruvian at Paris, a Critical, Historical, and Moral Work, containing an Account of the Voyage of a young Indian to France, at the beginning of the nineteenth Century; his Introduction and Adventures in that Country; his Criticism on the Manners, Usages, Customs, and Establishments of the French Nation; to which is added, the Particulars of his Return to Cusco, &c. enriched with historical Notes, by JOSEPH ROSNY, 4 vols. 18mo. Paris, 5 Fr.

The Peruvian Thorello, having arrived in France, travels through the southern departments, visits Lyons, &c. then repairs to Paris. While there, he resolves to see every thing that can gratify his curiosity, &c. at the same time, commits to paper the ideas that present themselves in consequence of the novelties that every where attract his attention. We are accordingly gratified with a description of the Tuilleries, the Palais-Royal, the ladies *of all kinds*, the fashions, the theatres, the Museum, the Institute, the National Library, the garden of plants, the prisons, the Invalids, the hospitals, and, in short, all the places of amusement or instruction, with which the French capital abounds.

At length, the faithful and affectionate Azara arrives in Paris, and finds her dear Thorello. The two lovers, after experiencing a number of adventures, determine to return to their native country; they accordingly set sail, and arrive in safety at Cusco.

This little work is drawn up in the form of letters, and will serve, particularly the three first volumes, as a guide to such strangers as are averse from entering into the dry details generally to be met with in mere books of description.

"Un Roman comme un Autre," &c. A Romance, like any Other, by Myself, Paris, 2 vols. 12mo.

The title is whimsical, and the work itself is written in imitation of Sterne.

"La Vengeance," &c. The Vengeance; translated from the German of Augustus Lafontaine, by W. A. DUVAL, 1 vol. 12mo. Paris.

Augustus Lafontaine, the author, has already attained considerable celebrity by his "Family Picture," &c. The present may be read without any danger, which is no small praise for a modern novel; but it will not add greatly to the reputation of the author.

"Bonheur et Vertu," &c. Happiness and Virtue, by P. L. LEBAS, Author of Anthony, or Crimes and Remorse.

The hero and heroine of this story are educated together by a clergyman, and persecuted by his vicar, by whom they are forced to leave that part of the country in which they were born and brought up. On their repairing to Paris, the young man finds great difficulty in earning a subsistence, and his sweetheart experiences many temptations in consequence of her beauty. Having, however, resisted all the allurements and seductions to which she was exposed, her virtue is at length rewarded by her union with her lover, who had taken an active part in the Revolution, and by that means obtained considerable advancement.

There is but little new or interesting, either in the plot, or situation of the parties.

"Roseide et Valmor," &c. Roseide and Valmor; or, the Victims of Pride.

This is said in the preface to be translated from the English of "Sir Horace Walpole!"

"Souvenirs de Mylady Cartemane," &c. Recollections of Lady Cartemane; or, the Manners of past Times, by ANTHONY DIANNYERE, an Associate of the National Institute.

Citizen Diannyère, the author of this novel, and a member of one of the first literary societies in Europe, is already known to the public by his Eloge on Condorcet, and a work on Political Economy. The purport of the present romance, as he assures us in his preface, "is to present a faithful description of some of the usages that prevailed anterior to the Revolution, and thus to inform such readers, as, being afflicted with the misfortunes of which they have been either the witnesses or the victims, imagine every thing was quite different under the *ancient government*—that far greater and more terrible evils then prevailed.

After this, he proceeds to relate, that so little respect was paid to female decorum, that several ladies, who had been well educated, were yet unfeeling enough to be present at the punishment of Damien. He also states some of the imposts to have been so ruinous, that

that the peasants were accustomed to pray for a hail-storm—that, their harvest thus becoming less abundant, the expences of gathering their grapes would also be diminished, and thus afford them a pretence for paying less to the state.

"Rosabelle; ou, la Caverne," &c. Rosabelle; or, the French Cavern, 1 vol. 18mo.

This is a publication of no reputation whatever, being entirely destitute of all the essential requisites of a romance.

"Le Conscrit; ou, le Billet de Logement," &c. The Conscript; or, the Soldier's Billet, by H. LEMAIRE, Author of La Pauvre Rentiere, 1 vol. 8vo. with Plates, Paris.

A young man of letters having been obliged to forsake his pen, and snatch up his sword, notwithstanding all his endeavours to escape the law of conscription, is sent to the barracks, and incorporated into a regiment then under orders to march to the frontiers. After a variety of vain and useless attempts to desert, this soldier, who had determined not to become a hero, sets out with his battalion to join the army of the Rhine. Happening one day, in the course of his march, to receive a billet entitling him to a night's lodging at a certain house, he began to flatter himself that he should find a pretty maid, good quarters, &c. He accordingly prepared a little compliment for the occasion. It being dark when he arrived, he presented his *billet* to a female whom he could not see; but to his inexpressible surprise, on uttering his high-flown eulogiums, the shrill sonorous voice of an old woman called out—Help! help! murder! and the poor recruit was immediately seized, and carried to the guard-house.

Soon after this, he discovers that the good old lady who had got him confined, was aunt to a beautiful and young female, being informed that a soldier intended to carry her niece a love-letter from her sweetheart, supposed that she had been lucky enough to intercept it. Having been liberated in consequence of the explanation that took place, in the morning the young lady in question is incited by curiosity to see the prisoner, and, falling in love with him, they are immediately married. Notwithstanding this, the bridegroom is obliged to join his *corps*, and, having distinguished himself in an engagement, he receives a commission.

This little romance may be considered as a petition to the French Government in favour of men of letters, who are in general more solicitous to enlighten their countrymen, than to defend their country.

CHILDREN'S AND SCHOOL-BOOKS.

"Cours de Cosmographie, de Chronologie," &c. A Course of Cosmography, Chronology, Geography, and Ancient and Modern History; divided into 125 Lessons, by MENTELLE, Member of the National Institute, 3 vols. 8vo. with Plates, and an Atlas consisting of fifteen coloured Maps, Paris.

This work consists of two parts:—the first contains cosmography, geography, and ancient history until the time of the crusades, and completes vol. 1. The second presents the continuation of geography and modern history up to the ninth year of the French Republic, and is divided into two volumes, one of which is dedicated to modern Europe, while the other contains Asia, Africa, and America.

"Le Nouveau Robinson," &c. The New Robinson Crusoe, a Work intended for the Amusement and Instruction of Children; translated from the German of M. CAMPE, 2 vols. 12mo. Geneva and Paris.

The author of the New Robinson Crusoe endeavours, throughout the whole of these two little volumes, to instruct children by exciting their curiosity. By interesting their feelings, he also attempts to generate in their breasts a noble enthusiasm for virtue and morality. His lessons are in the shape of dialogues between a father and his children, containing all the elementary knowledge necessary for infancy. In pursuance of an idea suggested by Rousseau, Robinson Crusoe is exhibited in his island, deprived of all the conveniences of life, but supplying these by his ingenuity and industry.

"Fables d'Esope," &c. The Fables of Esop, represented by means of prints; with an Explanation of the principal Events of his Life; engraved by the best Artists, and intended for the Instruction of Children of both Sexes, Paris, 2 vols. 4to. Price 8 Fr.

This edition of the Fables of Esop contains no less than sixty plates, which are engraved with great care.

"Abrégé de la Grammaire Française," &c. An Abridgment of the French

French Grammar, by M. de WAILLY, Member of the National Institute, eleventh Edition, revised and augmented by the Author himself, 1 vol. 8vo.

The late learned and virtuous De Wailly, a man of letters generally known and esteemed, was the author of this work, the success of which may be easily conceived by the number of editions through which it has passed. It is almost needless to add, that the merit of the Grammar is fully adequate to its success.

"Essai sur l'Othographie," &c. An Essay on French Orthography, &c. by HALY.

The difficulties of French orthography are well known, and much pains are taken in this little pamphlet to remove them. The author also gives rules for versification, and throws out a variety of new ideas for the decision of the learned.

"Le Guide des Humanistes," &c. A Guide to those who learn the Latin Language; or, the first Principles of Taste, developed in Remarks on the fine Verses of Virgil, and other good Poets, both Latin and French, a new Edition, Paris, 1 vol. 8vo.

It is the intention of the author to inspire the scholar, not with a taste for poetry only, but with the principles of that general taste, which teaches us to distinguish the good from the bad in any literary composition whatsoever.

He divides his book into three parts:—the first is dedicated to the examination of ideas that pervade every work; the second treats of the poetic style; and the last of cadence. This production contains but little that is new; it may, however, prove no less useful to youth.

"Metamorphoses d'Ovide," &c. The Metamorphoses of Ovid, adorned with 138 Prints, after the Designs of Sebastian Leclerc; to which is prefixed, a Life of Ovid, and an Abridgment of Poetic History, a Work destined for the Instruction of Youth, 2 vols. 4to. Paris, Price 12 Fr.

It is intended in the present work to arrive at the understanding through the medium of the eyes, these volumes being adorned with a prodigious number of prints, designed and engraved expressly for that purpose. The explanations are short, but comprehensive, and such as may be easily retained, and are calculated to make an impression on youth.

"Herbier Moral," &c. The Moral Herbal; or, a Number of new Fables, and other fugitive Poetry; to which is added, a Collection of Romances proper for Education, &c. by Madame DE GENLIS.

This is a new edition of a work composed for children, by the celebrated Madame de Genlis, who educated the Princes of the House of Orleans, and has been lately permitted to return to Paris.

"Le Jardin des Enfans," &c. The Garden of Children; or, Family Nosegays, &c.

A work totally unfit for children, and possessing all the thorns, without any of the sweets, of the rose.

"Histoire Elementaire, Philosophique, et Politique de l'Ancienne Grèce," &c. A History, Elementary, Philosophical, and Political, of Ancient Greece, from the Establishment of her Colonies, to the Reduction of Greece into a Roman Province; together with a Chronological Table, Map, &c. 2 vols. 8vo.

This work is drawn up in the manner of question and answer, and contains a variety of information relative to Ancient Greece. The philosophers, legislators, and men of genius, pass in review, and the author presents an historical and analytical notice of the doctrine of each. After treating of politics, he passes on to the arts and sciences, and contrives to convey to the pupil a tolerable idea of all that has been said respecting a country which has occupied during so many ages the attention of the civilised part of mankind.

"Abrégé des Hommes Illustres de Plutarque," &c. An Abridgment of the Illustrious Men of Plutarque, by Citizen ACHER.

Abridgments in general are attended with this great disadvantage, that they leave no traces behind them; and an Abridgment of Plutarch is perhaps less entitled to respect, than that of any author whatsoever. Citizen Acher, however, remarks by way of excuse, that no readable edition of Plutarch exists at this moment in France, that of Ricard being not as yet entirely published; Amiot's being too old, and Dacier, "who hated the Muses, and whom the Graces abhorred," being unfit for children, as it would infallibly corrupt their taste.

This is intended to consist of 3 vols. 12mo

12mo. but the two first only are as yet published.

"De l'Education des Filles," &c. On the Education of Daughters, by Fenelon, Archbishop of Cambray, &c. to which is added a Letter from the same Author to a Lady, on the Education of her only Daughter; and a Preliminary Discourse on some of the Changes that have taken Place in Respect to Education, &c. by J. S. Bourlet.

The name of Fenelon has undoubtedly contributed to the success of a work, which has already passed through several editions. It is written with great simplicity and precision, but no where exhibits the brilliant imagery of the author of Telemachus; good sense and discretion, however, every where prevail.

"Do not be afraid of any thing so much," say the good Archbishop, "as the vanity of young women; they are born with a violent desire to please; the road which conducts men to glory being shut to them, they endeavour to indemnify themselves by the charms of both body and mind. Hence arises that sweet and insinuating conversation; hence they aspire not only to beauty, but to all the internal graces, and are so passionately fond of dress. A cap, a bit of ribband, a lock of hair placed higher or lower, or the choice of any particular colour, are so many objects of importance to them. This species of excess is also carried higher in our nation than in any other. The changeable humour that prevails among us occasions a continual variety of fashions; to the love of dress, therefore, is superadded that of novelty, which has extraordinary charms on minds so disposed: in short, these two follies, in conjunction, mingle different ranks and degrees with each other, and produce the most fatal effects on female manners."

HALF-YEARLY RETROSPECT OF SPANISH LITERATURE.

WE submitted our last Retrospect to the public with a few general observations on Spanish Literature; the remarks we shall now make are merely those that naturally arise from the view of the productions within the last six months comprised in the subsequent catalogue.

Among the periodical works of Spain, the Historical and Political Mercury, and the Literary Memorial, are continued; but in this department, we observe no accession: without affecting to suppose the inundation that foams in torrents from the presses in our own country, and some neighbouring stat s, is always pure, and ever directed into right channels; yet, coinciding with the late General Washington, we consider opinion advantageously developed by these intruders, which, on a thousand occasions, remove the transient *vis inertiæ* of the mind, and give it activity and elevation.

In our last view, it was asserted, that many of the works were mere translations from the stock of other countries: this frequent borrowing abroad implies poverty at home; but when there is not only a deficiency in original works, but the productions themselves, instead of being drawn from he spring head, are translations of translations, it indicates, not only a want of genius in the country, but even a paucity of means to avail itself of general knowledge and improvement. In the publications arranged in this Retrospect, among the numerous translations, excepting from the French, we recollect only one from any modern language.

Under the title Archæology, Natural History, or Tactics, we have not been able to procure a single article; with respect to the former, we have before signified our regret, that the Saracenic Antiquities of that nation have been so long concealed. With regard to the second, Spain is a country peculiarly favourable to the pursuits of the naturalist. Mental application usually induces corporeal imbecility: the man of science resembling the midnight flame, his companion, a sudden gust destroys his activity and extinguishes his powers. With a form enervated by the studies of the closet, if he venture abroad to pursue his investigations under a clear sky, and in a friendly climate, he contemplates nature without being obstructed by those inclemencies to which his frame is obnoxious: this advantage he enjoys in Spain; in the irriguous vallies of the Pyrenees, sheltered by the excavations of the mountains the celebrated Tournefort explored the secrets of vegetation.

While the Prince of Peace was glittering in the blaze of military splendour; while the conquest of a new kingdom was meditated in the court of Madrid, and the integrity of the peninsula violated by the insurgents, Braganza was the project of female ambition—while gazettes extraordinary were ringing all the changes of martial triumph, it is singular that the eyes of the people should have been so little directed, and the pursuits of men of science in so small a degree diverted by these objects, that not one tactical work should have emanated from the press. To the observer of the progress of the mind, it indicates that the sentiments of the court of Spain do not at this day wholly guide the opinions of the people, and that some portion of that independent spirit is revived which glowed in the breasts of the Spaniards before the administration of Ximenes, at the commencement of the sixteenth century.

When we speak of the Drama in Spain, we refer to the country which first burst the pedant chains by which the poet had been dishonoured: the story of the Loves of Rodrigo and Ximena, given by two distinguished writers of that nation, diffused over Europe an energy of composition unattained even in the court of Leo X. We shall not degrade the classic age of Spain by an unworthy comparison with modern times; but we may express our satisfaction, that, in a state where the assiduity to polish has worn away all that is substantial in female education, a lady has distinguished herself as a dramatist, who may hold a respectable rank among the poets of her country.

The most important contributions from the Spanish press, are under the titles Anatomy, Chemistry, Pharmacy, Agriculture, and Jurisprudence. In our last Retrospect, it was stated, that the vaccine-inoculation had been noticed from the press, we have now the pleasure to announce, that the practice has been adopted by Spain; an account of a variety of cases has been published, and the mode of performing it has been so far simplified, that the parent is sufficiently instructed in the operation, without the necessity of having recourse to medical assistance.

Under Agriculture, it will be seen, that the system promoted by Mr. Arthur Young has drawn particular regard, which is especially desirable in a country where the new tillage can be introduced with such peculiar advantages from the felicity of soil and climate. Among the improvers of this class, we see with great pleasure the name of the Duchess of Alba, who (having under her controul the funds of the most opulent dukedom in Europe) is enabled extensively to contribute to the public good.

Jurisprudence may be defined the science of what is just and unjust, or of the laws, rights, and customs of man in society; many of the subjects might be confined to mere questions of art and locality. On the contrary, the publications of this class that have appeared in Spain, in general respect the great natural relations, duties, and interests of man: we are not fatigued with the technical and minute details on the limits of jurisdiction, and on the claims, or more correctly the usurpations of the privileged orders; but the patriotic jurist, taking an enlarged view of human wants, and adverting to the errors of past times, as obstructing the improvements of the present, suggests those changes which will relieve his countrymen from corporeal and mental oppression; and one adventurous writer, superior to the ecclesiastical and civil prohibitions on the disclosure of the public sentiment, regardless of the Censuras and Licencias of Consejos, and Ordinarios Prefatory to his own work, has recommended the liberty of the press, in imitation of the bold and enlightened maxims of British law.

The view we have taken of the recent literary transactions of Spain, has convinced us of the domineering influence of French councils, and of French principles, in that kingdom. This will appear the instant we reflect, that France is the fountain from which the numerous channels of the Spanish press are almost wholly supplied, and the French press is entirely under the direction of the constituted authorities. It was considered an object of great moment to England, on the accession of the Bourbons to the throne of Spain, that a separation of interests should subsist between the crowns of that family; but by the new order of things, the expedients of British policy for this purpose have been completely countervailed, and the maxims of the Consular court, which are so loudly proclaimed in the capital, are distributed, by the medium of the press, throughout the provinces of the Spanish empire.

If these changes be to that kingdom beneficial or injurious, and what relation they bear to the political and commercial interests of this country, are inquiries foreign to our present design.

AGRICULTURE.

"Curso Completo ó Diccionario Universal de Agricultura Teórica, Práctica, Económica, y de Medicina Rural y Veterinaria,

rinaria, escrito en Frances por una Sociedad de Agrónomos, y ordenado por el Abate Rozier; traducido al Castellano por D. JUAN ALVAREZ GUERRA, 34 rs." Complete View or Universal Dictionary of Theoretical, Practical, and Economic Agriculture, written in French by a Society of Agriculturists under the Direction of the Abbé Rozier; translated into Spanish by D. Juan Alvarez Guerra, 34 Reals. The Sr. Guerra is a Member in the Class of Agriculture of the Royal Economic Society of Madrid; the work has four plates illustrative of the subjects, which are directed to the most important agricultural inquires.

" Guia Veterinaria Original, por D. ALONZO y D. FRANCISCO DE RUS, Mariscales del Real Cuerpo de Guardias de Corps." Original Veterinary Guide, by D. Alonzo and D. Francisco de Ruz, Farriers of the Royal Regiment of Body Guards. This production extends to four octavo volumes; the first treats of the parts and proportions of the horse, on his diet, and on the several diseases to which he is subject, the cure of which is systematically explained; the second is confined to the more dangerous class of diseases, internal and external, to which domestic animals in general are exposed; the third comprizes a compendious anatomy of the horse, and a discourse on certain abuses to which he is liable; the fourth refers to the most successful method of preserving and improving the breed, and particular directions are given for the selection of the sire, and for the treatment of the mare.

" Semanario de Agricultura y Artes, tomo 9." Weekly Report of Agriculture and Arts, vol. 9th. Among other valuable articles, this publication contains the following:—The improvements of the Duchess of Alba on some of the family estates; the cultivation of vines, and the method of pressing the juice, and converting it into wine, in Malaga, S. Lucas Condado de Niebla & Xerez.

The Practice of Agriculture and Rural Economy of England, extracted from the Journies of Arthur Young.

Remarks on the Agriculture and Industry of Japan; on the Native and Exotic Plants in the Royal Gardens of Aranjuez. Practical Observations on the Climate of Spain, with the View to the Mode of Culture best adapted to it. Minute Observations on the Vaccine-pox, with Remarks by the Physicians of London, Paris, Vienna, &c. On the Medical Uses of Vital Air.

" Reflexiones sobre los Progesos de Agricultura y Pastoria." Reflections on the Progress of Tillage and Pasturage. This work explains the prevailing deficiency in the knowledge of soils, vegetables, and of the arts connected with their improvement; it represents the necessity of establishing public lectures on agriculture in all the institutions of the kingdom devoted to the education of youth. We shall be very happy to see this important intimation properly attended to in our own country, where we presume to possess much higher attainments in these branches of useful knowledge.

" Tratado de la Huerta; ó, Método de cultivar toda Clase de Hortalizas, por Dr. CLAUDIO BOUTELON." The Art of Gardening; or the Mode of Cultivating all Sorts of Hortulan Plants, by D. Claudio Boutelon. The author of this work is gardener to the Palace of Buen Retiro, and to the Royal Botanic Garden; he was assisted in the undertaking by D. Estebon Boutelon, under gardener, and manager of the woods in the Palace of Aranjuez. Both of them are Honorary Members of the Royal Society of Madrid, and Associates in the Institution for Natural History at Paris. The work is in a lexicographical form, and is the first of the kind that was ever published in Spain; it gives a description of each plant, of its varieties, of its usual mode of cultivation, of collecting the seed, of the enemies to which it is exposed, of the hot-house management of it, and of its economic and medicinal uses. 20 reals, boards.

ANATOMY, CHEMISTRY, AND PHARMACY.

" Tratado de Cirurgia y Medicina de D. PASCUAL FRANCISCO VIREY, M.D." Treatise on Surgery and Medicine, by D. Pascual Francisco Virey, M. D. This work is from a physician of the University of Valencia, and an Honorary Member of the Royal Institution of Midwifery; it extends to five quarto volumes; the first treats of symptoms; the second, of the several kinds of fevers, and their cures; the third and fourth compose an anatomical and chirurgical manual; and, in the fifth, the celebrated aphorisms of Hippocrates are practically explained.

Curso Completo de Medicina, que escribió en Latin el célebre Professor HERMAN BOERHAAVE, tom. 4 y ultimo; publicado el Dr. D. Juan Baptista Sandevilla." Complete Course of Lectures, from the Pen of the celebrated Professor Herman Boerhaave, vol. 4 and last published by Dr. D. Juan Baptista Sandevilla

This concluding volume comprises internal, acute, and chronic disorders, which form the second part of the Aphorisms of the celebrated original De Cognoscendis et Curandis Morbis.

"Supplemento a la Traduccion Castellana de los Elementos de Chímica de J. A. CHAPTAL." Supplement to the Spanish Translation of the Elements of Chemistry by J. A. Chaptal. This is taken from the third edition, published in Paris in 1796; into it are introduced the many important corrections and additions made by the author himself in the latest publication of his Elements, which extend to sixty different articles; among others, these treat of potash; marine-salt; the mode of making soap on a large and a small scale for private families; the best way of collecting the resinous juices of the pine; and on the analysis of a variety of animal substances.

"Apéndice à la Fisica del Cuerpo Humano; ó, Rudimentos Fisiológicos sobre los Funciones Sexuales, traducidos del Latin por Dr. D. JOSEPH COLL." Appendix to the Physical Description of the Human Body; or, Physical Rudiments of the Sexual Functions, from the Latin by Dr. D. Joseph Coll.

"Introduccion al Estudio de la Naturaleza y de la Medicina." Introduction to the Study of Nature and of Medicine, from the French, by Dr. FRANCISCO BONAFON. The original of this is in German, by M. Selle, physician to the King of Prussia, 8vo. 500 pages.

"Origen, Descubrimiento, y Progresos de la Vaccina; traducido del Frances por el Dr. D. PEDRO HERNANDEZ." Original Discovery and Progress of the Vaccine-pox; translated from the French by Dr. D. Pedro Hernandez. This work is by a Physician of the Royal College: the text is explained by plates correctly engraved. The author has divided his subject into two parts; the one treats of the history of the disease, and the other of the operative part; in the latter is pointed out the mode of inoculation, the qualities of the vaccine-fluid, and the treatment required during the complaint; to it is likewise added, a short account of the cases occurring in Spain; and to render this important discovery as useful as possible, directions are given for the operation so plain and minute, that it may be performed by parents or friends, where, from poverty, or remoteness of situation, medical assistance is not easily obtained.

Instruccion sobre los Medios de conservar la Salubridad, y purificar el Ayre de las Quadras en los Hospitales Militares de la Republica Francesa; dispuesto por la Junta de Sanidad del Departamento de la Guerra; traducido por el Dr. D. LEONARDO DE GALLI." Information on the Means of Preserving Health, and Purifying the Air of the Military Hospitals of the French Republic; arranged by the Board of Health of the War Department; translated by Dr. D. Leonardo de Galli.

"Descripcion de los Reales Baños de Armedillo; Analisis de sus Aguas, por Dr. PEDRO GUTIERRER Bueno Quimico en este Corte, un tom. en 4o. con dos Estampas, a 9 Rs." Description of the Royal Baths of Armedillo; an Analysis of their Waters, by Dr. Pedro Gutierrer, Chemist at Madrid, in 1 vol. 4to. with 2 Plates, 9 Reals. These Baths are five leagues from Calahorra, and three from Arnedo, and have been well-known from very high antiquity for the remarkable cures they have performed: their temperature is 42 degrees of Reaumur.

"Disertacion sobre el Recto Uso de las Suturas y su Abuso." Dissertation on the Use and Abuse of Sutures. This is a lecture read in the Royal College of Surgery of St. Carlos by D. ANTONIO F. COLANIN.

ASTRONOMY, MATHEMATICS.

"Quaderno 3o. de los Principios de Matemáticas Puras y Mixtas, a 6 Rs." Fasciculus 3d. on the Principles of Pure and Mixed Mathematics. This is from the pen of D. IGNACIO ROMAZA, and particular attention is paid to method and arrangement to facilitate the views of the student.

"Tratado Completo de Aritmética, ó Método para aprender a Contar por Principios, por D. JUAN GERARD, Presbitero, un tom. en 4o. a 11 Rs." Complete Treatise on Arithmetic, by Dr. Juan Gerard, Priest, 1 vol. 4to. 11 Reals.

"Conversaciones acerca de la Pluralidad de los Mundos, un tom. en 8vo." Conversations on the Plurality of Worlds, 1 vol. 8vo.

BELLES LETTRES, GRAMMAR, CRITICISM, LOGIC, AND RHETORIC.

"Principios Filosóficos de la Literatura; o, Curso Razonado de Bellas Letras, y Bellas Artes; Obra escrita en Frances por M. Batteux, de la Academia Francesa; traducida, ilustrada con Notas Criticas y los Correspondientes Apéndices sobre la Literatura Española por, D. AUGUSTIN GARCIA DE ARRIETA." Philosophical Principles of Literature; or, an an arranged Course of Belles Lettres, and of the Fine Arts; from the French of M. Batteux, of the Royal Academy, with Notes Critical and Explanatory, and with Appendices, applying the Subject to Spanish Literature, by D. Augustin Garcia de Arrieta. This is the fifth volume of the work; it treats on lyric poetry, on the didactic method, and on minor compositions; several supplements are subjoined by the translator: one on Hebrew poetry; another on Spanish lyrics; a third on the lyric drama; two more are devoted to the peculiarities of the Spanish language; an analysis is given of the poetics of Aristotle; and remarks are made on the distinction between false and genuine poetical taste.

"Coleccion Española de las Obras Gramaticales del Celebre Gramatico, FRANCES CESAR DU MARSAIS; ordenada para la Instruccion publica, con Aplicaciones y Exemplos Correspondientes a la Elocucion Castellana, y dedicada al Exc. Sr. Principe de la Paz, por D. JOSEPH MIGUEL ALEA." Collection in Spanish of the Grammatical Works of the famous Grammarian, Francis Cæsar du Marsais, with Examples of Elocution in the Spanish Language, dedicated to his Excellency the Prince of Peace, by D. Joseph Miguel Alea.

"Gramatica de la Lengua Castellana ajustada á la Latina, para facilitar su Estudio, por D. AUGUSTIN MUñOZ ALVAREZ, presbitero." Grammar of the Spanish Language and Rhetoric, accommodated to the Latin Construction, in order to facilate the Acquisition of it, by D. Augustin Muñoz, priest, 1 vol. 8vo. This is written by a Professor of the College of St. Michael Seville; and to it is subjoined an Appendix on the genius and idiomatic peculiarities of the language, with observations on its state at different periods, illustrated, with the assistance of the most celebrated authors, by D. JOSEPH GARCIA PEREZ DE VARGAS.

"Entretenimientos sobre las Ciencias, escritos en Frances, por el R. P. BERNARDO LAMI: traducidos é ilustrados por D. DOMINGO UGENA, presbitero." Dialogues on the Sciences, written in French by R. P. Bernardo Lami, translated and illustrated by D. Domingo Ugena, priest. This work has been very generally received, as a successful plan of instruction, in several universities and literary institutions.

"Frioleras eruditas y curiosas por D. PEDRO MONTENGON." Learned and curious Trifles, by D. Pedro Montengon, 1 vol. 8vo. This work is not confined to the title, but contains remarks on many useful subjects, and the learned author has availed himself of the assistance of many able writers.

BIOGRAPHY.

"Diálogos de Frederico III. Rey de Prussia con el Dr. Zimmerman, Medico, traducido del Portugues." Dialogues of Frederic III. King of Prussia, with Dr. Zimmerman, from the Portugueze. Every anecdote connected with that heroic and enlightened Prince is interesting to the historian and the moralist, and these dialogues are particularly calculated to give an insight into his character and motives of action.

"Biblioteca Nueva de los Escritores Aragoneses que florencieron desde el Año de 1689 hasta el de 1753, por el D. FELIX DE LATASSAY ORTIN. New Library of the Arragonese writers who flourished from A. D. 1689, to 1753, by D.D. Felix de Latassa y Ortin." (v. infra.)

"Vida del Doctor Benjamin Franklin, sacada de Documentos autenticos, Eleva en el Frontispicio su retrato grabado por Dr. ANTONIO VAZQUEZ." The Life of Benjamin Franklin, L.L.D. from authentic Documents, with his Likeness in the Frontispiece, engraved by Dr. Antonio Vazquez.

"Biblioteca Nueva de los Escritores Arragoneses que floremcieron desde el Año de 1753 hasta el de 1795, Por el Dr. D. FELIX DE LATASSA Y ORTIN." New Library of the Arragonese Writers who flourished between the Years 1753 and 1795, by Dr. D. Felix de Latassa. This work is a continuation of the same subject, on which the author had previously published six volumes; the two first relate to the more early characters, and the four afterwards published to the modern ones.

CHRONOLOGY AND GEOGRAPHY.

"Plano de la Ciudad de Lima." Chart of the City of Lima.

"Mapa Geográfica de la Provincia y Costas de Buenos Ayres desde su Capital hasta la Isla Santa Catalina, en que se incluie el Rio Grande de S. Pedro." Geographical Map of the Province and Coasts of Buenos Ayres, from the Capital to the Island of St. Catalina, in which is comprized the Course of the Great River St. Pedro.

"Mapa de la Isla de la Jamayca." Map of the Island of Jamaica. This includes the roads that intervene between that Island and those of Cuba and St. Domingo: it has two separate plans, the one extends from the Port Antonio and the Bay

Bay of St. Francisco to the north of Jamaica; the other from Port Royal, or Kingston Bay, to the south of the Island.

"Plano de Charlestown, Capital de la Carolina Meridional, con una Mapa de la Costa que media entre esta ciudad y la de Sn. Augustin de la Florida, en América." Plan of Charlestown, the Capital of South Carolina, with a Map of the Coast that intervenes between that City and St. Augustin, of Florida, in America.

"Mapa del Reyno y Fronteras de Portugal, sacada de las Cartas Geográficas de PEDRO TIXEIRA y JACOBO CANTELLI." Map of the Kingdom and Frontiers of Portugal, formed on the Geographical Charts of Pedro Texeira and Jacobo Cantelli. In this map the delineator has consulted the general map of Spain, of Nicolas Bailleul, jun. and of Portugal, of Gregorio Fosman and Nicolas Fer.

"Mapa Geografica del Reino de Inglaterra." Geographical Map of the Kingdom of England. "Plano de la Bahia y Puerto de Plymouth." Plan of the Harbour and Port of Plymouth. "Plano del Puerto y Abra de Portsmouth, que comprehende las Radas y Surgideros de Spithead y de Santa Helena, con un Mapa en punto menor de todo la Isla de Wicht." Plan of the Port and Harbour of Portsmouth, which comprehends the Roads and Anchorage of Spithead and St. Helens, with an explicit Map of the whole of the Isle of Wight. "Mapa de Irlanda, con arreglo á Observaciones Astronomicas." Map of Ireland, with Astronomical Observations. By Dr. JUAN DE LA CRUZ.

"Mapa Topográfica de los Contornos de Fuenterabia—Gallia Vetus—Hispañia Vetus, cum Tabula Minore Africæ et Numidiæ." Topographical Map of the Vicinity of Fonterabia—Ancient Gaul—Ancient Spain—with a small Chart of Africa and Numidia. These maps are from the designs of D. JUAN DE LA CRUZ, and the two last are particularly intended to illustrate the Commentaries of Julius Cæsar.

"Plano de la Bahia de Algeciras y del Fondeadero de Gibraltaro levantado por el Xefe de Esquadra de la Real Armada D. VICENTE TOFINO." Plan of the Bay of Algesiras, with the Soundings in the Vicinity of Gibraltar, drawn by the Commodore of the Royal Fleet, D. Vincente Tofiño.

"Mapa de Egipto." Map of Egypt; in which are shewn the Mouths of the Nile, the Course of the River up to Cairo, with its Canals and Branches, until it pass the Monastery of La Ciur.

DRAMA.

"Agamemnon Vengado, Tragedia, por D. VICENTE GARCIA DE LA HUERTA." Agamemnon Revenged, a Tragedy, by D. Vicente Garcia de la Huerta.

"Sofonisba, Tragedia, en 8°." Sophonisba, a Tragedy, 8vo.

"Raguel, Tragedia, en 8vo." Raguel, a Tragedy, 8vo.

"Guzman el Bueno, Tragedia, por D. NICOLAS FERNANDEZ MORATIN, 8vo." Guzman the Good, by D. Nicolas Fernandez Moratin, 8vo.

"Hernan Cortés, Tragedia, de ALEXO PIRON, traducida del Frances." Hernan Cortes, a Tragedy, by Alexis Piron, translated from the French.

"La Misantropia Desvanecida, Drama en un Acto, escrito por AUGUSTO KOTZEBUE, 2 rs." Misanthropy cured, a Drama, in one Act, written by Augustus Kotzebue: this in continuation of a play, entitled "Misantropy and Repentance, by the same hand.

"El Duque de Viseo, Tragedia Nueva en tres Actos, por D. MANUEL JOSEPH QUINTANA, en 8vo. a 3rs." The Duke of Viseo, a New Tragedy, in three Acts, by D. M. Joseph Quintana, 8vo. 3 reals.

"Fulgencia, Comedia Nueva, en tres Actos, por D. VICENTE RODRIGUEZ DE ARELLANO." Effulgence, a New Comedy, in three Acts, by D. Vicente Rodriguez de Arellano.

"Clementina y Desormes, Comedia Nueva, en cinco Actos, por Mr. MONVEL, traducida por D. VICENTE RODRIGUEZ DE ARELLANO." Clementina and Desormes, a New Comedy, in five Acts, by Mr. Monvel, translated by D. Vicente Rodriguez de Arellano.

"La Virtud en la Indigencia, Drama Nuevo, en 4 Actos, en Prosa, traducido del Frances, por D. J. E. G." Virtue in Poverty, a New Drama, in four Acts, in Prose, from the French of D. J. E. G.

"Los Amantes Generosos, Comedia Nueva, en Actos." The Generous Lovers, a New Comedy, in five Acts. The original of this play is in the German, from that language it was, with alterations, translated into French, and from the latter it received its present form.

"Ali Bek, Tragedia Nueva Original, en cinco Actos, por Dona MARIA ROSA DE GALVEZ." Ali Bek, a New Original Tragedy, in five Acts, by Donna Maria Rosa de Galvez.

"Un

"Un Loco hace Ciento, Comedia Nueva, en un Acto, en Prosa, por Doña MARIA ROSA GALVEZ." One Fool makes Many, a New Comedy, in one Act, by Donna Maria Rosa Galvez.

"El Califa de Bagdad, Opera Comica, en un Acto." The Caliph of Bagdad, a Comic Opera, in one Act.

"Catalina; ó, la Bella Labradora, Comedia Nueva, en tres Actos, traducida del Frances, por Doña MARIA ROSA GALVEZ." Catalina; or, The Lovely Villager, a New Comedy, in three Acts, translated from the French, by Dona Maria Rosa Galvez.

EDUCATION.

"Diccionario de Hechos y Dichos Memorables de la Historia Antigua y Moderna, tres tomos en 8vo. a 48rs." The Beauties of Ancient and Modern History, lexicographically arranged, 3 vols. 8vo. at 48 reals. This is professedly designed to impress upon the minds of young persons the most important historical events, and it has been the endeavour of the composer to accommodate his style to this design.

"Verdadero Método para aprender las Lenguas Española y Francesa." The true Method of learning the Spanish and French Languages. This is a fasciculus of a much larger work, that will be interesting and instructive to linguists.

"Rudimentos de Lengua Latina, para Instruccion de la juventud, por Quadernos dosen casa mes." Rudiments of the Latin Tongue, for the Instruction of Youth, published by Numbers of two to each month.

"Atlas Elemental Antiguo, o Coleccion de Mapas, para enseñar a los Niños Geografia, con un Indice Alfabético de los Ciudades, Villas, &c." Elementary Atlas of Ancient Geography; or, A Collection of Maps for the Instruction of Children; with an Alphabetical Index of the Cities, Towns, &c. To this work is subjoined a Chronological Epitome of Antient History.

"Compendio de los Primeros Rudimentos, muy claros y breves para aprender á leer y escribir en Frances sinso corio de Maestro, por D. FRANCISCO SOLDEVILLA." Compendium of the First Rudiments of the French Language, given in a clear and short Way to learn it without a Master, by D. Francisco Soldevilla.

ANCIENT HISTORY.

"Anales de la Nacion Española desde el Tiempo mas remoto hasta la Entrada de los Romanos; sacados de Escritores, originales y Monumentos contemporaneos, por D. LUIS JOSEPH VELAZQUEZ M. DE VALDEFLORES." Annals of the Spanish Nation, from the earliest Time to the Roman Invasion, extracted from original Authors and contemporary Monuments, by D. Luis Joseph Velazquez M. de Valdeflores.

MODERN HISTORY.

"Descripcion Breve de toda España." Short Description of Spain. This work explains the foundation of its metropolitan and capital cities, the number of parishes in each archiepiscopal diocese, the rents, the period when the universities were established, and many curious particulars connected with its ecclesiastical history.

"Los Comentarios Reales que tratan del Origen de los Incas del Perú, de su Idolatria, Leyes y Gobierno en Paz y en Guerra; sus Vidas y Conquistas y lo que fué aquel Imperio y su Republica, antes que los Españoles pasaron á El; por el Inca GARCILASO DE LA VEGA." Royal Commentaries on the Origin of the Incas of Peru, their Idolatry, their Laws and Government in Peace and War; on their Conquests, and on the Nature of their Establishments previous to the Incursions of the Spaniards, by the Inca Garcilaso de la Vega.

"Histôria General del Perú; Trata de su Descubrimiento, y como lo ganaron los Españoles, las Guerras Civiles que hubo entre Pizarros y Almagros; sobre el Repartimiento de la Tierra, Castigo y Levantamiento de Tiranos y otros Sucesos Particulares; escrito por el mismo Inca GARCILASCO." General History of Peru; the Mode of Discovery and of Conquest by the Spaniards; the Civil Wars that subsisted between the Pizarros and Almagros; on the Division of the Country; the Destruction of the Tyrants, and other Transactions; by the Inca Garcilaso de la Vega. The two preceding treatises are written by a native of the country, who obtained a captain's commission in the service of his Catholic Majesty.

SACRED AND ECCLESIASTICAL HISTORY.

"Cronicon de Christiano Andricomio Delfo, traducido del Latin por D. LORENZO MARTINEZ MARCILLA." Chronicle of Christiano Andricomio Delfo, translated from the Latin by D. Lorenzo Martinez Marcilla. This work contains an account of the creation of the world; of the formation of man and the increase of his species; of the orig n and principles of monarchical government; of the origin, progress,

progress, and conclusion of the Mosaical law; of the birth, life, and miracles of Jesus Christ; of the origin and advancement of the Catholic church, and of its persecutions.

JURISPRUDENCE.

"Cartas sobre la Policia, por D. VALENTIN DE FORONDA, un tomo, a 8 rs." Letters on Internal Police, by D. Valentin de Foronda, 1 vol. 8 reals. Seven Letters or Essays are included in this production:—The first is merely introductory; the next is medical; the third division treats of the means of generating and preserving an abundance of the necessaries of life; the fourth, on useful institutions; the fifth, on criminal law; the sixth, on human industry; and the seventh is a metaphysical inquiry wherein the author contends, that in the human species the intellect of the female is equal to that of the male in its original powers and subsequent development. It is curious to observe, that in a country where for so many centuries the sex has been considered as slaves of state, the general spirit of revolution should have so far diffused itself, as to admit the public discussion of this question from respectable authority.

"Las Leyes ilustradas por las Ciencias Fisicas; ó, Tratado de Medicina Legal y de Nigiene hública, escrito en Frances, por el Ciudo FRANCISCO MANUEL FODERE, Medico del Hospital de Caridad de la Ciudad de Marsella, y traducido al Castellano, Tomo I. 13 rs." Law, as founded on the Physical History of Man; or, a Treatise Medico Juridical, written in French, by Citizen Francisco Manuel Foderé, Physician to the Hospital of Charity in the City of Marseilles, and translated into Spanish, Vol. I. 13 reals.

"Biblioteca Español Económico Politica." The Spanish Economical and Political Library. This is the commencement of an extensive work, intended to comprize extracts from the best economic writers, with critical and literary notes and observations on the laws relating to agricultural produce; also laws, mercantile and sumptuary. It will further dilate on patriotic establishments, or interior police, and other matters connected with the civil history of Spain.

"Instituciones del Derecho Público General de España, por D. RAMON LAZARO DE DON, Tomo III." Institutions of Public Right, as acknowledged in Spain, by D. Ramon Lazaro de Don, Volume III. 20 reals. In this publication is concluded, the detail of the duties and privileges of all the members of the state.

"Principios de Economia Politica, por HERRENSCHWAND; publicados en Londres; traducidos al Frances, y ahora al Castellano, por D. JUAN SMITH, Brigadier de la Real Armada." Principles, Politico-economical, by Herrenschwand; published in London; translated into French, and since into the Spanish, by D. Juan Smith, Brigadier in the Royal Fleet. This treats of population and agriculture, and on all the branches of labour connected with public prosperity. The publication appearing subsequent to the celebrated work of Adam Smith, has received the advantage of its assistance, and enters with impartiality into the comparative advantages and disadvantages of different countries.

MISCELLANIES.

"Modo de preservar de los Regos a las Personas Casas y Demas Edificios. Means of preserving Persons and Buildings from the Fatal Effects of Lightning, by D. P. GATELL, 2 reals." In it he treats on the most prudent conduct to be adopted on the approach of violent tempests.

"Desengaños Filosóficos, que en obsequio de la Verdad de la Religion y de la Patria ofrece la Público el D. D. VICENTE VALCARCE, 4 tomos, en 4to. Philosophical Detections, which in regard to Truth, to Religion, and to his Country, are submitted to the Public, by D. D. Vicente Valcarce, 4 vols. 4to. This long work is from the pen of the Dean of Valencia, to expose the vanity and fraud of the new philosophy, and to prevent the diffusion of principles so dangerous to order and religion.

"Estenografia." Stenography. This is originally taken from an English work; it is the first attempt of the kind to accommodate this art to the structure of the Spanish language, 16 reals.

"Carta Historica sobre el Origen y Progreso de las Fiestas de Toro en España, por D. NICOLAS DE MORATIN." Historical Letter on the Origin and Progress of Bull Feasts in Spain, by D. Nicolas Moratin. We are sorry to see this barbarous custom sufficiently countenanced in Spain to give rise to this publication, yet while the brutality of pugilism and of baiting the noblest and most useful animal with the canine species are practiced in our own country, we must abstain from any severity of remark on the ferocity of the southern kingdoms, if we would avoid self-condemnation.

"Calen-

"Calendario Gregoriano y Republicano Frances, para el Año de 1801, que comprehende Parte de los Anos 9° y 10° de la Era Republicana." Gregorian Calendar and French Republican, for the Year 1801, which comprises Part of the 9th and 10th Years of the Republican Æra. This was published on the occasion of the entrance of the French troops into Spain, to prevent irregularities and misconstructions with the purveyors, magistrates, &c.

NOVELS AND FUGITIVE PIECES.

"Menosprecio de Corte y Alabanzas de Aldea por el Ilmo y Rmo. S. D. ANTONIO DE GUEVARA, Obispo que fué de Mondoñedo un tomo, en 8°." The Preference of a Rustic to a Town Life, by the right Rev. Father in God, Antonio de Guevara, late Bishop of Mondoñedo, 1 vol. 8vo.

"El Bachiller de Salamanca; ó, Aventuras de D. Querubin de la Ronda." The Batchelor of Arts of Salamanca; or Adventures of D. Querubin, de la Ronda.

"Adelayda; ó, el Triunfo del Amor; escrito en Frances por Madama GENLIS, y traducido por Doña MARIA JACOBA CASTILLA XARAVA, un tomo, en 8°." Adelaide; or, the Triumph of Love; written in French by Madame Genlis, and translated by Donna Maria Jacoba Castilla Xarava, 1 vol. 8°. We have noticed a work by D. Valentin de Foronda, wherein the talents of the female mind are asserted and vindicated in the production we have just given; we have seen with pleasure this effort of a female writer, to indulge her country with a specimen from one of her own sex, acknowledged among the most elegant writers of the age.

"Jacinto en Madrid; ó, el Tiempo de Ferias, novela repartida en 29 Capitulos que contiene el Diario de un Petimetre, la Moda, el Bayle, la Musica, &c." Jacinto of Madrid; or, the Time of Fairs, in 29 Chapters, being the Diary of a Pétit Maître on Fashion, Antics, and Musical Taste.

"El Mundo al Revés, ó Contraverdades, dedicadas á los Hombres Pensamientos, Sueltos, ó Memoria para Servir a la Historia del Buen Tono y de la Buena Compañia." The World Turned Upside Down, dedicated to the Male Species—Batchelors Thoughts; or, Thoughts on the Haut Ton and Polished Society.

"Vida y Hechos de Juan Mayorazgo." Life and Adventures of Juan Mayorazgo.

"Avisos Baratos que da á sus Amigos, el Lic. D. JUAN ESCARMIENTO, sobre las Ferias de Madrid; en un Romance jocoso." Cheap Advice to his Friends, by the Licenciate D. Juan Escarmiento, on the Fairs of Madrid; a humorous Romance.

PAINTING, ENGRAVING, AND STATUARY.

"Retrato de Madama Bonaparte, Esposa del Primer Consul." Portrait of Madame Bonaparte, Wife of the First Consul. This is from an original, engraved at Paris.

"Estampa Fina que representa el Combate que dió la Esquadra Inglesa a la Division Francesa Surta en el Puerto de Algeciras, el dia 6 de Julio, de 1801." An Engraving of the Engagement between the English Squadron and a Division of the French Fleet, in the Bay of Algesiras, on the 6th July, 1801. This plate exhibits a fine marine view, and the artist has chosen the moment when the English ship of war was silenced, within sight of the camp of St. Roque.

POETRY.

"Poesias de Don GASPAR MARIA NAVA, Conde de Noroña, dos tomos, en 8°, 30 rs." Poems of Don Gaspar Maria Nava, Count of Noroña, 2 vols. 8vo. 30 reals. This includes Anacreontic compositions, odes, songs, and a philosophical poem on Death with others. The new part of this work is the second volume; the first had appeared some time, before.

"Elegia Latina, en Elogio de Don JOSEPH DE MASDEVALL." A Latin Elegy, in Praise of Don Joseph de Masdevall. This poem, like that of our celebrated countryman Dr. Armstrong, is of the didactic kind, and on a medical subject.

PUBLIC INSTITUTIONS.

The Royal Economic Society of Madrid is about to publish the Sixth Volume of its Transactions, and has publicly signified its approbation of a translation made by one of its associates Don DOMINGO AGLIERO Y NEYRA, of the Political Economic and Philosophical Essays of Count Rumford. It notices the general reception which the works of this valuable writer have met with in Germany, England, France, Switzerland, and other countries by which the pressing wants of human beings have been relieved, and the comforts of life have been secured. It particularly recommends the adoption of a great variety of his expedients for the public good, and it has separated the sale of the translation we have noticed from the

the other papers of the Society, to promote its more extensive circulation, and to render as clear as possible the subjects which appear to the Society to conducive to general improvement; plates are subjoined, expletive of the more important particulars.

The Royal Academy of St. Fernando, in the important department of Architecture, has, under the sanction of a royal mandate issued in September last, settled the mode of graduation and titular distinctions of the students, which hitherto had not been attended to with the same regularity as in the other professions.

THEOLOGY AND ETHICS.

"Noticia Histórica de los Mysterios y Santos de la Religion Christiana, segun el órden en que se celebran en España, adornada de estampas Correspondientes a la Festividad de cada Dia." Historical Intelligence of the Mysteries and of the saints of the Christian Religion, accommodated to the Way in which they are signalized in Spain, and decorated with Designs for each Feast-day. This publication is in a double form in 4to. at 14 reals, and in 8vo. at 8 reals.

"Meditaciones con la Regla Para vivir Bien, por el P. JUAN PEDRO PINAMONTE." Meditations with the Great Rule of Life, by P. Juan Pedro Pinamonte.

"Directorio Espiritual, escrito para Instruccion de Novicios del Real Monasterio Cisterciense de Nra Sra de Sta. Susana de la Trapa, y es Utilisimo para todas las Personas, asi Religiosas y Seglares, que desean aprovechar en el camino de la Perfeccion para lo qual se dan las reglas Necesarias, un tomo, en 8°. Lo da á luz el M. R. P. M. D. JUAN DE SADA." Spiritual Directory, written for the Instruction of the Novices of the Royal Cistercian Monastery of our Lady of St. Susan de la Trapa, most Useful for all Persons, both Religious and Secular, who wish to be directed in the High road to Perfection, 1 vol. 8vo. by M. R. P. M. D. Juan de Sada.

"De los Remedios de qualquiera Fortuna." The Remedies for every Misfortune. This work is from the Latin of Lucius Annæus Seneca, and was long ago translated by the celebrated FRANCISO DE QUEVEDO Y VILLEGAS, a voluminous, eloquent and entertaining writer, whose works have deserved attention, but we believe have never been seen in an English dress, excepting one infolded piece of humour, intitled "The Dream of the Skulls."

"Sermones, Panegiricos y Morales, del P. FR. SEBASTIAN SANCHEZ SOBRINO, de la tercera Orden de Penitencia de S. Francisco, Calificador del Sto Oficio, quatro tomos." Panegyrical and Moral Sermons of P. Fr. Sebastian Sanchez Sobrino, of the Third Order of Penitents of St. Francis, Qualifier of the Inquisition, 4 vols.

"Propeta Evangélico." The Evangelical Prophet; the 2d and last volumes, 29 reals the two. This particularly relates to the prophecies of Isaiah, and their connections with the Messiah is explained, in opposition to the crude notions that have been circulated by writers little conversant with the subject.

"Carta Pastoral del Ilmo Sr. Obispo de Salamanca, escrito con Motivo de la Entrada de las Tropas Francesas en su Obispado." Pastoral Letter of the Bishop of Salamanca, written on the Occasion of the Introduction of the French Troops into his Diocese. Either the merit of the treatise, or the popularity of the subject has occasioned a very extensive sale of this work.

"Sermones predicados en la santa Patriarcal Inglesa de Sevilla, en los Dias de S. Clemente y S. Fernando, de 1799 y 1800, por el P. MTRO. MANUEL GIL." Sermons preached in the Patriarchal Church at Seville, on the Public Days of St. Clement and St. Ferdinand, in the Years 1799 and 1800, by P. Maestro Manuel Gil.

TRADE, COMMERCE, ARTS AND MANUFACTURES.

"Arte de Relozes de Ruedas para Torre y Faltriquera, dos tomos, en 4°." The Art of Watch and Clock making, 2 vols. 4to. This work contains 53 plates, and enters into the detail of a very ingenious mechanical employment, which hitherto has been very little understood in Spain.

"Memorias sobre el Egipto." Observations on Egypt. This work remarkably shews the influence of France over her southern neighbours. It is intended to explain the importance of Egypt as an agricultural, mercantile, military and political dependance of France; it contains the plans of operations adopted by the French for the conquest of the country, and the progress already made in that important enterprize, in which the interests of all Europe were so materially concerned.

"Proyecto sobre el Comercio, presendao por Mr. Colbert á Luis XIV. y traducido por Don ALEXANDRO DE SILVA Y AYANZ."

Ayanz." Treatise on Commerce, presented by M. Colbert to Lewis XIV. and translated by D. Alexandio de Silva y Ayanz. This work appears to be published with the express view of introducing into Spain some of the commercial and political improvements of that distinguished statesman. The translator is a Commissary of War in the Spanish service.

"Miscelanea, por D. Valentin de Forronda." Miscellanies, by D. Valentin de Foronda. Herein we find a dissertation on the dignity of commerce; a comparison between two humane institutions in Paris and Victoria; a discourse on the utility that would arise from a Spanish East India Company; a letter on the improvement in a pneumatic view of dungeons and prisons; an account of the discovery of Platina; some epistolary essays on the mode of increasing public happiness; and on the liberty of the press, under certain restrictions.

Voyages and Travels.

"El Viagero Universal; ó, Noticia del Mundo Antiguo y Nuevo; obra recopilada de los mejores Viageros, por D. Pedro Estala, presbitero; Suplimento al Egipto." The Universal Traveller; or, Intelligence of the Old and the New World; compiled from the principle Travellers, by D. Pedro Estala, priest; with a Supplement on Egypt.

"Quaderno 39 de la Coleccion General de los Trages que usan las Naciones del mundo Describierto Arreglada a la edicion del Viagero Universal." Fasciculus 39th of the General Collection of Habits of all the Nations in the Known World, accommodated to the Work entitled the Universal Traveller. The present collection contains the habits of some remote islands and those of Nootka Sound, with others employed on the occasion of a triumphal entry: (v. infra continuation).

"Ensayo Cronológico para la História General de la Florida, por D. Gabriel de Cardenas y Cano." Chronological Essay for the History of Florida, by D. Gabriel de Cardenas y Cano. This work contains the discoveries and the principal operations in that country by the Spaniards, French, Swedish, Danish, English and other nations; with an account of the native Indians, their customs, genius, idolatry, government, and wars. This treatise likewise contains the voyages of certain adventurers by the North Sea, since A. D. 1512, when Florida was discovered, to the year 1722.

"Noticias Americanas." American Intelligence. This publication is in the way of dialogue and treats of the natural history of North and South America, and contains a scientific arrangement of the vegetable, animal, and mineral kingdoms in the western world. It has a variety of observations on the Indians of those countries and on their language; and some conjectures are hazarded on its original population. 14 reals boards.

"Piratas de América, traducido del Flamenco, por el Doctor de Buena Maison." American Pirates, translated from the Flemish, by Dr. de Buena Maison. In this work observations are made on the mode of defence proper for the West India coasts; some account is given of the most remarkable voyages, and of several islands, their productions, their inhabitants, and of their wars with the Spaniards and French.

"Querderno 40 de la Colleccion General, de los Trages que usan las Naciones del mundo Descubierto Arreglada a la Edicion del Viagero Universal." Fasciculus 40th of the Coutume of the newly discovered Nations and Islanders, accommodated to the Edition of the Universal Traveller." Among others, it introduces those of the Sandwich Islands, unfortunately distinguished by the massacre of Cooke, our valiant and humane countryman.

THE RETROSPECT OF AMERICAN LITERATURE.

This article which has regularly been transmitted to us from America, has, by accident, been detained on its passage. It is consequently obliged to be postponed, but will make its appearance in the Number of the Magazine which will be published on the first day of March.

GENERAL INDEX

TO THE TWELFTH VOLUME.

Edin-

Literature

Mill,

TO THE PUBLIC.

Persons who have lately been disappointed in their Applications for complete Sets or particular Volumes of the MONTHLY MAGAZINE, *are respectfully informed, that several Numbers which were out of Print have lately been reprinted, and complete Sets may be had in Twelve Volumes, handsomely half-bound, Price Seven Pounds; or any single Number or Volume may be had, at the Pleasure of the Purcha[...]*

Names of the Authors, Patentees, &c. that occur in this Volume.

Remarkable Persons deceased, of whom Biographical Memoirs are given in this Volume.

N. B. The other Names are to be seen in the General Index, by looking under the respective Letters of each Name.

Authors whose Names occur in the Supplementary Number.

Alphabetical List of Bankruptcies announced between the 20th of June and the 20th of December, 1801, extracted from the London Gazette.

Bull

END OF THE TWELFTH VOLUME.

www.ingramcontent.com/pod-product-compliance
Lightning Source LLC
Chambersburg PA
CBHW021221300426
44111CB00007B/392
* 9 7 8 3 7 4 1 1 1 7 2 4 4 *